personality
development

ELIZABETH B. HURLOCK

McGraw-Hill Book Company

New York   St. Louis   San Francisco
Düsseldorf   Johannesburg   Kuala Lumpur
London   Mexico   Montreal
New Delhi   Panama   Rio de Janeiro
Singapore   Sydney   Toronto

This book was set in Univers by Black Dot, Inc.
The editors were John Hendry and David Dunham;
the designer was Barbara Ellwood;
and the production supervisor was John A. Sabella.
The drawings were done by Vantage Art, Inc.
The printer and binder was R. R. Donnelley & Sons Company.

**personality
development**

1 2 3 4 5 6 7 8 9 0 D O D O P 7 9 8 7 6 5 4 3

Library of Congress Cataloging in Publication Data

Hurlock, Elizabeth Bergner, 1898–
  Personality development.

  Bibliography: p.
  1. Personality.   I. Title.
BF698.H818   1974   155.2′5   73–3369
ISBN 0-07-031447-0

contents

preface

So much is known about personality today that no one book could cover the entire field. In choosing which areas of information to concentrate on in this book, the author was guided not only by a personal interest in the development aspect of personality but also by a desire to meet the needs of students whose interest in personality is primarily in understanding how it develops rather than in theory analysis or personality measurement, both of which are likely to have been covered in other courses.

As scientific research in personality goes forward, there is a growing realization that the personality pattern of the individual is a product of learning through life experiences. That is the focus of this book, though at no time is the importance of the hereditary foundations for learning and for life experiences overlooked or minimized. Part I is devoted to the leading research studies on the meaning of personality, what it is, what techniques are used to mold it, and how persistent or subject to change it is.

Each chapter of Part II covers one of the leading personality determinants and presents research findings to substantiate its inclusion. While other determinants undoubtedly exist, the available research does not show that they are significant enough to justify more than a brief mention at this time. Future research may prove differently or may uncover new determinants which are not even being investigated today.

Part III is devoted to a relatively new approach to personality evaluation. In spite of popular as well as scientific interest in measuring human characteristics, the measuring rods for assessing personality are so inadequate and inaccurate that little confidence can be placed in their results. For that reason, Chapters 14 and 15 outline a different approach to evaluating personality—that of determining whether the individual's personality pattern is healthy or sick and how healthiness in various degrees affects personal and social adjustment. For readers who are not already familiar with the more traditional kinds of personality tests and their uses, a brief critical analysis is given in the introductory section of Part III.

The author has made no attempt to develop a new theory about personality. Instead, an attempt has been made to coordinate existing research information so that the reader can learn with relative ease and speed where the weight of evidence lies. An attempt has also been made to evaluate conflicting findings and to arrive at some tentative conclusion.

To avoid distracting the reader with superfluous footnotes or bibliographical citations, the author has used reference numbers in the text only when specific studies are mentioned or quoted. The bibliography for each chapter, given at the end of the book, is, however, an acknowledgement of the numerous books and articles used directly or indirectly in the preparation of the chapter.

The author wants to take advantage of this opportunity to thank those scholars whose works are listed in the bibliography for their contributions, through their research, their conclusions, and their theories, to the material presented in this book. The author likewise wishes to express sincere gratitude to her many colleagues in the areas of developmental, counseling, and clinical psychology for their suggestions, criticisms, and encouragement in the planning and writing of this book. They have been of invaluable help.

Elizabeth B. Hurlock

PART ONE **the meaning of personality**

Through the centuries, personality has been regarded as a practical force in determining success or failure in life. In every culture, stock traditional beliefs about this "mysterious aspect" of the individual have become embedded in the folklore and been passed on from one generation to another. By now, these traditional beliefs or "old wives' tales" have acquired such a halo of infallibility that few dare to question them. After all, it is claimed, if people have believed them all these years, they must be correct.

Traditional beliefs about personality are myriad. A few of the most widely known may be used to illustrate what traditional beliefs are and how they have affected the scientific study of personality.

The belief that personality is inherited is expressed in the saying, "He's a chip off the old block." The implication of this belief is clear. If the person has some socially undesirable traits, he inherited them from his parents, so forget about trying to change them. If he is stingy and sullen, he can't become generous and cheerful any more than he can change his eye color, his stature, or the size of his ears. The implication is that neither training nor desire to improve will be of any avail. The person is a prisoner of his genes. The acceptance of this belief discourages any motivation to try to improve the personality.

Closely related to this old wives' tale is the belief that certain personality traits automatically accompany certain physical traits. The person with red hair has a fiery temper, for example; or the person with a high forehead is a "brain." The implication is that, since the physical traits are inherited and thus not subject to change, the personality traits that accompany them are similarly implacable to change. Like the "chip off the old block" belief, this belief also discourages the individual from trying to improve his personality.

A third widely held belief is that personality changes automatically accompany body changes. Since body changes are a part of the developmental sequence over which the individual has no control, it is assumed that the accompanying personality changes are likewise uncontrollable. According to tradition, radical physical changes are accompanied by equally radical personality changes at two times during the life span: first, at puberty, when the child's body is transformed into that of an adult, and second, at old age, when pronounced physical changes throughout the body parallel the loss of the reproductive capacity. The child, it is believed, will automatically outgrow his undesirable traits. The improvement in his personality is regarded as a natural accompaniment of the physical improvements which, according to tradition, transform the ugly duckling of childhood into a beautiful swan at the time of sexual maturing. Physical deterioration in old age, it is similarly believed, is accompanied by personality deterioration. Old people, as a group, are then said to change for the worse. This old wives' tale suggests that changes in personality are nature's work and therefore inevitable. With its acceptance, people assume a hands-off policy and wait for the changes to occur. When it becomes apparent that the adolescent is not outgrowing his undesirable personality characteristics or that the elderly person is allowing himself to become unsocial in his attitudes and behavior because people treat him as if he were, it may be too late to provide the motivation and offer the help that we know is possible.

According to tradition, the law of compensation in nature holds equally for people. A dry summer will be compensated for by a rainy winter; a poor crop one year will be followed by a good crop the next year. A girl who is beautiful is expected to be "dumb"; a boy who is endowed with athletic prowess is not expected to have the intelligence necessary to be a good student. Good personality traits are balanced by undesirable ones, thus producing the "average" person. The harm in accepting this traditional belief is obvious. If a person believes that nature will provide him with desirable traits to compensate for the undesirable, he will have little motivation to take the initiative in personality improvement. Nor will he feel that he should oppose nature's "laws."

In spite of the halo of infallibility surrounding old wives' tales, some scientists have been curious enough and bold enough to attack them to see if they can stand up under the scrutiny of scientific examination. The old beliefs thus have some value in that they have been a spur to scientific research. Their value in this respect is detailed in Part One. In Chapter 1, What Personality Is, the scientifically accepted meaning of personality is presented and the reasons given for accepting this definition in place of the traditional idea that personality is a mysterious aspect of the person

that determines how he reacts to other people and how they react to him. The chapter explains why personality is considered so important to success in life and why people are more personality-conscious today than in the past. The explanation centers on such subjects as how people judge others and how they are in turn judged, the role of first and subsequent impressions, and the influence of stereotypes on impressions and judgments. Further, "character," "individuality," and "personality" are distinguished so that the reader will know, from the very beginning, the scientifically approved use of these terms.

To disprove the traditional belief that personality is some nebulous, mysterious quality, Chapter 2, The Personality Pattern, stresses that it is something that can be objectively observed in the speech and actions of the individual and measured with a relative degree of accuracy. The definition and explanation of the "personality pattern" offer additional proof that the popular conception of personality is far from correct. To disprove the traditional belief that personality is inherited, Chapter 2 describes the role played by learning as well as that played by heredity. The importance of learning is accented in examination of the elements that make up the personality pattern: the core, or the self-concept, and the different traits which, through learning, are related to and influenced by the self-concept.

Scientific investigations of how personality syndromes develop are relied on to refute the traditional belief and to show that common learning experiences and imitation of a parent, sibling, or other family member are far more likely to be responsible for family similarities than is heredity.

The traditional belief that physical and personality characteristics go hand in hand is so widely held that physical characteristics are commonly used to judge personality. As such, the physical characteristics become "symbols of self," as Freud pointed out many years ago. Questions about how accurate the symbols of self are in making personality judgments have aroused scientific curiosity and led to extensive research. In recent years, this research has branched out to include characteristics other than the physical which have been found to be symbols of self. Thus, the testing of this old wives' tale has unearthed a wealth of information formerly overlooked or ignored. In Chapter 3, Symbols of Self, some of the symbols most commonly used to judge personality are analyzed. These include such important symbols of self as clothing, speech, names, use of leisure time, and reputation.

Many traditional beliefs imply that the kind of personality a person develops as well as the outstanding traits in his personality pattern are determined by his genetic makeup—by what his parents were before him. Acceptance of this premise weakens any motivation the person might otherwise have to improve his personality. It also weakens the motivation of parents and teachers to try to guide and direct the development of personality in children during the early, formative years of their lives. One of the first scientists to attack the premise was Freud. His insistence on the importance of early experiences in determining whether the child would grow up to be a well-adjusted or a maladjusted adult opened up a whole new field of research. Notable among the many scientists who have since contributed information about the relative importance of heredity and environment in personality development are such cultural anthropologists as Ruth Benedict and Margaret Mead. Today, the weight of evidence is definitely on the side of environment, though few scientists ignore the important role played by heredity in laying the foundations on which the personality pattern will be built and in determining how the personality will be molded by environmental influences. In Chapter 4, Molding the Personality Pattern, a detailed explanation is given of the many factors, both hereditary and environmental, that contribute to the development of personality. The emphasis is on how environmental factors—imitation, identification, and child-training—influence the hereditary potentials, how they shape the person's charac-

teristic way of adjusting to life and determine what his self-concept will be.

Many traditional beliefs imply that personality changes inevitably accompany physical changes and occur only when there are physical changes. As early as the days of Hippocrates in ancient Greece, it was observed that some personality changes were man-made, that they resulted from changes in the environment and in the person's general health condition at times other than puberty and middle or old age. This early point of view was substantiated in modern times by Freud's pioneer work in psychotherapy and by research evidence from a multitude of other souces. Evidence that learning, not heredity, is primarily responsible for these personality changes is presented in Chapter 5, Persistence and Change. The conditions under which personality changes occur are discussed, and the kinds of change that can be expected—either qualitative or quantitative. Research scientists generally agree that the only valid way of determining persistence and change in the personality pattern is to make longitudinal studies—studies of the same people from the beginning to the end of the life span. Because of the practical difficulties involved in such studies, relatively few have been made. Those which are available, however, show that the traditional beliefs about the time of personality changes, the direction of the changes, and the causes of the changes are, like most traditional beliefs, more incorrect than correct. There is little evidence, for example, that a person automatically outgrows his undesirable traits at puberty and much evidence that if he changes for the better, it is his work, not nature's.

CHAPTER 1 what personality is

The importance of personality increases as social life becomes more complex. A "pleasing" personality has a "marketable value" in a complex society and is highly prized and sought after. In simple cultures, where the scale of social relations is low and behavior is regulated by age-old customs, personality is of less concern.

As late as the turn of the century, life in America was on a relatively simple scale. The child went to school to learn the three R's and perhaps get a smattering of purely cultural subjects. Extracurricular activities were almost nonexistent. After school, the child returned home to share in the household chores and do his lessons; recreations were home-oriented and playmates were mainly siblings. So it was with college and university students. They went to college to learn, though having a good time was not entirely ignored.

Social life, except among the elite, was largely limited to family gatherings, church socials, and contacts with neighbors. On the whole, work was an individual matter, with each breadwinner working for himself, whether in the role of farmer, craftsman, shopkeeper, or professional man. If he was employed by someone else, it was usually a relative or friend of the family. Mate selection, greatly influenced by parental pressure, was usually restricted to the confines of one's own community. And since a strong social stigma was attached to divorce, marriage was generally for life.

Today, all these conditions are changed; and, in practically every life role, personality is of major significance. Even before he finishes first grade, the school child knows that the most popular children are those with a "good" personality. In junior high school, both boys and girls realize that, on a date, a pleasing personality is more desirable than intelligence, scholastic achievement, stylish clothes, or money. They are well aware of the role personality plays in determining whether they will be leaders or followers in the extracurricular activities of the school.

With the growth of big business and the inevitable decline of individual enterprise, getting along well with one's fellow workers and making a good impression on the boss earn greater recognition than the quality of one's work. Reaching the top of the business ladder depends more on personality than on intellectual ability, as shown by the fact that those who graduate from high school or college at the top of the class are far less likely to reach the heights of business success than are those who "majored" in social or athletic activities.

With mate selection in the hands of the young people themselves and with the rise in geographic mobility, an agreeable personality is a greater asset in a mate than family connection or socioeconomic status. And, finally, with the stability of marriage constantly threatened by socially approved separation, divorce, and remarriage, personality plays a prime role in holding one's mate.

RECOGNIZING THE SOCIAL VALUE OF PERSONALITY

The changes in American life described above have endowed personality with high social value and have made Americans so personality-conscious that a good personality is believed to be a guarantee of happiness and success in life. Developing the personality is a major goal for many people. In this "swell guy" era, with its premium on quiet adjustment, as Gross writes, "intelligence, competence, sweat and ability are becoming mere base requirements for the chance to show your true mettle, through your personality" (79).

The young child is unaware of the social value of personality, but the older child and adolescent are extremely personality-conscious and highly motivated to improve themselves. The older child discovers how people feel about him from the way they treat him and from what they say about him. If he is accused of acting like a baby or is called a bum or a slob, he knows that he has faults—psychologists called them "personality weaknesses"—which he must change or eliminate if he is to win social approval. If he is accused of being lazy by teachers, of being mean by siblings, or of being naughty by parents, he acquires some insight into the image others have of him.

Adolescents report that self-improvement and developing a better personality are two of their chief concerns. They want to know how they can change personality traits that they believe are keeping them from achieving social success and acceptance. Coleman states that adults often forget how "personality-oriented" adolescents are (40).

The adult who sees people of lesser ability outpace him in business and social life has driven home to him, even more forcibly than the adolescent, the achievement value of personality. As a result, he is strongly motivated to improve his personality.

After examining their personalities, some people conclude that their shortcomings can be overcome merely by improving the personality pattern they now have. Others, more dissatisfied with themselves, are more ambitious. Their hope is to develop a wholly new personality pattern and they try to discover some easy way to do it—by reading books or newspaper columns on personality improvement, by asking friends for advice, or by trying to imitate a person who represents a model of success.

WHAT IS PERSONALITY?

What, you may ask, is this highly prized thing labeled "personality"? Is it something a few lucky people are born with, a gift from the gods? Or is it within the reach of everyone? If it can be acquired, then why doesn't everyone make it his business to develop the kind of personality that will bring him the success, popularity, and happiness everyone wants? If it can be acquired, you may wonder why so many people have personalities that bring them the things they do not want—failure, unhappiness, and lack of social acceptance.

The meaning of personality

The term "personality" is derived from the Latin word *persona,* which means "mask." Among the Greeks, actors used a mask to hide their identity on stage. This dramatic technique was later adopted by the Romans to whom *persona* denoted "as one appears to others," not as one actually is.

The popular, nonscientific definition of personality as the effect one has on others has two defects. First, it emphasizes only the manifest aspects of the intricate pattern of personality, the *expressiveness* of the individual. Second, in emphasizing only the objective aspects of personality, it does not indicate what the real personality is, the subjective or interior organization which is responsible for the expressive aspects (2, 164). As Hall and Lindzey (81) have pointed out, few words in the English language have a greater fascination for the general public than personality:

Although the word is used in various senses, most of these popular meanings fall under one of two headings. The first usage equates the term to social skill or adroitness. An individual's personality is assessed by the effectiveness with which he is able to elicit positive reactions from a variety of persons under different circumstances. It is in this sense that schools which specialize in glamorizing the American female intend the term when they refer to courses in "personality training." . . . The second usage considers the personality of the individual to inhere in the most outstanding or salient impression which he creates in others. A person may thus be said to have an "aggressive personality" or a "sensitive personality" or a "fearful personality." In each case the observer selects an attribute or quality which is highly typical of the subject and which is presumably an important part of the over-all impression which he creates in others and his personality is identified by this term. It is clear that there is an element of evaluation in both usages.

In 1937, Allport identified in the literature almost 50 definitions of personality (2). Today, there are doubtless more. Most of the early psychological definitions emphasized the expressive aspects of personality and ignored or only indirectly implied the interior organization that is responsible for the observable aspects. Woodworth, for example, defined personality as the "quality of the individual's total behavior" (185). According to Dashiell, an individual's personality is the "total picture of his organized behavior, especially as it can be characterized by his fellow men in a consistent way (45). Munn gave a more comprehensive analysis, pointing out that personality is the "most characteristic integration of an individual's structures and activities." It is *characteristic* in a dual sense because (1) it is unique, thus differentiating the individual from all others, and (2) it is fairly consistent, representing the *customary* integration of a particular individual's structures and activities (126).

These representative early psychological definitions stressed the *manifest* aspects of personality—what may be observed by others—though they implied that what a person is, how he thinks and feels, and what is included in his total psychological makeup will be revealed through his speech and behavior. Munn implied this especially when he referred to the "integration of an individual's structures and activities." None, however, spelled out the significance of fundamental and often unconscious drives and wishes stemming from what may be considered the *real* personality—the individual's evaluation of himself, what he wants to be, how he appears to himself and to others, and how he regards his relationship with others.

To fully understand what personality is, the intricacy of its structure, and its all-pervasive influence on the "quality of the individual's total behavior," one must understand its motivational aspects. This becomes apparent when one considers what a false impression one often gets from judgments based solely on the manifest aspects of personality: the individual's speech, behavior, and appearance.

Allport's definition

The deficiencies in the early definitions led to attempts to define personality in such a way as to include its motivational aspects as well as some of its other outstanding characteristics. Of these, the most widely accepted is the short but all-inclusive definition proposed by the late Gordon W. Allport of Harvard University. Most of the definitions accepted today are patterned on Allport's: "Personality is the dynamic organization within the individual of those psychophysical systems that determine his characteristic behavior and thought" (2). An analysis of the key words in this definition will show how comprehensive it is and how much stress Allport placed on motivation.

Organization   "Organization" emphasizes the patterning of the independent parts of the personality structure, each of which has a special relation to the whole. It points out that personality is not just a sum of traits, one added to another, but rather that the different traits or manifest aspects of the personality pattern are held together and influenced by a central core, called the "concept of self."

The distinction between the normal and abnormal personality is to be found in the degree of organization that exists. A normal, healthy personality is a highly correlative structured person. The abnormal personality, by contrast, shows *disorganization,* the severity of the abnormality being directly related to the degree of disorganization.

Dynamic   "Dynamic" refers to the constantly evolving or changing nature of personality. Not only does the personality become more complex in struc-

ture as the individual's physical and psychological characteristics develop, but from time to time and from situation to situation, there are changes in the structural organization. The changes are not radical nor are they necessarily permanent. They do not represent the appearance of new traits. They are, in effect, fluctuations in the intensity of traits already present. They are thus *quantitative* rather than qualitative changes. Radical changes, especially when they occur suddenly and persist, are generally indicative of mental illness, as will be discussed in Chapter 5, Persistence and Change.

The dynamic nature of personality accounts for the difficulty experienced in trying to measure it. By contrast, intelligence, which is relatively stable, can be measured quite accurately.

Psychophysical systems   A psychophysical system is composed of habits, attitudes, emotional states, sentiments, motives, and beliefs, all of which are psychological but have a physical basis in the individual's neural, glandular, or general bodily states. As Allport said, "This term reminds us that personality is neither exclusively mental nor exclusively neural (physical). Its organization entails the functioning of both 'mind' and 'body' in some inextricable unity" (2).

Psychophysical systems are not the product of heredity although they have hereditary foundations. They are the product of learning and they derive from the life experiences of the individual. They are complexes of many elements in mutual interaction. Sometimes they are latent or inactive in the organism. As such, they are "potentials for activity" (2).

Determine   The word "determine" emphasizes the motivational role of the psychophysical systems. Within the individual, these systems lie behind specific acts and influence the form they will take. Once an attitude, belief, habit, sentiment, or some other element of a psychophysical system has been aroused by a stimulus, either from the environment or within the individual, it provokes adjustive and expressive acts which are characteristic forms of expression of that individual. As Allport has explained, "All the systems that comprise personality are to be regarded as *determining tendencies.* They exert a directive influence upon all the adjustive and expressive acts by which the personality comes to be known" (2).

Characteristic   The adjective "characteristic" refers to the distinctiveness or uniqueness of the person's behavior as an expression of the pattern of his particular psychophysical systems. Since no two people, not even identical twins, have exactly the same life experiences, each person learns to respond to his environment in terms of his individual experiences, drives, and interests and the different psychophysical systems that have been built up as a result of learning. As Allport has explained, even the behavior and concepts which people apparently share with others are, in reality, individual. Some, of course, are less "idiosyncratic" than others but none lacks a "personal flavor" (2).

Behavior and thought   Together, behavior and thought are a "Blanket to designate anything whatsoever an individual may do" (2). And what the person does, mainly, is adjust to his environment, though he may also reflect on it. This means that the patterns of behavior, determined by the psychophysical systems within the individual, are not aimless, but are directed toward the specific goal of fitting the individual into the physical and social environments in which he lives.

While personality may be expressed in speech, in reactions to people and things, in mannerisms, in fantasy, and in other ways, all are consciously, subconsciously, or unconsciously directed toward the specific goal of enabling the individual to adjust to his environment. As Allport (2) emphasized:

Above all, adjustment must not be considered as merely reactive adaptation such as plants and animals are capable of. . . . Adjustment to the physical world as well as to the imagined or ideal world—both being factors in the "behavioral environment"—involves mastery *as well as passive adaptation.*

PERSONALITY VERSUS CHARACTER

Personality is often confused with "character." The two are not synonymous, however, and cannot be used interchangeably. Character implies a moral standard and involves a judgment of value (2).

When used in connection with personality, character relates to behavior that is regulated by personal effort and will. *Conscience,* an essential element of character, is a pattern of inhibitory conditionings which control the person's behavior, making it con-

form to the socially approved patterns of the group with which the individual is identified.

PERSONALITY VERSUS INDIVIDUALITY

"Individuality" refers to the uniqueness of personality. According to Allport, "Personality itself is a universal phenomenon though it is found only in individual forms." A person "has many attributes characteristic of the human species, and many that resemble his cultural fellows: *but he weaves them all into a unique idiomatic system.*" Individuality in the personality pattern is just as characteristic as is individuality in appearance. As Allport said, each person is a "unique and never-repeated phenomenon" (2).

Each personality pattern is unique in that it differs from all other patterns in the combination and organization of its constituent traits, in the strength of the different traits, and in its core—the person's concept of himself. While a person's attributes may be qualitatively similar to those of other people, each of his attributes differs *quantitatively* from those of others. You may, for example, find any number of brave men, but each man's bravery will differ quantitatively from that of the others. Figure 1-1 shows how different combinations of the same traits produce individuality.

People are commonly described as belonging to certain "types." One person may be said to be the "ambitious type," another the "morose type," and still another the "stingy type." While it is true that people resemble one another in some respects, this does not mean that they are alike in *all* respects. Each person is to some extent unique. He is an individual, even though in some respects he may be characterized as belonging to some common "type."

Individuality is apparent in the structural and behavioral differences of newborn infants. Some newborns are active, fretful, and prone to excessive crying; some are placid and serene. Some are scrawny and poorly developed while others look as if they might be several weeks old.

Individuality increases as children grow older. Inherent traits begin the process of maturation, and environmental influences, especially social conditions, begin to shape the personality pattern. The hunger drive, for example, is universal and demands satisfaction, but the methods used to satisfy the drive and the

High dominance and low hostility   High dominance and high hostility

Figure 1-1 Individuality in personality often results from different combinations of the same traits.

degree of restraint placed on it when it comes in conflict with other drives are different for each person and are responsible for individual differences in personality patterns.

Causes of individuality

Individuality is a product of both heredity and environment. As Allport pointed out, "Nature's method of sexual reproduction guarantees superlatively novel genetic equipment for every mortal that is born" (2). Each of the 46 chromosomes that appear in the newly formed cell which will eventually develop into a new human being contains approximately 30,000 genes or carriers of individual traits. The likelihood of a duplication of this hereditary endowment, Scheinfeld has estimated, is but 1 in 300,000,000,000,000 (147). The improbability of similarity in heredity has been stated thus by Allport (2):

No two human beings (with the possible exception of identical twins) have even the potentiality of developing alike, especially when to all these genetic differences we add the differences that will occur in the environments and experiences of each mortal person.

Whatever individualizing influences the environment may have, there is a hereditary basis for the personality pattern. As Shirley has pointed out, within every individual there is a core or nucleus of temperamental qualities characteristic of him alone. This nucleus has such a "degree of toughness" that, when "coupled with the dynamic forces of growth, it prevents the individual from ever becoming a complete puppet of the forces that play upon him" (157). The person inevitably reacts in his own individual manner to people, to things, and to other environmental influences.

The uniqueness of each individual's personality is thus derived from a combination of "A factors," or constitutional factors, and a great number of "B factors," or environmental factors, both of which vary from person to person. Furthermore, the effect of environmental stimulation is influenced by other factors, past and present, both constitutional and environmental.

Even when the hereditary endowment is identical, as in identical twins, the chances of an identical environment, of identical life experiences, and of identical reactions and interactions are believed to be zero. This point of view has been expressed thus by Carlson and Stieglitz (36):

We are what we are today, to a great degree, because of what happened to us in our yesterdays, and no two people have had identical sequences of yesterdays. Furthermore, the effect of all these experiences increases with age, because they accumulate.

HOW PERSONALITY CONSCIOUSNESS SHOWS ITSELF

Concern with personality manifest itself in many ways, two of which are especially important. The first is a desire to create a favorable first impression on others, and the second is a desire to judge accurately the personalities of others.

First impressions

A first impression gives others a clue to the personality pattern of the observed individual. They then pigeonhole him as a certain "personality type" and ascribe to him the supposed characteristics of that "type," whether they fit him or not. In addition, the first impression determines what others will expect of the individual, and their expectations, in turn, influence his behavior. As Asch says, "We look at a person and immediately a certain impression of his personality forms itself in us" (13). Thorndike labeled the tendency to form judgments about people on the basis of first impressions the "halo error" of judgment (173).

Subsequent observations and further contacts with the individual may strengthen and enrich a first impression or they may upset it. Several independent impressions of different traits may be added together to form an impression of the individual's total personality.

How first impressions are formed

A first impression may be based on physical appearance, facial features or expression, gestures, dress, name, nationality, race, what the person says and how he says it, what he does and how he does it, or some other physical or psychological characteristic which is identified in the mind of the observer with a certain personality type or stereotype. Figure 1-2 shows some of the many factors that contribute to first impressions.

One's first impression on meeting a person with red hair may be that he has a fiery temper, because, according to tradition, *all* redheads have hot tempers. Or one may regard the rotund body build of the endomorph as a sign that he is lazy. Names that are similar for members of both sexes such as Robin, Leslie, or Lynn, tend to arouse the feeling that the person so named lacks sex appropriateness. An unusual name, like Eula, Romeo, or Apollo, may create the impression that the person is "peculiar." Any

name that carries unpleasant associations, such as Adolph in post-World War II days, leads to unfavorable judgments of the person who bears it.

Many studies have reported on the role of clothing in impression formation. Certain styles or colors may give the impression that a man is not sex appropriate; certain combinations may suggest to others that he is unconventional or sophisticated or interesting. Knowing this, many people deliberately wear the kind of clothes that will create the impression they want to give (82, 145).

Not all characteristics have the same impression-creating value; some are basic and some are secondary. The basic ones are associated in the mind of the observer with such qualities as intelligence, warmth, and coldness—qualities that permeate the person's total behavior. Characteristics that are secondary in impression formation are more superficial; they may be noted only occasionally in the person's behavior—an infrequent temper flare-up or an unusual display of affection, for example.

Often people are not even aware of the role a quality plays in forming their impressions of others. In one experiment McKeachie asked college men to judge the personality patterns of two groups of girls, some of whom used lipstick and some of whom did not. Although none of the men mentioned lipstick as a factor in influencing their judgments, their ratings of the girls definitely reflected its effect. This shows, as McKeachie concluded, that "unnoticed cues may provide the basis for judgments." Further, it shows the influence of superficial qualities (121).

The significance of a particular physical or psychological feature may vary from person to person. In McKeachie's experiment, the men's stereotypes of girls who wore lipstick and of those who did not depended on the men's past experiences (121). To some men, the use of lipstick created the impression that a girl was "fast" or "not nice," while to others it was an indication that the girl was well-groomed. One person may associate "efficient," "orderly," and "skillful" with the basic quality of "quick," while another, as a result of his experiences, may associate being nervous, high-strung, and restless with quickness (13).

Attitudes toward particular qualities also vary from person to person. Attitudes are colored by experience and they have a marked influence on judgments. If a person likes people who are intelligent, for example, his first impression of someone who appears to be intelligent will be influenced by his favor-

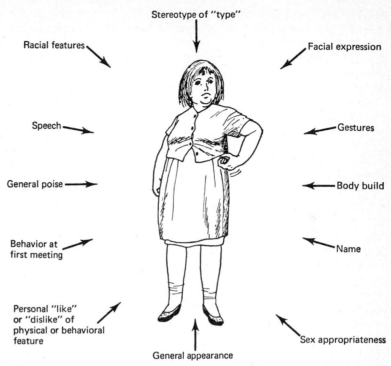

Stereotype of "type"

Racial features

Facial expression

Speech

Gestures

General poise

Body build

Behavior at
first meeting

Name

Personal "like"
or "dislike" of
physical or behavioral
feature

Sex appropriateness

General appearance

Figure 1-2 Some of the many factors contributing to the first impression a person makes on others.

able attitude. Similarly, certain trait words are viewed positively and others negatively. Such trait words as "sincere," "honest," "dependable," and "warm" are liked by most people, while "thoughtless," "rude," "spiteful," and "phony" are disliked because they are associated with disliked personality traits. Physical unattractiveness in the observed individual, it has been found, has more influence on the judgments of others than attractiveness (34). Also if the observer verbalizes his opinion of another, that too influences his first impression (114).

First impressions and reputation

Once an impression of an individual's personality has been formed, the individual gains the reputation of being a certain "type." He is then judged in terms of this reputation. Studies of social acceptance and prejudice demonstrate how difficult it is to change a reputation gained from first impressions. An individual may change his behavior, but that will not guarantee that the reputation he has acquired will automatically change. Only when the attitudes of others toward him change will his reputation change.

Attempts to improve the social acceptance of rejected and neglected children and adolescents have shown how difficult it is to change attitudes. Children who are disliked are avoided by their peers. And without direct experience with the disliked children, the peers have no opportunity to get to know them better and develop more favorable attitudes toward them. Teachers may try to provide such experiences and may even call attention to the improved behavior of the disliked children, but any attempt to force a closer association is only likely to intensify the unfavorable attitudes.

Similarly, prejudice against people identified with a disliked minority group is difficult to combat. Only when the prejudiced person voluntarily has direct personal contacts and pleasant experiences with individuals of the disliked group is he likely to change his unfavorable attitude toward the group and thus break down his prejudice.

Concern about first impressions

Adolescents are well aware of the role played by first impressions in the judgments others make of their personality. This awareness accounts, in part, for the adolescent's preoccupation with his appearance, his interest in clothes, his concern about physical features he regards as unattractive or sex inappropriate, and his desire to be like his peers in appearance, speech, behavior, and interests. Much of the anxiety an adolescent experiences in new social situations stems from his concern about whether he will create a favorable impression and gain the acceptance he craves.

Concern about first impressions is especially great in social encounters with members of the opposite sex. Because of his limited experience, the adolescent is unable to assess his ability to create a favorable first impression in situations where so much depends on having a well-developed repertoire of social skills. Many girls and boys shun situations in which they fear their social inadequacies might lead to an unfavorable first impression.

Adults, too, are concerned about creating a favorable impression on others. Many avoid community organizations or even refuse to attend church because they do not have the appropriate clothes or the money for contributions.

One of the reasons many men dread having to change jobs after age forty is the fear that their gray hair and other physical characteristics associated with the stereotype of "old" will work to their disadvantage. They are afraid that employers will get the impression that they are rigid, slow, and "too old to learn."

Judging others

The second important way in which personality consciousness shows itself is in the desire to judge others accurately. Success in any social situation, whether it be in the home, the school, the community, or the world of work, depends largely upon one's ability to get along well with people. Getting along with others is a two-way proposition: One must not only create a favorable first impression, but one must be able to assess others correctly so as to act in a way that will continue to impress them favorably. The ability to get along harmoniously with others becomes increasingly important as one approaches adulthood.

Studies of social acceptability and leadership reveal the crucial roles played by *social insight*—the ability to size up others—and *self-insight*—the ability to judge oneself accurately (47, 171). Before the child is 8 or 9 years old, he is rarely capable of perceiving the attitudes of others toward him. As a result, his social adjustments are poor and his friendships transitory (93, 103).

With age and social experience, the individual's social insight and self-insight improve; his social acceptance then increases and his friendships become more stable. Persons who are superior in social insight and self-insight are generally more popular and enjoy greater social acceptance than those who lag behind in these personality characteristics.

The ability to judge oneself and others accurately is an essential leadership quality. Even in childhood, the leader is able to assess his own abilities realistically and to evaluate the wishes of the group. He is a good judge of personality. In adolescence and adulthood, leadership is closely related to social insight. Other things equal, the individual who is best able to judge the group with which he is identified is most likely to achieve a leadership role.

Experience with many people in a variety of social situations contributes to the ability to size up the members of a group and predict what their wishes will be. Leaders are chosen, in part, because of their recognizable quality of "sensitivity" to other people.

Early attempts to judge others

Long before the modern approaches to the assessment of personality were developed, many attempts were made to study personality scientifically. However carefully controlled the techniques used in these early attempts were, they cannot justifiably be called scientific; instead, they must be looked upon as psuedoscientific. The three best known and most widely used methods in this category are physiognomy, phrenology, and graphology. The weakness of these methods and of many others is that they are based on the unsubstantiated belief that a close correlation exists between some measured characteristic and the personality pattern.

Physiognomy is a method of judging personality through the measurement and study of facial features. The underlying assumption is that certain physical features are closely correlated with certain personality traits. Following a sex and age group norm, the physiognomist uses such things as the distance between the eyes, the size of the ears in relation to the other features, the size and shape of the chin, and the color of the hair as clues to assess personality characteristics. The belief in physiognomy has been strengthened by widely accepted stereotypes. A person who is tall, has regular facial features, and moves with an air of self-confidence is viewed by others as a likely leader. He is "imposing" and "strong." The "gold-digger syndrome," including such personality traits as being conceited, demanding, and liking men's attention, is associated with high eyebrows, bowed lips, narrowed eyes, visible eyelids, and tilted head. Figure 1-3 illustrates how the phrenologist associates physical features with personality traits.

In *phrenology*, personality is judged by the size and shape of the skull. Elaborate techniques were devised to measure the skull. These measurements were then translated into personality characteristics believed to be associated with them. See Figure 1-4.

In *graphology,* the individual's handwriting is compared with norms which are supposedly associated with specific personality characteristics.

Obstacles to judging others

In everyday life people seldom hesitate to judge the personality patterns of those with whom they come in contact. But accurate judgments are very difficult for two reasons. First, the judgments are often based on the manifest aspects of the personality only and not on the real personality, and second, the judgments are influenced by cultural stereotypes.

REAL VERSUS MANIFEST PERSONALITY   One of the biggest obstacles to an accurate judgment of others is that their *real* personalities are often cloaked by

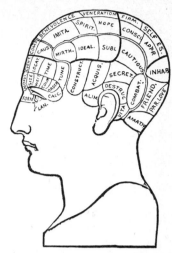

Figure 1-4   In phrenology, an attempt is made to determine the major personality characteristics of a person through the measurement of the size and shape of the skull. Note that the different areas of the brain were believed to control different functions and patterns of behavior. (Adapted from N. J. Hoffman: *The science of the mind applied to teaching.* New York: Fowler and Wells, 1887. Used by permission.)

socially approved behavior patterns. Their *manifest* personalities, on which first impressions are based, may be quite different from their real personalities. First impressions are thus superficial at best. Later contacts may provide a better insight into the real personality pattern. Not always, however. Some people have become so habituated to covering up their real motives and acting always in accordance with social expectations that they themselves do not know what their real personalities are like. Certainly, under such conditions, it is unlikely that observers would be able to judge them accurately.

In the young child, the real and manifest personalities are generally the same. As social contacts widen, however, the child learns to cloak socially inappropriate behavior in order to create a favorable impression on others. Each year, as he becomes more personality-conscious, his motivation to hide undesirable personality traits and behave in a socially approved manner grows stronger, and the cleavage between his real and his manifest personalities becomes greater. Only when the effort to mask the true personality is overdone and results in incongruous behaviors are observers likely to realize that the manifest personality is different from the real one.

How does a person cloak his real personality

Figure 1-3   The "science" of physiognomy is based on the assumption that certain physical features are closely correlated with certain personality traits. According to these beliefs, a person with a large head sticks to and carries out what he has commenced and can be fully relied upon. By contrast, a person with a small head supposedly is fitful and impulsive, like a weather vane that shifts with every changing breeze. (Adapted from O. S. Fowler: *New illustrated self-instructor in phrenology and physiognomy.* New York: S. R. Wells, 1877. Used by permission.)

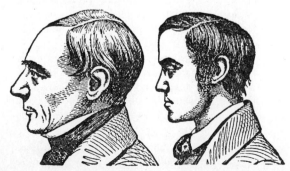

pattern? First impressions as well as subsequent judgments are generally based on appearance, speech, and behavior, and these are the areas where cloaks are most often employed to hide personality traits that might create an unfavorable impression. An individual who suffers from marked feelings of personal inadequacy may succeed in creating an impression of self-confidence and self-assurance by dressing in the latest style, by boasting of his achievements, by making derogatory remarks about others, and by behaving in an aggressive, self-assertive manner. The manifest personality of this person gives no indication that he feels inadequate.

Similarly, parental overprotectiveness, seemingly a sign of strong affection and well-developed "motherliness," may actually stem from feelings of personal inadequacy for the parental role or from a desire to reject a child who has not measured up to parental expectations. Also, prejudice and hostility are often expressions of feelings of personal inadequacy in which minority-group members are used as "scapegoats" (63, 97). Likewise, showing-off and clowning in social situations may be cloaks for feelings of inadequacy; the fat jolly person who is the life of the party is often trying to cover up how guilty he feels about overeating (63, 184).

INFLUENCE OF STEREOTYPES　The accuracy of personality judgments, especially first impressions, is greatly influenced by the observer's acceptance of cultural stereotypes. Stereotypes are accepted so uncritically that they even influence the individual's attitude toward himself and help to shape his own personality.

Stereotypes are a special category of concepts. They have the same general kinds of properties as other concepts and they serve to organize experiences, as do other concepts. They include a moral evaluation, a social class evaluation, and other evaluative comparisons of the individual groups which serve to form the basis of the stereotypes (50, 64, 179). They are crude overgeneralizations of some of the important variables of a group and are used as a convenient shorthand method of characterization (118, 150). A stereotype is evoked by a verbal symbol, such as "Sunday school teacher" or "whore." The verbal symbol mobilizes a complex of ideas and images, plus strong feelings, attitudes, and personal values (50).

Stereotypes may not be completely false, but most of them contain false elements. If one's stereotype of elderly people is developed largely from

observations of those elderly who, because of some physical or mental condition, require institutionalization, the stereotype contains many inaccurate elements (68, 181). Because of these false elements, stereotypes usually incorporate negative value judgments about the members of the stereotyped group. If any of the elements of the stereotype are valid, people tend to accept the stereotype as a whole and to act and make judgments in accordance with it (137, 174). When the stereotype of a group is unfavorable, it is likely to lead to prejudice if it contains references to physical, personal, or intellectual traits. As Vinacke has pointed out, however, stereotypes are by no means the only cause of prejudice. There are many other causes, some of which are more common than stereotyping (179). Perhaps the most common is unpleasant personal experiences.

How stereotypes are acquired　Stereotypes are learned at home, in school, and in the broader social contacts each individual has outside the home. Radio, television, movies, books, and jokes transmit culturally accepted stereotypes from one generation to the next. Characters on the screen are depicted as "types," jokes refer to racial, religious, or family-role "types," and books acquaint the child, from his earliest reading experiences, with the commonly accepted stereotypes of his culture. Fairy tales present a stereotype of the oldest child in the family as shrewd, mistrustful, and stingy, while the youngest is naive, good-natured, and poor (83, 149, 160). The stepmother of the fairy tale is cruel and designing (60, 83, 149, 160). From science fiction, the child acquires a stereotype of the scientist as an antisocial person completely wrapped up in his esoteric research (91).

Today, television is the master creator of stereotypes. Characters are presented as "types," and viewers come to think that people in real-life roles possess the same physical and psychological traits as the characters on TV. Fathers and teachers, for example, appear on the screen in such stereotyped ways that children expect their own fathers and teachers to be situation-comedy types (62).

Long before children think seriously about what their future occupations will be, they develop stereotypes of the people engaged in different occupations. In Figure 1-5, are shown present-day American stereotypes of bank presidents and butlers based on television characters (49).

Categories of stereotypes　Personality stereotypes contain both physical and behavioral traits which are regarded as characteristic of individuals belonging to rather broad categories.

Stereotypes based on *body build* label the fat person as easy-going, cheerful, and placid and the thin person as nervous, tense, and irritable. Those based on *facial features* emphasize the special relevance of skin texture, signs of aging, fullness of the lips, and facial tension in judging personality (47). Variations from the norm carry special meaning. The person with a high forehead is supposed to be highly intelligent, while the person with smaller-than-average ears is supposed to be stingy and miserly (91).

The traditional roles for different *family members* also serve as the basis of personality stereotypes. Because the role of the mother is to care for the child, the stereotype of her personality pattern consists of such traits as kindliness, understanding, helpfulness, and self-sacrifice. The television stereotype of the American mother often shows her as ineffectual and downtrodden (44). The father, by contrast, plays the role of provider, guardian, disciplinarian, and mentor. Personality traits associated with the traditional father role include sternness, authoritarianism, strictness, and punitiveness (111, 153, 176). By the time children reach adolescence, however, they have usually adopted the television and movie stereotype of the father as the "amiable boob of the situation comedies—the ineffectual but lovable bungler" (89).

Stepmothers, according to the stereotype presented in fairy tales and other stories, have personality patterns dominated by such traits as cruelty, selfishness, punitiveness, and craftiness (149, 160). The stereotype of the single woman is that of the bitter, frustrated, and friendless "old maid" (48). The henpecked-husband stereotype of the man married to a domineering woman is very similar except that his personality pattern is characterized by weakness and ineffectuality (168).

Because the prematurely born child plays the role of a helpless dependent, at least during the early years of his life, the stereotype of the premature is that of a physical and mental weakling. The only child is stereotyped as selfish, uncooperative, and aggressive—the "spoiled brat" personality pattern (27). Very similar is the stereotype of the firstborn (165).

Stereotypes about the personality patterns of different *national, regional, racial,* and *religious* groups are widely held. The Scots are tightfisted, the English are home-loving, taciturn, and introverted, the Jews are shrewd and crafty, the Negroes are carefree and irresponsible, the urban dweller is the city slicker and

Figure 1-5 Popular American stereotypes often originate from movies and television. These cartoon-like drawings were used in an experiment to determine how television influences children's occupational knowledge. (Adapted from M. L. DeFleur and L. B. DeFleur: The relative contribution of television as a learning source for children's occupational knowledge. *Amer. sociol. Rev.,* 1967, **32,** 777-789. Used by permission.)

the rural dweller is the country hick. People from the West Coast are breezy, and New Englanders are morose and taciturn.

Social class stereotypes classify middle-class people as conforming and striving, upper-class people as playboys, and lower-class groups as unambitious and careless. From a study of hypothetical rich and poor people, Luft concluded that "income, per se, is a significant variable in determining how one perceives persons. The data tend to support the idea that in our society, personality, like other commodities has a price associated with it" (115).

The *fraternity man* is stereotyped as gregarious, socially oriented, and unscholarly (112). The *perfect lover* is the Nordic-type male, daring, strong, and brave. *Bright* people are stereotyped as weak and eccentric, less handsome and less sociable than the dull or average (52, 109).

Stereotypes of people of *different ages* center mainly on the adolescent and the elderly. Teen-agers are regarded as rebellious, troublesome, and antisocial—as junior public enemies. Old people are stereotyped as has-beens—rigid, slow, ineffectual, worn-out, conservative. Typically, youth are the hope of the future while the elderly are awaiting life's end. In discussing the stereotype of the elderly, Wallin writes, "The public image of the oldster as an irritable, cantankerous, crotchety, eccentric individual who is narrow-minded, rigid, inept, amnestic, disruptive, deteriorated and decrepit needs to be revised" (180).

Occupation-related personality stereotypes are myriad. The professor is absent-minded; the politician is crafty; the artist is emotionally unstable (26). The artist may be activated either by "pure" motivations—not by a desire for material gain and a need to please superiors—or by some psychological disturbance (53).

The recent interest in science and in the training of more scientists has uncovered the fact that the scientist is sometimes thought of as a villainous character with a "Frankenstein personality," sometimes as a "savior of humanity," but most often as a person working in a bureaucratic society with pressures from all sides (91). He is a lonely "brain," so dedicated to his work that he does not know what goes on outside his laboratory (19, 124, 133). By contrast, doctors are stereotyped as assertive leaders, socially responsible and emotionally stable (11, 118).

Stereotypes of individuals identified with particular occupations relate appearance and personality. The country storekeeper has a friendly face; the bank president has a man-of-the-world look; the surgeon has a confident expression (151). The scientist has an absent-minded look, he wears a white coat and glasses, he is elderly or middle-aged, and he is either short and stout or tall and thin (122). The artist is stereotyped as unconventional in both appearance and behavior (26, 53).

Areas of influence of stereotypes In three areas stereotypes have special influence: judgment of others, judgment of self, and judgment of situations. How a person *judges others* is greatly influenced by his acceptance of cultural stereotypes, and his judgments, in turn, affect his attitudes toward others and his behavior.

Prejudice, hostility, and discrimination are common behavior patterns associated with judgments based on stereotypes. Hostility between racial and religious groups comes mainly from judging individuals in terms of the cultural stereotype of the group with which they are associated. Discrimination in the employment of elderly people and of women very often stems from the same cause, lumping everyone who belongs to an identifiable group together, regardless of individual distinctions. Family friction is intensified when any family member's role, whether it be that of the father, the mother, or a teen-age son or daughter, is judged in terms of the stereotype associated with

that role. Class antagonism based on social-class stereotypes is often a cause of labor unrest and even criminality.

Unfavorable *attitudes toward self*, which are expressed in poor personal and social adjustments, are often a reflection of unpleasant stereotypes. The stereotype of the fat person as one who is greedy, self-indulgent, and weak-willed encourages the individual who is fat to feel guilty and ashamed. He then tries to compensate for these unfavorable self-judgments either by withdrawing from the social group or by overemphasizing the favorable behavior patterns associated with the jolly fat person stereotype.

Resentment of the stormy teen-ager stereotype often leads adolescents to play the role associated with that label. When an individual notices in himself the physical changes commonly included in the stereotypes of middle- and old-age, he begins to think of himself as old. He worries, feels insecure, and comes to feel that his future as a member of society is bleak. These attitudes are expressed in unhappiness, loss of motivation to do what he is capable of doing, withdrawal from the social group, and poor personal adjustments.

Stereotypes color the individual's *judgment of a situation* and affect his characteristic method of reacting. If parents accept the stereotype of a "good parent" as one who is strict and authoritarian, they will not feel guilty if they cope with their children's misbehavior by using harsh corporal punishment. If they accept the stereotype of a "good parent" as one who is permissive and indulgent, however, they will judge the home atmosphere as happy only if the children feel free to express themselves openly.

Studies of vocational choice reveal a marked influence of stereotypes. Many young people reject science as a career because of the unfavorable stereotype of the scientist. Furthermore, girls often urge the boys they date to avoid scientific careers because they do not want to marry a person who, according to the stereotype, neglects his family, has few outside interests and social contacts, and is uninterested in financial rewards or fame (124, 151). Similarly, the cultural stereotype of the artist leads many parents to advise their sons against entering an artistic profession. Fathers especially are likely to regard male artists as sexually inappropriate (26).

Even before they reach adolescence, most boys and girls have acquired superficial, misleading, and highly glamorized stereotypes about the world of work from movies, television, and other mass media. As a result, many young employees become disillusioned vocational misfits.

Counteracting the influence of stereotypes Many stereotypes are learned early in life as part of the cultural heritage. They are presented in an authoritative way by parents, teachers, peers, and the mass media and are accepted uncritically. As time passes, they are reinforced by broader social pressures.

How firmly entrenched stereotypes may become has been demonstrated by several experiments designed to change them. In one experiment, "good mothers" who used traditionally approved methods of child rearing were advised to deal with some of their problems by substituting new, more democratic training methods for the traditional ones. The reasons for recommending the new methods were carefully explained and apparently understood. However, out of a group of 57 mothers, only 8 were willing to adopt the new procedures (30). In another experiment, questionnaires to determine graduate students' stereotypes of old age were administered before and after a course devoted exclusively to explaining the scientific facts about old age. At the end of the course, little change was found in the students' attitudes toward the elderly. Arnhoff and Lorge concluded that "whether dissemination of factual information, in and of itself, can change the negative attitude is still moot" (11). Sykes has suggested that before the belief in stereotypes can be changed, attitudes resulting from the stereotypes must be changed (169).

PERSONOLOGY

Because of the overriding importance of personality in everyone's life, scientists and laymen alike want to know more about it and how to control its development. This interest is not of recent origin. Historical records show that personality studies date back to the ancient Greeks. Through the ages the desire to understand what causes differences in personality has motivated investigative attempts, ranging from pure speculation to experiments involving the use of highly controlled measuring techniques.

Since World War I, scientific interest in personality measurement—rating the individual in relation to some standard or norm—has increased our knowledge and has motivated study in other areas. Scientists have tried to discover what personality is, what its determinants are, how it develops, why individual differences exist, and what constitutes a normal and an abnormal personality.

Since personality is very complex and is made up of many components, some of which are objective, observable, and measureable (e.g., physique, aptitudes, and habits) while others are subjective and therefore less easily studied and measured (e.g., motives, attitudes, and aspirations), methods of studying personality have not been limited to measuring the individual's characteristic behavior or the degree of his adjustment to different life situations. Instead, an attempt has been made to study the development of personality and the determinants of this development.

The systematic study of personality in all its aspects has been labeled "personology." This is not only one of the newest branches of psychological research but also one of the most active and productive branches. In addition, personology draws on many other fields of scientific research for information that will add to the understanding of personality. To date it has derived most of its material from psychology (normal, abnormal, clinical, developmental, differential, and social), the social sciences (especially sociology, gerontology, and anthropology), and medicine (psychiatry, psychosomatics, pediatrics, and geriatrics). Throughout this book, information derived from studies in all these areas will be used to interpret the meaning of personality, its development, the most important determinants of its development, and the characteristics and causes of normal and abnormal personalities.

SUMMARY

1 Personality consciousness in the American culture of today stems from the belief that a pleasing personality is a guarantee of success and happiness. Personality is of great significance in all areas of our complex society.

2 Early scientific concepts of personality emphasized the manifest aspects of personality, what may be observed by others. These early concepts came from the Greek word *persona,* meaning a mask used by dramatic actors to hide their own identity on the stage. This meaning is similar in many respects to the popular, unscientific concept of personality held by many today.

3 Present-day scientific concepts of personality stress the motivational as well as the behavioral aspects of personality. They emphasize not only how the individual appears to others but what he actually is and why he is as he is. Most of the scientific definitions of personality include the main points stressed by Allport when he said that personality is the "dynamic organization within the person of those psychophysical systems that determine his characteristic behavior and thought."

4 Character and personality are not synonymous. Rather, character is the moral aspect of personality or behavior that is controlled by "conscience."

5 Individuality refers to the uniqueness of personality which makes each person a "never-repeated phenomenon." It is observable in the appearance and behavior patterns of the newborn infant and becomes more pronounced with each passing year. Individuality is due more to quantitative differences in personality traits and to different combinations of traits than to qualitative differences in the traits. It is caused partly by hereditary differences resulting from differences in combinations of genes and partly by environmental factors that influence the unique hereditary potentials differently.

6 Personality consciousness shows itself in two outstanding ways: the person's desire to create a favorable impression on others and his desire to judge accurately the personality of other people.

7 First impressions, which are based on appearance, behavior, speech, and many other factors, result in a person being categorized as belonging to a certain personality "type" because he has some characteristics associated with that type. A person typed in this way develops a reputation which is used to judge him in the future and which, once established, is difficult or impossible to change. Knowing this to be true, most people try to create a favorable first impression.

8 Being able to judge others accurately is an aid to making good social adjustments and to receiving favorable judgments by others. The age-old interest in judging others accurately has led to many scientific and pseudoscientific methods of judging personality. Three of the earliest and most popular pseudoscientific methods were physiognomy—the judgment of personality from a study of facial features; phrenology—the judgment of personality from the size and shape of the head; and graphology—the judgment of personality from a diagnosis of the person's handwriting.

9 These attempts to judge personality and others of a more scientific nature have been hampered by two major obstacles. The first is the difficulty of distinguishing between the person's real personality, or what the person actually is, and his manifest personality, or the pattern of behavior he shows to others, cloaking his real motives and acting in accordance with social expectations in order to gain acceptance.

10 The second major obstacle to judging personality accurately comes from the acceptance of cultural stereotypes which influence the first impression the person makes of others, his opinion and treatment of them, and his opinion of himself.

11 Cultural stereotypes are acquired by social learning in the home, the school, the neighborhood, and the community at large and from the mass media. They cover a broad variety of people in different life roles. There are stereotypes of family members, of different occupations, of different religious, racial, national, and socioeconomic groups, and of different ages. False or partially false stereotypes about personality are so widely held and so deeply embedded in tradition that they are difficult to correct. Their influence distorts personality judgments and affects the individual's treatment of others as well as his attitudes toward self.

12 Because of the important role personality plays in the lives of all people and because of the strong desire on the part of psychologists and laymen to know more about personality and how to control its development, a new branch of psychology—*personology*—has developed. Research in personology covers all aspects of personality, supplemented by information from other areas of psychology, from the social sciences, and from medicine.

the personality pattern

The personality pattern is composed of traits, or specific qualities of behavior, which characterize the individual's unique adjustment to life as shown in his behavior and thoughts. The traits, however, are not merely added one to another. Rather, they are organized and integrated into a meaningful pattern. The definition of personality given in Chapter 1 emphasizes this by the use of the phrase "dynamic organization" (5).

The "core" or center of gravity of the personality pattern is the individual's concept of himself as a person as related to the world in which he lives. The quality of his behavior, expressed in the way he adjusts to people and things in his environment, is related to and, to a large extent, determined by his self-concept (27, 62, 93).

ROLES OF HEREDITY AND LEARNING

The personality pattern is founded on the individual's hereditary endowment. But it is not inherited. It is the product of learning during the course of prolonged social relationships with people both within and outside the home. As Anderson has pointed out, "Personality becomes organized around nodal points or experiences which have received particular emphasis and much reiteration" (13).

Three major factors are at work in determining the development of the personality pattern: *first,* the individual's hereditary endowment; *second,* early experiences within the family; and *third,* important events in later life outside the home environment (4). Thus the personality pattern is not the product of learning exclusively or of heredity exclusively. Instead, it comes from an interaction of the two. How different environmental influences affect personality development is illustrated in Figure 2-1.

Role of heredity

The personality pattern is inwardly determined by and closely associated with the maturation of the physical and mental characteristics which constitute the individual's hereditary endowment. Although social and other environmental factors affect the form the personality pattern takes, it is not instilled or controlled from without but evolves from the potentials within the individual. The principal raw materials of personality—physique, intelligence, and temperament—are the result of heredity. How they will develop will depend on environmental influences. This will be discussed in detail in Chapter 4, Molding the Personality Pattern.

The significance of the hereditary foundations in determining the personality pattern has been stressed by Rainwater (146):

Personality is formed from the interaction of significant figures (first the mother, later the father and siblings, later extrafamilial figures) with the child. The child brings to this interaction a certain biological constitution, certain needs and drives, and certain intellectual capacities which determine his reactions to the way in which he is acted upon by these significant figures.

In this interaction between hereditary and environmental factors, the individual selects from his environment what fits his needs and wants and rejects what does not. Therefore, the personality pattern develops from interactions with the environment which the individual himself has initiated.

One reason for stressing the role of heredity in the development of the personality pattern is to point up the fact that the pattern is subject to limitations. A person who inherits a low-grade intelligence, for example, cannot, even under the most favorable environmental conditions, develop a personality pattern that will lead to as good a personal and social adjustment as a person who inherits a higher level of intellectual ability.

Furthermore, recognition of the limitations imposed by heredity underlines the fact that people are not totally free to choose and develop the kind of personality pattern they want. Using intelligence again as an illustration: A person with a low-grade intelligence cannot develop the personality pattern of a leader even though he wants to do so and even though his desire gives him a strong motivation to try to develop the personality traits essential for leadership.

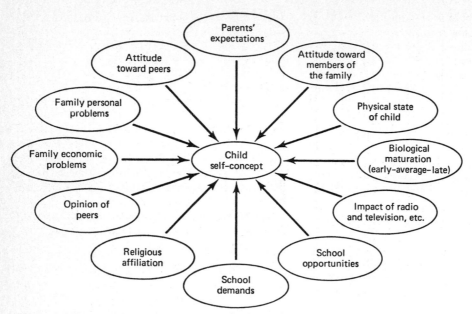

Figure 2-1 Different environmental influences, within and outside the home, that affect the developing self-concept. (Adapted from L. D. Crow and A. Crow: *Child development and adjustment*. New York: Macmillan, 1962. Used by permission.)

Role of learning

Learning, in its various forms, especially conditioning, imitation, and training, or learning under the guidance and direction of another, plays a prime role in the development of the personality pattern. Attitudes toward self, characteristic modes of responding to people and situations, attitudes toward the assumption of socially approved roles, and methods of personal and social adjustment, including the use of defense mechanisms, are learned through repetition and are reinforced by the satisfaction they bring. Gradually, the self-concept is built up and the learned responses become habitual, constituting the "traits" in the individual's personality pattern.

Social pressures within and outside the home determine what traits will be incorporated into the pattern. If a boy is encouraged to be aggressive, for example, because aggressiveness is considered a sex-appropriate trait for males, he will learn to react to people and things in an aggressive way. If, on the other hand, aggressiveness wins social disapproval or does not bring satisfaction, the person will try out other methods of adjustment until he finds one that meets his needs. He will then repeat it until it becomes a habitual form of behavior.

Knowing that learning plays a role in the development of the personality pattern is important for two reasons. *First,* it tells us that control can be exercised to ensure that the individual will develop the kind of personality pattern that will lead to good personal and social adjustments. This control will come from seeing to it that the person has learning experiences that will lead to a healthy self-concept and to socially approved modes of adjustment. As was stressed earlier, however, hereditary limitations must be considered in controlling the individual's learning experiences.

Second, it tells us that unhealthy self-concepts and socially unacceptable patterns of adjustment can be changed and modified. As in all learning, the sooner a change or modification is attempted, the easier it will be.

ELEMENTS OF THE PERSONALITY PATTERN

The personality pattern is composed of a core or center of gravity, called the "concept of self," and an integrated system of learned responses, called "traits." These are interrelated, with the core influencing the traits, which are the individual's characteristic methods of adjustment to life situations. To show the interrelationship, the pattern can be compared to a wheel in which the hub represents the concept of self and the spokes represent the traits. Just as the spokes of a wheel are held in position and, thus, influenced by the hub, so the traits are influenced by the concept of self.

The interrelationship is illustrated in Figure 2-2. If a person sees himself as a martyr, this self-concept, whether justified by facts or not, will have a profound influence on his behavior. In time, his behavior patterns will become so well learned from repetition that they will constitute his characteristic methods of adjustment and occur in a predictable manner. Others will then judge him as "feeling sorry for himself."

How the personality pattern develops and how the interrelationship between the concept of self and the different traits functions will now be examined in a detailed analysis of the two major elements of the pattern.

Concept of self

Many years ago, James called the core of the personality pattern, which provides its unity, the "self." Later, Freud referred to it as the "ego," and Sullivan used the phrase, the "self system" (75, 173). According to James, a person's self is the "sum-total of all that he can call his" (97).

In recent decades, what a person "can call his" has been spelled out in more definite and specific terms. It has been referred to as his "attitude toward self" (121), as an "organized configuration of perceptions of self" (139), as "those perceptions, beliefs, feelings, attitudes, and values which the individual views as part or characteristic of himself" (140), as the "organization of qualities the individual attributes to himself" (110), and as a "system of central meaning he has about himself and his relation to the world about him" (31).

Allport (5) has described the self-concept in this way:

The self is something of which we are immediately aware. We think of it as the warm, central, private region of our life. As such it plays a crucial part in our consciousness (a concept broader than self), in our personality (a concept broader than consciousness), and in our organism (a concept broader than personality). Thus it is some kind of core in our being.

How broad and all-inclusive the concept of self is has been emphasized by Jersild (99):

The self, as it finally evolves, is made up of all that goes into a person's experiences of his individual existence. It is a person's "inner world." It is a composite of a person's thoughts and feelings, strivings and hopes, fears and fantasies, his view of what he is, what he has been, what he might become, and his attitudes pertaining to his worth.

The importance of the self-concept in the personality pattern is evidenced by the labels usually given it. It is referred to as the core or center of gravity of the pattern (27) or as the "keystone of personality" (37). Its importance stems from its influence over the quality of a person's behavior and his methods of adjustment to life situations. As Lewin has pointed out, it gives "consistency to the personality" (117).

Figure 2-2 A person's concept of self influences his characteristic patterns of adjustment.

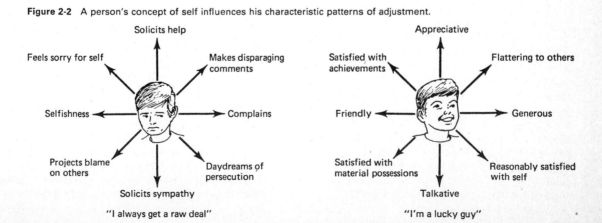

Stagner has emphasized the stability it contributes to personality (167).

Components of the self-concept

The concept of self has three major components: the perceptual, the conceptual, and the attitudinal. The *perceptual component* is the image the person has of the appearance of his body and of the impression he makes on others. It includes the image he has of the attractiveness and sex appropriateness of his body, the importance of the different parts of his body, such as his muscles, to his behavior and the prestige they give him in the eyes of others. The perceptual component is often called the "physical self-concept."

The *conceptual component* is the person's conception of his distinctive characteristics, his abilities and disabilities, his background and origins, and his future. It is often called the "psychological self-concept" and is composed of such life-adjustment qualities as honesty, self-confidence, independence, courage, and their opposites.

Included in the *attitudinal component* are the feelings a person has about himself, his attitudes about his present status and future prospects, his feelings about his worthiness, and his attitudes of self-esteem, self-reproach, pride, and shame. As the person reaches adulthood, the attitudinal component includes also the beliefs, convictions, values, ideals, aspirations, and commitments which make up his philosophy of life.

Kinds of self-concept

James was the first to suggest that a person has many "selves." The "real self," for example, is what a person really believes he is, his "ideal self" is the person he aspires to be, and his "social self" is what he believes others think of him and how they perceive him (97).

Recent studies reveal that the self-concept does indeed take different forms. Each form falls into one of four major categories which relate to the physical as well as the psychological self-concepts. The four categories of self-concept are the basic, the transitory, the social, and the ideal.

THE BASIC SELF-CONCEPT The basic self-concept corresponds to James's concept of the "real self"; it is the person's concept of what he really is. It includes his perception of his appearance, his recognition of his abilities and disabilities and of his role and status in life, and his values, beliefs, and aspirations.

The basic self-concept tends to be realistic. The person sees himself as he really is, not as he would like to be. Sometimes the basic self-concept is to the person's liking. More often, it is not. The person finds flaws in himself which make him unhappy and dissatisfied and which he would like to change. Even when the treatment he receives from others would seem to encourage greater self-acceptance, a person may cling to his basic self-concept.

THE TRANSITORY SELF-CONCEPT In addition to a basic self-concept, a person has a transitory self-concept. James first suggested this when he referred to the "self he hopes he now is" and the "self he fears he now is" (97). This means that a person has a self-concept which he holds for a time and then relinquishes.

Transitory self-concepts may be favorable or unfavorable, depending largely on the situation in which the person finds himself momentarily. They are generally influenced by some passing mood or emotional state or by a recent experience. They are transitory and unstable because they lack the perspective found in the basic self-concept.

A person who is well and happy, who is accepted by others, and who achieves what he has set out to do may have a transitory self-concept that is more favorable than his basic self-concept. Temporarily, he sees himself as the "self he hopes he now is." Changes in circumstances, in mood, and in achievement are likely to lead to a less favorable self-concept and he will then see himself as "he fears he now is" (97).

People differ in the frequency with which their behavior is guided and influenced by transitory self-concepts. Some experience frequent and intense fluctuations while others experience only slight and occasional shifts.

THE SOCIAL SELF-CONCEPT The social self-concept is based on the way the individual believes others perceive him, depending on their speech and actions. It is usually referred to as a "mirror image" (23, 98, 110, 183). If a child is constantly told that he is "naughty," he soon develops a concept of himself as a naughty child. If the social group regards members of a gang as "tough," they come to think of themselves as tough and act accordingly. The child whose parents are always telling him how bright he is develops a self-concept that contains some elements of false pride.

Social self-concepts may in time develop into basic self-concepts if the person believes that he is as others see him.

Since social self-concepts derive from social interactions, whether the concepts will be favorable or not depends on how the social group treats the individual. A person who as a child or adolescent was discriminated against because of his race, color, religion, or social class will usually have a far less favorable concept of himself than the person who was not subjected to such discrimination.

In early childhood, before the child is capable of assessing himself in terms of his abilities and disabilities, his needs and wants, his aspirations and values, he thinks of himself as he believes others think of him. His social self-concept is thus dominant. It is developed earlier than the basic self-concept and is the foundation for the basic self-concept. Only after the child is mature enough to understand and interpret the speech and actions of others is he able to judge the accuracy of his social self-concept and develop a basic self-concept.

People build up different social self-concepts, depending on the kinds of social groups—home, peer, or community—with which they are most often associated. A young child's social self-concept is influenced most by his relationship with his mother because he spends most of his time with her. How the different self-concepts are developed will be discussed later in the section, Hierarchy of Self-concepts.

The effect of the social self-concept on the behavior of the individual will depend largely on how important the opinions of others are to him *at that time* and on what person or persons are most influential in his life *at that time.* Jersild (99) has explained the matter in this way:

If a child is accepted, approved, respected, and liked for what he is, he will be helped to acquire an attitude of self-acceptance and respect for himself. But if the significant people in his life—at first his parents and later his teachers, peers, and other persons who wield an influence—belittle him, blame him and reject him, the growing child's attitudes toward himself are likely to become unfavorable. As he is judged by others, he will tend to judge himself.

Since the young child is most responsive to his mother, his social self-concept is largely based on her opinion of him or what he *believes* to be her opinion. His social self-concept may be transitory or per-

manent, depending on the consistency of the mother's treatment of him. In adolescence, the social self-concept is derived from the opinions of the peer group as a whole—the "generalized others" (149). In adulthood the effect of the self-concept on behavior is influenced by the strength of the person's desire to win the attention, approval, and acceptance of others. A man who is anxious to be a civic leader will be greatly influenced by the opinions of members of the community at large.

THE IDEAL SELF-CONCEPT The ideal self-concept is made up of perceptions of what a person aspires to be and what he believes he ought to be. It may be related to the physical self-image, the psychological self-image, or both. It may be realistic in the sense that it is within the reach of the person, or it may be so unrealistic that it can never be achieved in real life.

In childhood, the discrepancy between the ideal self-concept and the basic, the transitory, and the social self-concepts is usually large. Toward adolescence, the discrepancy normally diminishes as the other self-concepts become stronger and play a larger role in determining the person's image of himself. In adulthood, and certainly by middle age, the ideal self-concept usually has little impact on the person's concept of himself.

Almost everyone has an ideal self-concept in addition to his basic and transitory self-concepts. Whether the ideal self-concept is realistic or unrealistic is determined chiefly by whether the basic or transitory self-concept dominates. If the basic self-concept dominates, the ideal self-concept is likely to be realistic because the basic self-concept is founded on a more realistic appraisal of one's capacities and abilities. Whether an unrealistic ideal self-concept will be unrealistically high or low will depend on whether the transitory self-concepts are mainly favorable or unfavorable.

Development of self-concepts The newborn infant's state of consciousness is a "big, blooming, buzzing confusion" (97). The infant is not aware of himself as a person nor does he differentiate himself from environment. As Allport (5) has emphasized:

One thing is quite certain: the young infant is not aware of himself as a self. He does not separate the "me" from the rest of the world. And it is precisely this separation that is the pivot of later life. . . . The infant, though presumably conscious, lacks self-consciousness completely.

Gradually, because of the sensations he experiences from within his body and from his environment, he begins to differentiate between the two. This is the beginning of the long process of developing a concept of self. As Jersild (99) has written:

The development of self-awareness does not occur in all-or-none fashion which would enable us to assume that up to this point the child does not possess it but beyond this point he does. It is more likely that a child perceives different aspects of what he eventually calls himself with varying degrees of clarity at different times. . . . The process of self-discovery is actively going on at least as long as the child is developing or discovering new potentialities, and in a healthy person the discovery of self continues as long as he lives.

Each experience which helps to mold the self-concept has a definite sociocultural reference station. That is, it originates from and is influenced by the interaction of the individual and specific factors in the social and cultural environment in which he grows up. The various concepts of self, resulting from a wide variety of sociocultural interactions, are gradually fused into a generalized self-concept.

Hierarchy of self-concepts The organization of the different self-concepts acquired from a wide variety of experiences is hierarchical. As in all hierarchies, the foundations are laid first. Each new self-concept is interrelated with those which have already been formed and exerts an influence on others which are formed later.

The *primary* or first self-concept is shaped by the social experiences the person has in the home during his early years. As was stressed earlier, it is made up of many individual concepts, each resulting from different experiences with different people within the family group. The frequency and quality of the child's relationships with family members will determine how important a role they play in the formation of his primary self-concept. The primary self-concept in the hierarchy is, thus, a "mirror image" or a social self-concept.

As his social contacts increase, the child acquires other "mirror images" of himself. In the hierarchy of the self-concept, these are *secondary*. They are called secondary because they are formed later than the primary self-concept and are influenced by it.

The primary self-concept frequently determines the selection of situations in which the secondary self-concepts will be formed. For example, if in the home the child has developed a primary self-concept whose dominant elements support his feelings of self-importance, he will select as playmates those who treat him in much the way that the members of his family treat him. If the primary self-concept is dominated by feelings of personal inadequacy and inferiority, the child will seek out playmates whose attitudes make him feel more adequate or he will become a social isolate and try to avoid contacts with his peers.

Just about the time the child becomes mature enough to evaluate himself in relation to others, at the age of 5 or 6, his mental capacities have developed to the point where he is able to imagine things not immediately present. One way in which he expresses this ability is to imagine how he would like to be. This is the beginning of the development of the ideal self-concept, the concept of self that is different from and superior to the basic self-concept or the mirror images he does not find to his liking.

The ideal self-concept is, of course, influenced by concepts formed earlier. But what is more worth noting is that it becomes so closely interrelated with the other self-concepts that it forms an important part of the hierarchy and, in turn, influences earlier mirror images and basic self-concepts. A highly unrealistic ideal self-concept, for example, will increase a person's dissatisfaction with his mirror images and basic self-concept so much that he will become self-rejectant. This will have an adverse effect on his behavior and on his personal and social adjustments.

Because of its hierarchical and interrelated structure, the self-concept, once it is well developed, is very resistant to change. If a change is to be successful, it must start with the foundation concepts in the hierarchy, the mirror images, which have such a marked influence on the form the basic and ideal self-concepts will take.

Making a change in the mirror images can be done most successfully by changing the social milieu—the home, the school, or the community—in which the unfavorable mirror images were developed. This is not always possible, especially during the early years of life when the hierarchy of self-concepts is being formed. When the person is older and has greater personal control over his environment, it may be too late to make a radical change because by then the self-concept is well established. Persistence and change in the personality pattern will be discussed in detail in Chapter 5.

If a person is to be happy and well adjusted, all the self-concepts in the hierarchy must be integrated. How well integrated they will be will depend to a large extent on the degree of continuity in the sociocultural environments—the home and the people and groups outside the home—that give rise to the concepts.

When there is little continuity between the home and the rest of the environment, a person must shift from one self-concept to another. For example, if the child is the center of attention at home but is only a tiny figure in a large group at school, his concept of himself in the two environments will be radically different. If such discontinuities occur frequently, the person will find it difficult to form an integrated self-concept. He will make poor adjustments and be unhappy. He may try to avoid situations that contribute to his poor self-concepts or he may, by aggressive and even unsocial behavior, try to win the favor of peers or others who ignore or reject him. In either case, he is hardly likely to improve his social relationships or achieve an integrated self-concept.

Pattern of development   The various self-concepts described in the preceding sections develop at different times, depending on the individual's life experiences. But the pattern of development from one person to another is fairly predictable.

PHYSICAL AND PSYCHOLOGICAL SELF-CONCEPTS Physical self-concepts are usually acquired before psychological self-concepts. The child thus has an image of his physical characteristics before he is aware of his abilities and disabilities, his wants and needs, his roles in life, and his aspirations. In building up his physical self-concepts, however, the child is *not* emotionally uninvolved. In discussing the physical self-concept, Jersild has stressed that "the body image is not just a photographic impression: in common with all other aspects of the way in which a person views himself, it is likely to be colored by feelings and attitudes" (99). Emotions also intrude on the development of psychological self-concepts. In fact, this explains why physical and psychological self-concepts are so persistent and so difficult to change.

Gradually, the physical and psychological self-images fuse. When this happens, usually during late childhood, the feelings and attitudes accompanying the self-images will be fused also. Before the fusion, the young child perceives the physical and psychological aspects of himself as quite distinct. Each year, as his intellectual capacities develop and as his experiences broaden, new qualities and new potentials are added to his gradually fusing physical and psychological self-concepts. By late childhood, when the fusion is completed, he thinks of himself as one whole and single unit.

The *physical* self-concept begins to develop when the baby discovers the difference between himself and others. A fairly predictable pattern has been reported for the baby's self-discovery from looking at himself in a mirror. At the age of 18 weeks, the baby notices himself in the mirror. Between 22 and 23 weeks, he plays with his image as if it were someone else. This has been called the "playmate stage" of self-discovery. Between the sixth and seventh months, the baby tries to relate his mirror image to himself. This he does by repetitive activity, such as opening and closing his mouth, or by moving his hand or foot while observing his mirror image to see if there is a relationship between what he is doing and what he sees. The final stage, called the "coy stage," occurs around the ninth month when the baby seems to derive great pleasure from making faces and then laughing at them. By the time the child is a year old, his behavior shows true self-recognition. This is the basis from which his physical self-concept develops (56).

That a baby can distinguish himself from others even before he recognizes himself as a person is apparent in the shyness he shows in the presence of others (11). Shyness appears first around the age of 6 months and may be accompanied by crying if someone frowns or speaks harshly to the child. During the second and third years, the young child's awareness of the difference between himself and others is expressed in negativism and in many other ways (18, 99).

By comparing the size and shape of his own body with the bodies of other children and by hearing comments about his looks, the young child adds new meaning to his developing physical self-concept. Awareness of sex differences and of the clothing and hair styles associated with members of the two sexes comes around the age of 3 or 4 years (77, 143). Also at this time, the child begins to identify himself as belonging to a certain ethnic or racial group, basing his identification on such physical characteristics as skin color and hair. By the age of 5 years, he expresses his self-concept in ethnic terms, such as white, black, Italian, or Jewish. When a child has parents of different ethnic backgrounds, he may not be able to identify himself as belonging to a specific group (145).

Physical self-concepts change as bodily changes occur. When bodily changes are slow and relatively minor, as in later childhood and early adulthood, physical self-concepts remain fairly stable. At puberty, however, the individual's attention is focused on his rapidly changing appearance, and his physical self-concept changes from that of a child to that of an adult or near-adult. The person approaching old age likewise changes his physical self-concept. He may reluctantly give up thinking of himself as an adult in the prime of life and come to see himself as elderly and unattractive.

The *psychological self-concept* includes the person's attitudes toward his abilities and disabilities, his special aptitudes, his roles in life, his responsibilities, and his hopes and aspirations. This self-concept develops later than the physical self-concept. Before it can develop, the person must have sufficient reasoning ability to be able to assess his capacities and abilities in terms of socially approved standards and compare himself with others. Figure 2-3 shows how the psychological self-concept develops.

Social contacts with siblings provide the basis for the individual's first assessment of his abilities. The child compares himself—what he can do and how well he can do it—with both younger and older siblings.

Later, he compares himself with children outside the home. Still later, as an adolescent and as an adult, he compares his abilities with those of his classmates in high school and college, of his coworkers in the business world, and of members of the community with whom he comes in contact in social activities.

Concepts of the roles one is expected to play, of responsibilities, and of aspirations follow much the same pattern of development. They originate in the individual's relationships with his parents and teachers, and are later molded by contacts with peers, by reading, movies, television, and other forms of mass communication, and by members of the opposite sex for whom the individual has a romantic attachment. As was pointed out earlier, a girl who thinks scientists make "bad" husbands will encourage her boyfriend not to enter a scientific career. Similarly, men's aspirations are often influenced by the aspirations of their wives.

SOCIAL SELF-CONCEPTS   Early social self-concepts or "mirror images" develop in the home. Because the child's relationship with the mother is the first significant relationship in his life, what the mother thinks of the child, how she treats him, and how he interprets her treatment of him—all have a profound influence on how he thinks of himself. Should the mother be an unstable person, the young child will not only have a confused image of himself but will develop feelings of anxiety because he does not know where he stands in the mother's affection. Should he feel that his mother rejects him or prefers another sibling, his self-

Figure 2-3 The psychological self-concept develops from a person's comparison of himself with others.

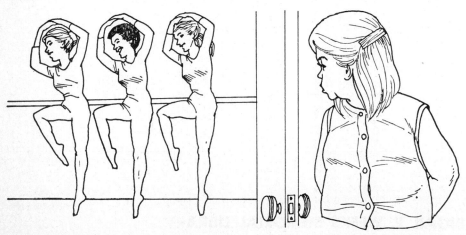

concept will be characterized by feelings of martyr-dom.

When the young child builds up social relation-ships with other family members, their treatment of him contributes to his developing self-concept. As a group, girls tend to develop less favorable self-concepts in the home than boys. The treatment that brings this about will be discussed in a later chapter.

The stability of the home also affects the de-veloping self-concept. If a child is suddenly deprived of his mother's love because of separation, the effect on his developing self-concept is more damaging than parental rejection. Regardless of the cause of the separation, he interprets it to mean rejection. The younger the child, the more damaging to his self-concept is family disorganization caused by death, desertion, or divorce (115, 164, 198). The arrival of a stepparent, especially a stepmother, may eliminate, minimize, or intensify the ill effects of disorganization, depending on the relationship between the child and the stepparent. The younger the child, the better the relationship is likely to be and the more favorable the effect on the child's developing self-concept (66, 164).

As the child comes in contact with more and more people outside the home, how they treat him, what they say to or about him, and what status he achieves in the group may strengthen the social self-concept developed in the home or may modify it in some other way. The attitudes of outsiders, as the child interprets them, exert a greater influence on his self-concept than the experiences he shares with them.

Both in the home and outside, the child learns that people have certain attitudes about members of the two sexes, about members of different races and religions, about the socioeconomic level of a person's family, and about people of different ages. He dis-covers that these attitudes are widely held and that they influence the way people act toward and treat those who are identified with the various groups. He thus learns the stereotypes of his culture and the social attitudes held toward those who fit into the stereotype patterns.

Stereotypes are not learned quickly. They may not be completely assimilated until late adolescence. At first, the child thinks of them as applying to others, not to himself. Only when he becomes aware of how others think about him does he consider himself in terms of the stereotypes or other culturally accepted attitudes. The child may know, for example, what the socially approved sex roles are by the time he is 5 or 6

years old. But this knowledge will not influence his developing self-concept until his own sex-role be-havior arouses approval or disapproval of others.

Similarly, he may recognize his ethnic identity or religious affiliation, but it will have little effect on his self-concept unless others express favorable or un-favorable attitudes toward it. Unfavorable social atti-tudes leading to discrimination and rejection will dam-age the child's self-concept, build up his resentment, and give rise to feelings of inadequacy.

Social-class discrimination affects the self-concept in the same way as ethnic or religious dis-crimination. It is likely to have a greater influence in adolescence and adulthood, however, than in child-hood.

By adolescence, the social self-concept or mir-ror image is essentially completed, though it may later change somewhat if the person's social experiences are markedly different from those previously en-countered. This point of view has been emphasized by Wylie (196):

By the time a child has reached adolescence he has formed a more or less precise image of what he and his culture expect of him as an adult. One of the principal problems for an adolescent then is to con-duct his life so that he has the feeling he is achieving this ideal image of himself.

Mirror images are of supreme importance in the development of the self-concept. *First,* formed early in life, they are the primary concepts of self. As such, they provide the foundations for later concepts of self. In addition, they influence the kinds of social relation-ships the person will select, and thus tend to be reinforced.

Second, as already mentioned, during the early years when the mirror images are being formed, chil-dren often misinterpret what others say or do. They get false impressions of what others think of them and misconstrue others' attitudes toward them. As a re-sult, their mirror images lead to unrealistic self-appraisals which, in turn, form the basis for unrealistic self-concepts.

Unfortunately, few adults are aware that chil-dren build up unfavorable self-concepts as a result of misinterpretations of adult attitudes. Few are aware of the lasting effects of the unfavorable self-concepts. And of even greater consequence, few adults try to control the development of children's self-concepts to ensure that they will be both realistic and favorable. The damaging effects of the haphazard, uncontrolled development of self-concepts based on mirror images acquired early in life have been pointed out by Jersild (98):

From an early age, without being deliberate about it, (the child) acquires ideas and attitudes about himself and others. These are woven into the pattern of his life. They may be true or false, healthy or morbid. Their development is left largely to chance. . . . A large proportion of children will move into adulthood troubled and unhappy about many things. Many will be afflicted by irrational fears which do not represent dangers in the external environment but unresolved problems within themselves. Many, as adults, will suffer from attitudes of hostility, vindictiveness, and defensiveness which are not a response to hostile forces in the outside world but represent attitudes carried over from unresolved childhood struggles. Many persons similarly will acquire persisting feelings of inferiority or other unhealthy attitudes regarding their personal worth which represent either an irrational estimate of themselves or a failure to accept themselves realistically as they are. In numerous ways there is a vast carry-over of unhealthy attitudes regarding self and others from childhood and adolescence into adult life.

BASIC SELF-CONCEPTS   It is perhaps impossible for a person to think of himself without being influenced to some extent by the mirror images he has of what he believes others think of him. It is difficult because he is usually forced to remain in the environment with the people who are primarily responsible for the formation of the mirror images—his parents, teachers, and peers.

To develop a basic self-concept that is free from the influence of mirror images, the person must do three things. *First,* he must become psychologically independent of those on whom he has depended for security. Only then can he evaluate himself realistically.

Second, he must make use of his abilities to think and make decisions for himself. These abilities develop with the growth of intelligence and with opportunities for decision making at home, in school, and in the peer group.

And, *third,* he must have broad social contacts with all kinds of people so that he can see himself as an individual, separate and distinct from the group with which he has been closely identified. Such contacts will provide him with a variety of standards against which he can evaluate his strengths and weaknesses.

How difficult it is to develop a basic self-concept, founded on one's actual abilities and status in life and free from the influence of others, has been revealed by studies of self-evaluation at different age levels. When the young child comes in contact with people outside the home, he frequently discovers a discrepancy between the way they treat him and his mirror image developed at home. As he compares his play skills, his ability to communicate, and his academic achievements with those of his age-mates, he often discovers a discrepancy between what he believed he was capable of and how outsiders rate him or how he rates himself. That early self-evaluations are usually less satisfactory than the mirror images built up in the home is shown in excessive boasting, which is evidence of the typical preschooler's need to strengthen his sense of self.

Even among elementary school children, self-evaluations have a low correlation with external criteria of their personality characteristics. Girls tend to overrate themselves, while boys usually underrate themselves at first and then improve their self-estimates slightly (153).

The "self-halo," the tendency to emphasize one's good traits and those correlated with popularity, decreases as the child becomes more socially aware. In its place comes a tendency to be self-critical, to be sensitive to the possibility of ridicule, failure, and loss of prestige, and to exaggerate the bad qualities one thinks one possesses. This tendency is especially strong at puberty when self-evaluations are usually the most negative (9). See Figure 2-4.

An accurate perception of one's status in the group and of how one's abilities compare with those of others does not come until the end of high school or even later. Girls tend to make accurate self-evaluations at an earlier age than boys (16, 17).

The difficulties experienced in making an accurate self-evaluation stem from the child's dependence on parents, teachers, and peers for security and status. By identifying himself with others—a process which Ausubel has labeled "satellizing"—the child gains a feeling of security. But at the same time, he tends to see himself through their eyes (16).

Only when the person reaches physical maturity and only if he can achieve a feeling of security about his ability to assume the adult role will he be able to "desatellize" himself and assess himself realistically

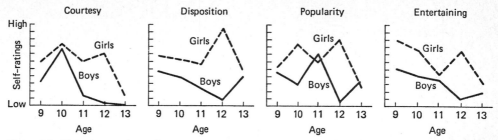

Figure 2-4 There is a tendency for pubescents to have a poor opinion of themselves. Because girls reach puberty sooner than boys, their negative self-evaluations occur earlier than do boys'. (Adapted from Sister M. Amatora: Developmental trends in preadolescence and in early adolescence in self-evaluation. *J. genet. Psychol.,* 1957, **91**, 89-97. Used by permission.)

without interference from social pressures and fear of social disapproval (172). When he acquires this psychological independence, he can free himself from the influence of the mirror images acquired earlier in life which have formed the foundation for his self-concept.

Developing a basic self-concept is a long and arduous task. It is never really completed because the concept must be changed and revised as a person's estimates of his abilities change. There is always a resistance to change, and the resistance is stronger when the change necessitates the acceptance of a less favorable self-concept than the already established mirror image. It is difficult, for example, for a child to revise his self-concept downward when he discovers that he is not the "all-perfect child" that his parents, grandparents, and other relatives had led him to believe he was. It is even more difficult for middle-aged and elderly people to maintain realistic self-concepts when family members, friends, and employers accept the social stereotype about the decline of abilities with age. As Strang (171) has explained:

The individual sets up defenses to preserve his present idea of himself. He rationalizes. He resists the impact of thoughts that would make it necessary for him to reexamine his self-concept.

IDEAL SELF-CONCEPTS Dramatic play, which begins around the age of 3 years and reaches its peak between 4 and 5, is the basis for the formation of an ideal self-concept. In his dramatic play, the child pretends to be someone he loves, admires, and would like to resemble. Later, from contacts with people he loves and admires, from stories, movies, television, and radio he builds up ideals. Then, by identifying himself

with them, he develops a concept of self as he would like to be—of the ideal self rather than the self-as-is.

The more dissatisfied a person is with himself and the more unsatisfactory the mirror images he has developed in his relationships with others, the stronger his motivation to develop ideal self-concepts. Each year, as he grows older and compares himself with others, he becomes increasingly aware of his shortcomings. To satisfy his desire to improve himself so that he can win success and popularity, he builds up ideal self-concepts which in themselves partially satisfy this desire and which also act as guides to the attainment of what he would like to be.

The development of ideal self-concepts follows a fairly predictable pattern (78, 128, 181). The young child has as his ideal a member of the family who, by comparison, seems superior to him. This is usually a parent, though it may be an older sibling who has been held up as a model. As his environment broadens, he selects his ideals or models mainly from outside the home. These may be people who are liked and admired by others and who seem superior to him—teachers, camp counselors, recreational leaders, or even successful and popular peers. Boys' ideals tend to come from the remote outside environment, while girls' ideals more often come from the immediate environment of the home and neighborhood (26).

By early adolescence, when crushes and hero worship are common, the ideal is usually a person other than a parent or teacher—someone who has a prestigious and well-recognized place in society. At the turn of the present century, adolescent ideals were usually political figures; now they come mainly from the entertainment world (50, 84, 192). They are almost always from the adolescent's own culture and from the higher socioeconomic groups within the culture (91, 192).

Some of the ideals used as models for the younger adolescent's ideal self-concepts are taken from books, movies, television, or even the comics. In discussing the role played by reading in the formation of the ideal self-concept, Strang (171) has explained:

Although fewer adolescents than might be expected report conscious identification with specific characters in fiction, it is possible that many youngsters draw upon various fictional sources for qualities which they may incorporate into their ideal selves. For example, they may get clues for solving their own problems of adjustment from characters who know how to get along with others (e.g., Antonia in Cather's My Antonia*), or those who have a good set of values (e.g., Kristin in Undset's* Kristin Lavransdatter*), or those who can transcend major tragedies in their lives (e.g., Jane Eyre in Bronte's* Jane Eyre*).*

The adolescent tends to be hypercritical, and it is not surprising that he soon finds flaws in his ideal. As a result, he develops a *composite* ideal made up of the physical and psychological traits he admires in different people and which he would like to possess. By this time, he is well aware of the values held by the group with which he is identified, and so these values are also embodied in the composite ideal. Since values change as the individual grows older, ideals likewise change. Regardless of the source of the ideal self-concept, and regardless of whether the concept is specific or composite, major emphasis is on superior ability, appearance, popularity, and socioeconomic status. The person or persons chosen as the ideal always have high prestige in the eyes of others.

An ideal self-concept is often a troublemaker. If it is unrealistic in the sense that the person has little hope of ever achieving in real life the qualities he hopes to achieve, he will be frustrated, disappointed, and disillusioned. This soon weakens his motivation to try to achieve a personality pattern like that of his ideal.

The more unrealistic the ideal self-concept, the harder it is for a person to see himself as he actually is and to form a concept based on his real abilities. If the person comes to think of his ideal self-concept as an image of what he actually is, he has difficulty not only in seeing himself realistically but also in seeing himself as others see him. Thus, the development of

mirror images as well as a basic self-concept becomes difficult.

Perhaps the most troublesome ideal self-concept is that based on a person or people whose characteristics are not admired or accepted by the larger social group. For example, if a teen-age girl admires a young woman whose popularity with boys comes from promiscuous sexual behavior and bases her ideal self-concept on the young woman, she may enjoy even less popularity than formerly and may develop a personality pattern that will make her a social misfit in the group with which she is striving to be identified.

DOMINANCE OF SELF-CONCEPTS   In the hierarchy of self-concepts, the various self-concepts are not separate and distinct but are so fused and interrelated that each influences the others and is, in turn, influenced by them. The psychological self-concept, for example, is influenced by the physical, the basic by the social and ideal, and the ideal, by the basic and social.

In this interrelationship, some of the self-concepts play dominant roles at one age and minor roles at another. Whether a certain concept is dominant or not is determined largely by the amount of satisfaction it gives the individual. And the degree of satisfaction a particular kind of self-concept gives is influenced largely by how it affects one's adjustment. This, in turn, is influenced to some extent by when it is developed in relation to the other kinds of self-concept. Since mirror images develop earlier than basic self-concepts, they help to pattern the kind of adjustment the individual makes. Should a person associate himself exclusively with those whose reactions to him are favorable, for example, he will develop such favorable mirror images that it may be difficult to match them with an ego-satisfying basic self-concept. Under such conditions, the mirror images will play a more dominant role in the hierarchy of self-concepts than the basic self-concept.

Similarly, if an ideal self-concept is built up early, before the child's imagination can be checked by his slower-developing reasoning ability, and if it is reinforced by the cultural belief that one can do or be anything he wants if he is willing to make the effort, the ego satisfaction from the ideal self-concept will so outweigh the satisfaction from mirror images or from self-concepts based on reality that the ideal will dominate.

While it can be safely predicted that the dominant self-concepts in the hierarchy will be those which give the person the greatest satisfaction, it is not easy to predict which these will be. It will depend largely on the person's experiences during the early, formative years. And experiences are more often a matter of chance than of guidance and control. For example, parents who treat the child in such a way that he develops extremely satisfying, but unrealistic, mirror images are making it difficult for him to develop realistic, and perhaps less satisfying, basic self-concepts. In the same way, parents who encourage the child to pretend that he is someone else in his play, and at the same time pressure him to aspire unrealistically high, encourage him to develop such ego-satisfying ideal self-concepts that he will be unable to match them with satisfying basic or social self-concepts. Even if one knows what kind of experiences the person has had during his early years, it is not easy to predict which self-concepts will be dominant because conditions in later life may alter the hierarchical pattern of his self-concepts.

If the individual is to be personally and socially well adjusted, the development of the self-concept cannot be left to chance. Parents and teachers must recognize that one of their prime duties is to control the development of the self-concept. Unless they assume this responsibility at the time the hierarchy of self-concepts is being formed, unfavorable self-concepts are likely to become so deeply rooted that later changes will be difficult or impossible.

NECESSITY OF FAVORABLE MIRROR IMAGES The young child should be encouraged to develop favorable mirror images. But if they are too favorable, he will have little motivation to try to improve. Furthermore, when he discovers that they are unrealistically favorable—when he compares himself with others and finds that he is not as great as he thought—it will be difficult for him to revise his self-image. Revision downward is always harder than revision upward and is more stubbornly resisted.

A child should be encouraged to develop a realistic ideal self-image, one which will motivate self-improvement, not one which will be impossible to live up to and, therefore, a source of frustration and of feelings of personal inadequacy. He should be encouraged to see himself realistically and to appraise himself in terms of those whose life patterns are similar to his. In this way he will not develop exaggerated feelings of inferiority or of superiority.

Guidance of this kind will help the child develop a hierarchy of self-concepts that will make for self-acceptance and reasonable self-satisfaction. Even more important, it will strengthen his motivation to try to improve instead of developing feelings of smug self-satisfaction or of hopelessness.

Discrepancies between self-concepts Studies of the effects of discrepancies between self-concepts in the hierarchy point up the results of chance development and the role that guidance could play. Discrepancies make fusion into a general self-concept difficult and are thus a primary cause of personality maladjustments.

DISCREPANCIES BETWEEN BASIC SELF-CONCEPTS AND MIRROR IMAGES When a discrepancy exists between a person's evaluation of himself and the concepts others have of him—between the basic self-concept and the mirror images —it leads to tension, difficulties in self-acceptance, and poor personal and social adjustments.

How great the tension will be depends partly upon the pressures put on the person to accept the evaluation of others in place of his own and how resistant he is to their evaluation. Tension is especially great when unfavorable evaluations are made by people in authority, such as parents, teachers, or employers, or by persons who have high prestige in the social group.

To relieve the tension and thus make self-acceptance possible, the person may devalue the source of the unfavorable evaluations, distort the evaluations, or deny his causal responsibility for the evaluations.

The tendency to discredit the source of the evaluations increases as the evaluations become more negative. The tendency to distort slightly unfavorable evaluations made by acquaintances or by people whose opinions are highly regarded leads the person to revise the evaluations upward so that he sees them in the best possible light. If the evaluations are made by people whom he regards less highly, he may try to ignore them.

DISCREPANCIES BETWEEN BASIC AND IDEAL SELF-CONCEPTS The discrepancy between what a person thinks he should be (his ideal self-concept) and what he thinks he is (his basic self-concept) should be relatively small. This does not mean that he should lack ambition or set his goals below his abilities. Instead, it means that he should choose goals that are within the realm of possibility, even though he may not achieve them for a long time. Children and young adolescents tend to be unrealistic in their aspirations, and so the disparity between their basic and ideal self-concepts is usually greater than in persons who are older, more mature, and more experienced.

The discrepancy between the basic and ideal self-concepts may also reflect the way the group or the individual evaluates certain traits. The discrepancy is greater in traits that are highly valued by the social group. For example, if high social value is attached to courage, a person who sees himself as somewhat timid and frightened will, in his ideal self-concept, see himself as the bravest of the brave. On the other hand, if low social value is attached to courage, as it may be for girls, that trait will have little effect on the formation of the ideal self-concept.

A large discrepancy between a person's real and ideal self-images will lead to poor personal and social adjustments. Sometimes the discrepancy may appear to be smaller than it actually is because the person uses defenses to cover up his unfavorable self-evaluations. He may, for example, deny that he is timid and frightened when his ideal self-concept stresses courage as one of his outstanding characteristics.

Even when defenses are used to lessen the discrepancy between basic and ideal self-concepts, the discrepancy is a disorganizing experience that leads to feelings of depression. As Lecky has pointed out, "All emotions can be traced directly to experiences which are interpreted by the individual as supports of or threats to one or more ideas of self" (116).

If the discrepancy between the basic and ideal self-concepts persists for too long, it will lead to personality disturbances and great unhappiness. The person will dislike himself and will behave in a way that will make others dislike him. In addition, he will suffer constantly from frustrations and humiliations because he sees himself falling far short of his ideal and is powerless to do anything about it. In time, he will develop marked feelings of inadequacy and inferiority which will further increase his dislike of himself and bring about even poorer social adjustments.

DISCREPANCIES BETWEEN PHYSICAL AND PSY-CHOLOGICAL SELF-CONCEPTS Some people are able to accept their psychological self-images but not their physical ones; in others, the reverse is true. Many adolescents who are dissatisfied with their looks are satisfied with their abilities in other areas, and vice versa. Similarly, the person approaching old age may have difficulty accepting the physical changes of aging but be self-acceptant so far as his abilities and disabilities are concerned. Or if he accepts the stereotype, he may believe that aging is a sign of mental deterioration.

At times in the life span when appearance is of great concern, in adolescence and early adulthood, or in situations where looks help to determine how successful a person will be, as in the selection of leaders or in courtship, an unfavorable physical self-image, even when the psychological self-image is satisfactory, will lead to poor adjustments and unhappiness. The greater the social value attached to physical or psychological characteristics, the more detrimental will be a discrepancy between the two self-concepts.

DISCREPANCIES BETWEEN SOCIAL AND IDEAL SELF-CONCEPTS There are times when a person sees himself through the eyes of others in a way which differs markedly from the way he would like to be. His resentment of others' judgments puts him on the defensive and encourages him to try to justify his behavior or devalue the source of the unfavorable judgments. The disparity between men's and women's concepts of the "ideal woman" is a good example of how such a discrepancy can prove to be a troublemaker. When a woman considers the ideal woman to be one who plays an equalitarian role in business, social, and home life, she will be frustrated, dissatisfied, and unhappy when she discovers that the significant men in her world regard the ideal woman as one who plays a submissive and inferior role. If she tries to fulfill their ideal, she will be unhappy; if she tries to live up to her own ideal, she will also be unhappy because their judgment and treatment of her will be unfavorable.

Stability of self-concepts   It is difficult for a person to see himself as he is when his self-concept fluctuates, as was pointed out in the discussion of transitory concepts. Only when the self-concept is relatively stable can a person develop a true sense of identity.

Some fluctuation and change are normal, however, especially during the early years of life when the self-concept is in its formative stage. As Jersild has pointed out, since the self-concept is composed of a person's thoughts and feelings and since thoughts and feelings are dynamic, changes are inevitable (98). Allport further emphasized the dynamic nature of the self-concept when, in discussing it as the "core of our being," he (5) said:

And yet it is not a constant core. Sometimes the core expands and seems to take command of all our behavior and consciousness; sometimes it seems to go completely offstage, leaving us with no awareness of self.

There are marked variations in the stability of the self-concept not only in different people but also in the same person at different times and under different circumstances. Tippett and Silber have reported four common kinds of variations in the stability of the self-concept.

First, variations occur in the self-concept over time. The self-concept may fluctuate either momentarily or over longer periods, as at puberty or late adolescence.

Second, variations may occur within the different self-image areas, such as ideal and basic. The physical self-image may vary at puberty, but not the psychological. Similarly, when a person goes to work, the work-role image may vary, but not the physical.

Third, variations may be found in the self-concept in different interpersonal situations. A person may see himself differently in the presence of his father, his mother, his teacher, and his best friend.

Fourth, variations occur within the different self-structures. The ideal self-concept may vary but the real or basic self-concept may remain stable, or vice versa (175).

The stability of the self-concept depends largely upon the integration of the primary self, formed early in life in the home, and the secondary self, formed later as the person's social horizons broaden. How great this integration will be is influenced by the continuity between the person's primary and secondary sociocultural environments and the consistency of the treatment he receives, especially in the home. The more stable the environment, the more sure a person is of what he thinks about himself and the more stable his self-concept.

The stability of the self-concept is also influenced by the discrepancy between negative and positive self-concepts. The smaller the discrepancy, the more stable the self-concept. A stable self-concept may be composed largely of either positive or negative self-concepts, depending mainly on the treatment

the person receives from others. A stable self-concept composed largely of positive self-concepts leads to self-acceptance and good adjustments. The person shows a high level of self-esteem; has few feelings of insecurity, inadequacy, and inferiority; exhibits little compensatory behavior of a defensive nature; is able to see himself as he believes others see him; and has better social acceptance.

A person with a stable self-concept composed largely of negative self-concepts or one with an unstable self-concept, due to a large discrepancy between negative and positive self-concepts, often develops a self-rejectant attitude. As a result, he makes poor personal and social adjustments. These are reflected in low self-esteem, uncertainly about self, belief that others have a poor estimate of him, withdrawal from social contacts, and the use of many defense mechanisms.

Studies show that the ideal self-concept tends to be less stable than the basic self-concept (71). Refer to the section entitled Discrepancies between Basic and Ideal Self-concepts for a more complete discussion of this.

VARIATIONS IN STABILITY The self-concept tends to be least stable during the early years of life when rapid physical and mental changes are taking place. A radical physical change that covers a relatively short period, at puberty, encourages instability, though normally this instability is only temporary. In discussing the effects of rapid physical and mental growth on the self-concept during puberty, Lively et al. (119) have written:

The acquisition of these new intellectual physical-social skills suggests that there will be a corresponding change in the personality of the child during this period of development. . . . Developmental changes in the child's conception of himself occur during these years.

During middle age, instability occurs once again when the reproductive function comes to an end. Usually it is not as severe as at puberty because the physical changes are less radical than earlier and because the stability achieved in adolescence has become more or less habitual.

Changes in environment are likewise responsible for changes in the self-concept. When radical environmental changes occur suddenly or when the different environments in which the person operates are inconsistent, the instability of the self-concept is especially marked. School experiences, for example, not only encourage children to become more realistic as they approach adolescence but they also provide new mirror images which may be quite at variance with the images acquired in the home.

At every age, instability in the self-concept is greatest among those with strong negative attitudes toward self. This instability is reinforced, to some extent, by rapid physical changes. The times when negative self-attitudes are most common coincide with the times when rapid physical changes elicit negative responses from the social group. Thus, negative self-attitudes and great instability of the self-concept become more pronounced at these times—at puberty, middle age, and old age.

EFFECTS OF STABILITY ON ADJUSTMENT Personal and social adjustments are greatly influenced by the degree of stability of the self-concept. A stable self-concept, even a negative one, gives the person a feeling of personal security. Lecky (116) has written:

The prime motive in all behavior is to preserve one's percept of one's self intact. To preserve the identity of self, self-consistency is necessary. Even a person who believes his "self" is stupid, bad, or evil will adhere to all percepts that bolster this belief and refuse to see or accept any percept that suggests he is clever, strong, or good. If he is not faithful to this picture of himself, he is threatened with loss of selfhood.

By encouraging the person to act in a predictable manner, a stable self-concept helps others to know what to expect of him. This is well illustrated in the reactions of young people from deprived environments. Those with stable self-concepts largely positive in nature can be counted on to behave in a socially approved manner in spite of environmental temptations to engage in delinquent behavior. They are "insulated" against delinquency. On the other hand, those whose relatively stable self-concepts are characterized by negative attitudes toward self can be "spotted" as potential delinquents even before their behavior becomes antisocial (173).

Unstable self-concepts lead to poor personal and social adjustments. A person who has disparate self-concepts is never sure which is the real "me." His inconsistent behavior gives him little ego satisfaction; it is so unpredictable that it antagonizes others and engenders unfavorable attitudes on the part of parents, teachers, and peers. These attitudes add to the instability of his self-concept and the deterioration in his personal and social adjustments.

Effects of self-concepts on behavior Whether stable or unstable, a person's self-concept is a motivating force in his behavior. The individual acts in accordance with how he sees himself at the moment. If he feels that he is misunderstood or discriminated against, he will act like a martyr. If he feels that people accept him, he will act in a friendly, cooperative way. Much unpredictable behavior can be traced to unstable self-concepts.

Because the self-concept is the dominant element in the personality pattern, it governs the individual's characteristic reactions to people and situations and determines the quality of his behavior. As Shane (159) has explained:

Children and adults are governed by the concept of self which they develop and make part of themselves. Thus we have boys and girls who assign to themselves the role of clown, good citizen, manager, shrinking violet, little demon, sage, feather-head.

Research studies from several areas of behavior illustrate how the concept of self, built up in the early years of life and reinforced by later experiences, influences the quality of the person's behavior and his characteristic reactions to people and to situations. Many school children work below their capacities because they have learned, at home or from members of the peer group, to think of themselves as "dumb." A child whose ability is limited may work beyond his teacher's expectations if he has a favorable self-concept characterized by feelings of competence and self-worth.

Studies of college students show that adjustment to college is influenced by how the student views himself when he comes to college and by the changes in his self-concept that result from changes in his environment (35).

Feelings of inadequacy, inferiority, unworthiness, or persecution stemming from specific environmental areas may become generalized and color the individual's entire self-concept. When this happens the person may have little resistance to pressures from members of the peer group to retaliate against those who have made them feel rejected or against society at large.

By contrast, adolescents who have a more favorable self-concept resulting from feeling accepted and loved at home, no matter how poor the home may be, are, as was mentioned above, insulated against pressures from the peer group to engage in delinquent activities. Reckless et al. (147) say that:

"Insulation" against delinquency is an ongoing process reflecting an internalization of non-delinquent values and conformity to the expectations of significant others. . . . It may be an outgrowth of discovery in social experience that playing the part of the good boy and remaining a good boy brings maximum satisfactions (of acceptance) to the boy himself.

Studies indicate that vocational decisions are ego-involved in the sense that people select vocations that will give them an opportunity to do work they are capable of doing and also provide maximum satisfaction. A person who is shy and retiring because he has a poor concept of his abilities, for example, will not select work that requires constant contact with people or entails a comparison of his work with that of coworkers. Similarly, if one feels most secure and happy in the environment in which he grew up, he will resist moving to another community even though a move might guarantee greater vocational success.

Traits

The personality pattern is a unified multidimensional structure in which the concept of self is the core or center of gravity (25). Into this structure are integrated many patterns of response tendencies, known as "traits," which are closely related to and influenced by the concept of self (158).

The major function of traits is to integrate lesser habits, attitudes, and skills into larger thought-feeling-action patterns. The concept of self, in turn, integrates the psychological capacities of the person and initiates action. In this role, the concept of self is the true core or center of gravity of the pattern.

Meaning of traits   Personality traits have been described and defined in many ways though most of the descriptions and definitions are similar in that they include certain common salient points. A trait has been described as an aspect or dimension of personality which consists of a group of related and consistent reactions characteristic of a person's typical adjustment (158).

All descriptions and definitions of traits emphasize that traits are *learned* tendencies to (1) evalu-

ate situations in a predictable way and (2) react in a manner which the person has found more or less successful in similar situations and when similarly motivated (158, 167). Since the person's characteristic ways of reacting are learned, each new reaction is influenced to some extent by the success the person has had in his previous adjustments to similar reactions. As a result, traits, while predictable, are not automatic acts which occur in exactly the same form every time they are aroused by the core of the personality pattern—the concept of self. Allport (5) has stressed the role of learning in bringing about slight variations in the predictable manner a person adjusts to situations:

Traits, unlike the "faculties" or "powers" of earlier psychology, are not "little men within the breast" who pull the strings of behavior. Traits are looser tendencies, each expression of a trait being slightly different because it confronts other determining conditions. Furthermore, after an act takes place, there is "feedback" to the nervous system, and in the future a trait will never be precisely the same as it was previously. Thus continuous flow is the primary fact. Yet we know that traits exist because, in spite of the continuous flow and change, there is considerable constancy in a person's mode of behavior. We can say that certain acts are characteristic of him. Traits underlie what is "characteristic" in conduct.

While traits are the product of learning, they are based on hereditary foundations and these foundations influence the form the trait will take. There is some evidence that certain traits are actually determined, or certainly favored, by hereditary predispositions. People who show the characteristic pattern of neurotic instability, for example, have various degrees of autonomic imbalance (122, 167). The intellectual capacity of a person, determined by his hereditary endowment, influences the way he perceives a situation and how he learns to react to it.

Characteristics of traits   Every trait has three characteristics: uniqueness, degree of likableness, and consistency. *Uniqueness* does not mean that a person has certain traits that are peculiarly his. It means that he has his own individual quantity of a particular kind of behavior. As Woodworth and Marquis point out, "Traits are 'dimensions' of behavior in which individuals differ" (195).

A trait is not something that is either present or

absent. Instead, like intelligence, it is distributed according to the curve of normal distribution. This means that a trait is present in all or almost all people, but in varying degrees. And in the curve of normal distribution, most people cluster around the mean or average in any particular trait.

The second characteristic of traits is *likableness*. Some traits, such as honesty, generosity, and trustworthiness, are liked by others, while some are disliked—rudeness, cruelty, and egocentrism, for example. These attitudes toward traits result from social learning in a particular cultural setting and are almost universal within a culture. Traits are liked or disliked because they contribute to social harmony or disharmony and add to the satisfaction or dissatisfaction experienced from being with a person who has the traits. A person who is generous not only contributes to the social well-being of others but is also a pleasant person to be with. By contrast, an egocentric person makes others feel uncomfortable because he is constantly talking about himself; he is likely to contribute to social disharmony by being uncooperative and refusing to carry his load.

The third characteristic of traits is *consistency*. This means that a person can be expected to behave in approximately the same way in similar situations. Consistency, like uniqueness, is relative. A person may be self-confident in a situation because he has mastered the skills needed to adjust to it and has experienced success in similar situations. But in situations requiring skills and modes of adjustment which he has not mastered so well or has had less success with in the past, he will show less self-confidence and may even show fear. Similarly, a person may be punctual in situations where punctuality gives him satisfaction, but not in situations where being on time is unimportant to him or is regarded as socially incorrect (88). These examples illustrate what Allport meant when he said that "perfect and rigid self-consistency is not to be expected" (5).

Traits versus habits   Emphasis on the consistency of behavior, which is characteristic of all traits, may lead one to believe that traits and habits are the same. Both, it is true, are learned patterns of behavior. Both are consistent in that in similar situations it is possible to predict that the person's behavior will be similar to his behavior in the past. And both imply that learning has resulted in behavior that occurs so automatically that the person does not have to

plan his act and is often not aware of what he is doing until after he has done it.

The major difference between habits and traits is that habits are narrow and limited determining tendencies while traits are more generalized determining tendencies. And because they are more generalized, traits are more variable in their expression than habits. Traits are often the result of the integration of several specific habits that have the same adaptive significance for the person.

An example will highlight the difference between a habit and a trait. Through parental guidance, a child learns specific polite habits. He learns to say "Thank you" for gifts, to say "Excuse me" when he inconveniences others, and to allow adults to pass through doors before him. He learns that such acts are socially approved and socially expected. He also discovers that they lead to greater social acceptance than other behaviors. In time, he sees the relationship between these specific habits and favorable social concepts. Consciously or unconsciously, he learns to act consistently in a manner in which polite acts play an important role. Then he is judged by others as a "polite person." One of his outstanding traits is "politeness" (5).

Common and unique traits   Within the personality pattern are both common and unique traits. The combination of the two contributes to the individuality of the person. Which will play a dominant role in the personality pattern varies greatly in different people and may even vary in the same person at different times in the life span.

Common traits are qualities that are found in most people within a cultural group, such as dominance, sociability, truthfulness, need for achievement, and generosity. However, among the members of the cultural group, common traits are found in varying degrees. These traits are the result of similar environmental influences, similar cultural values, and similar child-training methods. In other cultures, where values, child-training methods, and environmental conditions are different, other traits are common (7).

Unique traits are patterns of behavior which characterize a particular individual and may not be found or found to the same degree in other people. They are developed from unusual combinations of hereditary qualities, from personal experiences, and from the social environment with its cultural values (5, 167).

Unique traits are similar to the type which Allport has labeled "cardinal." They stand out so conspicuously and are so pervasive that they dominate most of the person's activities. They are the most significant traits so far as individuality and distinctiveness are concerned and may even be responsible for making the person famous (5). As Shaffer and Shoben have pointed out, "Only a few people can be rated as to the extent to which they are 'alarmist,' or 'chauvinistic,' or 'quixotic,' but when such an *individual trait* is prominent, it may be the most important feature of a person's character" (158).

Even common traits have a unique element, though this element is far less notable than in the unique traits. As was pointed out earlier, different people have varying amounts of the same traits. That this would be inevitable is explained thus by Frank (72):

Early in life the individual develops his or her idiomatic way of meeting the demands and opportunities of life and this forms his own pattern which governs his future behavior. Family, social life, schools and cultural traditions may block, hamper or impair the development of the individual or may aid it.

The uniqueness of common traits has been further emphasized by Allport (5);

No two persons ever have precisely the same trait. Though each of two men may be aggressive (or esthetic), the style and range of the aggression (or estheticism) in each case is noticeably different. What else could be expected in view of the unique hereditary endowment, the different developmental history, the never-repeated external influences that determine each personality? The end product of unique determination can never be anything but unique.

Number of traits Many attempts have been made to discover how many traits a typical personality pattern contains. To show what a gigantic task this is, Allport and Odbert in 1936 made a list of the words in the English language used to describe personality traits. They reported that 17,953 words were used for this purpose. Many of the words, however, were synonyms or were used to describe temporary rather than permanent trends in behavior (5).

More recently, by means of factor analysis, clusters or groups of personality traits have been

identified. It has been found, for example, that a person who is dominant in his relationship with others usually tends to be assertive, egotistical, vindictive, hard-hearted, and tough. The opposites of these qualities likewise tend to go together (37). If related qualities are grouped into clusters, the number of traits that must be considered in studying the personality pattern can be reduced and a more workable approach developed.

One of the best-known and most widely accepted classifications of personality clusters is that of Cattell (37). Starting out with 4,000 trait names, Cattell reduced the list to 171 by eliminating overlapping and rare qualities. Then, by factor analysis, he reduced the traits into clusters, dividing trait clusters into two categories: surface and source traits.

Surface traits are those which show the influence of environmental molding and which, therefore, vary in different cultures. *Source* traits are constitutional or environmental factors so basic that they apply in any culture and influence many different surface traits. Cattell identified 12 clusters of source traits and 20 of surface traits. These clusters are shown in Figures 2-5 and 2-6.

In spite of the usefulness of organizing the thousands of personality traits into a workable number of clusters, the practice has attracted four major criticisms. *First*, a "piecemeal analysis of personality may fail to reveal its integration, and may hide the interaction that each trait has with each other. A man who is 'dominant' and 'friendly' is a very differently organized person than one who is 'dominant' and 'hostile'" (158). *Second*, factor analysis can deal only with common traits, and thus the unique or "cardinal" traits that are so important to individuality are overlooked. *Third*, factor analysis does not tell the ways in which a trait or group of related traits express themselves. How, for example, does an aggressive person express his aggressiveness and how does a timid person express his timidity? *Fourth*, and perhaps the most serious criticism, factor analysis tells us what *is* without telling us *why*.

Even though experimenters may study and report rather specific clusters of traits, the important thing to remember is that the personality pattern is always composed not of a few but of many traits. Furthermore, the traits are extremely diverse. Realization of the breadth and complexity of the personality pattern will help you to understand why changing the pattern becomes increasingly difficult every year as

SURFACE TRAITS

Fineness of character
  a. Integrity, altruism
  b. Conscientious effort

    vs. Moral defect, nonpersistence
    vs. Dishonesty, undependability
    vs. Quitting, incoherence

Egotism, assertion, stubbornness
  a. Crude social assertion, exhibitionism
  b. Stubbornness, pugnacity, clamourness
  c. Rigidity, despotism, egotism
  d. Dictatorial, shrewdness
  e. Assertion, rivalry, conceit
  f. Eager self-assertion

    vs. Modesty, self-effacement, adaptability
    vs. Modesty, obedience to authority
    vs. Tolerance, self-effacement
    vs. Adaptability, friendliness, tactfulness
    vs. Naïveté, unassertiveness
    vs. Modesty, unassumingness
    vs. Lack of ambition

Boldness, independence, toughness
  a. Energy, boldness, spiritedness
  b. Independence, cleverness, confidence
  c. Lack of restraint, adventurousness
  d. Poised sociability, inertia, toughness
  e. Smartness, assertiveness, independence

    vs. Timidity, inhibition, sensitivity
    vs. Apathy, timidity, langour
    vs. Timidity, dependence, languidness
    vs. General inhibition, fearfulness
    vs. Introspectiveness, sensitivity, haste
    vs. Unsophistication, submissiveness, reverence

General emotionality, high-strungness, instability
  a. High-strungness, impulsiveness, anxiety
  b. Sthenic emotionality, hypomania, instability
  c. Intrusiveness, frivolity, neurotic instability
  d. Generally emotional, dissatisfied, intense

    vs. Placidity, deliberateness, reserve
    vs. Apathy, relaxation, deliberateness
    vs. Self-control, patience, phlegm
    vs. Deliberateness, seriousness, reserve
    vs. Content, placid, temperate

Liveliness, instability, verbal expressiveness
  a. Austerity, thoughtfulness, stability
  b. Verbal skill, interesting ideas, inquisitiveness
  c. Eloquence, affectedness, amusing conversationalism
  d. Creativity, wit, emotional color

    vs. Reserve, quiescence, naturalness
    vs. Playfulness, changeability, foolishness
    vs. Narrow interests, absence of flattery
    vs. Self-effacement, inarticulateness, naturalness
    vs. Dullness, banality, stability

Figure 2-5 Sample surface traits. (Adapted from R. B. Cattell: *Personality and motivation: Structure and measurement.* Yonkers, N.Y.: World, 1957. Used by permission.)

each of the traits in the network is reinforced by repetition.

PERSONALITY SYNDROMES

Since the time of Hippocrates it has been taken for granted that personality patterns conform to certain standards or "types." Classifying people according to type is a convenient and easy way to pigeonhole them, but few people fit the types precisely, whether they are types based on body build, glandular functioning, or behavior characteristics.

On the other hand, measurements of behavior characteristics have revealed that most personality patterns, while retaining an individual uniqueness, have some basic similarities. These similarities are due to cultural molding and to the use of similar child-training methods in the home and the school.

Today the medical term "syndrome" is commonly used to refer to personality patterns that show basic similarities. In medicine, syndrome relates to the pattern of predisposing causes of a disease, its symptoms, and its course. When applied to personality, it describes a specific kind of personality pattern which bears a resemblance to the personality patterns of other individuals who have had somewhat similar problems and have used somewhat similar methods of solving their problems (95). Syndrome refers to a cluster of symptoms which habitually occur together; it therefore indicates a higher level of organization than specific habits (167).

Clinical and test data, such as those of Cattell described above, have revealed characteristic abnormal as well as normal personality syndromes. Because of the practical value of discovering and treating personality abnormalities as soon as possible, most of the early studies were designed to identify abnormal syndromes. More recently, attention has been turned to normal children, adolescents, and adults. These studies have thrown light on the important influences that go to shape the personality pattern and have revealed how early shaping affects the adult personality pattern.

Abnormal syndromes

A number of syndromes characteristic of abnormal personality patterns have been identified and have proved valuable in the diagnosis of personality disorders. Three examples will illustrate the common elements in the syndromes.

The central feature of the *manic syndrome* is an affective stage of eagerness and joyous excitement. The association of ideas is rapid and uncontrolled, and thinking is flighty, though it is not illogical and may even be witty or sarcastic. The individual is easily distracted in the course of his associations by external stimuli and may exhibit a dreamlike looseness of ideas and logical connections. Memory and orientation to time, place, and identity are sound, but the individual does not recognize that his personality has changed. He often experiences fleeting hallucinations. The behavior pattern is characterized by talkativeness, overactivity, lack of restraint, and impatience. The person shows excessive enterprise, mischief, or facetiousness and may lose his sense of propriety in sexual as well as other matters (37).

SOURCE TRAITS

Cyclothemia (Outgoing, cheerful, adaptable)	vs. Schizothymia (Timid, withdrawn, hostile)
Emotionally mature (Realistic, self-controlled, stable)	vs. Demoralized (Unrealistic, evasive, changeable)
Hypersensitive (Self-pitying, excitable, demanding)	vs. Frustration tolerance (Self-controlled, stable emotionally, realistic)
Dominance (Assertive, conceited, headstrong)	vs. Submissiveness (Modest, self-critical, self-effacing)
Surgency (Cheerful, optimistic, sociable)	vs. Melancholic desurgency (Frustrated, pessimistic, shy)
Sensitive, imaginative (Kindly, idealistic, emotionally dependent)	vs. Rigid, tough (Hard, cynical, habit-bound)

Figure 2-6 Sample source traits. (Adapted from R. B. Cattell: *Personality and motivation: Structure and measurement.* Yonkers, N.Y.: World, 1957. Used by permission.)

The syndrome of the *psychopathic personality* includes such traits as unreliability, deceitfulness, egocentricity, improvidence, promiscuity, and extreme emotional shallowness, as shown in an inability to express anger, love, and other common emotions with the usual pattern of response. The individual may, however, possess superficial charm and give the impression of having sound mental health (37).

The syndrome of the *delinquent personality* includes strong drives, weak conscience, dissatisfaction, defensiveness, anxiety, tension, emotional immaturity, rebelliousness, and hypersensitivity. Many delinquents value present pleasures over future rewards and have little regard for the generally accepted norms of behavior. This combination of traits keeps the person in conflict with everyone and gives him a defense against a world which frightens and overwhelms him without providing adequate compensatory pleasure (52, 79, 90, 141). Adolescent delinquents have frequently been regarded as "problem children" at home and disciplinary problems in school. Studies of the personality patterns of "disciplinary students" show that they tend to be more flexible and less dogmatic than students who accept and follow the rules but that they have emergent value systems and beliefs which do not conform to those of the larger group. As rule breakers, they are showing a personality syndrome similar to that of the juvenile delinquent (48).

Normal syndromes

Among normal people, tests and clinical data have revealed personality syndromes resulting from similar training in the home and school, similar attitudes on the part of significant others, and similar cultural pressures.

One of the most fruitful areas of research has dealt with personality syndromes characteristic of people of different status positions within their families. Two normal personality syndromes have been found to be characteristic of the *only child*. Which of the two the child will develop will depend on whether he is overprotected and spoiled or is given opportunities to learn to get along with other people in spite of the absence of siblings.

The personality syndrome of the overprotected only child includes the characteristic traits of selfishness, self-centeredness, lack of cooperation, dependency on parents and teachers, chronic homesickness, and feelings of inadequacy in social situations, shown in shyness and withdrawal or aggressive attention-seeking behavior (5, 24). By contrast, only children whose home environment is more wholesome develop a personality syndrome characterized by self-confidence, slightly above average aggressiveness, independence, responsibility, gregariousness, and cooperativeness. Such children not only make good social adjustments but often assume leadership roles among their peers (24).

Parental rejection causes ego impairment, whether the rejection is real or imagined and whether it is expressed directly, by criticism, neglect, or antagonism toward the child, or indirectly, by perfectionistic demands, frequent separations from the child, and psychological detachment. Two typical personality syndromes have been identified. The first is characterized by aggressiveness, and the second, by submissiveness.

In the *aggressive syndrome* are usually found such traits as rebelliousness, hostility, jealousy, quarrelsomeness, suspicion, rationalization, projecting blame on others, lying, stealing, and truancy, and attention-seeking to compensate for the love the rejected individual feels he has been denied. Allport has identified six forms of aggressive behavior which are associated with this syndrome and which express the relative strength of the various traits. According to Allport, aggressive behavior is the expression of efforts to satisfy some desire, assertiveness in attacking a problem, enjoyment of fighting for fighting's sake, intent to injure as a by-product of competitive activity, sadism, or frustration (6). Toigo has identified two patterns of aggression. In the first, the person attempts by word or action to inflict harm on others, and in the second, the person expresses his aggression by taking the initiative, being forthright, and assuming leadership. The second is socially valued while the first is not (176).

The *submissive syndrome* includes such traits as inhibition, loneliness, seclusiveness, withdrawal, uncooperativeness, inactivity in social life, and perfectionism accompanied by strong feelings of guilt and personal inadequacy (5, 37, 158).

Interest in the *authoritarian personality syndrome* has developed from a concern with anti-Semitism and ethnocentrism. Studies reveal that prejudice is one element of this syndrome which develops because of extreme parental rejection or domination in childhood and is characterized by repressed hostility which may find expression in attacks on minority groups. In the authoritarian syndrome are such other traits as conventionality, suspiciousness, desire for power, concern over sex, conservatism, ethnocentrism, intolerance, dogmatism, destructiveness, and cynicism (2, 74, 152, 169). The authoritarian leader determines all the policies of the group, dictates the work tasks and work companions for each group member, allows personal bias to influence his praise or criticism of group members, and tends to remain aloof from group activities except when telling the group what to do (2, 152).

In the *prejudiced personality syndrome* are many of the traits found in the authoritarian syndrome. There is a generalized prejudiced attitude, however, not merely an antipathy toward a particular ethnic group; also there are extreme nationalistic sentiments and extropunitiveness—a tendency to project blame on others and to perceive the environment as threatening (105).

In contrast to the authoritarian and prejudiced syndromes is the tolerant personality syndrome. While many of the traits that go to make up this syndrome are similar to those of the authoritarian and prejudiced, they appear in different degrees (123).

The *independent syndrome* is characterized by such traits as originality, emotionality, creativity, and dependence on close relationships with people. The *yielder syndrome* has many of the traits found in the independent syndrome, but because of different values, people possess the traits in different degrees of intensity. Among the traits found in the yielder syndrome are optimism, efficiency, determination, patience, kindness, practical-mindedness, and dependence on the group for satisfaction (21). The yielder syndrome is characteristic of the person who is regarded as "conservative." In its extreme form, it is found most often among the less intelligent and the less well educated, and under such conditions, the person is usually anxious and insecure (127).

The *ascendant personality syndrome* is manifest in the person who upholds his rights and defends himself in face-to-face contacts, who does not object to being conspicuous and may even enjoy it, who through social initiative gravitates to positions of leadership, who enjoys social contacts, and who is extroverted and outspoken (86).

Rigidity is believed to be a generalized personality characteristic. It is a defense against anxiety arising from insecurity. To compensate, the individual uses various defense mechanisms and, therefore, behaves rigidly in any situation in which stress appears.

In the *rigid personality syndrome* are such traits as conservatism, inhibition, intolerance of disorder and ambiguity, resistance to change, social introversion, anxiety, and marked feelings of guilt (81, 150, 155).

Interest in the effect of social acceptance on personal adjustment, on adjustment to school, and on underachievement and dropping out of school or college has led to attempts to determine whether one specific trait or a syndrome of traits is responsible for social acceptance. Two opposing syndromes, the acceptance syndrome and the alienation syndrome, have been identified.

There are two kinds of *acceptance syndrome.* The first has been called the "aggressive" or "success-oriented" acceptance syndrome because the person whom it describes goes all out to get whatever he can for himself. The second is known as the "less aggressive" or "goodness-oriented" acceptance syndrome because the person is more interested in what he can do to bring satisfaction to the members of the group than in what he can do for himself. In both the aggressive and the less aggressive acceptance syndromes, characteristic traits include extroversion, cooperation, courtesy, unselfishness, truthfulness, frankness, temper control, resourcefulness, initiative, and willingness to conform to rules and regulations. All these traits make the person pleasant to be with because he contributes to the enjoyment of others (47, 108, 174, 182, 197).

Three *alienation syndromes* have been identified. They are quite distinct, though all include traits that make a person disliked by others. The first, known as the "recessive" alienation syndrome, is characterized by reserved, listless, and withdrawn behavior. The second, called the "socially disinterested" alienation syndrome, is that of a self-bound person concerned primarily with his own interests and welfare. People with the third kind of alienation syndrome, the "socially ineffective," cause trouble for others by being noisy, boisterous show-offs, by resisting authority and ignoring rules, regulations, or even laws, and by rejecting the accepted cultural mores regarding behavior, speech, and dress.

In general, the alienation syndrome is marked by such unsocial behavior as teasing and bullying, making unpleasant comments, being hypercritical, intentionally annoying people, lying and being sneaky, using alibis or projecting blame on others, and being sullen, sulky, and moody. People characterized by the socially ineffective syndrome are annoying to others, while those characterized by the recessive and socially disinterested are so distasteful that others have no desire to have anything to do with them (61, 67, 80, 174, 194).

Psychological interest in creativity has led to studies of the personality syndrome of persons described as "original" by the layman and as "creative" by the psychologist. Among the many traits regarded as elements of the *creative personality syndrome* are need for autonomy and independence, flexibility, nonconformity, playfulness, forcefulness, and aggressiveness. Creative people usually have a high level of aspiration, motivation, energy output, and self-discipline, and they are usually reserved and detached in interpersonal relationships. Contrary to the popular stereotype of the artist, who ranks high in creativity, there is little evidence that the creative personality syndrome leads to loneliness or maladjustment (15, 21, 36, 73, 94, 137).

DIFFERENCES IN PERSONALITY PATTERNS

Each personality pattern is unique in the sense that it differs in many respects from other personality patterns. As noted earlier, the differences are due partly to heredity and partly to environment. It is the uniqueness of the personality pattern that is responsible for individuality.

Five common ways in which personality patterns differ will be discussed in the following paragraphs: complexity, fluidity, accessibility, resistance to change, and centralization.

Differences in complexity Between the simple personality pattern of the young child or the mentally deficient adult and the complex pattern of the intelligent adult there are noticeable differences in complexity of personality makeup. Gradients of differences in the complexity of the concept of self as well as in the number and complexity of traits are apparent in individuals of different ages, intellectual levels, and cultural groups.

Differences in fluidity There are great differences in the rigidity of the organization of different personality patterns, ranging from markedly fluid to markedly rigid, but with most people falling between the two extremes. A fluid personality is characterized by the ability to adapt to new circumstances, by consistent attitudes and values, by social insight and self-insight, and by smooth adjustments to life. By contrast, the rigid personality is characterized by inconsistent or contradictory patterns of behavior, of attitudes, and of values, by poor social insight and self-insight, by poor adjustment, and by a tendency to break under stress.

Differences in accessibility Accessibility refers to one's "openness" to new stimuli and to the ability to communicate one's feelings to others. In the accessible personality, the real and manifest structures of the personality pattern are closely related.

A "closed" personality is characterized by relative inaccessibility to external stimulation, as shown by the individual's limited response to social stimuli, his rigidly restricted speech and behavior, and his inability to relate freely to others. In the closed personality, the gap between the real and the manifest personalities is wide.

Differences in resistance to change In general, resistance to change increases with age. Within the personality pattern, the core, or concept of self, is more resistant to change than are the traits. Those traits which are most closely related to defending the ego against threats from the environment, however, are more resistant to change than those which are least ego-involved.

Differences in centralization The term "centralization" refers to the degree of ego involvement in the organized systems or syndromes that constitute the traits of the personality pattern. In some personality patterns, many traits are ego-involved in that the behavior of the person is greatly influenced by his concept of self. The person who feels inadequate to meet life's challenges, for example, has a cluster of traits that includes defensiveness, irritability, nervousness, and anxiety. He behaves in such a way that others see him as lacking in self-confidence and as feeling martyred. The personality pattern that is less ego-involved has a constellation of traits which are expressed in sociability, geniality, frankness, and a generally relaxed attitude toward self and others.

Effects of differences

Differences in personality patterns help to explain why each personality is unique. They also throw light on the degree of stability of the patterns once they have been established.

In some personality patterns, a high level of integration results in all the person's acts being harmonized with his basic concept of self. In others, the integration is less complete, while in still others, the integration seems to be nonexistent. In the extreme form, lack of integration results in "split personalities," the "Dr. Jekyll and Mr. Hyde" structure, where there are two mutually inconsistent patterns but where, within each, there is integration (167).

Very high or very low levels of integration are relatively infrequent. Between the two extremes are varying degrees of integration and varying degrees of consistency in behavior. It is a well-known fact that people behave differently in different situations and under different circumstances. This inconsistency has been described in the old folk saying that a person is "house angel and street devil" or vice versa. Allport (7) has written:

Every parent knows that an offspring may be a hellion at home and an angel when he goes visiting. A businessman may be hardheaded in the office and a mere marshmallow in the hands of his pretty daughter.

What is the ideal level of consistency? The question is still unanswered, but there is agreement that above-average consistency leads to better adjustment than below-average. Extreme consistency is likely to lead to rigidity, while marked inconsistency leads to excessive flexibility. The individual whose personality is poorly integrated is overly influenced by the opinions and actions of others. He changes with every wind that blows, behaving in such a way that people regard him as unreliable and unpredictable. As a result, they judge him as having a "weak" personality.

SUMMARY

1 The personality pattern is composed of traits that are organized and integrated into a pattern in which the concept of self is the core or center of gravity. The pattern is founded on the person's hereditary endowment, which is shaped by environmental experiences in the home and, later, outside the home. It is thus possible to control the environmental forces to ensure the development of a desired personality pattern or to change a pattern that is likely to lead to poor personal and social adjustments.

2 The concept of self, the core of the personality pattern, is made up of beliefs and attitudes toward self. It consists of three major components: the perceptual, the conceptual, and the attitudinal. The self-concept takes many forms: the basic, which includes the person's perception of his appearance, abilities, role and status in life, values, beliefs, and aspirations; the transitory, or the concept a person holds of himself only temporarily before replacing it with another self-concept; the social, or "mirror image," in which the person sees himself as he believes others see him; and the ideal self-concept, or the person's perception of the kind of person he would like to be.

3 Different self-concepts develop at different times and in different ways, forming a hierarchy in which the basic self-concept is shaped by the person's social experiences in the home. Later self-concepts are influenced by those formed earlier. Only when the self-concepts in the hierarchy are integrated can the person be happy and well adjusted. Within the hierarchy are all kinds of self-concepts, some of which play a more dominant role in the integration than others.

4 The various self-concepts develop in accordance with a predictable pattern. Physical self-concepts develop earlier than psychological self-concepts. Early social self-concepts are developed in the home, with the mother playing a dominant role in their development. Later, the environment outside the home and the popular stereotypes relating to sex, race, and other factors contribute to the foundations laid in the home. The basic self-concept develops later than the social and is influenced by the social. Ideal self-concepts begin to develop in the preschool years; in adolescence they reflect the young person's dissatisfaction with the self-as-is. The sources for these concepts come first from the home and later from the larger environment.

5 Discrepancies between the self-concepts make fusion into a general self-concept difficult and lead to personality maladjustments. Fusion is especially difficult when marked discrepancies exist between the basic and ideal self-concepts or between the basic self-concept and mirror images. Fusion is less difficult, though serious enough to be recognized and avoided, when discrepancies exist between physical and psychological self-concepts or between mirror images and ideal self-concepts.

6 Personal and social adjustments are likewise threatened by instability of the self-concept. Only when a person has a relatively stable self-concept can he develop a true sense of identity. Instability is most common during the early years of life and when there are rapid physical and mental changes or rapid and radical environmental changes.

7 Self-concepts based on specific experiences often become general and affect the quality of the person's behavior in all situations. This fact highlights the important role guidance should play in the development of self-concepts to guarantee that they will be both healthy and stable.

8 The second important component of the personality pattern consists of the "traits," or patterns of response tendencies, which are integrated with and influenced by the self-concept. They are learned tendencies to react to environmental stimuli and are based on hereditary foundations. Traits differ from habits in that habits are narrow and limited behavior patterns while traits are generalized and, therefore, more variable in their expression.

9 Common traits are those which are found in most people in a cultural group. Unique traits are those which are characteristic of a given individual. Whether classified as unique or common, all traits have three characteristics: uniqueness, degree of likableness, and consistency.

10 Many thousands of traits are found in a typical personality pattern. Through factor analysis, traits have been grouped into clusters and thus a more workable approach to the study of personality patterns has been developed. Clusters have been classified into two groups: source traits and surface traits.

11 In spite of the uniqueness of each personality pattern, there are similarities between personality patterns owing to cultural molding and similar child-training techniques. Patterns that show basic similarities are known as personality syndromes. Personality syndromes have been identified among persons who are regarded as abnormal as well as among those whose adjustments to life are relatively normal.

12 Each personality pattern is unique in the sense that it is different from other personality patterns in complexity, fluidity, accessibility, resistance to change, and centralization. These characteristics contribute to the pattern's stability and integration, which, in turn, affect the kind of adjustment the person makes.

CHAPTER 3 symbols of self

Judgments of a person are greatly influenced by certain cues, or "symbols of self," that have significant meaning for members of the cultural group. Like all symbols, symbols of self are visible signs of something invisible. As such, they *suggest* something to the observer because of their association with what he can observe.

It is through symbols of self that a person tries to reveal to others qualities which he wants them to associate with him, but which he cannot or does not want to reveal directly. He knows, for example, that telling people he is rich would be considered boastful or in bad taste. But he can use indirect, less obvious techniques to reveal his wealth. He can wear expensive clothes, drive a high-powered car, and join exclusive clubs.

If symbols of self are to serve their purpose effectively, they must be visible. While people may be able to infer information from cues that are only implied or suggested, the surest way to guarantee that others will make the "right" inference is to use symbols that are clearly visible.

People will probably infer that a person who goes to college is bright. But if he goes to a "name" college and wins a Phi Beta Kappa key from that college, there is no doubt about his brightness. Similarly, people may infer that a girl is "feminine" if she spends most of her time with other girls and engages in play activities that are culturally defined as feminine. But more tangible cues, such as feminine clothes, the choice of feminine subjects of study in school and college, and preparation for a feminine occupation, will eliminate any doubt of her femininity.

The more tangible and concrete a symbol, the less likely it is to be misinterpreted. This point was emphasized by Ryan (198) in speaking of the symbolic value of clothes for children:

The child thinks in concrete rather than in abstract terms. It is much easier for him to attribute acceptance or rejection to something tangible such as possession of the uniform or symbol of the group than it is to attribute it to something intangible such as sportsmanship or friendliness.

Much the same point was made by Guitar (90) in regard to children's status symbols:

Status symbols for the young fall chiefly into the display area. Food and drink labels, family tree, proper address—all so important to their parents—carry little weight with the younger generation. What counts is what you wear, drive, or play.

To select cues that will not be misinterpreted, a person must know the significance of the symbols he uses. Unless a boy knows that old, dirty clothes signify to his peers that he is a "regular guy," he will have little incentive to revolt against parental pressures to be neat and clean.

Every cultural group has its own symbols by which it judges others. To use symbols as a means of communicating information about himself, a person must know what the symbols of a particular group are. In some tribal groups, for example, scarification of the face is a symbol of bravery. Bravery is highly valued, and the more scars the person has, the braver he is judged to be. In other cultures, scars on the face are interpreted as a carry-over of adolescent acne. And even though modern medicine has refuted the idea, many people still cling to the old wives' tale that acne is due to masturbation. So to some, scars on the face may be a symbol of having engaged in socially disapproved behavior. Figure 3–1 shows how symbols of self are used as a form of communication.

Socioeconomic classes also have distinguishing significant symbols. A youthful, stylish appearance plays a relatively minor role in the work and social lives of lower-class men and women, and so they have little incentive to try to hide their gray hair and wear the latest fashions as they approach middle age. Men and women of the middle and upper socioeconomic groups, on the other hand, are well aware of the social value of a youthful appearance in all areas of their life and they use every cue they can to encourage others to judge them as young, attractive, and up-to-the-minute in style.

People who are socially mobile must learn to interpret the symbols of self of the socioeconomic class they are trying to identify with. Eating *boeuf bourguignon* is characteristic of members of the upper and upper-middle classes, for example, while eating beef stew is characteristic of the lower classes. Until the socially mobile person learns the symbols and

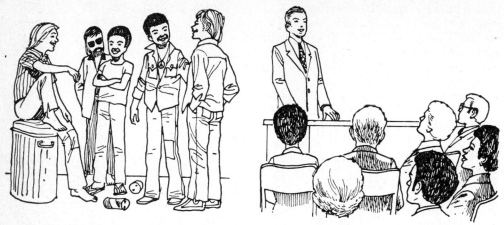

Figure 3-1 Symbols—such as style of dress—are used to communicate to the social group that a person possesses the qualities highly valued by the group at that age.

accepts them as his own, he will find identification with a higher class difficult (178).

Roles of symbols of self

Symbols of self play two roles. Not only do they influence one's judgments of others but they also influence one's concept of self.

Every member of a cultural group learns the meanings of the symbols of his group and applies them in making *judgments of others.* His impressions of others greatly affect his attitudes toward them and his treatment of them. The importance of symbols of self in this role varies according to how well the member of the social group—the one doing the judging—knows the other persons. If he does not know them, if they are newcomers, symbols of self carry a lot of weight. If he has known them a long time, the symbols have less influence on his judgments of them. In this connection, Ryan (198) has discussed the use of clothes as a symbol of self among adolescents:

The better known the individual, the less important are his clothes in determining popularity. For example, young adolescents in a small town who have known each other all their lives probably do not judge each other by clothing and therefore their clothes have little influence on their popularity or feelings of acceptance.

A person may not be aware that his judgments of others are affected by symbols of self. As Douty has pointed out, "Clothing may not be consciously perceived but its effect can be just as strong as though it

were" (64). In the same way, a person may not recognize that others' speech and use of the language influence his judgments.

Just as the individual uses the culture's symbols of self to judge others, so is he, in turn, being judged. The symbols thus influence the *development of the self-concept* and affect the personality. They become symbols of personal identity. The individual thinks of himself—and others judge him—in terms of those symbols. In addition, symbols of self contribute to the person's individuality and to his sense of distinctiveness. As such, they play a far more important role in personality development than most people recognize.

Common symbols of self

Since the cultural significance of a symbol of self must be learned before the individual can use it in judging others or appraising himself, age is one determinant of which symbols he will use. What he tries to communicate to others by the symbols he uses will depend on what is important at that time to him and to the group he is identified with. To the young child, going to school is a symbol of growing up. Being identified as a school child signifies to others that his babyhood days are over. Later, going to a particular school may be a symbol of belonging to the "right" group, and he will use the school uniform or a car sticker to make this identification manifest to all.

What qualities and characteristics people try to communicate by the use of symbols varies also from one culture to another. In the American culture, symbols are widely used to indicate identification with the "right" social group, individuality, maturity, autonomy, attractiveness, and sex appropriateness of appearance and behavior. All these are important in judging a person as "nice" or "well-adjusted."

In the following pages, the most common symbols of self in our culture will be described. Emphasis will be placed on what qualities are symbolized, how they are symbolized, and at what ages the symbols are used. In addition, a brief description will be given of how the symbols affect the person's concept of self; that is, how the judgments others make of the individual, as reflected in their attitudes toward him and the way they treat him, affect the way that he perceives himself.

CLOTHING

Long before a person becomes aware of the role physical appearance plays in the judgments others make of him, he discovers the symbolic value of clothing. Only if a marked physical defect focuses attention on the body does interest in the body develop as early as interest in clothes.

Jersild (121) has emphasized that clothing can symbolize many things which are important to a person and which he wants others to know:

An article of clothing which seems thoroughly objective in character may have tremendous subjective meaning. It may be an important protection of self, a means of self-defiance, of self-vindication, or it may be a means of communicating with others.

Once the symbolic value of clothing is recognized, the person tries to discover how clothes can be used to produce the effect on others he hopes to produce. This trial-and-error effort usually reaches a peak in early adolescence, the time when creating a favorable impression on others to gain social acceptance is so important.

Excessive interest in clothing, or greater interest than is normally shown by others of the same age and sex, is an indication of an unfavorable self-concept. Excessive interest is shown by talking constantly about clothes, reading about fashion to the exclusion of other subjects, wanting to be up-to-the-minute in style, and spending proportionally too much money on clothes. A scornful attitude toward clothes, shown by careless grooming, ignoring the prevailing styles, and dressing poorly when better clothes can be af-

forded, likewise indicates an unfavorable self-concept. Believing that others have a poor opinion of him, the person has a poor opinion of himself. Often he feels that society has shunned him, and he expresses his resentment in a contemptuous disregard for the kind of clothing that others consider desirable.

Qualities symbolized

Certain aspects of clothes give clues to the wearer's personality. In a study of the relationship between dress and selected measures of personality among women college students, it was found that those whose interest in dress centered on decoration were conscientious, conventional, conforming, nonintellectual, sociable, submissive, and sympathetic. Interest in economy in dress was found to be associated with a tendency to be responsible, conscientious, alert, efficient, precise, and controlled, while interest in comfort in dress was associated with a tendency to be self-controlled, socially cooperative, and sociable—the "controlled extroverts" (2).

Of the many qualities symbolized by clothing at various times in the life span, the following are the most important.

Autonomy   In late childhood and during most of adolescence, the individual uses clothes as a symbol of his independence. By wearing what his friends wear rather than what his parents want him to wear, he tells his peers that he is not "tied to his mother's apron strings." If parents favor conservative styles and colors and a neat appearance, the adolescent will symbolize his autonomy by wearing extreme styles and bright colors and assuming a casually sloppy manner of dress. In middle and old age, many people try to look younger than their years to counteract any impression others might have that they conform to the stereotype of old-age dependency.

Desire for attention   The desire to be noticed and to win the approval of others is universal. If being noticed is to have a positive effect on the person's self-concept, however, it must be favorable notice. Being noticed with disapproval makes a person feel inferior.

At an early age, the child discovers that his clothing attracts the attention of other children as well as adults. Favorable comments by adults and admiration or envy from other children contribute to the child's sense of self-importance. That is why the child is so eager to have new clothes and why he wants hand-me-downs to be altered or changed, even if only slightly, when they are given to him.

The adolescent appreciates the high attention value of clothing, but he knows that extreme styles, overornamentation, and too much jewelry win unfavorable attention and signify bad taste.

Clothes may also symbolize a desire not to be noticed. A person whose appearance deviates markedly from that of his peers—an obese child, for example—may be especially anxious to dress inconspicuously. The desire to be inconspicuous parallels the waning of physical attractiveness. As a result, well-adjusted middle-aged men and women tend to be more conservative in dress than they were in adolescence and early adulthood.

While conservatism in dress normally increases with age, a deviation from this pattern suggests to others that the person is unwilling to play the role the cultural group assigns to older people. Using clothes as a bid for attention in old age is a sign of poor adjustment and of rebellion against society's disregard for the elderly.

Identification   Throughout history the materials of which clothes are made, colors, and styles have been used to identify the wearer's role, status, or condition. "Clothes," as Hoult has explained, "play an important role in structuring the nature of interpersonal relationships" (113). Clothing, as an "outward sign of a way of life" (11) is a symbol of the wearer's status in the social group (141). When a person wants to be identified with a social group, he symbolizes his desire by "outward signs." A student dresses like a student; a businessman dresses in accordance with the stereotype of the businessman.

While today people can try to change their identification by dressing like members of the group with which they want to be identified, this was not always possible. At different times in history and in different countries, including America during the early Colonial days, sumptuary laws have been used to prescribe what people of various social classes could wear and prohibit them from copying the dress of members of other classes.

In Rome, at the time of the Emperor Aurelian, men could not wear yellow, white, red, or green shoes because by law these were reserved for women. Men were forbidden to wear garments made of silk, and only ambassadors to foreign lands were permitted to wear gold rings. In the reign of Edward III of England, sumptuary laws decreed that ermine and pearls, except for headdresses, might be worn only by members of the royal family and those nobles whose annual income exceeded one thousand pounds. In Puritan New England, the wearing of silver, gold, silk, laces, and beaver hats was prohibited by law because "excess of apparel among us is unbecoming to a wilderness condition and the professions of the gospel." Breaches of this law were punished as a form of witchcraft (116).

Belonging to a group he admires is a source of ego satisfaction to a child as well as to an adult. It makes little difference to the child if his clothes enhance his appearance or are in the latest style. As Ryan (198) stated:

The most important requisite of clothing, then, for the school child, is that it is sufficiently similar to other members of the group so that he is acceptable in this respect and is not ridiculed. Phrases such as "but all the others have . . ." or "nobody else has to wear . . ." are very familiar to every mother.

During adolescence a new meaning is associated with clothes. They become a badge of identity, creating the impression that the wearer is a member of the "right" group. Williams and Eicher (247) have reported that teen-age girls claim that the right clothing is needed to "get in" with the popular girls:

To adults, clothing and appearance may seem unimportant or, as emphasized by teen-agers, indicative of superficial and shallow values. However, if peer acceptance is important to an individual, dress and grooming can loom as crucial variables in the process of making friends and keeping them.

That the identification value of clothes is meaningful to adults may be seen in the widespread preference for white-collar jobs, even though blue-collar or "overall" occupations often pay more. It may also be seen in their willingness to go into debt or spend disproportionate amounts of money for clothes that will put up a "good front" and advance them socially.

Uniforms help to identify the wearers with specific roles. If the roles are prestigious, the judgments of others will be favorable. Even though boys and girls may rebel against wearing school uniforms, they like to wear them in public if the uniforms identify them with a prestigious school or college. Athletic uniforms identify the wearers with an activity that has high prestige in school and college life. Today, as Warburton (242) points out, the lab coat has taken on considerable symbolic value:

A neat, white, knee-length coat is universally recognized as the uniform of the scientist. . . . Just as we recognize a bishop by his mitre, or a burglar by his mask, we recognize a scientist by his lab coat. But in recent years the lab coat has become more than a mere workaday uniform. . . . Like spurs and shakos, the lab coat has been promoted to a new role: it is rapidly becoming not merely the uniform, but indeed the dress uniform *of the scientist. Dress uniforms are worn solely for symbolic and ceremonial reasons, not for practical purposes. . . . Scientists have momentarily achieved a position of high prestige, but in a democratic society (as in any other) prestige without symbols is but fleeting, while symbols without prestige may endure forever.*

Individuality   Although people like clothes that help to identify them with prestigious social groups, they also want to retain their individuality. As Bernard notes, "A girl should dress as the other girls do, but with just a touch of individuality" (22). This is true for boys, too, as well as for men and women.

Even the strong desire to be identified with his peers is not enough to make the older child or adolescent want to dress exactly like them. He wants his clothes to be just a little different so that he will be noticed, admired, or even envied. One of the major reasons for objecting to school uniforms is that they leave no room for individuality.

How much a person can express himself through his clothes and yet be identified with the group depends upon his level of acceptance in the group. The popular student can wear the most extreme styles as symbols of individuality and still arouse feelings of admiration and envy. But for the unpopular student, individuality in clothing is likely to be judged by others as bad taste or showing off. The greater the deviation from the styles worn by other members of the group, the more unfavorably the student is likely to be judged (84).

To win favorable social judgments, people who feel insecure in their status must conform to the fashions approved by the group, though they can individualize them to suit their own body builds or coloring. Achieving this favorable balance often means submerging personal likes and accepting the dictates of the fashion leaders.

Success   Regardless of age or sex, almost everyone wants others to think of him as successful. The meaning of "success" depends on what members of the group think is important. Adolescents value athletic success among boys and social success among girls. Boys who wear athletic uniforms with varsity insignia on them proclaim to all that they are successful athletes, while girls who wear clothes that identify them as among the "best dressed" proclaim their social success.

A person can symbolize socioeconomic success by wearing clothes made of superior material and designed by prestigious manufacturers, by having a large number of garments of each kind, and by wearing only the latest styles, which indirectly communicates the wearer's ability to discard old clothes and buy new ones as soon as the fashion changes. Which of these the individual will choose will depend largely on his socioeconomic status. Packard (178) has made the following distinctions:

The women of "old money" families (the true elite) tend to be relatively indifferent to swings in fashion; and their taste is oriented more to that of the British upper classes than to the French. . . . In contrast, the "new money" women (the unseasoned elite) are fascinated with high fashion as it is dictated by Paris. . . . As you move down into the range of the typical American woman, the aim is to follow whatever "smart" style is "sweeping the country." . . . In clothing as in other matters, the really rich prize age, while men well below them in status prize newness.

Success can also be symbolized by being a fashion leader. Leadership in any field is a symbol of success. If a person can be a style setter in his group, he will be judged by others as a leader and, as such, a successful person.

Sex appropriateness   The preschool child knows that others' judgments are greatly influenced by the sex appropriateness of his appearance. If a boy and girl wear "brother-sister outfits," the boy soon finds that other boys regard him as a sissy. The young child also discovers that certain colors are considered appropriate for boys and others for girls.

Because of cultural stereotypes, if a person wants to be considered sex-appropriate, he must wear the clothes that his group identifies with his sex. Even when the clothes worn by members of the two sexes are somewhat similar, the wearer's sex appropriateness is symbolized in color and style differences. Pants suits, for example, can be made "feminine" by the use of decorative buttons and other trimming and by the use of feminine blouses. See Figure 3–2.

Figure 3-2 Sex appropriateness can be symbolized by modifying the style of similar garments.

Sex appropriateness can also be symbolized by the way clothing is worn. Boys affect a sloppiness of appearance which is in direct contrast to the neatness identified as "feminine." Even in the business world, where good grooming is important, men adopt a more "casual" appearance than women.

Cosmetics, too, are symbols of sex appropriateness. As Wax (244) remarks:

Cosmetics help to identify a person as female in our culture and, generally speaking, as a female who views herself and should be treated as socially and sexually mature. The girl who wears cosmetics is insisting on her right to be treated as a woman rather than a child: likewise, the elderly woman wearing cosmetics is insisting that she not be consigned to the neutral sex of old age.

Maturity   The personal enjoyment and pride that the young child derives from wearing hand-me-downs associated with an older sibling are enhanced at adolescence when it is realized that certain styles can create the illusion that one is older and more mature than he actually is. The adolescent thus uses clothes to symbolize his maturity, which, he hopes, will result in more privileges.

Teen-age girls often go to extremes in style, in use of cosmetics, and in ornamentation of garments because they regard these as symbols of grown-up sophistication. Many teen-age boys also go through a stage of favoring "sophisticated" clothes in the hope of creating the impression that they are older than they are.

Effects of clothing on personality

Clothing symbolizes important characteristics of the wearer and influences the judgments others make of him. It influences the concept of self because the person tends to think of himself as others think of him. How greatly clothing will affect personality will depend on how well it symbolizes characteristics that the group regard as significant at that time. It will also depend on how well clothing meets the personal needs of the wearer at the time. When a person has a particularly strong craving for social acceptance, for example, his clothing may contribute to the poise and self-confidence he needs to make a favorable impression.

Girls with large body builds that are regarded by their peers as sex-inappropriate often select simple dark clothing in the hope that it will make their size less conspicuous. People who are sociable and want to attract attention favor bright colors and flamboyant designs. Those who are concerned about making a good impression often choose conservative colors and material with a small design. These facts have led to the conclusion that "the self is expressed through one's selection of clothing fabrics and that clothing items play a role in helping the individual to conform to an ideal self" (53).

That clothing suited to the needs of the individual helps him to achieve a favorable self-concept is well known to the layman, as shown by a large clothing company's advertisement in *The New York Times.* The ad said: "Psychoanalysis has helped some men to overcome obstacles and gain new confidence. So has good tailoring" (14).

The ego involvement of clothing has been noted by Hartmann. If clothes embarrass or humiliate the wearer or if they cause "swollen pride," they contribute to a distorted concept of self (96). Ordinarily, the wearer is quick to sense what others think of his clothes. This influences not only his attitude toward his clothes but also his attitude toward himself. Usually, the opinions of others reinforce the wearer's already-existing attitudes, whether they are favorable or not.

Morton (164) regards clothing as one of the chief determinants of personality:

For the vast majority of the human race, clothing plays a large part in making for happiness and success. . . . Clothes help to make us self-confident, self-respecting, jolly, free or they make us self-conscious, shy, sensitive, restrained. They determine how much we go into society, the places we go to, the exercise we take. They help us to get jobs and to hold them, to miss them and to lose them. . . . Clothes then make or mar us. They may enhance our personality or be so conspicuous as to subordinate us to them.

Effects of being well dressed
Studies reveal that people who are judged by others as being among the "best dressed" of their group feel "considerably better about themselves" than those who are judged as less well dressed. The "best dressed" are friendlier, more vivacious, and more talkative; they have a more active social life; and they are more popular and more likely to be selected as leaders (52, 133, 198). Knowing that they make a good impression on others, they are less self-conscious, less self-centered, and less anxious. Since they feel at ease, they behave in a natural, friendly way. As a result, they enjoy greater social acceptance than those whose behavior is judged less favorably (133, 198).

By adolescence, boys and girls recognize the value of clothing in making a good impression. As a result, they become extremely clothes-conscious and are willing to sacrifice other pleasures to buy the kind of clothes they want. They not only want to create the impression that they are well dressed, but they also want their clothes to tell others what "type" of person they are and what group they belong to.

Effects of being poorly dressed
Being poorly or inappropriately dressed can make a person feel uncomfortable and self-conscious. His uneasiness and lack of confidence adversely affect the judgments of others as well as his level of social acceptance. Feeling inadequate and inferior, he is likely to develop a self-rejecting attitude and to be shy, self-effacing, and uncooperative. He develops a defensive, nonparticipatory attitude toward social activities, claiming that they bore him. He develops a strong, almost fearful distaste of prominence and leadership roles and withdraws from any situation in which he might have to be in the spotlight (93, 133, 198).

Worrying about the impression he is making on others causes the poorly dressed person to become tongue-tied. He then gives the impression of being dull or bored. This accentuates his lack of social acceptance and intensifies his desire to be inconspicuous and to withdraw from the social situation as soon as possible. Occasionally a poorly dressed person will talk in a nervous and compulsive way to distract attention from his clothes, or he will apol-ogize for his own appearance and criticize that of others.

Only a person who is well known for his achievements, his wealth, or his social position can afford to be poorly dressed if he wants to be favorably judged. Even the most eminent person, however, cannot count on being favorably judged if others do not know of his achievements or recognize the symbols of his position.

Being poorly dressed over a long period is likely to give the person an inferiority complex. Should economic adversity or some other condition force a person to adopt a style of dress much below what he has been used to, it will lead to feelings of martyrdom in addition to feelings of inferiority. These feelings are responsible for some of the unfavorable attitudes toward self that are so prevalent among elderly people.

Fear of being unfavorably judged by others leads many adolescents and adults to use questionable devices to obtain the clothing they feel is essential to social approval. Many cases of shoplifting and petty thievery, especially among girls, have been attributed to the desire to obtain clothes, costume jewelry, and other aids to personal adornment which they or their parents cannot afford. Adults seeking advancement in the business world often borrow or spend beyond their means to buy expensive clothes.

Sex differences in effects
Clothes are a more common symbol of self for girls and women than for boys and men. This is not because appearance is a less important symbol of self for males, but rather because men's clothes are more standardized than women's. A man or boy can be well dressed with a rather limited wardrobe of well-selected clothes. Furthermore, men's styles change so slowly that men do not have to replace old garments with new ones every season.

Since men's and boys' clothes are more standardized in cut, materials, and colors than women's and girls', it is more difficult for males to use clothing to cover up their bad features and enhance their good ones. Their clothing thus serves as a symbol of their real selves, not of their ideal selves, as is so often true for females.

Feminine interest in clothes normally reaches a peak during adolescence and early adulthood—the time when success in courtship is of greatest concern. For men, by contrast, interest is greatest in middle age—when vocational achievements is usually at its height. As men approach retirement age, their interest in clothing ordinarily wanes. The value of clothing as a symbol of self declines rapidly as contacts with members of the business world, whose judgments are important to vocational success, come to an end. Since women do not usually withdraw from social life as early as men retire from business, their interest in clothes wanes more slowly. Even though they may be less active than when they were younger, favorable judgments of others are still important to them.

NAMES AND NICKNAMES

Names have always been used as symbols to identify people and to indicate status in the group, family connections, religious affiliation, occupation, and other personal details. This is true of primitive as well as civilized peoples.

It was Freud, however, who first emphasized that names are symbols of self in that they are representations of the personality pattern of the bearer and, as such, are used by others in making their judgments of him. Following this beginning, many studies have shown that names are not only a symbol of the personality of the bearer but are also a determinant of his personality (77, 156).

The symbolic role of names was stressed further by Freud in his explanation of the forgetting of names. Freud stated that the motivation for forgetting is to repress unpleasant associations with the person who bears a forgotten name. When the name touches off or is connected with some unpleasant association, the person may forget, distort, or falsify the name in a conscious or unconscious attempt to repress the unpleasant association (77).

While Freud's interpretation of forgetting is questioned by many psychologists today, it is a useful reminder of the symbolic value of names. If a person is known to others only by his name, they will judge him by it and endow him with the pleasant or unpleasant qualities which they associate with his name, whether the qualities fit him or not. Thus, his name may be either an asset or a barrier to his socialization.

Allport has referred to names as an "anchorage point of selfhood" (4). According to Helper, names are "personal labels" or "identity symbols" (105). They exert such a powerful influence on the judgments of others as well as on one's judgment of self that Murphy is justified in saying that "one of the most important parts of a person is his name" (165).

Why names are important symbols

A person's name is his only symbol of self which is permanent. The individual is given a name at birth and it remains with him throughout life. Even if people change their names, as girls do at marriage or as some people do when they dislike their names, the name-label that has been associated with them in the minds of others for so long continues to have its effect.

Unlike clothes, speech, and other symbols of self, names are peculiarly permanent. They cannot be changed without legal action, whether it be through marriage, adoption, or the direct initiative of the bearer. And since legal action cannot be taken before one reaches the age of legal maturity, any change before that time depends upon the willingness and consent of parents or guardians.

A person can, of course, change his nickname without legal action. But persuading others to accept the change is far from easy. If a group of boys label one of their classmates "Pudge" because he is overweight and clumsy, they are not likely to drop the name even if he goes on a diet and becomes slim.

When a person feels that his family name is embarrassing or humiliating, he may do something to try to free himself from its unpleasant associations. How emotionally difficult this is for a person is illustrated by the comment of a man whose family name was "Buggs." Changing his name, he said, was "not an easy step. In the church registers there are references to the Buggs going back to the year 1700" (147).

A person may try to conceal a disliked given name by using an initial or a nickname, by altering its spelling or pronunciation, or by changing the name completely. An unusual name may be substituted for a common one or vice versa. Walter may be substituted for Walto, Frances for Francesca, or Lee for Lurlene.

Disliked surnames are dealt with in much the same way. In a group of Chinese preschoolers, for example, Sui Fei Wong became Warren Wong and Chung Chan became Andrew Chang (56). These changes, it might be added, were in effect nicknames because they were used in school only to help the children avoid being identified with a national group against which, at the time, there was prejudice.

Changing the spelling or the pronunciation of a name often eliminates the embarrassment the name causes its bearer. The name, "Doome," for example, may be changed to "Dome," and the name "Rape" to "Rapé" (165). The surname "Christ" is less embarrassing if pronounced with a short *i* than if pronounced with a long *i*.

Name combinations

People judge a person by his full name as well as by its parts. Name combinations and the form the bearer uses when he writes his name are important symbols of self.

In a study of name styles and their relation to personality, it was reported that there are seven different ways in which a person with three names may use them as identity symbols. Each suggests certain things about the person's personality.

If John Jacob Brown signs himself "John Brown" or "John J. Brown" he will be judged as conforming to social customs and be thought of as having a conventional self-concept. If he uses "John Jacob Brown," he may be regarded as an exhibitionist with an exaggerated view of self or, if he is a weak and passive person, as one who is seeking to identify himself by a demonstrative display. If he omits his first two names and signs himself "J. J. Brown," he may be thought of as a restrained and reserved person, as one who wants to avoid revealing himself to others, or as one who dislikes his name or is embarassed by it. Using "J. Jacob Brown" suggests that he is striving for individuality and superiority. If he uses "Jr.," "III," or "IV" after his name it suggests to others an upper-class or close family identification and an awareness of status and tradition. The use of a title, such as "Dr.," "Col.," or "Professor," suggests that Brown plays an authoritative role in society and is regarded by others as a distinguished person (94).

Kinds of names

In almost every culture the individual has at least two names, his own personal name, or as it is sometimes called, his "Christian" or "given" name, and his surname or family name. If he has only two names, his personal name is known as his "first" name and his surname as his "last" name. If he has more than two names, the others are known as his "middle" name or names. The only name that is legally a surname is the last name. It is borne by all members of the individual's family and is not specifically his own.

One's *personal name* may be common or uncommon, depending on fads. At one time, "Pauline" may be "common," in the sense that many girls and women have this name, while at other times, it may be so infrequently used that it is "uncommon." The name "Anthony" became common in England at the time of the romance of Princess Margaret and Anthony Armstrong-Jones, now the Earl of Snowden (169).

In the American culture the *surname* is always the family name of the father if the parents are married. If they are not, the child's surname is that of the mother's family.

Middle names are selected by parents in the same way in which they select the first name. If a boy is to be called "Jr.," his whole name must be identical to that of his father.

Everyone has *kinship* names which symbolize his status in the family and his relationship to other family members. In his relationship to his parents, a boy's kinship name is "son"; in his relationship to his siblings, it is "brother"; in his relationship to his grandparents, it is "grandson"; and in his relationship to more distant relatives, it is "cousin" and "nephew." The warmth of one's relationship with family members is symbolized by what they call him and what he calls them. Calling one's mother-in-law "Mother Jones" symbolizes a warmer relationship than calling her "Mrs. Jones."

At some time in his life, almost everyone has one or more *nicknames.* These, like kinship names, are not legal names. They are names given to a person by members of his family or peer group, or in adulthood by friends or coworkers, which reflect the attitudes of others toward him. A nickname may be used for a short time and then be replaced by another, or it may cling to the bearer for the major part of his life.

Nicknames fall into a number of categories. "Pet" names, or names of endearment, generally originate in the home; *national* or *racial* nicknames derive from physical features, speech, or behavior patterns associated with the stereotypes of particular groups; *animal* names are based on physical characteristics, speech, or behavior associated with certain animals, such as "Pussy," "Rabbit," or "Hoss"; some names are derived from *physical traits* or *physical defects,* such as "Red," "Lanky," or "Fatso"; some are based on outstanding *personality characteristics,* such as "Tight," "Preacher," or "Happy"; some are *distortions of the real name,* such as "Debbie" or "Lizzie"; and some are made up from the *person's initials,* such as "SAP", "JAW," or "COW" (92, 165, 176).

As these classifications suggest, many nicknames are "verbal descriptions" of their bearers (80).

They may be complimentary, but more often they are verbal caricatures which emphasize some embarrassing physical or psychological trait. Whether they are disparaging or not will depend on how they originated, what associations they imply, and even on how they are spoken.

Nicknames often express an underlying emotional attitude of a particular group toward an individual. They may express the group's rejection of a reality situation the individual is unable to control. Color of hair, race, and build are "reality situations which may be painfully impressed upon the developing ego" by a nickname (92, 165).

A *title* may also be regarded as a kind of name. While in the United States social class distinctions are not indicated by such titles as "Count," "Earl," or "Prince," there are titles which symbolize the bearer's marital status (Miss, Mrs.) and profession (Dr., Reverend, or Professor).

Personal reactions to names

It is sometimes hard for the individual to know which of his names is a true symbol of self and which is used by others in their judgments of him. See Figure 3–3. The confusion of identity is well expressed in an old rhyme.

Mother calls me William
Auntie calls me Will
Sister calls me Willie
But Dad calls me Bill.

Figure 3-3 Confusion about identity arises when a person is called by different names.

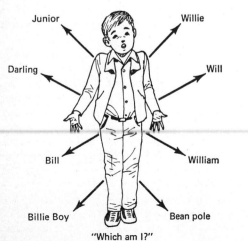

Junior

Willie

Darling

Will

Bill

William

Billie Boy

Bean pole

"Which am I?"

The confusion is multiplied when the person discovers that the meaning of his name or nickname may vary from one situation to another or from one user to another. When used by a parent, the name "Junior" is associated with pride; when used by a member of the peer group, it is associated with ridicule.

While a person may consider each of his names, separately, a satisfactory symbol of self, his name combination may carry unpleasant overtones or may open him up to considerable ridicule. A girl may be satisfied with the symbolism of the names "Jessie" and "May," but when they are combined with her surname to produce "Jessie May Berst," the symbolism is so unpleasant that she will hate her name. Similarly, an acceptable name combination, such as "Stanley Arthur Powell," may result in initials that encourage unfavorable judgments.

Reactions to specific names   As Flugel has remarked, "Few, if any, people are indifferent to their names" (75). We either like or dislike our names, and our attitudes are due mainly to the reactions of other people, not to the names per se.

Names are more often disliked for their associations than for the unpleasantness of their sounds. "Jack," for example, is liked because it is associated with a he-man image, while "Percy," which has a less harsh sound, is disliked because of its association with the stereotype of a "sissy." The once-favored name of "Adolf" has been shunned by the West Germans since World War II because of its association with Hitler (173).

Studies of likes and dislikes in *given* names have revealed that common names are preferred. Children and adolescents want to be as much like their friends as possible. Being different makes them feel both conspicuous and inferior. Only when they have passed through the self-conscious stage of early adolescence and are self-confident enough to want to attract attention to themselves do they like names that are unusual. Even then, they do not like names that are so different as to make them feel conspicuous (1, 31, 95, 105).

The most disliked given names are those which lend themselves to mispronunciation, misspelling, distortion, and ridicule; which are used for both sexes; which combine with the person's other names to produce initials or full names with unpleasant connotations; which are associated with unfavorable stereotypes, or with a minority, religious, or racial group; or which have disliked nicknames associated with them ("Lizzie" for Elizabeth) (3, 37, 42, 95, 165, 248).

When a name is so common that the bearer must use his surname or middle name or a nickname or Jr. to distinguish himself, he feels that he has lost his identity and comes to dislike his name. Similarly, rare names, such as "Elkanah" and "Seraphim," are disliked because they are difficult to pronounce and seem so outlandish to others that they encourage ridicule (95). Boys and men dislike having unusual names more than girls and women. However, women prefer the more common names for men and the more unusual ones for women (1, 66, 94).

The most disliked *surnames* are those which are difficult to pronounce or spell; which make the bearer feel inferior ("Small," "Little," or "Short") or embarrassed ("Fiddler," "Roach," or "Hogg"); which are associated with historical or stereotyped literary characters (St. George, who slew the dragon, or Simon, who was simple); and which sound "foreign," especially if they are associated with ethnic or religious groups that are subjected to prejudice (42, 95, 165).

Children and adolescents with stepfathers are often embarrassed because their surnames are not the same as their parents'. Even though they may not like their stepfathers, they usually want to change their names to avoid being different from their peers.

People in occupations where names are important symbols, such as acting and writing, often change their names in order to produce an aura of glamour or prestige (165). The well-known actress, Lauren Bacall, for example, was born Betty Joan Perskie—a far less glamorous name than the one she assumed for her stage career.

Disliked *middle names* are often hidden by the use of the initial only. Women are sometimes indifferent to their middle names as well as their surnames because they can drop the middle name when they marry and use only an initial for their maiden surnames.

Very few people like their *nicknames,* but there is little they can do about them. If they object, they are likely to be regarded as poor sports or as lacking in appreciation of the affection a "pet" name implies. The closer a nickname is to a verbal caricature, the more disliked it is.

Even though a person may have an affectionate relationship with members of his family, he often dislikes the *kinship* names they apply to him. A woman may object to her children calling her "Ma" or the "Old Lady" even though she knows it is done in an

affectionate, teasing vein. Fathers usually object to being called the "Old Man" or the "Boss" because they feel such names show lack of respect.

Most boys consider "Junior" a babyish name and most girls consider "Sis" derogatory. While a woman will not object to the formal kinship label "Mother" when used by her children, she is likely to object very much when it is used by her husband because she feels it implies that she is the children's mother, not his wife.

Children are known mainly by their first names, and so their surnames carry little meaning for them. Not until adolescence, when friends and acquaintances become more numerous and surnames are used by teachers and peers with increasing frequency, does the individual find his surname a matter of concern. In addition, it is not until adolescence that he is fully aware of the symbolic value of names or of the prejudice that comes from being associated with a minority or "foreign" group. From adolescence on, surnames are more important symbols of self than given names because in business and social life, people are known primarily by their surnames. At no time, however, are either given names or surnames unimportant to a person once he has learned that others judge him by them.

Symbolic value of names

The origin of the symbolic value of most names, as is true of the origin of stereotypes, is shrouded in mystery. Most symbolic values originated long ago and have been passed down to us by social learning.

Some symbolic values are relevant only to a small segment of a cultural group, such as names favored by a particular religious sect, but usually beliefs about the personality characteristic associated with names are universal within a culture. For example, among the Ashanti people in Africa, the boy's name "Kwadwo" is universally associated with a quiet, retiring, peaceful person while the name "Kwaku" is associated with the quick-tempered, aggressive troublemaker—the "bad boy" type (119).

In the American culture, the symbolic value of names comes from many sources—from historical, fictional, and religious figures, for example, and from leaders in the political, entertainment, or sports worlds whose activities are publicized in the mass media or known from personal experience. The symbolic value of a name, once established, is seldom eradicated from people's minds. People expect a person with a particular name to act "in character." "John" is thought of as trustworthy, while "Anthony" or "Tony" is thought of as sociable and glamorous. Girls bearing the name "Jane," "Agnes," or "Matilda" are thought of as plain, while "Violet" is expected to be sweet, shy, and completely feminine.

In a humorous discussion of the subject, Baker (13) pointed out some of the expectations commonly associated with names:

Juliet was deceiving herself when she insisted that there is nothing in a name. It is perfectly obvious that if the man under the balcony had been named John instead of Romeo she wouldn't even have opened the French windows for him. . . . A John has some slight option about his fate. He may, with great effort, transmute himself into a Jack, in which case he may wear sweaters, throw his pipe away, drive sports cars and engage in muscular activity. . . . Before his first change of diapers, the Irving knows that he is consigned to the intellectual life, doomed at worst to years with Nietzsche in the library stacks, at best to writing brilliantly denunciatory letters to the editors of elite magazines.

Qualities symbolized

As symbols of self, names are used by people to judge the personality characteristics of the bearer. The characteristics described below are most often symbolized by names.

Identification   The person's status within a social group is judged by the kind of name and the number of names he has. If he has a common name, he will be judged as belonging to the "common-man" category; if he has a "distinguished" name, he will be thought of as a distinguished person; if he has a name identified with a religious or ethnic minority, he will be identified with the stereotype of that group.

Kinship names and nicknames also serve as a form of identification. A woman who is called "Mother," "Mom," or "Mummy" is not only identified as playing the role of mother but is seen as the recipient of the respect and affection associated with that role. Further, the name "Mummy" suggests a close relationship between the child and his mother, while "Mother" suggests a more formal relationship.

The kind of nickname applied to a person identifies the kind of relationship he has with the group. A "pet" name suggests a close, warm relationship with family members or intimate friends; a complimentary nickname suggests a similar relationship with outsiders; and a verbal-caricature kind of nickname suggests a relationship marked by hostility, scorn, and even rejection.

The more names a person has, the more distinguished he is thought to be. If in addition to having more than two names, he has a title designating a prestigious occupation and is known as "Jr.," "III," or "IV," the identification as a distinguished person will be greatly enhanced.

Glamour   A person whose name is regarded as glamorous is automatically thought of as a glamorous person. Names which are unusual enough to be "interesting" but not funny or strange and those which are associated with members of the nobility in foreign countries, with glamorous people in the public eye, or with heroes and heroines of literature automatically endow the bearer with some element of glamour. It is difficult, for example, to think of a girl named "Olivia" or "Juliet" as a "plain Jane," while it is equally difficult to think of a girl named "Jane" as glamorous.

Personality type   Certain names suggest what people refer to as the introverted type—the quiet, shy, and socially withdrawn person. Others suggest an extrovert—the sociable, outgoing, and well-liked type. "Percy" and "Violet" are symbolic of the introvert, while "Susan" and "George" symbolize the extrovert. The "dependable type" is associated with "John" or "Ann," while the "adventuresome or unpredictable type" is associated with "Robin" or "Jo."

Individuality   Unusual names or name combinations suggest a person who is individualistic. "Jonathan Smith" suggests greater individuality than "John Smith," for example. Nicknames, even when they are verbal caricatures, imbue the bearer with an element of individuality in the judgments of others. One of the reasons titles are so meaningful to people is that they add a touch of individuality to even the most commonplace names. While individuality in names leads to favorable judgments, most people learn to dislike their names if they are too unusual.

Sex appropriateness   Everyone, from earliest childhood on, wants to be thought of as sex-appropriate. Having a sex-appropriate name goes a long way toward creating the impression in the minds of others that the bearer is a sex-appropriate person. It is hard to think of a boy as sex-appropriate if he is called "Percival" but easy if he is called "Robert" or "Ronald." Similarly, it is hard to think of a girl with a "hybrid name," one that is used for either sex, as truly feminine. If parents are disappointed because their daughter is not a boy, for example, and name her "Paula" for her father "Paul," she will be thought of as having both masculine and feminine characteristics. Names such as "Marion" or "Robin," which are used as often for boys as for girls, militate against judgments of sex appropriateness (80, 165, 248). See Figure 3–4.

A nickname that is applied to members of both sexes makes it difficult for people to think of the bearer as a sex-appropriate person. This is especially true of "pet" names. The person who is called "dear," "darling," or "sweetheart" by a family member may seem to others to be neuter. A verbal caricature, such as "Fatso" or "Greenhorn," fails to give others a cue to the sex of the bearer.

Popularity   How popular or how well accepted a person is may be symbolized by the name used in address by others, by the nickname applied to him, or even by the tone used in speaking his name or nickname. One who is liked by others is more often called by his first name, regardless of age, than by his surname. A more formal method of address suggests a distant relationship with others or even hostility. A person called by a complimentary nickname can be accurately judged as being liked by others.

Even when the first name or a flattering nickname is used to address a person, it does not automatically imply popularity. If the tone of voice used in address is cold and distant or if the name is spoken in a tone of ridicule or sarcasm, the implication is that the bearer of the name is unpopular (66, 165). Even a "pet" name habitually used in addressing a person may be said in such tones as to imply that the person is out of favor *at the moment.* A parent who calls his firstborn son "Junior," implying that the child is especially loved, may use such harsh, reproachful tones that his affection for the son is open to question.

Effects of names on personality

While most people think of names as a way of identifying others, there is evidence that names also have "a psychological aspect. . . . Names play a role of some

"Mommy, when other kids are around could you call me Bill instead of Billy?"

Figure 3-4 It is difficult to think of oneself as sex-appropriate when one has a name that lacks sex appropriateness. (Adapted from "The Family Circus." Register and Tribune Syndicate. *The Philadelphia Evening Bulletin,* Oct. 14, 1968. Used by permission.)

importance in our mental life, and may even influence our conduct in subtle ways which we fail to recognize" (75). Scientific evidence of the psychological effects of names on the bearer's self-concept is relatively recent, but there is historical evidence that as early as 2,000 B.C. people thought proper names had the power to determine the bearer's destiny (165).

The effect of names on personality, according to Hartman et al. (95) begins at birth and extends throughout life:

A child's name, like his somatotype, is generally a settled affair when his first breath is drawn, and his future personality must then grow within its shadow. A powerful mesomorphic boy must experience a different world from his puny counterpart; and, similarly, a boy who answers to a unique, peculiar or feminine name may well have experiences and feelings in growing up that are quite unknown to John or William. One would expect these different childhood experiences to be reflected in the subsequent personality. It is plausible, and confirmed by clinic experience, to assume also that some individuals are seriously af-fected as a result of a peculiar name.

Why names affect personality

Names affect the self-concept because the bearer real-izes that his name is a symbol to others of what he is and that they judge him in terms of what that symbol means to them. As McDavid and Harari have said, "People, like objects, tend to be judged by their labels" (156).

The name used in addressing a person tells him as well as others how the speaker feels about him. An intimate form of address suggests a liking for the person and a feeling that he is an equal or a subor-dinate. If a businessman calls his secretary by her first name, that implies that he likes her and considers her his subordinate. If, on the other hand, he refers to a superior officer in his company by the title "Mr." before his surname, he is symbolizing his respect for the officer's superior status.

Not only does the form of address tell how the speaker feels about the person but it also tells how he feels *at the moment.* If a superior officer in a business organization calls a subordinate "Tom," instead of his usual "Thomas" or "Mr. Jones," then Tom is justified in concluding that he is in the good graces of his superior *at that moment.* Similarly, when a mother calls her child by a pet name, he knows that the relationship between them is a good one. If she calls him by his given name on occasion, he may have reason to believe that at the time she is angry at him.

"Name calling" likewise gives the person a clue to how others judge him and feel about him—at least at that moment. The child, the adolescent, or the adult who is subjected to name calling by a sibling, a peer, or a spouse knows that the judgment made of him is unfavorable. If an adolescent is called a "baby," he knows that he is being judged as immature. If a hus-band calls his wife a "gold-digger," it tells her that he considers her grasping and demanding.

It must be stressed, however, that a name, per se, has little or no influence on a person's self-concept. Its influence is felt only when the person becomes aware of the social attitudes toward his name. A per-son may be liked by others because of his name, or his name may be liked because he is liked. In many cases, social attitudes toward names may be a case of "Which came first, the chicken or the egg?" (156).

When social attitudes toward a person's name or some part of it are positive, others' judgments and treatment of the person will probably be favorable. The bearer of the name, knowing or suspecting these positive social attitudes, will like his name and this will have a good influence on his behavior. People who like their names report that their names make them feel proud and that they have a feeling of importance when their names are mentioned (165).

The practical value of having a name that peo-ple usually like is that one may take advantage of the fact that if people know nothing about him except his name, they will expect him to be a nice person (165). Unlike someone else who has a name others tend to dislike, he does not have to be concerned about an unfavorable name reaction.

Evidence of effects on personality

A number of experimental studies have shown what effect names have on personality. While many studies have concentrated on neurotic tendencies, some have shown the favorable effects of names at different ages, especially during childhood and adolescence (156).

Among the Ashanti people in Africa, it is be-lieved that character is influenced by the day of the week on which the person is born. Therefore, it is customary to give the child a name associated with that day. This is known as his "soul name." Further-more, the Ashanti believe that, because one's name influences his personality, the child will grow up to have the personality traits associated with his name. Boys born on Monday are called "Kwadwo" and are expected to grow up to be quiet, peaceful people. Wednesday boys, traditionally called "Kwaku," are expected to grow up to be mischievous, quick-tempered, and aggressive. These social expectations influence the boys' self-concepts and, in turn, the quality of their behavior. Studies of juvenile court records of the Ashanti showed that very few boys with the name "Kwadwo" were listed. They had lived up to society's expectations. Many boys named "Kwaku" had likewise lived up to society's expectations and were listed in the court records (119).

People who dislike their names because they feel that their names lead others to view them un-favorably also tend to dislike themselves. They claim that they feel shy, self-conscious, sensitive, and em-barrassed when their names are mentioned or when they are introduced to strangers. They thus tend to shun social situations and to become self-bound and introverted. On the other hand, a positive relationship has been found between liking one's name and self-acceptance (24, 31, 222).

In a study of the relationship between the desirability of names and popularity, it was found that the "child who bears a generally unpopular or unattractive name may be handicapped in his social interactions with peers. . . . There may be a general tendency toward negative evaluation of infrequently encountered names" (156). McDavid and Harari have stressed that "socially undesirable names" inflict a handicap on children in peer-group popularity (156).

Continued embarrassment from disliked names often contributes to maladjustment. College students with eccentric names have more than their proportional number of flunk-outs, dropouts, and psychoneuroses. It has also been found that there is a greater likelihood of success in marriage if a man selects a wife with a common name (42). A woman with an uncommon name, it is said, may consider herself "odd" because she believes that others consider her odd. In addition, she may have been subjected to undue criticism, ridicule, or even ostracism because of her name and this may have fostered feelings of inadequacy and martyrdom (95).

Parents who give a child an eccentric name may be neurotic or "odd" themselves, and the unhealthy home climate and unfavorable parent-child relationships are likely, in time, to cause maladjustments in the child. The combination of unwholesome environmental conditions and an eccentric name is responsible for the effect the name has on personality (95).

Variations in effects of names on personality While there is no justification for saying that *all* unusual names will be disliked or that *all* disliked names will lead to personality maladjustments, there is a grain of truth in the statements. The *given* name, because it is used more than the surname during the early, formative years of life, is likely to have a more profound effect on personality than the surname. And since the foundations of the concept of self are laid in childhood, the given name influences the form these foundations will take.

The effect of a *nickname* on the self-concept depends not on the name alone but on what it implies to the bearer regarding the group's attitude toward him. If he interprets his nickname to mean that others are ridiculing him, he is likely to experience feelings of personal inadequacy and of resentment and hostility toward others and a general feeling of martyrdom. His nickname makes him "feel that he has committed some crime, either physically or actually" (176).

Not all nicknames are verbal caricatures, nor do all people react unfavorably to them. If a person

interprets his nickname to mean that he has the affection and acceptance of the group, it has a favorable effect on his personality. People who are very popular generally have nicknames, just as do those who are unpopular. However, a person is fortunate if his "name and/or personal characteristics do not suggest humorous, bizzare nicknames to the imaginative minds of his peers" (80). Because, as Garrison has stressed, "The nature of the nickname given a child and the use made of it may have a profound effect on the development of his personality" (80).

If the nickname is a term of endearment conferred on the person by a family member or intimate friend, its effect on his personality will depend not so much on the name itself as on the use made of it. Boys especially are self-conscious about being called by "pet" names in the presence of members of the peer group. Even adult men are often embarrassed when called by some name of endearment by their spouses. Under such conditions, it cannot fail to affect their self-concepts.

Much the same is true of kinship names. A boy may not object to being called "Sonny" in the presence of his family, but he will object to the use of this name in front of his peers. Similarly, a woman may not object when her husband refers to her as "Mother" in the presence of their children, but she will object when he calls her "Mother" in front of her friends. A man may react with amusement when a child or his wife calls him the "boss" at home, but outside the home, he resents it because he is afraid of being regarded by others as a tyrant.

The effect of a name on the concept of self will depend more on the *degree* of dissatisfaction the bearer experiences than on the fact that he dislikes it. Those who dislike their names tend to be less self-accepting and less well-adjusted than those who like or are indifferent to their names. The more they dislike their names, the more self-rejectant and the more poorly adjusted they are likely to be.

Need for care in name selection

A person's name is such a central symbol of self that great care should be exercises in selecting a name. This point has been stressed repeatedly by scientists who have studied the effects of names on personality. Allen et al. (3) write:

The choice of a given name to be bestowed upon the child is a matter of no little moment to him in his relations with other individuals, for an unfortunate selection may doom him to recurring embarrassment or even unhappiness.

Murphy (165) explains the psychological hazards faced by people with distressing names:

The names of individuals play an important role in the organization of their ego defense patterns and are cathected and utilized from the point of view of ego defenses in a manner similar to an organ or body part. . . . For some, the name may become part of the core of a severe neurosis. . . . The degree of pathological disturbance varies from exaggerated pride or exaggerated shame over one's name . . . to extremes of psychotic proportions.

It has been suggested from time to time that the child not be given a permanent name until "he has had time to investigate the world and determine what he would like to be" (13). This would, of course, eliminate many of the psychological hazards that come from having a disliked given name, but it is not at all practical. On the other hand, is there any doubt that a "parent might appropriately think twice before naming his offspring for Great Aunt Sophronia" (156)?

SPEECH

Speech is regarded as a symbol of self because it gives clues to the personality of the speaker. The symbolism of speech has been explained by Ellis: "Speech is the primary medium which all persons use to affect the society in which they live, and the main medium through which they are affected by that society" (73).

Speech tells others how the speaker thinks of himself, what his dominant interests are, how he feels about other people, and what his relationship with them is. As Shirley says, the "pattern of personality is clearly woven in the fabric of speech" (211). In addition, speech tells something about the emotional state of the speaker—whether he is happy or sad, frightened or calm, curious or apathetic, envious or appreciative, sympathetic or critical, or angry. As such, it is a "thermometer of emotional reactions" (211).

"Self-talk," Lipsett's label for the person's verbalizations about his own feelings and activities, is a prime symbol of self and of self-evaluation (145). The person who talks about his inferiority or inadequacy can be assumed to have a poor concept of self. The person who verbalizes his superiority, however, may

have a favorable self-concept, delusions of grandeur, or an unfavorable self-concept which he is attempting to hide. Penny (186) explains other ways in which we use speech in judging others:

In our everyday communication relationships we constantly make inferences, perhaps not always consciously, about the communicator's motivation from both what he says and how he says it. We observe . . . that he repeatedly returns to particular topics, that he selects some aspects of a topic and disregards others, that he uses a particular tone of voice or style of speech, and so on. From such data we may infer that he has a "one track mind," that he is biased, that he is being sincere or insincere. Probably most inferences of this kind are made automatically, on the basis of very limited data together with rather broad assumptions about human nature.

At a very early age, the child discovers that crying attracts attention to himself and influences the actions of others. After he learns to talk, he discovers that certain combinations of words, such as questions, criticisms, and boasting, have greater attention value than others. As he becomes able to interpret the reactions of others more accurately, he learns that some verbalizations bring favorable reactions while others do not. Later, when he discovers that people judge him by what he says and how he says it, he uses speech to create the impression he wishes to create.

The reactions of others to a speaker are influenced by the way they interpret what he says. This, in turn, affects the speaker's self-concept; a self-concept already established is either reinforced or modified by the reactions the speaker observes in others. As Penny (186) has explained it:

In a sense, the communicative act is an experiment in which the communicator gets more or less immediate feedback concerning others' evaluation of him and his communication procedures. Such feedback must constitute an important aspect of the socialization process.

Kinds of speech symbols

Many aspects of speech provide cues which can be used to judge the personality of the speaker. While the words used, pronunciation, and sentence formation are obvious cues, they are not nearly so useful as the content and form of speech, the purpose for which it is used, and the tone of voice of the speaker.

Content of speech At every age, from earliest childhood to the end of life, people tend to talk most about themselves, about their interests and aspirations, their likes and dislikes, their fears and joys. Thus, most speech is egocentric. Even when people do talk about other people or things, their own interests are dominant.

As children grow older, self-talk diminishes somewhat and "other-talk" makes its appearance as a regular part of their speech content. The more egocentric people are, however, regardless of age, the more they will talk about themselves. Most people talk less about themselves when they are with acquaintances and strangers than when they are with intimate friends and family members.

Older children, especially boys, discover that talking about tabooed subjects, such as sex and religion, attracts more attention from both peers and adults than talking about conventional topics. Telling off-color jokes and smutty stories is common among older boys and young adolescents who suffer from feelings of inadequacy in social relationships.

With advancing years, contacts with others decrease. The fewer contacts the person has with outsiders, the more likely he is to revert to the extremely egocentric speech of childhood. Old people, it has been found, talk almost exclusively about themselves, their health, financial problems, and living conditions, or about the treatment they receive from their families (100). Even in other-talk, they tend to relate everything to themselves and their interests and thus revert to talking about themselves (60, 129, 180).

The speech of girls and women at all ages, but especially in adolescence and old age, is more ego-involved than that of boys and men. Only when unfavorable reactions to their egocentric speech become apparent do they shift to more socially approved subjects.

Talking about personal problems suggests insecurity and a feeling of inadequacy to cope with the problems alone. Adolescents, who are faced with many problems that are new to them, talk to anyone they think can help them, often taking the same problem to several people. As they become more sure of themselves, they talk less about personal matters even to family members (67, 127).

Form of speech As a cue to the personality of the speaker, speech form is often more revealing than speech content. While certain forms are more common at particular ages, some prove to be so satisfying to the speaker that he continues to use them throughout life. Preferred forms are generally used with greater subtlety as the individual grows older, however, so that they cannot be so easily detected as in childhood.

An egocentric person who wants to be in the limelight uses different forms of speech to achieve this goal at different ages. The baby literally *cries* for attention. The young child asks *questions*, not so much because he wants answers but because he feels ignored or overlooked.

Adolescents and adults seeking to attract attention and convince others of their superiority use subtle forms of authoritative speech—commonly called "ex-cathedra speech"—and talk about any and every subject. They use long and *unusual* words, change the common *pronunciation* of words and the *tonal quality* of their voices to create the impression that they are better educated than their listeners, and go out of their way to express radical and *unconventional ideas* about controversial subjects.

On the surface, *bragging* and *boasting* suggest that the speaker feels secure and important. Most often, however, they are used to boost the speaker's failing courage. The more a person boasts and brags, the more likely it is that he is trying to cover up feelings of insecurity.

People who *complain* about their lot in life do so because they feel inadequate. Primarily, people complain about not having what the group with which they are identified considers important, whether it be good looks, material possessions, or skills. Older people who envy the health and vigor of younger people, for example, complain about their own poor health.

Criticism may spring from a sincere desire to help others, but it usually comes from the speaker's desire to cover up feelings of inadequacy and to convince others, as well as the speaker himself, of his capability. Poor students who have been called to task by parents and teachers, for example, are more critical of school than good students (123).

Making *derogatory comments* about people and things—often referred to as "name calling"—is a form of criticism which helps to give the speaker a feeling of superiority. Calling a person a "dumbbell" or "idiot" is ego-inflating for the name caller.

"Kidding," joking, and wisecracking—often called "chit-chat" or "banter"—are symbolic of the speaker's feelings of inadequacy. The speaker hopes to create the impression that he is poised and at ease. *Arguments,* in which each speaker champions his own point of view and tries to create the impression that he alone is right, likewise suggest feelings of inadequacy.

Similarly, *teasing* springs from feelings of inadequacy. When a person has been unfavorably compared with another, he often retaliates by teasing the other person. Boys who know that adults consider them sloppier, cruder, and less responsible than girls, retaliate by teasing girls. A man whose wife is successful in business or social life often tries to compensate for any feelings of inadequacy this may give him by teasing her, especially in the presence of others.

Tattling, which is especially common among young children, is a method of trying to cope with a situation in which the tattler feels inadequate. By tattling to a parent or teacher, the child hopes to elicit adult help. *Gossiping* behind a person's back is a way of retaliating against a person whom the gossiper regards as responsible, either directly or indirectly, for keeping him from achieving the status he hoped to achieve. The desire to impress others favorably is at the basis of *name dropping*—speaking in intimate terms about well-known and prestigious people in order to identify oneself with them.

The above discussion may seem to ignore the fact that the form of one's speech may and often does indicate good personal and social adjustment. Speech content and form which reveal an *interest in* and *sympathy for* others and their problems is symbolic of a socialized, outer-bound person. Similarly, *flattery* symbolizes admiration and respect for others. Only if flattery contains a suggestion of insincerity or an intimation that it is being used to gain an advantage for the speaker does it lead to unfavorable social judgments. Jourard has remarked that one of the characteristics of a healthy personality is *self-disclosure,* a willingness to talk to others about one's interests, feelings, and emotions (127).

Quantity of speech   The amount of talking a person does is as significant a cue to the understanding of his personality as are the content and form of his speech. Most people discover, even when they are children, that if they want to be popular they must contribute verbally to the group. They discover that the "Silent Sams" may be overlooked and ignored because they do not contribute to the group's enjoyment.

Since the popular female stereotype is that of a talkative person, girls try to convey the impression of being typically feminine by being gay and talkative, especially when they are with members of the opposite sex. Boys and men, on the other hand, try to symbolize their masculinity by talking little in the presence of members of the opposite sex, hoping to create the impression of being the "strong, silent type." Furthermore, since the popular stereotype of the upper-class person is that of a poised individual who can speak knowledgeably and well in any social situation, one who gives the impression of being tongue-tied in the presence of others is regarded as being immature or a member of a lower-class group or both.

One of the outstanding characteristics of the elderly is their silence. This does not come from mental deterioration, as is popularly believed, but from a strong feeling of insecurity and uncertainty about how others feel about them. They also want to avoid saying things that will lead others to regard them as old-fashioned.

Many people, from early childhood on, compulsively try to dominate any conversation in which they are involved. Their talkativeness is not so much an attention-getting device, but a defense against feelings of insecurity. If they talk constantly, they will not have to give opinions about topics they feel incompetent to discuss. Talking mainly about themselves and their own problems indicates their emotional instability and generally poor social adjustment.

At the opposite extreme are the nontalkers—the "Silent Sams." They are held back by a fear of making mistakes and creating an unfavorable impression or by the belief that they have nothing to offer that would be of interest to others. Children, adolescents, and adults are generally motivated by the former, while middle-aged and elderly people are more often motivated by the latter.

Quality of speech   The quality of a person's speech tells others more about his education and social-class identification than about his personality. However, since personality is influenced both directly and indirectly by education and social class, the quality of speech is too important a cue to be ignored. Speech quality has to do with the tonal quality of the voice, pronunciation, word selection, and sentence formation.

Not until adolescence is the individual fully aware of the effect the *tonal quality* of his voice has on the judgments others make of him. If the voice is loud, harsh, and grating, others will judge the speaker as crude. If it is well-modulated and pleasing to the ear, others will regard the speaker as "cultivated," and the tonal quality of his voice will thus enhance the attractiveness of the impression he makes.

As the typical male voice is lower-pitched and stronger than the typical female voice, a person's sex appropriateness after the puberty changes have taken place is judged by how closely his voice conforms to the norm. Even if a person is sex-appropriate in other respects, he will be judged unfavorably if his voice is sex-inappropriate.

In every culture, *pronunciation of words* is used as a symbol of the social-class identification of the speaker. The adolescent may try to imitate, often in an exaggerated way, the pronunciation of the members of the class he wants others to think he is identified with.

In an experiment made in New York City, it was found that at S. Klein, a store frequented mostly by lower- and middle-class patrons, fourth floor was most commonly pronounced "fawth flaw," while at the more exclusive Saks Fifth Avenue, the usual pronunciation was "forth flor," with a strong *r*. It was also found that people of the lower-middle class are most self-conscious about their pronunciation and try hardest to conform to the models of the upper classes (172).

Pronunciation likewise helps to identify the speaker with a geographic region or with an area of the community in which he lives. Because there are stereotypes of people who live in different areas, the speaker will be endowed, in the minds of others, with the qualities associated with the stereotype which he most closely represents.

Anyone who makes *grammatical mistakes* is identified as ignorant and uneducated. Also, since grammatical mistakes are more common among lower-class people, the person whose speech is grammatically incorrect is usually identified with the popular stereotype of the lower-class person.

Just as many members of the "old money" upper social classes dress simply, so do they speak simply. *Word choice* is thus a symbol of self. They often select words which are simple and forthright and avoid those which they regard as flowery (178).

Many regard the use of *slang* and *swear words* as in bad taste except among intimate friends of the same sex. A speaker who uses a great deal of slang and whose speech is overpunctuated with swear words is usually identified with the stereotype of the lower-class person.

Serious *speech defects,* such as lisping, slurring, and stuttering, make a person conspicuous. How others will react will depend largely upon their ages. Children and young adolescents usually regard speech defects as "funny" and laugh at them. Older adolescents and adults are sympathetic toward the person who has an embarassing speech defect.

Even when the speaker is not fully aware of the reactions of others, he is usually aware that his defect makes him different, and to him, this means "inferior." As a result, he withdraws from social activities or, if forced to be with others, he talks as little as possible. This creates the unfavorable impression that he is socially disinterested, that he feels superior to the peer group, or that he is self-bound.

How the use of *gestures* to supplement and emphasize speech will be interpreted will depend to a large extent upon the cultural group. In a culture where gestures are common and approved, their use will probably not affect social judgments. In the American culture, gestures usually identify the speaker with lower social-class groups or with some national group. In the case of the latter, judgments vary according to the social attitude toward the national group with which the speaker is identified.

Bilingualism   Bilingualism is a symbol of self in that it tells others something about the racial or national origin of the speaker. He will then be judged in terms of the qualities associated with the stereotype of the group with which his speech identifies him.

Bilingualism may come from a conscious effort of the individual to learn to speak in a foreign language as well as in the mother tongue. Usually, however, it comes from speaking a foreign language in the home—the mother tongue of one or both parents—and English outside. Because the language used in the home does not carry the same prestige as English in the peer group, the speaker is identified with a less prestigious minority group. Even after he learns to speak English, the bilingual person may retain a foreign accent, and this will prolong his minority-group identification. If the minority group is regarded with social disapproval, the bilingual person will be judged unfavorably.

In bilingual families where the cultural atmosphere is different from that of the majority, the person's adjustment to the cultural mores of the majority group may be impeded and his behavior may seem "different" to others (215). And even though the person eventually does assimilate the mores of the majority, his speech may continue to mark him as "different."

Other aspects of bilingualism also influence the judgment of others. While most children mispronounce words and make grammatical mistakes when they are first learning to talk, they speak reasonably correctly by the time they enter school. The bilingual child, however, continues to mispronounce English words and make grammatical mistakes until he is embarrassed or humiliated into making a conscious effort to speak correctly. By then, his concept of self may be permanently damaged. Furthermore, since incorrect speech is generally more common among lower-class people than among the middle and upper class, his incorrect speech will suggest lower-class identification to others.

Mental conflict, engendered by trying to think or speak in two languages, combined with fear of making mistakes in pronunciation and grammar, forces the bilingual person to speak in a slow, hesitating manner or to refrain from speaking whenever possible. As a result, he creates the impression of being uninterested in what others are saying, of being dull or ignorant, lacking in poise, or of having unsocial attitudes. None of these creates a favorable impression.

Effects of speech on personality

Children discover that they are regarded as "babies" if they continue to use baby talk after their peers have learned to communicate in a recognizable language. In the same way, adolescents and adults discover that they are judged by their speech and that judgments vary according to the speech of those with whom they are trying to communicate. The peer group, for example, may judge a boy favorably if he colors what he says with slang and swear words, while parents, teachers, and other adults will judge him unfavorably.

Awareness that speaking incorrectly, using socially unacceptable words, discussing tabooed subjects, and speaking with a foreign accent create unfavorable impressions makes the person who is guilty of these "linguistic sins" feel inferior and inadequate. Furthermore, anything that makes a person different from the people with whom he is associated encourages him to think of himself as inferior. And as speech is essential in all social relationships, it is an ever-present reminder to him and to others that he is different. That is why readily observable speech defects have such a damaging influence on the self-concept that most people with speech defects are somewhat maladjusted and self-rejecting.

Bilinguals also suffer psychological damage because of their inability to communicate with ease. Many become social isolates. Few become leaders in school or college activities, and many make poor social, emotional, and personal adjustments (10, 206, 215).

The extent of the psychological damage from bilingualism is related to the degree of social isolation it causes. People from a neighborhood where there are a number of others of the same national origin as they are less seriously affected than are those who are distinctly in the minority in their schools, jobs, and communities.

How long-lasting the effect of bilingualism will be and how seriously it will affect the person's self-concept will depend upon three factors: how aware the person is that he speaks with an accent, how aware he is of how others judge him because of his accent, and how successfully he can overcome his speech accent—the symbol of his identification with a minority group—and his "cultural accent"—the influence of the mores of a different culture. Getting rid of a cultural accent is as difficult as getting rid of a speech accent because both are based on deep-rooted habits, some of which have a strong emotional basis.

AGE

Every cultural group assigns specific roles to different ages and expects its members to conform to the pattern prescribed by the roles. The attitude of the group toward a person is then influenced by how useful to the group, how valued, and how prestigious the role for his age is. The person, in turn, accepts the cultural attitude toward his age and thinks of himself in terms of the cultural stereotype associated with it.

In primitive cultures, for example, the young male adult is extremely useful to the group because his strength makes him a good fighter, hunter, and fisherman—roles that are essential to group survival. When the major life pattern is centered around warlike pursuits, young men fill the most useful and prestigious roles (159, 197).

The meaning of age to a cultural group, then, will be determined by the age when people can best perform roles the group considers important. Because most cultures place higher values on peaceful than on warlike pursuits, more prestige is generally associated with advancing age, at least up to a point. What is true of a culture is also true of its formal bureaucratic organizations, such as the church, courts, business, army, schools, and universities, where high prestige is associated with seniority of rank.

The individual's age is thus used as a symbol of role status, and a person of a given age is expected to act in accordance with the patterns prescribed for his age role. As Walters et al. (241) have pointed out:

In thinking of developmental levels of children, parents ordinarily think of chronological age. . . . For example, if one hears that Mrs. Smith's daughter can't read, the first question which is likely to come to mind is, "How old is she?"

Cultural attitudes toward age

The social group evaluates age roles in terms of how appealing, how useful, how annoying, or how useless to the group's interests the roles are. For example, when the adolescent reaches adult size and appears to be fully developed, the cultural group tries to assign to him roles that are similar to those of the adult. The group discovers that the adolescent cannot be counted on to fulfill the roles and, as a result, takes an unfavorable attitude toward adolescence and regards it as one of the most troublesome and least valuable ages in the growing-up process (107).

For men, middle age is regarded by the cultural group as the peak age for success, achievement, and authority. It is, thus, a prestigious age. For women, by contrast, middle age marks the end of her reproductive and parental roles and is not a prestigious age.

As physical and mental decline progress, the social group regards the person as "old" and unable to carry out the important functions of the group. Status-giving roles in the home, in business, and in civic, social, and political life are then taken away from him and given to younger people. In return, he is offered roles of minor social usefulness or no role at all.

Symbols of age

Since the social group judges people in terms of age and since each age has a favorable or unfavorable stereotype associated with it, many people use symbols to create the impression that they belong to an age group that is more favorably judged than their

own. They falsify their age or refuse to reveal their age. An adolescent who wants to leave school or get married may claim that he is older than he actually is. A person approaching middle age knows that if he tells his real age his chances of getting a new job are slim. If he can achieve the appearance of a younger person, he may claim that he is several years younger than he actually is.

Of the many symbols that can be used to create the impression that one is of an age that will be favorably judged by others, those discussed in the following sections are the most common.

Appearance In our culture, young adulthood is looked upon as the most handsome age, and so adolescents try to look older than they are and middle-aged people try to look younger. To create these illusions, they diet, use beauty aids and plastic surgery, dye their hair, and wear clothes like those used by young adults.

In the business world, where the unfavorable attitude toward employing people whose appearance suggests that they are growing too old to be of value, many men and women do everything they can to look youthful. Others try to keep as active, alert, and interested as possible to avoid being associated with the stereotype of aging which stresses inactivity, rigidity, and narrowing of interests.

Autonomy Autonomy implies the ability to be self-directive rather than dependent on others for control. At every age, being able to do things without help from others is more favorably judged than being dependent. The child and the adolescent attach great value to the symbols of autonomy that tell others that they are old enough to do, say, and think as they please.

Autonomy in work is associated with a prestigious age. By the time a worker reaches the peak of his potential success, in middle age, he is usually more autonomous than he was when he was younger. As a result, many workers prefer jobs with independence in working hours and work programs because they feel that the more autonomy they have, the more likely they are to be judged as being at the peak years of success.

One of the major reasons elderly people want to remain in their own homes instead of living with their married children or in an institution is that they do not want people to associate them with the dependency that is part of the stereotype of the elderly. So long as they can maintain their independence, they feel that they will be identified with an age that has greater prestige than old age.

Activities   When adolescents look like adults in body structure and in dress, they are more likely to be treated as adults. If, in addition to looking like adults, they do the things that adults do, they feel that they have reached an age which is prestigious in the minds of others and will no longer be treated like children.

Many American adolescents today look upon smoking, drinking, driving a car, leaving school, having affairs or getting married, and even using narcotics as American puberty rites. These are the symbols of maturity which they believe will identify them in the minds of others as adults.

The tabooed pleasures of adulthood—especially drinking, smoking, driving a car, and engaging in sexual relations—are the ones many adolescents focus their attention on. If they do what adolescents are forbidden to do, they feel that this will eliminate any thought that they are still adolescents and will automatically class them with adults.

To symbolize their identity with a more prestigious age, many adolescents go to extremes in their use of maturity symbols. This they do in the hope of eliminating any suspicion in the minds of others that they are still minors. Excessive drinking, promiscuous sexual behavior, and using narcotics—all of which have attention value and all of which are identified with adults—are common among many adolescents who want to create the impression that they are older than their years. The more visible a maturity symbol is, the more successfully it will serve its purpose of identifying the individual with the adult age group. That is why most adolescent boys want to have their own cars and most adolescent girls insist upon the right to use cosmetics and to wear clothes like those in style for adult women.

A middle-aged or elderly person who rebels against the stereotype for his age often becomes infatuated with a younger person. Being seen with a younger person and doing things a younger person likes to do help to identify him with a younger age group. Furthermore, through associations with this group, he learns to dress, act, and talk like the members of the group. This further aids in his identification with them in the minds of others and leads to social judgments that he is younger than he actually is.

Effects of age on personality

Before a person's age can have any real effect on his personality, he must be aware of the cultural stereotype associated with his age and must apply that stereotype to judgments of himself. Being identified by the social group as a college student is more prestigious, for example, than being considered a teen-ager because the former implies a role designed to prepare a person to be useful to the social group while the latter carries the implication of being irresponsible, unreliable, and inclined toward destructiveness and antisocial behavior (107).

The more the person accepts the stereotype for his age, the greater will be the effect on his self-concept. When a person identifies himself as "old," he begins to worry, to feel insecure, and to believe that the best years are behind him. The more physical and psychological signs there are to make him realize that he is aging, the more readily he will accept the cultural stereotype of old age and the more anxiety, frustration, and stress he will experience.

The role the social group permits a person to play reinforces his attitude toward his age. Since this is determined more by the opportunities the group provides than by his abilities, the person is forced to accept the group's judgment. Although few adults show a reduction in social competence as they pass from middle age into the late fifties or early sixties, the social group regards them as too old to fill the roles they formerly filled and begins to deprive them of the opportunities to do so (99, 230).

When a person is forced to play roles that are not highly valued by the social group, he must revise his self-concept. Unless he is willing to accept the new roles and adjust to them, a deterioration in his self-concept will take place and will be reflected in unfavorable behavior. If he is willing to accept the stereotype of his age and adjust to the roles the social group associates with it, he will make better adjustments and be happier.

Just as children and adolescents judge themselves as older than their actual ages in the hope that others will grant them the privileges that go with being older, so older people tend to judge themselves as younger than they actually are. This they do to avoid thinking of themselves in terms of the unfavorable stereotypes associated with their actual ages.

A time does come, however, when older people must face reality and admit to themselves that they are aging. This time comes when certain objective factors, such as change in appearance, decreased physical and mental ability, forced retirement, or having grandchildren grow up to adulthood, focus attention on their actual age and make them accept the cultural stereotype.

Certain conditions hasten a shift in the aging person's concept of self. The more physical signs of aging a person has, such as graying hair, wrinkles, and impaired vision or hearing, the more readily will he admit to himself that he is "old." Role changes, such as retirement and widowhood, likewise hasten the shift. As Blau (27) has said:

It is the concept of self as old, and not the weight of his years as such, that constrains the older person to relinquish the photograph and reluctantly to substitute the mirror.

Once a person accepts the cultural stereotype of his age, it affects not only his self-concept but also the quality of his behavior. Many of the personality changes in the elderly are due not so much to physical and mental changes as to acceptance of the cultural stereotype of old age. Becoming socially withdrawn, for example, may stem from the way the social group treats the elderly rather than from lack of interest in social life. Henry and Cumming point out that, accepting the changes that go with being "old," the person "displays behavior characteristic of one who has withdrawn his investment from the world around him and reinvested it in himself" (106).

SUCCESS

Most people discover, long before they reach adulthood, that there is truth in the old saying that "nothing succeeds like success." As a result, they look for ways to express their success symbolically so that others will judge them favorably. As their reputation of being "successful" grows, so does the esteem and prestige they are given in the social group.

Most people want to be regarded as successful in areas that are important to others. And what is important to others varies from age to age and from one social group to another. The group, for example, does not consider it important for a child to be popular with members of the opposite sex. In fact, a child who is will probably be teased, scorned, and labeled "sissy" or "tomboy."

Similarly, children as a group do not consider house furnishings important. So long as they can be comfortable in the furniture in their homes and do not have to "be careful," they are satisfied. To adolescents, however, especially girls, the way the home is furnished is important and becomes increasingly so as the years pass. The home constitutes the background against which they are judged, and so they want it to be beautiful and impressive.

To members of the lower socioeconomic groups, having house furnishings that others admire and envy is not so important a symbol of success as having a car. Since members of the middle and higher socioeconomic groups use their homes more to entertain business associates and others whom they want to impress favorably, they regard home furnishings as important symbols of success and consider car ownership a mere necessity of modern life.

Symbols of success

To effectively play its role as a symbol of self, success must be visible. A person may communicate his success to others in various ways, some of which are crude and some extremely subtle. A child may boast and brag about how big his house is, how strong he is, or how much money his father makes. But when he discovers that this brings little prestige and much scorn, he learns to use more subtle methods. The adolescent and adult who want to tell others that they have a big home will complain about how much work is needed to run such homes; to proclaim their success in athletics, they will wear athletic insignia; and to show how successful the breadwinner of the family is, they will spend freely on status symbols.

The most common symbols of success are described in the following paragraphs.

Popularity Throughout life, popularity among one's peers is a symbol of good social adjustment, and good social adjustment is regarded as a symbol of success. Just as the older child wants to belong to a play gang, so does the adolescent want to belong to the crowd that has the fun. If he is not popular enough to be accepted in that crowd, he usually dislikes school and drops out for social rather than academic reasons. He regards himself as a social "failure," as do his classmates and teachers.

Among children and young adolescents, the more friends one has, the better. Before the high school days are over, number of friends is not so important as friends of the "right" kind. In adolescence, for example, being popular with members of the opposite sex is regarded as an important symbol of social success.

In adulthood, being popular enough to be identified with prestigious community organizations, having a wide circle of friends, entertaining and accepting invitations, and having one's name appear in the social columns of the newspaper—all are regarded as symbolic of success in the community's social life. Social participation, though it may be enjoyable, is often motivated primarily by its value as a symbol of success.

Leadership   A person who is selected as a leader is always popular and, in addition, has the respect and confidence of the other members of the group. Furthermore, since most people regard a leadership role as a certain sign of success, almost everyone, at some time or other, wants to symbolize his success by playing a leadership role. The more often a person is selected for leadership roles, whether in business or social life, the more successful he is judged to be.

Athletic achievement   The high prestige associated with sports in the American culture automatically ensures that "members of the team" are regarded as successful. Athletic achievement, however, is more symbolic of success for males, just as social success is more symbolic of success for females.

Both students and parents regard athletic success as more important than scholastic success, and so boys who are outstanding athletes are school "successes," even if their academic achievements are mediocre. In most schools and colleges, the dropout rate among successful athletes is practically zero (52, 61, 223).

Athletic achievement as a symbol of success does not end with graduation from school or college. In our culture, successful professional athletes earn salaries that enable them to live on a scale comparable to that of successful business executives. In addition, many receive so much publicity that they become "folk heroes" and serve as models for the ideal self among the young.

Educational achievement   The current American stereotype of the "brain"—the student who makes good grades—is often far from favorable. Only if a studious boy is outstanding in sports and a brainy girl popular with members of the opposite sex is the unfavorable stereotype likely to be forgotten (52, 76, 224).

That success in extracurricular activities is considered at least as important as grades is seen by the role this success plays in gaining admission to "name" colleges and in getting jobs in prestigious fields after college graduation. Academic success is thus judged as much by success in nonscholastic achievements as in strictly scholastic achievements.

Being a student in a prestigious school or college is likewise a symbol of success. Private schools and colleges tend to be selective in those they admit, and so it is assumed that only the best students will be there. Furthermore, since the tuition costs are high at private schools and colleges, the student's family is assumed to be well-off.

Regardless of how much interest students have in purely academic work, many want to be identified with a high school that stresses college preparation and with a college that stresses the liberal arts. Being in a vocational school or in a technical training school or college is not considered as prestigious or as symbolic of success as being in an institution that stresses the "less useful" subjects (212, 234).

Kind of occupation   In a democracy where hereditary titles do not exist, a person's occupation is a prime symbol of social status. And since occupational level and income usually go hand in hand, the higher his occupational level the more money the person will have for such status symbols as a home, clothes, and travel. The members of a person's family are likewise judged by his occupation because it determines their status as well as his in the social structure.

Even before adolescence, young people are aware of the prestige associated with different occupations by the cultural group. From then on, they judge others in terms of occupational prestige. Their judgments of their fathers' occupations affect their self-judgments because they know that their fathers' occupations reflect on them. When they themselves go to work, they know that they will be judged in terms of the symbolic value of their occupations, and this, too, affects their self-judgments.

The cultural stereotypes associated with different occupations were discussed in Chapter 1. The person is judged on the basis of his occupational stereotype whether it fits him or not. If the stereotype is complimentary, others will judge him favorably and vice versa.

The woman who works is judged in terms of her occupation just as a man is. Few women, however, are able to rise to leadership positions in prestigious occupations, and as a result, the working woman is usually less favorably judged than the working man. In addition, many people disapprove of mothers working, and so the employed woman who has children is likely to be less favorably judged than the woman who has no children even when they are in the same occupational category.

In a nation where practically every able person holds a job, anyone who is unemployed is looked upon with skepticism. If he is in a financial position to live comfortably without working, he is likely to be regarded as lazy, as not doing his share in the work of the community. While some may envy his affluence, most people will judge him as a "playboy" unless he devotes most of his time to volunteer community work.

If the unemployed person wants to work—if his unemployed status is involuntary—this symbolizes to others that he lacks the ability to get and hold a job. Should his unemployment force him to get financial assistance from family members or from the government, the unfavorable judgments of others will be colored by resentment. He soon gets the reputation of being a failure. The longer his unemployment persists and the greater the necessity of taking any job available, the more unfavorable his image becomes.

Money The world over, money and prestige go together. The more money a person has, the more successful he is judged to be.

When a person lives on an inherited income, whether it supplements what he earns or frees him from working, he is judged as coming from a successful family. "Old money" is thus a symbol of family success. By contrast, "new money," or money earned by the person himself, is regarded as a symbol of personal success (178). In every culture, greater prestige is associated with old money than with new, and the person with old money is more favorably judged.

Money in the bank or in stocks and bonds is not visible, and the person who wants to communicate to others the success that this represents must do so symbolically. There are two ways in which money can be used to symbolize success: boasting about how much one has or spending it on status symbols. The former, unless done very subtly, is considered in bad taste. This leaves the other alternative, spending.

Even a child recognizes the prestige value of money when he discovers that material possessions, so important to status, can only be obtained if one has the money to buy them. Later he learns that money helps to "buy" popularity in the form of material possessions, commercial amusements which he enjoys with his peers, and family status symbols. All these increase his social acceptability. He also discovers that leadership, like popularity, can be bought if one has enough money.

The older adolescent discovers that still other symbols of success have a price tag. If he wants to go to a name college, if he wants to go to a graduate or professional school to prepare for a prestigious occupation, if he wants to belong to the exclusive social and professional organizations of the community, if he wants to engage in the recreations that are popular with the upper-class adults of the community, he must have money to pay for them.

Perhaps most important of all, the adolescent learns that money and autonomy go hand in hand. If he has money, he can do much as he pleases. Financial dependency deprives him of his autonomy. Young adults who marry before they become self-supporting and older people who must get financial help from others are deprived of the status-symbol value of autonomy.

How much money a person needs to symbolize his success will vary from one age to another and from one group identification to another. In general, more is needed with each passing year.

Material possessions Material possessions are among the most universally used symbols of success because they are manifest. And many people are willing to spend more than they can afford to try to keep up with the Joneses and create the impression that they are as successful as they.

Which material possessions will best symbolize success depends on the age of the person and the group with which he is identified. To a child, a home and its furnishings are merely a place in which to live comfortably. To an adolescent or an adult, they are symbolic of the success of the breadwinner of the family, which is used to judge all family members. To a child, a car that is larger than the cars of his friends is symbolic of the family's success. To an adolescent or an adult, the number and make of the cars owned by the family are symbols of success. Having a car in a group where car ownership is not universal is also a symbol of success.

Club membership   The more exclusive a club and the more difficult it is to gain membership, the higher the prestige rating of those who belong. In high school and college, for example, some clubs, fraternities, and sororities are open to all, while others are open only to those who are invited to join. The latter carry greater prestige, and receiving an invitation to join is a symbol of social success. But the prestige value of membership varies even among the exclusive clubs. Some invitation-only clubs carry greater prestige than others and their members are judged as more successful. See Figure 3–5.

The status value of club membership is so impressed on many adolescents that they carry into adulthood the desire to be identified with the exclusive clubs of their communities. Adults who have not been members of exclusive clubs during their high school and college days are often especially anxious to be identified with the "right" community organizations. This identification is one of the rewards of occupational and social mobility.

Leadership in a club is a symbol of success. The more exclusive the club, the more symbolic of success

Figure 3-5   The more exclusive the club, the more it identifies its members with success.

is a leadership role. Since women have fewer opportunities to symbolize success in home and vocational areas than men, a leadership role in a community organization is a highly prized symbol of success for them. Men who fail to achieve vocational leadership also may try to compensate by getting elected to a leadership role in the community.

Use of leisure time   The success-symbol value of recreations is insignificant in young children because they ordinarily play alone or side by side in parallel play. Their play behavior tells little about how successful they are in social adjustments.

By school age, children are no longer satisfied with parallel and solitary play. They want to play with other children, and their success in being accepted in a gang serves as a symbol of their social success. In adulthood, likewise, social success is symbolized by the recreations the adult engages in and the people with whom he shares his leisure time. If he associates with people who are known to be community leaders, if he entertains and is entertained by them, if he joins the clubs they belong to and becomes an active participant in club activities, and if he engages in recreations that are commonly associated with upper-class people, such as golf, tennis, swimming, boating, or skiing, he is judged as a social success. As White (246) has explained:

The tendency to choose leisure activities on the grounds of membership in a particular social class begins in adolescence and becomes more pronounced in maturity. . . . As people get older and settle into the ways of the class to which they belong, they choose leisure activities which are congenial to their class. . . . Class differences are reflected by young people but are not fixed until maturity.

Regardless of age, the person who spends his leisure time alone or with members of the family is judged to be a social failure. Such people are commonly called "loners" and are regarded as maladjusted because they cannot get along well enough with other people to be acceptable to them in social situations. Even if the person prefers to spend his leisure time alone, he is regarded as "odd," because this is not the pattern of leisure-time behavior that is regarded as normal.

The person who falls back upon members of the family for leisure-time activities—whether he be a child or an adult—is regarded as a social failure. Knowing this, many children and adolescents refuse to participate in family social activities or to go to movies and athletic contests with their parents. They fear that their peers will judge them as so unpopular that they have no one outside the family to associate with.

In the lower social classes, leisure activities are largely family activities. Entertaining is done for the family instead of for outsiders. This proclaims to people in other social classes that the family members are social failures, that they lack friends with whom they can spend their leisure time.

Economic success can likewise be symbolized by leisure activities. The child or adolescent whose family can afford club membership will swim, play golf or tennis, and dance at the country club. When the young person's family lacks the resources to provide commercial amusements, he plays the games and sports that are available in the neighborhood, on the school or community-provided playgrounds, or at a Scout camp.

The adult is even better able than the child or adolescent to symbolize his economic success by his leisure activities. If he takes his exercise at a club, if he goes to the theater and opera for entertainment instead of to the movies, if he entertains or is entertained at parties that are reported on the society pages of the newspaper, and if he spends his vacations jetting to luxurious resorts here or abroad, no one can question his affluence.

If the adult spends his leisure time gardening, especially if he plants vegetables rather than flowers, if he spends his evenings watching television or goes to the movies only occasionally, if he visits friends and relatives during his vacations, and if he entertains mainly relatives and neighbors who bring "covered dishes" to provide refreshments, it is obvious to all that he is not an economic success (28, 63, 102).

Effects of success on personality

Because of the high prestige associated with success, it is not surprising that the degree of success the social group attributes to a person has a profound influence on his self-concept. Furthermore, the more prestige the group attributes to the area in which the person is successful, the more prestige value his success has and the more favorable the effect on his self-concept.

In the area of sports, for example, if the group attributes greater prestige to success in baseball than to success in track, then success will affect those who play baseball more favorably. In the area of occupa-

tions, a person in a blue-collar job may earn more money and be able to buy more prestige symbols than a person in a profession, but the prestige value of the blue-collar occupation is far less. Success in it brings a less favorable social judgment than success in a profession.

The more symbols of success a person has and the more visible the symbols are, the more favorable the judgments of others and, in turn, the more favorable the effect on the person's self-concept. Hidden successes may be ego-satisfying but they bring little if any influence on the judgments of others. Consequently, they have little influence on the person's social self-concept or mirror image. The effects of judgments of success on a person's self-concept and behavior will be discussed in detail in Chapter 10, Aspirations and Achievements.

REPUTATION

"Reputation"—the character commonly imputed to a person—is a symbol of self which others use to judge the individual. Their judgments, in turn, affect his self-concept. His *imputed* character may or may not be the same as his *real* character. However, the two are less likely to differ qualitatively than quantitatively.

The bright person, for example, is more likely to get the reputation of being a "brain" than of being a "dumbbell." While he may not be as bright as his reputation implies, he is bright enough to make others think that he is a "brain." Similarly, the selfish person may acquire the reputation of being a "tightwad," a reputation that is not entirely justified by his behavior, but he would be very unlikely to get the reputation of being a "big spender."

Conditions affecting reputations

Whether the reputation a person acquires is favorable or not will depend largely upon two conditions: social values and the personal frame of reference of those responsible for establishing the reputation.

Because *social values* differ from one group to another and even from time to time in the same group, judgments of reputation will depend to some extent upon how closely the person's behavior conforms to prevailing social values. In a school or college where good scholarship and good behavior are not highly valued by members of the peer group, the student who does good academic work and conforms to the socially approved patterns of adult behavior is likely to get the reputation of being a "brain," "teacher's pet," or "goody-goody." If, on the other hand, he follows the approved pattern of his peers by criticizing everything about school and neglecting his work in favor of athletics and other extracurricular activities, his reputation among his peers will be that he is a "good sport" or a "regular guy."

In a culture that attaches high prestige to money, material possessions, and identification with members of the higher socioeconomic groups, the person who possesses these symbols of social success will acquire a more favorable reputation than one who does not. Belonging to a group with high prestige increases the person's own prestige and contributes to his favorable reputation.

In judging people, or anything else, one tends to judge from one's own *frame of reference.* A person who likes blonds, for example, will judge blonds more favorably than brunets. As Northway and Detweiler have commented, "We see things not as they are but as we are" (175).

This means that people are judged more in terms of the judge's past experiences than in terms of personal relationships with the people themselves. Furthermore, since the judge's values are influenced by culturally approved values, people are judged more favorably if their appearance and behavior conform to the cultural values which the judge has accepted as his own. If, for example, a person values economic success more highly than intellectual attainment because this is a value of the group with which he is identified, he will judge a college professor less favorably than would a person who put higher value on intellectual attainment.

It is thus apparent that the reputation a person acquires is not dependent on his appearance or behavior alone but rather on *how* his appearance and behavior are judged by other people.

How reputations are acquired

Often those who make the judgments that determine a person's reputation are not aware that their judgments have any consequence at all. Reputations are acquired in many ways, but they are always the result of social judgments.

First impressions play an important role in the development of reputations. A person is judged by many factors: his appearance, his behavior, the people he is with, his resemblance to other people, his socioeconomic status, as determined by his clothing and manners, etc. (Refer to Chap. 1.) If the impression he makes is unfavorable, it will militate against any desire of the judge to get to know him better and to see if the impression is justified. If the impression is favorable, it will encourage further acquaintance, which will either strengthen or weaken the impression first made.

Appearance and behavior are central factors in first as well as subsequent impressions. As such, they serve as a basis on which the person's reputation is built. A good *appearance* creates favorable impressions and leads to favorable judgments.

When a person's *behavior* conforms to social expectations, he makes a good impression on others and is favorably judged by them. A child will get the reputation of being brave, for example, if he doesn't cry when he is hurt or frightened. A school-age boy may get the reputation of being friendly if he tries to make a new pupil feel at home.

Social *stereotypes* influence judgments and thus help to shape reputations. Prejudice against members of a minority group, for example, is often the result of judging them in terms of a stereotype rather than in terms of personal experiences. "Folkway prejudice" is a "general feeling of againstness" grounded in ethnocentrism which results in unfavorable reputations for those identified with a minority group.

Once people form an impression of a person, it affects their attitudes and behavior and serves as the basis for his reputation. His reputation then becomes a "halo" which colors subsequent judgments of him. It is, thus, a symbol to others of what he is (181).

Spreading of reputations

A reputation spreads among the members of a social group by "social contagion." Person A bases his opinion of person B on B's behavior, appearance, a stereotype, or some other cue and communicates his opinion to X, Y, and Z. When X, Y, and Z come in contact with B, their opinions of him, either consciously or unconsciously, are influenced by what A has said about him.

Children, for example, especially in the absence of an adult, are likely to comment with brutal frankness on the qualities of a playmate they dislike. To reinforce their dislike, they often label him with a derogatory nickname, such as "Crybaby" or "Stinky."

Their unfavorable comments and the derogatory nick-name influence the judgments others make of that child.

Adolescents and adults do the same. Much of their gossip centers on the characteristics and behavior of other people. Talking about a person helps to build up a halo for that person which colors the judgments others make of him (125).

People fall into the habit of thinking about a person in terms of his reputation without taking the trouble to discover if the reputation is a true symbol of his real self or if it relates only to one area of his behavior. In this way, a reputation based on a person's behavior in one area of life spreads to other areas. A child who gets the reputation of being a "crybaby" because he is afraid of big, boisterous dogs may be judged as a generally immature person, even though his behavior in other areas is much more mature than the behavior of those who are judging him.

How the halo effect of a reputation acquired in one area of behavior spreads and serves as a symbol by which others judge the person in other areas as well is illustrated by studies of students' ratings of the scholastic abilities of their peers. Popular students acquire the reputation of being "good students," while unpopular ones acquired the reputation of being either "poor students" or "brains" who have gotten their good grades by concentrating on their studies and neglecting extracurricular activities.

Similarly, a person who is a successful leader in one activity is often chosen for leadership roles in other, unrelated activities. As Marak puts it, the "authority" of a leader "extends to many areas not justified by his abilities, after the group members develop conceptions of him as a rewarding person" (150).

Persistence of reputations

How difficult it is to change a halo or an established reputation, which is so important as a symbol of self, is well illustrated in studies of popularity. Once a person gets the reputation of being a "good guy," he must do something to seriously antagonize others to change this reputation. It is most unusual for the popular person to "fall from grace." Similarly, even when a "bad sport" corrects the qualities that led to his unfavorable reputation, the halo clings and his reputation spreads. Jersild (123) explains how this happens:

A youngster who, for one reason or another, has received a bad reputation in the elementary grades may still be plagued by it in junior high school, for even though many of the children there are new to him, one first-class gossip from the former grade may be able to stir up doubts and suspicions against him.

The halo effect of reputation also leads to the persistence of leadership, especially in large social groups. A person who has gained prestige in a leadership role is better known to the group as a whole than are persons who have not served as leaders. Therefore, in deciding on a leader for a new activity, the group is almost certain to choose the person who has the reputation of being a successful leader in the past.

How can a person ever get rid of an unfavorable reputation? It is difficult, but it can be done, particularly if efforts are made before the halo effect takes over and before the person's self-concept is so damaged that he behaves in a manner that makes matters worse. Studies of popularity show that, once the halo effect becomes operative, members of the peer group are not likely to take the time or trouble to get to know the person well enough to discover whether his bad reputation is fair to him or not. Furthermore, members of the peer group can, either maliciously or unwittingly, do and say things that cause even greater harm.

A person may improve his reputation by trying to make a better impression on others. Changing his appearance and behavior may encourage others to judge him less unfavorably, but if his reputation stems partly from a stereotype of his minority-group status, little can be done to change that. If he has a nickname that calls attention to some distasteful characteristic, getting rid of the nickname, if possible, will erase a constant reminder of earlier unfavorable judgments.

Even if all these factors can be controlled, there is no guarantee that the unfavorable reputation will be forgotten or that the attitudes of others will change. Therefore, geographic mobility provides one of the best ways to free oneself of an unfavorable reputation. By moving to a new school, a new community, or a new job, a person may be able to "bury his background" and, with it, his old reputation.

Effects of reputation on personality

Awareness of the role reputations play in the judgments made by others comes slowly in childhood but rapidly during adolescence. Few children associate their nicknames or the treatment they receive from others with the fact that they have made an unfavorable impression on others and that this impression is becoming fixed as a reputation. During adolescence, however, the ability to perceive one's status in relationship to the status of other group members develops rapidly. It is then that the person fully appreciates the importance of his reputation as a symbol of self—for himself as well as for others. If others think of him as immature, he will think of himself as immature. If they think of him as bright, he will convince himself that he is bright even though he may have had some reservations about this before.

How great an effect an unfavorable reputation has on the self-concept is shown by evidence that, even after a person has buried his reputation by changing his school or job, he continues to think of himself in terms of his old reputation and continues to be influenced by it.

The psychological damage of being known as a "fatty" during the puberty fat period, for example, persists long after the fat has disappeared. Late-maturing adolescents who gain the reputation of being "kids" because they look and act younger than their age-mates show—even in middle age—the psychological damage that came from being treated in accordance with this reputation (126).

One of the most common examples of the persisting effects of reputation on the self-concept has to do with young people who were regarded as "stars" in their high school or college days. Not only do stars develop an aloofness that comes from feeling superior, but, even worse, they cannot adjust to being "average" when they get out into the larger world. If their adult achievements are not such as to prolong the reputation of being stars, they may develop the habit of reminiscing, of talking about the "good old days," or they may project the blame for their lack of adult stardom on someone or something else. Even as elderly people, they may continue to think and act as if they were the stars they were reputed to be when they were younger.

SUMMARY

1 Symbols of self are the cues by which a person is judged by others. They may, therefore, be regarded as symbols of personal identity. Symbols of self play two important roles: First, they influence one's judgments of others, and second, they influence one's concept of self.

2 Two conditions must exist if symbols of self are to play their roles successfully: First, they must be visible, and second, the person who uses them must know their significance. If either condition is missing, the symbols may be misinterpreted by others or ignored.

3 Clothing is an important symbol of self because it affects first impressions as well as subsequent judgments of a person. Among the qualities people try to symbolize by their clothes are autonomy, desire for attention, identity with a specific group, individuality, success, sex appropriateness, and maturity.

4 The well-dressed person is favorably judged by others, and this encourages him to judge himself favorably. The poorly dressed person is affected in just the opposite way.

5 Being poorly dressed over a period of time can lead to the development of an inferiority complex or can intensify one which already exists. There is a sex difference in the use and influence of clothes as symbols of self, with girls and women as a group being more affected than boys and men. This is not because judgments of males are less influenced by their appearance, but rather because the standardization of male clothing reduces its symbolic usefulness.

6 Almost as important as clothes as a symbol of self are names and nicknames—the identity symbols or labels by which people come to be known to others. These symbols are markedly influenced by the cultural stereotypes associated with names. That names and nicknames play an important role in self as well as in social judgments is shown by the person's attitude toward his individual names, his nickname, and his name combination. The person's reaction to his names is influenced not only by the cultural stereotypes associated with names but also by their usefulness in symbolizing personal or group identification, glamour, personality "type," individuality, popularity, and sex appropriateness.

7 The influence of names and nicknames on the self-concept comes not from the names per se but from the bearer's realization of the social attitudes toward his names. First and last names and nicknames have more influence on the self-concept than middle names, though their relative influence varies with the person's age.

8 Speech gives a clue to the personality of the speaker through its content and form, its quantity, and its quality, as shown in pronunciation, grammar, choice of words, and tone. Bilingualism adversely affects the quantity and quality of speech and often has a damaging effect on the person's social and self judgments.

9 Since every cultural group assigns specific roles to different ages and since roles vary in prestige, age is a prime symbol of self. To create the impression of belonging to a prestigious age group, a person may make use of such symbols of age as appearance, degree of autonomy, and activities engaged in.

10 The effect of age on the self-concept comes only with the person's awareness of how members of the social group regard his age and the roles they expect him to play. Being subjected to unfavorable social attitudes because of his age and being forced to play roles not to his liking have damaging effects on the self-concept. Since social attitudes toward age are markedly influenced by cultural stereotypes, the only way a person can escape the psychological damage that comes from unfavorable judgments of him because of his age is to try to create the impression that his age falls within the range that elicits favorable social judgments.

11 At every age, success is highly valued. The areas in which success is most highly valued vary according to age, sex, socioeconomic status, and cultural background. These factors also affect the way that members of the group judge the degree of success a person has achieved.

12 Some of the most commonly accepted symbols of success in our culture are popularity, leadership, athletic achievement, educational achievement, occupation, money, material possessions, club membership, and use of leisure time. The more symbols of success a person uses and the more manifest these symbols are, the more favorable the social judgments of him will be. The more favorable the social judgments, the more favorable the person's evaluation of himself.

13 Like his name, the reputation a person establishes is an important symbol of self because it becomes a label by which others judge him and by which he judges himself. Whether a person's reputation is favorable or not will depend on whether his behavior conforms to social values, which will color the judgments others make of him, and on the frame of reference of those who make the judgments. Consequently, a person may acquire a favorable reputation among members of one group but an unfavorable reputation among members of another, even though his behavior is similar in both groups.

14 Reputations are acquired from social judgments based on first impression, observations of behavior, and cultural stereotypes. A person's reputation quickly spreads among members of a social group and thus becomes a halo by which the individual is judged in many areas of life. Once an unfavorable reputation has been acquired, changing it is almost impossible except by geographic mobility which enables a person to bury his old reputation and establish a new one among members of a new social group.

15 The damaging consequences of an unfavorable reputation, so far as personality is concerned, come from the fact that it colors the judgments others make of a person and these judgments, in turn, color his evaluation of himself. Even when an unfavorable reputation has been buried and a new and more favorable one established, the person has become so accustomed to evaluating himself in unfavorable terms that he continues to do so.

molding the personality pattern

It has been said that personality development begins on the delivery table (42). If the definition of personality that emphasizes adjustment to environment is accepted, then one cannot believe that personality development begins before birth. The fetus does not adjust to the intrauterine environment; the environment adjusts to the developing fetus. This point of view is stressed by Allport (7):

The newborn infant lacks *personality, for he has not yet encountered the world in which he must live, and has not developed the distinctive modes of adjustment and mastery that will later comprise his personality.*

The "rudiments" of personality—the capacities for adjustment—are present at birth, Allport explains, but "only when the original stream of activity meets the environment, acting upon it and being acted upon by it, do the first habits, conscious desires, and incipient traits emerge" (7).

The newborn infant is not "merely a plastic blob of protoplasm waiting to be shaped in form and character by environmental pressures" (42). On the contrary, the infant enters the world equipped with certain capacities to adjust to the environment into which he is born (37, 48, 123). These capacities to adjust to the postnatal environment are affected by conditions in the prenatal environment, as will be discussed in detail in a later section, Maturation of Hereditary Potentials.

Furthermore, newborn infants are *differently equipped to adjust* to their environments. Differences in personality begin to appear during the first few days of postnatal life. Some newborn infants are active while others are passive; some cry excessively while others cry infrequently; some adjust quickly to their postnatal life while others adjust so slowly that survival may be threatened. These differences originate not so much from environmental factors as from inherent differences in adjustive capacities present at birth (7, 42, 93).

The variations in adjustive behavior suggest that the foundations for personality laid before birth, in the form of physical and mental capacities, influence the kind of adjustment the infant makes to postnatal life.

HEREDITARY POTENTIALS

Studies of the prenatal development of both infrahuman and human subjects reveal that the foundations of the capacities for adjustment to postnatal life are laid, in part, at the moment of conception. The foundations are then modified and new capacities for adjustment gradually unfold as development progresses throughout the 9 months of prenatal life.

The prenatal period is rightly regarded as a critical period in personality development, not because it is the time when the personality pattern is actually formed but because it is the time when the capacities which will determine what kind of adjustment the person will make to his postnatal life are established. It is also critical because it is the time when the attitudes of people who will play important roles in molding the newly created person's personality pattern are formed. While these attitudes often change later, the changes are more likely to be quantitative than qualitative.

At the moment of conception, the person's entire hereditary endowment, centered in the 23 chromosomes from the mother and the 23 chromosomes from the father, is established. Within these 46 chromosomes are thousands of genes or carriers of individual physical and mental traits which determine what his hereditary potentials will be. The person will never be able to add to or subtract from his hereditary endowment.

Significance of hereditary endowment

Neither the personality pattern nor the specific personality traits are directly controlled by the genes. Indirectly, however, the genes influence personality by affecting the quality of the nervous system, the biochemical balance of the body, and the structure of the body. The principal raw materials of personality—physique, intelligence, and temperament—are the foundations of personality which are genetically determined through structural inheritance. These raw materials are then patterned into personality characteristics by environmental influences.

Hereditary not only produces the raw materials from which personality will develop but it also limits development. Even with the best environmental conditions, innate capacities cannot develop beyond their potentials. Cattell et al. write that "all learning and adjustment is limited by inherent properties of the organism" (48). Education and guidance must take this fact into account as well as maturational trends.

It may be added that physical capacities—stature, energy, strength, attractiveness—and intellectual capacities are also "limited by inherent properties." The extent of the limitations on personality development, however, will be greatly influenced by the environment. A boy with a small body build, for example, is far more likely to develop an unfavorable self-concept if he grows up in an environment which values athletic success but disdains achievement in areas in which he can excel. Similarly, an unattractive girl will find her homeliness a much more severe limitation if she is the "ugly duckling" of a handsome family or of an exceptionally attractive peer group.

The hereditary endowment of a person, determined at conception, is the basis for individuality. As was stressed in Chapter 1, no two people have identical personality patterns. While identical twins have the same hereditary endowment because they develop from the same fertilized cell, environmental pressures produce different self-concepts, different traits, and different combinations of traits.

With the exception of identical multiple births—twins, triplets, quadruplets, etc.—all human beings have a hereditary endowment that is uniquely theirs. Even siblings inherit different chromosomes with unique gene combinations. And since the hereditary endowment influences the effect of the environment on the individual, no two personality patterns will be identical.

The fact that the hereditary endowment is established at the time of conception and is subject to only minor changes from environmental influences explains why some personality traits are more persistent than others. This matter will be discussed in more detail in Chapter 5.

ENVIRONMENTAL INFLUENCES

Some of the hereditary potentials of the individual will develop into forms that will meet with the approval of the group with which he is identified. Some potentials will be neglected, and still others will be discouraged from developing by social pressures. As Bühler has pointed out, "The succession of events which are of influence on a person's life are part of his history. They present a counter-agent to the individual's own dispositions, and they may be variously supportive of or detrimental to his own goal setting" (42).

The forms into which the hereditary potentials will develop will depend largely on the significant people in the individual's environment. It is they who determine what his physical and social environment will be. It is they who determine what opportunities the individual will have for learning and what limitations will be placed on these opportunities. While the cultural environment will provide him with approved patterns to imitate, it is the significant people in his life who will give him the training needed to mold his potentials and the motivation needed to call forth the effort to learn.

How markedly the environment influences the development of the personality pattern and how greatly environments differ is illustrated by Rennie et al. (172):

Take normally and identically endowed, newly born male triplets of an average middle-class family of Anglo-Saxon and Protestant extraction, place one for permanent adoption in another average middle-class family, place the second similarly in an average upper-class family, and the third in an average lower-class family, all three of these families likewise of Anglo-Saxon and Protestant extraction. Then observe them on a participant basis regularly over a period of years well into their adulthood. . . . What could we expect to observe as to the differences first in the conditioning and life experiences of these three boys?

From the very beginning we would find differences, some subtle and some gross, in patterns of feeding, training, rewarding and punishing, in modes of extending and withholding affection, in patterns of reaction to impulsive, aggressive and other forms of unacceptable behavior. As the boys grew toward school age there would be differences in the behavioral standards, life values and goal expectations defined for them, in the manner or emphasis of these definitions, and in the kinds of examples presented them as goal models. Moreover, there would be considerable differences in the patterns of intrafamily interactions, differences of paternal and maternal role performances, in sibling roles, in the qualities of family integration and mutual support, in the pressures of needs and wants against financial means, in the margins of flexibility and balance in the face of such life crises as illness, incapacitation, and death.

During their play with other boys we would find vast differences in their neighborhood environments, in the "codes of the street," in recreational facilities, in adult interest and supervision, in stimuli and opportunities for deviant behavior. There would be differences also among the three sets of parents, in the types of friends they chose, in their styles of relating themselves to such friends, in patterns of recreation during leisure hours, in their attitudes and outlook toward immediate and distant social settings, toward themselves and toward life itself.

As the boys grew toward the point of considering choices of career there would likely not only be different kinds of interests, aspirations and evaluations of self-adequacy among them but also different ranges of opportunity to be considered realistically in relation to their circumstances. . . . Would these differences in their sociocultural worlds be sufficiently weighty to have observable consequences for their personalities? Unfortunately there have been few personality studies made as yet of different social class groups. But those that have been made, usually involving comparisons of lower-class and middle-class children, are consistent in indicating that the answer is yes.

HOW THE ENVIRONMENT MOLDS PERSONALITY

The environment influences the personality pattern most notably in three ways: It encourages or stunts the maturation of hereditary potentials; it provides personality pattern models which the individual uses as a guide; and it either provides or denies needed learning opportunities.

Maturation of hereditary potentials

Through maturation, the hereditary potentials established at the time of conception will eventually devel-op. Some maturation occurs before birth and some after. Maturation, however, depends upon the environment, and so whether hereditary potentials will develop to their maximum will depend upon the kind of environment in which the individual grows and lives.

Maturation before birth   Studies of animal and human fetuses show that certain conditions in uterine life favor normal maturation while others retard the process or even distort the development of physical and mental potentials. Good physical and mental health on the mother's part are conducive to a favorable prenatal environment and to the normal maturation of hereditary potentials. The health of the mother influences the quality of nutritive substances, water, and oxygen transmitted through the placenta and umbilical cord to the fetal bloodstream from the maternal bloodstream (152, 186, 194).

Furthermore, the mental and physical health of the mother influences the quantity and quality of fetal activity in the latter part of the prenatal period (60). A moderate amount of fetal activity, characteristic of fetuses who are developing in a healthy prenatal environment, contributes to good postnatal adjustment (194, 220).

Unfavorable conditions in the prenatal environment, caused by maternal malnutrition, endocrine disturbance, infections, and severe emotional stress, interfere with maturation and produce developmental irregularities. If the irregularities are pronounced, and especially if the fetus's nervous system is affected, the individual's ability to make life adjustments may be permanently impaired.

In the prenatal environment, the *timing* of the disturbance rather than the disturbance itself is the crucial factor in determining interference with the normal pattern of maturation of hereditary potentials. Malnutrition, for example, does its greatest damage during the first three months of pregnancy. It is futile to correct the maternal diet after the first trimester in an attempt to prevent congenital abnormalities (117, 164, 220).

Maturation of hereditary potentials is generally slowed or halted for a short time after birth as the infant adjusts to the radical change from the environment inside the mother's body to the world outside. The effects of birth may be inconsequential and transitory or they may greatly affect the course of subsequent development (14, 117, 164). If birth is normal, the interruption in maturation will last only a week or so. If birth is difficult or if the brain or some other area of the body is injured, the interruption will be longer or development may be distorted. Whether birth injuries which distort the development of hereditary potentials have a temporary or permanent effect will depend largely upon how much damage is done to the infant's nervous system, especially his brain.

Prematurely born babies are more likely to suffer brain damage than full-term babies, because their skulls are too undeveloped to provide adequate protection for the brain during the birth process. As a result, the maturation of the hereditary endowment of prematures is more likely to be interfered with.

Maturation after birth　The postnatal environment, likewise, may encourage or stunt the maturation of hereditary potentials. "The milieu in which development occurs," Caldwell writes, "influences that development" (45). Bühler spells out the effect more specifically when she says that the person's hereditary endowment, both physical and psychological, is influenced by the person's motives and goals as well as by environmental and cultural forces (42).

The influence of the postnatal environment on the maturation of hereditary potentials is best shown by studies of children in culturally deprived areas of communities. Poor health and nutrition, neglect and lack of stimulation on the part of those responsible for encouraging and motivating the use of developing abilities, and lack of opportunity to develop abilities due to overprotection, institutionalization, and other causes—all show how detrimental an unfavorable environment is (11, 124, 177).

When a particular ability is maturing rapidly, an environment that discourages development is much more damaging than when the ability is maturing slowly. As in the prenatal environment, the *timing* of unfavorable conditions is the crucial factor. Loss of the mother through death or some other cause is most damaging if it occurs in the early years of life, for example, when the child is most dependent on the mother for providing an environment that will stimulate the development of his hereditary potentials (12).

The influence of the timing of unfavorable environmental conditions on personality development has been shown by a study of the effects of family size and density on young children. Children from large and closely spaced families have few contacts with the mother, owing to her preoccupation with the care of the home and older children, and they suffer some of the usual effects of maternal deprivation. They often tend to be lethargic, showing little interest in doing what they are maturationally capable of doing (214).

Studies of children of multiple birth and of those born prematurely also point up the influence of an unfavorable environment. The postnatal environment of children of *multiple birth* is very different from that of a singleton and is usually less favorable to the development of hereditary potentials. The singleton does not have to compete with another for parental affection and attention; he is not constantly pressured to associate and share his possessions with a sibling of his own age; he does not constantly see a replica of himself in a sibling who is dressed exactly as he is. The singleton learns to think of himself as an individual, not as a half or a third or a fourth of a whole. As he grows older he has a wider choice of roles; he is not forced at every turn to be like his sibling, whether his own needs are satisfied or not (42, 107, 186).

Equally as serious, parental attitudes toward multiples are less favorable than toward singletons. Many parents become anxious about their ability, financially and otherwise, to care for several children at one time, especially if the children are born prematurely—a characteristic of multiple births. In addition, many mothers become exhausted from overwork in caring for two or three infants. Not only does the emotional climate of the home deteriorate, but the children are deprived of the guidance and care they need for the development of their hereditary potentials (42, 186).

Few children who are *prematurely born* escape psychological damage stemming from unfavorable parental attitudes toward their early arrival. The beginnings of personality damage are seen in babyhood. While some prematures are gentle and have moderate affective reactions, most are petulant, shy, irascible, and negativistic. As they grow older, their behavior problems and nervous traits result in poorer personal and social adjustments than are usual for full-term children of the same age (42, 152, 176, 186).

Studies of prematures almost unanimously trace their personality problems to poor environmental conditions caused by unfavorable parental attitudes. Parental anxiety leads to overprotectiveness, which makes the child feel inadequate or resentful. In an effort to break down the restrictions placed on him, the child becomes aggressive or openly rebellious. Besides being overprotective, parents of a premature often push him to perform at the same level as the full-term child. This is not likely to be possible during the early years, and lack of self-confidence, accompanied by nervousness, is the inevitable result. These unfavorable personality traits in the premature child are intensified by the contrast between having too little expected of him at first and then, without adequate preparation, having too much expected too suddenly (42, 176).

Model of personality pattern

The second important way in which the environment influences the molding of the personality pattern is by providing models for the individual to follow. A model that is acceptable to members of the group with which the person is identified acts as a guide for him as well as for those who are responsible for training him to conform to social expectations. Figure 4–1 illustrates this.

Ryerson has remarked that a person's personality "lies safely within the boundaries defined by his culture" (183). Every cultural group decides what sort of personality pattern it wants in its members and then sets up norms of approved behavior. The culturally approved pattern is determined by what is best suited to successful adjustment in that cultural group.

The members of the group, especially the parents and teachers, are responsible for molding the child's personality pattern to conform to the group's standard. They do this *directly* by providing opportunities for learning, by preventing the child from learning what the group disapproves, by encouraging and rewarding him for learning what the group approves, and by rejecting or punishing him for learning what is unacceptable to the group. The older members of the cultural group show the new members what the "rewards of the game of life" are and convince him that he wants these rewards (183).

Indirectly, the cultural group influences the molding process by setting up models for the young to imitate and by making these models so prestigious that the young will want to imitate them. As Hilgard (105) has explained:

The process of growing up includes learning to behave in expected ways. We take on our group values without much reflection on them or without awareness that peoples of other cultures may not share these values. If our culture values cleanliness, promptness, hard work, then we tend to think of people as admirable if they exhibit these qualities. . . . Personality is a cultural product, but not exclusively so.

How closely a person is expected to conform to the cultural model varies from one culture to another. In some, a person may retain some individual qualities and still be socially acceptable; in others, the person is strictly regimented from the time of birth so that every member of the group fits into a carefully prescribed pattern with no deviations.

In the Soviet Union, for example, there are strong social pressures to shape each child into the pattern of the "ideal person" whose service is dedicated to the state rather than to individual gain. Since the rewards for conforming to the Soviet ideal are

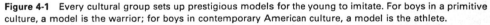

Figure 4-1 Every cultural group sets up prestigious models for the young to imitate. For boys in a primitive culture, a model is the warrior; for boys in contemporary American culture, a model is the athlete.

high, parents and teachers try to direct children's attitudes, sentiments, and beliefs toward this approved personality pattern (9).

Development of a basic personality type

Variations in the approved pattern of personality are found in different subgroups, but each culture attempts to mold in its members a basic pattern that conforms to the larger group's values. Common personality characteristics found in the majority of people in a cultural group constitute the group's *basic personality type,* which Kardiner (114) defines as

. . . that personality configuration which is shared by the bulk of the society's members as a result of the early experiences which they have in common. It does not correspond to the total personality of the individual but rather to the . . . value-attitude systems which are basic to the individual's personality configuration. Thus the same basic personality type may be reflected in many different forms of behavior and may enter into many different personality configurations.

The concept of the basic personality type, according to Allport (7), assumes:

a *that cultural tradition determines the lessons the parent will teach the child, and the way in which the lessons are taught;*

b *that different cultures have different ways of training the child—and different lessons to teach;*

c *that the child's early experience exerts a lasting effect upon his personality; and*

d *that similar experiences will tend to produce similar personalities within the culture.*

Figure 4–2 explains graphically how the basic personality type is molded. The relationship between cultural tradition and uniform child training, as Allport further explains, helps us to "understand why the personalities of the bushman and the American businessman are different. It also helps us to understand why one bushman is similar to another." It does not, on the other hand, "account for the differences between individual bushmen, or between individual businessmen" (7).

Differences between people within a cultural group due to variations in the basic personality type may be explained by the fact that (93):

Each person interprets and acts out the common cultural values within the framework of his own personal experiences and history; each puts upon these commonly held values the imprint of his own psychobiological capacities, abilities, and habits. To the degree that the individual within a given society is "normal," however, his most ego-involved attitudes and values are commonly shared by the majority of the other members of that society.

Influence of cultural values on basic personality type   Since the basic personality type approved by each cultural group is composed of traits that contribute to the successful adjustment of members of the group to its particular and unique life pattern, the basic personality patterns of no two cultures are identical. Noting this, Stendler writes, "As cultures differ, so do the personalities embedded in these cultures" (199).

Even cultures which are similar in many respects put varying degrees of emphasis on commonly held values. The French, for example, put more emphasis on thrift and individuality than Americans (199). The Germans put more emphasis on work and discipline than Americans. From the English point of view (71):

The well-brought-up child is expected to learn to control antisocial impulses and to be reserved. The American child is expected to develop a "marketable personality" with emphasis on ambition, getting ahead, popularity, initiative, and friendliness.

Figure 4-2   The basic personality pattern is molded through the interrelationship of cultural tradition and uniform child training. (Adapted from G. W. Allport: *Pattern and growth in personality.* New York: Holt, 1961. Used by permission.)

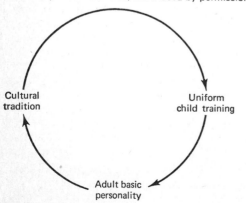

When a national group is composed of people from different countries, variations in the cultural values held by the group as a whole are quite marked. In America, the cultural system has two distinct parts: the general American culture and the various subcultures based on social class and/or ethnic group. Each subculture as well as the general culture has its own values and each attempts to mold in its members a basic personality pattern that will conform to its values.

The *American concept* of the "ideal person" puts high value on such qualities as personal output of energy, ability to adjust, mobility, optimism, competitiveness, fair play, cooperation, honesty, prestige, and efficiency. *Regional cultural values* differ somewhat in the emphasis placed on the general cultural values. In the Northeast, hard work and thrift are highly valued, with emphasis on mobility and change if they will lead to success. By contrast, in the Southeast, family solidarity is highly valued and mobility less so. Status or power based on kinship is more prestigious than that achieved by individual effort (82).

Clearly defined subgroup values set the model for the basic personality type to be molded in the young of the subgroup. *Middle-class values* emphasize self-control, getting ahead, and making the most of one's abilities and opportunities, even when this means denying present pleasures for future gains. By contrast, *lower-class values* stress immediate pleasures; and conformity to group standards is less highly valued than in the middle- or upper-class groups.

A study of altruism has shown how greatly social-class values differ. While people of all social classes feel obligated to reciprocate for the help given them, how much they will feel obligated to reciprocate depends on their social-class identification. Members of the lower class tend to believe that one should give only as much as one receives. Members of the middle class regard reciprocation as a social responsibility and feel that they should give more than they receive, especially to those less fortunate than they. The value of *noblesse oblige* is instilled in them from earliest childhood (28).

Other differences in admired personality traits within a cultural group may be based on *racial, ethnic, religious,* even *political* grounds. Three basic themes have been found to characterize the cultural values of Mexicans and Puerto Ricans: love and devotion to mother, submission and strong obedience to the father and other authority figures, and the superiority of the male over the female (73).

Effects of conformity to culturally approved pattern   The person whose personality pattern has been molded along lines approved by members of the cultural group with which he is identified has a far better chance for successful social adjustments and happiness than the one whose pattern is atypical for the group. The "rugged individualist" makes the poorest adjustments of all. He becomes a social misfit and this affects his self-concept unfavorably because he realizes how unacceptable his noncomformity is to the group with which he continues to be associated.

Difficulties in conforming to approved pattern   Some people find it easy to mold their personalities to conform to social expectations while others do not. An inherent tendency may make conformity difficult or impossible, as in the case of a boy with small stature and weak musculature who lives in a cultural group where high value is placed on physical strength and motor skills.

A person whose personality is molded according to the pattern approved by one cultural group and who then shifts to another cultural group with different values is ill prepared for conformity to that group's ideal. This may be a problem for immigrants or other geographically mobile persons.

Discontinuities in training have much the same effect. A child who is trained for a happy, carefree childhood, overprotected and freed from all except minor responsibilities, often finds it difficult to adjust to adult life where he is expected to be independent, to assume responsibilities, and to make decisions for himself (26).

Some people find conformity difficult because they do not approve of the cultural ideals of the group with which they are identified and prefer to conform to those of another group. Downwardly mobile people, for example, find it hard to relinquish middle-class values and accept lower-class values. This is one of the reasons why downward social mobility is such a traumatic experience, as will be discussed later.

In a culture where there are many subgroups and where values change rapidly and radically, as in America, it is difficult for parents and teachers to guide the child's development. The standards held in their own youth may not apply today just as the standards of today may not apply when the child reaches adulthood. In the home, the child's parents may have widely disparate values owing to differences in cultural background, religion, racial origin, socioeconomic status, or some other factor. The child is then confronted with a conflict in value patterns. The home pattern may be even further complicated by the presence of grandparents whose values are those of the older generation.

When the child goes to school, he is likely to encounter further conflicts in value systems. As most teachers come from middle-class backgrounds, there will be little discrepancy in values for the middle-class child. But should he come from an upper- or lower-class background, the discrepancy can be confusing. Then, too, the child's values may conflict with those of members of the peer group. To complicate the matter still further, peer values change and become increasingly sex-linked as children grow older. Among first graders, for example, the quiet, inconspicuous child is admired. Among third graders, such a child is overlooked or rejected, while the active, talkative, aggressive child is admired. By adolescence, there are not only shifts in values, but what is admired in a girl is not admired in a boy (134, 211). In addition, peer values become more at variance with parent and teacher values with each passing year. The individual must choose: He can accept adult values and lose status with his peers or he can accept peer values and risk endless conflicts with parents and teachers.

Vocational mobility may also require the adoption of new cultural values. Since each geographic area has slightly different values and each social group within a community has its distinctive pattern of values, a person who shifts from one locale or one social class to another must revise his old value system and acquire new values that will conform to those held by the group with which he is now identified.

Provision for learning

The third important way in which the environment influences the molding of the personality pattern is by providing opportunities for learning and pressures to motivate the person to take advantage of these opportunities. The shaping of the personality pattern from the hereditary potentials comes from learning. A person learns to behave in a culturally approved way and to think of himself as others with whom he comes in contact think of him.

Different kinds of learning are used in molding the personality pattern. Some are *self-initiated* in the sense that the learner takes the initiative in putting forth the effort needed to achieve an end result that he

feels is valuable to him. He is thus molding his own personality pattern, though environmental influences are felt through the reactions of other people to the behavior patterns he develops.

Some of the learning is *outer-directed* in the sense that the learner is instructed by someone else who, through approval or disapproval, motivates the learner to continue his practice until he has mastered the desired pattern of behavior. Outer-directed learning is called "training" because the activity is stimulated and directed by an outsider.

Conditions favoring learning How much and what a person learns will depend not alone on opportunities to learn and the method of learning used but also on the strength of the learner's motivation and his readiness to learn at the time the opportunities are presented. In addition, learning is greatly influenced by the attitudes and behavior patterns of those who direct the learning and by the model they present for the learner to imitate.

Even the most simple kind of learning cannot take place until the learner is in a *state of readiness*. The young child, for example, is not in a state of readiness for learning through following directions until his comprehension has developed to the point where he can understand what people tell him to do. This is a good deal later than the time at which he can learn by conditioning or imitation.

Regardless of the method used, learning must be *motivated* if it is to be effective. If the relationship between the learner and the person from whom he is learning is a positive one, his motivation to learn is likely to be high. A child will be more motivated to mold his personality after that of an older sibling whom he hero-worships than one whom he fears or dislikes.

Fear of loss of parental love or fear of punishment and satisfaction from approval and love are powerful motivating forces in learning at all ages, but especially in early childhood. As children grow older, approval or disapproval of the peer group provides the motivation to learn to conform to the group's standards of socially approved behavior.

It is not necessary for a person to *remember* the circumstances under which learning took place for early experiences to influence his personality pattern. Freud pointed out that, although early memories are usually submerged in the unconscious, they influence the quality of the person's behavior as he grows older as much as consciously remembered experiences (77).

This has been well illustrated by studies of crying in early childhood. Babies whose needs are promptly met cry much less than those whose needs are met less promptly and less consistently. Excessive crying leads to feelings of insecurity which, in time, become generalized. However, as children grow older, there is no evidence that they remember how their feelings of insecurity developed (122, 202).

With intellectual development, children are able to remember more, and their experiences leave an indelible impression on their personalities. Regardless of the kind of environment in which they grow up, people whose childhood experiences were mostly happy have an entirely different outlook on life from those whose memories of childhood center mainly on unpleasant experiences. Those with a preponderance of unpleasant childhood memories are more likely to be maladjusted.

RELATIVE IMPORTANCE OF HEREDITY AND ENVIRONMENT

The idea that hereditary potentials can be molded into any desired personality pattern was supported in the early part of this century by the teachings of John B. Watson. Watson claimed that a tiny, malleable creature, like a newborn infant, could be molded into anything the significant people in his environment desired (215).

Other scientists claimed, with equal strength of argument, that the newborn infant was "gene-controlled" and could scarcely be changed at all. This point of view is in line with the traditional belief expressed in the saying, "He is a chip off the old block."

Today there is little evidence that either point of view is correct. On the other hand, there is ample evidence that the form the personality pattern will take depends not solely on the training methods used or the kind of environment in which the person grows up but also on the hereditary potentials the person brings into the world with him (30).

Conditions affecting interaction of heredity and environment

The individual's potentials at the time of birth affect other people and the potentials themselves are affected in the relationships the individual has with significant people during the early years of his life. The molding of the personality pattern is thus a far more complex process than was previously believed, and many more elements are involved than would be true if the newborn infant were "merely a plastic blob of protoplasm" (42). Rainwater (170) has emphasized the complexity of the process:

Personality is formed from the interaction of significant figures (first the mother, later the father and siblings, later extrafamilial figures) with the child. The child brings to this interaction a certain biological constitution, certain needs and drives, and certain intellectual capacities which determine his reactions to the way in which he is acted upon by these significant figures.

In this interaction, significant people try to mold the child's personality into a culturally approved pattern. How they handle the child's basic drives and what expression of these drives they permit determine what sort of person the child will be.

The equipment for adjustment to his new environment that the child brings into the world with him will have a marked effect on how the significant people in his life react to him. If he is premature and his survival is threatened, if he is damaged by a long and difficult birth, or if some unfavorable condition in the prenatal environment produced physical or mental conditions that interfere with his adjustments, reactions to him will be very different from what they would be if he were a normal full-term child. Even a normal infant who is fussy and irritable will cause his parents more concern and anxiety than one who is calm and placid.

The parents' attitudes toward the child as a person and toward the role of parenthood also affect their relationship with him. If the child comes up to parental expectations, parental attitudes will be more favorable and parent-child relationships better than if the child is in some way disappointing to the parents.

Similarly, the attitudes of siblings, peers, relatives, and other adults, such as teachers and camp counselors, will be colored by what the child brings to their relationships. The happy, cooperative child wins friends among his peers while the aggressive, angry child is rejected. At school, the child who is well behaved and eager to learn will win the teacher's praise while the one who misbehaves and demands more than his share of attention will be regarded as troublesome.

The attitudes and behavior of other people toward the child will also affect the interactional pattern and thus influence the molding of his personality. A child who has learned to be aggressive at home will instigate relationships with people outside the home which are characterized by aggressive behavior. By contrast, the child who comes from a home where aggression is kept to a minimum will have friendly, cooperative interactions with outsiders.

Variations in relative importance of heredity and environment

The relative importance of heredity and environment in the molding of the personality pattern depends on at least three variables: the trait that is affected; the feature of the environment that is brought to bear on the developing trait; and the scope and intensity of the environmental forces.

Some *traits* are relatively stable; they vary little, regardless of environmental influences. Others are plastic and easily influenced by environmental conditions. Even the same trait may, in some people, be primarily the result of hereditary conditions, while in others, it is the product of environmental conditions. One person may be retiring and reclusive because of inborn qualities, for example, while another may become so because of conflict with his environment.

Thus, it is apparent that, in some traits, training outweighs the influence of heredity, while in others, the reverse is true. In general, however, the more directly a trait is bound to structural inheritance, the less it can be modified and changed by environmental influences.

The kind and intensity of *environmental influences* likewise affect the degree to which different traits will change. Whether the environmental influences are physiological, intellectual, or emotional will determine how much they can change different traits. Structural characteristics are usually more stable than traits that are more functional in nature (93, 194).

Value of knowing relative importance of heredity and environment

Knowledge of the conditions that affect the interrelationship of a person and his environment does not answer the question, Which plays a more important role in personality development, heredity or environment? The question cannot be answered in one word. In some aspects of the personality pattern, heredity is

more important; in other aspects, environment is more important.

For practical as well as theoretical reasons it would be extremely useful to be able to determine which influence is the more powerful. One practical application of such knowledge has been suggested by Jersild (112):

If children differ, by reason of their innate characteristics, in their tendency to be sensitive, to become hurt, to be yielding or to be defiant, to acquire attitudes of shame, to tolerate much or little pain and frustration, then we might assume that they differ in their innate tendencies to grow up as neurotic or healthy-minded individuals.

The relative importance of the two influences on personality cannot be determined once and for all because they may reinforce one another in their effect or they may conflict. The influence of the environment depends not on the environment alone but also on the person's hereditary endowment. As Allport put it, "The same fire that melts the butter, hardens the egg." Hereditary predispositions may influence environmental factors favorably or unfavorably, thus affecting the quality of personality molding: "Sometimes they (the raw materials of personality—physique, intelligence and temperament) accelerate the molding influence of the environment; sometimes they place limitations upon it; but always their force is felt" (7).

The form that the "raw materials" of personality take and their value to the person in making adjustments will be determined by the kind of environmental influences he is subjected to (30, 86). The constitutional quality of energy, vitality, or "pep," for example, may be harnessed and developed into one of the important qualities of leadership. Or, under less favorable environmental conditions, it may be turned into destructiveness, restlessness, or inattention, all of which will lead to poor adjustments and may even predispose the person to juvenile delinquency or adult criminality (83, 93).

WHEN PERSONALITY MOLDING BEGINS

The belief that the personality pattern is molded early in life is not new. In the sixteenth century, St. Ignatius claimed that if he could have the teaching of a child until he was 6 years old, nothing could undo the teaching (201). Freud, in the early part of the present century, emphasized the importance of the early years of life in determining the form the personality pattern would take. His theory was based on evidence that many of his patients who suffered from personality disturbances had had unhappy childhood experiences. These unhappy experiences, Freud postulated, came from the frustration of some natural impulse (77).

More recently, Watson and Gesell have come to the same conclusion, based on genetic studies of children from early babyhood (79, 215). Gesell et al., from studies of adolescents, concluded that "the foundation and most of the framework of the human action system are laid down in the first decade" (79).

Studies of poorly adjusted children, adolescents, and adults have substantiated these claims. Institutionalized babies, who suffer from emotional deprivation due to an absence of mothering during the first year of life, have been reported to be sad, depressed, apathetic; they lack animation and show signs of "mournful waiting" (39, 169). Young children subjected to undue thwartings become self-centered and reflective, live in a daydream world, or regress to infantile methods of meeting environmental situations (12, 75, 154, 171). Schizophrenia in adults usually has its roots in unfavorable early childhood experiences (11, 18, 163, 177).

Bartemeier (18) has pointed out that unfavorable early experiences have a profound effect on personality because the personality pattern is less fully organized then than it will be later:

Whatever emotional damage is inflicted on a child during the period of infancy has far greater effects upon the future character development than a similar damage inflicted at a later period when the personality has become more fully organized.

The damage from early experiences need not be permanent. Whether the damage will be eradicated or lessened or whether it will grow worse with the passage of time will depend partly on whether the conditions responsible for it change, partly on how long the person is subjected to the damaging effects of an unfavorable environment, and partly on what remedial steps are taken to correct the damage.

Why molding begins early

Molding of the personality pattern begins early in postnatal life because the capacity to learn develops early and is ready to function before the baby reaches

his first birthday. What happens in the early years of life, what kind of people the individual is associated with, what they expect of him, and how they try to enforce their expectations—all influence his developing personality and determine what sort of person he will grow up to be.

Whether he learns to be independent or dependent, for example, is determined by how his demands for independence are met even before he is 2 years old. If his demands lead to parental overprotection, he will become overdependent or hostile and willful. If the child is encouraged to be independent within the limits of his capacities, he will become autonomous and self-directive.

Even when unfavorable conditions in the early childhood environment improve as children grow older, memories of frustrations and unhappy experiences can never be entirely forgotten, nor will their effects on personality ever be completely eradicated. Once the molding begins, it is extremely difficult to change. If early molding favors the development of a healthy personality pattern, the individual is far less vulnerable to unfavorable environmental conditions which appear later.

Another reason molding begins early is that the baby enters the world with the hereditary endowment that will serve as the basis for the personality pattern. By the end of the second month of life, the baby begins to respond to other people in his own distinctive way, and in this interaction the traits of his personality pattern begin to take shape. As time goes on, changes in his personality pattern will primarily be changes in the strength of already-existing traits rather than the development of new traits.

HOW THE PERSONALITY PATTERN IS MOLDED

The cultural group sets the pattern for the approved basic personality and expects every member of the group to conform to it. In addition, the group lets every member know that conformity will be to his personal advantage. Thus, as Singh et al. have commented, "Personality is . . . shaped and changed by interactions with the culture in which the individual lives" (192).

In cultures where values are relatively static, the approved basic personality pattern likewise remains relatively static. Where values change frequently and radically, there will also be changes in the approved basic personality pattern. This, of course, does not mean changes in the total pattern but rather in certain aspects of it. Marked changes in moral values, for example, will be reflected in changes in the approved pattern for the character aspect of personality.

The culturally approved basic personality pattern is different for members of the two sexes. Whether a child will be molded along the lines set by the one model or by the other will be determined *not* by which of the models his parents or teachers consider the better, but by which one the cultural group considers appropriate for members of his sex. Crying, for example, will be tolerated among girls, but boys will be told that "boys don't cry."

Cultural influences usually determine the way in which a trait will be expressed. A middle-class cultural group will try to inhibit the expression of aggression, while a lower-class group will encourage it in boys as a symbol of masculinity. Similarly, the French emphasize learning to get along with people in the home while Americans emphasize learning to get along with people outside the home as well as inside it. Americans likewise put more emphasis on conformity to the group than the French (199).

Sources of molding

In the molding of the personality, the attitudes, feelings, and behavior patterns of the young are shaped first in the home and later reinforced or changed in the school, the peer group, and the community at large.

Some of the pressures that mold the personality pattern are applied consciously and some unconsciously. A mother may not be aware of her overprotectiveness or realize that it is affecting her child's self-concept. As Baumrind states, "With varying degrees of consciousness and conscientiousness, parents create their children psychologically as well as physically" (20).

The *family,* as the child's first social environment and as the social group with which he has the most frequent and closest contacts, is the most important source of personality molding. This has been stressed by Peck and Havighurst (167):

Each adolescent is just about the kind of person that would be predicted from the knowledge of the way his parents treated him. Indeed, it seems reasonable to say that, to an almost startling degree, each child learns to feel and act, psychologically and morally, as just the kind of person his father and mother have been in their relationship with him.

Within the home, the *mother* plays the central role in the molding process because she has more and closer contacts with the child than any other family member. However, the father, siblings, and other relatives contribute to the molding in proportion to the quantity and quality of their relationships with the child.

The influence of the *school* in the molding process comes from social pressures by teachers and members of the peer group. In the early years, the teacher plays the more important role, but in high school and college, the peer group is more influential.

Teachers sustain some of the child's home-grown attitudes, feelings, and behavior patterns; they reinforce others, deemphasize some, and create new ones. Attitudes toward self, toward others, and toward one's abilities and disabilities as compared with others are greatly affected by school pressures and the influence of teachers.

As early as the nursery school years, members of the *peer group* pass judgment on one another, showing approval or disapproval for different kinds of behavior, especially aggressive and sex-inappropriate behavior. By adolescence the influence of the peer group has increased to the point where it may surpass that of the home in determining the person's attitudes and behavior. In discussing the influence of the peer group, Martin and Westie (142) explained that the immediate group with which the young person is identified

. . . provides him with definitions of ingroups and outgroups and the "correct" feelings and behaviors in relation to their members. Under such circumstances, we find in our midst many Happy Bigots whose prejudices are born, not so much of personal psychological difficulties, but rather of the fact that their community and various groups inculcate, expect, and approve of their prejudices; personality factors probably serve primarily to predispose and to intensify or abate normative expectations.

Media of *mass communication*—books, magazines, newspapers, radio, television, movies, and comics—play a large role in shaping attitudes and beliefs and in structuring behavior patterns in accordance with the culturally approved values of the social group. These media help to reinforce values learned at home, in school, or in the peer group, and they serve as a means of learning new patterns.

How great an influence mass media have depends on where the individual lives. Persons brought up in a limited geographic or social setting may be aware of only the most generally accepted values of the culture. Mass media may help to free them from excessively narrow ideas and in this way help to mold their personality patterns. As a result, they may make better adjustments.

Religion helps to shape moral values and provides patterns for socially approved behavior. Children and adolescents brought up in homes where strict religious training prevails develop a more authoritarian personality pattern than those whose home environment puts less emphasis on religious training. Strict religious training usually reinforces strict, authoritarian child-training practices.

Whether the *occupation* in which a person is engaged affects his personality pattern or whether he selects an occupation to suit his personality is difficult to determine. Once in an occupation, a person usually tries to conform to the stereotype that is culturally associated with the people in it. Many years ago, Spranger (196) contended that the person's occupation molds the pattern of his personality:

No power in adult life molds a man so strongly as his vocation. The whole mentality of the agriculturist is entirely different from that of the stock raiser; the artisan differs from the clerk and the fisherman from the miner. Nature seems to stamp the soul with the special conditions under which he (man) wrests his livelihood from her.

More recent studies reveal that a person chooses an occupation that fits his needs and in which he feels at home. A person may decide to become a physicist, for example, because he believes that that profession will provide him the social isolation that he desires as a result of having felt "different" from earliest childhood. A person who had a well-supervised childhood and has been encouraged to help others and avoid danger may choose to be a clergyman. The well-regulated life and the conventional patterns of behavior that go with his occupation fit his needs (91, 186).

While a person's occupation unquestionably helps to mold his personality pattern, the molding is likely to be through reinforcement of personality characteristics which were already present and which were largely responsible for his choice of the occupation. It is questionable whether an occupation could bring about radical qualitative changes in a personality pattern because by the time a person is old enough to enter an occupation, his personality pattern is al-ready well formed. Consequently, it is safe to conclude that the molding influence results in *quantitative* changes by reinforcing traits already present.

Variations in reactions to molding influences

In some people, molding the personality pattern to conform to the culturally approved ideal is relatively easy. In others, it is more difficult, while in still others, resistance to the molding is so strong that little or no change occurs, regardless of the pressures to think, feel, and act as the group desires.

People who are insecure and anxious for group approval yield most easily to group pressures. If they feel that they can come close to the stereotype of the socially acceptable person, they will try to conform in every way in the hope of gaining social acceptance.

At all ages, people who are outer-directed, in the sense that they are strongly influenced in their thoughts, feelings, and actions by others, are more easily molded to a socially approved pattern than are those who are inner-directed and who decide what their actions will be without interference from others. In the outer-directed, the more prestigious the source of outside influences, the easier it will be to mold their personality patterns.

The person who is hardest to mold into a culturally approved pattern is the one who feels that his chances for social acceptance are so slim that it is not worth the effort to try to conform. Resentment against the group and against society at large often makes the person defiant. He thus resists any attempt by others to mold his personality and may retaliate by trying to develop socially disapproved characteristics. When good grooming and an attractive appearance are socially approved, for example, he bends backward to look sloppy and disheveled. If the social group tries to get him to obey its rules and laws, he may flout the rules and do what he pleases.

MOLDING TECHNIQUES

Two methods of learning are dominant in molding the personality pattern to conform to culturally approved standards: first, learning through guidance and control of behavior by another, and second, learning through imitation of the beliefs, attitudes, and behavior patterns of another. The first is an outer-directed method of learning and is commonly referred to as "child training." The second is self-initiated or inner-directed and is known as "identification."

During the preschool years, the molding comes primarily from child training in the home where the parents are responsible for the molding process. After the child enters school, identification gradually takes on more significance. No longer is the young person willing to be shaped by another. He wants to mold himself according to a pattern of his own choosing. However, at no time are pressures from members of the family and the social group completely absent.

In child training, culturally approved patterns are enforced directly by providing opportunities for the young to learn what the group wants them to learn and by limiting their opportunities to learn what the group does not want them to learn. Identification, by contrast, is an indirect way of enforcing culturally approved standards. By imitating the patterns of behavior of someone whose high status in the group is recognized, the person hopes to win the same kind of group approval and acceptance that his model has won. Unlike in child training, no one pressures the individual to behave as his model behaves; the imitation is voluntary, and in the young child may be subconscious. In older children, adolescents, and young adults, the imitation is consciously performed in the hope of winning the same social rewards as the person imitated.

It is impossible to say which plays the more important role in the molding of the personality pattern—child training or identification. The relative effectiveness of the two learning methods varies from one person to another and from one age to another. Furthermore, as has been pointed out, no two people react in the same way. In trying to explain individual differences in response even when similar personality-molding methods are used, Klineberg writes, "Many years ago Piéron spoke of the 'semi-permeable membrane' surrounding each personality, letting some experiences in, keeping others out. Every individual makes his own choice and his own interpretation of what his culture offers him" (116).

Child-training methods

Through its child-training methods, every cultural group tries to produce group members whose personality patterns conform to the standards of the culture. Thus the most important factor in perpetuating and stabilizing any human cultural group is the way it brings up its children.

The goal of child training is to mold the child so that he will be able to adjust to the traditional roles prescribed by the cultural group. However, in a constantly changing culture like our own, there is no single cultural pattern and there is no overall philosophy of child training. As a result, the methods used will depend upon the values and attitudes of the parents and teachers of each individual child. This means wide variations in specific training methods, even though all have the same aim: to produce a well-adjusted person.

Kinds of child-training methods
The child-training methods used in America today fall into three major categories: authoritarian, democratic, and permissive. *Authoritarian* methods are characterized by the use of strict rules and regulations to enforce the desired behavior. Under this method, it is not considered necessary to explain why the rules are important to the individual or to the social group. Failure to come up to expected standards is severely punished, but little or no recognition or praise is offered when the person does meet the expected standards.

Democratic methods emphasize the need for discussions, explanations, and reasoning to help the young understand why they are expected to behave in one way rather than another. When the person comes up to expected standards or shows that he is trying to do so, he is rewarded with parental or teacher approval. Punishment is used only when the person willfully refuses to do what is expected of him, and when it is used, it is relatively mild.

Permissive methods are not actually child training, though parents and teachers may regard them as such. The young person learns more by trial and error than by guidance. If he discovers that an act brings social disapproval, he will reject it in favor of another or still another until he hits upon one that brings him not only personal satisfaction but also the approval of the group. In reality, he is molding his own personality pattern without the guidance and help from others which those whose personalities are molded by authoritarian and democratic child-training methods have.

Variations in child-training methods Within each of the major child-training methods are many variations. Variations in the authoritarian method may range from reasonable restraints on antisocial behavior to rigid restraints that permit the child no freedom of action except that which conforms to prescribed standards. Democratic methods may range from careful planning of the child's activities so that his energies will be directed into approved channels to such extreme leniency that little or no control is exercised.

The kinds of control used to bring about the desired behavior also vary. Authoritarian child-training methods foster control through external force in the form of punishment. Democratic methods try to develop internal controls by educating the young person to behave in the approved manner and rewarding him with social approval.

Choice of child-training method

Since the turn of the century, dogmatic, authoritarian methods of training have in large measure given way to more democratic and permissive methods. There has likewise been a shift from the use of punishment to enforce an approved pattern of behavior to the use of education—discussions, explanations, etc.—to teach the young person to *want* to do what the social group expects of him.

These new approaches have accompanied a change in the philosophy of the nature of man. When it was believed that sinfulness was innate, cruel and punitive methods of child training were sanctioned. Now there is the belief, based on studies of learning, that young people will be "good" or "bad," depending on how they learn to behave. As a result, child-training methods have been considerably relaxed.

Even today, however, child training in America is very eclectic. There are marked variations in the methods used by different people and even the methods used by the same person from time to time. Those who use either the most restrictive or the most permissive methods are usually more consistent than those who operate between these extremes.

FACTORS INFLUENCING CHOICE OF CHILD-TRAINING METHODS Variations in the kind of child-training method used and in the way the training is enforced are influenced by a number of factors, each consistently related to certain characteristics of the parent or teacher whose responsibility it is to train the young or to certain characteristics in the young person himself.

There is a strong tendency for adults to use child-training methods *similar to those they were subjected to as children.* This is especially true of those brought up by authoritarian methods. *Younger parents* tend to be more democratic than older parents, but, in general, only if they rely upon child-training experts for advice rather than upon their own parents. Most parents tend to exert more control over *very young children* than over adolescents.

Parents who are better *educated* tend to be more democratic or permissive than those whose education is limited. *Education for parenthood* helps parents to understand the needs of children at different ages. This, in turn, influences the way they train their children. On the whole, the better the parent understands the child and his needs, the less authoritarian he will be.

Fathers who are *away from home* during the first year of a child's life have been reported to have little understanding of the developmental needs of the child and are thus overly strict in their training. *Mothers* generally have a better understanding of the child's needs than fathers and they tend to be less authoritarian. Children brought up in *monomatric homes*—homes where the mother takes exclusive care of the child—are usually better understood and enjoy more consistent child training than those brought up in polymatric homes where the care of the child is shared with another female (48).

Girls at every age are more restricted than boys and are expected to conform more closely to the socially approved patterns of behavior (66, 184). Parents from *rural* districts are, as a rule, more authoritarian in their methods of training children than parents from urban or suburban areas (216). *Black parents* tend to be more permissive than white parents from similar social classes (187).

Social-class differences in child training are great, although variations occur within every social class. As a rule, parents from middle-class socio-economic backgrounds are more authoritarian, more coercive, and less tolerant than parents from the lower classes. The latter, as a group, tend to be more permissive and also more inconsistent in their child-training methods. Since middle-class parents put such high value on getting ahead through achievements and social acceptance, they are more exacting in their expectations than lower-class parents (6, 144, 156, 170).

Within the middle-class group, parents who are better educated and enjoy a more favorable social status are more permissive (138, 144, 165). Social-class differences are reflected in the areas of behavior where greatest emphasis is placed. Middle-class parents are stricter about learning to control aggression and respecting the property rights of others while lower-class parents are stricter about masturbation, modesty, and the use of tabooed language (144, 170).

There are also social-class differences in the ways parents enforce the acceptance of cultural values by their children. Middle-class parents do so mostly by disapproval, by depriving their children of some privilege or the company of others, by stimulating feelings of guilt and shame in the child, and by threats of loss of parental love. Lower-class parents, on the other hand, use physical punishment, often very severe; shame and ridicule to "toughen the child up"; and rejection, or showing the child that they do not want to be "bothered with him" (96, 170). *Foreign-born parents* from every social class are more authoritarian than native-born parents (59, 115).

The adult's *concept of his role* influences the kind of child-training method used. Parents and teachers who hold to the traditional concept of their role exercise considerable restraint over the children under their care to guarantee that they will be successful. Teachers who hold to the authoritarian concept and are anxious to have their pupils adjust to a fairly rigid routine use commands, physical compulsion, and disapproval (123, 198).

The *personality pattern of the parent* influences the kind of child-training method used and the interpretation of this method. Women who show strong masculine tendencies exert more control over their children than do more feminine women (221). Parents who are inner-directed do what they think is right in training their children, while those who are outer-directed do what others think is right (221). Those who hold conservative opinions about social matters are usually more intolerant and authoritarian in the rearing of their children than those who are less conservative. Parents who tend to have radical opinions about social matters tend to be permissive in their child rearing (102). Fathers who are regarded as restrictive because of their authoritarian treatment of their children have been found to be submissive and suggestible and to suffer from feelings of inadequacy. By contrast, fathers who are regarded as permissive tend to be well-adjusted individuals who show marked flexibility, self-reliance, stability, and self-confidence (32).

The *personality of the child* also affects the method of child rearing his parents will use. Some children resist discipline of any kind and become negativistic toward all in authority; others submit to authority and try to conform. The extroverted child is more susceptible to social attitudes than the introvert and can more easily be conditioned to what his parents and teachers want him to do. As a result, it is easier to mold his personality pattern (70, 143, 185).

Influence of attitudes   The attitude of the person who trains the child and the attitude of the child toward the method used and toward the person who uses it are vital factors in molding the child's personality (69, 81, 99). There is, however, no convincing evidence that as an adult his personality will reflect the kind of training he received during his early years or that the effects of his early training will carry into the adult years. There is, for example, no real evidence that bottle feeding produces a less desirable personality pattern than breast feeding or that late toilet training is any more harmful to the developing personality than early toilet training (52, 58, 219).

It is apparent, therefore, that it is not the child-training method per se but the *total interaction* of the child and the person who uses the method that determines what effect it will have on his personality. Since the person is most vulnerable to outside influences during his early years, parental attitudes are more important at that time than later. Spock (195) has emphasized the early vulnerability of the child:

If the child is regularly shamed for his accidents, accidents in the general and in the sanitary sense, he acquires a sense of shame and unworthiness. If he is excessively dominated he becomes defiant or submissive. If he is constantly warned that the parent will no longer love him unless he behaves differently, his whole personality will be poisoned with uneasiness and antagonism.

Both the timing and the consistency of attitudes influence personality development. The *timing* of the attitudes of those who use the child-training methods is more important than the methods themselves. This means that the unfavorable attitudes of those whose responsibility it is to train the child produce more psychological damage at some times than at others.

The degree and extent of the damage depends on the frustrations the child experiences as a result of the attitudes at that particular stage in his development. Early frustrations may be so extensive, so severe, and so persistent that they cannot be offset by later compensatory gratifications. As a result, the damaging effect on personality is reinforced rather than diminished. When the young child is given an opportunity to learn to be independent, for example, he may be excessively shy and fearful as a result of overprotection at an earlier age.

Similarly, overpermissiveness, or the absence of frustrations, at a critical age can have far-reaching effects. A young person who was treated with great permissiveness as a child may have great difficulty learning to make adjustments outside the home where he is expected to obey the rules.

In the development of a wholesome personality pattern, *consistency* of attitude is as important as consistency of method. How parents and teachers apply the child-training method they think is best to achieve the goal of socializing the child will vary according to their attitudes at that time. These attitudes, in turn, will be influenced to a large extent by the circumstances of the moment, how they feel, how the child is behaving, and many other factors.

Effects of child training on personality

The knowledge that child training helps to shape personality is expressed in the old saying, "Spare the rod and spoil the child." The saying reflects some advice given in the Book of Proverbs: "Withhold not correction from the child: for if thou beatest him with the rod, he shall not die."

While it is true that few children die from beatings, it is also true that beatings usually inflict psychological damage that affects the whole personality pattern. This was stressed by Montaigne in his *Essays:* "I have never seen any effect in rods but to make children's minds more base, or more maliciously headstrong." Among scientists, the psychological damage of harsh child training was first recognized by Freud, who emphasized the effect of early training on adult personality (77).

Modern research studies have fully substantiated Freud's thesis. However, they have also shown that the effect of early experiences on the molding of the personality pattern is influenced to some extent by the hereditary endowment of the person. The interaction of heredity and environment has been stressed by Baumrind (20):

(the child's) energy level, willingness to explore and will to master the environment, and his self-control, sociability and buoyancy are set not only by genetic structure but by the regimen, stimulation and kind of contact provided by his parents.

Studies of authoritarian, democratic, and per-missive child-training methods have revealed what different effects they have on the child's developing personality pattern. The effects of strict, *authoritarian* training were recognized many years ago by Martineau (141):

I have a strong suspicion that the faults of temper so prevalent where parental authority is strong, and where children are made as insignificant as they can be made, and the excellence of temper in America, are attributable to the different management of childhood in the one article of freedom. Many children are irrecoverably depressed and unnerved for want of being convinced that anybody cares for them.

Modern studies show that authoritarian training methods produce a child who is quiet, well behaved, nonresistant, socially unaggressive, and restricted in curiosity, originality, and fancifulness (19, 43, 106, 110). As he grows older, he develops feelings of guilt about independent thinking and this impedes his social and emotional maturing. He learns to think of himself as worthless and, as a result, lacks confidence in his abilities. In time, this may develop into an inferiority complex which further militates against his achieving the success he is capable of.

Strict treatment and demands for rigid conformity in the early years of life often lead to the development of an "authoritarian personality" syndrome. (See Chapter 1 for a discussion of the characteristics of this syndrome.) A study of extreme conformists has shown them to be a product of rigid and punitive treatment in early childhood, which in time resulted in a generalized response of conforming (44, 52, 54, 123, 153, 157).

When antisocial behavior is strictly dealt with by harsh and punitive controls, it is likely to be driven underground. It will then seek new channels of expression, such as negativism, refusals, angry dependency on the frustrating person, defiance of those in authority, or displacement on some innocent victim, perhaps a pet or a member of a minority group. Overstrictness may make the child so submissive that he is less competitive and socially successful than other children. It may make him compulsively obedient but inwardly defiant. In addition it will undermine his confidence in his ability to make decisions and be independent.

On the other hand, overstrict control may push the person too far and thus motivate him to assert his independence. Feeling that his parents are against him, the child develops a generalized feeling of martyrdom which may be expressed in apathy and resignation but which is more often expressed in angry defiance of all in authority. This may eventually lead to delinquency, with the young person trying to prove to himself and to others that he is independent and will not allow himself to be dominated. Frank states the possibilities concisely: "The stricter the parents, the stronger may be the revolt and the more outrageous the 'hell-raising' or the more submissive conformity to parents and priggish self-justification" (75).

Democratic child training results in greater independence in thinking and acting and in a healthy, positive, confident self-concept. This leads to better personal and social adjustments and to more outgoing, active, and spontaneous behavior. As summarized by Sears et al. (187):

Mothers who love and accept their children, and who use love-oriented techniques of discipline rather than material or physical techniques, produce relatively more children with high conscience.

The favorable effects of democratic child training are seen also in the schools. Teachers who have a warm, friendly, and cooperative attitude get along well with children, and their pupils do better work and make better personal and social adjustments.

Extreme leniency, which characterizes *permissive* child training, is as detrimental to personality development as extreme authoritarianism. When too little control is exercised over his behavior, the child becomes insecure and confused. He feels unprepared to meet life's problems. Feelings of insecurity lead to fear, anxiety, a tendency to take advantage of parental uncertainty, and a feeling of contempt for parental "softness." The child interprets parental lack of control over his behavior as an indication that his parents care little about him.

Children brought up in homes where permissive child training is used become selfish and self-centered and show little compassion for others. They do not learn to conform to others, but imperiously expect others to conform to them. That this is poor preparation for good personal and social adjustments has been stressed by Jersild (112):

If children have not been disciplined in a manner that would put a curb on their expectations from others, they are due for some hard jolts as they may have

illusions concerning their own rights and a vague notion of omnipotence which will clash sooner or later with the realities of life. The overindulgent parent, likewise, may be so forebearing and so patient that the child demands from others a degree of patience and forebearance which they will not be able to give him.

That permissive child training is poor preparation for adult life has been further remarked by Aldridge (4) in his emphasis on how such training leads to delusions of grandeur and infallibility:

It is scarcely surprising that the offspring of this way of life, the beneficiaries of all this love and attention and self-sacrifice, should have grown up contemptuous of us or convinced that really we were dead all along and only they were alive. How could people be anything but dead or stupid or insane who had so little regard for their own needs, who asked so little for themselves? If we gave up our lives for them, it was only reasonable for them to suppose either that we did not value our lives or that they themselves must be terribly important to have provoked us to such fantastic generosity. So we taught them by our example and by our obsequious treatment of them to have no consideration or respect for adults and a grotesquely inflated respect for themselves.

VARIATIONS IN INFLUENCE OF CHILD-TRAINING METHODS Social-class differences in methods of child training and in value systems have resulted in class-distinguished personality patterns (144). Members of the upper classes put high value on family status and past accomplishments and relatively low value on individual striving and aggressiveness, and so it is logical that they would develop self-confidence, feelings of adequacy, and even feelings of self-importance regardless of their own personal achievements. Furthermore, because of the more permissive child-training methods used in upper-class homes, these characteristics are reinforced (132, 144).

Since lower-class parents tend to be inconsistent in child training, swinging from extremes of permissiveness to extremes of authoritarianism accompanied at times by harsh punishment, their children develop feelings of inadequacy and loss of self-confidence, which increase with age. In addition, lower-class children learn to be sly, secretive, and dishonest in order to avoid the punishment that inevitably follows nonconformity to parental wishes. Furthermore, because of the lower-class-value emphasis on aggressiveness, especially for men, boys are encouraged to develop a "bully" personality pattern (132, 144).

Middle-class values, with their emphasis on "doing," on individual achievement, encourage the development of striving and aggressiveness (144). Middle-class children are subjected to strong pressures to live up to parental expectations and to frustrate any opposing desires. Fearing that they will fall below parental expectations, they develop feelings of inadequacy, anxiety, and insecurity. These feelings are often accompanied by guilt and shame (6, 70, 170).

As middle-class children grow older, their personality patterns become even more class-distinguished. Neuroticism, characterized by anxiety symptoms, is more common among them than among adolescents from the upper and lower social classes. This suggests that mental health and social class are significantly related (172).

Sex differences in personality patterns reflect cultural values. The differences are in part at least the result of child-training methods. Even in the preschool years, mothers are stricter with their daughters than with their sons, and children usually interpret this to mean that boys are favored. This leads to a feeling of superiority on the part of boys and to resentment and a feeling of martyrdom on the part of girls. By adolescence, the effect is easily observed. Girls are more conforming than boys; they are quieter, more withdrawn, less aggressive, and less daring (66, 184).

Girls often bitterly resent being overprotected and treated too strictly, but have difficulty expressing their negative feelings and criticisms because they feel obligated to their parents. When severely punished or unjustly treated, however, they feel justified in expressing their feelings, even when this leads to family friction. At other times, they displace their resentments on others. This has been explained as one of the reasons for greater prejudice on the part of girls as compared with boys (8, 159).

The effects of child-training methods on personality vary also according to the family member who is in *control of the training*. There are four kinds of family control: "autonomic," or equalitarian, where control is shared by both parents; "wife-dominant," where control is in the hands of the mother; "husband-dominant," where control is in the hands of the father; and "conflict-in-power" where husband and wife are in conflict over which will control the training of the children. It has been reported that the lowest achievement and the highest anxiety occur when there is conflict in parental control. By contrast, the highest achievement and lowest anxiety are found among children from families of equalitarian control (205).

Essentials to a healthy personality pattern

To lay the foundations of a healthy personality pattern, child training must be both consistent and fair. Severity and laxity per se are not so damaging as lack of *consistency*. Consistency of training results in better integration of behavior and a more realistic approach to life, both of which contribute to good personal and social adjustments.

Changes in parental attitudes toward the child as he grows older often result in a change in child-training methods. Shifting to an entirely different method is often more damaging to the child's personality development than are inconsistencies in applying one method. Changes in child training come from two causes: First, parents may regard the child who rebels against parental protectiveness as less appealing than the helpless, dependent baby, and so they may adopt more authoritarian or more permissive methods of control. Second, parents may believe that, when babyhood is over, they must adopt stricter methods in order to teach the child to conform to social standards.

Children become increasingly sensitive to *fairness* or the lack of it as they grow older. If they think that they have been unfairly treated, they feel abused and become resentful not only toward those who they think have treated them unfairly but also toward all in authority.

Whether a child's grievances are justified or not, they affect his self-attitude as well as his attitude toward others. If the child interprets what others say or do as unfair and if he believes that he is a scapegoat or a victim of revenge or prejudice, the repercussions on his personality may persist even into adulthood.

When children or adolescents are expected to conform to more rigid or more restrictive standards than their friends, they feel that they are being unfairly treated. "The meaning to an individual of a certain amount of frustration," Klineberg writes, "will surely vary in relation to the amount of frustration to which he sees other individuals subjected" (116). The inevitable result of seeing oneself as a victim of unfairness is a feeling of martyrdom.

The *attitudes* of the people who are responsible for molding the child's personality pattern are as important to the development of a healthy personality as fairness and consistency. What parents, teachers, and other adults say and how they say it convey to the child their approval or disapproval, their friendliness or hostility, their interest or lack of interest, and other attitudes. Because of his limited knowledge and experience, however, the child may readily misinterpret what he hears and sees. A child may interpret a frown to mean that his mother is annoyed with him, whereas in reality, it may come from fatigue or a headache, something totally unrelated to him.

In the same way, children misinterpret words or read into them meanings that were not intended by the speaker. They often believe that they are unfairly blamed for something that their siblings were responsible for. Misinterpretation is often at the root of resentments which influence the child's attitude toward the mother and make him believe that she favors other children in the family.

Even older children, adolescents, and adults frequently misinterpret the speech, facial expressions, and behavior of others. A person may make judgments on the basis of too few cues or he may judge others' attitudes from his own narrow frame of reference. A person who is authoritarian, for example, is likely to judge the attitudes of teachers or others in authority as more authoritarian than they actually are.

Whether a person's judgments of others' attitudes are correct or not, they influence his concept of self. If a person believes that others like him and approve his conduct, the effect on his self-concept will be favorable, regardless of how they actually feel about him. On the other hand, attitudes interpreted as unfavorable will have a damaging effect on the self-concept.

Similarly, parents, teachers, and others in authority may misinterpret a child's attitudes. Parents may think the crying baby is being ornery while in reality he is trying to tell them he is hungry or cold. They may think the rebellious adolescent is showing signs of becoming a delinquent when he is merely trying to achieve a little more autonomy and develop more self-confidence.

A baby, a child, or an adolescent who feels that others understand him and his needs develops feelings of security and trust. If parents and teachers make no effort to understand, they are unwittingly paving the way for personality maladjustment in the child. Failure to understand the child's need for approval and love, even at the ages when overt demonstrations of affection are regarded as "babyish," deprives the child of the satisfaction of two of the strongest of human needs. Deprivation of affection leads to feelings of rejection, of being unwanted and unloved—feelings that are the basis of many personality disorders.

Identification

Identification, the second important molding technique, is often called "learning by imitation." More correctly defined, identification is the process by which a person takes over the values of another by imitation. It is the "tendency to view oneself as one with another person and to act accordingly" (203). Imitation is more limited than identification. It may refer to copying only one act, such as swinging a golf club or moving one's feet in a dance step.

In identification, the individual tries to duplicate in his own life the ideas, attitudes, and behavior of the person he is imitating. When young children identify themselves with parents, they use in their make-believe play the same kinds of behavior that their parents use in similar real-life situations. If a little girl is playing "mother" to her dolls or her peers, for example, she scolds, slaps, makes derogatory comments, or spanks to enforce her rules just as her mother does. This is certain to have some influence on her personality pattern. See Figure 4–3 for a graphic illustration of identification.

Identification may accompany child training in which the person learns through guidance and control. When a child identifies with an adult, he learns to

Figure 4-3 Personality molding through identification occurs when a person tries to duplicate the ideas, values, behavior, and attitudes of the person he admires.

do what the adult does as well as what the adult tells him to do. Learning by identification in the absence of child training, however, occurs when a person identifies with a popular hero or someone who has no control over him and no responsibility for training him.

Child training accompanied by identification is far more effective in personality development than training or identification alone. This is especially true in the case of young children. Landreth underlines this point: "Where there is no identification, parental admonitions are probably sounding brass and tinkling cymbals" (123).

Child training versus identification

Two major differences between child training and identification must now be reiterated. *First,* child training is outer-directed learning while identification is self-initiated and inner-controlled learning. In child training, a parent, teacher, or some other adult attempts to force a child to think, act, and feel in a manner that will conform to culturally approved standards. In identification, the child wants to think, act, and feel in a manner which he believes is representative of the standards of the cultural group as shown in the person he selects as his model. No external pressure is brought to bear to make him identify; any pressure involved comes from within himself.

The *second* major difference between child training and identification as learning methods responsible for molding the personality pattern is in the degree of motivation present. In child training, motivation to learn may be strong if punishment or praise is applied to force the learner to behave as society expects him to behave. But severe punishment and high praise are generally not sufficient to make him change his values or his feelings unless he wants to do so. He may, on the surface, appear to have changed, but, as has repeatedly been demonstrated in the case of prejudice, the new values and feelings may just be window dressing—brought out and displayed only when there is threat of punishment or social disapproval.

Identification is self-initiated learning, and so the person *wants* to learn. This supplies his motivation and explains why identification aids personality molding. That is also why young children who have not yet learned to respond to punishment or social disapproval may ignore a parental admonition unless they identify with their parents. Only as the child grows older and discovers the force of social disapproval will admonitions without identification provide adequate

motivation to learn to do something he does not want to do.

How motivation aids learning through identification is well illustrated by sex typing. Boys discover even before they enter school that "masculine" men are more admired than "sissies." Through identification with their fathers or some other male adult, they try hard to learn to be "regular boys." Social attitudes with regard to women's relative femininity are not quite so strong, and so girls are less strongly motivated to learn to be "typically feminine." As a result, boys are more firmly sex-typed at an earlier age than girls. Only when girls reach adolescence and discover that social approval is greater for those who are strongly "feminine" do they identify with typically feminine women and try hard to develop a corresponding personality pattern (27, 63, 78, 157).

Early recognition of importance of identification

The importance of identification in the molding of personality was first stressed by Freud. According to him, the child acquires the *ego-ideal,* a code of behavior made up of an accumulation of ideals, attitudes, and behavior patterns, as well as the *superego,* the punitive agent which enforces this code, from his parents (77):

When we were little children we knew these natures, we admired and feared them, and later we took them into ourselves. . . . Identification endeavors to mold a person's ego after the fashion of the one that has been taken as a model.

The implication of this theory is that *all* children identify with their parents and that it is, therefore, from imitating their parents that they acquire the cultural values that shape their personality patterns. The theory thus ignores the role played by child-training methods.

More recent studies have revealed that identification does not always occur. It occurs only when a positive affective tone or a reward value characterizes the relationship (63, 90). Identification, says Stoke, occurs when a person gives his "emotional allegiance" to an individual he admires and wants to resemble, whether that person be a parent, a teacher, a peer, or a popular hero (203). If there is no emotional allegiance, there will be no identification. The person will thus have no model to imitate, though he may learn the culturally approved values and patterns of behavior in other ways, such as trial and error or child training.

How much or how little a person will identify with another (the model) and pattern his behavior along the lines of the model will depend largely upon the kind of affective relationship that exists between them. A study of college students showed that the more affection a student had for a parent, the more he identified with the parent and the more he resembled that parent (87).

Conditions affecting identification

Certain conditions favor identification and others militate against it. Knowing what these conditions are will help one to understand why some children and adolescents do not identify and why, therefore, identification is not a universal method of molding the personality pattern.

CONDITIONS FAVORING IDENTIFICATION Studies of identification show that the following conditions are chief among those which encourage a young person to identify with another person and use him as a model.

The young person is treated with affection by the individual with whom he tries to identify.

The young person has an empathic understanding of the individual selected as a model.

The model gratifies the youth's needs.

The youth is acquainted with the model or knows about his prestige.

The young person enjoys being with the model for long periods of time.

The attitudes of significant people toward the model are favorable.

The role of the model is clearly understood and evokes a positive response from the young person.

The model is regarded as fair.

The model is of the same sex as the young person and behaves in a sex-appropriate manner.

The young person has a tendency to depend on others.

The model has a favorable attitude toward the youth.

The temperament of the model is compatible with that of the youth.

The youth has strong needs which coincide with the pattern of behavior of the model.

An older child or an adolescent often identifies with someone outside the home; the degree of his social acceptance has a marked influence on the degree of his identification. If he enjoys less than complete acceptance but sees the possibility of gaining complete acceptance, he will identify with the peer group in the hope of improving his social status. When his acceptance is low, however, he will conform to group standards only in public. The more he values membership in a group, the more highly motivated he is to identify with it and conform to its standards.

People who have a strong authoritarian tendency are likely to identify with "authority figures." Those who have a strong need for affiliation with their peers are more likely to identify with the peer group and conform to its standards.

CONDITIONS MILITATING AGAINST IDENTIFICATION When any one of the following conditions that militate against identification is present, identification is unlikely to occur. When two or more are present, identification is impossible.

First, among young children, lack of a consistent love object in the form of a parent makes it difficult for the child to identify with anyone. This condition often affects institutionalized babies and young children who are deprived of consistent care by one person or are subjected to inconsistent relationships with the person who cares for them. In the latter situation, the person who cares for the child sometimes provides him with the gratifications needed to bring about "emotional allegiance" but at other times rejects him, breaking or weakening any emotional bond that has been built up.

A second condition which militates against identification is the young person's hostility toward available model-candidates. Hostility toward a parent leads either to lack of identification or to breakdown of an already-established identification. In an older child or adolescent, hostility toward a parent may come from harsh and, to the young person, unfair discipline, or it may result from friction between the parents. The mother, for example, may criticize the father and condition the child against him.

A third and closely related condition is the youth's lack of admiration and respect for model-candidates with whom identification would normally take place. The so-called "generation gap" leads some young people to reject their parents' way of life and to express scorn and contempt for all who belong to the older generation. In this situation, Aldridge (5) explains, children and adolescents have no motivation to model their behavior after their parents:

They suffer the handicap of having formed their impressions of adulthood largely on their parents, and it is obvious that the example of their parents has in most cases given them little except strongly negative attitudes toward the possibilities of adult life. To the extent that they are certain of anything at all, they appear to be in agreement on one point: they do not want to become like Mother and Dad. The prospect of settling down in a dull job and a dull house, working to pay off the mortgage, seeking identity in reproduction, and then living for the children—with all that this implies in boredom, self-sacrifice, and generalized atrophy of the soul—fills them with a special kind of terror.

Even a young child's attitudes may be affected in this way, as illustrated in Figure 4–4. Once a child develops an aversion for the parent or the parental role, identification with any adult may be impossible for many years.

The personality pattern of the young person himself is a *fourth* condition which may militate against identification. One who is self-bound and introverted, who suffers from neurotic tendencies, such as feelings of martyrdom, may be unable to give emotional allegiance to anyone. By contrast, a normal, well-adjusted person can identify with another if the person with whom he wants to identify is reasonably receptive.

When circumstances make it difficult or impossible for a young person to identify with the kind of model he would normally identify with at his level of development, he may give his emotional allegiance to another kind. A child or adolescent who cannot identify with a parent, for example, may choose to model himself after a teacher, a relative, or a slightly older member of the peer group.

Sources of identification   The individual gives his emotional allegiance to different people at different ages. These people serve as the basis for his ideal self-concept, as was discussed in Chapter 2, and he tries to model his behavior after them. Shifts in the sources of identification follow a regular and predictable pattern unless interfered with by some environmental condition, such as institutionalization in babyhood or, later, the absence of the father from the home.

The young child identifies himself with the

"THAT'S why I'm never gonna get married!"

Figure 4-4 If a child develops an aversion for the role a parent plays, it weakens his desire to identify with the parent or any other adult and to learn to play an adult role. (Adapted from Ketcham's "Dennis the Menace." Publisher-Hall Syndicate. *The Philadelphia Evening Bulletin,* Nov. 26, 1969. Used by permission.)

mother because of his constant association with her and the emotional tie that develops between them. Later the boy shifts his emotional allegiance to the *father* while the girl continues to identify with the mother. Before he is old enough to go to school, the child may identify himself with an older *sibling,* especially one of the same sex, and try to imitate him.

After the child enters school, he begins to identify with a *teacher,* an *athletic instructor* or a *club leader.* Identification with the parent often continues, but in a slightly weakened form.

By late childhood, identification with the *peer group* often replaces the earlier identification with a parent or teacher. If there is identification with one member of the peer group, it will be with the leader who represents the interests and values of the child's gang better than any other member.

The adolescent identifies with a *young adult* of his own sex who appeals to the adolescent because of his glamour, achievements, or popularity. At first, the adolescent may have an erotic interest in the relationship; he may have a "crush" on the young adult or may hero-worship him. Later, the erotic element disappears, but the adolescent retains a strong liking and admiration for the model.

Children, and to a lesser extent adolescents, sometimes identify with fictional *characters* and try to model themselves along the lines set by these "heroes." Ordinarily the identification is short-lived, because it is more difficult to give one's emotional allegiance to a character in a book or on the screen than to a real person.

Shifts in sources of identification
Throughout childhood and adolescence, shifts in sources of identification occur frequently. They are due primarily to failure of the model to live up to expectations, pressures from significant people, greater personal satisfaction from other sources, and changes in values.

When the model to whom the child or adolescent gave his emotional allegiance *does not live up to expectations*—often unrealistically high expectations—the young person may shift to another model who seems, at the moment, to measure up better. This is illustrated in the child's shift from the mother to an outsider. When the child discovers that his mother is not the "big wheel" in the home that he once believed her to be, his desire to model himself according to her pattern is weakened. Similarly, a teacher often loses favor with the child if she shows favoritism toward a classmate or if she seems uninterested in his problems or unsympathetic.

Regardless of how strong an emotional attachment a boy may have for his mother, when *social pressures* are put on him by his father and by members of the peer group to identify himself with a male and to learn to play the role considered appropriate for members of his sex group, he will shift his identification. The impact of social pressures can be seen in "the taunts of 'sissy' or 'tomboy' hurled at young offenders who cross sex roles in play, in the ostracism of an adolescent who fails to conform to type, and the virtual rejection by both sexes of the extremely effeminate man or masculine woman" (203).

When children or adolescents are popular with their peers, they often find greater *satisfaction* from peer relationships than from relationships with their parents, their siblings, or their teachers. The adolescent who identifies with a small, select peer group—the adolescent clique—has an anchorage point for his personality development at a time when he is rebel-ling against adult authority and straining the emotional ties that made identification with a parent, teacher, or some other adult possible. As Blos has explained, "This belongingness to the group which becomes progressively important for the adolescent replaces family ties to some extent and thus prepares him for new conformities and identifications implicit in the group life of adults" (33).

When the child makes social contacts outside the home, he discovers the social and cultural *values* held by the broader social group. As his desire to "be someone" grows, he selects as his ideal a person who has some status and recognition in the social group. The importance of social status as a criterion in selecting the source of identification is shown by the fact that boys from the higher socioeconomic groups identify with their fathers more often than boys from the lower groups. The latter usually select a glamorous adult from outside the home as their ideal. Boys generally idealize adults whose prestige and high status in society come from occupational success, while girls idealize those whose status comes from social success and an attractive appearance (96, 203).

Influence of identification on personality
The molding of the personality pattern is directly influenced by child-training methods and indirectly influenced by identification. Since the foundations of personality are laid during the years when the environment is limited almost exclusively to the home—and the significant people in that environment are the parents—parental influence, especially that of the mother, is more pronounced and more persistent than any subsequent influence. According to Symonds, "If an individual possesses a healthy, stable, courageous and loving mother and father, the chances are that he will be a good student, a good worker, a good husband or wife, and a good citizen" (207).

The personality patterns of both boys and girls during the early years of childhood more closely resemble those of their mothers than their fathers. When personality disturbances occur, they too more closely resemble maternal personality disturbances. This tendency is due to the more constant contacts the children have with their mothers and to the closer emotional ties between them which favor identification.

Studies reveal that identification with parents affects the personality development of the child most notably in the areas of behavior, values, and attitudes

(97, 99). Through identification, the child learns *behavior patterns* similar to those of his parents. One study found that girls expressed anger in much the same manner as their parents. Girls who inhibited the expression of their anger had parents who were over-controlled and repressed, while those who expressed their anger impulsively in outbursts of temper had one or two impulsive parents. The effect of identification on sex-appropriate behavior has also been noted. When parents are strongly sex-appropriate in behavior, so are their adolescent sons and daughters. A girl who has a somewhat masculine mother tends to be less feminine than her peers unless the influence of the mother is counteracted by that of the peer group (99, 137, 138).

Older children and adolescents, especially those from the middle and upper classes, accept the *value systems* of their parents through identification with them and mold their own values along the lines of parental models. Middle-class boys and girls, for example, accept from their parents the values of achievement and mobility and apply these values to their academic and social lives (31). They accept the vocational values of their parents, as expressed in parental attitudes toward different kinds of work. If they are closely identified with their fathers, they may want to follow in their fathers' footsteps or enter occupations their fathers regard as rewarding. If they have little respect for their parents, they may choose occupations that are quite different from those in which the parents are employed or toward which the parents have a negative attitude, such as vocations in the artistic areas (65).

Many *attitudes* of children and adolescents are learned through identification with parents. Almost all studies of the subject report that the roots of prejudice can be found in parental attitudes which children learn even before they enter school (8). Unfavorable attitudes of pity and scorn toward old age are likewise learned through identification with the attitudes of parents. Linden (129) draws a connection between attitudes toward old people and attitudes toward persons in authority:

This debasement of the elder as the role model of authority has a tendency to diminish the importance of all authority. In addition, it gives the young rebel the illusion of possessing greater personal strength than is actually his endowment. . . . One of the results of this turn of events in the younger person is an exalted belief of his own capacity to destroy tradition, flout mores, and reject qualities of discipline that have been historically established and have through the ages withstood the test of application. Clearly the youngster can develop out of the experiences the point of view that he is a law unto himself, that his wishes are superior to the demands of society.

Older children and adolescents tend to identify with a parent they love and respect because of a particular trait or constellation of traits admired by the peer group. Male college students, for example, identify with their fathers on masculinity and with their mothers on friendliness, while female students identify with their mothers on femininity and general activity. Similarly, older children may imitate some of the behavior patterns of their parents but reject or ignore others.

Like identification with parents, sibling identification is important in personality molding during the early years in life. The firstborn child and the only child imitate their parents' behavior and thus are often more mature for their age than are children who imitate siblings. A secondborn child will try to keep up with the pace of an older sibling, especially if the older sibling is a boy. This has an "alerting" influence, causing the younger child to put forth more effort to overcome the mild frustration that results from not being able to do things as quickly or as well as the sibling. If the older sibling is a girl, the children are less competitive and more friendly with each other (118).

Outside the home, patterns of behavior learned from identification with siblings are reflected in peer relationships. Children with a male older sibling tend to be more competitive, ambitious, and enthusiastic in their peer relationships than those whose older sibling is a sister. Children with an opposite-sex sibling tend to be more friendly, more self-confident, and more cheerful than those with same-sex siblings (118).

Effect of unfavorable models for identification   Identification with a maladjusted model generally results in the young person's maladjustment as well (17, 104). Boys who identify with a father who is antisocial in his attitudes and behavior and who has a low-status job tend to duplicate his attitudes and behavior and to have low educational and vocational aspirations (175).

Maladjustment may also result from identification with a model whose characteristics and achievements are far beyond the capacities of the young person. The adolescent especially is likely to identify with a glamorous or talented adult and to become a frustrated idealist.

If a model does not conform to the standards of the cultural group, the person who imitates him will develop a personality pattern which is likewise unacceptable. Since cultural values differ for each age group, the child will be in for trouble if as an adolescent he clings to the model he identified with when he was young—a model who conformed to peer standards at the earlier age. Should a girl continue to identify with an older brother and become a "tomboy," the peer group will reject her as she grows older because she will not be sex-appropriate (118). Similarly, continuing to identify with a parent or teacher may result in a personality pattern that the peer group will scorn as "goody-goody" or as overconservative.

Sometimes children and adolescents identify with a peer group whose values, attitudes, and patterns of behavior deviate from the social norm, such as the adolescent "gang." The more emotional allegiance they give to this group, the more influence it will have on them and the more likely they are to develop personality patterns characteristic of the juvenile delinquent.

Unfortunately, not all heroes or heroines in the mass media are good models for the young to identify with and imitate. Characters in books, comics, movies, and television often represent values and attitudes that fall short of those approved by the group as a whole. And yet they are highly glamorized characters and young people continue to identify with them. How detrimental such models can be to personality development has been stressed by Wertham (217):

The result is a distortion of natural attitudes in the direction of cynicism, greed, hostility, callousness and insensitivity. This may express itself in the individual in overt acts, in fantasy, in dreams, in subtle personality changes, in a lowering of inhibitions or an alteration in the threshold of resistance to all kinds of injurious influences. . . . Harmful mass media influences are a contributing factor in many young people's troubles.

Effect of lack of identification   If the model-candidates available are not admired or loved or if an acceptable model is unstable in the sense that it is available only intermittently, the young person may not identify at all. In young children, lack of a person to identify with is usually caused by institutionalization where there is no stable substitute for the parent. In older children and adolescents, lack of identification may occur in a home broken by death, divorce, separation, or desertion; one parent is missing and the other is absent from home most of the day, working to support the family. If the missing parent is replaced by a stepparent, the child or adolescent may find it difficult to establish an emotional tie with the stepparent and thus may cut himself off from a readily available source of identification.

Achieving the emotional allegiance necessary for successful identification is generally harder for boys than girls. This is due partly to the father's absence from the home a good deal of the time and partly to the boy's preference for his mother, who usually is more "understanding" and tolerant than the father. The more dependent the child or adolescent, the more adversely he is affected by lack of identification. Firstborn children, it has been found, need to identify more than their later-born siblings because they tend, as a group, to be more dependent on their parents, especially on their mothers (99, 118, 147).

How early lack of identification affects the developing personality pattern has been shown in a study of 2-year-olds separated from their parents and placed in a residence nursery. They became very demanding of attention from members of the staff, showed intense and extreme expressions of hostility, and indulged in many antisocial activities. They were not satisfied to be near the staff members, but needed to be accepted by them. When the children were reunited with their parents, they continued to be aggressive and demanding, showing hostility toward their parents rather than affection.

The unfavorable effect on the children's personalities was due to the fact that the parents' absence upset the children's balance: Negative feelings toward everyday frustrations were increased without the compensation of affection. The balance could be restored only if a stable adult were available whom the children could identify with and substitute for the missing parents (100).

Among older children and adolescents, lack of identification has three common effects on personality. *First,* it interferes with sex typing. Lacking identification, both boys and girls are delayed in acquiring sex-appropriate behavior, interests, and attitudes. Girls, for example, tend to be more aggressive than the norm for their ages while boys tend to be less aggressive and to show more interest in feminine activities. As a result, they are scorned and rejected by their peers and develop unfavorable self-concepts.

The children's awareness of the unfavorable social attitude toward their sex inappropriateness leads to the *second* effect of lack of identification on the molding of personality: the tendency to behave in an antisocial way and to develop antisocial attitudes. The boys, for example, adopt exaggerated masculine behavior patterns to convince themselves and others of their masculinity. Because they associate "goodness" with femininity, they bend backward to be masculine and, in doing so, become "bad." Many delinquents, it has been found, have no fathers or other stable male adult models to identify with, and in their attempts to be "masculine" they become "bad" (15, 17, 191).

Third, lack of identification adversely affects social and personal adjustments. When children and adolescents lack the anchorage of security that normally comes with identification, they feel insecure, rejected, anxious, and unhappy. They show little interest in peer activities because they feel inferior, and their behavior is immature for their age. By contrast, as Rosenberg (179) notes:

Adolescents who report close relationships with their fathers are more likely to have high-esteem and stable self-image than those who describe their relationships as more distant.

Relative importance of child training and identification

From what has been said above, it is apparent that identification often plays a more important role in molding the personality pattern than child training. Identification is more important, for example, in learning appropriate sex roles; the young person can learn more from imitating a good model than from direct teaching. By identifying with an adult outside the home who conforms to the socially approved pattern of sex appropriateness, the young person learns the sex-appropriate pattern that is so essential to good social adjustments. As was stressed earlier, however, a combination of child training and identification is better than either alone because learning by one method is reinforced by the other. Equally important, identification provides motivation to learn, which is often lacking or weak when child training is used alone.

Identification plays an increasingly important role if parents relax their training of the child as he grows older. Furthermore, the rebellion of the older child or adolescent against parental and school dis-

cipline and the feeling that parents and teachers do not understand him or are unfair in their expectations and treatment make him resist direct training. Having someone to identify with fills the gap left by the decline in effectiveness of child training. At the same time, it provides the anchorage of security so essential to the development of a wholesome personality pattern.

Pressures to conform to the standards of the peer group are readily accepted by the young person because of the rewards in terms of social acceptance. So long as he feels that he is identified with a peer group, the young person will have the motivation necessary to learn the patterns of behavior approved by the group. As a result, he will, other things being equal, develop a wholesome personality pattern.

In both child training and identification, the changing developmental needs of the person who is being molded must be taken into account. Training methods suitable for a young child are not suitable for an adolescent. Inappropriate methods will lead to resentment, friction, and antisocial behavior, all of which will leave their disturbing mark on the adolescent's personality pattern. Similarly, prolonged identification with a parent leads to dependency and other immature patterns of behavior. The necessity of helping a young person change his source of emotional allegiance as he grows older has been stressed by Rybak (182) in a discussion of crushes—a normal pattern of behavior in puberty and early adolescence:

The main function of the adult in the crush or hero-worship relationship is to help the young person to learn from this experience, and then to gradually grow away from it into a more mature relationship.

It is obvious that the persons primarily responsible for molding the child's personality pattern should be well-adjusted people. As was remarked earlier, the attitude of the person who applies a child-training method is more important than the method itself.

Identification, unlike child training, permits the young person to choose the personality-molding agent. If his parents or teachers are poorly adjusted people, he can do little or nothing to change their training methods or their attitudes toward him. On the other hand, he can compensate by identifying with people who are well adjusted and who have wholesome attitudes toward themselves, toward him, and toward life. The importance of providing good models for young people to emulate has been pointed out by Havighurst (96):

(It) is clear that schools, churches, and youth-serving agencies influence the ideals of youth as much or more through the presence and behavior of teachers, clergy, and youth-group leaders as through their verbal teachings.

In conclusion, the following observations by an anonymous writer show how important a role identification plays in molding the personality pattern.

If a child lives with criticism, he learns to condemn.

If he lives with hostility, he learns to fight.

If he lives with fear, he learns to be apprehensive.

If he lives with pity, he learns to feel sorry for himself.

If he lives with jealousy, he learns to feel guilty.

If he lives with encouragement, he learns to be confident.

If he lives with tolerance, he learns to be patient.

If he lives with praise, he learns to be appreciative.

If he lives with acceptance, he learns to love.

If he lives with approval, he learns to like himself.

If he lives with recognition, he learns to have a goal.

If he lives with fairness, he learns to value justice.

If he lives with honesty, he learns the virtue of truth.

If he lives with security, he learns to have faith in himself and others.

If he lives with friendliness, he learns that the world is a good place in which to live.

SUMMARY

1 In spite of the commonly accepted belief that personality development begins at birth, there is evidence that conditions in the prenatal environment have a profound influence on the rudiments of personality—the capacities for adjustment—in the form of hereditary potentials. How hereditary potentials develop before and after birth is determined largely by the environment. This development, in turn, influences the personality pattern.

2 Evidence showing the role of environment in molding the personality pattern comes from studies of maturation of the hereditary potentials both before and after birth, from studies of models used for molding the personality pattern, and from studies of learning opportunities and motivation.

3 Studies of maturation show that unfavorable conditions in the prenatal environment may be damaging to later personality development if they occur at critical times in the prenatal period. Of these unfavorable conditions, maternal malnutrition, endocrine disturbances, infections, severe maternal distress, and birth injuries are the most common and most harmful.

4 Unfavorable conditions in the postnatal environment can likewise have a lasting and damaging influence on the personality if they occur at critical times in the developmental pattern. The effects of unfavorable environmental conditions are well illustrated in studies of multiple births and prematurity.

5 The second way in which the environment influences the personality pattern is by providing models for the person to imitate. This it does, directly, by providing opportunities for learning culturally approved patterns of behavior and by preventing the learning of disapproved patterns, and indirectly, by setting up prestigious models that the young will want to imitate. Every cultural group has an approved basic personality pattern which is based on the characteristics needed for successful living in that particular cultural group. Since each cultural group is unique in some respects, each has its own basic personality pattern.

6 The third major influence of the environment comes from the opportunities and motivation it provides for learning. Learning may be outer-directed, as in child training, or inner-directed, as in identification.

7 The question, which plays a more important role in personality development—heredity or environment—has, to date, remained unanswered. There is evidence that heredity is more important in some areas of the personality pattern while environment is more important in others.

8 Studies show that personality molding begins early in life and that the early years are the critical ones. Once the foundations are laid, environmental influences become less important with each passing year.

9 Environmental sources of personality molding include the family, the school, the peer group, mass media, religion, and the person's occupation. The relative importance of these molding sources varies from one age group to another and from one person to another.

10 Two kinds of learning are responsible for personality molding. The first is outer-directed learning and is known as child training. The second is inner-directed and is called identification.

11 Child-training methods are of three kinds: authoritarian, democratic, and permissive. Which will be used by parents and teachers depends largely upon the values, education, and socioeconomic background of the user, the users' conceptions of their roles, the personality of the parent or teacher and that of the child, and the attitudes of the users toward their roles.

12 Studies reveal that the effects of child training on personality differ greatly according to the method used, with democratic training producing far more favorable effects than either authoritarian or permissive. Regardless of the method used, to produce a healthy personality pattern, training must be both consistent and fair and the attitudes of those responsible for the training must be consistent and fair.

13 In identification, the young person selects a model he admires and respects and tries to imitate the model's attitudes and behavior. Identification is a less universal method of personality molding than child training be-

cause certain conditions in the environment as well as within the young person himself may make identification difficult or impossible.

14 The selection of sources of identification follows a predictable pattern, beginning in the home with the parents and then shifting to adults outside the home, older peers, or heroes from the child's culture. Which source of identification will be used will depend on how well the model lives up to the child's expectations, pressures from significant people, the satisfaction the child derives from identifying with the model, and changes in values.

15 As a molding influence, identification is often more effective than child training because the person's emotional allegiance to the model of his choice provides a strong motivation for him to learn the attitudes, values, and patterns of behavior he admires in the model. This motivation is often lacking in child training, especially in authoritarian training.

16 Just as a method of child training that is too authoritarian or too permissive can have damaging effects on personality, so can identification with a culturally disapproved model, especially one that is unsuited to the young person's existing stage of development. Equally as detrimental is having no model to identify with or inability to derive satisfaction from identification.

17 Studies of the relative importance of child training and identification as techniques in molding the personality pattern reveal that, though identification is often more effective than child training, a combination of the two, especially when child training is democratic, is better than either alone. As children grow older and as child training is gradually relaxed in the home and the school, identification becomes increasingly important.

persistence and change

Among the many traditional beliefs about personality are several that relate to persistence and change. Contradictory as these beliefs are, in the sense that some claim that the personality pattern is fixed while others claim that it changes at specific ages, they have endured and have had a marked influence on our thinking and behavior.

In this chapter we shall examine the scientific evidence regarding persistence and change in the personality pattern, but first it is important to know what the traditional beliefs are. It is also important to realize that the traditional beliefs have been given the stamp of approval by many psychologists on the basis of their observations of people over a period of time or their scientific studies of certain personality traits.

BELIEFS ABOUT PERSISTENCE

For centuries people have believed that the personality pattern persists in a relatively unchanged form throughout life and that if any change does occur, it will be slight. This belief is based on the assumption that the personality pattern is inherited, just as eye color or intelligence is. The popular saying, "He is a chip off the old block" is so widely held that few people question the possibility that the child may have learned certain patterns of behavior closely resembling those of a parent through constant association with that parent, especially when the child has a deep emotional attachment for the parent or regards him as a hero.

Some psychologists have found a parallel between persistence in personality and persistence in the level of intelligence. Studies of the constancy of the IQ over a number of years have demonstrated that the relationship between the child's mental age and chronological age remains constant; though there is a *quantitative* increase in intelligence up to the chronological age at which intellectual capacity stops growing, there is no *qualitative* increase (8, 134).

The assumption that personality, like intelligence, remains practically unchanged has been stressed by Kelly (103):

On the basis of available evidence, psychologists are not likely to anticipate marked changes in the intelligence of their friends—at least not until relatively late in life. . . . What about our expectations and anticipations regarding changes in those aspects of the individual which, for want of a better name, we call personality? Do we expect to find our former colleague pretty much the same sort of person that he was 15 or 20 years before, or are we prepared to find that he has changed markedly with the passing years? . . . Whether one is an extreme hereditarian, an environmentalist, a constitutionalist, or an orthodox psychoanalyst, he is not likely to anticipate major changes in personality after the first few years of life. Not only do psychologists of different theoretical persuasions tend to agree on this issue: it happens to be one on which the layman and the scientist share a common opinion.

Kelly (103) goes on to explain why people expect the personality pattern to remain constant:

Because of the need to believe in consistency of one's self from moment to moment and from year to year, we tend to infer an unwarranted degree of consistency in others. Some consistency is indeed necessary for social intercourse, and it is likely that, as a matter of convenience in remembering and dealing with our associates, we utilize stereotypy to a considerable degree and thus tend to infer greater consistency in others than may be the case. . . . While assuming that other adults are not likely to change, each of us, I suspect, wants to keep his theory sufficiently flexible to permit the possibility of change in himself— especially changes in the direction of his ego ideal! Even though in retrospect few of these desired changes may have occurred, it's comforting to think that one can change if one tries hard enough.

Origin of beliefs about persistence

The concept of persistence in the personality pattern dates back to the ancient Greek philosophers. Plato recognized that the personality of the individual prior to old age influenced his reactions to encroaching senility. "He who is of a calm and happy nature," he said, "will hardly feel the pressures of old age, but to him who is of an opposite disposition, youth and old age are equally a burden."

Among the Romans, Cicero emphasized the persistence of personality when he wrote in his *De Senectute*, "Those with simple desires and good dispositions find old age easy to take. Those who do not show wisdom and virtue in their youth are prone to attribute to old age those infirmities which are actually produced by former irregularities."

In the sixteenth century, St. Ignatius stressed the persistence of the personality pattern when he claimed that if he could have the teaching of a child until he was 6 years old, nothing could undo that teaching (193). Freud indicated that he, too, held this belief when he said that the foundations of personality are laid in the early years of life (66).

The acceptance of this traditional belief eliminates any motivation the person or his parents and teachers may have to change his personality, should it be such that it is leading to poor personal and social adjustments. Equally as damaging, its acceptance leads many people, adults as well as children and adolescents, to blame their parents for passing on to them, through their hereditary endowment, personality patterns that lead to poor adjustments and unhappiness. Blame leads to resentments, which, in turn, lead to poor family relationships.

BELIEFS ABOUT CHANGE

In spite of the popularly held belief that the personality pattern is inherited and therefore persistent, a contradictory belief asserts that changes in personality parallel radical physical changes. The two times in life when personality changes are believed to be inevitable are at puberty and old age.

It is popularly believed that the physical changes at puberty will lead to an improved appearance and that undesirable personality traits will be shed and replaced by desirable ones. The belief is expressed in such statements as "He will outgrow that when he becomes a man" or "She will be less shy (or less selfish or less boisterous) when she gets a little older." Schonfeld (181) says that many affluent parents train their children to enjoy a happy, carefree childhood and then are shocked when the children grow up to be irresponsible adolescents and adults:

Too many of today's affluent adolescents ask a girl to go steady and drop her if they find someone else who strikes their fancy. They come late for part-time jobs and drop them without notice, and they rush into marriage with no thought of how they are going to support the marriage. This irresponsibility has often been cultivated in the individual since early childhood. Yet parents and teachers are surprised when it does not miraculously disappear with adolescence.

Since the physical changes that accompany aging are, for the most part, changes for the worse, the belief has grown up that any personality changes paralleling the physical changes will be for the worse also. The stereotype of the elderly person as physically unattractive and ailing and as rigid, hypersensitive, and generally hard to live with is widely accepted (208).

Like the layman, many psychologists also believe that personality changes occur. However, they emphasize that changes result not from physical changes per se, as the traditional beliefs imply, but rather from social and environmental conditions, from the individual's effort to effect changes, and from professional guidance through psychotherapy. How social and environmental conditions can produce personality changes has been described by Davis and Havighurst (41):

We do not believe, in short, that the early personality is as irrevocable as the crack of doom. There certainly is no reason for a fatalistic view concerning man's ability to break the mold of his childhood learning. Admittedly, this learning often sets the pattern for many later responses toward people; even for one's life-long estimate of oneself. But new situations and new stimuli will change not only a man's behavior—they will change his belief in himself. Men have been saved from despair, and vice, and from even the deep shadow of insanity by a change in their opportunities, by a chance to work, or to gain social distinction; by finding someone who loved them, and had faith in their ability and courage; by the birth of a son or daughter, and the new responsibility and hope which it brought.

Rogers has explained how psychotherapy can bring about personality changes. The changes come gradually as the individual develops a new perception of self and thus adopts a new pattern of behavior. With changes in behavior come changes in the attitudes and behavior of other people toward the individual.

The person reorganizes his field of perception, including the way he sees himself. How he views the world—his "internal frame of reference"—will determine what his behavior will be. When the internal frame of reference is changed, either by therapy or by changed experiences, the person's characteristic manner of adjusting to life will likewise change (168). There is no definite proof that personality is more plastic in the early years of life. In fact, severe psychological stress is often more damaging in adulthood and thus causes greater changes in the adult's personality than the child's (193).

The danger of accepting the traditional beliefs that personality changes are an inevitable accompaniment of marked physical changes is that they stifle any motivation to try to change or curb undesirable traits. The individual himself—whether young or old—and his parents, teachers, counselors, and other associates tend to fold their hands and wait for nature to do its job. As a result, undesirable personality traits are reinforced through repetition.

MEANING OF PERSISTENCE AND CHANGE

Contradictory opinions, both traditional and scientific, about whether the personality pattern is persistent or subject to change leave one with a feeling of confusion: Does it change or doesn't it? Exactly what do the terms "persistence" and "change" mean?

Persistence

According to dictionary definitions, "persistence" means "enduring" or "constantly recurring." It does not mean that no change occurs but rather that certain traits tend to remain in an unchanged or relatively unchanged form, even in the face of training and social pressures. Allport stressed this meaning of persistence when he said, "The important fact about personality is its relatively enduring and unique quality" (3).

This means that you can expect a person who was excessively shy as a child to be a shy adult. Even if he modifies or controls his shyness somewhat and acts as if he has gained self-confidence, he will still feel ill at ease in the presence of others and will try to avoid situations in which he must meet and talk to strangers.

There is a persistence even in apparently inconsistent behavior. The predictable behavior of the proverbial "street angel-house devil" type of person is a good example. At home, he is persistently a "devil," in the sense that he is autocratic, selfish, and inconsiderate, while outside the home, he shows a different personality pattern—one that is aimed to win friends and impress people. Peck and Havinghurst (154) have stressed the persistence of inconsistent patterns of behavior:

Some individuals are markedly inconsistent—now considerate, now callously selfish; responsible here, irresponsible there. Such a pattern has its own "consistency," though. It is an enduring, predictable kind of pattern that sets the person off from other people of different character.

Persistence thus means that there are not likely to be revolutionary changes in the behavior pattern. No one remains *absolutely* consistent with respect to predominant forms of behavior. Instead, shifts are in the direction of behavior that existed at an earlier age, though the shifts are generally not pronounced and the forms of behavior may be much more subtle than when the person was younger (25, 137).

Change

"Change" means "to alter" or "to vary"; it does not necessarily mean that the alteration or variation will be complete. The personality pattern can change in some areas and remain persistent in others. Furthermore, change is not synonymous with "improvement." Change can be either for the better or for the worse.

While change is characteristic of the physique, physical features, and within limits, intelligence, the personality is more "fluid, or subject to change through influence of the environment" (25). However, it is important to emphasize that changes are more frequent and more pronounced in younger children than in older children and adolescents and far more frequent in childhood than in adulthood (114, 193). As a person approaches middle age, changes often do occur but this is not inevitable (151).

Kinds of change Changes are of two kinds: quantitative and qualitative. In *quantitative* changes, traits already present are strengthened or weakened. Undesirable traits usually become less undesirable because the person has a strong motivation to weaken such traits and conform to socially approved patterns.

The stronger the motivation to win social approval and acceptance, the stronger the motivation to strengthen desirable traits. If the person discovers that courteous behavior leads to the approval and acceptance he craves, he will become even more courteous than formerly. Similarly, discovery that cooperativeness is greatly admired by the social group will motivate him to do his share and even more.

Quantitative changes may create the impression that the person has changed his personality pattern. This impression is correct in the sense that there have been shifts in the traits, though there is no evidence that the shifts reflect a change in the core of the personality pattern—the self-concept.

In *qualitative* changes, an already-present trait, usually an undesirable one, is replaced by another trait, usually a desirable one. In the case of selfishness, for example, a qualitative change would mean that selfishness was eliminated and replaced with generosity. Sometimes, in qualitative changes, desirable traits are eliminated and replaced by undesirable ones. A person who was generous as a child may, as an adolescent, become selfish, self-centered, and stingy. Changes from desirable to undesirable traits are regarded as "danger signals" of poor adjustment or even of mental illness.

Quantitative changes are, for the most part, far more common and far more frequent than qualitative changes. Furthermore, they are usually in the direction of improvement. This is true throughout the major part of the life span, though quantitative changes often seem to be for the worse as people grow older (198).

Changes versus fronts   Changes may actually be only cloaks designed to gain greater social approval and acceptance. Instead of behaving in his characteristic manner, a person may behave as he knows people expect one to behave. A shy and fearful child may cover his shyness with a cloak of bombastic boasting and daredevil behavior in the hope that people will think he is brave and courageous. The stingy adolescent puts on a front of generosity when he finds that stinginess is a social handicap. The street angel-house devil puts on his angel cloak outside, where it is to his advantage to do so, but shows his devilish side at home where family members have to accept him no matter how outrageous his behavior. See Figure 5–1.

The use of fronts does not indicate that a change has taken place in the personality pattern. In situations where social approval and acceptance are not important, the person behaves in his characteristic manner (24, 36, 114, 136). Under stress, he will drop his cloak, even though by doing so he runs the risk of losing social approval and acceptance (198).

METHODS OF STUDYING PERSISTENCE AND CHANGE

If, then, personality is both persistent and subject to change, the logical questions are: How much change occurs and how much of the personality pattern remains persistent? When do changes occur and when does persistence take precedence over change? What produces change and what is responsible for persistence? In what direction do changes occur and how great are they? Do all personality patterns change equally or are some more persistent than others? And finally, are the changes in the real personality or the manifest personality?

While none of these questions has been fully answered, a growing body of scientific evidence sheds light on some of them, supplies some partial answers, and suggests what can be anticipated from further studies. The remainder of this chapter will be devoted to presenting the evidence that is now available.

Scanty information about persistence is not due to lack of interest in the subject or lack of awareness of its practical importance. Instead, it is due to the difficulties inherent in studying the problem.

If it were possible to use the *cross-sectional* method, observing and measuring persistence or change in representative samplings of people at different age levels throughout the life span, the answers to the questions raised above could be supplied relatively easily and quickly. But, as no two people are alike, even the best techniques in matching samples cannot produce valid information.

That the data obtained by the cross-sectional approach are not valid as evidence of either persistence or change has been emphasized by Kelly: "While the data provided by cross-sectional comparisons of different age groups are often highly provocative, they unfortunately are not adequate to permit firm conclusions regarding either developmental trends or intra-individual variability" (103).

The weaknesses of the cross-sectional method have been further emphasized by Owens (148):

Cross-sectional studies demand an excessive number of somewhat unlikely assumptions and are therefore

Figure 5-1 Changes in personality may merely be "fronts" used to win social approval when such approval is important.

open to varying and ambiguous interpretations. Prominent among the problems involved is that it is extremely difficult to secure comparable samples of the population at successive ages, and to be assured that they are in fact so comparable that it is something more than gratuitous to attribute all differences between them to a single variable such as chronological age.

Kuhlen and Pressey and Jones have pointed out another problem regarding the validity of the data obtained by the cross-sectional method. This problem is that, unless the sampling is so precise that the younger subjects may truly be assumed to be what the older subjects with whom they are compared were at the same ages, then age changes and cultural changes become almost indistinguishable (112, 158).

In the study of persistence, only the *longitudinal* method can provide valid results. Under this method the same individuals would be studied, preferably from birth to death, but certainly for a long enough period to see just how persistent the personality pattern is, when and how it changes, and what is responsible for the changes (16, 33, 130, 180, 191).

A number of studies have been made. But they have, for the most part, covered only part of the life span. To date, no study has traced the development of the personality patterns of a representative group of people from birth to death, though a small number have covered 30 or more years of the life span. The important studies using the longitudinal method will be discussed later in the chapter in the sections relating to evidence of persistence and change.

Methodological difficulties

Theoretically the longitudinal method can be used to obtain valid information about persistence and change in the personality pattern. But it presents practical problems which are extremely difficult and often impossible to cope with satisfactorily.

Subjects   While it may be relatively easy to study a group of young children year after year, especially in a small community where residency is stable, there is always the problem of being able to restudy the members of the group when they grow up and leave home for college, military service, marriage, or occupations that take them into other communities.

Terman, and later Oden, found this to be a serious handicap in their study of a group of gifted children whose intellectual and personality development they wanted to trace into adulthood and, later, into middle age (145, 204). The problem was solved, to some extent, by having the adults tested in their new communities, by paying their expenses to return to the home community for retesting, or by sending them material to fill out and return by mail.

Accurate records   Getting accurate records of the personality patterns of normal people over a span of years has proved to be a major obstacle to studies of persistence and change. One source of fairly accurate and readily available records is the medical and psychological histories of children who have suffered from some birth defect, especially brain damage.

Similarly, children suffering from maladjustments severe enough to bring them to clinics for therapy have accurate records kept of their characteristic behavior patterns over a span of years, often into adulthood. That is why many of the studies of persistence in the personality pattern have drawn on evidence from clinical cases (62, 73).

Methods of personality assessment Methods of assessing personality are still, to a large extent, in their experimental stages. Few are available for use in the preschool years when, if a longitudinal study is to be made, it must begin. It is essential to have an accurate assessment of the early personality pattern as a frame of reference for later studies. Furthermore, data relating to the personality traits of adults today were obtained years ago by methods no longer considered valid. This problem has been stressed by Kelly (103):

The paucity of longitudinal studies covering any major span of adult years is in no small part due to the fact that appropriate techniques of psychological measurement are themselves just coming of age.

Interpretation of assessments Even if the assessment of persistence or change over a period of, say, 10 or 15 or 20 years is made with the same tests or rating scales, the chances are that the interpretation of the follow-up tests or ratings will be made by a different person. This introduces a new variable. In studies extending over 50 or more years, it would be almost inevitable that someone else would have to interpret the follow-up studies made of the subjects when they reached middle life or later.

Kelly's study is a good illustration of this problem. In the original study, made in 1947, the interjudge reliability of the ratings ranged from .64 to .92 for 22 variables, with a median value of .75. The median correlation between these ratings and those made 4 years later, by different judges, was only .21, with a range from .00 to .43. Commenting on this, Kelly (103) remarked:

In brief, we are confronted with the situation that several judges looking at samples of behavior of a person at the same time agreed reasonably well, but that different judges looking at the samples of behavior of the same individual four years apart showed but little agreement in their ratings.

EVIDENCE OF PERSISTENCE

Popular and scientific interest has led to a number of studies to determine how persistent the personality pattern is. Some of the studies have traced persistence over a long period, some over only several years; some have concentrated on the early years of life, some on adolescence, and some on the adult years; some have studied persistence in normal personality patterns and some in abnormal patterns; some have made use of clinical techniques, some have used the case history approach, and some have used tests and rating scales.

Studies of short-term persistence

Some of the first studies of persistence were limited to short periods during the early years of life, a time when maturation and early learning experiences could be expected to produce changes in the personality pattern (177). One of the earliest studies, reported by Shirley in 1941, was based on a group of babies studied during the first 2 years of their lives. While marked consistency in behavior patterns was noted, no baby showed exactly the same behavior throughout the period. When shifts occurred, however, they were in the direction of the behavior pattern that had appeared earlier.

"Profile charts" for each baby on a number of personality characteristics likewise showed considerable consistency. While some of the characteristics were somewhat modified as time passed, they retained enough of their original content to be "identifying earmarks" by which the judges could identify the babies. One baby, for example, was distinctive for his "timorous crying." Later, his crying waned, but it was replaced by "apprehensive watching" of people and, still later, by hiding behind the mother and by refusing to play or to talk in the presence of a stranger (184).

More recent studies of short-term persistence have concentrated on children or adolescents and have covered a slightly longer period. Emmerich, in a study of preschool children, reported that "salient personality dimensions have high stability from ages 3 to 5, supporting the view that personality differences arise early in life and are maintained in essentially their original form." When changes did occur, they were mainly in the direction of improvement. Socially undesirable traits, such as aggression, dominance, and dependency, decreased while the more desirable trait of autonomy increased (56).

Because of the popular belief that there are radical changes in personality patterns as children pass through puberty and that these changes are inevitably for the better, several recent short-term studies of persistence at this time are especially useful. Such personality syndromes as reserved, somber, and shy versus expressive, gay, and socially easy or reactive, explosive, and restive versus phlegmatic, calm, and compliant were reported to be relatively unmodifiable. The passive versus domineering syndrome was less persistent, owing to psychosocial pressures. This study, made by Bronson, covered the ages from 5 to 16 years (28).

"Shirley's babies," who showed persistence in their personality patterns during the first 2 years of their lives, were restudied when they were 17 years old. Matching objective measurements and personality sketches with the original sketches was easy enough in most cases to justify the conclusion that their personality patterns had remained consistent (140).

A study of achievement strivings from the ages of 8 to 16 years revealed that this trait remained persistent throughout the period (61). Longitudinal surveys of child Rorschach responses in a group of children from 2 to 10 years and in one from 10 to 16 years revealed a consistency of ratings with some changes up to 16 years (5, 6).

Evidence from a longitudinal study showing that personality patterns remain persistent from 10 to 16 years, the time during which puberty changes occur, has been explained thus by Peck and Havighurst (154):

It has been found that most individuals tend to maintain the same attitudes and motives through the years. . . . The child who is deeply friendly and affectionate at ten, for instance, is most likely to show the same warm, trustful feelings for people at 16 and 17. Conversely, the child who is deeply cowed, submissive, and yet covertly resentful toward people at 10 is most apt to show just about the same reaction pattern at 17, even allowing for all the pressures and encouragement to become more independent as adolescence progresses. . . . Numerous details of attitude and behavior normally do change during the course of adolescent development, and allowance must be made for these maturational changes; but once such allowance is made for the changes "everybody" undergoes, it is remarkable how little alteration there is in the basic motive pattern of most adolescents.

Because of the accuracy of records kept of emotionally disturbed children, studies of persistence in their personality patterns are especially reliable. One study, reported by Zak et al., revealed that children who were found to be emotionally disturbed in the first grade functioned significantly less well as they went through the grades, as judged by classroom behavior, peer ratings, and achievement scores, than children who are emotionally stable. In fact, instead of "outgrowing" their emotional disturbances, they were worse by the time they reached the seventh grade (228).

Studies of long-term persistence

In recent years, studies of persistence, covering relatively small groups of subjects, have concentrated on older ages and have attempted to see if patterns that were persistent throughout childhood and adolescence remain so into adulthood. Long-term studies seek to show what changes occur in personality as environmental pressures become more varied, as social relationships expand, and as aspirations are affected by the maturation of intelligence and the broadening of experiences. Persistence of personality traits over a short period, in childhood or early adolescence, may mean nothing more than that the child has lived in a stable cultural and social milieu.

A brief description of a few of the long-term studies will be sufficient to show the trend of evidence and to supplement the results of studies of short-term persistence.

Dependent behavior, as shown in seeking help from others when under stress, has been reported to be persistent from the early school years into adulthood. Girls and women were found to show greater persistence in this trait than men because they were encouraged to be dependent while males were not (100). Persistence of striving for achievement and social recognition, through competence in intellectual or athletic attainments or through improved economic and cultural status, on the other hand, was greater among boys and men than among girls and women (100, 136).

A 40-year follow-up study of Terman's gifted group, begun in the early 1920s, has shown not only that specific personality traits persist as gifted individuals become adults but also that the poorly adjusted and well adjusted in childhood remain poorly and well adjusted in middle life (145). This finding has been corroborated by the findings of Havighurst and Slater and Scarr (85, 185).

A study of retired people revealed that those who were extroverted and socially oriented when they were adolescents showed similar patterns of behavior in their community-role behavior as elderly citizens. As King and Howell have commented, "The community role at 15-25 years of age seems to reflect the image of the late adult community role" (106).

One of the most extensive studies of persistence, in terms of span of time covered and number of subjects, has been reported by Kelly. Retesting a group of men and women 21 years after the original testing during their college years revealed that absolute changes in scores on personality test were very small. Kelly also reported consistency in the self-concept over this period, as reflected in self-ratings on ten dimensions, such as conventionality, intelligence, and quietness. While changes did occur in the personality pattern, they related to specific areas of personality and did not reflect any overall tendency to change (103).

Covering an even longer period, but with only a small number of subjects, Smith reported a comparison of ratings on thirty-five personality traits 50 years after the mother of the subjects had reported judgments about her six children in a diary. A 70 percent persistence was found after this 50-year period. However, there had been a general trend toward improvement over the years, with desirable traits improving and undesirable ones weakening (186).

An important long-term study of persistence, made at the University of California, has concentrated on the effects of deviant ages of sexual maturing among boys. By the time the early- and late-maturing boys had reached adulthood, the physical differences that had been so pronounced at puberty were largely gone, but the personality patterns, influenced by the treatment the boys had received from parents, teachers, and peers, persisted.

Those who had matured early were, as young men in their early thirties, responsible, enterprising, persistent in working toward a goal, self-controlled, dominant, and able to inspire confidence in others. These characteristics were similar to those they had shown in adolescence. By contrast, men who had matured late were rebellious, touchy, impulsive, and self-indulgent; they used many forms of compensatory behavior, and when they were hurt they sought encouragement and help until a fuss was made over them. In general, their behavior was a carry-over of the "little-boy behavior" of their adolescent years (98, 135, 139).

A study of the social participation in adult years of this group of early and late maturers revealed that there were persistent differences in adulthood just as there were in adolescence. Early maturers were more socially active and popular and more likely to play leadership roles, not only in adolescence but also in adulthood. As Ames commented, "Early-maturers tend to either become or remain socially active in adulthood, whereas late-maturers tend to either remain or become less socially active as a group" (7).

Because of the accuracy of records kept of brain-damaged and clinical cases, studies of maladjusted people have proved to be an especially useful source of information about persistence of the personality pattern. Records of patients in mental hospitals show that personality characteristics of psychotic patients have been stable from childhood. Those who as adults are excitable have been excitable since childhood, while those who are schizophrenic have been apathetic since childhood.

Adult psychotics are reported to have been social isolates as children and to have had few friends (116). As children, adult schizophrenics showed symptoms of withdrawal, such as shyness, listlessness, excessive daydreaming, and seclusiveness; they had little interest in others and few social relationships, and they suffered from many frustrations due to parental overprotectiveness, neglect, or indifference. Childhood schizophrenics, in short, develop into adult schizophrenics, even though clinical manifestations and their intensity may change (23, 64, 133, 147).

Poorly adjusted adolescents and adults, some of whom become juvenile delinquents and adult criminals, usually have a history of problem behavior in the home and school (15, 167, 196, 221). Figure 5–2 shows the relationship between nursery school behavior and later school adjustment. Those who as children do not conform to social mores fail to conform in adulthood also. This is shown in poor marital adjustment, with more broken homes and more divorces than found in the general population (166). Such indications of a disturbed life pattern suggest that "childhood behavior problems signal a high probability of adult difficulties" (166). Furthermore, as Westman et al. (221) have concluded:

Evidence contradicts the time-honored notion that

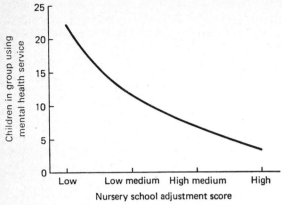

Figure 5-2 Because children with adjustment problems in nursery school tend to have adjustment problems in later school life, it is possible to project mental health service for them based on their nursery school adjustment. (Adapted from J. C. Westman, D. L. Rice, and E. Bermann: Nursery school behavior and later school adjustment. *Amer. J. Orthopsychiat.*, 1967, **37**, 725-731. Used by permission.)

children outgrow behavior problems seen in early life and supports the thesis that drastic shifts in manifest behavior tend not to occur during the first 18 years of life. Children with adjustment problems in nursery school tend to have adjustment problems in later school life, and these problems tend to be of the same order.

Follow-up studies of children and adolescents who made poor adjustments, as shown in family, social, and school life, and who suffered from feelings of personal inferiority, generalized tension, fears, and physical symptoms, showed that, in the early thirties, they suffered more from psychosomatic illness than did their age-mates who made good adjustments in childhood and adolescence. This suggests that poor adjustment is persistent (194).

In conclusion, then, it is obvious from evidence from short- and long-term studies, or from studies of well-adjusted and poorly adjusted people of different ages, that persistence is characteristic of the personality pattern and that this persistence carries through the major part of the life span. While some shifts do occur, especially in the early years of life, they are not so marked as is popularly believed. As Symonds (199) has emphasized:

These shifts in personality in childhood, adolescent, and adult years do not alter the main fact that there is a pronounced consistency in personality in most individuals throughout life.

When persistence develops

The debate over when the personality pattern becomes "fixed"—if it ever does—has gone on for centuries, as was pointed out earlier. Today, there are two opposing points of view. The first holds that the personality pattern does become fixed, but the age at which this is said to happen varies from one adherent of this point of view to another. The second point of view maintains that the personality pattern never becomes fixed but that changes are fewer and more difficult to make as the individual grows older.

Age of fixing of pattern Among those who adhere to the belief that the personality pattern becomes set or fixed at a certain age, James was among the first to state a specific age. Shortly before the turn of the present century, James (94) maintained that:

Already at the age of twenty-five you see the professional mannerisms settling down on the young commercial traveller, on the young doctor, on the young minister, on the young counsellor-at-law. You see the little lines of cleavage running through the character, the tricks of thought, the prejudices, the ways of the "shop," in a word, from which the man can by-and-by no more escape than his coat sleeve can suddenly fall into a new set of folds. On the whole, it is best he should not escape. It is well for the world that in most of us, by the age of thirty, the character has set like plaster, and will never soften again.

Since the time of James, the age has been lowered considerably. Thorndike pointed out, nearly half a century after James, "A person's nature at 12 is prophetic of his nature in adult years. . . . The child to whom approval is more cherished than mastery is likely to become a man who seeks applause rather than power, and similarly throughout" (206).

Most current opinions, based on studies of persistence, regard the first 5 or 6 years of life as the "critical period" in personality development. This is in line with the opinion of St. Ignatius expressed in the sixteenth century. This critical period is the time when the basic personality pattern is established and when many mild-to-severe personality disorders have their origin (14, 58, 73, 196, 221).

Follow-ups of children from 10 to 17 years, supplemented with reported data going back to their early years, led Peck and Havighurst to conclude that the first 10 years constitute the "critical period" in personality development. According to them, these data revealed a "characteristic personality and character pattern which was largely laid down by age ten and changed little thereafter. . . . This suggests that the child of each character type starts very early to develop along that type path, and that growth simply makes him more and more that kind of person" (154).

Not only do various studies state specific dates for the persistence of the total personality pattern but they also give specific dates for the persistence of individual traits. The first 5 years of school, for example, between the ages of 6 and 10 years, are regarded as the "critical time" to develop a motivation to master intellectual tasks. If the motivation is acquired then, it can be expected to persist into the adult years in the form of a desire to meet and master challenging problems (191).

Pushing the cutoff age a trifle later, some psychologists regard adolescence as the time when persistence begins. In one study, it was concluded that how the adolescent handles stress and adjusts to his new status will influence how he will adjust to old age because the patterns of adult attitudes and behavior are set in adolescence (160).

Variations in persistence

Individual differences have been noted in the degree of persistence of different aspects of the same pattern. Breckenridge and Vincent have written: "Some personalities are far more flexible than others, and change radically under radical changes of environment; others have a 'granite-like' quality which withstands the impact even of the most radical changes of environment" (25).

In a long-term study of women, marked differences were reported in the percentage of traits which fluctuated and those which persisted. In one woman, for example, 85 percent of the traits in her personality pattern persisted throughout her life, while in another, only 26 percent of the traits in her pattern were persistent (165).

Even where persistence is not pronounced and the person is regarded as "flexible," making changes in the personality pattern becomes increasingly difficult as age advances. Individual differences in flexibility in old age, however, suggest that the degree of persistence varies in old age just as in youth.

Variations within the personality pattern Areas of the personality pattern which

are largely determined by heredity are less subject to change than those built up through learning and influenced by environmental pressures. Intelligence, for example, which is largely determined by hereditary factors, is less likely to change than are attitudes (98).

Within the personality pattern, the most persistent area is the self-concept. As Breckenridge and Vincent have remarked, "Each personality preserves a central stability, a central core or focus or 'center of gravity' which does not change" (25).

The self-concept becomes stronger and more fixed with age because it is made up of attitudes, values, beliefs, and aspirations which are established early in life and which are strongly embedded by pressures from the social environment (30, 102, 155). Once this core becomes fixed, it will persist unless radical steps are taken to produce a change or unless the person is willing to make a great effort to effect a change (90, 196, 202).

As was pointed out in Chapter 2, most people resist making a change in their concept of self because stability of the self-concept gives them a feeling of security. Jersild (96) has explained the reason for this resistance:

The growing child has a strong tendency to preserve ideas and attitudes he already has formed. He strives in the presence of others and in his own eyes to be himself (as he sees himself) and to live in accordance with his concepts or attitudes regarding himself, whether these be true or false. He tries to be consistent with himself. He is likely to resist anything that is inconsistent with his own view of himself. It may even be difficult for him to see or hear or grasp the meaning of anything, favorable or unfavorable, that goes counter to his picture of himself.

The core of the personality pattern preserves the balance of traits within the pattern, and thus lends stability to the pattern. Though some of the individual traits are less stable than others, stability increases throughout childhood, and by the end of adolescence, most traits have become rather fixed.

Personality traits closely associated with biological structure are more stable than those which are principally influenced by experience. The least stable are those which involve social relations (103, 127, 145, 165). In the group studied by Smith, referred to above, the most stable traits included affection, attractiveness, brightness, conscientiousness, bossiness, carelessness, irritability, jealousy, spunkiness, and strength of will while the least stable were bravery, exactness, perseverance, quick temper, and shyness (186).

Traits that are traditionally sex-appropriate tend to be more persistent than others. For boys and men, for example, aggressiveness, drive for achievement, and self-assertiveness are especially persistent, while for girls and women, dependency, passivity, and drive for social prestige rank high in persistence (100, 209).

Causes of persistence

The chief causes of persistence in the personality pattern have been reported to be heredity, child-training methods, social environment, and repetition of experiences.

Heredity While the core of the personality pattern is a product of learning and is influenced by environmental factors during the early, formative years of life, certain traits are more influenced by heredity than others. Energy level, which expresses itself in strength of drive and peppiness, is, like intelligence, primarily a product of the person's hereditary endowment. Such traits can be counted on to be more persistent than those which are less influenced by heredity, such as attitudes and values (8, 137).

Heredity affects persistence in this way because the personality pattern is inwardly determined and closely associated with the maturation of inherent characteristics. The form the pattern will take is, unquestionably, influenced by social and other environmental factors. This means that the development of the personality pattern is not instilled in the person or controlled from without but evolves from the potentials within the person. As Rainwater has stressed, the child brings to his interaction with significant people in his life—parents, teachers, and peers—certain needs and drives and certain intellectual capacities which determine his reactions to the way he is acted upon by these significant people (161).

Since a person's hereditary endowment remains unchanged throughout life, except when some environmental condition or some unfavorable physical condition affects it, it determines the pattern of his maturation during the growth years and of his physical and mental decline in middle and old age. Maturation and decline have long-lasting effects on the person's self-concept and his relationships with others and are thus indirectly partly responsible for the persistence of certain aspects of his personality pattern.

Child-training methods There is little evidence that child-training methods per se have as permanent an influence on the personality pattern as some authorities have claimed (129, 144). On the other hand, there is ample evidence that the attitudes of parents toward the child and the way in which they enforce the child-training methods they use remain relatively constant. As a result, the child develops a firmly set concept of self and well-established patterns of adjustive behavior (129, 179). Parental overprotectiveness or overindulgence, for example, lead to ego weakness in the child. And since these parental patterns of child training tend to be repeated over and over again, they reinforce the ego weakness to the point where it becomes persistent (2, 28, 141, 171).

Studies of the defense and coping mechanisms used by adults have revealed that they are closely related to the family environment in childhood and remain relatively fixed aspects of the adult personality structure. Severe discipline in childhood, for example, leads to denials, guilt, and the use of defense mechanisms. Numerous conflicts in the family and avoidance of unpleasant situations lead to repressions, while excessive parental restrictiveness leads to displacements (217).

Peck and Havighurst have explained that "since the family influence is usually the same, whether in a stable or confused pattern," it is understandable that child training in the home would contribute to persistence of the person's adjustive behavior (154). They further emphasize how early child-training pressures lead to patterns of adjustment that become persistent as time passes:

The most powerful, most persistent attitudes, perceptual sets, and reaction patterns of adolescents appear to be those they have learned in the first 10 years of life through their emotionally paramount, moment-by-moment interactions with their fathers and mothers. "There's no place like home" is sheer unsentimental fact in a child's world.

Social environment The social environment, both in and outside the home, contributes greatly to the persistence of the personality pattern. The child's relationships with his parents, and later with his siblings, are relatively stable, and so he learns to see himself as he believes these significant people in his life see him. In time, the attitudes toward self which form the basis of his self-concept become relatively persistent, though they may change if the environment changes. As Stott has pointed out, the child's "basic personality structure—his individuality—very early begins to form as he, with his particular inherent temperamental nature interacts with the particular environment into which he is born" (196).

Furthermore, most parents and siblings tend to be consistent in their attitudes toward and treatment of the child. Parents show a marked consistency in their own personalities, and this influences the way they treat the child and their relationships with him. A mother, for example, who is calm or fussy, who hurries her child or allows him to do things at his own pace, is likely to persist from month to month or from year to year in her characteristic way of doing things for or with her child (184). This carries over into adolescence and reinforces the patterns laid down in the child's adjustive behavior during childhood (87).

Similarly, the child becomes accustomed to playing a certain role in his relationship with his parents and his siblings. If he comes from a small family, his role may be that of the "boss" if he is the firstborn or that of the "imitator" if he is the second-born (108). In a large family, he may be assigned the role of "mother's helper" if he is the firstborn, or the role of "baby of the family" if he is the last-born. In time, he learns to think of himself in terms of the role he has been assigned to play. And, because this role is generally constant, it contributes to the persistence of the self-concept (21).

It has also been reported that when a child is punished by parental rejection, he learns to be hostile toward his parents. His hostile behavior elicits hostility, counterpunishment, and further rejection from them. In time, a "vicious circle of maladjustment" develops.

The vicious circle is not limited to hostile behavior. Parental domination or sibling aggression elicits domination or aggression on the child's part. Unless steps are taken to break these vicious circles, the child's behavior patterns will become reinforced with repetition and develop into maladjustive behavior which may persist throughout life (42). This is illustrated in Figure 5-3.

Once the personality pattern or some dominant trait in that pattern has been established in the home, it tends to influence the individual to choose those people and situations outside the home which fit his needs and wants and to reject those which fail to give him satisfaction. If he has learned in the home to think

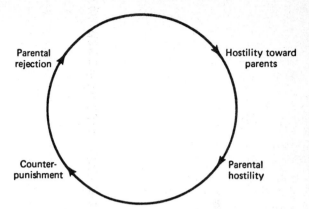

Figure 5-3 The vicious circle of maladjustment.

of himself as an important person, he will associate only with those peers who treat him as if they too think he is important and he will reject those who do not. He is thus selecting friends who treat him in accordance with his concept of himself and who reinforce his concept of himself as important. This selection from his environment of people and situations which are consistent with his concept of himself helps to explain the persistence of his personality pattern. The person who has learned to be friendly at home selects environments outside the home in which there are other people. This constant association with other people helps to preserve and increase his friendly attitudes and behavior. The person who is irritable and peevish, by contrast, arouses impatience and annoyance in others and the interaction produces an environment which fosters the continuation of his peevish ways. This relationship has been stressed by Roberts and Fleming (165):

Because personality development is an ongoing, dynamic process, inseparable from the life process, and because an individual becomes what he is through his interaction with the environment, the similarity between the personality characteristics of the same person at any two periods of his life is related to the continuity and similarity of the forces acting upon him.

Repetition of experiences Repetition of experiences strengthens foundations laid by earlier experiences of a similar nature. As in other kinds of learning, the more often the repetition, the more firmly established the pattern. Consequently, as long as the person's experiences and environment remain the same, there is a strong current of continuity in his personality traits.

Since the child learns to think of himself as he believes significant people in his life think of him, his self-concept reflects their attitudes and behavior toward him. Unless their attitudes and their treatment of the child change markedly, he will continue, year after year, to think of himself in terms of the foundations laid earlier. Under such conditions, his self-concept will remain unchanged and the behavior influenced by it will persist. Figure 5–4 shows how childhood role-playing influences adult behavior patterns.

The child also learns to play certain roles in the family, the school, and the play group. He may learn to play the role of "mother's helper" or of "model" for younger siblings. At school, he may learn to play the role of "teacher's pet" or of "class clown," and among his peers in the play group, of "leader" or "follower."

Whatever role the child learns to play, he will play it consistently unless changes in his environment permit him or force him to play other roles. Changing schools, for example, may force him to play the role of clown to attract the teacher's attention if he discovers that other children have already become the teachers' pets. (Refer to Chapter 2 and to Figure 2–2 for a discussion of the effect of role playing on the self-concept and a graphic illustration of its importance.)

An interesting example of the persistent effects of long-term role playing has been given by Mussen. Boys with "masculine" interests, Mussen reports, are less socially oriented in adolescence and in adulthood than those with more "feminine" interests. The latter, as a result of their greater interest and experience in social activities, develop stronger feelings of adequacy and more positive self-concepts. These effects on their personalities carry into adulthood and are constantly reinforced by the persistence of their feminine interests and social orientations (138).

The influence of reinforcement in learning to think of oneself in a particular way and in learning to behave in accordance with this self-concept is likewise illustrated in studies of maladjustment. As noted earlier, a vicious circle of maladjustment is set in motion. When a child is picked on by his playmates, he either retaliates aggressively or withdraws into a world of daydreams. Whichever response he makes, it tends to encourage his playmates to continue their original behavior and, in turn, his characteristic response. In time, this method of adjustment becomes habitual and carries over to other areas of his social life (42).

It is important to emphasize that what is learned during the early years of life may be merely a vague "feeling" or it may be a very specific pattern of behavior or a specific attitude toward self and one's relationships with others. What is learned can be just as persistent whether it is nebulous or specific, and often the former can be more harmful. This point of view has been expressed by Harsch and Schrickel (84):

Psychological effects which carry over from early infancy to childhood are probably vague dispositions to welcome human contacts, anticipating satisfaction, or to mistrust or fear adults as a result of inconsistent or unpleasant past treatment.

For example, even though a child may not remember the warm, loving care he received as a help-

Figure 5-4   The role played in childhood tends to be carried over into adult life.

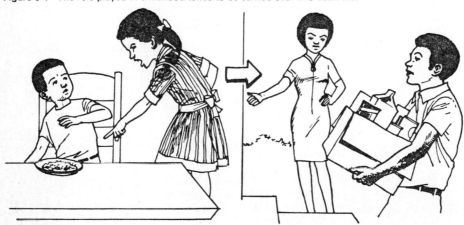

less baby, he has a vague feeling that he is loved and wanted. Unless there is a radical change in family attitudes toward him as he grows older, his early treatment will predispose him to behave in a loving manner toward the members of his family, and they will reciprocate with continued loving care. Instead of a vicious circle of maladjustment, there will be a circle of good adjustment. Through reinforcement, the child's habitual pattern of behavior will make him a sociable, lovable person.

CHANGES IN PERSONALITY

It is a rare person who is so completely satisfied with his personality that he has no desire to change it. The desire to change the personality for the better, to "improve" it, usually develops in late childhood when the child becomes aware, from what parents, teachers, and peers say to him, that they dislike some of his behavior. Such comments as "You're stingy," "You're the meanest kid I know," "You should be ashamed of yourself for picking on your little brother," or "You act like a baby" tell him that some of his characteristic methods of adjustment to people and situations do not win approval.

In time, the child puts two and two together and concludes that the reason he has fewer playmates than he would like is that people do not approve the way he acts. This conclusion is often confirmed by suggestions from parents and teachers that if he wants other people to like him, he will have to change his ways.

That older children recognize the relationship between their characteristic patterns of adjustment and their level of popularity is shown by their claim that they would like to be different or be like a peer who is more popular than they (4, 187). Unfortunately, far too many parents and teachers comfort them with the statement that they will "outgrow" the traits they do not like. This may soothe them for a while, but the dissatisfaction will flare up again, often with greater intensity, in adolescence when they look like adults but are still doing the things that made them unpopular when they were children.

During adolescence, the desire to be popular, not only with members of one's own sex but also with members of the opposite sex, is intensified. With this comes a reawakening of the old realization that a "nice" personality and popularity go hand in hand. For the first time, the individual becomes keenly aware

that personality has a "marketable value" and that it can "buy" popularity (126).

Discontent over personality generally reaches a peak between the ages of 15 and 16 years. It is stronger in boys than in girls and in members of the lower socioeconomic groups than in members of the higher groups (4, 37, 44). Figure 2–4 shows the generally poor opinions boys and girls have of themselves when they reach adolescence.

This dissatisfaction provides adolescents with a strong motivation to improve their personality patterns. They try to strengthen the qualities which they have discovered people like and weaken or cover up with fronts those which they have discovered militate against popularity. They thus make quantitative changes but rarely qualitative changes. As a result of their discoveries and their strong motivation to apply them to their own personalities, older adolescents usually have achieved enough improvement to be much more satisfied with themselves than when they were younger.

To achieve satisfaction, an adolescent must not only have a realistic self-concept but he must also be willing to accept this self-concept even when it falls below what he had hoped for. This means that the gap between the real and the ideal self-concepts must be as narrow as possible. Wylie (226) considers the closing of this gap one of the adolescent's chief tasks:

By the time a child has reached adolescence he has formed a more or less precise image of what he and his culture expect of him as an adult. One of the principal problems for an adolescent then is to conduct his life so that he has the feeling he is achieving this ideal image of himself.

Some adolescents know how they would like to improve their personalities and have a strong motivation to do so but they do not know how to go about it. They may, for example, try to model themselves along the lines of an extremely popular peer, not taking into consideration that hereditary differences or habits of long standing may make it impossible for them to revamp themselves so easily. Meeting failure because the gap between their real and ideal personalities is too large leads to discouragement. This, in turn, dampens their motivation to make what changes they can make and leads them to believe that there is nothing they can do.

When adolescents go out into the adult world, they realize that a "good" personality not only leads to popularity but that it is often a more important factor in business, professional, and social success than training and hard work. This increases their desire to improve their personalities.

That adults appreciate the "marketable value of personality" is evident in their reading books on "how to win friends and influence people," in their taking courses to improve their conversational skills and public speaking abilities, and in their trial-and-error, do-it-yourself attempts to improve their personalities. The more anxious the adult is to "better himself" economically and socially, the more personality-conscious he becomes and the more anxious he is to "improve" his personality.

Evidence of change in personality

A brief survey of a few of the many studies aimed at determining how much change takes place in personality and when this change occurs will indicate the vast amount of evidence that changes do occur in spite of the great tendency toward persistence.

In a study of children from nursery school age to puberty, it was found that ascendant behavior, whether in the form of domination, bossiness, or leadership, increases as social interactions increase, while submissive behavior remains relatively stable. Isolate behavior, on the other hand, gives way to more extroverted, social behavior (197).

During adolescence, students who go away to college have been reported to be less intolerant, authoritarian, and dogmatic after several years of college experience (9, 55, 123, 156). On the other hand, they show an increase in social and emotional maturity and often in feelings of insecurity if they are under parental pressures to get high grades or if they have been subjected to geographic or social mobility (18, 92, 195). There is also evidence of changes in attitudes and values at this time. According to Lehmann et al., "Although attitudes and values are instilled early in life, and are most easily modifiable in infancy and adolescence, it is readily evident that changes do take place from ages 18-22, or older" (118).

Studies reveal that personality changes in old age are quantitative rather than qualitative. Changes are, in a sense, exaggerations of lifelong traits. Aging is thus like applying a magnifying glass to the personality. With age, most people become more rigid in their thinking, more conservative in actions, more prejudiced, more opinionated, and more self-centered (51, 185, 186, 212). There is also evidence that the

marked sex differences in personality, characteristic of young people, tend to disappear in old age (83).

Modifications in a person's behavior may suggest that greater change has taken place in his personality pattern than is actually so. The core of the pattern, the self-concept, is relatively stable and is unlikely to change unless the person perceives shifts in the attitudes and treatment of significant people in his life. A person may, however, modify his behavior in response to social pressures in the hope of winning social approval. Thus, there are changes in the *manifest* personality but not in the real personality. (Refer to Chap. 2 for a discussion of real and manifest personalities.)

An individual's personality may, for example, be organized around a philosophy of life which maintains that security and success come only to the selfish opportunist. This egocentric outlook becomes bound up with the self-concept. The individual may, in the belief that it is "good for business," devote time to community welfare projects and contribute generously to community causes. This altruistic behavior seems to be in direct contrast to his usual "stinginess" and self-centeredness. On the surface, it looks as if he had "changed." In a stressful situation, such as a period of economic decline, his altruistic behavior may be replaced by behavior characterized by self-interest and self-protection. How the person reacts under stress is a good indication of whether there has been a real change in his personality or merely in the manifest aspect of it.

Characteristics of change in personality

Changes in the personality pattern fall into three major categories. *First,* some changes are for the better and some are for the worse. *Second,* some are quantitative and some are qualitative. And *third,* some occur slowly and some rapidly.

Better versus worse Personality changes for the better or for the worse reflect the kind of life adjustments the individual is making at the time. The more pronounced the changes, the more indicative they are of how the person is adjusting.

Successful adjustment at any age, for example, improves the self-concept and the person exhibits greater poise, self-confidence, and self-assurance. By contrast, failure or failure to come up to self-expectations leads to a deterioration in the self-concept and to feelings of inadequacy and inferiority which are expressed in antagonisms, defensive reactions, depression, and many other behavior patterns which lead to even poorer personal and social adjustments. These, in time, affect the self-concept even more unfavorably and lead to even poorer adjustments.

In normal people, personality changes for the worse frequently occur at puberty and middle age. The pubescent usually feels martyred. He is not up to par physically and he feels that parents and teachers are withholding privileges that, as a near adult, he is entitled to. In addition, he is discouraged because he realizes that he is not outgrowing his undesirable physical and personality characteristics.

Similarly with the middle-aged. When they see the deterioration in their appearance in the late forties and fifties, when they realize that many of their early aspirations will never be fulfilled, and when they recognize the growing unfavorable social attitudes toward them and their usefulness to society, it is understandable that their self-concepts deteriorate and that their behavior suggests a change for the worse in adjustments.

When pronounced changes, especially for the worse, occur at times in the life span when they normally do not occur, these changes should be recognized as danger signals. In late adolescence or young adulthood, a progressively more unfavorable self-concept, persisting and severe depression, or threats of suicide indicate that the person is making such poor social and personal adjustments that, unless remedial steps are taken and taken quickly, he will be headed for serious trouble.

Quantitative versus qualitative   Predominant modes of behavior tend to become less conspicuous as the person grows older. That is, undesirable traits become weaker and are overshadowed by the strengthening of more socially approved traits. There is little evidence that any revolutionary change occurs.

This means that qualitative changes, either the complete replacement of a desirable trait by an undesirable one or vice versa, do not normally occur even in the early years of life. For the most part, changes are quantitative: Characteristics already present are reinforced, strengthened, or weakened (25, 96, 103, 186).

A person who is shy, self-conscious, and self-

effacing in social situations may be less so in the presence of intimate friends than in the presence of strangers or those whom he regards as his superiors. But his behavior is consistent. He does not swing from being self-effacing to being boastful and bombastic. A person who is timid does not become a daredevil show-off, even though he might like to do so in the hope of winning greater social approval. He still thinks of himself as an inadequate person, even though he may temporarily cover up this concept of self with a cloak of bravery.

Do not conclude from what has been said that qualitative changes cannot and do not occur. They do. However, there is always a reason for the changes though it may not always be recognized. When a person alters his self-concept so radically that it affects the quality of his adjustments, the alteration is normally brought about by psychotherapy or by an alleviation or intensification of the environmental pressures that were responsible for the old self-concept. How these changes in the self-concept come about will be discussed later under the heading "Conditions Responsible for Personality Change."

Changes that occur in the self-concept or in some of the major areas of adjustment without any apparent reason are usually an indication of mental disease. In fact, in the diagnosis of mental disease, one of the criteria commonly used to determine whether a person is "normal" or "abnormal" is a marked change in his characteristic adjustment to life (84, 101, 183, 192).

A person who has always been careful of his money may become more or less careful as he discovers the social reactions to stinginess and generosity. If he is normal, he will probably be somewhat more generous, hoping to win greater social favor. If he is not normal, he may change into a spendthrift or he may vacillate between extreme generosity and miserliness. If a kind and loving father turns into a sadistic brute, it is logical to conclude that he is suffering from some form of mental illness. Men normally change somewhat in their attitudes and behavior toward family members as a result of business pressures, disenchantment with marriage and parenthood, financial worries, poor health, or any one of a number of other causes, but they do not change so radically unless they are mentally ill (43, 84, 183).

Slow versus rapid changes   Changes are regarded as slow if they are barely perceptible, while rapid changes are readily apparent to all. Normally, personality changes are slow and gradual. They are slow, even in childhood before the personality pattern has become well set, because every change involves the breaking of a previously learned habit and the learning of a new habit to replace it. This explains why personality improvement cannot take place overnight. While motivation provides the driving force to break old habits and learn new ones, doing so is always a slow, laborious process and may be impossible after the habits have been reinforced through repeated experiences.

One of the reasons why psychotherapy, whose major function is to help people revise unfavorable self-concepts so they can make better personal and social adjustments, is such a long drawn-out process is that it involves habit breaking and relearning. Normally, these changes, even with professional guidance, encouragement, and help, are slow.

Rapid changes at any age are danger signals. Changes of short duration are usually due to some artificial stimulation which temporarily causes the person to forget his real self-concept and see himself as he would like to be. Under the influence of alcohol, for example, a person who feels that he is a failure may forget his real self-concept and change from a depressed, defensive, self-reproachful person into a happy, carefree life-of-the-party type, fitting his ideal self-concept. A depressed and anxious adolescent may temporarily shed his unfavorable self-concept, which is expressed in maladjustive patterns of adjustment, by smoking marijuana or using other narcotics. So long as he is under the influence of a narcotic, he is a "changed" person.

Rapid personality changes which are persistent, on the other hand, are due not to artificial stimulants but to an endocrine or neurological upset. Brain injuries, tumors, and disturbances due to arteriosclerosis, cancer, or some other disease are normally accompanied by such readily apparent personality changes that other people wonder what is the matter with the person (151). Endocrine imbalance, often only temporary at puberty or at the climacterium in middle age, is accompanied by such rapid personality changes that even the person affected is aware that he is "not himself." When endocrine homeostasis is restored, however, there is no guarantee that he will revert to his former patterns of adjustment (10, 115, 151).

Since rapid changes in personality are far from universal even at the times when endocrine and neurological changes take place, it is quite possible that the physical, endocrine, or neurological condition per se is not responsible for personality changes. Instead, there is some evidence that people who have made relatively poor personal and social adjustments earlier are incapable of withstanding the effects of the normal bodily changes. They "crack" under the strain, and as a result, exhibit rapid changes in their personality patterns.

Variations in personality change

Just as there are marked variations in the degree of persistence of the personality pattern, so are there variations in the number and kinds of change that take place. For convenience, these will be discussed under three major headings: ages of change, kinds of people who change, and areas of the personality pattern that change.

Ages of change   While it is widely believed that the personality pattern is more plastic and, therefore, more subject to change in the early years of life, there is little definite evidence that this is always true. On the other hand, there is evidence that as one grows older the habit of thinking of oneself in a particular way and of acting in accordance with this self-concept becomes more firmly rooted and personality changes become more difficult (193). This does not mean that habits cannot be broken and replaced with other habits, but that it becomes increasingly difficult and requires a longer time as people pass from childhood into adolescence and adulthood.

Concepts of self and characteristic patterns of adjustment are most likely to change when people have a strong motivation to effect a change, when there are radical or rapid physical changes and when there is a marked change in the person's physical and social environment. Why these conditions bring about changes in the personality pattern will be explained in the next major section.

Kinds of people   In some people, the personality pattern has a "granite-like" structure which is impervious to the conditions that, in other people, do bring about changes (25). Those who are *other-directed*, who are highly susceptible to social pressures and the attitudes of significant people in their lives, change their self-concepts and patterns of adjustive behavior more often and more radically than inner-directed people—those who are governed more by their own values and goals. This variation is due to the fact that the other-directed person is more anxious to see himself and to have others see him in a favorable light (78).

Boys and men change their personality patterns more than do girls and women. Their environmental experiences are broader and more varied than those of girls and women, and they are subjected from early childhood to more social pressures to "improve" their personalities as an aid to business and social success. They thus have a stronger motivation to change (37, 126, 186).

Firstborns, whether male or female, are more dependent and more other-directed than later-borns and thus more susceptible to personality change (21, 78, 81, 108). *Exceptional* children, whether above or below the norm, are more resistant to pressures to change their personalities than are those closer to the norm. Exceptional children ordinarily see themselves as "different"—and children always interpret "different" to mean "inferior." People who perceive themselves as different tend to have very firmly fixed self-concepts and are thus relatively resistant to personality change (176).

People who develop the habit of using *defense mechanisms* to protect the self-concept from threats are less likely to change their personalities than those who see themselves realistically and do not feel the need to hide their real self-concepts. Attempts to get them to change their self-concepts not only are resisted but elicit a counterattempt on their part to get others to view them more favorable (13, 172).

At all ages, the more *stable the environment,* the fewer pressures there will be on a person to change his personality. Adolescents who remain in the family and neighborhood in which they grew up, for example, experience fewer pressures to change their personalities than those who go away to college (65). How stability of the environment affects change will be discussed in more detail in the next section.

People differ greatly in the degree of *motivation* they have to change their personalities. A person who is satisfied with himself as he is has little motivation to change. He will resist any advice or help offered him. This is apparent in the voluntary isolate who is satisfied to spend his time alone, doing as he pleases. He does not want to be made into a "social" person, no matter how hard others may try to influence him.

Areas of personality pattern   Some areas of the personality pattern are more subject to change than others; some are so rigid that change is practically impossible. Flexibility is, in part, related to age, with greater flexibility in young children than in adolescents and adults, and in part to differences in life experiences and the strength of the person's desire to change.

The part of the personality pattern least likely to change is the core, made up of attitudes, beliefs, values, and aspirations developed as a result of the person's relationships with others. The core, or self-concept, becomes stronger and more fixed with age. Change is easiest in young children, but even then, a sudden or radical change will cause emotional strain (25, 75, 114, 202).

Changes in the self-concept can and do occur in middle and old age. Persons who are convinced that they have been failures in life become discouraged, unhappy, and plagued with feelings of inadequacy and inferiority, though they may have been happy, confident, and optimistic when they were younger. Or the reverse may occur if things turn out better than had been expected (119, 143, 169, 209).

Some traits in the personality pattern remain stable, others fluctuate slightly, and still others change. The most variable traits are those which involve social relationships. As the individual's experiences broaden, he becomes increasingly aware of what traits are approved, and what are disapproved (25, 37, 48, 97, 137). Daring, for example, may be highly valued among members of a boys' gang during late childhood. It is not admired among girls, however, or among older adolescents. Instead, reasonable caution is admired. Being outspoken is usually synonymous with being truthful in childhood, but with being tactless in adolescence.

It is never possible to predict which traits will persist in a given person and which will change. How many traits will change and in what ways will depend on the life experiences of the person, his hereditary endowment, and his motivation to change. A trait such as honesty or self-confidence may persist in some people and fluctuate or change in others. A person may discover that honesty does not pay, and this may encourage him to be dishonest. Too many failures may weaken a person's self-confidence or even eradicate it, while unexpected successes may turn a person who previously lacked self-confidence into one who is arrogant and cocky.

Trying to change the entire personality pattern is not only difficult but dangerous. In every personality pattern there is a "point of fixity" beyond which change cannot be effected (205). Any attempt to force change beyond this point can upset the entire balance of the pattern and lead to maladjustments or even mental illness. While the point of fixity will vary from one person to another and in the same person from one age to another, it exists and must be recognized as a warning against any attempts to effect further changes (3, 103, 165).

Conditions responsible for personality change

Changes in personality do not occur of their own accord. Usually they are the result of multiple revisions in the thoughts and feelings related to the person's concept of self. If some structural disturbance affects the brain, such as a brain tumor, changes in personality can usually be traced to that one factor. But in a normal person, there are usually several causes of personality changes. These causes may or may not be interrelated.

If conditions are to be effective in bringing about personality changes, they must be operative at an early age. Attitudes, habits, and behavior patterns are established early in life and are firmly rooted in the personality pattern by the time a person reaches adolescence. They are then carried over into adulthood and become a way of life. As Gruen (80) has pointed out:

In most personality theories adulthood is viewed as the period of relative stability. It is presumed that, once adolescence is over, the personality structure no longer undergoes major changes and that the behavior of adults can be ascribed to underlying patterns laid down in childhood.

The personality pattern changes relatively little after people become adults. Therefore, adolescence, especially the latter part of adolescence, is regarded as a "critical age" in personality development. It is regarded as critical for two reasons. *First,* this is the time at which it is determined whether a person will be a mature, socially conscious, and resolute adult or will be immature, dependent, frustrated, and unsure of himself (34, 103).

Second, the personality pattern, already well set, is either well or poorly integrated by this time so far as any gap between the real and ideal self-concepts is concerned. The smaller the gap, the better the adjustments to adult life. Persons who have well-integrated personality patterns with stable and realis-

tic self-concepts make far better personal and social adjustments than those with unstable and unrealistic self-concepts (45, 65).

Of the many conditions responsible for personality changes, the following are reported to be most important: physical changes, changes in the environment, changes in significant people, changes in social pressures, changes in roles, strong motivation, changes in self-concept, and psychotherapy.

Physical changes Physical changes may come from maturation and decline or from illness, organic and glandular disturbances, injuries, or some other condition resulting from the person's life pattern but unrelated to the normal changes in the body structure. Marked physical changes, especially if they occur rapidly, do not give the person time to adjust smoothly; and, as a result, they have greater influence on his self-concept than slow or minor changes.

During periods of rapid physical change, physical and glandular changes upset the body homeostasis and, with it, the person's feelings of well-being. The person must then not only make physical readjustments but also change his concept of self so that it agrees with the social concept of a person of his age and the social expectations associated with his age. This requires psychological readjustments at the same time that organic and glandular readjustments are being made.

At puberty, for example, the young person must revise his physical self-concept and must adjust to this as well as to his new physical features, such as his increased size and the secondary sex characteristics that develop at this time. When the physical changes enable him to approximate his concept of his ideal self, the effect on his real self-concept will be favorable. The girl who in childhood was a "fatty" will have a much more favorable self-concept if she develops into a "graceful swan" at puberty than if she continues to be an "ugly duckling."

Similarly, physical changes in middle age, often rapid and upsetting to body homeostasis, necessitate a change in the self-concept, in feelings about self, and in attitudes toward one's abilities as they are affected by aging. When the person sees physical changes in himself, such as graying of the hair or loss of teeth, he begins to think of himself as "old" because he has learned to accept these changes as evidence of "oldness" in others. With this acceptance comes a tendency to worry, to feel insecure and useless, and to believe that the best years of life are over for him.

As his concept of self changes, it is reflected in changes in his characteristic patterns of behavior. He becomes anxious, frustrated, resentful, and stressful—changes for the worse which are readily apparent to all who knew him when he was younger. Personality changes are, thus, not a function of growing older but rather a function of a changed self-concept (42, 51).

Unfavorable changes in the person's physical condition, such as illness, overweight, glandular disturbances, or blindness, often result in personality changes because they affect the person's self-concept unfavorably. These physical changes are especially damaging if they occur after the person has learned to think of himself as a normal, healthy individual. Having to revise this self-concept and accept the fact that he is "handicapped" is the cause of the personality change (40).

Changes in environment Changes in either the physical or social environment may produce changes in the person's self-concept and, in turn, in his characteristic behavior. A change in environment, per se, will not guarantee an improvement in personality. In fact, the change may and often does have the opposite effect. Just moving to a new environment, for example, where the socioeconomic status of the people is superior to that of the people of the old environment will not automatically improve the child's, the adolescent's, or the adult's personality. Whether it does so or not will depend largely on how well the person is accepted in the new environment and how well the new environment meets his needs.

To have a favorable effect on the personality pattern, changes in the environment must do four things. *First,* they must improve the status of the person and, by doing so, enable him to feel more secure and adequate. *Second,* the changes must enable the person to be more in equilibrium with his environment in the sense that the environment meets his needs at that time. *Third,* the changes must enable him to come closer to his ideal. And *fourth,* by providing opportunities for broader social experiences with people of different cultural backgrounds and with different values and ideals, they must help the person see himself more realistically and revise his goals and aspirations in keeping with his abilities.

For most children and young adolescents, the physical and social environments do not change. Many live in the same neighborhood, go to the same school, play with the same members of the peer group, and have the same adults as neighbors year after year. Relations with family members, especially parents, are likewise persistent. As a result, opportunities to change their self-concepts by changing to environments better suited to their needs are very limited.

That is why studies of the effects of college attendance are so important as a means of throwing light on how environmental changes affect the personality pattern. While some changes unquestionably are due to intellectual maturation, most come from the fact that college tends to lift some of the repressions and frustrations young people experience in their homes and offers opportunities for them to learn to be independent (92, 216).

By breaking ties with his old environment, both in the home and in school, the college student can make a fresh start, profiting from his past mistakes and learning to adjust to new people and situations without the aid of parents and teachers. In addition, his broader and more diversified social contacts enable him to establish new values and revise his childhood values, to evaluate himself in relation to his new peers, and to play new and more mature roles than he played at home (45, 216).

Whether a changed environment will lead to an improvement of the personality pattern will depend largely on whether the personality moves toward equilibrium with its environment. "Psychological nomadism," which necessitates conformity to changing standards of behavior and shifting value systems, results in inward disturbances, leading to heightened emotionality and feelings of insecurity. Psychological nomadism is most likely to occur when one is socially mobile, when one goes away to college or into the armed services, with moves to different communities or neighborhoods in the same community, or when the home is disorganized (111).

At no time in life is equilibrium with the environment more important to personality improvement than in old age. When elderly people remain in an environment that is unstimulating and devoid of interests, they change for the worse and conform to the cultural stereotype of being crabbed, rigid, and hard to live with. For some older people, moving to communities that cater to the retired, where they will find people with interests similar to theirs, or to homes for the aged, where they will have the companionship of their peers, eliminates the feeling of being dependent, unwanted, and useless. As a result, many become happy and well-adjusted people.

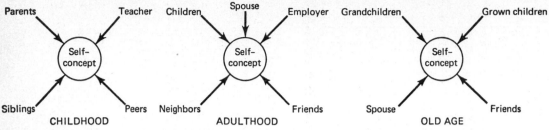

Figure 5-5   The significant people who play a role of importance in forming the person's self-concept change from one age to another.

How changes in the environment will affect the personality pattern depends not alone on whether the changes result in a movement of the personality toward equilibrium with its environment but also on when this movement occurs. At certain ages and stages of development, environmental changes are beneficial while at others they are detrimental. Parental divorce with its consequent radical changes in the pattern of family life, for example, is more detrimental to young children, whose lives are centered in the home, than to older children and adolescents, whose lives include peer relationships. If the death of a spouse coincides with the retirement of the remaining spouse and the problems, both economic and social, which retirement brings, it is far more damaging to the personality pattern than if it is earlier when the remaining spouse has more outside interests and a greater chance of remarrying.

Changes in significant people   When the significant people in an individual's life change, and when he tries to adapt his pattern of behavior and his attitudes, beliefs, values, and aspirations to theirs, changes in his personality pattern are inevitable. These changes may not be marked, nor are they always permanent.

From time to time throughout life, the people who are significant to a person change. As was explained in the discussion of the ideal self-concept (Chap. 2) and of identification (Chap. 4), the basis for the formation of this self-concept varies from one age to another. The extent to which changes in significant people bring about personality changes will depend on how much their attitudes, values, and so on differ from those of the individual. If there is a great disparity, he will be motivated to effect greater changes.

For example, in young adults, the significant people are usually spouses, employers, or successful community leaders. These people set the pattern the young adult tries to imitate and whose expectations he tries to conform to. The more they differ from him, the greater the gap between his ideal self-concept and his real self-concept, and the harder he will try to narrow the gap.

In old age, after people have retired, the most significant people in their lives are usually their grown children. If the attitudes of their grown children toward them are favorable, elderly parents will have little reason to change their self-concepts. If the attitudes are unfavorable, the amount of change the parents will want to make will depend largely upon the closeness of the parent-child relationship. Figure 5-5 shows the people who play important roles in the formation of the self-concept at different periods of life.

Changes in social pressures   As childhood progresses, the child becomes increasingly aware that some personality traits are admired while some are disliked. And since everyone normally has a strong desire to be accepted by those who are significant to him, he tries to change any personality trait that will militate against his being accepted.

Strong social pressures to conform to a socially approved personality pattern thus encourage changes in certain aspects of the personality. Traits which are likely to lead to social rejection, such as shyness, bossiness, aggressiveness, and greed, are more subject to change than those which are usually admired, such as affection, ambition, cooperativeness, and generosity.

The force of social pressures to change disliked traits has been emphasized by Thompson (205):

Only rarely does there occur a maverick, one whose life experiences somehow made him a rebel, rather than a conformist. But even then the degree of his deviation is not permitted to be unlimited. Beyond a certain point, society forbids his deviation, and few can survive that degree of disapproval.

Pressures to conform to the approved pattern are provided by the people who are significant in the person's life at the time. When a child is young he tries to conform to parental standards. Later, his peers' opinions provide the incentive to change.

Changes in roles Role changes result in status changes within the group. One's role may change because of a change in *age*. A child changes from being a dependent to being an economically independent person when he is old enough to become a wage earner. A change in one's role may also come from changes in *economic* conditions. A person who has been a generous sponsor of community projects may have to withdraw from this role when retirement or business reverses force him to count every penny he spends. Or a change in roles may be due to *affiliation with a new group.* A leader in one group may be a follower or even a neglectee in another.

If role changes result in a more favorable status, there will be a change for the better in the person's self-concept. Whether the changed role will have a favorable or unfavorable effect depends not so much upon what the new role is as upon how well it fits the person's needs and whether it has greater prestige in the eyes of the social group than the old role. Tuddenham has emphasized that one of the reasons for increased optimism in the group he studied over a period of 15 years was that their improved economic conditions allowed them to play more prestigious roles in the social groups with which they were identified (209).

Three conditions related to role changes are especially damaging to the personality pattern. The *first* is being prevented from making a change when one feels capable of doing so and when his peers are permitted to do so. The late maturer develops feelings of martyrdom, resentment, and inadequacy when people continue to treat him like a "kid" but extend the rights and privileges of the near adult to his earlier-maturing peers.

Second, changing roles is especially damaging to the self-concept if the individual is forced to play a role he does not want to play. Many women, it has been reported, resent having to give up a career to play the role of wife and mother, a role they enjoy less and one which carries little prestige (20, 49, 89).

Being unprepared for a role change is the *third* condition that contributes to personality damage. Middle-aged and elderly people who are unprepared economically and psychologically for the changed roles that advancing age will inevitably bring suffer far greater personality damage than those who are better prepared. Lack of preparation for aging may affect members of any socioeconomic group, but it is most likely to affect those of the lower groups. This has been stressed by Peck and Berkowitz (153):

Adjustment to the aging process comes most easily ... to upper-status people, but not primarily because they are economically advantaged. Lower-class people suffer genuine economic and social deprivations which handicap them as they grow old. At the same time, their ill-developed personalities also interfere with good adjustment at least as early as early middle age. The social-class differences in adaptability and adjustment, thus, are not only a matter of financial resources, but also of inner psychological resources.

Strong motivation When the motivation to improve the personality pattern is strong enough, changes can be effected. Ordinarily people are most strongly motivated to change those traits which they believe will improve their social relationships and earn them greater social acceptance. Even then, the changes are mainly quantitative; existing socially approved traits are strengthened and socially disapproved traits are weakened.

Outer-directed people are more susceptible to the opinions of others than inner-directed people. When the opinions of others are unfavorable, outer-directed people have a strong motivation to change their personalities to conform to the approved standards (13).

A person who perceives himself as "popular" has far less motivation to try to change his personality than one who perceives himself as "unpopular." However, if the unpopular person believes that his unpopularity is so great that nothing he can do will make him popular, he will have little motivation to try to improve his personality (37, 128, 205).

Children and young adolescents with a strong motivation to shed their dependence and become independent can do so if their motivation is not stifled. When mothers are unable to wait on their children hand and foot, the children have a strong motivation to learn to do things for themselves. Without this motivation, dependency persists and becomes a deeply rooted habit that carries into the adult years (21, 100, 180).

Elderly people who become socially disengaged and isolated from the pressures of the social group, due to retirement, failing health, economic problems, and other conditions, lack the motivation necessary to change or curb the undesirable personality traits associated with the cultural stereotype of the elderly. Rigidity, for example, is usually due more to lack of motivation to be adaptable than to mental or physical decline. Peck and Berkowitz (153) have written:

Many of the old assumptions about age-linked decline in general personality integration and adaptability may be untrue. Some middle-aged people cannot or will not learn much that is new but many can and do continue to adopt new ideas and new behaviors.

Changes in the self-concept   Since the self-concept is the core of the personality pattern and, as such, determines the kind of adjustment the person will make, a change in the self-concept will bring about a change in the entire personality pattern.

However, changing the self-concept is increasingly difficult as people grow older, and any change that is attempted must be made slowly and gradually to avoid upsetting the entire personality pattern. Even more important, people strongly resist any attempts by others to change their self-concepts and employ defense mechanisms to enable them to maintain their self-concepts intact.

Changing one's self-concept requires tremendous self-insight. This means that a person must be able and willing to see himself as he actually is, not as he would like to be or as others perceive him.

OBSTACLES TO CHANGING THE SELF-CONCEPT   It is very difficult for a person to see himself as he actually is. The *first* obstacle is an intellectual one. When a person becomes accustomed to behavior organized in a particular fashion, he may be unable to see that there are other ways of coping with a situation or problem. For example, if he has become accustomed to using aggressive physical or verbal attacks to get his way, it is hard for him to realize that you can "catch more flies with sugar than with vinegar."

The *second* obstacle is an emotional one. Many people resist thinking differently about themselves because they believe that will be admitting that they were wrong. If a person has always thought of himself as superior, he will hate to admit to himself or others that he is just an ordinary person. As Leeper and Madison (117) have explained:

. . . Discomfort bobs up to obstruct the thinking of any child or adult who faces the question of whether his

familiar picture of his real self is sufficiently accurate for the needs of his life.

In addition, a new concept of the real self may present to the individual some tendencies he has learned to fear. If he has learned to think of himself as a "follower" and this has brought him satisfaction, thinking of himself as having the ability to be a "leader" may bring out feelings of personal inadequacy. Leeper and Madison say, "New concepts about one's real self are almost certain to demand of the person some new kind of behavior that threatens to be uncomfortable, or embarrassing, even humiliating, and inevitably in some respects frustrating" (117).

A *third* major obstacle to getting a more accurate understanding of the real self is environmental. Sometimes the real self and the "mirror image" are contradictory. A person will find it very difficult to see himself as useful to society if racial, religious, sex, or age prejudice against him leads to social discrimination. Similarly, constant parental criticism of a person because he has not taken advantage of the opportunities his parents have given him make it difficult for him to think of himself as anything but a failure. A realistic self-appraisal which shows that he is doing as much as can be expected is quickly counteracted by unfavorable environmental pressures. Building up self-confidence and feelings of personal adequacy and security is practically impossible in such an environment.

CONDITIONS THAT FACILITATE CHANGES IN THE SELF-CONCEPT   The obstacles to gaining better self-insight described above may be offset to some extent by other conditions that facilitate changes in the self-concept. Many aids to changing the self-concept have been suggested; the following are the most important:

The use of introspection to see oneself as one actually is

An analysis of why one thinks of oneself in a particular way

A critical examination of one's behavior to see if it is creating an unfavorable impression on others

An objective comparison of oneself with others to see if one is inferior, superior, or equal

Self-disclosure to those for whom one has respect and confidence as a way of gaining new self-insight

Reading books that emphasize what contributes to success in life

Avoiding trying to model one's personality after the personality of an ideal

Changing one's aspirations when they are unrealistically high for one's potentials

Changing from an environment that fosters an unfavorable self-concept or, if this is impossible, ignoring the unfavorable aspects of the environment

Patient practice in trying to see oneself according to the new self-concept until one becomes accustomed to it, likes it, and accepts it

When the self-concept has been changed, it is essential to change the characteristic patterns of adjustment that are related to the old self-concept. Since many of these have become habitual through repetition and are used unconsciously, changing them may be as difficult as changing the self-concept. But unless they are changed, the person will continue to be judged unfavorably. And having this unfavorable mirror image constantly before him will militate against his liking and accepting his new self-concept. For example, a person who has developed a deeply rooted habit of inflating his ego by making disparaging comments about others will not be perceived favorably by them unless he changes this characteristic manner of behaving.

Use of psychotherapy Even though a person is strongly motivated, he may require professional help in changing his self-concept, learning to think of himself in a new way, and breaking destructive habits. A child or an adolescent, for example, may believe that he is brighter and more able than he actually is because of the way family members and intimate friends treat him. Later, when he goes to college or into the business world, his broadened social experiences should help him to revise his self-concept to a more realistic level. But by then the unrealistic self-appraisal may have become his habitual way of thinking of himself.

Psychotherapy is based on the assumption that a poorly adjusted person can make better adjustments if he is helped to develop a more favorable self-concept. Whether on an individual or group basis, psychotherapy helps a person to get better insight into the reasons for his unrealistically favorable or unfavorable self-concept, to realize how his self-concept affects the quality of his behavior, to recognize how irrational his self-concept and his behavior are, to achieve both the motivation and know-how to change his self-concept, to secure the guidance necessary to make this change without upsetting the entire personality pattern, and to change the conditions in the environment which contribute to an unfavorable self-concept.

A few examples of experimental attacks on the problem of changing the self-concept, through individual or group psychotherapy, will illustrate how effective it can be. An experiment in group counseling of junior high school boys resulted in better integration of their real and ideal self-concepts with the result that they were less tense and disturbed and more acceptant of themselves and others (32). People who feel inadequate to play a leadership role have been helped to change their self-concepts through training and experience in playing such a role. This resulted in a decrease in the discrepancy between their real and ideal self-concepts because they saw themselves playing a role they aspired to play in their ideal self-concepts (76).

Adolescent girls who feel "different" because they see themselves as unloved and unwanted at home and rejected by the peer group sometimes become unwed mothers. Psychotherapy with such girls during the pregnancy period can bring about changes in their self-concepts, making them feel more self-reliant, more self-confident, warmer, and less indulgent in their future relationships with members of the opposite sex (109).

Experimental attacks have been made on the strengthening of socially desirable personality traits and the weakening of undesirable ones. Specific training to increase the self-confidence of preschool children and to develop skills which their peers did not have made the children not only more self-confident but also more dominant in their relationships with children who had formerly dominated them (100, 128). Equally important, with their increased self-confidence in several skills, the preschoolers could be encouraged to try new tasks. It was thus apparent that their training became cumulative, and they changed from a pattern of nonascendant to ascendant behavior (125).

A study of isolate children—children who were unresponsive to others, who engaged in little free play, and who seldom spoke to anyone who was not smaller and younger than they—revealed that, after a period of psychotherapeutic treatment, they became less inhibited and participated in games and chose playmates of their own ages (50).

CONDITIONS MILITATING AGAINST EFFECTIVE-NESS OF PSYCHOTHERAPY A number of conditions militate against the effectiveness of psychotherapy as a means of improving the personality pattern.

The *first* is the age of the person. Even among children, the older the child, the less effective the treatment because the personality pattern has become more structured and the ego level more static. By the time a person reaches adulthood, his self-concept is so well-established and so stable that changing it takes a long time, perhaps years, very strong motivation, and the breaking down of the defenses he has established to protect himself from the emotional effects that a change in the self-concept, even a change for the better, is likely to bring.

The *second* is the hereditary predisposition of the person to behave in a certain way, the effects of early training, or conflicts with home influences. A person whose glandular condition predisposes him to be slow-moving and slow-thinking cannot be turned into an animated, life-of-the-party type. A person whose early interest patterns centered around creative play activities cannot easily be turned into a noncreative adult who fits well into an automated job and a rigorously scheduled pattern of living.

Third, some people tend to resist guidance whether it is for their benefit or not. Others who are more susceptible to guidance can effect personality changes more easily. An unsocial child, for example, may resist being changed into a social person because, from early experiences, he has found less satisfaction from group activities than from individual ones. Such resistance is often a warning signal that it would be best to stop trying to make the change. Otherwise, serious damage may be done to the person's self-concept by creating in him the impression that something is wrong with him because he chooses to be an individual. Resistance does not necessarily mean that he is going to develop into a poorly adjusted adult. As Harsh and Schrickel have remarked, "Independence need not make one an unsocial outcast, for in later years he may prove a leader among adults, while the school hero becomes a gas station attendant" (84). Similarly, the creative child, especially a boy whose father tries to change him into a "good businessman," may contribute far more to civilization and make a greater name for himself if he continues to be creative and resists attempts to make him be "practical."

The *fourth* and perhaps the most troublesome condition that militates against the effectiveness of psychotherapy as a way of bringing about changes in the personality pattern is the persistence of environmental pressures which affect the way the person views himself and his characteristic methods of adjusting. Since it is often impossible to get the individual out of his old, unfavorable environment and into a new one, psychotherapy tries to improve the environment in which the person presently lives. Should parents have unrealistically high aspirations for a child, for example, attempts are made to show them why their aspirations are unrealistic and why they should change their attitudes and treatment of the child. If a child is an isolate, the attitudes and treatment of his peers may help him to become more social or, as in a case described by Early, "Because the isolate's peers reinforce his approach behavior, it was conditioned when extinction might have occurred without reinforcement" (50).

How long do changes persist?

Naturally it is hoped that changes in the direction of improvement will persist indefinitely and that changes for the worse will be short-lived.

To answer the question, How long do personality changes persist? one must have evidence from longitudinal studies covering a long enough period in a person's life to know what happens to the changes when the person has new personal and social experiences and when his environment or the significant people in his life change. As already noted, there are only a few longitudinal studies covering the major part of the life span, and for the most part, they include only a small number of subjects.

A glance at a few studies carried over a relatively short period will suggest what one can reasonably expect. In a 5-year follow-up study of a group of nursery school children it was found that, in some cases, the changes persisted, while in others, they did not. The least persistent changes were those brought about in children who resisted making the changes (132). In a follow-up of children given psychiatric treatment for antisocial behavior, many showed improvement in their peer relationships and schoolwork. Others did not improve and some became delinquent (164).

Follow-ups of early- and late-maturing boys from puberty to the mid-thirties revealed that improvements in the personality patterns of the early maturers and changes for the worse in the late maturers persisted without appreciable change (7, 98).

Changes in college students as a result of their college experiences were still evident in follow-ups 4 to 5 years after graduation. As young adults, they were less conventional, less dogmatic, less authoritarian, and more tolerant than before they went to college (65, 109). Tuddenham's study of changes in personality after the "stormy" adolescent years showed that increased optimism persisted when follow-ups were made in the subjects' mid-thirties (209).

No studies have reported what happens to personality changes when the subjects later experience marked changes in their environment or in the attitudes of significant people. It is relatively safe to conclude, however, on the basis of evidence showing the conditions under which changes normally occur, that the changes will not persist. Instead, the subjects will probably revert to their former self-concepts and patterns of behavior or will change to a new personality pattern—the direction of the change being influenced by the kinds of changes that occur in the environment.

It is also relatively safe to conclude, on the basis of available evidence, that people who resist making a change in their personalities are more likely than others to revert to their former self-concepts and behavior patterns once the pressures to change have been relaxed. A person who prefers a nonsocial pattern may, during the years when being a social person is to his advantage, conform to social expectations and be social. As he grows older, the pressures to be social will not be so great as in childhood and adolescence. If he has not found the change to a social pattern of behavior satisfying, he will revert to the preferred pattern and think of himself as a voluntary "lone wolf."

PRACTICAL IMPLICATIONS OF PERSISTENCE AND CHANGE

However difficult the problem of determining the degree of persistence in the personality pattern and however inadequate the results of the studies to date, scientific interest in the problem has increased. Many new studies are being undertaken in an effort to answer some of the questions raised by earlier studies. Interest has been intensified by the practical implications of the problem. These have been emphasized by Roberts and Fleming (165):

To accept the idea that an individual is "born that way" and can do little about his personality characteristics breeds a defeatist attitude. On the other hand, to

believe that an individual can make of himself what he will may hold out false hopes of rebirth. Educators and psychologists need, therefore, to know what the possibilities for modification are and at what stages in development modification is most possible. All people working in the field of guidance, whether they be teachers, parents, psychologists, ministers, or counsellors, need to be discriminating about what changes it is sound to work for in helping people solve their personality problems.

A number of the practical implications of persistence and change in the personality pattern have been highlighted in the studies now available. Those discussed in the following sections are the most important.

Good foundations

If there is evidence that the personality pattern remains relatively persistent, with only minor changes, it is apparent that good foundations, which can stand the test of time and guarantee relatively good adjustments throughout life, must be laid. Good foundations include the establishment of a stable, realistic self-concept, the acceptance of this concept, and the development of socially acceptable patterns of behavior.

These foundations are far too important to be left to chance. Instead, the child should be carefully guided and directed throughout the early years of life. Parents and teachers can, if they take the time and trouble, discover what the child's self-concept is by listening to what he says about himself and what he says and does in the presence of others. If it is apparent that he is thinking of himself in an unfavorable way and if his behavior is such that it is leading to poor social adjustments, remedial steps should be taken at once to replace these poor foundations with more wholesome ones. Unfortunately, the weight of evidence does not indicate that this can readily be done.

Prediction of later adjustments

Persistence in the personality pattern makes it possible to predict what sort of person the individual will be in the future, what sort of adjustments he will make to life, and how he will behave in specific situations.

The prophetic character of the early personality pattern has been substantiated by scientific studies of persistence covering a considerable time period. If the fetus is very active, it tends to develop into a nervous, irritable, and hyperactive baby who changes little as he grows into adulthood (190). Children who are aggressive or dependent develop into aggressive or dependent adults. Children who are under pressure from parents and teachers to do good work in school can be expected to become compulsive workers in adulthood who suffer from "busy complexes" and feelings of guilt about taking time off for recreation (105, 160, 220). One can predict with a fair degree of accuracy that an early-maturing boy will make better adjustments to adult life than the late maturer (98).

In no area is the prophetic character of the early personality pattern greater than in the area of juvenile delinquency. Case studies of juvenile delinquents have shown that their antisocial behavior is not an overnight development. Most juvenile delinquents have been antisocial troublemakers since earliest childhood. It can, therefore, be predicted with reasonable certainty that antisocial troublemakers in the first grade of school are headed for juvenile delinquency and adult criminality unless remedial steps are quickly taken to change their personality patterns (73). If they do not express their unfavorable self-concepts in aggressive ways, they are likely to become anomic adults, schizophrenics, alcoholics, or drug addicts (12, 162).

On the other hand, it can be predicted that some children who grow up in culturally and economically deprived environments where juvenile delinquency and adult criminality are a way of life will not follow the delinquent pattern because they have been "insulated" against it. Insulation is achieved by the development of a favorable self-concept, fostered by parental love, respect, and trust; a socially acceptable pattern of adjustment, fostered by demands for conformity to reasonable rules and regulations; and a lack of tolerance for aggressive behavior combined with good parental models.

The treatment that makes the individual a law-abiding citizen in the home will make him a law-abiding citizen in the community, even when many of his associates are lawbreakers (176, 189). As Scarpitti et al. have explained, "The internalization of a favorable self-concept is the critical variable in the 'containment' of delinquency" (176).

It is far more difficult to predict which specific traits will persist and which will fluctuate or actually change (165). Those which are highly valued by the social group, such as honesty, courage, and generosity, will be more persistent, however, than those with low social value, such as timidity, cowardice, stinginess, and dishonesty. This means that, though it is

difficult to predict at an early age the exact adolescent or adult personality pattern, a general prognosis may be quite accurate (25, 184, 186, 204).

Early correction of maladjustments

Mental hygiene practice is based on three beliefs: that maladjustments become increasingly severe and increasingly resistant to correction over time; that changes in the personality pattern should be made early to avoid upsetting the personality structure; and that it is, therefore, important to recognize symptoms of maladjustment in their early forms and correct them before they become worse. These beliefs are based on knowledge of the principles of learning and of the difficulties involved in relearning (25, 57, 65, 127).

The insistence on early correction must not be misunderstood. It does not mean that no attempt should be made to change the personality pattern of maladjusted persons who are past the age when changes can be made relatively easily and successfully. Though the task is more difficult, changes can be effected at older age levels. In a study of the changes in attitudes and values associated with college attendance, Lehmann et al. (118) conclude:

It is . . . imperative that our colleges and universities . . . discard the notion that behavior characteristics are not their concern because it is too late to do anything about them. Just as the myth that intellectual development ceases after a certain age has been discarded, so should the notion that personality change is not possible for college students be discounted. . . . A college education, per se, is not instrumental in bringing about these changes, although college attendance might facilitate (them). Therefore, college faculties and administrators must realize that they are not necessarily providing a unique experience for their students but that maturation and the social environment might have more impact upon personality development than courses and formal academic experiences.

If there were evidence that changes could be made at any age with little or no difficulty or that changes naturally accompanied physical and mental maturation, then there would be no "best age" for attempting to make changes in the personality pattern. To date, there is little evidence to this effect.

Inner control of changes

Even when given guidance and help, a person must *want* to make changes in his personality and must be willing to put forth the effort needed to do so. No one can change his personality for him. As in all learning, the person can get information from others on how to learn in the best and most efficient way, but the practical application of this information is up to him. Changes cannot be imposed from without. They must be inner-controlled.

Inner control is hampered by two common obstacles. *First,* the person may believe that he will outgrow undesirable personality traits or that he has inherited the traits and can do nothing to change them. Either of these beliefs will weaken his motivation and limit the amount of effort he is willing to put forth. As Kelly has pointed out, "One *can* change if one tries hard enough," but weakened motivation militates against trying (103).

Second, the person may get discouraged if he expects to be able to make a change quickly. Learning and relearning are long processes, even when motivation is strong. If the person does not recognize this, his discouragement will weaken his motivation. Then he will not "try hard enough."

Persistence of environment and roles During the early, formative years of life, when the foundations of the personality pattern are laid, the person's environment remains relatively unchanged. Within his environment, the person is expected to play certain roles and these roles remain persistent. In the home, he may be expected to play the role of "big brother" to his younger siblings, and this he will be expected to do so long as he remains under the parental roof. If the peer group assigns him the role of "follower," its members will expect him to play that role and are not likely to assign him the role of "leader." These roles constrain him to follow a consistent pattern, and he comes to think of himself in terms of these roles.

If changes are to be made in the individual's personality pattern, his environment and his roles must be changed. Psychotherapists try to accomplish this by getting the significant people in the environment to adopt different attitudes toward the person, to treat him more favorably, and to assign him new roles. If they are successful, changes will take place. If they meet with resistance, the chances of a significant change in the personality pattern are negligible.

Dangers in radical change At any age, one or two traits that are proving to be a social or personal handicap can be modified without any real danger to the personality pattern. Trying to revamp the entire personality pattern so that it will conform to parental standards, match the personality pattern of an admired and successful person, or approximate the individual's own ideal self is extremely dangerous.

The personality pattern is an integrated whole, especially after the early years of childhood, and any attempt to change it radically can upset the balance. Here is what Breckenridge and Vincent (25) say:

The very stability of a central core of personality around which habits and attitudes achieve a working balance in any given personality proves to be the reason we cannot, or should not try to make over basic traits in any personality unless we have the help of highly trained specialists. To change any basic trait without due regard for the other traits, habits, and attitudes which balance this trait may be to invite disaster through a serious disturbance in the total personality balance.

Changes can be made with relative safety while the person is still young and while the self-concept is still in the process of formation. Even then, it is not the wishes of others that should be considered, but the person's own physiologic and psychologic constitution.

In every personality pattern, as was stressed earlier, there is a "point of fixity beyond which change cannot be effected" (165). The individual's personality pattern is uniquely his own. And while the pattern can be changed, it can also be upset if the delicate balance of the pattern is disturbed. The limits of change vary from one person to another and from one age to another in the same person. Consequently, it is impossible to change different personality patterns in the same degree.

SUMMARY

1 Traditional beliefs about personality persistence are based on the assumption that personality is inherited and, therefore, like other inherited traits, such as physique and intelligence, is subject to only minor change. Traditional beliefs about change are based on the assumption that physical and personality changes go hand in hand, with physical changes bringing about personality changes.

2 Persistence—which means enduring or constantly recurring—does not mean that the personality pattern is fixed, but rather that certain traits tend to remain in a relatively unchanged form. Change—which means to alter or to vary—is not synonymous with improvement because change can be either for the better or for the worse.

3 Quantitative changes, or changes of degree in different traits, are more common than qualitative changes, or the replacement of one trait with another. What appears to be a change in personality may merely be a front in the sense that the person cloaks socially undesirable traits to create a more favorable impression in the minds of others.

4 Because of practical as well as scientific interest in knowing whether the personality pattern is persistent or subject to change, many attempts have been made to determine with scientific accuracy just how persistent the personality pattern is. These attempts have been handicapped by the problem of methodology.

5 Only when the longitudinal method, which measures changes in the same group of people over a span of years, can be used is there reliable evidence of the degree of persistence that exists. Major obstacles to the use of this method include the difficulty of following the same subjects over a long period, keeping accurate records of any changes that occur and the possible reasons for them, and the assessment of the meaning of recorded evidence by different experimenters.

6 Because of these methodological difficulties, most of the studies of persistence and change have covered relatively short periods. Studies of short-term persistence are usually concentrated on years that are relatively easy to study, owing to the availability of the subjects: from the preschool years to junior high school, from junior through senior high school, or from high school through college. Many studies have concentrated on patterns of maladjustive behavior because of the availability of accurate clinical records.

7 The few studies of long-term persistence that have been made to date, like those of short-term persistence, show that relatively minor changes occur in either self-concepts or the person's characteristic method of adjusting to life. Persistence develops during the early years of life and is facilitated by the strength of the hereditary foundations, by the consistency of the child-training methods used, by the stability of the attitudes of the users of the child-training methods, by the stability of the social environment, and by repetition of experiences, especially in the roles played by the person in the environment.

8 Persistence varies within the personality pattern, with the self-concept more persistent than the traits and with the traits based on hereditary foundations more persistent than those due primarily to learning.

9 Long before childhood is over, most children want to change their personalities because they recognize what a handicap to favorable social judgments and to social acceptance unfavorable personality traits can be. This provides the necessary motivation to try to change the personality pattern. Some changes are for the better, and others are for the worse; some are quantitative and some are qualitative; and some occur slowly while others occur rapidly. Very rapid changes are usually regarded as danger signals of personality disorders.

10 Changes in personality are more frequent and more pronounced in the early years of life, in outer-directed as compared with inner-directed people, in members of the male sex, in firstborns, in different traits as compared with the self-concept; and in a changing as compared with a stable environment.

11 Many conditions have been reported to be responsible for personality changes. They include physical changes, environmental changes, changes in significant people in the person's life, changes in social pressures, changes in roles, strong motivation, changes in the self-concept, and the use of psychotherapy.

12 Longitudinal studies suggest that once a change has been made in the personality pattern it is likely to be persistent. However, persistence varies, depending on whether the person wanted to make the change or resisted it. Resisted changes tend to be transitory; the person reverts to his former self-concept and characteristic methods of adjusting to life.

13 The most important practical implications of knowing whether personality is persistent or subject to change are: the need to establish good foundations; the usefulness of being able to predict later adjustments on the basis of past adjustments; the desirability of correcting maladjustments early before they develop into habitual patterns of reaction; the need to understand that changes must be inner-controlled and cannot be imposed from without; the need to recognize that, so long as the social environment and the roles played by the person persist, there will be persistence in the personality pattern; and the necessity of understanding the dangers involved in trying to make radical changes in the personality pattern at any age, but especially after the early years of childhood.

PART **TWO** **personality
determinants**

In all sciences, theories are expounded, sometimes by recognized authorities and sometimes by relatively unknown scholars seeking to present the results of their thinking to the members of their profession or discipline. Theories are, for the most part, based on research studies, sometimes after years of painstaking experimentation and sometimes after only superficial experimentation.

If theories attract the attention of other scientists, they have great value. Their value is not only that they contribute new information but that they motivate other scientists to investigate the area of knowledge of the theory to prove or disprove it. Without new theories to stimulate further research, scientific knowledge would tend to become stagnant.

The many and often conflicting theories advanced to explain what determines the personality pattern have been a great spur to research in the area of personology. As Harsh and Schrickel[1] have said:

. . . No one theory of personality has accrued to it such a wealth of evidence as to pre-empt all others from the field. . . . The beginner in personality study has, then, this choice before him: he must decide which of the suggested orientations to personality theorizing promises maximum stimulation and guidance in his continuing effort to understand personality. It is not his problem at this point to decide which is the theory of personality.

Many of the theories expounded in the past followed the lead of Hippocrates, who believed that physical factors were the primary determinants of personality. In more recent times, theories based on research findings have stressed factors other than the physical. It would be impossible to review all the theories that have attracted scientific attention. Therefore, only the best known and most influential of those emphasizing the conditions that determine the pattern of personality will be discussed here.

From the time of the ancient Greeks, there have been theories to explain the relationship between

[1]C. M. Harsh and H. G. Schrickel, *Personality: Development and assessment,* 2d ed. New York: Ronald, 1958.

personality and the body.[2] Some theories assume that a particular body build, or "physique," is associated with a characteristic personality pattern. Other theories relate the personality pattern to the functioning of the body. Most of these theories, even those of the ancient Greeks, were derived from studies of abnormal body functioning or atypical physiques. Studying the abnormal was believed to offer a better opportunity to see just how the body affects the person's characteristic method of responding to environmental stimuli under normal conditions. This belief was based on the assumption that there is a quantitative rather than a qualitative difference between normal and abnormal. Studying the abnormal or atypical body under normal conditions would be similar to studying the normal body under a microscope.

Each of the theories in this group that has received widespread attention and acceptance has assumed that the body is primarily responsible for the personality pattern and has ignored social, cultural, and other environmental influences. Thus, they imply that the effect of the body on personality is direct and that any possible indirect influences, stemming from the person's attitude toward his body, can be ignored. A examination of a few of the best-known theories in this group will be sufficient to demonstrate their emphasis.

Kretschmer[3] evolved a theory of the relationship between physique and personality based on his observations of patients in mental hospitals. According to his theory, there are three main types of "habitus" or body build: the pyknic, the asthenic or leptosomic, and the athletic. A fourth type, the *dysplastic,* is a mixture of the other three.

According to Kretschmer's theory, the *pyknic* has a body build characterized by rounded contours; he has a short neck, fat face, broad trunk, and short arms and legs; and he has a tendency to put on weight. The *asthenic* is lean and angular, with long arms and legs, while the *athletic* is intermediate in build, with pronounced musculature. Kretschmer first observed exaggerated personality patterns associated with these body builds among mental patients. Schizophrenic patients were found generally to have the asthenic build while those suffering from manic-depressive psychosis were of the pyknic type.

The theory holds that similar personality patterns are found in the normal person, only in less exaggerated form. Asthenics tend to have autistic or introverted personalities. They draw away from social contacts, fail to react with normal emotions to members of the family and friends, are shy, sulky, lacking in humor, and are insensitive toward the feelings of others but oversensitive about the way others treat them. These people Kretschmer called the "schizoid type" or the "schizothyme."

Pyknics, by contrast, tend to be extroverted or "cyclic," with oscillation of mood and cycles of depression and elation alternating with normal mood states. In the elated state, they are jolly, cheerful, and sociable, but this mood is soon replaced by a state of depression in which they are quiet, calm, and moody. This type Kretschmer called "cycloid" or "cyclothyme."

Studies of photographs of college students and careful measurements of body builds led **Sheldon**[4] to classify people into three body types: endomorphs, ectomorphs, and mesomorphs. The *endomorph* is a heavy-set person; he tends to be obese and has a prominent abdomen and weak, flabby muscles. The *ectomorph* creates the impression of being fragile, weak and delicate because of his long, slender, and poorly muscled arms and legs, his delicate hair and skin, and a tendency to be stoop-shouldered. The *mesomorph,* by contrast, has a body build in which muscles and bones are prominent, thus creating the impression that he is strong and vigorous.

With each of these body types, Sheldon associated a distinctive personality pattern characterized by a constellation of traits. These three constellations he labeled viscerotonia, associated with endomorphs; cerebrotonia, associated with ectomorphs; and somatotonia, associated with mesomorphs.

The constellation of traits Sheldon associated with *viscerotonia* includes love of comfort, food, affection, and people; tendency to relaxation, sociability, conviviality; home-loving and placid. The pattern of *cerebrotonia,* associated with the body build of the ectomorph, is characterized by a predominance of restraint, inhibition, and desire for concealment and solitude, especially when troubled. The personality traits found among the mesomorphs, the *somatotonia*

[2]R. H. Major, *A history of medicine.* Springfield, Ill.: Charles C Thomas, 1954, vol. 1.
[3]E. Kretschmer, *Physique and character.* New York: Harcourt, Brace, 1926.

[4]W. H. Sheldon and S. S. Stevens, *The varieties of temperament.* New York: Harper, 1942. W. H. Sheldon, C. W. Dupertuis, and E. McDermott, *Atlas of man and a guide for somatotyping the adult male at all ages.* New York: Harper, 1954.

constellation, are bodily assertiveness; love of action, risk, and thrills; craving for muscular activity; aggressiveness; and lust for power.

The first recorded theory of the importance of bodily functioning on personality was that of **Hippocrates,**[5] who lived in Greece during the 5th century B.C. According to Hippocrates, people differ not only in body build but also in temperament. Variations, he explained, are the result of a persistent improper balance of the four body fluids or "humors": blood, black bile, yellow bile, and phlegm.

The "sanguine type" is characterized by a predominance of *blood* and is warmhearted, quick, pleasant, and emotionally excitable. *Black bile* is responsible for the "melancholic type," who is easily depressed and experiences slow, deep, and unpleasant emotions. Phobias or abnormal fears are attributed to a predominance of black bile. A predominance of *yellow bile* causes the "choleric type," who is easily angered and who experiences quick, strong, and unpleasant emotional excitement. The "phlegmatic type," who has a predominance of *phlegm,* has a personality constellation characterized by apathy and slow, weak, pleasant, and calm emotionality.

In recent years, medical knowledge of the endocrine glands, especially the effects of endocrine deficiency, has led to a number of attempts to explain personality in terms of the predominance of one or more of the glands of the endocrine system. Perhaps the best known of these theories is that of **Berman.**[6]

Starting out with medical evidence of the physical and psychological effects of deficiency of the different glands of the endocrine system, Berman attempted to show how personality characteristics were associated with hypo- or hyperfunctioning of the glands. Berman theorized that the typical feminine personality pattern, characterized by heightened emotionality, restlessness, and a craving for excitement and change, is a product of an excess of the hormone from the posterior lobe of the pituitary gland.

The typical masculine personality pattern, characterized by mastery of self and the environment, is by contrast the product of an excess of the hormone from the anterior lobe of the pituitary. People with a "magnetic personality," bubbling with vitality, have an excess of hormone from the thyroid glands. Berman[7] writes:

A restless, inexhaustible energy makes them perpetual doers and workers, who get up early in the morning, flit about all day, retire late, and frequently suffer from insomnia, planning in bed what they are to do the next day.

Antisocial behavior, in the form of juvenile delinquency and adult criminality, has been explained in terms of body build and chromosome makeup. According to **Sheldon,**[8] juvenile delinquents are endomorphic mesomorphs, with emphasis on mesomorphy. A report from a hospital for the criminally insane in Scotland has in more recent years given rise to a theory that genetic abnormality is linked to violent crimes. According to this theory, men who have an extra Y chromosome tend to be not only aggressive but also dull. This predisposes them to crimes of violence.

A theory of "organ inferiority" set forth by **Adler**[9] claims that a physical defect, whether it be lameness, blindness, or inferior stature, spurs the individual to compensate by developing a pattern of behavior that will relieve the tension and stress accompanying an inferiority complex caused by organ inferiority. He thus theorizes that the characteristic personality pattern of the person with an inferiority complex is due to physical, not psychological, causes.

One of the best-known of the theories that do not emphasize the role played by the physique or body functioning is that of **Freud.**[10] According to him, instincts are the propelling factors of personality. They drive behavior and also determine the direction that behavior will take. While the person can be activated by factors in the outside world, Freud claimed, these are less powerful driving forces than inborn instincts.

Freud claims that all human behavior is controlled by two basic general drives that are a part of the hereditary endowment. These two drives are *Eros,* the life instinct, and *Thanatos,* the death instinct. One very important aspect of Eros is the "libido," the drive that motivates all kinds of pleasure-seeking activities, everything generally called "love," such as self-love,

[5]Major, op cit.
[6]L. M. Berman, *The glands regulating personality.* New York: Macmillan, 1928.

[7]Ibid.
[8]Sheldon, op cit.
[9]A. Adler, *Individual psychology.* New York: Harcourt, Brace, 1924.
[10]S. Freud, *The standard edition of the complete psychological works of Sigmund Freud.* London: Hogarth, 1953–1962.

love for parents, love of mankind, and the love expressed in sexual union.

In the normal pattern of development, the object of affection shifts with age. But the normal pattern may be interfered with, and development is then arrested. Interference may come from the environment, as when a child's love for his mother is rejected, or it may come from within the person, as when lack of self-confidence motivates the person to cling to old and established patterns instead of trying to develop new ones.

When the normal pattern of libido shift is interfered with, it leads to personality problems, the type and severity of which depend on the kind of interference and its effect on the libido. The libido may be turned inward and directed into fantasies (introversion); it may cling to infantile love objects (fixation); it may be dammed up so that no expression occurs (repression); it may flow backward to earlier love objects (regression); or it may be directed into socially desirable, altruistic channels (sublimation). Freud maintained that neuroticism and personality disorders can be traced either to failure to advance to a mature stage in libidinal development or to regression to an earlier age where the individual derives greater satisfaction than he is able to derive from a more mature stage.

In an attempt to explain the emotional coloring of the personality pattern and the tendency to excessive anxiety which is at the basis of neuroticism, **Rank**[11] expounded his theory of the "birth trauma." According to this theory, the shock of birth creates a reservoir of anxiety which lays the foundation for anxiety throughout life. The anxiety created by the trauma of birth is accompanied by a desire to return to the safety and protection of the womb.

The separation anxiety experienced by every newborn infant Rank called the "primal anxiety." This, he claimed, is the most important element for the future development of the person and is also a source of potential neurosis as the person grows older. All that happens after the separation from the mother at birth is simply an expression of the primal anxiety.

As Rank expressed it, "The pleasurable primal state is interrupted through the act of birth." As a result of the anxieties initiated by the shock of birth, the person will, so long as he lives, have an unconscious yearning to return to the safety and security that the womb provided during the prenatal period.

In recent years, a number of social-psychological theories about personality determinants have attracted scientific attention. These theories stress influences that were largely disregarded in many of the psychoanalytical theories. **Freud**[12] stressed the decisive role the early years of life play in laying down the basic character structure of personality. By the time the child is 8 years old, he claimed, the foundations of the pattern have been so well formed that changes thereafter will be slight.

Adler,[13] like Freud, emphasized the early years, placing special emphasis, however, on such factors as order of birth and the degree of domination of parents resulting from the child's ordinal position. The firstborn, he contended, becomes the most conservative because he is most dominated by his parents. Furthermore, being dethroned from his position of center of attention by the arrival of a new baby gives the firstborn feelings of anxiety and insecurity. The lastborn of the family is less dominated by parents and more likely to be spoiled. He is apt to go through life expecting everybody to "baby" him. It is because of these early experiences, Adler claimed, that everyone develops a unique personality.

Horney[14] not only emphasized the importance of early social-psychological experiences in the shaping of the normal personality but she also explained how they can lead to neurosis. According to Horney, a neurotic personality develops primarily from mishandling by parents during the person's childhood. If the child is bullied, for example, intimidated, or rejected by family members on whom he is dependent for love and security, he will become oppressed by a "basic anxiety." Furthermore, the competitive nature of the culture in which he grows up encourages him to develop unrealistic conceptions of himself which, in his struggles to attain, further increase his basic anxiety.

Like Horney, **Sullivan**[15] has stressed that the basic motivations that help to shape the personality pattern are not instinctual, as Freud claimed, but come from the satisfaction of the child's biological needs and his seeking for security. If the child is praised, approved, and accepted by his parents, he experiences a feeling of well-being or "euphoria." Unpleasant experiences resulting from parental disapproval or rejection lead to early anxieties. Derived, or

[11]O. Rank, The trauma of birth. New York: Harcourt, Brace & World, 1929.

[12]Freud, op. cit.
[13]Adler, op. cit.
[14]K. Horney, Neurosis and human growth. New York: Norton, 1950.
[15]H. S. Sullivan, The interpersonal theory of psychiatry. New York: Norton, 1953.

secondary, anxieties then occur when dissociated thoughts and feelings threaten to alter the self-system. Since the self-system has within it tendencies for its own perpetuation, rigidity begins to characterize the personality pattern at an early age, making the occurrence of further anxiety states more likely. These may, in time, lead to neurosis.

Cultural anthropologists, like Benedict and Mead, have emphasized the dominant influence of social-cultural factors on the development of the personality pattern. Benedict[16] explained the influence of early experiences in her theory of "continuities and discontinuities." According to this theory, normal, healthy personality patterns develop when child training is continuous and when the child is not forced to behave or to think of himself in one way when he is young and then, as he reaches puberty, behave and think of himself in another way. Personality problems, anxieties, neuroses, and psychoses, according to Benedict, are in part the result of discontinuities in child training.

In addition to emphasizing the impact of parental child-training methods on the personality during the early, formative years, Mead[17] stressed the importance of training children to play culturally approved sex roles. Sex-appropriate behavior earns social approval and thus leads to a favorable self-concept.

The true value of the theories briefly outlined here lies in the motivation they have provided for further research into how the personality pattern develops and what factors affect its development. In Chapters 6 to 13, an attempt has been made to survey as many as possible of the research studies carried out to determine what factors in a person's life—either hereditary or environmental—are responsible for influencing his self-concept and his characteristic pattern of adjusting to life.

Chapter 6, Physical Determinants, emphasizes that physique and body functioning are without question directly responsible for personality development. However, modern research studies have pointed out that physical factors have an equal or even greater indirect effect. They influence the self-concept when the person compares his physique with that of his ideal, when he compares his physique with the culturally approved standards for sex-appropriate physiques, and when he becomes aware of the reactions of members of the social group to his physique.

While a few theories regard physical defects as important personality determinants—notably Adler's theory of organ inferiority—most have ignored the impact of physical defects. Research studies have shown that in childhood they have a direct influence on personality, and later on, they have an indirect influence through the effect they have on the attitudes of group members toward the handicapped person.

None of the important theories of personality determinants stresses the role played by intelligence. In Chapter 7, Intellectual Determinants, the reports of research studies in this area are examined to see if ignoring this determinant was justified. The examination has led to the conclusion that intellectual determinants are far too important to be ignored. Intellectual capacities, it is found, influence personality directly through the effect they have on the person's adjustments to life and his evaluation of his adjustments, and indirectly, through the effect they have on the person's self-concept via his awareness of how others judge him and his adjustments to life.

Also ignored in the major theories of personality determinants is the influence intellectual capacities have on the person's values, interests, morality, and humor—all of which are aspects of his personality pattern that affect his adjustment to life. While several theories of personality determinants, notably Sheldon's theory of somatotypes, have referred to the influence of physique on deviant moral behavior in the form of delinquency and criminality, none has pointed out that a morally deviant personality pattern may result from intellectual and social factors.

Rank, Horney, and Sullivan have indicated the influence of anxiety on the personality pattern, but none of the major theories has considered the role of the other emotions in determining personality. In Chapter 8, Emotional Determinants, research studies in this area have been reviewed to show how other emotions affect personal and social adjustments. The chapter stresses the direct effects of the emotions as well as the indirect, resulting from the way members of the social group react to the person's emotional behavior. Even more important, research studies have revealed that the dominant emotions developed by the person as a result of emotional and interpersonal experiences determine what his moods and temperament will be—aspects of his personality that color his characteristic adjustments to life.

[16] R. Benedict, *Patterns of culture.* Boston: Houghton Mifflin, 1934.
[17] M. Mead, *The cultural approach to personality.* In P. L. Harriman (ed.), *Encyclopedia of psychology.* New York: Philosophical Library, 1946, pp. 477–488.

In recent years, the important role the emotions play as personality determinants has been highlighted by studies of emotional deprivation, especially during the early, formative years. While some of the theories of personality have indirectly implied that anxiety comes from an unfavorable emotional climate in the home, none have emphasized the effect of the home on other emotions.

Some of the psychoanalytic theories of personality determinants, notably those of Freud and Adler, emphasize the role the family, or the "primary group," plays in personality development, but none refer to the role of social groups outside the home. This is also true of social-psychological theories of such cultural anthropologists as Benedict and Mead.

In Chapter 9, Social Determinants, the findings of research studies on the effects of social factors on the developing personality pattern are analyzed. Studies of the influence of social expectations, early social experiences both within and outside the home, social deprivation, social acceptance, the roles of leader and follower, and upward and downward social mobility—all show that social factors are strong personality determinants.

In an achievement-oriented culture, success and failure have a profound influence on personality, both directly, through the effect on the person's self-evaluation, and indirectly, through the evaluation others make of him. The major theories have either ignored or touched too briefly on this area to suggest what a significant personality determinant achievement motivation is.

Chapter 10, Aspirations and Achievements, covers the high points of the recent research in this area. It shows how aspirations are formed and explains why they tend to be unrealistic. Studies of achievement have shown that both success and failure are judged from the frame of reference of the individual himself. If he has high aspirations, what others judge as "success" he may judge as "failure" or "near failure." If his aspirations are low, he may look with pride upon what others judge a failure.

Valuable as these findings are to an understanding of how the self-concept develops, they are also useful as a source of evidence to counteract Adler's theory of organ inferiority. Unquestionably, some inferiority complexes are rooted in physical defects or physical weaknesses. But "organ inferiority" is by no means the only or even the chief cause of inferiority complexes. This has been amply proved by the many research studies of how aspirations influence the person's interpretation of his achievements as "successes" or "failures."

Freud first noted the importance of sex as a personality determinant and placed it in the spotlight of scientific attention. Later Mead emphasized that acceptance or rejection of the culturally approved sex role affects the person's personal and social adjustments. Recent studies, described and evaluated in Chapter 11, Sex Determinants, have substantiated the facts on which these theories were based.

None of the major theories of personality determinants mention that school or college may influence the developing personality pattern. And yet, in view of the amount of time young people spend in school and college and the emphasis placed on academic success or failure as a determinant of future life patterns, the school is secondary only to the home as an influence on how the person evaluates himself.

Chapter 12, Educational Determinants, explores some of the ways in which schools and colleges influence personality development. These include attitudes toward education and toward school as they are affected by early school experiences and by the attitudes of significant people in the child's life, attitudes toward the child and his treatment by teachers and peers, grades and academic honors, under- and overachievement, and the kind of school or college the person attends.

A number of theories of personality determinants, including some of the psychoanalytic and social-psychological theories, have emphasized the important role played by the family, especially parents, in shaping the personality pattern. There has also been emphasis on the roles played by child-training methods and ordinal position within the family.

Research studies in this area have been numerous and varied. The findings of many of the studies are summarized and analyzed in Chapter 13, Family Determinants. As a result of these studies, it is now apparent that family determinants are actually more important than the theories suggested and that many other areas of family life besides those stressed in the theories are crucial.

In conclusion, the reader is urged to note, in each chapter of this part of the book, how the theories of personality determinants have helped to broaden and increase our knowledge of the factors responsible for shaping the personality pattern. Try to imagine how limited the knowledge of personality determinants would be had there been no theories to spur scientific research.

physical determinants

It has been pointed out that the individual's "personal world" is central in the development of his personality. And "one object which is ever-present in this personal world is the body" (204). That the body influences personality is not a new concept. It goes back to ancient times. Today, however, there is even greater recognition of the influence of the body than in the past. It is now known that body size and functioning influence not only the quality and quantity of behavior, but also the "body image," or the way a person sees his body in relation to his ideal, in relation to the culturally approved pattern, and in relation to the way others see it.

Meyerson stressed this point of view when he claimed that the person's physique may influence behavior by mediating the effectiveness of the body as a tool for action or by serving as a stimulus to the self and others (159). This means, in brief, that the body influences the personality pattern both directly and indirectly.

Directly, the body influences personality by determining what a person can do and cannot do. Temporarily unfavorable physical states, such as fatigue, illness, or pain, will modify characteristic patterns of adjustment. Serious organic defects or weaknesses, especially those which affect the nervous system or the balance of the endocrine system, decrease the person's ability to make integrative adjustments to life; they present adjustment problems that differ markedly from those faced by people whose bodies function normally.

Indirectly, a person's adjustments to life are influenced by the way he perceives his body in relation to the bodies of others, his ideal as well as culturally approved standards, and by the evaluation of his physical abilities and disabilities by others. These perceptions shape his adjustive experiences. How this is done has been explained by Shaffer and Shoben (206):

A puny boy is likely to develop different preferred mechanisms than a strong, healthy child, because he has different experiences. Anxiety provoked by threatening diseases or disabling symptoms may lead to defensive or nonadjustive behavior. In such cases, a person's structure or physiology frustrates his mo-

tives, creates conflicts, and shapes the experiences through which he learns his adjustments. The precipitating events are physiological but the adjustive process is psychological.

Awareness of his physical superiority, inferiority, or equality thus influences the way a person evaluates himself because he knows that is how others evaluate him. As Thompson has pointed out, "Children may suffer emotionally from being a 'Shrimp,' 'Tubby,' 'Redhead,' or 'Bucktooth.' The taunt, 'Brown eyes turn around and tell a lie' can leave permanent psychological scars" (227).

In some areas, the direct influence of the physical determinants is greater than the indirect. This is true in the functioning of the endocrine glands. In other areas, the indirect influence is greater. Physical attractiveness, for example, does not directly affect the quality of a person's adjustments to life, but it has a profound indirect influence. The importance of the direct and indirect influences will be discussed in connection with each area of physical determinants.

TRADITIONAL BELIEFS ABOUT BODILY EFFECTS

There are many traditional beliefs about the influence of facial features, body build, and body functioning on personality. Aristotle claimed that different facial characteristics, such as the color and texture of the skin and hair; the quality of the voice; the condition of the flesh; and the build of the body are related to certain personality characteristics. Facial features, he claimed, are the most accurate bodily indications of personality.

Through the years, the tradition that specific personality characteristics are associated with different body builds grew up. The rotund build, for example, was associated with the good "mixer"—the easygoing person who gets along well with people, is diplomatic, and lively. By contrast, people with thin, lanky builds were believed to be moody, introverted, and unsocial. As Shakespeare expressed these traditional beliefs through Caesar:

Let me have men about me that are fat,
Sleek-headed men, and such as sleep o' nights.
Yond Cassius has a lean and hungry look;
He thinks too much, such men are dangerous.

Being able to classify people into personality types on the basis of facial features or body builds has a strong popular appeal because it provides an anchorage point for understanding and predicting behavior. As Hilgard has remarked, "If we know what to expect from fat people or from thin people or from red-headed people, then we can size up strangers and prepare ourselves to meet them on their own ground" (90).

Everyday observations of people reveal that there is a relationship between the body build of a person, his energy level, and his general health condition and the quality of his behavior. This has strengthened the traditional belief that there is a relationship between the body and the personality pattern.

This belief has been further strengthened by evidence from studies of atypical body builds and abnormal body functioning. Studies of the personality patterns of people with some atypical body condition, whether it be in structure or function, have revealed how close the relationship between the body condition and the personality pattern is (159). Even though present evidence indicates that the relationship is indirect rather than direct—in that the personality pattern is influenced by social attitudes toward the body defect—the relationship is strong enough to justify the belief that the body plays a role of major importance in personality development.

Personal observation and traditional beliefs about physical structures and functions and theories about how the body influences personality have stimulated scientific interest. As a result of research studies, there is evidence that body influences are as great as Aristotle claimed centuries ago, but that the influences are of a different kind than was formerly recognized. In the following pages of this chapter, the important findings of these studies will be reported, grouped according to kind of body influences.

BODY BUILD

Ever since the time of Hippocrates, there has been speculation about the relationship between the shape of the person's body—his body build in terms of height and weight—and his behavior. Many recent theories have likewise emphasized this relationship (109).

The influence of body build on personality is both direct and indirect. Whether the direct influence is greater than the indirect is still subject to question and controversy. In fact, it is closely related to the controversy over the relative importance of heredity and environment.

Many of the early theories about the determinants of personality stressed the direct influence of body build. And since body build is largely a product of heredity, it is logical that they would conclude that the personality patterns associated with particular body builds were likewise hereditary.

More recently, Sheldon, while stressing the relationship between body build and personality, emphasized the role of body build as a condition of adjustment to life. He thus suggested that the influence of body build on personality is both direct and indirect (207). That the indirect influence may be even more important than the direct has been suggested by Shaffer and Shoben (206):

Physique may well be one of the secondary determinants of personality, because it sets certain limitations to adjustive learning, and influences the social evaluations which a person receives from his fellows. A strong, muscular boy may develop self-confidence because he is successful in athletics, resulting in his acceptance by his schoolmates. A fragile and delicate youngster, under the conditions prevailing in our culture, has a more than average likelihood of learning to withdraw from social contacts. Perhaps all that is significant in the theories of physical habitus is adequately summarized by the old saying that a fat boy has to be good-natured because he can't fight and he can't run.

Direct influence

The direct influence of body build on personality is seen in the manner in which it determines what a person can and cannot do, his energy level, and his reactions to other people whose body builds are superior or inferior to his. In each instance, it helps him to evaluate himself either favorably or unfavorably.

Effect of body build on activities A person with a small, delicate body build or one with a heavyset, flabby body with little muscular development is handicapped in many sports which in childhood and adolescence have high prestige value. When he compares what he can do with what his age-mates can do, he is likely to develop feelings of inadequacy and inferiority—feelings which are reflected in unfavorable self-concepts.

How body build affects the person's activities has been shown in tests of strength and motor capacity. People with tall, thin body builds—the *ectomorphs*—have been reported to be superior to those with round, soft builds—the *endomorphs*—in speed, agility, and endurance. On the other hand, the *mesomorphs*—those with strong, muscular builds—are superior to both the endomorphs and the ectomorphs in activities involving speed, agility, and endurance. The excess weight of the endomorph and the insufficient strength of the ectomorph are a handicap in many activities in which they must compete with those whose bodies are strong and muscular (210).

The body build of the person affects his self-concept favorably if it permits him to do things that are prestigious as well as or better than others. It affects his self-concept unfavorably if what he can do has little prestige in the eyes of the social group. If he expends his energy on useful, prestigious activities, the effect on his self-concept will be more favorable than if he expends it in restless, random, meaningless activities that are annoying to others. The influence of body build is emphasized by Biller and Borstelmann (20):

A boy could have a very available masculine and nurturant father, as well as a mother who encouraged masculine behavior, but be limited in the development of a masculine adoption by inadequate or inappropriate physical status. Though mesomorphy per se is not sufficient to produce masculinity, a mesomorphic physique seems better suited for success in most masculine activities than one that is not, and parents and others seem to expect more masculine behavior from a mesomorphic boy than they do from a non-mesomorphic boy. . . . The tall and husky or mesomorphic boy may, even without the encouragement of parents, find success easier in masculine activities so that he is seen by others, and consequently learns to see himself, as very masculine. The frail ectomorph or pudgy endomorph may find such success difficult.

Effect of body build on energy level

Body build influences the person's energy level and this, in turn, affects the characteristic quality of his behavior. The endomorph, with his heavyset build, tends to be slow in his reactions, apathetic, and deliberate—the "easy-going type" who fails to see any necessity of hurrying or of becoming emotionally disturbed. In play, endomorphic children do not exert themselves any more than is necessary (32, 185). That this is directly related to their body builds has been emphasized by Davidson et al.: "The anxious mother of an endomorphic child may possibly derive some consolation from realizing that her failure to make the child as careful as she would like arises, not from her own shortcoming, but from the fact that the child is just not built that way" (55).

By contrast, a person with a thin, wiry build is usually nervous and excitable, often doing less and making more mistakes than the person who moves more slowly and deliberately. Between these two extremes is the person with a heavy, well-muscled body. He is both energetic and efficient. Because he is able to accomplish more with less effort, he generally develops a favorable self-concept which is expressed in dynamic, assertive, and dominant behavior.

Energy level follows a predictable pattern that is influenced not only by body build but also by age and health. The energy level of children is normally above that of adults. Furthermore, children seem to have more energy than they actually have because they do not know how to harness it for useful purposes or do not have opportunities to use their energy in work or play because of environmental restrictions. As a result, they expend it in restlessness and squirming (65, 141, 226).

When boys and girls reach puberty, with its rapid growth spurt, their energy level drops. Much of their time is spent in lolling around. As the puberty growth slows down, they resume their earlier activities, suggesting a rise in their energy levels (60, 72, 75, 149).

During the early years of adulthood, the energy level is high for both men and women. This is the time when, if their energy is harnessed and controlled, they can undertake activities which require prolonged periods of great energy expenditure and can achieve success because they have control over the use of their energy. As the body loses its strength and energy with aging, men and women find that the quality and quantity of their output decrease. This results in a tendency to react apathetically and deliberately, to show less enthusiasm for things they formerly enjoyed, and to withdraw from social contacts where they will have to compete with younger people.

The general health condition, whether physical or mental, likewise influences the energy level. When a person is not up to par physically, his energy level drops and this is reflected in listlessness and loss of enthusiasm. Much of the boredom pubescents show, for example, is due to the fact that rapid physical growth has temporarily sapped their energy.

How markedly energy level affects personality has been shown in studies of those whose energy level is low. Children with low energy level are shy, depressed, irritable, reserved, and unsocial. One of the causes for the irritability, stubbornness, depression, and other antisocial patterns of behavior characteristic of the elderly comes from decline in energy level with advancing age (22, 150).

Effect of body build on reactions to others   How a person reacts to others is greatly influenced by his body build compared with theirs. As Staffieri has pointed out, "The role of an individual's body configuration in social interactions and the effects of these interactions on self-concept is an important part of the total process of personality development" (219).

If a person is smaller or fatter than those with whom he is associated, he feels inferior. As a result, he is either shy and retiring, in order to make himself inconspicuous, or troublesome and obstreperous, in order to attract attention. If he is larger than the people he is with, but not too much larger, he will feel superior. Often he will express his feeling of superiority by bullying, teasing, and dominating those whom he regards as his inferiors.

Indirect influence

Indirectly, body build influences personality through *body cathexis*—the degree of satisfaction a person feels about himself because of some important aspect of his body (108). The indirect effect of body build has been found to be greater than the direct effect. If a person is satisfied with his body, his positive attitudes are expressed in self-confidence, self-assurance, and a generally wholesome self-concept. As Zion has written, "It appears that the security one has in one's body is related to the security with which one faces one's self and the world" (252).

Body cathexis occurs only when a person's body becomes important to him as a symbol of self. And this depends on when and to what degree the person becomes aware of social attitudes toward his body and the effect social attitudes have on the attitudes of others toward him. Only when he discovers that other people think that his body is important does he feel that it is.

Realization of the importance of the body as a symbol by which others judge the individual comes slowly. The young child realizes that his playmates judge him, but their judgment is based on play skills, not on body build. So long as he can play with them in such a way that he will be an enjoyable playmate, his body build is unimportant. Should he be so fat that he cannot keep up to the pace of group play, then he will realize that his body is important. Similarly, a slight deviation from the norm in height will not concern him because it does not affect his play skills or his popularity. Should he, on the other hand, be conspicuously taller than his classmates, he is likely to feel self-conscious and be concerned about whether his classmates and teacher think he is "dumb" because he is so much bigger than the other children in the class.

When the child reaches adolescence, he realizes for the first time that popularity is greatly influenced by appearance and that the size, shape, and sex appropriateness of his body affect his appearance. This realization makes his body important to him because he realizes that it is important to his peers. With this realization comes the full impact of body build on personality.

Sources of satisfaction   There are two sources of body cathexis: satisfaction with one's body because it is judged favorably by others and satisfaction because one's body compares favorably with one's childhood ideal.

JUDGMENTS BY OTHERS   How people judge the bodies of others depends on many factors. *First,* judgments are often based on a cultural stereotype about the "right" body build for members of the two sexes. In our culture, the "right" body build for males is tall, broad-shouldered, narrow-hipped, and well proportioned throughout. The cultural stereotype of the female body is one that is petite, slender, and with an hour-glass shape.

Second, the acceptance of traditional beliefs about the relationship between body build and personality type influences a person's judgments of the personalities of others. The belief that all leaders are larger than the norm for their sex group, for example, will influence the way a person judges the personality pattern of a tall person. Figure 6-1 shows the per-

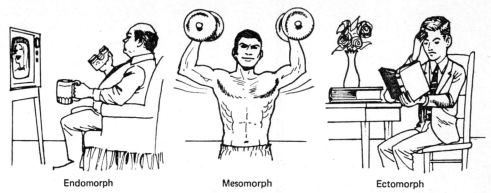

Endomorph   Mesomorph   Ectomorph

Figure 6-1 Personality patterns commonly associated with different body types.

sonality patterns many people associate with different body builds.

Third, judgments of others are influenced by the kind of personality the person has learned to associate with body weight. If he accepts the traditional belief that overweight and good-naturedness go hand in hand, he will judge a fat person as jolly. If from medical, psychiatric, and psychological reports, he has learned to associate fat with maladjustment, however, he will judge a fat person to be one who compensates for feelings of personal inadequacy by overeating.

The *fourth* body-build factor that influences people's judgments of the personality is body shape. Because babies and little children are top-heavy and chubby, it is logical that the association of immaturity and a childish build would develop. A person who tends to be chubby, even in old age, looks younger than a thin person, and this creates the impression in the minds of others that he is younger, both physically and psychologically, than he actually is. The puberty "fat period" creates the impression that the young pubescent is still a child—an impression that causes parents, teachers, and even peers to treat him as such.

Fifth, the belief that above-average size and above-average maturity go hand in hand leads to the judgment that big people are more mature than they actually are. In addition, little people are often judged as "childish." A small woman creates the impression that she is more dependent than a large woman, just as a small man is regarded as less mature and, hence, less equipped for leadership roles than a large man.

Sixth, most people associate the way a person expends his energy with both his maturity and his level of adjustment. People who do not harness their energy for a purposeful goal are regarded as "scatter-brained," while those who do are judged as "efficient"

and "well organized." Similarly, random expenditure of energy, in squirming, restlessness, and horseplay, is regarded as the "exuberance of youth"—a label which indicates a judgment of immaturity. As Eichorn (62) has explained:

Much of the exuberance and impulsivity of the late-maturer, however, may simply be that which is characteristic of most young animals. . . . Unfortunately, these patterns and attitudes, while perhaps appropriate and successful coping devices during childhood and early adolescence, may be maintained when they are no longer adaptive. Attitudes and behavior which were once a function of ability and status have become habitual and now reduce performance and status.

Awareness of judgments by others With social experience, older children and certainly adolescents learn on what basis people judge others. They then realize that they are being judged in the same way. For example, if they are given a derogatory *nickname* by their peers, such as "Fat Potato," "Bean Pole," or "Shorty," they know that their body builds do not conform to the approved pattern.

Critical comments by parents, teachers, and peers tell them how others feel about their bodies. A parent who is constantly telling a boy to "stand up straight" is implying that he will look taller and, hence, more sex-appropriate if he makes full use of his height. Similarly, comments about eating candy and other fattening foods suggest to the person that others think he is too fat.

How a person is *treated* by others gives a clue to how they feel about him. If a boy who is short is constantly turned down when he asks girls for dates, he will conclude, perhaps incorrectly, that girls think he is not "masculine" because he is so short.

Perhaps the most evident clue to how people feel about the child's body is *parental concern*. When a parent talks to a doctor, teacher, friend, or spouse about the child's or adolescent's height or weight, it tells the child or adolescent that something is wrong with him. This, in turn, suggests to him that he will be handicapped throughout life because his body build is not of the "right" type.

CHILDHOOD IDEAL   The second major source of satisfaction a person has with his body comes from a favorable comparison of his body as it is with the ideal body image he built up in childhood. While it is true that most people change their ideal body image as they grow older and as their experience broadens, the essential elements of the childhood ideal are usually persistent.

Far too often, childhood ideals are unrealistic. The child wants to be just the opposite of what he is or he wants to be like someone he admires, regardless of his hereditary potentials. If, for example, his father and mother are both short, the chances are that he has inherited the genes for shortness. Under such conditions, the chances of his being tall, like his ideal, are slight.

That childhood ideals affect a person's satisfaction with his body has been shown in studies in which adult men and women were asked to estimate their own bodies and to tell what they would like to change in them. For the most part, their estimates were less accurate than their estimates of the bodies of others. That they were biased by their childhood ideals was seen by the fact that men tended to see themselves as disproportionally "husky-looking" while women erred in the direction of believing they were more slender than they actually were. In addition, women wanted to lose weight while men wanted to gain weight. Most women wanted to change their bodies from the waist down while men wanted to change theirs from the waist up in the hope of coming closer to their childhood ideal (37).

Sources of dissatisfaction   Few people, after they realize what an important role body build plays in the judgments others make of them, are satisfied with their bodies. The more dissatisfied they are, the more damaging the effects on their personalities. Studies reveal three common and almost universal sources of dissatisfaction with one's body build:

deviations from the body build of age-mates, deviations from one's body ideal, and deviations from a culturally approved build.

DEVIATIONS FROM AGE-MATES   Boys and girls are hypersensitive to being taller or shorter, fatter or thinner, than their age-mates. Bayley (15) writes:

Being different from the group with whom one is thrown is always a possible hazard in social and emotional adjustments, but especially so during the adolescent years of growing into adulthood, when there seems to be a hypersensitivity to any deviations from the accepted norms. The physical differences which are thrust on some children by the mere differences of their velocities of maturing are among these hazards.

At any age, being different in height or weight is a psychological hazard. This is especially true of being overweight because social attitudes toward obesity are highly unfavorable. As most people know, to be fat and 40 is bad enough, but to be fat and 14 is even harder.

The effects of deviating from age-mates in body build is intensified by taunts and treatment that imply peer rejection. This is especially damaging in childhood, when the concept of self is being formed, and when tact is almost nonexistent. As Sontag has explained, "The unconscious cruelty of children toward anyone of them whose body does not conform to theirs in size, form, and function may be an important factor in the emotional adjustment of children lacking this conformity" (218).

DEVIATIONS FROM BODY IDEAL   Even though the body normally improves as the changes of puberty are completed, many people are still dissatisfied because their bodies do not come up to their childhood expectations. Some people adopt a more realistic body ideal, and some learn to use clothing to camouflage their bodies so that they more closely approximate their ideal. Unfortunately, far too many people retain such an unrealistic body ideal that even these adjustments are inadequate to bring them satisfaction. As a result, the gap between their real and ideal physical self-concepts is so wide that it has a detrimental effect on their self-concepts.

DEVIATIONS FROM CULTURALLY APPROVED BODY BUILDS   In a culture where gross size is a "must" for males and petiteness a "must" for females, any deviation from these culturally approved norms leads to personal dissatisfaction. Because Japanese-Americans, for example, are relatively small, many men of Japanese ancestry feel inferior. Even though the culturally approved female body build is petite, many American women of Japanese ancestry likewise feel that they are too short for the American norm (11).

Small boys and men and large girls and women have been reported to show poorer personal and social adjustments than those who more closely approximate the cultural norm. Boys are embarassed when they are with girls who are taller than they; it deflates their feelings of masculine superiority. Girls who are taller than boys have fewer dates than girls who are nearer the cultural norm. These unfavorable attitudes have a marked influence on personality development and carry over into adulthood (16, 122, 201).

Variations in dissatisfaction Studies of dissatisfaction reveal some predictable variations. Dissatisfaction varies according to age, sex, birth order, and personality pattern. Dissatisfaction also varies according to the parts of the body that deviate from the norms of the group.

AGE Adolescents are more concerned when their bodies deviate from the norm than are children because they have learned that body size plays an important role in adolescent social acceptance. This concern continues into adulthood. The adult knows that his appearance, which is greatly influenced by his body size, is important not only to social success but also to success in the business world. By middle age, concern increases when the body begins to become fat over the abdomen and hips. With retirement from business and gradual social disengagement with old age, concern about body build decreases.

SEX Body build, as an aspect of physical attractiveness, is more important in the social world of women and in the roles they play than it is for men. Consequently, from late childhood on, girls and women are more concerned about and less satisfied with their body builds. Because girls tend to have more unrealistic concepts of what they want to look like when they grow up than boys, the gap between their real and ideal self-concepts is wider. In addition, their self-concepts tend to be more definite and stable than those of boys, with the result that they are less likely to narrow the gap between their real and ideal body images (70, 73, 107, 108, 200, 204).

Males tend to accept or reject their bodies *in toto* while females make finer differentiations within their body images and like or dislike different parts of the body. Males are more concerned about height while females are more concerned about weight. While members of both sexes are concerned about the sex appropriateness of their bodies, it is of greater concern to females (16, 37, 70, 107).

Even though girls and women have more opportunity to improve their appearance by camouflaging with clothes the areas they do not like, they still find it difficult to close the gap between what they would like to be and what they know they are. Boys and men, on the other hand, find that clothes do little to improve their body builds so they compensate by trying to achieve success in some area that has high prestige value, such as sports.

Boys who find compensation through achievement impossible may use unsocial forms of compensation. Those with sex-inappropriate body builds, for example, have been reported to be more impulsive and troublesome than boys with sex-appropriate builds (109). Small boys tend to be more rebellious and more personally and socially maladjusted than those whose builds more closely approximate the norm (48). This is true also of late-maturing boys who are, for a time, smaller than their age-mates (106).

Studies reveal that many juvenile delinquents and adult criminals have distorted body images due to their culturally inappropriate body builds (48). This is especially true of boys of lower-class backgrounds who tend, because of poorer nutrition and physical care during childhood, to be shorter than their age-mates from more favored backgrounds. In addition, more pressures from family members and peers are put on them to be aggressive and show their masculinity. This often leads to delinquent behavior (127).

Another common form of compensation for culturally inappropriate bodies used by men is in the selection of a mate. Men with small builds usually marry women smaller than they or women of equal height. When they do not follow this pattern, it is usually because of economic or social considerations (16).

Similarly, girls and women, often engage in maladjustive behavior as a compensation for feelings of inadequacy resulting from inappropriate body builds. Tall girls, for example, are more impulsive and troublesome than girls who are small or of average size (48, 109). Obese women—like the overprotected—are often over-dependent and resentful toward those on whom they depend (110). Tall women sometimes choose short men as husbands so they can compensate for feelings of inadequacy by being the "head of the house" (16).

PERSONALITY PATTERN People who are outer-directed, who are concerned about the attitudes of others and are anxious to win social approval and acceptance, tend to be more affected by their body builds than the inner-directed.

BIRTH ORDER Firstborns are usually more affected by their body builds than later-borns. The greater anxiety and concern firstborns have about their body builds has been explained as part of the "firstborn syndrome" of insecurity and dependency (213).

PARTS OF THE BODY In general, the parts of the body people are most dissatisfied with are those which are least subject to change or camouflage. When a feature of the body cannot be changed, as is true of height, lack of conformity to the cultural ideal has a more damaging effect on personality than nonconformity in a part that can be changed. Dissatisfaction with sex inappropriateness, which is difficult to control, has a very damaging effect on personality.

Realization of how the social group, especially members of the opposite sex, feel about different areas of the body influences the person's attitudes toward those areas. If, for example, women know that men evaluate female attractiveness largely in terms of breast size and leg shape, they tend to be dissatisfied with their entire bodies if their breasts and legs do not come up to expectations.

Why body build influences personality

Ratings of people of different body builds at different ages have revealed a widespread tendency to associate certain personality characteristics with certain body builds. People with *endomorphic* builds (fat and heavyset) have been reported to be warm, kindly, cheerful, relaxed, softhearted, cooperative, low in tenseness and anxiety, and socially extroverted. They love comfort, recover rapidly from emotional upsets, are not sensitive to physical pain or verbal slights, and are not absorbed in fantasy.

Those with *ectomorphic* builds (tall and slender) are rated as detached, reserved, anxious, tense, shy, uncooperative, unaggressive, unsocial, and quiet. The

mesomorph (broad, muscular build) is rated as confident, energetic, enterprising, cheerful, social, self-assertive, dominant, independent, and possessing leadership qualities. As children, mesomorphs are often noisy, troublesome, and accident-prone. As they grow older and learn to harness their energies better, they become the outstanding athletes. And because of the high prestige attached to athletic success, they are popular and relatively well adjusted (50, 207, 236, 237).

The more definite the somatotype—the body-build type—the more marked the relationship between body build and personality (50). On the surface, this suggests that a hereditary factor is responsible for the relationship, but research studies do not substantiate such a conclusion.

The evidence shows that the characteristic personality patterns found in people of different body builds are due in part to social attitudes and to the roles their body builds permit them to play. If, for example, people believe that the ectomorph is "all skin and bones because he worries a lot," the person with such a build will incorporate this social evaluation into his own body concept. He then acts accordingly. He becomes a "worrier," and his behavior reinforces the social judgment (219).

Unquestionably, certain body builds predispose people to develop certain personality traits. A strong build, for example, predisposes a person to greater activity than a fat or a frail build. Furthermore, if people believe that certain personality traits accompany certain body builds, they provide opportunities and encouragement for the child to develop the traits traditionally associated with his build. The child with a mesomorphic build, for example, is given opportunities and encouragement to develop athletic skills because his parents believe that his build has destined him to be an outstanding athlete.

ATTRACTIVENESS

The strong influence of physical attractiveness on personality is not direct, but indirect, stemming from the favorable attitudes of other people toward those who are attractive. And since attractive people are attractive in varying degrees, the attitudes and treatment of others vary. The differences in treatment explain in part the differences in personality.

An attractive-looking person of any age is more appealing than one who is unattractive. "It is very rewarding," Brislin and Lewis write, "to be with someone who is physically attractive" (29). This is especially true in dating situations. A person who is attractive is more sought after for dates than the person who is homely.

In addition, people tend to be more tolerant in their attitudes and judgments of an attractive person. A pretty child, for example, is far less likely to be harshly criticized or punished for troublesome behavior than a homely child. In the business world, an attractive worker can be less efficient and less conscientious than an unattractive one and yet win a promotion.

Linden (135) discusses the relationship between attractiveness and lack of regard for the older person:

. . . We tend to place a considerable worth upon physical attractiveness and youthfulness. As a rule, these are symbols of pleasing packaging. As we grow older, the package changes, tending to deteriorate. It loses a certain freshness and desirability and thus becomes obsolete. Therefore, in our culture, in which the package possesses a value equal to or greater than its contents, the [aging] human facade . . . is not highly regarded.

Judgments of attractiveness

Whether a person is considered attractive or not is determined by the judgments others make of him. The person is first seen *in toto.* If the impression is favorable, the label "attractive" is then attached to him. If some feature stands out from the total pattern because it does not seem to fit, attention is focused on it first and this leads to the impression that the person is "homely." A nose that is too large for the other facial features, for example, leads to social judgments that the person is unattractive.

No single feature, per se, is either attractive or unattractive. Beauty depends on social judgments and these judgments are colored by cultural stereotypes. What one cultural group considers attractive, another may regard as homely or actually ugly.

In some cultures, fat is regarded as beautiful because it is associated with wealth. A person becomes fat because he can afford to eat as much as he wants. In our culture, in the past, fat was associated with being healthy and was admired. Today, it is associated with maladjustment and is judged as homely.

Furthermore, within a cultural group, standards of physical attractiveness change. At the turn of the

present century, ample feminine curves were considered attractive. Following World War I, during the "flapper era," curves were out and the flat-chested, flat-hipped female body was in. Today, the standard of an attractive female body is about halfway between these extremes—a pencil-slim body with unexaggerated curves.

Awareness of social attitudes Young children, unfamiliar with culturally approved stereotypes and unaware of how appearance affects social attitudes, are unconcerned about attractiveness. While the child does know that strangers comment favorably when he looks attractive and that parents are critical when he is unkempt, he associates this with his clothes rather than with his face or body. In addition, most adults are too tactful to comment about unattractive facial features, and they avoid overcomplimenting an attractive appearance in the belief that too much praise will make the child conceited.

Just as body build, unless it deviates markedly from the group norm, has little bearing on popularity among school-age children, so it is with attractiveness. Many children delight in being slovenly, dirty, and careless about appearance; they proudly display physical features which adults think homely, such as missing teeth and unmanageable hair which they refuse to have styled as long as the members of their gang do not criticize it. Disregard of appearance is partly a revolt against adult authority and, among boys, partly a way of showing their masculinity. Girls, who are more amenable to parental pressure, are usually neater and cleaner.

All of this changes at adolescence. Boys and girls discover that an attractive appearance increases their acceptance by members of the opposite sex as well as by members of their own sex. They discover that an attractive appearance helps them to make good first impressions. It gives them poise and self-confidence in social situations, thus helping them to meet more successfully the new social problems that all adolescents face. And they discover that their peers want the person they select as a leader to make a good appearance and to represent them to their satisfaction.

In the adult world, a person soon discovers that an attractive appearance is an aid in getting and holding a job and achieving vocational advancement. Young women find that it will help them to make a successful and enduring marriage.

With middle age comes the realization that maintaining a youthful appearance is as important to business and social success as is attractiveness. As a result, middle-aged people spend considerable time and money on beauty aids and clothes, on diets and drugs, and on exercises and camouflaged aids to their failing sensory capacities, such as contact lenses and hearing aids.

Dissatisfaction with appearance

The individual's awareness of the social values associated with appearance and his evaluation of the way in which his appearance compares with the cultural norm and with his own childhood ideal—these factors are responsible for the effect appearance has on personality. If the person's evaluation of his appearance is positive, it will give him satisfaction and he will develop a favorable self-concept. Relatively few people are satisfied with their appearance. The more dissatisfied they are, the more damaging the effect on the personality.

Sources of dissatisfaction   Some people are dissatisfied with one feature which they think mars their entire appearance. Others are generally dissatisfied, though they may be more critical of some features than of others. Dissatisfaction usually leads to worry, and the problem may be magnified out of all proportion.

Features that are most often worried about and cause the greatest dissatisfaction are those which are most often used by others to judge a person's personality. Among them are a nose that is too large or too irregularly shaped; teeth that are discolored, missing, or crooked; busts that are too small or too large; hair that is too curly or kinky; arms and legs that are too fat or too thin; skin that is acned or wrinkled; and facial hair that is overabundant in women or skimpy in men (37, 49, 136, 140, 201, 204).

Often the disliked feature has some unpleasant association, such as acne's traditional association with masturbation. Or the person may feel that a particular feature destroys the symmetry of his face, such as a prominent nose or teeth that are too large for the lips. He may feel that the feature falls below cultural standards, such as gray hair or wrinkles in a youth-oriented society. Or that the feature is sex-inappropriate, such as large hands and feet for women or small ones for men (37, 49, 201, 204).

The strongest dislikes are usually for features that cannot be camouflaged or changed. A girl may be

disturbed because even the most skillfully applied makeup does not camouflage her prominent chin. Or a man may be disturbed because there is nothing he can do to increase his meagre facial and body hair so that he will feel sex-appropriate.

On the other hand, features that are subject to change, sometimes at great cost or pain, cause less dissatisfaction and have a less damaging effect on the personality. From adolescence on, people spend more time, thought, and money on appearance because they believe that attractiveness is essential to success and, thus, to happiness and that attractiveness can be marred by even one disliked feature.

Reactions to dissatisfaction   One of the most common ways in which people who are dissatisfied with their appearance react is to select *clothes* to camouflage the parts of the body that fail to come up to cultural standards. A girl with small breasts, for example, can wear padded bras to make her breasts appear to conform to the prevailing sex-appropriate standards. Large feet can be made to appear smaller by wearing shoes with high heels. And height can be increased by wearing shoes with hidden lifts.

Cosmetics are an excellent camouflage for facial features that are not to the person's liking. Wax says that the purpose of cosmetics is to "manipulate one's superficial physical structure so as to make a desired impression upon others" (241). Hair can be curled or straightened to suit the person's preference; eyes can be highlighted by the use of mascara and false eyelashes; skin can be lightened or tanned by the use of creams and lotions; lips can be reshaped by the careful application of lipstick.

Crooked *teeth* can be straightened by braces in the young, and broken, missing teeth can be replaced by dentures. A *nose* that is too large or that is symbolic of a group against which there is prejudice can be improved by plastic surgery. *Wrinkles* and bags under the eyes can be removed by face-lifting. Many of the *scars of acne* can be removed by sanding away the outer layer of the facial skin.

Having to wear *glasses* bothers many people because they feel that glasses detract from their appearance and stereotype them as "studious." Girls are especially concerned if they have been brought up to believe that "boys don't make passes at girls who wear glasses." Today, people who must wear glasses, regardless of age or sex, are using contact lenses in rapidly increasing numbers.

Because an aging appearance is not considered attractive in the American culture, even middle-aged people try to camouflage or change all signs of aging. Wax (241) explains that women employ

. . . the techniques of grooming to conceal the signs of aging and to accentuate (and expose) the body areas where . . . appearance is still youthful. Some search hopefully for new techniques that will reverse the aging process in particular areas (e.g., "miracle" skin creams), others are shining examples of self-restraint and self-discipline (e.g., diet and exercise), and still others become virtuosos in the use of plastic devices of grooming (e.g., hair color rinses).

When an older man discovers that clothing does not conceal his aging appearance and that most beauty aids are considered sex-inappropriate, he often compensates by developing an I-don't-care attitude. This is an admission that he has failed in his attempts to influence the judgments of others favorably, not a sign that he is satisfied with his appearance.

Variations in dissatisfaction   Girls and women tend to be more dissatisfied with their level of attractiveness than boys and men, though this *sex* difference is not as marked as in dissatisfaction with body build. Furthermore, female dissatisfaction with attractiveness is concentrated mainly on specific features while male dissatisfaction concerns the total impression.

These sex differences are due largely to the roles members of the two sexes play and to social judgments of attractiveness. In business and social life, males are judged more by their ability than by their looks, whereas the reverse is true for women. A boy who is a good athlete will be well accepted by members of both sexes, regardless of his attractiveness, though being attractive is an added asset. A girl who wants to be popular must be good looking as well as a good dancer, a good conversationalist, and a member of a family with above-average socioeconomic status (37, 47, 181, 204).

Men are as concerned about looking "old" as women, but for a different reason. In men, concern centers on chances of promotion and keeping their jobs; in women, concern centers mainly on the attitudes of adolescent children toward their mothers' looks, a fear that their husbands will lose interest in them, and the possibility of losing leadership roles in

community affairs to younger and more attractive women.

There are predictable *age* differences in the degree of satisfaction people have with their attractiveness. As a general rule, the greatest satisfaction comes at ages when attractiveness is least important in social relationships. This means that during the major part of childhood and in the last years of life most people are fairly well satisfied with their looks. But during adolescence and most of the adult years, looks are important to success, and people are most dissatisfied with their looks at these ages.

Age differences are also found in what causes dissatisfaction with appearance. An adolescent girl, for example, may be dissatisfied because her breasts are too small. A middle-aged woman, on the other hand, may be dissatisfied because her breasts are too large. A pubescent is more concerned about the size of his nose in relation to his other facial features, while an adult is more concerned because the shape of his nose does not harmonize with his other facial features or because it identifies him with an ethnic or religious group against which there is prejudice.

Socioeconomic differences in degree of satisfaction with appearance stem from differences in life roles. During the adolescent years, when members of all socioeconomic groups are together in school, college, or the armed services, differences in satisfaction are minor. However, in adult life, when the roles of both men and women vary according to their socioeconomic status, differences in degree of satisfaction with appearance becomes much more pronounced.

Men of the lower socioeconomic groups, for example, are generally in skilled or semiskilled jobs where looks are unimportant. Similarly, their roles in community activities are usually limited to lodges or social clubs made up of men from the same kinds of occupations. For men of the middle and higher socioeconomic groups, on the other hand, appearance is very important to success in business, community, and social life, and they tend to be far more dissatisfied with their appearance.

Studies of social mobility show that one of the values a person must change if he is to be accepted by the higher-level group is that related to attractiveness of appearance. Thus, socially mobile people become looks- and clothes-conscious and spend proportionally more money on beauty aids and clothes than they did before they started their climb up the ladder (84, 180, 181).

Effects of attractiveness on personality

Realization that appearance plays an important role in social judgments inevitably affects the self-concept. If a person feels that his appearance is such that he will be judged positively, it will have a favorable effect on his personality. Few people, however, feel so. Most feel that their total appearance or some feature that mars their attractiveness is responsible for their not being as popular as they otherwise would be.

The more a person varies from the norm in physical attractiveness, the more he also varies in satisfaction and, thus, in the favorableness of his self-concept. Studies of the effects of acne illustrate how severely one unattractive feature can affect the self-concept. College students with acne score significantly higher on a neuroticism scale than those who are free from this skin blemish. Those of higher neuroticism also tend to develop acne at an earlier age (140). In discussing the effects of acne on personality, Kligman (116) states:

Teenagers who are acne sufferers frequently develop serious guilt problems. Teenage life is murderous anyway—there's the flux of contradictory emotions. The pressure on all of us for making good appearances is fantastic. There is enormous stress on beauty in America today and this helps to lower the self esteem of the acne victim.

One study has shown that an unattractive appearance may lead to deviant behavior. Not only are criminals judged to be below the norm in personal attractiveness, but the seriousness of their crimes is positively related to the degree of their unattractiveness. Burglars, for example, who engage in "behind-the-back" stealing, are contact-shy because of their unattractiveness. Robbers, who are bolder and who hold up their victims face to face, are 2 1/2 times more likely to be judged as attractive than are burglars.

Differences in attractiveness have also been found in criminals who commit sex crimes. Those who engage in illicit sexual relationships with adults are more attractive than those who victimize children. Corsini writes, "The more unattractive criminals seek out the presumably less critical children rather than their age peers" (49).

While physical unattractiveness does not, of course, necessarily lead to delinquent or criminal behavior, many unattractive people who are unable to improve their appearance enough to be reasonably acceptant of it do develop unfavorable self-concepts and unsocial patterns of behavior. Whether these will lead to withdrawal or aggression will depend upon their environments, the pattern of their lives, the kinds of relationships they have with family members, and a host of other conditions. For example, a child who has been criticized by his parents and nagged to improve his looks, and who interprets all this to mean that his parents reject him, often becomes hypersensitive about his appearance. He interprets the unfavorable attitudes of people outside the home to mean that they, too, reject him because of his looks. In time, he develops a generalized feeling of rejection which will be expressed in withdrawal or aggressive behavior.

At no time will an unfavorable self-concept be more damaging than in old age when physical attractiveness normally wanes and when other conditions, such as forced retirement, loss of community roles, and lowered income, intensify the belief of the person that he is being rejected because of his unattractiveness. Unquestionably, part of the personality change that so often accompanies aging can be traced to this.

HOMEOSTASIS

"Homeostasis" is the maintenance of a stable internal environment through a relatively steady temperature, a normal blood sugar level, an even rate of oxygen utilization, and a proper water balance. When any one of these conditions is upset, disturbances in homeostasis occur.

Direct and indirect effects

Homeostasis or lack of it has a pronounced effect, both directly and indirectly, on personality. Any alteration in the physiological state of a person will be reflected in behavioral changes which may be temporary or persistent, slight or major, depending on how great and how permanent the physiological changes are.

The *direct* effects of homeostasis are seen in the relaxed, poised, controlled, and socially acceptable behavior patterns of a person who is feeling well both physically and psychologically. Upsets in homeostasis are readily apparent in irritability following fatigue, indigestion, or some other uncomfortable state and in the temporary inability of a person to react normally after using alcohol and some of the narcotics.

Indirectly, homeostasis or lack of it may affect the personality through the way the person reacts to what he believes to be the attitudes and behavior of significant people in his life or to how close his body comes to his childhood ideal. For example, a person who is larger than the average for his age and sex group because of an excessive discharge of hormone by the pituitary gland will respond to his superior size in one of two ways. If his superior size is viewed favorably by others, he will react positively, and the upset in homeostasis will thus indirectly have a favorable effect on his self-concept. But if superior size is a social handicap, as it would be to a girl, the response will be negative, and the effect of the upset on personality will be unfavorable.

Similarly, bodily changes that are a normal accompaniment of aging will result in behavioral changes which the person senses or knows the social group looks upon with disfavor. Loss of skill, due to weakening of the muscles and changes in the central nervous system, and loss of control over the emotions, due to changes in the autonomic nervous system, lead to feelings of inadequacy. The aging person knows that the social group regards such changes as indicative of a decline in his usefulness to society.

Disturbances of homeostasis

Disturbances of homeostasis show how dependent good personal and social adjustments are on a balance in physiological functioning. To understand the relationship of homeostasis to the personality pattern, one must know what causes disturbances in homeostasis and be able to distinguish temporary disturbances and their effect on personality from permanent disturbances.

Causes of disturbances Dunbar has said, "The maintenance of homeostasis . . . is particularly difficult during a period of developmental change" (60). Disturbances in homeostasis may come from a physical condition or from a psychological state.

A *physical* condition, such as abnormal temperature or blood pressure, or the malfunctioning of an organ or gland, will disturb homeostasis and will be reflected in behavioral changes. Rapid or uneven growth at the time of the puberty growth spurt causes body instability, and the pubescent becomes irritable and uncooperative. Glandular changes in middle age, as the reproductive capacity wanes, likewise cause physical instability, and the person is nervous, tired, and sleepless.

Rises in blood pressure due to increased rigidity

in the walls of the aorta and central arteries; malnutrition due to poor eating habits, poverty, the use of dentures, or other causes; and decrease in amount and depth of sleep during old age—all contribute to disturbances in homeostasis which are responsible, in part, for behavioral changes at this time. Figure 6-2 shows decrease in amount of sleep during old age.

It is well known that a person's *psychological* state can have physiological reverberations. Any emotional upset, for example, disturbs the normal functioning of many of the internal organs of the body. The ambitious, aggressive "go-getter" in the business world, it has been reported, is especially susceptible to heart attacks because he lives under constant emotional strain that overtaxes his heart (172). The woman who is constantly tired may be suffering more from annoyance at the "easy life" her husband has as compared with hers—the "lazy-husband syndrome"—than from actual overwork (175).

Malnutrition at any age, but especially in old age, may be psychological in origin. Elderly people, for example, lose their motivation to prepare balanced meals when they must eat alone, and their loneliness often gives rise to emotional states which interfere with the proper digestion of the food they do eat.

Since marked physical changes at puberty, middle and old age, require role changes, they always have an emotional accompaniment, whether the new role is prestigious or not. Growing up means acquisition of the prestigious role of an adult, but even so, the emotional accompaniment upsets homeostasis. As Dunbar (60) has explained:

During this period the developing child experiences changes in body, changes in status including appearance and clothes, possessions and range of choice, and changes in attitudes toward sex and the opposite sex, all of which by necessity involve a changed parent-child relationship and changes in the rules and regulations to which the youngster is subjected.

Temporary and permanent disturbances Disturbances in homeostasis may be temporary or permanent. The longer the duration, or the more frequent the temporary disturbances, the more pronounced the effect on personality.

A common *temporary* disturbance to homeostasis in women is the menstrual period. For several days preceding and during this period, hormonal changes cause changes in blood pressure, body tem-

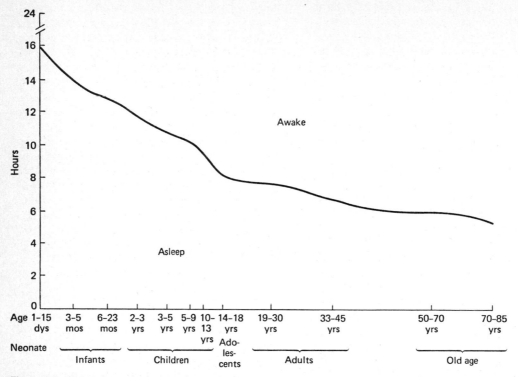

Figure 6-2 Decrease in amount of sleep as age progresses. (Adapted from H. P. Roffwarg, J. N. Muzio, and W. C. Dement: Ontogenetic development of the human sleep-dream cycle. *Science*, 1966, **152**, 604-609. Used by permission.)

perature, and basal metabolism and an accumulation of water which may press on nerve centers. It has been estimated that approximately one-half of all women regularly suffer from premenstrual tension which makes them nervous, irritable, and hard to work or live with (60, 163, 183). Unfavorable psychological states can accentuate the physical condition brought on by the hormonal changes. For example, if a girl or woman is identified with a group that regards menstruation as a sickness or "curse," her unfavorable attitude will accentuate the physical disturbances that normally accompany menstruation.

Some drugs, high fever, and alcohol are likewise responsible for temporary upsets in homeostasis. Heroin and marijuana produce a happy, dreamy state in which all the person's problems are forgotten. When the effects of the drugs wear off, the person becomes depressed, anxious, and guilt-ridden. Delirium, accompanying high fever, causes a change in personality characterized by a state of mental and emotional confusion. The person is irrational and irascible, with a tendency to resist aggressively any suggestions from others. As the fever subsides, so do the changes in behavior that accompanied it.

Permanent disturbances in homeostasis are reflected in relatively permanent personality changes. Such disturbances are usually the result of pronounced endocrine imbalance or deterioration of the tissues of the central nervous system. Deterioration of brain tissue may come from aging. A person suffering from senile dementia may merely show changes in mental abilities; he may become forgetful, rigid, and mentally confused. Or in more severe cases, he may become hostile and suspicious, anxious and depressed; he may experience delusions of persecution so extreme that he becomes afraid of people, shutting himself off from society and becoming a recluse (149, 163, 220).

Effects of homeostasis on personality

Since the time of the early Greek physicians, it has been recognized that disturbances to homeostasis affect personality. Today, the relationship has been substantiated by studies which show that behavioral changes accompany physical changes.

During periods of *equilibrium,* when homeostasis is maintained, people are "in focus"; they are happy and are making good personal and social adjustments. Upsets in homeostasis, due to physical or psychological causes, result in *disequilibrium.* The person is "out of focus"; he feels insecure, morbid, gloomy, and unhappy, and as a result, he makes poor adjustments (9, 75, 244).

The more pronounced the disturbance to homeostasis, the more behavioral changes there are, indicating the extent of the effect on the personality pattern. At puberty, when disturbances in homeostasis are accompanied by headaches, digestive upsets, a general feeling of fatigue, and other unfavorable physical conditions, there is a period of disequilibrium, often referred to as the "negative phase," when the maturing child feels insecure, uncertain, and confused. He expresses these feelings in moodiness, restlessness, irritability, rebelliousness, and generally unsocial patterns of behavior.

As growth slows down, these manifestations of maladjustive behavior disappear, as do the physical disturbances that accompanied rapid growth. There is then a period of equilibrium when the young adolescent's characteristic behavior is indicative of good personal and social adjustments (60, 75, 162, 183).

That behavioral changes are due to disturbances in homeostasis is further shown by the fact that when hormonal treatment is used to slow the speed of the physical changes, behavioral changes become less pronounced. This kind of treatment is sometimes used in middle age when the glandular changes that upset body homeostasis often result in personality changes similar to those at puberty (168, 228, 229).

A description of a few studies will illustrate how the personality pattern is affected by homeostasis or lack of it. *Anoxia* or reduction in the amount of oxygen in the inspired air, as in asthma, causes loss of self-criticism, emotional outbursts, and mental confusion (149). Alcock has remarked that "the asthmatic personality appears characterized by a high degree of emotional tension without appropriate release" (2). A drop in *blood sugar* level not only affects mental efficiency but also causes alterations in mood, increased irritability, and vague feelings of apprehension. When the blood sugar level rises above normal, depressive mental states occur (149, 163, 220).

An acute deficiency of *vitamin B complex* results in depression, increased emotionality, and hysteria (80). Serious malnutrition leads to reactions closely resembling psychoneuroses, with marked apathy, depression, irritability, general nervousness, and undependability. A marked deficiency of one element of normal nutrition, *salt,* may result in personality disturbances. High *blood pressure* frequently results in neuroticism (95, 163).

Severe *endocrine disorders* result in marked personality changes. A person suffering from hypothyroidism—a pronounced deficiency of the hormone from the thyroid glands—tends to be lethargic, apathetic, unresponsive, depressed, dissatisfied, and distrustful. A marked surplus of the thyroid hormone—hyperthyroidism—leads to excitability, anxiety, and extreme nervous tension. Unless these conditions are corrected by endocrine therapy, their effects on personality will be relatively permanent (149, 163, 183, 206, 212, 220).

Variations in effects Disturbances that upset homeostasis vary from one person to another and in the same person from one *age* to another. Studies reveal that periods of equilibrium and disequilibrium occur at predictable times. Whenever physical change is rapid, as in puberty and middle age, whenever a person is expected to assume a new role, as when he enters school or takes a job, and whenever changes in the environment, as in moving from one community to another, require a revision in the person's habitual pattern of living, disequilibrium and its damaging effects on personality can be expected.

There are also predictable ages of good and poor health. Illness is more common among children and elderly people than among adolescents and young adults (137, 209, 232). Minor physical disturbances, such as sleeplessness, nervousness, and tiredness, on the other hand, become increasingly more common with advancing age (154). See Figure 6-3.

At all ages, *sex* differences in disturbances to homeostasis are observed. Boys and men suffer more from frequent and serious illnesses than girls and women. The latter, however, suffer more from minor disturbances, such as sleeplessness and tiredness (149, 154, 183). (Refer to Figure 6-3.) On the other hand, women tend to handle the stresses of living better than men and to take better care of their health; thus, the disturbances to homeostasis are less pronounced and less often permanent in women.

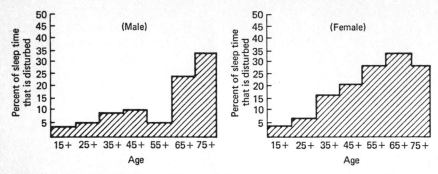

Figure 6-3 Disturbed sleep becomes increasingly more frequent as age advances. (Adapted from B. A. McGhie and S. M. Russel: The subjective assessment of normal sleep patterns. *J. ment. Sci.,* 1962, **108,** 642-654. Used by permission.)

The *environment* in which people live is partially responsible for the frequency and intensity of their homeostatic disturbances. Those who live in urban and suburban areas experience more stress and have more serious illnesses than those who live in rural areas (190). People who live alone, regardless of the environment, tend to suffer more from stress than those who live with other people—a condition that contributes to disturbances in homeostasis (42).

The *personality pattern* also has an effect on the frequency and intensity of homeostatic disturbances. Persons who are outer-controlled tend to suffer less from stress than those who are inner-controlled. The former are able to reduce their stress by communicating with others and getting a new perspective on the problems that concern them. The importance of communication has been noted by Dunbar: "The affective reaction to change is largely determined by the capacity to communicate. . . . Communication is a means of coping with anxiety which inevitably accompanies stress" (60).

PHYSICAL CHANGES

The body is constantly changing both on the exterior and on the interior. When changes are slow and gradual, they have relatively little effect on personality. But when they are rapid, the effect may be dramatic.

Physical changes are always accompanied by the necessity of changing one's life roles. Physical and role changes necessitate changing one's body image and the concept of one's abilities and one's status in the group. As the body changes from that of a child to that of an adult, for example, the young adolescent must change his concept of what he looks like, and he must adjust to new concepts of what his maturing physical and mental abilities mean to him and what his role as a near adult entails. The interaction of these different changes has been emphasized by Birren et al. (22):

Aging is a process of change involving all aspects of the organism. Its consequences range from altered structures and functions of the component tissues of the body to an altered relationship of the organism to its physical and social environment.

Whether changes will result in an improved self-concept or not will be determined by how the person reacts to the changes. This point of view has been stressed by Havighurst (85):

From middle age onward, the person confronts changes in the social environment and in his physical body which require readjustments on his part. Society does things to him, and his body changes negatively, but different personalities react differently to the same set of societal pressures and the same set of bodily changes.

Direct and indirect effects on personality

Physical changes have both direct and indirect effects on personality. The *direct* effects come from homeostatic disturbances and the resulting sapping of energy which influences not only what and how much a person can do but also his state of general well-being. If he feels listless and tired, he will be predisposed to emotional tension and emotional outbursts.

Physical changes affect personality *indirectly*

through the effect they have on the attitudes of significant people toward the individual, through the individual's own positive or negative reaction to the changes, and through his and others' attitudes toward his ability to play the role associated with his changed body. If a middle-aged person tries to dress and act like a teen-ager, for example, most people will react unfavorably to him because he is not playing the role associated with middle age.

Factors influencing effects of changes

How much influence physical changes have on personality will be determined primarily by the factors discussed in the following paragraphs.

Speed of changes Slow physical changes have relatively little effect on personality because they give the person and others time to adjust to his new body; they do not upset homeostasis or sap the person's energy; they give the person time to learn to play the new roles associated with his changed body; and most important of all, they give him time to revise his self-concept to include the changes. Rapid changes, by contrast, upset homeostasis, drain the energy, and allow no time for adjusting.

Rapid physical changes and personality disturbances characterize the pubertal "negative phase"—the period early in puberty when changes occur most rapidly. At this time boys and girls not only behave in a manner that makes others judge them unfavorably, but their behavior, combined with unfavorable social judgments, makes them judge themselves unfavorably (8, 60, 75, 183). This deterioration in the self-concept is illustrated in Figure 2-4.

The effects of rapid physical changes on personality may be obviated if hormone therapy is used to slow down the changes. In puberty, improvements are noted both in behavior and in self-concepts (183). In middle age, women receiving hormone therapy show few of the characteristic behavior patterns of the "climacteric storm," such as depression, emotional instability, and feelings of uselessness (81, 89, 169, 183). In old age, hormone therapy builds up health and vigor, thus retarding the unfavorable psychological effects the changes of aging bring (183, 216, 229).

Timing of changes When physical changes occur at times when other major adjustment problems must be met, the physical changes are harder to cope with and the effects on the personality are more pronounced. When a middle-aged woman must adjust to the "empty nest"—a home with no children left in it—she finds that the psychological problems resulting from changes in her accustomed role greatly aggravate her adjustment to the physical upsets of menopause. When a man must retire from his life work at the same time that the physical changes of aging require him to give up activities he formerly enjoyed, the problems of adjusting are multiplied.

People change physically at different times. As Johnston says, "The time clock which governs the developmental process is an individual one" (105). A change that makes a person different from his peers, even temporarily, makes adjustment to the change difficult because he feels conspicuous, embarrassed, and "inferior." Furthermore, others expect him to play the role associated with his changed appearance, regardless of his age or ability to play the role successfully. An early maturer, for example, is expected to act more like an adult than other boys or girls of the same age while a late maturer is treated like a "kid" because he looks younger than he actually is. According to Weatherley (242):

The late maturer must cope with the developmental demands of the junior high and high school period with the liability of a relatively small, immature appearing physical stature. His appearance is likely to call out in others at least mild reactions of derogation and the expectation that he is capable of only ineffectual, immature behavior. Such reactions constitute a kind of social environment which is conducive to feelings of inadequacy, insecurity and defensive "small-boy" behavior. Such behavior, once initiated, may well be self-sustaining.

Similarly, it is harder to grow "fair, fat, and 40" if one's associates are fair and 40 but not fat. Looking, feeling, and acting older than a spouse, a friend, or a coworker has an unfavorable effect on the self-concept.

Preparation for changes Adjustment to change is always facilitated by preparation. However, it is not the quantity of preparation that is important but the *quality*. Preparation based on faulty information or half-truths is worse than no preparation at all. It increases the tensions normally associated with change because it raises hopes and expectations which sooner or later will have to be adjusted to meet reality.

Inability to predict what the end result of changes will be, how long they will take, or how complicated they will be makes specific preparation impossible. A doctor can tell a woman what the normal pattern of menopausal changes is and what homeostatic disturbances most women experience, but he cannot tell her what *she* will experience except in a general way.

Even when people are prepared for the physical changes that occur at different times in the life span, few are prepared for the role changes and the changes in social expectations that accompany the physical changes. A man may be aware of the physical changes aging brings and know when to expect them, but he is not likely to be prepared for the social attitudes that will require him to withdraw from employment and from the active role he has played in community affairs.

If the unfavorable effects of ignorance or misinformation were temporary, the damage to the personality would be minor. Often, however, the effects are permanent and the damage great. Studies show that first menstruation can be such a traumatic experience for the unprepared girl that it can unfavorably color her attitudes toward the feminine role and endanger her ability to adjust to marriage and motherhood (169, 183).

Ignorance of the fact that the sex drive normally wanes with age and with the tensions of work, family responsibility, and economic competition drives many men to develop feelings of inadequacy because they fear they have lost their virility. Such feelings can be the foundation of a deep-seated inferiority complex which will affect their adjustments in all areas of life.

Social attitudes toward changes

What significant people in a person's life think about the changes that have taken place in his body will have a profound influence on what he himself thinks about the changes. If they make his body conform more closely to the cultural stereotype of attractiveness and sex appropriateness, social attitudes toward him will improve. The further he deviates from the cultural stereotype, the less favorably others will judge him.

In the American stereotype, youthfulness of appearance is a prime criterion of attractiveness. As facial and bodily changes destroy the image of youthfulness, social attitudes will inevitably be less favorable. That is why people use beauty aids and clothes to camouflage any feature that is associated with aging; that is why they diet, exercise, and get hormone treatments. See Figure 6-4.

It has been said that at middle age "men undergo a change in virility and women a change in fertility" (183). Since these qualities are highly valued by the social group, changes in appearance which suggest that they have been lost or diminished are bound to result in unfavorable social judgments and in the loss of prestigious social roles.

Effects on attractiveness, health, and body control

If body changes improve the appearance of a person, his health, and the control he has over his body, social judgments and self-judgments will be more favorable. When the transition to the adult body has been completed, the person is usually more attractive than he was earlier when lack of symmetry marred otherwise attractive features. As a young adult, he is normally at the peak of health and body control. Consequently, social judgments are likely to be more favorable than ever before.

The physical changes of middle and old age generally result in decreased attractiveness, failing health, and less control over the body, due to changes in the muscles, joints, and bones. The camouflages, the diets, and the exercises that worked so success-

Figure 6-4 When a person is aware of unfavorable social attitudes toward his waning attractiveness, it has an unfavorable effect on his self-concept. (Adapted from George Clark, "The Neighbors." Chicago Tribune-New York News Syndicate. *The Philadelphia Evening Bulletin,* April 20, 1967. Used by permission.)

"All this started on a bus when two young soldiers offered him their seats!"

fully when the person was younger now seem to have lost some of their effectiveness. Under such conditions, changes for the worse in the self-concept are almost inevitable.

Conformity to body ideal The body ideal includes good health, strength, and vigor as well as a youthful appearance. Because of the high cultural value placed on youthfulness, physical changes that make one look, feel, and act over 30 or so undermine the self-concepts of many people. In their attempt to approximate their body ideal, they dress and behave like younger people as long as they can. When clothes and beauty aids can no longer camouflage the tell-tale signs of aging and when health and vigor wane, they are forced to recognize how far they are from their ideal. The more rebellious they are in their attitudes and the less successful they are in clinging to the youthfulness they value so highly, the more dissatisfied they are.

Effects of physical change on personality

A changed body requires a revision of the body concept. If physical changes bring the person closer to his and the culture's ideal and result in more favorable social attitudes toward him, he will feel satisfied and will have greater poise and self-confidence.

Changes that cause the body to deviate from the ideal are unwelcome, and regardless of when they occur, they are damaging to the self-concept. If the pubescent grows too tall or too fat, the effects on his personality are just as upsetting as wrinkled skin and sagging muscles in middle age. This damage to the self-concept is shown in self-consciousness, withdrawal from social contacts, feelings of inadequacy, and a generalized feeling of inferiority.

When physical changes are rapid, especially if they are unwelcome changes, psychological adjustments cannot be made quickly enough to avoid permanent damage to the personality. The more attractive a person has been, the more he will rebel against losing his attractiveness as he grows older, and the stronger the emotional component of his response to signs of aging. Havighurst says, "We have invested a good deal of emotional capital in our physical attractiveness and this investment is going bad on us" (85).

Irregularities in the growth and functioning of different parts of the body also affect the self-concept and life adjustments. Unwelcome deviations, while always a handicap to a healthy self-concept, are especially damaging at times of rapid growth when attention is focused on the body changes that are taking place. Thus, deviant maturers are likely to make poorer personal and social adjustments than their normally maturing age-mates (68, 87).

Men and women who age faster than their contemporaries will be temporarily affected by this deviation. When their contemporaries catch up with them, any feelings of inadequacy they may have developed are likely to disappear or become less pronounced.

Another difficulty associated with body changes that affects personality is the social expectation that *role changes* will accompany body changes. Just as the physically mature adolescent is expected to act like an adult, so is the aging adult expected to act like a "senior citizen." If the person is satisfied with the role change and if he feels that he is performing the new role satisfactorily, his body changes will have a favorable effect on his personality. If the new role is less prestigious and less satisfying than the old one, the person will resist playing it even at the risk of arousing unfavorable social attitudes.

The self-concepts the person builds up as he goes through life are symptomatic of the kind of adjustment he will make to the physical changes of aging. As Havighurst has pointed out, "What old age will be like appears to depend partly upon physical constitution and partly upon the kind of life that has been led" (85). If a person has always had an unrealistic concept of his superiority or indispensability, aging will present a greater threat to his personality than if he had had a negative or more realistic self-concept.

BODY CONTROL

Good body control is a personal and social asset which contributes heavily to the person's self-concept. The effect of body control on personality may be direct or indirect. The *direct* effect comes from determining what the person can do and how well he can do it. The direct effect is also evident in motivation. When a person is self-conscious about his poor body control, he may be so concerned about unfavorable social reactions that he will lack the motivation to do what he is capable of doing.

Indirectly, body control influences personality through the effect the person's body control has on the attitudes of significant people in the social group. Because of the high social value placed on good body control, as shown in motor skills, strength, and speed, the person's self-concept is damaged by poor control.

Awareness of social value of body control

Even before the young child discovers the social value of good body control, he derives satisfaction from being his own master and from being able to do what he sets out to do without help. In his early peer contacts, the child discovers that social acceptance depends largely on his ability to do what his age-mates do and that leadership depends largely on superior play skills.

The schoolchild discovers that academic success is greatly influenced by the ability to do things which require skilled movements and that the confidence these build up encourages him to tackle new tasks. By adolescence, he is well aware that great prestige is attached to physical competence. Boys who excel in sports and girls who excel in social dancing are in the limelight of peer attention. Good body control is the key to social success.

In adult life, gracefulness and poise add to social success, while motor skills add to vocational success. At the basis of much of the feeling of inadequacy and self-consciousness noted among older people is the loss of body control which results from changes in the neuromuscular system and in the bones and joints—changes which are a natural accompaniment of the aging process.

Awkwardness

Awkwardness signifies a lack of control over the body. In judging awkwardness, one must compare a person's control with the norm for his age group. A child of 5 would be considered awkward if judged by adult standards, but when judged by standards for other 5-year-olds, he might have superior body control.

Causes of awkwardness Lack of body control may be due to environmental restrictions or parental overprotectiveness which have limited the person's *opportunities to learn* to coordinate the muscles of the body (27, 149, 183). It may also be due to the person's *body build*. People with flabby, fat bodies—the endomorphic build—tend to be relatively inactive and to spend their leisure time in passive amusements, such as reading and television watching, rather than in active games and sports. As a result, they do

not learn to coordinate their muscles as well as their ectomorphic or mesomorphic age-mates (149, 207, 210).

Rapid and uneven growth of the bones and muscles, hands, and feet at puberty upsets the patterns of coordination learned earlier. *Decline in energy* with advancing age, combined with neuromuscular changes, causes many elderly people to shun activities where skills are needed. Their skills begin to deteriorate and they lose the dexterity they formerly enjoyed. Writing seems like "too much work" to many older people, for example, and so they write less and their writing becomes slower and of poorer quality.

At any age, *emotional tension* disturbs motor coordination and leads to awkwardness. *Low-grade intelligence* makes the learning of skills difficult so that a person with below average intelligence can always be expected to be more awkward than his age-mates. This subject will be taken up in more detail in Chapter 7.

Awkwardness may be temporary or permanent. That due to emotional tension and to rapid growth is temporary. That due to aging, a physical defect, or any of the other common causes discussed above is likely to be permanent.

A tendency toward awkwardness is seen in many people who are either ambidextrous or left-handed. The person who is *ambidextrous* uses both hands equally well; he does not favor one or the other. The *left-handed* person prefers to do things with his left hand, though he may use his right hand for certain activities if he has been trained to do so. The tendency to be slightly awkward comes from the fact that non-right-handed people must use right-handed tools and follow right-handed models and instructions. Instead of learning to do things in the quickest and most efficient way for *them,* they learn by trial-and-error modification of right-handed methods. The ambidextrous person divides his learning between the two hands, and so neither hand becomes as skilled as it would if he were exclusively right- or left-handed (9, 149, 171, 182, 189).

Variations in awkwardness Even a person who has good body control will be awkward at times. Awkwardness is almost universal at the two *age* periods when body changes occur most rapidly: at puberty and in advancing age. The more rapid the changes, the more they will upset patterns of control learned earlier and the more awkward the person will be. A slowing down in speed of reaction and bodily movement with age likewise contributes substantially to awkwardness. See Figure 6-5.

At all ages, males are more awkward than females. This *sex* difference is due to the larger bodies of males, especially the hands and feet, which are more difficult to control, and to the quickness with which males typically try to do things (75, 92, 149, 183).

Evidence of *socioeconomic* differences in awkwardness is far from conclusive, although it has been suggested that awkwardness may be more common among members of the higher socioeconomic groups, particularly in adulthood. During childhood and adolescence, when members of all socioeconomic groups are in the same schools and are subjected to the same peer values of prestigious skills, such as sports for boys and dancing for girls, differences in awkwardness are negligible. Within every socioeconomic group, some members are awkward and some have good body control (47, 75, 149, 217).

In adulthood, the patterns of life for members of different socioeconomic groups begin to differ. Members of the lower groups usually go into vocations where manual skills are essential, while members of the upper groups go into vocations where such skills are of little value. Executives, for example, have little need for writing, and as a result, their handwriting deteriorates (123). Women of the lower socioeconomic groups spend more of their work and recreational time on activities which require skills and physical activity. Their need to control the movements of the body helps to ward off the awkwardness that normally follows lack of practice.

Effects of body control on personality

At all ages, good body control enhances the self-concept in two ways. *First,* it fosters the development of self-confidence, which is expressed in a calm assurance, poise, and a willingness to try new things in the belief that they can be mastered. In time, self-confidence becomes generalized and spreads to situations where motor control is not involved. *Second,* and more important, good body control encourages a feeling of security in social situations. This frees the person to turn his attention away from self and toward others, thus enabling him to make good social adjustments. He does not have to worry about how his body will function in social situations, whether he will be clumsy and do embarrassing things. The role of motor

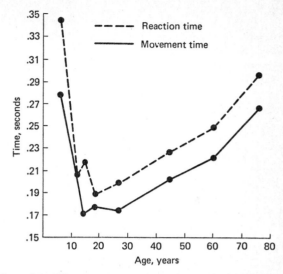

Figure 6-5 Differences in the speed of reaction at different ages. (Adapted from J. Hodgkins: Reaction time and speed of movement in males and females at various ages. *Res. Quart. Amer. Ass. Hlth. Phys. Educ. Recr.,* 1963, **34,** 335-343. Used by permission.)

control in the development of the self-concept has been stressed by Havighurst (84):

To an increasing extent, a child's conception of himself is tied up with the skills he has. . . . As a child becomes part of an activity group . . . he contributes certain skills, certain knowledge. He has an opportunity to test his skills against those of his peers. He adds to his conception of himself as his peers react to his skills.

The psychological damage of awkwardness comes from different experiences at different ages. A young child must depend on others to do things for him he would like to do for himself. This dependency is a source of constant irritation and frustration.

The older child who is unable to keep up with his age-mates is embarrassed and ashamed. As such upsetting experiences accumulate, he develops a generalized feeling of inadequacy and inferiority, and his self-concept is damaged by feelings of shame. In time, he is likely to develop an inferiority complex.

Children who fall below their age-mates in play skills experience social rejection or voluntarily withdraw from the play group to avoid the embarrassment that comes from being considered awkward and clumsy. They are thus not only deprived of opportunities to improve their body control but also confirmed in their belief that they are inferior.

Not realizing that rapid physical growth can disrupt patterns of coordination established when the body was smaller, the young adolescent will wonder if something is wrong with him when he spills or breaks things, trips over rugs, and stumbles over his own feet. Ridicule and criticism from others add to his embarrassment and increase his feelings of inadequacy.

Temporary loss of body control during periods of rapid growth has a far less damaging effect on personality than permanent loss of control. However, if temporary awkwardness goes on too long, as in the slow maturer at puberty, it can lead to a habitual concept of oneself as an awkward person even after the awkwardness has passed.

Decline in body control is one of the chief causes of the unfavorable self-concept that characterizes many elderly people. Feelings of inadequacy and inferiority arise when they compare themselves with younger people or with their own younger selves, and so they tend to shun motor activities and become dependent on others. As in young children, dependency in old age leads to frustration and unhappiness.

Since loss of motor control increases with advancing age, the damaging effect of awkwardness on the self-concept intensifies. Most elderly people are ashamed of their awkwardness. This encourages them to become socially disengaged, especially in situations where they must be with younger people who are likely to be critical of them or overprotective.

Left-handedness is often detrimental to good personal and social adjustment. Since manual dexterity affects the person's educational and vocational success, it influences his self-concept. When the cultural group tends to favor the use of the right and to regard the left-handed person as "different," the left-handed person's mirror image, or social self-concept, is certain to be unfavorable.

ACCIDENTS

Traditional beliefs about the cause of accidents are many and varied. An accident-prone person was born under an "unlucky star," he was not born with a "horseshoe around his neck," he has red hair which makes him impulsive and careless, and so on. While we have no scientific evidence to substantiate these beliefs, we cannot dismiss them lightly. They influence the person who believes them by allowing him to free

himself from any responsibility for an accident and by making him feel "martyred" or "hoodooed."

Accidents are most common from 4 to 15 years of age and after 65. They are more frequent and more serious among males than among females (176).

All accidents, however minor, leave psychological scars. Furthermore, the psychological scars are more permanent and more far-reaching in their effects than the physical scars unless the accident leaves a physical defect, such as a facial deformity or lameness. In such cases, the psychological damage of an accident is further intensified.

Causes of accidents

Among preschool children, accidents are usually due to lack of supervision and to the desire to explore something new without realizing its potential harm. Among older children, accidents come from the desire to win peer approval and attention by taking chances and defying safety rules. For boys, especially those who suffer from feelings of inadequacy and sex inappropriateness, bravery and daring have high value.

Many adults carry over childhood habits of reacting aggressively to dangerous situations or to laws regulating safety. As a result, they continue to have accidents. With age, caution usually replaces daring, but lack of body control and failing eyesight lead to an increase in accidents among the elderly.

Effects of accidents on personality

The effects of accidents on personality may be direct or indirect. The *direct* effects come from physical pain or discomfort, which makes the person feel sorry for himself, from believing that he was "born unlucky," or from embarrassment. The *indirect* effects come from two sources: *first,* how significant people in the person's life react—with sympathy or with accusations of carelessness—and *second,* how they interpret the cause of the accident—as "bad luck" or his fault.

The indirect effects, unless the accident leaves some permanent physical scar, are usually greater and more persistent than the direct effects. This is because significant people in a person's life are usually consistent in their reactions to his accidents and in their interpretation of the cause of his accidents.

For example, if the child's mother scolds him for being careless or for breaking a safety rule, he will have feelings of shame or guilt every time he has an accident. These feelings will be reinforced if his parents complain about the trouble and expense his accidents cause. Or if he is constantly told that accidents are "just bad luck," he will get into the habit of thinking of himself as a martyr—a habit which, in time, will become generalized and spread to every area of his life where his achievements fall below his hopes and expectations. These reactions of significant people will have very different effects on his self-concept.

Quite apart from the cause of accidents, certain effects on personality are predictable. Even when a person is not physically damaged by an accident, he is invariably psychologically damaged; the emotional shock of the accident makes him "lose his nerve," or become timid. The more accidents he has and the shorter the time interval between them, the more rapidly timidity will develop.

Timidity developed in accident situations often becomes generalized and spreads to other situations in which the person feels threatened. A child who has been psychologically damaged by accidents may be so timid at school that he lives in dread of being called on to recite. If he is an accident-prone child, this dread of being called on may become so severe that he will develop a school phobia and do everything within his power to avoid going to school. An adolescent or adult may withdraw from social situations, using such defense mechanisms as imaginary illness or invented prior engagements—a "busy" complex.

If accidents come from trying to impress others, the person lives in dread of having his peers think he has "turned yellow" or lost his nerve. He dreads even the possibility that they will dare him to do something dangerous with the taunt that he used to do such things, so why is he afraid to do them now?

Few children have enough understanding to appreciate the physical pain and mental anguish accident victims suffer. They tend to be unsympathetic toward a person who is hurt, laughing at the "funny" expression on his face or the "funny" position he is in. Should he cry out in pain, they are likely to call him a "baby." This adds to the other unfavorable effects of accidents on a person's self-concept, making him believe that he is a coward who cannot "take it" as others expect him to do.

PHYSICAL DEFECTS

It has been common knowledge throughout the centuries that people who suffer from physical defects recognize that they are different and that this tends to influence their behavior. The first scientific attention to the effects of physical defects on personality came from Alfred Adler in the early 1900s. In his theory of organ inferiority, Adler stated that neuroses and other manifestations of maladjustment are compensations for physical disabilities. When some part of the body is inferior, either morphologically or functionally, the theory claims, the person develops generalized feelings of inferiority which make him strive to compensate for the defect (1). Subsequent studies have revealed that *any* physical defect, however minor, is a "mental hazard."

Causes of physical defects

Some people are born with physical defects caused by an unfavorable condition in the prenatal environment or an injury during the birth process. Some physical defects are acquired through illness, accident, or aging. Some can be corrected or minimized, but many become more serious with the passage of time. Many conspicuous defects in adolescents and adults, for example, are carry-overs of relatively minor defects present at birth or acquired during the early years of life (52, 161, 199).

Some physical defects are psychosomatic in that they are caused by stress and unfavorable emotional conditions (120). Two common defects of this sort are obesity and some of the speech defects. Stuttering and slurring often come from prolonged emotional stress during the years when the child was learning to speak. Lisping in elderly people often begins when they start to wear dentures. The embarrassment caused by the speech defect only intensifies it (128).

Obesity is often psychosomatic rather than physical in origin (32, 205). Leckie and Withers write that the obese person is a "basically depressed person who eats to ward off his depression" (125). Studies of dieters show that those with good emotional adjustment are four times as successful in their dieting as those who suffer from emotional disturbances (205, 234).

Variations in frequency of defects

Few people at any age are completely free from physical defects. However, certain variations in the frequency and severity of defects are predictable. Physical defects are more common at certain *ages* than at others. Children have more defects than young adults, or at least more visible defects. With advancing age, the number and severity of physical defects increase (4, 6, 209).

Sex differences in physical disabilities are also predictable. Males have more physical disabilities than females because they have more accidents and are less likely to take care of themselves when injured or ill (6, 209). Girls and women are more concerned about defects which handicap them in social relationships, especially obesity and facial disfigurements, while boys and men are more concerned about those which limit their physical activities (192).

People from the lower *socioeconomic* groups tend to have more physical defects than have those from the middle and upper groups. This difference is due, in part, to better prenatal and postnatal care in the more favored socioeconomic groups and, in part, to their ability to afford corrective treatment, such as the straightening of crooked teeth (52).

Effects of physical defects on personality

Physical defects affect personality *directly* by placing limitations on what the person can do and thus restricting the areas within which he can develop a positive and realistic self-concept. *Indirectly,* the personality is affected by the way defects influence the attitudes and treatment of significant people. In general, physical handicaps requiring the use of crutches, leg braces, or wheelchairs are viewed more favorably and more sympathetically than obesity or facial deformities (168).

Direct effects of physical defects normally occur earlier than indirect effects. Even young children are aware of their inability to do things their playmates do, and if they know this is due to a physical handicap, they feel resentful and frustrated. Only if a defect does not prevent them from doing what their playmates do does it fail to have a direct effect on the self-concept.

Awareness of social attitudes toward defects is delayed because adults try not to let children know how they feel about defects and because the defects are unimportant in the peer group unless they interfere with the group's activities (21, 28, 97). Facial scars or broken teeth, for example, will go unnoticed unless they are very conspicuous. Even then, most children accept such defects in their playmates without judgmental comments or questions. Only after

they reach the looks-conscious age of adolescence, when the social group "virtually equates physical beauty with social survival, is disfigurement often short of tragic" (52). From then on, the indirect effects of physical defects on personality become as important as the direct effects, if not more so.

Numerous studies have been made of the direct and indirect effects of obesity on personality. Directly, obesity is a handicap in social relationships because the obese person is unable to keep up with his contemporaries. Indirectly, awareness of unfavorable social attitudes toward obesity makes the person feel inferior and socially scorned (32, 139). As time goes on, Atkinson and Ringuette have pointed out, "Massively obese individuals become more disturbed, perhaps because of both increasing self-dissatisfaction and cumulative adverse responses from others" (12).

Whether direct or indirect, the harmful effects of physical defects are far-reaching. The person who suffers from a physical defect, regardless of how minor it is, is faced with the normal adjustment problems of his age as well as the specific problems arising from the defect. He is thus extremely vulnerable to feelings of threat and to other sources of emotional instability.

Parental overprotectiveness of a child with a physical defect may interfere with his adjustment to school and his participation in extracurricular activities, causing him to be immature for his age and increasing his feeling of inadequacy and inferiority.

Physical defects that keep children from acquiring play skills deprive them of social contacts and make the children feel scorned or rejected by their age-mates. This leads to feelings of martyrdom, often intensified by the belief that they are rejected by their parents and siblings as well as their age-mates. With limited social contacts, children have few opportunities to develop their social sensitivity, and this further hampers their ability to make good social adjustments. As a result, they are forced to spend much of their play time alone; they develop few interests, have fits of boredom, and are envious of those who are socially accepted. Under such conditions, many physically handicapped children live in a fantasy world and become introverted and egocentric.

The damaging effects of physical defects begun in childhood increase with age and lead to poor personal and social adjustments in adult life—in work, marriage, and social life. A follow-up study of graduates from a school for crippled children showed that, as adults, they were socially very inactive, even though they had been socially active in their school days. This social inactivity in adult life was due, in part, to difficulties in getting around and, in part, to feelings of being unwanted. This led to personal dissatisfaction, unhappiness, and a tendency to be introverted and egocentric (52).

Factors influencing effects on personality Since people react differently to physical defects, the effects of defects on personality vary. One person may succumb to the obstacles his defect presents and accept nonexpression as his lot, while another may compensate by becoming highly competent in his chosen field. Individual reactions are influenced by a number of factors, the most important of which are described below.

AGE AT WHICH THE DEFECT IS ACQUIRED If crippling occurs early in life, the person usually adjusts better to the dependence it necessitates than if it occurs after he has learned to be independent (52). When a person has always had a facial disfigurement, it occupies a "central role in the development of his self-concept" (120). Should the disfigurement be acquired during adolescence or adulthood, when the social value of physical attractiveness is at a peak, it will have a more unfavorable effect on personality than if acquired in childhood when attractiveness is of less concern (52, 135). Any physical defect acquired after marriage is likely to be a greater obstacle to good marital adjustment than if it were present before marriage (69).

The development of physical defects is one of the greatest obstacles to good adjustment in old age. The necessity of wearing bifocals or a hearing aid or of using crutches is more of a blow to the person's ego than it would have been if it had arisen before other signs of aging appeared (43, 74, 94, 246).

KIND OF DEFECT People react more favorably to certain kinds of defects than to others, and their reactions have considerable impact on the individual's own reaction to his defect. People tend to react more favorably to physical than mental disabilities (100). They react more favorably to minor and to extremely serious defects and to nonfacial defects. The more distant the defect is from the person's face, the more favorable the social reactions (97, 121, 144, 155, 192).

SERIOUSNESS OF DEFECT The seriousness of a physical defect is determined by how much it restricts

a person's activities. A person who is blind or crippled, for example, has a more serious defect than the person who is deaf. The more the defect interferes with physical activities, the more difficult it is for the person to gain social acceptance. This is especially true in childhood when physical activity is essential to acceptance. By adolescence, girls can turn to nonphysical recreations and gain acceptance from their peers more readily than boys can.

Facial deformities, unless accompanied by some functional impairment, such as a cleft palate, would have little effect on the person's self-concept were it not for the unfavorable reactions of members of the social group toward the deformity. By contrast, obesity is very serious because it affects activities even though it is not as disfiguring as a facial deformity.

Only in old age will a defect that limits a person's activities not always be an obstacle to good personal adjustments. An elderly person may find that a disability that interferes with his activities is more of an asset than a liability in some situations. It may relieve him of the "necessity" of trying to appear young and sprightly. On the other hand, for some older people, as Kassel has explained, "disabilities . . . become status symbols, a means whereby they can obtain attention and control their families" (111).

CONTROL OF DEFECT Some physical defects can be corrected or minimized and others can be camouflaged by clothing or beauty aids. The more the defect can be controlled, the less revision the person will have to make in his body image and the less damaging the effect on his personality. Plastic surgery to remove scars and tattoos, for example, has been reported to aid their rehabilitation (174).

Plastic surgery to correct facial disfigurements or to delay or remove the appearance of aging from the face, hands, and arms also improves the person's self-concept. For example, facial drawings before and after surgery have revealed that the patients had a much improved image of themselves after successful treatment (30).

RECOGNITION OF BEING DIFFERENT Recognition by the person and by members of the social group that he is "different," and, as most would say, "inferior," increases the damaging effect of a physical defect on personality. Many amputee children resist the use of artificial limbs because they do not want to be even "more different" (39). A person who is so hard of hearing that he must wear a hearing aid is more readily recognized as different than one whose deafness is slight.

If the person suffers from such a serious defect that he is restricted to an environment where his peers suffer from a similar defect, as in schools for the blind, crippled, or deaf, he is less likely to realize how different he is than if his defect were less serious. When he is in constant contact with nonhandicapped people, he has a constant reminder of his defect. Children who are deaf or blind, for example, develop more personality disturbances when they are in regular schools than when they are in special schools (51, 52, 79, 93).

SOCIAL ATTITUDES   The attitudes of members of the social group, especially of such significant people as parents, siblings, teachers, and peers, have a marked effect on the attitude of the handicapped person toward his handicap and toward himself. If they pity him or feel sorry for him, he will feel sorry for himself and develop a feeling of martyrdom. If they reject him as a companion, he will experience all the negative attitudes toward self that come from social rejection, such as resentment, self-pity, and compensatory behavior. His behavior will then make him even less appealing and will increase his social rejection. Social attitudes are more favorable when the defect is slight or major than when it falls between these extremes. A slight defect generally does not prevent the person from doing what others do and it can usually be partially or wholly camouflaged. A major defect arouses pity and sympathy.

Social attitudes are also influenced by how well known the handicapped person is to members of the group. Once people become familiar with the disabled person they usually have a more favorable attitude toward him than they did when they first met him. In initial social interactions, many people feel uncomfortable in the presence of a person with a physical defect, especially when it is visible, and they terminate their social contacts with him sooner than they do with persons who are not handicapped. The most unfavorable social attitudes toward those who suffer from a physical defect are found in people with high ethnocentrism. They treat the disabled as an outgroup and reject them, just as they do people who belong to minority religious, racial, or socioeconomic groups (41).

Unfavorable social attitudes affect the person indirectly by making it difficult for him to gain social acceptance, by setting up barriers to work and marriage, and by making him feel that even members of his family reject him. Under such conditions, he can hardly have a favorable self-concept or find it easy to revise his body image even if the physical defect is corrected or camouflaged.

PERSONAL ATTITUDES   The person's attitude toward his defect, which is strongly colored by social attitudes, is the most important single factor in determining what effect the defect will have on his personality. A person with a facial disfigurement is likely to attribute his social rejection, for example, to the disfigurement. He does not realize that the rejection may be caused, in part, by his angry, aggressive behavior or that this behavior is a result of the way he himself feels about the disfigurement. Furthermore, when he compares himself with his ideal physical self he is even more dissatisfied with his face. He cannot believe that others view him more favorably than he views himself. This self-rejection increases the unfavorable effect of the disfigurement on his personality.

Some people develop strong feelings of guilt and shame about their defects. This makes them shy, withdrawn, and unsocial in their behavior. Others develop defensive reactions to compensate for feelings of insecurity and inferiority. Some people accept their disabilities at first and set realistic goals for themselves. Later, being frustrated by their limited achievements, they raise their goals to an unrealistic level, thus setting the stage for further frustrations.

Another common way of coping with physical defects is to refuse to acknowledge their existence and try to behave as if nothing were wrong. A child who is lame, for example, tries to play the same games and sports his age-mates play. He cannot keep up with them, and he is frustrated and resentful when they do not choose him as a team mate. Refusal to accept or even acknowledge handicaps is common among elderly people, especially men. Failing eyesight may make them slow and inaccurate in their work, but they are resentful when laid off from their jobs and hold a grudge against their employer and the younger person who replaces them. In time, they may develop a generalized feeling of martyrdom.

Perhaps the most unfavorable personal attitude toward a physical defect is dread of being ridiculed. Even when a person tries to ignore his defect, he learns that some people not only do not ignore it but treat it as a joke. People with speech defects, for example, are hypersensitive about talking becaus they discovered, as children, that others laughed at them or mimicked them (94).

HEALTH CONDITIONS

Good health contributes to good adjustment, and good adjustment in turn contributes to good physical and mental health. Poor health and illness, on the other hand, adversely affect personality through the unfavorable effects they have on social and personal adjustments. Poor adjustments often predispose the person to illness or intensify an already existing illness.

Poor health upsets body homeostasis, and a person who is not up to par physically suffers from heightened emotionality. He becomes nervous, fretful, irritable, and subject to anxiety and stress. By contrast, good health helps to maintain body homeostasis and this, in turn, makes the person feel better, both physically and psychologically, even when beset by the stresses, anxieties, and depressions that everyone normally encounters.

Variations in health conditions

Few people go for any great length of time without having some illness. Some people, however, have more than is usual for their age levels; that is, they are *illness-prone.* Their tendency to have more illness may be due to a hereditary weakness, to a poor prenatal environment, or to conditions in their personal lives.

Among children, home training is partially responsible for illness-proneness. Children brought up in strict, authoritarian homes tend to be nervous and tense. This state of uneasiness interferes with good eating and sleeping habits and makes them susceptible to illness. Excessively lax home training encourages illness-proneness by not promoting good health habits (52, 91, 149, 185).

Some of the poor health that illness-prone people experience is *imaginary.* They discover that feeling under the weather excuses them from doing things they do not want to do or things they do not do well. They learn to "enjoy poor health" because it enables them to avoid irksome responsibilities without feeling guilty. Among older people, imaginary illness is sometimes used to get attention and sympathy (111).

Many illness-prone people suffer from illnesses that are due more to psychological than to physical causes—*psychosomatic illness.* Certain psychosomat-

ic disorders in children, such as enuresis, asthma, allergic reactions, and diabetes, stem from parent-child tensions or are greatly aggravated by these tensions (52, 67, 149). Adolescents who have more than their share of problems and frustrations due to unsatisfactory romances, unpopularity, academic difficulties, and poor relationships with their families also have more than their share of illness (193).

Factors influencing variations in health conditions

Certain *age* differences in health conditions are predictable. Young children suffer from more frequent and more serious illnesses than older children and adolescents (199, 232). Typically, adolescence is a healthy period, though imaginary illness is common at this age (38, 232). Good health continues until middle age when illnesses, both major and minor, become more frequent. With advancing age, illnesses become even more frequent and more serious (53, 57, 78, 173).

Sex differences in health conditions favor females at some ages and males at others. Boys have more illnesses than girls during childhood. While both boys and girls experience relatively good health in adolescence, girls experience periodic disturbances, due to their menstrual cycle. Since illness is considered a sign of weakness, males—older boys, adolescents, and adults—often refuse to admit that they are not feeling well, and so they *seem* to be healthier than females. Girls and women, at any age, complain more about their health than boys and men, possibly because poor health is more socially acceptable among females. Imaginary illness is likewise more common among girls and women (57, 78). In old age, men not only have more frequent illnesses than women but their illnesses are more serious, as seen by the fact that they die earlier than women (52, 149, 195, 199, 232).

At every age, *social-class* differences in health conditions favor the upper and middle classes, owing largely to better nutrition and health care, both of which are influenced by economic factors. Evidence that elderly people of the lower classes complain less about their health than those of other classes may be explained, in part, by the fact that they have always suffered from relatively poor health and take poor health for granted (193, 196).

Of all the factors influencing differences in health conditions, *personality* is one of the most important. Poorly adjusted people, of whatever age, sex, or class, tend to suffer from more numerous and more serious illnesses than those who are well adjusted. In addition, they tend to overestimate their poor health and they are anxious and pessimistic about their chances of full recovery (88, 143, 157, 188, 193). For example, studies reveal that asthmatics suffer from personality problems characterized by emotionality and dependency. This increases and prolongs the physical disturbances asthma brings (24, 193, 243). Studies likewise show that people suffering from *any* form of chronic illness, whether physical or psychosomatic in origin, "display an emotional pattern that deviates from the normal" (170).

People who are well adjusted do not like to be ill. They try to avoid illness by reasonable health measures and by complying with the doctor's orders when they are sick. By contrast, the poorly adjusted "enjoy poor health" because of the attention it brings and the opportunity to avoid doing things they regard as disagreeable or difficult.

Effects of health conditions on personality

While health conditions, like the other physical determinants, affect personality both directly and indirectly, there is some evidence that the direct effects of health are more important and more persistent.

Direct effects   Of the many direct effects of health on personality, the three most common and most serious will be discussed. *First,* the person's health affects his appearance. Self-evaluations are greatly influenced by the attractiveness of the face and body. Good health tends to improve even a homely appearance. At all ages, the "glow of health" partially compensates for unattractive features and gives the face and body a pleasant appearance which others judge as attractive. Knowing that his appearance is attractive goes a long way toward giving the person self-confidence and self-assurance.

During illness, the "glow of health" vanishes and unattractive features lack any form of compensation. Furthermore, most people are disagreeable and out of sorts when they are not feeling well, and their grumpiness shows on their faces, further accenting the unattractiveness of their features. Should illness be accompanied by pain, the face has a drawn look which distorts even the most attractive features.

Knowing how the social group feels about physical attractiveness, the person who is ill will be even more concerned about the unfavorable effects of

his illness on his appearance. Especially in old age, when illnesses are frequent and prolonged, the realization that poor health detracts from the appearance adds to the other detrimental effects of illness on the self-concept.

The *second* direct effect of health conditions on personality is that they influence motivation. When the person is feeling well, his motivation to do what he is capable of doing is strong. As a result, he is reasonably satisfied with his achievements. When he is not feeling well, however, his motivation is low and he is dissatisfied because his achievements often fall below his capacities. Should poor health be prolonged, he may get into the habit of working below capacity, and continue to do so even when he feels better. He will then develop feelings of inadequacy and inferiority.

The *third* and perhaps most important direct effect of health conditions on the self-concept is that they limit what the person can do. When he is in good health, there are no limitations on what he can do, except those imposed by his own abilities and the social environment. If both of these are favorable, his achievements will come close to his expectations and he will be reasonably satisfied with himself.

Illness, on the other hand, limits activities and leaves the individual feeling frustrated, resentful, and martyred. A young child may enjoy the added attention he gets when he is unable to do things for himself, but an older child, an adolescent, or an adult will resent being restricted, especially if he is unsure of his status. Just as an adolescent may fear that limitations on his activities will lead to loss of social acceptance among his peers, so the adult may fear that they will mean lack of promotion or even loss of his job.

Indirect effects   The indirect effects of health conditions on personality come from the attitudes of members of the social group, especially significant people in that group, toward the person's health. If the individual is in good health, looking well and full of zest, if he wants to do what he is capable of doing, and if his emotional states are normal, social reactions to him will be positive. Favorable social attitudes will increase his social acceptance and, as a result, add to a favorable concept of self.

Studies show that the attitudes of significant people toward a person's illness greatly affect his self-concept. If parents regard the illness of a child as a family calamity, blaming him for being careless or for violating a family health rule, and complaining about the money and personal sacrifices his illness entails, he is bound to feel guilty and emotionally disturbed (10, 91).

Similarly, among older people, family attitudes toward their illnesses have a marked effect on their attitudes. Those who have the resources necessary to provide for their care without placing too great a burden on their families make the best adjustments to their illnesses (78, 196).

Evidence of effects on personality

There is ample evidence that good health has a favorable effect on personality while poor health, whether physical or psychosomatic in origin and whether real or imaginary, has a damaging effect. Many personality changes result from poor health conditions and persist even after the illness has been cured or its severity lessened. This is especially true during childhood, when personality is in its formative stage. In fact, many personality disturbances in adolescents and adults trace their origin to illness during the early childhood years (149, 222).

Regardless of the nature of the illness or the age of the person experiencing it, any illness reduces the scope of the person's world. It encourages him to be egocentric and selfish, it causes frustrations which may make the person aggressive and cantankerous or withdrawn, it leads to heightened emotionality, and it makes the person feel martyred. In older people, illness often encourages regression to an earlier period of their lives when they were healthier and happier (222).

Even tiredness, caused by poor health, overexertion, frustrations, or boredom with one's role in life, leads to personality changes which often become persistent if the conditions responsible for the tiredness persist. Constant tiredness may turn a happy, well-adjusted person into an unhappy, poorly adjusted one.

A number of studies show how marked an effect certain illnesses have on personality. Persons suffering from diabetes experience tension and anxiety which cause frustration when they try to conform to the demands of their social environments. As a result of frustration, they become aggressive, often turning their aggressions outward on others (52).

Physical disturbances caused by the female menstrual cycle often lead to emotional instability accompanied by a tendency to be irritable, depressed, out of sorts. This heightened emotionality is reflected in poor social adjustments and a decrease in work, both of which influence the woman's self-concept and the attitudes of other people (149, 163, 183, 247).

Some of the predisposition to irritability and crabbiness in old age may be traced to changes in the blood sugar level caused by the body's inability to withdraw glucose from the bloodstream and store it in tissues which have been damaged by the aging process (163, 173, 203).

Since illness in old age has such damaging effects on personality, it has been suggested that one of the best preparations for old age is health measures designed to prevent chronic and progressive diseases which impair the efficiency and happiness of the elderly and, as such, contribute to unfavorable personality changes (196). This suggestion could well be applied to *all* ages. Preventing illness and keeping the person in a state of good health would do much to ensure the development of a wholesome personality, good personal and social adjustments, and happiness.

SUMMARY

1 The body is an important personality determinant because of its direct influence on the quantity and quality of a person's behavior and its indirect influence through the way the person perceives his body as a source of self-evaluation. Traditional beliefs about the influence of facial features, body build, and body functioning, some of which trace back to the time of Aristotle, have stimulated scientific interest in the effect the body has on personality. Today, evidence from scientific studies suggests that the indirect influence is even greater than the direct influence.

2 Body build influences personality directly by determining what the person can and cannot do, what his energy level will be, and what his reaction will be to those whose body builds are superior or inferior to his. Indirectly, body build influences personality through body cathexis, or the degree of satisfaction the person experiences because of his body. This indirect influence has been reported to be even greater than the direct, because body build is a symbol of self by which others evaluate the person and by which he, in turn, evaluates himself.

3 Physical attractiveness has little direct influence on personality, but the indirect influence that comes from the attitudes of others toward the person's attractiveness or unattractiveness is great. People like to be associated with attractive people; their treatment of an attractive person is favorable and has a positive effect on his self-concept.

4 Homeostasis, or the maintenance of a relatively steady internal environment, affects personality directly through its effects on the quality of the person's behavior and, indirectly, through the way others judge his behavior. How pronounced these effects are has been highlighted by studies of the behavioral effects of unfavorable physical or psychological conditions that produce states of disequilibrium.

5 Rapid and pronounced physical changes upset homeostasis and affect personality directly through their influence on the person's characteristic patterns of adjustment. Indirectly, the effect of body changes comes from the attitudes of others toward the changes and what roles the social group will allow the individual to play as a result of his changed appearance. The effect of body changes on personality vary according to the speed of the changes, the timing of the changes in relation to similar changes in other members of the social group, how much preparation the person has had for the changes, social attitudes toward the changes, the effect of the changes on the person's attractiveness, health, and body control, and how closely the changes conform to his body ideal.

6 The direct effect of body control on personality comes from its influence on what the person can and cannot do. The indirect effect comes from the judgments others make of him based on the degree of control he has over his body. Awkwardness, which is caused by rapid growth, lack of opportunity to learn to coordinate the body, body build, emotional tension, low-grade intelligence, etc., is damaging to the self-concept because it leads to unfavorable personal and social judgments. How damaging awkwardness is to personality has been highlighted

by studies of people who are ambidextrous or who are left-handed.

7 Whether accidents are due to lack of supervision, poor muscle coordination, the person's desire to attract attention by engaging in daredevil stunts, or some other cause, they are damaging to the person's self-concept. The damage comes partly from the unfavorable judgments of others but mainly from his own unfavorable self-judgments, which lead to a generalized feeling of insecurity and inadequacy colored by a feeling of martyrdom if he believes that his accidents are due to "bad luck."

8 The first scientific recognition of the effects of physical defects on personality come from Alfred Adler's theory of "organ inferiority." Today, there is ample evidence that *any* physical defect is damaging to the self-concept, although the extent of the damage varies according to when the defect was acquired, the seriousness of the defect, social attitudes toward the defect, how much the defect can be controlled or camouflaged, and how aware the person is of being different. Physical defects affect personality directly by their effect on the person's behavior and, indirectly, by the attitudes of members of the social group toward the person who suffers from a physical defect.

9 Health conditions, which vary according to the age, sex, socioeconomic status, and birth order of the person, affect personality directly through their influence on what the person can do, how well he can do it, and how his appearance is affected by his health. The indirect effect comes from the attitudes of significant people as they are influenced by how good or how poor the person's health is, whether they believe his poor health is real or imaginary, and how much his health interferes with his activities and his relationship with others. At all ages and among members of both sexes, good health is a personality asset while poor health is a liability.

intellectual determinants

Intelligence provides the person with the capacity to meet and solve the problems that adjustment to life requires. How he uses his intellectual capacity will determine how successful his adjustment will be. The quality of his adjustment is, in turn, a major factor in his personality development.

Directly, intellectual capacities influence the kind of adjustment the person makes to his environment, to people, and to himself. As his intellectual capacities develop, the person constantly alters his awareness of the world and his perceptions of people, of situations, and of himself. He learns that he must transform his native impulsive behavior into orderly, patterned conduct that conforms to social expectations if he wants to win social acceptance and approval.

Indirectly, intellectual capacities influence the judgments other people make of the person. Their judgments affect his self-judgments because they determine what role the social group will permit him to play and how it will treat him. The person whom the social group regards as "bright," other factors equal, has more influence over others than the person who is looked upon as "average" or "dull." People respect his judgments and are willing to be influenced by him in a way they would not be influenced by one whose intellectual capacities they regarded as "inferior."

Knowing that the capacity for adjustment increases each year, the social group sets up standards for the level of adjustment it expects the person to achieve at different ages. These standards are "developmental tasks," or learning experiences which will enable the person to adjust to the social expectations for his age. The brighter a person is, the more the group expects of him, not only in the immediate present but also in the future. As Landreth has explained, the statement, "That boy will go far," suggests that "brightness at one period represents behavior potential, and this is *predictive* of future performance" (142). How well the individual lives up to social expectations will have a marked effect on his self-concept.

The person's awareness of his adjustive ability also influences his self-concept. If a child recognizes that he is superior in schoolwork, he will have a favorable self-attitude unless he discovers that his superiority has little prestige value or is actually regarded with contempt by his age-mates. Similarly, if an elderly person recognizes that he is "slipping" mentally, he will develop an unfavorable self-attitude, which will be accentuated by the social group's recognition of his slipping and by the group's assignment to him of roles below those he formerly had.

While adjustments are influenced both directly and indirectly by the level of the individual's intellectual capacities, there is evidence that, even in elementary school, the indirect influences are slightly greater than the direct. D'Heule et al. write: "As early as the 3rd grade, academic achievement is related to how the child perceives his world and how he relates to it, and this relation is somewhat independent of mental ability" (65).

INTELLECTUAL DEVELOPMENT

For approximately one-half of the normal life span, increases in mental capacity enable the person to adjust to his environment with greater and greater success. Then, beginning in about the mid-forties, decreases in mental capacity, normally preceded by physical declines, lessen the individual's capacity for adjustment.

While all people follow much the same pattern, the rate of development and decline varies sharply. Not all children reach the same point in physical and mental development at the same age nor do all adults begin to decline physically and mentally at the same age or at the same rate.

Furthermore, in the same person, physical and mental traits develop at different rates, reach maturity at different ages, and then start to decline at different ages and at different rates. While a person is usually consistent in his rate of development in the sense that he is generally early or late in reaching critical periods in the growth cycle, irregularities in rate of growth, both physically and mentally, are not uncommon (17, 91).

When irregularities are pronounced, for example when intellectual development is far ahead of physical development, the many adjustment problems that the person must face will have a profound effect on his personality. To illustrate, very bright children always find it difficult to make satisfactory social adjustments. Children of their own intellectual level, but several years older, regard them as too young to play with because of their smaller size, while normally intelligent children of their own size and age have few interests in common with them.

Pattern of development of general intelligence

Since the kind of adjustment a person makes is governed by his intellectual capacity, one cannot measure or predict the quality of the person's adjustment without knowing what his intellectual capacity is. This information comes largely from studies of intellectual growth based on standardized tests of general intelligence. The studies reveal an increase in general intelligence throughout the early years of life, with the rate of increase slowing during the adolescent years and coming to a standstill or a near standstill in late adolescence or early adulthood (17, 43, 74).

There are marked variations in the ages at which people reach their top capacity for intellectual functioning. For some, it may be 16 or 18 years, while for others, it may be 21 years or later. The higher the level of innate intellectual ability, the longer it will continue to grow (17, 43, 185). This is illustrated in Figure 7-1, which shows the leveling off of intellectual growth for people of different intellectual capacities, ranging from very low capacity to very high.

Throughout the growth years, children grow intellectually in their own, unique way, as Bayley has pointed out (17). Some are *labile* in the sense that their growth rate fluctuates markedly, sometimes being very slow and sometimes very fast; others are *stable,* manifesting a fairly steady progress without spurts or lulls; while still others show stability at certain ages and variability at others (17). Because of the fluctuations in rate of growth, it is difficult to predict what the mature intellectual level will be. Variations in the patterns of intellectual growth are shown in Figure 7-2.

After studying the intellectual growth of a group of children from 3 to 12 years of age, Sontag et al. reported that variations in a child's measured intelligence are usually greatest between the ages of 6 and 7 years. While a particular child may drop to a lower level at this time, the trend is definitely upward for most children. During the elementary school years, more children show gains than losses in intelligence quotients (IQ) scores, though the size of both gains and losses decrease with age. Furthermore, neither acceleration nor deceleration is limited to any one intellectual ability. Instead, all intellectual abilities seem to follow the same pattern (209).

From adolescence on, the pattern of intellectual growth is fairly consistent. Fluctuations in rate of growth are less marked than in the earlier years and predictions of what the mature level will be are more accurate (17, 43, 74).

After intellectual growth reaches its mature level, whether at age 16, 18, 20, or even later, the capacity for adjustment will change little over a span of about 30 or 35 years. There is some increment, as may be seen in Figure 7-2, but it is slight. Those of very high intellectual capacity may not reach their ceiling until 25 years of age or later, though the increase after the age of 20 is small (17, 174, 176).

During the adult years, measured intelligence varies little, suggesting that the stability that became apparent during the adolescent years increases with the passage of time (17, 34). Since most intellectual capacities remain at their peak until the mid-fifties or slightly later, the more mature person can adjust as

Figure 7-1 Levelling off of intellectual growth for people of different intellectual capacities. (Adapted from S. L. Pressey and R. G. Kuhlen: *Psychological development through the life span.* New York: Harper & Row, 1957. Used by permission.)

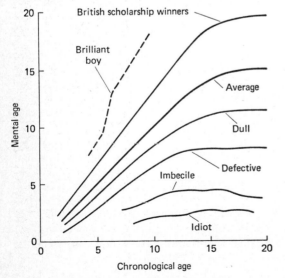

well as an adolescent and better than a child. It may take the person longer to learn as he grows older, but the quality of his learning does not suffer (17).

It is popularly believed that intelligence decreases with age, with decline setting in during the fifties. Studies of intellectual changes with age, using intelligence test scores, have borne out this belief (24, 33, 43). However, there is reason to question whether the data reported in the studies are accurate.

In the *first* place, most studies of the elderly use the cross-sectional method instead of the longitudinal method. This means that older people are compared with younger people who may have entirely different backgrounds and potentials. Schaie and Strother (199), using both cross-sectional and longitudinal approaches to study age changes in cognitive behavior in people from 25 to 70 years of age, write:

The most important conclusion to be drawn from this study is that a major portion of the variance attributed to age differences in past cross-sectional studies must properly be assigned to differences in ability between successive generations. Age changes over time within the individual appear to be much smaller than differences between cohorts. . . . The findings on longitudinal age changes suggest further that levels of functioning attained at maturity may be retained until late in life except where decrement in response strength and latency interferes.

Second, differences may be due to an error in sampling. Most studies of the elderly use institutionalized people who are readily available but who are more representative of the lower socioeconomic groups and of the less educated segments of the population than of the entire population. *Third,* the tests emphasize speed, which makes them favor younger subjects, and such material as practical information, which is more closely related to the interests of young adults than of the elderly. *Fourth,* the elderly do not have the same educational background as the young, nor are they accustomed to taking tests of the kind used to measure intelligence. And *fifth,* it is difficult to believe that the elderly have the same motivation for taking tests that younger people have.

A decrease in intellectual capacities with aging may be due to disuse. It has been reported that those of higher IQs and higher education, who use their intellectual capacities more than those of lower IQ, show less mental decline with age (24, 175, 176, 217, 230).

Or a decline may be due to brain damage from

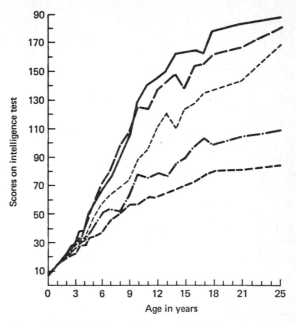

Figure 7-2 Individual growth curves of intelligence as measured by tests given to five males at intervals up to 25 years of age. (Adapted from N. Bayley: Research in child development: A longitudinal perspective. *Merrill-Palmer Quart.*, 1965, **11**, 183–208. Used by permission.)

some physical cause or to poor general health. It has been reported that the greatest mental decline comes just before death—the "imminence-of-death factor" —and generally lasts for less than 20 months. In most cases, this decline can be attributed to failing health which eventually causes death (22).

There is evidence that elderly people learn less than they are capable of because they underestimate their abilities or accept the cultural stereotype that they are too old to learn "new tricks" (143, 199). On the other hand, "Bright people do not become dull at 60 nor do dull people become moronic at 60" (238). The decline is far less dramatic than is popularly believed, except where there is brain deterioration or damage (24, 33, 43, 143).

Motivation to use one's intellectual capacities at all ages and opportunities to do so are important in preventing mental decline with aging, as Parker (178) explains:

Psychological aging is not to be measured in terms of capabilities alone, but in the use to which they have been applied from early age through all the years of maturity. This consists of a blending of a desire to learn, the ability to wonder and to derive satisfaction and pleasure therefrom, a diversity of interests, and the will to make the necessary effort.

No one specific pattern of mental decline is characteristic. The age at which decline begins, the speed of the decline, and its continuity, once it begins, vary greatly from one person to another. In general, the decline in mental efficiency is slower and less intense among those of the higher intellectual levels and among those whose health is good (24, 92, 178).

Patterns of development of specific intellectual capacities

The various intellectual capacities follow their own individual developmental patterns—patterns that are distinct and yet, in their major aspects, similar. In addition, the capacities reach maturity at different ages and start to decline at different ages and at different rates.

The developmental patterns impinge on personality because they affect the kind of adjustment the individual is able to make at different ages. This, in turn, influences the attitudes of other people toward him, his treatment by them, and the roles they permit him to play. If the social group expects the person to learn some developmental task, such as reading or controlling his aggressiveness, before he has developed the intellectual capacities essential for the task, his self-concept will be unfavorably affected because (1) he will think of himself as a "failure" and (2) the social group will judge him negatively.

Studies of the intellectual development of the same individuals over a period of years have found no evidence that intelligence is an integrated capacity which grows by steady accelerations. Instead, as Bayley (17) writes:

Intelligence is a dynamic succession of developing functions, with the more advanced and complex functions in the hierarchy depending on the prior maturing of the earlier simpler ones (given, of course, normal conditions of care). . . . Intelligence is a complex of separately timed, developing functions.

Not only do different mental functions develop at different rates but the independence of the functions increases with age (17). In the pattern of intellectual development, for example, memory precedes reasoning, with concrete reasoning developing earlier than abstract reasoning (17). Any mental ability that involves verbal ability improves with age. This is shown in tests of practical judgment, information,

disarranged sentences, and synonyms-antonyms (174, 176).

The rate of decline of intellectual abilities likewise varies. And as is true of differences in rate of growth, the differences in rate of decline are responsible for some of the adjustment problems people experience as age advances.

Studies have emphasized the normal patterns of growth and decline and the differences in the patterns from one mental ability to another. The mental abilities discussed below have received the most attention in scientific research.

Memory   The ability to remember what has been learned develops early and reaches its peak during late adolescence. Memory for concrete material, however, develops earlier than memory for abstract material. The more meaningful the material is to the learner, the more easily he will learn it and the longer he will remember it (108, 199).

Decline in memory of previously learned material—*forgetfulness*—is one of the criteria commonly associated with the cultural stereotype of the elderly. Studies of memory in the elderly have shown that there is less forgetting of old than of new material and that different kinds of material are subject to different degrees of forgetting (87). Memory of general information, numbers, and vocabulary, for example, shows little decline with age while memory of material that tends to be meaningless to the learner shows a more rapid decline (46, 185, 201, 219).

Forgetfulness may be largely a matter of lack of motivation on the part of elderly subjects in a test situation. If they see no point in remembering meaningless material such as nonsense syllables, they are likely to be inattentive. This militates against learning and, in turn, against remembering. Meaningful material, such as words and numbers, which are in constant use in daily life, show little loss through forgetting as people grow older (132, 199, 201). Subjects in their late sixties showed the least decline in memory in the area of words, as measured by vocabulary tests (199).

The tendency to *reminisce*—to forget or ignore the present and to recall the past—is characteristic of elderly people who are unhappy in their present status or who suffer from brain deterioration and cannot remember what they have just learned (219). The less immediate memory they have, the more they reminisce (33, 133).

Memory plays an important role in the kind of adjustment a person makes to life. Remembering people's names, for example, aids social acceptance. Being able to remember what one is expected to do leads to efficiency and the reputation of being a "well-organized" person. Reminiscing, in either adulthood or old age, makes a person "tiresome," lowering others' judgments of him and rendering him less acceptable.

Reasoning The ability to tackle new material and to solve new problems, the "capacity to understand and to apply a fresh method of thinking," known as "reasoning," reaches its peak in the twenties and then begins to decline. However, the speed and amount of decline vary according to the mental capacities of the person, with the ablest experiencing only slight decline and the duller, more decline (17, 33, 199).

Studies show that, in novel decision-making situations where old patterns of behavior are inapplicable, elderly people find it difficult to adopt a new approach; they tend to fall back on established modes of behavior (24). Most elderly people exhibit only a limited ability to perform on an abstract level (33, 156).

Since good adjustment requires that one be able to adapt to new people, new situations, and new problems, faulty reasoning is damaging to the personality. A person who can think independently will make far better adjustments than one who becomes overly cautious of his thinking and creates the impression of being rigid. Equally as serious, lack of capacity for abstract reasoning leads to lack of creativity; the person is afraid to think independently for fear of making mistakes. As a result, the quality of his achievements declines even though the quantity may not (24, 33, 144, 156, 176).

In a culture that changes rapidly, such as our own, the ability to adjust to new situations is essential to success in all areas of life. The person who lacks the reasoning ability to make these adjustments, whether he be young or old, will be far less successful than his other potentials may indicate.

Learning Adjustment at all ages requires learning. The more slowly and less efficiently the person learns, the poorer his adjustment.

Incidental or *latent learning* contributes to adjustment because it enables the person to acquire bits of information he has not set out to learn but which he may find useful later. It aids vocational success as well as social success.

There is evidence that learning increases as intellectual growth progresses and that it improves with use and training. Much depends on what is to be learned, however. If the situation requires learning new techniques, the difficulty of learning increases as age advances. As Lehman has explained in relation to the elderly, "To learn the new they often have to unlearn the old and that is twice as hard as learning without unlearning. But when a situation requires a store of past knowledge, then the old find their advantage over the young" (144).

In any learning situation, especially when new material must be integrated with previously learned material, elderly people are less efficient than younger. The elderly are more cautious and thus require more time to integrate their responses; in addition, they are more likely to become confused or "muddled," which causes them to make mistakes or to fail to organize the material in a logical manner (33, 37, 199).

Effective learning is greatly hampered by *rigidity*—"the tendency to perseverate and resist perceptual change, to resist the acquisition of new patterns of behavior and to refuse to relinquish old and established patterns" (199).

Contrary to popular belief, rigidity is not limited to older people nor do all older people become rigid. At any age, when a person's values are threatened, his intense emotional involvement inhibits his ability to adapt to new situations. Since rigidity is less common among people of higher intellectual levels, they can adjust better to the stresses imposed by the changes required to adjust to new situations (33, 151, 199). Degree of rigidity varies markedly, however, owing largely to individual differences in mental ability and schooling (33, 151, 199).

The most damaging consequence of mental rigidity is that it prevents the person from adapting readily to new situations—a quality essential to good adjustment and to favorable social judgments. Rigidity also inhibits the expression of originality and creativity and blocks even a highly intelligent person from achieving his potential level of vocational success. The feelings of inadequacy that poor achievement and limited success give rise to further endanger the person's adaptability.

CONDITIONS INFLUENCING INTELLECTUAL CAPACITIES

How a person uses his inherited intellectual capacities determines the quality of his adjustments. And the quality of his adjustments affects his self-concept, the attitudes of others toward him, and thus his personality. Maturation provides for the development of all inherent traits, including intellectual traits, but the use made of them is the person's own responsibility (17).

Timing is central in the development of intellectual capacities. Learning is best when what is offered educationally is consistent with the learner's state of readiness or his level of maturity. The development of his basic intellectual endowment is influenced, favorably or unfavorably, by socioeconomic, cultural, and other factors not only during the growth years but also in maturity.

Intellectual growth comes from many varied and complex factors in addition to inherent capacities for growth. Of the many conditions that influence the development of intellectual capacities, the physical condition of the person, the use he makes of his intellectual capacities, his education, motivation, early home experiences, emotional states, and personality are the most important.

Physical condition

At all ages, the person's physical condition affects the use he makes of his intelligence. A child with a relatively low energy level will have fewer interactions with his environment than one with a higher energy level. Ordinarily, a low energy level adversely affects learning and adjustive behavior. Childhood diseases and malnutrition during the growth years are sometimes responsible for variations in IQ as well as for variations in adjustive behavior (5, 60).

The slowing down of the muscular responses and of the nervous system processes with increasing age adversely affects intellectual and adjustive behavior not only in test situations but also in everyday life. The mental effort required in reasoning is often a barrier to its use with advancing age, especially among those in failing health (24, 156, 185).

Use of intellectual capacities

How much use is made of intellectual capacities is markedly influenced by social-class identification (103, 142). Parents of the upper and middle social classes provide more opportunities for the child's intellectual development than those of the lower social classes. Even more important, they encourage the child to make use of these opportunities (40, 59, 111). Many scientists believe that opportunities to learn and en-

couragement are primarily responsible for IQ differences between white and Negro children, rather than a hereditary factor, as others claim (43, 74, 111, 121).

Jensen, in commenting on environmental influences, agrees that they are, in part, responsible for differences in achievement. As he explains, "Many other traits, habits, attitudes and values enter into a child's performance in school besides just his intelligence, and these noncognitive factors are largely environmentally determined, mainly through influence within the child's family" (222).

Furthermore, social expectancy influences the use people make of their intellectual capacities. Those who are recognized as intelligent are expected to have more "social power" in decision-making situations than are those who are less intelligent. Boys and men, in most cultures, are expected to use their intellectual capacities more than girls and women and are given more opportunities and more encouragement to do so (55, 103, 238).

Intellectual capacities increase longer and decline later and more slowly if the person continues to be mentally active. Elderly people who continue to work or who have intellectually stimulating recreations are reported to have more normal brain functioning, to make better adjustments, and to do better on intelligence tests than those who retire and allow themselves to become mentally inactive (53). The decline is hastened by mentally unstimulating work and by an unstimulating home and social environment (160, 174, 176).

Education

Higher education makes people less conforming in their attitudes, less authoritarian and more resentful of formalized authority, freer to criticize, more tolerant of nonconforming ideas and behavior in others, and more cognizant of the kinds of adaptation necessary in complex situations (53, 172, 199).

The more education a person has, the later the onset of mental decline and the slower the decline. These results are due in part to the greater exercise of intellectual abilities among the better educated and in part to the higher intelligence of those who have more education (17, 53, 185, 199).

Motivation

Motivation affects how and how much one uses his intellectual capacities. Sources of motivation vary with age. Children are often motivated by a desire to win parental approval or avoid disapproval and punishment.

Adolescents are generally motivated to use their intellectual capacities by a desire to go to college—which may be regarded as a status symbol or as a way of having fun or of furthering vocational and social goals. They use their intellectual capacities most effectively in school subjects that they think will help them to achieve their goals.

In general, lack of motivation is more responsible for mental decline than is physical deterioration. Compulsory retirement deprives many elderly people of a motivation to keep mentally alert. That lack of motivation is partially responsible for mental decline in old age was shown by a study in which elderly subjects were offered cash prizes for improvement in a test situation. All improved with practice (132).

Early home experiences

Two aspects of early home experiences have a profound influence on the person's ability and motivation to make the most of his intellectual capacities. The *first* is the kind of discipline used in the home. In test situations, children whose parents are demanding in their discipline do better than those whose parents are inconsistent and overanxious. Children whose parents

are unconcerned about discipline do poorly on tests (135). According to Baldwin et al. (15):

The democratic environment is most conducive to mental development; when it is non-indulgent, it is conducive to intellectual growth in all its aspects. The least stimulating sorts of environments seem to be the highly indulgent or the highly restrictive ones.

The *second* aspect of early home experiences that influences the development of intellectual capacities is the emotional climate of the home. Emotional climate depends on many conditions, such as kind of discipline used, interfamily relationships, and economic conditions. A favorable home climate ordinarily results in an increase in IQ scores over time, and vice versa (17, 32, 185). This effect is illustrated in Figure 7-3, which shows changes in general intellectual ability for three children over a period of 16 years.

Emotional states

Many people fail to make the most of their intellectual capacities because of emotional problems. This is true at all ages and all levels of intelligence; it is most pronounced at the higher intellectual levels (217).

General emotional tension—"free floating anxiety"— militates against the efficient use of such intellectual capacities as memory and reasoning. The per-

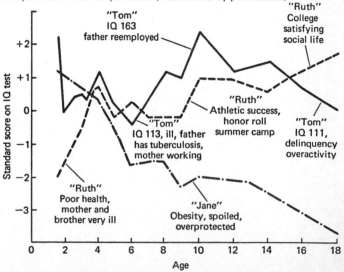

Figure 7-3 Some effects of home climate and family influence on the child's intellectual abilities, as measured by standard intelligence tests. (Adapted from S. L. Pressey and R. G. Kuhlen: *Psychological development through the life span.* New York: Harper & Row, 1957. Used by permission.)

son who is constantly worried and anxious functions below his intellectual potentials generally and works below his capacities. As he approaches learning situations, he is tense and unsure of himself. This lack of self-confidence adversely affects his performance in test situations as well as his ability to learn (129, 209).

Many adults fail to reach the level of achievement that their intellectual capacities and training would justify because of "intellectual inhibitions" stemming from family, personal, and social problems which give rise to anxiety and frustrations. There is evidence that some of the so-called decline in mental abilities with advancing age stems from anxiety and other unfavorable emotional states which make it impossible for the elderly person to do what he is capable of doing. Many older people, for example, view tests as a threat. This makes them suspicious and frightened, conditions which prevent them from putting forth their best efforts (92).

Personality pattern

The ability to learn is greatly influenced by such personality characteristics as anxiety, rigidity, negativism, hostility, and inflexibility (64). Strong *anxiety* makes it difficult for the learner to adjust to new situations. He becomes so concerned about his personal problems and his adequacy to meet new demands that he thinks about himself instead of the task to be mastered. In addition, he is less capable of improvising in a new situation where old and familiar techniques are inefficient or inapplicable (108).

Like anxiety, *rigidity* interferes with learning by making it difficult for the learner to adjust to new situations. *Negativism,* which is aroused by a threatening situation, leads to a defensive attitude that stifles motivation to learn.

Hostility is expressed in asocialization, or low social responsibility, and in low academic motivation. Underachievers are often satisfying an unconscious feeling of hostility against family members who demand academic success. Hostility affects academic work as early as the third grade and becomes progressively more detrimental to achievement as the student goes through high school and college (75, 82, 115). *Inflexibility,* or unwillingness to see other points of view, is closely correlated with lack of self-confidence and feelings of insecurity (129, 138).

While people who have the personality characteristics described above can deal with situations re-

quiring the recall of previously learned material, they have difficulty in situations involving new material. Such personality characteristics distinguish college students with reading difficulties. These students have difficulty getting started on a task, they are afraid to tackle anything new, they lose interest in a task when they hit a snag, and they are often rugged individualists who want to do as they wish, not as the group wishes.

DEVIANT INTELLIGENCE

Since intelligence aids adjustment, it would be logical to assume that the more intelligence a person has, the better his personal and social adjustments and the more satisfactory his personality development.

Studies of deviant intelligence—intelligence that is higher or lower than the norm—have not shown this assumption to be entirely correct. High-grade intelligence does not always ensure a healthy self-concept nor does low-grade intelligence always have a damaging effect. The effects of deviant intelligence on personality depend upon a number of factors, the most important of which are acceptance of the cultural stereotypes of people with deviant intelligence, social attitudes toward deviant intelligence, attitudes of significant people toward a person whose intelligence deviates from the norm, the person's awareness of others' attitudes, and his awareness of the extent of his deviation.

Stereotypes of deviant intelligence

Most people are at or near the norm in intelligence, and so it is not surprising that anyone whose intellectual development is very superior is regarded as "different" and "odd." Nor is it surprising that unfavorable cultural stereotypes have grown up about them and that the stereotypes have persisted in spite of highly publicized scientific information that contradicts them. These stereotypes affect attitudes toward those of deviant intelligence.

The popular belief that nature compensates for superiority in one area by inferiority in another area has led to a stereotype of the very bright in which "extraordinary mental proficiency is usually accompanied by physical frailty, early and drastic decline of abilities, insanity, and other compensatory deficiencies" (229). Hand in hand with this stereotype is the "beautiful but dumb" combination and its counterpart, the bright but unattractive. The stereotype of unattractiveness derives not so much from the very bright person's unattractive features, but from his lack of attention to conventional grooming, his disregard of fashion's dictates and beauty aids, and the necessity of wearing glasses due to "physical frailty."

The extremely bright person, according to the cultural stereotype, is a "loner," difficult to get along with. He is neither popular nor likely to be selected as a leader, even though his superior intellectual capacities might be of value to the activities of the social group. Nor is he likely to be a success in life, not because of lack of capacity but rather because he has difficulty getting along with people.

The stereotype of the person of low-grade intelligence has developed from the "fools" or "jesters" of medieval times. According to this stereotype, the stupid person says and does things to make others laugh at him, rather than with him, because he is too stupid to know the difference.

If the social group accepts the cultural stereotype of high intelligence as synonymous with maladjustment, labeling the very bright person a "brain," "curve raiser," or "egghead," he will have less prestige and, hence, less influence in the group than if the stereotype were more favorable. Similarly, acceptance of the stereotype of dullness as synonymous with being a fool leads to unfavorable social attitudes toward the dull person.

Social attitudes In the United States, identification with the majority means normalcy (157, 206). And as the IQ of the majority hovers around 100, those of deviant intelligence belong to the "minority." Like other minority groups, intellectual minorities are regarded with suspicion and disfavor. Since social attitudes toward brightness and dullness differ sharply, they will be discussed separately.

ATTITUDES TOWARD BRIGHTNESS While attitudes toward brightness are, on the whole, more favorable than attitudes toward dullness, they are by no means uniformly favorable but differ from group to group. They differ, for example, from one *school* to another and from one group within a school to another group. In a school that puts high value on going to college, the attitudes toward bright students will be more favorable than in a school where most of the students take jobs as soon as they graduate. If the popular members of the class put low value on intellectual

achievements, the general social attitude toward bright students is likely to be negative.

In the middle and upper *socioeconomic* groups, brightness is generally more highly valued than in lower socioeconomic groups. Superior intelligence and academic achievement are generally less valued among *girls* than among boys, and social attitudes toward bright girls are less favorable. As one bright high school girl explained, "If you're taller than the boys, it's bad enough, but if you're brighter, it's fatal" (212).

In general, brightness is more valued in *adolescence* than in childhood. Recognizing that education and vocational success are closely related and that higher education is limited to those who are bright enough to get into college, most adolescents place a higher value on intelligence than they did earlier. In fact, most adolescents place a higher value on intelligence and intellectual achievement than they are willing to admit. This is evident when they state that academic achievement is one of their major "problems" and when they rate intelligence high as a criterion in choosing a life mate (1, 2, 13).

Social attitudes are less favorable toward *very high* intellectual ability than toward moderate brightness. While peers may admire those who are bright, they often regard those who are *very* bright as "threats." They feel uncomfortable with the very bright because, by comparison, they themselves feel stupid and dumb. Furthermore, acceptance of the cultural belief that high intellectual ability and abnormality go hand in hand makes the peer group suspicious of everything the very bright person says or does.

Knowing that they are considered "different" or strange, the very bright are uneasy about what others think of them. This makes them feel inadequate in social relationships and thus intensifies the popular belief that they really are "strange." Furthermore, having little in common with their peers, many very bright children and adolescents concentrate their energies on intellectual pursuits. This they do, in part, because they find such pursuits more satisfying than the play of their peers and, in part, because they hope to win social acceptance in a peer group where intellectual achievement is highly valued.

As adults, those who are viewed by the social group as "intellectuals" or "eggheads" are aware of the unfavorable cultural stereotype of the very intelligent. Some try to disprove the stereotype because they feel socially isolated. Others become intellectual snobs as a form of compensation. This attitude leads them to engage in unsocial behavior, which tends to increase their unfavorable social image.

ATTITUDES TOWARD DULLNESS The social attitude toward those who are dull is usually one of scorn and annoyance. People are impatient with them because they are slow to learn and quick to forget; they tend to be more awkward than their age-mates and, hence, are not as skillful in games; they are slow in seeing the point of a joke and laugh only after everyone has stopped laughing; and they fail to recognize how limited their abilities are. Their classmates grow impatient with them because teachers must take time to reexplain what the rest of the class has already learned. Often parents and teachers accuse dull children of being "lazy" or "bad" and punish them for failing to learn.

By junior or senior high school, the dull person is usually so convinced of his dullness and aware of the unfavorable cultural attitude toward dullness that he becomes hypersensitive. Often he leaves school to avoid the constant embarrassment and humiliation his dullness causes. Some dull children and adolescents, however, will not admit, even to themselves, that they are dull. They blame their poor academic achievement on lack of interest in school, on the teacher's dislike of them, or on some other cause. In this way, they free themselves of the feelings of inferiority but substitute for them feelings of martyrdom.

Those who are *severely mentally retarded,* as in the case of idiots and imbeciles, are rejected as companions by their age-mates, but they are less likely to be ridiculed and blamed for their stupidity than those who are only slightly retarded. People generally feel sorry for them and for their families.

Attitudes of significant people

The attitudes of significant people, especially family members, have more influence on the self-concept of the person of deviant intelligence than do the attitudes of members of the social group as a whole. The closer the social relationship between the person and others, the more their attitude toward him will affect his self-concept.

Many parents of very bright children set unrealistically high goals for them and expect them to excel in *every* area of life. When the children fail to live up to such high expectations, parents accuse them of being lazy or of not taking advantage of their opportunities, often provided at great personal sacrifice to the parents.

Once bright children and adolescents get the reputation among their teachers and classmates of being "brains," the reputation becomes a halo by which they are judged in the future. As is true of parents, teachers and classmates expect them to be superior in all areas and are critical and punitive if they are not.

Since parents, especially mothers, evaluate themselves in terms of their children, having a mentally retarded child is stressful and ego-deflating. The more retarded the child, the lower the mother's self-esteem. Many parents are malevolent toward a retarded child, or even toward one who is not as bright as the other children of the family. They reject the child, adopt a hostile attitude toward him, and are excessively punitive. The more ambitious parents are for their children, the more malevolent they are toward the slow learner (52, 117).

Family members are often embarrassed by the behavior of a dull or retarded child. Older children and adolescents may be ashamed to have their peers come to their homes if the retarded sibling is present. If parents believe that something they did was responsible for a child's backwardness, they compensate for their feelings of guilt by becoming overprotective. As a result, the child is not motivated to be independent and probably becomes even more helpless than the level of his intelligence would justify.

Awareness of attitudes of others

Very young children do not know whether they are bright, dull, or average. Only after they enter school and have opportunities to compare their intellectual achievements with those of other children of their own age do they recognize variations in intelligence. If their school emphasizes competitive grades based on achievement, children become aware of their intellectual capacities sooner than if the school judges progress in terms of individual capacities. By junior high school, and certainly by senior high school, most boys and girls are apprised of how they compare with others intellectually.

When children become aware that others consider them "bright," they learn that brightness sets them apart and affects the attitudes of their teachers and peers. If their teachers expect more of them than of their classmates and if their classmates regard them as "brains" or "curve raisers," they will evaluate themselves in terms of these largely unfavorable labels.

If children are very retarded and hear their parents or neighbors refer to them as "dull" or "slow," they learn that they are different from their siblings. However, they do not appreciate the significance of their handicap until they have an opportunity to assess their abilities in relation to those of their age-mates. If the intelligence deficit is not severe enough to require placing the child in a special class or in an institution for the mentally retarded, he soon discovers that his academic achievements are inferior to those of his classmates and that, no matter how hard he tries, he cannot keep up to their pace. He also discovers that his classmates have an unfavorable attitude toward him because of his slowness. If he is put in a vocational school in junior or senior high school, he knows that his teachers judge him as "different."

Most dull children have such poor social insight that they fail to recognize how dull they actually are and how unfavorable the social attitudes toward them are. Therefore, their self-concepts are not as seriously damaged as they would be if the extent of the unfavorable social evaluations were fully appreciated.

Awareness of extent of deviation

Some children tend to *overestimate* their intellectual capacities because they have little basis for comparison. If a bright child is in a class with children of average ability, he may get the idea that he is brighter than he actually is because, in comparison with his classmates, he seems very superior. Or if the teacher consistently gives him A's because his work is the best in the class, he feels that he has even further evidence of his superior ability. In high school, college, or graduate school, when he runs into stiffer academic competition, he may lose his motivation to do what he is capable of doing. Then he may feel guilty because he has fallen below his own or others' expectations or he may blame others for not appreciating his abilities as he sees them.

If he comes to realize that his intellectual abilities are lower than he formerly believed, he may withdraw from situations where comparisons with others will be unfavorable to him or he may use rationalization to explain why he has fallen below expectations. It is not uncommon for students who believe they are brighter than they are to take easy courses, to enroll in courses in which they have little competition, or to go to colleges where competition is in their favor.

Dull children likewise overestimate their abilities. Their teachers may feel sorry for them and give them higher grades than their work merits because they have "tried," or they may have such poor self-insight that they do not see themselves as they actually are.

Just as some people overestimate their intellectual capacities, so do some *underestimate.* If parents expect too much of a child and express their disappointment by accusing him of not being serious enough or not working hard enough, the child may, in self-defense, come to believe that he is unable to do better. Or if a child is constantly compared with an older sibling, he may believe that he has less ability than he actually has because he cannot do what the older sibling does. The same situation may occur in school if he is younger than his classmates or if he is handicapped by an unstimulating home environment.

Underestimating their intellectual capacities leads people to set goals far below their capacities. They may claim they can never get into college, so why try? When they realize that they could have achieved more if they had not underestimated their capacities, they react in various ways. Some blame others for not giving them an opportunity to do what they were capable of doing. Some say they did not really want to do better. Others belittle intellectual achievements, becoming anti-intellectual; some joke about their "stupidity"; and some, of course, deprecate the poor quality of their work and feel guilty about it. This guilt is intensified by the knowledge that their parents and teachers are disappointed in them.

Effects on peer relationships

The effect of deviant intelligence on peer relationships depends more on the behavior of the deviant than on that of his peers. Most people, for example, react favorably to a moderately bright person, provided he behaves in a socially acceptable way. They respect his abilities, have confidence in his decisions, and often put him in leadership roles. However, should the bright person be "bored" with the activities his peers enjoy and belittle their "stupidities and inanities," he will be resented and will get the reputation of being "stuck up." If, in addition, he shows contempt for classmates who are slow learners, he is likely to be isolated by the rest of the class.

A bright boy or girl may enjoy intellectual pursuits, spend most of his time in school and college on his studies, and win high scholastic honors. Academic achievement is ego-satisfying, but it brings no honor to the group as a whole, as does achievement in sports and other extracurricular activities. Classmates resent the "brain's" lack of "group spirit" and show it. In addition, they resent having his superior achievements set a standard that they are expected to live up to. They regard him as a "curve raiser" who makes it difficult for them. This adds to the lack of social acceptance that other patterns of unsocial behavior on his part give rise to.

On the other hand, if a bright person looks upon his superior intellectual ability as a legacy from his ancestors and feels a responsibility to use his intellect for the benefit of others as well as himself, and if he tries to do his share or more to add to the enjoyment of the activities his peers engage in, his relationships with them will be good. By making himself more like his peers, he can counteract the cultural belief that his intellectual superiority makes him "different."

Dull people are considered "pests" because they make things difficult for the rest of the group. In school, they are slow learners and often spend their time "cutting up," disturbing those who want to learn. In social activities, they are clumsy and awkward in games, are slow to see the point of jokes, and have little to contribute to the conversation. In business or industry, they make more mistakes than their coworkers, are slow in their work, and often have to ask others to help them with problems they feel inadequate to cope with alone. Perhaps most irritating of all, they have such poor social and self insight that they do not realize they are unwelcome in the social group. By trying to force themselves into group activities, they further antagonize their peers.

Thus, it is the behavior of the bright or dull person himself that determines the kind of relationship he has with his peers, not the behavior of his peers. The bright person can control his behavior and have good or bad relationships with his peers, depending on how he behaves. The mentally deficient person cannot control his behavior because he lacks the necessary social and self insight to behave in a manner that will win social acceptance.

Effects on behavior

Since the interests and behavior of the person of deviant intelligence differ from the average, they in-fluence the attitudes of others and, therefore, affect his adjustments, especially in interpersonal relationships. What effect does deviant intelligence have on the person's behavior?

Recreational interests   Studies reveal that bright children prefer activities that tax their intellectual capacities, such as make-believe play, sports that require skills, collecting, card games, and any form of play that requires "thinking" (147, 164, 228). They show little interest in the simple neighborhood games of hide-and-seek, cops and robbers, or tag because they consider them "childish." Their reading, movie, and radio and television program preferences likewise reflect a greater maturity of interests than those of their less intellectually able peers (14, 228).

Having little interest in the play activities of their peers, very bright children and adolescents spend more time in solitary than in social play (228). And as most of the social contacts of childhood and adolescence center around play, those who are extremely bright often find too few congenial companions to make social contacts enjoyable. As a result, they spend much of their leisure time reading, working at their hobbies, listening to music, or watching the better-quality television programs (14, 228).

The recreational interests of those of different intellectual levels become even more disparate in adulthood. Commercial sources of recreation, such as movies, professional sports, dance halls, radio, and television appeal especially to those of the average or below-average intellectual levels, while reading, study, music, art, and hobbies appeal to those of the upper levels (104, 161). Since adults of the higher intellectual levels favor activities in which contact with others is not all-important, they tend to become self-sufficient in the use and planning of their leisure time. By contrast, those of lower intellectual levels become more dependent on others for entertainment (104, 161).

Achievements   Very bright children do better work in school, enjoy their work more, and are better adjusted to the school situation than those of lesser abilities (190, 200). They excel in language facility, resourcefulness, creative imagination, sustained attention, and breadth of attention. Even more important, they possess greater *intensity* of mind than less intelligent students (29, 181).

When very bright students are critical of their schools or colleges and dislike the work there, it is generally because they find the work dull or unchallenging. They are often bored, especially in classes where they are held back by less able students or where teachers discourage creative work by rewarding memory work.

In adult life, very bright people are more likely to be successful and to achieve fame than their less intelligent contemporaries. There is little evidence to justify the traditional belief that "early ripe, early rot," or that the very bright burn themselves out quickly and develop postadolescent mediocrity (216). However, both in school and in business, they may fall short of achieving what they are capable of. As Terman and Oden have pointed out, "Intellect and achievement are far from perfectly correlated" (217).

The failure of very bright people to reach their full potential may be due to lack of motivation caused by insufficient emotional satisfaction from achievement, an unstimulating home and school environment, unfavorable social attitudes toward achievement which encourage bright people to work below capacity in the hope of gaining acceptance, encouragement by parents and teachers to concentrate on intellectual activities at the expense of social and emotional development, and unfavorale self-concepts which result in lack of self-confidence, perseverance, and integration toward goals. In addition, some set unrealistically high levels of aspiration for themselves and if they fail to reach the goals, feel inadequate and inferior. Strang has remarked, "If their ego-involvement is great, the threat of failure may have a disorganizing effect on their performance" (212).

In school, the dull or mentally retarded are handicapped by language limitations, faulty reasoning and lack of imagination, and poor integration of mental activities. They do their best in shopwork and other activities requiring motor coordination. However, such work does not enable them to pass from one grade to another, and they are often forced to repeat grades. This makes them dislike school.

Since many children with below-average intelligence must go to schools that lack the facilities necessary for teaching them, they do not have the opportunity to develop the potentials they possess. As a result, they are handicapped vocationally in adult life and are forced to work in the lowest level of semiskilled or unskilled jobs or to live on unemployment benefits.

Social acceptance In school, those who are bright and academically successful have little in common with many of their classmates; they limit their close friendships to those whose abilities are similar to theirs. They are, however, on amiable terms with their less able classmates and are, on the whole, liked and respected. In fact, moderately bright boys and girls are generally significantly above the average in social acceptance. Strang writes that "it is the atypical gifted child who withdraws markedly from social contacts" (212).

By high school and college, bright students are usually socially and emotionally more mature than their classmates. They not only make good social adjustments but are often selected as leaders. This enables them to acquire social skills and social insight, both of which contribute to popularity and leadership roles in adult life. It has been found that those who are bright hold more positions of leadership and responsibility in adult life than do college graduates as a group (217).

By contrast, those who are dull make poor social adjustments. They are generally unpopular and rarely play leadership roles. The brighter the members of the group with which they are associated, the more unpopular they are (52, 136, 168, 191). Their handling of interpersonal relationships is poor because of their limited social and self insight, and their emotional behavior is immature as compared with that of their peers. They tend to be egocentric and emotionally uncontrolled, giving way to emotional outbursts at unpredictable times (198).

Dull children in regular school classes have a low social status. Their classmates claim that they are nuisances, that they talk too much and disturb the class, and that they cannot keep up in the games the rest of the group enjoys. The antisocial behavior of dull children is often a compensation for their feelings of inadequacy in academic and social situations. As they are socially isolated by their classmates, they lack opportunities to learn to improve their behavior. The older they get, the less accepted they are. Even when they associate with other dull children, their behavior is immature and they form few lasting friendships. When they try to assume leadership roles, they tend to be autocratic and "bossy," much as preschoolers are in their early attempts at leadership.

Dull adolescents and adults generally limit their social contacts to members of the family and neighbors. They rarely belong to community organizations. When they do, they attend meetings infrequently and seldom participate in the organizations' activities (198).

Markedly deviant intelligence leads to social isolation. Those who are very intelligent or very dull are not likely to be very popular with their age-mates. The disparity between them and their peers makes it almost impossible to establish satisfactory relationships and friendships.

From extensive studies of children and adolescents, Hollingworth has concluded that intelligence far above or far below the average tends to isolate people both psychologically and socially. Isolation, and its unfavorable consequences, occurs earlier for the very dull, because their intellectual deviation is more obvious and affects their interpersonal relationships when *others* perceive the deviation. On the other hand, exceptional deviation in the direction of superiority does not affect social relationships until the superior person *himself* feels that he is superior and acts in accordance with this feeling.

The *optimal* intelligence, Hollingworth claims, lies above the average, in the 130-150 IQ range. Within this range, she says, the person "comprehends more clearly but not too much more clearly, than the majority of his fellow men and women and becomes accepted as a leader." His vocabulary, interests, and ambitions still have enough in common with those of his contemporaries to permit and warrant cooperation.

Above 150 IQ, mutual rejection begins to appear between the deviant person and nearly all his contemporaries. He then turns to solitary pursuits or to the companionship of older people. This psychological isolation and lack of contact with peers results in eccentricities among very bright. In spite of this, many very bright people do develop favorable personality patterns. High intelligence carries with it compensatory functions, such as social and self insight, that help the person overcome such personality hazards as self-sufficiency, timidity, and a tendency to dominate (110).

Effects of deviant intelligence on personality

Deviant intelligence inevitably leaves its mark on the personality pattern. As has been stressed above, this is not because of deviant intelligence per se but rather because of the attitudes of the social group toward the deviant. And, as noted, the attitudes of the social group are influenced by the way the person behaves.

The effect on the self-concept is greatly influenced by how the person with deviant intelligence *believes* others feel about his being different and how they treat him while he is still young and in the process of developing a concept of himself as a person. If they think of him as "different," he will think of himself in that way too. This makes it difficult for him to behave normally, and to express his feelings toward people in a friendly way. His behavior thus reinforces the unfavorable social attitudes.

Effects of brightness Those who are bright, but not so bright that they are psychologically isolated, are usually well liked and respected by parents, teachers, and peers. Recognition of these attitudes gives them the self-confidence necessary to use their intellectual capacities to make good personal and social adjustments. They like people and are generally full of vitality, independent, resourceful, forceful, cooperative, humorous, dependable, free from feelings of inferiority, and sensitive to the approval and disapproval of others. Often, however, they have more nervous symptoms than those of lesser intelligence.

Most bright people have a strong desire for success and, instead of drifting, show a strong integration toward the goals they set. Contrary to popular opinion, they have "common sense." Unlike their peers of lesser intelligence, their levels of aspiration are usually realistic in the sense that they are within their potentials.

Those who are bright feel adequate to meet the demands society places on them and they believe that they stand well in the eyes of others. Being superior to their peers in emotional stability, responsibility, ambition, independence, and persistence, they are often chosen for leadership roles. Few are maladjusted (147, 149, 155, 181).

Recognizing their intellectual superiority sometimes encourages very bright persons to dominate, to be "bossy." When this happens, they are likely to be regarded as a "threat" by their less able peers. Since they often feel superior to their peers and intolerant of those who are less able, they may show a smugness which antagonizes others. As a result, they may be rejected as friends.

In adult years, very bright men and women, as a group, make better personal and social adjustments than those of average or below average intelligence. Studies of the very bright show that they are introspective, thoughtful, creative, adventuresome, and concerned with problems, meanings, and values. They have a wide range of interests, especially in the theoretical and aesthetic areas, and engage successfully in them. Because of their greater mental facility, they have a greater command over themselves.

Like the very bright at the younger age levels, they tend to be dominant in social situations, or at least not submissive. In fact, they are often critical and rebellious. They show few signs of maladjustment and are less tense, anxious, and given to feelings of insecurity than those who are less bright. They suffer less from depression and are less often authoritarian in their attitudes and behavior than the popular stereotype of the very bright claims. In general, they tend to be quite mature for their age.

Markedly superior intelligence affects personality development unfavorably by creating special problems not encountered in those who are merely bright. These problems result in the development of a personality pattern which includes several or most of the following traits: *negativism* toward institutionalized authority because the person perceives that it is often irrational or erroneous in its operation, *intolerance* because the person has observed over time the relatively inept thinking of others, *habits of chicanery* which enable the person to enjoy his unconventional or esoteric interests in a world unadapted to him, *emotional conflicts* about right and wrong, *solitary pursuits* and the companionship of older people, *self-sufficiency*, and the tendency to *dominate situations*. Most of these personality characteristics are the result of social and psychological isolation which come when the person has little in common with his peers (110, 147, 202, 227).

One study sought to determine how college professors felt about being identified with the unfavorable social stereotype of the "intellectual." Questioned about their feelings regarding their status in the social group, many of the professors claimed that they were ill at ease socially, that they did not mix well, and that they were not very approachable. Many claimed that they were snobbish about their intellectual superiority, though they also felt frustrated, had inferiority complexes, and suffered from a loss of self-respect. They explained their feelings as due to unfavorable social attitudes toward their role and the low prestige associated with it as shown by their comparatively low salaries. Some felt the need to conform to the social stereotype to prove that they actually were "intellectuals," while others were anxious to disprove the stereotype because they felt socially isolated. Those who

did the most creative work were least influenced by a minority-group complex. Those who accepted the negative stereotype developed minority-group complexes and did the poorest work (202).

SEGREGATION OF THE VERY BRIGHT What opportunities the cultural group provides for the intellectual development of those who are very bright plays as important a role in their personality development as the cultural stereotype. If very bright children are kept in the regular classroom with little or no attention to their special needs, they will not develop fully intellectually nor will they be motivated to develop the qualities of creativity and leadership which those of superior intellect normally possess. Instead, as they grow older, they will show intellectual sterility and rigidity.

If a sterile environment and lack of motivation turn them into low achievers, they become anxious and feel guilty for falling below their own and others' expectations. They often develop a compulsive defense anxiety and a habitual disorganized procedure in thinking. If, in addition, they try to gain popularity at the cost of developing their intellectual capacities, their feelings of guilt will be greatly increased, especially if they do not gain the social acceptance they crave.

Frequently, average classmates regard the very bright child as a "freak." Under such conditions, the development of a healthy self-concept is practically impossible. As Pressey (182) has pointed out:

The budding young scientist or scholar may be isolated or may associate only with a friend who is also considered "odd" or may belong only to an anemic subject club of no prestige in the community. . . . The teacher (perhaps made uncomfortable by keen questions) may even criticize his intense interest, and the other youngsters may call him sissy or odd. For him there is frustration, not the furtherance of cumulative success.

Isolating the very bright from their less well endowed contemporaries may stimulate their intellectual development and increase their self-confidence. However, it may also reinforce unfavorable social attitudes toward them and encourage their own snobbishness. If special classes emphasize intellectual excellence and ignore social and emotional development, the very bright child or adolescent may develop a personality pattern that makes good adjustment to life difficult. Jersild (122) writes:

*A person with towering intelligence may do spectacu-
lar things but unless his brilliant intellect is supported
by other qualities of mind and heart, his achievements
may actually not count for much. . . . There may be a
magnificent scope in what his mind can encompass in
his inquiries, for example, into the mysteries of human
endeavor, but unless he combines cleverness with
courage he will not be among those who become
heroes in the search for truth.*

The more isolated, socially and psychologically,
the very bright person is from his more average peers,
and the more constant his contacts with those whose
abilities are similar to his, the more likely he is to
develop personality maladjustments that will inhibit
his ability to use his intellectual capacities and achieve
up to his potentials. Isolation is especially damaging at
times when boys and girls are normally learning how
to get along with their age-mates, as during the "gang
age" of late childhood or during the high school years.

Effects of dullness   Although no personality
traits are peculiarly characteristic of the dull, those
who are dull do develop a personality pattern that is
quite distinct in *emphasis* (119). All people show some
egocentricity, timidity, and repression, but the mentally retarded possess these traits to a pronounced degree. As a result, these traits give a characteristic
quality to their personality pattern.

How markedly different the personality pattern
of the mentally retarded is from that of people of
normal or superior intelligence varies and depends on
a number of factors: when his mental retardation was
recognized, how people treat him, and how able he is
to recognize his inferiority and realize that it is fundamentally responsible for the way people react to him.

As has been noted, the dull person has poor
self insight and social insight. Because of his inability
to comprehend situations as quickly or as accurately
as those of normal intelligence, he says and does
things which make others think of him as a "pest" or a
"boob." Even worse, his poor insight makes it difficult
for him to recognize that he is responsible for the way
people treat him or to realize that their treatment of
him is derogatory. As a result, he continues to act in a
way that makes others reject him.

Those who are not so drastically retarded have
more social and self insight. When they recognize that
they cannot keep up with their peers in academic work
or extracurricular activities and cannot appreciate or
adjust to their peers' interests, they become aware

that they are "different." This leads to feelings of
inadequacy and inferiority. In time, they develop personality traits associated with marked feelings of inferiority, such as shyness, apathy, lack of ambition, and
resentments which are often expressed in aggressiveness and hostility toward those who have rejected
them.

SEGREGATION OF THE VERY DULL   Unless a
child's mental retardation is marked, parents are often
slow to recognize it. Or if they suspect that their child
is dull, they may believe that he will "outgrow" it.
Under such conditions, they resist any suggestion that
he be segregated from children who are brighter than
he, either at home or in school. By the time they are
willing to acknowledge his dullness, the child has
already encountered many failures and developed
feelings of inadequacy and inferiority. Furthermore,
the parents, disappointed because their unrealistic
aspirations for the child have gone unfulfilled, are
likely to reject him.

The longer the very dull child is permitted to
remain in classes with normal children, the more psychological damage he will receive from their treatment
of him—their ridicule and rejection. If the teacher
regards his poor schoolwork as an indication of laziness and his countless failures as proof that he is "not
trying," the psychological damage will be intensified.
As Sarason and Gladwin say, this is likely to "launch
the child into any new social situation with two strikes
against him" (198).

By the time mental retardation is recognized
and the child is put in a special class with other
mentally retarded children, the damage to his personality may be permanent. According to Sarason and
Gladwin, "No amount of intelligent dedication on the
part of teachers of special classes can erase the fact
that their pupils have been declared unfit to participate
with their peers in an activity which society inflexibly
demands of all its members at a certain age" (198).

Even though severe psychological damage may
have been done, the child is at least relieved of a
constant reminder of his inferiority once he has been
put in a special class where, by comparison with his
new classmates, he does not seem inferior. He becomes more mature and more emotionally stable than
retardates who are kept in regular classes. Through
the development of a healthier self-concept, his academic achievements often exceed his mental-age expectancy.

For those who are so mentally retarded that

institutionalization is wise or necessary, separation from their families has damaging effects on their personalities. This is especially so if they are old enough to recognize what a drastic change institutionalization will mean in the pattern of their lives. Institutionalization encourages overt conformity to the institutional culture at the expense of individuality, excessive phantasizing, avoidance and fear of new problem-solving situations, excessive dependence on the institutional culture, and greater rigidity than is normally found among the mentally retarded (52, 198).

MAJOR AREAS OF ADJUSTMENT AFFECTED BY INTELLIGENCE

The level of development of intellectual capacities and the way they are used affect the individual's adjustment to life and thus determine how greatly they will influence his personality.

Level of development refers not simply to IQ but also to the fact that intellectual capacities develop or decline at different times and at different ages. Imagination develops earlier than reasoning, for example, and this affects the quality of the child's adjustment. The child allows his imagination to run wild because he lacks the reasoning capacity which, as he grows older, will act as a check on the imagination. As a result, he builds up an unrealistic self-concept which, if markedly out of line with his capacity, will lead to self-rejection with its accompaniment of poor personal and social adjustments.

Similarly, a decline in reasoning power with advancing age may cause an elderly person to misinterpret the treatment he receives from others. He may develop a feeling of martyrdom with its accompaniment of poor adjustment. The feeling of martyrdom will be accentuated if the person also has vivid memories of past achievements, perhaps exaggerated and romanticized because of a decrease in critical ability.

Of the many areas in which intellectual capacities influence the kind of life adjustment the person makes, the three discussed here—values, morality, and humor—will be sufficient to illustrate how important the intellectual determinants are in personality development.

Values

Values are a "precipitate of behavior: they are established predispositions of behavior" (154). They are what is attractive to a person, the essence of what he seeks in an object, a person, or even himself (154). As such, they operate as criteria for making judgments between alternative courses of action and they directly influence the quality of the person's behavior and decisions. As a rule, the person adopts those values which help him to achieve the ends he desires and which are, at the same time, sanctioned by the group with which he is identified. His values are thus influenced by and are a reflection of his personality.

People differ in their values, and so it is not surprising that their judgments of the same object, person, or situation differ and that they behave differently in the same or similar situations. Each individual develops values which seem important to him and which guide his life. As Jersild (122) has explained:

The individual seeks to live as though living had value. . . . To the best of his ability and according to his lights, he seeks that which, from his point of view, is better rather than worse, that which enhances life instead of negating it, that which furthers his purposes so far as he has formed them, furthers his desires as far as he knows them. The search for value is inherent in the business of living. True enough, what a person seeks may not be what is best for him. His values may be false or harmful as judged in terms of what might best further his own growth and enrich his life. But from his point of view they are values none the less.

Development of values Values are developed by direct learning and by identification. The child learns, through the training he receives at home, in the school, and in Sunday school, and through imitating his parents and teachers, the culturally approved values of the social group with which his family is identified.

The older child learns the values of the peer group, of neighbors, and of the larger world, as presented in the mass media of communication—movies, radio, television, newspapers, magazines, and books. Some of these are the same as those learned at home and some are radically different.

The values the person learns from different environmental sources will depend partly on his intellectual level and partly on such factors as social pressures to accept some values and reject others, the way the values are presented to him, and the relationship he has with the persons whose values he accepts. If he grows up in a home where moral standards are lax and materialism is strong, he will develop values quite different from one who grows up in a home and neighborhood where great emphasis is placed on strict moral standards and spiritual values. In a large family the child must learn values that make for successful living in such a family: conformity to family patterns, cooperation, and "staying in line." In the small family, on the other hand, self-expression and individualism contribute to the family's vitality and are usually encouraged (32, 66).

In one study it was found that the attitudes of others toward the values of career- and homemaking-oriented women had a marked influence on how the values affected the women's personalities. Career-oriented women put great importance on "doing"—a value that is regarded by many as selfish and egocentric. By contrast, homemaking-oriented women favored "being"—a value that implies unselfishness and concern for others (226).

The kind of relationship a person has with teachers and friends likewise affects the values he learns. How he feels about school and how much importance he places on education is influenced not alone by his intellectual level or his achievements but also by how his teachers and classmates treat him. The more favorably his teachers treat him and the more popular he is with his classmates, the more readily he will accept their values, even though they may conflict with the values learned at home (167).

Variation in values   Every *cultural group* has its own values which have been developed over time to fit the pattern of life of the group and the temperament of the people who make up the group. Once established, group values are passed from one generation to another through the child-training methods used in the home, through the schools, through the personal contacts of group members, and through the mass media.

A comparison of national concepts of the "desirable life" shows how cultural values differ. Western cultures, as exemplified by Norway and the United States, regard flexibility, many-sidedness, enjoyment in action, and individualism as important values, but put little stress on social responsibility. By contrast, Eastern cultures, such as those of India, China, and Japan, stress conservatism, social withdrawal, self-sufficiency, self-control, conservation of what has been achieved, and sympathetic concern for others (140, 166).

The *social classes* within a cultural group also have distinct values. The upper class in the American culture, for example, stresses family background and leisure pursuits; the upper-middle class is oriented toward upper-class values and, in addition, stresses money and community position; the lower-middle and lower classes, seeing little opportunity to advance, emphasize living for the moment and enjoying what one has (51, 177).

The values parents seek to instill in their children conform closely to the social class with which they are identified. Working-class parents emphasize honesty and neatness, the "poor but honest" person who is respectable even if he is not respected by the social group as a whole. By contrast, middle-class parents put more emphasis on responsibility and inner control, both of which are essential if the person is to get ahead in life (240).

Since the prescribed pattern of life is different for members of the two *sexes,* every social class has a separate set of values for males and females. In the upper social groups, boys and men are expected to be "gentlemen," while in the lower classes, they are expected to be more aggressive and dominating. In both the upper and lower social classes girls and women are expected to be less aggressive and dominating than boys and men (21, 38, 159).

Changes in values   As the child grows older and comes in contact with people from different cultures and socioeconomic backgrounds, he often revises or changes the values he learned at home. Furthermore, his own life experiences give him a new perspective on the values he accepted uncritically as a child, and may lead to a revision of values.

Members of the middle class, for example, sometimes find that honesty is a handicap to popularity and they are willing to help their friends who are in an academic predicament by cheating (19, 211, 218). Members of the lower class, encouraged at home to be honest, frequently discover that honesty does not "pay" outside the home (38, 218). Many girls, brought up to regard virginity as a high moral value, discover that intercourse during the engagement period is expected by men and approved by their female peers.

In adulthood, changes in living patterns and broadened experiences may alter the relative importance of many of the values of the younger days (116). Good manners, courtesy, love, and courtship, for example, are highly esteemed by adolescents

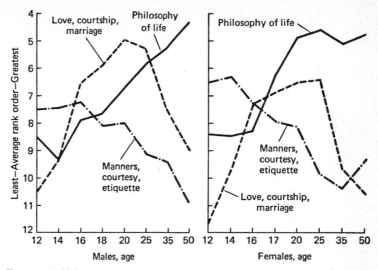

Figure 7-4 Values change with age. (Adapted from F. K. Shuttleworth: The adolescent period: A graphic atlas. *Monogr. Soc. Res. Child Developm.*, 1949, **14,** No. 1. Used by permission.)

while a philosophy of life has low value. By middle age, the relative position of these values change (224). This is illustrated in Figure 7-4.

The more rigid the personality of the person, the less change there will be in his values, even when his environment and experiences change radically. A person who is flexible, on the other hand, will alter his values readily if he feels that a change will result in better adjustments and greater happiness.

SOME AREAS OF VALUE CHANGE Value changes at different ages in the life span have been examined in a number of research studies. To illustrate how and when the changes occur, what is responsible for them, and how they affect life adjustments, four areas of value change will be discussed: work, the new and different, religion, and the use of money.

Work Young children have quite favorable attitudes toward work. They like to help at home, doing chores which many adults regard as "drudgery," and they feel important when they are praised for their achievements. They look forward to going to school and are at first challenged by what they are expected to learn. The brighter the child, the more favorable his attitude toward schoolwork.

By the end of the second grade, attitudes toward schoolwork begin to worsen, and by the age of 10 most children have developed a dislike for anything

that might be considered "work," whether it be their home duties, their schoolwork, or even difficult reading and sports practice (91, 221).

Before adolescence, children discover that liking work is just not "the thing to do." Furthermore, they discover that doing good work in school or in any except the most prestigious extracurricular activities does not add to their popularity. This antiwork attitude, reinforced by the values of the social group, affects vocational choice and, later, vocational satisfaction and success.

Studies of vocational values reveal that, in addition to being a means of earning a living, work represents a source of prestige and social recognition, a stepping-stone to a higher status, a basis for self-respect and a sense of worth, an opportunity for social participation, a source of intrinsic enjoyment, and an opportunity for creative expression (148, 232). In discussing what work means to the adult male worker, Pressey (183) says:

For most men, work is the center of their lives; it determines the resources for living for themselves and their families and their socioeconomic status, and has multiple meanings for them—as a basis for self-respect and the respect of others, a locus of social relationships during work and at the lunch hour, an activity often in itself enjoyable.

In adulthood, members of the higher classes

tend to have more favorable attitudes toward work than members of the lower classes. Undoubtedly, this is due in part to the greater interest and prestige inherent in the work done by the former. With experience, many adults put less emphasis on the amount of money earned and more on the amount of freedom their work gives them, its prestige, and their personal satisfaction in the work. As they approach retirement or find themselves unemployed, they discover what work really means to them. As a result, they put high value on it, often to the point of glorifying it.

A survey of attitudes toward work at different ages shows that they have a marked influence on life adjustments. The antiwork attitude of children and adolescents, causing them to shun their duties and try to shift responsibilities to others, leads not only to underachievement in school and college but also to a frictional relationship with parents, teachers, and peers.

Adults who persist in this attitude will be vocational underachievers just as they were educational underachievers. They will be dissatisfied not only on the job but also in their family and community life because they will not be able to have the status symbols they want. On the other hand, a prowork attitude and a vocation that fits in with the values a person holds will lead to good adjustment to the job and satisfaction both to the worker and to his employer (148, 160, 232).

Those who place high value on work find it difficult to make satisfactory adjustments to retirement. No substitute activities, such as hobbies and community services, can match the satisfaction they formerly derived from work.

The new and different To a child, anything that is new, whether toys, clothing, or a pet, has allure. He likes it just because it is new and different from what he is accustomed to, not because it is better. The same values hold in adolescence when the tendency toward faddism is a definite indication of the appeal of newness per se. Constant changes in clothing and hair styles, in patterns of behavior, speech, and manners, and even in beliefs show how willing adolescents are to accept the new and discard the old.

Willingness to accept new ideas and to act on them makes the adolescent seem radical to the adult because, as the adult views the situation, the adolescent accepts the ideas without weighing their value. In reality, much of the so-called radicalism of youth is an expression of revolt against what they regard as the conservatism of the older generation. According to Flacks (83), young people raised in democratic, egalitarian families

. . . find it difficult to accommodate to institutional expectations requiring submissiveness to adult authority, respect for established status distinctions, a high degree of competitiveness, and firm regulation of sexual and expressive impulses. They are likely to be particularly sensitized to acts of arbitrary authority, to unexamined expressions of allegiance to conventional values, to instances of institutional practices which conflict with professed ideals.

The so-called conservatism of the older generation is usually not mental rigidity, as is popularly believed, but the result of changed social values. Many adults, with increased experience, discover that the old often has an advantage over the new and untried. Consequently, they cling to old values until there is evidence that the new are superior.

From the point of view of adjustment, accepting the new just because it is new and rejecting the old just because it is old militates against stability—an essential to good adjustment. On the other hand, unwillingness to accept the new merely because it is new likewise militates against good adjustment. Only when a person accepts values and clings to them so long as they meet his needs, but is willing to change them when his needs change, can he be stable and well adjusted. Faddism makes stability impossible just as rigidity makes good adjustment impossible.

Religion Religious interests and observances vary greatly from one period of life to another owing to changes in religious values. To young children, going to Sunday school or church, hearing religious music or stories, and participating in different forms of worship and holiday observances are satisfying and awe-inspiring (131, 141).

As the novelty of the religious observances wears off and as reasoning ability and knowledge increase, older children begin to question what they formerly believed and to put less value on religion. Going to Sunday school and church then provides opportunities to be with friends and religious holidays primarily mean freedom from school (7, 91, 98, 141).

In adolescence, skepticism and doubt tend to undermine religious values (18, 94). And although young adulthood is often referred to as the least religious period in the life span, many young adults find new, perhaps nonreligious, values in religion—values associated with their parental and social roles. Being active in the church sets a good model for children to imitate and gives adults prestige in the community as well as opportunities to associate with the social groups they would like to be identified with. Packard (177) writes:

Going to church is a deeply felt, soul-searching experience for many millions of Americans. . . . For the majority of American Christians, however, going to church is the nice thing that proper people do on Sundays. It advertises their respectability, gives them a warm feeling that they are behaving in a way their God-fearing ancestors would approve, and adds (they hope) a few cubits to their social stature by throwing them with a social group with which they wish to be identified. And even those who take their worshiping seriously often prefer to do it while surrounded by their own kind of people.

With the approach of old age, once again religious values change. Going to church and engaging in religious observances are now motivated by a personal need rather than by a desire to win social approval or to identify with a prestigious social group. If the older person found personal satisfaction in religion when he was younger, he will continue to find it when he is older. If the only satisfaction he found was social, however, his interest in religion will decline as he grows older and as the social need is of less importance (58).

Religious values play an important role in personal and social adjustments. Personally, they contribute to a feeling of stability and security by giving the individual a permanent anchorage point. It has been shown that during the years when religious values are relatively less esteemed—in adolescence and early adulthood—the person suffers from strong feelings of insecurity and instability.

Socially, if the person behaves in such a way as to show that he accepts the group's religious values, whatever they may be, his social image will be enhanced and the group's judgment of him will be favorable. If members of the peer group put little value on religion, he will be judged more favorably by them if he does likewise.

Money Values relating to money change with experience in the use of money and with realization of the role of money in personal and social adjustments. However, money contributes to some end that is important to the person at every age.

To the young child, money is a means of getting things his parents do not give him, mainly sweets. After he goes to school, the child who has money to spend as he chooses for things the peer group regards as important gains prestige in the eyes of his peers.

For the adolescent, money contributes to two important ends: independence and social status. In planning for his future, therefore, it is not surprising that the adolescent is more concerned about how much a job pays than about the nature of the work, how interesting it is to him, or what opportunities it offers for future advancement. To the young adult, as to the adolescent, money is primarily a means of acquiring prestige symbols and fulfilling his need for entertainment.

The person does not view money as a source of security until he experiences the problems related to lack of money. So long as he is a minor and lives under the parental roof, he will be taken care of even if the breadwinner of the family is unemployed. Social security and other aids guarantee him this security.

When adults discover that satisfying their desire for prestige symbols often means buying on installment and being constantly in debt, they begin to change their attitudes about budgeting and saving money. This is hastened by the anxiety that comes from fear of losing their jobs, being unable to pay their debts, and having to ask their families or friends for help.

Middle-aged people worry about unemployment, the difficulties of getting another job and the financial distress they would face if the family breadwinner should die or be invalided. They place high value on savings and on spending money wisely and low value on spending freely for what they now regard as "extravagances." By the time people reach the sixties and are facing retirement, the value of money as a source of security reaches its peak. To the elderly, the value of money lies not in the prestige symbols or pleasures it will buy but in the security and independence it will provide.

Money values affect personality through the effect they have on personal and social adjustments. If the person has enough money for the prestige symbols he craves and if he can feel reasonably secure in his ability to maintain an independent status, the effect on his self-concept will be favorable. One of the conditions that leads to negative self-concepts in old age is lack of money for these very important personal needs.

Since one of the bases for social judgment is the

amount of money the individual has for status symbols and recreations, the more money he has, other things equal, the more favorably he will be judged by members of the group with which he is identified and the greater will be his chances of social acceptance. Furthermore, since the person's self-concept is a mirror image of the way significant people in his life judge him—or the way he believes they judge him—money is a means of improving the self-concept or of damaging it.

Morality

Every cultural group has its own mores or standards of approved behavior. Certain acts are "right" because they further the welfare of the members of the group, and others are "wrong" because they are detrimental to the welfare of the group. The most important mores are incorporated into laws with specific penalties for breaking them. Others persist as customs, which are as binding as laws, but without specific penalties.

The individual's intellectual capacities affect his response to the group's moral standards. The moral behavior of the individual, in turn, is closely related to his adjustment to life, to the judgments others make of him, and to his judgments of himself. In general, the more closely his behavior conforms to the moral standards of the group with which he is identified, the more favorable will be the effects on his personal and social adjustments.

If a child violates the mores of the group, he is excused on the ground that he is too young to understand or to know the mores. However, by the time he reaches adolescence, he is considered capable of understanding and abiding by the mores, and if he fails to do so he will earn an unfavorable reputation among the group members, make himself vulnerable to punishment or threats of punishment, and develop feelings of guilt. Conformity to the group's mores, on the other hand, will lead to group approval and personal satisfaction.

The person learns, from his personal experiences, that it is to his advantage to conform to standards of behavior set by the group, even though he may not at all times agree with the standards. As Wiggam (234) explains:

Intelligent individuals know that right conduct is simply intelligent conduct—the conduct that gets the best results. . . . They tend to choose the right conduct simply because they see it as the course of action that produces the best consequences. An intelligent child or adult discovers he can get what he wants in life more easily and surely by honesty than by deception.

Development of moral codes   No one is born knowing what the cultural group considers right or wrong. This he must learn. Even more important, if he wishes to win group approval, he must be motivated to choose, from different potentials for action, that which will satisfy his own needs and at the same time conform to group standards.

Learning what the group approves of is a long and difficult process—a process that depends on the maturation of intellectual capacities, especially the capacities for remembering, associating what one learns with previously learned facts, and weighing the merits against the demerits of the different choices. Hemming (106) writes:

Moral development is the process in which the child acquires the values esteemed by his community, . . . acquires a sense of right and wrong in terms of these values, and . . . learns to regulate his personal desires and compulsions so that, when a situational conflict arises, he does what he ought to do rather than what he wants to do. . . . Moral development is the process by which a community seeks to transfer the egocentricity of the baby into the social behavior of the mature adult.

A moral code is based on moral concepts which have been learned gradually over a long period. The fundamental concepts are learned in the home by direct teaching and imitation, motivated by threats of punishment and promises of reward. Later, these homegrown concepts are broadened and reinforced by learning from teachers, from adults in authority, and from peers.

Because of his intellectual immaturity, the young child cannot understand why certain things are right and others wrong. He learns to act as he is expected to without knowing why. Gradually, with increasing mental ability, he can see common features in apparently dissimilar situations. Then he can apply what he has learned in one situation to another situation. Specific moral concepts gradually become more general, more abstract, and more extensive.

As the individual grows older and as his social contacts broaden, he learns new moral concepts and generalizes old moral concepts to apply to new situations. By adulthood, he can apply moral concepts to an increasing range of conflicting life situations. In addition, he can ascribe different degrees of rightness or wrongness to acts, judging some as less wrong and some as more wrong. By this time, the person's moral code, based on concepts learned in childhood and adolescence, is well formed. Any change in it is likely to be merely a shift in emphasis rather than the development of new concepts. When a shift occurs, it is largely in the direction of more conventional morality. This is especially true in the areas of morality that relate to sex behavior.

INFLUENCE OF INTELLIGENCE ON DEVELOPMENT OF MORAL CODES The person's ability to develop a moral code to guide his behavior is greatly influenced by his intellectual capacities, though other factors may aid or retard the development. The brighter the person, the more able he is to understand the moral concepts he learns, to perceive the situations in which they apply, and to profit from experience. The short attention span which is characteristic of people of low intelligence is related to impulsive behavior. Poor reasoning power results in lack of foresight and planning which, if combined with impulsiveness, often leads to behavior that violates the moral standards of the group. At every age, those of high IQ tend to be more mature in their moral judgments and behavior than those of the lower intellectual levels.

Immoral behavior is by no means found only in persons of low intelligence. On the other hand, socially unapproved methods of meeting life's problems are more common in them (179, 189, 195). Deceit, for example, offers a means of solving difficulties which a person of limited intellectual capacity is more likely to use than a person of higher intelligence. The latter can adjust to his difficulties without being deceitful, although there is no guarantee that he will have the motivation to do so. He may find it easier to cheat than to be honest. And since he is clever, he will be able to cheat without detection more often than those who are less clever.

Conflicts in moral codes Developing a moral code to guide behavior is not a matter of simple learning. It is difficult because of the conflicts in moral codes a person encounters as his social horizons broaden.

First, conflicts arise when the person discovers that the moral concepts he learned in the home are not necessarily accepted outside the home, especially by his friends. If classmates think it is all right to cheat, the child is tempted to follow their example even though he knows that his parents and teachers regard cheating as "wrong."

Second, while children and adolescents may agree with parents, teachers, and other adults in a general way about what is right and what is wrong, they evaluate certain kinds of behavior differently. Cheating, for example, is far less wrong to schoolchildren than to members of the older generation.

Third, within a cultural group, everyone may accept the same moral code in a general way but subgroup interpretations of different aspects of the code may vary greatly. People from the lower socioeconomic groups tend to be more arbitrary and authoritarian in their interpretation of moral concepts while those from upper-middle- and upper-class backgrounds distinguish various degrees of wrongness in an act such as cheating.

Fourth, when a young person observes inconsistencies between what adults do—parents, teachers, or people in the mass media—and what they tell him he should do, he is confused.

Fifth, while similar moral concepts are learned by boys and girls during childhood, girls discover at adolescence that boys are permitted to do certain things which they are not allowed to do. The confusion that this causes is intensified by the girls' feeling that such treatment is not fair.

Sixth, when a concept conflicts with practical life pressures, the person is confused about which course of action to follow. A child may learn that it is "wrong" to fight. However, if his social contacts are largely with persons who believe that fighting is all right, he will have to either place himself at their mercy or violate his code and stand up for his rights.

Seventh, moral concepts are not necessarily mutually consistent. There may, for example, be a conflict between the concepts of truthfulness and loyalty. This means that a person may have to choose between telling a lie and sparing the feelings of a friend or telling the truth and hurting his friend's feelings.

Eighth, even though a person may know what moral concepts are approved by his group, he sometimes has difficulty knowing when and how to apply them. He knows that lying is "wrong." But if his mother does not punish him for lying, whereas his father does, it is hard for him to know when lying is permissible and when it is not.

And *finally,* confusion arises because of changes in cultural attitudes. In the past, it was considered "wrong" for women to smoke, especially in public.

Similarly, moral concepts relating to sex behavior, especially that of women, were far less permissive a generation ago.

EFFECTS OF CONFLICTS Regardless of the source of the moral conflicts the person faces, the resulting confusion affects learning and acceptance of a moral code in three ways. First, it *slows down the learning process.* If the home code and the peer code conflict, for example, the young person must decide which to follow. Whichever he decides in favor of, he must revise at least some of his moral concepts.

Second, a conflict in moral concepts *raises doubts about the fairness of the concepts.* The young child does not question the justice of the rules laid down by his parents, though he may try to evade them. Later, when he discovers that inconsistencies exist between the moral concepts he is expected to accept and those of his friends, he begins to question the fairness of the home concepts. Rebellion against moral concepts on the basis of their fairness generally reaches a peak in adolescence.

The third effect of a conflict in moral concepts is that it *increases the difficulty of making moral decisions.* A person does not know what decision to make if he is confused about what the social group considers right and what it considers wrong. The decision will be influenced partly by the person's knowledge of the relative values the group places on different kinds of behavior and partly by what is most important to him personally. If honesty is more highly esteemed by the group than cheating and generosity more esteemed than selfishness, he will try to act in accordance with both these values, but will be influenced by the particular situation at the moment. Many juvenile delinquents do socially disapproved things when they are with a gang which they would not do if alone in the hope of maintaining status in the gang (145, 186).

Discrepancies between moral codes and moral behavior Although each person is consistent in trying to live up to what he believes is right, at no age is there such a thing as absolute consistency between the person's moral code and his behavior. As Pressey and Kuhlen have pointed out, "There are no separate groups of saints and sinners. Most people are sometimes honest, sometimes not, sometimes helpful, sometimes not—average in virtue as in other traits" (185).

This means that discrepancies between moral codes and moral behavior are not limited to juvenile delinquents or adult criminals. Instead, they occur even in those who believe themselves to be law-abiding citizens and who have such a reputation among their peers.

CAUSES OF DISCREPANCIES Discrepancies between moral knowledge and behavior are due to a number of different conditions. Sometimes the person is unable to perceive the relationship between the moral standards he has learned and the situations in which they apply. Sometimes the moral training the person has received is faulty, incomplete, and confusing, owing to negative parental attitudes or parental ignorance of group values. Most often discrepancies between behavior and knowledge are due to emotional and motivational factors. Many of the acts of juvenile delinquents, for example, are motivated by anger at the way they are treated. They strike out in retaliation, doing things they know are wrong. Often people intentionally do things they know are wrong for a particular purpose, such as winning favor from others or avoiding punishment. Cheating may be motivated by a desire to get grades that come up to unrealistic parental expectations or to ensure that one is promoted along with his friends.

Few people, even young delinquents or adult criminals, are so ignorant of right and wrong that they cannot do what society expects of them. On the other hand, there is evidence that many people who feel inadequate or inferior are motivated to behave in a socially unacceptable way by feelings of resentment, hostility, defiance, and suspiciousness (93, 145, 186, 203).

Effects of morality on personality Moral or immoral behavior has no effect on personality until the person is intellectually mature enough to understand the attitude of the social group toward his behavior. A baby does not realize that an act is wrong unless he is punished for it. Even then, he may fail to understand why he was punished. Furthermore, he has no feeling of guilt from wrongdoing because he has not yet learned a moral code by which to judge his behavior.

As time passes, the person gradually learns what society expects and how it judges him when his behavior falls short of expectations. At the same time, he is learning to judge his own behavior in terms of a moral code he has developed through experience and moral teaching. If he feels that his behavior falls short of this code, he will have feelings of guilt. If his behavior comes up to expectations, both his own and the group's, he will be satisfied with himself.

The influence of moral expectations on the self-concept will depend on a number of conditions: whether the person is forced, by fear of punishment, to conform or whether he wants to conform because of the personal benefit he will derive from doing so; the attitude of the person who requires him to conform and the method used to enforce conformity; and whether he feels secure in his moral beliefs and in his ability to translate these beliefs into actions.

If a person feels unsure of his ability to make moral judgments that will win group approval or if he is uncertain of his ability to carry out decisions in ways that will be approved by the group, he will bolster himself up by rigid and authoritarian moral standards or he will lean on external standards of right and wrong rather than on his own convictions. In any situation in which a moral decision must be made, such a person is likely to be plagued by uncertainty and doubt. By contrast, the person who learns a socially acceptable code of moral values and accepts this code as a guide to his behavior is more secure, more confident of his ability to live up to the code, and more likely to be a "comfortable" and well-adjusted person.

EFFECTS OF GUILT AND SHAME   If the person realizes that his behavior falls short of group expectations or personal standards, he will have feelings of *guilt* and his reaction to these feelings will affect his self-concept. Before the age of 5 or 6 years, the child has few if any feelings of guilt, although he may become frightened when caught in a wrong act and try to rationalize his behavior or project the blame on someone else. The older child, however, is deeply concerned about social disapproval when his behavior falls short of expectations. In self-protection, he tries to find a scapegoat to blame for his misbehavior. Rather than feeling guilt, he feels *shame* when caught in an act which he knows is wrong. Only after the person learns to feel personally responsible for controlling his behavior instead of relying on external pressures, such as disapproval, punishment, or threat of punishment, is he capable of experiencing true guilt.

Feelings of guilt may lead the person to change

his attitude about the "wrongness" of certain behavior. If the person decides not to cheat when tempted to do so, he usually becomes more rigid in his attitude that cheating is wrong. If he decides that he will cheat, he is likely to become more tolerant toward cheating. This is a method he uses, unconsciously, to reduce the feelings of guilt which would otherwise follow his cheating (10, 137, 195, 205, 211).

Occasional feelings of mild guilt are not likely to have a permanent effect on the self-concept. They may make the person ashamed of himself and more realistic about the standards he sets for his behavior. Frequent feelings of guilt, however, resulting from recurring failure to live up to one's standards, are damaging to the self-concept. They make the person lose confidence in his ability to achieve what he sets out to do, even though no one but himself may know of his failure.

EFFECTS OF INTOLERANCE   A person's intolerance of others' shortcomings affects his personality by creating feelings of self-superiority. These feelings are reflected in the quality of his behavior and thus influence the attitudes of others.

The older child, for example, is contemptuous of those who do anything his group considers wrong, such as cheating or smoking. His moral standards are rigid and unalterable and his attitude toward those who do not conform is characterized by extreme intolerance. This self-righteousness makes the child smug and self-satisfied; it compensates for some of the feelings of inadequacy he experiences when his own conduct falls below the lofty standards he has set. The more often he falls below these standards, the more intolerant he is toward the transgressions of others and the more satisfaction he derives from their punishment. These are ego-building experiences for him.

Intolerance toward moral shortcomings usually reaches its peak in adolescence. At this age, intolerance of others' shortcomings parallels intolerance of personal shortcomings and makes the adolescent, for the time at least, cynical about all people. Since no one seems to conform to his ideals, he has a poor opinion of everyone, including himself. Normally, the adolescent becomes more liberal and more tolerant as his social experiences broaden. If this does not happen, his intolerance will eventually contribute to the development of the authoritarian personality syndrome. Refer to Chapter 2 for a discussion of this syndrome.

Humor

Freud was the first modern psychologist to point out how humor affects personality. According to his theory of wit, the pleasure that humor gives is due to discharge of psychic energy. Through humor, the person gratifies forbidden impulses, either sexual or hostile. Humor allows the person to revert to childish behavior, to rebel against authority. Further, humor gives the person freedom to criticize himself or members of the group with which he is identified. Laughter, accompanying the perception of the comic, is a form of emotional discharge and, as such, serves as a catharsis (85).

To distinguish between perception of the comic in oneself and in others, Allport has labeled the former a "sense of humor" and the latter a "sense of the comic." A sense of humor, therefore, is the ability to see oneself objectively and to be amused by one's inferiorities, jealousies, and unsocial desires. It is, in short, the ability to laugh at oneself. A sense of the comic, according to Allport, is a "cruder" source of mirth in which enjoyment is derived from the inferiorities of others—inferiorities which make the observer feel superior (5).

Intelligence and humor It is popularly believed that humor is a mark of intellectual superiority and that the higher the person's intelligence, the greater his wit and humor. This is one of the reasons for the high social value placed on humor.

There is no doubt that intelligence and humor are closely related. What a person perceives as comic depends upon his memory of past experiences and his ability to link them with new experiences as well as upon other mental and nonmental factors (63, 99, 239). The person must learn the significance of different social roles, for example, before he can perceive the humor in a situation in which a person of authority finds himself in a predicament. Furthermore, much of the humor in jokes and even simple puns depends upon the person's comprehension of language—which is closely correlated with intelligence.

What the person perceives as comic gradually changes as his intellectual abilities increase. The shift is from the concrete and obvious to the subtle and abstract, from slapstick to wit. Understanding the subtle humor and hidden hostility expressed in cartoons, for example, requires greater intellectual ability than understanding the rowdy pie-throwing comedy and overt physical hostility of slapstick (45, 196, 239).

Subjective humor—perceiving the comic in oneself—is more likely to be found among those of higher intellectual levels because it depends upon considerable self-insight. A person who has a sense of proportion concerning his own qualities is able to perceive their incongruities and absurdities and to laugh at them just as he would laugh at them in another person (5, 63, 239).

Factors influencing perception of the comic Reactions to comic situations, whether they relate to others or to the person himself, are greatly affected by factors other than intelligence. The *mood* and the *emotional* condition of the person at the time the comic situation arises are central to his reaction. It is difficult to see humor in anything when one is worried or angry, for example. Similarly, the general *physical condition* of the person, his *social* and *personal relationship* in the situation in which the comic appears, and the *attitudes* of members of the group toward the source of the comic affect the person's reaction.

As important as intelligence in the perception of the comic is the *personality pattern* of the individual. One who feels insecure and inadequate can rarely perceive the comic in situations in which he himself is involved. This is especially true in adolescence when, characteristically, the individual is so sensitive to the opinions of others that one of the last things he wants to do is put himself in a position in which others might ridicule him. Allport (5) states:

In adolescence, insight is but rarely attained, not because the youth is unmindful of himself as is the young child, but for the opposite reason, in his intense seriousness he lacks perspective. There are feelings of acute self-consciousness and of inferiority, largely because a sense of proportion has not developed. His failures and eccentricities do not amuse him; he is much more likely to weep about them than to laugh. In some adolescents, to be sure, this condition of storm and stress is much less marked than in others.

Failure to perceive the comic in a joke or cartoon does not necessarily imply inability to understand it. Instead, the person may deny understanding because the humor in the situation is distressing to him. As Levine and Redlich have pointed out, "The fact that such apparently innocuous stimuli as humorous cartoons can provoke such defensive reactions attests to the fact that humor actually taps deep preconscious conflicts" (146). This means that a person who lacks a sense of humor often has too many conflicts and anxieties to be able to enjoy the comic elements of a situation.

Expressions of humor Humor is generally, though not always, accompanied by smiling and laughing. Laughter may have a happy tone or it may be harsh or grating, as in the laughter of ridicule or gloating. Some laughter has a malicious quality: Laughing in triumph over an opponent, laughing at one's own "superiority," or laughing at another's discomfort is quite different—in both meaning and tone—from laughing *with* another person (5, 56, 108).

Among children, most laughter is good-natured, though there may be some gloating over the person who arouses the laughter. Among adolescents and adults, on the other hand, laughter frequently has a strong element of gloating, which affects its tone. Furthermore, because of its tension-releasing quality, laughter is often louder and longer than the humor of the situation would seem to justify. This is true of children's laughter also, but to a lesser degree (91, 101, 193).

Not all humorous situations evoke laughter nor does all laughter indicate that something humorous has been perceived. A person may laugh, for example, because others are laughing or because he wants to "break the ice" and put others at ease in a social situation.

In a comic situation, the person may smile instead of laugh. Or he may not show his amusement by any facial expression at all. How he reacts to humor is largely influenced by the situation and by the people involved in it. If he believes that smiling or laughing will be regarded as socially inappropriate or in bad taste, he will refrain from any expression, no matter how humorous he perceives the situation to be.

Effects of humor on personality
Because of the high social value attached to humor, everyone likes to think that his appreciation of the comic is at least equal to that of others. People rarely admit that they do not understand a joke because they do not want to feel inferior in a quality that has such high prestige value. Instead, they pretend that they perceive the comic and laugh when their peers laugh. Even children, Jersild writes, spend much time and effort trying "to discover what makes people laugh, and how to gauge timing and emphasis to bring out the comic in what they do and say" (123).

INDIRECT EFFECTS The indirect effects of humor on personality come from the reactions of others toward the person's expression of humor. Studies reveal that one of the traits that contribute most to social acceptance at all ages is a "sense of humor," meaning the ability not only to "take a joke" but also to see the comic in situations in which others are involved (55, 63, 91).

The person who gains the reputation of being a good sport or having a "sense of humor" can count on favorable reactions from others and social acceptance. Knowing that others judge him favorably, the person tends to judge himself favorably.

Humor is an invaluable aid in social situations. Wisecracking, telling humorous jokes or stories, poking fun at others, or telling amusing stories about oneself break down social barriers and compensate for shyness. By eliciting favorable reactions from others, they contribute greatly to the individual's feelings of self-importance.

DIRECT EFFECTS What the person considers humorous and what he laughs at tell what function humor serves in his life and what aspects of his personality are most influenced by his perception of the comic. A person who feels inadequate is likely to concentrate on humor which bolsters his own ego at the expense of others, while the person who feels more adequate can enjoy humor in which the joke is on him.

Similarly, since much humor is linked to repressed emotions, what a person considers humorous and what kind of humor he concentrates on give clues to the source of his repression, whether it be anxiety, hostility, or sex. People who use humor to attack others are usually unable—for one reason or another—to use direct methods of attack. As Levine and Redlich have pointed out, "By making others laugh, they exhibit both their own strength and their own weakness" (146).

Humor affects the personality directly in three important ways. First, it makes the person feel superior and thus compensates for any feeling of inadequacy he may have; second, it is a means of releasing tension, especially tension from pent-up anxieties and hostilities; and third, it helps the person develop and accept a more realistic self-concept. The first and second are the most common; the third is the least common, but the most important.

Feelings of superiority What makes the person feel superior varies with age and is influenced at every age by the person's ability to understand not only the humor in a situation but also the attitudes of others toward the form the humor takes. At all ages, feelings of superiority come from being able to ridicule others because of their frailties, inferiorities, failures, or predicaments.

There are many forms of humor which contribute to the person's feeling of superiority. Babies and young children quickly discover the fun of annoying adults by blowing bubbles in the cup of water or milk they are given to drink, by splashing their bath water, and by throwing things after they have been picked up and handed to them. Older children find it amusing to tease animals and younger siblings and to annoy teachers by clowning, cutting up, and making their classmates laugh. Being the instigator of the humor, receiving the spotlight of attention, more that compensates for any punishment they may receive.

Feelings of superiority can be experienced vicariously by identification with characters in the comics, in movies, or on the television screen. Slapstick comedies in which the hero successfully defies or outwits authority figures are especially humorous to children and young adolescents.

Tension release   Making jokes at another's expense often provides a socially accepted means of getting even with an "enemy" and is thus a substitute for unapproved direct aggression. Humor also helps to reduce or eliminate feelings of martyrdom if one can turn the tables and put another in the role of martyr. Teasing, pranks, and practical jokes are generally motivated by hostility, even though not always recognized as such by the person who engages in them. As Jersild (123) has pointed out:

The "pay-off" in a practical joke is that someone is humiliated or made to look ridiculous or is left at a loss, as when a child is given an empty box for a present, or a present of a baby carriage is given to two people who are being married in their sixties. . . . Such practical jokes may contain a coarse element of humor but their main character is that they express hostility, more or less thinly disguised.

It is especially gratifying to the practical joker if the butt of his pranks is a person in authority who he believes has treated him unfairly. In a study of cartoons it was found that those regarded as more amusing contained a greater element of hostility. Furthermore, the more intelligent subjects were better at finding hidden hostility in the cartoons than the less intelligent (196).

Humor is an outlet for general emotional tension as well as tension resulting from specific emotional experiences. A person who is worried, frightened, or angry or who is frustrated in his work, his homelife, or his social relationships finds satisfaction in a hearty laugh. The release of tension not only serves as a form of body catharsis, by clearing his system of pent-up emotional energy, but also enables him to get a better perspective on the situation that gave rise to his emotional state. Tension release is greater when shared with others than when experienced alone.

Realistic self-concept   A sense of humor enables the person to laugh at weaknesses, frailties, and failures in himself just as he would laugh at them in others. It enables him to get a better perspective of himself, to develop self-insight, and to see himself realistically. Although he may not like what he sees, a sense of humor can go a long way toward increasing his self-acceptance and adding to his psychological maturity. As Allport says, a sense of humor is "an almost invariable possession of a cultivated and mature personality" (5).

The person who is able to laugh at his own incongruities and absurdities can learn to accept himself as he is and be satisfied to strive for achievable improvements. He is able to acknowledge his weaknesses and problems, to view them as less than overwhelming, and to continue to be self-acceptant. A sense of humor about oneself thus exerts a powerful and positive influence on the personality pattern.

SUMMARY

1 Intellectual capacity influences personality directly through the kind of life adjustments the individual makes and indirectly through the judgments others make of him on the basis of his intellectual achievements. Their judgments of him, in turn, affect his evaluation of himself.

2 Knowledge of the normal pattern of intellectual development is essential to understanding the effects of intellectual capacities on behavior. While all people follow much the same pattern of general intellectual development, marked variations in rate of development give rise to adjustment problems.

3 Special intellectual capacities likewise follow predictable patterns of development, with

individual variations in their rates. These variations, too, give rise to adjustment problems of major or minor severity, depending on how markedly they deviate from the norm. The effects are especially serious in the case of deviant memory, reasoning, imagination, and learning.

4 Variations in the rates of intellectual development are due to such factors as physical condition, the use the person makes of his intellectual capacities, early home experiences, emotional states, and the personality pattern.

5 Deviant intelligence, markedly above or below the norm, affects personality both directly and indirectly. The direct effect comes from the influence deviant intelligence has on the person's characteristic pattern of adjustment to life, while the indirect effect comes from the judgments others make of the person. These judgments are often colored by cultural stereotypes, by social attitudes toward those of deviant intelligence, by the attitudes of significant people in the person's life, especially parents and teachers, by the person's awareness of the attitudes of others toward him, and by his awareness of how greatly his intellectual capacities deviate from those of the people with whom he is associated.

6 At every age, deviant intelligence affects peer relationships. Peers react to the person according to the way he responds to them and the way he adjusts to different situations. The person's awareness of his peers' feelings affects his personality.

7 In most instances, intelligence that is markedly below the norm has a less damaging influence on personality than intelligence that is markedly above the norm. Those who are very dull usually fail to recognize how negatively others feel about them or how severely their dullness affects their adjustments. Deviant intelligence affects recreational interests, achievements, and the degree of social acceptance the person enjoys. These effects come not so much from deviant intelligence per se as from the attitudes of members of the social group toward the person's behavior and attitudes.

8 Intelligence affects adjustment in many areas of behavior. A survey of three areas—values, morality, and humor—serves to illustrate the broad influence of intelligence on personality. Values are developed by direct learning and identification. The development of conflicting values, owing to disparities between values learned at home, those based on social and cultural pressures, and those based on personal preferences and needs, affects the kind of adjustment the person makes in his personal life and in his social relationships. His resolution of the conflicts, which depends on his intellectual capacities, affects his personality. Changes in values result from intellectual growth and broader life experiences. Changed values toward work, toward the new and different, toward religion, and toward money, for example, meet changed needs at various times in the life span. They affect the person's life adjustments and, in turn, his personality.

9 Intellectual capacities play an important role in moral behavior and influence the kind of adjustments the person makes. His adjustments, in turn, influence the judgments others make of him as well as his evaluations of himself. Only when a child is young is the social group tolerant of violations of the codes of the group. This tolerance comes from the belief that he does not yet have the intellectual maturity to learn what the group expects. By the time he reaches adolescence, he will be unfavorably judged if his moral behavior falls short of the group's codes.

10 Learning a moral code is complicated by the number of different codes the person encounters in his environment, the inconsistencies between people's moral codes and their behavior, and changes in moral codes as new patterns of behavior become socially acceptable. These conflicts not only slow down the individual's learning, but they make moral decisions difficult. As a result, there is often a discrepancy between a person's moral knowledge and his moral behavior. A pronounced discrepancy leads to unfavorable social and self judgments. This is primarily why a person's morality has such a marked impact on his personality.

11 Early scientific recognition of the influence of humor on personality is attributed to Freud's explanation of how humor affects a person's behavior, how it affects the self-concept, and how it is used as a source of emotional catharsis. Allport contributed to the scientific explanation by distinguishing between a sense of humor and a sense of the comic, showing how each affects social and self judgments.

12 Other studies have shown how intelligence determines the person's ability to perceive the comic in others as well as in himself and have emphasized the role of factors other than intelligence, such as the person's physical condition, his personal and social relationships, and his personality pattern.

13 Humor affects personality indirectly through the reactions of other people toward the person's expression of humor. It affects personality directly by making the person feel superior, by providing release from tensions resulting from anxiety and hostility, and by helping the person to develop and accept a realistic self-concept.

CHAPTER 8 emotional determinants

Emotions, whether fleeting or persisting, color the individual's perception of himself and his environment and affect his behavior. By determining what his characteristic pattern of adjustment to life will be, they affect his personality.

A person who habitually feels frustrated, for example, will be more hostile and impulsive than one who approaches people and environmental obstacles with more optimism and self-confidence. One who is habitually jealous will be suspicious of whatever others say or do.

Emotions can add pleasure to a person's life and motivate action that improves his social and personal adjustments. Or they can make life painful and be a handicap to adjustments. If strong and frequent, emotions can play havoc with a person's physical well-being by upsetting body homeostasis. They can, likewise, interfere with normal mental functioning, causing the person to perform far below capacity and to make more mistakes. Because of the close tie-in between achievement and the self-concept, the person feels inadequate, guilty, and embarrassed if his performance falls short of his own and others' expectations. An adolescent who is awkward and clumsy, or who does not do things in the socially approved manner, suffers from embarrassment and ego-deflation. The woman who runs out of some food or drink when she has guests is embarrassed because she is afraid of making an unfavorable impression (121, 153).

Not only do emotionally toned experiences affect the person's self-concept at the time they occur but memories of experiences continue to leave their mark. The greater the discrepancy between the real and ideal self-concepts, the more likely the person is to try to repress memories of unpleasant experiences. This he does in the hope of eliminating the damage they do to his concept of self.

The intensity and duration of an emotion determine how it will affect the personality. Emotional responses, pleasant and unpleasant, vary from moderate satisfaction and a vague uneasiness at one extreme to euphoric joy and a disorganized state of panic, dominated by fear or anger, at the other.

EFFECTS ON PERSONALITY

Emotions have both direct and indirect effects on personality. The direct effects come from physical and mental disturbances, while the indirect effects come from the reactions of members of the social group toward the person who is experiencing the emotion. If the emotions are unpleasant, such as fear and jealousy, or if they are strong and uncontrolled, they are damaging to the personality pattern. If they are pleasant and if they are controlled in such a way as to do little harm to the person's physical and mental well-being, they have a favorable effect on the personality pattern.

Direct effects

Directly, the emotions affect the individual's physical and mental functioning and his attitudes, interests, and values.

Even a mild emotion causes some *physical* imbalance or upset in homeostasis. A slight upset in homeostasis is usually therapeutic in the sense that it jolts the person out of any state of lethargy he may have fallen into and acts as a general tonic for his entire system. Severe upsets in homeostasis caused by strong and persistent emotions disorganize the person's normal patterns of behavior. If the emotions are expressed overtly, the person will then experience a state of relaxation. But if the emotion is inhibited, the person is likely to experience functional physical disorders, psychosomatic disturbances, delusions, hallucinations, and other symptoms of personality maladjustment.

Such physical disturbances as chronic exhaustion, digestive disorders, insomnia, headaches, high blood pressure, heart trouble, allergic reactions, skin diseases, and peptic ulcers are often related to emotional upsets. General nervousness, especially in children, often leads to speech defects in addition to other disturbances.

With advancing age, the effects of the emotions on physical well-being increase. The younger person is able to expend energy that has been mobilized for emotional responses in work, play, or strenuous exercise, but the elderly person does not have these outlets. The physical disturbances caused by intense emotions are thus prolonged.

Mental disturbances brought about by emotional upsets result in decreased mental efficiency. Under stress, the person is unstable and unpredictable and his performance is inconsistent, especially when reasoning is involved.

Studies show how detrimental anxiety and frustration are to learning complicated skills, such as reading and arithmetic (117). When reasoning is required, as in a digit-symbol substitution test, the effects of anxiety on mental efficiency are especially pronounced (10, 150). Anxiety affects people differently, however. Those who are normally low in anxiety are stimulated by an anxiety-provoking situation and motivated to do better; those who are already high in anxiety are hampered in their learning (15, 118, 151, 152, 162).

Frustration has much the same effects as anxiety. It keeps the person from doing what he is capable of doing and curbs any expression of creativity. Children suffering from frustrations play in a less constructive way than their abilities would justify. They cannot concentrate on what they are doing and, as a result, regress to a less organized and less mature form of play (47).

Another important direct effect of the emotions on adjustment is their coloring of the person's *interests, attitudes, likes,* and *dislikes.* People who have more likes than dislikes have healthier, more positive attitudes and make better personal and social adjustments than those who are ruled by their dislikes. Positive attitudes, built up from pleasant experiences, facilitate adjustments (12, 94).

The motivational power of love has a profound effect on behavior (94). The child who loves his mother wants to do things to please her, he likes what she likes, and he decides, when several alternatives are present, in favor of the one most likely to win her approval. So it is with adolescents and adults in their relationships with members of the opposite sex. A person in love develops interests and attitudes similar to those of the loved one. These influence his behavior and affect his adjustments to life. The similarity of the personality patterns of people who have been happily married for a long time may be partially explained by this fact (94).

Indirect effects

The indirect effects of the emotions on personality come partly from the judgments others make of the emotional behavior of the individual and the way they treat him and partly from the kind of emotional relationship he is able to establish with them. People tend to *judge a person* more favorably if he keeps his negative and unpleasant emotions under control. They would rather be with a person who is happy and cheerful than with one who is sad, depressed, disparaging, and complaining. A person who dwells on his "bad luck" or who attacks others indirectly by cutting or sarcastic jokes makes people feel uncomfortable. The old saying, "Laugh and the world laughs with you, weep and you weep alone," expresses the attitude of most people toward such emotional expressions.

Frequent and intense emotional outbursts, especially when there is no apparent justification for them, lead to the judgment that the person is "immature." On the other hand, a person who conceals his unpleasant emotions and tries always to behave in a socially approved manner, may also be immature. He bottles up the energy engendered by the emotion and stifles its normal expression. This pent-up energy smolders inside him for hours or days, leading to "moodiness," general nervous tension, or such specific nervous mannerisms as nail-biting and eye-blinking.

The second important indirect effect of emotions on personality comes from the person's ability or inability to establish *emotional relationships* with others. Social relationships are greatly influenced by the emotional linkage between people—the "empathic complex"—which occurs when two people find interests in common and when the needs in one person's life are met by his relationship with another person.

Children develop an emotional linkage with certain significant people in their lives—parents, siblings, grandparents, teachers, peers, or adults in the neighborhood—because these people serve some need in their lives. A pompous person may be ridiculed by others, but he may appeal to a shy child because he has qualities the child admires and wishes he himself had. By identifying himself with such a person, the child may fulfill his own need for self-importance.

Some people, as a result of harmful early experiences in the home or with members of the peer group, are unable to show others how they feel about them. This places a barrier between them and those they would like to have as friends. They are unable to establish a close, intimate relationship in which they can talk freely about their problems, exchange confidences, and show affection—all of which are essential elements of the empathic complex. Instead, their social relationships are marked by an "apartness" or aloofness in which no emotional linkage exists. Others view such people as cold, unfriendly, and withdrawn (5, 28, 33, 65).

At any time in life the person who feels rejected is in danger of becoming self-bound, unable to be friendly or to express affection for others. The most critical time, however, is early in life when the social environment is so limited that the individual is unable to seek substitute sources of emotional linkage. Almost as critical is old age, when social horizons narrow and social contacts are limited mainly to family members, neighbors, or old friends. Those who feel rejected become "misers" in their affection. They are afraid to invest positive feelings in people because they have discovered that such feelings are not likely to be returned.

Lack of interest in others and lack of positive displays of affection are bound to lead to further rejection or neglect. Studies reveal that at all ages one of the outstanding characteristics of those who are popular is their "friendliness," the quality of being outgoing and able to form emotional linkages with others (33, 88, 98).

Scientific evidence of effects of emotions on personality

As far back as 400 BC, Hippocrates tried to explain the dominance of certain emotional patterns as resulting from an imbalance in one of the five fundamental body humors—blood, black bile, yellow bile, phlegm, and the nervous humor. For example, a person with predominance of black bile would have a melancholy temperament; he would be persistently sad, easily depressed, slow, unpleasant, and undemonstrative (80, 166).

Modern scientific studies have not only disproved the existence of body humors but have, as we have seen, gone far in explaining what does determine the personality pattern. Studies of relatively recent origin are pointing the way to an understanding of how the emotions, as determined by both environmental and physical factors, influence personality and, even more important, how the damaging effects can

be controlled. Pressey and Kuhlen (138) explain that the impact of emotionality on life adjustments is probably greatest during the early years of life:

Habit patterns and personality, including patterns of emotional response, become more rigid and harder to change with increasing age.... [This] leads to the view that experiences having emotional impacts are psychologically important in inverse order to the age of the subject; i.e., the younger the person, the more constructive or damaging the experience may be.... In general, early emotional experiences may be of greater total significance than those occurring later in life, but other critical periods may exist and should be identified.

In the remaining pages of this chapter, we shall discuss a number of modern studies of the effects of the emotions on personality. Our discussion will include the following topics: dominant emotions, emotional balance, emotional deprivation, excessive love, emotional expressions, emotional catharis, and emotional stress.

DOMINANT EMOTIONS

Although everyone experiences the whole gamut of emotional responses, some people tend to experience a predominance of the pleasant emotions and others a predominance of the unpleasant. This predominance is reflected in the personality. The apprehensive person is full of fear; even his joy is tinged with uncertainty. The cheerful person is usually happy; even when sad or frightened, he can see the brighter side of things.

Temperament versus mood

The predominance of a particular kind of emotional reaction—the person's "prevailing emotional state"—determines his temperament. *Temperament* is that aspect of personality which is revealed in the tendency to experience moods or mood changes in characteristic ways (80). The outstanding quality of temperament is that it tends to be persistent and, as such, discloses which emotions play a dominant role in the person's life.

A *mood* is a temporary emotional reaction. Mood and temperament may reflect similar emotions, but temperament colors the person's characteristic method of adjusting to life while mood colors only his present pattern of adjustment (182).

Because of the persistence of temperament, we can predict how a person will react to a given situation with a fair degree of accuracy. We may not know what his mood will be at a particular moment, but if he has a cheerful disposition, or temperament, we can be fairly sure that he will not be terribly annoyed over a minor obstacle. Instead, he will take the bad with the good and not allow the bad to ruffle him excessively.

By contrast, the person who has a bad disposition can be counted on to react with anger out of all proportion to the nature of the obstacle. He can also be counted on to express his anger as he has habitually expressed it in the past—by flying off the handle in a temper tantrum, by attacking others bodily or verbally, or by thrusting the blame for the obstacle on his pet scapegoat, whoever or whatever it may be.

While moods predispose the person to react in much the same way as temperament, the reactions are less predictable. Unlike temperament, moods are fleeting; they do not represent the person's habitual manner of emotional reactivity. Instead, they are determined by the emotional state that has been aroused at the time.

Causes of dominant emotions

Early in the twentieth century, there were attempts to explain emotional predominance in terms of endocrine imbalance. The explanations followed closely the belief of Hippocrates that dominant emotions came from an imbalance of the body humors. A hypothyroid condition, one in which the amount of secretion from the thyroid glands is below normal, was believed to be responsible for the temperamental pattern described by Hippocrates as "phlegmatic." A hyperthyroid condition, one in which the amount of thyroxin in the bloodstream is above normal, was thought to make the person nervous and high-strung, similar to the pattern attributed by Hippocrates and his followers to a predominance of the nervous humor (80, 123).

Today, evidence points to environmental influences, especially child-training methods and early parent-child relationships, as primarily responsible for the predominance of the emotional patterns that constitute the person's temperament. Physical factors, however, such as general health and endocrine imbalance are not ignored (144). The predominance of certain unpleasant emotional states, particularly depression, are believed to be related to endocrine imbalance (129).

If a child is brought up in a restrictive home environment where little emotional warmth is shown, where parental expectations are beyond the child's capacities and lead to constant feelings of failure, and where substitute sources of socialization and love are lacking, he is likely to experience an overwhelming number of unpleasant emotions. This will lead to unhappiness and a predisposition to respond to future situations with unpleasant emotions. In time, this pattern of response will become habitual.

How the person will express his emotions will depend on what he has learned is socially approved in his culture, what he has found from experience brings him the greatest personal satisfaction, and what is the quickest and most expedient way of getting the end result he desires. The young child, for example, learns to cry for a purpose, either to get what he wants or to gain sympathy and attention. As he grows older, he learns that crying is regarded as an infantile form of behavior. He learns, then, to withhold his tears, even when he is in pain or suffering from some strong frustration. Similarly, he learns when it is considered appropriate to respond emotionally with a pleasant smile, a gentle laugh, or a loud guffaw.

Through *conditioning,* or learning by association, the person comes to respond emotionally to a wide variety of stimuli which originally failed to call forth any response. This is illustrated in Figure 8-1. Since conditioned responses depend on the person's ability to understand the situation in which the conditioning occurs, fears and anxieties, as Pressey and Kuhlen have pointed out, "may arise at any age from childhood to old age, only to wane in significance as familiarity, understanding, and skill in dealing with them are developed" (138).

Conditioned emotions do not remain static. Instead, they spread to people, objects, and situations similar to those with which they have become associated. Harlow states that "the initial love responses of the human being are made by the infant to the mother or some mother surrogate. From this intimate attachment of the child to the mother, multiple learned and generalized affectional responses are formed" (71).

Generalized emotional responses, resulting from the spread of conditioned emotions, are at the basis of *preferences,* or likes and dislikes. In time, they may become organized into patterns of emotional preference, or *attitudes.* If attitudes are highly charged

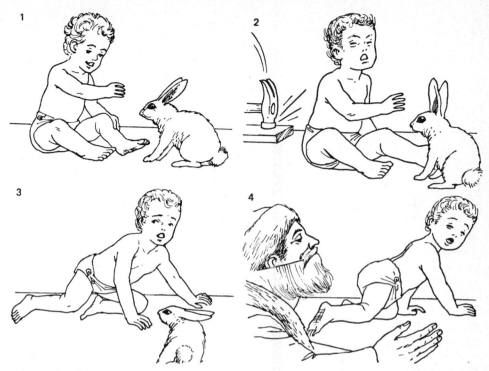

Figure 8-1 Through conditioning, a child learns to react emotionally to a wide variety of stimuli which formerly failed to call forth emotional responses. (1) Response to a rabbit before conditioning. (2) An unconditioned stimulus in the form of a loud, metallic sound is presented simultaneously with the rabbit several times. (3) This results in a conditioned fear of the rabbit. (4) A generalization develops of a conditioned fear to stimuli which resemble the rabbit in shape, color, form, or texture. (Adapted from G. G. Thompson: *Child psychology,* rev. ed. Boston; Houghton Mifflin, 1962. Used by permission.)

with emotion and resistant to change, they are known as *prejudices* and have a powerful influence on the person's thoughts and actions.

When attitudes are accompanied by excessive emotions, they often lead to a neurotic response pattern, called a *complex.* A person with a "mother complex," for example, has such an exaggerated emotionally toned attitude toward his mother that he is incapable of making normal adjustments to other people, especially to members of the opposite sex.

Changes in dominant emotions

Since emotional predominance is largely fostered by physical, environmental, and psychological factors, and is not the result of inheritance, changes in "disposition" may occur at any age. They are most frequent during the early years of life, before emotional patterns have become habitual.

The three most common causes of changes in the dominant emotions are environmental changes, physical changes, and changes in intellectual capacities. With *environmental changes,* the different treatment the person receives may readily bring about a revision in his self-concept, in his reactions to others, and in his outlook on life. These will undoubtedly influence the pattern of his emotional expression.

A child who has been accustomed to having the mother's undivided attention may bitterly resent her preoccupation with a new sibling. He shows his resentments at the changed treatment he receives by frequent and intense outbursts of anger and jealousy; he thus changes from a happy, calm child into a tense and irascible one.

The happy, carefree adolescent may turn into a bored, unhappy, resentful, and dour adult. If a man feels that he has been deposed in his wife's affection by her preoccupation with household duties and the care of children, he will suffer from resentment and frustration and a feeling of martyrdom and jealousy— all of which will change his disposition. Changes in a woman's disposition may occur if her role as wife and mother provides little personal satisfaction.

Physical changes, especially when they are pronounced and when they coincide with environmental changes and changes in social expectations, bring about radical changes in temperament, either temporary or permanent, depending on how the person adjusts to them. The moodiness of the pubescent may disappear once his body has been transformed into that of an adult. However, if he makes poor adjustments in adolescence, his moodiness may persist and he may become an anxious, gloomy, guilt-ridden adult.

While changes in temperament during old age may result, in part, from the general physical decline that accompanies aging, negative social attitudes toward the aging account for some of the changes. The tendency toward apathy, loss of enthusiasm, emotional unresponsiveness, and irascibility come partly from the person's realization of changed social attitudes toward him and toward his usefulness to society (20, 34, 49).

With changes in *intellectual capacities* come changes in interests and increased social and self insight. The happy-go-lucky schoolchild may readily develop into an anxious one if his parents pressure him to achieve academic success or if his peers begin to regard him as the class clown. Cole and Hall write: "It may suddenly strike a third-grade child that schoolwork is competitive, and this new idea may generate in him a feeling of shame because he has thus far puttered happily about at the bottom of the class" (40).

Effects on personality

How well the individual adjusts to life depends partly on which emotions predominate and how he expresses his dominant emotions.

One great difference between a person who is emotionally disturbed and one who is well adjusted is that, in the former, the negative or unpleasant emotions are more frequent and intense while, in the latter, the positive and pleasant emotions are dominant. A predominance of fear, anger, suspiciousness, and jealousy results in feelings of insecurity which lead to maladjustment and unhappiness. Persistence of this pattern of unpleasant emotions is likely to lead to paranoia. A predominance of affection, happiness, joy, and love, on the other hand, leads to feelings of security which help the person approach his problem with self-confidence, react to minor obstacles with equanimity, and retain his emotional balance even when he encounters severe obstacles. He makes good personal and social adjustments, is well liked, and generally makes a success of whatever he undertakes. Because of his pleasant disposition, people like to have him around. He is often selected for leadership roles because people feel that he will represent them well.

The way in which a person expresses emotions likewise influences his adjustments. The person who expresses his negative emotions, for example, with focus and direction will be better adjusted than the person whose negative emotions are generalized. This is seen in anxiety and hostility, both of which are generalized emotional states that result in negative attitudes toward people and in neurotic, maladjustive behavior.

Dominant emotions are revealed in *facial expression* as well as in overt behavior. Even when the face is in repose, it tells whether the person is cheerful, shy, or troubled. Often the facial expression tells the story of the person's feelings about himself and his environment more eloquently than his actions. It affects the judgments others make of him and their reactions to him. How they treat him influences his concept of self and intensifies the predominant emotional pattern that has been fostered by his other life experiences.

EMOTIONAL BALANCE

If the well-adjusted person is the one who has had the most pleasant emotional experiences, would it not be good child-training policy to see that the child has a happy, carefree, untroubled childhood? The answer is No. The well-adjusted person is one who has learned to face adversity.

Children who are protected from anything that is unpleasant and who are not required to conform to socially approved standards of behavior are ill prepared to meet the frustrations, disappointments, and other hardships they will encounter when they grow older. Parents cannot shield the schoolchild from all the realities of life, nor can they expect society to permit the older child to do as he pleases. The more permissive and over-protective parents are, the less well prepared the child will be to face life alone.

Everyone needs a reasonable number of unhappy experiences to build up *tolerance,* to learn how to meet problems and confront obstacles without going to pieces emotionally. Tolerance can be achieved only when the person learns to deal with negative emotions, as well as positive ones, and to react to unpleasant situations in a way that meets the approval of the social group and at the same time fills his own needs. And he must be able to do these things alone without the help of parents, teachers, or peers (167).

Tolerance is "mental health insurance"—a psychological protection against life's hazards. It can come only if the child is given opportunities and motivation to learn to cope with unpleasant emotional experiences.

Forms of emotional tolerance

Frustration, fear, jealousy, and envy—these are the four unpleasant emotions which everyone will inevitably face and must learn to tolerate.

Throughout life, the individual will confront obstacles, both within the environment and within himself in the form of limited abilities, which will prevent him from doing what he wants to do. These obstacles will prove frustrating to him. If he learns *frustration tolerance* from a reasonable number of frustrating experiences in early life, however, he will be able to cope with later obstacles so that they will not turn him into a maladjusted person.

While the baby and the young child can be shielded from frightening experiences, a time will come when the child must leave the protective environment of the home. If he has not learned *fear tolerance* of new and strange experiences, he will be afraid to step outside his front door alone. An overprotected child often experiences "school phobia," an abnormal and irrational fear of school due to his lack of experiences in dealing with people, environments, and activities outside the home (95, 105). Similarly, lack of social experience prevents a person from developing sufficient fear tolerance to withstand stage fright or embarrassment.

Jealousy leads to deep resentments against others, feelings of martyrdom, and a desire to retaliate. The sooner the person learns *jealousy tolerance,* the sooner he will be able to adjust to situations in

which he is not "Number One." This is particularly difficult for an only child, who has never had to share parental attention and affection with a sibling, or for any other child who has been in the limelight of favor or has had his every wish gratified. Sooner or later, he will have to compete with others on equal terms. The person who has not learned to tolerate jealousy will be plagued with unhappy feelings about himself which can only lead to personal and social maladjustments.

So long as the young child has things that are more or less like those of his siblings or playmates, he is satisfied. Before childhood is over, however, he recognizes differences in quality and comes to appreciate the social value of material possessions. When this happens he becomes envious if a sibling or peer has something better than he has. *Envy tolerance* learned early in life frees the individual from a powerful, potentially destructive motivating force. The envious adult goes hopelessly into debt trying to keep up with the affluent Joneses; he complains about his bad luck, cries on your shoulder, and covets your material possessions. Uncontrolled envy can seriously warp his personality.

Acquiring mental health insurance

Emotional balance, which is an essential element of mental health insurance, can be promoted in four ways. *First* and foremost, the child must be allowed to confront a reasonable number of unpleasant emotional experiences along with an abundant supply of pleasant ones. Parents often deprive themselves of what they need in order to buy things for their child and spare him the pangs of envy that they fear will damage his personality. A woman may neglect her husband and devote her time to meeting the instant wants of her child so that he will not be jealous of the father. Such measures are self-defeating.

Stagner (166) emphasizes the necessity of experiencing both pleasant and unpleasant emotions:

A boy or girl who has no fear or suspicion whatever of other people is not too well prepared for life in our competitive culture. Furthermore, we can sympathize with others only if we have had experience in some degree similar to theirs. A person who has never encountered any misfortunes cannot truly appreciate the position of those who suffer. An ideal child-rearing program, therefore, would give the growing personality a sufficient breadth of emotional situations, but not an excess. A child plunged into excessively stimulating surroundings before he has acquired the sense of reality and perspective necessary to keep his balance must inevitably develop an unstable personality.

The most significant part of the above statement is the warning given in the words "sufficient breadth of emotional situations, but not an excess." The environment should be controlled to ward against an excess of either the pleasant or the unpleasant.

The *second* way to promote emotional balance is to help the child understand why he cannot always express his unpleasant emotions as he would like to. This may be difficult when the child is very young, but it cannot be put off. It must be done before the child develops the habit of expressing himself in ways that will win social disapproval.

A young child has too limited a vocabulary to comprehend the full meaning of such an explanation as "Daddy and I can't afford to buy two new tricycles and that is why we are giving you the old one that your big brother has outgrown and getting him a new one." Even if the child cannot understand the meaning of the words, however, he will understand that there is some reason why he cannot express his jealousy or envy without restraint.

Sometimes gestures and acting out a situation will make words seem more meaningful to the child. As his comprehension increases, he can be taught to find satisfaction in activities that do not arouse an excess of the emotions he has not yet learned to tolerate. If he becomes frustrated when he tries to construct a block structure that is far too complicated for his stage of development, he can be shown how to construct a simpler one.

Third, whenever it is possible to do so, prepare the child for an unpleasant emotion in advance— before it is aroused and gets out of control. It is a well-known psychological principle that any stress situation can be met better if the person is prepared for it ahead of time. For example, a child can better tolerate the frustration of having to leave his play and come to supper if he is warned that supper will be ready in 10 minutes. Preparation also helps to reinforce the child's understanding that reason, not whim, requires him to tolerate unpleasant emotions.

To counteract any tendency the child may have to believe that whim or "meanness" is behind the adult's requirement that he control his unpleasant emotions, the adult should see to it that an unpleasant emotion is replaced with a pleasant one as soon as possible. This is the *fourth* way to promote emotional balance. It will not only wipe out any suspicion of "meanness" but it will also wipe out memories of the situation that gave rise to the unpleasant emotion. If a child is jealous of a new baby, a period of play with the mother while the baby takes a nap will go a long way toward counteracting any idea the child may have that the mother prefers the baby to him. Counteracting the unpleasant emotion immediately prevents the child from mulling over and exaggerating the circumstances and beginning to think of himself as misunderstood and mistreated—thoughts which lay the foundation for a martyr complex.

EMOTIONAL DEPRIVATION

Studies of emotional deprivation have increased our understanding of the role emotions play in personality development. A deficiency of emotional experiences, pleasant ones especially, during the early years of life leads to poor personal and social adjustments.

Meaning of emotional deprivation

Emotional deprivation means that, because of environmental obstacles, the person is denied stimulus objects which arouse emotional reactions. As the term is used by psychologists and sociologists, it refers mainly to love reactions, though in its broadest sense, it refers to any kind of emotional reaction.

Some children grow up in environments which deprive them of opportunities to experience the unpleasant emotions. As was stressed earlier, this keeps them from developing tolerance or mental health insurance. Other children have plenty of opportunities to experience the unpleasant emotions but are deprived of opportunities to experience the pleasant ones. It is to this second group that the term "emotional deprivation" is ordinarily applied.

Deprivation of love

Deprivation of any emotion is harmful to the personality, but deprivation of love is especially damaging (68). As Jersild says, "There is something emotionally satisfying about being loved, and there also is something very practical about it" (87). Harlow speaks of love as "a wondrous state, deep, tender and rewarding" (71). Love includes not only the condition of being loved but also the act of loving. If it is to contribute positively and maximally to personality development, it must be developmentally appropriate in terms of quality, quantity, and method of expression.

In the early years of life, the child tries to behave in such a way as to gain parental warmth and acceptance. Later, he learns behavior patterns which bring him parental approval and, at the same time, provide him with effective ways of gratifying his own needs. This frees him from some of the vulnerability that emotional dependence brings. Emotional warmth from love likewise serves to stimulate intellectual development (68).

Deprivation of an affectionate relationship is most damaging in early childhood. Deprivation at this time may come from institutionalization of the baby or child, owing to the economic or marital status of the parents, the health of the baby or mother, the death of one or both parents, or some other cause. A child may be rejected or neglected by his parents because they favor a sibling or have other things to do. Some parents believe that showing affection for the child will "spoil" him and make him feel too important. "Under-the-roof alienation"—as this kind of deprivation is called—is more common in the American culture than deprivation due to institutionalization (13, 21, 111, 187). Figure 8-2 shows some common causes of deprivation of love.

Many adults experience deprivation of love, especially in old age and after the death or divorce of a spouse. Deprivation can be almost as damaging to the self-concept in adulthood as in childhood.

Just as a child can suffer under-the-roof alienation, an adult may continue to live with a spouse but be "emotionally separated" from him. In many such cases, the individuals try to compensate for their own deprivation of love by focusing their affection on a child or by having extramarital love affairs.

Unmarried adults, too, experience deprivation of love, whether their failure to marry is due to choice or inability to attract a member of the opposite sex. Devotion to aging parents or to the children of relatives and friends rarely compensates for lack of an enduring affectionate relationship with a member of the opposite sex.

In old age, as in childhood, the major source of affection is normally the family. Even elderly people who are happily married and have interests of their own are rarely able to achieve emotional independence from their children. But in many cultures, the elderly are psychologically, if not economically, rejected by their children and grandchildren. This dep-

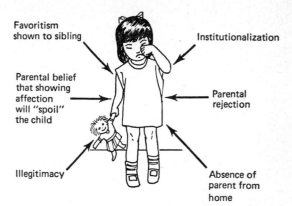

Figure 8-2   Some common causes of deprivation of love.

rivation of affection is especially damaging when failing health, loss of a spouse or former friends, or the necessity of moving into an institution or into the home of a family member brings about social isolation from nonfamily members who might otherwise supply the elderly person with some of the affection he needs and craves.

Deprivation of other pleasant emotions

Although studies of emotional deprivation have concentrated on the causes and effects of deprivation of love, studies in related areas show that psychological damage also results from a lack of opportunities to experience other pleasant emotions.

Curiosity is a pleasant and valuable emotion. It enables the person to discover new meanings and thus to broaden his interests and activities. It prevents boredom and stagnation by providing new avenues for thought and action. It is valuable because it supplies the motivation for learning and creativity. Without it, there would be little progress.

While the stifling of curiosity is harmful for people of all intellectual levels, it is especially so for those who are bright and creative and who are likely to make the greatest contribution to society. It is most damaging during the early years of life.

Many children and adolescents are deprived of opportunities to experience curiosity by a parent or teacher who is afraid they will be harmed, who finds their explorations annoying and destructive, or who feels that they will be unfavorably judged by others. Many children ask questions and get no answers or they are ridiculed and criticized.

Children may be deprived of stimuli to call forth curiosity, owing to an intellectually sterile environment or one which is planned for persons of greater or lesser intellectual capacities. As was pointed out in Chapter 7, very bright or very dull children who are kept in classes planned for those of average intelligence tend to develop a mental rigidity, feelings of boredom and frustration, and a generalized resentment against all in authority. They become apathetic and develop an "I don't care" attitude which stifles their motivation to do what they are capable of (36, 69, 106, 180).

Many people of all ages are deprived of experiencing the *happiness,* joy, or elation that comes from achievement. This deprivation may be due to environmental obstacles but more often it is the result of unrealistic levels of aspiration. A person may aspire above or below his capacities because he does not know what his true capacities are. Unrealistically high aspirations may also be due to pressures from parents, teachers, or even peers.

Unrealistically high levels of aspiration inevitably lead the person to feel that he is a failure because his achievements have not come up to his own or others' expectations. Under such conditions, what he does achieve will give him little satisfaction and certainly no happiness. Instead, it will lead to feelings of inferiority. If the person himself is realistic about his abilities but is pressed by parents, teachers, or others to do more than he is capable of, he will add resentments to his feelings of inferiority.

When lack of achievement is due to environmental obstacles, the person feels frustrated even if he has been able to achieve a moderate degree of success. Knowing that he could have done more and better, had he not been obstructed, makes him more angry than happy with what he does accomplish. How failure or achievements below one's capacities affect the self-concept will be discussed in detail in Chapter 10, Aspirations and Achievements.

Effects of emotional deprivation on personality

Deprivation of love results in "emotional starvation." Like the person who is hungry for food, the person who is starved for affection becomes irritable, unreasonable, and cantankerous. He shows his emotional hunger as he shows his physical hunger by emotional symptoms that vary from mild irritability to severe psychoses or by misbehavior that, as he grows

older, may reach the level of delinquency or adult criminality (13, 140).

Deprivation of opportunities to love and be loved delays the normal patterns of physical and mental development. This, in turn, affects the personality. Some of the specific effects of emotional deprivation have been reported to be:

Physical, as seen in listlessness, emaciation, loss of appetite, quietness, general apathy, and psychosomatic illnesses

Social, as revealed in handicaps in learning how to get along with people, lack of responsiveness to the advances of others, lack of cooperation, and hostility

Emotional, as shown in lack of emotional responsiveness and interchange (the empathic complex), feelings of insecurity, resentments as expressed in asocial behavior, restlessness, anxiety, temper tantrums, and many other forms of maladjustive behavior (4, 31, 35, 140, 164, 187, 194)

The older child or adolescent may push himself in intellectual and scholastic pursuits to gain acceptance by parents and teachers, or he may be so disturbed that he is unable to function and thus appears to be retarded. He may experience physical complaints which interfere with health and growth. Or he may develop nervous mannerisms, especially speech disorders. As he grows older, he may turn to delinquency as a substitute for emotional satisfaction.

The effects of deprivation of love on the personalities of older people will depend on how rejected they feel. Elderly people who have been institutionalized feel more rejected than those who live in their own homes or in homes of their grown children, even though they may suspect that their children resent having to care for them. A feeling of rejection leads to self-pity, anxiety, irritability, and negativism at any age.

Long-term effects on personality
While it was formerly believed that deprivation of love during the early, formative years would lay the basis for adult personality disorders, it is now questioned whether this is necessarily true. Permanent psychological damage may be obviated by favorable conditions either before the deprivation occurred or before the damage becomes too severe. As Bowlby et al. have emphasized, the assumptions that children who "experience institutionalization and similar forms of

severe privation and deprivation in early life *commonly* develop psychopathic or affectionless characters are incorrect" (31).

On the other hand, while a satisfying babyhood will not necessarily compensate for economic privation or other unfavorable conditions in the person's later life, it does provide a tentative—and probably persisting—character structure. As Harlow (71) points out:

Human affection does not extinguish when the mother ceases to have intimate association with the drives in question [for food, water, contact, etc.]. Instead, the affectional ties to the mother show a life-long, unrelenting persistence and, even more surprisingly, widely expanding generality.

One of the most common long-term effects of deprivation of affection on personality is *emotional insecurity*—a feeling of not belonging and of being unable to count on the affection of significant people. When babies sense a lack of consistency in the love relationship with their mothers, they cry excessively and show other symptoms of nervousness (143). When children recognize an inconsistency in their parents' child-training methods, with swings from punitiveness to permissiveness, they are unsure of the parents' affection. Their heightened emotionality is expressed in temper tantrums, irritability, nervous mannerisms, such as nail-biting, thumb-sucking, and speech defects.

Much of the adolescent rebellion against authority stems from emotional insecurity which had its origin in an unstable affectional relationship with parents during the childhood years. The person who never felt emotionally secure tends to be anxious and rebellious. He feels threatened, and this puts him on the defensive whenever there is any indication that his rights might be taken away from him. This defensive attitude may lead to a generalized rebellion against authority during the adolescent years.

Emotional insecurity in adolescence shows itself in a craving for the acceptance and affection of peers of both sexes. The adolescent tries to win this security by conforming as closely as possible to the standards of the peer group. One of the reasons for going steady and marrying early is that the adolescent is trying to compensate for unstable emotional relationships experienced at home (101).

Variations in effects on personality
The severity and persistence of the effects of deprivation of love depend largely on the extent of the deprivation, when it occurs, how long it lasts, and whether a satisfactory source of love can be substituted for a normal, but unavailable, source.

If the deprivation of affection is very slight in *extent,* the desire for affection is sharpened (28, 75, 97, 101). Children who must compete with their siblings for the mother's time and love become more friendly and eager to please. They seek more attention and affection from teachers and other adults than do children whose deprivation at home is extreme (97).

Pronounced deprivation of affection results in emotional starvation and intellectual torpor. Deprivation of affection accompanied by intellectual stimulation, however, leads to autism, or "emotional refrigeration," in which the person shows little or no interest in people and is cold, withdrawn, and distant (164).

The effects of deprivation of love on personality depend also on *when* it occurs. The child is most vulnerable from 6 months to 4 or 5 years of age. If the baby is separated from the mother before he becomes accustomed to her child-care technique, he will adjust to the new situation provided that he is cared for by *one person* (35, 194).

During the "critical period" of separation, between the last half of the first year and the age of 5, the child who has no stable source of love is unable to learn to identify with or associate love with another person normally. As a result, he develops into an "affectionateless" person or an aggressive one who demands attention and affection from others. On the other hand, if separation from the mother, or a mother substitute who has provided a stable source of love, occurs after the critical period, the child can generally adjust to the change, understand why it has occurred, and form satisfying new emotional relationships (35, 194).

A 19-day study of 2-year-olds in a residence and day nursery showed that those who were separated from their mothers completely were more upset by the separation than those who were separated during the day only, while their mothers worked. The children in residence responded by constantly seeking the mother, crying and shrieking; in their relations with staff members, they were demanding and hostile. They indulged in more autoerotic practices and showed more regression in sphincter control and more illness than those in the day nursery. Furthermore, the residential children were more anxious to identify with the nurses and other adults at the nursery than those who were there only for the day. When first reunited with the mother, the residential children showed little affection. Even a long time after the reunion, they tended to be aggressive, ambivalent toward the mother, and hostile toward the father and siblings (79).

There is little evidence that separation from the father during the "critical period" leads to any permanent damage. Since few young children develop an intense affectional attachment for their fathers comparable to that for their mothers, the separation results in no significant deprivation of affection (13, 35, 143).

Older children and adolescents deprived of a stable source of affection react differently from younger children, but the effect on their personalities is equally damaging. Loss of a parent, due to death or divorce, causes a typical grief reaction, accompanied by feelings of insecurity and inferiority (13, 28). If both parents are lost by death before the person is 14 or 15 years old, he feels inadequate, insecure, unwanted, and "different" (4, 28).

Under-the-roof alienation, or deprivation of affection because of parental neglect, rejection, or favoritism, is even more damaging to an older child or adolescent than deprivation due to parental death or divorce. The alienated person avoids social relationships outside the home because he has not found them satisfying in the home. He feels inferior and incapable of loving and being loved, and he develops a generalized hostility toward people (4, 17, 28).

Rejection by the peer group after having once experienced the satisfaction of acceptance has much the same effect on the older child or adolescent as deprivation of love at home. If, in addition to rejection by the peer group, his parents do not find him "satisfactory," he is deprived of two of the major sources of security and emotional satisfaction needed for the development of a healthy personality.

How long deprivation of love lasts influences its effect on the personality pattern. A short period of deprivation is more harmful in babies and young children than in those who are old enough to find a satisfactory substitute source of love (35, 79, 194). Among 2-year-olds, a separation from their mothers for only 19 days was reported to have "devastating" effects on children's personalities (79).

Boys who suffer under-the-roof alienation from their fathers are relatively little affected by the alienation until they are 4 to 7 years old. Before then, their mothers supply them with all the affection they seem to need. However, if alienation from the father continues into late childhood and early adolescence,

when boys normally identify with their fathers, the damage to their personalities is great, leading at times to juvenile delinquency (13).

Much of the psychological damage of deprivation of love can be eliminated if a *satisfactory substitute* source of love can be found (13, 35). Institutionalized babies, for example, have been reported to show none of the effects of deprivation of love if one person cares for them. Under the care of one person, they are assured of a stable source of affection and an understanding of their individual needs (142).

Older children and adolescents turn to the peer group for emotional satisfaction. If they are accepted by the group, the affection they find in peer relationships may compensate for lack of parental affection. Many adolescents, especially girls, find a member of the opposite sex a satisfactory substitute source of affection. For others, a crush on a teacher or an older member of their own sex serves as a satisfactory substitute. An adolescent who feels rejected both by his family and by the peer group is likely to get emotional satisfaction wherever he can, whether it be by joining a juvenile gang or by daydreaming.

In middle and old age, many people find that to some extent pets serve as a satisfactory substitute for the stable source of affection they were accustomed to before the death or divorce of a spouse or the departure of their children.

EXCESSIVE LOVE

Too much love leads to excessive mothering, or overprotectiveness, and is as bad psychologically as too little (25, 156).

As early as the turn of the century, Freud asserted that too much "parental tenderness" accelerates the child's sexual maturity, awakens a "disposition for neurotic diseases," spoils the child, and makes him unable to be satisfied with smaller amounts of love in later life (61). This point of view was echoed by John B. Watson, who in the 1920s warned that too much "mother love" was damaging to the child's personality development (186).

Later studies demonstrated that babies and young children showered with too much parental affection developed personality patterns that ill-fitted them to face life alone (143, 156). During World War II, the long-term effects of excessive mothering became the focus of scientific concern when it was found that more young men were being rejected by the armed services for psychological than for physical reasons. Strecker brought to public attention the damage caused by "momism" and "smother love" when he reported that overprotective mothers turn their sons and daughters into immature, dependent adults (171, 172).

Further research has justified Strecker's claims about the psychological damage of too much affection, especially during the early, formative years. The person who is smothered with affection by overdemonstrative and oversolicitous parents is likely to turn inward because he lacks motivation to express affection for others. Such a person focuses his attention on himself, becoming spoiled, selfish, and self-centered (13, 68, 111). In time, he may rebel against such treatment and begin to rebuff demonstrations of affection, not only from his mother but from anyone else who tries to show affection for him (171, 172). This leads to a generalized rebellion against authority and a negativistic attitude toward others (21, 156).

The overmotherd child who does not rebel is likely to become submissive, gullible, conservative, and lacking in aggressiveness, self-confidence, and leadership qualities. He depends on others for attention, affection, approval, and encouragement in everything he undertakes, and he is lonely and unhappy when away from those who supply the affection he craves (61, 78, 92).

The emotionally dependent person rarely achieves up to capacity. In school, the parent-dependent child looks to his teachers for special attention, approval, and affection. If he does not receive it, he does poor work and thus becomes even more dependent on his parents for affection. He also tends to become intellectually rigid and to have difficulty adjusting to new situations and people.

Parents who smother their child with love generally have unrealistically high levels of aspiration for him, and so he develops strong feelings of guilt, inadequacy, and resentment when he falls below their expectations. He may wind up biting his nails, stuttering, blinking his eyes, etc. He generally lacks emotional control, has a low level of frustration tolerance, and is afraid to act his age because of lack of self-confidence.

The firstborn child is more likely to be the victim of excessive mothering than the later-born. And a boy is more likely to be overmothered than a girl (28, 32, 164). The firstborn child experiences a high-pitched emotional relationship with his mother at first. Normally the intensity of the relationship steadily dimin-

ishes as the family grows and as the child himself begins to assert his natural desire for independence (97). Excessive mothering is more common in the upper socioeconomic groups and among mothers who have experienced marital adjustment problems or who were deprived of affection in their own childhood (156, 171, 172).

Balance between deprivation and excesses of love

Note that too much *mothering,* rather than too much love, is largely responsible for the damaging effects to personality discussed above. More often than not, however, too much love leads to overprotectiveness or excessive mothering. The two do not necessarily go together, but they usually do.

Children and adolescents, like adults, want love but they want it to be *developmentally appropriate;* that is, they want to be treated in accordance with their ages and interests. While the baby wants close, personal contacts with the mother or mother surrogate, the young child begins to rebuff physical demonstrations of affection. By the time he reaches school age, he is embarrassed by such demonstrations and is afraid that his peers will consider him a baby if his mother kisses him in public or greets him with a hug.

The child and adolescent do not reject parental love, but the way parents *express* their love. Love must be expressed in ways that meet the children's needs at that age, especially the needs for attention, interest, understanding, and sympathy. Unfortunately, parents, grandparents, and other adults often interpret the rejection of their expressions of affection as rejections of *them.*

Many adolescents feel deprived of parental love, while many parents feel that their adolescent children no longer love them. The constant complaint of adolescents that their parents "don't understand" them indicates that they want parental expressions of love to be tailored to meet their more mature developmental status.

A healthy medium—not too much and not too little love—displayed in a developmentally appropriate form is needed for the development of a healthy personality pattern. This point of view has been emphasized by Garrison (65):

Love seems to be a two-way affair and grows best when it is both given and received. A constant rejection in the home may leave the child's capacity for giving forth affection undeveloped, or may cause him to seek affection from individuals outside the home. Overaffection and indulgence may have as undesirable effects as lack of affection or rejection. . . . There is, therefore, the danger that overaffection for one or both parents will tend to exclude affection for children of the child's own age level.

Just what constitutes this happy medium cannot be determined arbitrarily. It depends on the individual child, on his age, on his level of development, on the source of affection, and many other factors. However, his behavior will tell if he is getting enough, too much, or too little affection.

As has been pointed out, an occasional and slight frustration of the person's desire for affection, attention, and dependency strengthens the drive and motivates the person to behave in such a way that he will be rewarded by expressions of affection (97, 156). It also motivates the child to work more effectively. In learning tasks, the child who experiences occasional withdrawal of affection performs more efficiently than one who is accustomed to constant approval and unalloyed demonstrations of affection (75).

After the critical period of deprivation of love has passed, an occasional separation from the mother—as when the child goes to nursery school or kindergarten—helps to prevent rigidity and to motivate the child to seek substitute sources of emotional satisfaction among his peers and other adults. There is special danger of not separating the mother and child early enough or often enough if the mother has neurotic needs of her own that make her overprotective (97, 156).

EMOTIONAL EXPRESSIONS

How the person expresses his emotions affects his personality both directly and indirectly. The *direct* effect comes from the ability of emotional expression to clear the system of the excess energy aroused to meet the situation that stimulated the emotion. The person may run away and hide when frightened, fight when angry, or laugh uproariously when happy or amused.

If he can clear his system of the excess energy, he will feel better both physically and mentally because homeostasis can be restored. Unless the energy aroused to meet the situation is cleared from his system, the upset in homeostasis will persist, with

damaging effects to his physical and mental well-being.

Indirectly, emotional expressions affect the personality pattern by influencing the judgments others make of the person. If he expresses his emotions in a manner that conforms to socially approved standards, he will be judged favorably, and this will provide him with a good mirror image of himself. If he has a temper tantrum, social disapproval will make him feel embarrassed and ashamed.

Even the child knows that unbridled expression of his emotions, such as the expression of joy in uproarious laughter, is frowned on by his parents. He knows that if he hits, bites, or screams when he is angry, he will by punished. Later, he discovers that he is considered babyish if he expresses his emotions without some restraint. Hilgard (80) writes:

It is necessary to suppress much emotional expression. Such suppression is encouraged by civilization. To be civilized is to be moderate in behavior, not to "lose one's head," not to "fly off the handle." We consider imperturbability, the ability to "take it," a virtue. While we admire emotional sensitivity in the form of social warmth and tenderness, we think it should be exercised with restraint. We admire temperance in all things over free indulgence.

Learning how to control the expression of their emotions is regarded by many adolescents as one of their most difficult problems. And yet they realize that they must if they are to create the impression that they are grown-up and if they are to win the attention and approval not only of their peers but of adults as well (66, 154, 169, 181).

Learning emotional control

"Control" does not mean elimination or suppression of normal emotional expression. It means learning to express the emotions in a way that will meet the approval of the social group and at the same time give the individual maximum satisfaction and minimum homeostatic disturbance.

To achieve these ends, the person must, *first,* learn to approach emotion-arousing situations in a logical, rational way. Instead of immediately interpreting a remark as an insult, he should assess it rationally and determine whether the speaker intended to be insulting or was merely tactless. This rational approach is a way of controlling the stirred-up mental state that triggers the physical preparation for action.

Second, the person must learn to substitute socially approved and personally satisfying expressions for impetuous overt expressions that may cause even further upset. Instead of pulling something apart to see how it works, the person can satisfy his curiosity by asking for an explanation or by reading a book that will supply the explanation.

The *motivation* to learn how to express emotions in a socially approved way is supplied by the significant people in a person's life. Social pressure to control fear has been explained thus by Jersild (87):

By virtue of the premium that is placed on not being afraid, of not revealing that he is afraid, the child may be driven to the point that one of his fears is the showing of fear. Many children, at quite an early age, get the idea that it is shameful to be afraid. . . . By the time they are adult, . . . they are so afraid at the thought of revealing fear that they do not dare to appeal for help. By a tragic twist of logic, some people see themselves not as frightened persons but as brave people who have the courage to go it alone.

That most people, regardless of age, show better control of their emotions outside the home than inside demonstrates that social pressures motivate control. We know that we can count on the acceptance and affection of family members even in an emotional outburst, but we are less certain of understanding and acceptance outside.

Variations in approved expressions

If there were only one approved method of expressing each emotion, learning emotional control would be greatly simplified. Since there is not, everyone must learn what is approved in the group with which he is identified. Approved expressions vary from culture to culture. The American Indian, for example, is trained not to express his emotions. To the non-Indian, he seems unemotional. Similarly, Sinhalese children are taught from earliest childhood to "overcontrol" their emotions (170).

Within a culture, patterns of approved emotional expression vary from one social class to another. In the United States, the lower social classes ordinarily encourage boys to be overtly aggressive as a sign of manliness, but they discourage overt expressions of aggression in girls. Middle-class families, by contrast, pressure children of both sexes to inhibit expressions of aggression (22, 28, 32).

Most cultural groups, regardless of social class,

religious, or sex identification, disapprove of overt expressions of the emotions, especially the unpleasant ones. As a result of social pressures, the emotions are "driven underground." As Jersild (87) has stated:

The child learns to disguise his feelings, or to hide them, or to express them in devious ways. Many children also learn to disapprove of themselves for having intense feelings. But they cannot rid themselves of their inborn (and essential) tendencies to be frightened, angry, grief-stricken, and ashamed. . . . They are under pressure to play false with their feelings. . . . A child [may be] seething with resentment against his elders, but, instead of showing this directly, he breaks bottles on a public highway as though it were "just for fun." . . . Children are under pressure also to conceal their emotions from themselves, to play false with themselves. . . . This appears noticeably in connection with feelings springing from grief, sorrow, pain, or anxiety so acute that the individual feels helpless and feels like breaking into tears.

There is a more tolerant social attitude toward the expression of pleasant emotions, but even they must be expressed with restraint to win social approval. A person can laugh with others so long as he does not laugh so loud that he attracts attention, but if he laughs alone, people are likely to question his sanity.

Variations in emotional expressions

Within a cultural group, individual variations in emotional expression are due primarily to age and past experiences. Among newborn infants and young babies, the patterns of emotional response vary mainly in the strength with which emotions are expressed, and this is due to variations in general health condition (29).

Gradually, as the person experiences the influence of learning and cultural and environmental pressures, the behavior accompanying different emotions is individualized. In meeting anger-provoking situations, for example, some people are aggressive and assertive; some are withdrawn and insecure; some feel sorry for themselves; some hit back, to show that they will not be "bossed"; and some turn their energy into constructive work (32, 66).

The way in which people express affection likewise varies according to age and past experience. The older the child, the more likely he is to express his affection verbally rather than physically. At all ages, however, girls are more overt in their expressions of affection than boys (28, 115, 183).

In discussing emotional expression in old age, Banham (20) remarks:

The emotions of old people are characterized by paucity rather than overabundance of affective energy. The form of their behavior tends to narrow, like a stream in a drought, into a channel rather than to brim over into general hyperactivity and tension.

Some elderly people meet frustrations by withdrawing from the life around them and living in a world of fantasy; they become apathetic and show little emotional responsiveness. Others become excitable and regress to immature forms of behavior, such as temper tantrums. Still others continue to express their emotions in normal ways, though their overt acts are likely to be more specific, less varied, and less appropriate to the occasion than those of younger people (34, 49, 76, 191).

Variations in expression also occur within the individual. No one follows a consistent pattern at all times. How a person reacts to an emotion-provoking stimulus depends on his physical condition at the time, on the interests and activities that are preoccupying him when the stimulus is presented, on the social group with which he happens to be, on his mood, etc.

In a fear-provoking situation, for example, a person will be less able to control and direct his fear responses if he is hungry, alone, and emotionally disturbed about other things than if he is in top physical and psychological shape and with someone in whom he has confidence. Figure 8-3 shows three of the ways the same child may respond to a fear-provoking stimulus.

Studies reveal that the intensity and form of expression of aggression in children vary according to the time of day, the setting, and the familiarity of the children with one another. The better the children know one another, the more aggressive they are and the more they express their aggression in bodily and verbal attacks. When no adult is present to protect them, children express their aggression less overtly (115, 160, 183).

Repression of emotional expressions

Strong control over the overt expression of the emotions is often necessary to avoid social disapproval and win the reputation of being "mature." But it drives emotional energy underground and leads to *moodiness*. Moodiness refers to moods engendered by the unpleasant emotions only, not to those engendered by happiness and joy.

The repression of such emotions as fear, anger, jealousy, and envy makes the person morbid and gloomy and leads to socially disapproved patterns of behavior—extreme laziness, vacillation, lack of interest in people and things, and preoccupation with self. Lack of concern for others and self-preoccupation are largely responsible for the characteristic surliness and rudeness of people who are in a "bad humor."

Very often, moodiness is accompanied by nervous mannerisms, such as face-twisting, pulling at some article of clothing, lip-sucking, and eye-blinking. It even affects speech, causing the person to stutter slightly or slur his words. These nervous mannerisms come from the pent-up energy that normally would be expressed in some overt action appropriate to the emotion that is being repressed.

Moods are temporary, lasting for minutes, hours, or occasionally days. While they last, the person is stirred up both physically and psychologically.

Figure 8-3   Three common ways a child may respond to a fear-provoking stimulus.

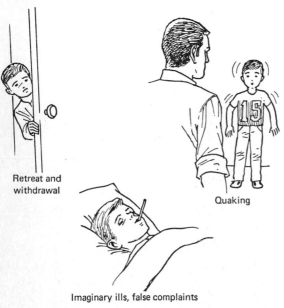

Retreat and withdrawal

Quaking

Imaginary ills, false complaints

They affect the personality *directly* by upsetting body homeostasis and thus decreasing physical and mental efficiency.

The *indirect* effects of moodiness are far more harmful and long-lasting. The person who is in a "bad humor," for example, is regarded as an unpleasant person to be with. While some people may sympathize with him because he has reason to be jealous or angry, they will soon lose patience with his surliness and rudeness. If his angry mood persists or recurs frequently, others will avoid him.

Even if the person has enough control to inhibit socially unacceptable behavior patterns, his facial expression will still reveal the mood he is in. If he is in a jittery mood, due to repression of fear, for example, he will have a "scared rabbit" look which others can readily detect.

Aftereffects of repression When a mood ends, body homeostasis is restored and the person is again able to function physically and psychologically in his normal way.

However, *how* the mood ends is important. Some moods simply dissipate or die out. Others smolder and end in an emotional outburst or some other pattern of socially disapproved behavior. Only when moods die out, as a result of lack of reinforcement, are the aftereffects of intense emotional repression favorable. Moods seldom end this way because the moody person tends to react to new environmental stimuli in a manner that reinforces the already-existing mood, thus strengthening it instead of giving it an opportunity to die out.

Some examples of common aftereffects of emotional repression will illustrate why moods are damaging to the personality.

EMOTIONAL BLOWOUTS An emotional outburst frees the body of the pent-up emotional energy and the mind of the pent-up mental states that keep a mood alive. If the emotion whose expression has been repressed is too strong or if its expression is repressed for too long, the person may "explode" emotionally, responding much more violently than the stimulus would seem to justify. Others will judge him unfavorably, regarding his outburst as a sign of emotional immaturity. The person himself will feel inadequate, ashamed, and guilty.

Studies of homicide and attempted suicide cases find that many are the result of frustrations so frequent and so intense that the person can no longer

repress his expression of anger. Whether he will turn his aggressions inward or outward will depend partly on the child-training methods he was subjected to and partly on his status in the cultural group (17, 192).

REGRESSION Venting the emotions by regression, or reversion to earlier patterns of behavior, is most common in children and young adolescents, though it is sometimes used by the elderly.

Because of the high social value placed on emotional maturity, any form of emotional expression that is characteristic of an earlier age level will meet with social disapproval and have a damaging effect on the person's concept of self.

DISPLACEMENT Repression of emotional expressions frequently results in displacement, or turning the pent-up emotional energy against a scapegoat. Children who in public appear to have good control over their emotions often turn their hostilities toward their parents, especially their mothers, when they encounter some strong frustration of their needs outside the home. In the elderly, grief due to the death of a spouse or some close friend is sometimes expressed in an irrational hostility toward living persons, especially relatives or others in the immediate environment (20).

The person who uses displacement as a way of clearing his system of pent-up emotional energy may feel better, both physically and psychologically, but his recognition of the unfavorable social attitudes toward his unsportsmanlike behavior quickly counteracts these favorable effects. He then tries to justify his behavior by *rationalization,* or giving a plausible explanation for it, often finding, however, that his excuses are regarded as rather flimsy by others. Or he may try to *camouflage* his displacement behavior. To get the social group to laugh at a person he is jealous of, he makes jokes about the "victim" or gives an exaggerated imitation of his walk or speech.

ESCAPE BY FANTASY A socially desirable but personally undesirable aftereffect of emotional repression is *escape* into a fantasy world. There the person can fight to his heart's content against someone who has angered him or release his repressed fear by performing brave deeds.

By escape into the world of fantasy, the person does nothing to win the disapproval of the social group because no one is aware of his make-believe exploits. He can damage his personality greatly, however, by building up an ideal self-concept which is far removed from his real self-concept. The wider the gap between the two, the greater the damage to his personality.

SUBLIMATION   The least commonly experienced aftereffect of emotional repression is sublimation, turning pent-up emotional energy into useful, constructive channels, such as playing on the school team, working for some just cause, or doing something creative.

Effects of emotional control on personality

Control of overt expressions of the emotions will have a favorable effect on the personality only if it fulfills two conditions. *First,* the method of expression used must meet the needs of the individual and give him satisfaction, and *second,* it must meet the approval of the social group. In many situations, only one of these conditions is met, and the effect on the personality is damaging. A person may gain satisfaction through a temper outburst, for example, but he will be dissatisfied with the unfavorable social attitude toward his outburst. Or, he may gain satisfaction from knowing that members of the social group approve his temper control, but he will be dissatisfied with the upset to physical and mental homeostasis the pent-up anger causes.

If control over the expression of emotions is wholesome, it will "produce certain valued consequences. These consequences include the riddance of undesired tensions, or the attainment of desired ones, and the maintenance and enhancement of other values. These other values include such things as self-respect, one's job, friendships, etc." (89). Unwholesome control, on the other hand, occurs when the person does not "respond emotionally as he is supposed or expected to, and when his emotionally-provoked behavior endangers his health, safety, his position, or anything else which he or society deems important" (89). If control over emotions is such that it makes the person nervous, jittery, and edgy, it will damage his physical and psychological well-being. This, in turn, will adversely affect his relationships with others. Furthermore, while he may be judged more favorably by the social group if he controls his emotions, he will experience feelings of guilt, cowardice, or even of martyrdom because he has allowed himself to be taken advantage of.

How to achieve wholesome control over the expression of the emotions—a control that will satisfy the needs of the person and at the same time come up to socially approved standards—has been explained by Jourard (89):

The healthy personality displays neither immediate expression nor chronic suppression of emotion exclusively. Rather, he displays a capacity to choose between the alternatives of suppression and expression. When it will not jeopardize important values, he will express his feelings freely, in an almost unrestrained fashion: he may laugh with gusto, cry without restraint, express anger with intense verbal outpour. If other values would be endangered by such emotionality, he is capable of suppressing his feelings and carrying on whatever instrumental behavior is in process at the time of the emotional arousal. . . . In the long run, this regime of selective suppression and release insures that the person will not suffer from the effects on his body and on his ability to perform produced by prolonged emotional suppression; and he will not needlessly endanger his job, his reputation, his self-respect, and other important values, by heedless emotional explosions. In short, he can suppress when he chooses, and he can let go when he chooses —and it is he who does the choosing.

EMOTIONAL CATHARSIS

Most people learn to repress the overt expressions of emotions that would lead to unfavorable social judgments. But, as has been stressed above, the physical and mental preparation for emotional expression persists. Unless the bodily changes and mental states that accompany this preparation for action are made use of, they will play havoc with the person's physical and psychological well-being.

Just as pent-up body wastes are harmful, so are the pent-up preparations for action that accompany the emotions. Consequently, to restore homeostasis, the body and mind must be purged. This purging is known as "emotional catharsis"—the freeing of the body and the mind of the preparations for action that normally accompany the arousal of an emotion.

Early recognition of catharsis

As early as the fourth century, BC, Hippocrates recognized the harmful effects of unexpressed emotions on the body and worked out a technique for relieving them through the use of cathartics. The most important of these were steam baths and exercise. Through the centuries, it has been known that strenuous physical exercise goes a long way toward relieving pent-up energy just as a hearty laugh or a "good cry" will make a person feel more relaxed.

It was not until the turn of the twentieth century, however, that physical catharsis was recognized as only partially effective. Freud, making use of modern scientific knowledge of the relationship between the mind and the autonomic system, which is responsible for preparing the body for action during emotional states, stressed that emotional catharsis involves more than merely relieving the body of pent-up energy. It also involves satisfying the strong urges of the needs which, when thwarted by the restraints of civilized life, are fundamentally responsible for emotional stress.

Forms of emotional catharsis

Today it is recognized that successful purging of the mind and body of pent-up emotional energy requires both physical and mental catharsis. Neither one is adequate by itself. Only when both are used can physical and mental homeostasis be restored.

Physical catharsis Like taking a laxative to clear the body of waste products that are causing headaches, listlessness, and pain, purging the body of pent-up emotional energy provides only temporary relief. It does not get at the root of the trouble. The constipated person must correct his eating habits or he will have to resort to laxatives again and again. Similarly the emotionally distressed person must deal with the mental aspects of his emotional upsets as well as the physical. Purging the body of pent-up physical energy is essential, but it is only the beginning of the process of emotional catharsis.

Of the many cathartics used to purge the body of pent-up emotional energy, the most common are strenuous physical activity in work or play, laughing, crying, giggling, sex play and sexual intercourse, steam baths, massages, and calisthenics. Which will be used will depend upon the life experiences of the person. Some are more effective than others. Some may not be available to the person and some may be socially disapproved. A young person may be prevented from strenuous physical work by child labor laws or by overprotective parents. A person who is unattrac-

tive to members of the opposite sex may lack opportunities for petting, necking, or sexual intercourse. A physically handicapped person may not be able to engage in strenuous work or play. Crying is regarded as immature except, perhaps, at funerals. Giggling and uninhibited laughter are regarded as immature or in bad taste. Sex play with members of the same sex is taboo, and with members of the opposite sex is frowned upon, except, perhaps, during the engagement period and after marriage.

Thus, the person's choice is limited by what is possible for him to use and what the social group considers appropriate. If one uses methods that are socially disapproved, he will feel guilty.

Mental catharsis The fundamental principle of mental catharsis is to bring the underlying causes of emotional disturbance out into the open, analyze them and subject them to reality testing to see how justified they are, and then find satisfactory ways of giving them expression. Strong drives which cannot be expressed because of their conflict with social codes are at the basis of emotional stress.

To satisfy these drives via mental catharsis, the person must be willing to talk about himself to others. Through *self-disclosure* he brings the underlying causes of his disturbance out into the open and, even more importantly, he subjects them to *reality testing* by getting another person's opinion of them (90, 136).

Children who have been brought up in a relatively open and democratic environment express their feelings rather freely. They criticize persons who they think have treated them unfairly by name calling, ridiculing, and making disparaging comments. If they feel their achievements are superior, they boast about them. With their friends, they air the gripes they have about their families, teachers, and others in authority. Discovering that their friends have similar gripes goes a long way toward helping them to get a better perspective. Much the same is true of adolescents. If they can talk over a problem with an intimate friend, thus verbalizing what has disturbed them, they see it in a new light. It does not seem so bad as it did before.

Many children, however, do not have friends to confide in or parents and teachers who take time to listen to their problems. Those brought up under authoritarian child-training methods have learned not to talk freely even with friends. The result is that many people have no confidant to whom they can express their repressed feelings.

Adolescents often inhibit self-disclosure among

their peers because they do not want to create an unfavorable impression by talking about how their parents restrict their activities. Nor do they want their peers to think that they are unsure of themselves and incapable of handling their own problems. They thus cut themselves off from their major source of emotional catharsis.

Studies of older adolescents and adults reveal how difficult self-disclosure is. As a general rule, the greater the degree of intimacy between the disturbed individual and the "target person"—the person with whom he is willing to discuss his problems—and the greater his respect for the target's judgment, the more free the self-disclosure will be. Ordinarily people are also more willing to discuss their problems with members of their own sex than with members of the opposite sex (53, 90, 181).

The degree of intimacy that one has with others, either family members or outsiders, is closely related to proximity in age. Adolescents and young adults, for example, are more willing to discuss their problems with siblings and peers than with parents and teachers. They feel that the generation gap makes it impossible for those who are older to understand their problems or be sympathetic toward them (52, 53, 63, 70, 81).

The nature of the problem that disturbs the person has a marked influence on his willingness to discuss it and his choice of a target person. The more personal the problem, the less willing he is to discuss it at all. Adolescent boys find discussing with their mothers such problems as sex, petting, and misbehavior much more difficult than discussing problems related to their work, their relatives, or how they dress. Girls find talking to their fathers about sex and petting much more difficult than talking about jobs, eating habits, or political and civic issues (52).

If self-disclosure is to be of value as an emotional cathartic, it must be more than merely blowing off steam. It must include not only a disclosure of what is disturbing the person but also an opportunity to look at it realistically, to get a trusted person's objective point of view about it, and to subject it to reality testing. While blowing off emotional steam will give temporary relief, it will not help the person see his problem realistically and objectively.

People who lack a readily available person to turn to as a target for self-disclosure often use substitute forms of mental catharsis. They may express their pent-up emotions in a *daydream,* fighting imaginary verbal battles with those who have frustrated them or telling an imaginary confidant things they would never tell a real person. This, too, may give temporary relief, but it has not long-term value because it does not help them to subject their problem to reality testing nor does it provide them with a new perspective. Most likely, it will make a bad situation worse by encouraging them to exaggerate the source of the emotional tension.

For some, *literary expression*—writing for the school or college newspaper or writing to a community or national newspaper—helps let off emotional steam and, at the same time, encourages them to assess objectively what they have written before they submit it for print. If the papers print comments or replies from others, this may further help them to see their problem objectively and realistically.

A few people, especially adolescent girls, find that keeping a *diary* helps to clarify their thoughts and feelings about problems that disturb them. This, like daydreaming and mere verbalizing, provides no opportunity to get an objective view of the problem, and so is not usually successful.

Effects of catharsis on personality

No one can expect to go through life without some emotional tension. However, the well-adjusted person learns to face his problems objectively, develops a tolerance of the unpleasant emotions, and learns that he can justifiably be angry, frightened, envious, or jealous at times without feeling guilty or inadequate. As Hilgard (80) has pointed out:

When a person can experience emotionally charged impulses without anxiety and guilt because he has achieved a proper balance between expression and control, he is then emotionally healthy. He finds it possible to accept his emotional impulses as natural, and to handle their expression in ways that are socially acceptable.

Emotional catharsis contributes to good adjustment both directly and indirectly. The *direct* effects of catharsis come from releasing the pent-up emotions and allowing physical and mental homeostasis to be restored. When the person is in a state of equilibrium, owing to the restoration of homeostasis, he can then see himself and his problems more realistically.

Indirectly, emotional catharsis affects the personality by enabling the person to behave in a manner that will win favorable reactions from members of the social group. To a large degree, it frees him of the nervousness and jitteriness which create the impression that he is immature. It goes far toward wiping out any tendency he may have to view himself and his relationships with other people in a distorted light, thus making him less prone to verbalize unfavorable attitudes and beliefs. And perhaps most important of all, it helps to eliminate the facial and bodily expressions of unpleasant emotions which others use as cues in judging him.

Since "self-disclosure is basic to mental health," as Pederson and Higbee state, emotional catharsis that is complete, in the sense that it makes use of both physical and mental catharsis, indirectly helps to bring about a healthy personality pattern which is a guarantee of favorable social reactions (136).

EMOTIONAL STRESS

Emotional stress is a *generalized* state of heightened emotionality which eventually becomes habitual. In some people, stress may come mainly from fear, while in others, it is a result of conflicts that give rise to anger, jealousy, envy, or some other unpleasant emotion. Stress is rarely characterized by a predominance of the pleasant emotions.

Stress differs from mood in that a mood is a temporary state of heightened emotionality which normally subsides after a relatively short time. Unless the preparation for action that accompanies a mood is expressed, however, a mood may persist and develop into stress.

Stress is more damaging to adjustment than moods because it is persistent. The person who is in a "bad mood" will be nervous and on edge, but these conditions will end when the mood passes. Not so with stress. The nervous mannerisms and the expression of stress on the face become habitual. Even when there is no apparent reason for stress, it will still be present, though in a less severe form than when there is a known reason.

Effects of stress on personality

Directly, stress affects the physical and mental well-being of the person by keeping him in a constant state of readiness for action related to the emotion that dominates his stress. Chronic anxiety, for example, brings about an overproduction of the adrenal steroids and they, in turn, inhibit growth by acting to antagonize the growth hormone from the pituitary gland. If chronic anxiety is present during the growth years, it may result in abnormal growth, especially in stunted growth (123, 166).

A disturbance to physical and mental health, as occurs in stress, affects the quality and quantity of the person's achievements and thus affects his self-concept. If, in addition, the pattern of his growth is upset, the unfavorable effects on his self-concept will be intensified.

Since stress affects the quality of the person's behavior, it *indirectly* influences his personality through the reactions it calls forth from others. A person who has learned to fear others acts in a defensive way, showing timidity and anxiety. Others react either by ignoring or by ridiculing him because of his immature behavior. Similarly, a person who learns to act aggressively when frustrated in what he wants to do becomes hostile toward others. They react to his hostility by rejecting him. In both examples, the person's stress is intensified.

No one who suffers from emotional stress makes good personal and social adjustments. Nor is he happy, realizing how far short he falls of his capacities and of the expectations of the significant people in his life. People with low self-esteem are more adversely affected by stress than those with high self-esteem. Positive self-attitudes and "stress tolerance" are related (155).

Persisting intense stress may motivate the person to go to excesses in the hope of relieving it. He may try to dull intense feelings of insecurity by overeating or using drugs. Or he may try to prove his adequacy by compulsively engaging in reckless or self-destructive activities, such as drinking or even criminal behavior. Women who experience severe stress during the menstrual period, when they are already undergoing an upset in homeostasis, have been reported to be more prone to commit suicide (177). How excesses affect personality will be discussed in detail in Chapter 14, Sick Personalities.

Sources of stress

Stress comes from conflict. It occurs when the attainment of a goal is threatened by an environmental obstacle outside the person or by a physical or psychological obstacle from within him. How a person responds to obstacles is influenced by what he has learned will give him the greatest satisfaction.

External obstacles may derive from parental child-training methods that keep the person from expressing a strong drive, such as curiosity or aggression, for fear of punishment or loss of parental love. They may come from peer rejection, which thwarts the person's desire for acceptance and companionship. They may come from religious or moral restrictions on activities the person would like to engage in. Or they may come from group criticism and ridicule, which make the person feel inadequate to do what he wants to do.

Internal obstacles may derive from a physical handicap, such as blindness, or a chronic physical disturbance, such as asthma, which frustrates the person and prevents him from doing what he wants to do. Most often, internal obstacles are psychological. The person with unrealistically high levels of aspirations, for example, will suffer repeated failure in his attempt to reach his goals. An excessively strong feeling of obligation to the family, an internalized puritanistic moral code, and obsessions of many kinds are further examples of internal psychological obstacles.

Constant conflict over the satisfaction of drives results in a more or less steady state of heightened emotionality. Before the bodily changes that normally accompany emotions have subsided and before body homeostasis is restored, another conflict occurs and the bodily preparation for action is triggered once again. The person is in an almost continuous state of readiness for action. As a result, he responds to emotion-provoking stimuli with greater intensity than a normal well-adjusted person would.

Common forms of stress

In some people, emotional stress takes the form of anxiety, while in others, the stress is dominated by frustrations, jealousies, and envies. In some, the emotions are expressed in overt actions, but in most, the expressions are inhibited or displaced. These variations contribute to the unique quality of each individual's personality pattern.

A brief description of anxiety, frustration, jealousy, and envy will show how differences in stress affect behavior. Note how each particular kind of stress affects the person's characteristic patterns of adjustment differently and thus contributes to individuality.

Anxiety Anxiety has been described as a "painful uneasiness of the mind concerning impending or anticipated ill: it represents a danger or threat within the individual rather than an external danger" (87). In anxiety, the disturbing stimulus does not physically precede or accompany the emotional state but is anticipated or expected to occur in the future. The response to this anticipated danger or threat is apprehension, uneasiness, or foreboding from which the person cannot immediately escape. Even more important, anxiety is accompanied by a sense of helplessness due to the person feeling blocked and unable to find a solution to his problem.

Anxiety differs from fear and worry, though it develops from them. It is vaguer than fear. Unlike fear, it does not come from a present situation which can be perceived but from some situation the person anticipates. Anxiety is more often stimulated by qualities within the person than by external stimuli. Frequently, the person is unaware of the conditions within himself which make him uneasy.

Like worry, anxiety is generally due to imaginary, often irrational, causes rather than real ones. Anxiety differs from worry, however, in two important respects: *First,* worry is related to specific situations, such as examinations, parties, or money problems, while anxiety is a generalized emotional state; *second,* worry comes from an objective problem while anxiety comes from some subjective problem.

CAUSES OF ANXIETY Feelings of inadequacy may come from any one of a number of common causes, such as parental overprotectiveness, which results in the person's inability to handle his problems successfully without help; criticism and belittling attitudes of significant people toward the person's achievements, which make him question his abilities; unrealistically high levels of aspiration, which cause the person to suffer repeated failure and undermine his self-confidence.

A person with a well-developed feeling of insecurity faces even the normal uncertainties of life and the problems associated with adjusting to new situations with little confidence that he can handle them successfully. As a result, he often fails, thus adding to his lack of self-confidence and increasing his anxiety.

Mild anxiety may be greatly intensified by identification with threatening characters in the mass media, especially on the movie or television screen. That mass media presentations cause anxiety is strongly questioned, but there is little doubt that they can intensify an already-existing state of anxiety (11, 77). As Wertham has put it, "A child's mind is like a bank.

Whatever you put in you get back ten years later with interest" (188).

Experiences that undermine self-confidence and make the person feel inadequate lead to anxiety. Students who in the past received grades below their expectation face a test situation with greater anxiety than those whose achievements were nearer their goals and who, as a result, have greater confidence in their ability to meet new challenges successfully (18). Older people who recall embarrassing experiences that occurred in their youth often shun social situations and refuse to talk in public for fear of future embarrassments (83, 153).

At certain times during the life span, stress is almost universal. "Stress periods" commonly occur when radical physical changes take place, as at puberty or middle age, and when the pattern of life changes radically, as after the death of a spouse, divorce, or retirement. Stress is also common when there is a family crisis or business reversal. A person who suffers from feelings of inadequacy will meet life's challenges with far greater anxiety than one whose past successes have given him self-confidence.

VARIATIONS IN ANXIETY   Anxiety varies in quantity and quality from one person to another and within the same person from one time to another. Shaffer and Shoben write, "Anxieties vary greatly in intensity from a mere qualm in a transient situational conflict to a permeating distress that may affect all of a person's social adjustments" (158).

Those who *worry more than usual,* especially during periods of adjustment when worry is common, are more likely to develop anxiety than those whose worries are less frequent and less intense. *Sex* differences in anxiety are not so great as are the methods members of the two sexes use to handle anxiety. Girls defend themselves against anxiety by daydreaming and expressing feelings of inferiority while boys handle their anxieties by being rebellious and engaging in annoying activities (62, 100, 120). The more *intelligent* the person, the more likely he is to suffer from anxiety and to resort to defense mechanisms to decrease his self-dissatisfaction (62, 137). *Birth order* affects anxiety through its effect on dependency. Since firstborns and only children tend to be more dependent than other children, their anxiety is greater both in amount and in intensity (7). Anxiety is higher among members of the *minority group* at all ages because of the feelings of inadequacy engendered by prejudice. Regardless of

social, religious, racial, or economic group status, people who are *popular* feel more secure and, consequently, less anxious than those who lack social acceptance (117, 134, 152, 153).

EFFECTS OF ANXIETY ON PERSONALITY   Anxiety affects personality through its effect on behavior. How the person judges his own behavior and the satisfaction he gets out of it determines how he will evaluate himself. This evaluation of self forms the core of his self-concept. His behavior likewise affects the judgment others make of him and their treatment of him. Indirectly, the judgment and treatment of others influence his self-judgments.

When an anxious person speaks, for example, he often breaks his speech with "ah," "er," "um," and other nonspeech variants. Others get the impression that he is unsure of himself and make unfavorable judgments of him (42).

Mild anxiety may be a source of motivation to improve. An anxious student is motivated to prepare his work before he goes to class and the anxious worker is motivated to do the best he can in the hope of retaining his job.

Anxiety of great strength may motivate some people to greater achievement. Most often, however, it leads to vacillation and indecision, thus lowering the level of achievement. Furthermore, the actions of a highly anxious person and his mixture of overconcern and underconcern often seem irrational to others and even to himself. Jersild (87) writes:

One of the marks of an anxious person is that he tends to overdo or to underdo. A slight affront or criticism may send him into a rage, or he may have what seems like an excess of calm when there really is something to get emotional about, as though he were under duress to put a tight lid on his feelings.

An anxious person often behaves in a manner that is curiously "out of character," as when a usually friendly person shows streaks of cruelty or when the "best boy in town" commits a brutal act that no one is able to understand (86). As Shaffer and Shoben (158) have explained:

[When a person] behaves irrationally, and contrary to his own best interests, his need to escape from anxiety is likely to lie at the root of it. . . . There is no specific effective adjustment to anxiety. When you are anxious, you are merely stirred up, unhappy, and driven to do something when there is really little to do.

Anxiety is therefore primary evidence of a lack of adjustment and is a key concept in the study of adjustive difficulties.

Anxiety may be expressed in ways apparently unrelated to the emotional state that has given rise to it. In discussing adolescent anxiety, Hornick remarks, "One of the commonest paths of anxiety in adolescence is acting out, acting up, or just plain action" (82). In Figure 8-4 are shown some of the ways anxiety is expressed by adolescents.

At any age, the person expresses mild anxiety in readily recognizable ways; he is worried and depressed or unaccountably edgy and nervous, he becomes angry very easily, or he gets his feelings hurt easily. The anxious person is easily influenced by what others say and do; he tends to be gullible. In addition, he often feels that he is misunderstood and is highly sensitive to criticism.

Strong anxiety may be so cloaked that it is not easily recognized. The highly anxious person, for example, may be a boisterous show-off, secretly trying to convince himself and others that he has no doubts about his ability to do anything he wishes. He may, on the other hand, appear to be bored and restless, going from one activity to another and being ill at ease when alone.

Because the anxious person always has a vague

Figure 8-4 Some of the common ways adolescents respond to anxiety-producing stimuli. (Adapted from L. D. Crow and A. Crow: *Adolescent development and adjustment,* 2d ed. New York: McGraw-Hill, 1965. Used by permission.)

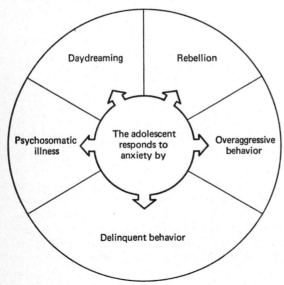

threat hanging over him, he never seems to be able to enjoy what he is doing. Instead, he is restless and is always trying to find something new or different which will "blunt the sharp edge of anxiety" (86). Consequently, he is dissatisfied with himself and he creates an unfavorable impression on others which, as a mirror image, helps to intensify the unfavorable concept he has of himself.

Frustration Frustration is a state of emotional stress which is characterized by confusion, annoyance, and anger. It occurs whenever goal-seeking behavior is interfered with (166). The person is aware of his inability to satisfy his drives and his failure to reach the goals he has set for himself, and so he feels helpless and suffers from injured pride (192).

CAUSES OF FRUSTRATION The barriers that give rise to frustration may come from obstacles in the physical or social environment, from deficiencies within the person himself, or from a conflict between opposing or incompatible motives. The *environment* of the school, planned to meet the needs of children of average intelligence, often proves to be frustrating to both bright and dull children. The adult who derived keen enjoyment from sports and outdoor activities when he was young may find confinement to an office desk so frustrating that he makes a poor adjustment to work and is constantly looking for a new job where he will be able to engage in the activities he formerly enjoyed.

Demands by people in the environment place even greater barriers in the way of satisfying drives. When parents and teachers insist that a child do what they think best rather than what he wants to do, the child suffers from frustrations. By the time he reaches adolescence, annoyance and anger may dominate his usual pattern of response to all in authority. Frustration is at the basis of much of the revolt so characteristic of the adolescent years.

Frustrations frequently come from excessive demands the person places on himself. Personal *deficiencies*—physical shortcomings, lack of intellectual ability, or skills inadequate to enable him to do what he wants to do—all place barriers in the way of goal satisfaction. The adolescent whose vocational aspirations are too high for his intellectual capacities, whose social aspirations are blocked by lack of physical attractiveness and social skills, and whose aspirations for independence are thwarted by economic dependence experiences constant tension.

Many frustrations trace their origin to a *conflict in motives.* When a young person is confronted with a conflict between wanting to go along with his friends in their forbidden activities and wanting to do what he knows is morally right, he meets with frustrations every time a choice must be made. A girl experiences stress when she must choose between being popular with boys and petting to extremes she disapproves of, just as a boy experiences stress when he masturbates to gain relief from sexual tension, knowing that masturbation is socially disapproved.

VARIATIONS IN FRUSTRATION People differ greatly in their *frustration thresholds*—the level of tension below which they can think rationally and act effectively. Not only does the frustration threshold differ for different people but it varies in the same person from time to time and for different needs. Shaffer and Shoben (158) have discussed the variation of the same need at different times:

A housewife "needs" her house to be very neat, orderly and clean. In the forenoon, her three-year-old son might spill a glass of milk, leave his toys in disarray and scatter magazines all over the newly-cleaned living room. Her reaction at that time is one of mild anger, followed by efficient attempts to set things straight. At five-thirty in the afternoon, the child repeats his efforts at messing up the house. This time the mother "explodes"—she spanks the child, hurls some chinaware herself, and is unable to begin preparation for supper until she has vented all the tension the mess has provoked.

At all ages, people from the lower *socioeconomic* groups have their needs thwarted or only partially met more often than those from other groups. They thus suffer more from frustration, which is expressed in hostility and often in aggression (103). *Girls and women* have greater social restraints on their behavior, and they suffer more from frustration than boys and men (103, 122, 154). With advancing *age,* frustrations are less troublesome than they were earlier. Whether this is due to a general dulling of emotionality or to the elderly becoming more self-bound and thus less influenced by external conditions or to some other cause is not known (27, 49).

Reactions following frustration vary also according to the intensity of the frustrating experience, how the person perceives the situation, what social restrictions there are on his behavior, and what methods of expression he has previously found to be satis-

factory in coping with his frustrations. Moderate frustration usually strengthens the person's drive because a goal that is hard to reach seems to be more attractive than one that is easy to reach. If the drive is weak, however, and the barriers seem insurmountable, frustration generally decreases effort. If the drive is strong, insurmountable barriers generally lead to disorganized behavior.

EFFECTS OF FRUSTRATION ON PERSONALITY How a person reacts to frustrations influences the judgments of others and, in turn, the way he judges himself. Furthermore, a person's manner of reacting to frustrations tends to be consistent, and so he soon acquires the reputation of being an immature or a mature person.

One of the commonest and earliest-to-appear patterns of reaction to frustration is *aggression* in which the frustrated person strikes out at an offending person or object, either physically or verbally and with varying degrees of intensity. While most aggression is *extrapunitive,* in the sense that it is directed toward others, some is *intropunitive,* or directed toward the person himself. Most often, however, aggression is *displaced.* Instead of attacking the person or obstacle responsible for the frustration or blaming himself, the aggressive person directs his attack toward an innocent person or group (82, 86).

Even intense frustration may not be expressed directly or displaced because the channels for expression are blocked by fear of punishment or social disapproval. The frustrated person then *withdraws* into himself and becomes inactive, inattentive, and apathetic. He gives the impression that he either is indifferent to frustrations and lacking in emotional responsiveness or is "weak" or "spineless."

Some people *regress* by not "acting their ages" when faced with frustrations. They long for the good old days when they felt capable of meeting life's challenges and were not frustrated by feelings of inadequacy. The married woman who feels incapable of meeting the responsibilities of home and family runs home to mother for help. The man, feeling that running home to mother is "childish," goes to his pals where he can get his gripes off his chest as he did during the gang days of childhood.

Frustration from thwarted drives has long been regarded as a precipitating factor in personality maladjustment. But there has not been universal agreement about exactly how the personality is affected because frustrations are not expressed in just one way. Freud placed emphasis on regression to infantile modes of response as the usual reaction to frustration (61). Jung contended that continual thwarting resulted in a turning inward of the libido or life urge, thus causing the person to become self-centered and reflective rather than overtly expressive—characteristic behavior of the extrovert (91). Adler maintained that thwarting leads to compensation in which the person is motivated to overcome barriers either by overt behavior or by symbolic expression in fantasy (2). More recently, Lewin has claimed that the person who encounters seemingly insurmountable barriers will insulate himself from his environment by withdrawing into himself and showing the characteristic behavior of the introvert (107).

These and similar observations of the behavior of people in frustrating situations have emphasized two things: *first,* that there are marked individual differences in the way people react to frustration, with each person learning a pattern of behavior which he has found to fit his needs best, and *second,* that most patterns of behavior learned in frustrating situations result in maladjustive forms of behavior.

It is important to recognize, however, that frustration does not always lead to maladjustment. Some people try to relieve the emotional stress caused by continued frustration by making a rational attack on the problem. If they fail, they will probably resort to the use of defense mechanisms, such as rationalization, projection of the blame on others, and fantasy, or some other stress-relieving mechanism. Under such conditions, maladjustive behavior develops with its unfavorable effects on personality.

Jealousy and envy As forms of emotional stress, jealousy and envy have much in common with anxiety and frustration. Jealousy and envy come from feelings of insecurity and inadequacy in situations the person regards as crucial to his happiness and welfare, as anxiety does. Both involve hostility, as frustration does. Both keep the person in a more or less constant state of emotional stress, as do anxiety and frustration. And both are expressed in behavior patterns combining the usual expressions of anxiety and frustration.

Jealousy and envy are separate and distinct emotional patterns, though they usually occur together. They are directed against people only, unlike anxiety and frustration, which may be directed also against objects. In jealousy, three people are involved,

while in envy, only two are. Jealousy generally develops earlier than envy and it develops because the person *is unable* to understand meanings and values. Envy, on the other hand, develops because the person *is able* to understand meanings and values.

In jealousy, anxiety is usually stronger than frustration though both contribute something to the jealousy pattern. In envy, the reverse is true; frustration is stronger than anxiety though certain characteristics of anxiety are involved in the envy pattern. The patterns of response are often difficult to distinguish, especially when the stress comes from a combination of envy and jealousy.

As in anxiety and frustration, people discover from past experience what methods of expressing jealousy and envy provide the maximum of satisfaction and the minimum of social disapproval. Consequently, each person has his own way of expressing these forms of emotional stress, and this contributes to the unique quality of his personality pattern.

JEALOUSY Jealousy grows out of fear and anger. The jealous person feels that he has been deprived of something that is rightfully his and that he is incapable of defending himself against this threat to his security. Jealousy develops over a period of time, beginning in babyhood; it may gradually become a generalized form of stress which, if intense, can play havoc with the person's physical and mental well-being.

Causes of jealousy Most babies, because of the constant care and attention their helplessness demands, develop a proprietary attitude toward the mother. Often before they can find a satisfactory substitute for the affection and attention they expect the mother to supply, they find themselves displaced by a newly arrived sibling. Not understanding why this newcomer has usurped the status they regarded as rightly theirs, they become angry at the interloper and lose the sense of security they formerly enjoyed.

The anger and sense of insecurity of the young child are intensified when he observes that older siblings get privileges denied him, that a sick sibling gets more time and attention than he, and that his father becomes the center of his mother's attention when he is at home. Experiences of this kind soon convince the child, too inexperienced and too immature mentally to understand them, that every family member is a threat to his security. This both angers and frightens him. If parents hold up an older sibling as a model for the child to imitate, they unwittingly increase the child's jealousy by implying that they favor the older sibling.

At school, if the child does not receive from his teacher the affection and attention that he has been accustomed to receiving at home, he feels insecure. To safeguard his security, he may take a proprietary attitude toward the teacher and the children he selects as playmates. While jealousy normally wanes when the child makes good adjustments to school, it often flares up again in adolescence when he is faced with the difficulties and uncertainties of dealing with members of the opposite sex. The strong desire for popularity, combined with feelings of insecurity, causes the adolescent to be jealous of those who are more popular than he or whom he regards as a threat to his popularity.

Before adolescence is over, the person may develop the habit of being jealous—a generalized pattern of viewing everyone as a threat. Many adults do not know why they feel uneasy about people and unable to trust them. Their reactions are so habitual that they fail to recognize the underlying jealousy that gives rise to their stress. As Jersild (87) has explained:

Among adults, the degree of jealousy a person exhibits frequently bears little relationship to his relative status or power as compared with others. The person who has "arrived" and has achieved the outward semblance of success will sometimes begrudge the recognition bestowed upon an underling, much as a big hound bristles when his master pets a forlorn poodle.

Effects of jealousy on personality The intensity of jealousy determines how greatly it will upset physical and mental homeostasis and undermine the person's feeling of security. Indirectly, jealousy affects personality by inviting unfavorable judgments from others, especially when the person expresses his jealousy in socially disapproved ways.

A person who is obsessed with a fear of losing his place in the affections of another and who experiences the anger and feelings of helplessness that accompany extreme frustration often imagines situations which keep him in a constant state of emotional turmoil. Others recognize this and judge him unfavorably.

Regardless of how the individual expresses his jealousy, either in physical or in verbal aggression, he is likely to be judged as immature. Most people, even young children, sense the unfavorable social attitudes toward their jealousy. This adversely affects their self-attitudes and is damaging to their self-concepts.

ENVY Like jealousy, envy develops from anger and fear. It differs from jealousy in that the immediate stimulus is a possession of another person—a quality of that person, such as intelligence or skill in sports, or a material possession, such as clothes or a car. Envy is a form of covetousness, of wanting what someone else has, not so much because of the possession itself but because it is highly valued by the social group.

Normally envy develops later than jealousy because it depends upon the ability to recognize values and know the relative amount of social prestige attached to them. Envy often gives rise to jealousy. A man who had no feelings of jealousy toward a classmate who was regarded as a "brain" may, as the years pass, envy the "brain's" financial success, his manner of living, and his status in the community and also come to be jealous of him.

Like jealousy, envy may be either sporadic or continuous. It may occur only when the envied person gets a new car, has a new honor bestowed upon him, or announces the birth of a new son. On the other hand, it may become an obsession. A person who suffers from feelings of inadequacy, insecurity, or inferiority can interpret anything others have as superior and consequently never really be free from envy.

Effects of envy on personality Obsessive envy is far more upsetting to physical and mental homeostasis than sporadic envy. Indirectly, envy affects personality through its influence on behavior and how the social group judges this behavior. If envy motivates the person to secure things others have, and to secure them by socially approved actions, the person will be favorably judged by members of the social group. If he resorts to socially disapproved actions, and succeeds in their not being discovered, he is likely to feel guilty. If his actions are discovered, he will be judged unfavorably and will feel ashamed.

Inability to relieve the emotional tension of envy in direct action may lead to indirect, usually verbal, modes of expression. Some people express their envy by complaining about their lot, feeling sorry for themselves, and thus hoping to win the attention and sympathy they crave. Others defend themselves against feelings of inadequacy by rationalizing their lack of material possessions on the grounds that they have had "bad luck."

Others defend themselves by the "sour grapes mechanism," making critical and disparaging remarks about the very material possessions they crave. By so doing, they relieve themselves, temporarily at least, of the emotional stress of envy. Still others displace their reactions, blaming others for their lack of success. Whatever form of expression envy may take, it is not easily camouflaged and is likely to be detected. And as envy is not a socially approved emotional reaction, the envious person is unfavorably judged by others, and consequently makes unfavorable judgments of self.

SUMMARY

1 Emotions are important personality determinants because they affect personal and social adjustments. This they do directly by coloring interests, attitudes, likes, and dislikes and by upsetting homeostasis. A mild homeostatic upset has a therapeutic effect, but a strong upset impedes physical and mental efficiency.

2 The direct effect of the emotions on personality comes from social judgments based on how the person handles his emotions and from his ability to establish emotional relationships with others.

3 Scientific evidence of the effect of emotions on personality traces back to Hippocrates, who explained persisting emotional patterns in terms of the domination of one of the five body humors. Today, scientific evidence emphasizes the role played by environmental factors in determining the dominance of specific emotional patterns, although physical influences, mainly the dominance of one of the endocrine glands, are likewise recognized.

4 Modern scientific studies distinguish between temperament—the person's prevailing emotional state—and mood—a temporary state of emotional reactivity. Because of the persistence of temperament, a person's typical reactions can be predicted more accurately than his specific actions, which may be influenced by his mood at the time. Today it is recognized that a person's dominant emotions, which are responsible for his temperament, are due not to an imbalance of the body humors or of the endocrine glands, as was formerly believed, but to a combination of physical and environmental conditions. It is also recognized that temperament can and does change, owing to environmental and physical changes and to changes in intellectual capacities.

5 Emotional balance, in which the pleasant emotions outweigh the unpleasant, is essential to good personal and social adjustment and to happiness. Unless the person develops a tolerance or ability to "take it" without going to pieces when he encounters obstacles and unpleasant experiences in which fear, anger, envy, and other negative emotions are aroused, he can be neither well adjusted nor happy. Development of the ability to tolerate unpleasant emotional experiences is, thus, regarded as mental health insurance.

6 Emotional deprivation, which occurs mainly with pleasant emotions, such as love, happiness, and curiosity, has long-term effects which lead to poor personal and social adjustments. How seriously emotional deprivation will affect personality varies according to the amount of emotional deprivation the person experiences, how long the deprivation lasts, at what age it occurs, and whether or not a satisfactory substitute source of the deprived emotion is supplied.

7 Since deprivation of love has such a devastating effect on personality, it is commonly believed that the more love the person receives, the happier and better adjusted he will be. Studies of excessive love, however, especially when it is not expressed in a developmentally appropriate way, show that it encourages dependency. A balance between deprivation and excess of love, when the scale is tipped slightly on the side of excess, leads to better adjustment and greater happiness because such a balance permits the person to learn to cope with temporary deprivation of love successfully.

8 How the person expresses his emotions affects his personality directly through the restoration of homeostasis, achieved by clearing the system of the excess energy the emotion gives rise to, and indirectly through its effect on the judgments of others. The way in which the person expresses his emo-

tions depends upon the patterns approved by members of the cultural and social groups with which he is identified and upon his motivation to learn to conform to these approved patterns.

9 Too much control over emotional expression leads to moods which affect, temporarily, the person's adjustments. Judgments of members of the social group as well as self-judgments are influenced by how moods end. Whether they end in an emotional outburst, regression, displacement, or fantasy, the effects on social and self judgments are unfavorable. If they end by sublimation or by dying out through lack of reinforcement, the effects on personality are more favorable.

10 It has long been recognized that the damaging physical and mental effects of repressing emotional expressions can be eliminated by catharsis. To purge the body and mind of pent-up emotional energy, physical catharsis that uses up excess energy must be accompanied by mental catharsis that enables the person to get better self-insight and understanding of his problem.

11 Fundamental to emotional catharsis is self-disclosure, which not only permits the blowing off of emotional steam but also enables the person to see his problem realistically enough to counteract the unfavorable emotions which might otherwise be aroused. Emotional catharsis, thus, both directly through its restoration of homeostasis and indirectly through its effect on the person's characteristic pattern of adjustment, has a favorable influence on personality.

12 Emotional stress—a generalized state of heightened emotionality which eventually becomes habitual—affects personality directly by disturbing physical and mental homeostasis, and indirectly by adversely affecting behavior. All stress comes from conflict over the satisfaction of drives due to environmental obstacles or physical and psychological obstacles from within the person. Stress may take different forms, the most common of which are anxiety, frustration, jealousy, and envy.

13 Anxiety is a state of mental uneasiness resulting from conflict in which fear is aroused. Mild anxiety may motivate appropriate behavior, but intense anxiety usually results in disorganized behavior. Frustrations, arising from conflicts in which anger is aroused by obstacles to goal-seeking behavior, may lead to aggressiveness, to withdrawal, or to regressive behavior, depending on which the person finds meets his needs best. All lead to poor personal and social adjustments.

14 In jealousy and envy, a feeling of insecurity and inadequacy is accompanied by hostility. Jealousy occurs when there is a threat to ego-satisfaction from a third person. Envy, involving only two people, is a form of covetousness. The person wants some thing or quality another has because the possession is highly valued by the social group. Both lead to upsets in physical and mental homeostasis and to unfavorable social judgments. Their effects on personality are, thus, both direct and indirect.

social determinants

The social group expects every person who belongs or wants to belong to the group to conform to its standards. It judges him according to his ability to come up to these expectations, decides whether to accept or reject him, and, if accepted, how much acceptance to grant him. A college fraternity, for example, expects a member or prospective member to conform to the popular image of a "fraternity man"—to be gregarious, to avoid the appearance of studying too much, and to achieve preeminence in extracurricular rather than curricular activities (131).

Since what a person can learn depends upon his developmental level, the social group sets *developmental tasks,* or learning experiences, which the person is expected to master at an age when most people of that age are capable of mastering them. During the elementary school years, the individual is expected to learn to get along with his age-mates and to play an appropriate sex role; during adolescence, he is expected to learn to get along with members of the opposite sex, as well as with members of his own sex, and to behave in a socially responsible way; during the adult years, both men and women are expected to emancipate themselves from their parents, to be emotionally and economically independent, and to accept civic and social responsibility (97).

In general, every social group expects its members to do two things: to learn to be "socialized" and to learn to play an approved social role. In becoming *socialized,* a person must learn what the social group considers "proper" performance behavior and must use "fronts" to cover up thoughts and feelings which the group considers unacceptable. He must, for example, learn not to look bored no matter how bored he may be. He must learn not to talk about tabooed subjects and not to look pleased when a person is hurt or is beaten in a game.

A *social role* is a pattern of customary behavior which has been defined by members of the social group and which is expected of every member according to the position he holds in the group, whether it be that of father, housewife, student, friend, leader, citizen, or whatever. Social roles are learned by the person and are internalized so that, in time, they become self-expectations as well as social expectations.

A person whose behavior comes up to social expectations and who tries to play the social role prescribed for him by the group can be assured of reasonable approval and acceptance. Living up to group expectations increases the individual's self-esteem. A nonsocialized person who does not measure up to social expectations, either because of ignorance of what the expectations are or because of willful disregard of them, will win the disapproval of the group and be rejected by its members. Knowing that others do not have a favorable opinion of him, the person is unlikely to have a favorable opinion of himself.

EARLY SOCIAL EXPERIENCES

No one is born social, unsocial, or antisocial. Attitudes toward people and toward social activities are determined early in life by the kinds of experiences the person has. While it is true that attitudes are not static, changes are more likely to be quantitative than qualitative. For example, an antisocial person may become less antisocial as a result of positive social experiences, but he is unlikely to become a social person.

The persistence of attitudes toward people and social experiences does not substantiate the traditional belief that some people are "born social" and some are not or that they are "born introverts" or "born extroverts," as Jung suggested (111). Instead, likes and dislikes for people and social experiences are learned by conditioning. And, as is true of all conditioning, likes or dislikes learned in specific situations soon become generalized and spread to similar situations.

A little girl whose older brother is a tease or bully may be conditioned to dislike him and develop a hostile, frictional relationship with him. Because her experiences with her brother have been unpleasant, and because she develops the habit at home of fighting back when he teases or bullies her, she is likely, in time, to transfer her hostile attitude to all boys and even to girls who are bossy or critical of her. As Bain has pointed out, "When the child enters school, he begins to reap the rewards or suffer the ills which flow from the first six years of life" (13).

The reason for the consistency of social attitudes and behavior patterns is that children who develop favorable attitudes toward social experiences when they are young have a strong motivation to seek social contacts. It is through their social contacts that they are able to learn what the social group considers appropriate behavior and to learn how to act so that their behavior will be favorably judged by others.

If, on the other hand, the child's early social experiences are unpleasant, he is likely to develop an unfavorable attitude toward social experiences and to shun them. By so doing, he deprives himself of valuable learning experiences. He acquires the reputation of being a "square" or a loner because he does not know how to do what his age-mates do or because he shuns social activities.

Importance of learning opportunities

A person must have opportunities to learn how to behave in a socially approved way. If his attitudes toward people and social experiences are favorable, he will have the necessary motivation to take advantage of the learning opportunities. But motivation alone is not enough. His learning must be guided and controlled so that he will learn *how* to behave in a manner that will win social approval and acceptance. To be successful, guidance must help him learn how to get along with people and how to adjust his interests and desires to those of the members of the group with which he is identified. While a child may learn, through trial and error, how to behave in a socially accepted way, he may, before he is finally successful, have to do a lot of learning and unlearning. He may, for example, go through periods of being bossy, a poor sport, or a "crybaby" before he discovers that the methods he is using to make contacts with others are not socially acceptable.

Studies show that guidance contributes significantly to socialization. When preschool children play together without adult supervision or without the adults who are present actively seeking to guide them, their relationships are considerably more hostile than when they are supervised and provided guidance in playing together in a friendly, cooperative way (142, 158, 200, 222).

Since the basis for social contacts outside the home in early childhood is the play group, the child must be accepted by members of the play group if he is to have continued opportunities to learn to be social. Guidance from adults aids acceptance in many ways. It helps the child learn to play in a cooperative manner, helps him to acquire skills that make his play more enjoyable to his age-mates, and equally important, helps him learn to play in a sex-appropriate manner.

One of the areas in which guidance can help the child to acquire skill is communication. In any play group, communication is essential to group belonging. Just talking is not enough; the child must talk about topics that interest his friends and he must talk in a manner that wins their approval. Without guidance, the child may talk almost exclusively about himself, which is boring to other children, or he may constantly boast, ridicule others, or make derogatory comments, which is ego-inflating but irritating to playmates.

Kind of early experiences

Enjoyable social experiences, especially during the early, formative years of life, help to ensure the development of positive social attitudes. If a person enjoys his social contacts, he will want to repeat them. If not, he will tend to shun people and deprive himself of valuable learning experiences. Even worse, he will tend to exaggerate the unsatisfactory experiences and convince himself that he prefers being alone.

Although people of any age may find their social experiences unpleasant, young children, as a group, are most likely to find them emotionally disturbing. Their limited experiences in the home, however pleasant they may have been, have not prepared them to meet strange people in strange settings alone. Even school-age children and adolescents often find many of their social experiences unpleasurable, both in the home and outside. In their recall of early experiences in school and at play, adults remember being teased and bullied by older children, being made to feel inadequate by their playmates, being criticized and ridiculed by peers, teachers, and other adults, being embarrassed by the reactions of others to what they did or said, and being forced to do things they did not want to do (33, 219).

Home experiences The home and the family provide the child's first social environment and determine what his first attitudes toward people and social activities will be. As Warnath concludes, "The home thus appears indeed to be a seat of learning for the development of social skills and perhaps of the desire to participate in activities with other individuals" (224).

No one specific aspect of family life is responsible for the formation of social attitudes and patterns of behavior. Child-training methods, the parent-child relationship, the child's position in the family structure—all these, as well as other factors, shape attitudes and affect behavior.

The kind of *child training* used in the home has a pronounced influence on later social adjustment. Children brought up by democratic methods, for example, make better social adjustments outside the home and have more favorable attitudes toward people and social activities than children brought up by authoritarian methods. Those brought up by permissive parents who indulge them and permit them to do much as they please develop feelings of inadequacy about their abilities and tend to become inactive and to withdraw from social situations (44, 181). Furthermore, both authoritarian and permissive child training tend to make children dependent on adults. Unable to stand alone, they get the reputation of being immature—a reputation which almost always leads to a low social status in the peer group.

Only when children have a satisfactory *relationship with their parents* can they enjoy social contacts outside the home. Only under such conditions, also, can they have healthy attitudes toward people and learn to function in groups composed of their peers. Children who feel rejected by their parents often carry an attitude of martyrdom outside the home and are unable to function in a way that will gain acceptance by others. It has been found that the adolescents who are most popular and most active in the social affairs of their schools and colleges have a warm and friendly feeling toward their families. When they were young, their parents not only encouraged them to participate in social activities outside the home but guided their social learning experiences (61, 224).

Relationships outside the home are influenced by the person's *position in the family*. An only child or one whose siblings are widely separated from him in age or are of a different sex tends to be more withdrawn outside the home than one whose siblings are near him in age or are of the same sex. The child who has no siblings of the opposite sex, however, has more difficulty associating with opposite-sex children

outside the home than one who has opposite-sex siblings (14, 121, 196, 197).

Experiences outside the home

Young children are more accustomed to social relationships with adults than with children, even if they have siblings, and so it is not surprising that they carry into outside situations the patterns of behavior they have found effective at home. They often ignore other children but try to win the attention of adults through glances, questions, comments, and urgent requests for overt notice (80). Many young children, it has been reported, are more influenced by adults outside the home than by parents or other relatives (80).

Social attitudes and behavior are greatly influenced by the children with whom the child associates. When his playmates are older than he, he strives to keep up with them and, by doing so, develops more mature patterns of behavior than his agemates. If the older children tend to boss him, he may become a meek follower or develop unsocial patterns of behavior. If he is older than his playmates, he will try to boss them. In either situation, he is learning to behave in a way that will make good social adjustments with his age-mates difficult as he grows older. If all his early playmates are of his sex, he may have difficulty later making social contacts with playmates of the opposite sex. Many prejudices come from imitating the prejudices of playmates. And the use of threats, fear, or shame to obtain a goal is often learned by imitation.

In spite of the fact that early social contacts outside the home are often characterized by aggressive attacks, including fighting, studies show that with guidance and supervision young children each year make more and more affectionate responses to their playmates and fewer aggressive ones (142). The child thus derives greater satisfaction from social relationships and is encouraged to seek further contacts with his peers.

Effects of early social experiences on personality

If reasoning ability were better developed at the time the foundations for socialization are being laid, the child would be able to avoid the conditioning stemming from early social experiences. He would recognize how irrational it is to assume, on the basis of one or more unpleasant experiences, that all future experiences will also be unpleasant. Once the conditioning occurs, however, it affects his subsequent relationships.

If the conditioning has stemmed from pleasant experiences, the child will respond to people in a warm, friendly manner and win their affection. This will strengthen his belief that all social experiences are pleasant and increase his desire to have friends and to participate in social activities. It will also motivate him to learn to behave in such a way that the pleasant experiences will be repeated.

Just the opposite happens when conditioning is based on unpleasant experiences. Instead of assuming that a frightening experience is just an occasional thing, as a more mature person would do, the young child concludes that *all* social experiences are frightening and tries to avoid them as much as possible. If the unpleasant experiences are marked by teasing, bullying, and other aggressions toward him, he will want to retaliate in kind.

As was stressed earlier in the discussion of the empathic complex (see Chap. 8), reactions between people are influenced by the emotional linkage between them. If a person likes people, the emotional linkage between him and others will be marked by a predominance of the pleasant emotions, and vice versa. How he reacts to them will affect how they treat him and how they judge him. If he reacts positively to others, they will like him and accept him. And their acceptance will have a favorable influence on his self-concept.

Like any act that is repeated over and over, behaving in a social, unsocial, or antisocial way becomes habitual in time. The person thus builds up a reputation based on his characteristic method of adjusting to people. If he behaves in a social manner, he becomes known as a good mixer, a good sport, a likeable fellow, a warm and friendly person. He soon becomes aware of how the social group feels about him, and this affects the way he feels about himself.

SOCIAL DEPRIVATION

Being deprived of opportunities for social contacts, like being deprived of affection and love, can play havoc with the personality pattern. As Mussen et al. have said, a child's lack of peer group contacts, because of geographic isolation, family restrictions, unfavorable social attitudes on the part of the child, or some other condition, "may result not only in im-

mediate unhappiness, but also in subsequent difficulties in interpersonal relationships" (165).

Social isolation is especially damaging to the personality in a culture which places high value on popularity. The damage comes in part from lack of opportunities to learn to participate in social activities and in part from the feelings of inadequacy which the deprived person feels in comparison with his agemates. Some of the effects of social deprivation on personality will be discussed in detail below.

Lack of opportunity for social contacts is by no means limited to the early years of life. Adults who are geographically mobile or who live in rural or suburban areas and young parents who are unable to afford help with the care of children may be cut off from the social contacts they formerly relied upon as a source of pleasure and ego satisfaction. For young women, especially, having to rely mainly on family members for social activities is difficult to accept and adjust to. It reminds them of their unpopular peers in school and college who had few friends and spent most of their time in solitary activities or with family members. Although men suffer less from social deprivation than women, because they usually have some social contacts in their jobs, they, too, judge themselves unfavorably when they are unable to continue the social contacts they enjoyed before marriage and parenthood.

Social deprivation is extremely damaging to the personality in old age. Owing to retirement and a letup in home responsibilities, older men and women have less to occupy their time. Those who have been content to rely on family members for social contacts find that even these are no longer available when grown children move away and relatives pass on. Many elderly people suffer as severely from social deprivation as from emotional deprivation because the two go hand in hand.

While social isolation leads to poor morale and mental disorganization at any age, it is particularly harmful to the elderly. Poor health, retirement, economic problems, unfavorable social attitudes toward the elderly, and other factors not present at earlier ages narrow their chances of ever ending their social isolation. As a result, mental illness and deviant behavior increase with advancing age (98, 138, 210).

Since social deprivation is damaging to the self-concept, one might conclude that the more opportunities the person has for social activities, the better adjusted and the happier he will be. However, just as too much love can be almost as damaging psychologically as too little (see Chap. 8), so it is with too many opportunities for social contacts. People who learn to overrely upon others will be unhappy when circumstances make it impossible for them to have the social contacts they crave. To avoid being alone, they look for companionship wherever it is available, regardless of congeniality of interests and values. As a result of indiscriminate sociability, they fail to develop healthy social attitudes. Even worse, they are unstable in their interests and values, changing them according to the people they happen to be with in the hope of winning acceptance. This makes them insecure and leads to social judgments of immaturity.

A middle-of-the-road situation in which the person has a reasonable number of both social contacts and opportunities to learn to tolerate social deprivation so that he can become self-sufficient will lead to healthier social attitudes. It will forestall much of the discontent, unhappiness, and poor mental health social deprivation can cause. This middle-of-the-road situation cannot be achieved when geographic isolation and poor health make social contacts extremely difficult or impossible. That is why institutional living is often better for the elderly than living in their own homes or with grown children. Living among peers provides opportunities for contacts with persons of similar and congenial interests and values.

Variations in effects on personality

How damaging social deprivation is to the personality pattern depends on many conditions, the most important of which are the age at which the deprivation occurs, how long it lasts, what causes it, how extensive it is, and how much the person wants and needs social contacts.

Social deprivation is most damaging to two *age* groups—the very young and the elderly. At neither period is the individual self-sufficient and occupied with duties and responsibilities. The young child who is deprived of the companionship of adults or other children gets into mischief. His behavior is socially disapproved, he is unfavorably judged by others, and so he judges himself unfavorably. Social deprivation makes the elderly person self-bound and selfish, tendencies which likewise lead to unfavorable social and self judgments.

By contrast, those who have duties, responsibilities, and interests to keep them occupied and those who are intellectually able to spend the time that they are alone in solitary recreations or daydreaming are far less likely to behave in a manner that will win social disapproval. For that reason, the damage to their personalities comes more from their own reactions to social deprivation (their lack of deprivation tolerance) than from the unfavorable reactions of others.

Just as deprivation of love varies in its effect according to *how long it lasts,* so does social deprivation. A short period of social deprivation whets the person's appetite for social contacts and motivates efforts to win the attention and acceptance of anyone who is available for such contacts (170). Young children and elderly people who have little of interest to fill their time tend to overestimate even short periods of social deprivation. Therefore, they are more damaged by them than older children, adolescents, and busy adults (78, 114).

The *cause* of a person's social deprivation may be external or internal. Some causes can be better controlled than others. Geographic isolation is easier to control than isolation due to social rejection. As a general rule, social deprivation among the younger age levels is due primarily to obstacles within themselves, and among the older age levels, to environmental obstacles.

The *extent* of social deprivation varies markedly. A child who is popular in the peer group may experience an occasional deprivation of social contacts when he is ill or away on a trip with the family. Another child of the same age may experience very extensive social deprivation if he is unpopular even though he is in an environment where there are plenty of opportunities for social contacts.

Deprivation is far more damaging to the person who *wants and needs social contacts* to be happy than to one who is self-sufficient or who voluntarily withdraws. When an elderly person decides on his own to withdraw from social or business activities, for example, he is far happier and better adjusted than when disengagement is involuntary. The more unwilling he is to retire from business or social life, the more martyred he feels when retirement is forced on him.

In summary, regardless of variations, social deprivation always has an adverse effect on personality. Loneliness, feeling martyred or rejected, and being forced to become self-sufficient, which makes the person self-centered and selfish—all are damaging to the self-concept. The more value the social group puts on social participation and popularity, the more damaged the person is psychologically by social deprivation. If deprivation is extensive and prolonged, it inevitably leads to unhealthy social attitudes and mental illness (78, 101, 118).

SOCIAL ACCEPTANCE

How much influence the social group exerts over a person at any age is greatly affected by two conditions: first, how acceptable he is to the group and, second, how important group acceptance is to him. The more acceptable a person is to the group, the closer his relationship with group members and the more influence they exert over him. The more value the person places on group acceptance, the more willing he is to be influenced by the group. However, he is more influenced by the leader and the most popular members of the group than by those whose status in the group is marginal (30, 96).

Levels of social acceptance

Social acceptance, or popularity, ranges from very high, as in the case of the *star* whom almost everyone likes and wants to claim as a friend, to very low, as in the case of the *social isolate* whom no one claims as a friend. Few people fall into these extremes. It is just as unusual for a person to be liked by everyone as it is for a person to be rejected by everyone.

Most people fall somewhere between these two extremes. Some, the *fringers,* are just on the line of acceptance. They are in a precarious position, always running the risk of losing what acceptance they have gained by doing or saying something that might turn others against them. Then there are the *climbers* who have acceptance in one group but want to gain acceptance in a higher group. Like the fringers, they are in the uncertain position of not knowing just how well accepted they are or how quickly they may lose the ground they have gained in their upward climb.

In the below-average categories of acceptance are those who voluntarily withdraw from the group because they gain little satisfaction from contacts and activities with the people who make up the group. They are the *voluntary isolates.* By contrast, some are *involuntary isolates* who crave contacts with members of the group but are not accepted by them. This lack of acceptance may take the form of rejection because they say or do things to make others dislike them or it may take the form of neglect or of being overlooked when they are not actually disliked by group members but are so shy, withdrawn, and nondescript that they

have little to offer. Involuntary isolates may, thus, be *rejectees* or *neglectees* depending on how the members of the group feel about them.

Some involuntary isolates are victims of circumstances over which they have little control. This is often true of women who, as a result of changes in the patterns of their lives after marriage, find themselves cut off from contacts with their former friends because of a move to a new community or restrictions on their activities caused by home responsibilities. Elderly people who are handicapped by poor health or lack of money may be forced against their will into social isolation.

More people, at every age, fall below the average in social acceptance than above the average. Within each sex group, males are more likely to be below average in acceptance than females. Why this should be so is still unproven, though it may be because girls are expected by the social group to behave "properly," while boys have more freedom. Furthermore, females place a higher value on popularity than males, and so girls have a stronger motivation to learn to behave in a manner that will ensure social acceptance (70, 195).

Conditions favoring social acceptance

Conditions that affect the individual's level of social acceptance may be divided roughly into two major categories: personality traits and nonpersonality influences.

Personality traits No one need be a paragon of perfection to be popular. In fact, many people who possess disliked or disapproved personality traits are far better accepted than those who possess few undesirable traits but whose desirable traits are weak and inconspicuous.

A person may compensate for disliked traits by being an active participant in socially approved group activities, by being a good conversationalist, and by exhibiting social know-how. Another person, with many desirable traits, may lose the advantage these traits give him by being a boring conversationalist.

Social acceptance comes from the response people make to the *total* personality pattern rather than to specific traits. Therefore, outstanding traits overshadow weaker traits. Bonney has written, "A socially good personality is a positive achievement: it is not simply the result of avoiding the bad" (26).

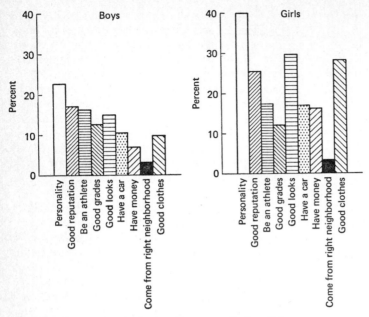

Figure 9-1 Importance of role played by personality in social acceptance as compared with nonpersonality factors. (Adapted from J. S. Coleman: *The adolescent society.* New York: Free Press, 1961. Used by permission.)

Figure 9-1 compares the role of personality and nonpersonality traits in social acceptance.

As was discussed in Chapter 2, certain constellations of personality traits lead to social acceptance—the acceptance syndromes—and others lead to social rejection—the alienation syndromes. The acceptance syndromes are made up of socially admired traits. In the alienation syndromes are traits which make the person disliked, which lead to social rejection, because the person is regarded as a pest or a nuisance, or to social neglect because the person has nothing to offer to the group.

Regardless of which form the alienation syndrome takes, people who are unpopular have either an inferiority or superiority complex. Those with a *superiority complex* are generally rejected because their behavior is aggressive and annoying to others. Those with *inferiority complexes,* on the other hand, are generally neglected and are "social islands" unto themselves in any group situation. They have such neutral personalities that they attract neither favorable nor unfavorable attention. Furthermore, unpopular people are self-bound and self-centered in the sense that they are too preoccupied with their own interests and problems to be concerned with the affairs of others. They are attention-demanding and resent having the attention of the group centered on anyone else.

One outstanding characteristic of every unpopular person is that he has a poor self-concept and suffers from feelings of insecurity and inferiority which stem from the belief that he makes a failure of whatever he undertakes. His poor self-concept may be expressed in the behavior patterns characteristic of a person who has a superiority complex and is trying to convince himself and others that his abilities are greater than is apparent or in behavior patterns characteristic of a person who feels inferior and inadequate to meet the challenges of life. Because of his poor self-concept, the person lacks self-confidence and self-respect. As a result, he is poorly adjusted and socially immature, displaying patterns of behavior that are characteristic of younger ages. This has a damaging effect on his interpersonal relationships.

Nonpersonality influences   Certain nonpersonality influences are at least in part responsible for the development of personality traits that lead to acceptance, rejection, or neglect. A brief discussion of a few of these will indicate their effect.

There is little relationship between the degree of

social acceptance people enjoy and the degree to which they *accept others.* Some people are sociable, companionable, or even chummy in the sense that they like close, personal contacts, while others prefer to keep their distance and are considered aloof. Some people form friendships easily while others form them slowly. Younger people, on the whole, form friendships more easily and are less discriminating in the choice of friends than older people.

A person may accept many people as friends but be accepted by only a few. Or he may be accepted by many and show an accepting attitude toward few. This is often true of stars. One of the major reasons a star does not reciprocate many friendship choices is that he is afraid of alienating people by showing an interest in others or he is afraid of being accused of favoritism.

Whether a person is accepted or rejected and the degree of acceptance he enjoys depend in part on the *group* and on the *kind of people* available for him to associate with. The group determines whether he "fits" and is congenial enough to be accepted. Adults of working-class backgrounds, for example, feel out of place in community organizations that are dominated by members of the middle and upper social classes. They feel that they are not accepted as equals by the majority.

First impressions play a central role in determining acceptance by the social group. If the person creates the impression of being disinterested in people and in group activities, the group members are likely to ignore him. If he creates the impression of being overanxious to be accepted, this will be interpreted as aggressiveness and will militate against his acceptance. Only when he shows a balance between the two will the first impression be favorable.

First impressions are greatly influenced by *appearance.* The most popular people at any age conform to group norms in dress and appearance. In time, the impression a person makes on others develops into a *reputation.* If favorable, a reputation aids social acceptance; if unfavorable, it militates against it.

Good health, which enhances personal attractiveness, vitality, and endurance, predisposes a person to be active in group affairs. Furthermore, a healthy person is likely to be a happy, cheerful person, and this contributes to social acceptance. Poor health tends to make the individual socially maladjusted and thus leads to rejection or neglect.

Social acceptance in childhood and adolescence is greatly influenced by the *family* and relationships with family members. The most popular young people, on the whole, come from small families where democratic control prevails. Only children tend to be less popular than middle children and those with siblings, but more popular than firstborns or last-borns (29, 195). Popular adolescents have warm, friendly feelings toward their families, are on friendly terms with their siblings, and quarrel less than those who are unpopular. When parents encourage or require their children to participate in social activities with them, they contribute to their children's social difficulties (63, 182).

Studies show that *socioeconomic status* has a marked influence on social acceptance. As Mussen et al. (165) have pointed out:

Economic factors may partially account for the relatively poor social standing of lower-class children. Poverty may mean poor health, poor clothes, and little participation in social activity. Any of these factors may reduce the child's opportunities for establishing stable peer relationships, and may thus handicap him in learning good social techniques. Moreover, the lower-class child's awareness of his lack of social know-how may produce feelings of inferiority and inadequacy and hence withdrawal from social interactions.

Geographic proximity to those of similar interests and values contributes to but does not necessarily ensure social acceptance. Newcomb puts it this way: "Propinquity is a facilitator but not a sufficient condition for the development of positive attraction" (174). Should a person's personality pattern or behavior be distasteful to the group, close contact with the group will not guarantee acceptance, but may lead to further rejection. Nor is *length of residence* in one area essential to social acceptance. It has been reported that many of the most popular children and adolescents come from families which have made many moves. It is *what* the person is that determines people's reactions to him, not how long they have known him (174, 178).

Persistence of sociometric status

Sociometric status, or the position the person has in a group, is persistent, although it may vary from one group to another. This means that the popular tend to remain popular, the disliked continue to be disliked, and the neglected find themselves on the outside, no matter how long they are associated with the group (66).

Persistence in sociometric status begins at the preschool level when children consistently choose the same playmates day after day. From then on, social acceptance scores are almost as constant from year to year as intelligence scores. This is true even when groups are shuffled, as occurs when children go from elementary to junior or senior high school (60, 142). Most young boys and girls who have friends continue to have friends in adolescence while those who are friendless continue to be friendless (60, 70, 104, 142). A study of middle-aged women revealed that those who were most popular had been popular during their high school days while those who were disliked or neglected had also been disliked or overlooked in high school (142). Thus it is evident that unpopularity "cannot be lightly dismissed as a 'passing phase'" (70).

At all ages, the stars and the neglectees have the most stable sociometric status. Those who are popular seldom "fall from grace." Those who are least liked and rejected tend to have the most unstable sociometric status. They tend to be more disliked or to acquire more enemies the more often they come in contact with people, and they do not acquire new friends to compensate for the number of enemies they acquire (70, 104).

Reasons for persistence   The reasons for the persistence of sociometric status are clear. The *personality characteristics* that lead to acceptance, rejection, or neglect tend to remain stable or to intensify slightly as the person grows older. The fundamental *values* by which people judge others likewise remain stable except at adolescence when there is a change from childish to more mature values.

Within a group, a person acquires a *reputation* based on his behavior. This reputation tends to follow him from year to year and from one social group to another. Even if the person changes and his behavior becomes more social, his reputation rarely changes, especially in adolescence and adulthood.

The stability of sociometric status is somewhat influenced by the *stability of the social group* with which the person is identified. Sociometric status may vary from group to group, but on the whole, it remains stable because the person carries his acceptance or alienation syndrome with him whatever group he is in.

Close and frequent *contacts* may cause a person's status to improve or to deteriorate, depending on how others react to him. However, changes will be slight and will not shift the person from a status of acceptance to one of rejection or the reverse.

One of the chief factors contributing to persistence of sociometric status is the person's interest in and attitude toward *social participation*. If the individual wants to be accepted, he will be motivated to develop socially approved traits and modes of behavior. A study of high school students' social participation was followed up 15 years later by Jones (108). The persistence of popularity was explained in this way:

The pattern of social interaction represented by participation in extracurricular high school activities provided many adolescents with social roles they found intrinsically congenial and likewise useful as a step toward other kinds of satisfying interpersonal relationships. They were thus motivated to repeat these experiences.

Awareness of social status

"Sociempathic ability," the ability to perceive one's own and others' sociometric status, is at the basis of the influence that social acceptance has on personality. It determines the quality of the person's behavior, his adjustment to social situations, and his social effectiveness (10, 96).

Up to the age of 4 or 5 years, the child is not clearly aware of how others feel about him. Consequently, he is relatively uninfluenced by the degree of social acceptance he enjoys. After that age, he gradually becomes aware of how people feel about others and also about him. This awareness he shows by such comments as "She doesn't like me so I don't like her." In addition, the child begins to recognize levels of preference. He recognizes that some children are liked better than others, some are disliked, and some are ignored. Similarly, he realizes that some people like him, some dislike him, and some ignore him (10, 60).

Each year, as his social horizons broaden and as his opportunities for social contacts increase, the young person's sociempathic ability improves. The *accuracy* of this ability helps to determine how much and what type of influence the group will have on him. If he believes, even incorrectly, that everyone likes him, he will develop a pattern of behavior quite different from that which he would develop if he believed everyone disliked him.

Variations   in   sociempathic   ability
The ability to perceive one's own status in the group is generally slower in developing than the ability to

perceive the status of others. The reason for this is that a person can be more objective in his reactions to other people than he can be in his reactions to himself. Furthermore, as most people learn to cover up their true feelings about another person in the person's presence, what they say and do may not be a true indication of how they feel about him.

Other factors equal, there is a close relationship between sociempathic ability and *intelligence.* The brighter the person, the more accurate is his ability to perceive his status and that of others in the social group. The mentally retarded are the poorest in sociempathic ability (157, 221). *Girls,* age for age, are superior to boys in this ability. During adolescence, both girls and boys can predict ratings of their own and of others' social status better when the ratings are made by girls (10).

A person who craves *affiliation* with a group is more accurate in his estimation of his popularity than one who does not care about acceptance and, as a result, is less interested in and aware of his popularity status (73, 221). And, finally, awareness of sociometric status varies according to the *degree of social acceptance* the person enjoys. One who is better accepted has closer and more frequent contacts with others and is thus better able to perceive how others feel about him. Lacking close contacts with others, the unpopular are usually unaware of how unpopular they are. The very popular tend to underestimate their popularity just as the unpopular overestimate theirs. The ability to recognize indifferent attitudes is even poorer than the ability to recognize acceptance and rejection (87, 157).

Methods of perceiving sociometric status Even the young child can get an idea of how others feel about him by their *tone of voice* and *facial expression.* The *treatment* he receives from others is an even better indication of how they feel. Teasing and bullying, mimicking his actions and speech, ridiculing his appearance or behavior, and laughing at his mistakes—all are clear-cut proofs that they do not like him.

How much *influence* a person has on others is further evidence of how they rate him. If they ask for and accept his advice, he can be sure that they rate him high. The *number of friends* a person has, even when the degree of intimacy with these friends varies, is an indication of his social acceptance. Addressing him by his given *name* suggests a greater social distance between him and others than using a nickname.

Using the family name suggests the greatest social distance (150).

Descriptive terms applied to a person show that person how others stereotype him and evaluate him. A person who is labeled a showoff, a pest, a brain, a good guy, or a big wheel has no difficulty in knowing in what category he has been pigeonholed (221).

Effects of social acceptance on behavior

People judge a person by his behavior, and their judgments have a profound influence on his judgments of self and thus, indirectly, on his personality.

People who know they are accepted move *toward* others, those who are ignored move *away* from others, and those who are disliked and rejected move *against* others. People who feel welcomed and respected in a group are much more likely to respond in a congenial and friendly spirit than those who sense disregard, hostility, or criticism. The behavior of disliked people may be the result of lack of social acceptance rather than the cause of it. Or it may be the result or cause of a vicious circle—the more the person is disliked, the more unacceptable his behavior, and the greater the dislike becomes.

How much influence social acceptance has on behavior depends on two conditions: how secure the person feels in his status in the group and how important social acceptance is to him. If a person feels *secure* in his status, he will feel free to act as he wishes and will not be greatly influenced by suggestions from others. The insecure person will be afraid to express himself until he sees how others are behaving and then he will follow the crowd. The strength of the *affiliation motive,* or how anxious the person is to be accepted by the group, likewise affects the degree to which his behavior is influenced by the group. The stronger the person's motivation to gain status and, hence, the greater his dependence on the group, the greater his susceptibility to influence from group members, especially those with high status (208, 214).

Specific behavior patterns A brief look at some of the specific ways in which sociometric status affects behavior will illustrate its motivating power. The degree of social acceptance a person enjoys influences his *emotional warmth* toward others. Popular people are able to display their emotional reactions toward others quite freely and overtly. The inability of the unpopular to join the group emotionally makes them "emotional outsiders" and increases their unpopularity.

Popular people show good *emotional control*; that is, they know when and how to express their emotions so that their behavior will win the approval of the group. Many unpopular people try to win the attention and sympathy of others by *overresponding, complaining,* or *seeking help.* While this behavior puts them in the limelight, the attention they get is usually unfavorable and unsympathetic.

The more popular the person the higher his level of *social participation.* Those whose popularity is high generally dominate the activities of the group and its membership (209). Social participation provides opportunities to improve social skills that contribute to even greater acceptance. One of the most important social skills the popular person has an opportunity to learn is *social insight,* or the ability to put oneself in the "psychological shoes" of another and perceive things from his frame of reference. Those who are least popular are least accurate in their judgments of others with the result that they frequently say and do things to make others dislike them (76, 106).

Social acceptance is related to good *achievement* while social rejection or neglect is related to poor achievement. Popular children and adolescents are generally good students, not necessarily because they are brighter but because they are happier and better adjusted. Those who are unpopular have negative attitudes toward their work and often drop out of school or college (209). As Havighurst and Neugarten remark, "Many a boy or girl drops out of school at the first opportunity, not for lack of academic ability, or for failure to meet the school's requirements, but for failure to gain acceptance into the peer group" (98).

Desire for social acceptance leads to *conformity* to the group. The greater the desire, the greater the conformity. Social conformity takes two forms: "acquiescence," or agreement with expressed group opinion rather than with that held by group members, and "conventionality," or concurrence with the mores, attitudes, and tenets of the cultural group.

Conformity to group standards varies not only according to desire for social acceptance but also according to actual level of acceptance (37). Characteristically, high conformity reflects an insecure social status. Strang (207) emphasizes this fact:

Conformity may be the price one pays for safety. An early-acquired fear of making mistakes may create enough anxiety to prevent an adolescent from being different from the rest of the group. An early-acquired fear of losing the love of one's parents, which in childhood led to model behavior, may also be manifested in conformity to group standards; it may survive as a fear of losing group acceptance.

Should a person enjoy less than complete acceptance but sees possibilities of gaining this acceptance, he will show a high degree of conformity because he is motivated by a desire to improve his status in the group. If his acceptance is low, however, he will conform only in public and then only to forestall complete rejection. He has little motivation to conform to the standards of a group that rejects him or accepts him only provisionally (12, 194).

Reasonable conformity is a socializing force which enables a person to learn patterns of behavior that will guarantee social acceptance. It is a source of potential danger for one whose desire for social acceptance is so strong that he is willing to conform to the standards of *any* group that will accept him. Should he be accepted by an antisocial group, such as a gang of juvenile delinquents, conformity to the group can lead to serious trouble.

Nonconformity is as detrimental to social acceptance and mental health as extreme conformity. The person who refuses to conform, regardless of his reasons for doing so, finds himself in the position of a social outcast. This deprives him of learning experiences, and even more important, it is damaging to his self-concept. If no one likes or accepts him, it is hard for him to like and accept himself.

Effects of social acceptance on personality

How much effect social acceptance has on the self-concept depends upon two factors: how aware the person is of his level of acceptance and what his affiliation motive is. Social convention leads people to hide their true feelings, and so it is often difficult to know what one's acceptance status is. Or one may be fully aware of his status but try to hide it from others and deny it to himself because of the negative effect it has on his self-esteem.

The influence of level of acceptance on personality is also proportional to how much a person wants to be accepted. A person with strong interests of his own, for example, will be far less concerned about the impression he makes on others and the degree to which they accept him as a friend than will a person who measures his worth in terms of what others think of him and how well they accept him.

Variations in effects with levels of acceptance

Being accepted is always ego-inflating while being rejected is always ego-deflating. Therefore, acceptance to any degree may be regarded as favorable to the self-concept while nonacceptance is damaging.

A person who is *well accepted* is cheerful, happy, and secure. Being accepted gives him an identity as a person, thus separating him from those on whom he was dependent when he was younger, especially parents, teachers, and siblings. Knowing that others like him gives him self-confidence and self-esteem. As a result, he develops social skills which facilitate social relationships and thus increase his acceptance.

A person who is self-confident and secure feels free to be original and creative; he is not fettered by social pressures as the less well accepted are. He feels that he is being supported in his originality by the approval of the group. Knowing that he is well liked also gives him confidence to attempt to influence others and to make suggestions for activities that will lead to group enjoyment. Because of this, he is likely to be selected for a leadership role. Of even greater significance, the person who feels secure is mentally free to turn outward and become interested in people and things instead of being self-bound.

Since others have a favorable concept of him, the well-accepted person develops a positive concept of himself, and this leads to self-acceptance. He is satisfied with his life, optimistic about his future plans, and confident of his chances for success. Well-accepted people usually have broader cultural and intellectual interests and a greater drive and zest for life than do those who are less well accepted.

People whose acceptance is very high, as is true of the stars, are more colorful, more outgoing, more involved with people than with things, more flexible about their impulses and their roles, and more active and daring than those who are only moderately popular. However, they often fail to establish close relationships with people. They do not want to offend anyone by selecting a few for special favors, but primarily they tend to be somewhat aloof and thus fail to show the emotional warmth that is essential to close personal relationships. This aloofness usually comes from a feeling of superiority, though this feeling is not great enough to militate against the high degree of acceptance they enjoy.

The effect of social isolation depends on whether the person's isolation is voluntary or involuntary and whether he is rejected or merely neglected. The person who is *rejected* when he wants to be accepted develops resentments not only against those who have rejected him but against people in general. He is often depressed and unhappy, showing his resentment by bossing or picking on others; he may develop defense mechanisms, blaming his lack of acceptance on some scapegoat or developing a "sour-grapes" attitude toward social activities. As has been explained before, some who are socially rejected become juvenile delinquents or adult criminals.

In discussing the effect of social rejection on the adolescent, Coleman states that a young person will not "sit still while his self-evaluation is being lowered by the social system of the school." If he fails to gain status in activities other than social, he will "take his psychological self and his energies elsewhere, leaving only a physical self in the school." This he does by engaging in solitary activities or by affiliating himself with a deviant subgroup (46).

The person who *voluntarily isolates* himself from others because he has little in common with those available for him to associate with feels that he is different; he may know or suspect that others regard him as different. And because being different is usually interpreted to mean being inferior, the voluntary isolate very often develops an inferiority complex.

People who are not totally accepted or rejected—the *fringers*—live in a state of uncertainty. As a result, they are hypersensitive to what others say and do; they feel insecure and ill at ease, never sure whether they will say or do something to make their situation worse. Their insecure status motivates them to conform in the hope of increasing their acceptance or, at least, not losing what they have. This state of uncertainty is also characteristic of *climbers* and *neglectees*. Both are unsure of how they stand in the group and how their behavior may aid or militate against improved acceptance. Their behavior reflects lack of self-confidence, which leads to unfavorable social judgments.

The marginal status of most fringers, climbers, and neglectees leads to the development of maladjustive personality characteristics: restlessness, excessive self-consciousness, irritability, moodiness, and lack of self-confidence (119).

Although different kinds of social isolation have different effects on personality, certain effects are almost universal. Social isolates are conformists, fearing that any deviation from the approved social pattern will elicit further rejection. They tend to be self-bound and thus increase their social isolation. They often try to compensate by engaging in attention-getting, aggressive, hostile behavior. They are discontented and unhappy and usually have a pessimistic outlook on life—a condition that further increases their isolation (75, 96, 173).

When social isolation occurs is almost as consequential as the fact that it has occurred. If it comes in childhood and adolescence when the desire for peer companionship is intense, it will be more damaging to personality development than if it first occurs in adulthood. An adult can always fall back on family members for companionship while, for a young person, the generation gap makes such companionship unsatisfactory.

Furthermore, social isolation at the time when the concept of self is being formed leads to the development of personality traits that adversely affect the person's future social adjustments as well as his self-concept. It may also lead to *anomie,* or social dysfunctioning and group alienation, based on the belief that the group has little interest in its members and their activities (37). Should social isolation occur later in life, after the person has become basically socialized, the effects on personality will be less damaging.

Improving social acceptance Because of the relationship between social acceptance and personality development, improving acceptance is a means to better mental health, better personal and social adjustment, and greater happiness. Since more people at every age are socially isolated, either voluntarily or involuntarily, than are socially accepted, it appears that the number of failures in interpersonal relationships—in school, community, business, and family life—is increasing (136, 138).

Furthermore, there is evidence that shifts in the degree of social acceptance enjoyed by those whose popularity is low are likely to be downward rather than upward. Thus, to avoid the damaging effects of even greater unpopularity on personality, parents, teachers, and the individuals themselves must take positive steps. It is too great a risk to sit back and hope that all

will work out satisfactorily. While a person's social acceptance may and sometimes does improve, this is far less common than many hope and believe (66, 96, 229).

Improving social acceptance is difficult at any age. The older the person and the longer he has been unpopular, the harder it is for him to increase his popularity. Strang (207) has emphasized the difficulties involved for young adolescents:

It is difficult to help a socially rejected or lonely adolescent. A "pep talk," superficial reassurance urging him to join a club or go to a party, may intensify his feelings of social inadequacy. . . . Sometimes, when the cause is quite obvious, the adolescent can be tactfully helped to make desirable changes in his appearance and acquire some of the social techniques that will make him more acceptable. . . . For more deep-seated personality problems, expert counseling or group psychotherapy are means by which lonely adolescents and those who have never learned to relate themselves to other persons may be helped to form closer ties.

If social acceptance is to be improved, it can be done most easily and most successfully early in life before the person acquires a poor self-concept, unhealthy attitudes toward other people and social activities, and an unfavorable reputation. Unfortunately, many parents and teachers do not recognize poor social adjustments in a child until it becomes apparent that he is a social isolate. Parents, especially, have the tendency to overestimate their child's social acceptance or to project the blame for his lack of acceptance on other children.

METHODS OF INCREASING ACCEPTANCE Attempts have been made to increase the social acceptance of children and adolescents with varying degrees of success. One approach has been to give the group an *opportunity to know* an unpopular person better in the hope that, with increased contact, members of the group will find him more congenial and will then be willing to accept him. If things can be so arranged that the situation will enable the unaccepted to receive recognition from the group, this will help to increase his chances for acceptance (90, 136).

Another approach has been to try in a subtle way to change the *attitudes of the group members* toward the person who is unpopular so as to make them more receptive of him. Class discussions of how unfair it is to reject a person just because he belongs to a different racial or religious group, of how girls feel when they are teased and rejected by boys, and of how popularity affects the person's attitudes toward school help to make young people more understanding and more tolerant of those they have treated as outcasts (142, 188).

When it is obvious that a person is socially unacceptable to a group because he has nothing in common with the group members and is unable to develop skills, interests, or values that will make him acceptable, he should be encouraged or helped to find *another more compatible group.* That this is far from easy has been explained by Elkins (63):

It is easier to adjust the academic requirements to the needs of the youngster than it is to adjust the social needs of the child to the group in which he is a misfit or to attempt to adjust the social responses of the group to such a child.

The best and surest way to increase the social acceptance of a person who is ignored or rejected is to *change the person.* He can strengthen the traits which contribute to acceptance, weaken those which lead to neglect or rejection, and change his self-concept, his attitudes toward the group, his relationship with group members, and his general attitude toward social activities.

The person's attitudes reflect the concepts the group members have of him and their treatment of him; therefore it is not easy or always possible to change these concepts, even though the person changes his patterns of behavior. Once a person's reputation for being a certain kind of person becomes firmly established, the concepts the group members hold of him are highly tenacious. If the person is a voluntary isolate, for example, he acquires the reputation of being odd or different, both of which are synonymous with being inferior. If he is an involuntary isolate, he is regarded as a pest or a square, labels that will make later social acceptance difficult if not impossible. Refer to Chapter 3 for a more complete discussion of the difficulties encountered in trying to change reputations.

Studies show that when a person can be helped to acquire social skills and competence in activities favored by the group, he will be better accepted. As Bretsch writes, "One avenue of promoting better adjustment on the part of school pupils is that of teaching them social skills which will enable them to function effectively in social situations" (35).

Other effective avenues include the correction of annoying mannerisms that create an unfavorable impression; acquisition of patterns of behavior that are admired by others, such as cheerfulness, cooperativeness, and conformity to social expectations; learning to look and act in a sex-appropriate way; and the development of greater social and self insight to enable the person to behave in a manner that is appropriate to the situation, thus becoming group-oriented instead of self-bound.

PREJUDICE AND DISCRIMINATION

Involuntary social isolation, whether from neglect or rejection, is ego-deflating at any age. When it occurs through no fault of the person himself but because he is identified with a particular racial, religious, sexual, or socioeconomic group, it is a bitter pill to swallow.

The victim of prejudice experiences not only the effects on personality normally associated with involuntary social isolation. He also develops a bitter resentment toward all who have been responsible for his isolation. This may in time spread to people in general.

Meaning of prejudice

"Prejudice" is a constellation of attitudes that cause, support, or justify discrimination. It is a form of *prejudgment* in which anyone who is identified with a group against which there are unfavorable social attitudes is looked upon with disfavor and distrust and is regarded as inferior. It is not based on what kind of person he is or what he does or says, but on his identification with a group. He is thus judged in terms of already-existing attitudes or prejudged in the sense that a judgment of him is made before he is assessed as an individual (5, 76, 77, 218).

In the constellation of attitudes that constitute prejudice, three elements stand out. *First,* there are widely accepted beliefs concerning the people against whom prejudice is directed. These beliefs are rarely based on personal experience but on stereotypes concerning the appearance, the behavior, and the personal qualities of all people who belong to a specific group. Like most stereotypes, these are passed down from one generation to another in a cultural group and are learned by each successive generation as part of the social learning.

Second, the stereotyped beliefs are accompanied by emotions. This emotional accompaniment ranges from cold indifference or distaste to bitter and violent hostility. In many instances, prejudice is a form of displaced hostility or of repressed aggression directed against a scapegoat group in order to resolve or avoid one's own grievances.

The *third* element in the constellation of attitudes that constitute prejudice is the belief that one should treat those against whom there is prejudice in some particular way. The kind of treatment that is endorsed varies from person to person and ranges from indifference to avoidance, from the exclusion of the members of a group against whom there is prejudice from some or all of the larger group's activities to active persecution (4, 48).

It is important to recognize the difference between prejudice and *preference*. A person may prefer being with people who have interests and values in common with his and with whom he feels "at home" to being with people whose interests and values are different from his. This does not mean that he dislikes those who are different or feels superior to them. It merely means that, given a choice, he will associate with people whom he finds congenial.

Unlike prejudice, preference contains no hostility. The social gap resulting from preference is due to a "comfort differential" or a feeling of greater "at homeness" with a particular group. Thus, while preference leads to social isolation for those who are different, the quality of the isolation is quite distinct from that which comes from prejudice because it contains no attitudes of hostility and no feeling of superiority.

While both prejudice and preference cause a person to discriminate against others in the sense that he rejects their companionship, there is a vast difference in the behavior found in the two situations. In the case of preference, the person selects from those who are available for him to associate with the people he finds most congenial and he then ignores the others. However, he does not attempt to make them feel uncomfortable or unwanted by being rude and discourteous or by hurting their feelings or showing his superiority. Usually he is kind and courteous, although he may indirectly let them know that he does not want their companionship by showing an interest in others while in their presence.

Prejudice, like all attitudes that develop early in life, may become so habitual that people are not aware of being prejudiced until a situation arises that tests their objectivity, such as the entry into a neighborhood of members of a different racial or religious group.

Nor is prejudice always apparent in the behavior of those who are prejudiced. It comes to the fore primarily in times of stress, inconvenience, or disturbance of the normal pattern of life. Prejudice against older workers, for example, is far less obvious during economic prosperity, when there are plenty of jobs available, than during recessions when there is unemployment and the elderly are discriminated against in favor of younger workers.

Meaning of discrimination

"Discrimination" involves acting categorically rather than individually. Although in popular usage the term includes such things as failure to include in group activities those with whom the person feels little in common, we shall use it here only in its strict sense—that is, in relation to prejudice. Specifically, this means that when a person discriminates against others it is because he looks upon them as belonging to a group against which he is prejudiced; he feels justified in treating them in a manner which he considers appropriate for all members of the group to which they belong.

Discrimination following prejudice differs from discrimination following preference in two major ways. Discrimination following prejudice consists, *first,* of treating a person on some basis other than individual merit and, *second,* of treating the person in such a manner that one's hostility is expressed in behavior that does physical or psychological harm to the person. Instead of ignoring a person he does not find congenial, the prejudiced person often goes out of his way to try to cause harm. The prejudiced person usually rationalizes his negative feelings and the unsocial behavior engendered by his prejudices. Otherwise, he would suffer feelings of guilt and remorse over his unfounded attitudes and unsportsmanlike behavior (4, 8, 48).

Since discrimination is based on attitudes which constitute the roots of prejudice, it is logical that discrimination would develop later than prejudice. Studies of the origins of prejudice and discrimination reveal that while awareness of differences between people of different races and of the two sexes is apparent in children's behavior by the time they are 4 years old, awareness per se does not constitute prejudice (123, 124, 163, 205). This is illustrated in Figure 9-2.

Only when the child learns the social attitudes toward those he perceives as different will prejudice develop. Prejudiced behavior, or discrimination, occurs slightly later (4, 8, 163, 205). By the time children enter first grade in school, the seeds of prejudice, sown earlier, are already taking root (47, 212). As Giles has stressed, "Little children, on first coming to school, have the words and sometimes the feelings of prejudice" (82).

Common targets of prejudice and discrimination

In a so-called "classless society" where social-class distinctions are not officially recognized, each individual is motivated to prove his equality with or superiority to other people. This gives rise to prejudice. When an individual or a group deviates from the norms of society in attitudes, behavior, appearance, or goals, there is usually prejudice. When there is no deviation, there is no prejudice.

Those who deviate are regarded as belonging to an outgroup or a minority group. The *minority group* is a subgroup in a larger society whose members are subject to prejudice, discrimination, segregation, or even persecution at the hands of another subgroup, the majority group. The *majority group* may not be numerically greater than the minority; its superior status comes from the fact that it has control over the economic, political, and ideological mechanisms of social stratification. As a result, the majority group is able to keep the minority group from achieving comparable status in society (94).

The roles played by minority and majority groups in the American culture can be illustrated by male and female roles. While there are numerically more females than males at all ages from earliest childhood, females are the minority group in the sense that the control of political, economic, social, and cultural life is in the hands of males. Even though women may have more money than men, owing to inheritances from fathers and husbands, they have little say in the running of the businesses and corporations in which their money is invested. This control is in the hands of men, as is true of all other areas of American life.

Prejudice and discrimination are, as Martin and Westie say, "part of the normative order of American society" (144). A few examples will show how widespread prejudice is in a culture that prides itself on being classless and democratic. *Women,* though statistically the majority group, are forced by tradition to play the minority-group role. There is discrimination against them in many areas of American life—in

"Me 'n' Jackson are exactly the same age. Only he's different. He's LEFT-HANDED!"

Figure 9-2 Awareness of differences does not necessarily constitute prejudice. (Adapted from Ketcham's "Dennis the Menace." Publisher-Hall Syndicate. *The Philadelphia Evening Bulletin,* Jan. 6, 1970. Used by permission.)

schooling, in government, and in business, industry, and the professions.

Old people, though far more numerous today than in any other era in history, are regarded as an outgroup and are subjected to prejudice and discrimination in employment, housing, community affairs, and other areas of life because the American culture is oriented toward the young, with high value placed on speed, efficiency, strength, and beauty.

A *single person,* especially a single woman, has always been regarded as a deviant, perhaps an unwilling one, in the American culture and has been a victim of prejudice and discrimination. Like the woman who wants to enter a "masculine" occupation, the girl who is not engaged or married by her late teens or early twenties is not conforming to the role expectations of the social group.

Rural people in an urban environment are regarded as "country hicks" by city people just as city people in a rural setting are regarded as "city slickers." Prejudice against the rural student and worker militates against their acceptance in urban schools or businesses where they are a minority group. Only when they are willing and able to divorce themselves from their rural interests, values, patterns of behavior, and appearance are they freed from the effects of prejudice and discrimination.

Because economic, social, and political power is in the hands of the upper social classes in all countries, members of the *lower social classes* are treated as a minority group, even though they are a majority statistically (99). One of the motivations for social mobility is the desire to escape the prejudice and discrimination directed toward lower social-class membership. In a democracy, where social-class membership is determined mainly by occupation, prejudice against certain *occupations* is linked to their lower social-class identification.

There is greater prejudice against some *national* groups than against others. In one study, university students gave higher prestige ratings to people from such national groups as the Americans, British, Swiss, and Canadians than to those from Iraq, Jordan, Lebanon, and Egypt (116). A person identified with a national group that has little prestige is subject to greater prejudice and discrimination than one who is identified with a national group with greater prestige.

In *ethnic-group* discrimination, there tends to be greater prejudice against those whose skin is the darkest. There is, for example, greater prejudice against blacks than against Indians or Orientals. Even within an ethnic group, degrees of prejudice and discrimination exist. Black people from Africa and from the West Indies are likely to experience less prejudice than those from the United States (47, 77, 176).

Prejudice against *religious groups* varies also. In general, prejudice against members of the Jewish faith is greater than against those of the Catholic faith, and within the Catholic faith, prejudice is greater against the Irish Catholics than against the French, Italian, and Spanish Catholics (178, 217). One of the reasons for prejudice against people of different religions is that they have different *values*. This is well illustrated in the high value placed on academic success by members of the Jewish faith. They are regarded by their Protestant and Catholic peers as curve raisers and brains—labels which clearly show that at least some of the prejudice against them is based on a difference in values (151, 178).

A person who is *stigmatized* or who believes that he is degraded in the eyes of others, is likely to be the target of prejudice (69). In many communities, children of divorced parents or of unmarried parents are stigmatized and subjected to discrimination. One of the reasons children do not want a mentally deficient sibling to remain in the home is that they do not want to be identified with someone who is a mental deviant (134, 190).

Another common target of prejudice and discrimination is the *newcomer* in a school, neighborhood, or community. He is in the role of a minority-group member because every one else is acquainted and a participant in established activities based on common interests and values. If the group is a closely knit one, like a childhood gang, an adolescent clique, or an adult social club, a newcomer is likely to face the prejudice and discrimination characteristically shown to outgroup members. If the groups are not closely knit or if they are in need of more members to function successfully or of new talent to provide new interests, the newcomer may be welcomed.

Effects of prejudice on personality

Prejudice is damaging to the personality of the person who is prejudiced as well as to that of the target person against whom prejudice is directed. It affects the values, moral concepts, symbols, and behavior of both. In speaking of the effect of prejudice on children, Arter has pointed out that "prejudice and discrimination potentially damage the personalities of all children—the children of the majority group in a somewhat different way than the more obviously damaged children of the minority group" (8).

Effects on person discriminated against How much prejudice and discrimination will affect the personality of the target person will be greatly influenced by his awareness of his rejection. Level of awareness varies with age and with the overtness of the expression of prejudice. Long before childhood is over, the person is aware of how others feel about him and is capable of interpreting the meaning of much of their behavior toward him.

Derogatory labels, such as "nigger," "kike," "brain," or "sissy," have a heavy emotional loading and are used to let the person who is being rejected know how others feel about him. The reaction of the person who is the target of prejudice is likewise emotionally loaded and more intense than it would be had the rejection occurred without the accompanying label. The emotional loading intensifies the rejected person's unfavorable attitude toward self and toward the group with which he is identified.

Studies show that, as a result of the prejudice experienced from whites, Negro children develop unfavorable attitudes toward themselves and their race and assign more negative roles to Negroes than to whites (47, 81). The same is true of old people. Because they live in a culture that puts high prestige on youthfulness, they associate themselves with an inferior status and develop unfavorable self-concepts.

The victim of prejudice and discrimination is always psychologically damaged. Allport (4) has emphasized the damage to the child:

A child who finds himself rejected and attacked on all sides is not likely to develop dignity and poise as his outstanding traits. On the contrary, he develops [ego] defenses. Like a dwarf in a world of menacing giants, he cannot fight on equal terms. He is forced to listen to their derision and laughter and submit to their abuse.

Because adolescence is an especially insecure and sensitive age, prejudice and discrimination at this time can produce even more psychological damage than in childhood. Why this is so has been explained by Friedenburg (74):

Adolescents lack reserves of self-esteem to sustain them under humiliating conditions. . . . Adolescents are dreadfully concerned about society's appraisal of them and of their worth. . . . They cannot easily assimilate an attack on their dignity or worth, for it produces not merely resentment but intense anxiety. The self is threatened while still ill-defined and in its early stages of construction.

Psychological damage from prejudice and discrimination takes many different forms. The target person learns to *hate himself* and his group because he feels that others hate him and the group with which he is identified. This leads to hostile and bitter attitudes toward those who have perpetrated the discrimination and toward all members of the group with which they are identified. In time, he may come to believe that the whole social environment is hostile.

As a result of feeling that he is hated, the target person often develops *aggressive behavior patterns.* Frequently, his hostility is expressed in *antisocial behavior,* characteristic of the juvenile delinquent or the adult criminal. One who cannot reconcile himself to being neglected or rejected because of his identification with an outgroup may try to gain status by affiliating himself with a group that wants to retaliate against those who make him and his group feel ashamed, inferior, resentful, and hostile. That leads to juvenile delinquency or adult criminality.

To compensate for feelings of inadequacy, the target of prejudice and discrimination may establish

higher levels of *aspiration* than his age-mates who are not subjected to such treatment. More often, however, realizing the general helplessness of his position, he becomes lethargic and submissive. In school, the child or adolescent who has been subjected to prejudice may have little academic aspiration because he knows his prospects for vocational advancement or vertical social mobility are slight. In time, he becomes indifferent to success and does not strive to work up to capacity.

A person who has been subjected to prejudice may try to meet his frustrations by being *conventional* and *authoritarian* or by being *derogatory* toward those who have discriminated against him. He may develop strong *respect for authority,* power, and "toughness," thus intensifying his feelings of inadequacy and reinforcing his willingness to submit to authority, even though resentfully.

To defend his ego, the person may do a number of things. The most common ego defenses are an obsessive concern about one's minority-group status, withdrawal, passivity, protective clowning, a strengthening of ingroup ties, and a hatred of self and of one's group. None of these lead to good personal or social adjustments and, as a result, they cause further damage to the personality—damage that may be so severe that mental disorders develop.

VARIATIONS IN EFFECTS OF BEING DISCRIMINATED AGAINST Prejudice and discrimination affect people differently. A person who feels *insecure and rejected at home* will react with greater emotional intensity to discrimination outside the home than a person who feels that his home is a place where he can retreat from prejudice. A person who has gained *some social acceptance* is less damaged by derogatory labels than one who has found little or no acceptance among his age-mates.

People subjected to *authoritarian child-training* methods sometimes react aggressively to prejudice and sometimes submissively. As a general rule, those from the *lower social classes* react aggressively and those from the middle and upper classes, submissively. *Girls* as a group smart more severely under what they regard as rude and humiliating treatment from the majority group than boys. But they have been trained to be less aggressive than boys, and so are frustrated in their desire to retaliate.

Those who are *segregated* from their peers, owing to prejudice against them, regardless of its source, are more damaged psychologically than are those who are not segregated. In speaking of the effects of racial segregation, Williams and Byars (228) have emphasized:

If society communicates to the Negro child that he is a second-rate, subservient individual, it is probable that he would come to view himself as an inferior person. There is no social institution that emphatically communicates to the Negro that he is an inferior individual more than segregation does.

There are individual differences in the way people *react to prejudice.* Some withdraw from the social group, some develop aggressive defense reactions, and some turn their hostility against society in general and engage in antisocial acts. Few accept discrimination as a challenge to show others their true worth.

Effects on persons who discriminate The person who is prejudiced and shows it by discriminating against others is likewise damaged psychologically, but in a different way from the person who is discriminated against. In general, the effect is to increase the intensity of the personality traits that predisposed him to be prejudiced.

By inflating his ego at the expense of others, by being intentionally rude to those whom he regards as his inferiors, he gets a false sense of his importance in the group and develops a superiority complex. Prejudice makes a person rigid, intolerant, cruel, vindictive, and extremely egocentric. Such a person shuns responsibilities whenever possible so that he will not be blamed if things go wrong; he accepts the conventional mores of the social group and dislikes all who deviate from them; and he is willing to conform to group opinion that he does not agree with in the hope of improving his status in the group.

Even when a person recognizes that prejudice conflicts with good sportsmanship or his religious training, he often clings to his old emotion-laden beliefs. This is partly because prejudice fills an underlying personal need and partly because it is the "thing to do." As Allport states, prejudice may be a "psychological crutch" used by immature and "psychologically crippled" people or it may come from a desire to conform to group expectations (4).

If a conflict develops between a person's moral and religious values, on the one hand, and his desire to inflate his ego and conform to group expectations on the other, he is likely to rationalize his prejudices and try to justify his attitude and behavior by claiming that "everyone does it" or that the minority-group people he has known are "typical" of the group with which they are identified. An employer, for example, may try to justify his prejudice against older workers by claiming that the ones he employed in the past were "typical" of all old people in that they were slow, accident-prone, and set in their ways.

Combating prejudice

Because of the psychological damages of prejudice to everyone concerned, many attempts have been made to modify or eliminate it. These attempts have met with varying degrees of success. Like overcoming social isolation, overcoming prejudice is a thorny problem.

All attitudes with an emotional weighting are persistent. They resist modification, and even when modified, tend to return to their original form and intensity when new experiences seem to reinforce earlier beliefs.

The younger the person is, the more susceptible he is to change. It is more difficult to modify prejudice in adolescence than in childhood and more difficult in adulthood than in adolescence. Far more important than age in determining the ease or difficulty of change, however, is the person's reason for being prejudiced. A prejudice that fulfills psychological needs is deep-seated and harder to change than one that is learned because it is the socially accepted pattern of behavior and "everyone feels that way."

METHODS USED TO COMBAT PREJUDICE A critical survey of the methods used to combat prejudice will show why they have not been entirely successful and what might be done to improve them.

Because prejudice places a barrier between the person who is prejudiced and the person against whom the prejudice is directed, each tends to view the other across the barrier with a hostile eye. The logical way to get rid of the hostility is to *get rid of the barrier.* This has been done by bringing members of hostile groups in contact with one another, either directly or indirectly, in schools, in recreation centers, in jobs, or in the armed services. With further acquaintance and with opportunities to get to know one another, the hostile groups may become less hostile or they may become more hostile, depending on their shared experiences (25, 186).

Another way of breaking down the barrier between hostile groups is to help the members of each group to *understand* why the members of the other group behave as they do and why they have different interests and values. Attitudes can be modified more successfully through discussion than through persuasive forms of communication, such as lectures, though a combination of the two gets better results than either alone. Since attitudes are a product of learning, new information must be given, understood, and accepted by a person before he is willing to change one attitude for another (156, 159). Figure 9-3 shows how a film showing and discussion helped to change ethnocentrism in a group of high school students.

Since prejudice stems from stereotypes, extensive *contact with many people* in a group does more to break down prejudice than intensive contact with a limited number of people in the group. In the case of prejudice against people of a given religious faith or ethnic group or against old people, the wider one's contacts with members of the group the more apparent it will be that they do not all conform to a stereotype but that each is an individual, different from others in the group in many ways.

Ideally, the use of stereotypes in mass media should be abandoned. This would help to eliminate many of the prejudices that stereotypes give rise to or intensify. It is not likely to happen, however. Depicting people in stereotyped appearances, roles, and patterns of behavior has become the traditional method of expressing humor or identifying characters on the screen. The method has been so successful that anyone who suggests its abandonment is likely to be regarded as ridiculous. That is why it is essential that people realize that *stereotypes are not characteristic* of everyone or of anyone, and that each person should, in fairness, be judged as an individual.

Prejudice *must be made "unfashionable"* if it is to be minimized or eliminated. Because everyone is influenced to some extent by the group with which he is identified, a person cannot be expected to be tolerant if his friends and associates think that discriminating against others is the right thing to do. That making prejudice unfashionable helps to reduce its severity has been shown in the case of college students. As a result of an emphasis on tolerance and liberalism in the classroom and on the campus, most college students become less prejudiced (186).

When prejudice is a tradition in a social or national group, it is unrealistic to expect the group members suddenly to become tolerant. Therefore,

other approaches to the problem of combating prejudice are likely to be more fruitful. *Changing the person against whom prejudice is directed* is most likely to get good results. If people are to be accepted, they must divest themselves of as many as possible of the insignia of a minority-group status. This means that people of minority religious, racial, or socioeconomic groups must accept the values and behavior patterns of the majority-group members. It means that people from rural areas must become "citified" if they want to be accepted in an urban environment just as the urban

Figure 9-3 Attempts to lessen ethnocentrism among high school students by film showing and by film showing followed by discussion. (Adapted from L. L. Mitnick and E. McGinnies: Influencing ethnocentrism in small discussion groups through a film communication. *J. abnorm. soc. Psychol.*, 1958, **56**, 82–90. Used by permission.)

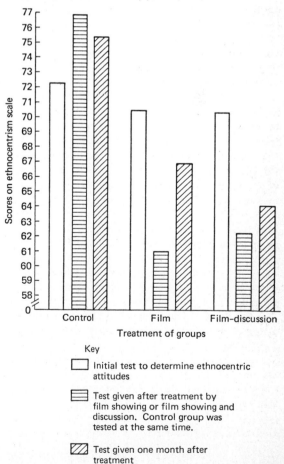

Key

☐ Initial test to determine ethnocentric attitudes

☰ Test given after treatment by film showing or film showing and discussion. Control group was tested at the same time.

▨ Test given one month after treatment

person must become a "suburbanite" if he wants to be accepted in a suburban environment.

In discussing the problem of combating racial prejudice—one of the most widespread forms of prejudice in our culture—Mussen et al. (165) have pointed out the difficulties:

Apparently both personality and situational factors are involved in changes in race attitudes. . . . Prejudice may be reduced by educational measures, such as encouraging contacts between members of various races. Such measures may often be effective with well-adjusted children whose prejudices are simply a reflection of prevalent stereotypes. On the other hand, where prejudice is a function of deep-seated psychological disturbances, such measures will not be effective or may even strengthen the prejudice.

GROUP STATUS

In any social group, no matter what its size, status varies from member to member. Some are leaders while others are followers. Some are satisfied with the status they have while others are dissatisfied and wish to attain a status that is more to their liking.

Within a group, the interaction of the members becomes stabilized in a pattern consisting of a hierarchy of statuses and roles. Each status has its own expectations, responsibilities, and loyalties. The person is judged by the other members of the group in terms of how successfully he plays the role associated with his status.

The role the person plays within a group, whether it be that of leader or follower, influences his personality. This it does *directly* by providing him with opportunities to develop certain personality traits that are essential to playing his role successfully. Eventually the person develops a "follower personality syndrome" or a "leadership personality syndrome."

Indirectly, status influences personality through the reaction of significant people to the role the person plays. In every social group, even among young children, the role of leader is more prestigious than that of follower. Consequently, reactions of the members of the group are more favorable to those playing leadership roles.

Status of leader

A leader is a member of a social group whom others are willing to follow because he has demonstrated his mastery in social relationships. In addition, he is able to elicit positive reactions toward himself from the group members because they recognize that he can contribute better than the other group members to satisfying the needs of the group as a whole. Most important of all, the leader has the potential ability to get others to act in a certain way.

Leadership may be positive or negative in direction in the sense that it may lead to socially approved or socially disapproved behavior on the part of group members. The leader is able to achieve his control over the behavior of the group members because of the emotional reactions he can arouse in them. The more loyal they are to him and the more the group accepts him as its leader, the greater will be his power over the members' behavior.

Kinds of leader Leaders can be divided roughly into two categories: the authoritarian and the democratic. The *authoritarian* leader is a bully, a tyrant, or a despot who is able to maintain his status only when the group is very large or when he can win and hold the respect of the group as a whole, even if he is not popular or liked by the group members. He wins respect mainly by satisfying the needs of the group members or by his show of power. The authoritarian leader is self-oriented in that he is anxious, aggressive, and has a driving need to be in the center of the group at all times.

The *democratic* leader, by contrast, is more sensitive to others and more prone to seek group sanction for his decisions. He shows a concern for the interests and feelings of the group members by asking for their opinions, and he is not likely to give direct orders. He leads on the basis of self-confidence, he has a clear perception of the requirements of the situation, and he can play the role of follower as well as of leader. He is "group-oriented" and uses a participatory style of leadership. In this way, he sets the tone for group interests and values.

The social distance between the authoritarian leader and his followers is relatively great. This usually leads to better work by the followers; it keep the leader from becoming emotionally involved with the followers and thus enables him to make decisions free from bias; and most important of all, it creates a halo for the leader, which enhances his prestige among the followers and facilitates his influence over them.

Small groups, as a general rule, have more democratic leaders than large groups. The larger the group, the more leadership skill is needed and the more likely it is to be authoritarian. In a large group, more demands are placed on the leader, and the wishes of the individual members must be subordinated to the accomplishment of group goals. Democratic leaders are generally better liked than authoritarian leaders.

The younger the group members, the more likely they are to accept authoritarian leadership. As they grow older and as their needs change, leadership then becomes a function of the situation, and democratic leaders prove to be more flexible. Because lower-class group members tend to be more aggressive and less cooperative, leaders must use more authoritarian methods to keep the group together than is necessary in groups made up of middle- and upper-class people.

Factors influencing leadership status

How much power a leader has over the behavior of others and how much his role affects his self-concept depend on a number of factors. The most important are the person's motivation to be a leader, his feelings of adequacy for the leadership role, how he achieved the leadership role, how persistent the role is, and how wide the scope of his leadership is.

MOTIVATION TO BE A LEADER While most people would like to have the prestige associated with being a leader, many feel inadequate for the role or are unwilling to assume the responsibilities that leadership brings. Some lack a strong motivation to be leaders because they can meet their needs for recognition and power by status symbols with less effort and personal sacrifice. Those who have a strong drive to be leaders may be motivated by a desire for recognition and self-expression or by a desire to compensate for feelings of inferiority.

The significance of motivation in determining not only the person's desire to be a leader but also the kind of leader he is has been illustrated by several studies of executives in business and industry. The main distinction between successful and unsuccessful executives is that the unsuccessful are afraid of power or are unable to detach themselves emotionally from their subordinates. When afraid of power, the unsuccessful executives show it in three ways: by rigid control, by convention-bound control with no innovations, and by aggressively erratic mood swings from domineering to affable, or by being either "against the boys or with them."

The stronger motivation of successful execu-

tives is shown in their willingness to pay the price in terms of pressure on their health, worry, lack of time for recreations and family life, loneliness, hard work, continuous interruptions of personal plans, and fear of making wrong decisions. One of the heaviest prices a leader must pay for his role is the willingness to accept authority and to accept the responsibility for failure as well as for success (7, 17, 45).

ADEQUACY FOR LEADERSHIP ROLE To be a successful leader, a person must feel that he is adequate for the role he is expected to play. Adequacy comes not from a general leadership ability but from a combination of the attributes of the leader and their relationship to the attributes of the other group members. DeHaan (52) has written:

Leadership is not a unitary trait or ability but, rather, it is made up of personal abilities and traits (which in some way make a person prominent and, thereby, eligible for the position as head of a group) plus consistent performance as a socioemotional specialist and a task specialist.

According to DeHaan, a "socioemotional specialist" is one who is sensitive to the needs and feelings of others, who can give and receive affection, release tension, achieve agreement in a group, and facilitate a feeling of group solidarity. A "task specialist" is one who specializes in the task engaged in by the group (52).

Since the interests and needs of groups vary, depending on the makeup of the group and the age of its members, effective leaders and leadership techniques also vary. All leaders, however, must possess certain qualities. In the first place, they must embody the *group's ideal*. This they can do by conforming closely to the norms of the group and by being able and willing to adopt its traditions and values. Because they represent the group in the eyes of society, they must have qualities that are esteemed by others as well as by the group they are identified with.

While *popularity* alone will not guarantee leadership, it is most unusual for a leader to be disliked by a majority of the group members. Being socially acceptable, leaders are more socially active than followers. This enables them to learn many of the skills essential to a leadership role.

To feel adequate for their roles, leaders must be *well adjusted*, both personally and socially. Their *intelligence* should be above the norm for the group but not so much above the norm that they are out of step with group interests. If the group is interested in *motor skills,* leaders must possess superior skills to feel adequate. Leaders must also make an *attractive appearance* to win the esteem of the group members. Most leaders come from the higher *socioeconomic* groups. This gives them prestige not only in their own group, but also in other groups, and enables them to dress better and to take advantage of opportunities to learn social skills—all of which adds to their feeling of adequacy for a leadership role (43, 107, 141).

A feeling of adequacy for leadership is greatly enhanced by training for leadership and successful leadership experience. These, in turn, depend to a large extent upon *early experiences,* especially those in the home. Firstborn and only children are usually given more opportunities to develop leadership ability than those in other sibling positions. Those brought up in homes where democratic child-training methods are used are more likely to develop leadership ability and confidence in themselves than those from homes where authoritarian training is used (233).

ACHIEVEMENT OF LEADERSHIP ROLE A leadership role is usually achieved in one of three ways. In the *formal* method, the person achieves his leadership role through an election in which he receives more votes from the members of the group than his opponents. In the *informal* method, no voting takes place, but the person is regarded as the leader by a majority of the group members. In the *appointment* method, the leader is designated by a person in authority without the consent or approval of the group members. The person who makes the appointment may be a group member, as when the president of an organization chooses a committee chairman, or he may be an outsider, as when teachers, camp counselors, or athletic coaches assign leadership roles (17, 38, 43, 172).

PERSISTENCE OF LEADERSHIP ROLE Nothing better convinces a person of his adequacy for leadership roles than persistence of leadership. If he is elected or appointed to one leadership role after another, he is justified in assuming that people consider him adequate for the role and he is, therefore, justified in considering himself adequate.

Whether the person will continue to play leadership roles from one year to another depends on two conditions: the stability of the group with which he is identified and his adaptability. Similarly, leadership is not likely to persist under two conditions: if the leader is appointed to fill a gap caused by the withdrawal of a leader chosen by the group and if the leader fails to meet the needs of the group (42, 171, 172).

Since leadership tends to become persistent, at every age a few stand out as the recognized leaders while the rest are relegated to role of followers. There are a number of reasons for this. The qualities that contribute to effective leadership tend to be persistent; they have become part of the leader's personality pattern. The leader has certain learning opportunities that are denied followers, and so he develops better social insight, superior social skills, and greater self-confidence. Persistence in leadership is also aided by the halo that is accorded the leader. Members of the group attribute to him, whether justified or not, the qualities they admire. If he is able to live up to their ideal, his prestige grows and his halo becomes more firmly fixed.

SPREAD OF LEADERSHIP Some leaders are "task specialists." Their leadership abilities make it possible for them to be leaders in only one area—sports, intellectual pursuits, social activities, or some other area where special abilities are required. Others are "general leaders" in that they can perform their role satisfactorily in a wide variety of activities. A college leader, for example, may be a successful football captain, an outstanding class president, and an effective chairman of the committee for the senior prom.

If a person has learned, from child-training methods used in the home and from experiences with the peer group, how to be adaptable and cooperative and if he has acquired traits that will add to his acceptance by different kinds of people, he will be able to play an adequate leadership role in a wide number of activities, though he may be more successful in some activities than in others. Even more important, the person who has a strong motivation to be a leader is willing to make sacrifices to learn how to lead in different areas.

After playing a leadership role successfully in one area, the person gains prestige in the group and is accorded a halo. With subsequent successes, his prestige and halo grow. In time, the group comes to think of him as the "great man" type of leader and elects or appoints him to leadership roles in a variety of activities. As a result of learning experiences, strong motivation, and prestige acquired from past successes, he becomes a general leader rather than a task specialist.

Effects of leadership status on personality If a person wants to be a leader and achieves this status, his ego is satisfied. The more prestigious the activity in which he plays a leadership role, the more ego-inflating his success. The high school football captain, for example, will have a more favorable self-concept than the president of the science club. Furthermore, if others feel that he is qualified to be a leader and select him for that role, he accepts the view that he is considered superior. This gives him self-confidence, a willingness to assert himself, and a controlled aggressiveness, all of which are essential to successful leadership. He develops what is commonly called a "dynamic personality."

That the desire to be a leader is a strong motivating force which must be given expression if the person is to be happy and well adjusted is seen in the fact that many people are willing to work hard and make many personal sacrifices to achieve their goal, even if it is not reached until they are middle-aged or elderly. Leaders in professional societies, business, government, or the armed forces must often wait many years before achieving this status but they feel that the status is worth it (128).

The person who wants to play a leadership role but fails will become bitter and resentful and full of self-doubt. Repeated failures to achieve a leadership role contribute heavily to an inferiority complex.

The thwarting of any desire is likely to intensify it. Consequently, the person who wants to lead but is deprived of opportunities to do so will glorify the leadership role. When this happens, his unfavorable attitudes toward self as well as toward those who have been successful in achieving the goal he craves will become stronger. His social relationships will be marked by jealousy and envy and he will be unfavorably judged by others.

The wider the scope of a person's leadership, the more positive the effect on his self-concept. He will feel that he is an important person because a wide variety of groups rely on him to lead them. By contrast, the task specialist has less ground for feeling important, especially if the area in which he is a leader has little prestige in the eyes of the larger peer group.

A leader is perceived as "different" from followers by members of the group, and this gives him the courage to be somewhat deviant. He is thus able to make a contribution to the group which he could not make if he were dominated by a strong desire to conform, as followers are. As a result of his contribution, he gains further prestige. This strengthens his leadership role as well as the favorable opinion the group members have of him.

As was pointed out earlier, the leader conforms more closely to the group's ideal than do any of the followers. Because of this, the group tends to put the leader on a pedestal and to look up to him as a superior person. Very often, the leader's aloofness makes him distant, unattainable, and emotionally restrained—the cool "big wheel." This pattern, once developed, usually remains persistent and contributes to the typical leadership personality syndrome. This syndrome is more characteristic of female than of male leaders, though it is found in leaders of both sexes.

The aloofness so characteristic of the successful leader often results in loneliness and a tendency to be self-sufficient, even to the point of being egocentric. One whose leadership status is not only persistent but also widespread may in time develop a feeling of personal superiority, regarding himself as superior to his followers, just as they regard him as superior. His feeling of superiority, unless well cloaked, will be expressed in behavior patterns that antagonize the followers. No longer will he be regarded as the group's ideal, but as an autocrat and tyrant.

Knowing how quickly the members of the group will change their attitude toward him if he develops delusions of grandeur and begins to dominate them, the leader usually tries to keep a sense of balance about his abilities and does not allow his superior status to go to his head. If a leader becomes aware that his followers are losing faith in him—if he hears grumblings of discontent, his suggestions are challenged, or if his decisions are criticized—his self-confidence gives way to feelings of insecurity. These feelings may be expressed in rigid conformity to patterns of behavior approved by the group members or in attempts to maintain control by authoritarian methods.

Regardless of how the beset leader attempts to retain his status, once the group begins to lose confidence in him he will not retain it for long. When a person is deposed from his leadership role, he develops a feeling of inadequacy. In addition, he is usually resentful toward those he believes were responsible for deposing him and toward the person who is chosen to take his place.

When a person is deposed from a leadership role not because of anything he has done but because the interests and values of the group have changed, his resentment will be intensified by the belief that he has been unfairly treated. An older person removed from his position of leadership in business, industry, or community affairs, for example, often feels bitter toward the group and resentful of the person who replaces him. He expresses his resentment by criticizing the group and the new leader, by making few contributions to the group, or by withdrawing from it.

Adjusting to the role of follower is difficult because of the resentments the deposed leader experiences. Strong and persistent resentments damage the personality by leading to feelings of martyrdom and, possibly, to voluntary social isolation accompanied by loneliness and self-centeredness.

Status of follower

Leaders and followers have much in common, though they differ in certain important respects. Followers, like leaders, are accepted members of the social group with which they are identified. Some followers are more popular than their leaders, while others are not. Many people are popular because they are fun to be with but they lack the essential qualities of a leader or the motivation to be a leader. The difference between leaders and followers is not that leaders are more *popular* but that they assume *responsibility for reaching group goals* while followers do not.

Leaders analyze a situation and *initiate action* while followers wait until the action has been initiated and then cooperate in reaching the goal. Most leaders do as much or more *work* than followers. However, it is a matter of the quality, not the quantity of the work done that differentiates the leader from the follower.

While leaders are superior in the *personality traits* essential for the leadership role, such as self-confidence, initiative, and cooperativeness, many followers are likewise superior in these traits. Followers who are popular, for example, have good social insight, but their social insight is not so good as that of the leaders.

Leaders tend to be more *authoritarian* in their attitudes than followers, but many followers are bossy and domineering. The difference between the two is that leaders do not arouse the resentments of the group members by their authoritarian attitudes so long as they are able to fill the needs of the group. Followers, by contrast, do not and cannot fill the group's needs and are likely to win disfavor by their authoritarian behavior.

The outstanding difference between leaders and followers is *motivation*. As noted earlier, leaders have a strong desire to lead and are unhappy and poorly adjusted if this desire is not fulfilled. Their motivation is high. Followers who possess leadership qualities might become leaders if their motivation to do so were strong enough.

Kinds of followers Some people are followers because they do not want to be bound by the responsibilities that a leader must assume. They are "contented" followers who voluntarily select this role. Others are followers because they lack the qualities needed to be leaders and are, as a result, involuntarily forced into the role of follower. They are usually the "discontented" followers.

Some followers contribute little to the group and its activities; they play a passive role, just going along with the crowd. They are the "hangers-on." Other followers make real contributions to the group by carrying out the responsibilities the leaders assign to them. They are content to do the work and let the leaders take the credit for any success they achieve. They are the "constructive" followers.

Destructive followers are the "tearer-downers." Their negative attitudes and behavior and their criticism of the leader and his policies have a bad influence on group morale. Destructive followers usually have a strong motivation to play the role of leader. When they fail, they are bitter and vindictive toward those who have achieved the status they crave. If they are able to win the approval of other disgruntled followers, they may become troublemakers in the group and thus get revenge against the leader whose status they envy.

Any large group, whatever the age of its members, is likely to have some followers in each of these categories. Consequently, the role of the leader becomes more difficult as the size of the group increases. Small groups, on the other hand, are likely to be made up of people with similar interests, attitudes, and values. With no troublemakers in the ranks, the role of the leader is easier.

Effects of follower status on personality How the role of follower affects personality depends on two conditions: first, whether or not the person wants to be a follower, and second, how he is treated in that role. Many people, as was stressed above, are followers by *choice*. Some doubt their ability to be leaders and prefer not to be placed in a leadership role for fear of failure. They feel inadequate for the role of leader and try to meet their need for recognition by acquiring status symbols of various kinds and by working hard on the tasks assigned them in the group in the hope of improving their acceptance. Frequently they rationalize their feelings of inadequacy by claiming that they do not want to pay the price of hard work and personal sacrifice that leadership entails. If they can convince themselves that this is so, it will go a long way toward eliminating their feelings of inadequacy.

A person may not want to be a leader, but at the same time, he expects the *treatment* he receives from the leader to be fair and ego-satisfying. Neither the child nor the adult wants to be bossed. Having to submit to authoritarian domination develops hostilities which damage the personality pattern and encourage aggressive behavior. Under more democratic leadership, followers are generally content to give the leader credit for the group's success. This does not make them feel inadequate, especially if they are popular and find satisfaction in group approval.

In fact, followers can usually establish closer friendships with those whom they find congenial than can leaders. Followers can receive affection and esteem without worrying about how others in the group will react to it and they can reciprocate without fear of being criticized for "playing favorites." For most people, this more than compensates for the prestige of leadership, with its accompaniment of apartness.

If followers are satisfied with the quality of leadership they are subjected to, they are willing to carry their share of the load in group activities. Consequently, they do not suffer from feelings of inadequacy nor do others regard them as shirkers. Being a happy, contented follower can thus have a more favorable effect on personality than being a successful leader who experiences the anxieties, uncertainties, and loneliness that leadership engenders.

SOCIAL MOBILITY

Very few people in contemporary American culture remain static in their social relationships. Most people go from one social group to another as the patterns of their lives change and as the groups with which they have been identified break up.

Likewise, very few people are satisfied with the social groups with which they are identified. Instead, they want to be identified with groups that have greater social prestige or are made up of people with whom they feel they will be more congenial.

As a result of these conditions, people in America are on the move, not only geographically but socially. This is bound to affect the patterns of their lives and their personalities. Consequently, social mobility, which may or may not be accompanied by geographic mobility, may be regarded as an important social determinant of personality.

Meaning of social mobility

"Social mobility" is the process of changing one's status by movement within a social group or from one social group to another. Within a social group, a person's status may change from fringer to involuntary isolate, from climber to leader, or from leader to follower. Or a person may move from one social group to another. A child who has little in common with the members of one gang may join another whose members are more congenial, for example, or a woman who resigns from professional organizations after marriage may join the social organizations of her community.

A person can go from one social group to another without moving his place of residence, but if he moves his place of residence or of business, the chances of retaining social contact with his former group are slim, especially if the geographic distance is great.

Since social mobility involves a change in the position the person occupies in the social structure, it automatically means a change in his social relationships. The change in social relationships will, in turn, affect his personality. This it does *directly* by affecting the satisfaction he receives from his status, and *indirectly* by affecting the way members of the social group react to him. If there is to be a minimum of psychological damage from social mobility, the person must be willing and able to give up the persons, objects, and ideas associated with his former status and recognize and assimilate those associated with his new status.

Kinds of social mobility

In *horizontal* social mobility, there is a movement from one group to another within a social stratum. In *vertical* social mobility, there is a movement from one social stratum to another. This movement may be either ascending or descending (226, 232). In ascending or *upward* social mobility, as the label implies, the person climbs up the social ladder. That is why he is called a "social climber" or a "climber." In descending or *downward* social mobility, the person goes down the social ladder and is generally referred to as a "slider" or a "skidder," depending on the speed of his descent.

There is a widespread belief in the American culture that anyone can go from the bottom to the top of the social ladder if he is willing to work hard, make personal sacrifices, and take advantage of the opportunities a democratic society makes available to its members. This "rags to riches" ascent, however, applies to very, very few people. Most who rise do so gradually, going up one rung of the social ladder in each generation.

Ascending the ladder is more difficult today than in past generations, largely because it can be done only through extensive training or higher education and mainly in situations where new economic enterprises open up. It can be achieved more easily when accompanied by geographic mobility which enables the person to "bury his past," to eliminate the stresses of family and old friends, and to advance vocationally.

Descent on the social ladder is likewise usually slow—one rung of the ladder in a generation. While some do skid headlong from the top to the botton, they are as scarce as those who climb rapidly from the bottom to the top.

Conditions contributing to social mobility

Horizontal mobility is usually the result of geographic mobility. It occurs when a person or family moves from one community, neighborhood, or group to another on the same level for personal or vocational reasons. It is less common in the lower than in the middle and upper social classes because lower-class people whose work is not highly specialized can usually find work in the area in which they live. People of the middle and upper social groups, who engage in more specialized work, move from place to place to take advantage of new opportunities.

Among the lower social-class groups, moves are generally from rural to rural or from urban to urban areas, with living conditions in the new environment similar to those in the old. In the middle-class groups, moves are almost always toward the larger urban centers or the suburbs surrounding them (59, 192, 232).

In *upward mobility*, the person has a strong motivation to improve his status. This motivation is intensified by proddings from his family and friends and from the realization that, in a democracy, improvement is possible. To achieve a higher status, the person must not only be motivated but must possess certain personality characteristics, the two most important of which are aggression and a sense of identity. If he is to win acceptance from and make a favorable impression on those who have more power and status than he, his aggression must be in the right amount and properly directed. He must behave in such a way that he will not be regarded as a "pusher." As Davis says, "His must be an effective, but congenial and disarming aggression" (51).

Achieving a sense of identity with those with whom the person wants to be associated is far from easy. The upwardly mobile person may be *in* a group but not *of* it. Without an opportunity to associate with people in the group that he wants to be identified with, he is deprived of opportunities to learn their interests, patterns of behavior, and values (132). As Davis has commented, "If a child associates intimately with no one but slum adults and children, he will learn only slum culture" (51).

Other personality characteristics needed to carry out the drive to upward social mobility include:

A high energy level, shown in a willingness to work hard and to concentrate skills in activities that will bring the best results

A strong desire for achievement accompanied by a willingness to work and a belief in one's ability to succeed

Willingness to take risks when opportunities present themselves

Willingness to be geographically mobile and to break ties with family and friends if this will help achieve one's goal

The ability to establish good social relationships with people

Orientation toward the future and willingness to sacrifice present gratifications to achieve future goals

High personal standards and values which will lead to behavior that is admired by those of higher social groups

A realistic self-concept accompanied by self-acceptance and self-confidence

The more intelligent the person, the more likely he is to be given an opportunity to be upwardly mobile. Very bright boys, for example, can achieve academic success which enables them to achieve vocational success. And with vocational success they have opportunities to associate with members of the higher social groups. Very bright girls who go on to college have opportunities to meet young men of a social status superior to that of their families. This provides them with opportunities to marry above the socioeconomic level of their families (220).

Movement up the social ladder can be achieved by occupational success and advancement, marriage to a higher-status person, inheritance of wealth, a fortunate investment of money that has been inherited or earned, association with and acceptance by people of higher status, transfer of church membership to a higher-status church, purchase of a home in a better residential area and use of money to purchase status symbols, the adoption of the customs, symbols, and values of a higher-status group, and perhaps other ways as well. Usually a combination of several of these is employed for upward mobility among men, while marriage to a higher-status or upwardly mobile man is the usual method for women (29, 178, 179, 220).

The personality syndrome of the *downwardly mobile* person is characterized by such traits as generally poor motivation, dissatisfaction, lack of drive and energy, greater concern for security or just getting by than for achievement, and orientation toward the present, with refusal to sacrifice for the future. Downwardly mobile persons have not internalized the cultural values and standards of behavior of the larger group; as a result, they are at the mercy of their impulses. Because they are dissatisfied with themselves, they create unfavorable impressions on others and have difficulty making friends (1, 51, 203).

The most common conditions that lead to downward mobility are:

Lack of adequate education or training to hold a position equivalent to that of the father

Lack of intelligence, motivation, or other qualities needed to hold a position equivalent to that of the father even though adequate opportunities for training have been available

Incompetence in a chosen occupation

Transfer of membership to a lower-class church

Prolonged unemployment or loss of business

due to poor health or unfavorable business conditions

Immigration from a foreign country and the necessity of accepting employment at a lower occupational level

In the case of women, marriage to men of lower occupational statuses than those of the fathers (2, 65, 178, 203)

Effects of social mobility on personality

Social mobility in any form leaves its mark on the personality of the mobile person. The mark varies in severity and persistence according to the kind of mobility, but it is practically always disturbing. As Bossard has commented, "Mobility has its advantages, but I wouldn't wish them on anyone" (29).

Effects of horizontal mobility   While horizontal mobility may mean a financial improvement for the family, an opportunity to bury the past, and a chance to gain a higher social status, it also means breaking old friendships and establishing new ones, adjusting to the mores and social life of a new group, and disrupting the schooling of children and adolescents. Until adjustments to the new environment are made, there is generally a period of loneliness and dissatisfaction and a longing to return to the old environment.

Studies of new children in neighborhoods have shown how difficult a situation they face. Many such children are teased, bullied, or ignored by those who make up the established groups. It is unusual for the members of the group to take the initiative in making contact with a new child. If he wants to gain acceptance, he must take the initiative, generally by winning the attention and interest of one child in the group. However, this is often interpreted as "pushiness" and it increases the group's tendency to ignore or reject him (235).

The difficulty of becoming accepted in a new group varies with age and environment. Adolescence and young adulthood are, on the whole, the most difficult periods in life for horizontal mobility because, at those ages, cliques are already established and newcomers not only are unwelcome but are often regarded as potentially disturbing influences and threats to those in power.

In rural and suburban communities, there is more "neighborliness" than in urban centers, and acceptance in a new group is easier to achieve. Rural and suburban families usually have more in common than urban families. However, should the person move into a housing development in an urban center, assimilation into the group is relatively easy because of the homogeneous nature of the environment.

In no case is acceptance into a new group achieved quickly. Nor is acceptance, once achieved, likely to be as complete as that which the person was accustomed to in his old group. As a result, he will experience the psychological damage that comes from social neglect or social rejection. This damage is greater for those who are used to high social acceptance or who anticipated higher acceptance in the new group than they are able to achieve.

Psychosocial isolation and loneliness lead to anxiety, dogmatism, and personality disorders of a minor or major degree. Anxiety depends mainly on the time when the environment is disrupted, while dogmatism is primarily a result of frequency of disruption. Most studies of mobility show that geographic mobility and various personality disorders go together. Thus, it can be said that the "basic effects of geographic mobility are disruptive in nature" (206).

Effects of vertical mobility Vertical mobility, whether upward or downward, is likewise psychologically damaging. It is a socially disruptive force, putting the person in a marginal position because he is torn from his social roots and has trouble establishing integrative social relationships. He must learn new values and standards as well as new patterns of behavior, and this is difficult because he is not well enough accepted by the group he aspires to affiliate with to know what their values and standards are or what behavior they consider appropriate.

Even when he can meet these social dilemmas successfully, the psychological scars acquired in the adjustive process persist and leave their mark on his self-concept. While the psychological scars are unquestionably greater in the case of downward social mobility, the upwardly mobile person is not entirely spared.

UPWARD MOBILITY Upward social mobility may satisfy a strong drive for achievement and even a neurotic drive to "show" those who did not accept the person when he was younger. But its effects are often far from pleasant and its influence on the self-concept

may be highly detrimental. Even though the upward climb may be admired and envied by others, it is not always a happy story for the person involved.

The *timing* of upward social mobility is a prime determinant of its effect on personality. When social mobility begins early in life, before a healthy personality pattern has developed, it can play havoc with self-concept. Upwardly mobile parents often drive their children to do better work in school, to be identified with the "right" crowd, and to behave in a way that will win acceptance in prestigious groups and reflect favorably on the parents. The home atmosphere is characterized by constant emotional stress.

When the drive for upward social mobility begins early and persists into the adult years, personality maladjustments are a common result. It has been said that "living up to the Jones's often results in following them all the way to a mental hospital." While social mobility striving is, of course, not directly responsible for mental illness, the tensions it causes and the disruption of social relationships resulting in loneliness and feelings of insecurity are not conducive to normal reactions in any crisis situation. The climber has less frustration tolerance than the static person, who has a higher degree of personality integration and is thus less subject to mental illness.

Of the many psychological scars resulting from upward social mobility, two—feelings of insecurity and feelings of social isolation—are especially damaging to personality.

Insecurity   Feelings of insecurity are almost universal among the upwardly mobile. While they also afflict the person who is static, they are generally related to situations for which the individual has been unprepared or in which he has met with failure. For the mobile, by contrast, insecurity becomes a generalized feeling; it affects all aspects of life, but is most damaging in the area of social relationships.

Generalized insecurity comes from the necessity of giving up old friends and associates and relinquishing the values that have served as lifetime guides. The mobile are identified neither with the old nor with the new. They lack firm ties with the group they are leaving behind and have not been able to establish similar ties in the new group.

Insecurity results in a number of patterns of behavior that influence personality. *First,* it leads to overconformity. The person is afraid to be different in appearance, speech, beliefs, or actions because he does not know how others will react (24). However, as

Ellis and Lane have remarked, this does not always result in being like those with whom the person wants to be identified (65):

While the upwardly mobile may depart significantly from the modalities of behavior generally observed in the lower class, their prior learning experiences result in only a segmental assimilation of the varied norms and values that make up the middle-class subculture. With the passage of time and continued social contacts with middle-class reference individuals, these subcultural discrepancies tend to disappear, though it is questionable whether the upwardly mobile ever develop a fully middle-class outlook on the world around them.

Accompanying overconformity is a loss of individuality and of the feeling of freedom to be socially critical. The person feels compelled to accept uncritically what others say or do. Associated with this is a rejection of family and community traditions and a desire to identify with the traditions of the new group.

Second, since the upwardly mobile are often denied status among the upper-class groups, they are likely to become exceptionally status-conscious; status and status symbols become crucial to them. A person with high mobility aspirations, for example, is usually willing to sacrifice interesting work for a job that pays well. He is very much aware of the kinds of behavior required to play the "social game"; he learns the proper "etiquette," joins the "right" organizations, and associates only with those who are in a position to help him advance. He is careful to engage in the proper amount of conspicuous consumption in an effort to keep up apperances without being overly ostentatious, and he takes pride in knowing, either personally or vicariously, members of the elite. As Blalock has said, "The extremely status-conscious person lives and acts as though status considerations are of the utmost importance. They are to him the essence of social interaction" (23).

Motivated by the same feeling of insecurity that is responsible for status consciousness is, *third,* the tendency to be hostile to those of inferior status or of a minority group. Among Jews, for example, those who are mobile tend to turn against those who have clung to the orthodox Jewish traditions. The more strongly motivated the person is to strive for a higher status, the more prejudiced he is likely to be (4, 201).

Social isolation Feelings of social isolation almost always beset the upwardly mobile. A person must terminate social ties with family members and former friends if he wants to climb the social ladder. As acceptance by the new group is likely to be slow, the person feels friendless and shut off. Even though his isolation may be caused by neglect, not rejection, he is nonetheless in a marginal status, belonging neither to the old group nor to the new. Should he cling to his old friends, he will feel superior to them and ill at ease. But he cannot allow himself to develop close personal contacts with members of the new group until he is sure that they belong to the "right" group.

Upward mobility weakens family ties, especially those relationships involving intergenerational family members. However, the mobile person's affection for his mother remains much more steady than that for his father and siblings (2, 93, 203).

DOWNWARD MOBILITY People who are forced to move downward in the social hierarchy develop feelings of inferiority and inadequacy. They feel frustrated and think of themselves as failures. In addition, they isolate themselves socially because they have little in common with those in their new occupational status and find it difficult to accept their values, interests, and patterns of behavior. Since they feel superior to the people in the new group, they are prejudiced against them. This not only affects their interpersonal relationships adversely and increases their social isolation, but it leaves the marks of being prejudiced, as discussed earlier, on their personalities.

Like the upwardly mobile, the downwardly mobile—the sliders or skidders—lack firm ties to any social group. Therefore, their status is that of "marginal men," torn from their social roots and unable or unwilling to establish themselves in the new group. This status is a constant source of frustration to the sliders or skidders and has a damaging effect on their self-concepts.

Among young sliders or skidders, there is the hope and expectation of returning to their former groups. This minimizes some of the psychological damage they would otherwise experience. Older sliders or skidders, however, realize that they have little hope of regaining their old status. Consequently, the psychological damage of downward mobility is far greater for them. Studies of men approaching middle life have emphasized how damaging sliding can be for those whose age is a barrier to regaining their former status. This damage may be reflected in poor marital and family relationships, in nervousness and psychosomatic disorders, and in a tendency toward suicide, homicide, and other crimes (34, 187, 203, 227).

The frustration resulting from social sliding and the realization that an uphill pull is impossible are difficult to tolerate. As Porterfield and Gibbs have explained, climbers and sliders, owing to their feelings of insecurity, have less frustration tolerance than the static (187).

Studies reveal that suicide is especially common among men of the upper classes who slide or skid socially. It is more common after the men reach middle age—when the chances of returning to their former status are recognized as slim. While the cases described in these studies may be exceptional, they emphasize the serious psychological damage that downward social mobility inflicts on people in this category (187, 203, 227).

SUMMARY

1 The social group judges a person in terms of his conformity to group expectations regarding proper performance behavior and role playing. Social judgments then serve as the basis for self-evaluation. In this way the social group influences the self-concept.

2 Whether the person becomes social, unsocial, or antisocial depends not upon heredity but on early social experiences in the home and outside. These early experiences provide the individual opportunities to learn to be social and the motivation necessary to do so. If early experiences are favorable, he will become a social person; if unfavorable, an unsocial or antisocial person.

3 Social deprivation is especially damaging in a culture that puts high value on popularity because it deprives the person of opportunities to learn to behave in a socially approved way and weakens his motivation to take advantage of any learning opportunities that occur. Regardless of when social deprivation occurs, it affects personality unfavorably, though the effects are most serious in the early years of life and among the elderly because of the greater dependency on others at these ages. The major damage from social deprivation is that it makes the person selfish and self-centered and en-

courages him to believe that he is a martyr. Too many social contacts are also damaging because they deprive the person of opportunities to learn to be self-dependent and self-reliant.

4 The degree of influence the social group has on personality development depends not alone on how well accepted the person is but also on how much social acceptance means to him. Regardless of a person's attitude toward social acceptance, he will be placed in a category of social acceptance by the group. Categories of social acceptance range from the very high—the star, whom everyone likes—to the very low—the social isolate, who is neglected or rejected by everyone. Few fall into these two extremes; most cluster around the average, with more below the average than above. Climbers and fringers are statuses of uncertain acceptance. Some social isolates are voluntary in that they prefer their own company to that of others; most are involuntary in that others do not like them even though they crave social acceptance.

5 What status the person has in the social group depends partly on his personality and partly on such nonpersonality factors as appearance, health, and geographic proximity to the group. Every degree of social acceptance affects the person's self-concept; the most damaging effects coming from the status of involuntary isolate and the least damaging from the status of star. These effects come only when the person is aware of the status he has achieved in the social group.

6 Because lack of social acceptance has such a damaging effect on personality and because most people fall below the average in acceptance, many methods to help people improve their acceptance have been tried. The most promising methods to date are those which help the person change his characteristic patterns of behavior so that he will conform more closely to the group's ideal and help him bury an unfavorable reputation, by geographic mobility if necessary.

7 Prejudice with its accompaniment of discrimination is damaging to the person who discriminates against others as well as to the person against whom the prejudice is directed. In both, the damage comes from a distortion in the self-concept. The usual targets of discrimination are members of minority groups—so-called because they lack power in the social group as a whole, not because of their numerical inferiority. The most common targets of prejudice and discrimination are females, the elderly, and members of racial, religious, and socioeconomic groups that are regarded by members of the majority group as inferior.

8 Combating prejudice is difficult because it is an attitude that is heavily weighted with emotion and, like all emotional attitudes, is resistant to change. That is why no satisfactory method of combating prejudice or of eliminating discrimination has yet been found.

9 The status the person holds in the group, whether leader or follower, influences his personality directly through the satisfaction or dissatisfaction he derives from his status and the opportunities his status affords for learning to be socialized. The indirect effect comes from the judgments others make of him on the basis of his status. Playing the role of leader or follower is due not to one factor alone but to a constellation known as the leader syndrome or the follower syndrome.

10 Owing to the opportunities leadership offers the person to acquire social skills needed for the leadership role and owing to the halo that surrounds the role, leadership persists and tends to spread to areas of behavior in which the person has only limited ability. Whether the effect on personality of being a leader or a follower will be favorable or not depends more on the person's attitude toward the roles and the satisfaction he derives from playing them than on the roles themselves. Being a contented follower leads to a more favorable self-concept than being a dissatisfied leader who feels inadequate for the role.

11 Social mobility, whether horizontal or vertical, upward or downward, affects personality by disturbing the customary pattern of the person's life. Regardless of what form it takes, it leads to anxiety, insecurity, and feelings of social isolation. The upwardly mobile person, in addition, becomes an overconformist and is status-symbol conscious while the downwardly mobile person feels guilty and ashamed.

CHAPTER 10 aspirations and achievements

In an achievement-oriented culture like our own, a person is judged by what his achievements are, how they compare with those of others, and how early in life he is able to attain them. If they are in an area that is highly valued by the social group, he will be more favorably judged than one who achieves more, but in a less prestigious area.

The earlier in life the achievements are attained, the more favorably the person is judged. The student who graduates from college at 16 or 18 is regarded as a "boy wonder." This is the label applied to the man who makes his millions before he is 40 or who is the youngest person to be chosen for a high-status position in government, business, industry, or the professions.

In time, the person comes to expect certain achievements of himself and he sets goals for their quality and quantity and timing. If his achievements come up to the goals he has set, he will be satisfied and happy. If not, he will feel like a failure, and the effect on his self-concept will be damaging.

The effects of achievement on personality are both direct and indirect. *Directly*, the effects come from how the person evaluates himself and, *indirectly*, from his realization of how others evaluate him. Of the two, the direct effects have greater impact on personality, because normally the person expects more of himself than others expect of him and thus judges himself more harshly than others do.

The effects come not from achievements per se, however, but from the achievements-aspiration relationship. That is why aspirations must be understood to be able to appreciate how success or failure affect the self-concept.

ASPIRATIONS

In everyday usage, ambition and aspiration are nearly synonymous and are often used interchangeably. *Ambition* means an eagerness or an ardent desire to achieve a particular end—rank, fame, honor, superiority, or power. *Aspiration* means a longing for and striving after something higher than oneself or one's present status. This longing may be ennobling or uplifting or it may be unwarranted or presumptuous.

The subtle distinction between "ambition" and "aspiration" is in the latter's emphasis on "something higher than oneself or one's present status." In aspiration, the motivation for achievement is improvement, while in ambition the motivation is the end result itself. This also explains why achievement per se does not always bring satisfaction to the person.

A person who is ambitious will be satisfied with his achievements if they are recognized and lauded by others. By contrast, a person who aspires to better himself or to achieve financial, social, or academic success above that which he has achieved to date will be satisfied only when his achievements come up to the goals he has set, regardless of how others view his achievements.

When used in this sense, aspirations are the goals a person sets for himself in tasks which have intense personal significance or in which he is *ego-involved.* Success in these tasks raises his self-esteem while failure leads to chagrin and feelings of inadequacy. The person confidently expects to achieve his goals in these ego-involved tasks and strives hard to achieve them. If he does achieve them, he will interpret his achievement to mean success. If he falls short of his goals, he will regard his achievement as failure.

If he did not expect to succeed, he would not be disappointed nor would he feel that he had failed. Instead, he would accept the results in a philosophical manner. On the other hand, when a person sets a goal, he usually knows what he wants. He is aware of the effort needed to reach his goal and knows at least some of the barriers he will have to overcome. Also, he has some expectation of the satisfaction he will derive from reaching his goal, even though he may not always be consciously aware of it.

In summary, then, aspirations must be considered from three points of view: *first,* what performance or aspects of it the individual considers important and desirable, or what he wants to do; *second,* how well he expects to perform, especially in the important aspects of the activity; and *third,* how important the performance is to him, either as a whole or in its different aspects (57).

For example, a man considers it important to do his job well. However, some aspects of the job, such as turning out more work of a better quality than his coworkers, are more important to him than other aspects, such as getting along well with his boss or having a pleasant relationship with his coworkers. He regards this goal of more work and work of a higher quality as more important than developing an efficiency technique which would enable him to accomplish more work in less time and with less effort. Therefore when he finishes a certain amount of well-done work per day, he is satisfied and feels that he has done a good day's work.

If working in an atmosphere of harmony is more important to him than doing a prescribed amount of work, however, he may turn out as much work as he had anticipated but be dissatisfied because he has had to work under pressure and ignore all social contacts with his coworkers. He may also be dissatisfied because he senses that he has set up a standard of output which his coworkers resent having to match. The more they resent him and the more cool and unfriendly they are, the more dissatisfied he is because he has fallen so far short of his goal of having them like him.

Motivation in aspirations

Behind all aspirations is the fundamental human need for achievement. Many years ago, Adler recognized the significance of this when he emphasized that everyone has a "life plan"—a purpose or goal—which determines his reactions. This life plan, Adler maintained, is generally developed early in life as a result of certain relationships between the person and his physical-social environment. This is especially true when the person suffers from a physical defect or inferiority. A person with a small physique or a physical blemish, such as a facial scar, usually unconsciously sets up a life plan or goal which will overcome or at least compensate for his defect. Thus, according to Adler, the person's aspirations are determined by a felt inferiority in some physical or social relationship.

In well-adjusted people, the driving force behind the need for achievement, or the "will to power," is adjusted to reality; it is integrated with social drives and leads to reasonable satisfaction through achieve-ment. In poorly adjusted people, it is unrealistic and unrelated to social drives, thus leading to failure and maladjustive behavior. Furthermore, while the well-adjusted person generally tries to compensate for failure or weakness by excelling in activities in which his ability is greatest, the poorly adjusted overcompensates or tries to excel where he is weakest in an attempt to deny his weakness (2).

Lewin puts less emphasis on the innate need for achievement and more on cultural pressures. He suggested that the social environment plays a more important role in determining what a person's aspirations will be than some weakness, which Adler contended was the motivating force behind all aspirations (145). Modern interpretations follow the lines set by Lewin and emphasize the social and cultural determinants of aspirations, as will be explained later in the chapter.

Kinds of aspirations

While all aspirations are strivings for something beyond the person's present status, there are different kinds of aspirations, depending on the function they serve in the person's strivings. Roughly, aspirations can be divided into three major categories, positive and negative, immediate and remote, and realistic and unrealistic.

Positive and negative aspirations
Negative aspirations center on the goal of avoiding failure while positive aspirations are oriented toward achieving success. If a person's aspirations are positive, he will be satisfied and regard himself as a success only if he improves his present status. If his aspirations are negative, they will center on maintaining his present status and avoiding a downward slide in the social scale. Like Pollyanna, the "glad girl," he will be happy if things get no worse than they are.

Most people have positive aspirations because they give greater satisfaction and greater feelings of self-importance from achievement. Only when a person has had a history of failures is he likely to be satisfied with negative aspirations.

Immediate and remote aspirations
From early childhood, people set goals for what they want to achieve. At first these goals are *immediate,* as when the baby purposefully reaches for a toy held before him, confidently expecting to grasp it. With

growth of intelligence, especially the capacity to imagine things not immediately present, the child starts to plan for the future, setting goals for "when I go to school" or "when I am grown up." These *remote* goals are generally less realistic and more fanciful than immediate goals. They are also more vital to the person than his immediate goals because they relate to areas of life which are especially important to him, such as his looks, his lifework, his future mate, or his personality. Consequently, remote goals hold greater potential danger for the self-concept than immediate goals.

Middle- and upper-class children, far more than those from lower social classes, are trained to set goals for the future and to deprive themselves of immediate pleasures that would handicap them in reaching their goals. By contrast, a child brought up in a family where the life philosophy is to enjoy today and let tomorrow take care of itself will concentrate on immediate goals and have few aspirations for the future.

Immediate aspirations derive mainly from the person's wishes at the moment, from success or failure in the immediate past, and from the social pressures placed on the person as he forms his aspirations. Remote aspirations are influenced by these factors and also by interests and aptitudes, cultural pressures, and past successes and failures in related areas. Thus, unlike immediate aspirations, which are little influenced by circumstances other than those present at the moment, remote aspirations are complex patterns involving a variety of peripheral factors.

HIERARCHY OF ASPIRATIONS   In time, remote goals fit together into a plan for the person's life, a plan which he believes will be desirable. Each goal contributes to the plan, but within the hierarchy of goals, some serve as the foundation for the plan while others do little more than add a bit of extra satisfaction to the total achievement.

Failure to achieve one of the fundamental goals in the hierarchy may upset the entire pattern. If the plan for a person's life hinges on going into a particular vocation, such as law, and he has planned his whole future around this career, including his marriage, his place of residence, his community role, and the plans he has for his children, then failure to be accepted by a law school will require a complete revision of his other goals. But if one of the minor goals in this hierarchy, such as his place of residence,

is not reached, the failure will have far less effect on his life plan and, therefore, will be less ego-damaging.

People who have had a number of failures in setting unrealistic remote goals may develop the habit of living in the present in order to protect themselves from the disappointment and ego damage that come from failure.

Realistic and unrealistic aspirations

Some aspirations are realistic in that the person is justified in expecting to achieve the goals he sets for himself. Far too many, however, are unrealistic because the person lacks the potentials to achieve the goals, no matter how strong his motivation and how hard he may work and sacrifice. Unrealistic aspirations are thus an index of the person's wishful estimate of his ability rather than of his real ability. Realistic aspirations, by contrast, are based on unbiased assessments of the person's ability.

All people at some time or other engage in wishful thinking. For those who keep it under control, it provides a strong source of motivation to achieve the wished-for goals in real life. For those who allow their imaginations to run wild, however, it leads to unrealistic aspirations and inevitable failure. Even a person who habitually sets realistic goals may be unrealistic at times, especially when his emotions are involved. For example, in setting his vocational goals, the young person often thinks in terms of the prestige of the vocation rather than his abilities.

CAUSES OF UNREALISTIC ASPIRATIONS   The chief causes of unrealistic aspirations are uncontrolled imagination, the mass media, traditional beliefs, and ignorance due to inexperience.

Uncontrolled imagination   Because imagination develops earlier than reasoning, the young child has difficulty distinguishing between what he actually experiences and what he imagines. With the development of reasoning and the accumulation of experience, the person learns to distinguish between reality and unreality. If imaginary experiences are more pleasurable than real ones, however, he may lack the motivation to make the distinction. In time then, he will develop the habit of wishful thinking and this will color his aspirations.

The mass media   While some people use the mass media as a form of relaxation and entertainment, others use them as an escape from unpleasant reality.

People who habitually use the mass media for escape come to identify with the characters portrayed and accept their values and behavior patterns as models. Eventually, they give up trying to find realistic and lasting solutions to their problems and tend to view everything, including themselves, their abilities, and their goals in an unrealistic manner. See Figure 10-1.

Traditional beliefs In America, and to some extent in all democracies, there is a belief that a person can become anything he wants if he works hard and takes advantage of his opportunities. This belief has been fostered in the minds of the young by real-life success stories as well as by the "rags to riches" or Cinderella theme of many books, movies, and television shows.

Ignorance due to inexperience Many unrealistic aspirations may be traced to ignorance on the part of the aspirant, ignorance that comes from inexperience. Studies of vocational choices, for example, show that up to 17 years of age, young people make "fantasy choices" owing to ignorance of their own capacities and of what vocations require in the way of ability and training. Only after they are 17 years of age or older and have had counseling or some work experience do their choices tend to become realistic (172, 216, 222).

EFFECTS OF REALISM ON PERSONALITY Realistic aspirations lead to success, satisfaction, and self-esteem. Unrealism generally leads to failure accompanied by feelings of guilt, embarrassment, shame, and unworthiness.

The person who is unrealistic about what he wants to be and do usually finds it "burdensome . . . to live up to this assumed role, to keep the pose, to live as if he were or had to be something he is not cut out to be" (122). The more unrealistic the person is in his thinking, the greater will be the gap between his aspirations and achievements. This is where unrealism has its most damaging effect on personality.

Many years ago, Samuel Butler emphasized that aspirations for unrealistic goals are troublemakers unless one takes into account two important rules of life. As he explained it:

There are two great rules of life, the one general and the other particular. The first is that everyone can, in the end, get what he wants if he only tries. This is the general rule. The particular rule is that every individual is, more or less, an exception to the rule.

The effect of unrealistic aspirations on the self-

Figure 10-1 Unrealistic aspirations are often fostered by mass media which emphasize the Cinderella theme of the poor girl who marries a young man of wealth and assured position.

concept will depend to some extent upon how well the person can take failure. Failure may act as an incentive to greater effort or it may discourage further attempts and, in so doing, lead to feelings of personal inadequacy. Also the person's frustration tolerance will, in part, determine the effect of failure on the self-concept. The person whose frustration tolerance is very limited will be psychologically crushed when he is unable to achieve what he has aspired to.

How aspirations develop

As a rule, children and young adolescents are less realistic in their aspirations than older persons. By the time people complete their education, whether at the end of high school, college, or graduate school, most are "ambitious" but not unrealistic in their vocational aspirations.

There is little evidence that the need for achievement wanes as the person approaches middle age, even though he has not achieved success by that time. There is, on the other hand, evidence that most people become more realistic as they grow older and become more experienced (136, 178).

Unfortunately, far too many people who lower their goals and make their aspirations more realistic as they grow older think of themselves as failures. This has a very damaging effect on their self-concepts. The fallacy of their thinking has been stressed thus by Whitman (235):

Many middle-aged men and women feel like failures when they aren't failures at all. They are merely using the wrong tape measure. They look at themselves in their 40s and 50s and take their measures by the standards of childhood dreams and ambitions. These standards are as ill-fitting to their present stature as the trousers or the dresses they wore when they were youngsters. Childhood dreams are wonderful for children: but when we keep clinging to them in our middle years, they can make failures of us all. This is not because the childhood dreams are wrong—it is rather that we misunderstand their function. . . . *Somewhere in the middle years we must let go of the dream. We must, in our maturity, recognize the dream for what it really is: a childhood spur to get us on our way, a goal.*

The relative stability of the childhood environment and the child-training methods of parents leads the child to develop a habit of aspiring either realistically or unrealistically. By adulthood, the individual has developed, often unconsciously, feelings of personal inferiority or superiority, depending on how successful or unsuccessful he has been in achieving his goals over the years. As Shaffer and Shoben have pointed out, "As a result of his early experiences . . . each person adopts a *style of life* which is the core of his character" (194).

Even more important, the person develops the habit of forming his aspirations in a characteristic way. He may, for example, habitually allow himself to be swayed by others in the choice of his goals; he may aspire to achieve what others think he should achieve rather than what he himself thinks he is capable of. The way in which he forms his aspirations affects his behavior and has a profound influence on his personality. If he is unable to live up to expectations and yet is unable to revise his aspirations without conceding defeat, the effect on his self-concept can be devastating.

Factors that influence aspirations

Studies show how unrelated many aspirations are to the person's abilities and interests. Many unrealistic aspirations, as noted above, are based on the expectations of other people. Of the many factors responsible for the formation of aspirations, the most common are intelligence, sex, interests, values, family pressures, group expectations, cultural traditions, competition with others, past experiences, the mass media, and personal characteristics.

INTELLIGENCE People who are bright have more realistic aspirations at all ages than those of average or below-average intelligence. They are better able to recognize their own shortcomings and the environmental obstacles that stand in the path of goal achievement. Those who are less bright tend to overestimate their abilities, and since they do not recognize the unrealistic nature of their aspirations, they do not revise them as they gain more experience.

Bright adolescents tend to set vocational goals that are in keeping with their interests, abilities, and opportunities for training. They are also attracted to unusual and unconventional jobs. Those who are less bright are more influenced by wishful thinking about what they regard as glamorous and prestigious (58, 113, 219).

SEX Boys and men generally feel a greater need for achievement in schoolwork, athletics, and vocational advancement than girls and women. As a result, they tend to set aspirations above their capacities in these areas. In the areas where achievement is more important for girls and women, as in social life and marriage, they tend to have more realistic aspirations than boys and men. Girls, as adolescence progresses, become more realistic about vocations than boys of the same age because they recognize that they must fit their vocations into their marriage plans (49, 75, 220, 236).

In adulthood, sex differences in aspirations are even more marked than in childhood and adolescence. Men's aspirations concentrate on achievements while women's concentrate on personal attractiveness and social acceptance. Furthermore, women are more concerned about their husbands' success than about their own (21, 220).

INTERESTS What a person is interested in will influence much of what he does. Thus, a person's interests affect his immediate goals as well as his more remote ones. A boy who is interested in sports and who has discovered the prestige associated with success in sports competition will have stronger and more clearly defined aspirations in athletics than in academic work where success brings little acclaim.

Some interests are closely related to abilities while others derive from social pressure or the desire for prestige. Studies show that interests related to abilities are the most satisfying. If a student has an aptitude for mathematics, his interest in that subject will be stronger and more persistent than if it were forced upon him by social pressures (174). Interest in love and marriage among teen-agers is fostered by the mass media and by peer pressures. If girls look upon early marriage as a way to establish themselves as women or as the "thing to do," the satisfaction they receive from running a home and raising a family will be far less than if their marriage filled a need for love and sharing not fulfilled by other social contacts.

Aspirations that develop from and are closely related to interests that satisfy some need in the person's life are more likely to persist than those related to transitory interests. Also, aspirations that develop from interests related to the person's abilities are more likely to be realistic than those fostered by social pressures (174).

As interests change, the aspirations rooted in these interests likewise change. For example, the boy whose aspirations during school and college centered on athletic success will, in adulthood, shift his aspirations for success to business and community affairs.

VALUES As was stressed in Chapter 7, values are a reflection of the person's home training, cultural background, and philosophy of life. They influence the intensity of the person's interests and give an emotional tone to his aspirations. In areas where values are strong, as in vocational and mate selection, aspirations are generally higher, less realistic, and less related to the person's capacities than in other areas.

The role of values in determining what the person's aspirations will be, how strong they will be, and how realistic they will be has been illustrated by studies of vocational and mate selection. Unfavorable vocational stereotypes tend to steer young people away from certain vocations, while favorable ones tend to attract them, even though they may be ill fitted for the more prestigious vocations by temperament, ability, and training (112, 216, 232).

In mate selection as well, values often lead to unrealistic aspirations. Girls more than boys aspire to an "ideal" mate rather than a real person. The result is that many girls find that they must lower their goals and choose from those who are available if they want to marry.

FAMILY PRESSURES Aspirations are often influenced by pressures from members of the family, mainly parents, but also siblings and other relatives, especially grandparents. Pressures for high achievement, the "great expectations syndrome," begin early and become stronger as the child approaches adolescence.

Parents commonly expect a child who is proficient in one area to be equally proficient in other, totally unrelated areas. A child whose marks are at the top of the class in mathematics, for example, is expected to have equally high marks in English and physical education; one who is good in track is expected to be equally good in football or baseball.

Sometimes parental pressures on children stem from the belief that a person can do anything he wishes provided he tries hard enough. Sometimes they stem from the parents' own unfulfilled aspirations for themselves; parents want their children to go a few steps ahead of them on the vocational and social ladders. And sometimes these aspirations stem from competition with other parents: If my child outdoes yours, that is a feather in my cap. Child and Beacon (45) have described how common this motive is:

Mothers in the park compete over teething schedules, time of rolling over, sitting up, smiling, etc., and anxiously consult publications which give developmental norms. This competition between parents (often in the presence of the children) continues throughout the preschool years with regard to nearly every aspect of motor and verbal development.

Within families, greater pressure is placed on only children than on children with siblings. And if there are siblings, greater parental pressure is placed on the firstborn. Parental pressure on the firstborn is reinforced by pressure from relatives, especially grandparents, and from siblings.

Among young children, mothers are more influential in their children's goal setting than fathers. As children grow older, fathers become more influential, especially in the case of boys. Only when the mothers have more education or a higher social status than the fathers do they have more influence on the aspirations of older children and adolescents. Working mothers have more influence than stay-at-home mothers on the aspirations of both boys and girls.

GROUP EXPECTATIONS   Like parents, the group with which the person is identified expects certain things from him. The person is thus motivated to aspire to achievements that will conform to the group's expectations. Cronbach (57) writes:

The standard set by one's group affects his goals. A person who thinks of himself as a normal member of a group will strive for the attainments characteristic of that group. . . . Wherever a person can, he decides how well he should be doing partly by noticing what others are doing. . . . Keeping up with one's group is necessary for self-respect.

With increasing age, the person is more influenced by the group and less by the family. In general, the group expects more of the person in adulthood than in childhood or adolescence and more at middle age—the peak years for achievement—than in old age. Teachers and members of the peer group have more influence on educational, vocational, and social aspirations during later childhood and adolescence than do family members.

Aspiration levels are inversely related to the *prestige* of the reference group. This means that as the prestige of the group with which the person is identified, or wishes to be identified, increases, his relative aspiration level decreases, and vice versa. So long as the person does as well as or better than members of his reference group, his motivation for greater achievement weakens (57, 95, 190).

The person's *status within a group* likewise influences the effect the group has on his aspirations. If a person feels that he belongs to a group, or if his status is marginal and subject to improvement, he will aspire to standards of behavior that will win the group's approval and acceptance. As noted above, "Keeping up with one's group is necessary for self-respect" (57). Those who fail to come up to group standards or to their own aspirations, which are influenced by the standards of the group, will suffer the most because they will be isolated from the group in which they sought acceptance.

CULTURAL TRADITIONS   The traditions that influence a person's aspirations are closely related to the culture's social structure and form of government. In cultures with class systems and authoritarian forms

of government, people are discouraged from developing aspirations that will make them unhappy when they discover that they cannot go outside their own class no matter how able they may be or how hard they may try. They are, however, encouraged to aspire to go to the top in the class in which they were born.

In democratic societies where rigid class systems do not exist, where going from one social class to another is possible and relatively common, people are encouraged to aspire high and are lauded for doing so. From earliest childhood, they are told that everyone can be a "success," that they are living in a "land of equal opportunity" where to "strive is to succeed" (6).

Unfortunately, cultural traditions in democratic societies often encourage aspirations that are unrealistic in form and strength; they do not point out the personal and environmental obstacles that may make the attainment of goals impossible. They do not, for example, stress the obstacles that certain minority groups, including women, will encounter in their attempts to rise vocationally. Nor do they take into account the fact that not all people are endowed by heredity with equal potentials for success.

COMPETITION WITH OTHERS   Even before the child enters the competitive world of the school where he is encouraged by his parents to aspire to stand at the top of his class, to be on the prestigious athletic teams, and to be identified with the leading crowd, he aspires to do what an older sibling or a neighborhood playmate does. He discovers that his parents are more pleased with achievements in some areas than in others, and this encourages him to aspire high in those areas.

Later he discovers that the social group rewards those who come out on top—he finds that there are even prizes for pinning the tail on the donkey at birthday parties—and this encourages him to develop the habit of aspiring to do things better than others in the hope of winning group approval and group rewards.

Many parents believe that, to be a success in adult life, their children must be trained to strive for high achievement. Child and Bacon (45) discuss child training in this light:

It is likely that much of this training, as performed by parents and teachers, is quite consciously motivated by the intention of preparing children to take effective parts in the life of contemporary American society, in which motives for achievement in adults play so important a part. To be quite lacking in motivation for achievement might be even more maladaptive in American society than to have an orderly strong and compulsive need for achievement which is expressed in inappropriate ways. Respect for the importance of achievement training in our society, then, simply gives us more reason for looking with a critical eye at the details of this training, seeking to understand where and how it is exerted successfully, where unsuccessfully, and with what effects on general mental health.

With experience, most people discover that competition with those who are superior rarely leads to success. As a result, they lower their aspirations when competing with superiors and tend to raise them when competing with their equals or with persons who do not come up to their level. By adulthood, the pattern of aspiring to what others aspire to has become a well-established habit. Thus, aspirations are more often influenced by competition with others than by individual interests, abilities, and needs.

PAST EXPERIENCES Two conditions related to past experiences influence aspirations. The *first* is praising and rewarding a person for his efforts rather than for his achievements. If the child who is not bright but who tries hard is praised by parents and teachers for his efforts, he will not realize how limited his abilities are. Since he does not learn to assess his abilities accurately, he will believe that he can do whatever he wants to do if he puts forth enough effort. This encourages him to aspire unrealistically high.

The *second* condition is the number and intensity of the frustrations the person has encountered. Whether frustrations come from the person's ineptitude or from environmental obstacles, their influence on his goal setting will depend on his capacity to tolerate frustration. The better he can tolerate frustration, the more realistic his aspirations will be.

If a person is to learn to aspire realistically, his past experiences should include a balance of successes and failures. A childhood marked by repeated successes will not necessarily guarantee good adjustment and happiness. The conditions that made these successes possible may not persist as time passes. As a result, the person is then less well equipped to tolerate frustrations and disappointments than is one who has experienced both failures and successes

and who has learned to evaluate his abilities more accurately.

THE MASS MEDIA By presenting patterns of life that are better than those most people have and implying that anyone can improve his lot in life and himself as a person, the mass media encourage people of all ages to set unrealistic, sometimes romanticized, aspirations for themselves. Young people, particularly children, tend to be gullible, owing to ignorance and lack of experience, and so they are especially susceptible to the influence of mass media.

While more emphasis was placed on encouraging the achievement motives of the reading and viewing audience in the past, the mass media today have a strong and sometimes subtle impact. Through incidental learning and identification with what he sees and hears, the person is influenced indirectly in his goal-setting behavior. Indirect appeals are often stronger than direct ones because the person is unaware of how they are influencing him and so does not resist them.

Mass media influences on goal setting are effective also because they imply that "everyone does it" or that it is the "thing to do." Whether the pattern of behavior is depicted on the screen or in print, the person assumes that it has the stamp of approval of the social group. This strengthens his desire to accept it as the pattern for his own aspiration.

The effect of mass media on aspirations is by no means limited to the young. Adults are also influenced. This is illustrated in the unrealistic aspirations many middle-aged people have for retirement. They romanticize retirement, seeing it as it is pictured in advertisements for annuity funds or for real estate in "colonies for the retired." Masserman (152) has described the mass media's picture of the retired man in present-day America:

He is generally pictured in our advertising arts as at least modestly wealthy and somewhat as a foot-loose playboy. His wife is never gray—she has interestingly platinum blonde hair and displays a remarkably well-preserved figure. And the two of them—provided, of course, they subscribe in time to the selflessly offered largess of the Rugged Individualist Retirement Insurance Company—can go gaily about the country, rootless as to place or family, living in a trailer, and fishing or golfing with well-preserved tan and vigor, anywhere from the golden coast of California to the enchanted keys of sunny Florida.

PERSONAL CHARACTERISTICS   Aspirations are greatly influenced by such personal characteristics as foresight, frustration tolerance, ability to delay gratification of wishes, self-esteem, ambition, and temperament. In setting vocational aspirations, for example, most people take into account their own temperaments, even though they may not realize they are doing so. A person who is adventuresome may aspire to success in a risky or dangerous line of work while one who is timid will choose an occupation that does not require physical or psychological daring. Those who have strong ambitions aspire to high-prestige occupations while the less ambitious aspire to occupations that are stable and secure.

Self-esteem is a function of the correlation of the person's ideal and real self-concept. The more they coincide, the higher the self-esteem. People with high self-esteem try to protect themselves from negative self-evaluations by learning to overlook or minimize objective failures and by exaggerating and concentrating on their successes. People with low self-esteem, on the other hand, are likely to exaggerate their failures. To avoid the embarrassment of failing to come up to group expectations and the pain of poor self-evaluations, they lower their aspirations, thus increasing their chances for success.

Strength of aspirations

Not all aspirations are of equal strength, nor is it possible to predict which of a person's aspirations will be strong and which will be weak. Certain kinds of aspirations are usually stronger than others, however, and predictions based on knowledge of these aspirations are likely to be reasonably accurate.

Remote aspirations are usually stronger than immediate ones because they deal with experiences in the distant future and are not seriously affected by current successes or failures. Even though immediate aspirations may be revised upward or downward with great frequency, according to how successful the person is, remote goals based on wishful thinking remain firm.

Positive aspirations which center on the hope of achieving success are usually stronger than negative aspirations based on the desire to avoid failure. While people want to avoid failure with its damaging effects on the self-concept, they normally put more emphasis on achieving success unless a series of past failures has made them failure-conscious.

Very rarely are realistic aspirations as strong as unrealistic ones. Realistic aspirations are a product of reasoning, while unrealistic ones are a product of imagination and have an emotional accompaniment which adds to their strength as motivating forces.

Aspirations which are verbalized or communicated in some manner to others become stronger than those which the person keeps to himself. By telling others what he hopes to accomplish, the person puts himself on the spot; he must make good or he will lose the esteem of those in whom he has confided. A person who aspires to lose 20 or 30 pounds and announces his intentions to his friends must stay on his diet or run the risk of being accused of having no will power.

Normally, aspirations based on the person's interests and values are stronger than those which come from pressures from others, even though they be people whose esteem and acceptance the person is anxious to win. Since aspirations are influenced at every age by pressures from the social group, however, what the social group considers important will lead to stronger aspirations than what the group considers unimportant.

Aspirations for goals that are difficult to achieve are stronger than those for goals that are less difficult. Whether in a laboratory experiment or in a real-life situation, the more effort the person must exert to achieve a goal, the stronger his aspiration will be. Aspiring to get into a very exclusive fraternity or an exclusive club will have a stronger motivating force than aspiring to get into a fraternity or club that is less exclusive or open to everyone (87, 165).

LEVEL OF ASPIRATION

The person's level of aspiration is the discrepancy between the goal he has already reached and the goal he hopes to reach. It differs from aspiration in that aspiration does not indicate how close the person is to achieving his goal. It is merely what he hopes to reach and what he is aiming for.

The gap between the goal the person has already reached and the goal he hopes to reach may be small. Under such conditions, his level of aspiration is realistic because the chances are very good that he will be able to reach his goal. When the gap is large, on the other hand, the level of aspiration is unrealistic; the person's chances of reaching the aspired-to goal grow slimmer and slimmer as the gap between the achieved and the hoped-for goal grows wider.

Levels of aspiration that are unrealistic may be either unrealistically high or unrealistically low. In the former, the gap is so great that the chances of reaching the desired goal are slim. In the latter, the gap is often *very* small; the level of aspiration is unrealistically low because the person needs to put forth relatively little effort to close it.

Most people are prodded into aspiring unrealistically high from earliest childhood. By adolescence, or even before childhood is over, they automatically aspire to goals far beyond their reach. Figure 10-2 shows how parents encourage the development of this habit.

When levels of aspirations are habitually unrealistically low, the trouble can usually be traced to the person himself rather than to pressures from parents, teachers, or members of the peer group. The person who has experienced many or severe failures tries to protect himself against future failures by setting his aspirations so low that the chances of experiencing another failure are reduced to a minimum.

Unrealistically high aspirations are not necessarily a source of damage to the self-concept; they may be a source of motivation and of ego-inflating pleasure. They are, in reality, a kind of wishful thinking which will not cause psychological damage so long as it remains a form of play. By contrast, levels of aspiration are a potential troublemaker. Because their focus is on the gap between achievement in the past and hoped-for achievement in the future, they are no longer a form of play. They are a serious measuring rod by which the person measures his achievements—his failures and successes. It is because of this function that levels of aspiration can and often are damaging to the self-concept.

When the gap between the person's achievements and his hoped-for goal is large, his self-concept will be severely damaged if he fails to reach the goal. He will think of himself as a failure, and if he has told others what his hoped-for goal is, they too will judge him as a failure. As a result, his subjective judgment will be reinforced by the objective judgments of others.

If it were not for the gap between the person's aspiration and his present and potential achievements, aspiring high would be commendable. It would act as a source of motivation and lead to achievements of which the person and those who are significant to him could be proud. But when the person's level of

"Choose your own career, Son. You can be a brain surgeon, banker, diplomat . . ."

Figure 10-2 Parents often encourage their children to aspire unrealistically high. (Adapted from Clark's "The Neighbors." Chicago Tribune-New York News Syndicate. *The Philadelphia Evening Bulletin*, April 1, 1965. Used by permission.)

aspiration is taken into consideration, high aspirations must be viewed in an entirely different light.

Methods of determining levels of aspiration

Since levels of aspiration are potential troublemakers, it is not always wise to encourage high aspirations until one knows how failure in a particular situation would affect the person. While failure to reach any goal is ego-deflating, failure to reach a goal that is highly important can be very damaging. Goals vary in importance according to the degree of personal satisfaction they bring and according to the amount of prestige the social group associates with them.

The person's former achievements are a good indication of future performance in the same or similar areas. This information can be supplied either by the person himself or by people who know him well. A student's grades can be obtained from the student or from school records and teachers' estimates. Objective tests can also be used to supply information about past as well as potential achievements.

Equally as important to know and far more

difficult to learn is the person's aspiration for a particular situation or for his life in general. This must be known to determine how great the gap is between his past and potential achievements and his aspirations. Some people are quite willing to discuss their aspirations; others will disclose them only if the person in whom they are confiding will disclose similar information to them. It is a case of "I'll tell you if you tell me" (125).

Most adolescents and adults are reticent about telling what their aspirations are. They have learned from experience not to disclose too much of a personal nature to others. Some are held back by a fear that others will regard their aspirations as an indication of delusions of grandeur, while others want to avoid unfavorable future social reactions if they fail to achieve their goals (125).

To some extent aspirations may be determined by laboratory studies, studies of wishes at different ages, studies of ideals, and studies of New Year's resolutions. None of these methods is completely satisfactory, but when a person is unwilling to disclose his aspirations, they are helpful. Even more important they provide indirect ways of learning the person's characteristic way of aspiring for the immediate as well as for the remote future. A brief discussion of these techniques will show how they contribute to discovering whether the person's level of aspiration is such that it can be a troublemaker for his self-concept.

Laboratory studies

Experimental studies of levels of aspiration have been limited mainly to measuring immediate goals where possible success is within reach. In such experiments, the person is given some task of moderate difficulty in which he is not skilled, such as canceling letters, tossing pennies, throwing darts, or doing exercises in arithmetic. He is told what score he made on his first trial and then asked what score he expects to make on the next one.

In this way, the subject in the experimental setup defines his own standards; he tells what he aspires to reach and then tries to come up to his expectations. While people react differently in these experimental procedures, most set goals above their past records and most are confident that they can reach their goals. Because there would be slight satisfaction for the person if he could see little improvement with further trials, he usually places his goal slightly higher after each successful trial and lowers it after a failure (57, 145, 153).

Experiments of this kind give clues to the person's method of reaching a goal and to his method of attacking barriers that stand in the way of achievement. They indicate how much effort he is willing to put into an activity to reach his goal and how he reacts to success or failure. These are only clues, however, not positive evidence that he *always* reacts in the same way. As in any laboratory experiment, conditions are of necessity different from those found in real-life situations. Consequently, the person's reactions may not be the same as in real life, even though the two situations have much in common.

More remote goals can be studied less successfully by laboratory techniques. They must, therefore, be ascertained mostly from what the person says he would like to do rather than from direct observation. Since most adolescents and adults tend to be guarded about disclosing their aspirations to people that they do not have close personal and emotional ties with, this information must be obtained indirectly.

One way of telling whether the person has high or low achievement motives is to have him tell a story about a picture shown to him. For example, if his story centers on a character who is trying to improve in some aspect of his life, such as getting a better job or becoming more popular, it is generally concluded that his own characteristic method of aspiring is reflected in what he says about the main character of his story (57, 145, 153).

Studies of wishes

Studies of wishes at different ages give important clues to the remote as well as the immediate wishes of the person. The young child expresses a desire for material possessions, such as toys, clothes, or sweets. By the time he goes to school, his wishes center on personal achievement, self-improvement, and greater social acceptance. By adolescence, wishes concentrate mainly on things that are culturally valued, such as status symbols, attractiveness of appearance, financial success, and popularity. These wishes serve as a basis for aspirations not only for the immediate present but also for the more remote future (50, 209, 234).

Studies reveal that people of the same age levels wish for much the same things. Almost every adolescent wishes to be more attractive in appearance, to be more popular with members of both sexes, and to improve his relationships with members of his family. Since many young people lack the socioeconomic status, the cultural background, and the personal characteristics needed to attain their wishes, however, there are wide variations in the gap between already-achieved goals and hoped-for goals and in the likelihood of reducing the gap.

With knowledge of the person's past performance and potential behavior in areas where his wishes are strongest, it is possible to predict whether he will achieve his goals. Used in this way, studies of wishes can be a fruitful source of information about the kind of adjustment the person is likely to make and the degree of self-satisfaction he is likely to experience.

Studies of ideals Studies in which people are asked to name their ideal person—one whom they admire or hope to model themselves after—give important clues to levels of aspiration. Knowledge of a child's ideal may indicate what he hopes to be when he grows up and sometimes even what he hopes to be in the relatively near future.

The potential damage to the self-concept in aspiring to be like an ideal comes from the fact that the person's chances of success are usually very slim. Unless he selects as his ideal a person whose abilities and personal characteristics are similar to his own, his level of aspiration is almost sure to be unrealistic.

Studies of New Year's resolutions Almost everyone at some time in life resolves that he will do something to bring about self-improvement, such as going on a reducing diet, or that he will refrain from doing something that is detrimental, such as losing his temper in public. Because New Year's Day is by tradition the time to turn over a new leaf, most resolutions are made at that time.

In many resolutions, the aspirations for improvement are specific. They spell out in detail what the person hopes to achieve and when. A resolution, for example, may be to lose 20 pounds by this time next year. Resolutions often reflect standards set by parents, teachers, or members of the peer group—standards which the person has accepted as his own.

A study of New Year's resolutions of 11- and 12-year-olds showed that most of the resolutions were based on standards the young people had accepted from members of the social groups with which they were identified. Most of their resolutions centered on home life, family relationships, school success, character and personality traits, and social relationships. The young person whose New Year's resolution is "to

tell the truth," "not to nag, contradict, or annoy my parents," or "not to fight with my sister" shows what his aspiration for the future is and in what area of his life he feels that he has fallen short of his own and others' expectations (239).

Resolutions, like wishes, may be realistic or unrealistic, depending on how close or how remote they are from present abilities and the person's potentials) A person who resolves to lose 20 pounds may have a realistic aspiration or an unrealistic one, depending on present weight, attitudes toward eating, and many other variables.

Resolutions, more often than wishes, are overtly stated. A person usually tells members of his family, his intimate friends, and sometimes even those whom he knows only slightly what he has resolved to do. If he achieves his goal, they will judge him favorably and this will reinforce his ego satisfaction that comes from knowing that he has achieved his goal.

Value of knowing level of aspiration

Imperfect as each of the methods described above is for determining the person's level of aspiration, each is valuable because it focuses the person's attention on the kind of aspiration he has set and makes him aware that he may have developed the habit of aspiring unrealistically high or unrealistically low.

Equally important, the evidence obtained about the person's characteristic method of aspiring helps him understand why he is often dissatisfied with himself, sometimes to the point of self-rejection. Realization of the cause of self-dislike will help him revise his habitual method of aspiring and learn to take into consideration his abilities and potentials when he sets his aspirations in the future. He must, however, learn to tackle his problems independently and make his appraisals with a minimum of outside help and guidance.

Knowing a person's past achievements and his potentials for future achievements may not be enough to predict his chances for success. It is essential to know also the strength of his motivation and other factors that compensate for limited ability and contribute heavily to achievement. This has been emphasized by Hilgard (109):

We must be cautious about assuming that because a person is able to announce his goal and to strive toward it we have then a complete picture of his motivation. Prestige-seeking, self-protection, and other goals inevitably enter to distort the clear picture of why a person is doing what he is doing.

ACHIEVEMENTS

Success in mastering the developmental tasks set by the social group will bring the person happiness, social recognition, and success with new tasks which are dependent on the foundations laid earlier. Before the child enters school, for example, he is expected to learn to walk and talk and take care of his bodily needs. Before he reaches legal adulthood, he is expected to handle his affairs without help from adults and to be emotionally independent of his parents (100). If a person comes up to group expectations, he is regarded as a success. If not, he is judged a failure. In time, he learns to think of himself as the group thinks of him and to regard himself as a success or failure. His awareness of the group judgment of him has a powerful influence on his self-judgment.

When the group expects more of a person than he is capable of, he sets his aspirations too high and is regarded as a failure both by the group and by himself. When, by contrast, group expectations are below the person's capacities, his achievements will be successes in the judgment of the group, though they may be regarded as failures by him if his own aspirations are above group expectations. The closer group expectations and personal aspirations are to a person's capacities, the greater the likelihood that his achievements will be regarded as successful both by him and by the group.

Factors contributing to achievement

Aspirations are only the beginning of a chain of activities that lead to successful or unsuccessful achievement. Success must be won by the person's own efforts, though help and guidance from others often make the achievement of a goal easier or even possible. Nor is ability alone enough to achieve success. The person must use his ability in the right way and at the right time.

A number of elements contribute to the complex process that leads to successful achievement—the "achievement syndrome." The person must have *training* under the guidance of an experienced person

to know how to make the best possible use of the abilities he has. He must also have *experience,* which comes with age and opportunities to enjoy wide and varied activities (55, 184).

Firstborn children, if has been found, have higher achievement drives than later-borns owing to the greater involvement, encouragement, and urging of their parents. They also have more parental guidance and help and, because of the close parent-child relationship, are more likely to use their parents as models to imitate. This accounts, in part at least, for their greater achievements (17, 46, 186).

Past achievements and the amount of satisfaction associated with them help to form the person's attitudes toward achievement in different areas. Studies show that attitudes toward work, for example, are strongly influenced by past achievements and by how well these achievements meet the person's needs. If the person has a strong need for dominance, having to work under someone instead of working independently will be frustrating and irritating, even though the quality of his achievements may be high enough to give him satisfaction (44, 56, 84, 136).

To achieve success in any activity at any age, the person must be *flexible*—willing to adjust to new roles and undertake new activities even if they are not necessarily to his liking. A boy must adjust to the approved male role even though he might prefer to play the feminine role. In work, the person must learn to adjust to the demands of his job even though it may not be exactly what he wanted or hoped for.

The person must also be *independent* of others to the extent that he can make his own decisions and carry them out successfully without having to rely upon the advice, guidance, or help of others (44). While firstborns tend to be more dependent and conforming than those who are later-born, they often compensate for this by their stronger motivation to achieve success in whatever they undertake. Closely related to independence is *risk taking*. To achieve success in any area, the person must be able and willing to take certain risks, hoping that they will turn out to his advantage (228).

Unquestionably, the central element in the achievement syndrome is *motivation*. The person must not only desire success, but he must be willing to sacrifice time, effort, and immediate pleasures to achieve higher goals and greater success in the future.

Whether the person will be willing to make such sacrifices will depend largely upon his evaluation of the goal. This has been discussed by Oden in her

40-year follow-up study of the attitudes of gifted boys and girls. In explaining the difference between "A" men, or those most successful in vocational status, and "C" men, or those least successful, Oden pointed out that there is no universal yardstick for measuring success. People differ in their attitudes depending on the prevailing patterns of the culture and their individual philosophies of life (163):

The correlates of success are not possessed exclusively by the A's, for there are no factors favorable to achievement that are not also found among some, albeit a minority, of the C men, but the magic combination is lacking. It should not be overlooked that a few of the C men have deliberately chosen not to seek "success," expressing a preference for a less competitive way of life with greater opportunity for personal happiness and freedom to pursue their avocational interests. In any case one must conclude, as was done in the 1940 study of success, that intellect and achievement are far from perfectly correlated, and that emotional stability and a composite of the personality traits that generate a drive to achieve are also necessary for outstanding achievement among intellectually gifted men.

Motivation to achieve, whether academically, socially, or vocationally, is stronger among firstborns, among those from small families, and among those from mother-dominated homes, homes with democratic control, and homes where good parent-child relationships prevail (1, 28, 161, 203). It is likewise greater when the person is satisfied with what he is doing. Studies show that the greatest motivation and satisfaction come from a job which gives the person a feeling of achievement, responsibility, growth, advancement, earned recognition, and enjoyment from the work itself (162, 230).

The reason motivation plays such a positive role in achievement is that it produces a stressful situation for the person. To resolve the stress, he uses greater effort and thus improves his performance. Only when the stress is so strong that it prevents concentration on the task at hand and keeps the person from using his abilities to their greatest advantage is motivation not a major positive factor in achievement.

Influence of early foundations on achievement

While the factors that make up the achievement syndrome contribute to goal attainment at any age, they are especially influential during the early years of life. Past successes, for example, have more influence on the achievement drive when the person is young than when he is older and has learned to take successes in stride. The same is true of failures. A young child may be so crushed by failures that he has no desire to attempt a task similar to one in which he has previously failed. As he grows older, he takes failures more philosophically, though at every age they have some impact on the achievement drive.

The first 5 years of the child's school experience, between the ages of 6 and 10 years, have been called the "critical period" in the development of the achievement drive. As Sontag and Kagan have pointed out, "High levels of achievement behavior at that age are highly correlated with achievement behavior in adulthood" (200).

This does not, of course, mean that the achievement drive is fixed and does not change later. There is ample evidence that it will change if conditions in the person's life that contribute to the drive are markedly altered. A person who has achieved top academic success in elementary school may, in junior or senior high school, experience a number of academic failures or near failures. Even if he wants to do as well as he did earlier, he may be handicapped by stiffer competition or by lack of help from his parents. Not being at the head of his class as he was in elementary school may dampen his motivation to achieve what he is capable of achieving.

Even when a change in the achievement drive does occur as the person grows older, there is little evidence that it will be a radical change. A person who has a strong achievement drive as a child, for example, is highly unlikely to make a complete about-face later in life. He is likely to continue to want to do his best. Furthermore, since the factors that contribute to the achievement drive tend to persist, they reinforce the developing drive so that, in time, it becomes habitual.

Obstacles to achievement

Many people who are willing and able to work are kept from achieving what they are capable of by obstacles over which they have no control. For the most part, these obstacles are *environmental*—primarily unfavorable social attitudes based on sex, race, religion, or age. Women, for example, rarely achieve the success they are capable of in areas outside of homemaking. Prejudice against women exists in many occupations and in executive positions in the occupations in which they have been accepted.

Work dissatisfaction which contributes to poor achievement can come from other environmental factors than discrimination and unfavorable social attitudes. Studies show that workers' dissatisfaction comes mostly from factors peripheral to the job, such as work rules, seniority rights, wages, and fringe benefits (162, 230).

Academic achievement is often adversely affected by lack of social acceptance. Those who are well accepted perform better than those who are neglected and much better than those who are actually rejected. Poor academic work is common among those who are resentful because they do not receive the social acceptance they crave (160). Although some students try to compensate for lack of social acceptance by high academic achievement, this is a far less common source of motivation than is social acceptance.

Successful achievement is likewise hampered by *subjective* or personal factors. Theoretically, these are more easily controlled by the person than the objective or environmental factors discussed above. In practice, however, they are so often the result of pressures from significant people—pressures to aspire unrealistically high—that the person is unable to control them. In addition, anxiety stemming from trying to achieve in unfamiliar situations or in situations which are associated with failure in the past militates against good performance even when the person is strongly motivated to achieve.

Poor achievement may come from the person's unfavorable attitude toward self, from poor health, from lack of motivation, and from many other subjective factors. Many people, for example, accept the belief that, with age, they will reach a plateau in their achievements from which they will inevitably go to lower levels as advancing age makes them less and less capable. This attitude deprives them of the motivation to work up to their capacities.

In conclusion, many factors, both objective and subjective, obstruct achievement. When the person knows or suspects that he is capable of achieving more than he actually has, he feels guilty, ashamed, and embarrassed if he believes that the fault lies within himself. If he believes that his lack of success stems from obstacles put in his path by members of the social group, he feels resentful and martyred. In either case, his personality will be damaged.

MEANING OF SUCCESS AND FAILURE

A person's attitudes toward his achievements and the degree of satisfaction he derives from them have a more far-reaching effect on his self-concept than the achievements themselves. If he is pleased with his achievements, he will think of himself as a success and this will bring him satisfaction and happiness. But if his attitudes toward his achievements are so negative that he thinks of himself as a failure, he will be dissatisfied and miserable.

Success and failure can be judged objectively or subjectively, depending on the frame of reference. To others, a person may be a success even though, to himself, he is a failure. He may have achieved more than any of his family or friends, he may have done better than anyone ever dreamed that he would, but he still may not be satisfied.

Subjective failure, or the individual's belief that he is a failure because he has not measured up to his own hopes and expectations, has a more damaging effect on the self-concept than *objective failure,* or failure so judged by others. Objective failure is especially damaging when the judgment is made by persons who are significant to the individual.

Similarly, *subjective success* is more ego-inflating than *objective success* though both contribute to a favorable self-concept and a sense of personal satisfaction. If a person believes that he is a success, even though the judgments of others do not corroborate his judgment, he can be happy and satisfied so long as he is ignorant of or disregards objective judgments. If he is sensitive to the judgments of the group members, however, he will be dissatisfied and will try, through rationalization, projection, or some other defense mechanism, to convince himself that his judgment is more accurate than theirs.

Success

Success comes in two varieties: satisfied and dissatisfied. Some people are satisfied with their successes but many are not. If they reach their goals, dissatisfied people believe that they have set their goals too low or have chosen the wrong goals. Even when they achieve status in the group because of their successes, they are still dissatisfied.

Satisfaction from success How much satisfaction a person derives from successful achievement depends not on the success alone. It depends also on his attitude toward the activity in which he has been successful. His attitude is largely determined by the values he associates with the activity, the prestige of the activity, the way in which significant people regard his success, the monetary rewards, and his own aspirations.

VALUES The values associated with different activities depend on what the group considers important. From earliest childhood, a person learns what the culturally approved values are and accepts them as his own. As a result, successful achievement in highly valued activities brings greater social recognition and approval as well as greater personal satisfaction than equal achievement in less valued activities.

Because of the high value placed on being married, the unmarried person is often judged to be a social failure. This is less true of men than of women, but unmarried men rarely escape unfavorable social judgments of some kind. Even when an unmarried woman makes a success of her chosen career, she is looked upon by others, women as well as men, as a failure if she does not have an ever-ready partner for social activities. These unfavorable attitudes have an adverse effect on self-judgments.

For both men and women, but especially for women for whom child rearing is a primary responsibility, success is judged by how well their children succeed. That is why parental aspirations for children are so high and why parental pressures on children to live up to expectations are so strong. A child who achieves more than his age-mates, scholastically, athletically, or socially, is regarded as a success and his parents, in turn, are regarded as "good parents." And because of the high value placed on parenthood, especially for women, it is inevitable that the child's achievement affects the parent's self-concept.

PRESTIGE OF ACTIVITY The more successful a person is in an activity with high prestige, the more favorable the reaction of the group, the greater his satisfaction, and the more positive the effect on his self-concept.

In a social group where political participation is a source of prestige, the officeholder who climbs high on the political ladder derives great satisfaction from his success. Holding an office is more prestigious for a middle-class man or woman than for one from the lower-class group and, as a result, gives the middle-class person more satisfaction.

ATTITUDES OF SIGNIFICANT PEOPLE The young child who lacks the critical ability to assess his achievements accurately accepts the attitudes of parents, teachers, siblings, and peers. If these significant people think he has been successful, he does also.

Personal dissatisfaction with achievements in schoolwork, sports, social activities, and other tasks is often tempered for both children and adolescents by favorable attitudes toward these achievements on the part of those whose opinions they value. The reverse is also true, and it applies to adults as well, but to a lesser extent. Men have been reported to be dissatisfied with the progress they make in their jobs when they feel that their wives and children are dissatisfied. This is at the basis of much job dissatisfaction and of much of the labor turnover (71, 165, 220).

MONETARY REWARDS In a culture which places high value on money and the status symbols money can buy, the monetary rewards for achievement have a prime influence on how much satisfaction the person derives from his achievements. Many people from earliest childhood become accustomed to receiving some reward for their achievements—a piece of candy, a new toy, or some special treat. By adolescence, part of their satisfaction from successfully completing high school or gaining admission to a prestigious college is a car or a trip to Europe.

One of the reasons women derive less satisfaction than men from successful achievement in business, industry, and the professions is that their earnings are lower than men's even when their duties and resonsibilities are similar. It is most unusual for married career women to earn as much as their husbands, though with the added burden of homemaking, they work harder and work longer hours. Their achievements are relatively unrewarded as compared with their husbands'. Figure 10-3 shows the average personal incomes for men and women in the same occupational groups. Note that in each occupational group women have lower monetary rewards than men.

Similarly, one of the reasons elderly people develop a "failure complex" is that their social security benefits or their earnings, if they are fortunate enough to have a job, are comparatively low. When they compare their income from these sources with their earnings at the peak of their careers, the late forties and early fifties, it is not surprising that they regard themselves as failures.

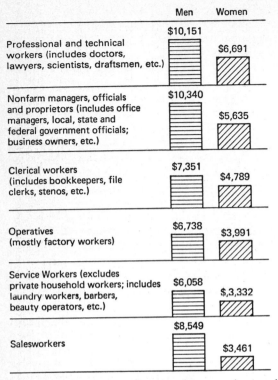

	Men	Women
Professional and technical workers (includes doctors, lawyers, scientists, draftsmen, etc.)	$10,151	$6,691
Nonfarm managers, officials and proprietors (includes office managers, local, state and federal government officials; business owners, etc.)	$10,340	$5,635
Clerical workers (includes bookkeepers, file clerks, stenos, etc.)	$7,351	$4,789
Operatives (mostly factory workers)	$6,738	$3,991
Service Workers (excludes private household workers; includes laundry workers, barbers, beauty operators, etc.)	$6,058	$,3,332
Salesworkers	$8,549	$3,461

Figure 10-3 Average annual earnings for men and women in the same occupational groups. (Adapted from Report by the Women's Bureau, Washington, D.C., 1970.)

PERSONAL ASPIRATIONS The dominant factor in determining the person's satisfaction with his achievements is the discrepancy between what he has achieved and what he had hoped to achieve. In discussing a group of students, Allport emphasized that a common cause of inferiority complexes was the gap between aspiration and achievement (3):

Feelings of inferiority cannot be taken as an index of actual inferiority. One notices, for example, that over one-half of the students have at one time or another suffered a sense of intellectual inferiority, an absurd situation from the factual or objective point of view. Over half the group cannot be below the average in intelligence; statistically, they cannot be inferior. . . . Inferiority feelings obviously are not based on factual inferiority but are subjective phenomena, engendered entirely by the ratio that obtains between success and aspiration.

Studies of unhappy marriages have shown that disillusionment, which is generally at the basis of dissatisfaction, usually comes when the transition is made from engagement to marriage. This is because romanticism causes young people to have unrealistic aspirations for "living happily ever after," as happens in the fairy tales of childhood (107, 214).

Because much of the discrepancy between aspiration and achievement comes from unrealistic approaches to life situations, the romantic idealist is more likely to experience disappointments and disillusionments with self and with others than the hard-headed pragmatist. Johnson has concluded that maladjustment follows a three-step sequence: from idealism to frustration to demoralization (124).

Dissatisfaction with success On the whole, people tend to be dissatisfied with their achievements. Dissatisfaction leads to a number of characteristic patterns of behavior, most of which have detrimental effects on the self-concept. *Directly,* dissatisfactions make the person think of himself as inadequate and inferior; *indirectly,* they affect him adversely by creating an unfavorable impression of him in the minds of others.

Some people who are dissatisfied with their achievements have a *compulsion to work harder.* In skilled performances, this usually leads to an increase in quantity of work but an impairment in quality and a greater variability of performance. A compulsion to work harder may lead to a *busy complex,* a tendency to feel rushed and pushed all the time. This is almost always accompanied by a feeling of guilt if the person takes time off to do anything not directly related to the activity in which his goals are so high. The student who is dissatisfied with his grades, like the businessman who is dissatisfied with his status on the business ladder, is constantly under pressure to do more and better work.

In time, such straining to advance leads to stress which may result in a physical or mental breakdown or in psychosomatic and psychological disorders. It often does not bring the satisfaction the person craves. Jersild writes, "The person who has a compulsion to compete because of lack of assurance of his worth often discovers that even when he has won a triumph he still has to go on competing because he has proved nothing to himself" (121).

It is very common for a person who is dissatisfied with his achievements to *blame* others or to become *hypercritical* of them. A wife may criticize and nag her husband when he does not achieve the success she had hoped for. Or parents may be disappointed and critical of their children when they fail to come up to parental expectations.

Dissatisfaction with one's own achievements is often expressed in *defense mechanisms.* The person may state aspirations below his abilities in the hope of winning attention and approval from others when his achievements surpass the stated aspirations. He may blame his failure on someone else, thus freeing himself of a feeling of guilt. If he blames himself, he further intensifies his dissatisfaction.

Dissatisfaction is most often expressed in *escape mechanisms.* Daydreaming, alcoholism, overeating, or the use of drugs—all serve to lessen the anxiety and self-reproach the person experiences when his achievements fall short of his aspirations. Juvenile delinquency and adult criminality may be a cloak for self-dissatisfaction which is expressed in an attempt to "show others" or to gain attention and notoriety—to become famous for misdeeds rather than good deeds.

When a person is dissatisfied with his life and what he has done with it, he may seek immediate gratifications to compensate for a long-range fulfillment which he believes he will never experience. This leads to different forms of *pleasure seeking,* such as "wine, women, and song." If the dissatisfaction is so great that no escape mechanism can be found, he may attempt *suicide.* Refer to Chapter 9 for a more complete discussion of this matter.

Effects of success on personality

The person who feels that he has been successful is proud of his achievements, satisfied with himself, and reasonably happy. This goes a long way toward building a favorable self-concept. It also raises self-esteem and builds self-confidence so that he attacks new problems with the belief that he can handle them successfully.

Tasks in which the person achieves success are more satisfying, more attractive, and more challenging than those in which he encounters failure or disappointment. He is motivated to repeat the former and avoid the latter. Since people like to do things in which they are successful or in which they anticipate success, they are more interested in such activities and more willing to put effort into them. Some people derive their greatest satisfaction from working hard to do a job well, while others get their greatest satisfaction from emulating a successful model (54, 77).

In addition to the personal satisfaction the person derives from success, his achievements tell him that his behavior is appropriate and that, therefore, there is no need to change. This acts as a stabilizing influence on behavior. Consequently, the successful person tends to be more relaxed than the one who experiences failure. This absence of stress makes it possible for him to enjoy his success.

One of the most valuable effects of success is that it encourages the person to be more realistic about his goal setting. Success shows him what he can do and suggests the limitations of his capacities. Because of the satisfaction he derives from success, he learns to "play it safe" in that he assesses new tasks in terms of his capacities before he sets his aspirations and thus limits his goals to those he has a reasonable chance of reaching. This behavior is more characteristic of intelligent, well-adjusted people than of those who are less able and poorly adjusted.

Studies reveal that many adolescents change their career goals in college when they realize that obstacles arising from personal, social, or economic limitations are likely to prevent them from attaining the lofty goals they set earlier (74, 146). Note in Figure 10-4 that these changes are much more common among those of lower socioeconomic status.

Figure 10-4 Changes in career goals during the college years of students with low-class background as compared with a representative sample of students. (Adapted from R. A. Ellis and W. C. Lane: Social mobility and career orientation. *Sociol. soc. Res.*, 1966, **50**, 280–296. Used by permission.)

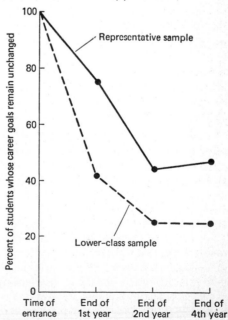

Indirectly, success enhances the self-concept by increasing the person's prestige in the eyes of others and adding to his social acceptance. That is why most successful people like to have their achievements known to others. The child or adolescent who is successful in schoolwork, in athletics, in dramatics, or in his social relationships wins the admiration and respect of others. The more prestige associated with the activity and the more people who know about his successes, the greater the admiration and respect of the group.

This is true also of adults. The man who makes a success in business, industry, or a profession or the woman who is successful in social and community affairs is looked up to and admired. Furthermore, success at any age puts the person in line for a leadership role. Each new success adds to the person's prestige and this, in turn, improves his self-concept.

Too much success early in life may weaken the person's motivation to do his best. It may cause him to lose some of the strong drive to achieve that occasional success engenders. After reaching a leadership role in their chosen occupation, many young adults "let down" in the sense that they lose their motivation to go beyond their present level of success.

Extraordinary success may prove to be more detrimental than helpful to social relationships, arousing jealousy and resentment among those who are less successful. As Child and Bacon (45) point out:

The outstandingly successful achiever may earn the hostility of his less successful contemporaries. The taunting cry of "mother's boy," "teacher's pet," or the like, is on occasion a reflection of the fact that one person's achievement is not necessarily pleasing to everybody, and that the immediate social environment provides some realistic motivation which is in conflict with the desire for outstanding achievement.

When a person surpasses his associates, he is sometimes judged in terms of the "robber baron" stereotype which associates dishonesty with success. Many people wonder whether the successful businessman has made his money honestly, and sometimes teachers and classmates wonder whether the superior student has cheated or had parental help.

Knowing that this suspicious attitude prevails makes the successful person uneasy. It may also lead to some of the undesirable personality characteristics that minority-group members develop when they know that social attitudes toward them are unfavorable. In addition, the person who is very successful is made to feel guilty because he has risen above the rest of the group. This detracts from the prestige he would otherwise get from his achievements and thus lowers his satisfaction. Child and Bacon (45) write:

Tradition of political equality and of humility can be so stated, and are on occasion so stated, that they would tend not only to interfere with the achievement strivings which are encouraged by other aspects of our culture but even to make a person feel positively guilty if he had been outstandingly successful in such strivings.

Failure

When a person fails to achieve what is expected of him, what he expects of himself, or what he is capable of achieving, his status and prestige in the eyes of the group fall and his attitude toward self deteriorates. His unfavorable self-attitude is reinforced by unfavorable group attitudes. Furthermore, when self-esteem is lowered by failure in areas which the person and the group consider important, the self-concept is damaged.

Whether failure is objective or subjective, it may be acknowledged or grandiose. In *acknowledged* failure, the person recognizes that his abilities and the conditions confronting him will never permit him to achieve the goals he has set or which the group expects him to reach. In *grandiose* failure, on the other hand, the person does not want to admit his limitations. He believes that someone or something outside himself has blocked his achievement and he becomes embittered because of his paranoid beliefs (197). Figure 10-5 illustrates different kinds of failure.

Causes of failure A number of interrelated causes contribute to failure. One which contributes a large share is *lack of ability*—mental, physical, or both. Many young people lack the intellectual capacity to do the work expected of them in school, and many adults lack the ability to come up to expectations in their work.

Even those who have the ability to succeed may fail because of *lack of training* or inferior training. Many a potential champion in sports, for example, loses out to those who have less ability but superior training. Educational deficiencies resulting in a lack of basic skills often make it difficult for older workers to adjust to technological changes and take on new jobs.

Subjective   Objective   Acknowledged   Grandiose

Figure 10-5 Failure can be of different kinds.

More failures come from *lack of motivation* than from lack of ability or training. A student who does not see the value of a school subject to his present or future life is likely to have so little interest in it that he is not motivated to study. Similarly, the "round peg in the square hole" in the business world has little interest in his work and little motivation to succeed in his job.

Even with strong motivation, a person may fail in what he undertakes because of *unrealistic aspirations* which force him to tackle tasks for which he has neither ability nor training. The person who "reaches for the moon" is doomed to failure, regardless of his desire to succeed.

A person whose aspirations are realistic may meet failure if his path is *blocked* by prejudice because of his sex, religion, racial origin, or some other condition over which he has no control. Teen-age and old workers, except when business is booming, find jobs difficult to get. Unemployment or employment below one's capacities is regarded as failure not only by the worker but also by the social group. This is destructive of the person's self-esteem and, in turn, of his self-concept. How detrimental unemployment can be to the self-concept has been stressed by the *Report of the President's Council on Aging* (178):

For workers in their middle years, unemployment can be tragic. Family responsibilities are likely to be at their height and the need to accumulate social security credits for adequate benefits upon retirement and to build up savings for old age are most urgent. Unemployment during these years undermines not only the worker's morale but the security of his dependents as well.

Dissatisfaction from failure The effect of failure on the self-concept depends on how the person reacts to it. People react differently and even the same person reacts differently from one situation to another. Failure is never a happy experience for anyone.

A person who *expects* to fail, who sets out with the belief that he cannot hope to succeed, will be far less damaged psychologically than the person to whom failure comes as a surprise. High school seniors who expect to be in glamorous jobs by the time they reach middle age have negative self-evaluations when they find themselves in occupations far below their aspirations (138). People who enter marriage with romantic ideas about it are often disenchanted and bitter when their marriages do not come up to their hopes and expectations (111, 173).

If a person feels that he made a *wrong choice of goals,* as in occupational or marital choice, his attitude toward his failure will be intensified. This is especially true as he grows older and realizes that changing goals is difficult if not impossible.

People who have learned *failure tolerance* so that they can accept an occasional failure as a step-ping-stone to ultimate success, or who have experienced so many failures that they are immune to them, developing an "I don't care" attitude, are far less disturbed by a failure than those who have always experienced success. A person who has gone through many periods of unemployment, for example, will be far less disturbed by being laid off a job than the person who has never been unemployed (43, 178).

Failure in activities that have high *value* for the person, either because they have prestige in the social group or add to the person's self-esteem, will be more distressing than failure in activities that have less value to him. For men, failure in business is more ego-deflating than failure in marriage. For women, the opposite is true, because they value success in marriage more highly than business success. Having a child who is physically or mentally defective is interpreted by many women as failure in parenthood (223).

Social expectancy of success makes failure a bitter pill. Since women are expected to be better parents than men, having children who fall below social norms is more distressing and embarrassing to mothers than fathers. In general, the effect of group expectancy is greater in the case of failure than in the case of success. The more a person admires the members of a group and the more anxious he is to live up to group expectations, the more damaging failure is to his self-esteem (207).

When failure is *known to the group,* the damage to the person's self-concept is far more severe than when the failure is known only to the person himself or to a small group of relatives and intimate friends. A defective child in an institution, for example, has far less impact on parental self-esteem than a defective child in the home.

A person's *self-esteem,* which is greatly influenced by the attitudes of other people, affects his reactions to failure. People with low self-esteem are extremely vulnerable to the effects of failure and tend to withdraw from situations where failure is likely to occur.

A person with high *achievement motivation,* as shown in a strong need to gain status in the eyes of others through achievements, will be anxious about possible failure and will be emotionally disturbed if he fails to come up to the standard he or the significant people in his life have set for him. A person with low achievement motivation, by contrast, will be less anxious and less likely to be upset by failure.

Reactions to failure   How a person will react to failure is more difficult to predict than how he will react to success. Reactions are greatly influenced

by whether the failure is acknowledged or grandiose, as described above (82).

EMOTIONAL ACCOMPANIMENT OF REACTIONS Since failure always involves an element of frustration in that a goal has not been achieved, the reaction has an emotional accompaniment. The person who acknowledges that he has failed because he aspired too high for his abilities usually becomes angry at himself. Or if he believes that he had the ability to succeed but was hindered by obstacles placed in his way by others, he will be angry at those he blames for obstructing him.

Children confronted with failure often make exaggerated emotional responses, such as crying, sulking, pouting, whining, or being destructive. Along with these emotional reactions go immature behavior —retreat from the task, demands for help, or rationalization. If failures are persistent, behavior becomes disturbed and disorganized. If, on the other hand, the failures are balanced by successes, behavior is more rational.

Many children are ashamed of their failures and suffer from feelings of guilt, especially when they know their parents and teachers expected them to succeed. Since these emotional reactions are strongest and most upsetting when others know about the failures, children are often motivated to conceal their shortcomings from others.

Emotional reactions to failure usually change in form as people grow older, but the impact on behavior and on the self-concept tends to increase as they become aware of the responses of others. In discussing the adolescent's emotional reactions to failure, Jersild (121) writes:

Shame of a wrath-producing sort is especially likely to occur if the adolescent again and again is thrust into situations where he fails. Some adolescents face such conditions day after day, at home and at school. Failure has a bitter taste. It has been called a kind of psychic poison. Failure is no less bitter to an adolescent just because, as seen by someone else, it was his own fault that he failed. Indeed, failure that the youngster blames in whole or in part upon himself is probably often the most bitter of all. Moreover, failure does not lose its sting just because it is repeated again and again. There are large numbers of adolescents who at school or at home are repeatedly reminded that they have failed to live up to what is expected of them. When we consider how frequently, in the lives of many adolescents, the experience of failure is repeated, without any good coming from it, it is easier to understand why it is that some young people lash out in acts of vandalism and other forms of violence or go about sullenly as though consumed with hate.

In time, repeated failures may lead to a deadening of the emotional reactions experienced earlier. In their place will be a sense of futility, a defeatist attitude. This protects the person from making further efforts to achieve his goal which, as before, may merely lead to another failure. Drinking and drugs are aids to the deadening of the emotional reactions to failure.

A person's emotional reactions to failure color his attitudes toward the activity in which the failure occurred. The activity becomes distasteful; the person dreads it and tries to avoid it in the future. Dislike for school and for certain subjects is closely related to the number, frequency, and severity of the failures the student experiences. Occasional failures may stimulate the student to work harder but they seldom make him like the subject any better. Repeated failures in a number of subjects almost always lead to a dislike for school and everything connected with it. This dislike often leads to truancy or dropout as soon as the compulsory age limit has been reached. This matter will be discussed in more detail in Chapter 12, Educational Determinants.

COMMON FORMS OF REACTION It is difficult to predict how a person will react to failure, but certain reactions are quite common. In one way or another, each of these common reactions eliminates some of the unfavorable effects that failure normally has on self-esteem.

When confronted by failure, some react with *self-negation,* or decreased self-evaluation. This may be verbalized in such a statement as, "This shows I might not be so good." Others react with *self-affirmation,* without any change in their self-evaluation. They say, in effect, "This is too difficult for anyone to do." As a general rule, people high in anxiety react more aggressively to the possibility of failure than those who are less anxious (117).

Because failure, even when mild and known only to the person himself, is a blow to self-esteem, many people use *escape mechanisms* to avoid situations that might lead to failure. Some people learn, from past failures, not to set a goal when they are unsure of success. Others learn that the best way to

avoid failure is not to strive for success in situations where the chances of failure are great. As Child and Bacon stated, "In some people the avoidance of failure is highly generalized, so that a dominant motive may be that of protecting oneself against failure at the cost of withdrawing from a great variety of activities in which failure is a possible outcome" (45).

Escape from situations involving failure or the threat of failure often seems cowardly to the person. This lowers the self-esteem he is trying to bolster by avoiding failure. Therefore, the person who uses escape mechanisms usually develops a *defensive attitude,* rationalizing his reasons for doing so or projecting the blame on others. Many people who are unemployed become defensive and thrust the blame for their unemployment on an "unfair employer."

If all failures become grandiose, if the person comes to believe that they are the result of blockings by others, he may develop a hostile, antagonistic attitude toward people in general. If he becomes embittered by these paranoid beliefs, he will develop a *martyr complex.* Public failure, which is even more damaging to self-esteem than private failure, tends to increase the use of defense mechanisms and lead to the development of a martyr complex (14, 197).

Failure may serve as a source of *motivation.* In some, it may be just what is needed to jolt them out of the state of complacency that was responsible for their failure in the first place. In others, it will have just the opposite effect, reinforcing their belief that they cannot succeed no matter how hard they try and thus weakening motivation.

Most people react to failure by *changing their goals.* Some set new goals very cautiously, even below what they have previously accomplished, thus showing that they lack confidence in their ability to succeed in the future. Some give up entirely, or would give up were it not for pressures put on them by others to try again. Still others retain the same optimistically high goals in the belief that present failures are not true indications of their capacities or that these failures resulted from obstacles that in the long run can be overcome.

Refer to Figure 10-4 for a graphic illustration of how students change their career goals during their college years. Note that the lower-class students who had the same career goals on entering college as other students tend to change their goals when they realize that their chances of success are less than they originally believed.

The well-adjusted person is usually willing to

lower his estimates of his ability when he realizes that he has aspired too high. This he does without feeling frustrated, angry, or inferior. In addition, he does not use compensations to explain his failures. The less well-adjusted person, who is more sensitive to failure, also generally changes his goals when he experiences repeated failure. But instead of accepting the fact that he was aspiring too high, he becomes unsure of himself and of his abilities and may raise his goals unrealistically high or set them unrealistically low.

Frequently, the poorly adjusted person convinces himself and tries to convince others that his failures were not his fault but resulted from his being blocked by others. Under such conditions, he is more likely to raise than to lower his aspirations after failure.

Effects of failure on personality

Failure is always ego-deflating. No one likes to fail, even though he may have anticipated it. Failure undermines self-esteem and self-confidence and, in time, destroys the person's belief that he can do anything at all well. This weakens his motivation to attempt even what he is capable of doing.

While failure is always damaging to the self-concept, the severity and extent of the damage will be greatly influenced by many conditions, including the following:

The degree of dissatisfaction the person experiences and how he habitually reacts to failure

How important the activity in which he failed is to the person

Whether or not significant people in his life and those whose esteem he values expect him to succeed

Whether his failure is known to others or only to himself

Whether he realizes how far below his potential his achievement has been

Whether he blames himself or someone else for his failure

Regardless of these variations, the person who thinks of himself as a failure is unhappy, self-rejectant, embarrassed, and ashamed because he believes that others look down on him. He also feels guilty because he feels that he has not lived up to the expectations of the significant people in his life.

Severe and frequent failure causes stress and anxiety. These emotional states make it difficult for the person to do the best he is capable of either in work or in social relationships. Repeated failure causes stress and anxiety so intense and so persistent that it may lead to psychosomatic illness or to a defeatist attitude which is reflected in a sense of futility. It strengthens the person's belief in his inadequacy and intensifies his poor personal and social adjustments.

Allport has explained the severe damage to personality of repeated failure as contrasted with occasional failure which the person can usually cope with to his immediate satisfaction (3):

If a straightforward adjustment is possible, the problem is met and solved, at least temporarily. And if a direct solution is unsuccessful and variations in the method of attack do not succeed, the failure is sometimes minimized, repressed, or rationalized out of the way. Often, however, when failures are recurrent and serious they cannot be so easily disposed of. A tension not relaxed by fulfillment is present in a latent state and always ready to cause trouble whenever the desire for the unattainable goal returns. As a result a deepseated sense of deficiency may develop and be steadily aggravated. . . . As failures multiply, the source of difficulty becomes the focus of attention and concern. The sufferer feels habitual uncertainty or fear in the face of those situations that threaten to reveal to himself and others his own weakness and ineffectuality. This condition is the famous inferiority complex. . . . Few people need to have explained to them the discomfort caused by feelings of inferiority.

Even though the well-adjusted person may realize that his level of aspiration is too high and be willing to lower it, replacing unrealistic aspirations with more realistic ones requires an emotional adjustment. As Jersild (121) has explained:

The emotional experience connected with this process of revising hopes and facing up to personal limitations has not been studied systematically. There are, however, findings suggesting that many persons are still not reconciled, as adults, to decisions they made during late adolescence or to makeshift adaptations they made then to the realities of life. . . . For example, many adults say they would choose a different occupation from the one they did choose if they had a chance to live youth over again. And divorce statistics indicate that many persons are not reconciled, at least the first time, to the fact that the mate they chose during late adolescence or early youth turned out to be a little less perfect than the creature they had pictured in their dreams.

Only when a person is willing to change his goals or when he finds means of reaching the goals he has set for himself so that he can experience success instead of failure can he hope to eliminate the psychological damage that failure always brings.

Value of failure   Even though failures undermine self-confidence and play havoc with self-esteem, they can and should be valuable learning experiences. From failure, the person should become more realistic about his assets and the boundaries of his abilities. He should learn what he is capable of doing successfully and what is beyond his capacities.

Many people, unfortunately, do not react to failure in this way. They are deprived of the valuable learning experience that failure can provide because their attitudes toward themselves are unrealistic. They believe that they have more ability than they actually have and they look for a scapegoat to blame for their failures.

Much of the value a person should derive from failure is counteracted by the unfavorable attitudes of significant people toward the failure. If he has tried hard to succeed but still has not lived up to the group's expectations, he feels guilty and ashamed. If he believes that the failure occurred through no fault of his but because of some barrier placed in his way, his unfavorable self-attitudes are coupled with the belief that he is being martyred. In time, he is likely to develop a "failure complex"—the expectation of failure in whatever he attempts and resentment toward any and all who he believes are responsible for blocking him.

While occasional failures, if approached realistically, can be valuable learning experiences, *repeated failures* are always detrimental, especially when they come close together without an occasional success in between. Each failure lowers the person's self-esteem and usually weakens his motivation to try again and again until success is finally achieved. The more convinced the person is that he is incapable of success in anything he undertakes, the less motivation he will have to try to succeed.

It must be recognized that no one can escape failure. An occasional failure is inevitable. For that reason, everyone should develop *failure tolerance,* or the ability to withstand the effects of failure and to profit by it. If the person has had enough experience with success to have a reasonable amount of self-confidence and if he has learned to assess his capacities realistically, then he will be able to tolerate occasional failures without having them damage his self-concept.

When, on the other hand, the person sets unrealistic aspirations, when he is constantly subjected to unrealistic expectations on the part of others, or when he cannot escape from an environment that is too difficult for him to cope with successfully, he will have little opportunity to develop failure tolerance.

Perhaps at no time is failure tolerance more valuable than during the early vocational period. The worker who feels that he is a failure because he does not earn as much or receive as rapid promotion as some of his age-mates often develops an unfavorable attitude toward his abilities. This seriously damages his chances for future success. The young college graduate or the young professional who does not realize, for example, that skilled high school graduates may make more money in their twenties and early thirties than he may become so discouraged that it interferes with his potentials for future success. If he can tolerate the "lean years" when, in comparison with his less-educated contemporaries he seems to be a failure, he will normally eventually outstrip them in earning power and prestige.

AGE OF ACHIEVEMENT

Most people set dates for achieving things that are important to them at that time. The preschooler sets a time for being able to ride a bicycle, for crossing the streets alone, or for being able to swim. The adult sets a time when he expects to be the foreman or manager in his work or have a specified sum of money saved.

Children and, to a lesser extent, young adolescents, think that, once they are grown up, they will have many years to achieve their important goals. As they approach adulthood, however, they become increasingly aware that the years for achievement are shorter than they originally thought. They come to realize that social attitudes toward those who show physical signs of aging are unfavorable and that they must achieve their goals before the social group places obstacles in their way.

They discover further that the social group regards the years between 20 and 40 as the critical age for achievement and that, if they have not made a reasonable success of their lives by the time they reach 40, the chances of being able to do so later grow slimmer with each passing year. They therefore set a deadline for their achievements and judge themselves as successes or failures in terms of what they have achieved when they reach this deadline.

Just when a person will reach the peak of achievement—in both quality and quantity—will depend on how hard he is willing to work to gain his goal, how willing he is to make the necessary sacrifices in time, effort, and personal pleasures to ensure success, and, most critical of all, the area in which he is striving to succeed. Unless he takes these factors into account, he is almost certain to fall short of his expectations and be dissatisfied with his achievements.

The age at which peak achievement is normally reached varies from one area to another. Peak achievement comes earlier in sports, for example, than in engineering or the sciences. Artists, likewise, "hit their stride" earlier than scientists or people in the business or professional worlds (66, 140, 141, 142). In every area, women tend to reach their peak achievement earlier than men—not because they are more precocious but rather because social barriers make it impossible for them to achieve as great success as men of comparable ability (140, 160).

Personal satisfaction from achievement

A person may be satisfied with his achievements before they are recognized by the social group. This is because he reaches his goal when, or perhaps before, he expected to reach it. If he receives the promotion he had hoped for earlier than he had anticipated, his "promotion satisfaction" will be greater than his "job satisfaction" and will affect his self-concept favorably.

In business, industry, and the professions, most workers experience the greatest satisfaction with their work and with their work achievements in the late forties and early fifties. During the sixties, they experience a sharp drop in vocational satisfaction because they realize that they have passed the peak achievement mark (156 , 188).

Satisfaction from achieving goals in areas other than work is likewise great. The woman whose children have lived up to her expectations feels that she is a success in her role of parent just as the woman who is chosen for numerous community committees feels that she is a success in her role as clubwoman. If these goals are reached at the age when the woman aspired to them, the satisfaction from achievement will be intensified.

Since middle age is traditionally the time when peak achievement occurs, those who enter middle age with a history of past failures or mediocre successes are likely to experience considerable trauma and stress and to think of themselves as failures. When they can look back on former achievements with satisfaction and pride, they regard themselves as successes.

Social recognition of achievement

Group recognition of achievement, which adds greatly to the satisfaction derived from achievement, comes later than personal satisfaction. It may come in the form of increased earnings, social awards, or leadership roles in the areas where achievement has been outstanding. Employers recognize peak achievement from the mid-forties to the mid-fifties by increasing the employees' wages at this period. The *earnings* of both men and women reach their peak at the age when, according to tradition, men and women reach their peak of achievement.

Social awards take many forms. The slang label "Wonder Boy," the designation "Father of the Year," or "Cake Baker of the Year," the award of an Oscar for outstanding performance in a movie—all are social awards. Studies of Nobel Laureates who have great prestige in their own fields as well as among the lay public reveal that social recognition comes later than the satisfaction the winners themselves had from their early achievements. As a group, they publish earlier, longer, and at a greater rate than persons who do not win this public recognition. However, after receiving the laureates, their production generally falls off, not because they are resting on their laurels but because the social demands made on them are often excessive (240).

Leadership roles, as a sign of social recognition for achievement, generally come later than personal satisfaction from achievement. The social group assigns such roles only after people have demonstrated their ability to lead and have gained prestige by doing work that is superior to that of their age-mates (140).

Lehman (140) has given the following explanation of why it is that social recognition of achievement through the assignment of leadership roles comes later than personal satisfaction and other kinds of social recognition:

The condition for creativity and originality, which can be displayed in private achievement, comes earlier than those social skills which contribute to leadership and eminence and which inevitably must wait, not upon the insight of the leader himself, but upon the insight of society about him. This may be a part of the reason why leaders of all kinds (most of whom are not highly original thinkers or artists) are usually not permitted to lead until they are over 50. It is worth noting also that today's leaders are older, on the average, than in previous epochs.

Effects of age of achievement on personality

One of the most damaging aspects of failure is not achieving success and social recognition when the person hoped and expected to do so. The dissatisfaction the person experiences is intensified by the realization that others with whom he has competed may have achieved success and social recognition earlier than he.

Many people have unrealistic aspirations about when they will reach goals which they are perfectly capable of reaching—but at a somewhat later time. The athlete who hopes to win an Olympics gold medal when he is 16 might more realistically set his goal for the age of 19. So long as the person realizes that reaching the goal he has set will take time and effort and that social recognition of his achievement is usually later than the achievement itself, he will not think of himself as a failure. Many people, however, are unrealistic about the time, effort, and planning needed to win success and recognition, and that is why even successful achievement coming later than the person hoped can be damaging to the self-concept.

By contrast, one of the greatest sources of satisfaction is achieving success and social recognition earlier than anticipated and earlier than one's competitors. Under such conditions, the effect on the self-concept is favorable. It may be so favorable as to lead to delusions of grandeur and a superiority complex—a situation that will, in time, counteract favorable social judgments, prove damaging to the self-concept, and put the person in a position where he will try to justify his delusions.

SUMMARY

1 At all ages people are judged by how their achievements compare with those of their peers. The person whose achievements in highly valued areas are superior in quantity and quality is favorably judged by the social group. However, whether favorable social judgments will lead to favorable self-evaluations will depend on whether the person's achievements come up to his own aspirations.

2 Aspirations are the ego-involved goals a person sets for himself. The more ego-involved his aspirations are and the more they relate to areas of behavior that are important to him, the greater will be their influence on his personality. Aspirations may be positive (to achieve success), negative (to avoid failure), immediate (to achieve a goal in the near future), remote (to achieve a goal in the remote future), realistic (within the person's capacity), or unrealistic (beyond the person's capacity).

3 What kind of aspirations the person develops is greatly influenced by such factors as intelligence, sex, personal interests and values, family pressures, group expectations, cultural traditions, competition with others, past experience, the mass media, and personal characteristics. Since the environment during the early, formative years of life is relatively stable, these factors reinforce the person's characteristic method of aspiring until it becomes habitual. The motivating power of aspirations varies, with remote and unrealistic aspirations tending to be stronger motivating forces than immediate and realistic aspirations. Negative aspirations are generally weaker in motivating strength than positive aspirations.

4 Level of aspiration—the discrepancy between the goal the person has already reached and the goal he hopes to reach—affects personality in terms of the size of the discrepancy. The discrepancy plays a more important role in determining what effect aspirations have on personality than do the aspirations themselves. Attempts to discover how people characteristically aspire to a desired goal have been made in laboratory studies (which must concentrate mainly on immediate aspirations) and in studies of wishes, ideals, and New Year's resolutions (which can indicate remote aspirations far more successfully than can laboratory approaches). Knowing the person's characteristic method of aspiring, one can tell whether the person is aspiring in ways that will lead to successful achievement, with its favorable effect on the self-concept, or to failure, with its damaging effect on the self-concept.

5 Achievements can be judged objectively, by comparing the person's achievements with those of his peers, or subjectively, by comparing the person's achievements with his level of aspiration. This means that he can be objectively a success and subjectively a failure or vice versa.

6 Many factors are responsible for achievement. These include training, experience, past achievements, flexibility, independence, risk taking, and motivation. Of these factors, motivation is by far the most important. Obstacles to achievement may come from the environment, but more often they come from personal factors, such as unrealistic levels of aspiration.

7 A person may be satisfied with his achievements or dissatisfied with them, depending on whether or not they come up to his expectations. How satisfied he is depends also on the value he attaches to the activity in which he achieves success, the prestige the social group attaches to the activity, the attitudes of people who are significant in his life, the monetary or other rewards he receives, and most important of all, whether it comes up to his expectations.

8 Dissatisfaction with success because his achievements fall below expectations affects the person unfavorably. It encourages him to become a compulsive worker in the hope of achieving his goal, to develop a busy complex which leads to feelings of guilt when he takes time off for any activity unrelated to his goal, to blame others and use defense mechanisms to free himself from feelings that he is a failure, or to escape into a world of fantasy where he can achieve his goal without interference from any source. All these affect the self-concept unfavorably and overshadow the favorable social judgments others make of him if they regard his achievements as successes.

9 Failure is damaging to personality because of unfavorable social judgments and self-evaluations. How severely failure will damage the personality depends on whether the person is judged to be a failure by others or only by himself. The most damage comes when he is so judged both objectively and subjectively. Whether failure is subjective or objective, it may be acknowledged or it may be grandiose, the person projecting the blame for his failure on others. In grandiose failure, resentment and bitterness add to the negative feelings about self that accompany acknowledged failure.

10 Failure, like success, is due to many causes. These include lack of ability, lack of adequate training, lack of motivation, unrealistic aspirations, or realistic aspirations that are blocked by environmental obstacles. The degree of dissatisfaction the person experiences from his failures varies according to whether he expects to fail or to succeed, whether he believes he made a correct or wrong choice of goals, whether he has developed failure tolerance, whether the members of the social group expect him to succeed or fail, whether the group knows of his failure, and how high his achievement motivation is.

11 All failure has an emotional accompaniment which colors the person's reactions to his failure and to the situations in which the failure occurred as well as other related situations. While personal reactions to failure are difficult to predict, common reactions include self-negation, self-affirmation, the use of defense or escape mechanisms, motivation and expectations for future successes, and the changing of goals.

12 Even though failure is always ego-deflating and thus affects personality unfavorably, it is valuable as a learning experience provided it is not too frequent or too severe. Its value comes from encouraging the person to aspire more realistically, to acquire the skills needed for successful achievement, and to learn to tolerate failure.

13 At what time in his life the person achieves success or failure likewise influences his personality. If he achieves success when he hoped to do so, it will have a far more favorable effect than if it comes later.

Furthermore, how closely he conforms to the timetable for achievement established by the social group likewise influences his reactions to his achievements. Falling below his own expectations or the timetable of the social group becomes increasingly damaging to his self-concept with advancing age because he realizes that time to catch up is running out and that his chances of reaching his goal grow slimmer each year.

sex determinants

It has been common knowledge since the days of Adam and Eve that sex makes the world go round. However, no one before Freud had verbalized so frankly and completely the importance of sexuality in the person's life or had shown so convincingly the role sexuality plays in personality development. Thorpe and Schmuller remark, "It was Freud who broke out of the nineteenth-century jail that had concealed the part that sex experiences play in the etiology of the emotionally disturbed person" (208).

Since the turn of the century, numerous studies have shown that sexuality is equally important in the personality development of the normal person. They have also made clear the role of sexuality in areas of personality not fully examined or even mentioned by early researchers in this field.

The major emphasis of the post-Freudian studies has been to point out that what effect sex has on personality depends largely on the person's attitudes toward and interest in sex, on his attitudes toward his own sex and the sex role he is expected to play, on the way he regards sex differences, on how he is affected by sex antagonism, and on what his attitude toward his own sex behavior is. They have emphasized that sexuality per se does not appreciably affect personality. Instead, only when sexuality affects the person's self-concept does it become a major factor in shaping his personality.

EFFECTS OF SEXUALITY ON PERSONALITY

Sexuality affects personality both directly and indirectly. Present evidence indicates that the indirect influences are stronger and more pervasive than the direct. But as Scheinfeld has written, "The most important of all influences on behavior is a person's sex, *both directly and indirectly*" (183).

Direct effects

The direct effects of sexuality come from the sex hormones produced by the gonads, or sex glands. In the male, these are the testes; in the female, the ovaries. The gonads of both sexes produce both of the sex hormones, androgen and estrogen, but in different quantities. The male gonads produce more androgen—the male hormone; and the female gonads, more estrogen—the female hormone.

The sex hormones influence the growth rate of the individual, the body formation and functioning, and the quality of behavior. When the balance of estrogen and androgen is normal, the male becomes masculine in appearance and behavior while the female becomes feminine. When the balance is disturbed, the male becomes effeminate and the female, masculine. Boys who were castrated before puberty, for example, as was done in some of the European countries to preserve their soprano voices for the church choirs and in some of the Asiatic countries to prepare them to play the role of eunuch in the harems of the wealthy, became feminine in appearance and behavior. Girls whose ovaries are removed before puberty—because of some diseased condition, say—tend to look and act masculine.

Normally, from the moment of conception, males and females follow different patterns of development. The differences have a profound influence, both directly and indirectly, on personality. Even before birth, males have more difficulty in adjusting to their prenatal environment than females. This is shown by the larger percentage of miscarriages among male fetuses and by the fact that more male fetuses are damaged by the prenatal environment and develop physical or mental abnormalities that handicap their adjustment to postnatal life (143, 158, 183).

From birth until death, males and females take quite different developmental roads. Ordinarily, for example, males are bigger and physically stronger than females. There are marked differences in the exterior of the body and in its functioning after puberty. And the pattern of physical decline for members of the two sexes differs. While it is impossible to separate environmental influences from hereditary endowments completely, there is evidence that the male intellectual and temperamental capacities are innately different from those of the female, just as their body build and functioning are different (119, 146, 183).

Differences in behavior are due in part at least to hormonal differences: the sharpest differences in behavior as in appearance coincide with the time in life when the sex organs are functioning most actively and when the production of the hormone appropriate for the person's sex is greatest. In females, this time is from puberty to the menopause, or from about 13 years of age to about 45. In men, the period when the gonads are most active is from puberty to the climacteric, or from about 14 to 55 years of age.

Before puberty, sex differences in appearance are very slight and behavioral differences are generally the product of learning and social pressure. After the menopause, women become less feminine in appearance and behavior while men, after the climacteric, become less masculine.

That hormonal factors are directly responsible for the effects sexuality has on personality is likewise apparent in boys and girls who are deviant maturers and in men and women who reach the "change of life" earlier or later than their peers. Among early maturers, sex interests, sex behavior, and sex attitudes are more mature than among average or late maturers of the same age. The varying rate of the changes that accompany the gradual decrease in the sex hormones with advancing age is likewise responsible for causing men and women to behave in a way that proclaims them as "sexually old" sooner or later than their peers (34, 183, 195).

Indirect effects

The indirect effects of sexuality are in large measure responsible for the personality differences between the sexes which are found in all cultures.

While sexuality influences personality indirectly in many ways, three are outstanding. The *first* has to do with the effect of cultural influences on the sex drive; the *second* concerns the influences resulting from the attitudes of significant people toward the individual because of his sex and their treatment of him; and the *third* concerns the molding of the personality pattern to conform to a socially approved pattern.

Cultural influences   The hormonal level unquestionably helps to determine individual differences in the sex drive, responsiveness to this drive, and sex practices. However, learning experiences which shape the person's attitudes toward all matters pertaining to sex appear to be the primary influence in determining not only the pattern of the person's behavior but also the strength of his expressions of the sex drive. And it is the pattern of the person's behavior that is at the basis of self-evaluations as well as the evaluations of others.

Significant people   How people react to a person because of his sex contributes tremendously to how he evaluates himself and how he feels about himself. Parental attitudes, for example, are almost always reflected in parental behavior. The child sooner or later senses or knows from chance remarks made by his parents or relatives or from the way his parents treat him if he is of the sex his parents had hoped for. Whether he interprets parental behavior correctly or not, it affects his attitudes toward himself. How his siblings react to him and how they treat him also influences his self-concept. In addition, when antagonism between the sexes among peers is strong, the child's reaction to his sex has a strong impact on his self-concept.

Social pressures   Even before babyhood is over, social pressures are brought to bear on the child to behave in a sex-appropriate manner and to think of himself as the cultural group thinks of individuals of his sex. In the molding process, as was stressed in Chapter 4, the cultural group, consisting first of the family, later of the peer group, and still later of the community, provides the person with opportunities and encouragment to learn to behave in a manner it considers appropriate. In addition, it deprives him of opportunities to learn to behave in a manner considered appropriate for members of the other sex.

INTEREST IN SEXUALITY

How much interest a person has in sexuality is a measure of the influence it will have on his personality. When interest is strong, the person becomes preoccupied with matters relating to sex. He may be excessively concerned about sexual behavior, opinionated about the superiority of one sex over the other, or anxious about proving to himself and others how sex appropriate he is. When interest in sex is low, matters relating to sex will be of little concern to the person and will have little influence on his personality.

Cultural emphasis on sexuality

A report in *Time Magazine* (209) explains why present-day Americans are more sex-conscious than any other people in the world:

An erotic renaissance (or rot, as some would have it) is upon the land. Owing to a growing climate of permissiveness—and the Pill—Americans today have more sexual freedom than any previous generation. . . . From stage and screen, printed page and folk-rock jukeboxes, society is bombarded with coital themes. Writers bandy four-letter words as if they had just completed a deep-immersion Berlitz course in Anglo-Saxon. In urban America, at least, the total taboos of yesteryear have become not only acceptable but, in many circles, fashionable musts as well. As Dr. William Masters (Human Sexual Response) *has suggested, "The '60s will be called the decade of orgasmic preoccupation."*

Effects of interest in sexuality on behavior

The cultural emphasis on sexuality encourages people of all ages to be more preoccupied with sexuality than they might otherwise be. Even among children, talking about sex is the "thing to do." It not only increases their interest in and knowledge about sex but helps them to identify with the social group and win the reputation of being "good sports."

Studies show that sex and sex organs are among the favorite conversational topics of older children. When they are with their peers, they feel freer to discuss such topics than when they are with adults (59). Adolescents in high school and college claim that it is much more difficult to discuss sexual matters with their parents than with their peers either of their own or of the opposite sex. When they are with intimate friends of their own sex, however, they talk about more personal matters, such as sexual feelings and attractions, than when they are with members of the opposite sex (18, 52, 60, 80).

"Smutty" stories and jokes about sex are likewise popular topics of conversation from late childhood on. By middle age, people talk about sex less, however, and many feel embarrassed or disgusted by "dirty" jokes and references to sexual matters (164).

The comic books read by young people and the movies or the television programs they watch often have a sex theme. Even if not, they show what is appropriate in appearance and behavior for members of the two sexes. Movies and television programs, for example, show the young person how he should act in a love situation. They set a model for him and one which he expects the person he is in love with to conform to as well. Popular media also stimulate a desire to engage in the kind of behavior portrayed. Erotic scenes, which have little effect before puberty, arouse many responses in the adolescent and young adult. These range from sentimental feelings to a desire for similar experiences (134, 209).

When sex play, either homosexual or heterosexual, and masturbation are the "thing to do" among members of a peer group, the young person engages in such activities whether or not they give him pleasure and even when he knows they are strongly disapproved of by parents and other adults. The same is true of petting and premarital intercourse in adolescence. In many cases, interest in sexual activities is far weaker than interest in being popular and in being regarded as one of the crowd (52, 134). Stagner (199) makes this comment:

There is considerable social pressure, particularly upon the adolescent, to become sexually sophisticated, i.e., to have (and be able to talk about) sexual experiences. This is a general phenomenon, but it is particularly true in situations where a large number of unmarried young people are gathered together, as in any army barracks or a college dormitory, and other comparable conditions. One of the main amusements of such groups consists of sitting in smoked-filled rooms telling stories of sexual conquests. But the unfortunate youth who cannot tell such stories or does not even know the vocabulary involved is subject to an extraordinary amount of ridicule and teasing. Under such circumstance, his early moral training, fears, etc., may break down and he will seek experiences in order to avoid criticism. . . . The whole social situation is so arranged as to keep sex constantly in the foreground of the adolescent's attention, and to place premiums of various kinds upon sexual sophistication as well as penalties upon ignorance.

Variations in interest in sexuality

In spite of the cultural pressures, people vary in the amount of interest they have in sexual matters, in the areas of interest, and in the wholesomeness of the interest. *Age* differences are especially marked, with the peak of interest coming in adolescence and early adulthood. It is now believed that this peak does not subside as early as was formerly thought, especially among women. Sometimes there is a revival of interest in sexuality at middle age. In men, the increased interest is due mainly to a desire to prove to themselves and to others that they are still young and virile. In women, the increased interest has been explained as due to removal of fear of pregnancy after the menopause (46, 117, 158, 220).

Even in old age, interest in sexuality does not die down as quickly as was formerly believed. In fact, there is ample evidence that people continue to be interested in sex into the sixties or even seventies, though the interest is unquestionably weaker than it was at middle age. This matter will be discussed in more detail later in the chapter (70, 79, 178, 203).

Sex differences in interest in sexuality are more qualitative than quantitative. While fear of social disapproval and pregnancy inhibits the full expression of sexual interest, the relaxing of moral standards regarding sex behavior, for women as well as for men, and the safeguard offered by readily obtained contraceptive devices have made girls, especially, far less inhibited than they were in past generations (23).

Among girls and women, interest in sex is concentrated more on making a successful marriage than on the personal satisfaction they derive from sexual expression. They often use sex as a means to an end. If they can win a husband who closely approximates their "dream man" by engaging in sexual behavior, they feel that the means justify the end. They are motivated by the "Cinderella tradition" to make as successful a marriage as they can (53, 124).

Boys and men, by contrast, are often more interested in sexual gratification than in marriage. This is shown by the fact that men, as a group, marry later than women and they more often marry "down" (22, 124). In addition, boys and men feel that expressions of sex are a way of proving their masculinity. That is why adolescent boys boast about their "sexual conquests" or visit houses of prostitution and why men often are more eager than women to have large families and more sons than daughters. To many males, these are visible insignia of their virility.

Differences in interest in sexuality are clearly apparent among the *socioeconomic* classes. Men of the lower classes are more interested in women as sexual partners than as social or intellectual partners. This is shown by the fact that a larger proportion of

their leisure activities are shared with men and other women than with their wives (117, 134, 154). Women of the upper and middle socioeconomic groups are interested in sex partly as a form of personal fulfillment and partly as a means to a prestigious status in society. By contrast, many women of the lower social classes regard sex as a source of "trouble" and children as a penalty for sex. This attitude may change as the use of contraceptives becomes more widespread (134, 166, 169, 213).

The better *adjusted* people are, both personally and socially, the more wholesome their interests in sexuality (38, 88). Even among children, the less well adjusted are more influenced by comics and television shows which emphasize sex than are the well adjusted (11, 25, 178). Poorly adjusted people, as they grow older, are not only relatively more preoccupied with sex, but they engage in more forms of deviant sex behavior, such as masturbation, rape, and homosexuality (38, 117, 134).

Effects of interest in sexuality on personality

How interest in sexuality will influence personality depends on how it affects behavior and how the individual and significant people in his life judge him because of the way he behaves. While it is true that interest in sexuality varies, the person and others as well judge his sexual behavior in terms of the approved standards of the group with which they are identified.

Directly, interest in sexuality affects the person's self-concept in two ways: first, through the effect it has on his behavior and, second, through the way he evaluates himself because of his behavior. For example, if a boy is brought up in a family that places high value on displays of masculine virility, the more sexually aggressive he is, the better satisfied he will be with himself.

The person evaluates himself in terms of the culturally accepted values of sex as he understands them. The *Time Magazine* (209) report on sex as a spectator sport states:

Erotic art often unduly celebrates sexual prowess to the exclusion of such qualities as tenderness, patience, courage, humor or honesty. If sex is universally regarded as the ultimate status symbol, as Playboy and the pornocrats suggest, many responsible adults will wind up feeling cheated and alienated; at the same time, and ironically, the aim of sex will become mental rather than sensory.

Indirectly, interest in sexuality affects the self-concept through the judgments made of the person by people who are significant in his life. An older person whose interest in sexuality is expressed in behavior similar to that of his younger years judges himself favorably because he feels that he is still virile, youthful, and sexually competent. If his spouse finds satisfaction from his sexual advances, this will reinforce his favorable self-concept. If he feels that his grown children regard such behavior as "not nice" or as a sign of depravity, however, it will have just the opposite effect (5, 79). In explaining how older women react to the judgments younger people make of their continued interest in sexuality, Kassel (113) writes:

To many people it is abhorrent to visualize grandparents or even parents past the childbearing age enjoying the pleasures of sexual intercourse. Older women, recognizing this attitude, repress their sexual desires and develop psychological conflicts and consequent guilt.

ATTITUDES TOWARD SEXUALITY

That attitudes toward sexuality, sex behavior, sex differences, and sex roles are a product of the culture in which the person grows up is evidenced by studies of both primitive and civilized peoples and of members of social classes within the same cultural group. The child learns, directly, from teaching and, indirectly, from imitation to regard sexuality as significant people in his life regard it.

As these significant people change—from parents to teachers, to peers of the same sex, and finally to peers of the opposite sex—the person's attitudes will probably change. But like all attitudes, the basic attitudes toward sex, established in the home during the early years of childhood, dominate later attitudes. The harm that comes from an unwholesome attitude toward sexuality is twofold: Once established, the attitude is highly resistant to change, and equally as serious, its effect on the person's concept of himself as a person can lead to poor personal and social adjustments.

What is an unwholesome attitude toward sexuality? For example, the person has learned to think of

his sexual organs and their function as something to whisper about. He has learned to think of touching his sexual organs or those of someone else as wicked and depraved. He has learned to think of the strong urge that makes a person want to come in close contact with a person of the opposite sex as one of "man's baser instincts." He has learned to think of the marital relationship as a "necessary evil" to be endured only for the sake of having children. If he has learned to think this way, he will endow his own feelings with these beliefs and will think of himself as a person who has "base instincts" and "animal cravings."

In time, he will convince himself that he must cover up such feelings if he is to win and hold the respect of members of the social group and he will believe that he must rationalize to himself and to others *any* sexual behavior that gives him enjoyment. He soon associates himself as a person with the feelings of shame and guilt that stem from his sexual interests, drives, and behavior. This affects his attitude not only toward the sexual aspect of self but also toward his entire self.

Rosenfeld (176) explains that as cultural attitudes change, toward greater or less permissiveness in the relations between the sexes, so do individual attitudes:

A quick look around confirms that a startling transformation is already taking place in our attitudes toward sex. . . . In fact, where sex is concerned it is hard to say any more what is "normal" and what is not. All sorts of behavior which only a few years ago were considered wrong, or at least questionable, now seem reasonable. . . . Sex in the movies leaves little to the imagination. And if sex is talked about much more openly these days, there is no reason to doubt that it is practiced much more uninhibitedly too. On the college campus, where a goodnight kiss at the dormitory door was once considered a bit wicked, premarital sex—while not indulged in universally—is now taken for granted.

While conventional views on sexuality still predominate throughout the nation, there is evidence that the change in attitudes that is taking place is occurring first among college students—the leaders of the next generation—especially in public and non-church-related private colleges (150, 197). There is also evidence that the greatest change in attitudes toward sexuality is occurring among members of the younger generation in the upper and middle socioeconomic groups. In the lower groups where standards of sex behavior have always been more permissive, there is less evidence of change (24, 74, 171).

Responsibility for the change in attitudes has been attributed to the contact of members of the armed forces with cultures where different standards of sex morality prevail; to the "Pill," which makes fear of pregnancy less of a deterrent force; and to the content of mass media presentations, especially magazines, movies, and television. As one irate mother put it: "The movies today are a far cry from Shirley Temple. I wonder how far they will go" (150).

Origin of attitudes

Attitudes toward sexuality are acquired along with knowledge about sex. The amount and accuracy of the information one receives are not as important in the shaping of attitudes as the way in which the information is given.

Refusing to answer a child's questions on the ground that he is "too young" to understand or that "one doesn't talk about such things" may lay the foundation for an unwholesome attitude. Many a child, given an answer to the question, "Where does a baby come from?" will forget what he was told, largely because it was explained in unfamiliar words. But he is not likely to forget the *way* in which he was told, the expression on the face of the person who gave him the information, and the ease or difficulty the person seemed to have in talking to him about the matter.

If these behavior symbols suggest to the child that the person who gave him information regards sexuality as a natural phenomenon, related to love, marriage, children, and a happy family life, he will learn to think of it in that way too. If, on the other hand, the symbols suggest that sexuality is something to be whispered about and that it is embarrassing and not altogether "nice," then he will think of it in that light. Mussen et al. state: "The most important part of sex education depends not on biological instruction *per se*, but upon the demonstration of healthy attitudes on the part of parents, teachers, and other influential adults" (147).

Sources of information Studies reveal that the source of the child's first information about sex matters is far less important than the attitude of the person who gives him the information. It is generally agreed that *parents*, especially parents of the same sex as the child, should be the best source of information. It is also agreed that some parents are incapable of giving this information accurately because of their own limited knowledge, their inability to communicate with the child, or their unhealthy attitudes, which color unfavorably any information they may provide (147, 170, 215).

Most studies of the information parents give their children about sex emphasize that it is far from adequate. One study reported that only 60 percent of the girls interviewed had been prepared for puberty and 10 percent of the boys informed about nocturnal emission or masturbation. Relatively few had been given information about intercourse from their parents, as shown in Figure 11–1. On the whole, the most complete and accurate information about sexuality came from reading (194). Difficulties in parent-child communication, especially about sex matters, increase as boys and girls approach puberty (60).

Parents who surround sexuality with mystery and taboos, who establish a "conspiracy of silence" in the home, whet the child's curiosity to learn more than his parents are willing to tell him. At the same time, the child gets the impression that there is something very wrong and harmful about sexuality that his parents are trying to protect him from.

Even when correct information is given to the child, it may be biased by the informer's negative attitudes to such an extent that the child learns unhealthy attitudes along with the facts. A mother who is unhappily married, for example, may readily distort the facts about reproduction because of her own dissatisfaction with her role as wife and mother.

Another source of unhealthy attitudes about sexuality is poor toilet-training practices. Young children generally associate their sex organs with their organs of elimination. If toilet training is accompanied by punishment which develops in the child feelings of guilt, shame, and anxiety, these feelings may be associated with sex also.

If the child's curiosity about sex is not satisfied in the home, he will seek information outside the home. While the chances of getting more misinformation from outside sources than from the home are great, this is far less damaging than the unwholesome attitudes that are being built up.

Much of the sex information children get outside the home comes from *suggestive pictures* in comics or in surreptitiously obtained pornography, from *dirty stories and jokes,* and from snatches of peer

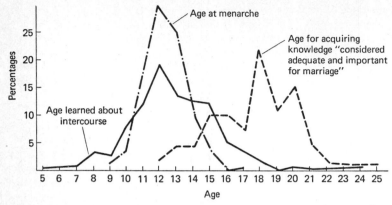

Figure 11-1   Ages at which adolescents learn about important areas of sexuality from their parents. (Adapted from G. Shipman: The psychodynamics of sex education. *Family Coordinator*, 1968, **17**, 3–12. Used by permission.)

gossip. Such information is usually given in whispers and is accompanied by demands for secrecy, embarrassed giggles, and sneers.

When a child does not understand all he hears in dirty jokes or stories or all he sees in suggestive pictures, he is likely to ask his friends to fill him in. His questions are generally met with a roar of laughter and taunts of "lily-white," "innocent," or "pure." This leaves him in the same state of doubt and confusion he experienced when he tried to get information from his parents. Believing that he is being deprived of something his friends know, he develops a feeling of martyrdom combined with feelings of inferiority and inadequacy.

Even *books on sex education*, written for the purpose of providing accurate information in a straightforward, unembarrassed manner, do not necessarily guarantee wholesome attitudes. Many children, brought up on stories about the stork or the way doctors bring babies in their satchels, find the coldly stated facts and unadorned drawings of pregnancy and childbirth a shock. Unless they have someone to interpret the content of such books in a sympathetic way, they are likely to develop feelings of revulsion and fear—feelings which are difficult to overcome later.

While some *schools* have sex education courses or combine sex information with courses in biology or hygiene, these are generally given so late in the child's school career that he has already accumulated a large fund of misinformation. One of the most common arguments against giving sex education in the schools is that the teachers assigned to teach the courses are often not qualified to do so without fostering unwholesome attitudes in the children. "Even with training, some opponents of sex education say, many teachers are either reluctant to teach this subject or are unqualified to do so because of 'sexual hang-ups' of their own" (215).

A certain amount of every child's information about sexuality comes from *direct exploration* of his body and the bodies of his playmates. A popular game of preschoolers, "playing doctor," enables the child to examine the body of a playmate as part of his role. It is not uncommon for older children or even young adolescents to play "being married." This gives them opportunities to experiment with their sex organs, either by handling them or by trying to fit the penis into the vagina.

Those who do not try to hide their explorations under the cloak of a game may display their sex organs to their companions, compare the size and development of their organs with those of their friends, challenge their companions to match their prowess in the toilet, peep at members of the opposite sex in the bath or on the toilet, and teach their less sophisticated companions how to masturbate.

Adult attitudes toward sexual exploration vary from amused tolerance to shocked outrage. While one parent may encourage kissing games as a way for children to learn what kissing is like or to break down barriers between members of the two sexes at parties, another may regard such games as vulgar, bad taste, or "putting bad ideas into children's heads." How significant people in the child's life, especially his mother, feel about sexual play and exploration determines how he will feel about it. From the time the child is 3 or 4 years old, social pressures play an increasingly important role in determining what his attitudes will be.

Effects of attitudes toward sexuality on personality

From early childhood to senility, the person is confronted with problems that relate directly or indirectly to sexuality. How he meets these problems is greatly influenced by the attitudes toward sexuality developed early in life and, in turn, affects the way he evaluates himself and views himself in relation to other people. Breckenridge and Vincent have voiced a warning about unhealthy attitudes toward sex (30):

Whatever the child's experience with sex, his adolescent and adult life can be normal and fulfilling only under one condition. He must not grow up with the feeling that sex and everything connected with it are nasty and dangerous.

Allport has likewise stressed that attitudes established early in life determine the adolescent's handling of the problems the developing sexual drive give rise to (3):

The ripening sexual impulses, for example, will be met within the framework of pre-existing attitudes and fears, and will be affected by traits acquired well before the onset of puberty. . . . Sex in normal lives never stands alone, it is tied to all manner of personal images, sanctions, tastes, interests, ambitions, codes, and ideals. . . . In any two personalities, sexuality never seems to play the same role. Its attachments, its significance, and the conduct associated with it are the most individualistic of all the phenomena of mental life. In spite of its biologically uniform aspects, in its psychological organization it is a remarkably idiosyncratic matter.

Sex attitudes and behavior are, in their turn, influenced by the person's self-concept. A person who feels inferior and inadequate may try to bolster his unfavorable self-concept by sexual behavior that will prove to himself and to others that he is a sex-appropriate person. He may try to outdo others in the number of his "sexual conquests" or he may engage in sexual behavior that will win the admiration if not the respect of his peers. Early marriage, for example, is often motivated by a desire to prove that one is grown-up or is capable of winning a marriage partner sooner than one's peers.

Back of the desire to win the attention and affection of members of the opposite sex during the "dangerous age" of middle age is a growing feeling of personal inadequacy resulting from the physical and psychological signs of approaching old age. For men and women in the "dangerous age," sex is a form of reassurance, an insignia of youthful vigor and attractiveness which helps to dispel any doubts they may have about their personal or sexual adequacy.

For those with marked feelings of personal inadequacy, preoccupation with sex is a danger signal of poor adjustment. "Overemphasis on sex," writes Strang, "is characteristic of the 'neurotic personality of our times'" (204). The sex addict—the person who shows a compulsive quest for sexual gratification—uses sexuality as an escape from feelings of inadequacy or inferiority. Often sexual gratification compensates for his inability to achieve his hoped-for goals in work or interpersonal relationships.

The way in which the person meets the sex problems that arise at different ages will determine how he evaluates himself. Unfavorable attitudes toward sexuality are often at the basis of frigidity in women and impotency in men. These not only affect the person's marital adjustments but also his self-concept; an impotent male feels inadequate as does a frigid female. Successful handling of sex problems contributes to a self-acceptant attitude which is essential to a well-adjusted personality.

ATTITUDES TOWARD OWN SEX

Developing a healthy attitude toward one's own sex and toward other people of the same sex is a problem everyone must face. Failure to solve it successfully can prove a serious handicap to personal and social adjustment. By the time the child is 4 years old, and often earlier, he is aware not only that there are two kinds of people in the world but also that specific labels are given to them. He recognizes the two sexes mainly on the basis of differences in hair styles and clothing. At the same time, he knows the label people apply to him and this enables him to identify himself with other people of the same sex as he.

This knowledge is not without its emotional accompaniment. When the child learns that people have different labels, he also learns that greater prestige is associated with one label than with the other. Thus he begins, very early in life, to think of himself and others who bear the same label as he in one way and of those who bear a different label in another way.

Cultural attitudes toward males and females

The child deduces from what people say or do that the cultural attitude toward one sex is more favorable than toward the other. It is an unusual child who reaches adolescence without knowing that within the cultural group the male sex is the preferred sex and that boys and men have many advantages that girls and women do not.

One of the earliest and most obvious cues which supply children and adolescents with this knowledge is *parental favoritism*. This favoritism toward the male child, especially on the part of the mother, is shown by indulgent reactions to the misbehavior of the favored child, by taking his part in sibling quarrels, by holding him up as an example to be imitated, by giving him first rights in any situation where a choice must be made, and by greater concern when he is sick or injured and greater pride and satisfaction when his achievements are recognized by others. As is true of parents, *siblings*, especially males, favor boys over girls, and so do other *relatives*.

The belief established in the home that boys are better liked by the social group than girls is reinforced by the attitudes and treatment of *peers* and *teachers*. Boys often tease and bully girls but hesitate to treat classmates of their own sex in this way for fear of retaliation. Many teachers, without meaning to play favorites, tend to be more lenient and more understanding of boys' misbehavior and poor schoolwork.

Discipline in childhood and social attitudes toward *moral codes* in adolescence and adulthood provide unmistakable clues to how society feels about members of the two sexes. Within the home, parents, particularly mothers, tend to be stricter with girls. By adolescence, the "double standard" of moral conduct is in full force. According to this standard, many things are considered "wrong" for girls but not for boys while practically nothing that girls may do is considered wrong for boys.

The double standard is reinforced by the greater *autonomy* given boys at all ages. Members of both sexes interpret this to mean that parents believe boys are more capable than girls of handling their social affairs. Furthermore, girls discover that they are not welcome at many social functions unless they are accompanied by boys while boys are welcome under any condition. This suggests to both boys and girls that boys are more highly valued in *social life*. Further evidence is provided by the fact that society grants boys and men the privilege of *selecting partners* for dating and marriage.

Denying girls certain *learning experiences* which are given to boys also serves as a cue to tell members of both sexes how the social group feels about them. In play, in school, and in preparation for a vocation, boys are encouraged to learn certain skills and to study certain subjects which are considered inappropriate for girls. While girls are not necessarily denied opportunities to learn or study these things, they are discouraged from doing so. At the same time, they are encouraged to learn less prestigious things that are generally regarded as "feminine."

Work discrimination, as shown by granting a disproportionate share of prestigious positions to men, by giving men higher pay than women for the same work, and by showing a preference for male employees at all ages in jobs where males and females compete, but especially after 40—adds to the realization that men are the favored sex in the business and professional worlds. Finally, the *mass media* with their emphasis on the achievements of men throughout history in war, in art, in literature, in music, and in science, with their emphasis on the achievements of men today in all areas, and with their tendency to report women's achievements mainly in the areas of the performing arts, beauty, and fashion—all imply that the social group thinks more highly of men than women.

Influence of cultural attitudes on behavior

Awareness of the cultural attitudes toward members of the two sexes leaves its mark on behavior. One of the first reactions to the realization of how the social group feels about the two sexes is a *wish* on the part of girls that they could belong to the male sex. Studies of children's attitudes, as disclosed in their drawings and verbalizations, show that girls prefer the male role and masculine activities to those considered appropriate for their own sex. By contrast, boys hardly ever express a desire to be a girl or to play the girl's role (16, 34).

As girls grow older, most of them realize that they must accept the female role if they are to be reasonably happy and well adjusted. However, that does not change their unfavorable attitude toward other girls. It has been found that this attitude becomes increasingly negative after the ninth grade (90).

At no age do most males show a preference for the female role or a wish that they had been born girls. Their preference for their own sex is reflected in their favorable attitude toward other boys as well as toward themselves. By the time boys reach the eighth grade, they have a more positive attitude toward girls than they did earlier, though this is likely to be directed at a particular girl rather than girls in general (90).

In some women, recognition of disparate social attitudes toward the two sexes and a feeling of being trapped by an unwanted role *undermine self-respect* and lead to a tendency to *derogate the female sex*. Adler labeled this response the "masculine protest." It includes the dissatisfaction women have with their own sex, their striving to achieve the male role in society, and their attempts to revenge themselves on society for having been born women (1).

The masculine protest makes women aggressive in their behavior and attitudes. They derive pleasure from dominating men, especially in the love relationship, from putting men at a disadvantage, and from ridiculing them. Their aggressiveness may also lead to a competitive attitude toward men, to a preference for a career rather than home activities, to a desire to dress like men, to a belittling of men's achievements, and to a lack of affection for or romantic feeling about men. These reactions are similar to those of other minority-group members who strive or overstrive to get what the social group has denied them (1, 71, 153).

Very few boys and men protest against being males or playing the male role. If any psychological harm comes from recognizing their favorable position, it is in the form of unwarranted feelings of superiority.

Female acceptance of the obstacles created by society's "sexist" attitudes stifles girls' and women's *motivation* to achieve success. The effect is much the same as that experienced by other minority-group members. Their desire to strive for success is deadened and they feel bitter and resentful toward the members of the social group who have blocked them. Many women with abilities and training equal to those of successful men must accept jobs with less respon-

sibility, less pay, and less prestige. Many adjust to the inevitable by selecting vocations which men do not want to enter because of the low pay or low prestige, such as teaching in the schools, home economics, library work, nursing, social service, or office work. Others withdraw from competiton with men completely and accept roles men cannot fill—those of wives and mothers. By so doing, they eliminate the frustrations that a career woman faces and, at the same time, build up their egos by convincing themselves and others that their participation in home, social, and community activities contributes to their husbands' success.

The favorable social attitudes toward males affects boys' and men's motivation to achieve success in a quite different way. It often weakens their motivation to put into their work the effort they are capable of. They thus become business or professional underachievers. As they approach middle age when they should be at the peak of their achievement, they often feel guilty or ashamed. Some develop a feeling of martyrdom, blaming their families for placing obstacles in their way, such as expecting them to spend time and energy on home responsibilities or objecting to a move to a new community which would have meant a step up on the vocational ladder.

Effects of cultural attitudes on personality

Constant reminders of the prevailing cultural attitudes toward members of the two sexes cannot fail to leave their mark on the individual's personality pattern through the influence they have on the self-concept. Each sex group is affected differently.

Influence on male self-concepts Under most conditions, boys sense or know that they are favored above girls in the home, in the school, and in society at large. However, if a boy feels that his parents find his sisters less troublesome than he and more helpful in the home, this is damaging to his self-concept. As Hartley (92) has explained:

He cannot compete, for the moment, with any hope of success. Is it to be wondered at that he later fiercely asserts and desperately defends a superiority to which his claims must be constantly validated? The girl can apparently slip easily and confidently into the intimate world of the household from the beginning, with a ready-made place and function that create a sense of worth. *The boy, falling out of infancy's haven, must wait and aggressively strive to prove himself.*

If, on the other hand, the boy feels secure in his favored status, this tends to make him cocky, arrogant, and demanding, especially in situations in which females are involved. Furthermore, because he feels superior to females, and because society has, for centuries, granted members of his sex rights and privileges withheld from members of the female sex, the boy does all within his power to maintain this superiority with minimum trouble and effort. One way to do this is to shut women out, to close doors to them in order to avoid having to compete with them.

To make their arguments for withholding equal opportunities from women seem like selfless sacrifice instead of selfishness and fear of finding themselves not the superior people they want to believe they are, many boys and men complain of the hard role men must play in life in comparison with the easy role they have made possible for women. They back this up with arguments about keeping their noses to the grindstone to provide laborsaving devices for the home so that their wives can have an easy life, with freedom to do as they please, while they, the husbands, must follow the dictates of tyrannical employers.

Influence on female self-concepts

Just as a superior role in the social group contributes to a feeling of superiority in boys and men, so an inferior role contributes to the development of feelings of inferiority in girls and women. Many high-achieving girls and women fail to see the justice of being treated as inferior, and so they react with anger and resentment, as does anyone subjected to derogatory treatment.

Whether this anger is expressed outwardly in "masculine protest" or suppressed behind a cloak of docile femininity, it will affect the personality adversely. The damages will be intensified as the years pass and the evidences of discrimination grow. Note what Allport (3) has to say on this subject:

The higher rate of inferiority feelings among women no doubt reflects the disadvantage they feel in a "man's world." Over and above whatever handicaps they have as individuals they have extra restrictions placed upon them, especially in economic and moral spheres of activity. . . . Girls have a harder time to make satisfactory positions for themselves in their environments, and for this reason suffer more com-monly feelings of inferiority. . . . In the home, the only niche allotted them in previous times, women did not have such exaggerated feelings of inferiority. It was their world, freely granted them by men. Few of the sex left the niche to compete in the "world of men." Nowadays it is the world of men in which women are living and competing, a world of standards intrinsically alien to them as women. Slowly these standards are being modified to include them. As this occurs, as women are admitted on equal terms, the ratio of inferiority feelings may be equalized. No doubt the change will also [lower] the percentage of girls preferring to be boys.

When a feeling of inferiority is well developed, the woman loses respect for herself and for members of her sex. In the lower social classes where the attitude toward women tends to be far less favorable than in the middle and upper classes, many girls grow up in homes where the role of women is so low and so scorned that they lose respect for themselves as people. When this happens, they become easy prey to the lure of money and glamour often associated with a life of prostitution. Harsh and Schrickel write that "prostitutes are seldom sex-obsessed but more often are women who have a low regard for the female role; thus they experience little difficulty in offering themselves up as sex objects" (91).

ATTITUDES TOWARD SEX DIFFERENCES

No one denies that males and females are different in appearance, bodily functions, attitudes, interests, values, and patterns of behavior. But how much of the difference is due to heredity and how much to environmental factors, such as social pressures, social expectations, and limitations on learning experiences? Brown and Lynn have stated that the psychosexual status of the person at birth is undifferentiated. The infant is psychosexually plastic and capable of developing along a variety of lines (36).

From the evidence now available, it appears that the physical differences between the two sexes are, in most instances, the result of heredity, while the major psychological differences are the result of environmental factors. As Hilgard (98) has explained:

Because the sexes are anatomically and physiologically unlike, it is easy to infer that as adults the differences in behavior between them correspond to their different biological organizations. Actually the situation is much more complex. Whether the man or the woman wears lace or highly colored clothes depends upon the styles current at the time. A series of historical accidents determined that men become bank clerks, women, cashiers in stores; men, telegraph operators, women, telephone operators.

Even in areas where sex differences are especially marked, such as interests and patterns of behavior, there is much overlapping. Some men show traits that are generally associated with women and some women show traits that are regarded as masculine. It would be just as difficult to find a man who is 100 percent masculine as it would be to find a woman who is 100 percent feminine.

Differences versus inferiorities

Differences do not mean inferiorities. Whether they are regarded as insignia of inferiority or of superiority depends upon one's frame of reference and upon cultural values. Throughout history, men have been the favored sex in most cultures. It has, therefore, become traditional to use the male stereotype as a frame of reference. Any deviation from this stereotype is then judged as inferior. Cultural values are determined largely in terms of the most prestigious group in the culture. Since this group is composed of males, cultural values put heavy emphasis on qualities that are "typically male." For example, every culture considers strength, bravery, adventuresomeness, and aggressiveness as admirable traits because they are characteristic of the virile male.

Regardless of hereditary potentials, children are trained to conform to these cultural ideals and strong pressure is put on them to develop the traits the social group expects them to have. While members of both sexes will be admired for their sex appropriateness, those who have the greatest prestige are the male possessors of the qualities that are typically masculine.

The ability to reason is a good example of how group pressures influence the development of admired personality traits. Even before the days of the intelligence test, reasoning was regarded as a "higher" mental ability than memorizing. Boys were encouraged to develop the ability to reason while girls were discouraged from developing it either by limiting their learning opportunities or by labeling those whose reasoning ability competed with men's as

"masculine women." As a result, men developed this ability and were judged as "superior." Women, on the other hand, were encouraged to develop the ability to memorize and were then judged as inferior because they possessed a trait that had less prestige. Men, having the ability to reason well developed, were considered better suited to deal with situations where decisions had to be made. As a result, they were given roles superior to those of women because these roles demanded the ability to reason which men possessed to a higher degree (34, 91, 114, 139).

Awareness of sex differences

Sex differences affect personality only when the person is aware of the differences and of how the social group feels about them. Most children are aware of the physical differences between the sexes by the age of 4 years. Girls are generally able to identify physical sex differences sooner than boys; and children with two parents, sooner than those with one parent. Boys, as a rule, catch up with girls in their ability to identify physical sex differences by the time they reach puberty (26).

Awareness of mental differences between the sexes, as shown in differences in academic abilities, interests, and aptitudes, does not always come until the school begins to encourage children to take certain courses of study and plan to enter vocations which they are told are appropriate for masculine or feminine interests and abilities.

In schools where academic achievement is not publicized to the pupils, few children actually know that mental sex differences exist. When they do know it, they know that the differences are generally favorable to girls. However, they do discover, shortly after entering elementary school, that the two sexes have different interests. They learn that boys prefer games and sports to dramatic play, comics and movies with adventure themes to those with family-life themes, and active to creative play.

They note that adults differ in their interests, just as children do. Mothers, they find, show a greater interest in sedentary activities, in making things, and in talking to people, while fathers want to do things away from home, such as fishing, hunting, and playing golf, and have less interest in reading, going to the movies, or watching television than mothers have.

Awareness of sex differences generally reaches its peak at the time of puberty when the changing body of the pubescent leads to a preoccupation with all things related to sexuality, including physical and mental differences between the sexes. This awareness increases each year as members of the two sexes go their separate ways, show different interests, and engage in different patterns of behavior.

Awareness of the social attitudes toward sex differences comes late, paralleling awareness of mental sex differences. During childhood, physical differences are not great enough, in appearance or strength, to make the differences in social attitudes readily noticeable. However, as children become aware of differences in interests and abilities, they learn that there are disparate social attitudes toward those of males and females.

Effects of sex differences on attitudes and behavior

General concepts of superiority and inferiority, acquired from cultural attitudes toward sex differences, influence the person's attitudes toward members of both sexes and his behavior in situations where members of both sexes are represented. According to Ausubel, "From an early age boys learn to be contemptuous of girls and their activities; and although girls retaliate in kind by finding reasons for deprecating the male sex, they tend to accept in part the prevailing view of their inferiority" (9).

As boys become more masculine in appearance and in patterns of behavior, they become more and more confirmed in their favorable attitude toward the male sex and their unfavorable attitude toward the female. Girls develop increasingly unfavorable attitudes toward themselves and toward members of their own sex; these attitudes are accentuated by the periodic discomforts and incoveniences of menstruation and the realization that girls' strength is far inferior to that of boys of the same age. Thus, the cultural belief that physical differences between the sexes make women the "weaker" sex is reinforced.

Strang (204) describes boys' attitudes toward girls at the junior high school level:

The attitude they generally present to the world in the seventh, and sometimes in the eighth, grade is "Nuts to girls." Socially they seem to avoid girls. At school dances they are likely to let the girls dance with one another while they discuss things like baseball scores. . . . The highlight of the evening for the boys is when they can pull down the decorations and break the *balloons which have been used to give the school gym "atmosphere." On leaving the dance, most of them go off in groups that are exclusively masculine.*

Because many men perceive women as inferior, they develop an *authoritarian attitude* toward them, as people in general do toward all groups they regard as inferior. In men of the middle and upper classes, many of whom try to hide their feelings of superiority behind a "veneer of equalitarianism," this feeling of superiority may be expressed in an *attitude of chivalry.* An attitude of chivalry places positive values upon "deference" and "protectiveness" toward women, it encourages certain formalized rules of conduct toward women, and it stereotypically conceives of women as physically fragile, morally pure, and intellectually naive. At least in the masculine mind, this justifies putting women in a subordinate position.

Attitudes toward sex differences established in childhood soon become *generalized attitudes* toward all members of the opposite sex and all members of one's own sex. Related to beliefs of male superiority there develops in boys and men an intolerance of traits that hint at femininity in men or of men who fall short of a virile ideal. This is accompanied by admiration for rough, aggressive, and strong-willed super-masculinity. At the root of this *antifemininity* is authoritarianism, which is characteristic of those who are prejudiced and who feel superior to anyone who is different (2).

Antifemininity, or supermasculinity, expresses itself in many ways. It may take the form of neglect of health, keeping up a pace that overtaxes the strength and endurance of even the healthiest male, and pushing oneself regardless of how one feels to avoid being thought of as weak. It may take the form of refusing to acquire social skills, such as polite manners or the ability to carry on a social conversation, to dance, or to be tactful.

The principal way men express antifemininity is in their treatment of women. Cloaking their feelings behind a superficial equalitarianism, many men block the advancement of women in business and industry, claiming that it "goes against nature to place women in positions of authority over men." Some men do not want their wives to work outside the home because they belive it reflects unfavorably on their masculinity (114). Others habitually criticize and make derogatory comments about women, including their wives and daughters.

A common way men express antifemininity in

the home is to insist on making all the major decisions for the family, especially those relating to economic matters. Supermasculine men also object to helping out in the home on the ground that all work in the home is "woman's work." Even in an emergency, such men help grudgingly and blame their wives for being inefficient (138).

Effects of sex differences on personality

Because of differences in hereditary endowment and cultural pressures throughout the early, formative years, boys and girls have developed quite different personality patterns by the time they reach adolescence. The effects of sex differences on personality are greatly increased by the kind of behavior boys and girls display as a result of having accepted the cultural attitudes about the meaning of these differences. The characteristic patterns of behavior associated with accepting these attitudes is damaging to both sexes, but in different ways.

Several specific examples will show how certain kinds of behavior, stemming from the cultural attitudes toward sex differences, influence the self-concepts of members of the two sexes. One of the earliest behavioral effects of these attitudes is the *withdrawal* of boys from play with girls. As social pressures are put on boys to stop playing with girls, the boys learn to think of themselves as superior. Since the boys will not play with them, the girls learn to think of themselves as inferior and unworthy of the rights and privileges boys are given.

As boys withdraw from play with girls, they seem to feel that they must show their superiority by treating girls with *disdain*. This leaves its mark on the girls' attitudes toward their own sex while coloring their attitudes toward boys. As the conviction of their superiority grows, boys change from friendly playmates to haughty, aloof, and supercilious rivals. They behave as if they must convince themselves and others of their superiority by aggressive attacks on girls. Consequently, if they do not ignore girls or treat them with disdain, they tease, bully, and play crude jokes on them.

Boys belittle girls' play, their interests, skills, and activities. They call girls names to make them angry and, if the girls fight back, they feel justified in "defending" themselves. If they have some of their pals to help them out, they generally come out ahead. Since boys are encouraged by the culture to be ag-

gressive and to fight, as a way of showing their masculinity, while girls are discouraged from fighting because it is not ladylike, boys tend to come out ahead in the battle of the sexes. This increases their belief in their superiority. Even in name calling and practical-joke playing, girls are more inhibited by social pressures than boys. The result is that they can rarely match boys in these areas where boys have the advantage of practice and of opportunities to learn new names and new pranks from older boys. So, once again, girls find themselves outdone by the boys. This is just another indication to them and to the boys of their inferiority.

However the battle of the sexes is met, at home or outside the home, girls generally lose in one way or another. This increases their feelings of inferiority and resentment and at the same time increases the boys' feelings of masculine superiority. The stronger the sex antagonism and the longer it lasts, the greater damage it does to the self-concepts of members of both sexes.

Since girls and women suffer from *discrimination,* because of their sex, in school, in the home, and in business, many develop a "minority-group complex." At the root of this complex is the belief that they have been singled out for unfair and differential treatment. It expresses itself in many ways, the most common of which are being hypercritical of members of their own sex, having misgivings about women's participation in professions, disliking or refusing to work under a woman, and wishing that they had been born men. Those who are less vocal in their expressions of martyrdom and less aggressive in their behavior, develop a chip-on-the-shoulder attitude which makes them unpleasant to be with.

Thus it is apparent that the cultural stereotypes about superiorities and inferiorities due to the physical and mental differences between the sexes play havoc with the personalities of members of both sexes. On the surface, it appears that women are more damaged psychologically than men. However, as was stressed in the discussion of the effects of prejudice and discrimination (see Chap. 9), those who feel superior and discriminate against those whom they regard as their inferiors are likewise damaged, but in a different way.

SEX APPROPRIATENESS

One of the worst stigmas that can be attached to a boy or man is the label "sissy" or "hen-pecked." It suggests that the male is not sex appropriate in the sense that he is not conforming to the expectations of the social group or to the stereotype members of the social group have of a typical male. Figure 11–2 shows these cultural stereotypes.

While little girls who are tomboys may find that social reactions to them are more colored by tolerance and amusement than by scorn, they discover that if they want to avoid the social stigma of being a "crowing hen" or a "tomboy," they must learn to look, act, and think "like girls."

Being sex inappropriate is thus a personal and social handicap, though, as Koch (120) explains, it is regarded as a greater handicap for males than for females:

There is evidence that it is more serious in our culture for the boy to deviate from the male type than for the girl to deviate from the female type. In others words, a sissy is more frowned upon than is a tomboy. Since a "man is known by the company he keeps," it will be viewed by the culture as important that a boy's companions be predominantly male.

While the social group will tolerate a girl's deviation from the approved pattern of appearance and behavior more readily than a boy's, toleration does not win social approval. Instead, it merely wards off social rejection. This is just as true in adolescence and adulthood as in childhood. To win the approval of members of the social group, people must conform to the group's stereotype of the sex-appropriate person for their sex.

A "henpecked husband," for example, may be well adjusted and happy in his role as a subservient member of the husband-wife team, but he will be poorly regarded by others. And so will his wife. Tolchin (210) points out some of the deeper implications that may be involved in the relationship:

The woman who becomes top sergeant in her home—barking commands at her submissive husband—has won a battle but lost a war. This Thurber-like female, still smarting from childhood feelings of belonging to an inferior sex, has succeeded in fulfilling an infantile desire to become the master of a man. . . . But she has surrendered her chances for emotional growth and the satisfaction of rearing children who feel emotionally secure. . . . In addition, she is usually aware of her inability to assert properly the authority that once belonged to her husband.

Meaning of sex appropriateness

The disparate, sometimes opposing, characteristics and behavior patterns attributed to males and females have been incorporated into the approved masculine and femine stereotypes. Those who conform to the stereotypes win social approval and acceptance, while those who do not are disapproved and rejected. Children are trained from earliest childhood to conform to the standards considered appropriate for their sexes. By the time they reach adulthood, they normally have developed into sex-appropriate adults.

Since personality traits, attitudes, emotions, and behavior patterns are largely a product of cultural traditions and customs, they vary greatly in the differ-

Figure 11-2 In every culture, there is a stereotype of male and female that is approved by the social group.

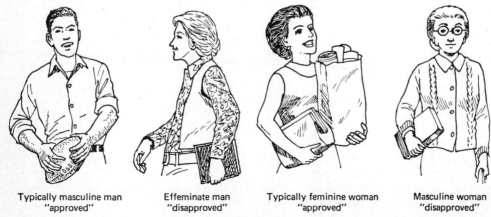

Typically masculine man
"approved"

Effeminate man
"disapproved"

Typically feminine woman
"approved"

Masculine woman
"disapproved"

ent cultures and even among the members of different social classes in the same culture. For example, the approved stereotype of a "gentleman" in many of the European countries during the eighteenth century would be considered a sissy today. Within our own culture, overt expressions of competitiveness and aggressiveness, especially among males, are more highly approved in the lower than in the middle and upper socioeconomic groups.

Stereotypes of sex appropriateness also differ from time to time within a culture. The shifts in what is considered appropriate generally follow changes in the life pattern of males and females within the cultural group. After World War II, early marriages, larger families, and the high cost of living drove many women into the labor market. This has been responsible for a gradual change in the stereotype of what is sex appropriate for the married women. Similarly, the shortage and high cost of domestic help have meant that many men are called upon to help out in the home. As a result, men who help their wives with domestic chores are no longer generally regarded as sissies.

Awareness of sex appropriateness

By the time children are able to identify physical characteristics that belong to one sex or the other, they are aware that certain kinds of behavior are also associated with members of the two sexes. Between the fourth and fifth years, most children realize that some things are considered right or appropriate for boys and others for girls. Preschool children, Brown says, "become fully aware of the fact that the world is divided into two groups of people and that, depending on whether one belongs to one group or the other, different behavior patterns are expected accordingly" (34).

Between the ages of 8 and 11 years, boys and girls have quite explicit ideas concerning appropriate behavior for members of the two sexes. Boys in this age group gave the following description of what they considered appropriate for boys (92):

They have to be able to fight in case a bully comes along; they have to be athletic; they have to be able to run fast; they must be able to play rough games; they need to know how to play many games—curb-ball, baseball, basketball, football; they need to be smart; they need to be able to take care of themselves; they should know what girls don't know—how to climb, how to make a fire, how to carry things; they should

have more ability than girls; they need to know arithmetic and spelling more than girls do.

The list of things the boys considered appropriate for girls indicates that they had a far less favorable stereotype of the girl than of the boy (92):

They have to stay close to the house; they are expected to play quietly and be gentler than boys; they must not be rough; they have to keep clean; they cry when they are scared or hurt; they are afraid to go to rough places like rooftops and empty lots; their activities consist of "fopperies" like playing with dolls, fussing over babies, sitting and talking about dresses; they need to know how to cook, sew and take care of children, but spelling and arithmetic are not as important for them as for boys.

Once boys and girls form a concept of sex appropriateness, anyone who deviates from it will be ridiculed or regarded with suspicion. Girls who prefer mathematics, science, and geography to the more "feminine" subjects, such as languages, art, and music, are often considered "oddballs" by their peers and unfeminine by adults. If they show a preference for "masculine" games and sports, they may find that neither boys nor girls will play with them.

Confusion about sex appropriateness In our culture, sex appropriateness is more clearly defined for boys than for girls, and the cultural pressure to adhere to the stereotype for their sex is stronger for boys. Boys thus find it relatively easy to learn what is sex appropriate for them. But both boys and girls experience some confusion about what is sex appropriate for girls.

This confusion has been increased by the radical changes that have been taking place over the past 30 or 40 years in our concepts of female sex appropriateness. Models of what is appropriate for girls and women are much less clear-cut than they formerly were and they overlap in many respects with the models for men and boys. In play, girls of today are not limited to dolls and "fopperies." The "sex bar" that prevented girls from playing boys' games has been lowered. Goodenough (83) writes:

A boy is not likely to be a Dale Evans, but a girl often becomes a Roy Rogers, or any of his masculine colleagues. Boys are rarely glamour girls, but many little girls fall eagerly into the roles of space men or masculine rough riders.

The model of appropriate woman's work is also blurred when children see some mothers working outside the home and others not. They may be equally confused about what is appropriate work for men and women when they see their fathers doing the dishes, helping with the baby, and hanging out the family wash and their mothers fixing the plumbing, washing the car and cutting the grass. A major source of confusion is lack of appropriate models in the home. According to Seward, "Sex models in the home must be appropriate *so long as society persists in stereotyping sex roles.* Domineering mothers and ineffectual fathers are likely to produce a younger generation of tomboys and sissies" (189).

Development of sex appropriateness

Learning to be sex appropriate is a slow process, covering a long period of development. The learning comes principally from direct instruction stemming from child training in the home and school, identification with and imitation of models in the environment, and information provided by the mass media.

Child training Training children to develop sex-appropriate patterns of behavior is universal. The greater the difference in adult sex roles, the more emphasis the culture will place on this kind of training. In our culture, where the training of children is largely in the hands of women in both the home and the school, there is a tendency to minimize learning concepts of different sex roles and to emphasize what women consider important behavioral and personality characteristics, regardless of the sex of the child. As a result, boys are often "emasculated" (57).

Take the trait of aggressiveness as an example. Women feel that the expression of aggressiveness should be limited and should take forms that are in general regarded as more appropriate for women than for men. As a result, boys learn the individual features of the mother's or teacher's aggressiveness rather than the typically masculine patterns of aggression. This makes them less aggressive than is generally considered appropriate for members of the male sex.

In democratic child training (see Chap. 4 for a description of child-training methods), less emphasis is placed on sex appropriateness of behavior than in authoritarian training. For males, authoritarian child training emphasizes dominance, learning how to be

the master of the home who provides for his family and is a strict disciplinarian and who tolerates no weakness in himself or others. The sex-appropriate traits such training attempts to develop are ruggedness, determination, assertiveness, and strong will power. By contrast, the female is trained to be weak in all these traits and to conform to the ideal of a sweet, submissive, morally controlled person who knows and keeps her place in the home.

Identification Sex appropriateness is also learned by identification with a like-sexed *parent, older sibling, or peer.* Through "role practice" in their make-believe or dramatic play, children learn to act, speak, and even think as their models do. In this way, they get the "feel" of behaving in a sex-appropriate manner.

Because fathers are more concerned about sex-appropriate behavior in their sons than mothers are about sex appropriatenss in their daughters, fathers reward their sons when they play and act like "regular boys" and punish them by their scorn, ridicule, and disapproval for sex inappropriateness. Thus, boys have a stronger motivation to imitate masculine behavior patterns than girls have to imitate feminine patterns. This speeds up the learning process for boys.

For young children of both sexes, the mother is the first source of identification because she is the most gratifying and most affectionate person the child has contact with. This is an appropriate model for girls but not for boys. As a result, boys must shift from a feminine to a masculine model in their early years. For most boys, the desire to be sex appropriate is strong enough to motivate them to make the shift successfully. For some, however, it is difficult because of lack of emotional interchange with the father or because of the father's absence from the home.

If the girl's relationship with her mother is less warm and less rewarding than her relationship with her father, she will have less desire to "learn to be a girl" than if the relationship with the mother were more positive. Furthermore, if the mother is unconcerned about sex appropriateness or if she presents a model that embodies some masculine and some feminine characteristics, this will retard the girl's learning of the appropriate feminine role.

While parents are the prime models for sex appropriateness, the child also tends to imitate the behavior patterns and manner of speaking of an older sibling. If that sibling is of the opposite sex and close enough in age to become a playmate, this will result in sex inappropriateness. This is more true of girls than of boys because parental attitudes are less strict when girls imitate boys than when brothers imitate their sisters.

The influence of peers is usually greater than that of siblings, especially for boys. As boys and girls begin to separate and to form friendships with members of their own sex, peer pressures to develop sex-appropriate patterns of behavior are strong. Since acceptance is crucial to both boys and girls, they become sensitive to what is "masculine" and what is "feminine" and highly motivated to learn to behave in a sex-appropriate way. By adolescence, sex appropriateness is well established through peer pressures.

Mass media   From the mass media young people learn what the social group considers sex appropriate. Stagner (199) describes the media's pervasive influence:

Girls identify themselves with movie stars and seek to be sexually alluring by every device known to modern advertising. . . . Social evaluation of success and failure are closely linked with sex. The man who uses the right soap, hair tonic, or shaving lotion will win a beautiful bride and get a job in her father's firm.

In the comics, sex appropriateness is often represented by the exaggerated drawing of the secondary sex characteristics of males and females and by the use of different forms of speech for members of the two sexes (11, 228). Even school textbooks present children with models of what the group considers sex appropriate. And since children accept the material in their textbooks as more authoritative than the material they read in other books "just for fun," the textbooks have a more profound influence on their concepts.

Areas of sex appropriateness

The child learns not only a general concept of sex appropriateness but also specific concepts related to various aspects of life. As the *body* changes during puberty, one of the pubescent child's greatest concerns is whether his body will now conform to the stereotype of what he has learned is appropriate for his sex. Similarly, at middle age, people are concerned about the decrease in feminine characteristics in women and masculine characteristics in men.

As the child is learning what is considered sex appropriate in body build and general appearance, he also learns that certain *clothing* is considered appropriate for members of each sex. He discovers, in addition, that properly selected clothing goes a long way toward covering up physical characteristics which are sex inappropriate and enhancing those which are sex appropriate.

Long before their elementary school days are over, children learn that some *names* are considered masculine while others are considered feminine. If their names or nicknames fail to conform to these stereotypes, they become self-conscious and develop feelings of inferiority. (Refer to Chap. 3 for a more complete discussion of names.)

While he is learning to talk, the child learns that his *speech*—what he says and how he says it—also reveals his sex appropriateness. Speech that contains slang, bombastic phrases, and swear words, that refers to sex and elimination, conveys the impression that the person is a "real boy" or a "he-man." Dirty words are a symbol of sex appropriateness in boys just as polite phrases are considered sex appropriate for girls (See Chap. 3.)

Sex-appropriate interests in and attitudes toward *education* are learned soon after the child enters school. In elementary school, it is more acceptable for girls to be good students than for boys. Boys who study and come to school with their lessons prepared are apt to get the reputation of being sissies. This attitude persists even into college, where a "gentleman's C" is often more respected than a hard-earned A. Girls who are good students may win peer respect but not necessarily peer acceptance or popularity with the opposite sex. In fact, many boys regard intellectual interests in girls as an indication of lack of femininity (175, 191).

Certain *achievements* are considered appropriate for boys and others for girls. Success in an area that is approved by the social group, as was stressed in the preceding chapter, is far more ego-inflating than success in an area that has little prestige. The same is true of sex appropriateness. Success in an activity that is considered sex appropriate for the achiever is far more ego-satisfying than the same success would be in an "inappropriate" activity (200).

Long before they go to school, children learn that certain *interests* are labeled masculine and others feminine. In play, for example, boys discover that some very appealing toys, such as dolls, tea sets, and makeup kits, are for girls only. While girls are given more latitude in their play interests, they too discover that some toys and games are not considered appropriate for them.

Until recently, an *interest in sex* was considered far more appropriate for males than for females. It was considered masculine to tell dirty stories, to look at sex pictures, and to read or talk about sex. Even today, with the relaxing of the double standard, "nice" girls and women are not supposed to express an interest in sex qua sex, to experiment just for the sake of proving how feminine they are, or to talk about sex except to female friends.

Although more women work today than ever before and hold many jobs that were traditionally regarded as masculine, sex labeling of *vocations* continues. Law, medicine, and engineering are "masculine," while teaching, nursing, and social work are "feminine." Women are expected to be interested in playing subservient roles while men are expected to be interested in achieving leadership roles—all in the same vocations. Furthermore, girls are expected to regard any vocation they select as a stopgap between school and marriage while boys are taught to regard a vocation as a means of providing for a family and offering the family an opportunity for upward mobility.

The area in which sex appropriateness is most important is *personality*. People discover, through social acceptance or rejection and from social approval and disapproval, what traits are considered appropriate for members of the two sexes. Boys discover, for example, that if they are kind, sympathetic, and thoughtful of others they may be admired by adults but are likely to be labeled as sissies by their peers. Similarly, boys and girls discover that aggressiveness is disapproved and disliked in girls but that it is not only admired in boys but frequently leads to leadership roles for them (93, 94, 175).

For the most part, sex differences in socially approved traits are less marked in adulthood than earlier. Many of the differences are in degree rather than in quality. With advancing age, the differences in sex-appropriate personality traits become less and less pronounced (18, 91).

Effects of sex appropriateness on personality

People who are not sure they measure up to the cultural stereotype of sex appropriateness or who believe that others feel they do not measure up become anxious and concerned. They try to prove to themselves and to others that they are sex appropriate. Since men are supposed to be big and strong, not subject to fatigue, illness, or any limitations on their activities, they constantly disregard warning signals of poor health to avoid being considered unmanly. This "suicidal cult of manliness" is one of the major reasons that men die earlier than women.

In addition to trying to prove their sex appropriateness, people try to inhibit or deflect any tendencies that might lead to social judgments of sex inappropriateness. The boy who is forced into business because his father thought his desire to be a musician was unmasculine and the girl who is persuaded to give up her career by a husband who feels that a woman's place is in the home are often unhappy, poorly adjusted people. "Marginal women,"—those who are torn between acceptance and rejection of the traditional beliefs of sex appropriateness—often suffer the psychological ravages of instability, conflict, anxiety, resentment, and self-hate. This is especially true of career women and of those who try to play simultaneously the traditional role of wife and mother and the modern role of career woman (138).

Some boys and men, like some girls and women, prefer the characteristics of the opposite sex to those considered appropriate for their own sex. They are beset by many conflicting emotions when they try to decide whether to follow their own inclinations or to try to please others. This conflict situation in men results in a "feminine protest," which is expressed in a derogatory attitude toward everything considered "masculine," whether it be appearance, attitudes, interests, or patterns of behavior. In women, it results in a masculine protest, described earlier.

This situation, for both males and females, leads to a rebellion against being forced into a pattern they do not like or feel incapable of adjusting to successfully. In addition, it leads to a defensive reaction toward their own sex-inappropriate behavior, which is often expressed in aggressiveness. Even when they conform outwardly to the sex-approved patterns, they often rebel inwardly. This results in ambivalence accompanied by tensions, anxieties, and resentments. It is from these feelings that the greatest personality damage comes.

By contrast, those who measure up to the standards of sex appropriateness for the groups with which they are identified feel adequate and satisfied in this area of their life. Other things equal, they know that they are favorably judged by others, and this enables them to evaluate themselves favorably. The doubts, uncertainties, anxieties, and other negative feelings experienced by those who have reason to doubt their sex appropriateness do not plague them and, consequently, they can be self-satisfied and self-acceptant.

SEX ROLES

Sex roles are the basic patterns of life assigned to the individual by the social group with which he is identified. The group prescribes for members of both sexes the approved patterns of behavior for different ages and under different conditions. These roles are based on the traditional belief that the two sexes differ and, therefore, should learn to play roles in keeping with the differences.

The prescribed sex roles vary within a large cultural group according to the cultural background and social-class status of the group members. They likewise differ from one cultural group to another, though here the differences are based on the belief that sex differences are of prime importance in areas of life that are crucial to the cultural group itself. In a predominantly warlike culture, for example, the approved sex role for men concentrates on warlike pursuits, as compared with money-earning pursuits in a culture where wars are infrequent and the attainment of things the culture values depends on the amount of money available.

Prescribed roles for members of the two sexes remained relatively static for many centuries. Parents and teachers knew exactly what their children would be expected to do and how they would be expected to do it at different periods in their life span. Training the young for the sex roles they would play throughout life was thus a relatively easy task. This is not the way it is in many cultures today. Changes in patterns of living due to the shift from a rural to an urban culture and from hand skills to modern technology have produced a number of changes in the approved sex roles.

Traditional versus developmental sex roles

Throughout the centuries, the prescribed roles for the two sexes were very different, with the role for boys and men regarded as more difficult and more danger-

ous than that for girls and women and, therefore, more prestigious. The *traditional* roles were based on the assumption that males were physically stronger and mentally superior and should play the dominant role, even though it might subject them to more danger and lead to earlier death. This role emphasized the "instrumental" nature of the male's contribution in the sense that it was he who was supposed to adapt to the requirements of the external environment.

The traditional role for women was regarded as inferior to that of the male. This was justified on the ground that females were believed to be incapable of playing as difficult and as dangerous a role as men. The female role emphasized "expressiveness"; that is, members of the female sex were expected to be responsible for emotional warmth and harmonious relationships in the home or in any social group with which they were identified.

The woman was expected to gain satisfaction from achievements by "proxy"—or through identification with a father, husband, or male relative—while the male gained satisfaction through his own achievements. The female role was thus other-oriented while the male role was self-oriented (121, 128).

As patterns of living have changed, many cultures have gradually adopted new sex-role expectations. The new roles have been labeled "developmental," "equalitarian," or "egalitarian." All embody the belief that the differences between the sexes are far less marked than was formerly believed and not particularly important for successful living in the modern urban technological culture (128, 162).

The male and female roles, while still different, are not "dominant" and "subservient." Their value to the social group as a whole is regarded as more equal. Perhaps the central change has been to make the female role more self-oriented. Expressed in another way, the equalitarian concept of the female role is similar to the male role in its major aspects and in its major emphasis.

Acceptance of approved sex role

Knowing what is sex appropriate does not guarantee that a person will be willing to accept the approved sex role or play the role consistently. How much obligation the person feels he owes the group will influence his willingness to live up to its role expectations. And how well he conforms to these expectations will influence his adjustment to the group and his acceptance by its members.

Difficulties in accepting approved sex role Some of the difficulties the individual encounters in accepting and playing the approved role for his sex are personal and some are environmental.

Americans tend to *idealize* the concepts of the different sex roles. The resulting discrepancy between the idealized concept and the real often leads to conflicts, tensions, and resentments. The role of wife and mother, for example, is often idealized by little girls as they play with their dolls. This idealized mother-role concept tends to grow stronger as the girls get older and begin to read romantic stories, view romantic pictures, and listen to romantic music. By the time they are ready to marry, they are likely to have such a highly romanticized concept of the role of wife and mother that they will undergo severe psychological trauma when circumstances force them to accept a realistic concept. Boys also idealize the role of the adult male and often find the real role far less glamorous and satisfying than they had expected.

The overlap of the approved male and female sex roles in our culture today results in *confusion,* not only for boys and girls but also for adults. Winick (227) relates some of the areas of overlap in which sex distinctions are disappearing:

Sex roles have become substantially neutered and environmental differences increasingly blurred. Our Age of the Neuter begins to leave its mark on young people in their very tender years. Gender-linked colors like pink and blue for children's clothing are yielding to green, yellow, and other colors that can be used for either Dick or Jane. . . . The hair of little girls is shorter and that of little boys is longer. . . . Other kinds of his-her appearances are chic for young people. . . . Reading habits of young people are less related to gender than they were a generation ago. . . . School curricula are offering fewer subjects which are unique to each sex and both sexes learn some subjects, for example, typing.

Confusion about the approved sex role is intensified when a person is *trained* for one role and then suddenly expected to play another. For example, girls are made dependent by parental sheltering, but when they marry, they are expected, literally overnight, to shift from the sex role of daughter to the sex role of wife—a role that demands far more independence and self-reliance than the daughter role. The woman who must adjust to the role of wife and mother after playing the role of businesswoman and then, later, to no clearly defined role when she becomes a widow with grown children, has great difficulty accepting and playing her roles successfully. Male roles, from childhood on, are, in contrast, much more stable and subject to fewer abrupt and drastic changes.

Motivation to accept the role considered appropriate for one's sex is strong only if the personal satisfaction and social prestige attached to the role are great. This explains why few boys or men wish that they had been born female and why many girls and women lack a strong motivation to play the traditional female role. See Figure 11–3.

DIFFICULTIES FOR WOMEN When girls approach adolescence, they discover many disadvantages to the approved female role which they were formerly unaware of. When they begin to feel the pinch of the "double standard," they realize that the female role is less rewarding than the male. While they want marriage and a family, many also want the independence and status offered by a career.

The college-trained woman, who feels that she is "different" from other women, wants to play a role that includes achievements related to her special interests, abilities, and training in addition to the achievements of the traditional wife and mother. For her, the developmental or equalitarian concept of the female role has great appeal. However, she often finds the difficulties confronted in trying to play that role insurmountable. Mead (138) describes her predicament:

So, we have the paradox of having women educated like men and of according them all the rights of men, except one—the right to dedicate themselves to any task other than homemaking. Whether they are good cooks, bad cooks or indifferent cooks, good mothers or irritable mothers, they are expected to regard homemaking as the ultimate career and the needs of a husband and a few children as sufficient for the most gifted and ambitious among them.

One of the chief difficulties educated women face in accepting the traditional female role is *value change.* Schooling develops many values which the woman must renounce and replace if she is to find any feeling of satisfaction in the traditional female role. Speaking of women college graduates, Levin (125) comments:

For the majority, in time, the satin-circled diplomas mark descent from ivory towers to park playgrounds, push-button kitchens, supermarkets and finished basements. The road from Freud to Frigidaire, from Sophocles to Spock, has turned out to be a bumpy one. Many young women—certainly not all—whose education plunged them into a world of ideas, feel stifled in their homes. They find their routine lives out of joint with their training. Like shut-ins, they feel left out ... The reason a college-bred housewife often feels like a two-headed schizophrenic is this: she used to talk about whether music was frozen architecture; now she talks over frozen food plans. Once she wrote a paper on the Graveyard Poets: now she writes notes for the milkman. Once she determined the boiling point of sulphuric acid; now she determines her boiling point with the overdue repairman.

Unquestionably, accepting traditional values about the use of leisure time is a major problem for educated women who are forced to accept the traditional female role. Having become accustomed to spending their leisure time with friends, in social activities of various kinds, in sports, either as active participants or spectators, or in community organizations, they find it difficult to adjust to being a "homebody" whose free time is spent primarily with family members and neighbors.

In trying to fill the traditional female role, the woman who prefers the equalitarian role may lose many of the qualities that made her outstanding and happy. She may occasionally be complaining and bitter. If she cannot or will not accept the values associated with the traditional role, she is likely to be anxious and deeply disturbed. Much of the *fatigue* women suffer from is not caused by overwork but by the tension produced by frustrations (149).

Even more damaging to the personality is the feeling of *futility* that often accompanies psychological fatigue. Many women who made the decision to accept the traditional role of wife and mother when they were too immature and inexperienced to know what the role actually meant feel caught in a web from which they see no chance for escape. By the mid-thirties or forties, many have completed their role of caring for young children, and each year after that their feeling of usefulness in the family decreases. According to Kiell and Friedman, "The rewards of housewifemanship are frustration and lowered self-esteem. Plowed under is the healthy self-concept [developed] before marriage" (116).

The more highly educated women are, on the

"You used to WORK before you were married, didn't you, Mommy?"

Figure 11-3 The implication that the female role in the home is less prestigious than that outside the home often weakens women's motivation to play this role. (Adapted from Keane's "The Family Circus." Register and Tribune Syndicate. *The Philadelphia Evening Bulletin,* Oct. 24, 1969. Used by permission.)

whole, the greater the dissatisfaction with the traditional female role and the greater the difficulty in accepting it. Many who have tried to accept the traditional role would like to shed it but realize that they have little chance of making a change to a role they would find more congenial. As a result, they tend to glorify the role they *might* have played and this increases their discontent.

DIFFICULTIES FOR MEN In spite of the advantages and prestige attached to the male role, not all boys or men are able or willing to accept it. For most, however, the preference for this role grows stronger and stronger as boys discover the favorable social attitudes associated with it. As Ausubel says, "The male counterpart of a 'tomboy' who relishes sewing and reads girls' books is indeed a rarity" (9).

On the other hand, some boys lack the *physique* and *strength* to be "regular boys" or to engage in rough-and-tumble games that people regard as masculine. Others have some special *talent* that absorbs their time and interest. If this talent lies in the area of art—an area that many people consider feminine—

these boys will prefer their artistic activities to those considered more appropriate for males.

By the time boys reach adulthood and marry, they may find themselves forced to play the role of *mother's helper* or family dishwasher and handy-man—roles which they regard as "woman's work." Many men resent being "mother's helper," but willingly take on household jobs which they regard as masculine, such as repairing appliances, mowing the lawn, or shoveling snow. Only if child care provides an outlet for their masculinity, as guides and companions to their children, do men find the father role satisfying.

Effects of sex roles on personality

A willing and wholehearted acceptance of one's socially-approved sex role contributes to social acceptance and a favorable self-evaluation. These lead to good social adjustments and happiness. Failure to fulfill role expectation leads to unfavorable social judgments, lack of social acceptance, and poor personal adjustment. Adolescent boys with "feminine" interests have been reported to be poorly adjusted, showing tendencies toward neuroticism. These patterns are in part due to the conflicts they experience between playing the role they want to play and the role the social group expects them to play (35, 96, 224).

How far-reaching and troubling can be the woman's unwillingness to accept her sex role is indicated by how the members of her family are affected. There is ample evidence that it leads to poor marital adjustments as well as to disturbances in the mother-child relationship which play havoc with the psychological development of her children (8, 12, 36, 152).

The mother who does not want to be a mother rejects her child, either consciously or unconsciously. The child senses this and suffers all the psychological damage of rejection. Anna Freud (71) discusses the "unwilling mother" in this statement:

None who has had even a short acquaintance with child welfare work will deny that there are "bad mothers." . . .*It is too much to expect [a mother to] fulfill her task if she has not taken on the role of motherhood voluntarily, if it has been forced upon her. That leaves on one side, classed as "unwilling," all those mothers who never meant to have a baby, or did not mean to have it at the particular time when pregnancy occurred. The reasons for their unwillingness may be external ones: financial difficulties, lack of their own home, or of space, the burden of too many earlier children, illegitimacy of the relations with the child's father. There are emotional reasons such as lack of affection for the husband which is extended to his child. Or, the reasons, rationalized merely on the surface by external conditions, may lie much deeper in the mother's nature. There are many women who are incapacitated for motherhood by virtue of their masculinity. They may wish for children for reasons of pride and possessiveness, but their humiliation at finding themselves female, their longing for a career, their competitiveness with the husband preclude any real enjoyment of or with the infant.*

When a strong preference for the role of the opposite sex and a rejection of the role for one's own sex persist, they become habitual and almost impossible to change. Unfavorable social attitudes toward the person who persists in playing the role approved for members of the opposite sex are likely to lead to personality maladjustments. *Sex-role inversion*—identification with and adoption of the psychological identity of the opposite sex, in which the person thinks, feels, and acts in a manner typical of the opposite sex—affects the entire personality structure. The person becomes a "psychosomatic misfit" whose body is characteristic of one sex but whose personality is characteristic of the other. In female sex-role inversion, the woman tries to be as masculine as possible.

Since the role of wife and mother is *the* socially approved role for women, the woman who does not fill this role, whether out of choice or necessity, soon becomes aware of the unfavorable social attitudes directed toward her. As a result, she takes an unfavorable attitude toward herself. Furthermore, in most families it is expected that any unmarried daughter will assume responsibility for the care of aging parents. This adds a feeling of martyrdom to an already unfavorable self-concept. As a result, the woman develops a personality pattern marked by resentment toward and envy of those who have been able to assume the traditional role. Should she later have an opportunity to marry, she is likely to develop feelings of guilt for deserting her parents (43, 58).

In contrast, the unmarried man does not feel embarrassed or ashamed at not accepting the traditional male role of husband and father. Little if any social stigma is attached to the role of bachelor. Rather, the bachelor who has made a success in his vocation is much sought after by women of all ages. If, in addition, he is attractive looking, he acquires a romantic halo which makes his role seem far more glamorous than that of the man who has accepted the traditional male role.

SEXUAL BEHAVIOR

Attitudes toward sexual behavior are a reflection of the attitudes of the significant people in one's life and of the social group with which one is identified. In childhood, most people learn to associate shame and fear of punishment with any behavior related to sex. They are made to feel guilty about engaging in any sex-related activity and to be anxious about the consequences.

Also in childhood, people learn what is considered "normal" and, therefore, "right" and what is considered "abnormal" and, therefore, "wrong" or "depraved" in sexual behavior. These early attitudes are often modified as people acquire more knowledge about sexuality and as their contacts widen. However, the effects of early learning experiences are never completely eradicated.

Variations in attitudes toward sexual behavior

Until recently there was a strong tendency in the American culture to condemm all sexual behavior except in marriage. Masturbation, sex play with members of the same or of the opposite sex, and premarital and extramarital intercourse were forbidden activities and anyone who engaged in them developed feelings of guilt and shame.

Today, especially among the *younger* generation, the attitude toward sexual behavior is far more tolerant and permissive. Many members of the older generation, and some of the younger as well, "still cling to the Puritan ethic of sex, even though today's best-selling novels, the best-attended movies, and many of the new magazines would suggest otherwise" (150).

Actually, the change has been more in *attitudes* than in behavior itself. For example, we have little evidence that there has been an increase or decrease in the number of people of different ages who engage in masturbation, but we do know that most people take a more tolerant attitude toward masturbation than they did in the past (118, 134, 170). Similarly,

premarital intercourse in not appreciably more widespread than formerly, though the attitudes toward it are more tolerant, especially when it is engaged in because of love rather than because of curiosity or conquest (150, 173). People who have gone to college, whether of the older generation or the younger, are more liberal in their attitudes toward sexual behavior than those with less *education*.

Attitudes toward sexual behavior differ markedly from one *social class* to another. Members of the lower socioeconomic groups have a strongly disapproving attitude toward all forms of sexual behavior except sexual intercourse. Many regard masturbation, homosexuality, petting, and necking as perversions and punish those who engage in such behavior with social disapproval and ostracism (118, 134, 166, 170). Among lower-class males, sexual relations with members of the opposite sex are frequent and open. Men boast of their "conquests" and regard them as status symbols (171).

In middle-class groups, attitudes toward sexual intercourse are less tolerant and toward other forms of sexual behavior, more tolerant. The attitude toward masturbation, for example, is more tolerant than among members of the lower classes, though disapproval is strong. Sexual intercourse outside marriage, especially among middle-aged and elderly, is regarded as a "sin." Petting to a climax and prolonged kissing is tolerated, though often frowned upon as "dangerous" and likely to lead to intercourse. There is also a tendency, especially among girls and women, to romanticize love and to regard the "cave-man" tactics of lower-class men as "vulgar" or even an indication of sexual perversion (53, 69).

Variations in attitudes toward sexual behavior are also found among people of different *religious faiths*, regardless of social class. In general, people of the Jewish faith, though still strict, are more permissive in their attitudes toward sexual behavior than those of the Protestant and Catholic faiths. The most permissive are those with no religious affiliation, and the least permissive, the Irish Catholics (54).

Although attitudes toward sexual behavior have changed in recent generations, *girls* and *women* of all ages are less tolerant than men and boys. Even with the relaxation of the double standard and the availability of the new contraceptives, members of the female sex are still stricter in their attitudes toward their own sexual behavior and that of other members of their sex than males are toward theirs (66, 150, 197).

Finally, variations in attitudes are notable among people of different degrees of *personal adjustment*. In both sexes at all ages, those who are best adjusted and those who have the most wholesome attitudes toward sexuality as an important aspect of life have the healthiest and most tolerant attitudes toward sexual behavior. This does not mean that they favor permissiveness in their own sexual behavior or in that of others but rather that they are more tolerant and less punitive than are those who are less well adjusted (69, 171, 272).

Forms of sexual behavior

In spite of the social restrictions and unfavorable social attitudes, few boys and girls reach adulthood or even adolescence without having engaged in some form of behavior related to sex. This behavior varies markedly from person to person but it follows a predictable pattern, with certain forms normally common at one age and other forms at other ages.

Since few forms of sexual behavior are entirely approved by the social group, engaging in sexual behavior is bound to affect the person's self-concept. The more his behavior deviates from that of others of the same age and the same socioeconomic and sex groups, the more unfavorably he will be judged and the more damaging the judgments will be to his self-concept.

A brief survey of the patterns of sexual behavior that are common at different ages in the life span and the attitudes of members of the social group toward these patterns will serve to show how the person who engages in them will be affected by social reactions. Only when social reactions are favorable will there not be psychological damage even when personal reactions to sexual behavior are pleasurable and satisfying.

One of the earliest forms of sexual behavior is *exploration*. Curiosity always leads to exploration but exploration can take many forms. It may be purely intellectual, leading the child to ask questions or to read books to get answers to the questions he is afraid to ask, or it may be manipulative, in which the child explores his own sex organs or those of others. In general, children and adolescents who are unable to satisfy their curiosity indirectly by an intellectual approach do so by a direct approach involving manipulative techniques. Furthermore, group pressures encourage the direct approach. If everyone is doing it, the child or adolescent will follow the group even though his curiosity has been satisfied already by indirect methods.

When children are taught that such behavior is "wrong" and forbidden, they usually carry it out in secret with constant fear of being caught and punished. In time, they come to experience feelings of anxiety and guilt whenever they engage in these forbidden activities.

The most common form of sexual behavior in children is *masturbation*. While there is little evidence that masturbation is physically harmful to children, social attitudes toward it are so unfavorable that most children develop feelings of guilt and shame and many suffer from acute anxiety caused by fear of what *might* happen to them as a result of masturbating.

The peak of masturbation generally comes during the pubertal years when the body is changing and when the sex drive is still diffuse. At this time there is also an increase in *homosexual* play. Both masturbation and homosexual play precede any erotic feelings from physical contacts with members of the opposite sex. This is also the time when *crushes* and *hero-worship* are common.

When boys and girls become sexually mature at puberty, the sex drive is normally turned to members of the opposite sex. This leads to a decrease in masturbation and homosexual play and an increase in *heterosexual play* in the form of necking, petting, and attempts at premarital intercourse. As the sex drive increases with sexual maturing, it is not uncommon for boys to try to force girls into sex play which many find offensive or frightening. This *aggressive sex play*, which is more likely to occur after boys have been drinking, when they are alone in cars with girls, or when they are on dates with younger girls or girls of a lower socioeconomic status than they, usually reaches its peak at 18 years of age.

Many girls resist aggressive sex play by force. If they are in love, however, if they feel adequately protected against pregnancy, and if they believe that the boys are serious about marrying them at some later date, their reactions are more likely to be positive than negative. The difference in attitudes toward sex play in the two sexes does not mean a difference in the strength of the sex drive. Instead, it means that girls are more inhibited by fear of strong social disapproval or possible pregnancy.

During the adult years, the patterns of sexual behavior differ somewhat for members of the two sexes. The male sex drive tends to weaken with the passage of time, owing primarily to psychological causes—anxiety about financial and vocational problems, overwork, or disenchantment with marriage—rather than to physical causes. Whether the female sex drive will weaken also depends mainly on psychological causes. If the woman is overworked by child care and household responsibility, if she is trying to carry a double load of work inside the home and outside, if she is disenchanted with marriage, or if she fears more pregnancies, the sex drive will gradually weaken somewhat, as does the male sex drive.

That psychological factors play an important role in the sexual activity of men is well recognized. As men approach middle age and many of the sources of anxiety that plagued them earlier are removed or lessened, they show a renewed interest in sexual behavior. This sometimes drives them to seek new sexual partners in extramarital affairs or to divorce their wives and marry younger women who they believe will meet their sexual needs more adequately.

The effect of psychological factors on the female sex drive is shown in a number of ways as well. As women reach the menopause, they realize that pregnancy is unlikely, and this removes the inhibitions they formerly had. When younger women believe that they have a "safe" contraceptive, they engage in intercourse more frequently (174).

There is little evidence that the sex drive weakens to the point where interest and participation in sex behavior dies out in old age. Instead, when the person is in good health, interest and participation in sexual behavior persists unless unfavorable attitudes on the part of the persons involved inhibit them. Only when there is a decline in health conditions does the strength of the sex drive decrease from physical causes (160).

That the sex drive is still present in old age, though weaker than in younger adults, is seen by the fact that older people continue to engage in sexual activities. What forms of sexual activity they will engage in depends to some extent upon the pattern of life the people follow and the forms that were most satisfying to them when they were younger. Older people who are widowed, for example, are far less likely to engage in extramarital sexual relationships than younger people. Unless they remarry, they are more likely to turn the energy from the sex drive into masturbation, erotic daydreams, or an erotic attachment to a younger person. It may even take the form of

sexual recrudescence—a foolish infatuation for members of the opposite sex which motivates the elderly man to want to make love to any or all young girls he comes in contact with or to rape or molest female children or young adolescents. In elderly women, it usually takes the form of being infatuated with or marrying men young enough to be their grandchildren.

Management of the sex drive

How the sex drive affects personality is influenced more by how the person manages the drive than by its strength. If the person uses healthy means of controlling it and if he expresses it in patterns of behavior that are socially approved, the effects will be beneficial, and vice versa.

As Freud pointed out long ago, suppression of the sex drive, especially during the early years of life, often leads to neuroticism in later life (72). Constant suppression of the sex drive, regardless of the reasons for doing so, leads to chronic sexual tension which is expressed in unhappiness, a sense of frustration, or sexual fantasies. All of these interfere with the person's ability to concentrate on the task at hand and to make good social adjustments.

It has been recognized for many years that unhealthy forms of sexual behavior and sex perversions may occur if sex objects appropriate to the person's age and status are not available. For example, adolescent boys and girls who are segregated from members of the opposite sex for long periods in all-male or all-female schools or camps and adults who are geographically isolated from members of the opposite sex because of imprisonment or the demands of their vocations often turn to socially disapproved forms of sexual behavior, such as masturbation, homosexuality, rape of children, or sexual contacts with animals.

Whether the person will suppress his sex drive, express it in socially approved behavior, or resort to socially disapproved behavior will depend largely on his attitude. If he believes that all forms of sexual behavior are depraved, he will have marked feelings of guilt and shame whenever he engages in it in any form. In time, these feelings will have an inhibitory effect on the sex drive.

If he has a more wholesome attitude toward sexuality and sexual behavior, he will be able to manage the sex drive in such a way as to satisfy his own desires while conforming to socially approved patterns of behavior. As Kirkendall has said, "Sexual behavior is primarily a psychological rather than a physical pattern" (119). Under such conditions, it can be managed by proper attitudes.

A study by Ellis of people's reasons for engaging in extramarital relations has revealed that while such behavior is disapproved by most people, the reasons for engaging in it may be either healthy or unhealthy. Among the "healthy" reasons cited for such behavior are the desire for sexual variation, love enhancement through the excitement of new romances and love experiences, adventure-seeking to relieve the monotony of married life and its problems, sexual curiosity, and sexual deprivation due to the sickness or absence of the spouse. In some groups, "wifeswapping" or having extramarital relations is not only accepted but even approved.

"Unhealthy" or emotionally disturbed reasons given for engaging in extramarital relations are low frustration tolerance, as in the case of excessive drinking, hostility toward the spouse, self-deprecation resulting from perfectionistic demands on the spouse which lead to feelings of inferiority, attempts to bolster self-esteem by affairs with a less perfectionistic person, ego bolstering by winning the favor of others in such affairs, escapism from family difficulties, and marital escapism versus separation or divorce (66).

These healthy and unhealthy reasons for engaging in extramarital relations are not limited, Ellis claims, to members of the male sex. Women engage in such relations and for the same reasons as men. The major difference between the two sexes is that women engage in extramarital relations less often than men, not because of lack of need or desire but rather because of fear of unfavorable social judgments if their affairs should become known or fear of pregnancy (66).

Some people find the sex drive especially difficult to manage. When they attempt to control it, they build up many tensions and become preoccupied with sexual activities. As Kirkendall has stressed, a "sexually promiscuous person is often a conflict-ridden or psychologically maladjusted person" (119). Overemphasis on sex is characteristic of the neurotic personality (110).

By contrast, the well-adjusted person has less difficulty managing his sex drive. He thus experiences fewer tensions and achieves a balance between sex and other interests. Consequently, he makes better personal adjustments and better adjustments to marriage.

Variations in management of the sex drive People who mature early are, on the whole, apt to engage in sexual behavior more frequently and to have a greater interest in sex than late maturers. People who as children learned that parents and other significant people in their lives regarded all forms of sexual behavior as "not nice" or "wicked" tend to make greater efforts to control the sex drive than those whose childhood experiences with sex were less associated with feelings of guilt and shame.

Most important of all, differences in people's concepts of themselves influence how they handle the sex drive. If the person has a marked feeling of personal inadequacy, he may use the sex drive to prove to himself and to others that he is adequate by engaging in sexual behavior that will be regarded as a symbol of masculinity or femininity. When a person's management of the sex drive conforms to his moral values, however, he will be able to respect and accept himself in a way which he cannot if his behavior falls below these values.

Effects of sexual behavior on personality

Because of the marked interest in sexuality among people of all ages and the high value placed on sexual behavior as a symbol of masculinity or femininity, it is understandable that the quality and quantity of the person's sexual behavior will have a profound influence on his self-concept. At no time is this more true than during the adolescent and adult years and at no period has it been more true than it is today.

The effects of sexual behavior on the self-concept are both direct and indirect. The *direct* influences come from the way the person evaluates himself in relation to his sexual behavior, and the *indirect* from the judgments others make of him because of this behavior. Many of the direct effects, resulting from the person's self-evaluations, are markedly influenced by social judgments which have a profound impact on his self-evaluations.

From earliest childhood, the indirect influences come from social attitudes toward the person's sexual behavior. The child who is criticized, shamed, or punished for engaging in sex play will soon think of himself as a "bad" person and will be ashamed. If his curiosity is strong enough to drive him to try to satisfy it anyway, and it usually is, he will live in constant dread of being discovered and punished. This will further intensify his unfavorable self-judgments.

Even sexual behavior that is sanctioned as a part of marriage indirectly affects the self-concept. If the wife, for example, gives evidence of not finding the marital relationship satisfying, the husband will consider this an indication of her failure to live up to the expected role. Should he then seek satisfaction in extramarital relations and should these become known to others, his self-evaluation will be greatly affected by how others evaluate this behavior.

Knowing how members of the social group feel about sexual behavior in middle-aged or elderly people influences the older person's evaluation of himself when he engages in such behavior. It is not uncommon for men and women, as they grow older, to wonder if they are "sex perverts" because they crave and enjoy sexual behavior as much as or even more than they did when they were younger. Even the mild flirtations of elderly men and women with younger persons of the opposite sex often lose much of their ego satisfaction when the elderly persons see the looks of amusement or disgust on the faces of others or hear comments about "a sign of senility."

Because judgments made by others serve as reference points by which the person judges himself, the most serious psychological damage of the indirect effects comes from the kind of standards others encourage the person to establish as a means of evaluating himself. It is in this way that the direct effects on personality are influenced by the indirect effects of sexual behavior. The girl who has been subjected to aggressive sex play on a date and who reacts to it with fear and disgust will wonder if she has created the impression that she is a "loose woman" who invites such behavior or if she is an "iceberg" because she resists aggressive advances. Bernard (20) writes:

When the norms forbade all extramarital sex relations, a girl or woman could easily refuse male requests. When the norms are permissive, she has nothing to hide behind. If she does not wish to engage in sex relations . . . she is left in an exploitable position. If in the past she had to say no to safeguard her self-respect, she must now say yes for the same reason—to avoid the dreaded epithet "frigid."

Both men and women evaluate themselves in terms of the satisfaction their marital relations give their spouses. How important this is in self-evaluation has been explained by Clark and Wallin (47):

Women's lack of sexual gratification has repercussions for their husbands as well as for themselves. In a culture that stresses the equality of marital partners and the right of both to sexual enjoyment, it is to be expected that husbands will tend to suffer some guilt in urging an activity they know is not pleasurable to their wives. Added to the guilt, and accentuating it, may be feelings of inadequacy engendered in husbands by the thought that the fault is or could be theirs.

Because a strong sex drive in women is often regarded as unfeminine, the woman who shows a keen interest in sexual behavior or who frankly derives satisfaction from it is often regarded as "oversexed." Consequently, if the woman's sex drive increases in strength and her husband's decreases, she feels guilty and ashamed. Her desire for sex play and intercourse tends to increase his feelings of masculine inadequacy and, at the same time, to increase his wife's feelings of guilt and shame.

Regardless of how they cope with the problem, men who feel sexually inadequate and women who feel that they are oversexed are psychologically damaged. This comes not from the effects of sexual gratification per se but from the realization that the social group judges members of the two sexes by standards which they have accepted to judge themselves. Only when their self-judgments conform to the social standards they have accepted will these judgments have a favorable effect on their self-concepts.

SUMMARY

1 The direct influence of sexuality on personality comes from the effects of the sex hormones which influence body form and functioning and the quality of the person's behavior. The indirect influence, which is greater than the direct, comes from three sources: the effect of cultural influences on the sex drive, the attitudes of significant people and their treatment of the person because of his sexuality, and the molding of the personality pattern to conform to a socially approved pattern of sex appropriateness.

2 The amount of interest a person has in sexuality is important in determining how much influence it will have on his personality. In spite of cultural pressures which encourage an interest in all matters relating to sexuality, interest varies in both amount and degree of wholesomeness. The variations depend on such factors as sex, age, and socioeconomic status.

3 Attitudes toward sexuality are learned in conjunction with the acquisition of knowledge about sexuality. Whether they will be wholesome or not depends largely on how sex information is given. Once learned, these attitudes are subject to only minor changes as the person grows older. That is why they have such a profound influence on how the person meets sexual problems. How he meets these problems, in turn, affects his personality directly through his self-evaluation and indirectly through the evaluation members of the social group make of him.

4 One of the principal sexual problems the person must face is that of developing a healthy attitude toward his own sex and toward other people of his sex. Because the attitudes in most cultures are more favorable toward members of the male sex, the person is influenced by these cultural attitudes in evaluating himself in relation to members of the other sex. Many females show their acceptance of the unfavorable social attitude toward their sex by wishing that they were males, by letting it undermine their self-respect, and by derogating members of the female sex in general. Acceptance of cultural attitudes toward members of the two sexes affects both males and females unfavorably.

5 Cultural attitudes likewise influence people's attitudes toward sex differences in physical and mental characteristics. Because the male sex has been the favored sex throughout history, it has become traditional to interpret male characteristics, whether physical or mental, as superior to the female and more prestigious. Acceptance of these traditional cultural attitudes toward sex differences results in encouraging males to evaluate themselves favorably and females to evaluate themselves unfavorably. This, combined with the treatment accorded members of the two sexes by the social group, strengthens the favorable self-evaluation of males and the unfavorable self-evaluation of females.

6 A person is considered sex appropriate if his appearance, behavior, attitudes, interests, and values conform to those traditionally associated with members of his sex. Because greater social pressure is placed on boys to be sex appropriate, it is easier for them to learn their approved sex role. Furthermore, females encounter greater confusion about just what are the standards of sex appropriateness for their sex. This slows down the learning process and weakens their motivation to learn.

7 Learning to be sex appropriate comes from child training and from identification with persons of the same sex in real life or in the mass media. How great an influence being sex appropriate will have on the self-concept depends on how sex appropriate the person is in areas that are highly valued by the social group, such as appearance, speech, names, interests, achievements, and personality traits. People who conform to social expectations in these areas are regarded more favorably than those who do not and this influences their self-evaluations.

8 Every cultural group prescribes sex roles which it expects members of the two sexes to accept and follow. In cultures where change is slow, it is relatively easy for children to learn how to play the roles they are expected to play. In cultures where changes take place rapidly, as in the American culture, learning to play the approved sex role is difficult. The difficulty is increased for girls by confusion about just what the approved sex role is—whether the traditional role or the more modern equalitarian role.

9 Learning what is the approved sex role does not necessarily provide the person with the motivation to accept it. This is most obvious among members of the female sex, especially women who have been college trained and who often prefer the equalitarian, or the developmental, role to the traditional female role.

10 How willing and able the person is to conform to the approved sex-role pattern influences personality through the person's evaluation of self. This is reinforced by social attitudes toward the person based on how closely he conforms to social expectations. Sex-role inversion, or the adoption of the psychological identity of the opposite sex, is a strong indication that the person has rejected the approved sex role for his sex. This leads to unfavorable social judgments and thus to negative self-judgments.

11 Because of the high social value associated with the role of wife and mother, unmarried women experience great psychological damage. Unmarried men, who encounter less disfavor in any event, can counteract unfavorable social judgments by successful achievement in their vocations. As women have few means of counteracting unfavorable social judgments, they develop feelings of failure accompanied by psychological damage.

12 The effect of sexual behavior on the self-concept comes from the person's attitude toward sexual behavior and the attitudes of significant people in his life. These attitudes are greatly influenced by early childhood experiences with sexual behavior and by the way significant people reacted to them. Attitudes vary according to the person's age, social class, religious faith, educational background, sex, and personal adjustment.

13 The person who expresses his sex drive in socially approved patterns of behavior judges himself more favorably than one who engages in the disapproved forms of expression. This is because the latter recognizes that others are judging him unfavorably. Equally important, when a person finds that he gains little personal satisfaction from using socially approved forms of expression, the favorable effects of approval by the social group are partially counteracted by his unfavorable evaluation of himself.

educational determinants

Next to the home, schools and colleges are the chief determinants of what a person thinks of himself and of what his habitual patterns of behavior will be. Solomon stressed this point when he said, "The school-room must be looked upon as a force secondary in importance only to the home in the development of human personality" (206). The preeminent role of the home was noted thus by Parker (164):

Boys and girls are not delivered as raw materials at the school door. They are already products—products of five or six years of processing in their homes. More and more we realize that what the school can do to develop a child's potential is limited by what the home has already done, and is doing, to him and for him.

Nevertheless, the school's role as a shaper of personality is formidable. Next to parents, teachers have more influence on the development of a child's personality than any other group of people. The teacher-child relationship has its greatest impact in the child's early school years when teachers normally play the role of surrogate parents during the time the child is away from home (206). As the child grows older, the teacher's influence decreases. This is true also of parental influence. However, by the time the decrease in teacher—and parental—influence begins to be felt, the foundations of personality are well laid.

During his early, formative years, the child has two worlds—the world of the family and the world of the school. If these worlds are similar, in that the values held by parents and teachers are consistent, the expectations of parents and teachers coincide, and their ways of guiding the child's development are similar, one will reinforce the other. If, on the other hand, the values, expectations, and guidance in the two worlds are dissimilar or conflicting, the child will be confused. If teachers put high value on studying and parents put low value on it, for example, the child will be torn between the two, not knowing which standard to accept as his own.

There are a number of reasons why educational institutions play such a significant role in personality development. *First,* all children must attend school, regardless of their personal preferences. *Second,* the school's influence comes early in life when the self-concept is being formed. While the compulsory age for school beginning varies somewhat for different states and different countries, most children are in school by the time they are 6 years old and some are in preschools by the time they are 2 or 3.

Third, children spend more time in school than in any other place outside the home. As they reach the adolescent years, they spend more of their waking time in school than in the home. *Fourth,* school provides the only real opportunity children have for getting ahead in life and, if this matters to them and their family, the school will influence personality by offering them a chance to become a "success," which is ego-inflating.

And, *finally,* school provides the person's first real opportunity to appraise himself and his abilities realistically, free from parental help or bias. Away from home, in an environment where he is judged on his merits, he learns how he stands in relation to his age-mates and how people, unbiased by personal ties, feel about him and judge his acts as compared with those of his peers. Just as the young child's self-concept is a mirror image of what he believes his parents think of him, so is the older child's self-concept a mirror image of what he believes his teachers and classmates think of him.

ATTITUDES TOWARD EDUCATION

A person's reaction to any situation, whether it be at work, at school, or in social activities, affects his adjustment to the situation, and his adjustment influences his concept of himself as a person. There is a circular reaction between the child's or adolescent's personality and his school: His personality largely determines his adjustment to school and his adjustment to school greatly influences his concept of self.

The student's attitude toward his school or college affects both his academic and nonacademic adjustments. His academic achievement and his adjustment to the extracurricular activities of school or college influence the judgments his teachers, class-mates, and parents make of him. These judgments affect their treatment of him, and the way he is treated shapes his judgment of himself.

Students who have favorable attitudes toward education usually work up to their capacities and make good adjustments to school. Those with unfavorable attitudes, by contrast, tend to become underachievers. In addition, they make little effort to adjust to school or to their teachers, classmates, studies, and the extracurricular activities or rules of the school. Many rebel against going to school and regard themselves as "martyrs" because the law requires them to attend. Working below their capacities increases their poor adjustment to school. In time, they begin to think of themselves as less able than they actually are. This dampens any motivation they might otherwise have had to do the work they are capable of doing.

Once formed, attitudes toward school are difficult to change. If a child thinks of himself as a "poor reader" or a "reading problem," for example, he cannot be motivated to improve his reading until he can be persuaded to change his self-concept. Instead, he puts up a "Gibralter-like resistance to learning" (35).

Early attitudes toward school

Whether school experiences will have a constructive and integrative effect on the student or a detrimental one will depend not on the school situation alone but also on what the student brings to school in the way of attitudes and behavior patterns. That is why his early attitudes toward school are so crucial.

Studies show that, typically, the American child looks forward to going to school. To him, going to school is a symbol of growing up. Families help to build up this favorable attitude in the belief that it will make the child's adjustment to school easier. Unfortunately, parents often paint school in such unrealistic ways that the child's experiences there do not come up to his expectations. However, because school is a new and exciting experience and because teachers do all they can to make the adjustment to school easier, the child generally has a favorable attitude *at first*. This favorable attitude usually persists through the first grade.

By the time the child reaches the second grade, he has had enough experience to know how far from reality his romanticized concept of school was. Estvan

and Estvan (78) explain the change in attitude that takes place after the first grade:

A general notion about school seems to be acquired early in life and for first graders the institution has undoubtedly a high place in their scale of values. As children grow older, they develop more extensive and refined concepts which enable them to discriminate in their perception of the objective features of school and, particularly, of the educational processes. This development is marked by a greater sensitivity to the social aspects of school life, and by a devaluation of the worth of the institution as a whole. . . . This lessening of enthusiasm for school may also be an outcome of the kinds of experiences the child has had in school some of which, apparently, have not kept the original flame burning as brightly as before.

As the child moves through the grades, his attitude toward school gradually deteriorates. Parental assessments of children's reactions to school, based on age and sex, indicate that dislike for school increases from 6 to 15 years of age (154). See Figure 12–1. Stemming from this unfavorable attitude is

Figure 12-1 Unfavorable attitudes toward school develop early in the child's school career. (Adapted from Keane's "The Family Circus." Register and Tribune Syndicate. *The Philadelphia Evening Bulletin*, Nov. 10, 1969. Used by permission.)

"Why does Mommy always say 'Have a good day'? She KNOWS we're going to SCHOOL!"

boredom with schoolwork and a general antagonism toward school—a resentment of the restrictions the school imposes and of the treatment received from teachers and school authorities. Estvan and Estvan (78) note some of the reasons for the deterioration:

It appears that children are not as fond of school as adults would like them to be. The fault does not lie in their disregard for learning as such. Rather, it seems to be based on the kinds of things pupils do in school, the way they get along with others, and the evaluation made of their efforts. If we may judge from their comments, many children do not find school activities very interesting compared with a steadily increasing diet of movies, television, travel experiences. School is "work" and not very stimulating at that.

Attitudes of older students

The typical American adolescent's attitude toward high school or college is no more favorable than that of the elementary school child. However, the adolescent realizes that education is a means to an end, both socially and vocationally. He has, according to Joseph, a "begrudging respect for education coming from external, societal pressures rather than internal regard" (122).

Forced by external pressures to recognize the value of education, the adolescent is willing to make sacrifices in time and effort to earn good grades. If he is motivated to move up the social ladder, he will be willing to work hard at his courses of study and to participate in extracurricular activities. This does not mean that he has suddenly developed a gung-ho attitude toward school. The young adolescent complains about school in general, about the restrictions school places on him, the homework he must do, the courses he is required to take, the way the school authorities run things, and the way his teachers teach (122).

Much the same holds true for college students. They want what college can give them both socially and vocationally. But, for many, the means to the desired end can be a long and unsatisfying period of forced labor. Like the child who thinks of the last day of school before vacation as a "red-letter day," so the college student often feels that he is at last gaining his freedom when his degree is conferred upon him.

Reasons for attitude deterioration

If an adolescent enters high school or college with an *unrealistic concept,* believing that he is going to have nothing but good times, he is in for a rude awakening.

Communities provide so many fun things for young people to do that schools and colleges cannot hope to compete with them as a source of entertainment. Mathematics, for example, cannot compete with a Western or a love story on TV, nor can Latin or ancient history compete with a date in the family's new car. The *curriculum* of the high school and college often seems so pedantic, old-fashioned, and irrelevant to the real world that students rebel at the thought of wasting their time on something they claim will never do them any good and will never be used in their daily lives (52, 54).

Even subjects that they can see some practical use for may be *taught* in a way that seems so boring that students feel they are wasting time that might better be spent on something that would be more interesting. When it is the thing to do to grumble and criticize everything and everyone connected with a school or college, the *morale* of any educational institution can sink to such a low level that it will reinforce already-existing unfavorable attitudes.

The leading cause of the deterioration in students' attitudes toward education is the constant reminder, through *grades* and *teacher comments,* of academic and personal shortcomings. The day in, day out pressure to perform well and the necessity of competing make schoolwork a "drag" for most students a good deal of the time.

Factors influencing attitudes toward education

Individual attitudes toward education vary from a strong interest and absorption in studies to an equally strong dislike for school in general or for the teacher, certain subjects, or the school rules in particular. These variations in attitude are due in large part to many factors which are operative to different degrees in the lives of all students. The most influential are described in the following paragraphs.

Sex Girls as a whole and at every age have more favorable attitudes toward school than boys. As a result, they do better work, cause less trouble for their teachers, and rebel less against school rules and expectations. Student rebellions, for example, are rarely initiated and carried out by girls.

Child-training methods The kind of child training used in the home determines what attitudes and behavior patterns the child will learn. These, then, are carried from the home to the school where they determine the quality of the child's behavior and the kind of adjustment he makes. If the child has developed a hostile attitude toward his parents, he will usually transfer this to his teacher and to all in authority at school. If he has learned to be timid because of authoritarian child-training methods at home, he will be timid with his teachers and classmates.

Parents who supervise their children's activities in a democratic, positive, encouraging manner help to develop adaptive behavior in their children. This, in time, becomes a generalized pattern that not only leads to success in school but fosters a favorable attitude toward school (235). When the relationship between students and their parents and other family members is a happy, cooperative, and democratic one, young people are encouraged to develop a feeling of responsibility and a wholesome attitude toward what must be done. As Cottle says, "Good parents produce good students" (57). When, on the other hand, parents show little interest in their children or in their schoolwork and when there is little exchange of affection or mutual respect, children have little motivation to do things to please their parents. Their schoolwork suffers, and they come to dislike school. Any unfavorable parent-child relationship, whether it be characterized by overindulgence, rejection, overprotection, or domination, is likely to "cripple the child's chances of adjusting successfully to the school situation, either socially or scholastically" (158).

Parental attitudes also affect children's interest in specific school subjects. For example, many parents believe that boys should like mathematics and other "masculine" subjects and do well in them. But they can see little reason for girls to study any subjects that will not add to their social attainments. Under these conditions, girls and boys come to think of themselves as "odd" if they are interested in what their parents regard as sex-inappropriate subjects (174). When parents are too authoritarian, children tend to develop resentments against school which, in time, may be expressed in student rebellions. When parents are too permissive, they encourage in their children an attitude of indifference toward school and academic achievement.

Home influences　Within the home, *parents* exert more influence on the child's attitude toward school than other family members. What parents think of school and its worth to the young person in the present as well as in the future will largely determine

his interest in education and his attitude toward it. When parents feel that a college degree is necessary, they encourage their child to continue his education through college or even through graduate school. In this way, they help to develop in the young person a strong motivation to stay in school, even though he may find it boring and question its usefulness (56, 96, 231).

Another aspect of parental influence is the attitude parents have toward teachers as a group and toward teaching as a profession. Most parents feel that teaching is all right for girls but inappropriate for boys. Many think of teachers, particularly male teachers, as ineffectual people who could not succeed in any vocation outside the cloistered walls of the academic world. They cannot help communicating this attitude, either directly or indirectly, to the child, and, in effect, encourage him to feel the same way.

Since young children tend to identify with an older sibling, they often adopt his attitude toward school, especially when he is of the same sex as they. If they learn to think unfavorably about school in imitation of an older sibling, their adjustment to school is likely to be difficult from the very start.

Unfortunately, unfavorable attitudes toward education—of parents, siblings, and other relatives—are communicated to the child before he has had any opportunity to form an unbiased judgment of his own. As Stone and Church (209) have pointed out:

Some of our negative feelings about education are early communicated to our children, making it difficult for them to approach school with the enthusiasm that is developmentally so timely. Quite early, adults (especially men) convey to children (especially boys) that school is to be spoken of disparagingly, that it is something of a penal institution, that it is less an opportunity than a forced drudgery, and that real life ends at the schoolhouse door.

Family influences on attitudes toward education are not limited to childhood, nor do they come only from parents and siblings. They may also come from one's spouse. A study of women's ambitions reveals that, in the area of education, women are more ambitious for their husbands than for themselves; this influences both husbands' and wives' attitudes toward education (224).

Social class　Parental attitudes toward education vary according to social class. *Middle-class* parents put great emphasis on the value of schooling and academic achievement as stepping-stones to vocational and social mobility. They also encourage conforming behavior in the classroom (195, 211).

Many *lower-class* parents feel that much of the work the child does in school has little relevance to what he will be doing after he leaves school and they, therefore, regard schooling as a waste of time. In addition, they believe that it is part of the teacher's job to maintain order in the classroom and so they do not feel responsible for encouraging the child to conform to school rules and regulations as middle-class parents do (124, 238).

Parental attitudes toward homework likewise vary. Many lower-class parents, for example, allow the child to play, read comics, or watch TV whether he has completed his homework or not. By contrast, middle-class parents as a rule insist that the child finish his homework, even if this leaves him no time for doing things he would like to do (26, 239).

In most schools and colleges, the "leading crowd" represents a particular social-class group. The other students tend to accept the attitudes, interests, and values of the leaders even when they differ from those learned at home. Lower-class boys attending a predominantly middle-class school, it has been reported, do not devalue education but adopt a more positive attitude similar to that of their middle-class peers (52, 238).

Religion The attitudes of parents toward education vary according to religious affiliation. Jewish parents, for example, put more value on education and expect higher academic achievements from their children than Protestant and Catholic parents. They regard educational achievement as essential to vocational and social success. Jewish parents teach their children these values at an early age, and as a result, Jewish children on the whole tend to have more positive attitudes toward education than children from Protestant and Catholic families (50, 162, 163).

Ethnic group Of the ethnic groups in America, studies to date report that black and Italian parents have the least favorable attitudes toward education. This is especially true of those from the lower socioeconomic groups. Because of discrimination, black parents have traditionally seen little possibility of their children being able to rise on the vocational and social ladders. Consequently, they have seen little value in

education and have conveyed this attitude to their children (14, 162, 163).

Peers Part of the unfavorable attitude many boys and girls develop toward school and college is peer-instigated. In speaking of the large number of "unwilling" college students, Hechinger declares, "It would be naive not to expect a kind of peer-group compulsion: but it would be even more unrealistic to think that the academic, scholarly life is really loved and sought by all of this huge mass" (99).

Even if a student likes school, he soon discovers that this is not the thing to do. Liking school and doing good academic work make him different, and to his age-mates, "different" is synonymous with "inferior." Consequently, to become one of the crowd, he must stop distinguishing himself with good grades and claim not to know the answers when called on in class; he may even go out of his way to get into trouble in the hope that a public reprimand will win the sympathies of his classmates and create the impression that he is a "good guy."

The influence of peers on boys' and girls' attitudes toward school can be illustrated by replies adolescents gave to the question, "How would you most like to be remembered in school?" Boys were asked to tell whether they would prefer to be remembered as an athletic star, a brilliant student, or most popular. And girls, as a brilliant student, a leader in extracurricular activities, or most popular. Boys showed an overwhelming preference for being remembered as athletes or as most popular, while girls showed an overwhelming preference for being remembered as leaders in extracurricular acitvities or as most popular. Relatively few boys or girls claimed that they wanted to be remembered as brilliant students (51). Coleman (51) commented on the significance of their replies:

The relative unimportance of academic achievement . . . suggests that these adolescent subcultures are generally deterrents to academic achievement. In other words, in these societies of adolescents those who come to be seen as the "intellectuals" and who come to think so of themselves are not really those of highest intelligence but are only the ones who are willing to work hard at a relatively unrewarded activity. The implications for American society as a whole are clear. Because high schools allow the adolescent subcultures to divert energies into athletics, social activities, and the like, they recruit into adult intellectual activities people with a rather mediocre level of ability. In fact, the high school seems to do more than allow these subcultures to discourage academic achievement: it aids them in doing so.

The status the student has in the peer group determines to a large extent how much his own attitudes toward education will be influenced by those of the group. A fringer or one who is neglected can always see the possibility of improving his status if he conforms closely to the standards of the group with which he wants to be identified. Only when the person's status is so secure that he knows everyone admires him, as is true of the "stars," or when it is hopeless, as is true of the rejected, can he afford to show his interest in academic matters without fear of loss of status. Under such conditions, his attitudes toward education will be influenced by factors other than peer pressures.

Personal adjustments   Well-adjusted people normally adjust with reasonable success to any situation in which they find themselves, even when the situation is not of their choosing or not to their liking. This is in direct contrast to those who are poorly adjusted and who show their annoyance and antagonism by grumbling and criticizing or by working below capacity.

Studies of students of all ages indicate that they react to school in accordance with these patterns. The poorly adjusted become the complainers, the troublemakers, and the underachievers. The well adjusted make it their business to adapt to the school situation, which they recognize as essential to their preparation for a successful future. Even though they find many subjects uninteresting and difficult, they try to do their best work. They accept the restrictions school rules impose on them as contributing to the welfare of other members of the school community and try to conform to the expectations of both school authorities and classmates (114, 180).

Effects of unfavorable attitudes on behavior

The effects of attitudes on behavior are highlighted by studies of persons who have unfavorable attitudes toward school or who actually dislike it. The effects are not limited to poor academic achievement but include

unsatisfactory personal and social adjustments as well (114, 186, 237). Among the most common patterns of behavior characteristic of those who dislike school are grumbling and criticizing, under- and overachievement, school phobia, truancy, dropping out, and school misdemeanors.

Grumbling and criticizing   Harris states that the child's or adolescent's grumbling about school often "reflects no more than the widespread and thoroughly American characteristic of unfavorable criticism of his institutions" (94). If it is the thing to do, even those who secretly enjoy their academic work will criticize their school or college. This kind of follow-the-crowd behavior usually reaches its peak during the adolescent years, the time when young people are most unsure of themselves and find that criticizing others helps to bolster their self-confidence. Eventually, those who originally criticized because it was the thing to do come to believe their criticisms and convince themselves that they do not like school or college any better than their friends do.

Underachievement   Underachievement, or working below one's tested abilities, may come from laziness, lack of motivation, unfavorable attitudes toward the activity in which the underachievement occurs, or a number of other causes. Unfavorable attitudes, however, are among the most common and most damaging causes, for, once established, they are very difficult to change.

When a student works below capacity, he often fails or does low-grade work in a subject which he could succeed in if he were willing to put in more time and effort. He may fall short in one area or in all. Failing to do good work in reading and English is especially harmful because these two subjects are basic to success in most other subjects. When the student fails in reading and English, he is likely to develop into a general school failure (81).

Once a student starts to work below capacity, the tendency to do so often becomes habitual. He convinces himself that he is doing the best he can, and this kills any motivation he might have to improve. The result is that underachievement becomes chronic.

Overachievement   In overachievement, the student does more than is expected of him on the basis of his abilities. This he does by working longer and harder than is justified, by getting help from parents and peers, or by cheating. He gives the impression of being extremely conscientious, and his teachers usually think that he is a more able student than he actually is.

On the surface, overachievement would seem to be motivated by a great liking for school. In reality, overachievers often have as unfavorable attitudes toward school as underachievers. Overachievers usually have strong feelings of inadequacy. But lacking a source of compensation for these feelings—achievement in sports or other extracurricular activities—they try to convince themselves and others of their adequacy by becoming "good" students.

If school achievements guaranteed peer approval and acceptance, the overachievers' attitudes toward school would improve. But peer reaction toward good academic work is usually not favorable, even though that of teachers and parents may be, and so the overachievers' attitudes may worsen.

School phobia   Intense dislike of school is often expressed as fear of being away from the protection and security of the family. Usually the child refuses to go to school or refuses to stay there if he is forced to go. He uses any ploy that works to gain his goal.

Some cases of school phobia develop from unpleasant school experiences. Most, however, are homegrown in that the child has become so emotionally attached to his parents, especailly his mother, that he feels anxious and insecure when away from her. He may not actually dislike school, but he is afraid to be away from the protection he has learned to depend on at home.

Truancy   Truancy differs from school phobia in three respects. *First,* the truant rarely tries to give an excuse for leaving school; he merely runs away. The child suffering from school phobia gives an excuse for leaving school, and if this excuse does not bring the desired result, he uses another and still another until he is permitted to leave.

Second, the truant usually does not go home when he leaves school, while the child who suffers from school phobia does. The truant engages in some activity in the community which he finds more pleasurable than the activities of the school from which he has escaped. And *third,* there is no fear of school or the school situation in truancy as there is in school phobia; the truant merely dislikes school (76, 154).

Dropping out   Many children and adolescents who dislike school but who, for one reason or another, are afraid to be truants wait until they reach the legal school-leaving age and then drop out. In one study where students gave their reasons for dropping out, they claimed that the teachers were dull and boring—"the same old thing over and over"—and that the school was "indifferent" and "punitive" (234).

Many students drop out for social rather than academic reasons. When they are not accepted by their classmates or by the classmates whose acceptance they crave, they develop such a dislike for the entire school situation that they want to escape from it. Some who achieve marginal acceptance find that they lack the financial resources to participate in the social activities their classmates enjoy.

School misdemeanors   Dissatisfied students at every age tend to be poor school or college citizens, and so it is common for them to be troublemakers as well as grumblers. While these two ways of expressing dissatisfaction do not always go hand in hand, they usually do.

The form troublemaking will take varies from group to group and from age to age, ranging from cutting up in the classroom to annoy the teacher to seizing a college building. Regardless of its form, the misdemeanor is an expression of dissatisfaction with the educational system and an attempt to get revenge against those who are in control of the educational environment.

Among young children, school misdemeanors consist mainly of disturbing the teacher and the other students by whispering, cutting up, and distracting others from their work. Older students, in high school and college, become bolder in their attempts to get even with an educational institution that frustrates and annoys them; they engage in vandalism, willful breaking of rules, and open defiance of the teachers and school administrators. Campus riots are, fundamentally, an expression of student dissatisfaction with and dislike of the way they are being educated.

Effects of attitudes toward education on personality

A person's attitudes toward education affect the kind of adjustments he makes to school or college. And his adjustments are expressed in behavior patterns which both he and others use in evaluating him. Thus, his attitudes affect his personality, and the influence is both direct and indirect.

The *direct* influence comes from the person's studies and from the interpersonal relationships he has with teachers and other students. In these relationships he gains an understanding of people, of situations, and most noteworthy of all, of himself—an understanding that could never be obtained in the narrower and more homogeneous social environment of the home. Studies show that students who have had 2 or more years of college are more flexible, more democratic, more understanding of others, and less authoritarian in their attitudes than those who have been exposed to the democratizing effects of college life for a shorter time (27, 114, 237).

The kind of education the person receives likewise influences his personality pattern. Students who major in liberal arts subjects are less rigid, less conforming, and less authoritarian than those who major in technical subjects (27, 150, 237). Education also helps to develop new interests, which encourages the person to be less self-bound and more alert to environmental stimuli. Studies of older people disclose that those whose educational opportunities were limited have fewer interests, less understanding of and tolerance for others, and a greater tendency to be self-bound than those who in their youth had greater educational opportunities. The more education the older person has had, the more mentally alert he is likely to be, the better adjusted, and the happier (97).

By far the most important direct effect of education on personality comes from the opportunity it gives the student to evaluate himself in terms of his age-mates. This he does through his grades, through the way his teachers and classmates treat him as compared with others, and through his social and other extracurricular achievements as compared with his classmates. How these comparisons affect the person's concept of self will be discussed in detail later in this chapter.

There are several ways in which attitudes toward education affect the self-concept *indirectly*. Education as a status symbol has a profound influence on the self-concept via the favorable judgments made by members of the social group. While neither education nor educators have the high prestige in this country that they have in most other countries, there is prestige associated with academic achievement and with the attainment of a high school diploma or a college degree.

When a person adjusts well to the school or college environment, both academically and socially, he is judged favorably by others in the educational institution as well as by his parents and family members. Similarly, if he achieves leadership in extracurricular activities he will win more positive judgments than one who lacks acceptance or achieves only marginal acceptance.

While peers may admire a child's bravery when he breaks rules or plays truant, they sooner or later judge him as a misfit or "pest." Adults, whether parents, teachers, or school administrators, likewise judge him negatively. That most dropouts feel compelled to rationalize their not getting a diploma or collge degree is evidence that they know or suspect that people judge them unfavorably and suspect that their reason for not finishing their course of studies was that they were intellectually unable to do so. Even young children who experience school phobia quickly become aware of the unfavorable attitudes their behavior brings. They know that their classmates regard them as "crybabies" and treat them with suspicion.

Because of the severe damage to personality that can come from years of poor adjustment to the school situation, it is essential to find out how and why unfavorable attitudes toward education develop. Why is it that at all ages and among members of both sexes attitudes toward education are predominantly unfavorable?

Many conditions, personal, social, and environmental, influence the student's attitudes and affect his adjustment to his educational experiences. The remainder of this chapter will be directed toward an analysis of the following conditions: readiness for school, early school experiences, the emotional climate of the school or college, teachers' attitudes and behavior, academic success, extracurricular activities, peer acceptance, school subjects, and kind of school.

READINESS FOR SCHOOL

The beginning of a school career is a radical departure from the child's established pattern of life. Some children adjust easily to the change and enjoy it. But for many it is a time of stress because they are not prepared for what the school expects of them. If a child is ready for school or an adolescent for high school or college, he will make satisfactory adjustments and his attitude toward the educational situation in which he finds himself will be favorable. If he is not ready, his adjustments will be poor and his attitudes unfavorable.

Should a child be held back when he is ready, should he not be permitted to enter school or advance to a grade where the studies are more suited to his abilities, he is likely to be bored. This will lead to as unfavorable an attitude as being expected to do work for which he is not yet ready.

Starting age

Schools in America are planned for children to start their formal education at the chronological age of 6 years, and so children who enter school above or below this age are likely to have adjustment problems which 6-year-olds do not encounter. These problems are mainly social and emotional, and they stem partly from boredom and partly from the fact that under- or overage children are regarded by their classmates as "dumb" or "too old" (17, 97).

Children who enter first grade at 6 years of age or 6 plus a few months have better attendance records, make better personal and social adjustments to school, and are better able to meet the tensions and restrictions imposed on them by the school environment than younger children. The latter tend to fall below the level of their class academically and often develop nervous mannerisms, speech defects, dependency on the teacher, school phobia, and other indications of maladjustment. Frequently, they have to repeat the grade. This leads not only to a negative attitude toward school but also to unfavorable judgments of their abilities by parents, teachers, and classmates—judgments that have harmful effects on their self-concepts (17, 143, 159).

It is commonly believed that school readiness is aided by nursery school and kindergarten experience. Unquestionably, preschool does help the child know what to expect when he enters first grade, but this advantage may be counteracted by boredom. The similarity between the preschool and first-grade programs aids adjustment but encourages boredom.

Physical readiness

There is evidence of a fairly close relationship between the child's physical development and his readiness for school. Delayed physical development is usually accompanied by delayed mental development, delayed strength increase, and poor muscular coordination. A child who functions below the norm of his classmates mentally and who is unable to compete on a par with them in games and sports makes poor academic as well as poor social adjustments (121, 186).

A study of school readiness and body configuration—the physique or total form of the body and the relationship of the different parts of the body to one another—has shown that between the ages of 5 and 7 years there is a striking reorganization of the child's body form. There is a marked difference in the figure of a child under 5 years of age, that of one who is 5 to 7, and that of one who is between 7 and 9.

The figure of the "intermediate" child, 5 to 7 years of age, is characteristic of one who is ready for school. By contrast, the figure of the child under 5 is characteristic of one who is psychologically and physically too young for school, while that of a child between 7 and 9 years is characteristic of one in the early grades of elementary school (202).

Studies of body build and school readiness provide evidence that, to be ready for first grade, the child needs an overall developmental age of 6 years and 6 months. The overall developmental age refers to physical as well as mental age. Furthermore, because of the close correlation between mental and physical age, the child who is physically immature tends to be mentally immature also, even though his IQ score falls within the normal range (186, 202).

Children who succeed in first grade tend to be more mature physically than those who fail. According to Simon (202):

Physcial maturity is more than skin-deep: it is reflected not only in superficial body features but in the maturational status of the central nervous system, which in turn underlies such behavior as readiness to submit to restraints and the application to tasks.

Lack of physical readiness likewise hampers adjustment to school during adolescence. The late maturer, who looks more like a child than a near adult, or the very bright child, whose physical development has not kept pace with his mental development, finds that he is not ready for the social life that is so crucial in the junior and senior high school years.

Furthermore, the late maturer's age-mates regard him as a child and exclude him from their activities (see Chap. 6). Such rejection, as will be discussed in detail later in this chapter, is likely to make him dislike school. A late maturer may try to compensate for lack of social acceptance by winning scholastic honors, but more often he loses the motivation to do good academic work and, as a result, becomes an underachiever. This leads to parent and teacher disapproval which adds to his feeling that the whole school situation is hostile.

Early maturers, by contrast, are ready for the social life of high school and college before they are intellectually ready for the academic work. They may have few interests in common with their classmates and feel that they are too old for the extracurricular activities their classmates enjoy. They then regard the treatment they receive in school and the lessons they are expected to master as "kid stuff." Even worse, knowing that many of their age-mates think of them as "dumb" because they are so much larger and more mature looking than the average adds to their unfavorable attitudes toward school.

Psychological readiness

The child who is psychologically ready for school is able to be independent of adult aid and guidance, consistent with his age; he can adjust socially to strangers, whether they be teachers or classmates; he accepts the fact that there is a prestige hierarchy among his classmates in which some children are favored above others by both teachers and peers, and that his status in this hierarchy may not be high; and he is mentally ready to learn what the first grade demands. He must also be emotionally mature enough to accept without becoming disturbed the restrictions every school demands, no matter how permissive it may be, and he must be able to control his emotions, especially anger, fear, and jealousy.

Children subjected to authoritarian child-training methods at home tend to be less mature for their age than those brought up by democtatic methods. On the other hand, children brought up under very permissive child-training methods do not learn to conform to rules and regulations imposed by others and so they find adjustment to school difficult. The only child, unless he has had some preschool experience, is often handicapped in the area of social relationships. While he generally makes the adjustment to school successfully, it takes him longer than it does children with siblings (15, 138).

Since learning to read is one of the principal components of the first-grade curriculum, the child who is ready to read makes better adjustments to school than one who is not ready. Reading readiness is greatly enhanced by good family relationships and by a home environment that shows a respect for and an interest in the printed word. While high intelligence contributes greatly to reading readiness, an interest in reading and a motivation to learn to read are also important factors.

Many late-maturing boys and girls of average or above average intellectual ability are psychologically unready for high school or college. Their psychological development, in terms of interests, attitudes, and emotional control, has been held back by delayed puberty. Since the curriculum is planned for the intellectual development of students, not for their psychological maturity, late matureres are capable of doing the required academic work, but have problems in the area of social relationships. To their classmates, they seem "young" for their years.

Early maturers, by contrast, give the impression of being older and more socially sophisticated than their classmates, even though their intellectual achievements may not be superior. They are often dissatisfied with their social relationships in school because they regard their age-mates as too young for them. Many early maturers develop unfavorable attitudes toward school or college owing to boredom and to feeling that they are out of step with their classmates (48, 121).

Effects of readiness on adjustments

Adjusting to any new situation is likely to be upsetting to a child, an adolescent, or an adult. However, if a person is physically and psychologically ready for the new experience, he will adjust to it in time. When he is not ready, his poor adjustment will be reflected in emotional tensions and behavior disorders of greater or lesser severity.

In most children, the strain of beginning school is shown by an increase in behavior problems both in school and at home. Some cry when it is time to go, cling to the mother, or even vomit their breakfasts. Others seem abnormally quiet and worried but show no outward signs of emotional tension. This is not a foolproof indication of their greater readiness for school; it is most often an indication of their characteristic method of responding to an emotion-provoking situation. Children who react explosively to school at first may, in the long run, make better adjustments than those who appeared to be calm but were actually inhibiting the expression of strong emotions (141).

Similarly, students who go through a period of homesickness at the beginning of college may react by crying, telephoning their parents daily, or keeping their bags packed in readiness to leave. Or they may react by quietly withdrawing from other students.

Adjustment to first grade does not guarantee quick, easy, or even satisfactory adjustment to higher grades. Each new school in the education hierarchy differs in some respects from the previous one. Adjusting to junior high school, for example, where the student lives at home, is much easier than adjusting to college, where the methods of teaching vary from one class to another, the curriculum contains many new areas of study, and the student may be living away from home. Every period of transition leaves a mark on the person's behavior. Because he feels insecure and unsure of himself in the new situation, he is self-conscious, aggressive, or withdrawn. None of these leads to good social or academic adjustment.

A person who is self-conscious tends to be tense in social situations. This causes him to overreact either by being too happy for the occasion or by flying into unreasonable bursts of temper. He is sensitive and reserved, especially when he is with people who he feels do not understand him or might ridicule him. He may express his discomfort by assuming an attitude of aloofness and indifference, or it may be expressed in bravado or supercilious scorn. Some people who are unsure of themselves in social situations become aggressive, as if trying to convince others as well as themselves that they are poised and self-confident.

Effects of school readiness on personality

The child who is physically and psychologically ready to enter school approaches the new situation with a poise and self-confidence that facilitate his adjustment. His successful adjustment increases his poise and self-confidence.

By contrast, the child who is physically or psychologically unready feels inadequate to meet the problems and challenges his new environment provides. Unless he has someone to help him, he will be at a loss to know what to do. Consequently, his adjustments will fall short of his own expectations and of those of his parents, teachers, and classmates.

Most teachers recognize that adjustment to school is difficult and try to ease the way for the children in their care as much as possible. Many high schools and most colleges have a "freshman orientation" week to help the entering students make a good transition to the new educational environment. The child or adolescent who adjusts quickly and successfully finds that others react to him favorably. This makes him view himself favorably, and his attitude toward school and toward education will be positive. In speaking of the young child's adjustment, Breckenridge and Vincent (35) say:

If the child is quick to smile, to obey orders, and to learn school routines, he often experiences a renewal of mothering affection from his kindergarten or first grade teacher. If he is troublesome to have in the group of children, slow to fit into the routine and not particularly lovable, he may exact rebuke and a further sense of isolation from the adult world.

At first, the child's schoolmates may be as emotionally disturbed as he by the new school situation. Consequently, they are too concerned with their own feelings and adjustment problems to notice him. But as they adjust, they begin to notice anyone who is lagging behind. They label him "baby" if he cries when things go wrong and are resentful if he demands too much of the teacher's time. Much the same situation exists among adolescents in high school and college.

EARLY SCHOOL EXPERIENCES

Just as early social experiences in the home and neighborhood influence the child's attitude toward people and social life, so do early school experiences influence the student's attitude toward the school situation and toward education in general. Even when early school experiences are pleasant and result in a favorable attitude, later experiences may be so unpleasant as to bring about a reversal.

Knowing this, some parents go all out to present school as a great and exciting adventure. They romanticize and glamorize college. Teachers, too, try to make the child's introduction to school easy and pleasant, believing that this will foster a favorable attitude and lead to good academic and social adjustments. The role teachers and school administrators play in freshman orientation for high school or college is designed to lead to the same goal.

Since children and, to a lesser extent, adolescents have a glamorized concept of what their new educational experience will be, they are often disappointed and disillusioned by their early experiences. In addition, they often suffer from embarrassment because they say and do things that their classmates ridicule or their teachers criticize. They are often humiliated by being made to feel different or inferior, and they are often angered by being discriminated against and rejected not because of what they do but because of what they are.

While some of the early experiences are unquestionably unpleasant in themselves, many *seem* to be so because they differ markedly from experiences in the home or neighborhood. The child who has been accustomed to being the center of attention at home feels neglected at school when he must share the teacher with thirty classmates. Similarly, the college student, accustomed to being at the top of his high school class and a leader in extracurricular affairs, feels lost and alone on the huge, impersonal college campus.

Effects of early school experiences on personality

The effects of early school experiences on personality are not limited to the time when the child enters school. They are felt whenever he must adjust to a new school or a new kind of school. The child who shifts schools when his family moves to a new community or the adolescent who goes away to college will have to adjust to a school situation which may differ radically from the one he left behind.

Success in adjusting to one school situation does not automatically guarantee success in adjusting to others. That is why early school experiences may affect the self-concept at any age, not just when the child begins his school career.

A school situation that meets the student's needs and comes up to his expectations will be pleasing to him. He will make good adjustments and be favorably judged by his teacher and classmates. Under such conditions, his early school experiences will prove to be ego-inflating. Or just the opposite may happen in a school situation that the student dislikes. In addition to feeling resentful at having to be in such a situation, he may feel that he is a martyr because he is unable to escape.

Regardless of how students react to early school experiences which they regard as unpleasant,

their personalities are damaged. The greatest damage comes from being forced to remain, year after year, in an environment which they believe is hostile to them. When their parents are punitive because of their poor school performance, their feeling of martyrdom is intensified.

If students who dislike school because of unfavorable early experiences drop out as soon as they reach the legal school-leaving age, they will develop feelings of inadequancy and inferiority in addition to their other negative feelings about themselves. If their parents are disappointed or angry with them, or if they find it difficult to get and keep a job, their feelings of self-dissatisfaction will increase.

EMOTIONAL CLIMATE OF SCHOOL OR COLLEGE

Most parents and school authorities think of the physical environment of a school or college as an all-important factor in determining how good the institution is. Impressive buildings, up-to-date equipment, athletic teams that win intercollegiate championships, and a "name" faculty are the criteria used by most people in judging the quality of education the students will receive.

While a good physical environment is necessary, the psychological environment of the school is just as important, if not more so. The advantages of a good physical environment can be counteracted by a teacher who dislikes his job or who dislikes teaching the kind or number of children assigned to him. His negative attitude toward his role as a teacher and toward his pupils will be reflected in his treatment of them and will cause them to be nervous, tense, and antagonistic toward all the school has to offer.

An emotional climate that promotes good mental health in every student and good morale among the students as a group is essential to favorable attitudes toward school and to good school adjustments. It is through the effect on their adjustment that the emotional climate affects students' personalities.

In explaining how a healthy emotional climate in the classroom can improve the students' self-concepts, Hilliard (108) emphasizes the following points:

School should be a place where children are not afraid to express the feelings they have: where mistakes can be made without embarrassment; where tears and disturbances are no disgrace; where encouragement and sympathy are offered when needed. There should be fun and laughter and perhaps even a bit of teasing. School should be a place where children are sure of warm human understanding.

Conditions responsible for emotional climate

Just as the emotional climate of the home is determined largely by parents, so is the school climate determined largely by *teachers.* What kind of person the teacher is, how he is perceived by the students, how he perceives his role and his relationships with his students, and how closely he conforms to the cultural stereotype of a teacher or to the student's concept of an ideal teacher—all are important in determining how and how much the teacher will influence the emotional climate of the classroom.

A favorable teacher attitude will be reflected in a healthy emotional climate. The teacher who is contented in his role and secure in his ability to do his job cannot help communicating his affectional warmth and happiness to his students. The teacher's attitude is contagious, spreading throughout the classroom.

Even though older children and adolescents have fewer contacts with each teacher as they progress through the grades into high school and college where the academic work is departmentalized, the contacts they do have influence their feelings about the various subjects and about academic life in general. One of the complaints students have about the emotional climate of the college is that it is so impersonal. Classes are so large that the professor knows only a handful of students and is, in any event, many students feel, more interested in research and writing than in teaching (226).

Policies relating to curriculum, extracurricular activities, and other aspects of the life of the school and college, as formulated by the *administration,* affect the institution's overall emotional climate. When students are treated like children and given little say about the courses they take or the rules that govern their school lives, they regard school policies as paternalistic and resent them bitterly. The school that is child-centered, in the sense that its policies are made primarily to serve the interests and needs of the pupils, has a far more wholesome emotional climate.

One aspect of administration policies that especially influences the emotional climate of the school is the *kind of discipline* that prevails throughout the institution and has the sanction of the administration. Schools and colleges which favor authoritarian discipline create a far less favorable emotional climate than those which take a more democratic approach. An unsatisfactory emotional climate likewise results from overpermissiveness. Just as children, in time, resent extreme parental permissiveness, so they resent and lose respect for teachers who are so permissive that they allow the classroom to become a bedlam.

By contrast, students of all ages, from kindergarten to graduate school, whose academic and social lives are governed by rules that they understand and respect develop a favorable attitude toward those in authority. If they are represented by classmates on disciplinary boards, they feel that they are being governed fairly and justly. This goes a long way toward promoting a healthy emotional climate not only in the classroom but in the instituation as a whole.

A highly *competitive atmosphere* in a school or college has an unsettling effect on the institution's emotional climate. Whether this excessive competiton is in academic work, sports, or other areas, it encourages students to vie with one another instead of working together cooperatively. For example, competition for high grades and a place on the honor roll or the dean's list breeds resentment on the part of those who try but fail and a smug self-satisfaction on the part of those who succeed.

Whether the highly competitive atmosphere is due to the students themselves, to parents who pressure their children to get ahead, or to teachers who believe that strong competition motivates students to work up to capacity, it is detrimental to the emotional climate of the school. Only those students who reach the top have a liking for school.

The emotional climate of the school or college is influenced by the degree of *harmony* that exists among the students. In a class or school where the students are democratic and each member is friendly with other members, even though there are also close friendships, the emotional climate is far healthier than where tightly knit cliques compete for leadership and where some students are made to feel unwelcome and excluded. In colleges and universities where some of the members belong to prestigious or exclusive fraternities and sororities while others have no such social connections, snobbishness and discrimination often play havoc with the academic and social atmosphere.

Effects of emotional climate on behavior

A healthy emotional climate is conducive to good performance. The majority of students feel a strong motivation to work up to capacity, to participate in extracurricular activities, and to conform to rules and regulations even though they may from time to time grumble and criticize.

Just the opposite is true when the emotional climate is unhealthy. Student *morale* deteriorates and motivation to work or take part in extracurricular activities lags. There is a close correlation between poor morale and *troublesome behavior.* Among young children, poor morale goes hand in hand with grumbling, breaking rules, and cutting up. Among adolescents, poor morale is more likely to be expressed in *attempts at reform* and protest, though complaining, criticizing, and rule breaking are also common. *Disciplinary problems* make the teacher's job more difficult, and the meting out of punishment leads to further deterioration in classroom morale.

An unwholesome school or college emotional climate makes students *nervous, anxious, and jittery.* This upsets their academic performance, especially in test situations. Younger students often develop reading problems and nervous mannerisms, especially speech disorders, while older students experience a persistent fear of failure. When students are nervous and anxious, they tend to be aggressive and quarrelsome. Their relationships with teachers as well as with classmates are colored by unpleasant emotions, and the unwholesome psychological climate worsens.

Effects of emotional climate on personality

Emotions are contagious in that people tend to imitate the emotional states of those with whom they are associated. The emotional climate of the school thus has a marked influence on the student's emotional states and, through them, on his personality. If he is with people who are tense and anxious, owing to competitiveness, poor personality adjustments, or other conditions in their lives, he will become tense and anxious also. In time, this may become his habitual pattern of reacting to life.

The student, as child and adolescent, spends many years in an educational environment. Whatever the emotional climate, he develops the habit of reacting to people and situations in ways which provide relief from his frustrations and annoyances. If the climate is unwholesome, the student is likely to become a constant grumbler, critic, or troublemaker.

If, by contrast, the emotional climate of the institution is wholesome, the long years the student is required to spend there are often adequate to counteract any unfavorable emotional patterns of behavior established in the home. Thus the wholesome emotional climate of the school has a therapeutic effect on his personality.

While the emotional climate of educational institutions can affect the personality pattern at any age, the early school years are the most critical. *First,* in the early years, the child ordinarily has one main teacher, and his entire day, except for recess and the lunch period, is usually spent in one classroom. Even his classmates are the same throughout the day. There is literally no escape if the emotional climate of the classroom is unwholesome.

Second, at the beginning of his school career, the child is far more susceptible to the influence of the teacher than he will be later. This will be explained in more detail in the next section. In the early grades, the teacher is chiefly responsible for the emotional climate of the classroom.

Third, emotional states are contagious, and the young child is extremely susceptible in this respect. Later, as his social horizons broaden and as he goes from one teacher to another for different subjects, he is less influenced by any one personality than he was when he spent the whole day with one teacher whom he regarded as a surrogate parent.

Finally, during the early part of the child's school career, his personality pattern is still in the process of being molded. At this time, *all* influences, whether favorable or unfavorable, affect his personality more than they will later when the pattern has been well established. The adolescent is far less susceptible to psychological damage from a maladjusted teacher than is a child in the elementary school.

TEACHER ATTITUDES AND BEHAVIOR

The teacher's influence on the young person's personality development is second to that ot the parents because the personality pattern is already partially formed when the child enters school and because the child spends less time at school and has a less intimate relationship with the teacher. However, the teacher's influence is second *only* to that of parents.

The influence of the teacher's attitudes and behavior on the student's personality pattern comes from two major sources: the kind of relationship that exists between the teacher and student and the effect of the teacher on the emotional climate of the school. The *emotional climate* was discussed in detail in the preceding section.

The *relationship between teacher and student* is determined in part by the teacher's attitude toward the student and in part by the student's attitude toward the teacher. These attitudes depend on how the teacher and the student perceive each other. When the teacher perceives the young person as a troublemaker or as a disinterested, lackadaisical student, her attitude toward him will, understandably, be far less positive than if she perceived him as a cooperative, interested learner.

If the student has a hostile attitude toward the teacher, it will be reflected in his interactions with the teacher and will influence her attitudes toward him and her treatment of him. His hostile attitude may be due to pressures from parents, siblings, and peers, to unpleasant experiences with the teacher, to dislike of the subject she teaches or the way she teaches it, or to the acceptance of unfavorable stereotypes of teachers as given in mass media.

While teacher-student relationships normally become more formal and less warm as students continue their education (see Figure 12–2), some students find their relationships with specific teachers pleasanter and more satisfying than their relationships with their parents. Some identify so strongly with a teacher that they try to model their behavior as well as their looks and dress after those of the teacher. This is especially common among girls during the "crush stage" in early adolescence (43, 47, 149, 242).

Factors influencing teacher-student relationships

Of the many factors in the American educational situation which influence teacher-student relationships, the most widespread and most significant are discussed in the following paragraphs.

Cultural stereotypes of teachers

When the cultural stereotype of the teacher is positive, as it is in many foreign countries, it engenders respect for the teacher on the part of the students. It also engenders self-respect and self-confidence in the teacher. This leads to a far more satisfactory teacher-student relationship than that which exists in a culture, like our own, where the portrayal of teachers in the mass media is disparaging (10, 49, 193). Cultural attitudes toward teachers in the United States and in Russia are compared in Figure 12–3.

Discussing the influence of mass-media image making, Schwartz (193) comments:

The motion picture industry, in perpetuating the unsympathetic image of the educator in literature, is taking advantage of a portrayal which has apparently been accepted by a majority of the mass audience. The important element is that the image of the educator which is perpetuated by the mass media can be a strong force influencing the images held by the general public.

Indirectly, the unfavorable cultural stereotype of the teacher affects students' attitudes toward teaching as a career, and this reinforces the negative concept they have of teachers as people. Teachers sense or know how their students feel about them and about

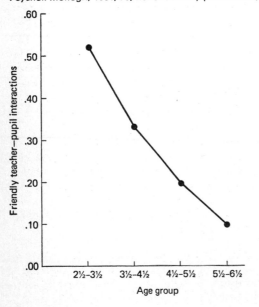

Figure 12-2 Friendly interactions with teachers decrease as children grow older, as shown in observation periods. (Adapted from H. R. Marshall: Relations between home experiences and children's use of language in play interactions with peers. *Psychol. Monogr.*, 1961, **75**, no. 5. Used by permission.)

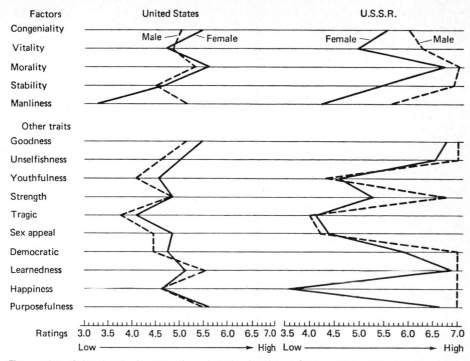

Figure 12-3 Cultural attitudes toward teachers in the United States and Russia, as indicated by student ratings. (Adapted from G. Gerbner: Images across cultures: Teachers in mass media fiction and drama. *School Review,* 1966, **74,** 212–230. Used by permission.)

their profession—a realization that colors their reactions to their students.

Favoritism Many students perceive their teachers as "playing favorites." This they resent, just as they resent parental favoritism toward a sibling. Few teachers recognize that they are showing favoritism and even fewer will admit it if it is called to their attention, but students themselves often get the opposite impression.

While the expression of favoritism, even in its mildest form, is an individual matter, certain children and adolescents are more likely to be favored by their teachers than others. Students who make *good grades* are usually favorites partly because it is ego-satisfying to teachers to have students do well and partly because good students are ordinarily cooperative members of the class, causing little or no trouble.

Students who are *dependent* on their teachers, asking for help with their lessons and with extracurricular activities, give their classmates the impression

that teachers prefer them and spend more time with them than with those who are more independent.

Even though many teachers try to help the educationally and socially deprived children in their classes, these students believe that teachers prefer students from higher *socioeconomic* backgrounds. Some teachers definitely show a preference for those from more favorable home backgrounds because they find them more promising and more talented students.

Boys tend to be more troublesome in the classroom than girls and to have less interest in doing their schoolwork well. As a result, teachers often show a preference for girls. It is not surprising, then, that girls perceive their teachers as more friendly toward them than do boys, who often feel rejected and "picked on" by their teachers.

Attitude toward students Students sense very quickly their teachers' attitudes toward them and their interest or lack of interest in them.

Studies reveal that student ratings of teachers as good or poor are based more on the teachers' interest in and treatment of the students than on teaching techniques. "Good" teachers like their students, are interested in them as people, encourage them to work up to capacity and to conform to school rules, are personally secure and self-assured, and are the leaders of the classroom group.

By contrast, teachers rated as poor are perceived by students as hostile and indifferent, unfriendly and punitive in their attitudes, lacking in understanding of young people and their capacities and needs, primarily concerned with their own affairs, and weak and vacillating in situations where leadership is needed. Since they seem to be unsure of themselves and of their ability to handle students, students take advantage of them, work below capacity, and cause trouble in the classroom (45, 120, 213).

Teaching techniques When students feel that their teachers are boring, that classes are dull and uninspiring, and that what they are expected to learn has little relevance to their daily lives, they are tempted to "stir up a little excitement." They develop an antagonistic attitude toward the teachers who seem boring to them and dislike the subjects taught by these teachers. In addition, they have little motivation to study.

Teaching techniques may be regarded as boring because they are too advanced or too simplified for the age or intellectual level of the majority of the class members. Young and inexperienced teachers tend to use too advanced teaching techniques while older teachers tend toward the other extreme. Students who are avid comics readers or television watchers often find the subject matter of their textbooks and classes dull by contrast.

Classroom control Just as children and adolescents resent authoritarian control in the home and strict and punitive parental attitudes, so do they resent such control and attitudes in the classroom. They regard ultrapermissive and vacillating disciplinarians as weak and ineffectual and show contempt for them, ridiculing them behind their backs and boasting about how easy it is to "get away" with things.

Even though they may rebel against rules, especially if they regard them as unfair, most children and adolescents have more respect for teachers who require them to conform to rules and regulations. If young people have a voice in setting up the rules and if they serve on committees that handle school disciplinary problems, they regard such procedures as democratic and fair and the teachers who follow them as good sports. Under such conditions, a student-teacher relationship marked by understanding and respect develops.

Personal adjustment of the teacher
The well-adjusted teacher is far more respected and liked by students than the poorly adjusted, and a warmer student-teacher relationship is possible. Studies of the personal adjustments of teachers have led Heil and Washburne to conclude that teachers are of three types. The first, "turbulent" teachers, are blunt, impulsive, tense, and unpredictable; they tend to express their feelings and thoughts in verbal and physical aggressions. The second, equally as harmful to the psychological well-being of students and to the emotional climate of the classroom, are the "fearful" type. Such teachers are insecure, helpless, dependent, and defensive. Not only do they fail to win the respect of their students but, even worse, students sense their insecurity and quickly take advantage of them. The third type are better in most respects for students and for classroom climate. These are the "self-controlled" teachers. Sensitive to the attitudes of others, at the same time they want things ro run smoothly and they expect their students to conform to school regulations. Even though they sometimes tend to be rigid, they command greater student respect than the other two types (100).

Effects of teacher-student relationships on students' personalities

The kind of relationship that exists between teacher and student and the way the student perceives that relationship have a *direct* effect on the student's self-concept. If a student believes the teacher dislikes him and if he interprets the teacher's words and actions to mean that she is rejecting and "picking on" him for whatever he says or does, he will come to think of himself as a martyr. By contrast, a student who does his work conscientiously, works up to capacity, causes no classroom disturbance, and does not demand too much of the teacher's time and attention, is perceived favorably by the teacher and is able to establish a satisfying teacher-student relationship. If he sees himself as a "good" person, as he believes his teacher sees him, this will have an ego-inflating effect on his self-concept.

Indirectly, the teacher-student relationship influences the student's personality in two ways: through its effect on the emotional climate of the classroom and through its effect on student achievement. An important factor in determining what the emotional climate of the classroom will be is the kind of relationship the teacher has with students. Even if the teacher's relationship with only a few students is unfavorable, the entire classroom climate can be affected adversely. This is especially true if the poor relationships involve popular students or if the majority of students side with and sympathize with a student or students who they believe have been treated unfairly by the teacher.

The second way in which the teacher-student relationship indirectly influences the student's personality is through the effect the relationship has on the student's motivation for academic achievement. When the student perceives the relationship as warm and friendly, his achievements are far better than when he perceives the relationship as hostile, punitive, or rejectant. Many underachievers are the product of a hostile teacher-student relationship.

The effects are greatest during the early school years when the personality pattern is still in the formative stage and when the teacher is more instrumental in the child's life than she will be later. Furthermore, the relationship may have the effect of reinforcing a pattern set in the home—or of modifying it if the teacher-student relationship differs markedly from the parent-child relationship. Solomon declares: "A child with both stable parents and stable teachers is fortunate. Conversely, emotional problems are aggravated when a child with unstable parents is exposed to unstable teachers" (206).

There is further evidence of the influence teacher-student relationships have on the student's personality. Patterns of behavior, developed as a result of learning to view himself through the eyes of the teacher, carry over into the student's relationships with people outside the school. The impulsive teacher sets a model for impulsive behavior in her students, while the experienced, reflective teacher sets a model for stable, self-assured behavior and positive personal relationships outside the school (134, 242). Farnsworth (79) writes:

What a teacher is and does is more influential on students than anything he may say. It is sometimes a shock to teachers to realize how much their students are concerned with what they do, say, read, wear, enjoy, and their manner and behavior generally.

ACADEMIC SUCCESS

Although many students and parents regard academic success as less prestigious than success in sports, social life, and other extracurricular activities, few people hold academic success in such low regard that it goes unrecognized and unapplauded. Like success in any other area, academic success is ego-satisfying.

Symbols of academic success

Academic successes are symbolized in various ways, all of which are visible to others. While the symbols of academic success differ from one school to another and from one age group to another, some are so universally used that they are readily recognized. As such, they serve as the cues by which a person is judged. Among the most common symbols of academic success are promotion, grades, honors, higher education, and diplomas and degrees.

Promotion   Being promoted from one grade or rank to another at the end of the school year is taken for granted by most students and is not markedly ego-inflating. But not being promoted is definitely ego-deflating. The child who is a repeater feels inferior, inadequate, ashamed, and stigmatized when he returns to the classroom in which he spent the preceding year and finds himself associated with classmates younger than he. The same ego-deflating experience occurs when college students are forced to repeat courses and are unable to graduate with their classmates.

How ego-deflating it is not to be promoted is modified to some extent by the reason for not being promoted and by the reactions of significant people. Repeating because of academic failure is always ego-deflating regardless of the student's age. It tells the student as well as his classmates, parents, and family friends that he is not as bright as his age-mates. Even if parents approve of the child's repeating a grade, he is still harmed by the negative judgments of others.

Repeating the first year in any new school, whether it be elementary school, high school, or college, is less damaging than having to repeat a later year. The reason for this is twofold: *First,* more students fail at this time, owing to adjustment difficulties, than later, and so the repeater is more likely to have company in his misery: *second,* friendships and other social ties are not so well established then as they will be later and, consequently, the student will not feel so cut off socially when he sees his classmates go ahead while he stays behind (44, 89).

Being accelerated or "skipping a grade" is an ego-inflating experience. It proclaims to all that the student is judged by his teachers to be brighter than his classmates. Even though acceleration presents many problems of social adjustment, the satisfaction of being favorably judged and of escaping boring, low-level academic work compensates, to a large degree, for the social problems the student encounters.

Grades   The purpose of grades is to tell the teacher the success of his teaching and to tell the student the success of his learning in relation to that of other students. However, as Pickup and Anthony (172) say, grades may serve other purposes:

In the typical educational context, the process of returning marks to pupils on completion of a task is not merely informational. The situation contains a number of demands which may affect the subsequent motivational state of the pupil. . . . A good mark may be considered a reward and a poor mark a punishment.

Studies show that teachers often grade on the basis of either general impressions or the student's "halo" (103, 187, 188). How damaging and unfair this is to the student has been emphasized by Russell and Thalman (187):

Boys and girls are meeting success or failure in many of our nation's schools on the basis of the mark which the teacher gives to them in recognition of some unknown quantity of hidden ingredients. Serious and permanent damage to a pupil's personality can result from continued failure in school: and if the mark results from a personality conflict between the teacher and the pupil, the act is cruel and unjustified.

Grades influence the student in many ways. They affect his attitude toward particular school subjects and toward school and education in general, and so they determine in large part whether he will be an achiever or an under- or overachiever. They also influence the quality of his school behavior. A student who makes good grades is rarely a troublemaker unless his grades fall far short of his expectations. By contrast, poor grades, especially when the student believes they are undeserved, very often lead to poor school citizenship and actual troublemaking.

Grades influence the student's concept of self by telling him how others judge him and how he rates in relation to others. They also affect the amount of time and energy he can expend on social activities, and this will determine how sociable he becomes.

The influence of grades on the self-concept is apparent in the way students react to poor grades. Some react by being ashamed and refusing to tell others what grades they received for fear of being unfavorably judged. Others try to shift the blame for their poor grades to their teachers, parents, or siblings. Still others try to minimize the value of grades. Symonds (213) indicates the many ways in which grades affect the self-concept:

Marks make a tremendous difference to a pupil. They influence his estimate of himself; they serve as a sign to him that he is liked or disliked; they determine whether he is to remain with classmates or instead to become (what he considers) an outcast and forced to join a group of strange pupils in another class. They indicate success or failure; they determine promotion; they indicate the probability of future success; they influence his parents' attitudes toward him. Marks help to determine whether a pupil thinks of himself as successful, smart, or as a failure, an outcast, stupid or a nitwit.

Academic honors   Selection for the honor roll or the dean's list, prizes and awards, merit scholarships, election to a scholastic honor society, graduation from college magna or summa cum laude—all help to reinforce the ego satisfaction that comes from high grades, which are the chief basis for academic honors. The ego satisfaction a student gets from academic honors is greatly reinforced by the approval and pride shown by parents and teachers. Many parents regard their child's academic success as a source of personal gratification and prestige. Still others, as Rothney and Koopman (185) explain, regard it as a way to improve social and economic status.

Education is a means of raising one's social status in America. A child or youth who can do well in school, win a scholarship or enter a college, can raise the status and inflate the egos of members of his family. Doing well in school can reflect glory on the parents. And if the glory is supplemented by the financial gain of a scholarship, parents and relatives are doubly pleased. In view of these social and financial rewards it is not unusual to find the gifted child pushed, prodded, coaxed and bribed to get good marks or to show other evidence that he is a successful student.

The attitude of peers toward academic honors varies according to how the student gets his honors and how much he contributes to the school in other areas. If a student works so hard to win honors that he has no time left to devote to anything else or if he wins them by taking "gut courses," getting help from parents and teachers, or cheating, he will be far less favorably judged by his peers than one who not only earns honors but also contributes to his school's prestige in extracurricular affairs. The honor student cannot fail to know how his classmates feel about him. This, in turn, cannot fail to affect his self-concept, even if he tries to convince himself that any unfavorable reactions spring from envy and jealousy.

Higher education   Not too long ago, a high school diploma was regarded as a symbol of prestige. Today, the decline in prestige associated with high school and even college graduation is due to the widespread availability of educational advantages. The more common they are, the less prestige associated with them.

Going to graduate or professional school, on the other hand, is prestigious because, to date, the percentage of students who continue their education after graduating from college is relatively small. The smaller the number and the keener the competition for available space in graduate or professional schools, the greater the prestige for those who are accepted. The prestige is enhanced if the student is accepted by one of the more esteemed schools.

The effects of higher education on the student's self-concept is greatly influenced by whether members of his family and his friends go on to college or to graduate school. If he is merely doing what everyone else is doing, going to college is not an ego-inflating experience unless he goes to a more prestigious college. On the other hand, if he is one of the first in his family to go on to higher education, it is ego-inflating. To let others know that he is a college student or in a professional training school, the person boasts about his achievements; uses identity symbols, such as blazers or ties in his college colors, stickers on his car, or writing paper with the college seal; and wears clothes and hair styles that proclaim his "college student" status.

While most students become more liberal and more tolerant as a result of their college experience, many also develop delusions of superiority. This is expressed in snobbishness toward those who have not had the advantages of higher education or who have gone to less prestigious colleges. Snobbishness is especially marked among students whose families and high school friends have not attended college. Accompanying their feeling of superiority is a hypercritical attitude toward people they consider their intellectual inferiors. In spite of this, many feel socially insecure and have the personality characteristics of the socially mobile person. Refer to Chapter 9 for a discussion of the effects of social mobility on personality.

Diplomas and degrees   For most Americans, the epitome of academic success is having a degree from a college or a professional training school, such as a degree in law, medicine, engineering, or theology. The higher the degree, the fewer people there are who have it and, hence, the greater its prestige. A diploma or degree is not satisfying to most people as a symbol of knowledge but as a symbol of eligibility for a job—a "union card" which guarantees that the holder will be able to get and hold a good job.

The attitudes of significant people have a great influence on how valuable a person regards a diploma from high school or college. Middle-class students consider diplomas more important than lower-class students because of the attitudes of their parents and peers (30, 73, 104). For example, there is a close relationship between completion of a college course on the part of parents and their children. This suggests that young people's values are markedly influenced by parental values (73, 104).

The effect of having or not having a diploma or degree on the person's self-concept is governed by two major factors: the people he is with and how important he views these insignia of academic success. If he is with *people* who have diplomas or degrees and he has one, he will feel that he is their equal, or if he has won his diploma or degree from a better-known and more prestigious school or college or with honors, he will feel that he is their superior. If he is with people who lack these marks of academic distinction, he will have feelings of personal superiority. On the other hand, if he lacks a diploma or degree and is with people who do, he will feel inferior.

When adults feel inadequate because they do not have a diploma or degree, they usually react in one of several ways, each of which serves to lessen their feelings of inadequacy. They try to minimize the value of a degree by talking about how many people reach the top of the ladder without one, or they ridicule the "long hairs" and the "intellectuals" as "impractical dreamers." Others project the blame for not completing their schooling on their family's poor financial status or lack of willingness to help. Still others—and this group is gradually increasing in numbers—return to high school and college, usually at night, to get their diplomas or degrees while carrying on the responsibilities of adult life. By so doing, they are trying to eliminate the cause of their feelings of inferiority and inadequacy.

EXTRACURRICULAR ACTIVITIES

Success in extracurricular activities contributes more to the student's self-concept than academic success. While academic failure is embarrassing and humiliating, failure in extracurricular affairs is even more so. More students drop out of school and college because they have failed to achieve a place for themselves in the extracurricular life of their schools and colleges than because they have failed academically.

Furthermore, failure in extracurricular life produces more emotional tension and more unhappiness than failure in academic work. The student who is an extracurricular "nobody," even though he may have some friends, is far more unhappy than the academic "nobody."

Reasons for importance of extracurricular activities

There are two reasons why extracurricular activities are so important to students—why they play such a crucial role in determining students' self-concepts. *First,* people judge students more favorably if they achieve success in extracurricular activities than if they achieve academic success, and *second,* the personal satisfaction derived from extracurricular activities is greater than that derived from academic success and produces a more favorable self-attitude.

Judgments by others Even though teachers may place higher value on academic success than on success in extracurricular activities, the majority of the students, school administrators, parents, and members of the community do not. In high school and in college, the lion's share of acclaim goes to those

who are outstanding in extracurricular activities, such as sports and dramatics. Being a football captain, a class president, or playing the leading role in a dramatic performance is more impressive to most members of the social group than being on the honor roll or the dean's list.

While extracurricular activities vary in prestige, a student who is active in *any* extracurricular activity is more favorably judged by parents and peers—the most significant people in the student's life—than the one who shuns such activities to outstrip his classmates in grades and academic honors. While teachers may feel that scholastic success is more important, most students place relatively low value on the opinions of their teachers.

The reason students judge those who are outstanding in extracurricular activities more favorably is that they regard the athlete, the debater, the actor, etc. as good "school citizens" who contribute something of value to the school group as a whole. By contrast, they regard those who devote their time and energies to getting high grades and scholastic honors as self-centered, egotistical, and generally unsocial. Only when outstanding students are also active in extracurricular affairs can they win the favorable opinion of their peers.

Personal satisfaction The student's personal satisfaction from extracurricular activities comes not from the favorable judgments of others alone but also from the pleasure the student himself gets from these activities. This pleasure is greatly enhanced by the fact that no one is forced to participate in extracurricular activities he dislikes or has to work under intense pressure to secure favorable ratings. Unlike in his academic work, the student can choose those activities which give him the greatest ego satisfaction and the greatest opportunity to excel.

In addition, as the student's interest in academic work declines, extracurricular activities make the school situation bearable. By the second grade, as was pointed out earlier, the decline in interest in and satisfaction from academic work is accompanied by an increased interest in the nonacademic activities the school offers, such as music and art. By high school, the student's enjoyment from school comes more from his participation in extracurricular activities than from his studies and classroom work.

Under such conditions, the student's success or failure in these activities largely determines what his attitude toward school will be and how he will adjust to school. This holds true for college also, even though most college students try to show enough interest in their work to make good grades in their courses as a stepping-stone to a good job after graduation.

That success in extracurricular activities has more influence on the student's self-concept than does success in academic work is shown by the fact that more students drop out of school for social reasons than for academic reasons. If they feel that they are "nobodies" in the sense that they have distinguished themselves in no prestigious area, they are often anxious to leave an environment which reminds them constantly of their inferiority and inadequacy.

Variations in effects of extracurricular activities

Success or failure in extracurricular activities affects boys and girls somewhat differently. Being outstanding in sports is more important for boys than for girls, while the reverse applies to social activities and dramatics (126, 197).

Since leadership roles in extracurricular activities are more often held by middle- and upper-class students than by those from the lower socioeconomic groups, failure to hold such roles is more ego-deflating to the former than to the latter. However, as participation in extracurricular activities is open to all students, members of the lower socioeconomic groups and those from minority racial and religious groups feel inadequate if they fail to win a place for themselves in these activities. Their feeling of inadequacy adversely affects their attitudes toward school, their adjustments, and, most serious of all, their self-concepts.

By contrast, students who do relatively poor academic work but achieve success in sports, music, dramatics, or other prestigious extracurricular activities develop a liking for school and work hard on their studies so that they will be able to participate in these activities. If they win distinction and acclaim for their achievements in extracurricular activities, it goes a long way toward eliminating any unfavorable effect poor academic work would otherwise have on their self-concepts.

PEER ACCEPTANCE

In schools where extracurricular activities play a primary role in school life, being socially accepted and enjoying a feeling of belonging are essential to liking school. No child or adolescent can have a favorable attitude toward any situation where he sees others having fun but knows that he is not welcome.

Peer acceptance affects the student's attitude toward school in proportion to the emphasis the school places on extracurricular activities. Schools that emphasize preparation for college regard scholarship as more relevant to the student's needs than sports, dramatics, and so on. Colleges that are very competitive for high-grade students regard scholarship as the most relevant area of accomplishment. This does not mean that peer acceptance is unimportant in these schools and colleges, but that the student's attitude toward school is less dominated by whether or not he is socially accepted.

Variations in peer acceptance

At all levels in the educational hierarchy, certain students are more likely than others to enjoy only marginal acceptance or to be rejected. They are the ones who are most likely to develop unfavorable attitudes toward school. Students who belong to *minority* religious, ethnic, or socioeconomic groups generally experience poor peer acceptance. Furthermore, they learn early in their school careers that the rewards school has to offer, in the form of grades, prizes, favors by teachers, offices held in school activities, and acceptance by their classmates, are reserved mainly for those of the majority groups. Even if they try to identify with these groups, they generally find their acceptance poor.

Students who are *physically handicapped* and unable to engage in the active play of their classmates soon discover that they are left out of the activities their classmates enjoy. While they may participate in the less active social affairs of the school, such as the clubs, bands, and religious organizations, these are not the prestigious organizations and they do not contribute much to social acceptance.

Living at a distance from the school and having to be *transported* decreases the student's chances for participating in the extracurricular activities of the school, and this, in turn, lessens his chances for social acceptance. In the junior and senior high schools and in college, this has a very unfavorable effect on the student's attitudes toward education.

The students who are likely to have the poorest peer acceptance are those who *deviate* markedly in physical development, mental ability, and to a lesser extent, age. Because children judge age in terms of size, and adolescents, in terms of physical maturity, children who are large for their age are expected by their classmates to be brighter than they, and early maturers are expected by their classmates to be more grown-up in behavior as well as brighter. If large children or early-maturing adolescents are not placed in a class where they resemble the other students in appearance, their classmates will regard them as "dumb," and this will militate against their acceptance. Marked deviations in intelligence, as was explained in Chapter 7, likewise affect the peer acceptance of students of all ages.

Socially mobile students, especially during the adolescent years, often enjoy less peer acceptance in their new schools than they did in the schools from which they came. In part, this is due to differences in interests and values, but mainly it is due to the fact that the gangs, cliques, or crowds in the new school are already formed, and a newcomer, unless he has something special to offer, finds it difficult to penetrate the psychological walls that surround these tightly knit social entities. Refer to Chapter 9 for a more complete discussion of the social problems of mobile people.

In a study of high school students, it was reported that four kinds of student behavior affect both teacher and peer acceptance:

Adaptive-academic type (A-a) in which the student is consistently and predominantly committed to the academic work of the classroom

Adaptive-social type (A-s) in which the student meets the demands of the school but engages in considerable work-avoidance activities

Maladjustive-active type (M-a) in which the student rejects the work of the school and actively displays disruptive behavior—the "troublemaker"

Maladjustive-passive type (M-p) in which the student rejects the work of the school but does not try to disrupt the work of the classroom

The most liked is the (A-a), or the adaptive-academic type, and the least, the (M-a), the maladjustive-active or "troublemaker" type who is disliked by both teachers and peers. Students show a preference for other students who are most like themselves. Troublemakers, for example, usually show a preference for other troublemakers. Among the student group as a whole, however, the boys prefer the (A-s), or work-avoidance students, while the girls prefer the (A-a), or the "good student" type (170).

Effects of peer acceptance on school adjustment

Students who are well accepted by their peers develop a favorable attitude toward school. This attitude is expressed in academic achievements that enable the student to be promoted with his classmates and to participate in the extracurricular activities that occupy the social life of the school or college. Unaccepted students, by contrast, develop such negative attitudes toward everything in the school situation that they have little motivation to do the work they are capable of doing. They often become troublemakers to retaliate for their lack of acceptance, and many become truants and dropouts when they find their lack of peer acceptance intolerable.

While some students always find it difficult to gain peer acceptance, others could be accepted if they learned to behave in a more socially approved way. One of the major social obstacles for very bright children and adolescents, for example, is their feeling of superiority. This is quickly recognized by their peers and resented so much that they reject the very bright as friends. Since students at all ages must experience peer acceptance to some extent if they are to enjoy being in school and are to have a wholesome attitude toward the school situation, one of the greatest problems for educators is to help students to be liked by their classmates. This is not easy, as was pointed out in Chapter 9.

Effects of peer acceptance on personality

Since peer acceptance or lack of it affects behavior, it also affects the judgments of others. The student who is accepted by his peers judges himself favorably because he knows that others judge him well enough to accept him as a friend. He has reason to believe that he is a worthy person. Constant reinforcement of this belief by teachers and peers as he goes through school builds up a favorable self-concept and counteracts unfavorable self-concepts developed at home.

If, on the other hand, the child lacks acceptance, it is hard for him to judge himself positively. If teachers tend to reject him, as his classmates do, this not only reinforces the effect of peer judgments of his inferiority and inadequacy but builds up the child's resentments against teachers as well as classmates. As the student's negative attitudes toward himself are reflected in his behavior, classmates and teachers are further alienated. Day in and day out exposure to such an environment can have devastating effects on the child's personality.

Another way in which peer acceptance or rejection affects the student's personality is the amount of happiness or sadness engendered by peer relationships. In adulthood, a person can escape from situations where it is obvious that he is not wanted. This is not true during the school years. Daily exposure to an environment where social rejection is readily apparent gives the student plenty of opportunity to develop the habit of being unhappy, a habit which, by the end of the compulsory school years can be so firmly rooted in the personality pattern that it may never be uprooted. A habit of being happy can just as easily be developed by the student who is accepted by his peers.

SCHOOL SUBJECTS

School subjects influence the student's personality both directly and indirectly. *Directly,* they affect (1) his characteristic pattern of responding to people and situations, and (2) his view of different school subjects and areas of life as sex appropriate or inappropriate (as masculine or feminine). *Indirectly,* they influence his personality through the effect they have on his attitude toward school and education in general. His attitude then affects his adjustments and the way he judges himself as well as the way others judge him.

Factors influencing attitudes toward school subjects

Many studies have been made of the way students of different ages react to the various subjects taught in schools and colleges and, to a lesser extent, of the way the subjects affect students' self-attitudes and reactions to school or college. These studies reveal that an unfavorable attitude toward one subject often leads to an unfavorable attitude toward all other subjects and toward school in general. The major factors influencing student attitudes and behavior are discussed below.

Nature of school subject Certain school subjects tend to make the student somewhat rigid and intolerant in his attitudes and characteristic approach to life situations while others encourage him to be more tolerant and understanding. Mathematics and science, for example, because they are exact and pre-

cise, encourage the student to approach everything in a way that conforms to a prescribed pattern; at the same time, they stifle any tendency the student might have to be creative and original. Students who major in these subjects, or who show a greater interest in them because they excel in them or feel that the subjects will be useful in later life, are more influenced by them than students who merely take them as required courses.

Courses in literature, music, art, and languages, by contrast, encourage the student to be more creative by emphasizing the expression of likes and dislikes and the evaluation of the works of others. Courses in the social sciences, such as government, psychology, and anthropology, help the student to understand people as well as himself, and this encourages a more liberal, tolerant point of view with respect to people and life in general.

Method of teaching The subject matter of a course, in many cases, has less effect on the student's personality than the way the course is taught. Just as children brought up in authoritarian homes develop a rigidity and intolerance in their characteristic approach to life, so do students in schools where an authoritarian pattern of teaching prevails. The student who is expected to learn only what the teacher wants him to learn and to give the teacher the answer she expects to receive becomes accustomed to responding in this way. In time, this pattern of response becomes habitual.

Teachers who encourage students to approach a subject in a critical way and who, in their grading, reward originality as well as accuracy provide a learning environment in which students develop the habit of responding in a more liberal, creative manner. This helps to counteract any tendency students might have to become rigid and intolerant.

Even subjects which traditionally lead to a precise and exact approach to things, as is true of science and mathematics, can be taught in a manner that encourages inventiveness and flexibility. On the other hand, any subject, even literature or art, can be taught in a manner that will lead to an illiberal and intolerant approach.

Mastery of school subject A student who does well in a subject usually likes it, especially if the grade he receives is up to his expectations. A low or failing grade inevitably makes the student dislike the subject. Good grades are always ego-inflating just as poor grades are always ego-deflating. The effects of mastery of a subject, as symbolized by the grades received, are intensified by the attitudes of parents and teachers.

There is a traditional belief, held by most parents and many educators, that a student who does well in one subject can and should do equally well in all subjects. This belief is based on the assumption that there is a general mental ability that can be applied with equal ease to all tasks. It is assumed, therefore, that a student who does well in mathematics is able to do equally well in reading, spelling, foreign languages, or history.

Scientific studies based on the results of intelligence and aptitude tests show that this belief is unjustified. It is a rare student who does equally well, or equally poorly, in all school subjects (91, 216). However, like most traditional beliefs, this one persists and has its effect on parents' and teachers' expectations.

Awareness of these expectations influences the student's expectations and he, too, expects to do equally good work in all his subjects. Failure to do so leads to unfavorable judgments by the student as well as by parents and teachers. These judgments are reflected in the student's self-attitudes.

Effort involved in mastery   How much time and effort the student must invest in the mastery of school subjects also influences his self-concept. Most students, long before they reach the high school age, develop an antiwork attitude—a negative attitude toward anything that requires "excessive" time and effort. If they can master a school subject easily and with minimum effort, they will like it. On the other hand, they usually dislike subjects they have to work hard on, regardless of what grades they get.

Most students who are not as bright as their age-mates dislike school in general and those subjects which require hard work in particular. If, to guarantee being promoted with their classmates, they must sacrifice play time to study, their antiwork attitude will grow and, with it, their dislike of the more demanding subjects.

An antiwork attitude is one of the common motivations for cheating. If a student can get reasonably good marks by copying another student's work, using notes in an examination, or getting help from a classmate or parent, he is tempted to take the easiest way out and thus save himself the time and effort needed to do the work alone.

Many students develop an antiwork attitude toward school because they come from homes where they are given few responsibilities and where the parental philosophy of child rearing emphasizes a "happy, carefree childhood." Having to work to master their lessons seems to be a punishment, and this they resent.

Not only does an antiwork attitude lead to dislike for school subjects and school in general, but it also fosters a feeling of martyrdom. The student who has this attitude has to invest his energy in things he does not enjoy to ward off the constant threat of being deprived of doing what he wants to do if he fails to come up to parents' and teachers' expectations. No wonder he feels that he is being martyred.

Usefulness of subject   The student's feelings of martyrdom are intensified when he has to study subjects he can see no use for, either now or in his adult life. How, he questions, can Latin or ancient history help him to be a successful businessman? Or what use will he ever have for algebra or geometry in these days of the computer?

Failure to do good work in a "useless" subject does far less damage to the self-concept than failure in a "useful" one. Failure in Latin, for example, while ego-deflating has a less damaging effect on a student's self-concept than failure in reading. Knowing how important reading is in school as well as daily life, the student who is a poor reader is far more damaged psychologically than one who does poor work in a subject he considers unnecessary to success.

As a school subject, reading is a barometer of students' attitudes and adjustment. Good readers have pride in their achievement, are favorably judged by themselves and others, and make good personal and social adjustments in school. Poor readers, by contrast, realize that they are unfavorably judged because of their failure in an important area of learning. They develop feelings of inadequacy which are expressed in social withdrawal, especially if reading failure results in lack of promotion, or in aggressive, cocky, and hostile attitudes toward authority—attitudes which increase their dislike for school, intensify their poor adjustment, and encourage unfavorable judgments by teachers and classmates (140, 159, 175, 233).

Poor readers experience not only poor social adjustments but also poor personal adjustments. Failure to learn to read well impairs their motivation to work up to capacity in any subject. Being recognized by teachers and classmates as "poor readers" undermines their self-confidence and sense of personal worth. Anxiety about their ability to do the work required of them not only in reading but in all classes where reading is a major tool leads to nervous mannerisms which further damage their feelings of personal security and worth. And, because they feel inadequate, they dislike reading and all subjects dependent on it.

Sex appropriateness of subject

Even though all children study the same subjects during the elementary school years, they know that parents and peers expect boys and girls to like and do better work in different subject matter areas. Each year, as children advance through the grades, social expectations based on sex-appropriate criteria become more clearly defined and more forcibly imposed on them.

Traditionally, boys should like science and mathematics and should do well in them because they will prove to be useful in adult life. Girls, by contrast, are expected to like and do well in languages, literature, art, music, and English because, in their adult lives as wives and clubwomen, these subjects will be useful to them. Furthermore, they can use these subjects in the careers that are open to women, in teaching, social work, or office work.

These cultural beliefs about the sex appropriateness of school subjects are transmitted to children at an early age by their parents and are later reinforced by teachers and classmates. Most parents, for example, think there is little need for girls to study mathematics beyond the simple arithmetic foundations. They consider it "odd" for girls to want to study higher mathematics and try to impress upon them the value of studying subjects that will be more useful to them in adult life.

Children accept these parental values and make them their own. By the time they reach the age when they are given a choice in the subjects they may study, their interests in and attitudes toward different subjects conform very closely to the traditional beliefs based on sex appropriateness (84). A girl may exhibit a real talent for mathematics, but, as Poffenberger and Norton note, "Self-concepts in regard to mathematical ability are well established in the early school years and it is very difficult for even the best teacher to change them in spite of the fact that potentiality is much in evidence" (174).

When a student likes and does well in a sex-appropriate subject, his favorable self-concept is strengthened because he knows the reactions of the social group will be favorable. Liking and doing well in a sex-inappropriate subject, by contrast, brings less favorable social judgments and makes the student wonder if he is, indeed, an "oddball."

Peer attitudes

By the time children reach the "gang age" of late childhood, their attitudes, values, and behavior are influenced more by their peers than by their parents and teachers. Peer attitudes toward school subjects carry great weight. While they vary from one school to another and from one grade to another, depending largely on the likes and dislikes of leaders and popular class members, the student is vastly influenced by them.

Students who select subjects that are in vogue or who like the preferred courses in a required curriculum, are judged more favorably by their peers than those who deviate from the popular choices. At no time is this more true than in early adolescence when deviation from peer choices in any area marks the person as "different" (meaning "inferior"). Pressey (177) explains how an interest in science may affect a student if science is not fashionable among the popular members of the peer group:

The budding young scientist or scholar may be isolated or may associate only with a friend who is also considered "odd" or may even belong to an anemic subject club of no prestige in the community. . . . The teacher (perhaps made uncomfortable by keen questions) may even criticize his intense interest and the other youngsters may call him sissy or odd.

Degree of choice

By junior or senior high school, students are given some choice in the subjects they will study. They may, for example, select the college preparatory or the vocational program and, within each, they have some choice of subjects. In college and graduate school, students have even greater latitude. The opportunity to make one's own decisions, to exercise one's autonomy, is ego-boosting at any age.

The range and amount of choice in course selection granted the student influences his concept of himself. The less choice he has, the more likely he is to think of himself as a martyr and to feel that the school or college authorities regard him as too immature to make a wise selection. Withheld autonomy damages the student's concept of self, makes him critical of the subjects he is required to take, and lowers his motivation to do his best.

KIND OF SCHOOL

Just as the kind of home the child grows up in plays a deciding role in determining what sort of personality pattern he will develop, so does the school or college. The kind of school he attends shapes his patterns of behavior and his concept of himself as a person both directly and indirectly.

Direct influence of kind of school

The kind of school or college the student attends molds his personality pattern by the values it stresses, by the courses of study it provides and how they are taught, by the kind of teachers it employs, and by the method of discipline sanctioned by the school authorities. Year in and year out exposure to these molding influences is intended to prepare the student for the kind of life he is expected to live as an adult.

Different kinds of schools and colleges, for example, stress the development of different *values*. Special schools for the physically and mentally handicapped emphasize training for independence within the limits of the children's capacities. Public schools, as Packard (162) points out, stress "middle-class" moral and social values:

The public schools of America are in general not only dominated by upper-middle-class thinking but make intensive—if unwitting—efforts to reinforce values cherished by such classes. . . . The school also stresses that all right-thinking citizens concern themselves with social problems, government policies, and world affairs. Typically, the father of a lower-class youngster takes either a dim or indifferent view of all such preoccupations.

The influence of the *kind of teacher* the student has comes partly from the values and attitudes the teacher stresses in the teaching of subject matter and partly from the student's identification with the teacher. A radical teacher in high school or college, for example, can encourage a student to develop radical attitudes and values by the way he teaches the subject matter of his course and by creating the impression that he is a reformer of the ills of the world. If he seems more glamorous than the more prosaic teachers,

the student will identify with him and want to follow in his footsteps (226).

The student's personality is also influenced by the *courses of study* which he likes and in which he is most successful. As explained earlier, some subject matter, per se, tends to make the student more rigid and authoritarian in his approach to life than other subject matter, though the way a course is taught is more of a determinant than the subject matter itself.

The prevailing philosophy of *discipline* in a school or college is another factor that influences the student's personality. Strict, authoritarian discipline, in either home or school, encourages the development of an authoritarian personality pattern, characterized by rigidity, intolerance, and lack of creativity. Democratic discipline, on the contrary, encourages the development of tolerance, understanding, and creativity.

Indirect influence of kind of school

The indirect influence on personality stemming from identity with a specific school or college comes from the way in which people, particularly those who are significant to the student, regard the institution and how much prestige it has.

The halo that surrounds a prestigious school is transferred to the student, and people judge him accordingly. Baltzell declares, "It is more advantageous, socially and economically, to have graduated from Harvard, Yale, or Princeton with a low academic standing than to have been a Phi Beta Kappa at some less fashionable institution" (20).

Most students, by the time they begin to think seriously of their future vocations, believe that they have a better chance of getting to the top of the vocational ladder if they are graduates of prestigious schools and colleges. That they are right has been borne out by studies which show that, almost without exception, the most successful businessmen, industrialists, professional men, and executives had their academic training in prestigious colleges, and many, also, in prestigious preparatory schools (20, 162, 163). Realization that the chances for future success are enhanced by identification with a prestigious educational institution also influences how students view themselves.

In conclusion, then, it is apparent that the effect of a school or college on the student's personality comes not so much from whether the education he receives there fits his needs and is suited to his abilities as from how he and other people view the institution. If it conforms to his expectations and is a source of ego satisfaction and ego inflation because of its prestige, he will be proud to be identified with it.

If, on the other hand, he views it as a less prestigious institution than he had aspired to being associated with, he will be embarrassed or actually ashamed of his identification with it. Association with such an educational institution fosters feelings of personal inadequacy. If the student graduates from the school or college, he will be identified with it for life. Only by transferring to an institution that he can be proud of will the damaging effects on his personality be eradicated.

Even when embarrassment and shame are unwarranted, the very fact that the student experiences these negative feelings is justification for trying to change his attitudes and, if this fails, getting him to shift to another institution. While rationalization and other defense mechanisms may reduce the impact of negative feelings on the self-concept to some extent, the reduction will not be great enough to ensure the development of positive attitudes toward self and to restore the motivation to work up to capacity.

SUMMARY

1 Next to the home and parents, schools and colleges and teachers have the greatest influence on personality development. The principal reasons for the schools' and teachers' impact are that children attend school during the early years of life when the personality pattern is being formed; they spend more time in school than in any other place except the home; educational institutions provide young people with opportunities to achieve their goals; and they give children their first opportunities to assess their strengths and weaknesses realistically.

2 How great an influence educational institutions have on personality development is largely determined by the student's attitudes toward schools and colleges, toward his teachers, and toward the value of education. At first, these attitudes are usually favorable, but gradually they deteriorate as a result of ego-deflating experiences in school and peer-group pressures. There are, however, marked variations in attitudes toward education depending on the sex of the student, the child-training methods he had been subjected to in the home, the social class with which his family is identified, the ethnic and religious backgrounds of his family, and his own adjustment to school.

3 When attitudes are favorable, the student usually works up to capacity, enjoys his school experiences, and has a warm, friendly relationship with his teachers and classmates. When attitudes are unfavorable, the student usually works below capacity; he grumbles, complains, and criticizes school; and he may even develop such a fear of school that he refuses to go. Dislike for school or college often leads to truancy, to dropping out, or to remaining and misbehaving as a way of getting revenge.

4 Studies reveal that certain conditions encourage the development of unfavorable attitudes while others encourage favorable ones. If a child is physically and psychologically ready to enter elementary school or if an older student is ready to enter high school, college, or graduate school, his attitude tends to be far more favorable than if he is unready, either physically or psychologically. Since readiness affects the kind of adjustment the student makes to academic work, to extracurricular activities, and to his teachers and classmates, the quality of his adjustment is the basis on which he is evaluated by others and on which he evaluates himself.

5 Physical and psychological readiness determine in large part the kind of early experiences the student has in a new educational environment, whether it be nursery school, a school to which he has transferred, or graduate school. The more favorable these early experiences are, the more favorable the student's attitudes and, in turn, the better his adjustment.

6 Attitudes toward an educational institution are greatly influenced by the emotional climate of the institution. The conditions most responsible for a school's emotional climate are the teachers' attitudes toward the teaching role and toward the students, the administrative policies regarding discipline and the curriculum, and the degree of competitiveness and harmony among the students.

7 The emotional climate of an institution affects the motivation students have to work up to capacity, their classroom behavior, and their general emotional reactions. It is through these behavior patterns that the emotional climate of a school or college influences personality by affecting the student's self-evaluation and the evaluation others make of him. The influence of the emotional climate is greatest during the early years when the self-concept is being formed.

8 Student-teacher relationships, which are dependent on the teacher's treatment of the student, on the student's attitude toward a particular teacher, on cultural stereotypes of teachers as a group, and on the teaching and disciplinary techniques the teacher uses, affect the student's attitudes toward specific subjects as well as toward education in general. These attitudes, in turn, affect the quality of the student's academic work—the basis for self and social evaluation.

9 Because academic success is highly valued by most adults, the degree of success a student achieves affects his personality via self and social evaluations. Every student becomes aware of how successful or unsuccessful he is in this area by academic symbols of success: promotion, grades, honors, and diplomas and degrees. How significant people in the student's life react to these symbols of success influences how he reacts.

10 To many students, success in extracurricular activities is more important than success in educational activities. This is a reflection of the attitudes of parents and peers—the most significant people in the student's life. Success in extracurricular activities reinforces favorable attitudes toward school and favorable self-judgments. It compensates in part for unfavorable attitudes toward school. Failure in extracurricular activities, on the other hand, is regarded by most students as more ego-deflating than failure in academic activities and is therefore more damaging to the self-concept.

11 The effect of success in extracurricular activities is greatly influenced by the amount of peer acceptance the student enjoys. Students who are poorly accepted because they belong to minority religious or ethnic groups, because they are physically handicapped, or because they deviate from their classmates in mental ability, socioeconomic status, or classroom behavior experience poor peer acceptance and develop negative attitudes toward school. Their dislike of school leads to poor school adjustment with its damaging effects on personality.

12 School subjects affect personality directly by influencing the student's characteristic pattern of response to people and situations, and indirectly by influencing his attitudes toward school, which, in turn, affect his school adjustment. How the student reacts to school subjects depends on how relevant he feels they are, how they are taught, how successfully he masters them, how much time and effort he must expend on them, how sex appropriate he thinks they are, how his peers react to them, and how much choice he is given in their selection.

13 When children realize that different kinds of schools and colleges are judged differently by the social group, the kind of school or college he attends affects his personality. This it does indirectly through the judgments others make of him because of his identification with the school or college and, directly, through the interests, attitudes, and values he acquires via his identification with teachers and classmates and via the subject matter of his courses of study. Thus, the effect of a school or college on the student's personality comes less from the education he receives than from how he perceives the educational institution with which he is identified.

CHAPTER 13 family determinants

Of all the conditions that influence personality development, relationships between the individual and the members of his family unquestionably rank first. By contrast with the home, the school is indeed secondary.

The home is the person's primary environment from the time he is born until the day he dies. While it may change over the years, owing to relocation, marriage, divorce, death, and birth of new members, the family unit and the pattern of living that meets the needs of its members remain relatively constant.

Most people think of the home influence as limited to the childhood years. They regard parents and siblings as the only family members who exercise a cardinal influence. These beliefs have been totally disproved. There is ample evidence that family influences are ruling determinants of what the person's concept of self will be in adult life as well as in childhood and that spouses and offsprings exert as strong an influence as parents and siblings in the early years of life.

WHY FAMILY INFLUENCES PREDOMINATE

Scientific studies of the family in a wide variety of cultures have revealed why it has such impact on the developing concept of self in childhood and why this impact persists relatively unchanged throughout the life span. Of the many reasons reported, the four discussed below are universal.

Time spent in the home

Family influence on personality is greatest when the major part of one's time is spent in the home and with members of the family. The amount of time you spend with a person is one of the chief determinants of how significant that person will be in your life and how much influence his attitudes, values, and behavior will have on your behavior and on your attitude toward self.

At certain times in life a person normally spends more time in the home and with members of the family than at others. These predictable times are during the preschool years, before the child's environment has broadened to include much more than his immediate neighborhood, and again in old age, when the person retires and spends more time at home than in the community setting. It is recognized that during the adult years women, even married working women, spend much more time in the home than men.

Control over behavior

Family members exert more control over a person's behavior than any other person or group of persons. In childhood, teachers, baby-sitters, and grandparents are only surrogate parents who act temporarily *in loco parentis.* Within a family group, even when it is considered equalitarian, husband and wife have more control than do children, and in some areas of family life the wife has more control than the husband, and vice versa. Wives usually control child training, for example, while husbands control money matters.

The prestige associated with a positon of authority facilitates the influence the person in the position has over the behavior of another person. Even more important, however, is the permanency of the control. A teacher, for example, is in control of the child's behavior for only a few hours a day five days a week during the school year. This contrasts with parental control which extends from year to year during the first 18 or 21 years of the person's life.

Emotionally toned relationships

While a child or adolescent may have a strong emotional attachment to a teacher or a friend or a sweetheart, this attachment rarely has the permanency that family relationships have. As long as it lasts, it may exert a strong influence on the person's concept of self, but when it ends, its influence declines rapidly.

The persistence of family relationships reinforces the effect of the emotional tie. Even when a family relationship is broken by death, its influence on the family members who survive may be greater than it was during the lifetime of the deceased member (27). For example, a boy may hero-worship a dead father to the point where he tries, as he grows up, to reproduce in his own life all the behaviors and attitudes that he attributes to his father.

Early social experiences At the time when the foundations of the personality pattern are being laid, the child's primary social experiences take place in the home. That is why, as Glasner states, "Personality is formed in the first instance within the womb of family relationships" (82). It is from these early experiences that the child acquires his attitudes, values, and patterns of social behavior. Warnath remarks that "the home thus appears indeed to be a seat of learning for the development of social skills, and perhaps of the desire to participate in activities with other individuals" (228).

Since the child's early social experiences are mainly with his parents, it is they who play the dominant role in molding his personality pattern. Bishop (23) expands on this statement:

The pattern of personality development in the young child is established primarily within the framework of his relationship with the parents. During the child's earliest years the parents constitute the chief social influence which the child experiences. The techniques which the parents employ in the treatment of the child, i.e., the incentives they offer, the frustrations they impose, their methods of control, together with the character of their general attitudes toward him serve as formative forces on the child's behavior. Habit patterns are forged as the child assimilates and internalizes these learning experiences, which interact with, and are conditioned by, his biological individuality. Later, the determining nature of parental roles is supplemented by forces from other parts of the environment. Nevertheless, all through the formative years, the particular quality of the parent-child interaction is a significant factor in the establishment of permanent motivational and personality attributes.

The persistence of these early foundations can be observed in the personality patterns of college students. When parents are rejecting, their adolescent children are reported to be glum, suspicious, timid, insecure, anxious, introverted, and tense. When they are loving, their children become extroverted, warm, conscientious, composed, and happy. When they are neglectful, their children become serious, retiring, aloof, and anxious (202).

Security of environment

To be happy and secure, a person must feel that he has an anchorage ground, a place to which he can go with his joys and triumphs as well as with his sorrows and defeats. Without this haven, he feels cut adrift, inadequate, and unhappy. The importance of the home to the child's feeling of security has been emphasized by Bossard and Boll (27):

Home is the place the child comes back to with his experiences. It is the lair to which he retreats to lick his wounds: the stage to which he returns to parade the glory of his achievements: the refuge he finds in which to brood over his ill treatment, real or fancied. Home, in other words, is the place to which one brings the everyday run of social experience, to sift, to evaluate, to appraise, to understand, or to be twisted, to fester, to be magnified, or ignored, as the case may be.

Studies show that family breakups due to death or divorce are traumatic for every family member, both spouse and children. Self-concepts are damaged and patterns of life are inevitably upset (86, 95, 126). Loss of a spouse is especially unsettling among the elderly because they regard the spouse as their chief source of emotional security (116).

INFLUENCE OF FAMILY ON PERSONALITY DEVELOPMENT

Directly, the family influences personality development by molding and by communication. Indirectly, the influence comes from identification, from unconscious imitation of attitudes, behavior patterns, etc., and from the mirror image of self one develops by viewing oneself through the eyes of family members.

Direct influences

Through the child-training methods they use, parents attempt to *mold* their children to conform to the culturally approved pattern of the social group with which they are identified. How this is done was described at length in Chapter 4. The powerful influence parents have in shaping the personality patterns of their children has been recognized by college students who, in retrospective reports of the training they received during their childhood and early adolescence, claimed that they felt their parents were largely responsible for their dominant personality characteristics. Strict, demanding, punitive, and inhibiting parents, for example, encourage their children to depend on external controls to guide their behavior. As a result, when the children are outside the orbit of direct parental influence, they tend to be impulsive (101, 116, 121, 203). How different child training methods influence the personality pattern is illustrated in Figure 13-1.

Attempts to mold the personality patterns of family members are by no means limited to parents. Older children, adolescents, and even young adults try to mold their parents, siblings, and other relatives according to their concepts—often unrealistic—of what these family members should be. The adolescent, for example, is often highly critical of his mother and attempts to "reform" her so that she will more closely approximate his concept of what a mother should be. Nor it is unusual for middle-aged adults to try to mold their aging parents to fit their ideas of what elderly people should be.

Communication is a direct method of personality transmission by which family members try to influence the personality development of other members. Parents transmit attitudes and values by telling their children how they should feel and behave in different situations or by pointing out the qualities in other people, things, and situations that their children should value.

Adolescents and young adults try to make their parents more tolerant by criticizing their narrow-mindedness and by emphasizing the good qualities of the people or social groups against whom their parents and grandparents are prejudiced. Much of the criticism that goes on in the family circle is an attempt to get family members to change their characteristic patterns of adjustment.

Indirect influences

By *identification* with someone who is admired and loved, a child, an adolescent, or even an adult tries to mold his own personality after that of the other person. (See Chap. 4 for a detailed discussion of identification.) While identification may be with people outside the home, especially during the "crush stage" of adolescence, it is usually confined to family members. Furthermore, it is most common during the early years of life.

When a child identifies with a parent, he develops a personality pattern similar to that of the parent. His attitudes toward self and others will lead to good or poor personal and social adjustments depending on whether the parent is a well- or poorly adjusted person.

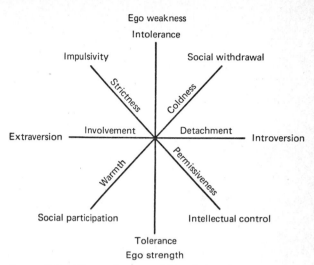

Figure 13-1 Effects of parent-child relationships on the child's personality pattern. (Adapted from P. E. Slater: Parental behavior and the personality of the child. *J. genet. Psychol.*, 1962, **101**, 53–68. Used by permission.)

Children sometimes identify with a young uncle or aunt or with an older cousin, but most often they identify with an older sibling. The little boy tends to identify with an admired older brother who treats him as a pal. An older sister who is popular and attractive to members of both sexes may become a little girl's idol, provided the older sister has a kindly attitude toward her.

There is a tendency to imitate people with whom one is constantly associated even in the absence of a strong emotional attachment. This *unconscious imitation* occurs more often in children and young adolescents than in adults. A child who is associated day after day with playmates who cheat in games is far more likely to develop the habit of cheating than if he associated with children who believed in fair play. Since the young child's associations with parents and siblings are so close, he imitates them more than he does his playmates.

Studies reveal that both children and young adolescents acquire patterns of behavior similar to those of family members. Living with parents who are nervous, anxious, and lacking in a sense of humor makes children highly nervous and subject to frequent outbursts of temper (48, 152, 203). By contrast, children with warm, affectionate, interested parents usually become social and gregarious people, showing an interest in and affection for persons outside the home as well as in it (71, 169).

The effect of unconscious imitation on the personality pattern is not limited to children or young adolescents, though its greatest impact is during the early, formative years. A person who lives with a nagger very often becomes a nagger himself, even though he was not earlier. In a family, one nagging parent can initiate a pattern of nagging that spreads to all the other family members (65). Or a happy, cheerful spouse can set a pattern that will be imitated by the children as well as by the other spouse. These patterns become more pronounced as time passes, and so spouses tend to resemble each other more and more as they grow older (39, 116).

One of the principal ways in which the family influences a person's self-concept is through a *mirror image* of himself, or how he believes the members of his family regard him. The family thus becomes the "looking glass" in which the person sees himself. He judges the attitudes of his parents and siblings and significant others by the way they treat him. Jourard and Remy (111) say this about the mirror image:

The self may be said to be made up of reflected appraisals. If these were chiefly derogatory . . . then the self dynamism will itself be chiefly derogatory . . . . It will entertain disparaging and hostile appraisals of itself. . . . It is, therefore, the parents and significant others, brothers, sisters, or nurse, who determine the nature of the self-dynamism. . . . [The self] tends very strongly to maintain the direction and characteristics given to it in childhood.

The more significant a family member is to an individual, the greater will be his influence on the person's mirror image. A child who believes that his mother disapproves of him because she constantly criticizes the way he behaves or talks will develop an unfavorable self-concept from his associations with her. This may be partially counteracted, however, by the hero worship of a younger sibling or by the pride his father shows in his achievements. Similarly, it is difficult for elderly people to have favorable self-concepts when their children and grandchildren treat them in a way that they can interpret to mean only one thing—that they are a troublesome burden to the rest of the family.

Variations in family influence on personality

There is evidence that family relationships affect the personality patterns of the various family members differently. A person who is quiet, introverted, and *socially withdrawn* is more influenced than is one who is extroverted and socially active. The former tends to brood over any unpleasant relationship, such as friction between parents or between siblings, while the extrovert has enough outside interests to turn his attention to other people when he finds relationships in the home unpleasant.

A person who is in *poor health*, regardless of age, is more influenced by family relationships than one who is healthy. He is less active socially and thus more dependent on the family. In addition, a person who is in poor health tends to brood more and to exaggerate situations that would be seen in their true perspective if he were feeling better. A sick person may interpret a casual remark as a criticism, for example, while a healthy person would let it pass unnoticed.

Because girls and women spend more time in the home and with family than do boys and men, there is a *sex* difference in the effect family relationships have on personality. This difference is well illustrated in in-law relationships and grandparent-grandchildren relationships. Wives, it has been reported, are more influenced by their relationship with their mothers-in-law than with their fathers-in-law. Husbands are less influenced by their relationships with in-laws of either sex than are wives (64).

Age differences in the effect of family relationships on personality are closely related to the amount of time people of different ages spend in the home and with family members. The more time spent in the home, the greater the influence of family members and vice versa.

The influence of *different family members* on the personality pattern of the individual depends on such conditions as the age of the person at the time, the amount of control a particular family member has over the person, the amount of time spent with the family member, and the emotional tie between the person and the family member.

In most homes, mothers spend more time with their children, have more control over them, and express their affection more overtly than fathers. As a result, mothers exert more influence over the child's developing personality. A comparison of children from *monomatric* families, or families where the child is under the exclusive care of the mother, with those from *polymatric* families, where the care of the child is shared with another female, has revealed that, at the age of 6 months, babies from monomatric families are less irritable and easier to handle. At 1 year, they exhibit personality traits that make them better adjusted, both personally and socially, than babies from polymatric families. They are more active, are more emotionally responsive in their interactions with their mothers, and make social contacts with people outside the home more easily. They show the basic personality traits of well-adjusted people (35).

The monomatric relationship leaves its mark on the mother's personality as well as the baby's. The mother who assumes full care of her baby and continues to do so after the helpless months of babyhood are passed is more understanding and tolerant of childish behavior than is the mother who has shared her maternal duties with another female. She provides a healthier home climate for all family members. In addition, she feels more confident of her ability to perform her maternal role successfully, and this adds to her self-confidence and poise.

The effect of sibling relationships on the personality pattern of the siblings involved varies according to their age, the control exerted by one sibling over another, and the affection that exists between them. Younger siblings are, as a rule, more influenced by older siblings than the reverse because the younger tends to hero-worship the older and tries to imitate him. Siblings of the same sex tend to have close emotional ties, while those of the opposite sex often have a frictional relationship because the boy develops a feeling of superiority, which his sister resents (121, 237).

Of all relatives outside the immediate family, grandchildren and grandparents have the greatest influence on each other's personality patterns. Grandmothers have more influence on and are more influenced by grandchildren than grandfathers. Grandmothers and grandchildren spend more time together, grandmothers exercise greater control over the grandchildren, and the emotional tie between the two is stronger than that between grandfathers and grandchildren (155, 179).

In summary, then, while it is evident that family relationships have a marked influence on the personality patterns of all family members, the influence is far from equal. That is why, in considering the effects of the family, one must remember that they vary according to the kind of relationship that exists and the family members who are involved.

In the remaining sections of this chapter, some of the most important family relationships and the ones that have received the greatest research attention will be discussed. It is believed that this résumé of the evidence will support the statement at the beginning of the chapter that family relationships play a role second to none in the development of the self-concept. First, a brief discussion of the effects of the home's emotional climate on the personalities of family members will serve to emphasize the pervading influence of family relationships.

EMOTIONAL CLIMATE OF THE HOME

While the emotional climate of the school has a strong influence on personality, as was discussed in Chapter 12, it is much less important than that of the home. *First,* the individual spends a relatively short time in school as compared with the time spent in the home, and *second,* the school affects only the child or the adolescent, not the parents, the grandparents, or other relatives.

It is true that the effect of the emotional climate of the school can carry over to the home. But this effect can be counteracted or minimized by the emotional climate of the home, or if the two are similar, they may reinforce each other. On the other hand, the home climate is a prime determinant of the child's adjustments to school. And the emotional climate of the school can do little to change the effect of the home on his pattern of adjustment.

Effects of home climate on personality

The emotional climate of the home *directly* influences the person's characteristic pattern of behavior and his characteristic adjustment to life. If the home climate is favorable, the individual will react to personal problems and frustrations in a calm, philosophical manner and to people in a tolerant, happy, and cooperative way. If the home climate is frictional, he will develop the habit of reacting to family members and outsiders as well in a hostile or antagonistic way.

Indirectly, the home climate influences the person by the effect it has on his attitudes toward people. If the child perceives his mother as showing favoritism toward a sibling, he develops an attitude of resentment toward people in positions of authority. Many who become radical nonconformists do so because their resentment of parental authority has developed into a resentment against *all* in authority.

Conditions contributing to a favorable home climate

When family members are capable of *empathy* or of putting themselves in the psychological shoes of other family members and viewing situations from their frame of reference, they behave in such a way as to make family relationships pleasant and harmonious. As Lee (129) has explained:

If you can learn a simple trick, Scout, you'll get along a lot better with all kinds of folks. You'll never really understand a person until you consider things from his point of view. . . . until you climb into his skin and walk around in it.

When everyone in the family realizes how an aged parent feels about having to move into the home of a married daughter and tries to make him feel welcome, for example, harmonious relationships will be possible and the home climate will be far pleasanter than if empathy were lacking.

Empathy is greatly aided by *communication* between family members. The breakdown in communication between parents and adolescent children contributes heavily to home friction. Many parents face a dilemma when they must choose between allowing their teen-age children to communicate freely and imposing the rule that "if you can't say something nice, don't say anything at all." Duvall (63) writes:

Communication has it advantages. It ventilates feelings, fosters mental health, encourages active interaction between members of different generations, and gives the individuals a sense of being heard and understood. The danger of a policy of open candid communication is that it allows teen-agers to express unpleasant, seemingly disrespectful attitudes and feelings. . . .Today the emphasis is on freer expression of real feelings in the family. This paves the way for the closer companionship that is so highly valued. But it also makes for more overt unpleasantness and expressed hostility between family members. . . . The problem is shall they be allowed to criticize their parents and air their real feelings or should they be silenced for the sake of peace and quiet around the house?

A good home climate, fostered by communication between family members, is possible when there is *respect for the opinions* of others. Even if family members disagree, mutual respect helps to reduce friction.

Open communication and respect for the opinions of others usually lead to *reasonable expectations* among family members. When the mother communicates to the members of her family why she needs their help more when she takes a second job and works outside the home as well as in, they show that their expectations for her contribution to family life are reasonable by assuming some of the duties she previously carried. If a person tries to conform to unreasonable expectations, friction is almost inevitable, and certainly tension and discontent will rise.

Whether *togetherness*—or acting together as a unit—will improve the home climate will depend on how well it meets the needs of family members. Young children want to be a part of the family group because it gives them a feeling of security. Before childhood is over, however, they derive their greatest satisfaction from their contacts with members of the peer group. By adolescence, as the young person "lives more and more in a society of his own, he finds the family a less and less satisfying psychological home" (49).

Among adults, togetherness meets the needs of some family members more than others. The companionship of spouses, children, and relatives is more important for women than men. Adults who come from families with strong traditional religious values, as is true of those of the Catholic and Jewish faiths, stress togetherness more than those of Protestant faiths or those whose interest in religion is weak (52, 131, 157, 183).

When the time spent together is pleasurable for everyone, such as the family dinner accompanied by stimulating conversation, it contributes to a happy home climate. Another positive aspect of togetherness is described by Bossard (26):

Family rituals, meaning prescribed family ways of doing things together, build up a feeling of rightness and happiness through participation. By nature, ritual in family living is the same as ritual in religion, and the history of religion shows that those with the most elaborate and pervasive rituals are those that best retain the allegiance of their members. It is really very easy to understand this: all it means is that people can best be held together by doing things together.

Too much togetherness can intrude on the *independence* of family members and can thus be harmful. While most people believe they are capable of handling more independence than others give them credit for, a reasonable amount of independence keeps them from feeling that they are being "bossed" or "regimented." There would be less friction between mothers and teen-age daughters, for example, if the daughters were given more autonomy in choosing their own clothing. The right clothing means so much to teen-age girls that they often regard lack of independence in this area as no independence at all.

Independence can be carried to the point where it jeopardizes family stability, however. At any age, to feel secure, one needs *stability* in his pattern of living and in his relationships with significant people. Especially during the early years of life, a frictional home climate, with constant threats of disruption due to the divorce or separation of parents, can be so damaging to the personalities of children that they develop serious personality disorders. All family members are affected adversely, but those who are very young are particularly vulnerable. This matter will be discussed later in the section dealing with deviant families.

Damaging as lack of stability in the pattern of living is to the home climate, lack of stability, or inconsistency, in family expectations is even more so. The child who does not know what is expected of him or the adult who is unsure of the role he is expected to play usually vacillates between one possibility and another. This vacillation, through its influence on family relationships, disrupts the pattern of family living.

Some friction is inevitable in family life. How disagreements are expressed, however, will determine whether the home climate will be favorable or not. The most common ways of *expressing disagreements* are criticism of the opinions and actions of others, attempts to reform another's behavior or change his attitudes and beliefs, nagging, ridiculing, and—a far less common method—discussing different points of view in a calm, rational, and objective way to help others understand them.

There are also a number of ways of trying to solve a disagreement and, thus, ending a conflict: calling a temporary truce by changing the subject, having one family member give in for the sake of peace and harmony, and compromising, with each family member modifying his point of view somewhat after he sees and understands the points of view of the other members.

Only the last method—compromise—will lead to a favorable home climate. While a truce or a cooling-off period will help temporarily, the friction is almost sure to recur. Giving in to another's demands for the sake of harmony is likely to encourage bullying

tactics. The person comes to believe that he can dominate by "making a fuss." This always leads to a deterioration in the home climate.

Criticizing and ridiculing are ego-deflating for the person attacked, and he bitterly resents them. In his resentment, he retaliates, and this strains the family relationship. How criticism of a family member affects the home climate is illustrated in Figure 13-2.

Conditions contributing to an unfavorable home climate

Friction always upsets family homeostasis and disturbs the emotional climate of the home. Even if the friction concerns only two family members, it rarely remains isolated. Rather, it spreads to all family members as they take sides with those who are directly involved.

The major personality damage of friction is ego-deflation. In anger, people say and do things with an intensity and vindictiveness quite alien to their usual peaceful selves. Feelings are hurt and people see themselves in an unfavorable light through the eyes of other family members.

Figure 13-2 Criticism of family members has a damaging effect on the home climate. (Adapted from Lichty's "Grin and Bear It." Publisher-Hall Syndicate. *The Philadelphia Evening Bulletin,* Nov. 11, 1966. Used by permission.)

"I don't cook this right! I don't bake that right! Why don't you get out and do your protesting in the street like other kids!"

The more crucial the problem or situation from which the friction springs, the more damaging it will be to the home climate and to the family members involved. For example, when a parent disapproves of an adolescent's choice of friends, especially friends of the opposite sex, the rift between parent and adolescent is likely to be insurmountable. An adolescent regards his friends as about the most important thing in his life and he resents any criticism of them.

Favoritism, or behavior that suggests a preference for one family member over all the others, inevitably leads to friction and a resentment of those involved in the preference relationship. Just as a child resents parental preference for a sibling, so does a husband resent his wife giving the children more time and attention than she gives him.

Often, what appears to be favoritism is not favoritism at all. One family member may simply require more attention than another—the helpless baby, for example, or the sick schoolchild.

It is logical for people to prefer someone who shows a great interest in them over another who seems cold and unresponsive. If a man feels that overt expressions of affection for his children, especially his sons, are unmasculine, the children are likely to interpret this to mean lack of interest or love. They then turn to their mother. Similarly, if daughters are more affectionate toward their fathers than are sons, it is understandable that the father would show a preference for the daughters.

Those who are the object of preference often react with a smug self-satisfaction that antagonizes other family members. If, in addition, they try to take advantage of their favored position by expecting more privileges, this infuriates those who are not the favorites to the point where they often gang up against the family members involved in the preference relationship. The result is a "house divided" —a situation which cannot fail to lead to an unfavorable emotional climate.

Feelings of inadequacy for the role one is expected to play in the home makes him unsure of himself and vacillating in his behavior. In addition, he is hypersensitive to any criticism that ensues when his behavior does not come up to the expectations of other family members. A girl, for example, who does not play as feminine a role in the family as her parents think she should is hypersensitive about being criticized or reproved for her "tomboyish ways."

When a person is hypersensitive about criticism, he becomes resentful of those who criticize.

Furthermore, if he feels inadequate for his role and uncertain about what to do, he approaches every situation in a trial-and-error way. Other family members then do not know what they can expect from him and what is expected of them. As a result, criticism becomes more common, and the friction increases.

A clash over opposing *interests* and *values* can bring about a deterioration in the home climate unless family members show mutual respect and understanding. The larger the family group and the greater the age difference between the members of the group, the greater the likelihood of friction over differences in interests and values.

Older children and adolescents, for example, have interests that differ so greatly from those of their parents and grandparents that being together for holiday celebrations is sometimes "boring" for all concerned. Similarly, young adults find that they have little in common with their middle-aged parents, just as middle-aged people have little in common with their elderly parents.

There is an even wider disparity in the values of family members of different age groups. For example, adolescents regard cheating as a far less serious moral problem than their parents and grandparents. Young adults tend to place less value on saving money for emergencies than their parents and more value on having a car and other items which their parents regard as "unnecessary luxuries." See Chapter 7 for a more complete discussion of values and interests.

One *poorly adjusted* family member can spoil the home climate for all family members, especially if the role played by that member is central in the family constellation. A poorly adjusted mother is more disruptive than a poorly adjusted father. The firstborn sibling, who has a closer relationship with the mother and who is assigned the role of mother surrogate in the care of younger children, can, if he is poorly adjusted, spoil the home climate more readily than a poorly adjusted later-born sibling.

A family member who shows his maladjustment by being moody and morbid casts a spell of gloom over the entire home environment. One who feels that he has been martyred and goes around with a chip on his shoulder sets a pattern which other family members often imitate. This is evident in the jealousy that spreads from a child to a sibling or even to a parent. The generalization of maladjustive states from one family member to all family members comes from unconscious imitation, not from identification.

Authoritarian control by a person in authority is

deeply resented, even though this resentment may not be verbalized or overtly expressed for fear of punishment. Instead, it is often displaced on an innocent victim. This arouses further resentments which lead to a frictional relationship and a poor home climate. For example, when an older sibling is put in the role of surrogate parent and is given authority over younger siblings in the parent's absence, the older sibling tends to be "bossy" in his control and this leads to a frictional relationship with the younger siblings.

Lack of emotional warmth in family relationships is interpreted by most family members to mean lack of interest and affection or, if it is marked, rejection. It may mean any of these, or it may reflect a characteristic pattern of reacting to *all* people, not only family members, a belief that showing affection will break down respect for those in authority, a belief that showing affection for boys will turn them into "sissies," and so on.

Whatever its cause, lack of emotional warmth breaks down family cohesiveness and predisposes family members to engage in frictional behavior. On the other hand, families that maintain stable, consistent, and warm relationships, with mutual trust and approval on all sides, have a wholesome home climate. This leads to ego strength on the part of all family members (168).

From this review, it is apparent that many conditions can spoil the emotional climate of the home. It is also clear that an unfavorable emotional climate is most damaging to those family members who, through necessity, spend a major part of their time in the home. It should be emphasized again, however, that the degree of psychological damage caused by an unfavorable home climate varies markedly, with persons who are quiet, withdrawn, and introverted likely to be damaged more than those who are extroverted, involved in interests outside the home, and concerned more with things than with people.

Regardless of these individual differences, no family member escapes some psychological damage from an unfavorable home climate. This damage comes mainly from the fact that the person imitates the patterns of behavior he is constantly subjected to in his relationships with people rather than from the direct effects alone.

As some of the conditions that lead to an unfavorable home climate affect the family member directly, as well as indirectly, through their effects on his self-concept, these will be discussed in more detail in the remaining sections.

ORDINAL POSITION

According to tradition, the ordinal position of the person in his family—the order of his birth in relation to his siblings—has a marked influence on his personality. Fairy tales depict the firstborn, for example, as uncertain, mistrustful, shrewd, stingy, and wealthy—a characterization which suggests a personality pattern that leads to poor personal and social adjustments. By contrast, the lastborn has the favored position; as a result, he is secure, open, confiding, generous, good-natured, humane, and generally well adjusted. While he may be naive or even stupid, he is depicted as a pleasanter person.

Scientific interest in the effects of ordinal position on personality began with Freud, who claimed that the person's "position in the sequence of brothers and sisters is of very great significance for the course of his later life" (77). Adler emphasized that each position provides a predictable personality pattern, with that of the middle and last child more favorable than that of the firstborn (3). Rank likewise emphasized that the lastborn has a more favorable position, as far as personality is concerned, than the firstborn (178).

More recent scientific studies have shown what effects ordinal position has on personality and have shown that these effects are due to the "psychological position" of the person in the family rather than to ordinal position per se. The firstborn, for example, is "brought up while the others grow up" (42). He is likely to be the victim of excessive parental demands and expectations, while later-born children grow up in a more permissive and relaxed atmosphere. In addition, later-borns have siblings to identify with and are thus freed from some of the pressures and expectations that come with almost exclusive adult identification (87, 139, 229).

Effects of ordinal position on personality

The psychological position of a person in the family, resulting from his order of birth, affects his self concept both directly and indirectly. The *direct* effect comes from the role the person is expected to play in the home and what different family members expect of him. To conform to these expectations, he is molded, from earliest childhood, into the pattern that family members want him to follow.

When children are unable to conform to parental expectations, they often become anxious, resentful and rebellious. This frequently leads to behavior problems. The behavior ratings for children of different ordinal position show that the first-born and middle children present more problems for their parents than do those born later (200).

Another effect of birth order that directly affects the developing personality pattern comes from the competitiveness between siblings that develops as a result of different parental expectations. Realizing that the firstborn has a favored position in the family, especially if he is a boy, and realizing that this gives him special opportunities for success, siblings constantly compete, either as individuals or in various relationships of alliance, for a comparable place of significance and success in the family.

Indirectly, ordinal position influences the self-concept (1) through the effect that competitiveness and rivalry among siblings has on the home climate and (2) through the way the individual's behavior in relation to social expectations is judged by the people who are significant in his life. If the lastborn child of the family feels that he is being slighted in favor of the firstborn, this can lead to a frictional relationship with the firstborn and resentments against the parents. If, on the other hand, he hero-worships the firstborn and the firstborn treats him favorably, the home climate is likely to be sunny.

Sex differences in effects of ordinal position on personality

Family expectations and family pressures to conform to these expectations differ for members of the two sexes. In general, the differences are most pronounced in adolescence.

Reports of sex differences in personality due to ordinal position indicate that firstborn girls tend to be more bossy at home, while second-borns are more bossy at play (216). Such behavior is more common among girls with sisters than those with brothers. In addition, firstborn girls are more aggressive toward adults than later-born girls and more defiant of adult authority; they demand more attention; and they are comparatively overactive, irritable, tense, and somewhat shy in the presence of strangers. They have more problems at all ages than do later-borns (121, 197).

When a firstborn girl is replaced in parental affection and attention by a later-born boy, parental hopes and aspirations shift to him. This leads to resentment on the girl's part, which further increases her problems and intensifies the conditions that affect her personality unfavorably.

Sex differences in this regard are less apparent in later-born children. Since later-borns recognize that parental hopes and expectations are centered more on the firstborn, whether a boy or a girl, than on them, they feel less pressed to achieve unrealistic goals and are usually subjected to a more relaxed method of child rearing.

Long-term effects of ordinal position on personality

Reports indicate that the effects of birth order on personality do not end when the person begins to spend more time outside the home than in. The effects tend to be more persistent in the later-born than in the firstborn, however (27, 199, 216).

High school teachers identify firstborns as superior students not because of higher levels of intelligence but because of stronger motivation, seriousness, adult orientation, and susceptibility to external pressures. As Bradley and Sanborn have pointed out, "High achievement later in life may be as much a matter of favorable experiences as it is of anything else" (30). This has been substantiated by Altus and others who report that, within families, more firstborns achieve success in adult life than later-borns (7, 54, 139, 193).

A study of the relationship between ordinal position and adjustment to marriage further emphasizes the long-term effects. In the family of his childhood, the person learns to play a given role related to his ordinal position. For the man, the best position, from the point of view of later marital adjustments, is that of the oldest brother with younger sisters. For the woman, the best position is that of a younger sister with older brothers.

When the ordinal positions are reversed, that is, when the husband is the younger brother of older sisters and the wife the older sister with younger brothers, the wife is likely to try to "boss" her husband the way she "bossed" her younger brothers. When both husband and wife are firstborns, they carry into adulthood personality patterns characterized by bossiness and a tendency to feel superior. The result is a frictional marital relationship (91).

"Typical" personality patterns

Children of different birth order are exposed to social environments that differ radically and to different parental expectations, and so it is understandable that their personality patterns would vary. Since our culture favors no uniform way of bringing up children of different ordinal positions, however, there are no distinct personality types or syndromes that inevitably accompany a given birth-order position.

On the other hand, certain personality patterns are found so frequently among people of different birth orders that they may be regarded as typical of those ordinal positions.

Personality pattern of firstborns

Studies have repeatedly pointed out that the typical firstborn enjoys a number of advantages. These advantages are largely responsible for the personality pattern that is so characteristically found among firstborns. On the whole, achievement is greater among first- than among later-borns in the same family (102, 147). As Schachter (193) has explained:

The repeated findings of a surplus of first-borns among eminent scholars appears to have nothing to do with any direct relationship of birth order to eminence but is simply a reflection of the fact that scholars, eminent or not, derive from a college population in which first-borns are in a marked surplus.

Because the "dice are loaded in favor of firstborns," they achieve more than their later-born siblings (7). The ability to achieve more comes from their strong motivation to make the most of their innate abilities. Among the many traits fostered in firstborns by parental guidance and pressure to achieve success are conscientiousness, seriousness, conservatism, a sense of responsibility, and stronger emotional ties and greater loyalty to the family. All these contribute to the achievements which make their parents proud of them and their siblings envious of them (7, 30, 98, 137, 139, 191, 221).

However, these desirable personality traits of firstborns are usually accompanied by other traits that lead to less favorable personal and social adjustments than are characteristic of later-born siblings in the same family. Like the desirable traits, they, too, are the product of parental overprotectiveness and parental pressures to achieve.

Studies reveal that firstborns tend to be more conforming and dependent than later-borns; they are more affiliative, especially in stress situations; they are more susceptible to group pressures and more withdrawn and introverted; they have less frustration tolerance and are prone to angry outbursts; they are more fearful of pain and frightening situations; and they are often anxiety-ridden because they are afraid of not being able to live up to adult expectations (19, 37, 50, 92, 197, 231).

Firstborns who achieve greater success than their later-born siblings tend to be bossy, selfish, self-centered, and spoiled. They show their feelings of superiority about their achievements by derogatory comments and criticisms of others. But in spite of their feelings of superiority, they continue to suffer from feelings of insecurity which developed early in life when they were replaced by younger siblings in their parents' attention and concern. That insecurity is a common characteristic of firstborns is shown by the fact that they tend to marry earlier than their later-born siblings as a way of reducing anxiety and overcoming the feelings of insecurity they have carried with them from childhood (7, 161, 191, 206, 229, 238).

That feelings of insecurity are responsible for much of the poor personal and social adjustment characteristically found among firstborns has been explained in this way by Montagu (145):

The first-born does seem to take rather a beating. For a year or more he is emperor of the universe. Everything exists to cater to his needs. . . . Then more or less abruptly the halcyon existence is terminated, or at least considerably changed, by the eruption into it of a brother or sister. . . . Really, can one wonder that the first-born is often what parents frankly call a "mess"!

Personality pattern of lastborns

The typical personality pattern of the "baby of the family"—the lastborn child— resembles in some respects the pattern of the firstborn but differs enough in other respects to justify Adler's claim that the youngest children of the family "bear unmistakable signs of the fact that they have been the youngest" (3).

The personality characteristics typically found in both the lastborn and the firstborn trace back to quite different origins. The firstborn, for example, is pushed and prodded to achieve what his parents expect of him and have sacrificed to make possible for him. By contrast, the baby of the family is likely to be pampered and spoiled by siblings as well as parents, and little is expected of him. Both become self-centered, selfish, and bossy, but for different reasons (27, 103, 199).

Other personality characteristics of the lastborn which resemble those of the firstborn are dependency, affiliative need, lack of self-confidence, lack of frustration tolerance, resentfulness, defiance of authority, and a tendency to be troublesome. Dependency in the lastborn comes from being pampered and waited on by siblings, while dependency in the firstborn comes from being pampered and waited on by adults. Having played the "little brother role" in childhood, the lastborn gets into the habit of needing pals; this motivates him to join gangs, and later, school or college fraternities. The affiliative need in the firstborn comes from his constant association with adults (12, 54, 121, 230).

Lack of self-confidence in the firstborn is the result of too many parental pressures and unrealistic expectations. In the lastborn, it is the result of pampering. Lack of frustration tolerance in the firstborn is the result of always having help from adults in coping with problems he is unable to handle alone. In the lastborn, it comes from relaxed parental discipline and the tendency of all family members to be tolerant in their attitudes toward the "baby's" temper outbursts.

Resentfulness, defiance of authority, and a tendency to be troublesome in the firstborn comes from being overly regimented and subjected to intense pressure to live up to parental expectations. It is a form of revolt against parental domination. In the lastborn, by contrast, these characteristics develop when the child feels left out of family activities because he is "too young," when he is not given the privileges other children are given, and when he has to use their cast-off clothes, toys, and other equipment, which he interprets as parental rejection. Such feelings may and often do lead to a martyr complex.

In contrast to firstborns, most lastborns have relatively weak achievement motivations. They are not pressed to achieve, nor do most families sacrifice to provide them with the opportunities provided firstborns. As a result, they are less anxious and less likely to be guilt-ridden. Little is expected of them, and so they have little reason to worry or feel guilty about not being successful.

Because of the relatively permissive upbringing most lastborn children are subjected to, they do not learn to harness their imagination for creative tasks. Instead, they tend to use their imagination for daydreaming or identification with heroes in mass media. Firstborns, by contrast, are more creative (92, 98).

In their attempts to mimic their older siblings—attempts which often result in failure—many lastborn children develop feelings of inadequacy and lack self-confidence. Few firstborns are plagued with feelings of inadequacy, not because they are more able to achieve what they set out to do, but because they receive more help from parents.

In direct contrast to firstborns, who give the impression of being mature or "old for their age" owing to their constant contacts with adults, being expected to assume mature responsibilities at an early age, and their high motivation to succeed, lastborns give the impression of being immature or "young for their age." This is due to their more constant contacts with siblings than with adults, not being expected to assume responsibilities, and their weak motivation to succeed.

Perhaps the characteristics that most commonly differentiate lastborns from firstborns are their extroverted, social behavior and their tendency to be optimistic and happy. These traits derive from the same set of circumstances that make lastborns appear young for their age. They have more opportunity to learn to get along well with other young people, and since less is expected of them than of firstborns, they can enjoy life without feeling guilty or anxious about success.

Even though lastborns, like everyone else, have undesirable personality characteristics, these are outweighed by the desirable. Therefore they make better personal and social adjustments and are less likely to be unhappy and maladjusted. In comparison with firstborns, fewer lastborns suffer from mental disorders, and fewer dislike themselves to the point where they contemplate or commit suicide (54).

Personality patterns of middle-borns The typical personality pattern of second-born or middle children in a large family is a product of the treatment such children receive and of parental expectations for them. By the time the second child arrives, parents are less anxious about their ability to cope with problems arising from baby care. With the arrival of each new baby, they are more and more confident, and the amount of time they have to devote to each child decreases progressively. Each child is less overprotected and less dependent. Also, with the parents more relaxed, a warmer parent-child relationship is possible, which makes the later-born children more extroverted and fun-loving.

On the other hand, second-born and middle children use the firstborn as a pacemaker. When they are unable to keep up to the pace he sets and when he rejects them as playmates because they are "too young," they are likely to feel inadequate and resentful. These negative feelings are intensified if the older child tries to lord it over them. Even when this happens, they are motivated to show him that they are not "babies." This is especially true in the relationship of a younger boy with an older sibling who is also a boy. Koch (121) declares:

The male sibling keeps the sib on his toes. It isn't that the male has greater skill or knowledge but rather that he, by the challenge he presents, stimulates or alerts his sib more than does a girl. Jealousy of him because he tends to be favored by his mother may also spark the alerting.

Finding relatively little satisfaction from the companionship of the older sibling and from parents who have little time to devote to them, second-borns and other middle children become less family-oriented and more peer-oriented. From their peer relationships they develop personality traits that lead to good personal as well as social adjustments. As a result, they are usually more popular with their peers than are first- or lastborns.

Second-borns and middle children usually accomplish less in life and are less successful academically and vocationally than their older siblings. They also tend to be less creative. While this may not concern them greatly when they are young, as they approach adulthood they often become jealous of the older sibling whom they perceive as the parental pet and whose greater opportunities they bitterly resent. As a result, a frictional relationship often develops between them and the firstborn. They then ally themselves with a younger sibling who also feels that he has been discriminated against in favor of the first-born.

In conclusion, it is evident that the position a person has in his family, owing to the order in which he was born, does leave a mark on his personality. Furthermore, the personality pattern associated with each position contains desirable as well as undesirable traits, and it is impossible to claim that any position is "best." From the evidence, one might tentatively say that the position of the middle child is more favorable than that of the first- or lastborn child in a family of three or more children. In a family of two children, the position of the second-born seems to be more advantageous for personality development.

Since ordinal position remains constant and family members are consistent in the way they treat the person who holds a given position, chances are that the personality pattern will be so well molded by the time the child reaches the age where he is more influenced by peers and teachers than by parents and siblings that it will change little even though there are marked environmental changes in his life. That is why

Freud was justified in saying that the position a person has in "the sequence of brothers and sisters is of very great significance for the course of his later life" (77).

SIZE OF FAMILY

The kind of family a person grows up in or lives in as an adult is influenced by its size and composition in terms of the people who live under the same roof and are interrelated in their patterns of living. The size of the family influences the personality pattern both directly and indirectly.

Directly, it determines what role the person will play in the family constellation, what kind of relationship he will have with other family members, and to a large extent, what opportunities he will have to make the most of his native abilities. *Indirectly,* family size influences the personality pattern through the kind of home climate fostered by families of different sizes and by the attitudes of the most significant members of the family toward the person.

According to popular belief, the larger the family the more frictional it will be. This has been explained mathematically by Bossard and Boll. They say that the number of interpersonal relationships in a family can be determined by the following formula:

$$X = \frac{Y^2 - Y}{2}$$

where X is the number of interpersonal relationships and Y is the number of family members.

In a 3-member family, for example, where there are a mother, a father, and a child, there will be 3 interactional systems. If, however, there are 3 children, 1 grandparent, and 2 parents, that is, 6 people living under the same roof, the number of interpersonal relations will increase to 15 (27). This formula is illustrated in Figure 13-3.

In spite of variations in home conditions that influence the amount of friction, the traditional belief about the relationship between family size and family friction is usually correct. Family friction tends to be stronger and more persistent in families of four or more members than in those of only two or three members (27, 64, 68).

Effects of family size on personality

Only children develop a different personality pattern from those who spend the formative years of their

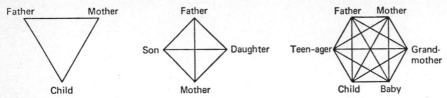

Figure 13-3 The larger the number of family members, the larger the number of interpersonal relationships.

lives in a family with one or two siblings, and they differ from children who are members of large families, including relatives who are a permanent fixture in the family constellation.

It is not size per se that is primarily responsible for the differences, but other conditions that develop as a result of family size. When a family is large, for example, the work load is large, and it becomes much more important that all family members do their share. Furthermore, it is impossible for parents to devote as much time and attention to each child as is possible in a small family.

In addition, because of economic restrictions, it is rarely possible in a large family to give all the children the material possessions, educational and recreational advantages, and opportunities for social contacts that children from small families enjoy. People who grow up in large families often feel deprived, and many develop feelings of martyrdom and of resentment against the father for not earning enough to provide them with the advantages their friends have.

The *kind of association* that exists between family members has a great impact on their personalities. This is determined more by how parents feel about their roles as parents and how satisfied they are with the number of children they have than by size itself. When parents want a large family, they have a warmer association with their children and accept the responsibilities a large family brings more cheerfully than if they want only one or two children. Parents' attitudes toward the number of children they have are also influenced by how soon the children come after marriage and by how much time there is between each new child's arrival. According to Freedman and Coombs (76):

Those who have their children very quickly after marriage find themselves under great economic pressure, particularly if they married at an early age. Opportunities for education or for decisions involving present sacrifices for future gains are difficult. They are less able than others to accumulate the goods and assets regarded as desirable by young couples in our society. They are more likely than others to become discouraged at an early point and to lose interest . . . in the competition for economic success.

Other conditions equal, parents will have a stronger desire for a large number of children if the husband-wife relationship is good than if it is strained (44, 170, 175).

Another aspect of the connection between family size and personality is the amount of *understanding* and *empathy* found in families of different sizes. As was emphasized earlier, the ability of a family member to identify with another and to understand his interests, values, and points of view will go a long way toward producing a healthy home climate. In a small family, parents have time to empathize with their children and to communicate with them. In a large family, there is less time, and, also, as the number of children increases, the gap between the generations grows wider. This combination of conditions tends to lead to less warmth and less understanding in the large family.

While most of the relevant studies have concentrated on the effects of family size on the personality patterns of children, there is evidence that family size also influences the personalities of parents and even grandparents. If a man regards having a large family as a symbol of virility, for example, the effect of a large family on his self-concept will be favorable. If he regards a large family as a millstone around his neck, preventing him from making the vocational success he was capable of, the effect on his self-concept will be negative. Even when a woman wants a large family, if the children come so close together that she feels overburdened with work, she may begin to feel that she is a martyr (163).

Most grandparents like to boast about how many grandchildren they have. This is especially true of those who have had smaller families of their own than they had hoped to have and who can limit their relationships with their grandchildren to the "fun-seeking role." If having a large number of grandchildren means that they must act as surrogate parents or must make financial sacrifices to help with the care and education of the grandchildren, attitudes of pride may be replaced by feelings of being imposed upon (155).

Effects of different-sized families on personality

No one family size can be considered "ideal" as far as the effect on personality is concerned. Tuckman and Regan conclude that "conditions for personal growth and development may be more favorable for some aspects in smaller families and for others in large families" (222). A good deal of evidence has been collected, and that relating to four different family sizes will now be examined.

One-child families   The two common stereotypes of the only child depict him in such an unfavorable light as to imply that he could not hope to be a success in life or to be happy. According to the first, he is a "spoiled brat," selfish, egocentric, and antisocial. In the second, he belongs to that category of people known as "mice"—sensitive, withdrawn, dependent on others, and generally unsocial. While the "mouse" may not be as unsuccessful in adjusting to people as the "spoiled brat," he tends to "hide his light under a bushel" and to become a loner. As a result, his chances of being happy and well-adjusted are slight.

The unfavorable traditional beliefs about only children were corroborated by early scientific studies. G. Stanley Hall (93) wrote in 1907:

Being an only child is a disease in itself. The only child is greatly handicapped. He cannot be expected to go through life with the same capacity for adjustment that the child reared in the family with other children has.

More recent studies agree that the only child develops a distinctive personality pattern. This is often called the "only-child syndrome." However, there is ample evidence that the kind of personality pattern the only child develops, even though "distinctive," has many characteristics that lead to good personal and social adjustments (4, 33, 222).

Among the *favorable* characteristics of the only-child syndrome is maturity of behavior, especially control over the emotions. This is due to constant contact with adults and imitation of adult behavior patterns. Since only children are spared the rivalries, name calling, and conflicts so characteristic of families with several children, they do not develop jealousies and envies, nor are they made to feel inadequate by constant comparison with siblings (4, 219). In describing the greater maturity of the only child, Messer (143) writes:

The only child seems older, more serious than his peers. Often this stems from the fact that the only child has never been allowed to be a child in the real sense of the word. The mature adult has within his personality a piece of childhood and a piece of adolescence as well as a preponderance of maturity. But, as an adult, the only child seems to have an overweighting of maturity.

Like the favorable personality characteristics the only child develops, his *unfavorable* characteristics are a product of the home environment.

Many only children are lonely in the sense that they lack companionship with their peers and the opportunity to play with other children. They are overexposed to adults and underexposed to children. Underexposure to peers encourages them to feel cheated of what their peers have, with the result that they become envious and jealous of those who have siblings.

The loneliness of only children encourages the habit of daydreaming, which usually weakens their motivation to achieve what they are capable of achieving and almost always makes social adjustments difficult. Deprived of opportunities to learn to get along with real people at the preschool age when their peers are learning social skills, they seem unsocial to their peers later when they have opportunities for companionship. This point is emphasized by Messer (143):

The only child is at a decided disadvantage with children who are growing up in the rough-and-tumble atmosphere of larger families. And so he prefers to be with older people whom he knows how to manipulate. He can ingratiate himself with adults, but his tactics don't work with children.

The only child is the apple of his parents' as well as his grandparents' eye. Not only is he given what he wants but he is subjected to a less rigid discipline than is essential in a home with several children. This encourages him to be selfish and self-centered—

personality characteristics that militate against good social adjustments outside the home.

An adult-oriented child becomes a dependent person, both physically and emotionally. He tends to lack self-confidence in his abilities because he is constantly measuring himself against adults instead of against his peers. As the comparison is rarely in his favor, he is likely to develop feelings of inadequacy.

An only-child family affects the personalities of the parents as well. Tolchin remarks that "the emotional investment of parents in an only child is 100 percent" (219). Consequently, they are willing to make financial investments to give the child every possible advantage and opportunity, but they expect more in return than they would of any other child, even a firstborn.

If the only child lives up to the parents' expectations, they feel that they have done a good job and this is ego-inflating. When parental expectations are unrealistically high or when parents put excessive pressure on the only child to live up to reasonable expectations, the child may revolt and show little appreciation for what they have done. He may even go out of his way to defy parental as well as all adult authority.

The mother's personality is more strongly affected by having an only child than the father's. The mother claims more credit when the child is a success than does the father, and she feels more acutely that she has been a failure when the child does not live up to expectations. In addition, as the mother's role comes to an end sooner when the only child grows up and leaves home than is true of mothers of several children, the mother of the only child suffers more from role deprivation, and this has a deleterious effect on her personality. This matter will be discussed in the section dealing with family roles.

Small families In the American culture, a "small family" is one that has two or three children. Most small families are "planned" families insofar as the number of children, the timing of the arrival of the first child, and the spacing of subsequent children are concerned. Since the children are wanted, the parent-child relationship is usually warm and wholesome. This contributes to a healthy home climate. In a small family, democratic control usually prevails, permitting each family member to develop his own interests and talents and thus encouraging creativity and individuality.

Most small families are economically secure enough to give all children opportunities to prepare themselves for adult life, though the firstborn, as was stressed earlier, often gets most of these advantages. However, as few parents can provide advantages for their children without personal sacrifice, parents of small families tend to put great pressure on their children and accuse them of not being appreciative if they fail to live up to parental expectations. Children develop strong feelings of anxiety, and their achievements are not as ego-satisfying as they might otherwise be.

In a small family, parents can devote enough time to the care and guidance of each child to ensure that failures will be kept to a minimum. This builds up self-confidence and self-assurance and eliminates the feelings of inadequacy that come when a child is left to meet his problems alone. Unlike the only child, every child in a small family can count on having someone to be with whose interests are similar to his. And even though his relationships with his siblings may be frictional, he learns to compete as well as to cooperate with age-mates. This helps him to adjust to social situations outside the home and leads to a self-confidence which the only child lacks.

In spite of the many conditions that favor the development of desirable personality characteristics in the small family, the child must "pay the price for this in the form of problem-creating circumstances" (27). Perhaps the chief of these is the competition for parental attention, affection, and approval. This leads to jealousy and envy, especially against the firstborn, who is usually perceived to be the parents' favorite. A home environment that encourages jealousies and envies is damaging to the self-concept of all its members.

If children in a small family are spaced several years apart, parents are able to give each child enough attention and help to encourage him to be dependent. While not as dependent as the only child, the child from a small family tends to be dependent enough to show the unmistakable signs of an overprotective upbringing. This, combined with the jealousies and animosities apparently endemic to small families, encourages a feeling of personal inadequacy to meet problems alone. It also results in poor frustration tolerance, because the child becomes accustomed to having his parents meet and solve his problems for him.

In spite of the unfavorable traits that customarily develop in children who grow up in a small family, the favorable outweigh the unfavorable more than they do in the case of the only child. As a result, the personality pattern molded by a small-family environment will, typically, favor better personal and social adjustments.

The home climate of the small family may not be as pleasant for parents and other relatives as that of a one-child family. But there are compensations. Parents experience greater feelings of usefulness and a greater challenge to try to understand each child, to help him develop his individual abilities, and to see that each feels loved and wanted so that none will be psychologically damaged by suspicions of parental favoritism.

The feeling of being useful to her family is as ego-satisfying to the mother as the feeling of being able to provide several children with opportunities to develop their interests and abilities is to the father. For both parents, having several children who measure up to their expectations is more ego-satisfying than having just one do so. Furthermore, the chances of having one child measure up to parental expectations is greater in the small family than in the one-child family where all depends on one child.

Medium-sized families Medium-sized families in the American culture have four or five children. They seem to provide a happy medium between small and large families, enjoying the good characteristics fostered by both small and large families and, at the same time, counteracting the unfavorable characteristics.

The child who grows up in a medium-sized family never has a reason to feel lonely because he always has siblings around. Nor does he have to feel neglected or rejected by hypercritical parents; he can gang up against his parents with a sibling who feels much as he does. In addition, having enough siblings for constant companionship provides learning experiences which will help him make good social adjustments outside the home.

Except in times of economic depression, parents of medium-sized families can usually provide opportunities for each child to develop his abilities. But since this can be done only with parental sacrifice, perhaps with the mother taking a second job outside the home, there is less likelihood that parents will force these opportunities on a child who shows little or no interest in them. As a result, the child is freed from pressures to live up to parental expectations, regardless of his abilities.

To avoid a chaotic home climate, a medium-sized family must have reasonable discipline and must enforce rules on all family members. This trains the child, from his earliest days, to conform to a pattern that will make life pleasanter for all—a habit which will lead to favorable judgments by people outside the home.

And as the burden of work involved in living in a medium-sized family is too much for parents to carry alone, every child learns to be a cooperative member of a working team. This, combined with conformity to group expectations of approved behavior, will help to develop a personality pattern that will lead to good social and personal adjustments.

In any family, parental favoritism always causes resentment among the children who are not favored and feelings of superiority on the part of the one who is the favorite. As family size increases, so does the tendency to have favorites. Favoritism has an unfavorable effect on the home climate as well as on the personality patterns of all the children.

One of the leading causes of unwholesome personality traits is variation in the abilities of siblings. Even when a child is superior to his siblings in some ability, his successes may not receive the recognition from parents and siblings that those of another sibling receive. A girl who is outstanding in science, for example, may not receive as great recognition as a brother who is a good athlete. Lack of recognition militates against the development of self-confidence that success normally brings, and leads instead to a feeling of resentment.

How a medium-sized family affects the personality pattern of the parents will depend on how satisfied they are with the size of the family and how adequate they feel about performing their parental roles. If the mother feels that she is overworked by having so many children, she will probably feel martyred. If, on the other hand, she has the willing cooperation of all family members, she will enjoy her role and have pride in the affection and cooperation of her children.

In the same way, a father may have great pride in his children and their achievements if they appreciate the hard work and sacrifices he makes for them. It is ego-satisfying to him to have others recognize their successes. When his children are critical of him or when they gang up against him and show a preference for their mother, however, he feels that he is both a failure as a parent and a martyr.

Large families Families with six or more children are considered "large" in our culture. They tend to be more common in the lower than in the middle and upper socioeconomic groups. Thus, some of the unfavorable personality effects reported to be associated with large families may be due to socioeconomic factors, not to family size per se. Furthermore, as having a large number of children is often unplanned for and unwanted, parental attitudes tend to be less favorable in large than in smaller families. This influences the home climate, and through it, indirectly, the personality pattern of every family member.

In a large family, parents have too little time to overprotect or indulge any child. Children therefore learn to be independent and mature in their behavior at an earlier age than in smaller families. If all the work entailed in bringing up a large family is to be done, every child must learn at an early age to be cooperative and to carry his share of the load. The child who grows up in a large family never has to be lonely. And with a number of siblings to choose from, he can usually find at least one who is congenial and companionable. As a result, he learns to be social and to enjoy social activities.

The large family does, however, encourage certain personality characteristics that hamper good personal and social adjustments. To keep the home climate reasonably calm and harmonious, parents must usually assume authoritarian control. Typically, this kind of control reaps a harvest of resentment and rebellion. An accompaniment of authoritarian control is regimentation of the children, which stifles individuality, and the assignment of roles that lead to rebellion if the children do not like them.

Often older siblings, especially the older daughters, are expected to assume the role of surrogate mother. This the girls resent because it deprives them of opportunities to participate in social activities with their friends. The resentment is damaging to their personalities as well as to the personalities of younger siblings, whom they often treat with less consideration, more impatience, and less affection than the youngsters receive from the mother. The younger siblings feel rejected and experience all the damaging personality effects that rejection gives rise to.

Unless the family income is high, children who grow up in a large family are of necessity deprived of many of the material possessions and social and educational advantages their peers have. This gives rise to jealousies and envies which often foster the development of a martyr complex. Parents may, through severe personal privation, provide the children with the opportunities that their peers have. But if the children

do not take full advantage of these opportunities or show adequate appreciation, their parents are likely to make them feel guilty and ashamed.

Lack of adequate supervision and guidance, especially when the mother must work to help meet family needs, leads to undisciplined behavior in school, antisocial behavior outside of school, and personality maladjustments. The problem is greater for children from large families than for those from smaller families. Consequently, children who grow up in large families tend to make poorer personal and social adjustments.

How having a large number of children affects the personalities of parents depends largely upon how they feel about the size of the family—whether they wanted a large family and planned for it. In general, the personality effects are likely to be unfavorable. Both parents feel overworked and deprived of the material possessions and opportunities for recreation that their friends with smaller families enjoy. While they may not feel martyred, they often envy friends who have fewer home duties and responsibilities.

Many men whose vocational success falls below their aspirations blame the family for their lack of success. They maintain that they are overworked at home and so cannot do as well on their job as they otherwise could. They often claim that they cannot afford to shift to new jobs that might offer greater long-run opportunities because their primary concern must be job security, even if that means lower pay.

Living under a constant threat of economic insecurity makes parents anxious and fearful. Under such conditions, it is difficult to be relaxed and happy or to create a healthy, rewarding home climate. Consequently, the problems that are normal in a large family are intensified and the emotional strain become overwhelming. As Stöckle has pointed out, families up to six children are not likely to overtax the physical and emotional strength of parents. Families above that number inevitably do (210). When economic conditions make it necessary for the mother of a large family to work outside the home, her physical and emotional strength are likely to be overtaxed to the point where her frustration tolerance reaches the breaking point.

FAMILY COMPOSITION

Directly, the influence of family composition on personality comes from the kind of people there are within the family for the individual to identify with and the kind he selects as his source of identification and imitation. A boy who selects his mother as a model to imitate will develop into an effeminate man, even though there was a father in the home and he might have selected him if there had been a warmer father-son relationship.

Indirectly, the composition of the family affects the personality pattern through the effect it has on the home climate. If a man resents the presence of his mother-in-law in the home as a permanent resident, he is likely to have a frictional relationship with her that will make the home climate unpleasant for all.

Another indirect influence comes from the effect produced by the judgments other family members make of the individual and his achievements. If a grandmother believes that children should spend time at home on studies or home duties, she is likely to be hypercritical of their watching television by the hour. Expressing her disapproval in term of their "laziness" or "selfishness" will affect their self-concepts unfavorably and will make them resentful because they are criticized for doing what their friends do.

Variations in family composition

A *nuclear* family is composed of the parents and children, whereas an *extended* or elongated family consists of the nuclear family plus relatives who live under the same roof with the nuclear family. The family members may all be *singletons,* or some may be singletons while others are *multiple births*—twins, either identical or nonidentical, triplets, quadruplets, or even quintuplets.

Some families may have *both parents* in the home and others may have only *one parent* or one natural parent and a *stepparent.* All the children may be of one *sex,* or they may be of both sexes in varying numbers. There may be small *age* differences between the children and between them and their parents or large age differences. In an extended family, the age differences may be very great.

Extensive research has thrown light on the influence family composition has on the personality patterns of family members. A description of several variations in composition will serve to show what effects they have.

Nuclear versus extended families

Friction is more likely to occur in an extended than in a nuclear family and to be more severe and more persis-

tent. This is due to the wider range of ages, which leads to one of the most common causes of family friction—differences in needs, interests, aspirations, and values.

If authoritarian control is used to maintain peace and to ensure at least outward respect of the young for the elderly family members, antagonism smolders under the surface only to break out later in frictional relationships among other family members. That is one reason why an extended family, consisting of three or more generations, is a hazardous form.

Psychological damage can also come from the financial privation that is common in an extended family. When parents must assume financial responsibility for elderly relatives, they often have to cut back on many of the material possessions and social and educational advantages they want for themselves and their children. It often means that family members must crowd themselves into a home meant for a nuclear family and that each member must assume some responsibility for the care of the elderly relatives. These situations build up resentments, especially among the children and adolescents of the family. Knowing or sensing how their children and grandchildren feel, older people often feel guilty for placing such a burden on their families.

The psychological damage to extended family members is greater in mobile than in static families. When members of the younger generation have been able to move up the vocational and social ladders, they are often embarrassed by and ashamed of the relatives who have not climbed up with them. So long as the relatives remain in their own homes, the members of the mobile younger generation are not so readily identified with them by outsiders as they are when they live under the same roof.

It is not inevitable that the extended-family situation will have unfavorable effects on the personalities of family members. The effects, whether favorable or unfavorable, will depend on the emotional warmth that exists between the members of the nuclear family and the relatives, how much the relatives upset the pattern of life of the nuclear family, how much financial privation their presence causes, and a host of other conditions.

Invasion by outsiders

Whether the family is nuclear or extended in its composition, family members become adjusted to it in time and accept it as the expected pattern for them.

Anything that upsets the homeostasis of family living upsets every family member and requires new adjustments to the changed situation.

A common source of upset in family homeostasis is invasion by outsiders. The outsiders may be guests—"paying," who live with the family for an indefinite period, or "invited," who spend a relatively short time with the family—baby-sitters who take care of the home and the children while the parents are away or while the mother is ill, servants who come in occasionally to clean or do household chores, or stepparents who become a permanent part of the family pattern.

Except for stepparents, the influence of outsiders is usually only temporary. The children of the family tend to regard them as intruders, however, and to resent their presence. This leads to negative attitudes and friction. While there are outsiders in the home, children are expected to be on their good behavior, and when they fail to come up to the expectations of the outsiders, they are often criticized or reproved by their parents or looked upon with scorn or disapproval by the intruders.

Even when outsiders are liked by all family members, they inevitably upset family homeostasis by crowding the home, disrupting the normal schedule, and adding to the work and responsibilities of all family members. Knowing that the outsiders will be there for only a short time, family members are not motivated to try to adjust to them. As a result, the home remains upset until the outsiders leave. That is why frequent or prolonged invasions by outsiders can be very damaging to the personalities of all family members.

Even though the intrusion of a stepparent is likely to be permanent, most children, especially when the natural parent is still alive, cannot or will not accept this fact and adjust to it. Instead, they regard the stepparent as a temporary intruder.

When the stepparent assumes a role of authority over them, it intensifies the children's resentments and hostilities. This, in turn, sets the stage for frictional relationships with the stepparent and disrupts the home climate. It is not surprising that many children with stepparents think of themselves as martyrs, that stepparents feel inadequate because they cannot handle the situation better, and that the natural parent feels guilty for having brought into the home a person who has disrupted the lives of all and has caused so much unhappiness (28, 70, 114).

Age variations in family composition

The greater the age differential among family members, the less cohesiveness there is likely to be and the greater the chance for friction. If the older family members can remember their younger years and empathize with the younger members, however, they can bridge the generation gap which is at the basis of much of family friction. Young people cannot do this because they have not lived long enough to know what it is like to be older. Thus the responsibility for frictional relationships between the generations, with their damaging effects on personality, is primarily in the hands of adults or adolescents who are approaching adulthood.

Family friction is by no means limited to extended families. In any relationship, a difference in ages great enough to produce different frames of reference on life in general can be expected to cause friction. It can also be expected to cause divisiveness, as seen by the lack of interest in doing things together or the inability to "speak the same language."

In a family where there is a wide age gap between husband and wife, for example, there is often far less congeniality than when the age differential is smaller. The older spouse tends to develop a feeling of superiority, and the younger, a feeling of inferiority and of inadequancy about his ability to perform his role successfully (27). When there is a large age gap between children in a family, friction may be kept to a minimum by parental threats of punishment if the older sibling teases and bullies the younger. However, there will be word battles and name calling. The damaging effects of these will be intensified if the older sibling is appointed parent surrogate with control over the younger sibling and the privilege of disciplining him if he does not obey.

Older parents tend to be stricter than younger parents. As a result, their children often develop personality problems due to parental inhibition of childish impulses. By contrast, the permissiveness of younger parents may encourage children to do much as they please, even if this involves unsocial or antisocial behavior (211).

Another aspect of age variations within the family that influences personality is the judgment others make of a family member's appearance and behavior. As teen-agers tend to be critical of anyone who looks old, for example, they are far more likely to be critical and ashamed of parents who look old enough to be their grandparents than of parents who look younger. If their parents try to dress or act as if they were younger than they actually are, teenagers criticize them for not looking and acting their age.

Unfavorable judgments affect the self-concept adversely. The more significant the judgment-maker is to the person being judged, the more destructive his unfavorable judgment will be. Thus, parents of hypercritical adolescent children often develop feelings of inadequacy about their parental roles and build up resentments against their children—negative feelings that are harmful to the emotional climate of the home and to their personalities.

Since adolescents are identified with their parents in the minds of their peers, those who are ashamed of their parents develop feelings of inadequacy and inferiority. In addition, they feel guilty because they do not show their parents the love and appreciation that their parents expect.

Sex variations in family composition

Normally, in any family, whether nuclear or extended, both sexes are represented but in varying numbers. As the age of family members advances, the more likely it is that the female sex will predominate.

Sex variations affect family relationships in a number of ways, each of which has an impact on the self-concepts of all family members. A family with all female children, for example, tends to be more frictional than one with all male children or a combination of the two sexes (17, 91). When boys predominate, it is common for them to tease and bully their sisters. Frictional relationships affect not only the home climate but also the personality patterns of all who are involved in the friction. Of even more far-reaching consequence, the frictional relationships between siblings of the two sexes often become habitual patterns of adjustment.

Nonfrictional sibling combinations also influence the personalities of children and adolescents. Boys, especially when they are older than their sisters, are stimulating and security-taxing to their sisters. As a result, girls learn to be more self-confident and poised and to take teasing without having their feelings hurt. Boys who have older sisters tend to be quiet and withdrawn, depending more on others than on themselves. When they have older brothers they are more poised, more self-confident, and less dependent (197, 229).

Boys brought up in homes where the firstborn is a girl or where girls predominate are likely to be more "sissified" than when the firstborn is a boy or when boys predominate. Girls, on the other hand, are far more likely to become tomboys when the firstborn is a boy or when boys predominate. In other words, both boys and girls tend to identify with siblings who hold important positions in the home either because of their ordinal position or their majority status.

Just as the early school years are dominated by female teachers, so the early years in the home are dominated by females—mothers, grandmothers, and female baby-sitters. Even when the father is in the home, the care of the children is left to females. Under such conditions, many boys develop personality characteristics that are more feminine than masculine. Refer to Chapter 11 for a more complete discussion of why this is true.

The sex composition of the family affects adults as well as children. In a family with male children only, the mother may be a queen or a drudge, depending on the example set for the sons by the father. Similarly, in a family with all daughters, the father may be the adored idol or public enemy No. 1; if his daughters feel that he is unsympathetic to them or unfair to the mother, they may gang up against him.

In an extended family, especially as parents and grandparents grow older, female members tend to predominate, primarily because females have longer lifetimes. If a maternal grandmother makes excessive demands on the mother, her husband and children will resent being neglected in favor of the elderly parent. This leads to a frictional home climate and motivates the husband and male children to withdraw from family activities as much as possible (46). How this affects family members is illustrated in Figure 13-4.

With retirement, a man is at home more than at any time since his preschool years. Whether the home is dominated by female relatives or he lives alone with his wife, his identification is mainly with females rather than with men, as during his school and working years. It has been reported that as men grow older they tend to become more feminine in their interests and activities, a tendency that leaves a mark on their personalities (117).

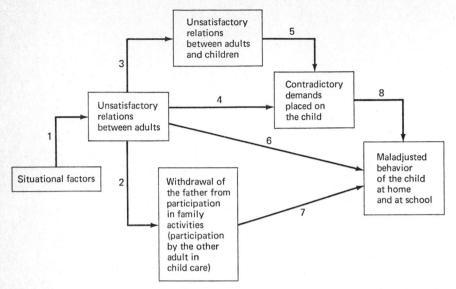

Figure 13-4 Conflicting demands in the home lead to a poor home climate, and this is reflected in the child's adjustive behavior in the home and at school. (Adapted from A. W. Clark and P. Von Sommers: Contradictory demands in family relations and adjustments to school and home. *Hum. Relat.*, 1961, **14**, 97–111. Used by permission.)

Singletons versus multiple births

The majority of families are made up of members who were born as singletons. Some, however, contain one or more sets of twins, either identical or nonidentical, while few contain a set of triplets, quadruplets, or even quintuplets.

From the moment of birth, children of multiple birth and singletons are subjected to quite different family attitudes, expectations, and treatment. This is true outside the home also, but to a lesser extent. As Koch puts it, "The play of forces, biological and social, upon twins is rather different in many respects from that which molds the singleton" (122). Whether this different play of forces will favor or hamper good adjustment and the development of favorable self-concepts depends on a number of factors.

One of the most common causes of unfavorable parental attitudes toward children of multiple birth is the extra work, extra anxiety, and extra financial strain their care entails. In one study, for example, all but three of the twenty-five mothers questioned emphasized the hardships caused by having children of multiple birth. Whether multiple birth will lead to such unfavorable attitudes or not will depend on how eager parents are to have children and on whether they have realistic concepts of the parental role. If multiple births

are the firstborn children of a family, parental attitudes are likely to be less favorable than if the children are born after the parents have learned, from experience, how to take care of babies and have discovered the gratifications as well as the hardships of parenthood.

The typical but by no means universal parental attitude toward children of multiple birth is expressed in a jingle by an anonymous writer quoted by Scheinfeld (195):

The Joy (?) of Twins
Drudgery that's double or more
Laundering until your hands are sore;
Tangle of lines with soggy things drying,
Day and night chorus of yelling and crying,
Endless chores and no end of expenses.
Worries that drive you out of your senses,
Every one bothering you with questions,
Every one giving you crazy suggestions,
Husband complaining you're no kind of wife,
Everything mixed up in your life.
If I know who to blame for twins, I'd sue 'em.
Those who want twins *are* welcome *to* 'em.

While children of multiple birth are often the

center of social attention, especially if they are very much alike in appearance and dress, other conditions are far less ego-inflating for them. If they are identical or if they are of the same sex but nonidentical, children of multiple birth are expected to look and act alike. This discourages the development of individuality. The twin who is stronger or more aggressive, for example, becomes the "boss" and sets the pattern the other is expected to follow, whether it meets his needs or is to his liking. If this leads to a frictional sibling relationship, the psychological damage that comes with frustrations of identity and individuality increases. In time, the weaker twin develops feelings of inferiority, and the stronger, feelings of superiority. There is evidence that these effects persist throughout life.

Children of multiple birth have little reason to feel lonely, especially during the preschool years, whereas singletons, even those with older siblings, are often lonely because their older siblings regard them as too young to be congenial playmates. The advantages of not being lonely are often counteracted, however, by the absence of stimulation that comes from trying to win the attention and favor of an older sibling (119).

In spite of the ready availability of playmates, twins engage in more solitary play than singletons. This may be due to their desire to establish their identity, to frustrations resulting from being forced to play together, or to lack of learning how to be cooperative from play with older and more experienced playmates.

The few available studies of triplets, quadruplets, and quintuplets have put little emphasis on the effects of multiple birth on personality. They suggest that the effects on parental attitudes as well as on the children themselves are similar, though stronger, than in the case of twins. It can thus be concluded that the larger the number of children making up the multiple birth, the greater the likelihood of psychological damage, just as there is evidence that the likelihood of physical damage is greater (127, 146, 163, 195, 198).

While studies of the effects of multiple births in a family where there are singletons have not, to date, been made, it would be logical to conclude that all the damaging effects of favoritism would be operative. The special attention given to twins by outsiders and the greater attention parents must give them to meet their physical needs would almost surely be interpreted by singleton siblings to mean that they were being rejected in favor of the twins.

Furthermore, since children of multiple birth are constantly together, they make little effort to affiliate with their other siblings. This their siblings further interpret as rejection. In addition, the extra work, fatigue, and frustration parents experience in caring for twins have an adverse effect on the home climate and add to the psychological damage done to the other siblings.

FAMILY ROLES

In every family, regardless of its size and composition, each member is expected to play a certain role. Each role is clearly defined by family members and contributes to a harmonious living arrangement for all family members. Lehrman says that the family is a "structure made up of the interrelated roles assigned to its various members" (130). Some family roles are traditionally prescribed, while others are prescribed by individual families to meet their particular needs. Some roles are inflexible while others are flexible. Some are even chosen by individual family members, with or without the approval of the other members.

There are, for example, traditional roles for the mother, the father, the child, and the grandparents. If these roles do not meet the needs of a given family or of a member of the family, the other family members may agree that they should be modified or even radically changed.

If a mother decides to go to work outside the home and her husband and children agree and are willing to assume some of the home duties she formerly performed, this change in the traditional mother role will not affect her or any family member adversely. Similarly, while the traditional role of the child in the home emphasizes help to the family, how this help is given is often determined by the needs of the individual family. In a large family, the help will usually take the form of performing home chores or caring for younger children, while in a small family it will take the form of supplying companionship to the parents and playing with younger siblings while the mother is occupied with home chores.

Roles may be voluntarily selected by family members to meet their own needs and interests, regardless of how other family members feel about them. Or members may play more than one role. A woman who wishes to work outside the home may play the double role of working wife.

Effects of family role-playing on personality

Role-playing in the family affects the self-concept both directly and indirectly. In both instances, the effect is great because of the cross influences of each family member's attitudes and behavior on every other member.

Directly, role-playing affects the self-concept by determining how the individual feels about the role he is expected to play and how well he believes he plays it. Knowing what is expected of him by other family members gives him a standard by which to judge his performance. A husband, for example, expects to be dominant in family decision making and he knows that this is the traditional role for him to play. But if his wife works outside the home, she may make some of the decisions about the family budget, and this will lead him to judge himself as not playing his role successfully.

Indirectly, the effect of role-playing comes from its influence on the home climate and from how family members and outsiders judge the individual's success in playing the role the social group expects him to play. When all family members agree on a concept of the mother role, for example, they use this concept to judge the mother and her performance of her role.

If a working mother is judged unfavorably by the members of her family for "shirking" her maternal duties, she feels anxious and guilty. Similar unfavorable judgments by friends and neighbors will further damage her self-concept (84).

Unfavorable family judgments of the way a member plays his role affect his personality indirectly by giving rise to a frictional home climate. If a grandmother is criticized by her grandchildren for the way she treats them when she plays the surrogate-mother role and by her married children for her "old-fashioned ideas" about child rearing, she interprets this to mean that she has failed in her role. If, on the other hand, she plays her role as surrogate mother in a manner that pleases the grandchildren, they will judge their mother's role-playing by comparing it with the grandmother's. This may give rise to a frictional mother-child or mother-grandmother relationship.

Once a person learns to play a certain role in the home, it becomes habitual and is carried outside the home in his relationships with other people. In a study of children's play, it was found that the "family-group hierarchy is reproduced in the play hierarchy" (215). This reinforces the learning. A girl who learns to play the surrogate-mother role in the home continues to play it outside the home in her play with other children. As she grows older, she shows a "motherly" approach to all younger children. She is then judged by outsiders as a responsible, trustworthy person.

If a girl learns to play the tomboy role in the home where she is the only girl in a large family of boys, she will quickly learn that boys and girls outside the home reject her as a playmate because they regard her behavior as sex inappropriate. The unfavorable judgments of outsiders may reinforce unfavorable family judgments or they may counteract some of the favorable family judgments.

Factors influencing role-playing

A host of factors influence the role the person plays in the family and how he plays it. They are, therefore, central in determining how his role-playing will affect his self-concept. The most influential factors are covered in the following pages.

Attitude toward role The person's attitude toward the role he is expected to play affects how he plays the role and how he feels about being expected to play it. In general, the person tends to think that the roles others are expected to play are superior to his. The grass on the other side of the fence always seem to be greener.

A mother of an only child may feel that the mother of a larger family is much more fortunate than she, and vice versa. Similarly, a man tends to regard his wife's role as easier than his, while she regards his as not only easier, in terms of time and effort, but more self-fulfilling and glamorous.

When a person has a negative attitude toward the role he is expected to play, he will have little motivation to play it and, when forced to do so, will feel imposed upon and will play the role only half-heartedly. Family members and outsiders will then judge the person and his role-playing unfavorably.

Concept of role The person's concepts of the roles he and other family members are expected to play influence his attitude toward his own role-playing as well as his attitude toward theirs. If he and they play their roles in accordance with his concepts, self-evaluations and evaluations of and by others will be positive, and the home climate will be harmonious.

Unfortunately, people usually have unrealistic, highly romanticized concepts of different family roles based mainly on the way the roles are presented in the mass media. A highly romanticized concept of the role of "wife" or "mother," for example, may lead to disenchantment with the real role.

Since the stepmother is stereotyped in fairy tales and the mass media as "wicked," it is not surprising that a child with a stepmother regards her with suspicion and resents her authority over him. Furthermore, if his real mother is dead, he is likely to have a highly romanticized concept of what she was like. He then uses this as a frame of reference by which to evaluate his stepmother, to her inevitable disadvantage. The home climate is thus severely damaged and, with it, the personalities of all family members.

Social attitudes toward family roles

The attitudes of family members toward their roles are greatly influenced by social attitudes—attitudes held by the community. Both are based largely on mass media stereotypes.

While social attitudes toward stepparents have been unfavorable for many years, there is, unfortunately, a growing tendency for social attitudes toward the roles of grandparents, parents, children, and adolescents to be equally unfavorable. Children are depicted in the mass media as "brats," adolescents as "impossible to live with" because they "know it all," and parents as ineffectual, child-dominated muddlers. Such concepts cannot fail to affect the attitudes of family members toward one another as well as toward themselves. Crowther (51) writes:

Something amazing is happening to the conventional image of Mom (short for American mother) in recent films. It is being severely "dumped on," to use a contemporary phrase. Mother is being presented as a boy's (or a girl's) worst friend. . . . Suddenly he is confronted by the accumulating idea that mothers are without infallible wisdom and, indeed, can be bad for a kid. And fathers have not come off much better in all the films, though they have usually been subordinate to the mothers and sometimes even victimized by them—all of which makes for further implications of the nefariousness of Mom.

Unfavorable social stereotypes of unmarried adult family members, especially the women who are depicted as "old maids," lead to unfavorable family attitudes toward them. Studies of married and unmarried women have found no evidence of personality distortion among the unmarried (13, 41, 177). However, knowing how others feel about their unmarried state does affect their self-concepts as well as their happiness.

Satisfaction from role

The amount of satisfaction the person derives from playing the role he is expected to play in the family affects his attitude toward it. This, in turn, affects his success in playing the role and how he as well as other family members judge him.

Satisfaction from family role-playing comes from many sources, the most important of which are the feeling that one's role is important to the family, that family members appreciate one's contribution to the family's physical and psychological welfare, and that one is prepared to play his role successfully.

Parents of young children feel that their roles are *important* to the well-being of their children and that they are both needed and appreciated. As children grow older and spend more time outside the home, parents begin to feel "useless." This feeling reaches a peak when the children leave home for college or homes of their own.

A person cannot feel *appreciated* if he is constantly criticized by other family members. Stoodley (212) explains how a mother feels in this situation:

As children grow up they naturally start to pick up ideas as to who is the "big wheel" in their family. More often than not it isn't Mother. Perhaps they go to a school where the teachers are women, but the principal is a man. Perhaps they see that the jobs they consider important are occupied mostly by men. Or perhaps they merely absorb the sentiments of their social milieu which associates prestige with some specific kind of expertness, whether it be that of the certified public accountant, the skilled mechanic or the physician.

Regardless of what role a person tries to play, he will derive little satisfaction from it if he feels *unprepared* to play it successfully. A young wife who has been trained along lines unrelated to the roles of wife and mother feels inadequate to cope with the duties and responsibilities these roles entail. If, in addition, she has an unrealistic, glamorized concept of the roles, her dissatisfaction with her new situation will be intensified. Figure 13-5 shows how lack of preparation for a family role affects the individual's attitude toward it.

The Neighbors   *By George Clark*

"I didn't know a new baby could overcrowd a house with his belongings in his first few days."

Figure 13-5 Lack of preparation for a family role often leads to dissatisfaction and disenchantment. (Adapted from Clark, "The Neighbors." Chicago Tribune—New York News Syndicate. *The Philadelphia Evening Bulletin,* Aug. 27, 1969. Used by permission.)

Choice of roles People resent being forced to play a family role that is neither of their choosing nor to their liking. When the firstborn daughter is expected to play the mother-surrogate role, regardless of how this may interfere with her studies or social life, she regards it as "unfair" and projects her resentment on the siblings she is forced to take care of.

One of the reasons "shotgun" marriages, or marriages entered into solely to legitimize the status of an unborn child, are hazardous is that the man resents being forced into a marriage that he had not contemplated and does not want, either because he does not love the girl or feels that marriage at this time will jeopardize his educational and vocational future. The wife soon discovers this and, in time, so does the child. Under such conditions, there is little chance for a happy marriage and greater chance of a divorce with its damaging effects on the personalities of all involved (135).

Changed roles Changing one's role means breaking off habitual patterns of adjustment and learning new ones. And since learning new patterns of adjustment is easier and more effective when the motivation to do so is strong, successful role changing depends largely upon how satisfying the old role was and how eager the person is to learn a new one.

In the postparental period, when the last child of the family goes away from home, the roles of both spouses change. This means new adjustments to each other and adjustments to new recreations, new home duties, and new social activities. The effect of such role changes can be traumatic.

A common role change for men comes after retirement. Instead of working away from home, they work in the home, often sharing household duties with their wives. If they do not regard their new role as effeminate, it will not be damaging to their personalities. For many women, having someone to share their home responsibilities is ego-bolstering. See Figure 13-6.

DEVIANT FAMILY PATTERNS

In a culture where being different is widely regarded as being inferior, it is not surprising that people feel ashamed and embarrassed if their family patterns differ from those of the people with whom they associate. Among adults, such feelings are a carry-over from their childhood experiences.

No family pattern is "deviant" unless it differs from other families in the group with which the person is identified in some conspicuous way. Divorce and remarriage may be considered deviant in one social group while, in another, they are so common as to be regarded as normal. Similarly, in one group the majority of mothers may work outside the home, while in another, only one or two mothers do.

Being different affects people of all age levels, though the effects are greatest in late childhood and early adolescence. A brief discussion of a few deviant family patterns will illustrate what the effects are.

Solo families When one parent is absent, due to death, divorce, desertion, separation, or some other cause, the home becomes a "solo" home, with one parent, usually the mother, playing the role of both parents (117).

The solo home may be a source of embarrassment to all family members or it may be a source of pride. If the father's absence is due to divorce or desertion, it will usually be a source of embarrassment. If he is serving his country overseas in the armed forces or is engaged in an occupation that requires frequent and long absences from home, his absence will probably be a source of pride. Members of the social group judge the solo home by the same standards as family members, and so their judgments reinforce those of family members.

Since the child's personality pattern is largely molded during the early years of life, the parent's absence at this time leaves its mark on the child's personality. When the father is away from home, the mother tends to be more indulgent and less demanding in her child training. This encourages the child to be dependent and less mature than his age-mates—conditions that jeopardize his social relationships and lead to unfavorable social judgments.

Lacking a source of masculine identification, boys are more likely to be psychologically damaged by the father's absence from the home than are girls. By comparison with boys from homes where the father is present, boys from solo homes are usually more dependent and less sex appropriate in their behavior. Their poorer personal and social adjustments often lead to aggressive behavior and to poor schoolwork. As a result, they are unfavorably judged by others.

The personality effect of a solo home is not limited to children. It is felt by parents as well as other family members. The father will have feelings of guilt about neglecting his children, even if he supports them. He will be lonely and will envy fathers who can share their children's lives. And he may be ashamed if he feels that he is unfavorably judged by outsiders.

Many wives resent the extra burden of work and responsibility placed on them in a solo home. They are lonely and often try to compensate for their loneliness by attaching themselves emotionally to their elder sons, whom they come to regard as surrogate husbands. Even more common, they are almost always anxious about their ability to play both the mother and father roles successfully. They try to overcome these unfavorable effects, in many cases, by remarriage.

Divorced families Divorce normally eliminates some of the friction so damaging to the home climate. But unless the family lives in a community where divorce is common, such a rupture in the family pattern is likely to stigmatize all family members in the eyes of the social group.

In most cases of divorce, the care of the children is awarded to the mother, and the damaging effects of living in a solo home are compounded by the social stigma of being different or disgraced. Furthermore, as fathers are usually given visiting privileges by the court when the divorce is granted, children experience divided loyalties to their parents and develop feelings of insecurity, stemming from being in two homes and receiving different treatment from their two parents. Reconstruction of the family should one or both parents remarry further adds to the children's feelings of insecurity. They now have three or four parents to adjust to, and they feel quite different from peers who have only two parents.

Divorce often means downward social mobility for all family members because the income of the family must be divided to support two households. To avoid this or to minimize its impact, many divorced women work outside the home, turn the care of younger children over to a relative or servant, and expect the older children to assume heavier home responsibilities than their peers are expected to assume.

Figure 13-6 For many women, it is ego-bolstering to have their husbands share the home responsibilities with them. (Adapted from Clark, "The Neighbors." Chicago Tribune—New York News Syndicate. *The Philadelphia Evening Bulletin,* Nov. 14, 1966. Used by permission.)

"It's so nice now that Henry's retired. We're doing together all the things I'd planned."

Variations in the way family members adjust to divorce are greatly influenced by how much divorce upsets the accustomed pattern of family life, how the children adjust to a stepparent or stepparents if their natural parents remarry, how old children are when the divorce occurs, how common divorce and stepparents are among families they are associated with, and many other conditions.

That divorce is damaging to the personalities of many children is evidenced by a higher incidence of problem behavior and juvenile delinquency among children of divorced parents. It is also evidenced by their poorer personal and social adjustments, during both childhood and adulthood, in their schoolwork, their vocations, and their marriages.

Among parents, there are also marked differences in the personality effects of divorce. Some find divorce to be a happy solution to an unpleasant experience, and their personalities improve after the friction that led up to the divorce ends. If they remarry and find happiness in their new marriages, this also favors personality improvement. When, on the other hand, divorce leads to a radically changed pattern of life, to loneliness, and to social stigma in a group where divorce is frowned upon, the effect on personality will be damaging.

Widowhood   The status of a widow or a widower is not only deviant but also ambiguous in that the person is neither single nor a spouse. Widowhood almost always leads to poor self-evaluation. In discussing the problem role ambiguity gives rise to for women, Berardo (21) declares:

Women occupying widowhood status experience varying degrees of role ambiguity emanating from vague and contradictory normative expectations concerning appropriate behavior. . . . The period of widowhood necessitates a reorganization and reintegration of social roles suitable to a new status.

Whether widowhood is due to death or divorce, most people who are deprived of a spouse are lonely and are faced with many adjustment problems, personal, social, and economic. They may have to give up their homes and live in smaller quarters or with their children, and they will have to accept a social life involving primarily members of their own sex rather than members of both sexes as before.

A factor that contributes to the widow's unfavorable self-evaluation is the attitude of other married women. While they may sympathize with her, they also regard her as a potential threat to their marriages. Goode writes, "Wives, suspicious of her motives, misinterpret her most casual gestures toward their husbands. Husbands, meanwhile, assume she is in a perpetual state of tumescence" (159).

Widowed men experience few if any of these unfavorable social judgments. Since there are more widows who want husbands that there are widowers who want wives, and since widowers who want to remarry generally prefer younger women, widowed men are in a favored position. If they are well-off and personable, they are sought after. And this is ego-inflating for them.

Another condition that contributes to the widow's unfavorable self-concept is that she is often in an unfavorable economic position. This often means that she must receive help from her children. Having to accept a state of dependency after years of independence is a role change which is always ego-deflating. Few widowers find themselves in this position.

A final condition of widowhood that has a marked effect on personality is the attitude of members of the social group, especially younger members, toward the remarriage of older people. Many younger people regard the remarriage of older women with scorn or amusement. Their attitude toward the remarriage of older men is far more favorable. Awareness of these social attitudes inevitably affects the widow's self-evaluation unfavorably.

Disgraced families   Strong disapproval of some kinds of deviant family patterns make the family members feel "disgraced." In addition to the feeling of shame normally associated with deviance, they feel inferior. The family member who is responsible for bringing "disgrace" to his family will also feel guilty.

Most people who belong to a "disgraced" family are aware of the unfavorable social attitude toward them. The more disparaging they perceive the social attitude to be, as expressed verbally or in actions, the more damaged they are psychologically and the more negative their self-evaluation will be.

The home climate of any "disgraced" family is frictional. Every family member experiences social isolation to some extent and many of his social contacts are at a lower social level than he would like. He is rejected by the members of the social group with which he was formerly identified, or he withdraws because he feels ashamed. His involuntary isolation and the frictional home climate contribute greatly to his unfavorable self-evaluation and intensify the psychological damage of being identified with a "disgraced" family.

CRITERIA OF FAMILY DISGRACE Because of variations in social group and subgroup values, a family pattern that is regarded as a disgrace in one group may not be considered so in another. Furthermore, some individuals within a group may consider a family pattern disgraceful while others, with different values, may be willing to tolerate the pattern or even approve it.

In one group, for example, an unmarried daughter who is approaching her thirties is regarded as an "old maid"—a label that implies a stigma. The members of the group regard the woman as "odd" or "pathetic" and sympathize with her parents for having a daughter who is such an "ugly duckling" that no man wants to marry her. In another group, the woman may be admired for her achievements even though she may be pitied for having missed the roles of marriage and motherhood. In still another, she may be regarded as "lucky" to have escaped the hard work and privations marriage and parenthood bring.

Thus, the way the person perceives the deviant family pattern determines whether he regards it as disgraced or merely different. As a general rule, the fewer instances of similar deviant family patterns there are in a particular social group, the greater the likelihood of perceiving them as indications of disgrace. The larger the number, the more they are likely to be regarded as different but normal.

COMMON KINDS OF DISGRACED FAMILIES Remembering the pitfalls of making sweeping generalizations and the variations in criteria noted above, we can now discuss the family patterns that in the American culture are commonly regarded as disgraced.

In small communities, where marrying in the same faith is the usual pattern, an *interfaith* marriage, especially between members of two widely different religious faiths, is often regarded as a family disgrace. In urban or suburban areas, such marriages may be regarded as unfortunate, but family members do not feel that they have anything to be ashamed of even though they may have a somewhat apologetic attitude when they sense that people are critical of them (134, 182).

In the past, marrying a person with a different racial background was frowned upon and, in some instances, forbidden by law. Today, *interracial* marriages are gradually becoming more common, especially in the urban areas. Because interracial marriages are more readily apparent—owing to the differences in physical appearance of the spouses and their children—they are more subject to social evaluation than are interfaith marriages.

According to tradition, *defective children* are due to "bad blood" or to indiscreet behavior or lack of proper caution on the part of the mother during pregnancy. A woman who believes such traditions will feel both guilt and shame if her child is physically or mentally defective. Should her husband likewise believe them, he will blame her for not using greater caution during pregnancy, and she may blame him if there is any evidence that the child might have inherited the physical or mental deficiency from his side of the family.

Some people, mainly members of the older generation, regard *adoption* of a child as a form of family disgrace. They believe that adoption proclaims to the world that the father lacks virility or that God did not consider the parents capable of bringing up children properly or would have given them children of their own.

Among the younger generation, some strongly disapprove of adoption when it means accepting an illegitimate child. If the parents of the adopted child are not made known, it is assumed that the child was born out of wedlock. Even though adoption legalizes the status of the child, some people, even today, regard having an adopted child as a disgrace to the family. Under such conditions, the child, his adoptive parents, and other family members as well are regarded as disgraced.

In all social groups, having a *premarital pregnancy* is regarded as a family disgrace. The mother is looked upon as a "bad" woman who has brought disgrace upon herself, her child, her parents, and other family members. Her parents may receive sympathy from other family members and from members of the social group, but they also receive condemnation for not having instilled in their daughter the approved moral values of the social group.

Knowing how universal the social disapproval is and how it will reflect on all family members, the unwed mother often tries to avoid having the baby by having an abortion. Her parents are more likely to deal with the problem by insisting upon a marriage so that the child's birth will be legitimate. This is by no means always a successful solution, as Dame et al. (56) explain:

Premarital pregnancy imposes additional strains, both emotional and realistic, upon a marriage at a time when the couple has many adjustments to make. Therefore it constitutes a severe hazard unless both partners have considerable ego strength.

Regardless of how the problem of premarital pregnancy is met, it leaves psychological scars on the woman and all members of her family. If the abortion is successful, the mother-to-be suffers severe feelings of guilt for having "killed" her child. If the child is born, after a marriage to establish its legitimacy, most people will realize that it was premaritally conceived; their attitude toward the child and other family members will be almost as unfavorable as if it were illegitimate. That is why many families in this situation try to conceal the date of the child's birth or of the parents' marriage.

Because the father of an illegitimate child is generally unknown to outsiders, he and the members of his family escape the social condemnation that the mother and her family are subjected to. However, many men under such conditions feel guilty about the role they played in bringing disgrace to the woman and her family and about their unwillingness to assume responsibility for their actions. Many men feel that they have acted like cowards and reproach themselves for their unchivalrous behavior.

SUMMARY

1 The relationship a person has with his family is unquestionably the most important factor in his personality development. The influence of the family is great at all ages, not in childhood alone, though some family members exert greater influence at some ages than at others. The chief reasons for the family's dominant influence are the time spent in the home, the control family members have over the person's behavior, the emotionally toned relationship he has with his family, and the security the home environment affords.

2 The direct influence of the family on personality development comes from the child-training method used to mold the personality pattern and the communication of interests, attitudes, and values between family members. The indirect influence comes, first, from the person's identification with a family member he admires, respects, and loves and whom he either consciously or unconsciously imitates, and second, from the mirror image the family members provide for him to use to evaluate himself. Females, introverts, those in poor health, the very young, and the very old are most influenced by their relationships with their families.

3 The emotional climate of the home exerts an even greater influence on the personalities of all family members than does the emotional climate of the school. A favorable emotional climate in the home is aided by empathy, communication between family members, respect for the opinions of each member of the family, togetherness, and methods of coping with disagreements. An unfavorable home climate comes from friction between family members, favoritism, feelings of inadequacy for the roles family members are expected to play, clashes between family members with different interests and values, authoritarian control by parents, and lack of emotional warmth between family members.

4 The ordinal position, or order of birth, of the person in his family affects personality directly because of the role the person is expected to play, and indirectly, through the influence ordinal position has on the home climate. These influences vary for members of the two sexes. Once established, the effect of ordinal position on personality carries into adult life. Studies of the effects of ordinal position show that there are predictable, though not necessarily universal, personality syndromes for first-, last-, and middle-born children.

5 The size of the family influences personality directly by determining what role the person plays in the family constellation, and indirectly, by the kind of home climate characteristically associated with families of different sizes. Home climate, in turn, is influenced by how the family members, especially the parents, feel about the size of the family.

6 Just as ordinal position leads to the molding of personality syndromes that are characteristically found among those who hold specific positions in their families, so are there characteristic, but not necessarily universal, personality syndromes for only children and for those who have grown up in small, medium, and large families. Size of family affects the personalities of parents as well as children, with the effects of small families generally more favorable than the effects of large or one-child families.

7 Family composition affects personality directly through the kind of family members it supplies for sources of identification and imitation. Indirectly, as is true of family size, the influence on personality comes from the effect of family composition on the home climate and from the judgments different family members make of the individual. In composition, the family may be nuclear, composed of parents and children, or extended, composed of the nuclear family plus relatives who live under the same roof with the nuclear family. Within each kind of family, all members may be singletons, or some may be of multiple births of varying numbers. In the nuclear family, there may be two parents, one parent, or a parent and stepparent. The family, whether nuclear or extended, may be predominantly of one sex or it may contain members of both sexes in varying numbers. Age differences are greater in extended than in nuclear families. These variations have a marked influence on how harmonious or how frictional the home climate will be.

8 A common source of friction in the home climate is the invasion by outsiders for varying lengths of time. The invaders may be household help, guests, or stepparents. So long as they remain, friction persists and tends to increase, though it normally subsides when they leave.

9 Regardless of the size or the composition of the family, every member is expected to play a certain role. Roles may be traditionally prescribed or they may be selected by individual family members with or without the sanction of other members. If the person satisfactorily plays the role he is expected to play, this leads to favorable judgments by other family members and, in turn, to favorable self-evaluations, which influence personality directly. Indirectly, the personality effect of role-playing comes from the influence it has on the home climate.

10 How successfully the person plays his role in the family is influenced by his attitude toward the role, his concept of it, social attitudes toward it, the satisfaction he derives from playing the role he is assigned to play, and how much choice he is given in its selection. Changing roles, especially when the original role was to the person's liking, tends to lead to stress, which is damaging to the home climate and has an unfavorable effect on the personalities of all family members.

11 Being associated with a family that deviates in any noticeable way from other families in the social group leads to feelings of embarrassment and shame. Family deviance has an adverse effect on the home climate as well as on the self-concepts of all who are identified with the family. Among the common deviant family patterns are solo families, divorced families, families with stepparents, widowed families, and families that are disgraced because one or more family members behave in a way that is strongly disapproved by the social group. The more the family pattern differs from that of other families in the social group, the more unfavorable will be the social judgments of all family members and the greater the chances for a frictional home climate.

PART THREE evaluation of personality

Centuries before scientists dreamed of measuring intelligence, attempts were made to measure personality by such techniques as graphology, physiognomy, and phrenology. It was recognized that personality played an important role in the person's adjustment to life and an assessment of personality could be used to predict whether he would be a success or a failure.

In those early days, intelligence as a determinant of success or failure was largely unrecognized. Or if recognized, it was regarded as just one aspect of personality. Consequently, no serious attempts were made to measure intelligence and no techniques similar to those used to measure personality were devised.

Scientific studies of intelligence began just before the turn of the century. The first serious attempt to measure it was made by Alfred Binet and his collaborator Th. Simon in France in the 1890s. Their desire was to find a measuring rod that would pick out, among the children in the elementary schools of Paris, those whose intellectual capacities were so low that they would be unable to do the work of the regular school grades. The early intelligence tests were thus measures to predict potential failure.

Throughout the early years of intelligence testing in the United States, many of the research scientists who were working to devise intelligence tests suitable for the assessment of the intellectual capacities of all children, not just those who were potential academic failures, saw the possibility of developing scientific tests to assess personality. It was not until this country entered World War I, however, and psychologists were commissioned by the government to develop tests to pick out men whose intellectual capacity was too low to make them good soldiers that the motivation to develop a test for personality was strong enough to lead to action.

The motivation for designing the first personality test came from the desire to identify those men in the officers' training schools who had the personality characteristics essential to leadership. The fundamental assumption on which the first scientifically recognized personality test was based was that a good leader must be a well-adjusted person and that this could be determined by a standard test of personality.

Shortly before World War I ended, the first personality test, devised by R. S. Woodworth of Columbia University and known as the Personal Data Sheet or the "P. D. Sheet," made its appearance. While few who used this early test, including Woodworth himself, were satisfied with it, they saw its potentialities.

The major criticism of the P. D. Sheet was that it tried to test the person's total adjustment by a collection of items that were believed to be associated in some way or other with overall adjustment. It became apparent that personality includes too many characteristics to be measured by one test. This critical approach led to new tests devised to measure one or more specific personality characteristics, such as introversion and extroversion, which were claimed to be important determinants of success or failure in specific situations. These tests attempted to get specific reactions to specific situations. The results were then compared to see if there was individual consistency and to find certain personality syndromes, such as introversion, melancholy, or leadership. While the original P. D. Sheet was designed to select men in the armed services who had the potentials for leadership, tests were later developed to measure personality characteristics of children and adolescents.

The original tests' focus was negative rather than positive. Just as the original Binet-Simon tests of intelligence were designed to identify those who were potential academic failures, so the original personality tests were used to identify those who were poorly adjusted. It became obvious that this focus was unjustified and that future tests should take a more positive approach to the qualities they were attempting to measure.

Once the ground was broken and the pattern set for developing new and different tests of personality, interest in making personality tests equaled, if it did not surpass, interest in developing tests of intelligence. By the time of World War II, personality tests had become so numerous and their use so widespread in schools, colleges, business, and industry that they were automatically used as part of the testing program for all men who volunteered or were drafted for service in the armed forces.

Leaders in business and industry, as well as administrators in schools and colleges, saw in this new kind of testing many potential values for their own areas. Soon personality tests became as important in their testing programs as intelligence tests

were. The demand for personality tests to be used for people of all age levels and in a wide variety of activities was met as new personality tests began to appear in rapid succession. Some followed the traditional pattern set by Woodworth's P. D. Sheet of World War I, but many took radically new forms. Thus, just as the period from the turn of the century to the end of World War I can rightly be regarded as the "era of the intelligence test," so the time from the end of World War I to the present can be regarded as the "era of the personality test."

A brief survey of the many kinds of tests that have been devised to assess personality and the names of several in each category will serve to show how numerous and varied the tests are. It will also show how great the demand is for acceptable methods of determining what the personality pattern is and will highlight the popular belief that personality plays a more important role in the kind of adjustment the person makes to life than does any other aspect of his makeup.

In commenting on how great the popular interest in personality testing is and how widespread is its use, Gross[1] points out that "brain watching," as he calls it, or personality testing was, by 1962,

a more than $50,000,000-a-year business that has become one of the main determinants of your career, your job, your very place in society. With his tools, the question-and-answer tests (How many people do you hate very much? None? Over 50?), ink blots, other paper scalpels, and an extraordinary quantity of huckster bravado often unbecoming to his profession, he has convinced those who will pay for psychological information about their fellow men that he can reduce a man's "yes" and "no" answers and other test responses to the measurement of such human traits as radicalism, extroversion, aggression, happiness, and even latent homosexuality and a craving for early-morning Martinis.

The pattern set by Woodworth's P. D. Sheet during World War I, known as the *self-report inventory,* led to many inventories similar in their major aspects to the original. Today, this kind of test is the most numerous, though often one of the most criticized. Of the many inventories, the best known are the Bell Adjustment Inventory, Bernreuter Personality Inventory, Gordon Personal Profile, Cattell's Sixteen Personality Factor Questionnaire, Guilford-Martin In-

---

[1] M. L. Gross, *The brain watchers.* New York: Random House, 1962.

ventories, Guilford-Zimmerman Temperament Survey, and the Minnesota Multiphasic Personality Inventory (usually referred to as MMPI).

A large group of tests are designed to serve as *measures of interests and attitudes,* whether in different kinds of work, educational curricula, or recreational activities. Among the most commonly used tests in the interest category are the Strong Inventory, Kuder Preference Record, Thurstone Interest Schedule, and the Guilford-Schneiderman-Zimmerman Interest Survey.

Among the attitude tests are the Thurstone Scales (designed to measure attitudes toward Communism, capital punishment, and many other institutions, practices, issues, and groups of people, such as minority groups), the Minnesota Scale for the Survey of Opinion, and the Allport-Vernon-Lindzey Study of Values.

Projective techniques are among the most widely popularized and most controversial methods of assessing personality. Most of these have evolved from clinical techniques used in the diagnosis and treatment of psychiatric patients. The tests are given in structured tasks which permit the person an almost unlimited variety of possible responses with only brief, general instructions to guide him. This allows free play of the subject's imagination. The aim is to get a composite picture of the entire personality pattern, not just a measurement of separate traits. Among the best-known techniques in this category are the Rorschach Inkblot Test, the Thematic Apperception Test (usually referred to as TAT), and the Rosenzweig Picture-Frustration Study.

Closely allied to this category of tests are the *drawing and painting projective techniques,* used more for children than the tests listed just above. The best known of the drawing tests are the Manchover Draw-a-Person Test (often abbreviated to Draw-a-Person Test) and the *play techniques*, which make use of dolls and toys for the child to use to show his characteristic patterns of adjusting to the people and situations which they represent.

Verbal tests, as a kind of projective technqiue, were first used by Galton and Jung and were called "free-association tests." In these, the subject was told to give the first word that came to mind after hearing a stimulus word. It was believed that, on the basis of the words given by the subject, one could get a picture of his characteristic interests, attitudes, and frames of reference. The most widely used tests in this category are the Kent-Rosanoff Test and the Murray and Mor-

gan Word Association Technique. Verbal tests that are today winning greater favor than the original free-association tests are sentence-completion tests and story-completion tests. Of these, the most widely used is the Rotter Incomplete Sentence Blank.

Situational tests—tests to measure how a person reacts when placed in a specific situation, such as one in which he has an opportunity to cheat if he so desires—were for some time expected to prove to be a more accurate way of assessing characteristic patterns of adjustment than the paper-and-pencil tests and other technqiues had been. This hope never materialized. The only test in this category that has stood the test of time, and even it has limited usage because of the time and difficulty in administering it, is the Hartshorne and May Test of Honesty.

One of the earliest forms of personality assessment tests was the *rating scale*. At first, rating scales were used to assess a subject's characteristics by having a second person who knew the subject well pinpoint, on a scale of values from 1 to 5, how the subject rated in a number of traits, such as honesty, courage, or sociability, as compared with the norm of the population.

It was soon recognized that anyone who knew a person well enough to rate him on such a scale of values would be biased and would, as a result, give ratings which showed a "halo effect" rather than a true picture of his personality. It was then suggested that self-rating scales be used, in which the person himself indicated how he thought he stood in different traits in relation to the norm for the group. But the halo effect was even greater in self-ratings than it had been in ratings by others.

As an outgrowth of the early rating scales, several more subtle forms of ratings were devised which are believed to be less influenced by the halo effect. The two that are best known and most often used, especially in studies of the characteristic personality patterns of popular and unpopular people, are Moreno's Nominating Technique and Hartshorne and May's Guess Who Technique. In the former, subjects are asked to nominate persons whom they know for roles of friendship of various levels of intimacy. In the latter, subjects are asked to name, from members of their school classes, those who most closely resemble a hypothetic person described in the test.

At present, in spite of the tremendous amount of time, effort, and money put into devising tests to assess personality, no one is totally satisfied with the outcome. Every test has been subjected to critical attacks and every test has proved to be less valid as either a clinical or practical test than it had been hoped it would be. As Gross[2] has pointed out, the general opinion of psychologists is that there is "more sell than science in personality testing." He adds:

Many personality tests are bad thermometers and scores on such tests must be taken with a large, educated granule of salt. . . . In fact, not only academic psychologists, but many brain watchers themselves are equally skeptical—if only about the other fellow's test practices.

This skepticism about personality tests is based on widespread criticism that the tests are neither valid nor reliable. While it would be impossible to enumerate all the criticisms of specific personality tests, a few general criticisms will suffice to show what is responsible for the skepticism about and dissatisfaction with personality tests as they exist today.

Most personality tests can be given successfully only by highly trained specialists of whom there are too few to meet the current demand. When the tests are given by persons who lack adequate training, the findings are worthless or may even be damaging to the reputation and self-concept of the person who is tested.

Evaluation of the results of personality tests can be made only by well-trained specialists. The unavailability of enough specialists to make the evaluations thus limits the use of the tests.

Personality tests, even more so than intelligence tests, are far more useful as diagnostic techniques when given individually than when given to a group. Because individual testing is time-consuming, the use of personality tests is limited, or the use of group tests—which are far less valuable as diagnostic instruments—is forced.

Personality traits are not consistent enough to be measured except perhaps by a battery of tests to determine whether a pattern of behavior is characteristic of the person or characteristic of his behavior only in a specific kind of situation. Is he, for example, an honest person or is he honest in his business dealings only?

To date, determination of the validity of personality tests has shown extremely low correlations, even when such scientifically questionable methods as correlation with other tests or internal consistency are used. The question is asked, Do personality tests actually measure personality or some quality or qualities unrelated or only slightly related to what they are purported to measure?

Most personality tests offer excellent opportunities to cheat to those who want to appear in a favorable light or to those who want to create the impression that they are inferior or even abnormal for some desired goal, such as escaping duty in the armed services. No test to date has been able to cope with this problem. The more test-sophisticated the subject is, the better able he is to see to it that the test results will give the picture of his personality pattern that he wants to give.

Gross[3] has summarized the chief criticisms of personality tests in this way: "Personality test scores are really measuring several outside factors: intelligence, motivation, psychological sophistication, psychological defenses, tendency to lie."

Because of the widespread criticism of personality tests of all kinds, because of the doubts about whether the existing personality tests actually measure personality or some other characteristics of the subject, and because of the inability, to date, to develop a personality test in which personologists have confidence, either as a measuring rod or as a diagnostic technique, there is a gradual trend toward trying to evaluate personality by methods other than tests. While personality tests are still used, far less reliance is placed on their findings than formerly and more reliance is placed on other approaches.

These new approaches to the evaluation of personality consist of trying to set up norms or standards of what may be regarded as a "well-adjusted personality." This is done by observing and analyzing the characteristic behavior in different situations of those who are regarded by others as well-adjusted people, by a study of their achievements and their own reports of how they feel about these achievements, and by how they rate their satisfaction with themselves and with life in general.

Then, by observing a specific person's behavior, by examining information gained from reports by parents, teachers, peers and others about how that person behaves in situations which the personologist

---

[2] Ibid.

[3] Ibid.

is unable to observe, and by assessing reports by the person himself about how he behaves in different situations and why, the personologist attempts to evaluate the person's level of personal and social adjustment. No one is willing to say that this is *the best* technique, though there is general agreement that it is superior to existing personality tests.

Much the same approach is used to set up norms for poorly adjusted people—those who suffer to some extent, major or minor, from personality sickness. The characteristics of people with major personality sickness, first observed, analyzed, and recorded by psychiatrists, are today well known in the various forms of neuroses and psychoses. Personologists are following the pattern set by psychiatrists to determine the usual characteristics of people who suffer from milder personality sickness.

It is possible to compare the characteristic behavior of individuals with these norms and thus to assess their personalities and their level of adjustment. To supplement the findings of such a comparison and to give clues of what further evidence might be unearthed to broaden the diagnosis, personologists resort to some of the standard personality tests though they place far less reliance on tests than on other sources of information.

While this approach to personality evaluation is relatively new and is still in fact in an experimental stage, there is a growing feeling among personologists that this may be *the* way to evaluate personality because it is proving to be a better approach than the exclusive use of personality tests. There is also a growing feeling that this approach gives a more comprehensive picture of the total personality pattern than can be obtained from any single personality test or from even a battery of tests.

More important, this approach discloses evidence about what is responsible for any personality sickness the person may suffer from as well as evidence of the cause of the healthy personality pattern. This is not done by any of the standard personality tests available; their assessment of personality is limited to evaluating the degree of the person's adjustment and the characteristic patterns of behavior in which this adjustment expresses itself.

It is not considered worthwhile to discuss the standard tests of personality further in this text. Such a decision seems justified to the author and is based on two facts: *First*, personality tests are still in such an experimental stage that most personologists can feel little confidence in their validity as measuring rods,

and *second*, they are described, analyzed, and criticized in detail in so many textbooks in general psychology and measurement that the reader is already familiar with them or has ready access to information about them.

Chapter 14, Sick Personalities, is devoted to a comprehensive analysis of what constitutes a sick personality, how it affects the person's adjustments, both personal and social, what is responsible for it, how widespread sick personalities are, in what kinds of individuals or groups sick personalities are most likely to develop, and what the critical ages for personality sickness are. Because personologists have devoted considerable time and effort to pinpointing the danger signals of personality sickness, a large section of this chapter is devoted to explaining what the major danger signals are and why they are so regarded.

In Chapter 15, Healthy Personalities, contrasts are made between healthy and sick personalities to emphasize that the difference between them is quantitative, not qualitative. This was recognized many years ago by psychiatrists in their studies of normal and abnormal people.

Just as there are certain danger signals that enable personologists, or even laymen, to spot potential personality sickness, so there are signs that can be used to spot healthy personalities. Knowledge of these signs has come from extensive research studies of people of all ages whose behavior is regarded as "healthy."

How important it is to have a healthy personality is emphasized by evidence relating to the effect of a healthy personality on personal and social adjustment, on achievement, and on personal satisfaction and happiness. While this evidence is, of necessity, largely subjective, it is too significant to be ignored.

Since an untrained person is no more capable of helping another to acquire a healthy personality than he is of helping him to acquire a healthy body, no "do-it-yourself" suggestions will be given. Instead, evidence from research studies will be summarized to familiarize the reader with the approach of personologists, and an evaluation of their success or failure will be given.

In conclusion, it is hoped that the material presented in this section of the book will give the reader a more hopeful attitude toward the problem of evaluating personality than he may have had before from the widely accepted negative attitudes about assessment through the use of personality tests.

sick personalities

A **"sick" personality** is one in which there is a breakdown in the personality structure which results in poor personal and social adjustments. Just as in physical illness, the person does not behave as he normally does. As a result, there is an impairment in the way he adjusts to everyday life situations. The scientist regards such a person as "disturbed," "disordered," and in severe cases, "neurotic" or "psychotic." The layman says that he is "peculiar," "nutty," "off his rocker," "crazy," or whatever word is currently popular for describing those whose behavior deviates from the expected norm.

Deviant behavior stemming from personality sickness is labeled "problem behavior" by the scientists because it leads to problems of adjustment for the individual as well as for others with whom he comes in contact. The layman is more likely to call the individual a "problem child," a "problem teen-ager," or a "problem adult"—thus putting emphasis on the person rather than on his behavior. When the individual's behavior conforms to social expectations, he is labeled "normal" and his behavior is regarded as "normal behavior."

What the layman recognized as a "normal personality" is not necessarily a healthy personality. In fact, as Jourard has emphasized, "It is possible to be a normal personality and be absolutely miserable" (95). The person is considered normal by members of the social group if he plays his role according to social expectations, but unless he derives personal satisfaction from this role, he will likely in time develop a personality "sickness" (95).

A personality may seem to others to be healthy when, in reality, it is sick. This is true also of the person's physical condition. He may seem to be in the best of health while, actually, he is suffering from some minor or major illness which he is able to hide. This enables him to behave in a manner which makes others judge him as "healthy." When a person is suffering from a headache, for example, he can camouflage his true physical condition by forcing himself to be as efficient, as alert, and as pleasant as he is when he feels in the best of health.

The same is true of personality sicknesses. If a person is anxious to be favorably judged by others, he can camouflage feelings of inadequacy, of martyrdom, or of inferiority and behave in such a manner as to create the impression that he is a normal, well-adjusted person. Under stress, however, the camouflage often fails and the person reveals his real self. The selfish opportunist, whose outlook on life is egocentric, may, by altruistic behavior, be able to create the impression that he is more concerned about the welfare of others than about his personal well-being. But in stressful situations, his altruistic behavior disappears and is replaced by self-interest and protective activity. This is true of all forms of personality sickness that lead to maladjustment, regardless of how minor or major they may be (107).

DETERMINATION OF PERSONALITY SICKNESS

People tend to regard any behavior that is inconvenient or annoying to them as indicative of maladjustment and to regard the person who displays such behavior as maladjusted. The more inconvenient or annoying the behavior, the more likely it is to be considered indicative of a sick personality. "Problem children," for example, are those who behave in such a way that they annoy and inconvenience their parents, teachers, and other adults.

Many annoying and inconvenient behavior characteristics, such as temper tantrums, transitory lying and stealing, sex play, and overdependency, are not indicative of mental pathology, however, because they are normally found in all children at certain ages. Only if a child has an overabundance of such traits at one time, if they are unusually prolonged beyond the age at which they normally appear, or if they interfere with the child's adjustments to the point where it is impossible for him to participate satisfactorily in the activities of his age-mates can they be labeled problems and be regarded as danger signals of personality sickness.

The same is true of deviant physical symptoms. Excessive tiredness when a person overworks or works under emotional strain is not a true symptom of sickness unless it is prolonged beyond the time when rest and relaxation should cause it to disappear. Similarly, occasional headaches may be regarded as normal. But if headaches are persistent and intense, they may be regarded as danger signals of upsets in body homeostasis. As such, they are symptoms of physical illness.

Determination of physical or personality sickness, through diagnosis of its cause and recommendations for its cure, can best be done by a person who is professionally trained. If a layman tries to make a diagnosis, he is usually incorrect because he makes his judgment on the basis of criteria which, though relevant to him, may have little to do with reality.

Role of personologist

The person best suited to determine whether a personality pattern is sick or healthy is the personologist—a person "who has formulated an explicit and detailed concept of healthy personality" (95). The personologist is usually a psychologist, trained and specializing in the area of clinical psychology but with an interest in formulating standards of healthy personality patterns from studies of those whose adjustments are good as compared with those whose adjustments are poor. Extensive studies of persons who are functioning successfully and happily can provide data for standards of behavior patterns which are valued by members of the social group as well as by the individual, just as extensive studies of those who are functioning in deviant ways and are unhappy provide data for standards of behavior that indicate personality sickness.

When a standard of what constitutes a healthy personality pattern has been established, the personologist can compare the behavior of a particular person with the standard to see how well he conforms to it or how greatly he deviates from it. Any deviation can be regarded as an indication of personality sickness. The greater the deviation, the sicker the personality. Figure 14-1 shows the "healthy" limits for different traits and the deviations from these limits for an actual person.

The personologist cannot always determine quickly whether the personality pattern is healthy or sick. People camouflage their true feelings and put up fronts, but sooner or later, with repeated observations, the personologist can make a determination. This can be done best when people are under stress and when camouflages give way to behavior that is characteristic of their true feelings about themselves (24, 140).

Even more important, a single standard of what constitutes a "healthy" personality pattern cannot be used for judging all people. The personality profile of a highly creative person might lead one to suspect that he was "sick" because it deviates in certain respects from the profiles of those who are less creative. However, evidence of the kind of adjustments he makes may show that, because he is more insightful and more original in his thinking and behavior, he is as healthy as those who are less creative, if not more so. This highlights the fact that blanket diagnoses result in misjudgments.

Figure 14-1 By setting up standards for "healthy" limits for different traits, personality sickness can be diagnosed by finding how much a person deviates from these limits. (Adapted from S. M. Jourard: *Personality development: An approach through the study of healthy personality.* New York: Macmillan, 1958. Used by permission.)

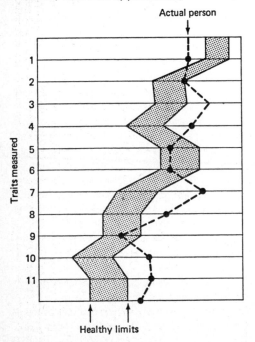

PREVALENCE OF PERSONALITY SICKNESS

Formerly, people who were mentally sick, like those who suffered from physical ailments, were kept at home. Only those who were so mentally sick that they could not be cared for at home were sent to hospitals —usually labeled "insane asylums"—for treatment.

Consequently few outsiders were aware of their illness and few people in general were aware of the prevalence and severity of personality sickness.

While those who remained at home were considered "strange" because their behavior failed to conform to expected patterns, only members of their families and close family friends understood how deviant they were. The family tried to keep them from coming in contact with outsiders as much as possible to avoid having other members of the family stigmatized by the prevailing belief that insanity "runs in the family."

All of this changed with the growth of mental health clinics in communities and in schools and colleges and with the widespread use of different forms of psychotherapy. Social attitudes toward personality sickness became more tolerant and more and more people began to seek the aid of personologists, often boasting that they were under the care of a psychiatrist.

The change in social attitudes came during World War II when popular attention was focused on the fact that more young men were rejected by the armed services for psychological than for physical reasons (193). At the same time the mass media began to disseminate scientific information regarding the patterns of behavior characteristic of sick personalities, as was done in the case of physical illness.

As a result of the change in social attitudes, the lay public has become alerted to the danger signals of personality sickness, just as it has become alerted to the danger signals of cancer and other physical diseases. Recognition that personality disturbances can be treated has brought the problem out into the open so that it is possible today to know how widespread personality sickness is.

Another factor that has contributed to the realization of the prevalence of personality sickness has been scientific emphasis on the importance of seeking remedial aid as soon as a pattern of behavior that is regarded as antisocial appears instead of waiting and hoping that the child or adolescent will "outgrow" it. Since parents and teachers are alerted to the danger signals of personality sickness today, they seek professional help for children who show symptoms of such sickness in the belief that, if it is treated early, the child will grow up to be a well-adjusted person (143).

In spite of the trend toward bringing personality sickness out into the open and treating it as soon as symptoms appear, many cases of personality sickness are overlooked or regarded as trivial because they do not annoy or inconvenience parents, teachers, or other adults. The child who causes no trouble may be suffering from as severe a personality sickness as the troublesome one, but he often goes unnoticed until the sickness is well developed. His sickness is then harder to treat than it would have been, had it been recognized in its earlier stages.

Parents are able to spot personality sickness in children earlier and more successfully than teachers. *First,* parents have more frequent contact with the child than does the teacher. Consequently, they have a better opportunity to observe the child's characteristic behavior in many situations. *Second,* the child tends to be on his good behavior in school and often camouflages behavior which is symptomatic of personality sickness. And *third,* the teacher has less personal interest in and concern about a child than parents and unless the child's behavior is disruptive in the classroom it often goes unnoticed (170).

Personality sickness is likely to be spotted more easily in young children than in older children, adolescents, or adults. There are two reasons why. Behavior disorders in young children are usually more annoying to other people than those which are common in older age groups, and young children have not yet learned how to camouflage their unsocial behavior. Thus, their sickness is not only more annoying to others but it is also more apparent.

CRITICAL PERIODS OF PERSONALITY SICKNESS

Illness can strike at any age. However, there are certain predictable "critical ages" when both physical and psychological illnesses are most likely to strike.

People are more susceptible to physical illnesses during times of stress, when the body is undergoing radical and rapid changes, as in the early and later years of the life span, or when the reproductive functioning changes, as at puberty and during the menopause in women and, to a lesser extent, during the climacteric in men (150). The prevalence of physical illness at times of rapid growth or radical changes in bodily functioning is due to upsets in body homeostasis that make the person especially susceptible to the effects of stress. He is more likely to succumb to physical illness at such times than when body homeostasis is better maintained.

Just as stress predisposes a person to physical illness, so it predisposes him to mental illness. While all sick personalities do not develop first during times of emotional or physical stress, most do. Far fewer develop at times when body homeostasis is maintained. Furthermore, during periods of stress, any forms of personality sickness already present are likely to be intensified and to develop into a characteristic pattern of adjustment.

Why the early years are critical

During his early years, the person is especially susceptible to the strains and stresses of life. His attitudes, habits, and behavior patterns are in the process of being formed and can easily be upset by strains from the environment or from within himself. Many personality difficulties found later in life have their origin in the preschool years, becoming permanent features of the individual's personality pattern. Rich (163) states:

It would appear that the things which happen to an individual during his childhood are important in determining the pattern of his later life. . . . It is in these early years that the essential methods are built up which the individual will use throughout his life in meeting difficult situations and frustrations. The forms in which they may be expressed may change under the various influences of the environment and of maturity, but the essential characteristics of the type of reactions will remain more or less fixed.

A common example of the persistence of maladjustive behavior that develops early in life is juvenile delinquency. Boys and girls who feel that they are not appreciated or loved at home develop hostile and defiant attitudes toward parents and toward all in authority. They become disobedient, troublesome, and unruly because of their unfavorable attitudes toward the treatment they receive. In time, this becomes a way of life. By adolescence, their personality sickness is so pronounced that successful treatment is often difficult or impossible (49, 52).

Why puberty is a critical age

Children who reach puberty with only minor personality sicknesses may become mentally sick at this time because they fail to establish their identity. They are dissatisfied with themselves as people and with the adjustments they make to others and to the goals they have set for themselves. Deviant maturers especially experience constant feelings of frustration from the

way they are treated by the social group in addition to having to cope with the normal problems that accompany the upsets in homeostasis that are characteristic of this period of rapid growth and change in bodily functions (49, 94).

Since the homeostatic disturbances of puberty persist into the early years of adolescence, when the social group expects more mature patterns of behavior, it is not surprising that severe psychiatric disorders sometimes occur and that minor disturbances to mental health are widespread. Success in school and in social life is so crucial to adolescents that failure in either is extremely upsetting. Their greater awareness of their abilities and weaknesses adds to the self-dissatisfaction which is fundamental to their personality sickness.

Why middle age is a critical age

The upsets in body homeostasis which accompany the menopause and the climacteric coincide with the changed roles middle-aged people are expected to play. In women, the change is from that of wife and mother to wife in an "empty nest" or to working wife, often in a job of little interest, which is frustrating and ego-deflating. In men, the change is from a role of authority in the home or in business to one of imminent retirement with decreased authority and prestige.

As is true of the critical period of puberty and early adolescence, personality sickness of minor or major severity is by no means a universal accompaniment of the stresses normally associated with middle age. Instead, there is ample evidence that when it does occur it stems from poor adjustments made earlier which have persisted and grown worse with the passage of time.

Those who break under the strain of adjustments to the changed roles of middle age have a history of unresolved problems and poor personal and social adjustments. If the stresses of middle age prove to be too severe for them to cope with, the already-existing personality sickness becomes worse and often necessitates institutionalization. (9).

Why old age is a critical age

Next to early childhood, old age is the most critical period for personality sickness. Aging brings with it a loss of resources—physical, social, economic, and psychological—and the person is less and less able to cope successfully with environmental changes, stresses, and changes within himself which old age inevitably brings.

If, in addition, the foundations for social, emotional, and personal adjustments laid earlier are poor, the elderly person is even less capable of coping. As a result, he is less happy and less satisfied with himself and with life in general than when he was younger. It is this lack of satisfaction that predisposes him to personality maladjustments of minor or major severity.

To avoid personality sickness, the elderly person must be able to satisfy his needs within the framework that life provides for him. When he must change his roles, owing to poor health and environmental pressures, he is likely to become maladjusted because the changes will rarely be to his liking or of his choice. When sources of self-esteem are cut off by retirement, by economic and health factors, and by unfavorable social attitudes toward him because of his age, the elderly person is predisposed to develop traits characteristic of the minority-group personality. Only if something can be done to restore his waning self-esteem can personality changes for the worse be avoided.

When elderly people become detached from the social group, either through choice or through rejection by its members, there is a loss of self-esteem and, with it, a tendency for personality sickness in one form or another to develop. The more important social contacts and acceptance are to a person, the more damaging their withdrawal will be to the self-concept in old age (29, 101).

Variations in effects of critical periods

Some people pass through the critical periods with very little damage to their personalities and what damage does occur may be only transitory. Others break under the strain and develop personality sicknesses. While some of these may be transitory, others leave their mark on the personality pattern and become the person's characteristic method of adjustment.

How successfully the person will pass through the critical periods will depend upon how healthy he is physically, how severe the strains are, how much help and guidance he has in meeting the strains that normally occur at these periods, and how healthy his personality is when the stresses occur. Just as a person in good physical health can withstand stresses better than one in poor physical condition, so can the person whose mental health is good.

CAUSES OF PERSONALITY SICKNESS

The causes of personality sickness fall into two major categories: physical and psychological. Some *physical* condition may in part at least account for the way a person reacts in different situations and for the kind of adjustment he makes to life in general. A study of American presidents and British prime ministers since the turn of the century has suggested that those who were seriously or persistently ill showed impaired judgment that resulted in maladjustive behavior which, in turn, affected their leadership roles (142).

A temporary upset in body homeostasis, due to a headache or a digestive disturbance, may lead to a temporary pattern of maladjustive behavior. When the upset ends, the person reverts to his former pattern of adjustment. On the other hand, a persistent illness often affects the person's characteristic pattern of adjustment to life. This frequently leads to a personality sickness. Glandular disturbances, asthma, or allergies (see Chap. 6) have been found to lead to patterns of adjustive behavior which deviate from the norm and lead to personal and social maladjustments.

Brain damage at any age can lead to personality sickness. Many of the personality disorders of elderly people are due, in part, to brain deterioration that has resulted from some physiological cause. These disorders are often intensified by unfavorable environmental conditions, but the basis for them is physical.

The fundamental *psychological* cause of personality sickness is anxiety which stems from self-dissatisfaction. The person is unhappy about himself and dislikes himself to the point where he becomes self-rejectant. He constantly wishes that he were different or that he could be like someone he admires and looks up to. Jersild (91) says:

Self-rejection includes chronic attitudes of self-disapproval and self-disparagement, self-distrust, feelings of being unworthy, not being deserving of satisfactions, reward, or success. In one of its most cruel forms, self-rejection includes severe guilt, viewing oneself as among the damned.

Self-rejection shows itself in a wide variety of behavior patterns. The person is self-critical and self-derogatory. He constantly condemns himself for his shortcomings which are often not shortcomings at all but he believes them to be because he expects to surpass all others. His self-regard vacillates with the attitudes of others toward him, or what he believes their attitudes to be.

He accepts the opinions and decisions of others, even though he has no justification for believing that they are any wiser than he. He feels that others view him with hostility and disparagement; he claims that people are against him, that they treat him unfairly, and that they belittle and disapprove of him.

Self-rejection shows itself also in distrust of one's own attitudes and feelings. It is evident when a person strikes a pose, pretending to be what he is not, and when he boasts and brags in an attempt to impress others. Very often, it is expressed in a grudging attitude toward self as shown by an unwillingness to spend money for clothes, self-improvement, or material possessions. When self-rejection is strong, it is sometimes expressed in various forms of self-destructiveness, such as taking reckless chances, inviting punishment, or doing things to bring disgrace upon oneself when, as Jersild remarks, "there is nothing to gain and everything to lose" (91). Many accidents occur among those who are self-rejectant.

The patterns of behavior described above lead to unfavorable social judgments and social rejection. The person's self-rejectant attitude is then intensified. As Jersild (91) said of adolescents:

The tragic thing about adolescents who severely reject themselves is that they often do things which cause others to confirm the low opinion they have of themselves. Deeper even than the tragedy of severe self-rejection is its pathos. The severely self-rejecting adolescent is his own enemy. He has taken unto himself all the unkindness of his heredity and all the harshness of his environment, and then he has added something more: everything is his fault and he is no good.

Self-rejection can develop at any age, though it tends to be stronger in adolescence than earlier because the adolescent is more aware of his shortcomings than the child and because social acceptance is more important to the adolescent. At all ages, boys and men tend to be more self-rejectant than girls and women (11, 155).

Nor is self-rejection an overnight development. Ordinarily, it begins at an early age and continues to develop unless remedial steps are taken to check it.

That self-rejection in adulthood is a carry-over from childhood has been emphasized by Jersild (90):

A large proportion of children will move into adulthood troubled and unhappy about many things. . . . Many, as adults, will suffer from attitudes of hostility, vindictiveness, and defensiveness which are not a response to hostile forces in the outside world but represent attitudes carried over from unresolved childhood struggles. Many persons similarly will acquire persisting feelings of inferiority or other unhealthy attitudes regarding their personal worth which represent either an irrational estimate of themselves or a failure to accept themselves realistically as they are. In numerous ways there is a vast carry-over of unhealthy attitudes regarding self and others from childhood and adolescence into adult life.

Causes of self-rejection

A person becomes self-rejectant when he is unable to gratify his needs and desires because of personal limitations or obstacles in his environment. This causes him to dislike himself and to be unhappy, both of which lead to some degree of maladjustment.

Of the many causes of self-rejection, the following are the most common and the most damaging: unrealistic expectations; environmental obstacles; unfavorable social attitudes; personal limitations; severe emotional strain; repeated failures; identification with maladjusted people; inability to get a proper self-perspective; poor childhood training; and lack of motivation. These are illustrated in Figure 14-2.

Unrealistic expectations Unrealistic self-expectations lead to a gap between the real self-concept and the ideal self-concept. Self-rejection due to unrealistic expectations can develop at any age but it is most likely during early adolescence when the person who has been encouraged to believe that he will outgrow his undesirable physical and mental characteristics finds that he has not done so. The disparity between what he had hoped to be and what he is persists or increases, thus prolonging his self-rejection. Many college students, for example, go to college with grandiose expectations only to discover that, when they meet stiff competition with other students, their expectations are not realized.

If, on the other hand, the person becomes more reality-oriented and less egocentric as he grows older

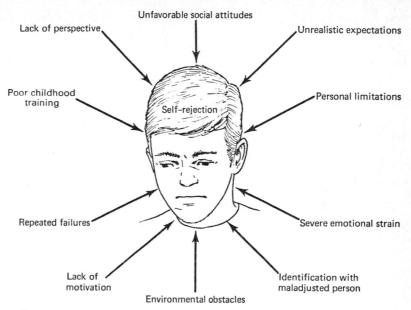

Figure 14-2 Some common causes of self-rejection.

and has more varied experiences, he will be able to see himself more realistically. This will help to close the gap between what he thinks he is and what he would like to be. When this happens, his self-rejectant attitude will diminish and he will be happier.

Environmental obstacles An environment that presents severe or repeated obstacles to the fulfillment of the person's interests, needs, and desires inevitably leads to self-dissatisfaction. The person learns to react to stressful situations in such a manner that he is unhappy and feels that he has been trapped by obstacles over which he has no control. This makes him feel resentful against those who he feels are responsible for trapping him.

The child or adolescent, for example, feels trapped when his place of residence or financial limitations make it impossible for him to attend a school or college where the academic work is better suited to his interests and abilities and where the students have more in common with him. In the same way, a woman who had planned to continue her career after marriage feels trapped when she discovers that carrying the double load of homemaking and career prevents her from achieving the success she felt she was capable of achieving.

How central a role environmental obstacles play

in self-rejection has been discussed by Lane (107) in terms of psychological malnutrition:

The human personality, as well as the body, is subject to malnutrition. Lacking essential nutrients and conditions for growth the personality develops crookedly. The greater number of malnourished personalities become dull. These cause us little trouble, grow up to do work we do not like to do. Others become neurotic. They don't think straight, are undependable and unpredictable, but are bothersome principally to their families and immediate neighbors. A smaller portion of malnourished become aggressive. They strike out, rarely back, in response to deprivation. They are the disorderly ones.

Unfavorable social attitudes Before unfavorable social attitudes can affect the person's self-evaluation so unfavorably that they will lead to self-rejection, the person must be able to recognize how unfavorable social attitudes toward him actually are. There is evidence that people who are unpopular tend to overestimate themselves and tend to perceive themselves less realistically than those who are popular. Consequently, they are not as severely damaged psychologically by unfavorable social attitudes as they would be if they had better self- and social insight.

The unfavorable attitudes that lead to social neglect or rejection often stem from the way the person behaves in social situations and the way he treats other people. If, for example, he thinks he is more important than others judge him to be, he will have interpersonal difficulties, and the attitudes of those with whom he comes in contact will be unfavorable.

Not all social rejection comes from unsocial behavior on the part of the person who is rejected. Some of it may be due to his identification in the minds of others with the kind of person they do not like or against whom they are prejudiced. The person is not rejected because of what he has done or said but rather because he is identified with a stereotype of a disliked group.

Some who are subjected to discrimination by members of the social group withdraw from the group and feel hurt. Others react more aggressively, demanding an opportunity to participate on equal terms. This often increases the unfavorable social attitude toward them and, with it, the unfavorable treatment by members of the group. Regardless of how the person reacts, discrimination is psychologically damaging because it leads to self-rejection.

Unfavorable social attitudes can lead to self-rejection at any time. Their effects are likely to be felt most, however, by people who have a history of poor adjustment. Many mental breakdowns in old age have their origin in personal maladjustments of long duration. The majority of such breakdowns are not due to brain damage but rather to social conditions which give rise to feelings of insecurity, inadequacy, and rejection. Elderly persons who have a history of maladjustment are least able to withstand the changed social conditions and social attitudes which almost all elderly people are subjected to (183).

Personal limitations   Personal limitations, either physical or psychological, force a person to see himself less favorably than he would like. Before this can lead to self-rejection, however, the person must be able to recognize his limitations by comparing himself with his age-mates. Long before childhood is over, most children are aware of their limitations as well as their strengths. The more emphasis the school places on grades and on competition in extracurricular activities, the more aware children are of their limitations. This is one of the reasons, as was emphasized earlier (see Chap. 12), that children's attitudes toward school become more and more negative. It is difficult to like a

situation that constantly reminds you of your limitations.

Many people learn to minimize the harm that recognition of their limitations does to their self-concepts by using defense mechanisms, such as rationalization, projection, and fantasy. These will be discussed in detail later in this chapter. If people can convince themselves that their limitations are not all that great, they can avoid some of the self-rejection they would otherwise experience.

If people are realistic about their limitations, the effect on their self-concepts can be so damaging as to make them self-rejectant. Strang (192) has given an example of a 16-year-old girl whose ultrarealism about her physical limitations caused her to experience an "apparently hopeless self-rejection." The girl verbalized her feelings in this way:

Why am I ugly? Everybody hates me for I am unbearable to look at. My teachers can't stand the sight of me and they fail me. My name is Gertrude so you can see that my face goes well with my name. I have a puss only my mother could love—(and even she doesn't).

Severe emotional strain   Severe emotional strain upsets body homeostasis and prevents the person from functioning adequately, either physically or mentally. No matter what the person does, whether he engages in activities that require motor skills or memory, reasoning, and other mental abilities, he realizes that he is falling short of his potentials. Recognition of his limitations predisposes him to be self-rejectant.

The athlete whose performance in competition is below his performance during practice and the student who "goes blank" on an examination for which he has spent hours in preparation cannot help being annoyed at themselves for their poor achievements. Knowing that they are capable of doing better leads to a self-rejectant attitude, even when they are able to convince themselves, in part at least, that their lack of success was due to causes over which they had no control.

Equally as important are the effects of severe emotional strain on happiness, though the degree of unhappiness will vary somewhat according to the kind of emotional strain experienced. If the emotional strain is dominated by jealousy or envy, it is likely to make the person more unhappy than if it is dominated by fear; in the former, the individual experiences resentments and feelings of martyrdom in addition to the emotional states themselves. And no one who is unhappy can be self-acceptant.

When severe emotional strain is transitory, the effects on personality are far less pronounced than when the strain is relatively persistent. Though the person may be self-rejectant while the transitory strain lasts, its detrimental effects will disappear when it subsides, and temporary self-rejection will probably be replaced by self-acceptance. When severe emotional strain is persistent, however, self-rejection becomes the person's characteristic pattern of adjusting to life.

Repeated failures   All people experience some failures in their lives. The usual reaction is to be self-rejectant. However, if a failure is followed by a series of successes, the effect of the failure on the self-concept will be only transitory.

When failures come repeatedly, without their damage to the self-concept being counteracted by the favorable effects of success, the person begins to think of himself as a failure and, in time, develops a failure complex. Since failure complexes tend to stifle the person's motivation to do what he is capable of, one who develops a failure complex usually becomes an underachiever in whatever he undertakes (60).

When a person's failure is known only to himself, self-rejection is less pronounced than when failure is known to others. If a student could keep his academic failures a secret, for example, the effects would be somewhat ego-deflating and would unquestionably lead to a measure of self-rejection. But knowing that his teachers and many of his classmates are aware of his failures adds to their ego-deflating effects. The more significant the people are who know of his failures and the more unfavorable their reactions to him, the more self-rejectant he will become.

Identification with maladjusted people   Regardless of age, people tend to imitate the attitudes, emotions, and behavior patterns of persons with whom they are associated. Children who are associated with a person who shows fear or has temper tantrums tend to imitate these patterns of emotional expression.

When a person admires and loves someone who has a self-rejectant attitude which expresses itself in maladjustive behavior, it is almost inevitable that he too will develop a self-rejectant attitude and some

form of personality sickness. The child is bound to be self-rejectant, for example, if his mother constantly complains about the sacrifices she makes for her children and the career she gave up to do things for the family. She sets a model of self-rejection which affects the child's attitude toward himself.

Uncritical imitation of a person who is admired and loved is more common in the early years of life than later. That is why identification plays a more important role in personality molding in childhood than it does as the person grows older (see Chap. 4). However, since maladjustive behavior is likely to persist, behavior stemming from rejectant attitudes toward self tend to persist into the adult years (64, 76, 100).

For children and, to a lesser extent, for adolescents, the heroes and heroines of the mass media supplement or replace parents, teachers, and other adults as objects of identification. If the heroes of comics, movies, and TV show a pattern of maladjustive behavior, the young person will tend to imitate that behavior (117, 180, 219). Figure 14-3 shows how a young child will imitate patterns of violent behavior he has viewed on the television screen. Even among his playmates, such patterns of behavior will arouse

Figure 14-3 Identification with maladjusted characters in mass media can lead to self-rejection caused by social rejection. (Adapted from Hesse, *St. Louis Globe Democrat.* Reprinted in *The Philadelphia Evening Bulletin,* Oct. 3, 1969. Used by permission.)

Hesse, St. Louis Globe Democrat

"Junior's been watching too much TV lately"

shock and scorn which will be expressed in social criticism, rejection, or punishment. Social reactions of this kind will lead to or will intensify a self-rejectant attitude in the child.

Lack of self-perspective   A person who is unable to see himself in an objective way is likely to minimize his strengths and exaggerate his weaknesses. The lack of perspective that leads to self-dissatisfaction and self-rejection may come from a number of conditions including lack of opportunities for contacts with people; inability to communicate with those who could help one understand oneself better, such as parents, teachers, and spouses; unwillingness to see oneself realistically; and distorted self-concepts encouraged by parents or other significant people. Regardless of the cause, lack of perspective usually leads to an exaggeration of weaknesses, which encourages self-rejection, rather than to an exaggeration of strengths, which encourages self-acceptance. Brandt (24) states:

Coming to know oneself and coming to like oneself are perhaps the most important tasks in growing up. Yet many people fail to master them. . . . Unhappiness, prejudice, failure, neurosis and even psychosis are the partners of inability to know and like oneself.

The person who is introverted, withdrawn, and anomic has difficulty communicating with others. He tends to keep his problems to himself and to exaggerate them to the point where he thinks of himself as a failure. This encourages him to be self-rejectant.

Poor childhood training   Children and adolescents who have been subjected to inconsistent or punitively authoritarian discipline in the home or school develop a concept of themselves as unworthy, "bad," or failures. When others see them as "naughty," "irresponsible," and "selfish," they are likely to perceive themselves this way.

Extremely permissive discipline likewise encourages self-rejection. The child or adolescent is permitted to do much as he pleases, and when he makes mistakes he must bear the blame for them. Similarly, when he does things that annoy and anger others, he must accept their criticism, scorn, or rejection. He often interprets his parents' or teachers' permissiveness to mean that they are too little interested in him and his welfare to be bothered to guide and advise him. Thus his feelings of inadequacy and self-rejection increase.

By contrast, those who are subjected to democratic discipline are spared many of the failures and rejections that occur when young people are permitted to do as they please. And, because the young person's opinions are asked and he is told why he is expected to do certain things and refrain from doing others, he can assume that those in authority have a favorable opinion of him. As a result, he feels justified in having a favorable opinion of himself.

How important a role poor training, whether in the home or the school, plays in self-rejection is well illustrated in the case of juvenile delinquents. Studies reveal that one of the universal characteristics of juvenile delinquents is self-rejection. These studies also show that they are almost always from homes where poor training, of a punitive, authoritarian, and inconsistent nature, prevails. Feeling unloved, unwanted, and unappreciated by their parents, they develop a self-rejectant attitude which encourages them to retaliate by doing things to hurt others (44, 64).

Lack of motivation   When the person lacks motivation to achieve what he is capable of, regardless of the cause, he develops feelings of guilt, shame, and personal dissatisfaction. Under such conditions, he cannot admire or respect himself and, thus, he becomes self-rejectant.

Should lack of motivation to achieve persist into the adult years, the person will be dissatisfied with himself because he will realize that he has even fallen behind people who are less able than he. His dissatisfaction will be intensified if members of his family or his vocational associates accuse him of being "lazy" or of "lacking ambition." The more anxious he is to win social esteem and recognition, the more damaging this will be to his self-concept. That this is true is seen by the fact that many nonachieving adults blame their lack of achievement on someone else, not on their own lack of motivation.

Significance of self-rejection

Two points about self-rejection are highly significant: *First*, it is at the root of most personality sicknesses, and *second*, it is controllable. As was pointed out earlier, self-rejection is not the only cause of personality sickness; there are sometimes physical causes. But even when physical causes or environmental conditions predispose the person to maladjustment, their effects on the self-concept are intensified by the self-rejectant attitude that develops from them.

Self-rejection is controllable, but it must be spotted early and dealt with by persons who are capable of helping the individual gain sufficient insight to recognize how unjustified much of his self-rejection is and how seriously it interferes with his achievements, his adjustments, and his happiness.

Unfortunately, many people believe that children and young adolescents are just "going through a phase" when they claim they do not like themselves or say they wish they could be like someone else. Studies show that young people do not outgrow these feelings. Instead, self-dissatisfaction becomes stronger, predisposing them to achieve less than they are capable of and leading to unfavorable judgments by members of the social group (24, 43, 221).

Failure to control self-rejectant attitudes is harmful at any age, but especially when the person is old enough and experienced enough to recognize how significant personality is in his life. The young adolescent is more damaged psychologically by self-rejection than the young child because he is more aware of the important role personality plays. By the time he is old enough to recognize this, the habit of being self-rejectant may be so deeply rooted that replacing it with a self-acceptant attitude is difficult or even impossible. Cosgrove (36) writes:

Too many of us carry the seeds of our own destruction within us; we harbor resentments that damage our relationship with others; anxieties about our own adequacy produce a need to protect our self-esteem. We feel impelled to adopt ridiculous or handicapping poses—we have to be the "big shot" in order to feel comfortable—we set for ourselves impossible goals to impress ourselves and others; our damaged self-esteem finds any criticism too hard to take; normal mistakes become magnified into personal disasters, and we can only become comfortable by blaming them on others. All of these attitudes are handicapping to us in our jobs and in our relationships with our family and friends.

MAJOR CATEGORIES OF PERSONALITY SICKNESS

Like physical illnesses, the innumerable varieties of personality sickness can be combined into major categories because they have certain features in common. It is widely recognized that there are two chief categories of sick personalities. The *first* consists of forms of behavior which are satisfying to the person but are socially unacceptable. The *second* consists of behavior patterns that are socially acceptable but not satisfying to the person who engages in them.

Socially unacceptable behavior patterns

Certain behavior patterns are disapproved by members of the social group because they are annoying, boring, in bad taste, or actually harmful to others. However, they are satisfying to the person who engages in them; they gratify some need or desire which has not been gratified by patterns of behavior that are socially approved.

A person may derive satisfaction from projecting the blame for his own shortcomings to someone else because this frees him from the feelings of shame, guilt, and self-rejection that shortcomings normally give rise to. But blaming another for one's shortcomings is regarded as poor sportsmanship and bad taste. It can also be harmful to the target of the projected blame; it encourages others to believe that he is responsible for mistreating the person or making him unhappy. This will damage the target person's image in the social group and may even make members of the group reject him.

Similarly, an elderly person who finds his life boring and ego-deflating may discover that he is happier and more self-acceptant when he ignores the present and lives mentally in the past. This encourages him to reminisce, recalling with strong emotional feelings his past successes and happinesses.

Reminiscing may satisfy the person's own needs and desires, but like all forms of personality sickness in this category, it does so at the expense of social approval and acceptance. The person who reminisces is regarded as annoying and boring by those who have to hear the tales of his past glories over and over again. They scorn him because they feel that he is trying to show off or win sympathy. And since he makes no effort to live in the present or to be interested in what others are doing, his egocentrism adds to their annoyance and boredom and makes them want to avoid him.

Jenkins (89) has classified into six categories the behavior problems of children and adolescents—patterns of behavior which are disapproved by the social group but which give the persons who engage in them a satisfaction not derived from more socially acceptable behavior:

Hyperkinetic or hyperactive reactions, such as distractability, restlessness, impulsiveness, and changeable moods

Withdrawing reactions, characterized by seclusiveness, detachment, and inability to form close interpersonal relationships

Overanxious reactions, as shown in chronic anxiety, self-consciousness, and approval-seeking

Runaway reactions, accompanied by furtiveness, inclination to steal, and association with delinquent gangs

Unsocialized aggressive reactions, as expressed in quarrelsomeness, physical or verbal aggressiveness, destructiveness, or hostile teasing of other children

Group delinquent reactions, as contrasted with individual unsocialized aggressiveness but expressed in much the same kind of behavior

Socially acceptable behavior patterns

The second major category of personality sicknesses consists of behavior patterns which are socially acceptable but which do not satisfy the needs and desires of the person who engages in them. A man who is an introvert and who prefers interests and activities which do not include other people can make himself psychologically sick by forcing himself to play the role of the "life of the party." Social judgments of him may be more favorable when he plays this role but he derives far less personal satisfaction from it than from the role of introvert.

The person whose behavior conforms to social expectations is regarded by the layman as well adjusted and "normal," regardless of how he feels about the role he is playing. Only when the person's needs and desires are satisifed by his characteristic pattern of adjusting to life and only when this pattern is socially acceptable can he be regarded as psychologically healthy, however. If he is satisifed with his adjustments to life and if members of the social group approve of them, his personality will be healthy.

Failure to fulfill either of these two essentials leads to self-rejection. When this occurs, the person becomes psychologically ill. Thus, regardless of the category in which a certain personality sickness falls, the fundamental cause for it is self-rejection.

DANGER SIGNALS OF PERSONALITY SICKNESS

Neither personality sickness nor physical sickness comes without some forewarning. In physical illness, the danger signals that warn the person that he is on the verge of illness may be unusual and excessive fatigue, general achiness, headaches, fever, or any one of many other common symptoms.

When the danger signals of physical illnesses were not as well known to the medical profession and the lay public as they are today, it was customary to ignore these forewarnings and assume that the person was only temporarily indisposed. It was often assumed that a good night's sleep was all that was needed to restore him to good health. Today, it is widely recognized that ignoring physical danger signals is hazardous. Doctors urge their patients to get in touch with them if they are not feeling up to par and to report what the symptoms are so that therapeutic treatment can be begun at once, hoping in this way to arrest the development of the illness.

This new approach is based on the medical knowledge that changes in physical condition usually mean trouble and that major trouble can often be averted if remedial steps are taken in time. This point of view has been justified by the decrease in serious and fatal illnesses at all age levels, but especially in infancy and childhood.

Personologists are equally aware of the necessity of discovering the common danger signals of mental illness and of informing the lay public of their findings so that mental illness, like physical illness, can be controlled in its early stages. Some of the danger signals are already so well known that parents, teachers, and others who work with young people or even adults can be on the lookout for them. It is also recognized that in the advanced stages personality sickness requires long and extensive therapy, usually in an institution and is not as responsive to treatment as in the early stages.

Purpose of danger signals

Every symptom that may be regarded as a danger signal of an incipient personality sickness serves one fundamental purpose—to protect the ego from unfavorable self- and social judgments and thus enable the person to like and accept himself. Each symptom tells the same story, namely, that the person is self-rejectant.

Washburn states that "just as an individual evolves many responses to protect his body, so he does to protect his ego" (206). He jumps out of the path of a speeding car, he protects himself against the elements, and he sits down to rest when he is fatigued. When his ego is threatened, he also uses a protective device of one kind or another, depending partly on the condition that led to the threat and partly on which device worked best for him in similar past experiences. For example, common methods of ego defense against negative social attitudes are devaluation of the source of the atttitudes, rejection of the attitudes, rationalization to explain why they exist, conformity, and underrecall, or intentionally misperceiving another person's attitude (93).

Number of danger signals

In diagnosing physical illness, doctors do not rely upon one danger signal alone unless it is very pronounced or persistent. Instead, they look for several related symptoms which together appear to be responsible for a particular illness. In diagnosing flu, they look for a syndrome of danger signals, such as fever, headache, tiredness, general achiness, and sore throat.

The same approach is used by the personologist in diagnosing personality sickness. He looks for a syndrome of related danger signals which seem to point to a particular diagnosis. The more related danger signals there are, the more confident he can be that his diagnosis is correct.

One of the obstacles confronting personologists is that they have so little clinical evidence of specific syndromes of danger signals for the various forms of personality sickness. In this respect, they lag behind the medical profession—not because personality sickness is less common or less dangerous than physical illness but because clinical work in this area is still in its infancy.

In spite of the relative lack of clinical evidence, there is enough evidence to justify the belief that every personality sickness, even the most minor one, is characterized by several related symptoms that may correctly be regarded as danger signals. A person who engages in excessive daydreaming, for example, also shows other closely related patterns of behavior, such as rationalization, in an attempt to bolster his ego and defend himself against any doubt that he is as able as he wants to be, and regression to an earlier stage in life when he was happier and more self-acceptant.

Variations in danger signals

Danger signals of personality sickness may appear at any *age*. Some are more important, more frequent, and more prophetic at one age than at another, while some are equally frequent and prophetic at all ages. This is true also of physical danger signals. Fever, for example, is more prophetic of serious physical illness in babies and young children than in older children, adolescents, and adults.

As an example of behavioral symptoms, cruelty, which is so common among young children and so dependent on their lack of understanding of how it affects others, cannot be considered as prophetic of personality sickness as it is among more knowledgeable adolescents and adults. Similarly reverie or excessive daydreaming is an almost universal characteristic during the early adolescent years, and so it is not regarded as a danger signal of self-rejection at that time. But if it persists in this excessive form into late adolescence or adulthood, the diagnosis would have to be reversed.

There are also *sex* differences in the kinds of danger signals most often observed. Girls and women, as a group, tend to exhibit less aggressive danger signals than men and boys. In the next section, where danger signals are discussed in detail, sex differences will be indicated wherever we have clinical evidence that such differences exist.

Danger signals vary considerably in degree of *rationality*. In a study of the devices used by elderly people to defend themselves against the problems of aging, Havighurst and Albrecht described two major groups of devices: the irrational and the rational.

Irrational ways of achieving self-acceptance consist of dwelling in memory and fantasy on pleasures and triumphs experienced earlier; regression to a stage in life when one was happier and better adjusted (for example, becoming dependent on others for help, attention, and companionship); hallucinations and "convenient forgetting" of unpleasant and threatening experiences (talking to lost loved ones, for instance, much as lonely children defend themselves against loneliness and feelings of neglect and rejection by playing with imaginary companions).

Rational defenses against the problems of aging

consist of taking an interest in clothes and grooming so as to make as attractive an appearance as possible; cultivating new friendships, new interests, and new leisure-time activities; learning to be independent of one's children; and avoiding excessive reminiscing about the "good old days" (75).

COMMON DANGER SIGNALS OF PERSONALITY SICKNESS

Danger signals of personality sickness take many different forms but all are alike in proclaiming that the person does not like himself and has a self-rejectant attitude. All are used, either consciously or unconsciously, to protect the injured ego or to ward off threats to the ego.

The person relies mainly on those signals which he has discovered, from past experience, best protect his ego from possible threat or serve to bolster it if it has already been damaged. If, as time goes on, he discovers that one technique does not work well anymore, he is likely to abandon it in favor of another.

Since most of the danger signals a person uses are recognized by others as symptoms of poor adjustment, they tend to lead to unfavorable social judgments. When the person recognizes these unfavorable judgments, he feels even more threatened and is motivated to continue to use the danger signals or search for new ones. His aim is to ward off the ego threats and become less self-rejectant.

Clinical studies of maladjusted children, adolescents, and adults have disclosed so many danger signals of personality sickness that it would be impossible to discuss them all. Therefore, only the most common and those most extensively investigated by clinical research will be discussed here. These include immaturity, regression, cruelty, antisocial behavior, defense mechanism, showing off, psychological painkillers, conformity, and suicide.

Immaturity

A person is judged as "immature" if his performance in some area of behavior falls below the standards set by his peers. A child who is slower than his age-mates in learning to speak in sentences and who continues to use baby talk long after the other children of his age are speaking well is regarded as immature in speech development.

Immaturity may be general or it may be limited to one or several areas of behavior. A person may conform to patterns of behavior common among his peers in most areas but fall below them in emotional control or in moral judgments and behavior. Or he may fall below the standards set by his peers in most of the important areas of behavior.

Most immature people, even young children, are aware of their immaturity and feel embarrassed and ashamed. If they cannot or will not behave in a manner considered appropriate for their age, they develop feelings of inadequacy. These negative self-attitudes are reinforced by the person's awareness of unfavorable social judgments made by peers and others. Realization of unfavorable social judgments should provide the necessary motivation for people to try to behave more maturely. If it does, self-judgments as well as social judgments will improve.

Some immature people are unable, for one reason or another, to behave in a manner that conforms to the standards for their age. Others—the majority, in fact—feel inadequate to do so. Immaturity is thus a danger signal of personality sickness. It tells others that the person does not like himself. He is self-rejectant in that he feels inadequate to act his age and knows that others have an unfavorable attitude toward him because his behavior falls below their expectations.

Common areas of immaturity *Irresponsibility,* or failure to assume the responsibilities expected of a person of one's age and level of development, is a prominent form of immaturity at all ages. The "let John do it" type of immature person shifts the responsibilities expected of him onto the shoulders of anyone who is available and willing to assume them. He tries to free himself from feelings of inadequacy by letting someone else carry the load which is rightly his but which he feels inadequate to carry.

Closely related to irresponsibility as a sign of immaturity is *dependency* on others. The child who is mentally and physically old enough to dress and feed himself but feels inadequate to do so becomes dependent on others to do these things for him. *School phobia*, as explained in Chapter 12 in connection with educational determinants, usually stems from excessive dependency on the mother, resulting in the young child's fear of facing the new experiences of school alone (86). Dependency on parents and the familiar environment of the home causes *homesickness* among older children and young adolescents away from home in camps, colleges, or the armed services. As Rose (168) explains:

Homesickness is a reaction to unsuccessful adjustment to a new social environment where there is a feeling either of frustration in the desire to be accepted or of inadequacy because of lack of the necessary social skills to keep pace with others. Longing for the home may indicate a desire for the attention and affection to which an individual was accustomed in his home or a need for help in establishing new contacts. In some cases the longing for the home seems to be only a rationalization for the desire to escape from the unsatisfactory present situation.

Homesickness is often intensified by the person's unrealistic or romanticized memories of home experience. In retrospect, the institutionalized elderly person sees his home as so superior to his present surroundings that he feels unloved, unwanted, and cut off from all the ties that served to provide him with a sense of security. Homesickness for him is just one of several danger signals of personality sickness and growing maladjustment.

Early marriages and *premarital pregnancies* are danger signals of immaturity. The person who marries while still dependent on his parents for support is looking for the emotional security that he feels is lacking in his home. Similarly, girls who become pregnant before marriage are poorly adjusted in the sense that they lack feelings of emotional security and are trying to compensate by having an affair (85, 118, 123, 135).

Regression

Regression is an attempt, either consciously or unconsciously, to return to an earlier stage of development in which the person felt happier and more secure. It signifies that he lacks confidence in his ability to cope with the situation in which he finds himself. To avoid behaving in a way that will make him dislike and reject himself, he tries to return to a stage where he can be more confident and, hence, more self-acceptant.

Many young children who are jealous of a new sibling attempt to return to the helplessness of an earlier age in the hope of regaining the sense of emotional security and the confidence they formerly enjoyed. They wait for someone to dress and feed them, cry and demand parental attention, and try to hurt the sibling whom they believe is responsible for their state of insecurity.

Realizing that regression evokes unfavorable social attitudes, older children, adolescents, and adults use more subtle forms than young children. They verbalize their wishes to return to the "good old days" when they were younger and make unfavorable comparisons between the present and the past. As Linden (114) remarks:

Where the future appears to be without promise, and the now is lacking in human relationships, the memories of pleasures and exploits of the past, exaggerated in retrospect, become the sedative that drives the present into discard.

Regardless of the person's age, regression in any form leads to unfavorable social judgments. Just as people become impatient with a young child who refuses to do what he is capable of doing, so they become exasperated with the older person who longs to return to an earlier day instead of trying to adjust to the present. Regression proclaims to others that he is not a well-adjusted person, and it is an important danger signal of personality sickness. See Figure 14-4.

Cruelty

According to adult standards, *all* young children are cruel at some time or other. They take pleasure in inflicting pain on other people and on animals. When the target of their cruelty cries out in pain, this intensifies their pleasure and makes them feel that they are in charge of the situation. Childish cruelty derives from feelings of inadequacy which children experience because of their inferior size and strength and their lack of skill in doing things that other people can do. Their helplessness is a threat to their egos and further increases their feelings of inadequacy.

With age and experience, most children learn that the temporary satisfaction and ego inflation which acts of cruelty provide are overshadowed by social disapproval and scorn. They then abandon cruelty in favor of more socially approved methods of ego inflation or they use more subtle techniques of cruelty. Regardless of how subtle their techniques are, people who continue to defend their egos by inflicting pain or discomfort on others are soon recognized as maladjusted.

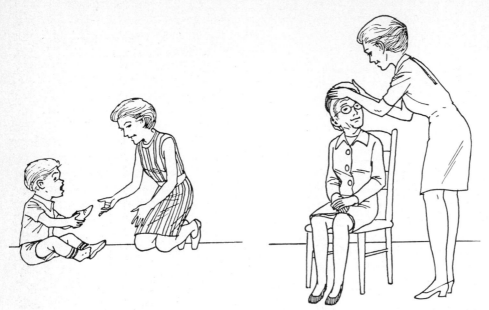

Figure 14-4 Regression to an earlier stage of helplessness to gain social attention at any age may be regarded as a danger signal of personality sickness. An elderly person who asks for help in a simple task may be showing such a danger signal.

Forms of cruelty Which forms of cruelty a person uses will depend upon which give him the greatest personal satisfaction and which avoid or minimize social disapproval. One of the most common forms is *bullying*—inflicting physical pain on an animal or another person who is smaller, weaker, or less able to defend himself. Since bullying is regarded as unsportsmanlike, it is generally abandoned as a form of ego inflation as children approach adolescence. However, some adolescents and even some adults continue to use it, though mainly on occasions when it is traditional to do so as in hazing ceremonies.

At all ages, bullying is more common among boys and men than among girls and women. This can be explained, to some extent, by the fact that boys grow up with the belief that they should be superior to girls. If, owing to either physical or mental limitations, they are inferior to some girls, one way they can ease their ego humiliation is to bully the girls. Boys who get ego satisfaction from pulling a cat's tail also get ego satisfaction from pulling a girl's hair.

While no available research studies have reported any relationship between a man's physical size and the likelihood of his being a bully, there is some evidence that many juvenile delinquents and adult criminals who attack women are small and sex inappropriate in body build (35, 64, 98).

When people abandon bullying as a form of ego inflation, they often substitute *teasing*. Teasing is like bullying, in that it is an attempt to hurt another as a way of increasing one's feeling of self-importance. It differs from bullying in that the hurt is psychological rather than physical. The psychological hurt comes from calling attention to, ridiculing, and encouraging others to laugh at some weakness or idiosyncrasy of the person who is being teased. It may be a physical feature, such as hair color; an interest that is regarded as sex-inappropriate, such as a boy's interest in art; or an affectional relationship, such as a child's affection for his teacher or a young adolescent's affection for a member of the opposite sex.

To hurt the person who is the target of the teasing, the teaser usually exaggerates, in a joking way, the feature selected for the focal point of the teasing and makes it seem so ridiculous that others will laugh at it. A boy who teases a girl because of her formal manners will say in an affected voice, "Oh thank you veddy much, dear Miss Jones."

Nicknames, as was pointed out in Chapter 3 in the discussion of symbols of self, very often originate in teasing. The boy or girl who is labeled "Red" or "Skinny" by his peers is teased for a physical feature that sets him apart from the rest of the group. Every time the person is called by this derogatory nickname, it hurts his ego and, at the same time, inflates the ego of the person who uses the label.

Many jokes are meant to be subtle ways of teasing others. The traditional family jokes about mothers-in-law, "meddling" grandmothers, and "inefficient" wives and the traditional religious and racial jokes are designed to do psychological damage to their victims.

Social attitudes toward teasing are less unfavorable than toward bullying because teasing is more subtle and does not do physical harm to its victims. Consequently, the teaser continues his teasing and finds it a satisfactory technique for ego inflation. However, like bullying, it is an indication, no matter how subtle it may be or how well camouflaged in good humor, that the person who uses it does so because he suffers from a self-rejectant attitude.

One of the commonest forms of cruelty the self-rejecting person uses to inflate his ego is *discrimination*. Discriminating against another person because of his religion, for example, hurts him in his social life, in his work, in school, and in other areas. He is treated as an inferior and is not given an opportunity to do what he is capable of doing. In addition, he is often rejected, teased, bullied, and taunted.

The person who does the discriminating is himself psychologically damaged in several ways, each of which increases his self-rejectant attitude and leads to even greater maladjustment. *First*, discrimination leads to unfavorable social judgments. The person soon becomes aware that members of the social group regard his behavior as unfair if not actually cruel. Realization of these unfavorable social judgments intensifies his self-rejectant attitude. *Second*, the person feels guilty and ashamed of his unfair and unsportsmanlike behavior, and this likewise intensifies his self-rejection. And *third*, the temporary satisfaction that inflicting psychological pain brings only widens the gap between what the person would like to be and his real self-concept and thus intensifies his self-rejection.

All the available research studies of prejudiced people, especially those who express their prejudices in discriminatory behavior, reveal that the people are maladjusted. Their dislike of others, which leads to their discriminatory behavior, stems from their dislike of self. The more they discriminate and the more cruel their discrimination is, the more obvious the danger signal of personality sickness (8, 129, 140, 220).

Antisocial behavior

Behavior is antisocial if it is hostile or damaging, either physically or psychologically, to the welfare of members of the social group. Such behavior may be conscious or unconscious. Only if it is conscious can it be regarded as a danger signal of personality sickness. Young children, for example, are too young and too unaware of values associated with material possessions to appreciate how antisocial their destruction of a cherished object belonging to another person is. Therefore, their destructiveness cannot justifiably be regarded as a danger signal of personality sickness because they are not trying to ease their self-rejectant attitudes by inflating their egos at someone else's expense.

If an adult intentionally leaves the radio turned on all night to annoy a neighbor, on the other hand, this is conscious antisocial behavior and can justifiably be regarded as a danger signal of personality sickness. The same is true if he intentionally parks his car in front of another person's garage so that the person cannot back his car out.

In spite of the personal satisfaction antisocial behavior brings to the self-rejectant person, it also brings social disapproval, scorn, and even punishment. These social reactions counter much of the personal satisfaction the person anticipated from the behavior. As Lorber (116) has pointed out:

Disruptive, attention-seeking actions produce, at best, merely insignificant and fleeting moments of social recognition and, in long range perspective, impair the positive development of rewarding interpersonal relations and satisfactory social living.

Antisocial behavior indicative of self-rejection Some forms of antisocial behavior are designed primarily to annoy others, some to put the self-rejectant person who feels neglected and inadequate into the limelight, some to bolster the person's ego by making him feel that he has gained the upper hand in a social situation, and some to defy existing rules and laws. The form used depends mainly on what the person has discovered from past experience bolsters his ego and minimizes his self-rejectant feeling.

Misdemeanors, such as breaking home or school rules, usually involve behavior that is troublesome and disruptive to members of the social group. The child or adolescent who cuts up in class is trying to make himself the center of peer attention and peer admiration. He knows he is poorly accepted by his peers and he hopes to improve his acceptance in this way. If he succeeds, his behavior will lead to greater self-acceptance.

Studies show that misdemeanors are more common among those who feel insecure and inadequate than among those who feel more self-acceptant. This further substantiates the evidence that misdemeanors are danger signals of personality sickness (13, 32, 198, 200).

When children and young adolescents discover that misdemeanors serve to minimize their feelings of self-rejection, they sometimes intensify their rebellion against authority and break laws, thus becoming *juvenile delinquents*. It is important to recognize, however, as Asuni has emphasized, that "not all delinquents are maladjusted and not all maladjusted are delinquent" (13).

Some juvenile delinquents are well-adjusted people in the sense that they have adjusted successfully to the social group with which they are identified and have accepted the values of this group as their own. While these values are not those of society at large, the group that accepts them does so because they fit the members' needs. So long as a person conforms to the social group's values and is accepted by the group, he does not suffer from personality sickness unless he feels anxious, ashamed, and guilty about identification with a group whose standards of behavior are not accepted by society at large (84).

Criminality in adulthood is even more likely to be a danger signal of maladjustment than is delinquency in adolescence. By the time the person reaches adulthood, he is aware of the seriousness of breaking laws and is far less likely to do so because his friends think it is the "thing to do" than is the adolescent. He not only knows that he is breaking the law but he wants to do so (2).

The criminal is motivated by a desire to retaliate for what he considers the wrongs society has inflicted on him. The lack of social acceptance, the feelings of personal inadequacy, and other conditions which led to feelings of inadequacy and self-rejection when he was younger are intensified as he grows older unless remedial steps are taken to help him change his self-concept and become more self-acceptant.

Studies of adult criminals reveal that in most cases there has been a history of misbehavior and delinquency dating back to their childhood years. As children and adolescents growing up, they became increasingly aware of the negative social attitudes toward them and this intensified their unfavorable attitudes toward themselves. If they were not maladjusted and self-rejectant they would not commit crimes, regardless of how their friends and business associates behaved (7, 64, 97, 139).

Defense mechanisms

A defense mechanism is a "constellation of related ideas by means of which the individual maintains, enhances, and defends himself. It provides a relatively enduring and general frame of reference that orients behavior when one perceives a threat to the self" (206). Whenever a person perceives himself as inadequate, he uses one or more defense mechanisms to provide a "protective attitude," thus minimizing or eliminating his feelings of inadequacy.

If defense mechanisms are to serve successfully as an ego protection, the person must be unconscious of his use of them. If he uses them consciously they may prove to be a threat to his self-esteem and thus destroy the acceptable self-picture he is trying to create.

The use of defense mechanisms begins early, often in the preschool years, when the young child recognizes that he is anxious, depressed, and unhappy because he is not behaving as he would like to behave or because others have a critical attitude toward him and his behavior. He develops a repertoire of defense mechanisms to protect his ego and, in time, selects from this repertoire those which he finds work best as ego protectors.

In spite of the satisfaction defense mechanisms provide, the satisfaction is only temporary; it does not actually correct the problem that gave rise to the use of the defense mechanisms. As when temporary corrective measures are taken for a physical illness, further corrective measures will have to be taken later, often stronger and more drastic than would have been needed if the earlier measures had actually gotten to the bottom of the trouble. This point is emphasized by Jourard (95):

When a person experiences pain, it is a signal that something is wrong with his body. If he utilizes pain as a signal, the person will take active steps to remove the causes of the pain, thus prolonging his life. If the person anesthetizes his pain, the factors which are responsible for the pain remain active: as soon as the drug or anesthetic wears off, pain is again experienced. . . . *The various mechanisms of defense are much like anesthetics; they may be effective in neutralizing or reducing the unpleasant emotions of guilt and anxiety, but they do nothing to remove the factors which are producing the threat. Consequently, the defensive person becomes addicted to defenses just as a pain-evader might become addicted to aspirin, codeine, serpisil, or alcohol. Neither person has the courage or ego strength to investigate the causes of the unpleasant feelings and to take the steps necessary to remove the causes. . . . In time, the habitual addict to defense mechanisms may display the clinical symptoms of neurosis and psychosis.*

Common forms of defense mechanisms

It has been known for a long time that people who feel inadequate use defense mechanisms to bolster their egos. In the Book of Proverbs, for example, it is said that "the wicked flee when no man pursueth." Shakespeare put into Hamlet's mouth the words, "The lady doth protest too much, methinks."

Freud and, later, Adorno et al. interpreted defense mechansims in a more scientific way. Freud, for example, explained how forgetting, projection, rationalization, sublimation, and other defense mechanisms are used by the self-rejectant person as forms of ego defense (57). Adorno et al. showed how the authoritarian person uses such defensive attitudes as projection and displacement (4).

Clinical studies reveal a wide repertoire of defense mechansims that are in common use by maladjusted people of all ages—people who are trying to ease the psychological discomforts that come from feelings of inadequacy and, by so doing, trying to be more self-acceptant. To date, we have no clinical evidence of which defense mechanisms are used most frequently or least frequently, and so no attempt will be made to discuss them in order of frequency of use or relative importance.

RATIONALIZATION Rationalization may be defined as "an explanation of one's own motives and behavior which has been selected from among many possible explanations, because it enhances and defends the individual's self-structure" (95). The person who rationalizes is motivated not to give a factual account of his real intentions but rather to explain his conduct in such a way as to protect his ego. The person is not consciously lying; he believes, or at least has convinced himself, that the explanation he gives for his behavior is true. He ignores other possible explana-

tions, selecting from those which are related to his behavior the one which will best protect his ego and will be most likely to win sympathetic reactions from others, thus minimizing any rejectant attitudes toward him they might otherwise have.

For example, a person who has not achieved the vocational success he aspired to and which his family and friends expected of him may rationalize his lack of success by explaining that he has been handicapped by a limited education, that he had to quit school or college to help out with family finances.

PROJECTION In projection, the person tries to explain or excuse behavior that falls short of his and others' expectations by thrusting the blame onto something or someone else. Projection may take a more subtle form, as when the person calls attention to the shortcomings of another in the hope of diverting attention from his own undesirable behavior. According to the old saying, "It is the poor workman who blames his tools." These "tools" may be people as well as inanimate objects.

Projection differs from rationalization in one major respect. In projection, the person thrusts the blame for his shortcomings onto a specific person or thing which he uses as a scapegoat, whereas in rationalization, he uses *any* plausible excuse. While rationalization may involve a scapegoat, the role of the scapegoat in causing the person's shortcomings is not highlighted as it is in projection.

As a source of ego defense, projection is more satisfying than rationalization because it makes the person feel that he has been victimized and shifts attention and blame from himself to someone or something else, thus freeing him from social blame and reproach. However, unless projection is very subtle, it is likely to be regarded as poor sportsmanship. As such, it will fail to achieve its purpose of improving social and self judgments. That is why people tend to use projection less frequently than rationalization after they become more conscious of social attitudes.

DISPLACEMENT In displacement, the person directs his resentments, stemming from feelings of inadequacy, martyrdom, or inferiority, against a person, object, or situation which is unrelated to the origin of his resentments. The individual thus relieves himself of the tensions that have intensified his self-rejectant attitude and so reduces his self-rejection.

The object of displacement is usually a smaller and more helpless person, an animal, or an inanimate object. The angry person who throws an ink bottle or kicks a chair is showing his resentments as much as the person who attacks an animal or a person smaller than he. The juvenile delinquent who attacks an innocent victim is often motivated by a desire to rid himself of pent-up resentments which have intensified his feelings of self-rejection.

Like projection, displacement is regarded as poor sportsmanship and leads to disapproval or rejection by members of the social group. As children grow older, they recognize these unfavorable social reactions and either abandon this defense mechanism or use it only when they feel that it will not win social disapproval, as in the case of a gang attack on an innocent victim or the telling of a joke about a family member when they feel certain that other family members will side with them instead of with the victim.

FANTASY   Blazer has defined fantasy as "an escape or defensive mechanism offering either solace or an illusionary release from unsatisfying reality or an imaginary satisfaction of wishes any actual gratification of which has been forbidden by repression" (22). Whenever fantasy is excessive for a person's age and level of development, it may be regarded as a danger signal of personality sickness. Shaffer and Shoben (174) have spelled out what "excessive" means in this context:

Although no one can give a precise definition of what is an "excessive" amount of fantasy, practical criteria can be applied to individual cases. Too great a dependence on daydreaming seems to be caused by the same factors that underlie the seclusive forms of defense. When fear, anxiety, or persistent frustration prevents active adjustment, daydreaming will be used. Fantasy plays a dual role as a direct satisfier of basic motives and as a compensation for thwarted attainments.

Even though a person may, through fantasy, bolster his ego by satisfying wishes that have remained unsatisfied in daily life, the attitudes of members of the social group toward him are unfavorable. The person who spends much of his time in a fantasy world neglects his duties and responsibilities. In addition, he creates the impression that he is completely egocentric because he makes no effort to become a part of the social group. While he does nothing to harm members of the group, as is done in projection

and displacement, he does nothing to contribute to their well-being or happiness. Negative social judgments of his egocentrism add to the unfavorable self-concept that he is trying to defend by the use of fantasy.

Forms of fantasy   Certain forms of fantasy are common at certain ages because they help to reduce the ego threats that people of those ages are especially likely to encounter. The white lies of childhood, resulting from the young child's desire to be more self-acceptant, are not conscious falsifications of the truth; instead, they are unconscious falsifications which serve to inflate the child's ego. The little boy who tells his parents made-up stories of his prowess on the baseball diamond has actually convinced himself that he is a baseball hero to compensate for feelings of personal or social inadequacy.

As children grow older, their developing intelligence and increased experience make it possible for them to distinguish between truth and untruth. Normally, therefore, lying as a form of ego defense will decline. When it persists, either consciously or unconsciously, it may be regarded as a danger signal of personality sickness and as a defense against self-rejection.

To defend themselves against the self-rejection that loneliness brings, many young children create imaginary companions with whom they play as they would like to play with real children. While this is a satisfactory solution to their problem when they are young, it is unsatisfactory as they grow older because it deprives them of opportunities to learn how to get along with real people.

Daydreaming is one of the most common forms of fantasy used as a defense mechanism. All kinds of daydreaming fall into two major categories: the "conquering-hero" daydream in which the dreamer tries to bolster his ego by seeing himself as a far more important person than he is in daily life, and the "suffering hero" or "martyr" daydream where he gains satisfaction through self-pity.

Borrowed fantasies, or ready-made daydreams based on the dreamer's identification with a hero in escape literature, movies, and television, are also effective ways of reducing self-devaluation and attitudes of inferiority. For the time, the person who imagines himself in the role of a ready-made hero feels like a hero. Blazer states that "through the process of identification we are enabled to incorporate these manufactured dreams into our own repertory, where they serve as models for more dreams of the same type'' (22).

Imaginary illnesses or *phantom handicaps* are used as a defense against doing things which the person feels inadequate for and which, if carried out, would increase his self-rejectant attitude. By imagining that he is unable to do them, for one physical reason or another, the person not only hopes to win social sympathy but also hopes, either consciously or unconsciously, to reduce or minimize his self-rejectant attitude. Of all forms of fantasy, phantom handicaps are least likely to arouse social disapproval and most likely to win sympathy.

SOUR-GRAPES MECHANISM Some people try to minimize ego threats by derogating the value of something they do not have or which they feel is out of their reach. This defense mechanism—so-called because it was used by the fox in Aesop's fable of the fox who said he did not want the grapes he had vainly tried to reach because they were ''sour''—is a device used, either consciously or unconsciously, to ward off the feelings of inadequacy that inevitably follow failure to achieve a desired goal. A high school student who fails to gain admission to the college of his choice may rationalize his failure by pointing out all the defects and weaknesses of the college that refused to accept him.

Most people sense the bitter resentment behind even the most subtle use of the sour-grapes mechanism and regard the person who uses it as a poor sport. The person sooner or later senses the negative social judgment, and this reduces the value of the mechanism for him.

POLLYANNA MECHANISM Similar in some respects but radically different in other respects from the sour-grapes mechanism is the Pollyanna mechanism—a defense mechanism named for the heroine of the 1913 novel *Pollyanna* by Eleanor Porter. The ''glad girl'' was irrepressibly optimistic, always able to see a silver lining in even the darkest cloud.

Like the person who defends his ego against threats by derogating what he cannot have, the person who uses the Pollyanna mechanism defends his ego by concentrating on the superior qualities of what he has to the point where what he cannot have seems unimportant. Furthermore, he diverts the attention of others from what he cannot get by concentrating on

what he has and, by so doing, tries, either consciously or unconsciously, to prevent them from judging him as a failure.

Unquestionably, the person who seems happy and contented with what he has creates the impression that he is a better-adjusted person than the one who adopts a sour-grapes attitude. On the other hand, social judgments may be unfavorable if the Pollyanna mechanism is used frequently enough to suggest that the person lacks ambition and is satisfied to be an underachiever.

COMPENSATION Compensation is an ego defense which reduces the person's feelings of self-rejection in two ways: *first,* by channeling his energies into an activity in which he can achieve success and thus eliminate some of the self-rejectant attitude that followed failure in another activity, and *second,* by diverting his attention as well as the attention of others from the activity in which he failed to the one in which he is a success. A businessman who is unable to achieve the vocational success he desires may compensate by becoming a community leader.

If not carried to excess, compensation may prove to be an effective way of defending the ego against threats that lead to self-rejection. The dangers of overcompensation have been described thus by Crow (39):

A compensatory activity may be unrealistic, such as exaggerated manner . . . or affected speech. The individual may tend to compensate for a defect by overaggressiveness, bullying, false submissiveness, or overzealousness in denunciation of social or individual inadequacies. These compensatory habits are expressions of the individual's denial to himself of his own inadequacy.

REPRESSION Repression is often referred to by the layman as ''convenient forgetting.'' The person forgets, either consciously or unconsciously, those things which remind him of his inadequacies. In this way, he eliminates some of the psychological distress that has led to self-rejection.

Were it possible to repress all memories of an unpleasant experience so that its ego-deflating effects could be eradicated, repression would prove to be a good defense mechanism. It would serve the person well and at the same time fail to arouse adverse social judgments. However, repression is rarely complete, and so some of the unrepressed memories express themselves in behavior that leads others as well as the person himself to feel that he is behaving in an irrational way. These judgments intensify his self-rejection instead of alleviating it.

DEVALUATION   Since one of the common causes of self-rejection is unfavorable social judgments, one way to defend the ego against such judgments is to devalue their source. This can be done either by minimizing the importance of the judgments or by trying to prove to oneself and to others that those who made the adverse evaluation were not competent to pass judgment or were prejudiced.

The child who is constantly criticized by an older sibling will quickly develop a self-rejectant attitude unless he can convince himself that the older sibling's criticism derives from jealousy or conceitedness.

Like projection and the sour-grapes mechanism, devaluation of the source of unfavorable judgments is likely to be considered poor sportsmanship. The worker who claims that the supervisor who criticizes his work is prejudiced is just as likely to be unfavorably judged by members of the social group as is the child who claims that a criticizing older sibling has delusions of grandeur. This then militates against the defensive value the devaluation would otherwise have.

Showing off

All young children show off to attract attention to themselves. They discover, partly by trial and error and partly by the encouragement they receive from doting parents, that when they say or do something to put themselves at the center of attention their feelings of neglect and rejection are replaced by the ego satisfaction that comes from being noticed, approved, or even applauded.

In spite of the ego satisfaction children receive from showing off, they learn, sooner or later, that social attitudes toward show-offs are unfavorable. In school, those who act on the impulse of the moment, who engage in horseplay, who break rules, or who repudiate authority are regarded by both peers and teachers as nuisances. The ego satisfaction they get from being in the limelight is thus reduced by unfavorable social attitudes.

If this kind of behavior persists, it may be regarded as a danger signal of personality sickness. Since most children are aware, certainly before they finish the second grade, that showing off is disapproved by teachers and peers, its continued use may indicate that they are socially as well as personally maladjusted.

Patterns of show-off behavior   One of the most common forms of showing off is *boasting* about one's achievements, possessions, and social contacts. Whether it is the child who boasts of his larger and better toys, the adolescent who boasts of his romantic conquests, or the adult who boasts of his important friends, often subtly by name dropping, the fundamental source of satisfaction is the ego inflation he hopes to achieve from the admiration of others. As was pointed out in Chapter 3 in the discussion of symbols of self, unless boasting is done very subtly, it is more likely to lead to social disapproval than to admiration. It then loses its value.

Clowning, in any situation and at any age, can be counted on to get a laugh. However, the laugh often turns to disapproval, scorn, or contempt. Even children soon become annoyed at the class clown's disruption of what they want to do and are contemptuous of his silliness and showing off. The "life of the party" discovers that the temporary social attention he wins does not effectively increase his social acceptance.

Making *derogatory comments* and *name calling* are show-off techniques that are often substituted for clowning. By adolescence, these techniques of ego inflation are both common and effective. If the person limits his use of them to people and situations his peers likewise criticize, such as teachers and the school, he wins far less social disapproval than if he directs them toward a member of the peer group or a popular adult.

The *daredevil* who takes unreasonable chances and defies authority has a marked feeling of personal inadequacy which he is trying to compensate for. By accepting dares and doing things that most of his peers are afraid to do, he hopes to win both admiration and acceptance. While both boys and girls engage in daredevil acts, they are far more common among boys. They are also more common among children than among adolescents, who have discovered that daredeviltry, like clowning, wins only temporary admiration and may lead to injuries (218).

Accident-proneness may be regarded as a danger signal of personality sickness. If a person has more than his share of accidents because of his tendency to show off and try to steal the limelight, it is an indication that he feels neglected, a feeling that encourages self-rejection. In speaking of accident-prone children, Dunbar says, "Children who feel hopeless about making themselves understood tend to do something to get attention, smash things or hurt themselves, until, if no one comes to the rescue, they get the habit" (49).

Defying authority, in the form of rules and laws laid down by parents, teachers, and law-enforcement authorities, is a common show-off technique. Some of the ways self-rejectant young people try to inflate their egos are by smoking, drinking, glue-sniffing, driving faster than the legal speed limit, and using narcotics. Since smoking is not forbidden by law, many adolescents substitute it for the more dangerous forms of showing off that may lead to conflict with the law (167).

Which form of defiance young people will use to inflate their egos will depend largely on what meets their personal needs best and which forms will have the greatest defiance value. As adolescent smoking is far more common and more widely accepted than formerly, it has lost much of its show-off value in favor of drinking, which is still disapproved by parents and teachers and governed by rules in many schools and colleges and by laws in the states. Here is one explanation of the present popularity of marijuana smoking as a form of show-off behavior (197):

Part of pot's attraction is "doing something illegal together." . . . To most psychiatrists, the increase in marijuana smoking represents not so much a search for new thrills as the traditional, exhibitionistic rebellion of youngsters against adult authority. Parents who are agreeable to students' drinking almost always boggle at drugs. "There is not much that students can do that is defiant," says a Boston psychiatrist. "They think with some degree of glee about what their parents would think if they knew they were smoking marijuana."

Psychological pain-killers

The attention value of using such techniques as drinking, smoking, and taking drugs to defy authority and their value as a means of inflating the ego lead some people to rely upon them to ease the psychological pain that comes from self-dissatisfaction and self-rejection. People discover, often by trial and error, that psychological pain can be eased by any technique that helps them to forget their troubles temporarily. This they may discover very early, even before they recognize the attention value of defying authority.

As psychological pains increase, many people follow the same path that they use for easing physical pain; they increase the frequency of use and the intensity of the pain-killer. Just as some people become addicted to the use of aspirin or codeine, so some become addicted to the use of psychological pain-killers.

Today it is recognized that a person who has become addicted to any technique to deaden the psychological pain of self-rejection is suffering from personality sickness. Instead of condemning him for weakness of will power, as was formerly done, most people approve the new trend, which involves finding out what is responsible for the personality sickness so that its cause can be eliminated and the use of pain-killers made unnecessary.

In many cases, the infrequent and moderate use of psychological pain-killers cannot correctly be regarded as a danger signal of personality sickness. The motivation for their use may be social—doing what everyone does—or merely the desire to attract attention.

On the other hand, their use may be regarded as a danger signal under three conditions: *first,* if they are used more often in solitude than in social settings; *second,* if they are used so frequently and with such intensity that they attract negative attention only—pity or contempt; and *third,* if they are used much more often by those who are not well liked or who are socially inadequate than by those who are popular and who make good social adjustments. "Addictions," write Stewart and Livson, "are not isolated habits but expressions of pervasive personality tendencies" (191).

Studies of people of different ages who are addicted to psychological pain-killers reveal that certain personality traits are characteristic among them. They are usually less popular and more rebellious, withdrawn, irresponsible, and easily dominated by parents or spouses than nonaddicts (185, 191). In describing the personality characteristics of the young male narcotic addict, Gilbert and Lombardi (62) write:

He appears to be the kind of irresponsible, undependable, egocentric individual who has a disregard for social mores, acts on impulse, and demands immediate gratification of his wants. He is impatient and irritable, lacks the persistence to achieve a goal, and will act out aggressively against authority or others who thwart his desires. This acting out may then be followed by feelings of guilt and depression which can only be alleviated by more drugs . . . . Thus, the use of drugs may seem to him to be the only realistic solution to his problems—at least it offers him a temporary relief from the pain of living.

Common psychological pain-killers

As is true of other danger signals of personality sickness, which form of psychological pain-killer the person will use will depend primarily upon which he has discovered from past experience eases his self-rejectant attitude and makes him feel more adequate and secure. He may, as a child, find that overeating serves as a psychological pain-killer and then discover later that alcohol or narcotics serve his needs better. Thus, as an adolescent or adult, he is likely to substitute the use of alcohol or narcotics for overeating.

Many children, when they have been good and have done things to please their parents, are rewarded with food, usually sweets. The better they are, the more sweets they are given. Sweets soon become associated with ego inflation. As time passes, the children turn more and more to sweets when they feel frustrated and depressed. Candy, cookies, ice cream sundaes—all these provide a psychological boost. In time, such children develop the habit of *overeating* and become obese. As a result of their overweight, they are unable to keep up the pace set by their less obese peers and so they are gradually rejected as playmates. This encourages more overeating and greater obesity.

When children reach adolescence, they find that obesity is a social handicap, especially in their relationships with members of the opposite sex. The more rejected they are socially, the more they turn to eating as a way of killing the psychological pain social rejection brings. As they reach adulthood, they often discover that obesity is a vocational, social, and marital handicap. By that time, overeating has become a habitual method of meeting all frustrations and all situations that make them feel self-rejectant. Consequently, except in rare cases where there is a glandular or some other physical cause, obesity is due to overeating. Either obesity or overeating may be regarded as a danger signal of personality sickness.

Every gang-age child or young adolescent who wants to defy authority and thus inflate his ego is tempted to smoke. Though *smoking* is not always a pleasant physical experience for him, it is an ego-satisfying one. The more social approval he wins from his peers for daring to defy adult authority, the more

quickly he will learn to associate ego satisfaction with smoking.

In mid-adolescence, he discovers that smoking is an accepted pattern of social behavior. He smokes when his friends smoke because it is the thing to do. This does not in any way indicate that he is suffering from personality sickness. "Social smoking" is a sign of good social adjustment because it indicates that the person is trying to conform to the mores of the group with which he is associated.

On the other hand, *excessive* smoking, especially in solitude, may be regarded as a danger signal of personality sickness. The person who smokes much more than his peers, and does so in solitude as well as when he is with members of the peer group, shows that he is engaging in an activity which he has discovered gives him psychological satisfaction whenever he feels depressed, frustrated, or annoyed. It gives him a "lift" when he feels self-rejectant.

"Chain smoking" or excessive smoking is often found among those who have a history of rebelling against social restrictions, in some cases since elementary school days. As they grow older, if they find that smoking eases some of the feelings of inadequacy and resentment they experience when they are frustrated and rebellious, they reach for a cigarette and smoke one after another until some of the emotional disturbance disappears.

Drinking usually starts as "defiant drinking"—a revolt against adult authority and a way of asserting one's independence of parents and teachers. Many adolescents, when they first start to drink, get little physical satisfaction from it but much psychological satisfaction. Not only do they feel that they are grown up and independent but they also feel that they are accepted members of the peer group. They find, from social drinking, that alcohol gives them a "lift" and helps them to forget their troubles. If they drink enough, they learn that alcohol anesthetizes them, temporarily at least, against all unpleasant situations.

Once they discover the psychological value of drinking, they may use it excessively and in solitude, as chain smokers use cigarettes. Drinking is no longer a social activity, to be carried out with their friends, but a psychological pain-killer. Whenever they feel depressed and unhappy, they take a drink. If this does not kill their psychological pain, they take another and still another. In time, unless therapeutic steps are taken, they slip into alcoholism—the excessive use of alcohol, usually in solitude, to help them forget their troubles or, as the saying goes, "to drown their sorrows." As such, it becomes a psychological pain-killer whose function is not to socialize the person but rather to ease the distresses caused by self-rejection.

Narcotics are used as a psychological pain-killer by many people, especially by members of the younger generation. Many discover from using marijuana that it gives them a psychological lift and makes them forget their troubles temporarily and feel more adequate. This use is, at first, social; people want to do what other members of their peer group are doing.

Having once discovered the pain-deadening effects of marijuana, many then rely on its use whenever they feel psychologically depressed. In time, they develop the habit of using it to inflate their egos and camouflage their problems, and like the chain smoker or the alcoholic, they use it in solitude, not as a social activity.

The danger of using drugs as ego inflaters lies in the fact that, while adolescents or young adults may initially use them as thrill promotors when they feel bored and inadequate, they may become addicted to their use whenever they want to kill the psychological pain that comes from self-rejection. Many maladjusted adolescents become habitual users before they reach the age of legal maturity (62, 127, 143).

Since narcotics are expensive and their general sale and use are illegal, some young people sniff glue to relieve their depressive states. However, many juvenile delinquents from all social classes steal to get the money necessary to buy narcotics, which they find more effective once they become accustomed to them (14, 141).

Sex differences in use of psychological pain-killers

Studies indicate that boys and men use all the psychological pain-killers, with the exception of overeating, more frequently and become more habituated or addicted to their use than girls and women. This is not necessarily or solely because boys and men are more self-rejectant than girls and women, but also because the use of cigarettes, alcohol, and narcotics wins less social disapproval for members of the male sex.

During the adolescent years, the use of these psychological pain-killers is often regarded as an insignia of masculinity. This increases their ego-inflating value for men. In contrast, females who use them may develop feelings of guilt. This does not mean that there are no female chain smokers, alcoholics, or drug addicts who, like members of the male sex, use psychological pain-killers when they feel depressed and unhappy about themselves. There is evidence that, just as the double standard for behavior is gradually breaking down, so the gap between the sexes in the use of psychological pain-killers is gradually narrowing.

Overeating to compensate for feelings of inadequacy is more prevalent among females than males. It is considered more sex-appropriate for females to eat sweets, and that is why there is more obesity due to overeating among women. Men who suffer from obesity usually overdrink.

As the double standard of moral conduct in the upper and middle socioeconomic groups is being abandoned, so is the use of overeating as a leading female psychological pain-killer. Women and girls of the upper and middle socioeconomic groups today are extremely weight-conscious and are turning more and more to masculine psychological pain-killers, especially excessive smoking and alcoholism. Younger women in the lower socioeconomic groups are also becoming weight-conscious, no longer accepting the traditional views about smoking, drinking, and the use of narcotics (28, 69, 127, 141, 148, 173).

Conformity

The degree to which a person conforms to the mores of the social group with which he is identified—in appearance, speech, and patterns of behavior—is an indication of how well adjusted he is, both personally and socially. Because conformity is intended to fulfill normative group expectations, the person who conforms to these expectations is favorably judged by members of the group. Consequently, he can judge himself favorably.

Too much or too little conformity can be judged only in terms of the norms of the age of the person who is being judged. At certain times, such as late childhood and early adolescence, overconformity is so characteristic that conformity must be almost obsessive to be regarded as a danger signal of personality sickness. Lack of conformity and a desire to assert individuality, on the other hand, are characteristically found in preschool children and older adolescents, especially college students, and are therefore signs of normal adjustment.

Causes of conformity Conformity is not per se a sign of personality sickness. Some people conform, even overconform, because they feel that it is to their personal advantage to do so. The adolescent may readily choose to conform in what he wears, says, and does because he hopes that this will increase his acceptance by members of the peer group.

Most conformity is a product of child training. By conforming to parental demands, the child reduces the anxiety he would experience if he were more independent in his thoughts and actions. In time, conformity becomes a generalized anxiety-reducing experience. The person then reacts to all authority, including the authority of group opinion, in much the same way that he learned to react to parental authority when he was a child. He has become conditioned to conform as a result of his childhood experiences. In discussing conformity-conditioning and the effects it has on the person's behavior, Shaffer and Shoben (174) write:

Conformity-conditioning is one of the devices, found in some form in every culture, by which society maintains its integrity, although often at some cost to the adjustments of the individual persons. . . . If an association between punishment and blame is made very frequently or very strongly, the conditioning generalizes. A person so conditioned then comes to react with fear and submission to any social criticism whatsoever, either expressed or implied. A generalized fear of criticism affects one's perception of other people's actions, just as all strong motives affect the way the world is perceived. Consequently, a person overconditioned to criticism sees slights and insults when none are intended, and in popular speech he is said to be "sensitive." We all have a moderate fear of social scorn, which perhaps is necessary for social control. A stronger degree of fear is disorganizing, because a person is so preoccupied with escaping it or combating it that he does not attend to the satisfaction of his other constructive social wants.

Overconformity When excessive conformity occurs at ages when it is not normally found, it is a danger signal of personality sickness. It shows that the person is suffering from feelings of personal inadequacy and is afraid to do or say anything that might draw the criticism and scorn of others. He may even question his own judgment and hold back from saying or doing what he would like for fear that he might be wrong while others are right. As a result, he has a

"guilt-motivated need to conform." He becomes a "compulsive conformist" who conforms even when it is against his own principles.

That this is a defense mechanism to ward off anxiety and to protect the ego against threats that will intensify an already-existing feeling of personal inadequacy is evident by the fact that many compulsive conformists limit their conformity to times when the group is present. They resent having to relinquish their own beliefs, principles, or autonomy. Hence, when they feel they will not be subject to criticism or scorn, they do or say as they wish.

Certain personality characteristics typically found among compulsive conformists indicate poor personal and social adjustments and thus justify regarding overconformity as a danger signal of personality sickness. Studies reveal that overconformists are rigid, vacillating, intolerant, submissive, lacking in frustration and hostility tolerance, low in interpersonal confidence, readily influenced by peers and authority figures, and compulsively afraid of all in authority. They adhere to orthodox religious beliefs and are lacking in creativity because they are afraid to be different (5, 20, 95, 138).

Underconformity Underconformity, in which a person refuses to conform to social expectations and often chooses a pattern of behavior diametrically opposite to that approved by the group, is a more evident danger signal of personality sickness than is overconformity. The underconformist is showing, by his appearance, his speech, and his actions, that he feels rejected by members of the social group and is "thumbing his nose" at them as a way, usually unconscious, of easing the psychological pain that social rejection brings.

Studies of the personality patterns of underconformists reveal that they have many of the same characteristics as overconformists (5, 95, 139). Instead of showing their self-rejectant attitudes in overconformity, in the hope of bolstering their egos and winning greater social approval and acceptance, they go to the opposite extreme and violate social expectations. They have learned from past experience that violating social expectations gives them greater satisfaction and is more ego-inflating, for the time being at least.

If persons who underconform grew up in a home environment where permissive child training prevailed and if they were in schools where teachers condoned rule violation, they did not develop the "guilt-motivated need to conform" that characterizes those who conform or overconform. Consequently, they believe that they can be laws unto themselves and do as they please, and they find that this kind of behavior gives them greater satisfaction.

Attitude toward conformity When a person conforms because he believes it is the right thing to do and will be to his personal advantage as well as contributing to the welfare of the group, his attitude may be regarded as "healthy."

When, on the other hand, he conforms because he is afraid not to, fearing punishment or social disapproval, his attitude is "unhealthy." If, in addition, he conforms against his better judgment and against his principles, this is further evidence of personality sickness.

Similarly, the attitude of the extreme nonconformist is unhealthy. Flouting mores and repudiating the views of the majority about what is right and best for all concerned shows a lack of respect for others as well as a lack of pride of self. The nonconformist's attitude is, if anything, even more unhealthy than that of the overconformist. As such, it is a danger signal of even greater personality sickness.

Suicide

It is a rare adolescent who does not, at some time or other, think of killing himself because he is a "failure" or because he believes the world is "unfair" to him. Relatively few adolescents go beyond talking, though some do try to commit suicide, if for no other reason than to frighten their parents or teachers into treating them better in the future.

When threats or suicide attempts occur frequently, they are one of the most serious danger signals of maladjustment. They not only show how self-rejectant the person is but also how hopeless he feels about his life situation. Sometimes suicide attempts are impulsive and sometimes premeditated (63, 66). Sometimes the person hopes that, by showing others how great his self-rejection is, he will get them to help with his problems and will, certainly, get them to treat him more sympathetically. Jacobziner (87) explains some of the other factors behind adolescent suicide attempts:

Suicide is, in most cases, a sudden precipitous reaction to a stressful situation resulting from frustration, depression, overt or masked anger, or a rebellious act against a restraining figure, a loved one. It is intended to frighten and to cause the restraining persons to change an attitude or behavior towards the victim. It is often intended as a warning to parents or loved ones, as an expression of dissatisfaction or displeasure with existing unpleasant situations, and as a plea for improved relationships.

Personality patterns of suicide victims Clinical studies of people of different ages who commit suicide, who attempt to do so, or who meet their daily problems by talking about suicide reveal that they all have one characteristic in common, namely, they are strongly self-rejectant. Sometimes this self-rejectant attitude comes from accumulated failures, often failures which they have convinced themselves are due to no fault of their own, and sometimes it comes from the loneliness which results not from environmental isolation but from social isolation.

Regardless of the cause of the self-rejectant attitude, the personality pattern associated with it is characterized by depression and anxiety; by feelings of extreme inadequacy and inferiority; by a belief that the situation is so hopeless that the person is completely helpless to cope with it and is, therefore, a martyr; by the belief that he is the victim of prejudice; by the belief that members of the social group consider him "useless"; and by marked feelings of guilt and shame which have led to self-contempt. Most people who are suicide-prone have long histories of gloominess, withdrawal, anxiety, and other problems. They have suffered from personality sicknesses which have grown progressively worse and have resulted in greater and greater self-rejection (61, 112, 153, 172).

Danger periods in suicide There are certain predictable times when suicide and suicide attempts are more likely to occur. These danger periods coincide with those times in the life span when adjustments are especially difficult and when emotional stress is most common. A person who is poorly adjusted finds it particularly difficult to adjust to the problems that are normal for persons of his age. When he sees his problems mounting, he becomes increasingly self-rejectant, feeling that he is even more of a failure than he was earlier.

Adolescence, with its myriad adjustment problems, is one of the peak danger periods. While the suicidal impulse may have developed earlier, often in later childhood, it is strongest between the ages of 14 and 18 years. This is the most difficult time in the adolescent span for the young person to adjust to his new status and to new social expectations. If he adjusts with reasonable success, suicide-proneness decreases (1, 16, 68).

For women, another critical period comes at middle age, usually between 45 and 54 years. This is a time when women have many difficult adjustments to make, owing to their role-status change as their children grow up and as they find satisfying employment difficult to obtain. The feeling of uselessness and futility which these adjustment problems give rise to intensify any already-existing maladjustment they may experience (59, 61).

Men, by contrast, do not reach a critical period until they face the problems that retirement gives rise to, at the age of 65 or later. If, in addition, they suffer from poor health and feel that their days of usefulness are over, they too experience a feeling of futility. This, combined with any existing maladjustment, predisposes them to think of suicide as the best solution to their problems (59, 61, 80). Figure 14-5 shows the critical periods for suicide and suicide attempts.

Variations in suicide-proneness
At all ages, *males* exceed females in suicide attempts and actual suicide. This is not because males are more maladjusted, but rather because they have been trained and encouraged, since earliest childhood, to be braver and to act more aggressively in stressful situations.

Suicide-proneness is most common among those who regard themselves as *failures*. Even when a person is objectively successful, he may believe that he is a failure because his achievements fall below his aspirations. Those who are objective failures, as shown in failing grades in school and college or in downward social or vocational mobility, are especially suicide-prone.

People who are *introverted* and *egocentric* are more suicide-prone than those who are more socialized. This is well illustrated by the preponderance of suicide notes which put stress on "I" (201). *Unstable* people of all ages are more suicide-prone than the stable (80).

Cultural attitudes toward suicide
Attitudes toward suicide vary from culture to culture. In some Oriental countries, suicide is regarded as a way of upholding personal and family honor; in most Occidental countries, it is regarded as a disgrace to the individual and to all members of his family.

Within a given culture, the more stable the group the less favorable the attitude toward suicide.

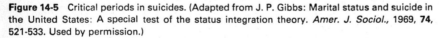

Figure 14-5 Critical periods in suicides. (Adapted from J. P. Gibbs: Marital status and suicide in the United States: A special test of the status integration theory. *Amer. J. Sociol.*, 1969, **74**, 521-533. Used by permission.)

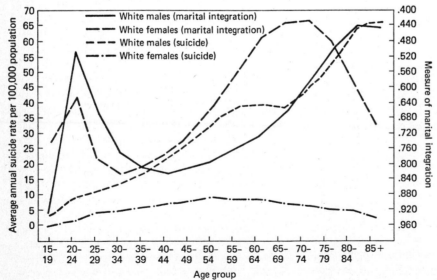

Stability is greater in rural areas and in middle-class families than in urban areas and in upper- and lower-class families. In the former, the attitude of the social group toward suicide is less favorable and more punitive than in the latter (145, 162). Attitudes also vary in different religious groups. The more orthodox the religion, other factors equal, the less tolerant the attitude toward suicide (48, 145, 162).

Since people in our culture are aware of the unfavorable social attitudes toward suicide, an unsuccessful suicide attempt increases their self-rejectant attitude. Where the attempt is successful, unfavorable social attitudes toward the suicide victim and toward other members of his family often lead to family "disgrace."

VARIATIONS IN PERSONALITY SICKNESS

According to tradition, the Quaker said to his wife,"All the world is queer save me and thee; and sometimes I think thee is a little queer." There is a lot of truth in this saying. Everyone has an assortment of foibles and crotchets, even the person who believes, like the Quaker, that he himself is completely immune. However, so long as the person's idiosyncrasies do not disturb his adjustments too much, he can be considered a relatively "normal" person.

It has been estimated by a number of authorities that from 4 to 6 percent of all children have "problem behavior" that points toward some form of maladjustment. Indications of maladjustment increase in frequency and intensity until, among the total population, the number of sick personalities begins to approximate, if not outstrip, the number of healthy ones (43, 109, 133, 179, 220). This is not surprising if, by sick, we mean any deviation from normalcy. In discussing emotional maturity, which is one of the major criteria of mental health, Menninger (132) comments:

Emotional maturity . . . is one of those ideal states and can only be measured by our deviations from it. We don't often get there entirely and totally and if we do, we have daily or hourly fluctuations from it.

How much personality sickness is estimated to exist at any age level—or how serious the sickness is in a particular person—will depend, to some extent, upon the criteria used in making the judgment. A parent, for example, may not regard a child as psychologically sick if he is quiet, withdrawn, hypersensitive, and obedient. But a personologist might regard him as emotionally disturbed and in dire need of diagnosis and treatment (17, 95).

Predictable variations

Although there are exceptions, certain variations in the frequency and severity of personality sickness are predictable. The factors responsible for the variations in frequency and severity are age, sex, socioeconomic status, family size, popularity, and kind of sickness.

Age Personality sickness is more likely to occur at ages when major physical, social, or environmental changes occur in the person's accustomed pattern of living. Such changes mean that the individual must break old habits and establish new ones. This is always accompanied by emotional tension stemming from a fear of inadequacy to make the transition successfully, and so the ego is especially vulnerable to any kind of threat.

Sex Personality sickness is more common among males at certain ages and among females at others. From late adolescence through middle age, neuroses and psychoses are more frequent among girls and women than among boys and men (55). Since these severe forms of sickness develop from the milder forms, it is quite likely that the milder forms are also more frequent among females at these ages.

In the elderly, personality sickness, in major and minor forms, tends to be more widespread among men. As was explained in relation to suicide, many men find the adjustment to retirement a very traumatic experience. Any self-rejection they experienced earlier is intensified if they believe that family members regard them as "useless" now that their wage-earning days are over (50, 70, 169, 183).

Socioeconomic status Personality sickness in all forms is more frequent among members of the lower socioeconomic groups than among the middle and upper groups. It is more common among members of the middle socioeconomic groups than among the higher groups.

The lower the socioeconomic status of the person, the more frustrations he experiences in both his personal and social relationships. Middle-class people suffer from extreme anxiety when they feel they are not getting ahead in school, business, or social life, and this makes them self-rejectant. That suicide is more common among lower- and middle-class people is evidence of the intensity of the self-rejectant attitudes (1, 48, 82, 161, 169).

Family size   One might expect to find more personality sickness in small families, especially the one-child, "spoiled brat" families, than in larger ones. But as a rule, this is not so. The reasons for becoming self-rejectant are fewer when family size is small enough to permit each member to have the love and attention he craves, and so the cause of personality sickness is not present to the same extent as in larger families (95, 109, 148, 170).

The beginning of a self-rejectant attitude can usually be traced to early home experiences. Normally, only children and firstborn children in larger families encounter such favorable and acceptant parental attitudes that they develop into well-adjusted people (179). If parental expectations are unrealistically high, however, and if the children are pressured to live up to such expectations and punished if they fail to do so, there is a likelihood that they will become self-rejectant and defensive.

Popularity   When a person is accepted by others, it is not difficult for him to be reasonably self-acceptant. When he is ignored or rejected, he becomes self-rejectant. How variations in popularity affect the extent to which people rely on fantasy as an ego booster has been discussed by Coleman (33). In this excerpt, he speaks of the mass media in particular:

Those who are in especially favored positions will not need to escape from the world in which they find themselves, and will turn to the world of mass media less often. Conversely, those in a particularly disadvantaged position will often use this way out of their unfavorable environment. . . . When an adolescent is in a system that fails to give him status and allow him a positive self-evaluation, [he] often escapes to a world where he need not have such a negative self-evaluation—the world of mass media.

Kind of personality sickness   While traits such as bossiness, belligerency, bragging, and bullying make people of all ages so unpopular that they cannot fail to develop a self-rejectant attitude, certain conditions in the person's life lead to variations in the kind of personality sickness he develops and in its degree of severity.

Havighurst, as was noted earlier, divides poor adjustment into two major categories, according to the methods the person uses to defend his ego. In the first, the "angry" form of personality sickness, the person has an attitude of general hostility and a tendency to blame others when things go wrong. In the second, "the self-hating" form, the person openly rejects himself and blames himself for his failures. This makes him unhappy and depressed to the point where he longs for death or even threatens to take his life (74).

SERIOUSNESS OF PERSONALITY SICKNESS

Just as physical illness is always serious, so is personality sickness. They should not be taken lightly—and for many of the same reasons, five of which are exceedingly important. *First*, either can and will become progressively worse unless it is diagnosed and treated by a person competent to do so. Just as good adjustment is cumulative, so is maladjustment. Every new experience is assimilated in terms of what has gone before.

Second, personality sickness is not outgrown. Since it does not show itself in pronounced forms in early childhood, it is often overlooked. Or, if it is apparent, parents and teachers far too often assume that the child will outgrow it and, consequently, take no action. Like a minor physical illness, it often becomes a major one if neglected. Bennett (18) declares:

Maladjustive behavior shows a tenacious tendency to remain maladjustive. Forms of activity that succeed in doing the individual far more harm than good remain in operation even in the face of the strongest psychotherapeutic efforts. Minor forms of maladjustive behavior become permanent fixtures in the totality of the individual's behavior and often remain throughout his lifetime. Small things, insignificant in themselves, pile up and add burdens to the day-to-day existence and drain efficiency.

Third, personality sickness spreads through conditioning and becomes general rather than specific. A person may become rebellious against overdomineering parents, and as time goes on, he will come to feel rebellious toward all in authority. He will become a nonconformist or will project his anger on innocent victims and become a sadist, getting great satisfaction from inflicting physical or mental pain on others, especially on those he should normally love.

Fourth, personality sickness leads to or exaggerates already-existing social rejection. A maladjusted person, regardless of what form his personality sickness takes, is not a pleasant person to be associated with. When a person senses or knows that social attitudes toward him are unfavorable, it is hard for him not to be self-rejectant.

The *fifth* and by far the most serious aspect of personality sickness is that it leads to unhappiness not only for the person who experiences it but for all with whom he comes in contact. This is partly because he knows that people are critical and rejectant of him, partly because he feels that he is mistreated and misunderstood, and partly because he is ashamed, either consciously or unconsciously, of the way his personality sickness expresses itself.

The unhappiness that comes from physical or psychological sickness tends to be cumulative and persistent. When a person is physically ill, annoyances and frustrations seem to pile up, one on the other, until he is so unhappy that he is unable to be cheerful or to get any pleasure from life. In time, he gets into the habit of responding to life situations in this gloomy way, and a permanent change takes place in his personality.

If the person who is physically or psychologically ill finds that flight into the world of fantasy helps him to be less self-rejectant, the habit of flight will grow. The feelings of resentment that encourage him to escape into the pleasanter world of fantasy will make his unhappiness even more intense when he is forced to be in the real world.

COPING WITH PERSONALITY SICKNESS

One of the most common traditional beliefs about personality, as has been stressed throughout this book, is that the person will outgrow undesirable personality traits and automatically develop desirable ones. Scientific evidence does *not* substantiate this belief. Instead, it shows that any trait, favorable or unfavorable, will be reinforced by repetition and will become a deep-rooted habit (43, 96).

In coping with personality sickness, personolo-gists must take the same approach that is taken by members of the medical profession in coping with physical illness. This consists of diagnosis to discover the cause of the illness, reports to the patient of the findings to make him aware of what is the matter with him and how minor or serious it is, prescription of whatever therapeutic measure is needed, and often change of environment—even hospitalization—if the personologist feels this is essential to a satisfactory cure.

Before treatment is begun, a diagnosis of the cause of personality sickness must be made. If the danger signals of personality sickness are not recognized by parents and teachers or by the person himself, the sickness may get a strong hold on the person before remedial steps are taken to correct it. Many children do not know the reason for their misconduct or why they do certain things that others regard as unsocial, such as bullying, teasing, or clowning. This is true also of adolescents and adults. They know that they are doing things that antagonize and lose the respect and acceptance of others but they do not know why they do them.

Diagnosis of personality sickness is difficult and time-consuming. Unfortunately, there are no diagnostic techniques for personality sickness today which can be used with the speed and efficiency of medical techniques. Nor can the major part of the diagnosis of personality sickness be made by laboratory technicians. Instead, the diagnosis must be made by trained personologists using techniques which are slow, difficult to apply, and usable only by highly trained therapists.

A complication encountered by personologists is the patient's reticence to discuss his personal problems when they are psychological in origin. He may feel that psychological problems are a stigma or he may not even recognize them as problems. The diagnostic process is slow until the personologist can establish rapport with the patient. Only then can he persuade the patient to talk freely about his problems and to try to recall early childhood experiences which may underlie the problems he is now finding an obstacle to good personal and social adjustments.

In personality sickness, far greater responsibility for the cure must be placed on the shoulders of the patient than in physical disease. Since there are no "wonder drugs" for psychological illness and since the use of drugs and other therapeutic treatments, such as shock therapy, are reserved mostly for acute cases, the personologist's role is limited mainly to diagnosing the cause of the sickness, making his patient aware of his findings, and prescribing the therapeutic technique he should follow. This often puts a heavier burden of responsibility on the patient than he is willing or able to assume.

Regardless of the form personality sickness takes, the fundamental cure consists of a change in the self-concept. No wonder drug or operative technique can be used to achieve this goal. Instead, it must come from the willingness of the person to make a change in the way he views himself and the way he would like to be. Only then can the sickness be cured. Strang (192) writes:

Successful therapy tends to narrow the gap between the "real self" and the "ideal self." Self-acceptance also seems to be increased by therapeutic counseling, in the course of which the client tends to acquire understanding, to become more secure, more self-accepting, less apologetic and self-condemnatory, more realistic in his self-appraisal, and more self-reliant. He may become able to change patterns in himself that he recognizes as undesirable.

To be able to achieve the goal of being less self-rejectant and more self-acceptant, many people need temporary or permanent aids. Two aids have been widely and successfully used to date. *First*, psychological pain-killers, in one form or another, may be used for a short period until the severity of the illness has subsided and the person is able to cope with his problems without this artificial aid. Margaret Mead (144) states, "We should not have to go through the day with a headache. We should not have to face unnecessary anxiety when a pill would relieve the tension. . . . It's very unhealthy not to face certain stresses."

The *second* aid is a change of environment. Just as physical illness is often cured more speedily and more completely by a change of environment, so is personality sickness. A person whose psychological environment is the source of constant frustrations, anxieties, and feelings of inadequacy cannot hope to be cured if he remains in that environment. His condition may improve, with psychotherapeutic treatment and cooperation on his part, but a cure is unlikely.

For example, a person who is constantly subjected to discrimination cannot hope to become a well-adjusted, self-acceptant person so long as he remains in an environment where he is constantly subjected to discrimination. Self-evaluation largely reflects the evaluations of others; if these are unfavorable, so will be the self-evaluation.

Unless members of the social group have a favorable attitude toward a person, remaining in the group will be psychologically damaging to him, and self-rejection will be the predicted outcome. That is why a change of environment is essential if a more healthy self-concept is to be achieved. When such a change is impossible, the obstacles to coping with personality sickness are almost insurmountable.

One cannot overstress the importance of recognizing that, unlike physical illness, which may develop with lightning rapidity, personality sickness normally develops gradually. This permits time for a diagnosis to be made to determine its cause and for remedial measures to be begun before it becomes worse. However, if its symptoms go unrecognized or if the person and members of his family believe that he will outgrow it and do not take steps to diagnose and treat it, the personality sickness may become so deep-rooted that later diagnosis and remedial treatment will be in vain.

SUMMARY

1 Sick personalities are those in which there is a breakdown in the personality structure that results in poor personal and social adjustments. Such personalities are usually labeled "disturbed" by the scientist and "peculiar" or "crazy" by the layman.

2 A so-called "normal personality" is not necessarily a healthy personality. Only when the person's behavior conforms to social expectations and, in so doing, provides him with satisfaction can it be called "healthy." Although "normal" and "abnormal" are used by the layman to describe the person's characteristic pattern of adjustment, they do not take into consideration the person's satisfaction with his behavior. The labels "healthy" and "sick" are more accurate.

3 Just as physical sickness can best be diagnosed by those trained in medicine, so personality sickness can best be diagnosed by those trained in personality diagnosis—the personologists. This is done by formulating a concept of personality health, based on studies of people who are judged to make

good personal and social adjustments, and then using this concept as a standard for comparing the behavior of others to see how well they conform to it or how markedly they deviate.

4 There is evidence that personality sickness is more widespread today than in the past. This may be because it is better recognized than formerly, because there are more records available of poorly adjusted people, or because the stresses and constant changes of modern life predispose people to personality sickness. While personality sickness can occur at any age, the most vulnerable times are when there are marked physical changes or when the person is expected to play radically different roles from those which he formerly played.

5 Personality sickness may come from a physical condition, either glandular or neurological, that upsets body homeostasis, but it generally comes from a psychological condition marked by anxiety which leads to self-rejection. Self-rejection comes from many causes. The most common are unrealistic aspirations; environmental obstacles that keep the person from doing what he wants and is able to do; unfavorable social attitudes; personal limitations of either a physical or psychological nature; severe and prolonged emotional strain; repeated failures; identification with maladjusted people; lack of perspective, which results in the person's exaggeration of his weaknesses; poor child training, especially when strictly authoritarian or overly permissive; and lack of motivation to be self-acceptant when the person falls below his own expectations. Self-rejection is controllable, but, unfortunately, few people know how to control it.

6 Personality sickness may take any one of a number of common forms. These are usually divided into two major categories: first, those which consist of behavior patterns that are satisfying to the person but are socially unacceptable, and second, those which consist of behavior patterns that are socially acceptable but not satisfying to the person.

7 As is true of physical sickness, personality sickness is preceded by signals which alert the person and those with whom he is associated that he is not in a healthy state. The value of these danger signals of personality sickness varies with the age and the sex of the person, though at any age and for members of either sex, they symbolize the fact that an unhealthy psychological state exists.

8 The most common of the danger signals of impending personality sickness, for people of all ages and both sexes, are immaturity of behavior and attitudes, regression to earlier patterns of adjustment which the person found more to his liking, cruelty, antisocial behavior, defense mechanisms, showing off, psychological pain-killers, under-and overconformity, and threats of or attempts at suicide.

9 Predictable variations in personality sickness are influenced by age, sex, socioeconomic status, family size, popularity, and the kind of personality sickness. Knowing these variations makes it possible to predict when and under what conditions personality sickness may develop for a given individual.

10 Personality sickness is a matter of grave concern for many reasons. Such sickness tends to become progressively worse unless it is diagnosed and treated by a competent person before it becomes pronounced; it is not "outgrown"; it tends to spread through conditioning and become general rather than specific; it leads to social rejection or it exaggerates already-existing social rejection; and it leads to unhappiness not only in the person who is psychologically sick but in all with whom he is closely associated.

11 There is little or no evidence that people outgrow personality sickness or that it cures itself in time, as often happens in the case of physical sickness. On the contrary, there is ample evidence that personality sickness, if neglected, tends to worsen and to spread to areas of the person's behavior where it did not exist earlier.

12 Because of the seriousness of personality sickness, an aggressive attack on it is essential. Such an attack involves diagnosing the cause of the sickness, reporting the findings of the diagnosis to the person to alert him about the cause and nature of the trouble, and prescribing therapeutic measures. Each of these steps is difficult. There are no "wonder drugs" for psychological sickness as there are for physical sickness and the person himself must assume a greater responsibility for following the prescribed pattern of treatment than is necesasary in physical sickness.

✝ **13** Because of these difficulties, temporary aids must sometimes be given in the form of psychological pain-killers or changes in the environment to avoid reinforcing the illness. Fortunately, psychological sickness normally develops fairly slowly, thus allowing time to cope with it, provided it is recongized early and provided remedial steps are taken before it becomes established.

CHAPTER 15 healthy personalities

People with healthy personalities are those who are judged to be well adjusted. They are so judged because they are able to function efficiently in the world of people. They experience a kind of "inner harmony" in the sense that they are at peace with others as well as with themselves (3, 79). As Frank has pointed out, "The core of a healthy personality is an image of the self that the individual can accept and live with, without feeling too guilty, anxious, or hostile, without being self-defeated or destructive of others" (49).

Jourard has defined a person with a healthy personality as one who "is able to gratify his needs through behavior that conforms with both the norms of his society and the requirements of his conscience" (73). There are thus two essentials to a healthy personality. The *first* is that the person must not only play his role in life satisfactorily but he must derive satisfaction from it. Satisfaction leads to the emotional state known as happiness or contentment. Without this, the personality cannot be healthy. A person who is chronically dissatisfied with himself and the role he is expected to play in life sooner or later develops a sick personality.

Satisfaction depends largely on whether the person's life pattern meets his needs, interests, and aspirations. When marriage comes up to his expectations, he will be satisfied. If, on the other hand, he feels that his role as parent does not come up to his expectations or that his vocational achievements fall short of his aspirations, even though he plays these roles to the satisfaction of members of the social group, he will be dissatisfied. Cavan has emphasized that "a well-adjusted person is able to satisfy his needs quickly and adequately within the system of controls and outlets provided by his culture" (26).

Maslow has described a person with a healthy personality as one who is "self-actualizing." By self-actualization Maslow means the process of fulfilling the potentials inherent in the person. This is possible only if he can gratify certain basic needs, such as physical satisfactions, safety, esteem, and love. When these basic needs are fully gratified, the person can then turn his energies into tasks that will enable him to fulfill his inherent potentials (85).

The *second* essential to a healthy personality is that the person must play his role in life to the satisfaction of others. He cannot behave in just any way that gives him satisfaction. Instead, he must act in ways that conform to the laws, customs, and moral codes which prevail in his social group and which he is expected to accept as behavioral guides. If he fails to act in accordance with these standards, his conscience will be disturbed. This will lead to feelings of guilt and shame, neither of which contributes to a healthy personality (73, 74).

NUMBER OF HEALTHY PERSONALITIES

It is far more difficult to determine the number of people with healthy personalities than the number who suffer from sick personalities. There are two major reasons for this.

The *first* is the comparative absence of records of people with healthy personalities. Records of those with sick personalities are available in mental institutions and mental health clinics and in school, college, and vocational reports. Even as rough and incomplete as these records are, they give some idea of what percentage of the general population is regarded as having sick personalities of minor or major severity.

Since no attempt is made to keep records of those who are judged to have healthy personalities, the only way to estimate how many fall in this category is to subtract the percentage of the population known to have sick personalities from 100 percent and thus have a rough estimate of the percentage regarded as pyschologically healthy. Certainly this method is far from reliable, just as is the method of determining the percentage with sick personalities. It is most unlikely that all those with sick personalities are accounted for in the available records.

The *second* reason for the difficulty in determining how many people have healthy personalities is the ambiguity about what constitutes a healthy personality. Many regard the person who is not troublesome and who makes reasonably good adjustments to other people and to life situations in general as healthy. But these criteria fail to take into consideration the essential requirement that the person's adjustment must also bring him satisfaction.

Others regard "healthy" as synonymous with "normal," "ideal," or "characteristic of the average" (86, 112). To still others, "healthy" means 100 percent healthy, the absence of any form or degree of sickness. As in physical health, it is questionable whether there is anyone who does not have some degree of psychological disturbance. This was stressed in the case of children by Thompson (120):

Normal adjustment is a relative thing. Every child suffers some anxiety, displays some behavior that is unacceptable to others, fails to reach some goals that are extremely important to him, and experiences some periods of what he calls unhappiness.

Thus, while it is difficult to establish even roughly how many people have healthy personalities, it is relatively safe to say that the number with healthy personalities still outweighs the number with sick personalities. It is also relatively safe to say that the percentage of people with healthy personalities is decreasing, since information about the number of sick personalities points to their increase. Of the many reasons given for the decrease in the number of people who are regarded as well adjusted, the following are most often suggested:

Increase in stress, owing to the quickening tempo of modern life

Increase in the use of automation, which militates against feelings of individuality and self-worth

Laxity of discipline and law enforcement, which eliminates the guidelines to behavior that are essential to feelings of security

Increased pressure for achievement

Increased pressure for popularity and social acceptance

Increased desire to get ahead, which means social mobility with its damaging effects on feelings of security and belonging

Rapid social change, which means ambiguity about the roles the person is expected to play, especially sex roles

Increase in number of elderly people who, because of unfavorable social attitudes toward them, often develop personality sickness

Breakdown in patterns of family life which could in the past be counted on to give feelings of security to every family member

Breakdown in religious interests and practices, formerly an important source of personal security

Increased coverage of crime and other antisocial patterns of behavior in the mass media

DIAGNOSING HEALTHY PERSONALITIES

Just as sick personalities can be diagnosed successfully only by those who are trained to do so, so can healthy personalities. External behavior alone does not tell the full tale. Both of the criteria described above must be considered: Is the person gaining satisfaction from the role he plays in life in addition to behaving in such a way that his characteristic patterns of adjustment meet social expectations?

Appraisals of healthy personalities, as is true of sick personalities, can best be made by personologists who have set up standards, based on studies of people who are regarded as well or poorly adjusted, to determine what the characteristics of a well-adjusted person are. These characteristics are then used as the norm by which a particular individual is evaluated. Tests, observations of behavior, self-reports by the person, and other diagnostic techniques are used to see how he compares with the norm for people who are judged to be well adjusted.

One point to emphasize about the norm for healthy personalities is that it is based on characteristics that are recognized and valued not by the layman alone but by personologists whose studies have provided them insight into what constitutes good or bad mental health.

From studies of people who make good personal and social adjustments, the personologist knows the characteristics of well-adjusted people in general, not of one specific well-adjusted person. This provides the basis on which he formulates an explicit and detailed concept of a healthy personality (73).

In determining the characteristics of a self-actualizing person, Maslow studied a sample of real people whom he judged to be self-actualizing to determine what characteristics they had in common. While not all the people whom he judged to be self-actualizing had all the characteristics, most of them had a majority of the characteristics.

All the self-actualizing people, for example, accepted themselves and others. All of them showed an interest in problems outside themselves and had some mission in life or some task they wanted to fulfill. All of them were autonomous in the sense that they were independent of environmental pressures in making decisions about their actions. And all showed some "imperfections" (85).

CHARACTERISTICS OF HEALTHY PERSONALITIES

From studies of people of all age levels, of both sexes, and of different socioeconomic and cultural backgrounds, personologists have identified a number of characteristics which are found in people who are well adjusted and who, therefore, have healthy personalities. Just as no one with a sick personality suffers from all forms of personality sickness, so does no one with a healthy personality have *all* the characteristics identified with those who are regarded as psychologically healthy.

Of the many characteristics of healthy personalities, the following are the most common: realistic self-appraisals, realistic appraisal of situations, realistic evaluation of achievements, acceptance of reality, acceptance of responsibility, autonomy, acceptable emotional control, goal orientation, outer orientation, social acceptance, philosophy-of-life-directed, and happiness.

Realistic self-appraisals

The well-adjusted person sees himself as he is, not as he would like to be. The gap between the real and the ideal self-concepts, so wide in those who suffer from personality sickness, is very much smaller among the well adjusted. Since the well-adjusted person can appraise himself, his abilities, and his achievements realistically, he does not need to use defense mechanisms to try to convince himself and others that his failure to come up to his expectations is the fault of others or of environmental conditions over which he has no control.

Nor does he have to use psychological painkillers to dull the distress and anxiety he suffers when he fails to come up to his expectations. This does not

mean that he is resigned to the inevitable, that he feels powerless in the face of overwhelming odds or has developed a defeatist attitude. It means simply that he is realistic.

The person who is realistic about himself does not have to try to devalue the source of unfavorable social evaluations in an attempt to prove to himself or others that the evaluations are incorrect or unfair. Instead, he accepts adverse evaluations as a form of constructive criticism and tries to improve qualities that others judge unfavorably.

If the well-adjusted person does not like what he sees in himself or what others see in him, he is ready and willing to change. By so doing, he finds it easier to accept himself and to be happy about himself. He can then regard himself as worthy, even if not perfect. As a result, he has a healthy regard for his rights and is willing to stand up for them should he be challenged.

Realistic appraisal of situations

A well-adjusted person does not expect to be perfect, nor does he expect the situations in which he finds himself to be perfect. He approaches situations with a realistic attitude, accepting the bad with the good. This does not mean that he has a defeatist attitude or that he projects the blame onto someone else when things are not to his liking. Rather, he is willing to do what he can to make the situation more to his liking. Such a person has a constructive approach to life.

In his realistic appraisal of situations, the well-adjusted person recognizes that no one can be a law unto himself—that he can do whatever he wants, when he wants. He realizes that there must be rules of conduct which protect the rights of others and himself, and he is willing to abide by them even when they are not entirely to his liking.

Unlike the maladjusted person, who shows a contempt for rules and laws and becomes antisocial, the well-adjusted person is realistic enough to recognize that by doing things that are in conflict with the expectations of others he is hurting himself as well as others. He realizes that the temporary satisfaction he might derive from antisocial behavior is more than offset by the unfavorable opinions of members of the social group toward him and their rejection of him. In short, he finds that it pays to be a law-abiding citizen rather than a troublemaker or lawbreaker.

The well-adjusted person's realistic appraisal of situations is shown by his realization that success is not handed to a person on a silver platter. He recognizes that success comes only with hard work, the willingness to make personal sacrifices, and pass up immediate pleasures in favor of the long-term gains he is striving for.

The person who is able to appraise a situation realistically recognizes that some situations are "work situations" and others are "play situations." He then knows when to work and when to play. The schoolchild who daydreams because school bores him or cuts up to win the attention of his classmates is just as poorly adjusted as the person who is such a compulsive worker that he feels guilty when he takes time off from work to relax. In both, maladjustment is shown by their inability to recognize that their behavior is annoying and harmful to others as well as to themselves.

A person who is well adjusted recognizes that, if he encounters environmental obstacles which are beyond his control, he will only meet defeat if he continues to fight against them. Under such conditions, the realistic approach to the situation is not to complain about it or develop a martyr complex, as the maladjusted person does, but to try to change the situation so that such obstacles will not be encountered. A very bright child in a school with children of average or below average intelligence is just as much a misfit as a trained and experienced executive in a minor clerical job.

When conditions make it impossible to change environments, a well-adjusted person will adjust to the inevitable and develop interests and activities to compensate for the lack of need fulfillment in his present environment. The bright child, for example, can develop intellectual interests and pursuits, often encouraged and directed by his teachers, to supplement the work given in his classes. The adult whose job provides too little interest and challenge to meet his needs can compensate by developing avocational interests that do.

Realistic evaluation of achievements

A well-adjusted person is able to evaluate his achievements realistically and to react to them in a rational way. This contrasts with the maladjusted person who regards his successes as a personal triumph which shows others his superiority over them. The maladjusted person allows himself to develop a superiority complex which he expresses in boasting, bragging,

and derogatory comments about those whose achievements fall below his.

In explaining how a well-adjusted person reacts to his successful achievements, Lawton remarks, "He does not magnify his successes or extend their application from the field in which they originally occurred" (79).

In contrast with the maladjusted person who regards his failures as a stigma, who allows himself to become embittered, or who projects the blame onto others, the well-adjusted person "draws lessons from his defeats" (79). He assesses them rationally to see where the blame lies instead of assuming that he was not at fault.

Nor does the well-adjusted person develop a martyr complex—feeling that he is the victim of bad luck or discrimination—or a defeatist complex, which leads him to believe that he will be a failure in whatever he undertakes. Instead, he is actively optimistic. Thompson (120) explains the effect of failure on well-adjusted children:

The child whose psychological adjustment can be considered within normal range "bounces back" from . . . disappointments and depressions. He continues to orient his behavior toward goals that promise to satisfy his needs, and he adjusts his goal-setting to the social demands of his culture.

The well-adjusted person assesses the tasks in which he has achieved success or failure, according to the judgments of others, to determine what his performance actually was. He tries to find out whether his success was really due to lack of competition, which made his achievement appear greater than it truly was, whether he had enough innate ability to achieve success with minimum effort, or whether he won it by hard work.

Similarly, he evaluates his failures realistically to see if they were actually failures *for him* or whether they were due to competition with persons whose abilities were greater than his. He also considers whether he tried hard enough and, if he did not, whether his lack of effort was due to laziness, fear of failure, or some other cause. In addition, he assesses his aspirations to see if they were realistic and, if not, he profits by his failure, setting his future aspirations at a more realistic level.

Whether achievements are successes or failures, the well-adjusted person does not rest on his laurels when he succeeds or give up when he fails. He accepts the outcome as a challenge to work harder and do better in the future. He thus profits by his successes as well as by his failures.

Acceptance of reality

One of the characteristics of a well-adjusted person is his willingness to accept reality instead of running away from it. While he may not like things as they are, he is realistic enough to know that he can either change them or change to a locale where things will be more to his liking.

In many areas, acceptance of reality is essential to a healthy personality. The person must learn to accept his *limitations,* either physical or psychological, if he cannot change them and to do what he can with what he has. He can also compensate for his limitations by improving those characteristics in which he is strongest. The poorly adjusted person, by contrast, develops a martyr complex, feeling sorry for himself or blaming himself or others for his limitations.

Every cultural group assigns a certain *role* to a person and expects the person to play it. The sex role, for example, is well defined. Since a person cannot change his sex, he must play the role approved by the social group if he wants to be socially accepted and self-acceptant. When a role can be changed, such as the vocational role, a well-adjusted person will change it if it is not to his liking. Clinging to a role that does not fill his needs if he can change it leads to feelings of martyrdom and of resentment against those who he feels are forcing him to play the role. Neither of these will contribute to a healthy personality.

A realistic person accepts the fact that life is often difficult. He recognizes that his successes and satisfactions to a large extent compensate for his failures and disappointments. As Lawton (79) states:

[*The well-adjusted person*] *would not change, even if he could, the fact that life is an endless struggle in which human purposes are hurled against external resisting forces, human and natural. He knows, and makes use of the knowledge, that in this struggle the person who fights himself least will have the most strength and the best judgment left for the outside battle.*

The person who accepts reality knows that no one can turn back the hands of the clock or skip over the present and land in the future. He knows that he must *live in the present*, even though he feels that the past or the future would be more to his liking. Lawton further declares that the well-adjusted person "partici-

pates with pleasure in the experiences that belong to each successive age level, neither anticipating those of a later period nor holding on to those of an earlier period" (79).

Children and adolescents often live in anticipation of the time when they will be grown-up; they can imagine all the pleasures and freedoms that adults enjoy but they have little recognition of the responsibilities that go with adulthood. It is also very common for middle-aged people to count the days until they can retire, when everything as they see it will be rosy. They do not realize the loneliness and economic hardship that old age often brings.

Similarly, many people who are disillusioned with the present yearn for the good old days. They spend their time in memories and fantasies, dwelling on the pleasures and triumphs of youth. How damaging this can be to good adjustment has been explained by Brien: "Nostalgia can become a drug, a form of self-abuse, a fantasy alternative time track, which excuses failures in the present" (16).

No matter how unpleasant the real world is, the well-adjusted person does not try to *escape* into a world of fantasy where he can have everything to his liking. Instead, he "accepts the authority of reality: that is, he finds the major satisfactions of life in accomplishments and experiences that take place in the real world and not in the realm of day-dreams and make-believe" (79).

This, of course, does not mean that a person whose personality is healthy does not at times engage in fantasy. It merely means that escape into the daydream world is not his characteristic pattern of adjusting to difficult or unpleasant real-life situations. When he does daydream, his escape is short and he returns to the real world to face the problems there.

Acceptance of responsibility

The "let-John-do-it" people are poorly adjusted. They are either too lazy to accept responsibility or they feel inadequate to do so. By contrast, the well-adjusted person is a responsible person. He feels confident of his ability to cope with life and its problems and to take responsibilities suited to his age and level of ability. Figure 15-1 shows a "let-John-do-it" boy who is only too willing to let his mother clean up after he has entertained his friends.

The well-adjusted person is enough of a realist to recognize that he should not accept responsibilities that he is unprepared to carry out successfully. He

Figure 15-1 Acceptance of responsibility is a sign of personality health, whereas avoidance of responsibility is a sign of personality sickness.

knows that by doing so he will not only win social disapproval for his failures but will undermine his self-confidence to the point where he will be hesitant to accept future responsibilities. He accepts the challenge of his abilities but he does not have a compulsion to overrate them.

The person who is well adjusted accepts responsibility in a number of areas. He accepts responsibility for *himself and for his behavior*. If things go wrong and if he is criticized, he accepts the blame and is willing to admit that he made a mistake. This contrasts with the poorly adjusted person who depends on others for help whenever he meets an obstacle or has to tackle a new problem and who blames others for his mistakes.

When a problem arises, the well-adjusted person accepts the responsibility for tackling that problem and trying to solve it. The well-adjusted person, according to Lawton, "attacks problems that require solution instead of finding means to evade them. He enjoys attacking and destroying obstacles to his development and happiness, once he has decided that they are real and not imaginary obstacles" (79).

Even though a well-adjusted person may "object to a particular *role* or position in life, so long as he must fill it he willingly accepts the responsibilities and the experiences that pertain to this role or position" (79). The girl who does not like her sex role but knows she cannot change it accepts the responsibilities that go with that role just as does the stepmother who may find the role she accepted when she fell in love with a widower with children not what she had anticipated. As one wife put it, "When you say Yes to a man you say Yes to the dishes."

When the well-adjusted person meets *obstacles* in the path he has decided to follow, he assumes responsibility for coping with these obstacles instead of expecting someone else to do so. He may ask advice or help if he does not know how to cope with them or feels inadequate to do so alone, but he does not relinquish his reponsibility to another as the poorly adjusted person does.

Acceptance of responsibility means that the well-adjusted person is *dependable*. People know they can count on him and on his word. If he says that he will be at a certain place at a certain time, they know he will be there unless he meets some situation over which he has no control. If he says he will do something, they know it will not only be done but that it will be done when he said it would.

This is in direct contrast to the poorly adjusted person who has an excuse for everything and who is chronically late in meeting appointments and in doing what he said he would do. As a result, his life is a maze of broken promises and unfinished business which, in time, leads to broken friendships when the people who had depended on him find that he is unreliable.

Autonomy

Closely related to acceptance of responsibility is autonomy. The well-adjusted person is not only independent in thought and actions; he is, in addition, self-directing and self-governing in that he charts the course of his life to meet his needs and wants. Says Barrett-Lennard, "He trusts and depends on his own capacities to organize and interpret the data of his experience. He freely steers his own course" (5).

Since he is self-directing, the well-adjusted person can respect himself as an individual who has selected his life pattern to meet his own needs and wants just as he can respect others, even though he may not approve the life patterns they have selected. This is in contrast to those who are afraid to be autonomous because of threats of social criticism or feelings of inadequacy when not conforming to the letter to the group pattern.

The well-adjusted person shows his autonomy in several ways. In *decision making*, he is able to "make important decisions with a minimum of worry, conflict, advice-seeking, and other types of running-away behavior. After making a choice, he abides by it, until new factors of crucial importance enter into the picture" (79).

Autonomy shows itself in *independence*. The autonomous person does not depend on others when he is capable of being independent. As Brower has explained, one of the characteristics of the well-adjusted person is the "degree to which he has resolved his dependencies and can function independently of social influences" (18). He is, thus, self-motivated.

Studies reveal that a major difference between well- and poorly adjusted old people lies in the greater degree of autonomy the former have been able to achieve. Instead of depending on grown children, relatives, or friends, the well-adjusted elderly person cultivates new friendships, new interests, and new leisure-time activities to take up the hours formerly devoted to home or vocational responsibilities. He directs his life to meet his needs and interests instead of expecting others to plan his affairs for him (62, 63).

While a well-adjusted person *conforms* to the mores of the group with which he is identified and so keeps abreast of changing ideas, interests, and activities, he does not feel that he must rubber-stamp everything other people wear, do, or say. Just as the overconformist or nonconformist shows signs of personality sickness, so the reasonable conformist shows signs of personality health.

Acceptable emotional control

Acceptable emotional control, as was stressed in Chapter 8, cannot be imposed by others. The person must assume the responsibility for keeping his emotions under control so that they will not hurt others or himself. For example, he must learn not to blow his top when he is angry or sink into a mood of deep despair when things do not turn out as he had hoped they would. In short, he must be able to meet frustrations without violence or destruction.

A well-adjusted person can live comfortably with his emotions. This is possible because he had developed, over a period, a degree of stress tolerance—anxiety tolerance, depression tolerance, and pain and privation tolerance. If this were not so, he would be constantly emotionally disturbed even though he might have learned to repress the expression of his emotions sufficiently that others regard him as emotionally mature.

In describing the emotional behavior of a well-adjusted person, Lawton (79) states:

He is able to show his anger directly when injured and to act in defense of his rights, with both indignation and action appropriate in kind and amount to the injury. He is able to show his affection directly and to give evidence of it in acts that are fitting in amount and kind to its extent. He can endure pain, especially emotional pain and frustration, whenever it is not in his power to alter the cause.

Goal orientation

Most people have goals they hope to reach. There are, however, two major differences between well- and poorly adjusted people in this respect. The *first* is that the well-adjusted set realistic goals while those who are poorly adjusted set more unrealistic goals than realistic ones. When the well-adjusted set goals which they later find are unrealistic, they are willing to lower them to more realistic levels.

The *second* major difference between well- and poorly adjusted people in goal-setting is that the well adjusted make it their business to acquire the knowledge and skills needed to reach their goals. Even if they encounter occasional setbacks, they do not give up. They improve their knowledge or skills or they lower their goals to more realistic levels. The poorly adjusted, by contrast, do not organize their time and effort to make the best use of their innate potentials. Instead, they fulfill their aspirations either by trying to get help from others or in fantasy.

The result is that a well-adjusted person is a well-organized one. He integrates his various functions and roles in life according to a consistent, harmonious pattern. He is thus able to make the best use of his time and effort, and this increases his chances of reaching his goals. This, of course, does not mean that he is a compulsive worker or that he is driven to achievements by someone else. The goals are set by him, rather than imposed upon him by others, and so he has a strong motivation to do all he can to achieve them.

Outer orientation

Well-adjusted people are outer-oriented while those who are poorly adjusted tend to be inner-oriented or self-bound. The former belong to the group known as "extroverts" while the latter are "introverts." Most young children are self-bound, largely because their helplessness makes them dependent on others to do things for them. As children acquire skills and knowl-edge, those who are well-adjusted start to turn out-ward. Boys tend to be slightly more extroverted than girls, and girls show a regressive trend toward in-troversion from the time they reach puberty.

Turning inward, a characteristic sign of poor adjustment, may be explained by the fact that at puberty and early adolescence, both boys and girls are less satisfied with themselves than they were earlier and than they will normally be later. This is especially true of girls who find it difficult to accept the approved feminine sex role after having enjoyed considerable freedom as children, when their role was more similar to that of boys.

When a person is outer-oriented, he shows an interest in people, situations, and things. He derives more satisfaction from social than from self contacts. This contrasts with the self-bound person, who shows more interest in self.

The well-adjusted person's interest in others is revealed in a number of ways. He is *unselfish* about his time, effort, and material possessions. He is willing to respond in any way he can to the needs of others and does not regard it as an imposition. The ability to *empathize* with others, to understand and to sym-pathize with them in happiness and sorrow without feeling envious of their successes or scornful of their failures, is common among the well adjusted and uncommon among the poorly adjusted.

Even more characteristic of the well-adjusted person is a well-balanced and mature capacity for loving and being loved. This does not mean a childish infatuation or a showering of affection on persons who show little interest in him, nor does it mean a demand for love and attention from those he admires regardless of how they feel about him. Rather, it means a mature, well-controlled giving and accepting of af-fection with those for whom there is mutual admira-tion, respect, and affiliation.

Interest in others helps the well-adjusted person to gain enough *perspective* on himself and his abili-ties, as compared with the abilities of his peers, to prevent the development of delusions of grandeur. The well-adjusted person is thus able to recognize and acknowledge his feelings and reactions. If he does not like what he sees, he is ready to change. This contrasts with the poorly adjusted person who regards himself as near perfect and who, as a result, has no desire or motivation to change.

Because he does not suffer from delusions of grandeur, the well-adjusted person is *flexible in his thinking*. He is not so opinionated that he believes he is always right and that those who disagree with him are always wrong. Instead, he is honest with himself and presents himself to others as he is. He has the humility to say, "I was wrong." If, on the other hand, he is proved right, he does not gloat over those who disagreed with him and say, "I told you so."

Since he has no delusions of grandeur, he is not cruel to others, as is so characteristic of the poorly adjusted. The well-adjusted person is *kind* in his reac-tions to others, even when they are unkind to him. This does not mean that he is always willing to turn the other cheek and ignore another's unkindnesses but that he regards them more with sympathy than with anger.

The outer-bound person, who likes and respects others, is willing to disclose to them his thoughts and feelings. A reasonable degree of *self-disclosure* is a common characteristic of well-adjusted people. This does not mean indiscriminate self-disclosure but rather self-disclosure to those the person likes and respects as friends. Poorly adjusted people, who tend to be emotionally unstable, often disclose more about themselves than do the emotionally stable, and they are more indiscriminate in the targets they select for self-disclosure. By contrast, lack of self-disclosure is common in those who are psychologically maladjust-ed and who suffer from different forms of personality sickness (72, 100).

The well-adjusted person discloses his thoughts, feelings, or aspirations only to those who he believes will be understanding and sympathetic and who will not blab to others. The persons to whom he is willing to talk freely will change from one age level to another and even within the same age level if he loses confidence in them (74, 75).

Some of the indications of the well-adjusted person's outer orientation have been summarized by Barrett-Lennard (5):

He genuinely appreciates and values others as he does himself. He is comfortable and open with them be-cause he is comfortable and open with himself. He is not guarded in a personal sense because he has nothing to hide. He does not distort himself to please others, nor does he use them as scapegoats for self-dissatisfaction.

Social acceptance

People with sick personalities are far less pleasant to be with than those whose personalities are healthy.

And since people with healthy personalities are more popular than those with sick personalities, they are happier and better satisfied with themselves.

Knowing that they are positively evaluated by others not only fosters a favorable self-concept in the well adjusted, but also leads to greater social participation. The well adjusted see themselves as adequate to meet social challenges, demands, and expectations, and so they are willing to participate in social activities and are highly capable of identifying with other people.

A person who is well accepted has no need for boasting, showing off, or other patterns of behavior characteristic of maladjusted people who are trying to win greater social acceptance. He can be natural, at ease, and friendly in his relationships with others, and all this increases his social acceptance.

The degree to which a person adjusts to others in the home, in school, in business, or in social life and the degree of harmony that exists in his interpersonal relationships are good indications of how well adjusted he is. Even though he may have little in common with those with whom he is associated, he makes it his business to get along with them if circumstances make it impossible for him to seek the companionship of persons whose interests are more similar to his and who would meet his needs better.

Philosophy-of-life-directed

Just as well-adjusted people are goal-oriented, so do they direct their lives by a philosophy which helps them to formulate plans to meet their goals in a socially approved way. This philosophy of life may be based on religious beliefs, it may be based mainly on what they believe is right because it is best for all concerned, or it may be based on personal experiences.

The poorly adjusted person does what he wants without considering others or he does what others urge him to do even if he knows that is considered wrong by the social group as a whole. By contrast, the well-adjusted person has a morality based on recognition of the greatest good for the greatest number and on the belief that he should follow the guidelines of his moral code even if that would make him unpopular with members of the peer group.

Many well-adjusted people have a philosophy of life that is influenced by, if not actually based upon, religious faith. They regard religion as a personal experience and accept the parts of their faith that meet their needs best. The poorly adjusted, however, tend to reject all religions and claim to be atheists or they cling to an orthodox faith that puts more emphasis on religious practices than on religious beliefs (27, 76, 82). For them, religion is often a crutch or an escape mechanism for feelings of insecurity and unhappiness (94).

Happiness

One of the outstanding characteristics of the well-adjusted person is happiness. This means that in the well-adjusted person happiness outweighs unhappiness and the person is an essentially happy person. By contrast, unhappiness dominates in personality sickness to the extent that the person often contemplates or attempts suicide (91).

Conditions contributing to happiness Three conditions contribute to the happiness of the well-adjusted person. All enhance the person's self-concept and lead to reasonable self-satisfaction. These conditions have been called the "Three A's of Happiness": Achievement, Acceptance, and Affection. Figure 15-2 shows the three A's of happiness.

ACHIEVEMENT Although it is popularly believed that a person can best be happy when he is free from responsibilities and thus "carefree," there is little evidence that this is true. Children who have no responsibilities are bored and unhappy; they suffer from feelings of personal inadequacy and inferiority because they have no accomplishments to be proud of or to be praised for (18, 60).

Adults who look forward to the day when they will be free from the cares and responsibilities life has imposed upon them find that, when the time comes for retirement or when the children are grown and

Figure 15-2 The three A's of happiness.

away from home, life is not as rosy as is had seemed in fantasies. Feeling useless and unwanted leads to unhappiness rather than to the happiness they had anticipated.

By contrast, achievements lead to a sense of personal satisfaction and pride. If the achievements are recognized by others, personal pride and satisfaction are greatly increased. Even when achievements fall below personal or social expectations, the person who is recognized for his efforts and is commended for them derives satisfaction and tries harder in the future.

Three factors influence the amount of satisfaction the person derives from his achievements. *First* the more closely his achievements match his expectations, the greater his satisfaction. If his expectations are unrealistic, the chances that his achievements will come up to his expectations are so slim that dissatisfaction is inevitable.

Second, satisfaction will be greater if the achievement is in an area that is valued by the person. If it is important to him to achieve success in social life, he will be dissatisfied with himself if he fails to do so, even though his achievements may be high in other, relatively unvalued areas, such as scholarship.

Since what is valued by a person is largely determined by the prestige it has among members of the social group, the *third* condition that influences the degree of satisfaction the person derives from his achievements is how members of the group with which he is identified, especially those who are significant to him, feel about his achievements. If the young child's mother is lavish in her praise of his being able to dress himself without help, this achievement will give him great satisfaction. As he grows older and people outside the home become more important to him, their attitudes will influence his satisfaction with his accomplishments.

ACCEPTANCE The more popular a person is, the more reason he has to be satisfied with himself and, in turn, to be happy. However, being popular with just anyone is not enough. Real self-satisfaction can come only from being popular with the people the person wants to be popular with. If he wants to be identified with the leading crowd in school, he will not be happy if he has to settle for the acceptance of a group that is looked down upon by the leading crowd and by the majority of his peers. Similarly, an adult who wants to be invited to the social affairs of the community

leaders will not be made happy by receiving invitations from those who have no social rating in the community.

Popularity is more desired at certain times in the life span than at others. Also popularity means more to some people than to others. It is more important to the average adolescent, for example, than to the young child or the elderly person, for whom family acceptance is more desired. Because females associate greater prestige with popularity than males, social acceptance plays a more important role in determining the degree of happiness females experience.

AFFECTION Even young children sense the affection others have for them. Each year, as their social perception increases, they are better able to know how much affection others have for them. If they feel that others love them, this goes a long way toward making them happy.

Conversely, the belief that others have little or no affection for them is at the root of much of the unhappiness poorly adjusted people experience. The young child who suffers from lack of love, owing to the absence of one or both parents or to parental rejection; the handicapped person who believes that he is a nuisance and, therefore, unloved; or the elderly person who feels that his days of usefulness to his family and to society have passed—all experience unhappiness because they believe they are unloved.

Popularity and affection from others do not necessarily go hand in hand. A person may have many friends because his family's prestige or money enable him to entertain or to have status symbols that arouse the envy of others, but that does not guarantee that he will be genuinely liked. People may like him for what he can do for them rather than for himself as a person.

As was stressed earlier, leaders are often respected and admired but not loved. This is largely because they do not want to establish any warm, close relationships but want to be on friendly terms with all. Others regard them as cold, aloof, and impersonal—traits which do not encourage others to show emotional warmth toward them.

As is true of popularity, affection from a person the individual wants to have a close, warm relationship with is far more important to his happiness than affection from someone who means little to him. The more significant a person is to another, the greater the happiness his affection will bring.

Variations in conditions contributing to happiness Not one of these three conditions leading to happiness—achievement, acceptance, or affection—will, alone, lead to happiness. The person who is popular will not be happy if he does not receive affection from those who are important to him, nor will he be happy if he is successful but unloved. The socially mobile person whose economic success is not accompanied by acceptance and affection derives little happiness from what he has striven so hard to achieve.

Relatively few people experience the three essentials to happiness in the degree they want to experience them. This is largely because they have unrealistic expectations. They want to achieve more than their ability or their willingness to work makes possible. Similarly, few are satisfied with being accepted and loved by those who will accept and love them. They aspire to friendships with those who do not find them congenial and to love from those who do not reciprocate their interest.

It thus becomes apparent that the person can be happy only when he has a realistic enough appraisal of his abilities and potentials to develop realistic aspirations and expectations. So long as his self-appraisals are unrealistic, his aspirations and expectations will be unrealistic and he cannot expect to be happy.

Studies of people who are happy reveal that one of the essentials of their happiness is prompt satisfaction of their needs. If one has a need to be loved, for example, waiting to find a person who loves one enough to propose marriage will not bring happiness. On the other hand, the young woman who has plenty of dates and is beseeched to go steady is happy because she is getting prompt satisfaction of her need at that time.

In the same way, a person who has a strong need for success will be far happier if he is successful when he is young than if he has to wait until middle or old age. While eventual success will, unquestionably, bring happiness, it will come only after years of disappointment.

Persistence of any unfilled need inevitably leads to unhappiness. If the person needs to be a success to be happy and if his aspirations are so unrealistically high that he never achieves as great success as he had hoped for, he will be persistently unhappy. In time, the habit of unhappiness will be so deeply rooted that, even though he may eventually achieve up to his expectations, he will be far less satisfied with them and, consequently, far less happy than if the habit of unhappiness had not marred the joy that normally accompanies success.

Thus, there is no one thing that will bring happiness nor is there persistent happiness throughout the life span. Happy people, as was pointed out earlier, however, have certain characteristics in common. A study by Wilson (134) concluded that:

The happy person is a young, healthy, well-educated, well-paid, extroverted, optimistic, worry-free, religious, married person with high self-esteem, high job morale, modest aspirations, of either sex and of a middle range of intelligence.

Perhaps the most telling characteristics in this list are modest aspirations, extroverted, healthy, and optimistic. If the person's aspirations are modest, he is not likely to be unrealistic and hence, not likely to fall below his aspirations and regard himself as a failure. As an extrovert, he is likely to be popular and to receive affection from others—two conditions essential to happiness. Being healthy contributes to happiness at any age. And, finally, an optimistic outlook on life is a healthy outlook without which it is difficult to be happy.

HEALTHY PERSONALITY SYNDROME

There is no one trait that leads to good adjustments to self, to others, or to life in general. On the other hand, many of the characteristics described above are found in those who are regarded as well-adjusted people. It is therefore possible to conclude that a cluster of characteristics make up the well-adjusted syndrome or the "healthy personality syndrome" (21).

Once again, it should be stressed that not every well-adjusted person has all these characteristics. Nor does the absence of one or more of them necessarily indicate poor adjustment. The one thing that is inevitably a part of this syndrome is that the person enjoys a kind of "inner harmony"; he is at peace with himself just as he is at peace with others. Bain (3) has summarized the main characteristics of the person with a healthy personality syndrome:

He thinks, acts, and feels according to what is expected and tolerated within his society. . . . He is both satisfied and stimulated by the life he leads. He has the

habit of happiness and the habit of making and break-
ing habits effectively. He is neither unduly frightened
by the future nor wedded to the past . . . . He has no
sense of sin but he profits by experience. He has a
sturdy sense of humor which laughs with people, not
at them. He knows his limitations and capacities and
acts accordingly. He has a fairly accurate judgment of
others and of what others think of him . . . . He makes
his goals and ideals consistent with his knowledge of
what is possible, and he is open-minded about the
"possible." He respects himself because he respects
others . . . . He wants an opportunity to realize his
own potentials so long as it does not prevent others
from doing the same.

CAUSES OF HEALTHY PERSONALITIES

No one is born with a sick or healthy personality. The
kind of personality pattern the person develops depends largely upon his life experiences. If these experiences are favorable, his personality will be healthy. If
they are unfavorable, the chances are that he will
develop a sick personality.

Healthy personalities, like sick personalities, result from both physical and psychological causes.
While both physical and psychological causes play a
major role, the psychological appear to be more important.

Physical causes

A healthy mind is normally found in a healthy body,
and so is a healthy frame of reference or outlook on
life. A person who is in good health, whose body is in a
state of homeostasis, and who suffers from only temporary and minor illnesses, is far more likely to have a
healthy attitude toward self and toward life in general
than the person who suffers from chronic illness,
whose homeostasis is upset by glandular imbalance
or other physiological conditions, or whose illness is
severe, even though only temporary.

Upsets in homeostasis at the times when the
body is undergoing radical changes—at puberty and
in middle age—always lead to a temporary tendency
to view life as gloomy and unsatisfying. If other conditions are favorable, however, when homeostasis is
restored, there will normally be a return to a healthy
outlook.

Since everyone has some physical defects, even
though they may be minor, everyone has the potential

of developing an unhealthy outlook on life and on
himself in particular. Whether he will do so or not will
depend on how much his defects interfere with his
being able to do what his peers do, how he himself
views his defects, and how the significant people in his
life view them.

One of the reasons healthy personalities are
often replaced by less healthy ones in old age is that
the person develops physical defects that handicap
him in what he wants to do. If he is forced to become
dependent on others, it is not surprising that his attitude toward self and toward life becomes distorted.

Psychological causes

Psychologically, the major factor contributing to a
healthy personality is self-acceptance. The person can
be self-acceptant only when stress, due to anxiety,
frustration, and other emotional states which affect
the self-concept adversely, is at a minimum. If the
self-concept is reasonably favorable, the person will
accept himself because he will like himself. If the
self-concept is unfavorable, he will reject himself or
accept himself only partially. Since self-acceptance is
so crucial to personality health, the conditions under
which self-acceptance occurs and how it influences
behavior will now be examined.

SELF-ACCEPTANCE

Self-acceptance is the "degree to which an individual,
having considered his personal characteristics, is able
and willing to live with them" (97). As Jersild (71) has
explained:

The self-accepting person has a realistic appraisal of
his resources combined with appreciation of his own
worth; assurance about standards and convictions of
his own without being a slave to the opinions of
others; and realistic assessment of limitations without
irrational self-reproach. Self-accepting people recog-
nize their assets and are free to draw upon them even
if they are not all that could be desired. They also
recognize their shortcomings without needlessly
blaming themselves.

Conditions favorable to self-acceptance

Many of the conditions that determine how much a
person likes and accepts himself are the opposite of

those which lead to self-rejection, as described in Chapter 14. The following are the most important: self-understanding; realistic expectations; absence of environmental obstacles; favorable social attitudes; absence of severe emotional stress; preponderance of successes; identification with well-adjusted people; self-perspective; good childhood training; and a stable self-concept.

Self-understanding   Self-understanding is a perception of self marked by genuineness, not pretense; realism, not illusion; truth, not falsehood; forthrightness, not deviousness. It is not merely recognizing facts but realizing the significance of facts.

Whether a person will understand himself will depend not on his intellectual capacities alone but also on his opportunities for self-discovery. He must have an opportunity to try out his abilities without being overprotected by others and he must be permitted to pit his skills and abilities against those of others to see where he stands in relation to them (20, 70, 97).

Lack of self-understanding may come from stupidity or ignorance; it may come from lack of opportunities for self-discovery; or it may come from the person's desire to see himself only as he would like to be, not as he actually is. If the person is blind to what he does not want to see, he is engaging in self-deception to cloak what he does see so that it will be to his liking.

Self-understanding and self-acceptance go hand in hand. The better a person understands himself, the better he can accept himself, and vice versa. Lack of self-understanding leads to a discrepancy between the person's concept of himself as he would like to be—his ideal self-concept—and the mirror image he has from his social contacts, which forms the basis for his real self-concept.

Realistic expectations   When a person's expectations for achievement are realistic, chances are that his performance will come up to his expectations. This will contribute to the self-satisfaction that is essential to self-acceptance.

Expectations are more likely to be realistic when the person formulates them himself rather than allowing others to influence him unduly. They are also more likely to be realistic when the person is sufficiently self-understanding to be able to recognize his limitations as well as his strengths. (See Chapter 10).

Goals may be realistic but the person may lack the knowledge or skills needed to reach the goals. For example, he may have the ability to play an administrative role in business or industry, but if he lacks a college education, he is not likely to be given an opportunity to demonstrate his potentials.

Only when the gap between the real and the ideal self-concepts, based on unrealistic expectations, can be narrowed down to the point where the ideal can be attained may the person hope to be self-acceptant. So long as a gap between the two exists, he will be self-rejectant to some extent.

Absence of environmental obstacles   Inability to reach goals that are realistic may come from environmental obstacles over which the person has no control, such as discrimination based on race, sex, or religion. When this happens, the person, knowing his potentials, finds it difficult to be self-acceptant. When the obstacles in his path are removed and when parents, teachers, peers, or employers encourage the person to achieve the success he is capable of, he can be satisfied with his achievements, provided his expectations are realistic.

Favorable social attitudes   Since the attitudes of members of the social group toward a person mold his self-attitudes, the person who experiences favorable social attitudes can be expected to be self-acceptant. Whether he will or not will depend to a large extent upon how realistic his aspirations for himself are and how well he understands his own strengths and weaknesses.

The three major conditions that lead to favorable social evaluations are, *first,* absence of prejudice against the person or the members of his family; *second*, possession of social skills the other group members value, especially social insight, which enables the person to put himself into the psychological shoes of another and understand how he feels; and *third*, willingness to accept group mores in dress, appearance, speech, and behavior.

Absence of severe emotional stress   Even when mild and transitory, emotional stress leads to upsets in physical and psychological homeostasis. Severe and persistent stress, as in a home or work environment where the emotional climate is poor, leads to such pronounced upsets that the person's behavior is markedly distorted and others become critical and rejectant of him. In addition, upsets in physical homeostasis that accompany emotional stress make the person work less efficiently and predispose him to feel so tired and listless or so emotionally keyed-up that he reacts negatively to people, regardless of how they react to him.

Absence of emotional stress makes it possible for the person to do his best and to be outer-oriented instead of self-oriented. Absence of stress also enables him to be relaxed instead of tense, happy instead of angry, resentful, and frustrated. These conditions contribute to the favorable social evaluations which form the basis for favorable self-evaluations and self-acceptance.

Preponderance of successes   A preponderance of failures leads to self-rejection, and a preponderance of successes leads to self-acceptance. A preponderance of successes may be quantitative or qualitative. In the former, the actual number of successes may outweigh the actual number of failures. In the latter, there may be a greater number of failures, but the successes are so much more important and meaningful that they outweigh the failures both in social and in self judgments.

Only when a person has unrealistically high aspirations is he not influenced considerably by social judgments of his successes and failures. Even under such conditions, some of the sting of failure is reduced by favorable social judgments of his successes. He then becomes more self-acceptant than he would be in the absence of these favorable social judgments.

Identification with well-adjusted people   The person who identifies with well-adjusted people is predisposed to develop positive attitudes toward life and thus behave in a manner that leads to favorable self-judgments and self-acceptance.

While identification may be strong at any age, it is especially so during the early, formative years when the person's outlook on life is being formed and when the foundations of personal adjustment are being laid. That is why a home environment that provides the child with a well-adjusted source of identification contributes to development of a healthy personality. Normally it is the mother who is most often chosen as a source of childish identification, and so her adjustment has a strong influence on the child's personality pattern.

Self-perspective   A person who can see himself as others see him has greater self-understanding

than one whose self-perspective tends to be narrow and distorted. An enlightened self-perspective facilitates self-acceptance.

Good childhood training   Although the kind of adjustment the person makes may change radically as his life progresses, the core of the self-concept, which determines what his adjustment to life will be, is laid in childhood. That is why good home and school training are so critical.

Democratic training leads to healthier personality patterns than authoritarian or overpermissive training. Democratic training, in which rules and regulations are explained to the child, suggests to him that he is respected as a person. The child thus learns to respect himself and assumes responsibility for controlling his own behavior within the framework of the rules and regulations set by those in authority.

Stable self-concept   A stable self-concept is one in which the person sees himself in the same way most of the time. Only if that self-concept is favorable will the person accept himself. If it is unfavorable, it will naturally lead to self-rejection.

An unstable self-concept, in which the person sees himself favorably at some times and unfavorably at others, fails to give the person a clear picture of what he really is. He is ambivalent about himself, accepting himself today and rejecting himself tomorrow. If the person is to develop the habit of self-acceptance, he must see himself in a favorable light often enough to reinforce the favorable self-concept so that self-acceptance will become habitual.

Effects of self-acceptance

The more a person accepts himself, the better his self and social adjustments. The person who makes good personal adjustments will be happy and successful. The one who makes good social adjustments will be popular, will enjoy social contacts, and will have a full and rich life. The importance of self-acceptance in adolescence has been stressed by Jersild: "The adolescent who realistically accepts himself has a treasure. Within his own world, the one with meagre talents who forthrightly appreciates what he has is richer than the one who is bountifully endowed but deplores himself" (71). This is true at other ages as well.

Studies reveal what a broad influence self-acceptance has in the person's life. For convenience, we shall group the effects of self-acceptance into two major categories—the effects on self-adjustment and the effects on social adjustments—and examine some of those which are most important.

Effects on self-adjustment The self-acceptant person does not think of himself as a paragon of perfection. Instead, he is able to *recognize his good features as well as his faults.* One characteristic of the person who is well adjusted is that he usually recognizes his good features before his faults and emphasizes them rather than his faults. As one person explained:"We all have to live with ourselves twenty-four hours a day and therefore we should think much of ourselves, at least enough to give confidence to our ego to improve ourselves" (119).

As a result of "thinking much" of himself, the person who is self-acceptant has *self-confidence* and *self-esteem.* He is more willing to *accept criticism* than the less self-acceptant person, who avoids facing the fact that he is in any way imperfect, as criticism implies. While the self-acceptant person may not like criticism, he accepts it and profits from it. He even makes *critical self-appraisals* which help him to recognize and correct his weaknesses.

Self-acceptance is accompanied by *personal security.* This encourages the person to believe that he can handle life's problems and that he is accepted by significant people in his life. It also encourages him to rely on his own principles and values to guide his actions rather than on the conventions and standards of others.

The self-accepting person evaluates himself realistically, and so he can *use his capacities* effectively, whether they are great or small. He keeps his levels of aspiration within the bounds of potential achievement. He accepts or even demands his proper *share of the good things of life* and does not take it for granted that he does not deserve them.

He will not always *defer to others* or allow them to take the things he wants without entering into competition to win or keep them. Furthermore, because of his realistic appraisal of himself, the self-accepting person is *honest* and does not have to pretend. As a result, he can get more pleasure out of life, not having to do things for devious reasons and not needing to pretend that he is something that he is not.

Even more important, the self-accepting person does not want to be someone else. He is *satisfied with himself*, though not so satisfied that he has no desire to improve. He would like to improve his good qualities and eliminate his bad qualities, but always within the framework of his own life pattern.

Jersild (71) has summarized the outstanding effects of self-acceptance on personal adjustments in adolescence:

> *Among the outstanding characteristics of self-accepting adolescents are spontaneity and responsibility for self. They accept the qualities of their humanity without condemning themselves for conditions beyond their control. They do not see themselves as persons who should be above anger or fear or devoid of conflicting desires, free of human fallibility. They feel they have a right to have ideas, aspirations, and wishes of their own. They do not begrudge themselves the satisfactions of being alive.*

Effects on social adjustments Acceptance of self is accompanied by *acceptance of others.* This, in turn, is usually, though not always, accompanied by *acceptance by others.* The self-accepting person feels secure enough to take an *interest* in others and to show *empathy*—the ability to transpose himself into the thinking, feeling, and acting of another. As a result, he makes better social adjustments than the person who is self-oriented because of feelings of inadequacy and inferiority.

The person who accepts himself is *tolerant* of others, overlooking their weaknesses and unkindnesses, while the self-rejecting person is likely to react in a hostile, antagonistic manner. The self-accepting person recognizes that he, too, has weaknesses which others do not like.

Tolerance of others is often accompanied by a desire to *help others.* Since the self-accepting person is not self-oriented and does not condemn others for their weaknesses, he is willing to lend a helping hand to those who need his help. As Brandt has explained, self-accepting people "are free to be themselves, to realize their own potentialities and to help others realize theirs" (15).

As a general rule, the more self-accepting the person, the more likely he is to be accepted by others. However, it must be remembered that many other factors enter into social acceptance. These were discussed in detail in Chapter 9.

PREDICTABLE AGES FOR PERSONALITY HEALTH

Under certain conditions, characteristically present at various ages, it is relatively safe to predict that the personality pattern will be healthy. When body *homeostasis* is normal, the health of the person is good and this predisposes him to be well-adjusted and happy. When life goes along on a fairly even keel and *no radical adjustments* must be made in one's accustomed pattern of behavior, the absence of strain and stress favors good adjustments. When one is in an age group which normally enjoys favorable *social attitudes,* it is relatively easy to be self-acceptant. And at the times in life when the person is most likely to be realistic about himself and his self-evaluations, he is most likely to be satisfied enough to accept himself.

It is not difficult for a *baby* or even a *toddler* to be well adjusted because most people love babies and toddlers and try to meet all their important life needs. Only if young children are constantly associated with a poorly adjusted person, especially a maladjusted mother, is personality sickness likely to develop at this early age. Figure 15-3 shows the relationship between the mother's behavior and the baby's happiness and general adjustive pattern.

Since *childhood* is a period of fairly slow and even growth, there is little to upset body homeostasis except a temporary illness. In addition, life in the home and in the school, once the initial adjustment to school has been made, is normally quite harmonious. Consequently, the pattern of adjustment established in the early years of life is not interrupted. If that pattern has been favorable, one can predict that the childhood years will be marked by relatively good adjustment and happiness.

The favorable social attitudes toward babies are often replaced by less favorable ones as children reach the rough-and-tumble age of childhood. This is especially true for boys, who are more difficult to handle and less willing to conform to adult standards than girls. This could adversely affect children's self-acceptant attitudes and their general pattern of adjustment and happiness were it not usually counteracted by favorable peer attitudes. Children who are well accepted by the peer group are far less influenced by unfavorable adult attitudes than are those who are poorly accepted by their peers. Usually, peer influence is paramount among older children.

During the years of *puberty* and *early adoles-cence,* a healthy personality is difficult to maintain even if the foundations laid in childhood were sound. The upsets in body homeostasis that accompany radical physical and glandular changes, the changed social expectations for the roles the young people will be expected to play, and the generally unfavorable social attitudes toward "teen-agers"—all contribute to make these years difficult for young people to adjust to.

With the approach of adulthood, the *older adolescent's* homeostatic upsets are over, his health is normally at its peak, his status in the social group is that of a near adult, he can look forward to the freedom and achievement of adult life, and social attitudes are more favorable than at any time since babyhood. This generally favorable situation encourages self-acceptance.

How healthy the *adult* personality pattern will be depends on the person's general health and life conditions, how successful he has been in reaching the goals he aspired to reach, how the significant people in his life as well as members of the social group feel about him, and—especially—the kind of foundations laid for good personal and social adjustments during the early, formative years of his life. The early years of adulthood are those in which self-acceptance is greatest and in which healthy personalities tend to thrive (7, 9, 18, 33, 88, 127).

Middle age, as was stressed in Chapter 14, is the beginning of a critical period for personality sickness. It is a time when there are not only upsets in homeostasis, as the reproductive glands gradually reduce their release of hormones, but also radical role changes, especially for women. Middle age is often a period of disappointment and hopelessness—disappointment because achievements have fallen far short of expectations and hopelessness because the chances of reaching youthful goals are growing slimmer with each passing year.

Most middle-aged people are aware of the gradually increasing unfavorable social attitudes toward them—in the family, in business, and in the community. They realize that people are beginning to regard them as "too old" for the roles they would like to play or which they formerly played. This, combined with the other negative factors just discussed, makes self-acceptance increasingly difficult.

Healthy personalities are harder to maintain in *old age* than at any other time in the life span. *All* of the conditions that militate against self-acceptance, discussed in relation to other periods in the life span,

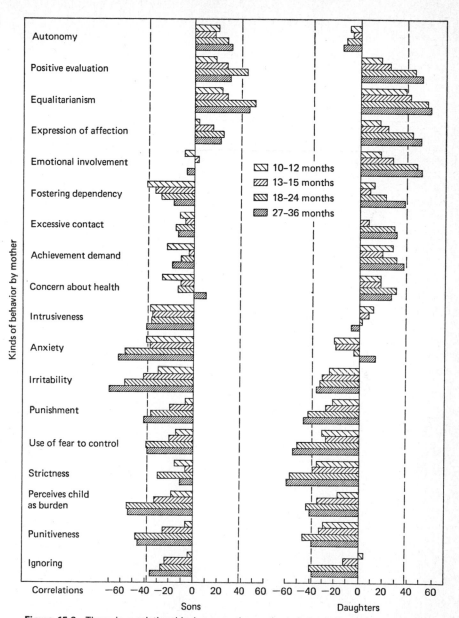

Figure 15-3 There is a relationship between the mother's behavior and the young child's happiness at four age levels. (Adapted from N. Bayley: Research in child development: A longitudinal perspective. *Merrill-Palmer Quart.*, 1965, **11**, 183–208. Used by permission.)

are present in old age, and all seem to be more powerful forces against self-acceptance than they were earlier (19, 21, 78, 168).

There is no time in life, for example, when the feeling of failure is likely to be more acute and persis-

tent than in old age. While a younger person who feels that he has been a failure can always hope that things will improve and that he will eventually succeed, the elderly person knows that time is running out on him and that the social group, which has put him into retirement, will not give him another chance to prove that he can be a success.

For a few of the elderly, life's circumstances and treatment provide reason for being self-acceptant; for most, there is ample reason for becoming self-rejectant.

In summary, it is apparent from this brief review that one of the principal factors influencing the health of the personality pattern is the social attitude that prevails toward people of a given age group. At any age, self-acceptance is easiest when the attitudes of others, especially those who are significant to the person, are favorable.

Almost as important as social attitudes in predicting at what age the personality is most likely to be healthy is the degree of self-understanding the person has. Self-understanding cannot be expected to be well-developed until the person approaches the adolescent years. By adolescence, most boys and girls are self-critical as well as self-admiring. They are self-understanding to the point where they can see themselves as they are, not just as they would like to be or as they are in the eyes of biased family members (15, 37, 43, 115).

AIDS TO ACHIEVING A HEALTHY PERSONALITY

Since a healthy personality is not a part of the person's hereditary endowment but is developed through learning and life experiences, almost everyone can have a healthy personality. Thus, it is something the person must acquire for himself. To do so requires motivation and know-how.

No one wants to be mentally sick. However enlightened people may be, there is still some social stigma attached to mental illness. Furthermore, life is more enjoyable and people are happier when they are physically and mentally healthy. There are few things people dread more than the prospect of being institutionalized, whether for physical or mental illness. Consequently, *motivation* to have a healthy personality is rarely a problem.

The major problem is to know how to achieve good health. Leaders in medical science devote considerable time to disseminating information about how to prevent physical illness and promote good health. This is done through the schools, colleges, and mass media in the hope of reaching the majority of the lay public.

Less is known about how to prevent mental illness and maintain good mental health, and so most people lack the necessary *know-how*. Thus, while their motivation may be strong, the second essential to achieving a healthy personality is often lacking.

There is little doubt that people would follow advice about how to achieve better mental health if such advice were readily available. However, personology is a relatively new science and specialists in the field are relatively few. Therefore, little has been done to disseminate the information that is available.

It is almost universally accepted among personologists that the key to good mental health is self-acceptance, while the chief cause of personality sickness is self-rejection. Therefore, it is obvious that the fundamental task is to help people learn how to be self-acceptant. Many suggestions about how to do this have been made, but because of the newness of the research in this area, no one has yet brought all this scattered information together. An attempt will be made to do so here.

Aids to self-acceptance

Of the many suggestions that personologists have made about how to achieve a healthy personality, those listed below have most often been suggested and emphasized (4, 9, 25, 30, 37, 42, 43, 57, 69, 74, 113). The primary aim of all these suggestions is to show the person how to close the gap between the real and the ideal self-concepts—an essential to self-acceptance.

No attempt has been made to rank the suggestions in order of value. *All* are inportant, though their relative importance varies, depending on the age, sex, socioeconomic status, and other conditions of the person. Some attempt has been made, however, to arrange them according to the areas of behavior they refer to.

Make sure that a foundation for a healthy self-concept is laid and see that early experiences reinforce this concept to ensure that it will become habitual.

Convince the person that he will not outgrow any undesirable personality traits he may have nor will his personality change for the better without effort on his part.

Be on the alert for the beginning of any personality disturbance, such as projecting blame onto others or drifting into the world of fantasy when things go wrong. At the first sign of personality disturbance, take immediate remedial steps to cure it so that it will not develop into a habit. Get advice from a personologist on how to do this.

If the personality disturbance does not respond to treatment in the person's present environment, such a radical step as change of environment may be essential.

Encourage and help the person to acquire good health and to live within his physical limitations. Help the person correct any physical defect, such as obesity, that will lead to unfavorable social and personal evaluations, show him how to camouflage those defects which cannot be corrected, and help him develop compensatory motor and mental skills to detract attention from his handicaps to his skills.

Make sure that the person's important needs, especially for achievement, acceptance, and affection, are met in forms suited to his age and level of development. When he is young, he should be assured that his parents want him, accept him as an individual, and will provide him with unwavering affection.

During the early, formative years of life, fair, firm, consistent, and loving discipline that takes into account the child's expanding ability for self-discipline should be used to instill in him socially approved moral values to use as guidelines for behavior that will be socially approved as well as self-approved.

When he goes astray in his behavior, the person should be given guidance, help, and encouragement to return to socially approved patterns of behavior.

Provide an environment rich in opportunities for learning how to live successfully with other people.

Help him to increase his social insight so that he will understand people better and be able to control his behavior in a way that will make them want to accept him.

Point out to him what makes people popular and give him guidelines on how to develop the characteristics that will make him acceptable to others.

Guide him in the development of a stable self-concept by helping him to close the gap between his real and ideal self-concepts.

Make sure that the self-concept, as it becomes stable, is also favorable.

Avoid encouraging a person to be overly ambitious.

Help him to develop such success factors as persistence, thoroughness, accuracy, curiosity, originality, leadership, pride in achievement, and creativity in his thinking.

Set a good example of personal and social adjustments and see that he has contacts with people who have socially approved standards and ideals which he is encouraged to live up to.

Encourage him to accept and conform to social expectations of different roles, especially the culturally approved sex role.

Provide him with opportunities for success, especially as soon after a failure as possible, to avoid the development of a "failure complex."

Help him to increase his self-understanding so that he has a better appreciation of his strengths and weaknesses.

Help him to develop stress tolerance to avoid the self-dislike that leads to self-rejection.

Make sure that he has a favorable self-image by stressing his potentials and by helping him to acquire the skills needed to achieve these potentials in real life, not in the fantasy world.

Let him know that the people who are significant in his life have faith in him, that they trust him and expect the best of him.

Be sure that he experiences the thrills of contributing to activities and goals which he feels are good, meaningful, and worthy.

Above all else, try to get him to be realistic about himself by helping him to close the gap between his real and ideal self-concepts. The following jingle, used by Gen. Alfred M. Gruenther (58), serves to show how this goal can be achieved:

Sometime, when you're feeling important,
Sometime, when your ego's in bloom,
Sometime when you take it for granted,
You're the best qualified in the room,
Sometime when you feel that your going,
Would leave an unfillable hole,
Just follow this simple instruction,
And see how it humbles your soul.
Take a bucket and fill it with water,

Put your hand in it, up to the wrist,
Pull it out, and the hole that's remaining,
Is a measure of how you'll be missed.
You may splash all you please when you enter,
You can stir up the water galore,
But stop, and you'll find in a minute,
That it looks quite the same as before.
The moral in this quaint example
Is do just the best that you can
Be proud of yourself, but remember,
There is no indispensable man.

SUMMARY

1 People with healthy personalities are judged to be well adjusted. This is because they can gratify their needs, interests, and aspirations through behavior that conforms to social expectations. A person with a healthy personality is thus one who is self-actualizing.

2 Even though it is far more difficult to determine the number of people with healthy personalities than those with sick personalities, owing to lack of records of well-adjusted people and ambiguity about the meaning of "healthy personality," there is a general feeling among personologists that a greater number of people have healthy personalities. On the other hand, there is a general belief that the percentage of people with sick personalities is on the increase.

3 Diagnosis of personality health, as is true of diagnosis of personality sickness, can best be done by personologists. When a diagnosis is to be made, two criteria are taken into consideration: the degree of satisfaction the person derives from the role he plays in life and how closely this role conforms to characteristics that are valued not by laymen alone but also by personologists.

4 From studies of people of different social and cultural backgrounds, personologists have identified certain characteristics which are almost universal in those whom they regard as well-adjusted, or as having healthy personalities. Some of the most important are the ability to appraise themselves realistically and to take a realistic approach to situations, the ability to evaluate their achievements realistically, acceptance of re-

sponsibilities, achievement of autonomy and acceptable emotional control, goal-orientation and outer-orientation, the ability to gain social acceptance, being philosophy-of-life-directed, and being happy. These characteristics are regarded by personologists as constituting the healthy personality syndrome.

5 Because happiness is, unquestionably, one of the principal characteristics of the healthy personality syndrome, extensive studies have been made to determine what factors are primarily responsible for happiness. These studies show that the three most important conditions contributing to happiness, regardless of age, sex, socioeconomic status, or any other variable, are achievement, acceptance, and affection, commonly referred to as the Three A's of Happiness.

6 Just as sick personalities may result from either physical or psychological causes, so may healthy personalities. Good physical health, which is accompanied by body homeostasis, contributes to a favorable concept of self. The major psychological cause of personality health is self-acceptance; this can occur only in the absence of stress when a state of inner harmony is possible. When a person has a reasonably favorable concept of himself, he can like and accept himself.

7 The conditions which contribute to self-acceptance are, in the main, the opposite of those which lead to self-rejection. The most important are self-understanding, realistic expectations, absence of environmental obstacles, favorable social attitudes, absence of severe emotional stress, a preponderance of successes, identification with well-adjusted people, self-perspective, good childhood training, and a stable self-concept.

8 The effects of self-acceptance are apparent in the kind of self- and social adjustments the person makes. And since self-acceptance contributes to social acceptance, it also contributes to better social adjustments.

9 Some of the major effects of self-acceptance on self-adjustment are apparent in the person's ability to recognize his faults, in his self-confidence and self-esteem, his willingness to accept criticisms from others, his ability to make critical self-appraisals and to correct weaknesses he recognizes in himself, his ability to be honest with himself as well as with others, his feelings of personal security, the ability to make effective use of his capacities, his refusal to defer to others, and his ability to be satisfied with himself so that he does not want to be someone else.

10 The effects of self-acceptance on social adjustments are equally important. The self-acceptant person accepts others, shows an interest in them, and can empathize with them. He is tolerant of their weaknesses and tries to help them. Because of these traits, his chances for social acceptance are increased, though other conditions over which he has little or no control may interfere with his social acceptance.

11 There are predictable ages for personality health because certain conditions characteristically present at these ages favor self-acceptance. When body homeostasis is normal, when no radical adjustments must be made in the person's accustomed life pattern, when there is, therefore, an absence of unusual strain and stress, and when social attitudes toward the age group with which the person is identified are favorable, the chances of personality health are greatest. The most favorable periods for personality health are babyhood, childhood, and early adulthood.

12 Although everyone wants to make good personal and social adjustments and be happy, many do not know how to do so because personology is a relatively new science and its findings have not yet been made available on a wide scale. Furthermore, achieving a healthy personality cannot be done by others. The responsibility is in the hands of the person himself. All that the personologist can do is provide the person with the know-how. This know-how is based on suggestions of how one can become more self-acceptant—the fundamental essential to a healthy personality.

bibliography

CHAPTER 1

1 Adams, J. D.: The egghead vs. the muttonhead. *The New York Times,* Nov. 23, 1958.

2 Allport, G. W.: *Pattern and growth in personality.* New York: Holt, 1961.

3 Allport, G. W.: Prejudice: Is it societal or personal? *Relig. Educ.,* 1964, **59,** 20–29.

4 Altus, W. D.: Birth order and scholastic aptitude. *J. consult. Psychol.,* 1965, **29,** 202–205.

5 Amidon, E.: The isolate in children's groups. *J. teacher Educ.,* 1961, **12,** 412–416.

6 Anastasi, A.: Heredity, environment, and the question "How?" *Psychol. Rev.,* 1958, **65,** 197–208.

7 Anastasi, A.: *Psychological testing,* 3d ed. New York: Macmillan, 1968.

8 Anderson, C. A.: The self-image: A theory of the dynamics of behavior. In D. E. Hamachek (ed.), *The self in growth, teaching, and learning.* Englewood Cliffs, N. J.: Prentice-Hall, 1965, pp. 1–13.

9 Anderson, N. H.: Likableness ratings of 555 personality trait words. *J. Pers. soc. Psychol.,* 1968, **9,** 272–279.

10 Armstrong, J. D.: The search for the alcholic personality. *Ann. Amer. Acad. pol. soc. Sci.,* 1958, **315,** 40–47.

11 Arnhoff, F. N., H. V. Leon, and I. Lorge: Cross-cultural acceptance of stereotypes towards aging. *J. soc. Psychol.,* 1964, **63,** 41–58.

12 Arnhoff, F. N., and I. Lorge: Stereotypes about aging and the aged. *Sch. Soc.,* 1960, **88,** 70–71.

13 Asch, S. E.: Forming impressions of personality. *J. abnorm. soc. Psychol.,* 1946, **41,** 258–290.

14 Ausubel, D. P., and H. M. Schiff: Some intrapersonal and interpersonal determinants of individual differences in sociempathic ability among adolescents. *J. soc. Psychol.,* 1955, **41,** 39–56.

15 Ausubel, D. P., H. M. Schiff, and E. B. Gasser: A preliminary study of developmental trends in sociopathy: Accuracy of perception of own and others' sociometric status. *Child Develpm.,* 1952, **23,** 111–128.

16 Axelrod, M: Urban structure and social participation. *Amer. sociol. Rev.,* 1956, **21,** 13–15.

17 Bader, I. M., and A. M. Hoffman: Research in aging. *J. Home Econ.,* 1966, **58,** 9–14.

18 Bealer, R. C., F. K. Willits, and P. R. Maida: The rebellious youth subculture: A myth. *Children,* 1964, **11,** 43–48.

19 Beardslee, D. G., and D. D. O'Dowd: The college-student image of the scientist. *Science,* 1961, **133,** 997–1001.

20 Bell, G. B., and H. E. Hall: The relationship between leadership and latency. *J. abnorm. soc. Psychol.,* 1954, **49,** 156–157.

21 Bertocci, P. A.: The psychological self, the ego, and personality. In D. E. Hamachek (ed.), *The self in growth, teaching, and learning.* Englewood Cliffs, N. J.: Prentice-Hall, 1965, pp. 14–26.

22 Binder, D.: West Germans see themselves as "good," Easterners as "bad." *The New York Times,* Feb. 5, 1967.

23 Blain, M. J., and M. Ramirez: Increasing sociometric rank, meaningfulness, and discriminability of children's names through reinforcement and interaction. *Child Develpm.,* 1968, **39,** 949–955.

24 Blumenfeld, W. S.: Some correlates of TV drama viewing. *Psychol. Rep.,* 1964, **15,** 901–902.

25 Bogardus, E. S.: Measuring changes in ethnic reactions. *Amer. sociol. Rev.,* 1951, **16,** 48–51.

26 Borg, W. R.: The effect of personality and contact upon a personality stereotype. *J. educ. Res.,* 1955, **49,** 289–294.

27 Bossard, J. H. S., and E. S. Boll: *The sociology of child development,* 4th ed. New York: Harper & Row, 1966.

28 Bowerman, C. E., and J. W. Kinch: Changes in family and peer orientation of children between the fourth and tenth grades. *Soc. Forces,* 1959, **37,** 206–211.

29 Bretsch. H. S.: Social skills and activities of socially accepted and unaccepted adolescents. *J. educ. Psychol.,* 1952, **43,** 449–458.

30 Brim, O. G.: The acceptance of new behavior in child rearing. *Hum. Relat.,* 1954, **7,** 473–491.

31 Bringmann, W., and G. Rieder: Stereotyped attitudes toward the aged in West Germany and the United States. *J. soc. Psychol.,* 1968, **76,** 267–268.

32 Bruch, H.: Developmental obesity and schizophrenia. *Psychiatry,* 1958, **21,** 65–70.

33 Bruner, J. S., and H. V. Perlmutter: Compatriot and foreigner: A study of impression formation in three countries. *J. abnorm. soc. Psychol.,* 1957, **55,** 253–260.

34 Byrne, D., O. London, and K. Reeves: The effect of physical attractiveness, sex, and attitude similarity on interpersonal attraction. *J. Pers.,* 1968, **36,** 259–271.

35 Caldwell, B. M., and J. B. Richmond: The impact of theories of child development. *Children,* 1962, **9,** 73–78.

36 Carlson, A. J., and E. J. Stieglitz: Physiological changes in aging. *Ann. Amer. Acad. pol. soc. Sci.,* 1952, **279,** 18–31.

37 Child, I. L., E. H. Potter, and E. M. Levine: Children's textbooks and personality development: An exploration in the social psychology of learning. *Psychol. Monogr.,* 1946, **60,** no. 3.

38 Chowdhry, K., and T. M. Newcomb: The relative abilities of leaders and nonleaders to estimate opinions of their own groups. *J. abnorm. soc. Psychol.,* 1952, **47,** 51–57.

39 Clifford, C., and T. S. Cohn: The relationship between leadership and personality attributes perceived by followers. *J. soc. Psychol.,* 1964, **64,** 57–64.

40 Coleman, J. S.: *The adolescent society.* New York: Free Press, 1961.

41 Colle, R. D.: Negro image in the mass media: A case study in social change. *Journalism Quart.,* 1968, **45,** 55–60.

42 Cooper, J. B.: Emotion in prejudice. *Science,* 1959, **130,** 314–318.

43 Copp, L. A.: A repertoire of perceptions of the professor's role. *Dissert. Abstr.,* 1968, **28** (9–A), 3474.

44 Crowther, B.: Poor Mom. *The New York Times,* Apr. 22, 1962.

45 Dashiell, J. F.: *Fundamentals of general psychology,* 3d ed. Boston: Houghton Mifflin, 1949.

46 Davies, J. D.: *Phrenology: Fad and science.* New Haven, Conn.: Yale, 1955.

47 Davitz, J. R.: Social perception and sociometric choice of children. *J. abnorm. soc. Psychol.,* 1955, **50,** 173–176.

48 Deegan, D. Y.: *The stereotype of the single woman in American novels.* New York: King's Crown, 1951.

49 DeFleur, M. L., and L. B. DeFleur: The relative contribution of television as a learning source for children's occupational knowledge. *Amer. sociol. Rev.,* 1967, **32,** 777–789.

50 Deutscher, I.: The stereotype as a research tool. *Soc. Forces,* 1958, **37,** 55–60.

51 Dienstfrey, H.: Doctors, lawyers, and other TV heroes. *Commentary,* 1963, **35,** 519–524.

52 Durr, W. K.: Characteristics of gifted children: Ten years of research. *Gifted Child Quart.,* 1960, **4,** 75–80.

53 Eiduson, B. T.: Artist and nonartist: A comparative study. *J. Pers.,* 1958, **26,** 13–28.

54 England, R. W.: Images of love and courtship in family-magazine fiction. *Marriage fam. Living,* 1960, **22,** 162–165.

55 Escalona, S. K.: Some determinants of individual differences. *Trans. N. Y. Acad. Sci.,* 1965, **27,** 802–816.

56 Eysenck, H. J.: The development of moral values in children. VII. The contribution of learning theory. *Brit. J. educ. Psychol.,* 1960, **30,** 11–21.

57 Feinberg, M. R.: Stability of sociometric status in two adolescent class groups. *J. genet. Psychol.,* 1964, **104,** 83–87.

58 Ferreira, A. J.: Family myth and homeostasis. *Arch. gen. Psychiat.,* 1963, **9,** 457–463.

59 Fielder, F. E.: A note on leadership theory: The effect of social barriers between leaders and followers. *Sociometry,* 1957, **20,** 87–94.

60 Fisher, H. H.: Family life in children's literature. *Elem. Sch. J.,* 1950, **50,** 516–520.

61 Fishman, J. A.: Negative stereotypes concerning Americans among American-born children receiving various types of minority group education. *Genet. Psychol. Monogr.,* 1955, **51,** 107–182.

62 Foster, J. E.: Father images: Television and ideal. *J. Marriage & Family,* 1964, **26,** 353–355.

63 Frenkel-Brunswik, E., and J. Havel: Prejudice in the interviews of children. 1. Attitudes toward minority groups. *J. genet. Psychol.,* 1953, **82,** 91–136.

64 Gardner, R. C., E. J. Wonnacott, and D. M. Taylor: Ethnic stereotypes: A factor analytic investigation. *Canad. J. Psychol.,* 1968, **22,** 35–44.

65 Garrison, K. C.: A study of the aspirations and concerns of ninth-grade pupils from

the public schools of Georgia. *J. soc. Psychol.*, 1966, **69**, 245–252.

66 Gerbner, G.: Images across cultures: Teachers in mass media fiction and drama. *School Review*, 1966, **74**, 212–230.

67 *Geriatric Focus* Report: Church attendance may decline with age, but religious interest and concern increase. Nov. 1965, **1**, pp. 2–3.

68 *Geriatric Focus* Report: Professional "stereotypes" hamper treatment of aged. 1966, **5**, no. 13, 1, 5–6.

69 Gilchrist, J. W.: Social psychology and group processes. *Annu. Rev. Psychol.*, 1959, **10**, 233–264.

70 Glick, P.C.: The life cycle of the family. *Marriage fam. Living*, 1955, **17**, 3–9.

71 Glueck, E. T.: A more discriminative instrument for the identification of potential delinquents at school entrance. *J. crim. Law Criminol. Police Sci.*, 1966, **57**, 27–30.

72 Gold, M.: Power in the classroom. *Sociometry*, 1958, **21**, 50–60.

73 Goldman, M.: Profiles of an adolescent. *J. Psychol.*, 1962, **54**, 229–240.

74 Gollin, E. S.: Organizational characteristics of social judgment: A developmental investigation. *J. Pers.* 1958, **26**, 139–154.

75 Gordon, L. V.: Personal factors in leadership. *J. soc. Psychol.*, 1952, **36**, 245–248.

76 Gottesman, I. L.: Heritability of personality. *Psychol. Monogr.*, 1963, **77**, no. 9.

77 Gray, R. M.: The personal adjustment of the older person in the church. *Sociol. soc. Res.*, 1957, **51**, 175–180.

78 Gronlund, N. E., and A. P. Whitney: Relation between pupils' social acceptability in the classroom, in the school, and in the neighborhood. *School Review*, 1956, **64**, 267–271.

79 Gross, M. L.: *The brain watchers*. New York: Random House, 1962.

80 Guilford, J. S.: Isolation and description of occupational stereotypes. *Occup. Psychol.*, 1967, **41**, 57–64.

81 Hall, C. S., and G. Lindzey: *Theories of personality*, 2d ed. New York: Wiley, 1970.

82 Hamid, P. M.: Style of dress as a perceptual cue in impression formation. *Percept. mot. Skills*, 1968, **26**, 904–906.

83 Handschin-Ninck, M.: Aellester und Jüngster in Märchen. *Prax. Kinderpsychol. Kinderpsychiat.*, 1956, **7**, 167–173.

84 Harris, D. B.: Sex differences in the life problems and interests of adolescents: 1935 and 1957. *Child Develpm.*, 1959, **30**, 453–459.

85 Hartman, A. A., R. C. Nicolay, and J. Hurley: Unique personal names as a social adjustment factor. *J. soc. Psychol.*, 1968, **75**, 107–110.

86 Hathaway, S. R., E. D. Monachesi, and L. A. Young: Rural-urban adolescent personality. *Rural Sociol.*, 1959, **24**, 333–346.

87 Havighurst, R. J.: The social competence of middle-aged people. *Genet. Psychol. Monogr.*, 1957, **56**, 297–375.

88 Hayes, M. L., and M. E. Conklin: Intergroup attitudes and experimental change. *J. exp. Educ.*, 1953, **22**, 19–36.

89 Hechinger, G., and F. M. Hechinger: *Teen-age tyranny*. New York: Morrow, 1963.

90 Henry, J.: Permissiveness and morality. *Ment. Hyg., N. Y.*, 1961, **45**, 282–287.

91 Hirsch, W.: The image of the scientist in science fiction: A content analysis. *Amer. J. Sociol.*, 1958, **63**, 506–512.

92 Hites, R. W., and D. T. Campbell: A test of the ability of fraternity leaders to estimate group opinion. *J. soc. Psychol.*, 1950, **32**, 95–100.

93 Horrocks, J. E., and M. E. Buker: A study of the friendship fluctuations of preadolescents. *J. genet. Psychol.*, 1951, **78**, 131–144.

94 Howard, P. J., and C. H. Morrell: Premature infants in later life: Study of intelligence and personality of 22 premature infants at ages 8 to 19 years. *Pediatrics*, 1952, **9**, 577–584.

95 Johnson, H. H.: Some effects of discrepancy level on response to negative information about one's self. *Sociometry*, 1966, **29**, 52–66.

96 Jones, M. C.: A comparison of the attitudes and interests of ninth grade students over two decades. *J. educ. Psychol.*, 1960, **51**, 175–186.

97 Kassof, A.: The prejudicial personality: A cross-cultural test. *Soc. Probl.*, 1958, **6**, 59–67.

98 Keniston, K.: Social change and youth in America. *Daedalus*, 1962, **91**, 145–171.

99 Kiker, V. L., and A. R. Miller: Perceptual judgment of physiques as a factor in social image. *Percept. mot. Skills*, 1967, **24**, 1013–1014.

100 Kirchner, W. K.: The attitudes of special groups toward the employment of older persons. *J. Geront.*, 1957, **12**, 216–220.

101 Kirchner, W. K., and M. D. Dunnette: Attitudes toward older workers. *Personnel Psychol.*, 1954, **7**, 257–265.

102 Kogan, N., and F. C. Shelton: Images of "old people" and "people in general" in an older sample. *J. genet. Psychol.*, 1962, **100**, 3–21.

103 Kohn, M.: The child as a determinant of his peers' approach to him. *J. genet. Psychol.*, 1966, **109**, 91–100.

104 Kuhlen, R. G., and E. Luther: A study of the cultural definition of the prime of life, middle age, and old age, and of attitudes toward the old. *J. Geront.*, 1949, **4**, 324.

105 Lambert, W. E., H. Frankel, and G. R. Tucker: Judging personality through speech: A French-Canadian sample. *J. Commun.*, 1966, **16**, 305–321.

106 Lane, B.: Attitudes of youth toward the aged. *J. Marriage & Family*, 1964, **26**, 229–231.

107 Lane, H.: The meaning of disorder among youth. *Education*, 1955, **76**, 214–217.

108 Lasswell, T. E.: Social class and stereotyping. *Sociol. soc. Res.*, 1958, **42**, 256–262.

109 Laycock, F., and J. S. Caylor: Physiques of gifted children and their less gifted siblings. *Child Develpm.*, 1964, **35**, 63–74.

110 Lazar, E. A., and C. Klein: What makes parents repulsive. *The New York Times*, Feb. 7, 1965.

111 Levin, P. L.: Putting down father. *The New York Times*, Mar. 21, 1965.

112 Levine, G. N., and L. A. Sussmann: Social class and sociability in fraternity pledging. *Amer. J. Sociol.*, 1960, **65**, 391–399.

113 Levy, D. M.: *Maternal overprotection*. New York: Columbia, 1943.

114 Loewenthal, K.: How are "first impressions" formed? *Psychol. Rep.*, 1967, **21**, 834–836.

115 Luft, J.: Monetary value and the perception of personality. *J. soc. Psychol.*, 1957, **46**, 245–251.

116 Marak, G. E.: The evolution of leadership structure, *Sociometry*, 1964, **27**, 174–182.

117 Markell, N. N., M. Meisels, and J. E. Houck: Judging personality from voice quality. *J. abnorm. soc. Psychol.*, 1964, **69**, 458–463.

118 Marsh, G. G., and J. L. Halberstam: Personality stereotypes of United States and foreign medical students. *J. soc. Psychol.*, 1966, **68**, 187–196.

119 Mason, D. J.: Judgments of leadership based upon physiognomic cues. *J. abnorm. soc. Psychol.*, 1957, **54**, 273–274.

120 McDavid, J. W., and H. Harari: Social desirability of names and popularity in grade school children. Paper presented at APA Convention, Chicago, 1965.

121 McKeachie, W. J.: Lipstick as a determiner of first impressions of personality: An experiment for the general psychology course. *J. soc. Psychol.*, 1952, **36**, 241–244.

122 Mead, M., and R. Métraux: Image of the scientist among high-school students. *Science*, 1957, **126**, 384–390.

123 Meyer, H. D.: The adult cycle. *Ann. Amer. Acad. pol. soc. Sci.*, 1957, **313**, 58–67.

124 Michael, D.N.: Scientists through adolescent eyes: What we need to know, why we need to know it. *Scient. Monthly*, 1957, **84**, 135–140.

125 Mohr, G. J., and M. A. Despres: *The stormy decade: Adolescence*. New York: Random House, 1958.

126 Munn, N. L.: *The evolution and growth of human behavior*, 2d ed. Boston: Houghton Mifflin, 1965.

127 Murray, H. A.: *Explorations in personality*. Fair Lawn, N. J.: Oxford, 1938.

128 Mussen, P. H., J. J. Conger, and J. Kagan: *Child development and personality*, 3d ed. New York: Harper & Row, 1969.

129 Nash, H.: Stereotyped associations to schematic faces. *J. genet. Psychol.*, 1958, **93**, 149–153.

130 Nedelsky, R.: The teacher's role in the peer group during middle childhood. *Elem. Sch. J.*, 1952, **52**, 325–334.

131 *New York Times* Report: Women increase majority in U. S. Nov. 12, 1956.

132 *New York Times* Report: Variation is found in life expectancy across the nation. July 8, 1965.

133 *New York Times* Report: Caricatures put scientists on pedestal. Dec. 12, 1969.

134 Niab, L. N.: Factors determining group stereotypes *J. soc. Psychol.*, 1963, **61**, 3–10.

135 Packard, V.: *The status seekers*. New York: Pocket Books, 1961.

136 Packard, V.: *The pyramid climbers*. New York: McGraw-Hill, 1962.

137 Pasamanick, B., and H. Knobloch: The contribution of some organic factors to school retardation in Negro children. *J. Negro Educ.*, 1958, **27**, 4–9.

138 Pinard, M.: Marriage and divorce decisions and the larger social system: A case study in social change. *Soc. Forces*, 1966, **44**, 341–355.

139 Pressey, S. L.: Not all decline! *Gerontologist*, 1966, **6**, no. 2.

140 Pressey, S. L., and R. G. Kuhlen: *Psychological development through the life span*. New York: Harper & Row, 1957.

141 Remmers, H. H., and D. H. Radler: *The American teenager*. Indianapolis: Bobbs-Merrill, 1957.

142 *Report of the President's Council on Aging.* 1963.

143 Riestra, M. A., and C. E. Johnson: Changes in attitudes of elementary school pupils toward foreign-speaking peoples resulting from the study of a foreign language. *J. exp. Educ.*, 1964, **33**, 65–72.

144 Rogers, C. R., and B. F. Skinner: Some issues concerning the control of human behavior. In D. E. Hamachek (ed.), *The self in growth, teaching, and learning.* Englewood Cliffs, N. J.: Prentice-Hall, 1965, pp. 94–120.

145 Ryan, M. S.: *Clothing: A study in human behavior.* New York: Holt, 1966.

146 Saegner, G., and S. Flowerman: Stereotypes and prejudicial attitudes. *Hum. Relat.*, 1954, **7**, 217–238.

147 Scheinfeld, A.: *Your heredity and environment.* Philadelphia: Lippincott, 1965.

148 Schupack, M. B.: Research on employment problems of older workers. *Gerontologist*, 1962, **2**, 157–163.

149 Schwartz, E. K.: A psychoanalytic study of the fairy tale. *Amer. J. Psychother.*, 1956, **10**, 740–762.

150 Secord, P. F., and E. S. Berscheid: Stereotyping and the generality of implicit personality theory. *J. Pers.*, 1963, **31**, 65–78.

151 Secord, P. F., W. Bevan, and W. F. Dukes: Occupational and physiognomic stereotypes in the perception of photographs. *J. soc. Psychol.*, 1953, **37**, 261–270.

152 Secord, P. F., W. F. Dukes, and W. Bevan: Personalities in faces. 1. An experiment in social perceiving. *Genet. Psychol. Monogr.*, 1954, **49**, 231–279.

153 Secord, P. F., and S. M. Jourard: Mother concepts and judgments of young women's faces. *J. abnorm. soc. Psychol.*, 1956, **52**, 246–250.

154 Secord, P. F., and J. E. Muthard: Personalities in faces. IV. A descriptive analysis of the perception of women's faces and the identification of some physiognomic determinants. *J. Psychol.*, 1955, **39**, 269–278.

155 Shaffer, L. F., and E. J. Shoben: *The psychology of adjustment*, 2d ed. Boston: Houghton Mifflin, 1956.

156 Sheikh, A. A.: Stereotypy in interpersonal perception and intercorrelation between some attitude measures. *J. soc. Psychol.*, 1968, **76**, 175–179.

157 Shirley, M. M.: The impact of the mother's personality on the young child. *Smith Coll. Stud. soc. Wk.*, 1941, **12**, 15–64.

158 Siegel, A.E.: The influence of violence in the mass media upon children's role expectations. *Child Develpm.*, 1958, **29**, 35–56.

159 Skorepa, C. A., J. E. Horrocks, and G. G. Thompson: A study of friendship fluctuations of college students. *J. genet. Psychol.*, 1963, **102**, 151–157.

160 Smith, W. C.: Remarriage and the step-child. In M. Fishbein and E. W. Burgess (eds.), *Successful marriage*, 2d ed. Garden City, N. Y.: Doubleday, 1955, pp. 328–349.

161 Snygg, D.: The need for a phenomenological system of psychology. In D. E. Hamachek (ed.), *The self in growth, teaching, and learning.* Englewood Cliffs, N. J.: Prentice-Hall, 1965, pp. 50–67.

162 Sorenson, R.: Youth's need for challenge and place in society, *Children*, 1962, **9**, 131–134.

163 Spaights, E.: Accuracy of self-estimation of junior high school students. *J. educ. Res.*, 1965, **58**, 416–419.

164 Stagner, R.: *Psychology of personality*, 3d ed. New York: McGraw-Hill, 1961.

165 Stewart, L. H.: The expression of personality in drawings and paintings. *Genet. Psychol. Monogr.* 1955, **51**, 45–103.

166 Stoodley, B. H.: The dynamics of the conscious and the unconscious. In D. E. Hamachek (ed.), *The self in growth, teaching, and learning.* Englewood Cliffs, N. J.: Prentice-Hall, 1965, pp. 27–39.

167 Strang, R.: *The adolescent views himself.* New York: McGraw-Hill, 1957.

168 Strodtbeck, F. L.: The interaction of the "henpecked" husband with his wife. *Marriage fam. Living*, 1952, **14**, 305–308.

169 Sykes, A. J. M.: Myth and attitude change. *Hum. Relat.*, 1965, **18**, 323–337.

170 Symonds, P. M.: Personality testing. *Rev. educ. Res.*, 1955, **26**, 274–278.

171 Taft, R.: The ability to judge people. *Psychol. Bull.*, 1955, **52**, 1–23.

172 Taylor, C., and G. G. Thompson: Age trends in preferences for certain facial proportions. *Child Develpm.*, 1955, **26**, 97–102.

173 Thorndike, E. L.: A constant error in psychological rating. *J. appl. Psychol.*, 1920, **4**, 25–29.

174 Triandis, H. C., and V. Vassiliou: Frequency of contact and stereotyping. *J. Pers. soc. Psychol.*, 1967, **7**, 316–328.

175 Tuckman, J., and I. Lorge: The projection of personal symptom into stereotype about aging. *J. Geront.*, 1958, **13**, 70–73.

176 Tuddenham, R. D.: Studies in reputation. I. Sex and grade differences in school children's evaluations of their peers. II. The diagnosis of social adjustment. *Psychol. Monogr.*, 1952, **66**, no. 1.

177 Udry, J. R.: Marital instability by race, sex, education, and occupation using 1960 census data. *Amer. J. Sociol.*, 1966, **72**, 203–209.

178 *U. S. News & World Report*: How women's role in U. S. is changing. May 30, 1966, pp. 50–60.

179 Vinacke, W. E.: Stereotypes as social concepts. *J. soc. Psychol.*, 1957, **46**, 229–241.

180 Wallin, J. E. W.: The psychological, educational, and social problems of the aging as viewed by a mid-octogenarian. *J. genet. Psychol.*, 1962, **100**, 41–46.

181 Wiggins, J. W., and H. Schoeck: A profile of the aging: U. S. A. *Geriatrics*, 1961, **16**, 336–342.

182 Williamson, R. G.: Dating, courtship, and the "ideal mate": Some relevant subcultural variables. *Family Life Coordinator*, 1965, **14**, 137–143.

183 Winick, C.: The Beige Epoch: Depolarization of sex roles in America. *Ann. Amer. Acad. pol. soc. Sci.*, 1968, **376**, 18–24.

184 Witryol, S. L., and J. E. Calkins: Marginal social values of rural school children. *J. genet. Psychol.*, 1958, **92**, 81–93.

185 Woodworth, R. S., and D. G. Marquis: *Psychology*, 5th ed. New York: Holt, 1947.

CHAPTER 2

1 Abu-Laban, B: Self-conception and appraisal by others: A study of community leaders. *Sociol. soc. Res.*, 1963, **48**, 32–37.

2 Adorno, T. W., E. Frenkel-Brunswik, J. D. Levinson, and R. N. Sanford: *The authoritarian personality.* New York: Harper & Row, 1950.

3 Ainsworth, L. H.: Rigidity, insecurity, and stress. *J. abnorm. soc. Psychol.*, 1958, **56**, 67–74.

4 Alexander, F.: The dynamics of personality development. *Soc. Casewk.*, 1951, **32**, 139–143.

5 Allport, G. W.: *Pattern and growth in personality.* New York: Holt, 1961.

6 Allport, G. W.: Prejudice: Is it societal or personal? *Relig. Educ.*, 1964, **59**, 20–29.

7 Allport, G. W.: Traits revisited. *Amer. Psychologist*, 1966, **21**, 1–10.

8 Alvarez, W. C.: Sexual life in the aging. *Geriatrics*, 1957, **12**, 141–142.

9 Amatora, Sister Mary: Developmental trends in pre-adolescence and in early adolescence in self-evaluation. *J. genet. Psychol.*, 1957, **91**, 89–97.

10 Amen, E. M., and N. Renison: A study of the relationship between play patterns and anxiety in young children. *Genet. Psychol. Monogr.*, 1954, **50**, 3–41.

11 Ames, L. B.: The sense of self of nursery school children as manifested by their verbal behavior. *J. genet. Psychol.*, 1952, **81**, 193–232.

12 Amos, W. E.: A study of self-concept: Delinquent boys' accuracy in selected self-evaluations. *Genet. Psychol. Monogr.*, 1963, **67**, 45–81.

13 Anderson, J. E.: Personality organization in children. *Amer. Psychologist*, 1948, **3**, 409–416.

14 Anderson, N. Y.: Likableness ratings of 555 personality-trait words. *J. Pers. soc. Psychol.*, 1968, **9**, 272 279.

15 Arasteh, J. D.: Creativity and related processes in the young child: A review of the literature. *J. genet. Psychol.*, 1968, **112**, 77–108.

16 Ausubel, D. P.: *Ego development and the personality disorders.* New York: Grune & Stratton, 1952.

17 Ausubel, D. P., H. M. Schiff, and E. B. Gasser: A preliminary study of developmental trends in sociopathy: Accuracy of perception of own and others' sociometric status. *Child Develpm.*, 1952, **23**, 111–128.

18 Banham, K. M.: Obstinate children are adaptable. *Ment. Hyg., N. Y.*, 1952, **36**, 84–89.

19 Berger, E.: Relation between expressed acceptance of self and others. *J. abnorm. soc. Psychol.*, 1952, **47**, 778–782.

20 Bills, R. E.: Self concepts and Rorschach signs of depression. *J. consult. Psychol.*, 1954, **18**, 135–137.

21 Barron, F.: The psychology of creativity. In F. Barron (ed.), *New directions in psychology*, vol. 2. New York: Holt, 1965, pp. 1–134.

22 Baugh, V. S., and B. L. Carpenter: A comparison of delinquents and nondelinquents. *J. soc. Psychol.*, 1962, **56**, 73–78.

23 Bell, H. M.: Ego-involvement in vocational decisions. *Personnel Guid. J.*, 1960, **38**, 732–736.

24 Bossard, J. H. S., and E. S. Boll: *The sociology of child development*, 4th ed. New York: Harper & Row, 1966.

25 Brandt, R. M.: The accuracy of self estimate: A measure of self concept reality. *Genet. Psychol. Monogr.*, 1958, **58**, 55–99.

26 Bray, D. H.: Attributes of ideal persons and of the self as conceived by some English secondary school children. *J. exp. Educ.*, 1964, **33**, 93–95.

27 Breckenridge, E. M., and E. L. Vincent: *Child development*, 5th ed. Philadelphia: Saunders, 1965.

28 Brodbeck, A. J., and H. V. Perlmutter: Self-dislike as a determinant of marked ingroup and outgroup preferences. *J. Psychol.*, 1954, **38**, 271–280.

29 Bronson, W. C.: Dimensions of ego and

infantile identification. *J. Pers.*, 1959, **27**, 532–545.

30 Brown, F. J.: *Educational sociology*, 2d ed. Englewood Cliffs, N. J.: Prentice-Hall, 1954.

31 Brownfain, J. J.: Stability of the self-concept as a dimension of personality. In D. E. Hamachek (ed.), *The self in growth, teaching, and learning.* Englewood Cliffs, N. J.: Prentice-Hall, 1965, pp. 269–287.

32 Butterworth, R. F., and G. G. Thompson: Factors related to age-grade trends and sex differences in children's preferences for comic books. *J. genet. Psychol.*, 1951, **78**, 71–96.

33 Caplan, S. W.: The effect of group counseling on junior high school boys' concepts of themselves in school. *J. counsel. Psychol.*, 1957, **4**, 124–128.

34 Carter, D. C.: The influence of family relationships and family experience on personality. *Marriage fam. Living*, 1954, **16**, 212–215.

35 Cartwright, R. D.: Self-conception patterns of college students, and adjustment to college life. *J. counsel. Psychol.*, 1963, **10**, 47–52.

36 Casbdan, S., and G. Welsh: Personality correlates of creative potential in talented high school students. *J. Pers.*, 1966, **34**, 445–455.

37 Cattell, R. B.: *Personality and motivation: Structure and measurement.* Tarrytown-on-Hudson, N. Y.: World, 1957.

38 Chase, P. H.: Self-concepts in adjusted and maladjusted hospital patients. *J. consult. Psychol.*, 1957, **21**, 495–497.

39 Chown, S. M.: Personality factors in the formation of occupational choice. *Brit. J. educ. Psychol.*, 1959, **29**, 23–33.

40 Cole, D. L.: The perception of Lincoln: A psychological approach to the public's conception of historical figures. *J. soc. Psychol.*, 1961, **55**, 23–26.

41 Coleman, J. S.: *The adolescent society.* New York: Free Press, 1961.

42 Combs, A. W.: New horizons in field research: The self-concept. *Educ. Leadership*, 1958, **15**, 315–319, 328.

43 Coombs, R. H.: Social particpation, self-concept and interpersonal valuation. *Sociometry*, 1969, **32**, 273–286.

44 Cottle, T. J.: Self-concept, ego ideal, and the response to action. *Sociol. soc. Res.*, 1965, **50**, 78–88.

45 Cowan, E. L., and P. N. Tongas: The social desirability of trait descriptive terms: Application to a self-concept inventory. *J. consult. Psychol.*, 1959, **23**, 361–365.

46 Crane, A. R.: Stereotypes of the adult held by early adolescents. *J. educ. Res.*, 1956, **50**, 227–230.

47 Cunningham, A.: Relation of sense of humor to intelligence. *J. soc. Psychol.*, 1962, **57**, 143–147.

48 Cummins, E. J.: Are disciplinary students different? *Personnel Guid. J.*, 1966, **44**, 624–627.

49 Dai, B.: A socio-psychiatric approach to personality organization. *Amer. sociol. Rev.*, 1952, **17**, 44–49.

50 Danzinger, K.: Choice of models among Javanese adolescents. *Psychol. Rep.*, 1960, **6**, 346.

51 Dean, D. G.: Romanticism and emotional maturity: A preliminary study. *Marriage fam. Living*, 1961, **23**, 44–45.

52 Dentler, R. A., and L. J. Monroe: Social correlates of early adolescent theft. *Amer. sociol. Rev.*, 1961, **26**, 733–743.

53 Deutsch, M., and L. Solomon: Reactions to evaluations of others as influenced by self-evaluations. *Sociometry*, 1959, **22**, 93–112.

54 Dien, D. S., and E. W. Vinacke: Self-concept and parental identification of young adults with mixed Caucasian-Japanese parentage. *J. abnorm. soc. Psychol.*, 1964, **69**, 463–466.

55 Dinitz, S., S. F. R. Scarpitti, and W. C. Reckless: Delinquency vulnerability: A cross group and longitudinal analysis. *Amer. sociol. Rev.*, 1962, **27**, 515–517.

56 Dixon, J. C.: Development of self recognition. *J. genet. Psychol.*, 1957, **91**, 251–256.

57 Dreger, R. M.: Spontaneous conversation and story-telling of children in a naturalistic setting. *J. Psychol.*, 1955, **40**, 163–180.

58 Ebaugh, F. G.: Age introduces stress into the family. *Geriatrics*, 1956, **11**, 146–150.

59 Eisenberg, L.: A developmental approach to adolescence. *Children*, 1965, **12**, 131–135.

60 Eismann, E. P.: Ego ideal maturation in late adolescence. *Dissert. Abstr.*, 1968, **28**, (10-B), 4294.

61 Elkins, D.: Some factors related to the choice-status of ninety eighth grade children in a school society. *Genet. Psychol. Monogr.*, 1958, **58**, 207–272.

62 Emmerich, W.: Personality development and concepts of structure. *Child Develpm.*, 1968, **39**, 671–690.

63 Engel, M.: The stability of the self-concept in adolescence. *J. abnorm. soc. Psychol.*, 1959, **58**, 211–215.

64 Epstein, E. M.: The self-concept of the delinquent female. *Smith Coll. Stud. soc. Wk.*, 1962, **32**, 220–234.

65 Escalona, S. K.: Some determinants of individual differences. *Trans. N. Y. Acad. Sci.*, 1965, **27**, 802–816.

66 Fast, I., and A. C. Cain: The stepparent role: Potential for disturbances in family functioning. *Amer. J. Orthopsychiat.*, 1966, **36**, 485–491.

67 Feinberg, M. R.: Stability of sociometric status in two adolescent class groups. *J. genet. Psychol.*, 1964, **104**, 83–87.

68 Fey, W. F.: Acceptance by others and its relation to acceptance of self and others: A revaluation. *J. abnorm. soc. Psychol.*, 1955, **50**, 274–276.

69 Fontana, A. F.: The effects of acceptance and rejection by desired membership groups on self-evaluation. *Dissert. Abstr.*, 1964, **25**, 3675.

70 Fouls, J. B., and W. D. Smith: Sex-role learning of five-year-olds. *J. genet. Psychol.*, 1956, **89**, 105–117.

71 Frank, G. H., and D. S. Hiester: Reliability of the ideal self-concept. *J. counsel. Psychol.*, 1967, **14**, 356–357.

72 Frank, L. K.: Introduction: The concept of maturity. *Child Develpm.*, 1950, **21**, 21–24.

73 Freedman, M. B.: Some theoretical and practical implications of a longitudinal study of college women. *Psychiatry*, 1963, **26**, 176–187.

74 Frenkel-Brunswik, E.: Patterns of social and cognitive outlook in children and parents. *Amer. J. Orthopsychiat.*, 1951, **21**, 543–558.

75 Freud, S.: *The standard edition of the complete psychological works of Sigmund Freud.* London: Hogarth, 1953–1962.

76 Fried, E.: Ego functions and techniques of ego strengthening. *Amer. J. Psychother.*, 1955, **9**, 407–429.

77 Gagnor, J. H.: Sexuality and sexual learning in the child *Psychiatry*, 1965, **28**, 212–228.

78 Glöckel, H.: A comparative study of the self-ideal in youth. *Child Develpm. Abstr.*, 1960, **34**, no. 649.

79 Glueck, S., and E. T. Glueck: *Family environment and delinquency.* Boston: Houghton Mifflin, 1962.

80 Goertzen, S. M.: Factors relating to opinions of seventh grade children regarding the acceptability of certain behaviors in the peer group. *J. genet. Psychol.*, 1959, **94**, 29–34.

81 Goins, A. E.: Rigidity-flexibility: Toward clarification. *Merrill-Palmer Quart.*, 1962, **8**, 41–61.

82 Goodchilds, J. D., and J. Harding: Formal organizations and informal activities. *J. soc. Issues*, 1960, **16**, no. 4, 16–28.

83 Grater, H.: Changes in self and other attitudes in a leadership training group. *Personnel Guid. J.*, 1959, **37**, 493–496.

84 Greenstein, F. I.: New light on changing American values: A forgotten body of survey data. *Soc. Forces*, 1964, **42**, 441–450.

85 Guerney, B., and J. L. Burton: Relationships among anxiety and self, typical peer, and ideal percepts of college women. *J. soc. Psychol.*, 1963, **61**, 335–344.

86 Guilford, J. P., and W. S. Zimmerman: Fourteen dimensions of temperament. *Psychol. Monogr.*, 1956, **70**, no. 10.

87 Hanlon, T. E., P. R. Hofstaetter, and J. P. O'Connor: Congruence of self and ideal self in relation to personality adjustment. *J. consult. Psychol.*, 1954, **18**, 215–218.

88 Harsh, C. M., and H. G. Schrickel: *Personality: Development and assessment*, 2d ed. New York: Ronald, 1959.

89 Harvey, O. J., H. H. Kelley, and M. M. Shapiro: Reactions to unfavorable evaluations of the self made by other persons. *J. Pers.*, 1957, **25**, 393–411.

90 Hathaway, S. R., and E. D. Monachesi: The personalities of predelinquent boys. *J. crim. Law Criminol. police Sci.*, 1957, **48**, 149–163.

91 Havighurst, R. J.: *Human development and education.* New York: Longmans, 1953.

92 Havighurst, R. J., and D. V. MacDonald: Development of the ideal self in New Zealand and American children. *J. educ. Res.*, 1955, **49**, 263–273.

93 Hawk, T. L.: Self-concepts of the socially disadvantaged. *Elem. Sch. J.*, 1966, **67**, 196–206.

94 Helson, R.: Personality characteristics and developmental history of creative college women. *Genet. Psychol. Monogr.*, 1967, **76**, 205–256.

95 Hilgard, E. R.: *Introduction to psychology*, 4th ed. New York: Harcourt, Brace & World, 1962.

96 Hillson, J. S., and P. Worchel: Self-concept and defensive behavior in the maladjusted. *J. consult. Psychol.*, 1957, **21**, 83–88.

97 James, W.: *Principles of psychology.* New York: Holt, 1890.

98 Jersild, A. T.: *In search of self.* New York: Teachers College, 1952.

99 Jersild, A. T.: Social and individual origins of the self. In D. E. Hamachek (ed.), *The self in growth, teaching, and learning.*

Englewood Cliffs, N. J.: Prentice-Hall, 1965, pp. 196–208.

100 Jones, M. C.: A study of socialization patterns at the high school level. *J. genet. Psychol.,* 1958, **93,** 87–111.

101 Jones, S. C., and D. J. Schneider: Certainty of self-appraisal and reactions to evaluations from others. *Sociometry,* 1968, **31,** 395–403.

102 Jorgensen, E. C., and R. J. Howell: Changes in self, ideal-self correlations from ages 8 through 18. *J. soc. Psychol.,* 1969, **79,** 63–67.

103 Jourard, S. M: Healthy personality and self-disclosure. *Ment. Hyg., N. Y.,* 1959, **43,** 499–507.

104 Jourard, S. M., and R. M. Remy: Perceived parental attitude, the self, and security. *J. consult. Psychol.,* 1955, **19,** 364–366.

105 Kassof, A.: The prejudicial personality: A cross-cultural test. *Soc. Probl.,* 1958, **6,** 59–67.

106 Katz, P., and E. Zigler: Self-image disparity: A developmental approach. *J. Pers. soc. Psychol.,* 1967, **5,** 186–195.

107 Keene, J. J.: Religious behavior and neuroticism, spontaneity, and world-mindedness. *Sociometry,* 1967, **30,** 137–157.

108 Keislar, E. R.: Experimental development of "like" and "dislike" of others among adolescent girls. *Child Develpm.,* 1961, **32,** 59–69.

109 Kent, D. P.: Social and cultural factors affecting the mental health of the aged. *Amer. J. Orthopsychiat.,* 1966, **36,** 680–685.

110 Kinch, J. W.: Experiments on factors related to self-concept change. *J. soc. Psychol.,* 1968, **74,** 251–258.

111 King, C. E., and W. H. Howell: Role characteristics of flexible and inflexible retired persons. *Sociol. soc. Res.,* 1964, **49,** 153–165.

112 Klausner, S. Z.: Social class and self-concept. *J. soc. Psychol.,* 1953, **38,** 201–205.

113 Koch, H. L.: The relation of certain formal attributes of siblings to attitudes held toward each other and toward their parents. *Monogr. Soc. Res. Child Develpm.,* 1960, **25,** no. 4.

114 Kohn, M.: The child as a determinant of his peers' approach to him. *J. genet. Psychol.,* 1966, **109,** 91–100.

115 Koppitz, E. M.: Relationship between some background factors and children's interpersonal attitudes. *J. genet. Psychol.,* 1957, **91,** 119–129.

116 Lecky, P.: *Self-consistency.* New York: Island Press, 1951.

117 Lewin, K.: *Field theory in social science.* New York: Harper, 1951.

118 Lieberman, J. N.: Playfulness. An attempt to conceptualize a quality of play and the player. *Psychol. Rep.,* 1966, **19,** 1278.

119 Lively, E. L., S. Dinitz, and W. C. Reckless: Self concept as a predictor of juvenile delinquency. *Amer. J. Orthopsychiat.,* 1962, **32,** 159–168.

120 Lodge, H. C.: The influence of the study of biography on the moral ideology of the adolescent at the eighth grade level. *J. educ. Res.,* 1956, **50,** 241–255.

121 Lowe, C. M.: The self-concept: Fact or artifact? *Psychol. Bull.,* 1961, **58,** 325–326.

122 Lund, F. H.: Biodyamics vs. Freudian psychodynamics. *Education,* 1957, **78,** 41–54.

123 Martin, J. G., and F. R. Westie: The toler-ant personality *Amer. sociol. Rev.,* 1959, **24,** 521–528.

124 Martin, W. E.: Learning theory and identification. III. The development of values in children. *J. genet. Psychol.,* 1954, **84,** 211–217.

125 Matteson, R. W.: Self-estimates of college freshmen. *Personnel Guid. J.,* 1956, **34,** 280–284.

126 *McCall's* Report: The empty days. Sept. 1965, pp. 79–81, 140–146.

127 McClosky, H.: Conservatism and personality. *A er. pol. sci. Rev.,* 1958, **52,** 27–45.

128 McDonald, R. L.: Effects of sex, race, and class on self, ideal-self, and parental ratings in Southern adolescents. *Percept. mot. Skills,* 1968, **27,** 15–25.

129 McIntyre, C. J.: Acceptance by others and its relation to acceptance of self and others. *J. abnorm. soc. Psychol.,* 1952, **47,** 624–625.

130 Mead, M.: *Male and female.* New York: Dell, 1968.

131 Muma, J. R.: Peer evaluation and academic performace. *Personnel Guid. J.,* 1965, **44,** 405–409.

132 Nahinsky, I. D.: The self-ideal correlation as a measure of generalized self-satisfaction. *Psychol. Rec.,* 1966, **16,** 55–64.

133 Oskamp, S.: Relationship of self-concepts to international attitudes. *J. soc. Psychol.,* 1968, **76,** 31–36.

134 Packard, V.: *The status seekers.* New York: Pocket Books, 1961.

135 Packard, V.: *The pyramid climbers.* New York: McGraw-Hill, 1962.

136 Parker, E.: *The seven ages of woman.* Baltimore: Johns Hopkins, 1960.

137 Parloff, M. B., L. E. Dalta, and J. H. Handlon: Personality characteristics which differentiate creative male adolescents and adults. *J. Pers.,* 1968, **36,** 528–552.

138 Paulsen, A. A.: Personality development in the middle years of childhood: A ten-year longitudinal study of thirty preschool children by means of Rorschach tests and social histories. *Amer. J. Orthopsychiat.,* 1954, **24,** 336–350.

139 Pedersen, D. M.: Ego strength and discrepancy between conscious and unconscious self-concepts. *Percept. mot. Skills,* 1965, **20,** 691–692.

140 Perkins, H. V.: Factors influencing changes in children's self-concepts. *Child Develpm.,* 1958, **29,** 221–230.

141 Peterson, D. R., H. C. Quay, and T. L. Tiffany: Personality factors related to juvenile delinquency. *Child Develpm.,* 1961, **32,** 355–372.

142 Phillips, A. S.: Self-concepts in children. *Educ. Res.,* 1964, **6,** 104–109.

143 Rabban, M.: Sex-role identification in young children in two diverse social groups. *Genet. Psychol. Monogr.,* 1950, **42,** 81–158.

144 Rabinowitz, M.: The relationship of self-regard to the effectiveness of life experiences. *Dissert. Abstr.,* 1966, **26,** 4800–4801.

145 Radke-Yarrow, M. J., and B. Lande: Personality correlates of differential reactions to minority group belonging. *J. soc. Psychol.,* 1953, **38,** 253–272.

146 Rainwater, L.: A study of personality differences between middle and lower class adolescents: The Szondi Test in culture-ant personality research. *Genet. Psychol. Monogr.,* 1956, **54,** 3–86.

147 Reckless, W. C., S. Dinitz, and E. Murray: Self concept as an insulator against delinquency. *Amer. sociol. Rev.,* 1956, **21,** 744–746.

148 Redmond, F. H.: Growth and development of the self-concept. *Dissert. Abstr.,* 1967, **28,** (2-A), 506.

149 Reeder, L. G., G. A. Donahue, and A. Biblarz: Conceptions of self and others. *Amer. J. Sociol.,* 1961, **66,** 153–159.

150 Rehfisch, J. M.: A scale for personality rigidity. *J. consult. Psychol.,* 1958, **22,** 11–15.

151 Rogers, C. R., and R. F. Diamond: *Psychotherapy and personality change.* Chicago: University of Chicago Press, 1954.

152 Rokeach, M.: Political and religious dogmatism: An alternative to the authoritarian personality. *Psychol. Monogr.,* 1956, **70,** no. 18.

153 Russell, D. H.: What does research say about self-evaluation? *J. educ. Res.,* 1953, **46,** 561–573.

154 Sarbin, T. R.: A preface to a psychological analysis of the self. *Psychol. Rev.,* 1952, **59,** 11–22.

155 Schaie, K. W.: Differences in some characteristics of "rigid" and "flexible" individuals. *J. clin. Psychol.,* 1958, **14,** 11–14.

156 Scharr, J. H.: Violence in juvenile gangs: Some notes and a few analogies. *Amer. J. Orthopsychiat.,* 1963, **33,** 29–37.

157 Schupack, M. B.: Research on employment problems of older workers. *Gerontologist,* 1962, **2,** 157–163.

158 Shaffer, L. F., and E. J. Shoben: *The psychology of adjustment,* 2d ed. Boston: Houghton Mifflin, 1956.

159 Shane, H. G.: Social experiences and selfhood. *Childhood Educ.,* 1957, **33,** 297–298.

160 Sherif, M., and H. Cantril: *The psychology of ego-envolvements.* New York: Wiley, 1947.

161 Shirley, M. M.: The impact of the mother's personality on the young child. *Smith Coll. Stud. soc. Wk.,* 1941, **12,** 15–64.

162 Shlien, J. M.: The self-concept in relation to behavior: Theoretical and empirical research. *Relig. Educ.,* 1962, **57,** suppl., 111–127.

163 Smith, G. M.: Six measures of self-concept discrepancy and instability: Their interrelations, reliability, and relations to other personality measures. *J. consult. Psychol.,* 1958, **22,** 101–112.

164 Smith, W. C.: Remarriage and the stepchild. In M. Fishbein and E. W. Burgess (eds.), *Successful marriage,* 2d ed. Garden City, N. Y.: Doubleday, 1955, pp. 328–349.

165 Smith, W. D., and D. Lebo: Some changing aspects of the self-concept of pubescent males. *J. genet. Psychol.,* 1956, **88,** 61–75.

166 Snyder, E. E.: Socioeconomic variations, values, and social participation among high school students. *J. Marriage & Family,* 1966, **28,** 174–176.

167 Stagner, R.: *Psychology of personality,* 3d ed. New York: McGraw-Hill, 1961.

168 Staines, J. W.: The self-picture as a factor in the classroom. *Brit. J. educ. Psychol.,* 1958, **28,** 97–111.

169 Starr, B. D.: Disciplinary attitudes of both parents and authoritarianism in their children. *Dissert. Abstr.,* 1965, **26,** (6), 3482.

170 Steinmann, A., J. Levi, and D. J. Fox:

Self-concepts of college women compared with their concept of the ideal woman and men's ideal woman. *J. counsel. Psychol.*, 1964, **11**, 370–374.

171 Strang, R.: *The adolescent views himself.* New York: McGraw-Hill, 1957.

172 Strodtbeck, F. L., J. F. Short, and E. Kolegar: An analysis of self-descriptions by members of delinquent gangs. *Sociol. Quart.*, 1962, **3**, 331–356.

173 Sullivan, H. S.: *The interpersonal theory of psychiatry.* New York: Norton, 1953.

174 Sutton-Smith, B., and B. G. Rosenberg: Peer perceptions of impulsive behavior. *Merrill-Palmer Quart.*, 1961, **7**, 233–238.

175 Tippett, J. S., and E. Silber: Self-image stability: The problem of validation. *Psychol. Rep.*, 1965, **17**, 323–329.

176 Toigo, R.: Social status and schoolroom aggression in third-grade children. *Genet. Psychol. Monogr.*, 1965, **71**, 221–268.

177 Torrance, E. P.: Some practical uses of a knowledge of self-concepts in counseling and guidance. *Educ. psychol. Measmt*, 1954, **14**, 120–127.

178 Torrance, E. P.: Changing reactions of preadolescent girls to tasks requiring creative scientific thinking. *J. genet. Psychol.*, 1963, **102**, 217–223.

179 Tuddenham, R. D.: Studies in reputation. I. Sex and grade differences in school children's evaluations of their peers. II. The diagnosis of social adjustment. *Psychol. Monogr.*, 1952, **66**, no. 1.

180 Turner, R. H., and R. H. Vanderlippe: Self-ideal congruence as an index of adjustment. *J. abnorm. soc. Psychol.*, 1958, **57**, 202–206.

181 Van den Daele, L.: A developmental study of the ego-ideal. *Genet. Psychol. Monogr.*, 1968, **78**, 191–256.

182 Van Kravelen, A.: Characteristics which "identify" the adolescent to his peers. *J. soc. Psychol.*, 1962, **56**, 285–289.

183 Videbeck, R.: Self-conception and the reactions of others. *Sociometry*, 1960, **23**, 351–359.

184 Volkman, A. P.: A matched-group personality comparison of delinquent and nondelinquent juveniles. *Soc. Probl.*, 1959, **6**, 238–245.

185 Walsh, A. M.: *Self-concepts of bright boys with learning difficulties.* New York: Teachers College, 1956.

186 Wattenberg, W. W., and C. Clifford: Relation of self-concepts to beginning achievement in reading. *Child Develpm.*, 1964, **35**, 461–467.

187 Weingarten, S.: Reading as a source of the ideal self. *Reading Teacher*, 1955, **8**, 159–164.

188 Wenkart, A.: Self-acceptance. *Amer. J. Psychoanal.*, 1955, **15**, 135–143.

189 Wernimont, P. F.: Intrinsic and extrinsic factors in job satisfaction. *J. appl. Psychol.*, 1966, **50**, 41–50.

190 Wheeler, D. K.: Development of the ideal self in Western Australian youth. *J. educ. Res.*, 1961, **54**, 163–167.

191 Williams, R. L., and H. Byars: Negro self-esteem in a transitional society. *Personnel Guid. J.*, 1968, **47**, 120–125.

192 Winick, C.: Trends in the occupations of celebrities: A study of news magazine profiles and television interviews. *J. soc. Psychol.*, 1963, **60**, 301–310.

193 Winkler, R. C., and R. A. Myers: Some concomitants of self-ideal discrepancy measures of self-acceptance. *J. counsel, Psychol.*, 1963, **10**, 83–86.

194 Witryol, S. L. and J. E. Calkins: Marginal social values of rural school children. *J. genet. Psychol.*, 1958, **92**, 81–93.

195 Woodworth, R. S., and D. G. Marquis: *Psychology*, 5th ed. New York: Holt, 1947.

196 Wylie, L.: Youth in France and the United States. *Daedalus*, 1962, **91**, 198–215.

197 Yamamoto, K. L: Creativity and sociometric choice among adolescents. *J. soc. Psychol.*, 1964, **64**, 249–261.

198 Yarrow, L. J.: Research in dimensions of early maternal care. *Merrill-Palmer Quart.*, 1963, **9**, 101–114.

199 Zander, A., and G. Rasmussen: Group membership and self evaluation. *Hum. Relat.*, 1954, **7**, 239–257.

200 Zimmer, H.: Self-acceptance and its relation to conflict. *J. consult. Psychol.*, 1954, **18**, 447–449.

CHAPTER 3

1 Adelson, D.: Attitudes toward first names: An investigation of the relation between self-acceptance, self-identity and group and individual attitudes toward first names. *Dissert. Abstr.*, 1957, **17**, 1831.

2 Aiken, L. R.: The relationships of dress to selected measures of personality in undergraduate women. *J. soc. Psychol.*, 1963, **59**, 119–128.

3 Allen, L., L. Brown, L. Dickinson, and K. C. Pratt: The relation of first name preferences to their frequency in the culture. *J. soc. Psychol.*, 1941, **14**, 279–293.

4 Allport, G. W.: *Pattern and growth in personality.* New York: Holt, 1961.

5 Alpenfels, E. J.: Status symbols of youth. *PTA Mag.*, 1966, **60**, no. 7, 4–6.

6 Amatora, Sister Mary: Free expression of adolescents' interests. *Genet. Psychol. Monogr.*, 1957, **55**, 173–219.

7 Ames, L. B.: The sense of self of nursery school children as manifested by their verbal behavior. *J. genet. Psychol.*, 1952, **81**, 193–232.

8 Anast, P.: Personality determinants of mass media preferences. *Journalism Quart.*, 1966, **43**, 729–732.

9 Angelino, H., L. A. Barnes, and C. L. Shedd: Attitudes of mothers and adolescent daughters concerning clothing and grooming. *J. Home Econ.*, 1956, **48**, 779–782.

10 Anisfeld, E., and W. E. Lambert: Evaluation reactions of bilingual and monolingual children to spoken language. *J. abnorm. soc. Psychol.*, 1964, **69**, 89–97.

11 Anspach, K.: Clothing selection and the mobility concept. *J. Home Econ.*, 1961, **53**, 428–430.

12 Arnhoff, F. N., and I. Lorge: Stereotypes about aging and the aged. *Sch. Soc.*, 1960, **80**, 70–71.

13 Baker, R.: Juliet was kidding herself. *The New York Times*, Apr. 20, 1967.

14 Barber, B., and L. S. Lobel: "Fashion" in women's clothes and the American social system. *Soc. Forces*, 1952, **31**, 124–131.

15 Bayley, N., and M. H. Oden: The maintenance of intellectual ability in gifted adults. *J. Geront.*, 1955, **10**, 91–107.

16 Becker, H. S.: Personal changes in adult life. *Sociometry*, 1964, **27**, 40–53.

17 Beilin, H.: The pattern of postponability and its relation to social class mobility. *J. soc. Psychol.*, 1956, **44**, 33–48.

18 Bell, W., and M. T. Force: Urban neighborhood types and participation in formal associations. *Amer. sociol. Rev.*, 1956, **21**, 25–34.

19 Bereiter, C.: Fluency ability of pre-school children. *J. genet. Psychol.*, 1961, **98**, 47–48.

20 Berger, B. M.: The new stage of American man: Almost endless adolescence. *The New York Times*, Nov. 2, 1969.

21 Bergler, E.: *The revolt of the middle-aged man.* New York: Wyn, 1954.

22 Bernard, J.: Teen-age culture: An overview. *Ann. Amer. Acad. pol. soc. Sci.*, 1961, **338**, 1–12.

23 Bernstein, B.: Language and social class. *Brit. J. Sociol.*, 1960, **11**, 271–276.

24 Blain, M. J., and M. Ramirez: Increasing sociometric rank, meaningfulness, and discriminability of children's names through reinforcement and interaction. *Child Develpm.*, 1968, **39**, 949–955.

25 Blaine, G. B.: Moral questions stir campuses. *The New York Times*, Jan. 19, 1964.

26 Blane, H. T., M. J. Hill, and E. Brow: Alienation, self-esteem and attitudes toward drinking in high-school students. *Quart. J. Stud. Alcohol*, 1966, **29**, 350–354.

27 Blau, Z. S.: Changes in status and age identification. *Amer. sociol. Rev.*, 1956, **21**, 198–203.

28 Bliven, B.: Using your leisure is no easy job. *The New York Times*, Apr. 26, 1964.

29 Bogart, L.: Adult talk about newspaper comics. *Amer. J. Sociol.*, 1955, **61**, 26–30.

30 Boroff, D.: American fetish: The college degree. *The New York Times*, Feb. 14, 1960.

31 Boshier, R.: Attitudes toward self and one's proper names. *J. indiv. Psychol.*, 1968, **24**, 63–66.

32 Bossard, J. H. S., and E. S. Boll: Marital happiness in the life cycle. *Marriage fam. Living*, 1955, **17**, 10–14.

33 Bossard, J. H. S. and E. S. Boll: *The sociology of child development*, 4th ed. New York: Harper & Row, 1966.

34 Botwinick, J.: Research problems and concepts in the study of aging. *Gerontologist*, 1964, **4**, 121–129.

35 Bowerman, C. E.: Adjustment in marriage: Over-all and in specific areas. *Sociol. soc. Res.*, 1957, **41**, 257–263.

36 Breckenridge, M. E., and E. L. Vincent: *Child development*, 5th ed. Philadelphia: Saunders, 1965.

37 Broom, L., H.P. Beem, and V. Harris: Characteristics of 1,107 petitioners for change of name. *Amer. sociol. Rev.*, 1955, **20**, 33–39.

38 Brough, J. R., and M. L. Reeves: Activities of suburban and inner-city youth. *Personnel Guid. J.*, 1968, **47**, 209–212.

39 Brown, D. G.: Sex-role development in a changing culture. *Psychol. Bull.*, 1958, **55**, 232–242.

40 Brown, R., and M. Ford: Address in American English. *J. abnorm. soc. Psychol.*, 1961, **62**, 375–385.

41 Bush, G., and P. London: On the disappearance of knickers: Hypothesis for the functional analysis of the psychology of clothing. *J. soc. Psychol.*, 1960, **51**, 359–366.

42 Cabe, P. A.: Name length as a factor in mate selection: Age controlled. *Psychol. Rep.*, 1968, **22**, 794.

43 Caillois, R.: *Man, play, and games.* New York: Free Press, 1961.

44 Carrow, Sister Mary A.: Linguistic functioning of bilingual and monolingual children. *J. speech hear. Disord.*, 1957, **22**, 371–380.

45 Catton, W. R.: What's in a name? A study of role inertia. *J. Marriage & Family*, 1969, **31**, 15–18.

46 Cavan, R. S.: *The American family*, 4th ed. New York: Crowell, 1969.

47 Chansky, M. N.: The attitudes students assign to their teachers. *J. educ. Psychol.*, 1958, **49**, 13–16.

48 Chown, S. M. and A. Heron: Psychological aspects of aging in man. *Annu. Rev. Psychol.*, 1965, **16**, 417–450.

49 Christensen, H. T., R. Andrews, and C. Freiser: Falsification of age at marriage. *Marriage fam. Living*, 1953, **15**, 301–305.

50 Clarke, A. C.: The use of leisure and its relation to levels of occupational prestige. *Amer. sociol. Rev.*, 1956, **21**, 301–307.

51 Cline, V. B., and J. M. Richards: A factor-analytic study of religious beliefs and behavior. *J. Pers. soc. Psychol.*, 1965, **1**, 569–578.

52 Coleman, J. S.: *The adolescent society.* New York: Free Press, 1961.

53 Compton, N. H.: Personal attributes of color and design preferences in clothing fabrics. *J. Psychol.*, 1962, **54**, 191–195.

54 Compton, N. H.: Body build, clothing and delinquent behavior. *J. Home Econ.*, 1967, **49**, 655–659.

55 Crow, L. D., and A. Crow: *Adolescent development and adjustment*, 2d ed. New York: McGraw-Hill, 1965.

56 Daley, R.: What's in a name? A lot if it's Sui Fei. *The New York Times*, Nov. 10, 1964.

57 Danzinger, K.: The child's understanding of kinship terms: A study in the development of relational concepts. *J. genet. Psychol.*, 1957, **91**, 213–232.

58 Davis, J. A.: Status symbols and the measurement of status perception. *Sociometry*, 1956, **19**, 154–165.

59 DeFleur, M. L.: Mass communication and social change. *Soc. Forces*, 1966, **44**, 314–326.

60 Denny, D., D. M. Kole, and R. G. Matarazzo: The relationship between age and the number of symptoms reported by patients. *J. Geront.*, 1965, **20**, 50–53.

61 Dentler, R. A.: Dropouts, automation and the schools. *Teachers Coll. Rec.*, 1964, **65**, 475–483.

62 Deutsch, M.: The role of social class in language development and cognition. *Amer. J. Orthopsychiat.*, 1965, **35**, 78–88.

63 Donald, M. N., and R. J. Havighurst: The meaning of leisure. *Soc. Forces*, 1959, **37**, 355–360.

64 Douty, H. I.: Influence of clothing on perception of persons. *J. Home Econ.*, 1963, **55**, 197–202.

65 Douvan, E.: Independence and identity in adolescence. *Children*, 1957, **4**, 186–190.

66 Drake, D.: On pet names. *Amer. Imago*, 1957, **14**, 41–43.

67 Dreger, R. M.: Spontaneous conversations and story-telling of children in a naturalistic setting. *J. Psychol.*, 1955, **40**, 163–180.

68 Dunphy, D. C.: The social structure of the urban adolescent peer groups. *Sociometry*, 1963, **26**, 230–246.

69 Dunsing, M: Spending money of adolescents. *J. Home Econ.*, 1956, **48**, 405–408.

70 Elkins, D.: Some factors related to the choice-status of ninety eighth-grade children in a school society. *Genet. Psychol. Monogr.*, 1958, **58**, 207–272.

71 Elliott, D. S.: Delinquency, school attendance, and dropout. *Soc. Probl.*, 1966, **13**, 307–314.

72 Elliott, F.: Shy middle graders. *Elem. Sch. J.*, 1968, **69**, 296-300.

73 Ellis, D. S.: Speech and social status in America. *Soc. Forces*, 1967, **45**, 431–437.

74 Fellows, L.: Schoolboy dress scored in Britain. *The New York Times*, Aug. 11, 1963.

75 Flugel, I.: On the significance of names. *Brit. J. med. Psychol.*, 1930, **10**, 208–213.

76 Fosmire, F. R.: The role of ego defense in academic reputation. *J. soc. Psychol.*, 1959, **49**, 41–45.

77 Freud, S.: *The standard edition of the complete psychological works of Sigmund Freud.* London: Hogarth, 1953–1962.

78 Friedlander, F.: Relationships between the importance and the satisfaction of various environmental factors. *J. appl. Psychol.*, 1965, **49**, 160–164.

79 Friedsam, H. J.: Reactions of older people to disaster-caused losses: An hypothesis of relative deprivation. *Gerontologist*, 1961, **1**, 34–37.

80 Garrison, K. C.: *Growth and development*, 2d ed. New York: Longmans, 1959.

81 Gesell, A., F. L. Ilg, and L. B. Ames: *Youth: The years from ten to sixteen.* New York: Harper & Row, 1956.

82 Gildston, P.: Stutterers' self-acceptance and perceived parental acceptance. *J. abnorm. Psychol.*, 1967, **72**, 59–64.

83 Glenn, H. M.: Attitudes of women regarding gainful employment of married women. *J. Home Econ.*, 1959, **51**, 247–252.

84 Glickman, A. S.: Clothing leadership among boys. *Dissert. Abstr.*, 1958, **18**, 682–684.

85 Glueck, S., and E. T. Glueck: *Family environment and delinquency.* Boston: Houghton Mifflin, 1962.

86 Goldstein, S.: Changing income and consumption patterns of the aged: 1950–1960. *J. Geront.*, 1965, **20** 453–461.

87 Gollin, E. S. Organizational characteristics of social judgment: A developmental investigation. *J. Pers.*, 1958, **26**, 139–154.

88 Goode, E.: Social class and church participation. *Amer. J. Sociol.*, 1966, **72**, 102–111.

89 Grosser, G. S., and W. J. Laczek: Prior parochial vs. secular secondary education and utterance latencies to taboo words. *J. Psychol.*, 1963, **55**, 263–277.

90 Guitar, M. A.: Status seekers, junior grade. *The New York Times*, Aug. 16, 1964.

91 Gunn, B.: Children's conceptions of occupational prestige. *Personnel Guid. J.*, 1964, **42**, 558–563.

92 Habbe, S.: Nicknames of adolescent boys. *Amer. J. Orthopsychiat.*, 1937, **7**, 371–377.

93 Hamid, P. N.: Style of dress as a perceptual cue in impression formation. *Percept. mot. Skills*, 1968, **26**, 904–906.

94 Hartman, A. A.: Name-styles in relation to personality. *J. gen. Psychol.*, 1958, **59**, 289–294.

95 Hartman, A. A., R. C. Nicolay, and J. Hurley: Unique personal names as a social adjustment factor. *J. soc. Psychol.*, 1968, **75**, 107–110.

96 Hartmann, G. W.: Clothing: Personal problem and social issue. *J. Home Econ.*, 1949, **41**, 295–298.

97 Havighurst, R. J.: *Human development and education.* New York: Longmans, 1953.

98 Havighurst, R. J.: The leisure activities of the middle-aged. *Amer. J. Sociol.*, 1957, **63**, 152–162.

99 Havighurst, R. J.: Body, self and society. *Sociol. soc. Res.*, 1965, **49**, 261–267.

100 Havighurst, R. J., and R. Albrecht: *Older people.* New York: Longmans, 1953.

101 Havighurst, R. J., and A. deVries: Life style and free time activities of retired men. *Hum. Develpm.*, 1969, **12**, 34–54.

102 Havighurst, R. J., and K. Feigenbaum: Leisure and life style. *Amer. J. Sociol.*, 1959, **64**, 396–404.

103 Heathers, G.: Acquiring dependence and independence: A theoretical orientation. *J. genet. Psychol.*, 1955, **87**, 277–291.

104 Hechinger, G., and F. M. Hechinger: *Teen-age tyranny.* New York: Morrow, 1963.

105 Helper, M. M.: Learning theory and the self-concept. *J. abnorm. soc. Psychol.*, 1955, **51**, 184–194.

106 Henry, W. E., and E. Cumming: Personality development in adulthood and old age. *J. proj. Tech.*, 1959, **23**, 383–390.

107 Hess, R. D., and I. Goldblatt: The status of adolescents in American society: A problem in social identity. *Child Develpm.*, 1957, **28**, 459–468.

108 Hickey, T., L. A. Hickey, and R. A. Kalish: Children's perceptions of the elderly. *J. genet. Psychol.*, 1968, **112**, 227–235.

109 Hoar, J.: A study of free-time activities of 200 aged persons. *Sociol. soc. Res.*, 1961, **45**, 157–163.

110 Hodge, R. W., P. M. Siegel, and P. H. Rossi: Occupational prestige in the United States: 1925–1963. *Amer. J. Sociol.*, 1964, **70**, 286–302.

111 Holmes, E.: Who uses consumer credit? *J. Home Econ.*, 1957, **49**, 340–342.

112 Horwitz, J.: This is the age of the aged. *The New York Times*, May 16, 1965.

113 Hoult, T. F.: Experimental measurement of clothing as a factor in some social ratings of selected American men. *Amer. sociol. Rev.*, 1954, **19**, 324–328.

114 Huffine, C. L.: Inter-socioeconomic class language differences: A research report. *Sociol. soc. Res.*, 1966, **50**, 351–355.

115 Hunt, L. A.: A developmental study of factors related to children's clothing preferences. *Monogr. Soc. Res. Child Develpm.*, 1959, **24**, no. 3.

116 Hurlock, E. B.: *The psychology of dress.* New York: Ronald, 1929.

117 Iverson, M. A.: Attraction toward flatterers of different statuses. *J. soc. Psychol.*, 1968, **74**, 181–187.

118 Jacobi, J. E., and S. G. Walters: Social status and consumer choice. *Soc. Forces*, 1958, **36**, 209–214.

119 Jahoda, G.: A note on Ashanti names and their relationship to personality. *Brit. J. Psychol.*, 1954, **45**, 192–195.

120 Jahoda, G.: Development of the perception of social differences in children from 6 to 10. *Brit. J. Psychol.*, 1959, **50**, 159–175.

121 Jersild, A. T.: *In search of self.* New York: Teachers College, 1952.

122 Jersild, A. T.: *The psychology of adolescence*, 2d ed. New York: Macmillan, 1963.

123 Jersild, A. T.: *Child psychology*, 6th ed.

Englewood Cliffs, N. J.: Prentice-Hall, 1969.

124 Jitodai, T. J.: Migrant status and church attendance. *Soc. Forces*, 1964, **43**, 241–248.

125 Johnson, E. E.: Student ratings of popularity and scholastic ability of their peers and actual scholastic performances of those peers. *J. soc. Psychol.*, 1958, **47**, 127–132.

126 Jones, M. C.: A study of socialization patterns at the high school level. *J. genet. Psychol.*, 1958, **93**, 87–111.

127 Jourard, S. M.: Age trends in self-disclosure. *Merrill-Palmer Quart.*, 1961, **7**, 191–197.

128 Kanous, R. A., L. E. Daugherty, and T. S. Cohn: Relation between heterosexual friendship choices and socioeconomic level. *Child Develpm.*, 1962, **33**, 251–255.

129 Kastenbaum, R.: On the meaning of time in later life. *J. genet. Psychol.*, 1966, **109**, 9–25.

130 Keislar, E. R.: The generalization of prestige among adolescent boys. *Calif. J. educ. Res.*, 1959, **10**, 153–156.

131 Kelly, J. A.: A study of leadership in two contrasting groups. *Sociol. Rev.*, 1963, **11**, 323–335.

132 Kent, D. B.: Social and cultural factors influencing the mental health of the aged. *Amer. J. Orthopsychiat.*, 1966, **36**, 680–685.

133 Kernaleguen, A. P., and N. H. Compton: Body-field perception differentiation related to peer perception of attitudes toward clothing. *Percept. mot. Skills*, 1968, **27**, 195–198.

134 Knupfer, G., and R. Room: Age, sex, and social class as factors in amount of drinking in a metropolitan community. *Soc. Probl.*, 1965, **12**, 223–240.

135 Koch, H. L.: The relation of certain formal attributes of siblings to attitudes held toward each other and toward parents. *Monogr. Soc. Res. Child Develpm.*, 1960, **25**, no. 4.

136 Kogan, N., and F. C. Shelton: Beliefs about "old people": A comparative study of older and younger samples. *J. genet. Psychol.*, 1962, **100**, 93–111.

137 Koppe, W. A.: The psychological meanings of housing and furnishings. *Marriage fam. Living*, 1955, **17**, 129–132.

138 Krippner, S.: Upper- and lower-class children's sentence completions and speech improvement. *J. clin. Psychol.*, 1965, **21**, 335–337.

139 Kunde, T. A., and R. V. Dawis: Comparative study of occupational prestige in three Western cultures. *Personnel Guid. J.*, 1959, **27**, 350–352.

140 Lane, B.: Attitudes of youth toward the aged. *J. Marriage & Family*, 1964, **26**, 229–231.

141 Laswell, T. E., and P. F. Parshall: The perception of social class from photographs. *Sociol soc. Res.*, 1961, **45**, 407–414.

142 Lay, C. H., and B. F. Burron: Perception of the personality of the hesitant speaker. *Percept. mot. Skills*, 1968, **26**, 951–956.

143 Lerea, L., and B. Ward: Speech avoidance among children with oral-communication defects. *J. Psychol.*, 1965, **60**, 265–270.

144 Levinson, H.: What work means to a man. *Menninger Quart.*, 1964, **18**, 1–11.

145 Lipsett, L. P.: A self-concept scale for children and its relationship to the children's

form of the manifest anxiety scale. *Child Develpm.*, 1958, **29**, 463–472.

146 Livson, N.: Parental behavior and children's involvement with their parents. *J. genet. Psychol.*, 1966, **109**, 173–194.

147 *London Times* Report: Buggs family changes its name. June 12, 1965.

148 Luft, J.: Monetary value and the perception of persons. *J. soc. Psychol.*, 1957, **46**, 245–251.

149 Mahler, L: Determinants of professional desirability. *J. soc. Psychol.*, 1961, **55**, 97–103.

150 Marak, G. E.: The evolution of leadership structure. *Sociometry*, 1964, **27**, 174–182.

151 Markel, N. N., R. M. Eisler, and H. W. Reese: Judging personality from dialect. *J. verbal Learn. verbal Behav.*, 1967, **6**, 33–35.

152 Marshall, H. R.: Relations between home experiences and children's use of language in play interactions with peers. *Psychol. Monogr.*, 1961, **75**, no. 5.

153 Martinson, F. M.: Ego deficiency as a factor in marriage: A male sample. *Marriage fam. Living*, 1959, **21**, 48–52.

154 *McCall's* Report: The empty days. Sept. 1965, pp. 79–81, 140–146.

155 McCarthy, D.: Language development. *Monogr. Soc. Res. Child Develpm.*, 1960, **25**, no. 3, 5–14.

156 McDavid, J. W. and H. Harari: Stereotyping of names and popularity in grade-school children. *Child Develpm.*, 1966, **37**, 453–459.

157 McDill, E. L., and J. Coleman: Family and peer influences in college plans of high school students. *Sociology of Education*, 1965, **38**, 112–126.

158 McInnes, J. H., and J. K. Shearer: Relationship between color choice and selected preferences of the individual. *J. Home Econ.*, 1964, **56**, 181–187.

159 Mead, M.: *Male and female*. New York: Dell, 1968.

160 Meltzer, H.: Workers' perceptual stereotypes of age differences. *Percept. mot. Skills*, 1960, **11**, 89.

161 Meyer, H. D.: The adult cyle. *Ann. Amer. Acad. pol. soc. Sci.*, 1957, **313**, 58–67.

162 Michael, G., and F. N. Willis: The development of gestures in three subcultural groups. *J. soc. Psychol.*, 1969, **79**, 35–41.

163 Middleton, D.: In Britain, names denote status and the more the better. *The New York Times*, July 5, 1960.

164 Morton, G. M.: Psychology of dress. *J. Home Econ.*, 1926, **18**, 584–586.

165 Murphy, W. F.: A note on the significance of names. *Psychonal. Quart.*, 1957, *26*, 91–106.

166 Musgrove, F.: The social needs and satisfactions of some young people. 1. At home, in youth clubs, and at work. *Brit. J. educ. Psychol.*, 1966, **36**, 61–71.

167 Nelson, D. O.: Leadership in sports. *Res. Quart. Amer. Ass. Hlth. Phys. Educ. Recr.*, 1966, **37**, 268–275.

168 Neugarten, B. L., and D. C. Garron: Attitudes of middle-aged persons toward growing older. *Geriatrics*, 1959, **14**, 21–24.

169 *New York Times* Report: Trends in Anthony in naming babies. July 15, 1962.

170 *New York Times* Report: Autonomy found to be chief goal of bright students. Oct. 19, 1964.

171 *New York Times* Report: Britain's best-dressed: The youthful mods. Feb. 24, 1965.

172 *New York Times* Report: New Yorkers show status by their Rs. Nov. 2, 1967.

173 *New York Times* Report: Once-proud name of Adolf shunned by West Germans. Jan. 19, 1969.

174 *Newsweek* Report: The divorced woman: American style. Feb. 13, 1967, pp. 64–70.

175 Northway, M. E., and J. Detweiler: Children's perception of friends and non-friends. *Sociometry*, 1955, **18**, 527–531.

176 Orgel, S. Z., and J. Tuckman: Nicknames of institutional children. *Amer. J. Orthopsychiat.*, 1935, **5**, 276–285.

177 Ostermeier, A. L.: Adolescent behavior as manifested in clothing. *Child Study Center Bull.*, State University Coll., Buffalo, 1967, **3**, 1–10.

178 Packard, V.: *The status seekers*. New York: Pocket Books, 1961.

179 Packard, V.: *The pyramid climbers*. New York: McGraw-Hill, 1962.

180 Parker, E.: *The seven ages of woman*. Baltimore: Johns Hopkins, 1960.

181 Pastore, N.: Attributed characteristics of liked and disliked persons. *J. soc. Psychol.*, 1962, **52**, 157–163.

182 Patterson, G. R., and D. Anderson: Peers as social reinforcers. *Child Develpm.*, 1964, **35**, 951–960.

183 Payne, E.: Musical taste and personality. *Brit. J. Psychol.*, 1967, **58**, 133–138.

184 Pear, T. H.: *Personality, appearance and speech*. London: G. Allen, 1957.

185 Pederson, D. M., and V. J. Breglio: Personality correlates of actual self-disclosure. *Psychol. Rep.*, 1968, **22**, 495–501.

186 Penny, R.: Age and sex differences in motivational orientation to the communicative act. *Child Develpm.*, 1958, **29**, 163–171.

187 Powell, M.: Age and sex differences in degree of conflict within certain areas of psychological adjustment. *Psychol. Monogr.*, 1955, **69**, no. 2.

188 Pressey, S. L., and R. G. Kuhlen: *Psychological development through the life span*. New York: Harper & Row, 1957.

189 Pryer, M. W., W. A. Flint, and B. M. Bass: Group effectiveness and consistency of leadership. *Sociometry*, 1962, **25**, 391–397.

190 Psathas, G.: Ethnicity, social class and adolescent independence from parental control. *Amer. sociol. Rev.*, 1957, **22**, 415–423.

191 Quay, H. C., and L. C. Quay: Behavior problems in early adolescence. *Child Develpm.*, 1965, **36**, 215–220.

192 *Report of President's Council on Aging.* 1961.

193 Riester, A. E., and R. A. Zucker: Adolescent social structure and drinking behavior. *Personnel Guid. J.*, 1968, **47**, 304–312.

194 Roach, M. E.: The influence of social class on clothing practices and orientation at early adolescence: A study of clothing-related behavior of seventh-grade girls. *Dissert. Abstr.*, 1962, **22**, 2897–2898.

195 Rogers, K. D., and G. Reese: Smoking and high school performance. *Amer. J. Dis. Children*, 1964, **108**, 117–121.

196 Rosencranz, M. L.: Social and psychological approaches to clothing research. *J. Home Econ.*, 1965, **57**, 26–29.

197 Roucek, J. S.: Age as a prestige factor. *Sociol. soc. Res.*, 1958, **42**, 349–352.

198 Ryan, M. S.: *Clothing: A study in human behavior*. New York: Holt, 1966.

199 Schaefer, E. S.: Children's reports of parental behavior: An inquiry. *Child Develpm.*, 1965, **36**, 413–424.

200 Scheinfeld, A.: *The new you and heredity.* Philadelphia: Lippincott, 1961.

201 Schneider, D. M., and G. C. Homans: Kinship terminology and the American kinship system. *Amer. Anthropologist*, 1955, **57**, 1194–1208.

202 Schonfield, D., and J. Trimble: Advantages of aging. *Proc. 20th Ann. Meeting Gerontol. Soc.*, 1967.

203 Schupack, M. B.: Research on employment problems for older workers. *Gerontologist*, 1962, **2**, 157–163.

204 Schwebel, A. I.: Effects of impulsiveness on performance of verbal tasks in middle- and lower-class children. *Amer. J. Orthopsychiat.*, 1966, **36**, 13–21.

205 Searls, L. G.: Leisure role emphasis of college graduate homemakers. *J. Marriage & Family*, 1966, **28**, 77–82.

206 Seeman, M.: The intellectual and the language of minorities. *Amer. J. Sociol.*, 1958, **64**, 25–35.

207 Seltzer, C. C.: Masculinity and smoking. *Science*, 1959, **130**, 1706–1707.

208 Semple, R. B.: New help for the 18,457,000 of us who are old. *The New York Times*, Feb. 5, 1967.

209 Sheppard, D.: Characteristics associated with Christian names. *Brit. J. Psychol.*, 1963, **54**, 167–174.

210 Shipley, S., and M. L. Rosencranz: Older women's clothing preferences. *J. Home Econ.*, 1962, **54**, 854.

211 Shirley, M. M.: *The first two years.* Vol. 3 *Personality manifestations.* Minneapolis: University of Minnesota Press, 1933.

212 Silverman, D.: An evaluation of the relationship between attitudes toward self and attitudes toward a vocational high school. *J. educ. Sociol.*, 1963, **36**, 410–418.

213 Slater, C.: Class differences in definition of role and membership in voluntary associations among urban married women. *Amer. J. Sociol.*, 1960, **65**, 616–619.

214 Slater, P. E.: Cross-cultural views of the aged. In R. Kastenbaum (ed.), *New thoughts on old age*, New York: Springer, 1964, pp. 229–236.

215 Soffietti, J. P.: Bilingualism and biculturalism. *J. educ. Psychol.*, 1955, **46**, 222–227.

216 Solomon, A. L.: Personality and behavior patterns of children with functional defects of articulation. *Child Develpm.*, 1961, **32**, 731–737.

217 Stewart, L., and N. Livson: Smoking and rebelliousness: A longitudinal study from childhood to maturity. *J. consult. Psychol.*, 1966, **30**, 225–229.

218 Stolz, H. R.: Shorty comes to terms with himself. *Prog. Educ.*, 1940, **17**, 405–411.

219 Stout, D. R., and A. Latzke: Values college women consider in clothing selection. *J. Home Econ.*, 1958, **50**, 43–44.

220 Stringer, L. A.: Parent-child relations in early school years. *Soc. Wk.*, 1964, **9**, 98–104.

221 Strongman, K. T., and J. Woosley: Stereotyped reactions to regional accents. *Brit. J. soc. clin. Psychol.*, 1967, **6**, 164–167.

222 Strunk, O.: Attitudes toward one's name and one's self. *J. indiv. Psychol.*, 1958, **14**, 64–67.

223 Sutton-Smith, B., J. M. Roberts, and R. M. Kozelka: Game involvement in adults. *J. soc. Psychol.*, 1963, **60**, 15–30.

224 Tannenbaum, A. J.: *Adolescent attitudes*

toward academic brilliance. New York: Teachers College, 1962.

225 Teele, J. E.: Correlates of voluntary social participations. *Genet. Psychol. Monogr.*, 1967, **76**, 176–204.

226 Terrell, G., and J. Shreffler: A developmental study of leadership. *J. educ. Res.*, 1958, **52**, 69–72.

227 Thompson, L. J.: Stresses in middle life from the psychiatrist's viewpoint. In C. B. Vedder (ed.), *Problems of the middle-aged.* Springfield, Ill.: Charles C Thomas, 1965, pp. 116–120.

228 Tiktin, S., and W. W. Hartup: Sociometric status and the reinforcing effectiveness of children's peers. *J. exp. Child Psychol.*, 1965, **2**, 306–315.

229 *Time* Report: Pop drugs: The high as a way of life. Sept. 26, 1969, pp. 68–78.

230 Tuckman, J., and I. Lorge: The projection of personal symptom into stereotype about aging. *J. Geront.*, 1958, **13**, 70–73.

231 Turner, R. H.: Some aspects of women's ambition. *Amer. J. Sociol.*, 1964, **70**, 271–285.

232 Udry, J. R.: Structural correlates of feminine beauty preferences in Britain and the United States: A comparison. *Sociol. soc. Res.*, 1965, **49**, 330–342.

233 Ulrich, G., J. Hecklik, and E. C. Roeber: Occupational stereotypes of high school students. *Voc. Guid. Quart.*, 1966, **14**, 169–174.

234 *U. S. News & World Report:* Changes in today's college students. Feb. 17, 1964, pp. 48–50.

235 *U. S. News & World Report:* How women's role in U. S. is changing. May 30, 1966, pp. 58–60.

236 *U. S. News & World Report:* Runaway problem of retirement: More and more older people. Aug. 5, 1968, pp. 76–78.

237 Vener, A. M.: Clothes tell a story. *The New York Times*, Aug. 28, 1959.

238 Vielhaber, D. P., and E. Gottheil: First impressions and subsequent ratings of performance. *Psychol. Rep.*, 1955, **17**, 916.

239 Walker, R. E., R. C. Nicolay, R. Kluceny, and R. E. Riedel: Psychological correlates of smoking. *J. clin. Psychol.*, 1969, **25**, 42–44.

240 Walster, E., and B. Walster: Effect of expecting to be liked on choice of association. *J. abnorm. soc. Psychol.*, 1963, **67**, 402–404.

241 Walters, J., F. I. Stromberg, and G. Lonian: Perceptions concerning development of responsibility in young children. *Elem. Sch. J.*, 1957, **57**, 209–216.

242 Warburton, F. E.: The lab coat as a status symbol. *Science*, 1960, **131**, 895.

243 Wass, B. M., and J. B. Eicher: Clothing as related to role behavior of teen-age girls. *Quart. Bull., Mich. Agri. Exp. Stat.*, 1964, **47**, 206–213.

244 Wax, M.: Themes in cosmetics and grooming. *Amer. J. Sociol.*, 1957, **62**, 588–593.

245 Wernimont, P. F.: Intrinsic and extrinsic factors in job satisfaction. *J. appl. Psychol.*, 1966, **50**, 41–50.

246 White, R. C.: Social class differences in the uses of leisure. *Amer. J. Sociol.*, 1955, **61**, 145–150.

247 Williams, N. C., and J. B. Eicher: Teenagers' appearance and social acceptance. *J. Home Econ.*, 1966, **58**, 457–461.

248 Winick, C.: The Beige Epoch: Depolariza-

tion of sex roles in America. *Ann. Amer. Acad. pol. soc. Sci.*, 1968, **376**, 18–24.

249 Yamamoto, K.: Development of ability to ask questions under specific testing conditions. *J. genet. Psychol.*, 1962, **101**, 83–90.

250 Yoshino, I. R.: The stereotype of the Negro and his high-priced car. *Sociol. soc. Res.*, 1959, **44**, 112–118.

251 Zagona, S., and L. A. Zurcher: An analysis of some psycho-social variables associated with smoking in a college sample. *Psychol. Rep.*, 1965, **17**, 967–978.

252 Zimmer, B. G., and A. H. Hawley: The significance of membership in associations. *Amer. J. Sociol.*, 1959, **65**, 196–201.

253 Zucker, R. A.: Sex-role identity patterns and drinking behavior of adolescents. *Quart. J. Stud. Alcohol*, 1968, **29**, 868–884.

CHAPTER 4

1 Adelson, J.: What generation gap? *The New York Times*, Jan. 18, 1970.

2 Albert, R. S.: The role of mass media and effect of aggressive film content upon children's aggressive reponses and identification choices. *Genet. Psychol. Monogr.*, 1957, **55**, 221–285.

3 Aldous, J., and L. Kell: Child-rearing values of mothers in relation to their children's perceptions of their mothers' control: An exploratory study. *Marriage fam. Living*, 1956, **18**, 72–74.

4 Aldridge, J. W.: In the country of the young. Part I. *Harper's Mag.*, Oct. 1969, pp. 49–64.

5 Aldridge, J. W.: In the country of the young: Part II. *Harper's Mag.*, Nov. 1969, pp. 93–107.

6 Alper, T. G., H. T. Blane, and B. I. Abrams: Reactions of middle and lower class children to finger paints as a function of class differences in child-training practices. *J. abnorm. soc. Psychol.*, 1955, **51**, 439–448.

7 Allport, G. W.: *Pattern and growth in personality.* New York: Holt, 1961.

8 Allport, G. W.: Prejudice: Is it societal or personal? *J. soc. Issues*, 1962, **18**, 120–132.

9 Alt, H.: Basic principles of child rearing in the Soviet Union: First-hand impressions of an American observer. *Amer. J. Orthopsychiat.*, 1958, **28**, 223–240.

10 Antonovsky, H. F.: A contribution to research in the area of the mother-child relationship. *Child Develpm.*, 1959, **30**, 37–51.

11 Apperson, L. B.: Childhood experiences of schizophrenics and alcholics. *J. genet. Psychol.*, 1965, **106**, 301–313.

12 Archibald, H. C., D. Bell, C. Miller, and R. D. Tuddenham: Bereavement in childhood and adult psychiatric disturbance. *Psychosom. Med.*, 1962, **24**, 343–351.

13 Auerbach, A. B.: Meeting the needs of new mothers. *Children*, 1964, **11**, 223–238.

14 Bacola, E., F. C. Behrle, L. deSchweinitz, H. C. Miller, and M. Mira: Perinatal and environmental factors in late neurogenic sequelae. *Amer. J. Dis. Children*, 1966, **112**, 359–374.

15 Bacon, M. K., I. L. Child, and H. Barry: A cross-cultural study of correlates of crime. *J. abnorm. soc. Psychol.*, 1963, **66**, 291–300.

16 Bailyn, L.: Mass media and children: A study of exposure habits and cognitive effects. *Psychol. Monogr.*, 1959, **73**, no. 1.

17 Barclay, A., and D. R. Cusumano: Father absence, cross-sex identity, and field-dependent behavior in male adolescents. *Child Developm.*, 1967, **38**, 243–250.

18 Bartemeier, L.: The contribution of the father to the mental health of the family. *Amer. J. Psychiat.*, 1953, **110**, 277–280.

19 Baumrind, D.: Effects of authoritarian parental control on child behavior. *Child Developm.*, 1966, **37**, 887–907.

20 Baumrind, D.: Child care practices anteceding three patterns of preschool behavior. *Genet. Psychol. Monogr.*, 1967, **75**, 43–88.

21 Baumrind, D., and A. E. Black: Socialization practices associated with dimensions of competence in preschool boys and girls. *Child Developm.*, 1967, **38**, 291–327.

22 Becker, L. J.: The changing moral values of students. *J. Home Econ.*, 1963, **55**, 646–648.

23 Behers, M. L.: Child rearing and the character structure of the mother. *Child Developm.*, 1954, **25**, 225–238.

24 Beier, E. G., and F. Ratzeburg: The parental identifications of male and female college students. *J. abnorm. soc. Psychol.*, 1953, **48**, 569–572.

25 Bell, R. R., and J. V. Buerkle: The daughter's role during the "launching stage." *Marriage fam. Living*, 1962, **24**, 384–388.

26 Benedict, R.: Child rearing in certain European countries. *Amer. J. Orthopsychiat.*, 1949, **19**, 342–350.

27 Bennett, E. M., and L. R. Cohen: Men and women: Personality patterns and contrasts. *Genet. Psychol. Monogr.*, 1959, **59**, 101–155.

28 Berkowitz, L., and P. Friedman: Some social class differences in helping behavior. *J. Pers. soc. Psychol.*, 1967, **5**, 217–225.

29 Berkowitz, L., and R.M. Lundy: Personality characteristics related to susceptibility to influence by peers or authority figures. *J. Pers.*, 1957, **25**, 306–316.

30 Bettelheim, B.: Where self begins. *Child & Family*, 1968, **7**, no. 1, 5–9.

31 Bieri, J., and R. Lobeck: Self-concept differences in relation to identification, religion and social class. *J. abnorm. soc. Psychol.*, 1961, **62**, 94–98.

32 Block, J.: Personality characteristics associated with the fathers' attitudes toward child-rearing. *Child Developm.*, 1955, **26**, 41–48.

33 Blos, P.: *The adolescent personality.* New York: Appleton-Century-Crofts, 1941.

34 Bossard, J. H. S., and E. S. Boll: *The sociology of child development*, 4th ed. New York: Harper & Row, 1966.

35 Bowerman, C. E., and J. W. Kinch: Changes in family and peer orientation of children between the fourth and tenth grades. *Soc. Forces*, 1959, **37**, 205–211.

36 Brody, J. E.: New mothers get advice on "blues." *The New York Times*, Feb. 25, 1968.

37 Brody, S.: Signs of disturbance in the first year of life. *Amer. J. Orthopsychiat.*, 1958, **28**, 362–367.

38 Bronfenbrenner, U.: The role of age, sex, class and culture in studies of moral development. *Relig. Educ.*, 1962, **57**, S–3, 8–17.

39 Bronson, G.: Critical periods in human development. *Brit. J. med. Psychol.*, 1962, **35**, 127–133.

40 Bronson, W. C.: Dimensions of ego and infantile identification. *J. Pers.*, 1959, **27**, 532–545.

41 Brown, D. G.: Masculinity-femininity de-

velopment in children. *J. consult. Psychol.*, 1957, **21**, 197–202.

42 Bühler, C.: The life cycle: Structural determinants of goal setting. *J. humanist. Psychol.*, 1966, **6**, 37–52.

43 Busse, T.V.: Child-rearing antecedents of flexible thinking. *Developm. Psychol.*, 1969, **1**, 584–591.

44 Byrne, D.: Parental antecedents of authoritarianism. *J. Pers. soc. Psychol.*, 1965, **1**, 369–373.

45 Caldwell, B. M.: What is the optimal learning environment for the young child? *Amer. J. Orthopsychiat.*, 1967, **37**, 8–21.

46 Caldwell, B. M., L. Hersher, E. L. Lipton, J. B. Richmond, G. A. Stern. E. Eddy, R. Drachman, and A. Rothman: Mother-infant interaction in monomatric and polymatric families. *Amer. J. Orthopsychiat.*, 1963, **33**, 653–664.

47 Carlsmith, L.: Effect of early father absence on scholastic aptitude. *Harv. educ. Rev.*, 1964, **34**, 3–21.

48 Cattell, R. B., G. F. Stice, and N. F. Kristy: A first approximation to nature-nurture ratio for eleven primary personality factors in objective tests. *J. abnorm. soc. Psychol.*, 1957, **54**, 143–159.

49 Centers, R., and M. Horowitz: Social character and conformity: A differential in susceptibility to social influences. *J. soc. Psychol.*, 1963, **60**, 343–349.

50 Chansky, N. M.: The attitudes students assign to their teachers. *J. educ. Psychol.*, 1958, **49**, 13–16.

51 Child, I. L., E. H. Potter, and E. M. Levine: Children's textbooks and personality development: An exploration in the social psychology of education. In W. E. Martin and C. B. Stendler (eds.), *Readings in child development*. New York: Harcourt, Brace & World, 1954, pp. 479–492.

52 Christie, R., and P. Cook: A guide to published literature relating to the authoritarian personality through 1956. *J. Psychol.*, 1958, **45**, 171–199.

53 Cianciolo, P. J.: Children's literature can affect coping behavior. *Personnel Guid. J.*, 1965, **43**, 897–903.

54 Clifford, E.: Discipline in the home: A controlled observational study of parental practices. *J. genet. Psychol.*, 1959, **95**, 45–82.

55 Cole, M., F. M. Fletcher, and S. L. Pressey: Forty-year changes in college student attitudes. *J. counsel. Psychol.*, 1963, **10**, 53–55.

56 Croft, I. J., and T. G. Grygier: Social relationship of truants and juvenile delinquents. *Hum. Relat.*, 1956, **9**, 439–466.

57 Davids, A., R. H. Holden, and G. B. Gray: Maternal anxiety during pregnancy and adequacy of mother and child adjustment eight months following childbirth. *Child Developm.*, 1963, **34**, 993–1002.

58 Davis, R. E., and R. A. Ruiz: Infant feeding method and adolescent personality. *Amer. J. Psychiat.*, 1965, **122**, 673–678.

59 Devereux, E. C., U. Bronfenbrenner, and R. R. Rodgers: Child-rearing in England and the United States: A cross-national comparison. *J. Marriage & Family*, 1969, **31**, 257–270.

60 Doty, B. A.: Relationships among attitudes in pregnancy and other maternal characteristics. *J. genet. Psychol.*, 1967, **111**, 203–217.

61 Douvan, E.: Sex differences in adolescent

character processes. *Merrill-Palmer Quart.*, 1960, **6**, 203–211.

62 Dreger, R. M.: Just how far can social change change personality? *J. Psychol.*, 1966, **64**, 167–191.

63 DuHamel, T. R., and H. B. Biller: Parental imitation and nonimitation in young children. *Developm. Psychol.*, 1969, **1**, 772.

64 Dunphy, D. C.: The social structure of the urban adolescent peer groups. *Sociometry*, 1963, **26**, 230–246.

65 Dyer, W. G.: Parental influence on the job attitudes of children from two occupational strata. *Sociol. soc. Res.*, 1958, **42**, 203–206.

66 Elder, G. H.: Structural variations in the child rearing relationship. *Sociometry*, 1962, **25**, 241–262.

67 Emery, F. E.: Psychological effects of the Western film: A study in television viewing. *Hum. Relat.*, 1959, **12**, 215–232.

68 Eron, L. D.: Relationship of TV viewing habits and aggressive behavior in children. *J. abnorm. soc. Psychol.*, 1963, **67**, 193–196.

69 Esty, J. F.: Early and current parent-child relationships perceived by college student leaders and non-leaders. *Dissert. Abstr.*, 1968, **29** (3–B), 1169–1170.

70 Eysenck, H. J.: The development of moral values in children. VII. The contribution of the learning theory. *Brit. J. educ. Psychol.*, 1960, **30**, 11–21.

71 Farber, M. L.: English and Americans: Values in the socialization process. *J. Psychol.*, 1953, **36**, 243–250.

72 Fast, I., and A. C. Cain: The stepparent role: Potential for disturbances in family functioning. *Amer. J. Orthopsychiat.*, 1966, **36**, 485–491.

73 Fernandez-Marina, R., E. M. Maldonado-Sierra, and R. D. Trent: Three basic themes in Mexican and Puerto Rican family values. *J. soc. Psychol.*, 1958, **48**, 167–181.

74 Ford, N. A.: Literature as an aid to social development. *Teachers Coll. Rec.*, 1957, **58**, 377–381.

75 Frank, L. K.: The concept of maturity. *Child Developm.*, 1950, **21**, 21–24.

76 Freedman, M. B.: The sexual behavior of American college women: An empirical study and an historical survey. *Merrill-Palmer Quart.*, 1965, **11**, 33–48.

77 Freud, S.: *The standard edition of the complete psychological works of Sigmund Freud.* London: Hogarth, 1953–1962.

78 Fryrear, J. L., and M. H. Thelen: Effect of sex of model and sex of observer on the emulation of affectionate behavior. *Developm. Psychol.*, 1969, **1**, 298.

79 Gesell, A., F. L. Ilg, and L. B. Ames: *Youth: The years from ten to sixteen.* New York: Harper, 1956.

80 Gewirtz, J. L.: A factor analysis of some attention-seeking behaviors of young children. *Child Developm.*, 1956, **27**, 17–36.

81 Gibson, H. B.: The measurement of parental attitudes and their relation to boys' behavior. *Brit. J. educ. Psychol.*, 1968, **38**, 233–239.

82 Gillian, J.: National and regional cultural values in the United States. *Soc. Forces*, 1955, **34**, 107–113.

83 Glueck, S., and E. T. Glueck: *Family environment and delinquency.* Boston: Houghton Mifflin, 1962.

84 Goodman, M. E.: Japanese and American

children: A comparative study of social concepts and attitudes. *Marriage fam. Living*, 1958, **20**, 316–319.

85 Gordon, R. A., J. F. Short, D. S. Cartwright, and F. L. Strodtbeck: Values and gang delinquency: A study of street-corner groups. *Amer. J. Sociol.*, 1963, **69**, 109–128.

86 Gottesman, I. I.: Heritability of personality. *Psychol. Monogr.*, 1963, **77**, no. 9.

87 Gray, S. W.: Perceived similarity to parents and adjustment. *Child Develpm.*, 1959, **30**, 91–107.

88 Greenfield, N. S.: The relationship between recalled forms of childhood discipline and psychopathology. *J. consult. Psychol.*, 1959, **23**, 139–142.

89 Grinder, R. E.: Parental child-rearing practices, conscience, and resistance to temptation of sixth-grade children. *Child Develpm.*, 1962, **33**, 803–820.

90 Guerney, B., L. Stover, and S. McMeritt: A measurement of empathy in parent-child interaction. *J. genet. Psychol.*, 1968, **112**, 45–55.

91 Guilford, J. S.: Isolation and description of occupational stereotypes. *Occup. Psychol.*, 1967, **41**, 57–64.

92 Hammer, M.: The relationship between recalled type of discipline in childhood and adult interpersonal behavior. *Merrill-Palmer Quart.*, 1964, **10**, 143–145.

93 Harsh, C. M., and H. G. Schrickel: *Personality: Development and assessment*, 2d ed. New York: Ronald, 1959.

94 Hartley, R. E.: A developmental view of female sex-role definition and identification. *Merill-Palmer Quart.*, 1964, **10**, 3–16.

95 Hartup, W. W., S. G. Moore, and G. Sager: Avoidance of inappropriate sex-typing in young children. *J. consult. Psychol.*, 1963, **27**, 467–473.

96 Havighurst, R. J.: *Human development and education*. New York: Longmans, 1953.

97 Hearn, J. L., D. C. Charles, and L. Wolins: Life history antecedents of measured personality variables. *J. genet. Psychol.*, 1965, **107**, 99–110.

98 Heider, G. M.: What makes a good parent? *Children*, 1960, **7**, 282–287.

99 Heilbrun, A. P.: Parental model attributes, nurturant reinforcement, and consistency of behavior in adolescents. *Child Develpm.*, 1964, **35**, 151–167.

100 Heinicke, C. H.: Some effects of separating two-year-old children from their parents. *Hum. Relat.*, 1956, **9**, 105–176.

101 Heinstein, M. I.: Expressed attitudes and feelings of pregnant women and their relations to physical complications of pregnancy. *Merrill-Palmer Quart.*, 1967, **13**, 217–236.

102 Henry, J.: Permissiveness and morality. *Ment. Hyg., N. Y.*, 1961, **45**, 282–287.

103 Hetherington, E. M.: Effects of paternal absence on sex-typed behaviors in Negro and white preadolescents. *J. Pers. soc. Psychol.*, 1966, **4**, 87–91.

104 Higgins, J.: Effects of child-rearing by schizophrenic mothers. *J. psychiat. Res.*, 1966, **4**, 153–167.

105 Hilgard, E. R.: *Introduction to psychology*, 4th ed. New York: Harcourt, Brace & World, 1962.

106 Hill, D.L., and R. H. Walters: Interaction of sex of subject and dependency-training procedures in a social-reinforcement study. *Merrill-Palmer Quart.*, 1969, **15**, 185–198.

107 Hill, O. W.: A twin study. *Brit. J. Psychiat.*, 1968, **114**, 175–179.

108 Hilliard, F. H.: The influence of religious education upon the development of children's moral ideas. *Brit. J. educ. Psychol.*, 1959, **29**, 50–59.

109 Hobbs, D. F.: Parenthood as a crisis: A third study. *J. Marriage & Family*, 1965, **27**, 367–372.

110 Hoffman, M. L: Power assertion by the parent and its impact on the child. *Child Develpm.*, 1960, **31**, 129–143.

111 Jakubczak, L. F., and R. H. Walters: Suggestibility as dependency behavior. *J. abnorm. soc. Psychol.*, 1959, **59**, 102–107.

112 Jersild, A. T.: *Child psychology*, 6th ed. Englewood Cliffs, N. J.: Prentice-Hall, 1969.

113 Kagan, J.: The child's perception of the parent. *J. abnorm. soc. Psychol.*, 1955, **53**, 257–258.

114 Kardiner, A.: *The psychological frontiers of society*. New York: Columbia, 1945.

115 Karr, C., and F. Wesley: Comparison of German and U. S. child-rearing practices. *Child Develpm.*, 1966, **37**, 715–723.

116 Klineberg, O.: Cultural factors in personality adjustment of children. *Amer. J. Orthopsychiat.*, 1953, **33**, 465–471.

117 Knobloch, H., and B. Pasamanick: Prospective studies on the epidemiology of reproductive casualty: Methods, findings, and some implications. *Merrill-Palmer Quart.*, 1966, **12**, 27–43.

118 Koch, H. L.: The relation of certain formal attributes of siblings to attitudes held toward each other and toward their parents. *Monogr. Soc. Res. Child Develpm.*, 1960, **25**, no. 4.

119 Kohn, M. L.: Social class and parental values. *Amer. J. Sociol.*, 1959, **64**, 337–351.

120 Koppitz, E. M.: Relationships between some background factors and children's interpersonal attitudes. *J. genet. Psychol.*, 1957, **91**, 119–129.

121 Kunz, P. R.: Religious influences on parental discipline and achievement demands. *Marriage fam. Living*, 1963, **25**, 224–225.

122 Lakin, M.: Personality factors in mothers of excessively crying (colicky) infants. *Monogr. Soc. Res. Child Develpm.*, 1957, **22**, no. 1.

123 Landreth, C.: *Early childhood behavior and learning*, 2d ed. New York: Knopf, 1967.

124 Lane, E. A., and G. W. Albee: Early childhood intellectual differences between schizophrenic adults and their siblings. *J. abnorm. soc. Psychol.*, 1964, **68**, 193–195.

125 Lazowick. L. M.: On the nature of identification. *J. abnorm. soc. Psychol.*, 1955, **51**, 175–183.

126 Lefkowitz, M. M., L. O. Walder, and L. D. Eron: Punishment, identification and aggression. *Merrill-Palmer Quart.*, 1963, **9**, 159–174.

127 Lehmann, I. J., and I. K. Payne: An exploration of attitude and value changes of college freshmen. *Personnel Guid. J.*, 1963, **41**, 403–408.

128 Lerman, P.: Gangs, networks and subcultural delinquency. *Amer. J. Sociol.*, 1967, **73**, 63–72.

129 Linden, M. E.: The older person in the family. *Soc. Casewk.*, 1956, **37**, 75–81.

130 Lindzey, G., D. T. Lykken, and H. D. Winston: Infantile trauma, genetic factors, and adult temperament. *J. abnorm. soc. Psychol.*, 1960, **61**, 7–14.

131 Lipset, S. M., and L. Lowenthal (eds.): *Culture and the social character*. New York: Free Press, 1961.

132 Lipsitz, L.: Working-class authoritarianism: A re-evaluation. *Amer. sociol. Rev.*, 1965, **30**, 103–109.

133 Littman, R. A., R. C. A. Moore, and J. Pierce-Jones: Social class differences in child rearing: A third community for comparison with Chicago and Newton. *Amer. sociol. Rev.*, 1957, **22**, 694–704.

134 Livson, N.: Parental behavior and children's involvement with their parents. *J. genet. Psychol.*, 1966, **109**, 173–194.

135 Lodge, H. C.: The influence of the study of biography on the moral ideology of the adolescent at the eighth grade level. *J. educ. Res.*, 1956, **50**, 241–255.

136 London, P., R. E. Schulman, and M. S. Black: Religion, guilt and ethical standards. *J. soc. Psychol.*, 1964, **63**, 145–149.

137 Lynn, D. B.: The husband-father role in the family. *Marriage fam. Living*, 1961, **23**, 295–296.

138 Maccoby, E. E.: The taking of adult roles in middle childhood. *J. abnorm. soc. Psychol.*, 1961, **63**, 493–503.

139 Macfarlane, J. W., L. Allen, and M. P. Honzik: *A developmental study of the behavior problems of normal children between twenty-one months and fourteen years*. Berkeley: University of California Press, 1954.

140 Marshall, H. H.: The effect of punishment on children: A review of the literature and a suggested hypothesis. *J. genet. Psychol.*, 1965, **106**, 23–33.

141 Martineau, H.: Quoted by S. M. Lipset and L. Lowenthal (eds.), *Culture and the social character*. New York: Free Press, 1961, p. 155.

142 Martin, J. G., and F. R. Westie: The tolerant personality. *Amer. sociol. Rev.*, 1959, **24**, 521–528.

143 Martin, W. E.: Effects of early training on personality. *Marriage fam. Living*, 1957, **19**, 39–45.

144 McArthur, C.: Personality differences between middle and upper classes. *J. abnorm. soc. Psychol.*, 1955, **50**, 247–254.

145 McCord, J., W. McCord, and E. Thurber: Some effects of paternal absence on male children. *J. abnorm. soc. Psychol.*, 1962, **64**, 361–369.

146 Mead, M.: *Male and female*. New York: Dell, 1968.

147 Medinnus, G. R.: Adolescents' self-acceptance and perceptions of their parents. *J. consult. Psychol.*, 1965, **29**, 150–154.

148 Michner, J. A.: The revolution of middle-class values. *The New York Times*, Aug. 8, 1968.

149 Midlarsky, E., and J. H. Bryan: Training charity in children. *J. Pers. soc. Psychol.*, 1967, 4, 408–415.

150 Milton, G. A.: A factor analytic study of child-rearing behaviors. *Child Develpm.*, 1958, **29**, 381–382.

151 Mischel, M.: Preference for delayed reinforcement: An experimental study of a cultural observation. *J. abnorm. soc. Psychol.*, 1958, **56**, 57–61.

152 Montagu, A.: *Prenatal influences*. Springfield, Ill.: Charles C Thomas, 1962.

153 Mosher, D. L., and A. Scodel: Relation-

ships between ethnocentrism in children and the ethnocentrism and authoritarian rearing practices of their mothers. *Child Develpm.*, 1960, **31**, 369–376.

154 Munn, N.: *The evolution and growth of human behavior*, 2d ed. Boston: Houghton Mifflin, 1965.

155 Munson, B. E.: Personality differentials among urban, suburban, town and rural children. *Rural Sociol.*, 1959, **24**, 257–264.

156 Murphy, E. B., E. Silber, G. V. Coelho, D. A. Hamburg, and I. Greenberg: Development of autonomy and parent-child interaction in late adolescence. *Amer. J. Orthopsychiat.*, 1963, **33**, 643–652.

157 Mussen, P. H., J. J. Conger, and J. Kagan: *Child development and personality*, 3d ed. New York: Harper & Row, 1969.

158 Mussen, P. H., H. B. Young, R. Gaddini, and L. Morante: The influence of the father-son relationship on adolescent personality and attitudes. *J. child Psychol. Psychiat.*, 1963, **4**, 3–16.

159 Nakamura, C. Y.: The relationship between children's expressions of hostility and methods of discipline exercised by dominant, overprotective parents. *Child Develpm.*, 1959, **30**, 109–117.

160 Nakamura, C. Y., and M. M. Rogers: Parents' expectations of autonomous behavior and children's autonomy. *Develpm. Psychol.*, 1969, **1**, 613–617.

161 Nash, J.: The father in contemporary culture and current psychological literature. *Child Develpm.*, 1965, **36**, 261–297.

162 Nikelly, A. G.: Maternal indulgence and neglect and maladjustment in adolescence. *J. clin. Psychol.*, 1967, **23**, 148–150.

163 Osterkamp, A., and J. D. Sands: Early feeding and birth difficulties in childhood schizophrenia: A brief study. *J. genet. Psychol.*, 1962, **101**, 363–366.

164 Pasamanick, B., and H. Knobloch: Retrospective studies of the epidemiology of reproductive casualty. *Merrill-Palmer Quart.*, 1966, **12**, 7–26.

165 Pavenstedt, E.: A comparison of the child-rearing environment of upper-lower and very low-lower class families. *Amer. J. Orthopsychiat.*, 1965, **35**, 89–98.

166 Payne, D. E., and P. H. Mussen: Parent-child relations and father identification among adolescent boys. *J. abnorm. soc. Psychol.*, 1956, **52**, 358–362.

167 Peck, R. F., and R. J. Havighurst: *The psychology of character development*. New York: Wiley, 1962.

168 Prothro, E. T.: Arab students' choices of ways to live. *J. soc. Psychol.*, 1958, **47**, 3–7.

169 Provence, S.: Disturbed personality development in infancy: A comparison of two inadequately nurtured infants. *Merrill-Palmer Quart.*, 1965, **11**, 149–170.

170 Rainwater, L.: A study of personality differences between middle and lower class adolescents: The Szondi Test in culture-personality research. *Genet. Psychol. Monogr.*, 1956, **54**, 3–86.

171 Reimanis, G.: Relationship of childhood experience memories to anomie later in life. *J. genet. Psychol.*, 1965, **106**, 245–252.

172 Rennie, T. A., C. L. Srole, M. R. Opler, and T. S. Langner: Urban life and mental health. *Amer. J. Psychiat.*, 1957, **113**, 831–837.

173 Rettig, S., and B. Pasamanick: Invariance in factor structure of moral value judgments from American and Korean college students. *Sociometry*, 1962, **25**, 73–84.

174 Riesman, D.: The college student in an age of organization. *Chicago Rev.*, 1958, **12**, 50–68.

175 Robins, L. N., H. Gyman, and P. O'Neil: The interaction of social class and deviant behavior. *Amer. sociol. Rev.*, 1962, **27**, 480–492.

176 Robinson, N. M., and H. B. Robinson: A follow-up study of children of low birth weight and control children at school age. *Pediatrics*, 1965, **35**, 425–433.

177 Roff, M.: Childhood social interactions and young adult psychosis. *J. clin. Psychol.*, 1963, **19**, 152–157.

178 Rose, A. M.: Parental models for youth. *Sociol. soc. Res.*, 1955, **40**, 3–9.

179 Rosenberg, M.: *Society and the adolescent self-image*. Princeton: Princeton University Press, 1965.

180 Rosenthal, M.J.: The syndrome of the inconsistent mother. *Amer. J. Orthopsychiat.*, 1962, **32**, 637–644.

181 Rush, W. S.: Some factors influencing children's use of the mass media of communication. *J. exp. Educ.*, 1965, **33**, 301–304.

182 Rybak, W.: Notes on crushes and hero-worship of adolescents. *Psychiat. Quart. Suppl.*, 1969, **39**, 48–53.

183 Ryerson, A. J.: Medical advice on child rearing: 1550–1900. *Harv. educ. Rev.*, 1961, **31**, 302–322.

184 Schaefer, E. S., and N. Bayley: Maternal behavior, child behavior and the interrelation from infancy through adolescence. *Monogr. Soc. Res. Child Develpm.*, 1963, **38**, no. 3.

185 Schaie, K. W.: Differences in some personal characteristics of "rigid" and "flexible" individuals, *J. clin. Psychol.*, 1958, **14**, 11–14.

186 Scheinfeld, A.: *Your heredity and environment*. Philadelphia: Lippincott, 1965.

187 Sears, R. R., E. E. Maccoby, and H. Levin: *Patterns of child rearing*. New York: Harper, 1957.

188 Sewell, W. H.: Social class and childhood personality. *Sociometry*, 1961, **24**, 340–356.

189 Shaw, M. C.: A note on parent attitude toward independence training and the academic achievement of their children. *J. educ. Psychol.*, 1964, **55**, 371–374.

190 Siegelman, M.: "Origins" of extraversion and introversion. *J. Psychol.*, 1968, **69**, 85–91.

191 Siegman, A. W.: Father absence during early childhood and antisocial behavior. *J. abnorm. Psychol.*, 1966, **71**, 71–74.

192 Singh, P. N., S. C. Huang, and G. G. Thompson: A comparative study of selected attitudes, values and personality characteristics of American, Chinese and Indian students. *J. soc. Psychol.*, 1962, **57**, 123–132.

193 Smith, L. M., and P. F. Kleine: The adolescent and his society. *Rev. educ. Res.*, 1966, **36**, 424–436.

194 Sontag, L. W.: Implications of fetal behavior for adult personalities. *Ann. N. Y. Acad. Sci.*, 1966, **132**, 782–786.

195 Spock, B.: *The pocket book of baby and child care*, rev. ed. New York: Pocket Books, 1968.

196 Spranger, E.: *Types of men*. New York: Stechert, 1928.

197 Stagner, R.: *Psychology of personality*, 3d ed. New York: McGraw-Hill, 1961.

198 Staudt, V. M.: Character formation is the teacher's business. *Education*, 1957 **77**, 198–202.

199 Stendler, C. B.: The learning of certain secondary drives by Parisian and American children. *Marriage fam. Living*, 1954, **16**, 195–200.

200 Stephens, W. N.: Judgments by social workers on boys and mothers in fatherless families. *J. genet. Psychol.*, 1961, **99**, 59–64.

201 Stevenson, I.: Is the human personality more plastic in infancy and childhood? *Amer. J. Psychiat.*, 1957, **114**, 152–161.

202 Stewart, A. H., I. H. Weiland, A. R. Leider, C. A. Mangham, T. H. Holmes, and H. S. Ripley: Excessive infant crying (colic) in relation to parent behavior. *Amer. J. Psychiat.*, 1954, **110**, 687–694.

203 Stoke, S. M.: An inquiry into the concept of identification. In W. E. Martin and C. B. Stendler (eds.), *Readings in child development*. New York: Harcourt, Brace & World, 1954, pp. 227–239.

204 Stone, F. B., and V. N. Rowley: Children's behavior problems and parental attitudes. *J. genet. Psychol.*, 1966, **107**, 281–287.

205 Straus, M. A.: Conjugal power structure and adolescent personality. *Marriage fam. Living*, 1962, **24**, 17–25.

206 Strickland, B. R., and D. P. Crowne: Conformity under conditions of simulated group pressure as a function of the need for social approval. *J. soc. Psychol.*, 1962, **58**, 171–181.

207 Symonds, P. M.: Essentials of good parent-child relations. *Teachers Coll. Rec.*, 1949, **50**, 528–538.

208 Taylor, P. H.: Children's evaluations of the characteristics of the good teacher. *Brit. J. educ. Psychol.*, 1962, **32**, 258–266.

209 Toman, W.: Family constellation as a basic personality determinant. *J. indiv. Psychol.*, 1959, **15**, 199–211.

210 Tryon, C., and W. E. Henry: How children learn personal and social adjustment. *Yearb. nat. Soc. Stud. Educ.*, 1950, **49**, pt. 1, 156–182.

211 Tuddenham, R. D.: The constancy of the personality ratings over two decades. *Genet. Psychol. Monogr.*, 1959, **60**, 3–29.

212 Tuma, E., and N. Livson: Family socioeconomic status and adolescent attitudes to authority. *Child Develpm.*, 1960, **31**, 387–399.

213 Von Mering, F. H.: Professional and non-professional women as mothers. *J. soc. Psychol.*, 1955, **42**, 21–34.

214 Waldrop, M. F., and R. Q. Bell: Effects of family size and density on newborn characteristics. *Amer. J. Orthopsychiat.*, 1966, **36**, 544–550.

215 Watson, J. B.: *Behaviorism*. New York: People's Institute Publishing Co., 1925.

216 Werner, E.: Milieu differences in social competence. *J. genet. Psychol.*, 1957, **91**, 239–249.

217 Wertham, F.: The scientific study of mass media effects. *Amer. J. Psychiat.*, 1962, **119**, 306–311.

218 White, M. S.: Social class, child rearing practices, and child behavior. *Amer. sociol. Rev.*, 1957, **22**, 704–712.

219 Whiting, J. W. M., and I. L. Child: *Child training and personality: A cross cultural study*. New Haven, Conn.: Yale, 1953.

220 Winestine, M. C.: Twinship and psychological differentiation. *Dissert. Abstr.*, 1965, **26**, 4082–4083.

221 Zuckerman, M., and M. Oltean: Some rela-

tionships between maternal attitude factors and authoritarianism, personality needs, psychopathology and self-acceptance. *Child Develpm.*, 1959, **30**, 27–36.

CHAPTER 5

1 Alexander, C. N.: Consensus and mutual attraction in national cliques: A study of adolescent drinkers. *Amer. J. Sociol.*, 1964, **69**, 395–402.

2 Allen, M. G.: Psychoanalytic theory of infant gratification and adult personality. *J. genet. Psychol.*, 1964, **104**, 265–274.

3 Allport, G. W.: *Pattern and growth in personality.* New York: Holt, 1961.

4 Amatora, Sister Mary: Developmental trends in pre-adolescence and early adolescence in self-evaluation. *J. genet. Psychol.*, 1957, **91**, 89–97.

5 Ames, L. B.: Longitudinal survey of child Rorschach responses: Younger subjects aged 2 to 10 years. *Genet. Psychol. Monogr.*, 1960, **61**, 229–289.

6 Ames, L. B.: Longitudinal survey of child Rorschach responses: Older subjects aged 10 to 16 years. *Genet. Psychol. Monogr.*, 1960, **62**, 185–229.

7 Ames, R.: Physical maturing among boys as related to adult social behavior. *Calif. J. educ. Res.*, 1957, **8**, 69–75.

8 Anastasia, A.: Heredity, environment, and the question "How?" *Psychol. Rev.*, 1958, **65**, 197–208.

9 Anderson, C. C.: A developmental study of dogmatism during adolescence with reference to sex differences. *J. abnorm. soc. Psychol.*, 1962, **65**, 132–135.

10 Andrus, R.: Personality changes in an older age group. *Geriatrics*, 1955, **10**, 432–435.

11 Angrist, S. S.: Role conception as a predictor of adult female roles. *Sociol. soc. Res.*, 1966, **50**, 448–459.

12 Apperson, L. B.: Childhood experiences of schizophrenics and alcholics. *J. soc. Psychol.*, 1965, **106**, 301–313.

13 Backman, C. W., P. F. Secord, and R. J. Peirce: Resistance to change in the self-concept as a function of consensus among significant others. *Sociometry*, 1963, **26**, 102–111.

14 Bain, R.: Making normal people. *Marriage fam. Living*, 1954, **16**, 27–31.

15 Baker, J. W., and A. Holzworth: Social histories of successful and unsuccessful children. *Child Develpm.*, 1961, **32**, 135–149.

16 Bayley, N.: The life span as a frame of reference in psychological research. *Vita Humana*, 1963, **6**, 125–139.

17 Becker, H. S.: Personal changes in adult life. *Sociometry*, 1964, **27**, 40–53.

18 Berdie, R. F.: Personality changes from high school entrance to college matriculation. *J. counsel. Psychol.*, 1968, **15**, 376–380.

19 Blaine, G. B.: Moral questions stir the campus. *The New York Times*, Jan. 16, 1964.

20 Blood, R. O.: Long-range causes and consequences of the employment of married women. *J. Marriage & Family*, 1965, **27**, 43–47.

21 Bossard, J. H. S., and E. S. Boll: *The sociology of child development*, 4th ed. New York: Harper & Row, 1966.

22 Botwinick, J.: Cautiousness in advanced age. *J. Geront.*, 1966, **21**, 347–353.

23 Bower, E. M., T. A. Shellhamer, and J. M. Daily: School characteristics of male adolescents who later became schizophrenic, *Amer. J. Orthopsychiat.*, 1960, **30**, 712–729.

24 Brandt, R. M.: Self: The missing link for understanding behavior. *Ment. Hyg., N. Y.*, 1957, **41**, 24–33.

25 Breckenridge, M. E., and E. L. Vincent: *Child development*, 5th ed. Philadelphia: Saunders, 1965.

26 Brody, E. M., and G. M. Spark: Institutionalization of the aged: A family crisis. *Family Process*, 1966, **5**, 76–90.

27 Bronson, G. W.: Identity diffusion in late adolescents. *J. abnorm. soc. Psychol.*, 1959, **59**, 414–417.

28 Bronson, W. C.: Central orientations: A study of behavior organization from childhood to adolescence. *Child Develpm.*, 1966, **37**, 125–155.

29 Brow, D. R., and D. Bystryn: College environment, personality and social ideology of three ethnic groups. *J. soc. Psychol.*, 1956, **44**, 279–288.

30 Bugental, J. F. T., and E. C. Gunning: Investigations into self-concept. III. Stability of reported self-identifications. *J. clin. Psychol.*, 1955, **11**, 41–46.

31 Bühler, C.: Clinical study of the reactions of the individual to his own age. *Geriatrics*, 1957, **12**, 439–443.

32 Caplan, S. W.: The effect of group counseling on junior high school boys' concepts of themselves in school. *J. counsel. Psychol.*, 1957, **4**, 124–128.

33 Carlson, R.: Stability and change in the adolescent's self-image. *Child Develpm.*, 1965, **36**, 659–666.

34 Cartwright, R. D.: Self-conception patterns of college students and adjustment to college life. *J. counsel. Psychol.*, 1963, **10**, 47–52.

35 Cattell, R. B., and R. W. Coan: Personality factors in middle childhood as revealed by parents' ratings. *Child Develpm.*, 1957, **28**, 439–458.

36 Cole, L., and I. N. Hall: *Psychology of adolescence*, 6th ed. New York: Holt, 1964.

37 Coleman, J. S.: *The adolescent society.* New York: Free Press, 1961.

38 Cox, F. N.: An assessment of children's attitudes toward parent figures. *Child Develpm.*, 1962, **33**, 821–830.

39 Crane, A. R.: The development of moral values in children. IV. Preadolescent gangs and the moral development of children. *Brit. J. educ. Psychol.*, 1958, **28**, 201–208.

40 Cruickshank, W. M., and G. O. Johnson (eds.): *Education of exceptional children and youth*, 2d ed. Englewood Cliffs, N. J.: Prentice-Hall, 1967.

41 Davis, A., and R. J. Havighurst: *Father of the man.* Boston: Houghton Mifflin, 1947.

42 Davitz, J. R.: Contributions of research with children to a theory of maladjustment. *Child Develpm.*, 1958, **29**, 3–7.

43 Dean, D. G.: Romanticism and emotional maturity: A further exploration. *Soc. Forces*, 1964, **42**, 298–303.

44 DeJung, J. E., and E. F. Gordon: The accuracy of self-role perception: A developmental study. *J. exp. Educ.*, 1962, **31**, 27–41.

45 Denmark, T., and M. Guttentag: The effect of college attendance on mature women: Changes in self-concept and evaluation of

student role. *J. soc. Psychol.*, 1966, **21**, 1–8.

46 Dreger, R. M.: Just how far can social change change personality? *J. Psychol.*, 1966, **64**, 167–191.

47 Dunbar, F.: Homeostasis during puberty. *Amer. J. Psychiat.*, 1958, **114**, 673–682.

48 Dunphy, D. C.: The social structure of the urban adolescent peer groups. *Sociometry*, 1963 **26**, 230–246.

49 Dyer, E. D.: Parenthood as a crisis: A re-study. *Marriage fam. Living*, 1963, **25**, 196–201.

50 Early, C. J.: Attitude learning in children. *J. educ. Psychol.*, 1968, **59**, 176–180.

51 Edwards, A. E., and D. B. Wine: Personality changes with age: Their dependency on concomitant intellectual decline. *J. Geront.*, 1963, **18**, 182–184.

52 Elkind, D.: Egocentrism in adolescence. *Child Develpm.*, 1967, **38**, 1025–1034.

53 Ellis, A.: Requisite conditions for basic personality change. *J. consult. Psychol.*, 1959, **23**, 538–540.

54 Ellis, R. A., and W. C. Lane: Social mobility and career orientation. *Sociol. soc. Res.*, 1966, **50**, 280–296.

55 Elton, C. F., and H. A. Rose: The face of change. *J. counsel. Psychol.*, 1968, **15**, 372–375.

56 Emmerich, W.: Continuity and stability in early social development. II. Teacher ratings. *Child Develpm.*, 1966, **37**, 17–27.

57 Engel, M.: The stability of the self-concept in adolescence. *J. abnorm. soc. Psychol.*, 1959, **58**, 211–215.

58 Escalona, S. K., and M. Leitch: Early phases of personality development. *Mongr. Soc. Res. Child Develpm.*, 1952, **17**, no. 1.

59 Exline, R. V.: Interrelations among two dimensions of sociometric status, group congeniality, and accuracy of social perception. *Sociometry*, 1960, **23**, 85–101.

60 Feinberg, M. R.: Stability of sociometric status in two adolescent class groups. *J. genet. Psychol.*, 1964, **104**, 83–87.

61 Field, S. C.: Longitudinal study of the origins of achievement striving. *J. Pers. soc. Psychol.*, 1967, **7**, 408–414.

62 Fish, B.: Longitudinal observations of biological deviations in a schizophrenic infant. *Amer. J. Psychiat.*, 1959, **116**, 25–31.

63 Frank, L. K.: Genetic psychology and its prospects. *Amer. J. Orthopsychiat.*, 1951, **21**, 506–522.

64 Freedman, A. M., and L. Bender: When childhood schizophrenic grows up. *Amer. J. Orthopsychiat.*, 1957, **27**, 553–565.

65 Freedman, M. B., and C. Bereiter: A longitudinal study of personality development in college alumnae. *Merrill-Palmer Quart.*, 1963, **9**, 295–302.

66 Freud, S.: *The complete psychological works of Sigmund Freud.* London: Hogarth, 1953–1962.

67 Gallagher, J. R.: The favorite teacher: A parent's enemy or ally? *Marriage fam. Living*, 1961, **23**, 400–402.

68 Gardner, D. B., G. R. Hawkes, and L. G. Burchinal: Noncontinuous mothering in infancy and development in later childhood. *Child Develpm.*, 1961, **32**, 225–234.

69 Geiken, K. F.: Expectations concerning husband-wife responsibilities in the home. *J. Marriage & Family*, 1964, **26**, 349–352.

70 Gesell, A., F. L. Ilg, and L. B. Ames: *Youth:*

The years from ten to sixteen. New York: Harper & Row, 1956.

71 Glaser, K.: Attempted suicide in children and adolescents: Psychodynamic observations. *Amer. J. Psychother.*, 1965, **19**, 220–227.

72 Glasser, P. H. and L. N. Glasser: Role reversal and conflict between aged parents and their children. *Marriage fam. Living*, 1962, **24**, 46–51.

73 Glueck, E. T.: A more discriminative instrument for the identification of potential delinquents at school entrance. *J. crim. Law Criminol. police Sci.*, 1966, **57**, 27–30.

74 Gould, R. E.: Suicide problems in children and adolescents. *Amer. J. Psychother.* 1965, **19**, 228–246.

75 Gowan, J. C.: Changing self-concept in exceptional children. *Education*, 1965, **85**, 374–375.

76 Grater, H.: Changes in self and other attitudes in a leadership training group. *Personnel Guid. J.*, 1959, **37**, 493–496.

77 Greene, J. E.: Alleged misbehaviors among senior high school students. *J. soc. Psychol.*, 1962, **58**, 371–382.

78 Greenberg, G. N., and G. H. Frank: Personality correlates of attitude change: The tendency to alter attitudes toward self in other-directed and inner-directed people. *J. gen. Psychol.*, 1967, **76**, 85–90.

79 Greenberg, H., and D. Fare: An investigation of several variables as determinants of authoritarianism. *J. soc. Psychol.*, 1959, **49**, 105–111.

80 Gruen, W.: Adult personality: An empirical study of Erikson's theory of ego development. In B. L. Neugarten (ed.), *Personality in middle and late life.* New York: Atherton Press, 1964, pp. 1–14.

81 Hall, R. L., and B. Willerman: The educational influence of dormitory roommates. *Sociometry*, 1963, **26**, 294–318.

82 Hall, W. E., and W. Gaeddert: Social skills and their relationship to scholastic achievement. *J. genet. Psychol.*, 1960, **96**, 269–273.

83 Hardyck, C. D.: Sex differences in personality change with age. *J. Geront.*, 1964, **19**, 78–82.

84 Harsh, C. M., and H. G. Schrickel: *Personality: Development and assessement*, 2d ed. New York: Ronald, 1959.

85 Havighurst, R. J.: *Human development and education.* New York: Longmans, 1953.

86 Havighurst, R. J.: Successful aging. *Gerontologist*, 1961, **1**, 8–13.

87 Heilbrun, A. B.: Parental model, attributes, nurturant reinforcement, and consistency of behavior in adolescents. *Child Develpm.*, 1964, **35**, 151–167.

88 Helson, R.: Sex differences in creative style. *J. Pers.*, 1967, **35**, 214–233.

89 Hobbs, D. F.: Parenthood as a crisis: A third study. *J. Marriage & Family*, 1965, **27**, 367–372.

90 Hood, J. J.: Consistency of self-concept in adolescence. *Dissert. Abstr.*, 1962, **22**, 2458–2459.

91 Huntley, C. W.: Changes in study of value scores during four years of college. *Genet. Psychol. Monogr.*, 1965, **71**, 349–383.

92 Izard, C. E.: Personality change during college years. *J. consult. Psychol.*, 1962, **26**, 482.

93 Jacobziner, H.: Attempted suicide in adolescence. *J. Amer. med. Ass.*, 1965, **191**, 7–11.

94 James, W.: *The principles of psychology.* New York: Holt, 1890.

95 Jersild, A. T.: *In search of self.* New York: Teachers College, 1952.

96 Jersild, A. T.: *Child psychology*, 6th ed. Englewood Cliffs, N. J.: Prentice-Hall, 1969.

97 Johnson, H. H.: Some effects of discrepancy level on response to negative information about one's self. *Sociometry*, 1966, **29**, 52–66.

98 Jones, M. C.: A report on three growth studies at the University of California. *Gerontologist*, 1967, **7**, 49–54.

99 Jourard, S. M.: Age trends in self-disclosure. *Merrill-Palmer Quart.*, 1961, **7**, 191–197.

100 Kagan, J., and H. A. Moss: *Birth to maturity: A study in psychological development.* New York: Wiley, 1962.

101 Kastenbaum, R.: Theories of human aging: The search for a conceptual framework. *J. soc. Issues*, 1965, **21**, no. 4, 13–36.

102 Katz, I.: Review of evidence relating to effects of desegregation on the intellectual performance of Negroes. *Amer. Psychologist*, 1964, **19**, 381–399.

103 Kelly, E. L.: Consistency of the adult personality. *Amer. Psychologist*, 1955, **10**, 659–681.

104 Kent, D. P.: Social and cultural factors affecting the mental health of the aged. *Amer. J. Orthopsychiat.*, 1966, **36**, 680–685.

105 Kinch, J. W.: A formalized theory of the self-concept. *Amer. J. Sociol.*, 1963, **68**, 481–486.

106 King, C. E., and W. H. Howell: Role characteristics of flexible and inflexible retired persons. *Sociol. soc. Res.*, 1964, **49**, 153–165.

107 King, G. F., and M. Schiller: Ego strength and type of defensive behavior. *J. consult. Psychol.*, 1960, **24**, 215–217.

108 Koch, H. L.: The relation of certain formal attributes of siblings to attitudes held toward each other and toward their parents. *Monogr. Soc. Res. Child Develpm.*, 1960, **25**, no. 4.

109 Kogan, W. S., E. E. Boe, and E. F. Gocka: Personality changes in unwed mothers following parturition. *J. clin. Psychol.*, 1968, **24**, 3–11.

110 Kramer, R.: The status of the boy: 1969. *The New York Times*, Mar. 30, 1969.

111 Krush, T. P., J. W. Bjord, P. S. Sindell, and J. Nelle: Some thoughts on the formation of personality disorder: Study of an Indian boarding school population. *Amer. J. Psychiat.*, 1966, **122**, 868–876.

112 Kuhlen, R. G.: Age differences in personality during adult years. *Psychol. Bull.*, 1945, **42**, 333–358.

113 Landau, G.: Restoration of self-esteem. *Geriatrics*, 1955, **10**, 141–143.

114 Landis, J. T.: Personality: A 1954 view. *J. Home Econ.*, 1954, **46**, 459–462.

115 Landsman, G.: Explorations in mental health programs for the aging. *Gerontologist*, 1963, **3**, 105–109.

116 Lantz, H. R.: Number of childhood friends as reported in the life histories of a psychiatrically diagnosed group of 1,000. *Marriage fam. Living*, 1956, **18**, 107–109.

117 Leeper, R. W., and P. Madison: *Toward understanding human personalities.* New York: Appleton-Century-Crofts, 1959.

118 Lehmann, I. J., B. K. Sinha, and R. T. Hartnett: Changes in attitudes and values associated with college attendance. *J. educ. Psychol.*, 1966, **57**, 89–98.

119 Levine, A. J.: A sound approach to middle age. In C. B. Vedder (ed.), *Problems of the middle-aged.* Springfield, Ill.: Charles C Thomas, 1965, pp. 40–43.

120 Lief, H. I., and W. C. Thompson: The prediction of behavior from adolescence to adulthood. *Psychiatry*, 1961, **24**, 32–38.

121 Lipscomb, I. F.: The effects of counseling, both group and individual, on changes in self-concept of high school sophomore girls of low socioeconomic background. *Dissert. Abstr.*, 1968, **28** (9–A), 3466–3467.

122 Lodge, H. C.: The influence of the study of biography on the moral ideology of the adolescent at the eighth grade level. *J. educ. Res.*, 1956, **50**, 241–255.

123 Long, B. H., E. H. Henderson, and R. C. Ziller: Developmental changes in the self-concept during middle childhood. *Merrill-Palmer Quart.*, 1967, **13**, 201–215.

124 Lopata, H. Z.: The life cycle of the social role of housewife. *Sociol. soc. Res.*, 1966, **51**, 5–22.

125 Lowenthal, M. F.: Social isolation and mental illness in old age. *Amer. sociol. Rev.*, 1964, **29**, 54–70.

126 Luft, J.: Monetary value and the perception of persons. *J. soc. Psychol.*, 1957, **46**, 245–251.

127 Macfarlane, J., L. Allen, and M. P. Honzik: *A developmental study of the behavior problems of normal children between twenty-one months and fourteen years.* Berkeley: University of California Press, 1954.

128 Manis, M.: Social interaction and the self-concept. *J. abnorm. soc. Psychol.*, 1955, **51**, 362–370.

129 Martin, W. E.: Effects of early training on personality. *Marriage fam. Living*, 1957, **19**, 39–45.

130 McClusky, H. Y., and G. Jensen: The psychology of adults. *Rev. educ. Res.*, 1959, **29**, 246–255.

131 McDermott, J. F.: Parental divorce in early childhood. *Amer. J. Psychiat.*, 1968, **124**, 1424–1432.

132 McKinnon, J. K. M.: Consistency and change in behavior manifestations. *Child Develpm. Monogr.*, 1942, no. 30.

133 Michael, C. M., D. P. Morris, and E. Soroker: Follow-up studies of shy, withdrawn children. II. Relative incidence of schizophrenia. *Ment. Hyg., N. Y.*, 1957, **27**, 331–337.

134 Michel, W.: Continuity and change in personality. *Amer. Psychologist*, 1969, **24**, 1012–1018.

135 More, D. M.: Developmental concordance and discordance during puberty and early adolescence. *Monogr. Soc. Res. Child Develpm*, 1953, **18**, 1–128.

136 Moss, H. A., and J. Kagan: Stability of achievement and recognition seeking behaviors from early childhood through adulthood. *J. abnorm. soc. Psychol.* 1961, **62**, 504–513.

137 Munn, N. L.: *The evolution and growth of human behavior*, 2d ed. Boston: Houghton Mifflin, 1965.

138 Mussen, P. H.: Long-term consequences of masculinity of interests in adolescence. *J. consult. Psychol.*, 1962, **26**, 435–440.

139 Mussen, P. H., and M. C. Jones: Self-conceptions, motivations and interpersonal attitudes of late- and early-maturing boys. *Child Develpm*, 1957, **28**, 243–256.

140 Neilon, P.: Shirley's babies after fifteen years: A personality study. *J. genet. Psychol.*, 1948 , **73**, 175–186.

141 *New York Times* Report: Tantrums called key to adult life. June 22, 1969.

142 Noel, D. I., and A. Pinkney: Correlates of prejudice: Some racial differences and similarities. *Amer. J. Sociol.*, 1964, **69**, 609–622.

143 Oberg, W.: Age and achievement: The technical man. *Personnel Psychol.*, 1960, **13**, 245–259.

144 O'Connor, N.: The evidence for the permanently disturbing effects of mother-child separation. *Acta Psychol.*, 1956, **12**, 174–191.

145 Oden, M. H.: The fulfillment of promise: 40-year follow-up of the Terman gifted group. *Genet. Psychol. Monogr.*, 1968, **77**, 3–93.

146 Offer, D.: *The psychological world of the teenager.* New York: Basic Books, 1969.

147 O'Neal, P., and L. N. Robins: Childhood patterns predictive of adult schizophrenia: A 30-year follow-up study. *Amer. J. Psychiat.*, 1958, **115**, 385–391.

148 Owens, W. A.: Age and mental abilities: A longitudinal study. *Genet. Psychol. Monogr.*, 1953, **48**, 3–54.

149 Packard, V.: *The status seekers.* New York: Pocket Books, 1961.

150 Packard, V.: *The pyramid climbers.* New York: McGraw-Hill, 1962.

151 Parker, E.: *The seven ages of woman.* Baltimore: Johns Hopkins, 1960.

152 Payne, D. E., and P. H. Mussen: Parent-child relations and father identification among adolescent boys. *J. abnorm. soc. Psychol.*, 1956, **52**, 358–362.

153 Peck, R. F., and H. Berkowitz: Personality and adjustment in middle age. In B. L. Neugarten (ed.), *Personality in middle and late life,* New York: Atherton, 1964, pp. 15–43.

154 Peck, R. F., and R. J. Havighurst: *The psychology of character development.* New York: Wiley, 1962.

155 Perkins, H. V.: Changing perceptions of self. *Childhood Educ.*, 1957, **34**, 82–84.

156 Plant, W. T.: Longitudinal changes in intolerance and authoritarianism for subjects differing in amount of college education over four years. *Genet. Psychol. Monogr.*, 1965, **72**, 247–287.

157 Pratt, K. J.: Motivation and learning in medieval writings. *Amer. Psychologist,* 1962, **17**, 496–500.

158 Pressey, S. L., and R. G. Kuhlen: *Psychological development through the life span.* New York: Harper, 1957.

159 Preston, C. E., and K. S. Gudiksen: A measure of self-perception among older people. *J. Geront.*, 1966, **21**, 63–71.

160 Raines, G. N.: Adolescence: Pattern for the future. *Geriatrics,* 1956, **11**, 159–162.

161 Rainwater, L.: A study of personality differences between middle and lower class adolescents: The Szondi Test in culture-personality research. *Genet. Psychol. Monogr.*, 1956, **54**, 3–86.

162 Reimanis, G.: Relationship of childhood experience memories to anomie later in life. *J. genet. Psychol.*, 1965, **106**, 245–252.

163 Rettig, R. S., and B. Pasamanick: Differential judgments of ethical risk by cheaters and noncheaters. *J. abnorm. Psychol.*, 1964, **69**, 109–113.

164 Rexford, E. N., M. Schlefer, and S. T. vanAmerogen: A follow-up of a psychia-

165 Roberts, K. E., and V. V. Fleming: Persistence and change in personality patterns. *Monogr. Soc. Res. Child Develpm.*, 1944, **8**, no. 3.

166 Robins, L. N., and P. O'Neal: Mortality, mobility, and crime: Problem children thirty years later. *Amer. sociol. Rev.*, 1958, **23**, 162–171.

167 Robins, L. N., and P. O'Neal: The adult prognosis for runaway children. *Amer. J. Orthopsychiat.*, 1959, **29**, 752–761.

168 Rogers, C. R.: Some observations on the organization of personality. *Amer. Psychologist,* 1947, **2**, 358–368.

169 Rose, A. M.: The mental health of normal older people. *Geriatrics,* 1961, **16**, 459–464.

170 Rosen, B. C.: Social class and the child's perception of the parent. *Child Develpm.*, 1964, **35**, 1147–1153.

171 Rosenthal, M. K.: The generalization of dependency behavior from mother to stranger. *J. child Psychol. Psychiat. and allied Disciplines,* 1967, **8**, 117–133.

172 Roth, R. M.: The role of self-concept in achievement. *J. exp. Educ.*, 1959, **27**, 265–281.

173 Ryan, M. E.: Social adjustment of kindergarten children ten years later. *Smith Coll. Stud. soc. Wk.*, 1949, **19**, 138–139.

174 Rybak, W.: Notes on crushes and hero-worship of adolescents. *Psychiat. Quart. Suppl.*, 1965, **39**, 48–53.

175 Sanford, N.: Personality development during the college years. *Personnel Guid. J.*, 1956, **35**, 74–80.

176 Scarpitti, F. R., E. Murray, S. Dinitz, and W. C. Reckless: The "good" boy in a high delinquency area: Four years later. *Amer. sociol. Rev.*, 1960, **25**, 555–558.

177 Schachter, F. F., A. Cooper, and R. Gordet: A method for assessing personality development for follow-up evaluations of the preschool child. *Monogr. Soc. Res. Child Develpm.*, 1968, **33**, no. 3.

178 Schaefer, E. S., and N. Bayley: Consistency of maternal behavior from infancy to preadolescence. *J. abnorm. soc. Psychol.*, 1960, **61**, 1–6.

179 Schaefer, E. S., and R. G. Bell: Patterns of attitudes toward child rearing and the family. *J. abnorm. soc. Psychol.*, 1957, **54**, 391–395.

180 Schaie, K. W.: A general model for the study of developmental problems. *Psychol. Bull.*, 1965, **64**, 92–107.

181 Schonfeld, W. A.: Socioeconomic affluence as a factor. *N. Y. State J. Med.*, 1967, **67**, 1981–1990.

182 Sears, R. E., E. E. Maccoby, and H. Levin: *Patterns in child rearing.* New York: Harper, 1957.

183 Shaffer, L. F., and E. J. Shoben: *The psychology of adjustment,* 2d ed. Boston: Houghton Mifflin, 1956.

184 Shirley, M. M.: The impact of the mother's personality on the young child. *Smith Coll. Stud. soc. Wk.*, 1941, **12**, 15–64.

185 Slater, P. E. and H. A. Scarr: Personality in old age. *Genet. Psychol. Monogr.*, 1964, **70**, 229–269.

186 Smith, M. E.: A comparison of certain personality traits as rated in the same individuals in childhood and fifty years later. *Child Develpm.*, 1952, **23**, 159–180.

187 Smith, W. D., and D. Lebo: Some changing aspects of the self-concept of pubes-

cent males. *J. genet. Psychol.*, 1956, **88**, 61–75.

188 Snyder, E. E.: Socioeconomic variations, values, and social participation among high school students. *J. Marriage & Family,* 1966, **28**, 174–176.

189 Sollenberger, R. T.: Chinese-American child-rearing practices and juvenile delinquency. *J. soc. Psychol.*, 1968, **74**, 13–23.

190 Sontag, L. W.: Implications of fetal behavior and environment for adult personality. *Ann. N. Y. Acad. Sci.*, 1966, **134**, 782–786.

191 Sontag, L. W., and J. Kagan: The emergence of intellectual achievement motives. *Amer. J. Orthopsychiat.*, 1963, **33**, 532–535.

192 Stagner, R.: *Psychology of personality,* 3d ed. New York: McGraw-Hill, 1961.

193 Stevenson, I.: Is the human personality more plastic in infancy and childhood? *Amer. J. Psychiat.*, 1957, **114**, 152–161.

194 Stewart, L. H.: Social and emotional adjustment during adolescence as related to the development of psychosomatic illness in adulthood. *Genet. Psychol. Monogr.*, 1962, **65**, 175–215.

195 Sticht, I. G., and W. Fox: Geographical mobility and dogmatism, anxiety and age. *J. soc. Psychol.*, 1966, **68**, 171–174.

196 Stott, L. H.: The persisting effects of early family experiences upon personality development. *Merrill-Palmer Quart.*, 1957, **3**, 145–159.

197 Stott, L. H., and R. S. Ball: Consistency and change in ascendance-submission in the social interaction of children. *Child Develpm.*, 1957, **28**, 259–272.

198 Stout, I. W., and G. Langdon: A report on follow-up interviews with parents of well-adjusted children. *J. educ. Sociol.*, 1953, **26**, 434–442.

199 Symonds, P. M.: What education has to learn from psychology. IX. Origins of personality. *Teachers Coll. Rec.*, 1960, **61**, 300–317.

200 Tannenbaum, A. S.: Personality change as a result of an experimental change of environmental conditions. *J. abnorm. soc. Psychol.*, 1957, **55**, 404–406.

201 Tannenbaum, D. E.: Loneliness in the aged. *Ment. Hyg., N. Y.*, 1967, **51**, 91–99.

202 Taylor, D. M.: Changes in the self-concept without psychotherapy. *J. consult. Psychol.*, 1955, **19**, 205–209.

203 Teicher, J. D., and J. Jacobs: Adolescents who attempt suicide: Preliminary findings. *Amer. J. Psychiat.*, 1966, **122**, 1248–1257.

204 Terman, L. M., and M. H. Oden: *The gifted child grows up.* Stanford: Stanford University Press, 1947.

205 Thompson, C.: Concepts of self in interpersonal theory. *Amer. J. Psychother.*, 1958, **12**, 5–17.

206 Thorndike, E. L.: Note on the shifts of interest with age. *J. appl. Psychol.*, 1949, **33**, 55.

207 Tryon, C., and W. E. Henry: How children learn personal and social adjustment. *Yearb. nat. Soc. Stud. Educ.*, 1950, **49**, pt. I, 156–182.

208 Tuckman, J.: Older people's judgment of the passage of time over the life span. *Geriatrics,* 1965, **20**, 136–140.

209 Tuddenham, R. D.: The constancy of the personality ratings over two decades. *Genet. Psychol. Monogr.*, 1959, **60**, 3–29.

210 Vaughan, G. M.: Ethnic awareness in rela-

tion to minority group membership. *J. genet. Psychol.*, 1964, **105**, 119–130.

211 Vedder, C. B., and A. S. Lefkowitz (eds.): *Problems of the aged.* Springfield, Ill.: Charles C Thomas, 1965.

212 Wallin, J. E. W.: The psychological, educational, and social problems in the aging as viewed by a mid-octogenarian. *J. genet. Psychol.*, 1962, **100**, 41–46.

213 Washburn, W. C.: Patterns of protective attitudes in relation to differences in self-evaluation and anxiety level among high school students. *Calif. J. educ. Res.*, 1962, **13**, 84–94.

214 Watson, R. I.: The personality of the aged: A review. *J. Geront.*, 1954, **9**, 309–315.

215 Wax, M.: The changing role of the home for the aged. *Gerontologist*, 1962, **2**, 128–133.

216 Webster, H.: Changes in attitudes during college. *J. educ. Psychol.*, 1958, **49**, 109–117.

217 Weinstock, A. R.: Family environment and the development of defense and coping mechanisms. *J. Pers. soc. Psychol.*, 1967, **5**, 67–75.

218 Weinstock, A. R.: Longitudinal study of social class and defense preferences. *J. consult. Psychol.*, 1967, **31**, 539–541.

219 Weller, L.: The relationship of personality and nonpersonality factors to prejudice. *J. soc. Psychol.*, 1964, **63**, 129–137.

220 Werner, E., and E. Gallistel: Prediction of outstanding performance, delinquency, and mental disturbance from childhood evaluations. *Child Develpm.*, 1961, **32**, 255–260.

221 Westman, J. C., D. L. Rice, and E. Bermann: Nursery school behavior and later school adjustment. *Amer. J. Orthopsychiat.*, 1967, **37**, 725–731.

222 Wheeler, D. K.: Expressed wishes of students. *J. genet. Psychol.*, 1963, **102**, 75–81.

223 Williams, A. F.: Social drinking, anxiety and depression. *J. Pers. soc. Psychol.*, 1966, **3**, 689–693.

224 Winkler, R. C. and R. A. Myers: Some concomitants of self-ideal discrepancy measures and self-acceptance. *J. counsel. Psychol.*, 1963, **10**, 83–86.

225 Witryol, S. L., and J. E. Calkins: Marginal social values of rural school children. *J. genet. Psychol.*, 1958, **92**, 81–93.

226 Wylie, L.: Youth in France and the United States. *Daedalus*, 1962, **91**, 198–215.

227 Yarrow, L. J.: Research in dimensions of early maternal care. *Merrill-Palmer Quart.*, 1963, **9**, 101–114.

228 Zak, M., E. L. Cowen, J. Rappaport, D. R. Beach, and J. D. Laird: Follow-up study of children identified early as emotionally disturbed. *J. consult. clin. Psychol.*, 1968, **32**, 369.

CHAPTER 6

1 Adler, A.: *Study of organ inferiority and its psychical compensation.* Washington: Nervous and Mental Disease Publishing Co., 1919.

2 Alcock, T.: Some personality characteristics of asthmatic children. *Brit. J. med. Psychol.*, 1960, **33**, 133–141.

3 Allport, G. W.: *Pattern and growth in personality.* New York: Holt, 1961.

4 Alpiner, J. G.: Audiologic problems of the aged. *Geriatrics*, 1963, **18**, 19–26.

5 Alvarez, W. C.: Sexual life of the aging. *Geriatrics*, 1957, **12**, 141–142.

6 Alvarez, W. C.: Are the old more likely to have automobile accidents? *Geriatrics*, 1961, **16**, 317–318.

7 Alvarez, W. C.: History of geriatrics goes back to 2500 B.C. *Geriatrics*, 1964, **19**, 701–704.

8 Amatora, Sister Mary: Developmental trends in pre-adolescence and in early adolescence in self-evaluation. *J. genet. Psychol.*, 1957, **91**, 89–97.

9 Ames. L. B., and F. L. Ilg: The developmental point of view with special reference to the principle of reciprocal neuromotor interweaving. *J. genet. Psychol.*, 1964, **105**, 195–209.

10 Angelino, H., and E. V. Mech: "Fears and worries" concerning physical changes: A preliminary survey of 32 females. *J. Psychol.*, 1955, **39**, 195–198.

11 Arkoff, A., and H. B. Weaver: Body image and body dissatisfaction in Japanese-Americans. *J. soc. Psychol.*, 1966, **68**, 323–330.

12 Atkinson, R. M., and E. L. Ringuette: A survey of biographical and psychological features in extraordinary fatness. *Psychosom. Med.*, 1967, **29**, 121–133.

13 Baldwin, D. C., and M. L. Barnes: Patterns of motivation in families seeking orthodontic treatment. *Int. Ass. Dent. Res. Abstr.*, 1966, **44**, 142.

14 Bartley, L., and J. Warden: Clothing preferences of women 65 and older. *J. Home Econ.*, 1962, **54**, 716–717.

15 Bayley, N.: Research in child development: A longitudinal perspective. *Merrill-Palmer Quart.*, 1965, **11**, 183–208.

16 Beigel, H. G.: Body height in mate selection. *J. soc. Psychol.*, 1954, **39**, 257–268.

17 Benedek, T.: Climacterium: A developmental phase. *Psychoanal. Quart.*, 1950, **19**, 1–27.

18 Bergler, E.: *The revolt of the middle-aged man.* New York: Wyn, 1954.

19 Bernard, J.: Marital stability and patterns of status variables. *J. Marriage & Family*, 1966, **28**, 421–448.

20 Biller, H. B., and L. J. Borstelmann: Masculine development: An integrative review. *Merrill-Palmer Quart.*, 1967, **13**, 253–294.

21 Billings, H. K.: An exploratory study of the attitudes of noncrippled children toward crippled children in three selected elementary schools. *Dissert. Abstr.*, 1967, **28**, (3–A), 958–959.

22 Birren, J. E., R. N. Butler, S. W. Greenhouse, L. Sokoloff, and M. R. Yarrow: *Human aging: A biological and behavioral study.* Bethesda, Md.: Dept. of Health, Education and Welfare, 1963.

23 Blank, A., A. A. Sugerman, and L. Roosa: Body concern, body image and nudity. *Psychol. Rep.*, 1968, **23**, 963–968.

24 Block, J.: Further consideration of psychosomatic predisposing factors in allergy. *Psychosom. Med.*, 1968, **30**, 202–208.

25 Bond, J. O.: The fragile male. In C. B. Vedder (ed.), *Problems of the middle-aged.* Springfield, Ill.: Charles C Thomas, 1965, pp. 150–156.

26 Brayshaw, A. J.: Middle-aged marriage: Idealism, realism, and the search for meaning. *Marriage fam. Living*, 1962, **24**, 358–364.

27 Breckenridge, M. E., and E. L. Vincent: *Child development*, 5th ed. Philadelphia: Saunders, 1965.

28 Breslin, H. B.: The relationship between the physically handicapped child's self-concept and his peer reputation. *Dissert. Abstr.*, 1968, **29** (4–B), 1493.

29 Brislin, R. W., and S. A. Lewis: Dating and physical attractiveness: Replication. *Psychol. Rep.*, 1968, **22**, 976.

30 Brown, A. M.: Surgical restorative art for the aging. In C. B. Vedder (ed.), *Problems of the middle-aged.* Springfield, Ill.: Charles C Thomas, 1965, pp. 172–182.

31 Brown, W. M. C., W. H. Price, and P. A. Jacobs: Further information on the identity of 47 XYY males. *Brit. med. J.*, 1968, **2**, 325–328.

32 Bruch, H.: Developmental obesity and schizophrenia. *Psychiatry*, 1958, **21**, 65–70.

33 Bull, K. R.: An investigation into the relationship between physique, motor capacity, and certain temperamental traits. *Brit. J. educ. Psychol.*, 1958, **28**, 149–154.

34 Burch, R. J., and D. Jackson: The greying of hair and the loss of permanent teeth in relation to an autoimunne theory of aging. *J. Geront.*, 1966, **21**, 522–528.

35 Busse, E. W.: Geriatrics today: An overview. *Amer. J. Psychiat.*, 1967, **123**, 1226–1233.

36 Byrne, D., O. London, and K. Reeves: The effect of physical attractiveness, sex, and attitude similarity on interpersonal attraction. *J. Pers.*, 1968, **36**, 259–271.

37 Calden, G., R. M. Lundy, and R. J. Schlafer: Sex differences in body concepts. *J. consult. Psychol.*, 1959, **23**, 378.

38 Cauffman, J. G.: Appraisal of the health behavior of junior high school students. *Res. Quart. Amer. Ass. Hlth. Phys. Educ. Recr.*, 19 ‾, **34**, 425–430.

39 Centers, L., and R. Centers: Peer group attitudes toward the amputee child. *J. soc. Psychol.*, 1963, **61**, 127–132.

40 Charles, D. C.: Outstanding characteristics of older patients. In C. B. Vedder and A. S. Lefkowitz (eds.), *Problems of the aged.* Springfield, Ill.: Charles C Thomas, 1965, pp. 15–23.

41 Chester, M. A.: Ethnocentrism and attitudes toward the physically disabled. *J. Pers. soc. Psychol.*, 1965, **2**, 877–882.

42 Chilman, C. S., and D. L. Meyer: Single and married undergraduates' measured personality needs and self-rated happiness. *J. Marriage & Family*, 1966, **28**, 67–76.

43 Christopherson, V. A.: Role modifications of the disabled male. *Amer. J. Nurs.*, 1968, **68**, 290–293.

44 Clarke, H., and A. L. Olson: Characteristics of 15-year-old boys who demonstrate various accomplishments and difficulties. *Child Develpm.*, 1965, **36**, 559–567.

45 Clifford, C., and T. S. Cohn: The relationship between leadership and personality attributes perceived by followers. *J. soc. Psychol.*, 1964, **64**, 57–64.

46 Cohen, J.: The effects of blindness on children's development. *Children*, 1966, **13**, 23–27.

47 Coleman, J. S.: *The adolescent society.* New York: Free Press, 1961.

48 Compton, M. H.: Body build, clothing and delinquent behavior. *J. Home Econ.*, 1967, **49**, 655–659.

49 Corsini, R. J.: Appearance and criminality. *Amer. J. Sociol.*, 1959, **65**, 49–51.

50 Cortés, J. B., and F. M. Gatli: Physique and self-description of temperament. *J. consult. Psychol.*, 1965, **29**, 432–439.

51 Craig, H. B.: A sociometric investigation of

the self-concept of the deaf child. *Amer. Ann. Deaf*, 1965, **110**, 456–478.

52 Cruickshank, W. M., and G. O. Johnson (eds.): *Education of exceptional children and youth*, 2d ed. Englewood Cliffs, N. J.: Prentice-Hall, 1967.

53 Curtis, H. J.: Biological mechanisms underlying the aging process. *Science*, 1963, **141**, 686–694.

54 Dalton, K.: School girls' behavior and menstruation. *Brit. med. J.*, Dec. 1960, pp. 1647–1649.

55 Davidson, M. A., R. G. McInnes, and R. W. Parnell: The distribution of personality traits in seven-year-old children: A combined psychological, psychiatric and somatotype study. *Brit. J. educ. Psychol.*, 1957, **27**, 43–61.

56 Davis, J. A.: Status symbols and the measurement of status perception. *Sociometry*, 1956, **19**, 154–165.

57 Denney, D., D. M. Kole, and R. G. Matazarro: The relationship between age and the number of symptoms reported by patients. *J. Geront.*, 1965, **20**, 50–53.

58 Dibiase, W. J., and L. A. Hjelle: Body-image stereotypes and body-type preferences among male college students. *Percept. mot. Skills*, 1968, **27**, 1143–1146.

59 Douglas, J. W. B., and J. M. Ross: Age of puberty related to educational ability, attainment and school leaving age. *J. child Psychol. Psychiat.*, 1964, **5**, 185–196.

60 Dunbar, F.: Homeostasis during puberty. *Amer. J. Psychiat.*, 1958, **114**, 673–682.

61 Dunphy, D. C.: The social structure of the urban adolescent peer groups. *Sociometry*, 1963, **26**, 230–246.

62 Eichorn, D. H.: Biological correlates of behavior. *62nd Yearb. nat. Soc. Stud. Educ.*, 1963, pt. 1, 4–61.

63 Eisenberg, L.: A developmental approach to adolescence. *Children*, 1965, **12**, 131–135.

64 Eisendorf, C.: Attitudes toward old people: A re-analysis of the item-validity of the Stereotype Scale. *J. Geront.*, 1966, **21**, 455–462.

65 Elliott, R.: Physiological activity and performance: A comparison of kindergarten children and young adults. *Psychol. Monogr.*, 1964, **78**, no. 10.

66 Elser, R. P.: The social position of hearing handicapped children in the regular grades. *Except. Children*, 1959, **25**, 305–309.

67 Farina, A., M. Sherman, and J. G. Allen: Role of physical abnormalities in interpersonal perception and behavior. *J. abnorm. Psychol.*, 1968, **73**, 590–593.

68 Faust, M. S.: Developmental maturity as a determinant in prestige of adolescent girls. *Child Develpm.*, 1960, **31**, 173–184.

69 Fink, S. L., J. K. Skipper, and P. N. Hallenbeck: Physical disability and problems in marriage. *J. Marriage & Family*, 1968, **30**, 64–73.

70 Fisher, S.: Sex differences in body perception. *Psychol. Monogr.*, 1964, **78**, no. 14.

71 Force, D. G.: Social status of physically handicapped children. *Except. Children*, 1956, **23**, 104–107, 132.

72 Frank, L. K. and M. Frank: *Your adolescent, at home and in school*. New York: Viking, 1956.

73 Fuller, G. B., and G. H. Lunney: Relationship between perception and body image among emotionally disturbed children. *Percept. mot. Skills*, 1965, **21**, 530.

74 Genshaw, J. K., and F. D. Maglione: Familiarity, dogmatism, and reported student attitudes toward the disabled. *J. soc. Psychol.*, 1965, **67**, 329–341.

75 Gesell, A., F. L. Ilg, and L. B. Ames: *Youth: The years from ten to sixteen*. New York: Harper, 1956.

76 Gording, E. J., and E. Match: Personality changes of certain contact lens patients. *J. Amer. Optometric Ass.*, 1968, **39**, 266–269.

77 Gordon, J. E.: Relationships among mothers' achievement, independence training, attitudes and handicapped children's performance. *J. consult. Psychol.*, 1959, **23**, 207–212.

78 Gray, R. M., J. M. Baker, J. P. Kesler, and W. R. E. Newman: Stress and health in later maturity. *J. Geront.*, 1965, **20**, 65–68.

79 Greenberg, H. M., L. Allison, M. Fewell, and C. Rich: The personality of junior high and high school students attending a residential school for the blind. *J. educ. Psychol.*, 1957, **48**, 406–410.

80 Greenberg, P., and A. R. Gilliland: The relationship between basal metabolism and personality. *J. soc. Psychol.*, 1952, **35**, 3–7.

81 Greenblatt, R. B.: Treatment of menopausal symptoms. *Geriatrics*, 1957, **12**, 452–453.

82 Hardyck, D. C.: Sex differences in personality changes with age. *J. Geront.*, 1964, **19**, 78–82.

83 Hartman, A. A.: Name styles in relation to personality. *J. gen. Psychol.*, 1958, **59**, 289–294.

84 Havighurst, R. J.: *Human development and education*. New York: Longmans, 1953.

85 Havighurst, R. J.: Body, self, and society. *Sociol. soc. Res.*, 1965, **49**, 261–267.

86 Heald, F. P., M. Dangela, and P. Brunschyber: Physiology of adolescence. *New Eng. J. Med.*, 1963, **268**, 192–198, 243–252, 299–307, 361–366.

87 Hellersberg, E. F.: Unevenness of growth in its relation to vulnerability, anxiety, ego weakness and the schizophrenic patterns. *Amer. J. Orthopsychiat.*, 1957, **27**, 577–586.

88 Henley, B., and M. S. Davis: Satisfaction and dissatisfaction: A study of the chronically-ill aged patient. *J. Hlth. soc. Behav.*, 1967, **8**, 65–75.

89 Hess, E., R. B. Roth, and A. F. Kaminsky: Is there a male climacteric? *Geriatrics*, 1955, **10**, 170–173.

90 Hilgard, E. R.: *Introduction to psychology*, 4th ed. New York: Harcourt, Brace & World, 1962.

91 Hinkle, L. E., W. N. Christenson, F. D. Kane, A. Ostfeld, W. N. Thetford, and H. G. Wolff: An investigation of the relation between life experience, personality characteristics, and general susceptibility to illness. *Psychosom. Med.*, 1958, **20**, 278–295.

92 Hodgkins, J.: Reaction time and speed of movement in males and females of various ages. *Res. Quart. Amer. Ass. Hlth. Phys. Educ. Recr.*, 1963, **34**, 335–343.

93 Holden, R. H.: Changes in body image of physically handicapped children due to summer camp experience. *Merrill-Palmer Quart.*, 1962, **8**, 19–26.

94 Horowitz, L. S., N. S. Rees, and M. W. Horowitz: Attitudes toward deafness as a function of increasing maturity. *J. soc. Psychol.*, 1965, **66**, 331–336.

95 Horwitt, M. K.: Nutritional problems in the aged. In C. B. Vedder and A. S. Lefkowitz (eds.), *Problems of the aged*. Springfield, Ill.: Charles C Thomas, 1965, pp. 172–178.

96 Humphreys, L. G.: Characteristics of type concepts with special reference to Sheldon's typology. *Psychol. Bull.*, 1957, **54**, 218–228.

97 Hunt, J.: On being disabled. *Personnel Administration*, 1968, **97**, 48–51.

98 Iliffe, A. H.: A study of preferences in feminine beauty. *Brit. J. Psychol.*, 1960, **51**, 267–273.

99 Ingwell, R. H., R. W. Thoreson, and S. J. Smits: Accuracy of social perception of physically handicapped and nonhandicapped persons. *J. soc. Psychol.*, 1967, **72**, 107–116.

100 Jaffee, J.: "What's in a name": Attitudes toward disabled persons. *Personnel Guid. J.*, 1967, **45**, 557–560.

101 Jamieson, B. D.: The influence of birth order, family size and sex differences on risk-taking behavior. *Brit. J. soc. clin. Psychol.*, 1969, **8**, 1–8.

102 Jersild, A. T.: *The psychology of adolescence*, 2d ed. New York: Macmillan, 1963.

103 Johnson, B., and H. A. Morse: Injured children and their parents. *Children*, 1968, **15**, 147–152.

104 Johnson, R.: How parents' attitudes affect children's illnesses. *Bull. Instit. Child Study, Toronto*, 1955, **27**, 5–8.

105 Johnston, F. E.: Individual variation in the rate of skeletal maturation between five and eighteen years. *Child Develpm.*, 1964, **35**, 75–80.

106 Jones, M. C.: Correlates of somatic development. *Child Develpm.*, 1965, **36**, 899–911.

107 Jourard, S. M.: *Personal adjustment*, 2d ed. New York: Macmillan, 1963.

108 Jourard, S. M. and P. F. Secord: Body-cathexis and the ideal female figure. *J. abnorm. soc. Psychol.*, 1955, **50**, 243–246.

109 Kagan, J.: Body build and conceptual impulsivity in children. *J. Pers.*, 1966, **34**, 118–128.

110 Kagan, J., and H. A. Moss: *Birth to maturity: A study in psychological development*. New York: Wiley, 1962.

111 Kassel, V.: Polygyny after 60. *Geriatrics*, 1966, **21**, 214–218.

112 Kaufman, I., and L. Heims: The body image of the juvenile delinquent. *Amer. J. Orthopsychiat.*, 1958, **28**, 146–159.

113 Keislar, E. R.: Experimental development of "like" and "dislike" of others among adolescent girls. *Child Develpm.*, 1961, **32**, 59–69.

114 Kiker, V. L., and A. R. Miller: Perceptual judgment of physiques as a factor in social image. *Percept. mot. Skills*, 1967, **24**, 1013–1014.

115 Kleck, R., H. Ono, and A. H. Hastorf: The effects of physical deviance upon face-to-face interaction. *Hum. Relat.*, 1966, **19**, 425–436.

116 Kligman, A. M.: Out damned spots. *Penna. Gazette*, Nov. 1967, p. 35.

117 Klopfer, W. G.: Psychological stresses of old age. *Geriatrics*, 1958, **13**, 529–531.

118 Krogman, W. M.: The physical growth of the child. In M. Fishbein and R. J. R. Kennedy (eds.), *Modern marriage and family living*. Fair Lawn, N. J.: Oxford, 1957, pp. 417–425.

119 Kurlander, A. B., S. Abraham, and J. W.

Rion: Obesity and disease. *Hum. Biol.*, 1956, **28**, 203–216.

120 Laird, J. T.: Emotional disturbances among the physically handicapped. *Personnel Guid. J.*, 1957, **36**, 190–191.

121 Lane, J. A.: Assessment of physically handicapped adult students in college. *Dissert. Abstr.*, 1968, **28** (9-A), 3511–3512.

122 Lantz, B.: Children's learning, personality and physiological interactions. *Calif. J. educ. Res.*, 1956, **7**, 153–158.

123 La Rieviere, J. E., and E. Simonson: The effect of age and occupation on speed of writing. *J. Geront.*, 1965, **20**, 415–416.

124 Larsen, V. L.: Sources of menstrual information: A comparison of age groups. *Family Life Coordinator*, 1961, **10**, 41–43.

125 Leckie, E. V., and R. F. J. Withers: Obesity and depression. *J. psychosom. Res.*, 1967, **11**, 107–115.

126 Lederer, H. D.: How the sick view their world. *Pastoral Psychol.*, 1957, **8**, no. 74, 41–49.

127 Lefkowitz, M. M., and J. Cannon: Physique and obstreperous behavior. *J. clin. Psychol.*, 1966, **22**, 172–174.

128 Lehrhoff, I.: Speech problems in children. *J. Pediat.*, 1958, **52**, 91–95.

129 Lemkau, P. V.: The influence of handicapping conditions on child development. *Children*, 1961, **8**, 43–47.

130 Lerner, R. M.: The development of stereotyped expectancies of body build-behavior relations. *Child Develpm.*, 1969, **40**, 137–141.

131 Lerner, R. M., and E. Gellert: Body build identification, preference and aversion in children. *Develpm. Psychol.*, 1969, **1**, 456–462.

132 Leventhal, T., and M. Sills: Self-image in school phobia. *Amer. J. Orthopsychiat.*, 1964, **34**, 685–695.

133 Levine, A. J.: A sound approach to middle age. In C. B. Vedder (ed.), *Problems of the middle-aged*. Springfield, Ill.: Charles C Thomas, 1965, pp. 40–43.

134 Lewit, D. W., and K. Virolainen: Conformity and independence in adolescents' motivation for orthodontic treatment. *Child Develpm.*, 1968, **39**, 1189–1200.

135 Linden, M. E.: Effects of social attitudes on the mental health of the aging. *Geriatrics*, 1957, **12**, 109–114.

136 Linn, E. L.: Social meanings of dental appearance. *J. Hlth. hum. Behav.*, 1966, **7**, 289–295.

137 Lipman, A.: Health insecurity of the aged. *Gerontologist*, 1962, **2**, 99–101.

138 Lopata, H. Z.: The life cycle of the social role of housewife. *Sociol. soc. Res.*, 1966, **51**, 5–27.

139 Lowrey, G. H.: Obesity in the adolescent. *Amer. J. pub. Hlth.*, 1958, **48**, 1354–1358.

140 Lucas, C. J., and A. B. Ojha: Personality and acne. *J. psychosom. Res.*, 1963, **7**, 41–43.

141 Maccoby, E. E., E. M. Dowley, J. W. Hagen, and R. Degerman: Activity level and intellectual functioning in normal preschool children. *Child Develpm.*, 1965, **36**, 761–770.

142 MacGregor, F. C.: Social and cultural components in the motivation of persons seeking plastic surgery of the nose. *J. Hlth. hum. Behav.*, 1967, **8**, 125–135.

143 Maddox, G. L.: Some correlates of differences in self-assessment on health status among the elderly. *J. Geront.*, 1962, **17**, 180–185.

144 Manheimer, D. I., and G. D. Mellinger: Personality characteristics of the child accident repeater. *Child Develpm.*, 1967, **38**, 491–513.

145 Manz, W., and H. E. Lueck: Influence of wearing glasses on personality ratings: Cross-cultural validation of an old experiment. *Percept. mot. Skills*, 1968, **27**, 704.

146 Marak, G. E.: The evolution of leadership structure. *Sociometry*, 1964, **27**, 174–182.

147 Marcus, L. M., W. Wilson, L. Kraft, D. Swander, F. Sutherland, and E. Schulhofer: An interdisciplinary approach to accident patterns in children. *Monogr. Soc. Res. Child Develpm.*, 1960, **25**, no. 2.

148 Martin, J. C.: Racial enthnocentrism and judgment of beauty. *J. soc. Psychol.*, 1964, **63**, 59–63.

149 Martin, P. C., and E. L. Vincent: *Human development*. New York: Ronald, 1960.

150 Master, A. M., and R. P. Lasser: Blood pressure after age 65. *Geriatrics*, 1964, **19**, 41–46.

151 Matthews, V., and C. Wootis: A preferred method for obtaining rankings: Reactions to physical handicaps. *Amer. sociol. Rev.*, 1966, **31**, 851–854.

152 McCully, R. S.: Fantasy productions of children with a progressively crippling and fatal illness. *J. genet. Psychol.*, 1963, **102**, 203–216.

153 McDavid, J. W., and H. Harari: Stereotyping of names and popularity in grade-school children. *Child Develpm.*, 1966, **37**, 453–459.

154 McGhie, B. A., and S. M. Russell: The subjective assessment of normal sleep patterns. *J. ment. Sci.*, 1962, **108**, 642–654.

155 Meissner, A. L., and R. W. Thoreson: Relation of self-concept to impact and obviousness of disability among male and female adolescents. *Percept. mot. Skills*, 1967, **24**, 1099–1105.

156 Merriman, J. B.: Relationship of personality traits to motor ability. *Res. Quart. Amer. Ass. Hlth. Phys. Educ. Recr.*, 1960, **31**, 163–173.

157 Meyer, A. E., R. Gotle, and W. Weitemeyer: Duration of illness and elevation of neuroticism scores. *J. psychosom. Res.*, 1968, **11**, 347–355.

158 Meyer, E., W. E. Jacobson, M. T. Edgerton, and A. Canter: Motivational patterns in patients seeking elective plastic surgery. *Psychosom. Med.*, 1960, **22**, 193–203.

159 Meyerson, L.: Special disabilities. *Annu. Rev. Psychol.*, 1957, **8**, 437–456.

160 Miller, A. R., and R. A. Stewart: Perception of female physiques. *Percept. mot. Skills*, 1968, **27**, 721–722.

161 Montagu, A.: *Human heredity*. New York: Harcourt, Brace & World, 1959.

162 More, D. M.: Developmental concordance and discordance during puberty and early adolescence. *Monogr. Soc. Res. Child Develpm.*, 1953, **18**, 1–128.

163 Morgan, C. T.: *Physiological psychology*, 3d ed. New York: McGraw-Hill, 1964.

164 Morgan, R. F.: The adult growth examination: Preliminary comparisons of physical aging in adults by sex and race. *Percept. mot. Skills*, 1968, **27**, 595–599.

165 Munn, N. L.: *The evolution and growth of human behavior*, 2d ed. Boston: Houghton Mifflin, 1965.

166 Mussen, P. H., and D. K. Newman: Acceptance of handicap, motivation, and adjustment in physically disabled children.

Except. Children, 1958, **24**, 225–260, 277–278.

167 Mysak, E. D., and T. D. Hanley: Processes in speech: Pitch and duration characteristics. *J. Geront.*, 1958, **13**, 309–313.

168 Nash, H.: Assignment of gender to body regions. *J. genet. Psychol.*, 1958, **92**, 113–115.

169 Neugarten, B. L., and R. G. Kraines: "Menopausal symptoms" in women of various ages. *Psychosom. Med.*, 1965, **27**, 266–273.

170 Neuhaus, E. C.: A personality study of asthmatic and cardiac children. *Psychosom. Med.*, 1958, **20**, 181–186.

171 *New York Times* Report: Left-handed find handicap grows. Aug. 2, 1959.

172 *New York Times* Report: "Go-getters" called more susceptible to heart attacks. Jan. 8, 1966.

173 *New York Times* Report: Ailments multiply as age exceeds 65. Feb. 4, 1966.

174 *New York Times* Report: Plastic surgery aiding prisoners. Mar. 27, 1966.

175 *New York Times* Report: Lazy husbands said to fatigue wives. Apr. 3, 1966.

176 *New York Times* Report: 5-to-14 age groups held mishap prone. July 6, 1967.

177 *New York Times* Report: Inheritance called strong among girls. Nov. 10, 1968.

178 Norris, A. H., and W. N. Shock: Age and variability. *Ann. N. Y. Acad. Sci.*, 1966, **132**, 591–601.

179 Over, R.: Possible visual factors in falls by old people. *Gerontologist*, 1966, **6**, 212–214.

180 Packard, V.: *The status seekers*. New York: Pocket Books, 1961.

181 Packard, V.: *The pyramid climbers*. New York: McGraw-Hill, 1962.

182 Palmer, R. D.: Development of a differential handedness. *Psychol. Bull.*, 1964, **62**, 257–272.

183 Parker, E.: *The seven ages of woman*. Baltimore: Johns Hopkins, 1960.

184 Peck, R. F., and R. J. Havighurst: *The psychology of character development*. New York: Wiley, 1962.

185 Peckos, P. S.: Nutrition during growth and development. *Child Develpm.*, 1957, **28**, 273–285.

186 Pressey, S. L., and R. G. Kuhlen: *Psychological development through the life span*. New York: Harper & Row, 1957.

187 Rafferty, F. T., and E. S. Stein: A study of the relationship of early menarche to ego development. *Amer. J. Orthopsychiat.*, 1958, **28**, 170–179.

188 Rahe, R. H., and R. J. Arthur: Life-change patterns surrounding illness experiences. *J. psychosom. Res.*, 1968, **11**, 341–345.

189 Reed, G. F., and A. C. Smith: A further experimental investigation of the relative speeds of left- and right-handed writers. *J. genet. Psychol.*, 1962, **100**, 275–288.

190 Reinhold, R.: Man's life span is linked to where he lives. *The New York Times*, May 3, 1968.

191 *Report of President's Council on Aging*. 1963.

192 Richardson, S. A., and J. Royce: Race and physical handicap in children's preference for other children. *Child Develpm.*, 1968, **39**, 467–480.

193 Robbins, P. R.: Personality and psychosomatic illness: A selective review of research. *Genet. Psychol. Monogr.*, 1969, **80**, 51–90.

194 Roffwarg, H. P., J. N. Muzio, and W. C.

Dement: Ontogenetic development of the human sleep-dream cycle. *Science*, 1966, **152**, 604–609.

195 Rogers, K. D., and G. Reese: Health studies: Presumably normal high school students. *Amer. J. Dis. Children*, 1965, **109**, 9–27.

196 Rose, A. M.: Class differences among the elderly: A research report. *Sociol. soc. Res.*, 1966, **50**, 356–360.

197 Rosen, G. M., and A. O. Ross: Relationship of body image to self-concept. *J. consult. clin. Psychol.*, 1968, **32**, 100.

198 Ryan, M. S.: *Clothing: A study in human behavior*. New York: Holt, 1966.

199 Scheinfeld, A.: *Your heredity and environment*. Philadelphia: Lippincott, 1965.

200 Schneiderman, L.: The estimation of one's own body traits. *J. soc. Psychol.*, 1956, **44**, 89–99.

201 Schonfeld, W. A.: Body-image disturbance in adolescents. *Arch. gen. Psychiat.*, 1966, **15**, 16–21.

202 Schreiber, E. H.: The relationship between personality characteristics and dental disorders in adolescents. *Dissert. Abstr.*, 1967, **28** (4–A), 1313.

203 Schwartz, A. N., and R. W. Kleemeier: The effects of illness and age upon some aspects of personality. *J. Geront.*, 1965, **20**, 85–91.

204 Secord, P. F., and S. M. Jourard: The appraisal of body-cathexis: Body-cathexis and the self. *J. consult. Psychol.*, 1953, **17**, 343–347.

205 Seltzer, C. C., and J. Mayer: A review of genetic and constitutional factors in human obesity. *Ann. N. Y. Acad. Sci.*, 1966, **132**, 688–695.

206 Shaffer, L. F., and E. J. Shoben: *The psychology of adjustment*, 2d ed. Boston: Houghton Mifflin, 1956.

207 Sheldon, W. H., C. W. Dupertuis, and E. McDermott: *Atlas of man: A guide for somatotyping the adult male at all ages*. New York: Harper, 1954.

208 Shipman, W. G.: Age of menarche and adult personality. *Arch. gen. Psychiat.*, 1964, **10**, 155–159.

209 Shock, N. W.: *Trends in gerontology*, 2d ed. Stanford, Calif.: Stanford, 1959.

210 Sills, F. D., and P. W. Everett: The relationship of extreme somatotypes to performance in motor and strength tests. *Res. Quart. Amer. Ass. Hlth. Phys. Educ. Recr.*, 1953, **24**, 223–228.

211 Simon, M. D.: Body configuration and school readiness. *Child Develpm.*, 1959, **30**, 493–512.

212 Simpson, S. L.: Hormones and behavior pattern. *Brit. med. J.*, 1957, **2**, 839–843.

213 Singer, J. E., and P. F. Lamb: Social concern, body size and birth order. *J. soc. Psychol.*, 1966, **68**, 143–151.

214 Slater, P. E., and H. A. Scarr: Personality in old age. *Genet. Psychol. Monogr.*, 1964, **70**, 229–269.

215 Smith, K. V., and D. Greene: Scientific motion study and aging processes in performance. *Ergonomics*, 1962, **5**, 155–164.

216 Sobel, H.: When does human aging start? *Gerontologist*, 1966, **6**, 17–22.

217 Solley, W. H.: Ratio of physical development as a factor in motor co-ordination of boys ages 10-14. *Res. Quart. Amer. Ass. Hlth. Phys. Educ. Recr.*, 1957, **28**, 295–304.

218 Sontag, L. W.: Some psychosomatic aspects of childhood. *Nerv. Child*, 1946, **5**, 296–304.

219 Staffieri, J. R.: A study of social stereotypes of body image in children. *J. Pers. soc. Psychol.*, 1967, **7**, 101–104.

220 Stagner, R.: *Psychology of personality*, 3d ed. New York: McGraw-Hill, 1961.

221 Stephens, W. N.: A cross-cultural study of menstrual taboos. *Genet. Psychol. Monogr.*, 1961, **64**, 385–416.

222 Stott, D. H.: Infantile illness and subsequent mental and emotional development. *J. genet. Psychol.*, 1959, **94**, 233–251.

223 Strongman, K. T., and C. J. Hart: Stereotyped reactions to body build. *Psychol. Rep.*, 1968, **23**, 1175–1178.

224 Symonds, P. M.: What education has to learn from psychology: IX. Origins of personality. *Teachers Coll. Rec.*, 1960, **61**, 301–317.

225 Talland, G. A.: The effect of age on speed of simple manual skills. *J. genet. Psychol.*, 1962, **100**, 69–76.

226 Thompson, G. G.: *Child psychology*, rev. ed. Boston: Houghton Mifflin, 1962.

227 Thompson, H.: Physical growth. In L. Carmichael (ed.), *Manual of child psychology*, 2d ed. New York: Wiley, 1954, pp. 292–334.

228 Thompson, L. J.: Stresses in middle life from the psychiatrist's viewpoint. In C. B. Vedder (ed.), *Problems of the middle-aged*. Springfield, Ill.: Charles C Thomas, 1965, pp. 116–120.

229 *Time* Report: Pills to keep women young. Apr. 1, 1966, p. 50.

230 Turberg, J.: An investigation of the association of maternal attitudes and childhood obesity and the self-concept of the obese child. *Dissert. Abstr.*, 1967, **28**, 243–244.

231 Udry, J. R.: Structural correlates of feminine beauty preferences in Britain and among the United States: A comparison. *Sociol. soc. Res.*, 1965, **49**, 330–342.

232 Valadian, I., H. C. Stuart, and R. B. Reed: Studies of illness of children followed from birth to eighteen years. *Monogr. Soc. Res. Child Develpm.*, 1961, **26**, no. 3.

233 Vedder, C. B., and A. S. Lefkowitz (eds.): *Problems of the aged*. Springfield, Ill.: Charles C Thomas, 1965.

234 Wagonfeld, S., and H. M. Wolowitz: Obesity and the self-help group: A look at TOPS. *Amer. J. Psychiat.*, 1968, **125**, 249–255.

235 Waldrop, M. F., F. A. Pederson, and R. Q. Bell: Minor physical anomalies and behavior in preschool children. *Child Develpm.*, 1968, **39**, 391–400.

236 Walker, R. N.: Body build and behavior in young children. I. Body build and nursery school teachers' ratings. *Monogr. Soc. Res. Child Develpm.*, 1962, **27**, no. 3.

237 Walker, R. N.: Body build and behavior in young children. II. Body build and parents' ratings. *Child Develpm.*, 1963, **34**, 1–23.

238 Walster, E., V. Aronson, D. Abrahams, and L. Rottmann: Importance of physical attractiveness in dating behavior. *J. Pers. soc. Psychol.*, 1966, **4**, 508–516.

239 Washburn, W. C.: The effects of physique and intrafamily tension on self-concepts in adolescent males. *J. consult. Psychol.*, 1962, **26**, 460–466.

240 Watson, E. J., and A. M. Johnson: The emotional significance of acquired physical disfigurement in children. *Amer. J. Orthopsychiat.*, 1958, **28**, 85–97.

241 Wax, M.: Themes in cosmetics and grooming. *Amer. J. Sociol.*, 1957, **62**, 588–593.

242 Weatherley, D.: Self-perceived rate of physical maturation and personality in late adolescence . *Child Develpm.*, 1964, **35**, 1197–1210.

243 Weiss, J. H.: Birth order and asthma in children. *J. psychosom. Res.*, 1968, **12**, 137–140.

244 Werboff, J.: Research related to the origins of behavior. *Merrill-Palmer Quart.*, 1963, **9**, 115–122.

245 Werner, A. A.: Sex behavior and problems of the climacteric. In M. Fishbein and E. W. Burgess (eds.), *Successful marriage*, rev. ed. Garden City, N. Y.: Doubleday, 1955, pp. 475–490.

246 Whiteman, M., and I. F. Lukoff: Attitudes toward blindness and other physical handicaps. *J. soc. Psychol.*, 1965, **66**, 135–145.

247 Wickham, W. W.: The effects of the menstrual cycle on test performance. *Brit. J. Psychol.*, 1958, **49**, 34–41.

248 Wiggins, J. S., N. Wiggins, and J. C. Conger: Correlates of heterosexual somatic preference. *J. Pers. soc. Psychol.*, 1968, **10**, 82–90.

249 Williams, M. C., and J. B. Eicher: Teenagers' appearance and social acceptance. *J. Home Econ.*, 1966, **58**, 457–461.

250 Wltryol, S. L., and J. E. Calkins: Marginal social values of rural school children. *J. genet. Psychol.*, 1958, **92**, 81–93.

251 Zahran, H. A. S.: A study of personality differences between blind and sighted children. *Brit. J. educ. Psychol.*, 1965, **35**, 329–338.

252 Zion, L. C.: Body concept as it relates to self-concept. *Res. Quart. Amer. Ass. Hlth. Phys. Educ. Recr.*, 1965, **36**, 490–495.

253 Zola, I. K.: Feelings about age among older people. *J. Geront.*, 1962, **17**, 65–68.

254 Zunich, M., and B. E. Ledwith: Self-concepts of visually handicapped and sighted children. *Percept. mot. Skills*, 1965, **21**, 771–774.

CHAPTER 7

1 Abel, H., and R. Gingles: Identifying problems of adolescent girls. *J. educ. Res.*, 1965, **58**, 389–392.

2 Adams, J. F.: Adolescent personal problems as a function of age and sex. *J. genet. Psychol.*, 1964, **104**, 207–214.

3 Albert, R. S.: The role of mass media and the effect of aggressive film content upon children's aggressive responses and identification choices. *Genet. Psychol. Monogr.*, 1957, **55**, 221–285.

4 Allinsmith, W.: Conscience and conflict: The moral force in personality. *Child Develpm.*, 1957, **28**, 469–476.

5 Allport, G. W.: *Pattern and growth in personality*. New York: Holt, 1961.

6 Altmeyer, A. J.: Economic status of older people and their need for economic security. *Geriatrics*, 1957, **12**, 201–202.

7 Amatora, Sister Mary: Home interests in early adolescence. *Genet. Psychol. Monogr.*, 1962, **65**, 137–174.

8 Ames, L. B.: Children's stories. *Genet. Psychol. Monogr.*, 1966, **73**, 337–396.

9 Anastasi, A.: Heredity, environment, and the question "How?" *Psychol. Rev.*, 1958, **65**, 197–208.

10 Aronson, E., and D. R. Mettee: Dishonest behavior as a function of differential levels of induced self-esteem. *J. Pers. soc. Psychol.*, 1968, **9**, 121–127.

11 Ausubel, D. P.: Relationships between shame and guilt in the socialization process. *Psychol. Rev.*, 1955, **62**, 378–390.

12 Back, K. W., and K. E. Davis: Some personal and situational factors relevant to the consistency and prediction of conforming behavior. *Sociometry*, 1965, **28**, 227–240.

13 Bailey, J. A., and R. V. Robertson: Students' and teachers' perceptions of students' problems. *Personnel Guid. J.*, 1964, **43**, 171–173.

14 Bailyn, L.: Mass media and children: A study of exposure habits and cognitive effects. *Psychol. Monogr.*, 1959, **73**, no. 1.

15 Baldwin, A. L., J. Kalhorn, and F. H. Breese: Patterns of parent behavior. *Psychol. Monogr.*, 1945, **58**, no. 3.

16 Baldwin, W. K.: The social position of the educable mentally retarded child in the regular grades in the public schools. *Except. Children*, 1958, **25**, 106–108, 112.

17 Bayley, N.: Behavioral correlates of mental growth: Birth to thirty-six years. *Amer. Psychologist*, 1968, **23**, 1–17.

18 Bealer, R. C., and F. C. Willets: The religious interests of American high school youth: A survey of recent research. *Relig. Educ.*, 1967, **62**, 435–444.

19 Becker, L. J.: The changing moral values of students. *J. Home Econ.*, 1963, **55**, 646–648.

20 Beilin, H.: The pattern of postponability and its relation to social class mobility. *J. soc. Psychol.*, 1956, **44**, 33–48.

21 Bennett, E. M., and R. L. Cohen: Men and women: Personality patterns and contrasts. *Genet. Psychol. Monogr.*, 1959, **59**, 101–155.

22 Berkowitz: B.: Changes in intellect with age. IV. Changes in achievement and survival in older people. *J. genet. Psychol.*, 1965, **107**, 3–14.

23 Bijou, S. W.: The mentally retarded child. *Psychology Today*, 1968, **2**, 46–51.

24 Birren, J. E.: Psychological aspects of aging: Intellectual functioning. *Gerontologist*, 1968, **8**, 16–19.

25 Bittner, J. R.: Student value profiles of state and church-related colleges. *Coll. Stud. Survey*, 1968, **2**, 1–4.

26 Blackman, L. S., and H. Kahn: Success and failure as determinants of aspirational shifts in retardates and normals. *Amer. J. ment. Defic.*, 1963, **67**, 751–755.

27 Blakely, W. P.: A study of seventh grade children's reading of comic books as related to certain other variables. *J. genet. Psychol.*, 1958, **93**, 291–301.

28 Blazer, J. A.: Fantasy and its effects. *J. gen. Psychol.*, 1964, **70**, 163–182.

29 Bledsoe, J. C., and I. D. Brown: The interests of preadolescents: A longitudinal study. *J. exp. Educ.*, 1965, **33**, 337–344.

30 Boehm, L.: The development of conscience of pre-school children: A cultural and sub-cultural comparison. *J. soc. Psychol.*, 1963, **59**, 335–360.

31 Boroff, D.: American fetish: The college degree. *The New York Times*, Feb. 14, 1960.

32 Bossard, J. H. S., and E. S. Boll: *The sociology of child development*, 4th ed. New York: Harper & Row, 1966.

33 Botwinick, J.: Research problems and concepts in the study of aging. *Gerontologist*, 1964, **4**, 121–129.

34 Bradway, K. P., and C. W. Thompson: Intelligence at adulthood: A 25-year follow-up. *J. educ. Psychol.*, 1962, **53**, 1–16.

35 Breckenridge, M. E., and E. L. Vincent: *Child development*, 5th ed. Philadelphia: Saunders, 1965.

36 Brodie, T. A.: Attitude toward school and academic achievement. *Personnel Guid. J.*, 1964, **43**, 375–378.

37 Bromley, D. B.: Some effects of age on the quality of intellectual output. *J. Geront.*, 1957, **12**, 318–323.

38 Bronfenbrenner, U.: The role of age, sex, class and culture in studies of moral development. *Relig. Educ.*, 1962, **57**, suppl., 3–17.

39 Bronson, W. C.: Central orientations: A study of behavior organization from childhood to adolescence. *Child Develpm.*, 1966, **37**, 125–155.

40 Brookover, W. B., S. Thomas, and A. Paterson: Self-concept of ability and school achievement. *Sociology of Education*, 1964, **37**, 271–278.

41 Brown, C. M. and L. W. Ferguson: Self-concept and religious belief. *Psychol. Rep.*, 1968, **22**, 266.

42 Burlingame, W. V.: An investigation of the correlates of adherence to the peer culture. *Dissert. Abstr.*, 1967, **28** (5–B), 2118–2119.

43 Butcher, H. J.: *Human intelligence: Its nature and assessment*. London: Methuen, 1968.

44 Butterfield, E. C., and E. Zigler: The effects of success and failure on the discrimination learning of normal and retarded children. *J. abnorm. soc. Psychol.*, 1965, **70**, 25–31.

45 Byrne, D.: The relationship between humor and the expression of hostility. *J. abnorm. soc. Psychol.*, 1956, **53**, 84–89.

46 Caird, W. K.: Memory loss in the senile psychosis: Organic or psychogenic? *Psychol. Rep.*, 1966, **18**, 788–790.

47 Calvert, J. F.: An exploration of some of the relationships between sense of humor and creativity in children. *Dissert. Abstr.*, 1968, **29** (4–B), 1494.

48 Campbell, E.Q.: The internalization of moral norms. *Sociometry*, 1964, **27**, 391–412.

49 Carlett, H. A.: A study of the fantasy behavior of children at three age levels. *Dissert. Abstr.*, 1965, **26**, 1167–1168.

50 Cartwright, R. D.: Self-conception patterns of college students, and adjustment to college life. *J. counsel. Psychol.*, 1963, **10**, 47–52.

51 Chase, S.: American values: A generation of change. *Publ. Opin. Quart.*, 1965, **29**, 357–367.

52 Chazan, M.: Factors associated with maladjustment in educationally subnormal children. *Brit. J. educ. Psychol.*, 1965, **35**, 277–285.

53 Chown, S. M., and A. Heron: Psychological aspects of aging in man. *Annu. Rev. Psychol.*, 1965, **16**, 417–450.

54 Clifford, E.: Discipline in the home: A controlled observational study of parental practices. *J. genet. Psychol.*, 1957, **95**, 45–82.

55 Coleman, J. S.: *The adolescent society*. New York: Free Press, 1961.

56 Coser, R. L.: Laughter among colleagues. *Psychiatry*, 1960, **23**, 81–95.

57 Cottle, T. J.: Self concept, ego ideal and the response to action. *Sociol. soc. Res.*, 1965, **50**, 78–88.

58 Covalt, N. R.: The meaning of religion to older people. In C. B. Vedder and A. S. Lefkowitz (eds.), *Problems of the aged.* Springfield, Ill.: Charles C Thomas, 1965, pp. 215–224.

59 Crandall, V. J., W. Katkovsky, and A. Preston: Parents' attitudes and behavior: Grade-school children's academic achievement. *J. genet. Psychol.*, 1964, **104**, 53–66.

60 Cravioto, J.: Malnutrition and behavioral development in preschool children. *Courrier*, 1966, **16**, 117–127.

61 Crowley, F. J.: The goals of male high school seniors. *Personnel Guid. J.*, 1959, **37**, 488–492.

62 Cummings, S. T., H. C. Bayley, and H. E. Rie: Effects of the child's deficiency on the mother: A study of mothers of mentally retarded, chronically ill and neurotic children. *Amer. J. Orthopsychiat.*, 1966, **36**, 595–605.

63 Cunningham, A.: Relation of sense of humor to intelligence. *J. soc. Psychol.*, 1962, **57**, 143–147.

64 Damarin, F. L., and R. B. Cattell: Personality factors in early childhood and their relation to intelligence. *Monogr. Soc. Res. Child Develpm.*, 1968, **23**, no. 6.

65 D'Heule, A., J. C. Mellinger, and E. A. Haggard: Personality, intellectual and achievement patterns in gifted children. *Psychol. Monogr.*, 1959, **73**, no. 13.

66 Domino, G.: Maternal personality characteristics of sons' creativity. *J. consult. clin. Psychol.*, 1969, **33**, 180–183.

67 Dubin, E. R., and R. B. Dubin: The authority inception period in socialization. *Child Develpm.*, 1963, **34**, 885–898.

68 Dukes, W. F.: Psychological studies of values. *Psychol. Bull.*, 1955, **52**, 24–50.

69 Dunlap. J. M.: The education of children with high mental ability. In W. M. Cruickshank and G. O. Johnson (eds.), *Education of exceptional children and youth*, 2d ed. Englewood Cliffs, N. J.: Prentice-Hall, 1967, pp. 143–193.

70 Dunsing, M.: Spending money of adolescents. *J. Home Econ.*, 1956, **48**, 405–408.

71 Durkin, D.: Children's concepts of justice: A comparison with the Piaget data. *Child Develpm.*, 1959, **30**, 59–67.

72 Durr, W. K.: Characteristics of gifted children: Ten years of research. *Gifted Child Quart.*, 1960, **4**, 75–80.

73 Duvall, E. M.: Family dilemmas with teenagers. *Family Life Coordinator*, 1965, **14**, 35–38.

74 Dye, N. W., and P. S. Very: Growth changes in factorial structure by age and sex. *Genet. Psychol. Monogr.*, 1968, **78**, 55–88.

75 Eckland, B. K.: Social class and college graduation: Some misconceptions corrected. *Amer. J. Sociol.*, 1964, **70**, 36–50.

76 Edwards, J. B.: Some studies of the moral development of children. *Educ. Res.*, 1965, **7**, 200–211.

77 Eisendorf, C.: The WAIS performance of the aged: A retest evaluation. *J. Geront.*, 1963, **18**, 169–172.

78 Eron, L. B.: Relationship of TV viewing habits and aggressive behavior in children. *J. abnorm. soc. Psychol.*, 1963, **67**, 193–196.

79 Eysenck, H. J.: The development of moral values in children. VII. The contribution of the learning theory. *Brit. J. educ. Psychol.*, 1960, **30**, 11–21.

80 Fein, L. G.: Religious observances and mental health. *J. pastoral Care*, 1958, **12**, 99–101.

81 Feldman, F. L.: Money: An index to personal problems in adolescents. *Marriage fam. Living*, 1963, **25**, 364–367.

82 Finger, J. A., and G. E. Schlesser: Nonintellective predictors of academic success in school and college. *School Review*, 1965, **73**, 14–29.

83 Flacks, R.: The liberated generation: An exploration of the roots of student protest. *J. soc. Issues*, 1967, **23**, no. 3, 52–75.

84 Ford, L. H.: Reaction to failure as a function of expectation for success. *J. abnorm. soc. Psychol.*, 1963, **67**, 340–348.

85 Freud, S.: *The standard edition of the complete psychological works of Sigmund Freud.* London: Hogarth, 1953–1962.

86 Friedlander, F.: Relationships between the importance and the satisfaction of various environmental factors. *J. appl. Psychol.*, 1965, **49**, 160–164.

87 Friedman, H.: Memory organization in the aged. *J. genet. Psychol.*, 1966, **109**, 3–8.

88 Friedmann, E. A., and R. J. Havighurst: *The meaning of work and retirement.* Chicago: University of Chicago Press, 1954.

89 Friesden. D.: Academic-athletic-popularity syndrome in the Canadian high-school society: 1967. *Adolescence*, 1968, **3**, 39–52.

90 Garrison, K. C.: A study of the aspirations and concerns of ninth-grade pupils from the public schools of Georgia. *J. soc. Psychol.*, 1966, **69**, 245–252.

91 Gesell, A., F. L. Ilg, and L. B. Ames: *Youth: The years from ten to sixteen.* New York: Harper & Row, 1956.

92 Ghiselli, E. E.: The relationship between intelligence and age among superior adults. *J. genet. Psychol.*, 1957, **90**, 131–142.

93 Glueck, E. T.: A more discriminative instrument for the identification of potential delinquents at school entrance. *J. crim. Law Criminol. police Sci.*, 1966, **57**, 27–30.

94 Goldman, R. J.: The application of Piaget's scheme of operational thinking to religious story data by means of the Guttman Scaleogram. *Brit. J. educ. Psychol.*, 1965, **35**, 158–170.

95 Gorelick, M. C., and M. Sandhu: Parent perception of retarded child's intelligence. *Personnel Guid. J.*, 1967, **46**, 382–384.

96 Gottsdanker, J. S.: Intellectual interest patterns of gifted college students. *Educ. psychol. Measmt.*, 1968, **28**, 361–366.

97 Gowan, J. C.: Changing self-concept in exceptional children. *Education*, 1965, **85**, 374–375.

98 Graebner, O. E.: Child concepts of God. *Relig. Educ.*, 1964, **59**, 234–244.

99 Graham, L. R.: The maturational factor in humor. *J. clin. Psychol.*, 1958, **14**, 326–328.

100 Green, R. F., and B. Berkowitz: Changes in intellect with age. III. The relationship of heterogeneous brain damage to achievement in older people. *J. genet. Psychol.*, 1965, **106**, 349–359.

101 Harsh, C. M. and H. G. Schrickel: *Personality: Development and assessment*, 2d ed. New York: Ronald, 1959.

102 Havighurst, R. J.: How the moral life is formed. *Relig. Educ.*, 1962, **57**, 432–439.

103 Havighurst, R. J.: Body, self and society. *Sociol. soc. Res.*, 1965, **49**, 261–267.

104 Havighurst, R. J., and K. Feigenbaum: Leisure and life style. *Amer. J. Sociol.*, 1959, **64**, 396–404.

105 Hecht, R. M., J. E. Aron, and S. Litzman: Let's stop worrying about aptitudes and look at attitudes. *Personnel J.*, 1965, **44**, 616–619.

106 Hemming, J.: The development of children's moral values. *Brit. J. educ. Psychol.*, 1957, **27**, 77–88.

107 Herriott, R. E.: Some social determinants of educational aspirations. *Harv. educ. Rev.*, 1963, **33**, 157–177.

108 Hilgard, E. R.: *Introduction to psychology*, 4th ed. New York: Harcourt, Brace & World, 1962.

109 Hoffman, M. L.: The role of the parent in the child's moral growth. *Relig. Educ.*, 1962, **57**, suppl. 18–23.

110 Hollingworth, L. S.: *Children above 180 IQ: Origin and development.* Yonkers, N. Y.: World, 1942.

111 Honzik, M. P.: Environmental correlates of mental growth: Prediction from the family setting at 21 months. *Child Develpm.*, 1967, **38**, 337–364.

112 Hood, J. J.: Consistency of self-concept in adolescence. *Dissert. Abstr.*, 1962, **22**, 2458–2459.

113 Horn, J. L., and R. B. Cattell: Age differences in primary mental ability factors. *J. Geront.*, 1966, **21**, 210–220.

114 Horrall, B. M.: Academic performance and personality adjustment of highly intelligent college students. *Genet. Psychol. Monogr.*, 1957, **55**, 3–83.

115 Hummel, R. H., and N. Sprinthall: Underachievement related to interests, attitudes and values. *Personnel Guid. J.*, 1965, **44**, 388–395.

116 Huntley, C. W.: Changes in values during the four years of college. *Coll. Stud. Survey*, 1967, **1**, 43–48.

117 Hurley, J. R.: Parental malevolence and children's intelligence. *J. consult. Psychol.*, 1967, **31**, 199–204.

118 Hurlock, E. B.: The adolescent reformer. *Adolescence*, 1968, **3**, 273–306.

119 Hutt, M. L. and R. G. Gibby: *The mentally retarded child: Development, education and guidance.* Boston: Allyn & Bacon, 1958.

120 Jaffee, J.: "What's in a name": Attitudes toward disabled persons. *Personnel Guid. J.*, 1967, **45**, 557–560.

121 Jensen, A. R.: How much can we boost IQ and scholastic achievement? *Harv. educ. Rev.*, 1969, **39**, 1–123.

122 Jersild, A. T.: *The psychology of adolescence*, 2d ed. New York: Macmillan, 1963.

123 Jersild, A. T. *Child psychology*, 6th ed. Englewood Cliffs, N. J.: Prentice-Hall, 1969.

124 Johnson, E. E.: Student ratings of popularity and scholastic ability of their peers and actual scholastic performances of those peers. *J. soc. Psychol.*, 1958, **47**, 127–132.

125 Johnson, G. O.: The education of mentally retarded children. In W. M. Cruickshank and G. O. Johnson (eds.), *Education of exceptional children and youth*, 2d ed. Englewood Cliffs, N. J.: Prentice-Hall, 1967, pp. 194–237.

126 Jones, M. C.: Correlates of somatic development. *Child Develpm.*, 1965, **36**, 899–911.

127 Jones, R. L., N. W. Gottfried, and A. Owens: The social distance of the exceptional: A study at the high school level. *Except. Children*, 1966, **32**, 551–556.

128 Jones, V.: Character development in children. In L. Carmichael (ed.), *Manual of child psychology*, 2d ed. New York: Wiley, 1954, pp. 781–832.

129 Jourard, S. M.: *Personal adjustment*, 2d ed. New York: Macmillan, 1963.

130 Kagan J., L. M. Sontag, C. T. Baker, and V. L. Nelson: Personality and IQ change. *J. abnorm. soc. Psychol.*, 1958, **56**, 261–266.

131 Kaluger, G., and C. J. Kolson: The speaking religious vocabularies of kindergarten children. *Relig. Educ.*, 1963, **58**, 387–389.

132 Kamin, L. J.: Differential changes in mental abilities in old age. *J. Geront.*, 1957, **12**, 66–70.

133 Kastenbaum, R.: On the meaning of time in later life. *J. genet. Psychol.*, 1966, **109**, 9–25.

134 Keislar, E. R.: Experimental development of "like" and "dislike" of others among adolescent girls. *Child Develpm.*, 1961, **32**, 59–69.

135 Kent, N. and D. R. Davis: Discipline in the home and intellectual development. *Brit. J. med. Psychol.*, 1957, **30**, 27–33.

136 Kingsley, R. F.: Prevailing attitudes toward exceptional children. *Education*, 1967, **87**, 426–430.

137 Knowlton, J. G., and L. A. Hamerlynck: Perception of deviant behavior: A study of cheating. *J. educ. Psychol.*, 1967, **58**, 379–385.

138 Koch, H. L.: The relation of certain formal attributes of siblings to attitudes held toward each other and toward their parents. *Monogr. Soc. Res. Child Develpm.*, 1960, **25**, no. 4.

139 Kohn, M.: The child as a determinant of his peers' approach to him. *J. genet. Psychol.*, 1966, **109**, 91–100.

140 LaGrone, C. W.: Sex and personality differences in relation to fantasy. *J. consult. Psychol.*, 1963, **27**, 270–272.

141 Landis, B. Y.: Religion and youth. In E. Ginzberg (ed.), *The nation's children.* Vol. 2. *Development and education.* New York: Columbia, 1960, pp. 186–206.

142 Landreth, C.: *Early childhood: Behavior and learning*, 2d ed. New York: Knopf, 1967.

143 Latimer, J. F.: The status of intelligence in the aging. *J. genet. Psychol.*, 1963, **102**, 175–188.

144 Lehman, H. C.: *Age and achievement.* Princeton: Princeton University Press, 1953.

145 Lerman, P.: Individual values, peer values, and subcultural delinquency. *Amer. sociol. Rev.*, 1968, **33**, 219–235.

146 Levine, J., and F. C. Redlich: Failure to understand humor. *Psychoanal. Quart.*, 1955, **24**, 560–572.

147 Levinson, B. M.: The inner life of the extremely gifted child, as seen from the clinical setting. *J. genet. Psychol.*, 1961, **99**, 83–88.

148 Levinson, H.: What work means to a man. *Menninger Quart.*, 1964, **18**, 1–11.

149 Liddle, G.: Overlap among desirable and undesirable characteristics in gifted children. *J. educ. Psychol.*, 1958, **49**, 219–223.

150 Luft, J.: Monetary value and the perception of persons. *J. soc. Psychol.*, 1957, **46**, 245–251.

151 Mangan, G. L., and J. W. Clark: Rigidity

factors in the testing of middle-aged subjects. *J. Geront.*, 1958, **13**, 422–425.

152 Marshall, H. R.: The relation of giving children an allowance to children's money knowledge and responsibility and to other practices of parents. *J. genet. Psychol.*, 1964, **104**, 35–51.

153 Marshall, T. F., and A. Mason: A framework for the analysis of juvenile delinquency causation. *Brit. J. Sociol.*, 1968, **19**, 130–142.

154 Martin, W. E.: Learning theory and identification. III. The development of values in children. *J. genet. Psychol.*, 1954, **84**, 211–217.

155 Mason, E. P., H. L. Adams, and D. F. Blood: Further study of personality characteristics of bright college freshmen. *Psychol. Rep.*, 1968, **23**, 395–400.

156 Maxwell, A. E.: Trends in cognitive ability in the older age ranges. *J. abnorm. soc. Psychol.*, 1961, **63**, 449–452.

157 McCammon, R. W.: The concept of normality. *Ann. N. Y. Acad. Sci.*, 1966, **134**, 559–562.

158 McDonald, F. J.: Children's judgments of theft from individual and corporate owners. *Child Develpm.*, 1963, **34**, 141–150.

159 Mead, M.: The changing American family. *Children*, 1963, **10**, 173–174.

160 Meltzer, H.: Attitudes of workers before and after 40. *Geriatrics*, 1965, **20**, 425–432.

161 Meyer, H. D.: The adult cycle. *Ann. Amer. Acad. pol. soc. Sci.*, 1957, **313**, 58–67.

162 Milgrim, S. A.: A comparison of the effects of classics and contemporary literary books on high-school students' declared attitudes toward certain moral values. *Dissert. Abstr.*, 1968, **28** (10–A), 3899.

163 Mills, J.: Changes in moral attitudes following temptation. *J. Pers.*, 1958, **26**, 517–531.

164 Moore, T.: Realism and fantasy in children's play. *J. child Psychol. Psychiat.*, 1964, **5**, 15–36.

165 Morgan, R. F.: Note on the psychopathology of senility: Senescent defense against the threat of death. *Psychol. Rep.*, 1965, **16**, 305–306.

166 Morris, C., and L. V. Jones: Value scales and dimensions. *J. abnorm. soc. Psychol.*, 1955, **51**, 523–535.

167 Morris, J. F.: The development of adolescent value-judgments. *Brit. J. educ. Psychol.*, 1958, **28**, 1–14.

168 Muma, J. R.: Peer evaluation and academic performance. *Personnel Guid. J.*, 1965, **44**, 405–409.

169 Nadeau, B. E.: Religious attitudes of parents and development of moral judgment in children. *Dissert. Abstr.*, 1968, **28** (8–B), 3463.

170 Nahinsky, I. D.: The self-ideal correlation as a measure of generalized self-satisfaction. *Psychol. Rec.*, 1966, **16**, 55–64.

171 Neisser, E. G.: Emotional and social values attached to money. *Marriage fam. Living*, 1960, **22**, 132–139.

172 Nelson, E. N. P.: Persistence of attitudes of college students fourteen years later. *Psychol. Monogr.*, 1954, **68**, no. 2.

173 Neuringer, C., and L. W. Wardke: Interpersonal conflicts in persons of high self-concept and low self-concept. *J. soc. Psychol.*, 1966, **68**, 313–322.

174 Nisbet, J. D.: Intelligence and age: Retesting with twenty-four years' interval. *Brit. J. educ. Psychol.*, 1957, **27**, 190–198.

175 Oden, M. H.: The fulfillment of promise:

40-year follow-up of the Terman gifted group. *Genet. Psychol. Monogr.*, 1968, **77**, 3–93.

176 Owens, W. A.: Age and mental abilities: A second adult follow-up. *J. educ. Psychol.*, 1966, **57**, 311–325.

177 Packard, V.: *The status seekers.* New York: Pocket Books, 1961.

178 Parker, E.: *The seven ages of woman.* Baltimore: Johns Hopkins, 1960.

179 Peck, R. F., and R. J. Havighurst: *The psychology of character development.* New York: Wiley, 1962.

180 Pflaum, J.: Nature and incidence of manifest anxiety responses among college students. *Psychol. Rep.*, 1964, **15**, 720.

181 Pielstick, N. L.: Perceptions of mentally superior children by their classmates. *Percept. mot. Skills*, 1963, **17**, 47–53.

182 Pressey, S. L.: Concerning the nature and nurture of genius. *Scient. Monthly*, 1955, **81**, 123–129.

183 Pressey, S. L.: Potentials of age: An exploratory field study. *Genet. Psychol. Monogr.*, 1957, **56**, 159–205.

184 Pressey, S. L., and A. W. Jones: 1925–1953 and 20–60 age changes in moral codes, anxieties, and interests, as shown by the "X–O Tests." *J. Psychol.*, 1955, **39**, 485–502.

185 Pressey, S. L., and R. G. Kuhlen: *Psychological development through the life span.* New York: Harper & Row, 1957.

186 Reckless, W. C., and S. Dinitz: Pioneering with self-concept as a vulnerability factor in delinquency. *J. crim. Law Criminol. police Sci.*, 1967, **58**, 515–523.

187 Reese, H. W.: Relationship between self-acceptance and sociometric choice. *J. abnorm. soc. Psychol.*, 1961, **62**, 472–474.

188 *Report of the President's Council on Aging.* 1963.

189 Rettig, S., and B. Pasamanick: Differential judgment of ethical risk by cheaters and noncheaters. *J. abnorm. soc. Psychol.*, 1964, **69**, 109–113.

190 Rice, J. P.: A comparative study of academic interest patterns among selected groups of exceptional and normal intermediate children. *Calif. J. educ. Res.*, 1963, **14**, 131–137, 144.

191 Ringness, T. A.: Self-concepts of children of low, average, and high intelligence. *Amer. J. ment. Defic.*, 1961, **65**, 453–461.

192 Ringness, T. A.: Emotional adjustment of academically successful and unsuccessful bright ninth-grade boys. *J. educ. Res.*, 1965, **59**, 88–91.

193 Roberts, A. F., and D. M. Johnson: Some factors related to the perception of funniness in the humor situation. *J. soc. Psychol.*, 1957, **46**, 57–63.

194 Rodgers, R. R., U. Bronfenbrenner, and E. C. Devereux: Standards of social behavior among school children in four cultures. *Int. J. Psychol.*, 1968, **3**, 31–41.

195 Roskens, R. W., and H. F. Dizney: A study of unethical academic behavior in high school and college. *J. educ. Res.*, 1966, **59**, 231–234.

196 Rubinstein, A. M.: The relationship between hostile attitudes and the appreciation of hostile jokes. *Dissert. Abstr.*, 1966, **26**, 4816.

197 Sampson, E. E.: Student activism and the decade of protest. *J. soc. Issues*, 1967, **23**, no. 3, 1–33.

198 Sarason, S. B., and T. Gladwin: Psychological and cultural problems in mental

subnormality: A review of research. *Genet. Psychol. Monogr.*, 1957, **57**, 3–290.

199 Schaie, K. W., and C. R. Strother: A cross-sequential study of age changes in cognitive ability. *Psychol. Bull.*, 1968, **70**, 671–680.

200 Schmuck, R.: Some relationships of peer liking patterns in the classroom to pupil attitudes and achievement. *School Review*, 1963, **71**, 337–359.

201 Schonfield, D., and B. A. Robertson: Memory storage and age. *Canad. J. Psychol.*, 1966, **20**, 228–236.

202 Seeman, M.: The intellectual and the language of minorities. *Amer. J. Sociol.*, 1958, **64**, 25–35.

203 Shanley, F. J.: Middle-class delinquency as a social problem. *Sociol. soc. Res.*, 1967, **51**, 185–198.

204 Shaw, M. C.: Note on parent attitudes toward independence training and the academic achievement of their children. *J. educ. Psychol.*, 1964, **55**, 371–374.

205 Shelton, J., and J. P. Hill: Effects on cheating of achievement anxiety and knowledge of peer performance. *Develpm. Psychol.*, 1969, **1**, 449–455.

206 Simonson, E.: The concept and definition of normality. *Ann. N. Y. Acad. Sci.*, 1966, **134**, 541–558.

207 Smith, D. C., and L. Wing: Developmental changes in preference for goals difficult to attain. *Child Develpm.*, 1961, **32**, 29–36.

208 Smith, J. F.: The psychology of moral egoism. *Dissert. Abstr.*, 1968, **28** (10 B), 4302–4303.

209 Sontag, L. W., C. T. Baker, and V. L. Nelson: Mental growth and personality development: A longitudinal study. *Monogr. Soc. Res. Child Develpm.*, 1958, **23**, no. 2.

210 Southern, M. L., and W. T. Plant: Personality characteristics of very bright adults. *J. soc. Psychol.*, 1968, **75**, 119–126.

211 Steininger, M.: Attitudes toward cheating: general and specific. *Psychol. Rep.*, 1968, **22**, 1101–1107.

212 Strang, R.: *The adolescent views himself.* New York: McGraw-Hill, 1957.

213 Strang, R.: Children's moral concepts: A tentative taxonomy. *Education*, 1964, **85**, 67–77.

214 Sugarman, B.: Social norms in teenage boys' peer groups. *Hum. Relat.*, 1968, **21**, 41–58.

215 Symonds, P. M.: What education has to learn from psychology. VI. Emotion and learning. *Teachers Coll. Rec.*, 1958, **60**, 9–22.

216 Terman, L. M.: The discovery and encouragement of exceptional talent. *Amer. Psychologist*, 1954, **9**, 221–230.

217 Terman, L. M., and M. H. Oden: *The gifted group at mid-life: Thirty-five years' follow-up of the superior child.* Stanford: Stanford University Press, 1959.

218 Thompson, O. E.: Student values in transition. *Calif. J. educ. Res.*, 1968, **19**, 77–86.

219 Thumin, F. J.: Reminiscence as a function of chronological age and mental age. *J. Geront.*, 1962, **17**, 392–396.

220 Trent, J. W., and J. L. Craise: Commitment and conformity in the American college. *J. soc. Issues*, 1967, **23**, no. 3, 34–51.

221 Tyler, L. E.: The antecedents of two varieties of vocational interests. *Genet. Psychol. Monogr.*, 1964, **70**, 177–227.

222 *U. S. News & World Report:* Can Negroes learn the way whites do? Mar. 10, 1969, pp. 48–51.

223 VanKrevelen, A.: Characteristics which "identify" the adolescent to his peers. *J. soc. Psychol.*, 1962, **56**, 285–289.

224 Vedder, C. B. (ed): *Problems of the middle-aged.* Springfield, Ill.: Charles C Thomas, 1965.

225 Vincent, E. L., and P. C. Martin: *Human psychological development.* New York: Ronald, 1961.

226 Wagman, M.: Interests and values of career and homemaking oriented women. *Personnel Guid. J.*, 1966, **44**, 794–801.

227 Walsh, A. M.: *Self-concepts of bright boys with learning difficulties.* New York: Teachers College, 1956.

228 Wang, J. D.: The relationship between children's play interests and their mental ability. *J. genet. Psychol.*, 1958, **93**, 119–131.

229 Warren, J. R., and P. A. Heist: Personality attributes of gifted college students. *Science*, 1960, **132**, 330–337.

230 Watley, D. J.: Career progress of merit scholars. *Nat. Merit Scholarship Corp. Res. Rep.*, 1968, **4**, no. 1.

231 Watson, G.: Some personality differences in children related to strict or permissive parental discipline. *J. Psychol.*, 1957, **44**, 227–249.

232 Wernimont, P. F.: Intrinsic and extrinsic factors in job satisfaction. *J. appl. Psychol.*, 1966, **50**, 41–50.

233 Whiteman, P. H., and K. P. Kosier: Development of children's moralistic judgments: Age, sex, I.Q., and certain personal-experiential variables. *Child Develpm.*, 1964, **35**, 843–850.

234 Wiggam, E. A.: Do brains and character go together? *Sch. Soc.*, 1941, **54**, 261–265.

235 Withey, S. B.: The influence of the peer group on the values of youth. *Relig. Educ.*, 1962, **57**, suppl., 34–44.

236 Wolfenstein, M.: Children's understanding of jokes. *Psychoanal. Stud. Child*, 1954, **8**, 162–176.

237 Yamamoto, K.: Creativity and sociometric choice among adolescents. *J. soc. Psychol.*, 1964, **64**, 249–261.

238 Zander, A., and E. VanEgmond: Relationship of intelligence and social power to the interpersonal behavior of children. *J. educ. Psychol.*, 1958, **49**, 257–268.

239 Zigler, E., J. Levine, and L. Gould: Cognitive processes in the development of children's appreciation of humor. *Child Develpm.*, 1966, **37**, 507–518.

240 Zunich, M.: Attitudes of lower-class families. *J. soc. Psychol.*, 1964, **63**, 367–371.

CHAPTER 8

1 Abel, H., and R. Gingles: Life goals of parents for children. *J. Home Econ.*, 1965, **57**, 734–735.

2 Adler, A.: *Problems of neurosis.* New York: Farrar & Rinehart, 1930.

3 Albert, R. S.: The role of mass media and the effect of aggressive film content upon children's aggressive responses and identification choices. *Genet. Psychol. Monogr.*, 1957, **55**, 221–285.

4 Alexander, I. E., and A. M. Adlerstein: Affective responses to the concept of death in a population of children and early adolescents. *J. genet. Psychol.*, 1958, **93**, 167–177.

5 Alexander, T.: Certain characteristics of the self as related to affection. *Child Develpm.*, 1951, **22**, 285–290.

6 Allinsmith, W.: Conscience and conflict: The moral force in personality. *Child Develpm.*, 1957, **28**, 469–476.

7 Allman, T. S., and W. F. White: Birth order categories as predictors of select personality characteristics. *Psychol. Rep.*, 1968, **22**, 857–865.

8 Allport, G. W.: *Pattern and growth in personality.* New York: Holt, 1961.

9 Alpenfels, E. J.: Status symbols of youth. *PTA Mag.*, 1966, **60**, no. 7, 4–6.

10 Alpert, R., and R. N. Haber: Anxiety in academic achievement situations. *J. abnorm. soc. Psychol.*, 1960, **61**, 207–215.

11 Ames, L. B.: Children's stories. *Genet. Psychol. Monogr.*, 1966, **73**, 337–396.

12 Anderson, J. E.: The relation of attitude to adjustment. *Education*, 1952, **13**, 210–218.

13 Anderson, R. E.: Where's Dad? Paternal deprivation and delinquency. *Arch. gen. Psychiat.*, 1968, **18**, 641–649.

14 Angelino, H., J. Dollins, and E. V. Mech: Trends in the "fears and worries" of school children as related to socioeconomic status and age. *J. genet. Psychol.*, 1956, **89**, 263–276.

15 Atkinson, J. W., and G. H. Litwin: Achievement motivation and test anxiety conceived as motive to approach success and motive to avoid failure. *J. abnorm. soc. Psychol.*, 1960, **60**, 52–63.

16 Ausubel, D. P.: Relationship between shame and guilt in the socialization process. *Psychol. Rev.*, 1955, **62**, 378–390.

17 Averill, J. R.: Grief: Nature and significance. *Psychol. Bull.*, 1968, **70**, 721–748.

18 Baldwin, A. L., and H. Levin: Effects of public and private success or failure on children's repetitive motor behavior. *Child Develpm.*, 1958, **29**, 363–372.

19 Bandura, A., and R. B. Walters: Aggression. *62d Yearb. nat. Soc. Stud. Educ.*, 1963, pt. 1, 364–415.

20 Banham, K. M.: Senescence and the emotions: A genetic theory. *J. genet. Psychol.*, 1951, **78**, 175–183.

21 Bartlett, C. J., and J. E. Horrocks: A study of the needs status of adolescents from broken homes. *J. genet. Psychol.*, 1958, **93**, 153–159.

22 Bateman, M. M., and J. S. Jensen: The effect of religious background on modes of handling anger. *J. soc. Psychol.*, 1958, **47**, 133–141.

23 Bell, E. C.: Nutritional deficiency and emotional disturbance. *J. Psychol.*, 1958, **45**, 47–74.

24 Berkowitz, L., J. A. Green, and J. R. Macaulay: Hostility catharsis as the reduction of emotional tension. *Psychiatry*, 1962, **25**, 23–31.

25 Berlyne, D. E.: A theory of human curiosity. *Brit. J. Psychol.*, 1954, **48**, 180–191.

26 Berlyne, D. E., and F. D. Frommer: Some determinants of the incidence and content of children's questions. *Child Develpm.*, 1966, **37**, 177–189.

27 Billig, O., and R. W. Adams: Emotional conflicts of the middle-aged man. In C. B. Vedder (ed.), *Problems of the middle-aged.* Springfield, Ill.: Charles C Thomas, 1965, 121–133.

28 Bossard, J. H. S., and E. S. Boll: *The sociology of child development,* 4th ed. New York: Harper & Row, 1966.

29 Bousfield, W. A., and W. D. Orbison: Ontogenesis of emotional behavior. *Psychol. Rev.*, 1952, **59**, 1–7.

30 Bowerman, C. E., and J. W. Kinch: Changes in family and peer orientation of children between the fourth and tenth grades. *Soc. Forces*, 1959, **37**, 206–217.

31 Bowlby, J., M. Ainsworth, M. Boston, and D. Rosenbluth: The effect of mother-child separation: A follow-up study. *Brit. J. med. Psychol.*, 1956, **29**, 211–247.

32 Breckenridge, M. E., and E. L. Vincent: *Child development,* 5th ed. Philadelphia: Saunders, 1965.

33 Bronson, W. C.: Adult derivatives of emotional expressiveness and reactivity-control: Developmental continuities from childhood to adulthood. *Child Develpm.*, 1967, **38**, 801–817.

34 Byrd, E.: Measured anxiety in old age. *Psychol. Rep.*, 1959, **5**, 439–440.

35 Casler, M.: Maternal deprivation. *Monogr. Soc. Res. Child Develpm.*, 1961, **26**, no. 2.

36 Cave, R. L.: A factorial comparison of creativity and intelligence. *Dissert. Abstr.*, 1968, **28** (10–B), 4293.

37 Chilman, C. S., and D. L. Meyer: Single and married undergraduate personality needs and self-rated happiness. *J. Marriage & Family*, 1966, **28**, 67–76.

38 Chittick, E. V., and P. Himelstein: The manipulation of self-disclosure. *J. Psychol.*, 1967, **65**, 117–121.

39 Clifford, E.: Discipline in the home: A controlled observational study of parental practices. *J. genet. Psychol.*, 1959, **95**, 45–82.

40 Cole, L., and I. N. Hall: *Psychology of adolescence,* 7th ed. New York: Holt, 1969.

41 Coleman, J. S.: *The adolescent society,* New York: Free Press, 1961.

42 Cook, M.: Anxiety, speech disturbances and speech rate. *Brit. J. soc. clin. Psychol.*, 1969, **8**, 13–21.

43 Coser, R. L.: Some social functions of laughter. *Hum. Relat.*, 1959, **12**, 171–182.

44 Cronbach, L. J.: *Educational psychology,* 2d ed. New York: Harcourt, Brace & World, 1963.

45 Crow, L. D., and A. Crow: *Adolescent development and adjustment,* 2d ed. New York: McGraw-Hill, 1965.

46 Cruickshank, W. M., and G. O. Johnson (eds): *Education of exceptional children and youth,* 2d ed. Englewood Cliffs, N. J.: Prentice-Hall, 1967.

47 Davis, J. M.: A reinterpretation of the Barker, Dumbo and Lewin study of frustration and aggression. *Child Develpm.*, 1958, **29**, 503–506.

48 Davitz, J. R.: Contribution of research with children to a theory of maladjustment. *Child Develpm.*, 1958, **29**, 3–7.

49 Dean, L. R.: Aging and the decline of affect. *J. Geront.*, 1962, **17**, 440–446.

50 Dimond, R. E., and D. C. Munz: Ordinal position of birth and self-disclosure in high school students. *Psychol. Rep.*, 1967, **21**, 829–833.

51 Douglas, V. I.: Children's responses to frustration: A developmental study. *Canad. J. Psychol.*, 1965, **19**, 161–171.

52 Dubbé, M. C.: What parents are not told may hurt. *Family Life Coordinator*, 1965, **14**, 51–118.

53 Dunbar, F.: Homeostasis during puberty. *Amer. J. Psychiat.*, 1958, **114**, 673–682.

54 Earle, A. M., and B. V. Earle: Early maternal deprivation and later psychiatric illness. *Amer. J. Orthopsychiat.*, 1961, **31**, 181–186.

55 Emmerich, W.: Variations in the parent role as a function of the parent's sex and age and the child's sex and age. *Merrill-Palmer Quart.*, 1962, **8**, 3–11.

56 Faw, V.: Learning to deal with stress situations, *J. educ. Psychol.*, 1958, **48**, 135–144.

57 Fawl, C. L.: A developmental analysis of the frequency and causal types of disturbance experienced by children. *Merrill-Palmer Quart.*, 1962, **8**, 12–18.

58 Feinberg, M. R.: Stability of sociometric status in two adolescent class groups. *J. genet. Psychol.*, 1964, **104**, 83–87.

59 Feshbach, S.: The drive-reducing function of fantasy behavior. *J. abnorm. soc. Psychol.*, 1955, **50**, 3–11.

60 Fraser, D. C.: Environmental stress and its effect on performance. *Occup. Psychol.*, 1957, **31**, 248–255.

61 Freud, S.: *The standard edition of the complete psychological works of Sigmund Freud.* London: Hogarth, 1953–1962.

62 Frost, B. P.: Anxiety and educational achievement. *Brit. J. educ. Psychol.*, 1968, **38**, 293–301.

63 Gardner, D. B., G. R. Hawkes, and L. G. Burchinal: Noncontinuous mothering in infancy and development in later childhood. *Child Develpm.*, 1961, **32**, 225–234.

64 Gardner, G. E.: Separation of the parents and the emotional life of the child. *Ment. Hyg., N. Y.*, 1956, **40**, 53–64.

65 Garrison, K. C.: *Growth and development*, 2d ed. New York: Longmans, 1959.

66 Gesell, A., F. L. Ilg, and L. B. Ames: *Youth: The years from ten to fourteen.* New York: Harper & Row, 1956.

67 Gilbert, D. C.: The young child's awareness of affect. *Child Develpm.*, 1969, **40**, 629–640.

68 Goode, W. J.: The theoretical importance of love. *Amer. sociol. Rev.*, 1959, **24**, 38–47.

69 Gowan, J. C.: Changing self-concept in exceptional children. *Education*, 1965, **85**, 374–375.

70 Haring, J.: Freedom of communication between parents and adolescents with problems. *Dissert. Abstr.*, 1967, **27** (11–A), 3956–3957.

71 Harlow, H. F.: The nature of love. *Amer. Psychologist*, 1958, **13**, 673–685.

72 Harsh, C. M., and H. G. Schrickel: *Personality: Development and assessment*, 2d ed. New York: Ronald, 1959.

73 Hartley, R. E.: Some safety valves in play. *Child Study*, 1957, **34**, 12–14.

74 Hartman, B. G.: Survey of college students' problems identified by the Mooney Problem Check List. *Psychol. Rep.*, 1968, **22**, 715–716.

75 Hartup, W. W.: Nurturance and nurturance withdrawal in relation to dependency behavior of preschool children. *Child Develpm.*, 1958, **29**, 191–201.

76 Havighurst, R. J.: Factors which control the experience of aging. *Gawein*, 1965, **13**, 242–248.

77 Hazard, W. R.: Anxiety and preference for television fantasy. *Journalism Quart.*, 1967, **47**, 461–469.

78 Heathers, G.: Emotional dependence and independence in nursery school play. *J. genet. Psychol.*, 1955, **87**, 37–57.

79 Heinicke, C. M.: Some effects of separating two-year-old children from their parents: A comparative study. *Hum. Relat.*, 1956, **9**, 105–176.

80 Hilgard, E. R.: *Introduction to psychology*, 4th ed. New York: Harcourt, Brace & World, 1962.

81 Holman, M.: Adolescent attitudes toward seeking help with personal problems. *Smith Coll. Stud. soc. Wk.*, 1955, **25**, 1–31.

82 Hornick, E. J.: Emergencies, anxiety and adolescence. *N. Y. State J. Med.*, 1967, **67**, 1979–1981.

83 Horwitz. E.: Reported embarrassment memories of elementary school, high school, and college students. *J. soc. Psychol.*, 1962, **56**, 317–325.

84 Horwitz, F. D.: The relationship of anxiety, self-concept, and sociometric status among fourth, fifth, and sixth grade children. *J. abnorm. soc. Psychol.*, 1962, **65**, 212–214.

85 Jegard, S., and R. H. Walters: A study of some determinants of aggression in young children. *Child Develpm.*, 1960, **31**, 739–747.

86 Jersild, A. T.: *The psychology of adolescence*, 2d ed. New York: Macmillan, 1963.

87 Jersild, A. T. *Child Psychology*, 6h ed.: Englewood Cliffs, N.J.: Prentice-Hall, 1969.

88 Jones, M. C.: Psychological correlates of somatic development. *Child Develpm.*, 1965, **36**, 899–911.

89 Jourard, S. M.: *Personality adjustment.* New York: Macmillan, 1958.

90 Jourard, S. M., and M. J. Landsman: Cognition, cathexis, and the "dyadic effect" in men's self-disclosure behavior. *Merrill-Palmer Quart.*, 1960, **6**, 178–186.

91 Jung, C. G.: *Collected works.* New York: Pantheon Books, 1953.

92 Kagan, J., and H. A. Moss: *Birth to maturity: A study in psychological development.* New York: Wiley, 1962.

93 Kahn, M.: The physiology of catharsis. *J. Pers. soc. Psychol.*, 1966, **3**, 278–286.

94 Keislar, E. R.: Experimental development of "like" and "dislike" of others among adolescent girls. *Child Develpm.*, 1961, **32**, 59–69.

95 Kennedy, W. A.: School phobia: Rapid treatment of fifty cases. *J. abnorm. Psychol.*, 1965, **70**, 285–289.

96 Kent, D. P.: Social and cultural factors affecting the mental health of the aged. *Amer. J. Orthopsychiat.*, 1966, **36**, 680–685.

97 Koch, H. L.: The relation of certain formal attributes of siblings to attitudes held toward each other and toward their parents. *Monogr. Soc. Res. Child Develpm.*, 1960, **25**, no. 4.

98 Kohn, M.: The child as a determinant of his peers' approach to him. *J. genet. Psychol.*, 1966, **109**, 91–100.

99 Kuhlen. R. G.: *The psychology of adolescent development*, 2d ed. New York: Harper & Row, 1963.

100 L'Abate, L.: Personality correlates of manifest anxiety in children. *J. consult. Psychol.*, 1960, **24**, 342–348.

101 Landis, J. T.: Dating maturation of children from happy and unhappy marriages. *Marriage fam. Living*, 1963, **25**, 351–353.

102 Landreth, C.: *Early childhood: Behavior and learning*, 2d ed. New York: Knopf, 1967.

103 Lawson, R., and M. H. Marx: Frustration: Theory and experiment. *Genet. Psychol. Monogr.*, 1958, **57**, 393–464.

104 Lenneberg, E. H.: Language disorders in childhood. *Harv. educ. Rev.*, 1964, **34**, 152–177.

105 Leventhal, T., and M. Sills: Self-image in school phobia. *Amer. J. Orthopsychiat.*, 1964, **34**, 685–695.

106 Levinson, B. M.: The inner life of the extremely gifted child, as seen from the clinical setting. *J. genet. Psychol.*, 1961, **99**, 83–88.

107 Lewin, K.: *A dynamic theory of personality.* New York: McGraw-Hill, 1935.

108 Lintz, L. M., R. H. Starr, and G. R. Medinnus: Curiosity rewards in children. *Psychol. Rep.*, 1965, **16**, 1222.

109 Lipsitt, L. P.: A self-concept scale for children and its relationship to the children's form of the manifest anxiety scale. *Child Develpm.*, 1958, **29**, 463–472.

110 Lövaas, O. I.: Effect of exposure to symbolic aggression on aggressive behavior. *Child Develpm.*, 1961, **32**, 37–44.

111 Maas, H. S.: Preadolescent peer relations and adult intimacy. *Psychiatry*, 1968, **31**, 161–172.

112 Maccoby, E. E., E. M. Dowley, J. W. Hagen, and R. Degerman: Activity level and intellectual functioning in normal preschool children. *Child Develpm.*, 1965, **36**, 761–770.

113 Macfarlane, J. W., L. Allen, and M. P. Honzik: *A developmental study of the behavior problems of normal children between twenty-one months and fourteen years.* Berkeley: University of California Press, 1954.

114 Mallick, S. K., and B. R. McCandless: A study of catharsis of aggression. *J. Pers. soc. Psychol.*, 1966, 4, 591–596.

115 Marshall, H. R.: Relations between home experiences and children's language in play interactions with peers. *Psychol. Monogr.*, 1961, **75**, no. 5.

116 Maw, W. H., and E. W. Maw: Nonhomeostasis experiences as stimuli of children with high curiosity. *Calif. J. educ. Res.*, 1961, **12**, 57–61.

117 McCandless, B. R., A. Castaneda, and D. S. Palermo: Anxiety in children and social status. *Child Develpm.*, 1956, **27**, 385–391.

118 McKeachie, W. J., D. Pollie, and J. Speisman: Relieving anxiety in classroom examinations. *J. abnorm. soc. Psychol.*, 1955, **50**, 93–98.

119 Medinnus, G. R., and J. M. Love: The relation between curiosity and security in preschool children. *J. genet. Psychol.*, 1965, **107**, 91–98.

120 Meissner, W. W.: Some anxiety indications in the adolescent boy. *J. gen. Psychol.*, 1961, **64**, 251–257.

121 Modigliani, A.: Embarrassment and embarrassability. *Sociometry*, 1968, **31**, 313–328.

122 Moore, S. G.: Displaced aggression in young children. *J. abnorm. soc. Psychol.*, 1964, **68**, 200–204.

123 Morgan, C. T.: *Physiological psychology*, 3d ed. New York: McGraw-Hill, 1964.

124 Moulton, R.: Oral and dental manifestations of anxiety. *Psychiatry*, 1955, **18**, 261–273.

125 Munn, N. L.: *The evolution and growth of human behavior*, 2d ed. Boston: Houghton Mifflin, 1965.

126 Nakamura, C. Y.: The relationship between children's expressions of hostility and methods of discipline exercised by dominant, overprotective parents. *Child Develpm.*, 1959, **30**, 109–117.

127 *New York Times* Report: Student drug use is laid to tension. Feb. 2, 1969.

128 *New York Times* Report: Tantrums called key to adult life. June 22, 1969.

129 *New York Times* Report: Doctors study link between changes in body chemistry and depression. Dec. 8, 1969.

130 Nighswander, J. K., and G. R. Mayer: Catharsis: A means of reducing elementary school students' aggressive behavior? *Personnel Guid. J.*, 1969, **47**, 461–466.

131 Otis, N. B., and B. R. McCandless: Responses to repeated frustration of young children differentiated according to need area. *J. abnorm. soc. Psychol.*, 1955, **50**, 349–353.

132 Packard, V.: *The status seekers.* New York: Pocket Books, 1961.

133 Paivio, A., and W. E. Lambert: Measures and correlates of audience anxiety. ("stage fright"). *J. Pers.*, 1959, **27**, 1–17.

134 Palermo, D. S.: Racial comparisons and additional normative data on the children's manifest anxiety scale. *Child Develpm.*, 1959, **30**, 53–57.

135 Peckos, P. S.: Nutrition during growth and development. *Child Develpm.*, 1957, **28**, 273–285.

136 Pedersen, D. M., and K. L. Higbee: Self-disclosure and relationship to the target person. *Merrill-Palmer Quart.*, 1969, **15**, 213–220.

137 Phillips, B. N., E. Hindsman, and E. Jennings: Influence of intelligence on anxiety and perception of self and others. *Child Develpm.*, 1960, **31**, 41–46.

138 Pressey, S. L., and R. G. Kuhlen: *Psychological development through the life span.* New York: Harper & Row, 1957.

139 Pressey, S. L., F. P. Robinson, and J. E. Horrocks: *Psychology in education*, 2d ed. New York: Harper & Row, 1959.

140 Provence, S.: Disturbed personality development in infancy: A comparison of two inadequately nurtured infants. *Merrill-Palmer Quart.*, 1965, **11**, 149–170.

141 Rathbun, C., H. McLaughlin, C. Bennett, and J. A. Carland: Later adjustment of children following radical separation from family and culture. *Amer. J. Orthopsychiat.*, 1965, **35**, 604–609.

142 Rheingold, H. L., and N. Bayley: The later effects of an experimental modification of mothering. *Child Develpm.*, 1959, **30**, 363–372.

143 Ribble, M. A.: *The personality of the young child.* New York: Columbia, 1955.

144 Ricciuti, H. N.: Social and emotional behavior in infancy: Some developmental issues and problems. *Merrill-Palmer Quart.*, 1968, **14**, 82–100.

145 Rose, A. M.: Class differences among the elderly: A research report. *Sociol. soc. Res.*, 1966, **50**, 356–360.

146 Rosen, B. C.: Social class and the child's perception of the parent. *Child Develpm.*, 1964, **35**, 1147–1153.

147 Rosenthal, M. J.: The syndrome of the inconsistent mother. *Amer. J. Orthopsychiat.*, 1962, **32**, 637–644.

148 Rosenthal, M. J., M. Finkelstein, E. Ni, and R. E. Robertson: A study of mother-child relationships in the emotional disorders of children. *Genet. Psychol. Monogr.*, 1959, **60**, 65–116.

149 Salzinger, K.: A method of analysis of the process of verbal communication between a group of emotionally disturbed adolescents and their friends and relatives. *J. soc. Psychol.*, 1958, **47**, 39–53.

150 Sarason, I. G.: The effect of anxiety and two kinds of failure on serial learning. *J. Pers.*, 1957, **25**, 383–392.

151 Sarason, I. G.: Test anxiety, general anxiety and intellectual performance. *J. consult. Psychol.*, 1957, **21**, 485–490.

152 Sarason, S. B., K. Davidson, F. Lighthall, and R. Waite: Rorschach behavior and performance of high and low anxious children. *Child Develpm.*, 1958, **29**, 277–285.

153 Sattler, J. M.: Embarrassment and blushing: A theoretical review. *J. soc. Psychol.*, 1966, **69**, 117–133.

154 Saul, L. J., and S. E. Pulver: The concept of emotional maturity. *Int. J. Psychiat.*, 1966, **2**, 446–460.

155 Schalon, C. L.: Effects of self-esteem upon performance following failure stress. *J. consult. clin. Psychol.*, 1968, **32**, 497.

156 Sears, R. R., E. E. Maccoby, and H. Levin: *Patterns of child rearing.* New York: Harper & Row, 1957.

157 Settlage, C. F.: The values of limits in child rearing. *Children*, 1958, **5**, 175–178.

158 Shaffer, L. F., and E. J. Shoben: *The psychology of adjustment*, 2d ed. Boston: Houghton Mifflin, 1956.

159 Shapiro, D. S.: Perceptions of significant family and environmental relationships in aggressive and withdrawn children. *J. consult. Psychol.*, 1957, **21**, 381–385.

160 Siegel, A. E.: Aggressive behavior of young children in the absence of an adult. *Child Develpm.*, 1957, **28**, 371–378.

161 Smith, M. E.: Childhood memories compared with those of adult life. *J. genet. Psychol.*, 1954, **85**, 321–335.

162 Smock, C. D.: Perceptual rigidity and closure phenomenon as a function of manifest anxiety in children. *Child Develpm.*, 1958, **29**, 237–247.

163 Smock, C. D., and B. G. Holt: Children's reactions to novelty: An experimental study of "curiosity motivation." *Child Develpm.*, 1962, **33**, 631–642.

164 Sontag, L. W., C. T. Baker, and V. L. Nelson: Mental growth and personality development: A longitudinal study. *Monogr. Soc. Res. Child Develpm.*, 1958, **23**, no. 2.

165 Southern, M. L., and W. T. Plant: Personality characteristics of very bright adults. *J. soc. Psychol.*, 1968, **75**, 119–126.

166 Stagner, R.: *Psychology of personality*, 3d ed. New York: McGraw-Hill, 1961.

167 Staudt, V. M.: Character formation is the teacher's business. *Education*, 1957, **77**, 198–202.

168 Sternlicht, M., and Z. W. Wanderer: Catharsis: Tension reduction via relevant cognitive substitution: An experimental demonstration. *J. gen. Psychol.*, 1966, **74**, 173–179.

169 Strang, R.: *The adolescent views himself.* New York: McGraw-Hill, 1957.

170 Straus, M. A., and J. H. Straus: Personal insecurity and the Sinhalese social structure: Rorschach evidence for primary school children. *Child Develpm. Abstr.*, 1959, **33**, no. 246.

171 Strecker, E. A.: *Their mothers' sons.* Philadelphia: Lippincott, 1946.

172 Strecker, E. A., and V. T. Lathbury: *Their mothers' daughters.* Philadelphia: Lippincott, 1956.

173 Taft, R.: The ability to judge people. *Psychol. Bull.*, 1955, **52**, 1–23.

174 Thompson, D. F., and L. Meltzer: Communication of emotional intent by facial expression. *J. abnorm. soc. Psychol.*, 1964, **68**, 129–135.

175 Thompson, G. G.: *Child psychology*, rev. ed. Boston: Houghton Mifflin, 1962.

176 Thorndike, R. L.: *The concept of over- and underachievement.* New York: Teachers College, 1963.

177 Tonks, C. M., P. H. Rack, and M. J. Rose: Attempted suicide and the menstrual cycle. *J. psychosom. Res.*, 1968, **11**, 319–323.

178 Tryon, A. F.: Thumb-sucking and manifest anxiety: A note. *Child Develpm.*, 1968, **39**, 1159–1163.

179 Vedder, C. B., and A. S. Lefkowitz (eds.): *Problems of the aged.* Springfield, Ill.: Charles C Thomas, 1965.

180 Wade, S.: Differences between intelligence and creativity: Some speculations on the role of environment. *J. creative Psychol.*, 1968, **2**, 97–101.

181 Walsh, A. M.: *Self-concepts of bright boys with learning difficulties.* New York: Teachers College, 1956.

182 Walter, D., L. S. Denzler, and I. G. Sarason: Anxiety and the intellectual performance of high school students. *Child Develpm.*, 1964, **35**, 917–926.

183 Walters, J., D. Pearce, and L. Dahms: Affectional and aggressive behavior of pre-school children. *Child Develpm.*, 1957, **28**, 15–26.

184 Walters, R. H., W. E. Marshall, and J. R. Shooter: Anxiety, isolation, and susceptibility to social influence. *J. Pers.* 1960, **28**, 518–529.

185 Watley, D. J.: Personal adjustment and prediction of academic achievement. *J. appl. Psychol.*, 1965, **49**, 20–23.

186 Watson, J. B.: *Psychological care of infant and child.* New York: Norton, 1928.

187 Wayne, D.: The lonely school child. *Amer. J. Nurs.*, 1968, **68**, 774–777.

188 Wertham, F.: The scientific study of mass media effects. *Amer. J. Psychiat.*, 1962, **119**, 306–311.

189 Whiteman, M., and I. F. Lukoff: Attitudes toward blindness and other physical handicaps. *J. soc. Psychol.*, 1965, **66**, 135–145.

190 Williams, F., and J. Tolch: Communication by facial expression. *J. Commun.*, 1965, **15**, 17–27.

191 Williams, J. E.: Some effects of institutional living on personality development. *J. Marriage & Family*, 1966, **28**, 331–337.

192 Wirt, R. D.: Ideational expression of hostile impulses. *J. consult. Psychol.*, 1956, **20**, 185–189.

193 Worchel, P.: Catharsis and the relief of hostility. *J. abnorm. soc. Psychol.*, 1957, **55**, 238–243.

194 Yarrow, L. J.: Research in dimensions of early maternal care. *Merrill-Palmer Quart.*, 1963, **9**, 101–114.

195 Young, F. M.: A comparison of the nervous habits of preschool and college students. *J. Pers.*, 1949, **17**, 303–309.

196 Zander, A.: Group membership and individual security. *Hum. Relat.*, 1958, **11**, 99–111.

197 Zeligs, R.: Children's attitudes toward annoyances. *J. genet. Psychol.*, 1962, **101**, 255–266.

198 Zuk, G. H.: The influence of social context on impulse and control tendencies in pre-adolescents. *Genet. Psychol. Monogr.*, 1956, **54**, 117–166.

199 Zweibelson, I.: Test anxiety and intel-

ligence test performance. *J. consult. Psychol.*, 1956, **20**, 479–481.

CHAPTER 9

1 Abegglen, J. C.: Personality factors in social mobility: A study of occupationally mobile businessmen. *Genet. Psychol. Monogr.*, 1958, **58**, 101–159.

2 Adams, B. N.: Occupation position: mobility and the kin of orientation. *Amer. sociol. Rev.*, 1967, **32**, 364–377.

3 Aldridge, J. W.: In the country of the young: Part II. *Harpers Mag.*, Nov. 1969, pp. 93–107.

4 Allport, G. W.: Prejudice: Is it societal or personal? *Relig. Educ.*, 1964, **59**, 20–29.

5 Ames, R. G., and A. F. Sakuma: Criteria for evaluating others: A reexamination of the Bogardus Social Distance Scale. *Sociol. soc. Res.*, 1969, **54**, 5–24.

6 Angrist, S. S.: Role constellation as a variable in women's leisure activities. *Soc. Forces*, 1967, **45**, 423–431.

7 Argyris, C.: Some characteristics of successful executives. *Personnel J.*, 1953, **32**, 50–55.

8 Arter, P. M.: The effects of prejudice on children. *Children*, 1959, **6**, 185–189.

9 Ausubel, D. P.: Ego development among segregated Negro children. *Ment. Hyg., N.Y.*, 1958, **42**, 362–369.

10 Ausubel, D. P., and H. M. Schiff: Some intrapersonal and interpersonal determinants of individual differences in sociempathic ability among adolescents. *J. soc. Psychol.*, 1955, **41**, 39–56.

11 Babchuk, N.: Primary friends and kin: A study of the associations of middle class couples. *Soc. Forces*, 1965, **43**, 482–493.

12 Back, K. W., and K. E. Davis: Some personal and situational factors relevant to the consistency and prediction of conforming behavior. *Sociometry.* 1965, **28**, 227–240.

13 Bains, R.: Making normal people. *Marriage fam. Living*, 1954, **16**, 27–31.

14 Baker, F., and G. M. O'Brien: Birth order and fraternity affiliation. *J. soc. Psychol.*, 1969, **78**, 41–43.

15 Barr, J. A., and K. H. Hoover: Home conditions and influences associated with the development of high school leaders. *Educ. Admin. Superv.*, 1957, **43**, 271–279.

16 Bayley, N.: Research in child development: A longitudinal perspective. *Merrill-Palmer Quart.*, 1965, **11**, 183–208.

17 Beer, M., R. Buckhout, M. W. Horowitz, and S. Levy: Some perceived properties of the differences between leaders and nonleaders. *J. Psychol.*, 1959, **47**, 49–56.

18 Bell, W.: Anomie, social isolation, and the class structure. *Sociometry*, 1957, **20**, 105–116.

19 Beloff, H.: Two forms of social conformity: Acquiescence and conventionality. *J. abnorm. soc. Psychol.*, 1958, **56**, 99–104.

20 Bendix, R., and F. W. Howton: Social mobility and the American business elite. *Brit. J. Sociol.*, 1957, **8**, 357–369; 1958, **9**, 1–14.

21 Berger, B. M.: The myth of suburbia. *J. soc. Issues*, 1961, **17**, no. 1, 38–49.

22 Berkowitz, W. R.: Perceived height, personality and friendship choice. *Psychol. Rep.*, 1969, **24**, 373–374.

23 Blalock, H. M.: Status consciousness: A dimensional analysis. *Soc. Forces*, 1959, **37**, 243–248.

24 Blau, P. M.: Occupational bias and mobility. *Amer. sociol. Rev.*, 1957, **22**, 392–399.

25 Bogardus, E. S.: Racial distance changes in the United States during the past 30 years. *Sociol. soc. Res.*, 1958, **43**, 127–134.

26 Bonney, M. E.: A study of constancy of sociometric ranks among college students over a two-year period. *Sociometry*, 1955, **18**, 531–542.

27 Bordeau, E., R. Dales, and R. Connor: Relationship of self-concept to 4-H Club leadership. *Rur. Sociol.*, 1963, **28**, 413–418.

28 Borgatta, E. F., R. F. Bales, and A. S. Couch: Some findings relevant to the great man theory of leadership. *Amer. sociol. Rev.*, 1954, **19**, 755–759.

29 Bossard, J. H. S., and E. S. Boll: *The sociology of child development*, 4th ed. New York: Harper & Row, 1966.

30 Bowerman, C. E., and J. W. Kinch: Changes in family and peer orientation of children between the fourth and tenth grades. *Soc. Forces*, 1959, **37**, 206–211.

31 Bowers, D. G.: Self-esteem and the diffusion of leadership style. *J. appl. Psychol.*, 1963, **47**, 135–149.

32 Brandt, R. M.: The accuracy of self estimate: A measure of concept reality. *Genet. Psychol. Monogr.*, 1958, **58**, 55–99.

33 Breckenridge, M. E., and E. L. Vincent: *Child development*, 5th ed. Philadelphia: Saunders, 1965.

34 Breed, W.: Occupational mobility and suicide among white males. *Amer. sociol. Rev.*, 1963, **28**, 179–188.

35 Bretch, H. S.: Social skills and activities of socially accepted and unaccepted adolescents. *J. educ. Psychol.*, 1952, **43**, 449–458.

36 Bringmann, W., and G. Reider: Stereotyped attitudes toward the aged in West Germany and the United States. *J. soc. Psychol.*, 1968, **76**, 267–268.

37 Brittain, C. V.: Age and sex of siblings and conformity toward parents versus peers in adolescence. *Child Develpm.*, 1966, **37**, 709–714.

38 Bryant, G. W.: Ideal leader behavior descriptions of appointed and sociometrically chosen student leaders. *Dissert. Abstr.*, 1968, **28** (9–A), 3497.

39 Bugental, D. E., and G. F. J. Lehner: Accuracy of self perception and group perception as related to two leadership roles. *J. abnorm. soc. Psychol.*, 1958, **56**, 396–398.

40 Burchinal, L., B. Gardner, and G. R. Hawkes: Children's personality adjustment and the socio-economic status of their families. *J. genet. Psychol.*, 1958, **92**, 149–159.

41 Cartwright, D. S., and R. J. Robertson: Membership in cliques and achievement. *Amer. J. Sociol.*, 1961, **46**, 441–445.

42 Cassel, R. N., and A. E. Shafer: An experiment in leadership training. *J. Psychol.*, 1961, **51**, 299–305.

43 Clifford, C., and T. S. Cohn: The relationship between leadership and personality attributes perceived by followers. *J. soc. Psychol.*, 1964, **64**, 57–64.

44 Clifford, E.: Discipline in the home: A controlled observational study of parental practices. *J. genet. Psychol.*, 1959, **95**, 45–82.

45 Coates, C. H., and R. J. Pellegrin: Executives and supervisors: Contrasting self-conceptions and conceptions of each

other. *Amer. sociol. Rev.*, 1957, **22**, 217–220.

46 Coleman, J. S.: *The adolescent society*. New York: Free Press, 1961.

47 Colle, R. D.: Negro image in the mass media: A case study in social change. *Journalism Quart.*, 1968, **45**, 55–60.

48 Cooper, J. B.: Emotion in prejudice. *Science*, 1959, **130**, 314–318.

49 Crowne, D. P., and S. Liverant: Conformity under varying conditions of personal commitment. *J. abnorm. soc. Psychol.*, 1963, **66**, 547–555.

50 Curtis, R. F.: Occupational mobility and urban social life. *Amer. J. Sociol.*, 1959, **65**, 296–298.

51 Davis, A.: Personality and social mobility. *School Review*, 1957, **65**, 134–143.

52 DeHaan, R. F.: Social leadership, *57th Yearb. nat. Soc. Stud. Educ.*, 1958, pt. 2, 127–143.

53 Dennis, W.: Causes of retardation among institutional children: Iran. *J. genet. Psychol.*, 1960, **96**, 47–59.

54 Dentler, R. A.: Dropouts, automation and the schools. *Teachers Coll. Rec.*, 1964, **65**, 475–483.

55 Douvan, E., and J. Adelson: The psychodynamics of social mobility in adolescent boys. *J. abnorm. soc. Psychol.*, 1958, **56**, 31–44.

56 Dresher, R. H.: Seeds of delinquency. *Personnel Guid. J.*, 1957, **35**, 595–598.

57 Dubin, E. R., and R. Dubin: The authority inception period in socialization. *Child Develpm.*, 1963, **64**, 885–898.

58 Duff, J. C.: Quest for leaders. *J. educ. Sociol.*, 1958, **32**, 91–95.

59 Duncan, O. D.: The trend of occupational mobility in the United States. *Amer. sociol. Rev.*, 1965, **30**, 491–498.

60 Dunnington, M. J.: Behavioral differences of sociometric status groups in a nursery school. *Child Develpm.*, 1957, **28**, 103–111.

61 Duvall, E. M.: Family dilemmas with teenagers. *Family Life Coordinator*, 1965, **14**, 35–38.

62 Elkin, F.: Socialization and the presentation of self. *Marriage fam. Living*, 1958, **20**, 320–325.

63 Elkins, D.: Some factors related to the choice-status of ninety eighth-grade children in a school society. *Genet. Psychol. Monogr.*, 1958, **58**, 207–272.

64 Elliott, D. S.: Delinquency, school attendance, and dropout. *Soc. Probl.*, 1966, **13**, 307–314.

65 Ellis, R. A., and W. C. Lane: Structural supports for upward mobility. *Amer. sociol. Rev.*, 1963, **28**, 743–756.

66 Emmerich, W.: Continuity and stability in early social development. II. Teacher ratings. *Child Develpm.*, 1966, **37**, 17–27.

67 Estvan, F. J., and E. W. Estvan: *The child's world: His social perception*. New York: Putnam, 1959.

68 Etzioni, A.: Lower levels of leadership in industry. *Sociol. soc. Res.*, 1959, **43**, 209–212.

69 Farina, A., J. G. Allen, and B. B. Saul: The role of the stigmatized person in affecting social relationships. *J. Pers.*, 1968, **36**, 169–182.

70 Feinberg, M. R.: Stability of sociometric status in two adolescent class groups. *J. genet. Psychol.*, 1964, **104**, 83–87.

71 Feshbach, N. D.: Sex differences in children's modes of aggressive responses to outsiders. *Merrill-Palmer Quart.*, 1969, **15**, 249–258.

72 Fiedler, F. E.: A note on leadership theory: The effect of social barriers between leaders and followers. *Sociometry*, 1957, **20**, 87–94.

73 French, E. G., and I. Chadwick: Some characteristics of the affiliation motivation. *J. abnorm. soc. Psychol.*, 1956, **52**, 296–300.

74 Friedenberg, E. Z.: *The vanishing adolescent.* Boston: Beacon Press, 1959.

75 Fromm-Reichmann, F.: Loneliness. *Psychiatry*, 1959, **22**, 1–15.

76 Gallagher, J. J.: Social status of children related to intelligence, propinquity, and social perception. *Elem. Sch. J.*, 1958, **58**, 225–231.

77 Gardner, R. C., E. J. Wonnacott, and D. M. Taylor: Ethnic stereotypes: A factor analytic investigation. *Canad. J. Psychol.*, 1968, **22**, 35–44.

78 Geschwender. J. A.: Status inconsistency, social isolation and individual unrest. *Soc. Forces*, 1968, **46**, 477–483.

79 Gesell, A., F. L. Ilg, and L. B. Ames: *Youth: The years from ten to sixteen.* New York: Harper & Row, 1956.

80 Gewirtz, J. L., and D. M. Baer: The effect of brief social deprivation on behavior for a social reinforcer. *J. abnorm. soc. Psychol.*, 1958, **56**, 49–56.

81 Gibby, R. G., and R. Gabler: The self-concept of Negro and white children. *J. clin. Psychol.*, 1967, **23**, 144–148.

82 Giles, H. H.: *The integrated classroom.* New York: Basic Books, 1959.

83 Goertzen, S. M.: Factors relating to opinions of seventh-grade children regarding the acceptability of certain behaviors in the peer group. *J. genet. Psychol.*, 1959, **94**, 29–34.

84 Gold, M.: Power in the classroom. *Sociometry*, 1958, **21**, 50–60.

85 Gondor, L. H., and E. I. Gondor: Changing times. *Amer. J. Psychother.*, 1969, **23**, 67–76.

86 Goode, E.: Social class and church participation. *Amer. J. Sociol.*, 1966, **72**, 102–113.

87 Goslin, D. A.: Accuracy of self-perception and social acceptance. *Sociometry*, 1962, **25**, 283–296.

88 Grace, H. A., and N. L. Booth: Is the "gifted" child a social isolate? *Peabody J. Educ.*, 1958, **35**, 195–196.

89 Greenberg, H., J. Pierson, and S. Sherman: The effects of single-session education techniques on prejudice attitudes. *J. educ. Sociol.*, 1957, **31**, 82–86.

90 Gronlund, N. E., and W. S. Holmlund: The value of elementary school sociometric status scores for predicting pupils' adjustment in high school. *Educ. Admin. Superv.*, 1958, **44**, 255–260.

91 Griffit, W. B.: Personality similarity and self-concept as determinants of interpersonal attraction. *J. soc. Psychol.*, 1969, **78**, 137–146.

92 Hagedorn, R., and S. Labovitz: An analysis of community and professional participation among occupations. *Soc. Forces*, 1967, **46**, 483–491.

93 Handel, G., and L. Rainwater: Persistence and change in working class life style. *Sociol. soc. Res.*, 1964, **48**, 281–288.

94 Harris, M.: Caste, class, and minority. *Soc. Forces*, 1959, **37**, 248–254.

95 Hartup, W. W., S. G. Moore, and G. Sager: Avoidance of inappropriate sex-typing by

young children. *J. consult. Psychol.*, 1963, **27**, 467–473.

96 Harvey, O. J., and C. Consalvi: Status and conformity to pressures in informal groups. *J. abnorm. soc. Psychol.*, 1960, **60**, 182–187.

97 Havighurst, R. J.: *Human development and education.* New York: Longmans, 1953.

98 Havighurst, R. J., and B. L. Neugarten: *Society and education.* Boston: Allyn & Bacon, 1957.

99 Hawk, T. L.: Self-concepts of the socially disadvantaged. *Elem. Sch. J.*, 1966, **67**, 196–206.

100 Heidensohn, F.: The deviance of women: A critique and an enquiry. *Brit. J. Sociol.*, 1968, **19**, 160–175.

101 Heyman, D. K., and F. C. Jeffers: Study of the relative influences of race and socioeconomic status upon the activities and attitudes of a Southern aged population. *J. Geront.*, 1964, **19**, 225–229.

102 Hicks, J. M.: The influence of group flattery upon self-evaluation. *J. soc. Psychol.*, 1962, **58**, 147–151.

103 Hodge, R. W., and D. J. Treiman: Class identification in the United States. *Amer. J. Sociol.*, 1968, **73**, 535–547.

104 Horrocks, J. E., and M. Benimoff: Stability of adolescent's nominee status, over a one-year period, as a friend by the peers. *Adolescence*, 1966, **1**, 224–229.

105 Izard, C. E.: Personality similarity and friendship: A follow-up study. *J. abnorm. soc. Psychol.*, 1963, **66**, 598–600.

106 Jahoda, G.: Development of the perception of social difference in children from 6 to 10. *Brit. J. Psychol.*, 1959, **50**, 159–175.

107 Johnson, R. T., and A. N. Frandsen: The California Psychological Inventory profile of student leaders. *Personnel Guid. J.*, 1962, **41**, 343–345.

108 Jones, M. C.: A study of socialization patterns at the high school level. *J. genet. Psychol.*, 1958, **93**, 87–111.

109 Jones, S. C., and D. J. Schneider: Certainty of self-appraisal and reactions to evaluations from others. *Sociometry*, 1968, **31**, 395–403.

110 Jourard, S. M.: *Personal adjustment,* 2d ed. New York: Macmillan, 1963.

111 Jung, C. G.: *Collected works.* New York: Pantheon Books, 1953.

112 Kagan, J., and H. A. Moss; *Birth to maturity: A study in psychological development.* New York: Wiley, 1962.

113 Kalish, R. A.: Of children and grandfathers: A speculative essay on dependency. *Gerontologist*, 1967, **7**, 65–69, 79.

114 Kastenbaum, R. (ed.): *New thoughts on old age.* New York: Springer, 1964.

115 Katz, I., and L. Benjamin: Effects of white authoritarianism in biracial work groups. *J. abnorm. soc. Psychol.*, 1960, **61**, 448–456.

116 Keehn, J. D., and E. T. Prothro: National preferences of university students from twenty-three nations. *J. Psychol.*, 1956, **42**, 283–294.

117 Keislar, E. R.: Experimental development of "like" and "dislike" of others among adolescent girls. *Child Develpm.*, 1961, **32**, 59–66.

118 Kent, D. P.: Social and cultural factors influencing the mental health of the aged. *Amer. J. Orthopsychiat.*, 1966, **36**, 680–685.

119 Kerckhoff, A. L., and T. C. McCormick:

Marginal status and marginal personality. *Soc. Forces*, 1955, **34**, 48–55.

120 Kipnis, D.: The effects of leadership style and leadership power upon the inducement of an attitude change. *J. abnorm. soc. Psychol.*, 1958, **57**, 173–180.

121 Koch, H. L.: The relation of certain formal attributes of siblings to attitudes held toward each other and toward their parents. *Monogr. Soc. Res. Child Develpm.*, 1960. **25**, no. 4.

122 Kohn, M.: The child as a determinant of his peers' approach to him. *J. genet. Psychol.*, 1966, **109**, 91–100.

123 Kutner, B.: Patterns of mental functioning associated with prejudice in children. *Psychol. Monogr.*, 1958, **72**, no. 7.

124 Lambert, W. E., and Y. Taguelii: Ethnic cleavage among young children. *J. abnorm. soc. Psychol.*, 1956, **53**, 380–382.

125 Lantz, H. R.: Number of childhood friends as reported in the life histories of a psychiatrically diagnosed group of 1,000. *Marriage fam. Living*, 1956, **18**, 107–109.

126 Laumann, E. O.: Friends of urban men: An assessment of accuracy of reporting their socioeconomic attributes, mutual choice, and attitude agreement. *Sociometry*, 1969, **32**, 54–69.

127 Lazerwitz, B., and L. Rowitz: The three-generation hypothesis. *Amer. J. Sociol.*, 1964, **69**, 529–538.

128 Lehman, H. C.: *Age and achievement.* Princeton, N.J.: Princeton University Press, 1953.

129 Lenski, G. E.: Trends in inter-generational occupational mobility in the United States. *Amer. sociol. Rev.*, 1958, **23**, 514–523.

130 Lesser, G. S.: The relationship between various forms of aggression and popularity among lower-class children. *J. educ. Res.*, 1959, **50**, 20–25.

131 Levine, G. N., and L. A. Sussmann: Social class and sociability in fraternity pledging. *Amer. J. Sociol.*, 1960, **65**, 391–399.

132 Liddle, G.: Overlap among desirable and undesirable characteristics in gifted children. *J. educ. Psychol.*, 1958, **49**, 219–228.

133 Litcher, J. H., and D. W. Johnson: Changes in attitudes toward Negroes of white elementary school students after use of multiethnic readers. *J. educ. Psychol.*, 1969, **60**, 148–152.

134 Long, B. H., R. C. Ziller, and E. E. Thompson: A comparison of prejudices: The effects upon friendship ratings of chronic illness, old age, education and race. *J. soc. Psychol.*, 1966, **70**, 101–109.

135 Lopata, H. Z.: The life cycle of the social role of housewife. *Sociol. soc. Res.*, 1966, **51**, 5–22.

136 Lott, B. E., and A. J. Lott: The formation of positive attitudes toward group members. *J. abnorm. soc. Psychol.*, 1960, **61**, 297–300.

137 Lowenthal, K.: How are "first impressions" formed? *Psychol. Rep.*, 1967, **21**, 834–836.

138 Lowenthal, M. F., and D. Boler: Voluntary vs. involuntary social withdrawal. *J. Geront.*, 1965, **20**, 363–371.

139 Luft, J.: Monetary value and the perception of persons. *J. soc. Psychol.*, 1957, **46**, 245–251.

140 Maddox, G. L.: Activity and morale: A longitudinal study of selected elderly subjects. *Soc. Forces*, 1963, **42**, 195–204.

141 Marks, J. B.: Interests, leadership and sociometric status among adolescents. *Sociometry*, 1954, **17**, 340–349.

142 Marshall, H. R.: Relations between home experiences and children's use of language in play interactions with peers. *Psychol. Monogr.*, 1961, **75**, no. 5.

143 Marshall, H. R., and B. R. McCandless: Relationships between dependency on adults and social acceptance by peers. *Child Developm.*, 1957, **28**, 413–419.

144 Martin, J. G., and F. R. Westie: The tolerant personality. *Amer. sociol. Rev.*, 1959, **24**, 521–528.

145 Martin, W. T.: The structuring of social relationships engendered by suburban residence. *Amer. sociol. Rev.*, 1956, **21**, 446–464.

146 May, S. H.: Purposeful mass activity. *Geriatrics*, 1966, **21**, 193–200.

147 Mayer, G. R., G. D. Krazler, and W. A. Matthes: Elementary school counseling and peer relations. *Personnel Guid. J.*, 1967, **46**, 360–365.

148 McCandless, B. R., C. B. Bilous, and H. L. Bennett: Peer popularity and dependence on adults in preschool-age socialization. *Child Developm.*, 1961, **32**, 511–518.

149 McCandless, B. R., and J. M. Hoyt: Sex, ethnicity and play preferences of preschool children. *J. abnorm. soc. Psychol.*, 1961, **62**, 683–685.

150 McDavid, J. W., and H. Harari: Stereotyping of names and popularity in grade-school children. *Child Developm.*, 1966, **37**, 453–459.

151 McDill, E. L.: Anomie, authoritarianism, prejudice, and socioeconomic status: An attempt at clarification. *Soc. Forces*, 1961, **39**, 239–245.

152 McKee, J. P., and A. C. Sherriffs: Men's and women's beliefs, ideals, and self-concepts. *Amer. J. Sociol.*, 1959, **64**, 356–363.

153 McNeil, J. D.: Changes in ethnic reaction tendencies during high school. *J. educ. Res.*, 1960, **53**, 199–200.

154 Medinnus, G. R.: An examination of several correlates of sociometric status in a first-grade group. *J. genet. Psychol.*, 1962, **101**, 3–13.

155 Mehlman, B.: Similarity in friendships. *J. soc. Psychol.*, 1962, **57**, 195–202.

156 Miller, K. M., and J. B. Biggs: Attitude change through undirected group discussion. *J. educ. Psychol.*, 1958, **49**, 224–228.

157 Miller, R. V.: Social status and sociempathic differences. *Except. Children*, 1956, **23**, 114–119.

158 Minturn, L., and M. Lewis: Age differences in peer ratings of socially desirable and socially undesirable behavior. *Psychol. Rep.*, 1968, **23**, 783–791.

159 Mitnick, L. L., and E. McGinnies: Influencing ethnocentrism in small discussion groups through a film communication. *J. abnorm. soc. Psychol.*, 1958, **56**, 82–90.

160 Montgomery, J. E., and J. Walters: The impact of social mobility on the family. In B. L. Bonniwell and R. L. Witherspoon (eds.), *Studies in social mobility*. Villanova, Penna.: Villanova University Press, 1966, pp. 25–34.

161 Moore, S. G.: Displaced aggression in young children. *J. abnorm. soc. Psychol.*, 1964, **68**, 200–204.

162 Moore, T.: Realism and fantasy in children's play. *J. child Psychol. Psychiat.*, 1964, **5**, 15–36.

163 Morland, J. K.: A comparison of race awareness in northern and southern children. *Amer. J. Orthopsychiat.*, 1966, **36**, 22–31.

164 Mosher, D. L., and A. Scodel: Relationships between ethnocentrism in children and the ethnocentrism and authoritarian rearing practices of their mothers. *Child Developm.*, 1960, **31**, 369–376.

165 Mussen, P. H., J. J. Conger, and J. Kagan: *Child development and personality*, 3d ed. New York: Harper & Row, 1969.

166 Mussen, P. H., and A. L. Parker: Mother nurturance and girls' incidental learning. *J. Pers. soc. Psychol.*, 1965, **2**, 94–97.

167 Naegele, K. N.: Friendship and acquaintances: An exploration of some social distinctions. *Harv. educ. Rev.*, 1958, **28**, 232–252.

168 Nakamura, C. Y., and M. M. Rogers: Parents' expectations of autonomous behavior and children's autonomy. *Developm. Psychol.*, 1969, **1**, 613–617.

169 Nam, C. B.: Nationality groups and social stratification in America. *Soc. Forces*, 1959, **37**, 328–333.

170 Neale, J. M.: Egocentrism in institutionalized and noninstitutionalized children. *Child Developm.*, 1966, **37**, 97–101.

171 Nelson, D. O.: Leadership in sports. *Res. Quart. Amer. Ass. Hlth. Phys. Educ. Recr.*, 1966, **37**, 268–275.

172 Nelson, P. D.: Similarities and differences among leaders and followers. *J. soc. Psychol.*, 1964, **63**, 161–167.

173 Neuringer, C., and L. W. Wandke: Interpersonal conflicts in persons of high self-concept and low self-concept. *J. soc. Psychol.*, 1966, **68**, 313–322.

174 Newcomb, T. M.: The prediction of interpersonal attraction. *Amer. Psychologist*, 1956, **11**, 575–586.

175 Niab, L. N.: Factors determining group stereotypes. *J. soc. Psychol.*, 1963, **61**, 3–10.

176 Noel, D. L.: A theory of the origin of ethnic stratification. *Soc. Probl.*, 1968, **2**, 157–172.

177 Northway, M. L.: Outsiders. In J. L. Moreno (ed.), *The sociometry reader*. New York: Free Press, 1960, pp. 455–470.

178 Packard, V.: *The status seekers*. New York: Pocket Books, 1961.

179 Packard, V.: *The pyramid climbers*. New York: McGraw-Hill, 1962.

180 Patterson, G. R., and D. Anderson: Peers as social reinforcers. *Child Developm.*, 1964, **35**, 951–960.

181 Pavenstedt, E.: A comparison of the child-rearing environment of upper-lower and very low-lower class families. *Amer. J. Orthopsychiat.*, 1965, **35**, 89–98.

182 Phelps, H. R., and J. E. Horrocks: Factors influencing informal groups of adolescents. *Child Developm.*, 1958, **29**, 69–86.

183 Phillips, D. L.: Social participation and happiness. *Amer. J. Sociol.*, 1967, **72**, 479–488.

184 Pierce-Jones, J.: Social mobility orientations and interests of adolescents. *J. counsel. Psychol.*, 1961, **8**, 75–78.

185 Pine, G. J.: Social class, social mobility and delinquent behavior. *Personnel Guid. J.*, 1965, **43**, 770–774.

186 Plant, W. T.: Changes in ethnocentrism associated with a four-year college education. *J. educ. Psychol.*, 1958, **49**, 162–165.

187 Porterfield, J. I., and J. P. Gibbs: Occupational prestige and social mobility of suicides in New Zealand. *Amer. J. Sociol.*, 1960, **64**, 147–152.

188 Reese, H. W.: Attitudes toward the opposite sex in late childhood. *Merrill-Palmer Quart.*, 1966, **12**, 157–163.

189 Rhine, W. R.: Birth order differences in conformity and level of achievement arousal. *Child Developm.*, 1968, **39**, 987–996.

190 Richardson, S. A., and J. Royce: Race and physical handicap in children's preference for other children. *Child Developm.*, 1968, **39**, 467–480.

191 Riestra, M. A., and C. E. Johnson: Changes in attitudes of elementary school pupils toward foreign-speaking people resulting from study of a foreign language. *J. exp. Educ.*, 1964, **33**, 65–72.

192 Rose, A. M.: Class differences among the elderly: A research report. *Sociol. soc. Res.*, 1966, **50**, 356–360.

193 Salmon, P.: Differential conforming as a developmental process. *Brit. J. soc. clin. Psychol.*, 1969, **8**, 22–31.

194 Savell, J. M., and G. W. Healey: Private and public conformity after being agreed and disagreed with. *Sociometry*, 1969, **32**, 325–329.

195 Schachter, S.: Birth order and sociometric choice. *J. abnorm. soc. Psychol.*, 1964, **68**, 453–456.

196 Schaefer, E. S., and N. Bayley: Maternal behavior, child behavior and their intercorrelations from infancy through adolescence. *Monogr. Soc. Res. Child Developm.*, 1963, **28**, no. 3.

197 Sears, R. R., E. E. Maccoby, and H. Levin: *Patterns in child rearing*. New York: Harper & Row, 1957.

198 Sewell, W. H., and A. O. Haller: Social status and the personality adjustment of the child. *Sociometry*, 1956, **19**, 114–125.

199 Sheikh, A. A.: Stereotypy in interpersonal perception and intercorrelation between some attitude measures. *J. soc. Psychol.*, 1968, **76**, 175–179.

200 Siegel, A. E., and L. G. Kohn: Permissiveness, permission, and aggression: The effect of adult presence or absence on aggression in children's play. *Child Developm.*, 1959, **30**, 131–141.

201 Silberstein, F. B., and M. Seeman: Social mobility and prejudice. *Amer. J. Sociol.*, 1959, **65**, 258–264.

202 Skorepa, C. A., J. E. Horrocks, and G. G. Thompson: A study of friendship fluctuations of college students. *J. genet. Psychol.*, 1963, **102**, 151–157.

203 Stacey, B.: Some psychological consequences of intergenerational mobility. *Hum. Relat.*, 1967, **20**, 3–12.

204 Stagner, R.: *The psychology of personality*, 3d ed. New York: McGraw-Hill, 1961.

205 Stevenson, H. W., and N. G. Stevenson: Social interaction in an interracial nursery school. *Genet. Psychol. Monogr.*, 1960, **61**, 37–75.

206 Stitch, T. G., and W. Fox: Geographical mobility and dogmatism, anxiety and age. *J. soc. Psychol.*, 1966, **68**, 171–178.

207 Strang, R.: *The adolescent views himself*. New York: McGraw-Hill, 1957.

208 Strickland, B. R., and D. P. Crowne: Conformity under conditions of simulated group pressure as a function of the need for social approval. *J. soc. Psychol.*, 1962, **58**, 171–181.

209 Sugarman, B.: Social norms in teenage boys' peer groups. *Hum. Relat.*, 1968, **21**, 41–58.

210 Tanenbaum, D. E.: Loneliness in the aged. *Ment. Hyg., N. Y.*, 1967, **51**, 91–99.

211 Taylor, F. K.: Display of dyadic emotions. *Hum. Relat.*, 1957, **10**, 257–262.

212 Taylor, R. G.: Racial stereotypes in young children. *J. Psychol.*, 1966, **64**. 137–142.

213 Terrell, G., and J. Shreffler: A developmental study of leadership. *J. educ. Res.*, 1958, **52**, 69–72.

214 Tiktin, S., and W. W. Hartup: Sociometric status and the reinforcing effectiveness of children's peers. *J. exp. child Psychol.*, 1965, **2**, 306–315.

215 Toigo, R.: Social status and schoolroom aggression in third grade children. *Genet. Psychol. Monogr.*, 1965, **71**, 221–268.

216 Trent, R. D.: The relation between expressed self-acceptance and expressed attitudes toward Negroes and whites among Negro children. *J. genet. Psychol.*, 1957, **91**, 25–31.

217 Triandis, H. C., and L. M. Triandis: Race, social class, religion, and nationality as determinants of social distance. *J. abnorm. soc. Psychol.*, 1960, **61**, 110–118.

218 Triandis, H. C., and V. Vassiliou: Frequency of contact and stereotyping. *J. Pers. soc. Psychol.*, 1967, **7**, 316–328.

219 Tulkin, S. R., J. F. Muller, and L. K. Conn: Need for approval and popularity: Sex differences in elementary school students. *J. consult. clin. Psychol.*, 1969, **33**, 35–39.

220 Turner, R. H.: Preoccupation with competitiveness and social acceptance among American and English college students. *Sociometry*, 1968, **23**, 307–325.

221 Van Krevelen, A.: Characteristics which "identify" the adolescent to his peers. *J. soc. Psychol.*, 1962, **56**, 285–289.

222 Walters, J., D. Pearce, and L. Dahms: Affectional and aggressive behavior of preschool children. *Child Develpm.*, 1957, **28**, 15–26.

223 Walters, R. H., W. E. Marshall, and J. R. Shooter: Anxiety, isolation and susceptibility to social influence. *J. Pers.*, 1960, **28**, 518–529.

224 Warnath, C. F.: The relation of family cohesiveness and adolescent independence to social effectiveness. *Marriage fam. Living*, 1955, **19**, 346–348.

225 Wedge, B.: Nationality and social perception. *J. Commun.*, 1966, **16**, 273–282.

226 Westoff, C. F., M. Bressler, and P. C. Sagi: The concept of social mobility: An empirical inquiry. *Amer. sociol. Rev.*, 1960, **25**, 375–385.

227 Wilensky, H. L., and H. Edwards: The skidder: Ideological achievements of downward mobile workers. *Amer. sociol. Rev.*, 1959, **24**, 215–231.

228 Williams, B. L., and H. Byars: Negro self-esteem in a transitional society. *Personnel Guid. J.*, 1968, **47**, 120–125.

229 Williams, J. E.: Acceptance by others and its relationship to acceptance of self and others. *J. abnorm. soc. Psychol.*, 1962, **65**, 438–442.

230 Witryol, S. M., and J. E. Calkins: Marginal social values of rural school children. *J. genet. Psychol.*, 1958, **92**, 81–93.

231 Wolman, B.: Leadership and group dynamics. *J. soc. Psychol.*, 1956, **42**, 11–25.

232 Yasuda, S.: A methodological inquiry into social mobility. *Amer. sociol. Rev.*, 1964, **29**, 16–23.

233 Zaleznik, A.: The human dilemmas of leadership. *Harv. bus. Rev.*, 1963, **41**, 49–55.

234 Ziller, R. C.: The alienation syndrome: A triadic pattern of self-other orientation. *Sociometry*, 1969, **32**, 287–300.

235 Ziller, R. C., and R. D. Behringer: A longitudinal study of the assimilation of the new child in the group. *Hum. Relat.*, 1961, **14**, 121–133.

CHAPTER 10

1 Adams, R. L.: Personality and behavioral differences among children of various birth positions. *Dissert. Abstr.*, 1967, **28** (5–A), 1697.

2 Adler, A.: *Individual psychology.* New York: Harcourt, Brace, 1925.

3 Allport, G. W.: *Pattern and growth in personality.* New York: Harper & Row, 1961.

4 Amatora, Sister M.: Home interests in early adolescence. *Genet. Psychol. Monogr.*, 1962, **65**, 137–174.

5 Anastasiow, N. J.: Success in school boys' sex-role patterns. *Child Develpm.*, 1965, **36**, 1053–1066.

6 Anderson, D.: What a high school class did with fifty years of life. *Personnel Guid. J.*, 1966, **45**, 116–123.

7 Anderson, D. G., and R. A. Heimann: Vocational maturity of junior high school girls. *Voc. Guid. Quart.*, 1967, **15**, 191–195.

8 Antonovsky, A.: Aspirations, class and racial-ethnic membership. *J. Negro Educ.*, 1963, **37**, 385–393.

9 Astin, A. W.: Personal and environmental factors associated with college dropouts among high aptitude students. *J. educ. Psychol.*, 1964, **55**, 219–227.

10 Astin, H. S.: Career development during the high school years. *J. counsel. Psychol.*, 1967, **14**, 94–98.

11 Bailyn, L.: Mass media and children: A study of exposure habits and cognitive effects. *Psychol. Monogr.*, 1959, **73**, no. 1.

12 Baird, L. L., and J. L. Holland: The flow of high school students to schools, colleges, and jobs. *ACT Res. Rep.*, 1968, no. 26.

13 Baker, L. G.: A comparison of the personal and social adjustments of 38 never-married women and 38 married women. *Dissert. Abstr.*, 1967, **28** (2–A), 465.

14 Baldwin, A. L., and H. Levin: Effects of public and private success or failure on children's repetitive motor behavior. *Child Develpm.*, 1958, **29**, 363–372.

15 Banducci, R.: The effect of mother's employment on the achievement aspirations and expectations of the child. *Personnel Guid. J.*, 1967, **46**, 263–267.

16 Barry, W. A., and E. S. Bordin: Personality development and the vocational choice of the ministry. *J. counsel. Psychol.*, 1967, **14**, 395–403.

17 Bartlett, E. W., and C. P. Smith: Child rearing practices, birth order, and the development of achievement-related motives. *Psychol. Rep.*, 1966, **19**, 1207–1216.

18 Beardslee, D. G., and D. D. O'Dowd: The college student's image of the scientist. *Science*, 1961, **133**, 997–1001.

19 Beilin, H.: The pattern of postponability and its relation to social-class mobility. *J. soc. Psychol.*, 1956, **44**, 33–48.

20 Bell, G. D.: Processes in the formation of adolescents' aspirations. *Soc. Forces*, 1963, **42**, 179–186.

21 Bennett, E. M., and L. R. Cohen: Men and women: Personality patterns and contrasts. *Genet. Psychol. Monogr.*, 1959, **59**, 101–155.

22 Bennett, W. S., and A. P. Gist: Class and family influences on student aspirations. *Soc. Forces*, 1964, **43**, 167–173.

23 Blackman, L. S., and H. Kahn: Success and failure as determinants of aspirational shifts in retardates and normals. *Amer. J. ment. Defic.*, 1963, **67**, 751–755.

24 Blai, B.: An occupational study of job satisfaction and need satisfaction. *J. exp. Educ.*, 1964, **32**, 383–388.

25 Blazer, J. A.: Fantasy and its effects. *J. gen. Psychol.*, 1964, **70**, 163–182.

26 Blood, R. O.: Long-range causes and consequences of the employment of married women. *J. Marriage & Family*, 1965, **27**, 43–47.

27 Bossard, J. H. S., and E. S. Boll: *The sociology of child development*, 4th ed. New York: Harper & Row, 1966.

28 Bowerman, C. E., and G. H. Elder: Variations in adolescent perception of family power structure. *Amer. sociol. Rev.*, 1964, **29**, 551–567.

29 Boyle, R. P.: The effect of the high school on students' aspirations. *Amer. J. Sociol.*, 1966, **71**, 628–639.

30 Brim, O. G., and R. Forer: A note on the relation of values and social structure to life planning. *Sociometry*, 1956, **19**, 54–60.

31 Brodie, R. D., and M. R. Winterbottom: Failure in elementary school boys as a function of trauma, secrecy and derogation. *Child Develpm.*, 1967, **38**, 701–711.

32 Brodie, T. A.: Attitude toward school and academic achievement. *Personnel Guid. J.*, 1964, **43**, 375–378.

33 Bronzaft, A. L.: Test anxiety, social mobility, and academic achievement. *J. soc. Psychol.*, 1968, **75**, 217–222.

34 Brown, R. G.: A comparison of the vocational aspirations of paired sixth-grade white and Negro children who attend segregated schools. *J. educ. Res.*, 1965, **58**, 402–404.

35 Bruce, G. D., C. M. Bonjean, and J. A. Williams: Job satisfaction among independent business men. *Sociol. soc. Res.*, 1968, **52**, 195–204.

36 Bühler, C.: The course of human life as a psychological problem. *Hum. Develpm.*, 1968, **11**, 184–200.

37 Burnstein, S.: Fear of failure, achievement motivation, and aspiring to prestigeful occupations. *J. abnorm. soc. Psychol.*, 1963, **67**, 189–193.

38 Butterfield, E. C., and E. Zigler: The effects of success and failure on the discrimination learning of normal and retarded children. *J. abnorm. Psychol.*, 1965, **70**, 25–31.

39 Callard, E. D.: Achievement motive in the four-year-old child and its relationship to achievement expectancies of the mother. *Dissert. Abstr.*, 1964, **25**, 3725.

40 Campanelle, T.: Motivational development of adolescents. *Education*, 1965, **85**, 310–313.

41 Cantril, H.: A study of aspirations. *Scient. American*, 1963, **208**, no. 2, 41–45.

42 Caro, F. G., and C. T. Pihlblad: Aspirations and expectations: A re-examination of the bases for social class differences in the occupational orientations of male high school students. *Sociol. soc. Res.*, 1965, **49**, 465–475.

43 Cavan, R. S.: Unemployment: Crisis of the common man. *Marriage fam. Living*, 1959, **21**, 139–146.

44 Chambers, J. A.: Relating personality and biographical factors to scientific creativity. *Psychol. Monogr.*, 1964, **78**, no. 7.

45 Child, I. L., and M. K. Bacon: Cultural pressures and achievement motivation. In P. H. Hoch and J. Zubin (eds), *Psychopathology of childhood.* New York: Grune & Stratton, 1955, pp. 166–176.

46 Chittenden, E. A., M. W. Foan, D. M. Zweil, and J. R. Smith: School achievement of first- and second-born siblings. *Child Develpm.,* 1968, **39,** 1123–1128.

47 Chown, S. M.: Personality factors in the formation of occupational choice. *Brit. J. educ. Psychol.,* 1959, **29,** 23–33.

48 Christensen, H. T.: Lifetime family and occupational role projections of high school students. *Marriage fam. Living,* 1961, **23,** 181–183.

49 Christensen, H. T., and M. M. Swihart: Postgraduate role preferences of senior women in college. *Marriage fam. Living,* 1956, **18,** 52–57.

50 Cobb, H. V.: Role-wishes and general wishes of children and adolescents. *Child Develpm.,* 1954, **25,** 161–171.

51 Cohen, E. G.: Parental factors in educational mobility. *Sociology of Education,* 1965, **38,** 404–425.

52 Coleman, J. S.: *The adolescent society.* New York: Free Press, 1961.

53 Cooper, J. B., and J. H. Lewis: Parent evaluation as related to social ideology and academic achievement. *J. genet. Psychol.,* 1962, **101,** 135–143.

54 Costello, C. G.: Need achievement and college performance. *J. Psychol.,* 1968, **69,** 17–18.

55 Crandall, V. J.: Achievement. *62nd Yearb. nat. Soc. Stud. Educ.,* 1963, pt. 1, 416–459.

56 Crisera, R. A.: A study of job satisfaction and its relationship to performance in the job situation. *Dissert. Abstr.,* 1966, **26,** 4793–4794.

57 Cronbach, L. J.: *Educational psychology,* 2d ed. New York: Harcourt, Brace & World, 1963.

58 Crowley, F. J.: The goals of male high school seniors. *Personnel Guid. J.,* 1959, **37,** 488–492.

59 Crowne, D. P., L. K. Conn, D. Marlow, and C. N. Edwards: Some developmental antecedents of level of aspiration. *J. Pers.,* 1969, **37,**73–92.

60 Dalta, L. E.: Family religious background and early scientific creativity. *Amer. sociol. Rev.,* 1967, **32,** 626–635.

61 Davids, A., and P. K. Hainsworth: Maternal attitudes about family life and child rearing as avowed by mothers and perceived by their underachieving and high-achieving sons. *J. consult. Psychol.,* 1967, **31,** 219–237.

62 Danesino, A., and W. A. Layman: Contrasting personality patterns of high and low achievers among college students of Italian and Irish descent. *J. Psychol.,* 1969, **72,** 71–83.

63 Dean, D. G.: Romanticism and emotional maturity: A further exploration. *Soc. Forces,* 1964, **42,** 298–303.

64 DeCharms, R., and G. H. Moeller: Values expressed in children's readers: 1800–1950. *J. abnorm. soc. Psychol.,* 1962, **64,** 136–142.

65 DeFleur, M. L., and L. B. DeFleur: The relative contribution of television as a learning source for children's occupational knowledge. *Amer. sociol. Rev.,* 1967, **32,** 777–789.

66 Dennis, W.: Creative productivity between the ages of 20 and 80. *J. Geront.,* 1966, **21,** 1–8. ʳ

67 Diedrich, R. C., and P. W. Jackson: Satisfied and dissatisfied students. *Personnel Guid. J.,* 1969, **47,** 641–649.

68 Dienstfrey, H.: Doctors, lawyers, and other TV heroes. *Commentary,* 1963, **35,** 519–524.

69 Duncan, O. D., A. O. Haller, and A. Porter: Peer influence on aspirations: A reinterpretation. *Amer. J. Sociol.,* 1968, **74,** 119–137.

70 Durig, K. B.: A study of social status and occupational choice among high school students. *Dissert. Abstr.,* 1968, **28** (9–A), 3777.

71 Dyer, W. G.: Parental influence on the job attitudes of children from two occupational strata. *Sociol. soc. Res.,* 1958, **42,** 203–206.

72 Eckland, B. K.: Social class and college graduation: Some misconceptions corrected. *Amer. J. Sociol.,* 1964, **70,** 36–50.

73 Elder, G. H.: Achievement motivation and intelligence in occupational mobility: A longitudinal analysis. *Sociometry,* 1968, **31,** 327–354.

74 Ellis, R. A., and W. C. Lane: Social mobility and career orientation. *Sociol. soc. Res.,* 1966, **50,** 280–296.

75 Empey, L. T.: Role expectations of young women regarding marriage and a career. *Marriage fam. Living,* 1958, **20,** 152–155.

76 Falk, L. L.: Occupational satisfaction of female college graduates. *J. Marriage & Family,* 1966, **28,** 177–185.

77 Feather, N. T.: Effects of prior success and failure on expectations of success and subsequent performance. *J. Pers. soc. Psychol.,* 1966, **3,** 287–298.

78 Ferguson, E. D.: The effect of sibling competition and alliance on level of aspiration, expectation and performance. *J. abnorm. soc. Psychol.,* 1958, **56,** 213–222.

79 Field, S. C.: Longitudinal study of the origins of achievement striving. *J. Pers. soc. Psychol.,* 1967, **7,** 408–414.

80 Finger, J. A., and G. E. Schlesser: Nonintellective predictors of academic success in school and college. *School Review,* 1965, **73,** 14–29.

81 Flaherty, Sister M. R., and E. Reutzel: Personality traits of high and low achievers in college. *J. educ. Res.,* 1965, **58,** 409–411.

82 Ford, L. H.: Reaction to failure as a function of expectancy for success. *J. abnorm. soc. Psychol.,* 1963, **67,** 340–348.

83 Frandsen, A., and M. Sorenson: Interests as motives in academic achievement. *J. sch. Psychol.,* 1968–1969, **7,** no. 1, 52–56.

84 Friedlander, F.: Relationships between the importance and the satisfaction of various environmental factors. *J. appl. Psychol.,* 1965, **49,** 160–164.

85 Garai, J. E., and A. Scheinfeld: Sex differences in mental and behavioral traits. *Genet. Psychol. Monogr.,* 1968, **77,** 169–299.

86 Geist, H.: Work satisfaction and scores on a picture interest inventory. *J. appl. Psychol.,* 1963, **47,** 369–373.

87 Geschwender, J. A.: Status inconsistency, social isolation, and individual unrest. *Soc. Forces,* 1968, **46,** 477–483.

88 Goodschilds, J. D., and E. E. Smith: The effects of unemployment as mediated by social status. *Sociometry,* 1963, **26,** 287–293.

89 Green, L. B., and H. J. Parker: Parental influence upon adolescents' occupational choice: A test of an aspect of Roe's theory. *J. counsel. Psychol.,* 1965, **12,** 379–383.

90 Greene, R. L., and J. R. Clark: Birth order and college attendance in a cross-cultural setting. *J. soc. Psychol.,* 1968, **75,** 289–290.

91 Gribbons, W. D., and P. R. Lohnes: Shifts in adolescents' vocational values. *Personnel Guid. J.,* 1965, **44,** 248–252.

92 Gysbers, M. C., J. A. Johnston, and T. Gust: Characteristics of homemaker and career-oriented women. *J. counsel. Psychol.,* 1968, **15,** 541–546.

93 Hall, R. L., and B. Willerman: The educational influence of dormitory roommates. *Sociometry,* 1963, **26,** 294–318.

94 Haller, A. O.: On the concept of aspiration. *Rural Sociol.,* 1968, **33,** 484–487.

95 Hansche, J., and J. C. Gilchrist: Three determinants of the level of aspiration. *J. abnorm. soc. Psychol.,* 1956, **53,** 136–137.

96 Hanson, J. T.: Ninth grade girls' vocational choices and their parents' occupational level. *Vocat. Guid. Quart.,* 1965, **13,** 261–264.

97 Hardin, E.: Job satisfaction and the desire for change. *J. appl. Psychol.,* 1967, **51,** 20–27.

98 Harrison, F.: Aspirations as related to school performance and socioeconomic status. *Sociometry,* 1969, **32,** 70–79.

99 Hartman, B. G.: Motives for college attendance. *Psychol. Rep.,* 1962, **22,** 783–784.

100 Havighurst, R. J.: *Human development and education.* New York: Longmans, 1953.

101 Havighurst, R. J.: Body, self, and society. *Sociol. soc. Res.,* 1965, **49,** 261–267.

102 Heber, R. F., and M. E. Heber: The effect of group failure and success on social status. *J. educ. Psychol.,* 1957, **48,** 129–134.

103 Hecht, R. M., J. E. Aron, and S. Lirtzman: Let's stop worrying about aptitudes and look at attitudes. *Personnel J.,* 1965, **44,** 616–619.

104 Heilbrun, A. B.: Parental identification and the patterning of vocational interests in college males and females. *J. counsel. Psychol.,* 1969, **16,** 342–347.

105 Henley, N. M.: Achievement and affiliation imagery in American fiction: 1901–1961. *J. Pers. soc. Psychol.,* 1967, **7,** 208–210.

106 Henton, J. M.: The effects of married high-school students on their unmarried classmates. *J. Marriage & Family,* 1964, **26,** 87–88.

107 Hermann, R. O.: Expectations and attitudes as a source of financial problems in teen-age marriages. *J. Marriage & Family,* 1965, **27,** 89–91.

108 Herriott, R. E.: Some social determinants of educational aspirations. *Harv. educ. Rev.,* 1963, **33,** 157–177.

109 Hilgard, E. R.: *Introduction to psychology,* 4th ed. New York: Harcourt, Brace & World, 1962.

110 Hill, G. B.: Choice of career by grammar school boys. *Occup. Psychol.,* 1965, **39,** 279–287.

111 Hobart, C. W.: Disillusionment in marriage and romanticism. *Marriage fam. Living,* 1958, **20,** 156–162.

112 Hodge, R. W., and D. J. Treiman: Class identification in the United States. *Amer. J. Sociol.,* 1968, **73,** 535–547.

113 Hollander, J. W.: Development of a realistic vocational choice. *J. counsel. Psychol.,* 1967, **14,** 314–318.

114 Hulm, C. L.: Effects of changes in job-satisfaction levels on employee turnover. *J. appl. Psychol.*, 1968, **52**, 122–126.

115 Hummel, R. H., and N. Sprinthall: Underachievement related to interests, attitudes, and values. *Personnel Guid. J.*, 1965, **44**, 388–395.

116 Hundleby, J. D., and R. B. Cattell: Personality structure in middle childhood and the prediction of school achievement and adjustment. *Monogr. Soc. Res. Child Develpm.*, 1968, **33**, no. 5.

117 Hunt, D. E., and H. M. Schroder: Assimilation, failure-avoidance and anxiety. *J. consult. Psychol.*, 1958, **22**, 39–44.

118 Jackson, P. W., and H. M. Lahaderne: Scholastic success and attitude toward school in a population of sixth graders. *J. educ. Psychol.*, 1967, **58**, 15–18.

119 Jencks, C.: Social stratification and higher education. *Harv. educ. Rev.*, 1968, **38**, 277–316.

120 Jennings, F. G.: Adolescent aspirations and the older generation. *Teachers Coll. Rec.*, 1964, **65**, 335–341.

121 Jersild, A. T.: *The psychology of adolescence*, 2d ed. New York: Macmillan, 1963.

122 Jersild, A. T.: *Child psychology*, 6th ed. Englewood Cliffs, N. J.: Prentice-Hall, 1969.

123 Johnson, L., and G. B. Strother: Job expectations and retirement planning. *J. Geront.*, 1962, **17**, 418–423.

124 Johnson, W.: The semantics of maladjustment. In L. A. Pennington and I. A. Berg (eds.), *An introduction to clinical psychology*. New York: Ronald, 1948, pp. 298–516.

125 Jourard, S. M.: *Personal adjustment*, 2d ed. New York: Macmillan, 1963.

126 Kandel, D. B., and G. S. Lesser: Parental and peer influences on educational plans of adolescents. *Amer. sociol. Rev.*, 1969, **34**, 212–223.

127 Katkovsky, W., A. Preston, and V. J. Crandall: Parents' attitudes toward their personal achievements and toward the achievement behaviors of their children. *J. genet. Psychol.*, 1964, **104**, 67–82.

128 Katz, F. M.: The meaning of success: Some differences in value systems of social class. *J. soc. Psychol.*, 1964, **62**, 141–148.

129 Kent, D. P.: Social and cultural factors affecting the mental health of the aged. *Amer. J. Orthopsychiat.*, 1966, **36**, 680–685.

130 Kent, N., and D. R. Davis: Discipline in the home and intellectual development. *Brit. J. med. Psychol.*, 1957, **30**, 27–33.

131 Kinnane, J. F., and Sister M. M. Bannon: Perceived parental influence and work-value orientation. *Personnel Guid. J.*, 1964, **43**, 273–279.

132 Koch, H. L.: The relation of certain formal attributes of siblings to attitudes held toward each other and toward their parents. *Monogr. Soc. Res. Child Develpm.*, 1960, **25**, no. 4.

133 Korman, A. K.: Task success, task popularity and self-esteem as influences on task-liking. *J. appl. Psychol.*, 1968, **52**, 484–490.

134 Kosa, J., L. D. Rachiele, and C. O. Schommer: The self-image and performance of socially mobile college students. *J. soc. Psychol.*, 1962, **56**, 301–316.

135 Krippner, S.: The educational plans and preferences of upper-middle class junior high school pupils. *Vocat. Guid. Quart.*, 1965, **13**, 257–260.

136 Kuhlen, R. G.: Needs, perceived need satisfaction, opportunities, and satisfaction with occupation. *J. appl. Psychol.*, 1963, **47**, 56–64.

137 Kuhweide, K., H. E. Lueck, and E. Tunaeus: Occupational prestige: A cross-cultural comparison. *Percept. mot. Skills*, 1968, **27**, 154.

138 Kuvlesky, W. P., and R. C. Bealer: The relevance of adolescents' occupational aspirations for subsequent job attainment. *Rural Sociol.*, 1967, **32**, 290–301.

139 LaGrone, C. W.: Sex and personality differences in relation to fantasy. *J. consult. Psychol.*, 1963, **27**, 270–272.

140 Lehman, H. C.: *Age and achievement*. Princeton, N. J.: Princeton, 1953.

141 Lehman, H. C.: The age decrement in outstanding scientific creativity. *Amer. Psychologist*, 1960, **15**, 128–134.

142 Lehman, H. C.: The most creative years of engineers and other technologists. *J. genet. Psychol.*, 1966, **108**, 263–277.

143 Leib, J. W., and W. N. Snyder: Achievement and positive mental health: A supplementary report. *J. counsel. Psychol.*, 1968, **15**, 388–389.

144 Levinson, H.: What work means to a man. *Menninger Quart.*, 1964, **18**, 1–11.

145 Lewin, K., T. Dembo, L. Festinger, and P. S. Sears: Level of aspiration. In J. McV. Hunt (ed.); *Personality and the behavior disorders*. New York: Ronald, 1944, vol. 1, pp. 333–378.

146 Lichtenberg, P.: Reactions to success and failure during individual and cooperative effort. *J. soc. Psychol.*, 1957, **46**, 31–34.

147 Ludwig, D. J., and M. L. Maehr: Changes in self-concept and stated behavior preferences. *Child Develpm.*, 1967, **38**, 453–467.

148 Luft, J.: Monetary value and the perception of persons. *J. soc. Psychol.*, 1957, **46**, 245–251.

149 Lunneborg, P. W.: Birth order, aptitude and achievement. *J. consult. clin. Psychol.*, 1968, **32**, 101.

150 Maccoby, E. E., W. C. Wilson, and R. V. Burton: Differential movie-viewing behavior of male and female viewers. *J. Pers.*, 1958, **26**, 259–267.

151 Martin, J. G., and F. R. Westie: The tolerant personality. *Amer. sociol. Rev.*, 1959, **24**, 521–528.

152 Masserman, J. H.: The psychodynamics of aging. *Geriatrics*, 1957, **12**, 115–122.

153 McClelland, D. C. (ed.): *Studies in motivation*. New York: Appleton-Century-Crofts, 1955.

154 McDill, E. L., and J. L. Coleman: Family and peer influences in college plans of high school students. *Sociology of Education*, 1964, **38**, 112–126.

155 Meade, R. D.: Realism of aspiration levels in Indian and American college students. *J. soc. Psychol.*, 1968, **75**, 169–173.

156 Meltzer, H.: Attitudes of workers before and after 40. *Geriatrics*, 1965, **20**, 425–432.

157 Mischel, W., B. Coates, and A. Raskoff: Effects of success and failure on self gratification. *J. Pers. soc. Psychol.*, 1968, **10**, 381–390.

158 Mowsesian, R., B. R. Heath, and J. W. M. Rothney: Superior students' occupational preferences and their fathers' occupations. *Personnel Guid. J.*, 1967, **45**, 238–242.

159 Mulvey, M. C.: Psychological and socio-logical factors in prediction of career patterns of women. *Genet. Psychol. Monogr.*, 1963, **68**, 309–386.

160 Muma, J. R.: Peer evaluation and academic performance. *Personnel Guid. J.*, 1966, **44**, 405–409.

161 Murherjee, B. N.: Birth order and verbalized need for achievement. *J. soc. Psychol.*, 1968, **75**, 223–229.

162 Myers, M. S.: Who are your motivated workers? *Harv. bus. Rev.*, 1964, **42**, 73–88.

163 Oden, M. H.: The fulfillment of promise: 40-year follow-up of Terman gifted group. *Genet. Psychol. Monogr.*, 1968, **77**, 3–93.

164 O'Shea, A. J.: Peer relationships and male academic achievement: A review and suggested clarification. *Personnel Guid. J.*, 1969, **47**, 417–428.

165 Packard, V.: *The status seekers*. New York: Pocket Books, 1961.

166 Packard, V.: *The pyramid climbers*. New York: McGraw-Hill, 1962.

167 Paris, B. L., and E. B. Luckey: A longitudinal study in marital satisfaction. *Sociol. soc. Res.*, 1966, **50**, 212–222.

168 Parker, A. W.: Career and marriage orientation in the vocational development of college women. *J. appl. Psychol.*, 1966, **50**, 232–235.

169 Parsons, O. A.: Status needs and performance under failure. *J. Pers.*, 1958, **26**, 123–138.

170 Pavalko, R. M., and M. H. Walizer: Parental educational differences and the college plans of youth. *Sociol. soc. Res.*, 1969, **54**, 80–89.

171 Pearlin, L. I., M. R. Yarrow, and H. A. Scarr: Unintended effects of parental aspirations: The case of children's cheating. *Amer. J. Sociol.*, 1967, **73**, 73–83.

172 Perrone, P. A.: Stability of values of junior high school pupils and their parents over two years. *Personnel Guid. J.*, 1967, **46**, 268–274.

173 Pineo, P. C.: Disenchantment in the later years of marriage. *Marriage fam. Living*, 1961, **23**, 3–11.

174 Poffenberger, T., and D. Norton: Factors in the formation of attitudes toward mathematics. *J. educ. Res.*, 1959, **52**, 171–176.

175 Powell, E. H.: Occupation, status and suicide: Toward a redefinition of anomie. *Amer. sociol Rev.*, 1958, **23**, 131–139.

176 Pressey, S. L.: Potentials of age: An exploratory field study. *Genet. Psychol. Monogr.*, 1957, **56**, 159–205.

177 Psathas, G.: Toward a theory of occupation choice for women. *Sociol. soc. Res.*, 1968, **52**, 253–268.

178 *Report of President's Council on Aging.* 1963.

179 Rezler, A. G.: Characteristics of high school girls choosing traditional or pioneer vocations. *Personnel Guid. J.*, 1967, **45**, 659–665.

180 Ringness, T. A.: Identification patterns, motivation and school achievement of bright junior high school boys. *J. educ. Psychol.*, 1967, **58**, 93–102.

181 Robinson, H. A., R. P. Connors, and G. H. Whitacre: Job satisfaction researches of 1964–65. *Personnel Guid. J.*, 1966, **45**, 371–379.

182 Rolcik, J. W.: Scholastic achievement of teenagers and parental attitudes toward and interest in schoolwork. *Family Life Coordinator*, 1965, **14**, 158–160.

183 Rose, A. M.: Factors associated with the life satisfactions of middle-class, middle-

aged persons. In C. B. Vedder (ed.), *Problems of the middle-aged*. Springfield, Ill.: Charles C Thomas, 1965, pp. 59–67.

184 Rosen, B. C.: Family structure and achievement motivation. *Amer. sociol. Rev.*, 1961, **26**, 574–585.

185 Rubin, Z.: Do American women marry up? *Amer. sociol. Rev.*, 1968, **33**, 750–760.

186 Rushing, W. A.: Adolescent-parent relationship and mobility aspirations. *Soc. Forces*, 1964, **43**, 157–166.

187 Safilios-Rothschild, C.: "Good" and "bad" girls in modern Greek movies. *J. Marriage & Family*, 1968, **30**, 527–531.

188 Saleh, S. D., and J. L. Otis: Age and level of job satisfaction. *Personnel Psychol.*, 1964, **17**, 425–430.

189 Sandeen, C. A.: Aspirations for college. *Personnel Guid. J.*, 1968, **46**, 462–465.

190 Schonfeld, W. A.: Socioeconomic affluence as a factor. *N. Y. State J. Med.*, 1967, **67**, 1981–1990.

191 Sears, P. S., and H. Levin: Levels of aspiration in preschool children. *Child Develpm.*, 1957, **28**, 317–326.

192 Seeman, M.: On the personal consequences of alienation in work. *Amer. sociol. Rev.*, 1967, **32**, 273–285.

193 Sewell, W. H., and V. P. Shah: Parents' education and children's educational aspirations and achievements. *Amer. sociol. Rev.*, 1968, **33**, 191–209.

194 Shaffer, L. F., and E. J. Shoben: *The psychology of adjustment*, 2d ed. Boston: Houghton Mifflin, 1956.

195 Silverman, D.: An evaluation of the relationship between attitudes toward self and attitudes toward a vocational high school. *J. educ. Sociol.*, 1963, **36**, 410–418.

196 Sivertsen, D.: Goal setting, level of aspiration and social norms. *Acta psychol.*, Amsterdam, 1957, **13**, 54–60.

197 Slotkin, J. S.: Life course in middle age. *Soc. Forces*, 1954, **33**, 171–177.

198 Smith, R. J., C. E. Ramsey, and G. Castillo: Parental authority and job choice: Sex differences in three cultures. *Amer. J. Sociol.*, 1963, **69**, 143–149.

199 Solomon, D.: The generality of children's achievement-related behavior. *J. genet. Psychol.*, 1969, **114**, 109–125.

200 Sontag, L. W., and J. Kagan: The emergence of intellectual achievement motives. *Amer. J. Orthopsychiat.*, 1963, **33**, 532–534.

201 Spady, W. G.: Educational mobility and access: Growth and paradoxes. *Amer. J. Sociol.*, 1967, **73**, 273–286.

202 Spaeth, J. L.: Occupational prestige expectations among male college graduates. *Amer. J. Sociol.*, 1968, **73**, 548–558.

203 Stacey, B. G.: Some psychological aspects of inter-generation occupational mobility. *Brit. J. soc. clin. Psychol.*, 1965, **4**, 275–286.

204 Stein, A. H., and J. Smithells: Age and sex differences in children's sex-role standards about achievement. *Develpm. Psychol.*, 1969, **1**, 252–259.

205 Steiner, I. D.: Self-perception and goal-setting behavior. *J. Pers.*, 1957, **25**, 344–355.

206 Still, J. W.: Man's potential—and his performance. *The New York Times*, Nov. 24, 1957.

207 Stotland, E., and A. Zander: Effects of public and private failure on self-evaluation. *J. abnorm. soc. Psychol.*, 1958, **56**, 223–229.

208 Stout, R. T.: Social class and educational aspirations: A Weberian analysis. *Personnel Guid. J.*, 1969, **47**, 650–654.

209 Strang, R.: *The adolescent views himself*. New York: McGraw-Hill, 1957.

210 Straus, M. A.: Deferred gratification, social class and the achievement syndrome. *Amer. sociol. Rev.*, 1962, **27**, 326–335.

211 Taylor, R. G.: Personality traits and discrepant achievement: A review. *J. counsel. Psychol.*, 1964, **11**, 76–82.

212 Teahan, J. E.: Parental attitudes and college success. *J. educ. Psychol.*, 1963, **54**, 104–109.

213 Terman, L. M., and M. H. Oden: *The gifted group at mid-life*. Stanford, Calif.: Stanford, 1959.

214 Theodorsen, G. A.: Romanticism and the motive to marry in the United States, Singapore, Burma, and India. *Soc. Forces*, 1965, **44**, 17–27.

215 Thistlewaite, D. L., and N. Wheeler: Effects of teacher and peer subcultures upon student aspirations. *J. educ. Psychol.*, 1966, **57**, 35–47.

216 Thompson, O. E.: Occupational values of high school students. *Personnel Guid. J.*, 1966, **44**, 850–853.

217 Tomeh, A. K.: The impact of reference groups on the educational and occupational aspirations of women college students. *J. Marriage & Family*, 1968, **30**, 102–110.

218 Torgoff, I., and G. Tesi: Effect of differences in achievement motivation and social responsibility on responses to moral conflict. *J. Pers.*, 1968, **36**, 513–527.

219 Torrance, E. P., and D. C. Dauw: Aspirations and dreams of 3 groups of creatively gifted high school seniors and a comparable unselected group. *Gifted Child Quart.*, 1965, **9**, 177–182.

220 Turner, R. H.: Some aspects of women's ambition. *Amer. J. Sociol.*, 1964, **70**, 271–285.

221 Ulrich, C., and R. K. Burke: Effect of motivational stress upon physical performance. *Res. Quart. Amer. Ass. Hlth. Phys. Educ. Recr.*, 1957, **28**, 403–412.

222 Ulrich, G., J. Hecklik, and E. C. Roeber: Occupation stereotypes of high school students. *Vocat. Guid. Quart.*, 1966, **14**, 169–174.

223 Van Der Veen, F., B. Huebner, B. Jorgens, and P. Neja: Relationships between the parents' concept of the family and family adjustment. *Amer. J. Orthopsychiat.*, 1964, **34**, 45–55.

224 Vroom, V. H.: Ego-involvement, job satisfaction, and job performance. *Personnel Psychol.*, 1962, **15**, 159–177.

225 Wagman, M.: Interests and values of career and homemaking oriented women. *Personnel Guid. J.*, 1966, **44**, 794–801.

226 Warriner, C. C., D. A. Foster, and D. K. Trites: Failure to complete as a family characteristic: A college sample. *J. educ. Res.*, 1966, **59**, 466–468.

227 Watson, D., and J. Siegel: Test anxiety, motive to avoid failure, and motive to approach success. *J. exp. Res. Pers.*, 1966, **1**, 236–243.

228 Weinstein, M. S.: Achievement motivation and risk preferences. *J. Pers. soc. Psychol.*, 1969, **13**, 153–172.

229 Wellington, J. A., and N. Olechowski: Attitudes toward the world of work in elementary schools. *Vocat. Guid. Quart.*, 1966, **14**, 160–162.

230 Wernimont, P. F.: Intrinsic and extrinsic factors in job satisfaction. *J. appl. Psychol.*, 1966, **50**, 41–50.

231 Wertham, F.: The scientific study of mass media effects. *Amer. J. Psychiat.*, 1962, **119**, 306–311.

232 Werts, C. E.: Paternal influence on career choice. *J. counsel Psychol.*, 1968, **15**, 48–52.

233 Wheeler, C. L., and E. F. Carnes: Relationships among self-concepts, ideal self-concepts and stereotypes of probable and ideal vocational choices. *J. counsel. Psychol.*, 1968, **15**, 530–535.

234 Wheeler, D. K.: Expressed wishes of students. *J. genet. Psychol.*, 1963, **102**, 75–81.

235 Whitman, H.: Let go of the dream. In C. B. Vedder (ed.), *Problems of the middle-aged*. Springfield, Ill.: Charles C Thomas, 1965, pp. 199–202.

236 Wilensky, H. L., and H. Edwards: The skidder: Ideological achievements of downward mobile workers. *Amer. sociol Rev.*, 1959, **24**, 215–231.

237 Worell, L.: Level of aspiration and academic success. *J. educ. Psychol.*, 1959, **50**, 47–54.

238 Wylie, R. C., and E. B. Hutchins: School-work-ability estimates and aspirations as a function of socioeconomic level, race, and sex. *Psychol. Rep.*, 1967, **21**, 781–808.

239 Zeligs, R.: Trends in children's New Year's resolutions. *J. exp. Educ.*, 1957, **26**, 133–150.

240 Zuckerman, H.: Nobel laureates in science: Patterns of productivity, collaboration, and authorship. *Amer. sociol. Rev.*, 1967, **32**, 391–403.

241 Zunich, M.: Children's reactions to failure. *J. genet. Psychol.*, 1964, **104**, 19–24.

CHAPTER 11

1 Adler, A.: *Problems of neurosis*. New York: Cosmopolitan Book Corp., 1930.

2 Allen, D. A.: Anti-femininity in men. *Amer. sociol. Rev.*, 1954, **19**, 591–593.

3 Allport, G. W.: *Pattern and growth in personality*. New York: Holt, 1961.

4 Altus, W. D.: Birth order and its sequelae. *Science*, 1966, **151**, 44–49.

5 Alvarez, W. C.: Sexual life of the aging. *Geriatrics*, 1957, **12**, 141–142.

6 Angelino, H., and E. V. Mech: Some "first" sources of sex information as reported by sixty-seven college women. *J. Psychol.*, 1955, **39**, 321–324.

7 Angrilli, A. F.: The psychosexual identification of pre-school boys. *J. genet. Psychol.*, 1960, **97**, 329–340.

8 Angrist, S. S.: Role constellation as a variable in women's leisure activities. *Soc. Forces*, 1967, **45**, 423–431.

9 Ausubel, D. P.: Ego development among segregated Negro children. *Ment. Hyg.*, N.Y., 1958, **42**, 362–369.

10 Axelson, L. J.: The marital adjustment and marital role definitions of husbands of working and nonworking wives. *Marriage fam. Living*, 1963, **25**, 189–195.

11 Bailyn, L.: Mass media and children: A study of exposure habits and cognitive effects. *Psychol. Monogr.*, 1959, **73**, no. 1.

12 Baker, L. G.: A comparison of the personal and social adjustments of 38 never-married and 38 married women. *Dissert. Abstr.*, 1967, **28** (2–A), 775–776.

13 Barclay, A., and D. R. Cusumano: Father absence, cross-sex identity, and field dependent behavior in male adolescents. *Child Develpm.*, 1967, **38**, 243–250.

14 Barry, H., M. K. Bacon, and I. L. Child: A cross-cultural survey of some sex differences in socialization. *J. abnorm. soc. Psychol.*, 1957, **55**, 327–332.

15 Beigel, H. G.: Body height and mate selection. *J. soc. Psychol.*, 1954, **39**, 257–268.

16 Beiliaukas, V. G.: Recent advances in the psychology of masculinity and femininity. *J. Psychol.*, 1965, **60**, 255–263.

17 Beilin, H., and E. Werner: Sex role expectations and criteria of social adjustment for young adults. *J. clin. Psychol.*, 1957, **13**, 341–343.

18 Bennett, E. M., and L. R. Cohen: Men and women: Personality patterns and contrasts. *Genet. Psychol. Monogr.*, 1959, **59**, 101–155.

19 Bergler, E.: *The revolt of the middle-aged man.* New York: Wyn, 1954.

20 Bernard, J.: The fourth revolution. *J. soc. Issues*, 1966, **22**, no. 2, 76–87.

21 Biller, H. B.: Father dominance and sex-role development in kindergarten-age boys. *Develpm. Psychol.*, 1969, **1**, 87–94.

22 Biller, H. B., and L. J. Borstelman: Masculine development: An integrative review. *Merrill-Palmer Quart.*, 1967, **13**, 253–294.

23 Birdwhistell, M.: Adolescents and the pill culture. *Family Coordinator*, 1968, **17**, 27–32.

24 Blaine, G. B.: Sex and the adolescent. *N.Y. State J. Med.*, 1967, **67**, 1967–1975.

25 Blakely, W. P.: A study of seventh grade children's reading of comic books as related to certain other variables. *J. genet. Psychol.*, 1958, **93**, 291–301.

26 Bledsoe, J. C., and I. D. Brown: The interests of preadolescents: A longitudinal study. *J. exp. Educ.*, 1965, **33**, 337–344.

27 Blood, R. O.: Long-range causes and consequences of the employment of married women. *J. Marriage & Family*, 1965, **27**, 43–47.

28 Boring, E. G.: The woman problem. *Amer. Psychologist*, 1951, **6**, 679–692.

29 Bossard, J. H. S., and E. S. Boll: *The sociology of child development*, 4th ed. New York: Harper & Row, 1966.

30 Breckenridge, M. E., and E. L. Vincent: *Child development*, 5th ed. Philadelphia: Saunders, 1965.

31 Brim, O. G.: Family structure and sex role learning by children: A further analysis of Helen Koch's data. *Sociometry*, 1958, **21**, 1–16.

32 Broderick, C. B., and G. P. Rowe: A scale of preadolescent heterosexual development. *J. Marriage & Family*, 1968, **30**, 97–101.

33 Brotman, J., and R. J. Senter: Attitudes toward feminism in different national student groups. *J. soc. Psychol.*, 1968, **76**, 137–138.

34 Brown, D. G.: Sex-role development in a changing culture. *Psychol. Bull.*, 1958, **55**, 232–242.

35 Brown, D. G.: Psychosexual disturbances: Transvestism and sex-role inversion. *Marriage fam. Living*, 1960, **22**, 218–227.

36 Brown, D. G., and D. B. Lynn: Human sexual development: An outline of components and concepts. *J. Marriage & Family*, 1966, **28**, 155–162.

37 Brown, M. H., and J. E. Bryan: Sex as a variable in intelligence test performance. *J. educ. Psychol.*, 1957, **48**, 273–278.

38 Bühler, C., A. Brind, and A. Horner: Old age as a phase of human life. *Hum. Develpm.*, 1968, **11**, 53–63.

39 Burchinal, L. G.: Sources and adequacy of sex knowledge among Iowa high school girls. *Marriage fam. Living*, 1960, **22**, 268–269.

40 Cameron, P.: Note on time spent thinking about sex. *Psychol. Rep.*, 1967, **20**, 741–742.

41 Carey, G. L.: Sex differences in problem-solving performance as a function of attitude differences. *J. abnorm. soc. Psychol.*, 1958, **56**, 256–260.

42 Child, I. L., E. H. Potter, and E. M. Levine: Children's textbooks and personality development: An exploration in the social psychology of education. *Psychol. Monogr.*, 1946, **60**, no. 3.

43 Chilman, C. S., and D. L. Meyer: Single and married undergraduates' measured personality needs and self-rated happiness. *J. Marriage & Family*, 1966, **28**, 67–76.

44 Christensen, H. T. and G. R. Carpenter: Timing patterns in the development of sexual intimacy: An attitudinal report on three modern Western societies. *Marriage fam. Living*, 1962, **24**, 30–35.

45 Christensen, H. T., and M. M. Swihart: Postgraduate role preferences of senior women in college. *Marriage fam. Living*, 1956, **18**, 52–57.

46 Christenson, C. V., and J. H. Gagnon: Sexual behavior in a group of older women. *J. Geront.*, 1965, **20**, 351–356.

47 Clark, A. L., and P. Wallin: Women's sexual responsiveness and the duration and quality of their marriages. *Amer. J. Sociol.*, 1965, **71**, 187–196.

48 Coleman, J. S.: *The adolescent society.* New York: Free Press, 1961.

49 Collier, M. J., and E. L. Gaier: The hero in the preferred childhood stories of college men. *Amer. Imago*, 1959, **16**, 177–194.

50 Cooper, A. J.: "Neurosis" and disorders of sexual potency in the male. *J. psychosom. Res.*, 1968, **12**, 141–144.

51 Cronbach, L. J.: *Educational psychology*, 2d ed. New York: Harcourt, Brace & World, 1963.

52 Crow, L. D., and A. Crow: *Adolescent development and adjustment*, 2d ed. New York: McGraw-Hill, 1965.

53 Dean, D. G.: Emotional maturity and marital adjustment. *J. Marriage & Family*, 1966, **28**, 454–457.

54 Dedman, J.: The relationship between religious attitude and attitude toward premarital sex relations. *Marriage fam. Living*, 1959, **21**, 171–176.

55 Deegan, D. Y.: *The stereotype of the single woman in American novels: A social study with implications for the education of women.* New York: King's Crown, 1951.

56 Deutscher, I.: The quality of postparental life: Definitions of the situation. *J. Marriage & Family*, 1964, **26**, 52–59.

57 Devereux, E. C., U. Bronfenbrenner, and R. R. Rodgers: Child-rearing in England and the United States: A cross-national comparison. *J. Marriage & Family*, 1969, **31**, 257–270.

58 Doty, C. N., and R. M. Hoeflin: A descriptive study of thirty-five unmarried graduate women. *J. Marriage & Family*, 1964, **26**, 91–94.

59 Dreger, R. M.: Spontaneous conversations and story-telling of children in a naturalistic setting. *J. Psychol.*, 1955, **40**, 163–180.

60 Dubbe, M. C.: What parents are not told

may hurt. *Family Life Coordinator*, 1965, **14**, 51–118.

61 DuHamel, T. R., and H. B. Biller: Parental imitation and non-imitation in young children. *Develpm. Psychol.*, 1969, **1**, 772.

62 Dunbar, F.: Homeostasis during puberty. *Amer. J. Psychiat.*, 1958, **114**, 673–682.

63 Dunn, M. S.: Marriage role expectations of adolescents. *Marriage fam. Living*, 1960, **22**, 99–111.

64 Dye, N. W., and P. S. Very: Growth changes in factorial structure by age and sex. *Genet. Psychol. Monogr.*, 1968, **78**, 55–88.

65 Ehrmann, W. W.: *Premarital dating behavior.* New York: Holt, 1959.

66 Ellis, A.: Healthy and disturbed reasons for having extramarital relations. *J. hum. Relat.*, 1968, **16**, 490–501.

67 Emmerich, W.: Parental identification in young children. *Genet. Psychol. Monogr.*, 1959, **60**, 257–308.

68 Empey, L. T.: Role expectations of young women regarding marriage and a career. *Marriage fam. Living*, 1958, **20**, 152–155.

69 Farnsworth, D. L.: Sexual morality and the dilemma of the college. *Amer. J. Orthopsychiat.*, 1965, **35**, 676–681.

70 Freeman, J. T.: Sexual capacities in the aging male. *Geriatrics*, 1961, **16**, 37–43.

71 Freud, A.: *Safeguarding the emotional health of our children.* New York: Child Welfare League of America, 1955.

72 Freud, S.: *The standard edition of the complete psychological works of Sigmund Freud.* London: Hogarth, 1953–1962.

73 Fryrear, J. L., and M. H. Thelen: Effect of sex model and sex of observer on the emulation of affectionate behavior. *Develpm. Psychol.*, 1969, **1**, 298.

74 Gagnon, J. H., and W. Siman: They're going to learn in the streets anyway. *Psychology Today*, July 1969, pp. 46–47, 71.

75 Gallagher, J. R.: That favorite teacher: A parent's enemy or ally? *Marriage fam. Living*, 1961, **23**, 400–402.

76 Garai, J. E., and A. Scheinfeld: Sex differences in mental and behavioral traits. *Genet. Psychol. Monogr.*, 1968, **77**, 169–299.

77 Gebhard, P. H.: Factors in marital orgasm. *J. soc. Issues*, 1966, **22**, no. 2, 88–95.

78 Geiken, K. F.: Expectations concerning husband-wife responsibilities in the home. *J. Marriage & Family*, 1964, **26**, 349–352.

79 *Geriatric Focus* Report: Sexual difficulties after 50. 1966, **5**, no. 5.

80 Gesell, A., F. L. Ilg, and L. B. Ames: *Youth: The years from ten to sixteen.* New York: Harper & Row, 1956.

81 Ginsberg, E.: The changing pattern of women's work: Some psychological correlates. *Amer. J. Orthopsychiat.*, 1958, **28**, 313–321.

82 Goldberg, S., and M. Lewis: Play behavior in the year-old infant: Early sex differences. *Child Develpm.*, 1969, **40**, 21–31.

83 Goodenough, W.: Interest in persons as an aspect of sex differences in the early years. *Genet. Psychol. Monogr.*, 1957, **55**, 287–323.

84 Gray, S. W.: Masculinity and femininity in relation to anxiety and social acceptance. *Child Develpm.*, 1957, **28**, 203–214.

85 Hacker, H. M.: Women as a minority group. *Soc. Forces*, 1951, **30**, 60–69.

86 Hall, E.: Ordinal position and success in engagement and marriage. *J. ind. Psychol.*, 1965, **21**, 154–158.

87 Hall, M., and R. A. Keith: Sex-role preference among children of upper and lower social class. *J. soc. Psychol.*, 1964, **62**, 101–110.

88 Halleck, S. L.: Sex and mental health on the campus. *J. Amer. med. Ass.*, 1967, **200**, 684–690.

89 Harrell-Bond, B. E.: Conjugal role behavior. *Hum. Relat.*, 1969, **22**, 77–91.

90 Harris, D. B., and S. C. Tseng: Children's attitudes toward peers and parents as revealed by sentence completions. *Child Develpm.*, 1957, **28**, 401–411.

91 Harsh, C. M., and H. G. Schrickel: *Personality: Development and assessment*, 2d ed. New York: Ronald, 1959.

92 Hartley, R. E.: Children's perceptions of sex preference in four culture groups. *J. Marriage & Family*, 1969, **31**, 380–387.

93 Hartley, R. E., and F. P. Hardesty: Children's perceptions of sex roles in childhood. *J. genet. Psychol.*, 1964, **105**, 43–51.

94 Hartup, W. W., S. G. Moore, and G. Sager: Avoidance of inappropriate sex-typing in young children. *J. consult. Psychol.*, 1963, **27**, 467–473.

95 Havighurst, R. J.: The leisure activities of the middle-aged. *Amer. J. Sociol.*, 1957, **63**, 152–162.

96 Heilbrun, A. B.: Conformity to masculinity-feminity stereotypes and ego identity in adolescents. *Psychol. Rep.*, 1964, **14**, 351–357.

97 Henton, J. M.: The effects of married high school students on their unmarried classmates. *J. Marriage & Family*, 1964, **26**, 87–88.

98 Hilgard, E. R.: *Introduction to psychology*, 4th ed. New York: Harcourt, Brace & World, 1962.

99 Hill, D. L., and R. H. Walters: Interaction of sex of subject and dependency training procedures in a social-reinforcement study. *Merrill-Palmer Quart.*, 1969, **15**, 185–198.

100 Hilliard, M.: *Women and fatigue: A woman doctor's answer.* Garden City, N.Y.: Doubleday, 1960.

101 Hobbs, D. E.: Transition to parenthood: A replication and an extension. *J. Marriage & Family*, 1968, **30**, 413–417.

102 Hurvitz, N.: Marital roles strain as a sociological variable. *Family Life Coordinator*, 1965, **14**, 39–42.

103 Irish, D. P.: Sibling interaction: A neglected aspect of family life research. *Soc. Forces*, 1964, **42**, 279–288.

104 Jahoda, M., and J. Havel: Psychological problems of women in different social roles. *Educ. Recal.*, 1955, **36**, 325–335.

105 Jersild, A. T.: *Child psychology*, 6th ed. Englewood Cliffs, N.J.: Prentice-Hall, 1969.

106 Johnson, M. M.: Sex role learning in the nuclear family. *Child Develpm.*, 1963, **34**, 319–333.

107 Johnstone, J., and E. Katz: Youth and popular music: A study in the sociology of taste. *Amer. J. Sociol.*, 1957, **62**, 563–568.

108 Jones, M. C.: Psychological correlates of somatic development. *Child Develpm.*, 1965, **36**, 899–911.

109 Josselyn, I. M.: Psychology of fatherliness. *Smith Coll. Stud. soc. Wk.*, 1956, **26**, 1–13.

110 Jourard, S. M.: *Personal adjustment*, 2d ed. New York: Macmillan, 1963.

111 Kammeyer, K.: The feminine role: An analysis of attitude consistency. *J. Marriage & Family*, 1964, **26**, 295–305.

112 Karen, R. L.: Some variables affecting sexual attitudes, behavior and inconsistency. *Marriage fam. Living*, 1959, **21**, 235–239.

113 Kassel, V.: Polygyny after 60. *Geriatrics*, 1966, **21**, 214–218.

114 Kenkel, W. F.: Traditional family ideology and spousal roles in decision making. *Marriage fam. Living*, 1959, **21**, 334–339.

115 Khatri, A. A., and B. B. Siddiqui: "A boy or a girl?" Preferences of parents for sex of offspring as perceived by East Indian and American children: A cross-cultural study. *J. Marriage & Family*, 1969, **31**, 388–393.

116 Kiell, N., and B. Friedman: Culture lag and housewifemanship: The role of the married female college graduate. *J. educ. Sociol.*, 1957, **31**, 87–95.

117 Kinsey, A. C., W. B. Pomeroy, and C. E. Martin: *Sexual behavior in the human male.* Philadelphia: Saunders, 1948.

118 Kinsey, A. C., W. B. Pomeroy, C. E. Martin, and P. H. Gebhard: *Sexual behavior in the human female.* Philadelphia: Saunders, 1953.

119 Kirkendall, L. A.: Toward a clarification of the concept of male sex drive. *Marriage fam. Living*, 1958, **20**, 367–372.

120 Koch, H. L.: The relation of certain formal attributes of siblings to attitudes held toward each other and toward their parents. *Monogr. Soc. Res. Child Develpm.*, 1960, **25**, no. 4.

121 Kogan, K. L., and J. K. Jackson: Conventional sex-role stereotypes and actual perceptions. *Psychol. Rep.*, 1963, **13**, 27–30.

122 Kotlar, S. L.: Middle-class marital role perceptions and marital adjustment. *Sociol. soc. Res.*, 1965, **49**, 283–293.

123 Kreitler, H., and S. Kreitler: Children's concepts of sexuality and birth. *Child Develpm.*, 1966, **37**, 363–378.

124 Kuhlen, R. G., and N. B. Houlihan: Adolescent heterosexual interest in 1942 and 1963. *Child Develpm.*, 1965, **36**, 1049–1052.

125 Levin, P. L.: Road from Sophocles to Spock. *The New York Times*, June 28, 1960.

126 Levinger, G.: Systematic distortion in spouses' reports of preferred and actual sexual behavior. *Sociometry*, 1966, **29**, 291–299.

127 Lloyd-Jones, E.: Women today and their education. *Teachers Coll. Rec.*, 1955, **57**, 1–7.

128 Lopata, H. Z.: The life cycle of the social role of housewife. *Sociol. soc. Res.*, 1966, **51**, 5–22.

129 Luckey, E. B., and G. D. Nass: A comparison of sexual attitudes and behavior in an international sample. *J. Marriage & Family*, 1969, **31**, 364–379.

130 Lynn, D. B.: Divergent feedback and sex-role identification in boys and men. *Merrill-Palmer Quart.*, 1964, **10**, 17–23.

131 Maccoby, E. E., W. C. Wilson, and R. V. Burton: Differential movie-viewing behavior by male and female viewers. *J. Pers.*, 1958, **26**, 259–267.

132 Marshall, H. R.: Relations between home experiences and children's use of language in play interactions with peers. *Psychol. Monogr.*, 1961, **75**, no. 5.

133 Mason, E. P.: Cross-validation study of personality characteristics of junior high students from American, Indian-Mexican and Caucasian ethnic backgrounds. *J. soc. Psychol.*, 1969, **77**, 15–24.

134 Masters, W. H., and V. E. Johnson: *Human sexual response.* Boston: Little, Brown, 1965.

135 McDaniel, C. O.: Dating roles and reasons for dating. *J. Marriage & Family*, 1969, **31**, 97–107.

136 McGee, L. C.: The suicidal cult of "manliness". *Today's Hlth*, Jan. 1957, pp. 28–30.

137 McKee, J. P., and A. C. Sherriffs: Men's and women's beliefs, ideals and self-concepts. *Amer. J. Sociol.*, 1959, **64**, 356–363.

138 Mead, M.: American man in a woman's world. *The New York Times*, Feb. 10, 1957.

139 Mead, M.: *Male and female.* New York: Dell, 1968.

140 Miller, H., and W. Wilson: Relation of sexual behavior, values, and conflict to avowed happiness and personal adjustment. *Psychol. Rep.*, 1967, **23**, 1075–1086.

141 Milton, G. A.: The effects of sex-role identification upon problem-solving skill. *J. abnorm. soc. Psychol.*, 1957, **55**, 208–212.

142 Minuchin, P.: Sex role concepts and sex typing in childhood as a function of school and home environments. *Child Develpm.*, 1965, **36**, 1033–1048.

143 Montagu, A.: *Prenatal influences.* Springfield, Ill.: Charles C Thomas, 1962.

144 Moser, A. J.: Marriage role expectations of high school students. *Marriage fam. Living*, 1961, **23**, 42–43.

145 Moss, J. J., and R. Gingles: The relationship of personality to the incidence of early marriage. *Marriage fam. Living*, 1959, **21**, 373–377.

146 Mussen, P. H.: Long-term consequents of masculinity of interests in adolescence. *J. consult. Psychol.*, 1962, **26**, 435–440.

147 Mussen, P. H., J. J. Conger, and J. Kagan: *Child development and personality*, 3d ed. New York: Harper & Row, 1969.

148 Nadler, E. B., and W. R. Morrow: Authoritarian attitudes toward women and their correlates. *J. soc. Psychol.*, 1959, **49**, 113–123.

149 *New York Times* Report: Lazy husbands said to fatigue wives. Apr. 3, 1966.

150 *New York Times* Report: Youth views seen shifting on sex. June 22, 1969.

151 Olsen, M. E.: Distribution of family responsibilities and social stratification. *Marriage fam. Living*, 1960, **22**, 60–65.

152 Orden, S. R., and N. M. Bradburn: Working wives and marriage happiness. *Amer. J. Sociol.*, 1968, **74**, 392–407.

153 Ovesey, L.: Masculine aspirations in women. *Psychiatry*, 1956, **19**, 341–351.

154 Packard, V.: *The status seekers.* New York: Pocket Books, 1961.

155 Packard, V.: *The pyramid climbers.* New York: McGraw-Hill, 1962.

156 Papanek, M. L.: Authority and sex roles in the family. *J. Marriage & Family*, 1969, **31**, 88–96.

157 Paris, B. L., and E. B. Luckey: A longitudinal study of marital satisfaction. *Sociol. soc. Res.*, 1966, **50**, 212–22.

158 Parker, E.: *The seven ages of woman.* Baltimore: Johns Hopkins, 1960.

159 Peck, R. F., and R. J. Havighurst: *The psychology of character development.* New York: Wiley, 1962.

160 Pfeiffer, E., A. Verwoerdt, and H-S Wang:

Sexual behavior in aged men and women. *Arch. gen. Psychiat.*, 1968, **19**, 753–758.

161 Pickford, J. H., E. I. Signori, and H. Rempel: The intensity of personality traits in relation to marital happiness. *J. Marriage & Family*, 1966, **28**, 458–459.

162 Podell, L.: Sex and role conflict. *J. Marriage & Family*, 1966, **28**, 163–165.

163 Poffenberger, T., and D. Norton: Factors in the formation of attitudes toward mathematics. *J. educ. Res.*, 1959, **52**, 171–176.

164 Pressey, S. L., and A. W. Jones: 1923–1953 and 20–60 age changes in moral codes, anxieties, and interests, as shown by the "X-0 Tests." *J. Psychol.*, 1955, **39**, 485–502.

165 Rainwater, L.: A study of personality differences between middle and lower class adolescents: The Szondi Test in culture-personality research. *Genet. Psychol. Monogr.*, 1956, **54**, 3–86.

166 Rainwater, L.: Some aspects of lower class sexual behavior. *J. soc. Issues*, 1966, **22**, no. 2, 96–108.

167 Rollings, E. M.: Family situations of married and never-married males. *J. Marriage & Family*, 1966, **28**, 485–490.

168 Reese, H. W.: Attitudes toward the opposite sex in late childhood. *Merrill-Palmer Quart.*, 1966, **12**, 157–163.

169 Reevy, W. R.: Adolescent sexuality. In A. Ellis and A. Abarband (eds.), *The encyclopedia of sexual behavior*. New York: Hawthorn, 1961, pp. 52–67.

170 Reevy, W. R.: Child sexuality. In A. Ellis and A. Abarband (eds.); *The encyclopedia of sexual behavior*. New York: Hawthorn, 1961, pp. 258–267.

171 Reiss, I. L.: The sexual renaissance: A summary and analysis. *J. soc. Issues*, 1966, **22**, no. 2, 123–137.

172 Riesman, D.: Permissiveness and sex roles. *Marriage fam. Living*, 1953, **21**, 211–217.

173 Robinson, I. E., K. King, C. J. Dudley, and F. J. Chine: Change in sexual behavior and attitudes of college students. *Family Coordinator*, 1968, **17**, 119–123.

174 Rodgers, D. A., and F. J. Ziegler: Changes in sexual behavior consequent to use of noncoital procedure of contraceptives. *Psychosom. Med.*, 1968, **30**, 495–505.

175 Rosenberg, B. G., and B. Sutton-Smith: The measurement of masculinity and femininity in children: An extension and revalidation. *J. genet. Psychol.*, 1964, **104**, 259–264.

176 Rosenfeld, A.: Challenge to the miracle of life. *Life Mag.*, June 16, 1969, pp. 39–50.

177 Rosenkrantz, P., S. Vogel, H. Bee, I. Broverman, and D. M. Broverman: Sex-role stereotypes and self-concepts in college students. *J. consult. clin. Psychol.*, 1968, **32**, 287–295.

178 Rubin, I.: The "sexless older years": A socially harmful stereotype. *Ann. Amer. Acad. pol. soc. Sci.*, 1968, **376**, 86–95.

179 Rubin, I., and L. A. Kirkendall: *Sex in the adolescent years*. New York: Association Press, 1968.

180 Rubin, Z.: Do American women marry up? *Amer. sociol. Rev.*, 1968, **33**, 750–760.

181 Ryan, M. S.: *Clothing: A study in human behavior*. New York: Holt, 1966.

182 Rybak, W.: Notes on crushes and hero-worship of adolescents. *Psychiat. Quart. Supp..*, 1969, **39**, 48–53.

183 Scheinfeld, A.: *Your heredity and environment*. Philadelphia: Lippincott, 1965.

184 Schell, R. E., and J. W. Silber: Sex-role discrimination among young children. *Percept. mot. Skills*, 1968, **27**, 379–389.

185 Searls, L. G.: Leisure role emphasis of college graduate homemakers. *J. Marriage & Family*, 1966, **28**, 77–82.

186 Sears, R. R., E. E. Maccoby, and H. Levin: *Patterns of child rearing*. New York: Harper & Row, 1957.

187 Segal, B. E.: Male nurses: A case study in status contradiction and prestige loss. *Soc. Forces*, 1962, **41**, 31–38.

188 Sessoms, A. D.: An analysis of selected variables affecting outdoor recreation patterns. *Soc. Forces*, 1963, **42**, 112–115.

189 Seward, G. H.: *Sex and the social order*. New York: McGraw-Hill, 1946.

190 Seward, G. H., and W. R. Larson: Adolescent concepts of social sex roles in the United States and the two Germanies. *Hum. Develpm.*, 1968, **11**, 217–248.

191 Sexton, P. C.: Schools are emasculating our boys. *Child & Family*, 1967, **6**, no. 1, 56–58.

192 Shaffer, L. F., and E. J. Shoben: *The psychology of adjustment*, 2d ed. Boston: Houghton Mifflin, 1956.

193 Shainess, N.: Images of woman: Past and present, overt and obscured. *Amer. J. Psychother.*, 1969, **23**, 77–97.

194 Shipman, G.: The psychodynamics of sex education. *Family Coordinator*, 1968, **17**, 3–12.

195 Shock, N. W.: The physiology of aging. *Scient. American*, 1962, **206**, no. 1, 100–110.

196 Slovic, P.: Risk-taking in children: Age and sex differences. *Child Develpm.*, 1966, **37**, 169–176.

197 Smigel, E. O., and R. Seiden: The decline and fall of the "double standard." *Ann. Amer. Acad. pol. soc. Sci.*, 1968, **379**, 6–17.

198 Sporakowski, M. J.: Marital preparedness, prediction and adjustment. *Family Coordinator*, 1968, **17**, 155–161.

199 Stagner, R.: *Psychology of personality*, 3d ed. New York: McGraw-Hill, 1961.

200 Stein, A. H., and J. Smithhells: Age and sex differences in children's sex-role standards about achievement. *Develpm. Psychol.*, 1969, **1**, 252–259.

201 Steinmann, A., and D. J. Fox: Male-female perceptions of the female role in the United States. *J. Psychol.*, 1966, **64**, 265–276.

202 Stevenson, H. W., G. A. Hale, K. T. Hill, and B. E. Mody: Determinants of children's preferences for adults. *Child Develpm.*, 1967, **38**, 1–14.

203 Stinnett, N., and J. E. Montgomery: Youths' perceptions of marriages of older persons. *J. Marriage & Family*, 1968, **30**, 392–396.

204 Strang, R.: *The adolescent views himself*. New York: McGraw-Hill, 1957.

205 Strodtbeck, F. L.: The interaction of the "henpecked" husband with his wife. *Marriage fam. Living*, 1952, **14**, 305–308.

206 Sutton-Smith, B., and B. G. Rosenberg: Manifest anxiety and game preferences in children. *Child Develpm.*, 1960, **31**, 307–311.

207 Taylor, P. T.: Children's evaluations of the characteristics of the good teacher. *Brit. J. educ. Psychol.*, 1962, **32**, 258–266.

208 Thorpe, L. P., and A. M. Schmuller: *Personality: An interdisciplinary approach*. Princeton, N.J.: Van Nostrand, 1958.

209 *Time* Report: Sex as a spectator sport. July 11, 1969, pp. 61–66.

210 Tolchin, M: Wife who wins battles may find she lost war. *The New York Times*, Mar. 24, 1960.

211 Torrance, E. P.: Changing reactions of preadolescent girls to tasks requiring creative scientific thinking. *J. genet. Psychol.*, 1963, **102**, 217–223.

212 Turner, R. H.: Some aspects of women's ambition. *Amer. J. Sociol.*, 1964, **70**, 271–285.

213 Udry, J. R.: Sex and family life. *Ann. Amer. Acad. pol. soc. Sci.*, 1968, **376**, 25–35.

214 *U.S. News & World Report*: Advice to businessmen on health and retirement. Mar. 7, 1966, pp. 62–67.

215 *U.S. News & World Report*: Why the furor over sex education. Aug. 4, 1969, pp. 44–46.

216 *U.S. News & World Report:* Woman's changing role in America. Sept. 8, 1969, pp. 44–46.

217 Vener, A. M., and C. A. Snyder: The preschool child's awareness and anticipation of adult sex roles. *Sociometry*, 1966, **29**, 159–168.

218 Vroegh, K.: Masculinity and femininity in the preschool years. *Child Develpm.*, 1968, **39**, 1253–1257.

219 Wagman, M.: Interests and values of career and homemaking oriented women. *Personnel Guid. J.*, 1966, **44**, 794–801.

220 Wallin, P., and A. L. Clark: Religiosity, sexual gratification, and marital satisfaction in the middle years of marriage. *Soc. Forces*, 1964, **42**, 303–309.

221 Walters, J., D. Pearce, and L. Dahms: Affectional and aggressive behavior of preschool children. *Child Develpm.*, 1957, **28**, 15–26.

222 Walters, P. A.: Promiscuity in adolescence. *Amer. J. Orthopsychiat.*, 1965, **35**, 670–675.

223 Ward, W. D.: Process of sex-role development. *Develpm. Psychol.*, 1969, **1**, 163–168.

224 Webb, A. P.: Sex-role preferences and adjustment in early adolescents. *Child Develpm.*, 1963, **34**, 609–618.

225 Werner, A. A.: Sex behavior and problems of the climacteric. In M. Fishbein and E. W. Burgess (eds.), *Successful marriage*, rev. ed. Garden City, N.Y.: Doubleday, 1955, pp. 475–490.

226 Whalen, R. E.: Sexual motivation. *Psychol. Rev.*, 1966, **73**, 151–163.

227 Winick, C.: The Beige Epoch: Depolorization of sex roles in America. *Ann. Amer. Acad. pol. soc. Sci.*, 1968, **376**, 18–24.

228 Witty, P. A.: Studies of children's interests: A brief summary. *Elem. Educ.*, 1960, **37**, 469–475.

229 Yourglich, A.: Explorations in sociological study of sibling systems. *Family Life Coordinator*, 1964, **13**, 91–94.

230 Zuk, G. H.: Sex-appropriate behavior in adolescence. *J. genet. Psychol.*, 1958, **93**, 15–32.

CHAPTER 12

1 Adams, B. N., and M. T. Meidam: Economics, family structure, and college attendance. *Amer. J. Sociol.*, 1968, **74**, 230–239.

2 Agras, S.: The relationship of school phobia to childhood depression. *Amer. J. Psychiat.*, 1959, **116**, 533–536.

3 Alexander, C. N.: Ordinal position and social mobility. *Sociometry*, 1968, **31**, 285–293.

4 Allen, E. A.: Attitudes of children and adolescents in school. *Educ. Res.*, 1960, **3**, 65–80.

5 Allen, G. B., and J. M. Masling: An evaluation of the effects of nursery school training on children in the kindergarten, first and second grades. *J. educ. Res.*, 1957, **51**, 285–296.

6 Allport, G. W.: Prejudice: Is it societal or personal? *Relig. Educ.*, 1964, **59**, 20–29.

7 Altus, W. D.: Birth order and its sequelae. *Science*, 1966, **151**, 44–49.

8 Amatora, Sister M.: School interests in later childhood. *Education*, 1960, **81**, 32–37.

9 Ames, R.: Physical maturing among boys as related to adult social behavior. *Calif. J. educ. Res.*, 1957, **8**, 69–75.

10 Anderson, H. H., G. L. Anderson, I. H. Cohen, and F. D. Nutt: Image of the teacher by adolescents in four countries: Germany, England, Mexico and the United States. *J. soc. Psychol.*, 1959, **50**, 47–53.

11 Anderson, J. A., and J. C. Follman: Attitudes of dropouts toward school. *Psychol. Rep.*, 1968, **23**, 1142.

12 Astin, A. W.: Personal and environmental factors associated with college dropouts among high aptitude students. *J. educ. Psychol.*, 1964, **55**, 219–227.

13 Auster, D., and J. Moldstad: A survey of parents' reactions and opinions concerning certain aspects of education. *J. educ. Sociol.*, 1957, **31**, 64–74.

14 Ausubel, D. P.: Ego development among segregated Negro children. *Ment. Hyg., N.Y.*, 1958, **42**, 362–369.

15 Axtell, J. B., and M. W. Edmunds: The effect of preschool experience on fathers, mothers, and children. *Calif. J. educ. Res.*, 1960, **11**, 195–203.

16 Bach, M. C.: Factors related to student participation in campus social organizations. *J. soc. Psychol.*, 1961, **54**, 337–348.

17 Baer, C. J.: The school progress and adjustment of underage and overage students. *J. educ. Psychol.*, 1958, **49**, 17–19.

18 Baird, C. L.: The role of the teacher of six and seven year-old children. *Brit. J. educ. Psychol.*, 1968, **38**, 323–324.

19 Baird, L. L.: The achievement of bright and average students. *Educ. psychol. Measmt.*, 1968, **28**, 891–899.

20 Baltzell, E. D.: *Philadelphia gentleman*. New York: Free Press, 1958.

21 Beardslee, D. C., and D. D. O'Dowd: The college-student image of the scientist. *Science*, 1961, **133**, 997–1001.

22 Beichman, A.: Will teacher be the new drop-out? *The New York Times*, Dec. 7, 1969.

23 Beilin, H.: Teachers' and clinicians' attitudes toward the behavior problems of children: A reapprasial. *Child Develpm.*, 1959, **30**, 9–25.

24 Bene, E.: Some differences between middle-class and working-class boys in their attitudes toward education. *Brit. J. Sociol.*, 1959, **10**, 148–152.

25 Bernard, J.: The fourth revolution. *J. soc. Issues*, 1966, **22**, no. 2, 76–87.

26 Blakely, W. P.: A study of seventh grade children's reading of comic books as related to certain other variables. *J. genet. Psychol.*, 1958, **93**, 291–301.

27 Bloom, B. S., and H. Webster: The outcome of college. *Rev. educ. Res.*, 1960, **30**, 321–333.

28 Bonney, M. E., and E. L. Nicholson: Comparative social adjustments of elemetary school pupils with and without preschool training. *Child Develpm.*, 1958, **29**, 125–133.

29 Bordua, J. D.: Educational aspirations and parental stress on college. *Soc. Forces*, 1960, **38**, 262–269.

30 Boroff, D.: American fetish: The college degree. *The New York Times*, Feb. 14, 1960.

31 Boshier, R., and P. N. Hamid: Academic success and self-concept. *Psychol. Rep.*, 1968, **22**, 1191–1192.

32 Bossard, J. H. S., and E. S. Boll: *The sociology of child development*, 4th ed. New York: Harper & Row, 1966.

33 Bower, E. M., and J. A. Holmes: Emotional factors and academic achievement. *Rev. educ. Res.*, 1959, **29**, 529–544.

34 Bowerman, C. E., and J. W. Kinch: Changes in family and peer orientation of children between the fourth and tenth grades. *Soc. Forces*, 1959, **37**, 206–211.

35 Breckenridge, M. E., and E. L. Vincent: *Child development*, 5th ed. Philadelphia: Saunders, 1965.

36 Brodie, R. D., and M. R. Winterbottom: Failure of elementary school boys as a function of traumata, secrecy and derogation. *Child Develpm.*, 1967, **38**, 701–711.

37 Bronzaft, A. L.: Test anxiety, social mobility, and academic achievement. *J. soc. Psychol.*, 1968, **75**, 217–222.

38 Brookover, W. B., S. Thomas, and A. Paterson: Self-concept of ability and school achievement. *Sociology of Education*, 1964, **37**, 271–278.

39 Brown, A. W., and R. G. Hunt: Relations between nursery school attendance and teachers' ratings of some aspects of children's adjustment in kindergarten. *Child Develpm.*, 1961, **32**, 585–596.

40 Bühler, C.: School as a phase of human life. *Education*, 1952, **73**, 219–222.

41 Campbell, R. J.: Coeducation: Attitudes and self-concepts of girls at three schools. *Brit. J. educ. Psychol.*, 1969, **39**, 87.

42 Carter, H. D.: Over-achievers and under-achievers in the junior high school. *Calif. J. educ. Res.*, 1961, **12**, 51–56.

43 Chansky, N. M.: How students see their teacher. *Ment. Hyg., N.Y.*, 1958, **42**, 118–120.

44 Chase, J. A.: A study of the impact of grade retention on primary school children. *J. Psychol.*, 1968, **70**, 169–177.

45 Cheong, G. S. C., and M. V. DeVault: Pupils' perceptions of teachers. *J. educ. Res.*, 1966, **59**, 446–449.

46 Chopra, S. L.: A comparative study of underachieving students of high intellectual ability. *Except. Children*, 1967, **33**, 631–634.

47 Christensen, C. M.: Relationships between pupil achievement, pupil affect-need, teacher warmth, and teacher permissiveness. *J. educ. Psychol.*, 1960, **51**, 169–174.

48 Clarke, H., and A. L. Olson: Characteristics of 15-year-old boys who demonstrate various accomplishments or difficulties. *Child Develpm.*, 1965, **36**, 559–567.

49 Clarke, J. H.: The image of the teacher. *Brit. J. educ. Psychol.*, 1968, **38**, 280–285.

50 Cohen, E. G.: Parental factors in educational mobility. *Sociology of Education*, 1965, **38**, 404–425.

51 Coleman, J. S.: The adolescent subculture and academic achievement. *Amer. J. Sociol.*, 1960, **65**, 337–347.

52 Coleman, J. S.: *The adolescent society*. New York: Free Press, 1961.

53 Coleman, J. S.: Athletics in high school. *Ann. Amer. Acad. pol. soc. Sci.*, 1961, **338**, 33–42.

54 Coleman, J. S.: Teen-agers and their crowd. *PTA Mag.*, 1962, **56**, no. 7, 4–7.

55 Condon, M. E.: Extracurricular activities of physically handicapped children. *Personnel Guid. J.*, 1958, **37**, 53–54.

56 Cooper, J. B., and J. H. Lewis: Parent evaluation as related to social ideology and academic achievement. *J. genet. Psychol.*, 1962, **101**, 135–143.

57 Cottle, T. J.: Family perceptions, sex role identity and the prediction of school performance. *Educ. psychol. Measmt.*, 1968, **28**, 861–886.

58 Crowder, T., and J. J. Gallagher: The adjustment of gifted children in the regular classroom: Case studies. *Except. Children*, 1957, **23**, 353–366, 396.

59 Cruickshank, W. M., and G. O. Johnson (eds.): *Education of exceptional children and youth*, 2d ed. Englewood Cliffs, N.J.: Prentice-Hall, 1967.

60 Cummins, R. E.: Research insights into the relationship between teachers' acceptance attitudes, their role concepts and childrens' acceptance attitudes. *J. educ. Res.*, 1960, **53**, 197–198.

61 Dale, R. R.: Pupil-teacher relationships in co-educational and single-sex grammar schools. *Brit. J. educ. Psychol.*, 1966, **36**, 267–271.

62 Dansereau, H. K.: Work and the teen-ager. *Ann. Amer. Acad. pol. soc. Sci.*, 1961, **338**, 44–52.

63 Davidson, H. H., and G. Lang: Children's perceptions of their teachers' feeling toward them related to self-perception, school achievement, and behavior. *J. exp. Educ.*, 1960, **29**, 107–118.

64 Demos, G. M.: Attitudes of student ethnic groups on issues related to education. *Calif. J. educ. Res.*, 1960, **11**, 204–206.

65 Denmark, F., and M. Guttentag: The effect of college attendance on mature women: Changes in self-concept and evaluation of student role. *J. soc. Psychol.*, 1966, **69**, 155–158.

66 D'Heurle, A., J. C. Mellinger, and E. A. Haggard: Personality, intellectual and achievement patterns in gifted children. *Psychol. Monogr.*, 1959, **73**, no. 13.

67 Diedrich, R. C., and P. W. Jackson: Satisfied and dissatisfied students. *Personnel Guid. J.*, 1969, **47**, 641–649.

68 Doris, J.: Test anxiety and blame assignment in grade school children. *J. abnorm. soc. Psychol.*, 1959, **58**, 181–190.

69 Drasgow, J.: Underachievers. *J. counsel. Psychol.*, 1957, **4**, 210–211.

70 Dudek, E. Z., and E. P. Lester: The good child facade in chronic underachievers. *Amer. J. Orthopsychiat.*, 1968, **38**, 153–158.

71 Duncan, O. D., A. O. Haller, and A. Portes: Peer influence on aspirations: A reinterpretation. *Amer. J. Sociol.*, 1968, **74**, 119–137.

72 Dutton, W. H.: Another look at attitudes of junior high school pupils toward arithmetic. *Elem. Sch. J.*, 1968, **68**, 265–268.

73 Eckland, B. K.: Social class and college

graduation: Some misconceptions corrected. *Amer. J. Sociol.*, 1964, **70**, 36–50.

74 Elder, G. H.: Achievement motivation and intelligence in occupational mobility: A longitudinal analysis. *Sociometry*, 1968, **31**, 327–354

75 Elkins, D.: Some factors related to the choice-status of ninety eighth-grade children in a school society. *Genet. Psychol. Monogr.*, 1958, **58**, 207–272.

76 Elliott, D. S.: Delinquency, school attendance, and dropout. *Soc. Probl.*, 1966, **13**, 307–314.

77 Epperson, D. C.: Some interpersonal and performance correlates of classroom alienation. *School Review*, 1963, **71**, 360–376.

78 Estvan, F. J., and E. W. Estvan: *The child's world: His social perception.* New York: Putnam, 1959.

79 Farnsworth, D. L.: Emotions and learning. *Harv. educ. Rev.*, 1955, **25**, 95–104.

80 Finlayson, D. S., and L. Cohen: The teacher's role: A comparative study of the conceptions of college educated students and head teachers. *Brit. J. educ. Psychol.*, 1967, **37**, 22–31.

81 Fitzsimmons, S. J., J. Cheever, E. Leonard, and D. Macunovich: School failure: Now and tomorrow. *Develpm. Psychol.*, 1969, **1**, 135–146.

82 Flaherty, Sister M. R., and E. Reutzel: Personality traits of high and low achievers in college. *J. educ. Res.*, 1965, **58**, 409–411.

83 Flanders, N. A., B. M. Morrison, and E. L. Brode: Changes in pupil attitudes during the school year. *J. educ. Psychol.*, 1968, **50**, 334–338.

84 Frandsen, A., and M. Sorenson: Interests as motives in academic achievement. *J. sch. Psychol.*, 1968–1969, **7**, no. 1, 52–56.

85 Gallagher, J. J.: Peer acceptance of highly gifted children in elementary school. *Elem. Sch. J.*, 1958, **58**, 465–470.

86 Gerbner, G.: Images across cultures: Teachers in mass media fiction and drama. *School Review*, 1966, **74**, 212–230.

87 Gesell, A., F. L. Ilg, and L. B. Ames: *Youth: The years from ten to sixteen.* New York: Harper & Row, 1956.

88 Goldworth, M.: The effects of an elementary school fast-learning program on children's social relationships. *Except. Children*, 1959, **26**, 59–63.

89 Goodman, E.: A study of certain aspects of the social-emotional adjustment of non-promoted elementary school children. *Dissert. Abstr.*, 1968, **28** (10–A), 3997–3998.

90 Gregersen, G. F., and R. M. W. Travers: A study of the child's concept of the teacher. *J. educ. Res.*, 1968, **61**, 324–327.

91 Haggard, E. A.: Socialization, personality and academic achievement in gifted children. *School Review*, 1957, **65**, 388–414.

92 Hand, H. C.: Girls' choices of high school subjects. *J. Home Econ.*, 1960, **52**, 659–661.

93 Handler, M. S.: Professor sees education oversold as cure-all. *The New York Times*, July 18, 1969.

94 Harris, D. B.: How children learn interests. *49th Yearb. nat. Soc. Stud. Educ.*, 1950, pt. 1, pp. 129–135.

95 Harrison, F.: Aspirations as related to school performance and socioeconomic status. *Sociometry*, 1969, **32**, 70–79.

96 Harrison, F. I.: Relationship between home background, school success, and adolescent attitudes. *Merrill-Palmer Quart.*, 1968, **14**, 331–344.

97 Havighurst, R. J.: *Human development and education.* New York: Longmans, 1953.

98 Hechinger, F. M.: On cheating. *The New York Times*, Jan. 31, 1965.

99 Hechinger, F. M.: There are too many unwilling students. *The New York Times*, Dec. 14, 1969.

100 Heil, L. M., and C. Washburne: Characteristics of teachers related to children's progress. *J. teacher Educ.*, 1961, **12**, 401–406.

101 Heilbrun, A. B., and D. B. Waters: Underachievement as related to perceived maternal child rearing and academic conditions of reinforcement. *Child Develpm.*, 1968, **39**, 913–921.

102 Hemmerling, R. L., and H. Hurst: The effect of leisure time activities on scholastic achievement. *Calif. J. educ. Res.*, 1961, **12**, 86–90.

103 Henry, J.: Permissiveness and morality. *Ment. Hyg., N. Y.,*, 1961, **45**, 282–287.

104 Herriott, R. E.: Some social determinants of educational aspiration. *Harv. educ. Rev.*, 1963, **33**, 157–177.

105 Hess, R. D., and H. Goldman: Parents' views of the effect of television on their children. *Child Develpm.*, 1962, **33**, 411–426.

106 Hill, J. P.: Similarity and accordance between parents and sons in attitudes toward mathematics. *Child Develpm.*, 1967, **38**, 777–791.

107 Hill, J. P., and R. A. Kochendorfer: Knowledge of peer success and risk of detection as determinants of cheating. *Develpm. Psychol.*, 1969, **1**, 231–238.

108 Hilliard, P.: *Improving social learning in the elementary school.* New York: Teachers College 1954.

109 Hilliard, T., and R. M. Roth: Maternal attitudes and the non-achievement syndrome. *Personnel Guid. J.*, 1969, **47**, 424–428.

110 Hoffman, L. W., S. Rosen, and R. Lippitt: Parental coerciveness, child autonomy and child's role at school. *Sociometry*, 1960, **23**, 15–22.

111 Horowitz, E.: Reported embarrassment memories of elementary school, high school and college students. *J. soc. Psychol.*, 1962, **56**, 317–325.

112 Hurlock, E. B.: The adolescent reformer. *Adolescence*, 1968, **3**, 273–306.

113 Hymes, J. L.: *Behavior and misbehavior: A teacher's guide to action.* Englewood Cliffs, N.J.: Prentice-Hall, 1957.

114 Jarrett, W. H., and A. O. Haller: Situational and personal antecedents of incipient alienation: An exploratory study. *Genet. Psychol. Monogr.*, 1964, **69**, 151–191.

115 Jensen, V. H.: Influence of personality traits on academic success. *Personnel Guid. J.*, 1958, **36**, 497–500.

116 Jersild, A. T.: *The psychology of adolescence*, 2d ed. New York: Macmillan, 1963.

117 Jersild, A. T.: *Child psychology*, 6th ed. Englewood Cliffs, N.J.: Prentice-Hall, 1969.

118 Johnson, C. J., and J. R. Ferreira: School attitudes of children in special classes for mentally retarded. *Calif. J. educ. Res.*, 1958, **9**, 33–37.

119 Johnson, E. E.: Student ratings of popularity and scholastic ability of their peers and actual scholastic performances of those peers. *J. soc. Psychol.*, 1958, **47**, 127–132.

120 Johnson, O. G.: The teacher's role in providing a climate to grow in. *J. nat. Educ. Ass.*, 1957, **46**, 233–236.

121 Jones, M. C.: Psychological correlates of somatic development. *Child Develpm.*, 1965, **36**, 899–911.

122 Joseph, T. P.: Adolescents: From the views of members of an informal adolescent group. *Genet. Psychol. Monogr.*, 1969, **79**, 3–88.

123 Kagan, J.: The child's sex-role identification of school objects. *Child Develpm.*, 1964, **35**, 1051–1056.

124 Kandel, D. B., and G. S. Lesser: Parental and peer influences on educational plans of adolescents. *Amer. sociol. Rev.*, 1969, **34**, 212–223.

125 Kelly, P. H.: An investigation of the factors which influence grammar school pupils to prefer scientific subjects. *Brit. J. educ. Psychol.*, 1961, **31**, 43–44.

126 Kniveton, B. H.: An investigation of the attitudes of adolescents to aspects of their schooling. *Brit. J. educ. Psychol.*, 1969, **39**, 78–81.

127 Koch, H. L.: Children's work attitudes and sibling characteristics. *Child Develpm.*, 1956, **27**, 289–310.

128 Koch, H. L.: The relation of certain formal attributes of siblings to attitudes held toward each other and toward their parents. *Monogr. Soc. Res. Child Develpm.*, 1960, **25**, no. 4.

129 Kowatrakul, S.: Some behaviors of elementary school children related to classroom activities and subject areas. *J. educ. Psychol.*, 1959, **50**, 121–128.

130 Kramer, R.: The state of the boy, 1969, *The New York Times*, Mar. 29, 1969.

131 LaPouse, R., and M. A. Monk: Fears and worries of a representative sample of children. *Amer. J. Orthopsychiat.*, 1959, **29**, 803–818.

132 Leavitt, J.: Teacher-pupil relationships. *J. educ. Res.*, 1959, **29**, 210–217.

133 Leventhal, T., and M. Sills: Self-image in school phobia. *Amer. J. Orthopsychiat.*, 1964, **34**, 685–695.

134 Levin, H., T. L. Hilton, and G. F. Leiderman: Studies of teacher behavior. *J. exp. Educ.*, 1957, **26**, 81–91.

135 Levine, G. N., and L. A. Sussmann: Social class and sociability in fraternity pledging. *Amer. J. Sociol.*, 1960, **65**, 391–399.

136 Levinson, B. M.: The inner life of the extremely gifted child from the clinical setting. *J. genet. Psychol.*, 1961, **99**, 83–88.

137 Lewis, G. M.: Interpersonal relations and school achievement. *Children*, 1964, **11**, 235–236.

138 Livson, N.: Parental behavior and children's involvement with their parents. *J. genet. Psychol.*, 1966, **109**, 173–194.

139 Lundin, R. W., and C. R. Sawyer: The relationship between test anxiety, drinking patterns and scholastic achievement in a group of undergraduate college men. *J. gen. Psychol.*, 1965, **73**, 143–146.

140 Lynn, R.: Temperamental characteristics related to disparity of attainment in reading and arithmetic. *Brit. J. educ. Psychol.*, 1957, **27**, 62–67.

141 Macfarlane, J., L. Allen, and M. P. Honzik: *A developmental study of the behavior problems of normal children between*

twenty-one months and fourteen years. Berkeley: University of California Press, 1954.

142 Marine, E.: School refusal: Who should intervene? (Dogmatic and treatment categories). *J. sch. Psychol.,* 1968–1969, **7,** no. 1, 63–70.

143 Marshall, H. R.: Relations between home experiences and children's use of language in play interactions with peers. *Psychol. Monogr.,* 1961, **75,** no. 5.

144 Mayer, G. R., B. Salzer, and J. H. Cody: The use of punishment in modifying student behavior. *J. spec. Educ.,* 1968, **2,** 323–328.

145 McArthur, C.: Personalities of public and private school boys. *Harv. educ. Rev.,* 1954, **24,** 256–262.

146 McDavid, J.: Some relationships between social reinforcement and scholastic achievement. *J. consult. Psychol.,* 1959, **23,** 151–154.

147 McGee, H. M.: Measurement of authoritarianism and its relation to classroom behavior. *Genet. Psychol. Monogr.,* 1955, **52,** 89–146.

148 Mead, M., and R. Métraux: Image of the scientist among high school students. *Science,* 1957, **126,** 384–390.

149 Medley, D. M.: Teacher personality and teacher-pupil rapport. *J. teacher Educ.,* 1961, **12,** 152–156.

150 Meyer, G. R., and D. M. Penfold: Factors associated with interest in science. *Brit. J. educ. Psychol.,* 1961, **31,** 33–37.

151 Meyer, W. J., and G. G. Thompson: Sex differences in the distribution of teacher approval and disapproval among sixth-grade children. *J. educ. Psychol.,* 1956, **47,** 385–396.

152 Millar, T. P.: The child who refuses to attend school. *Amer. J. Psychiat.,* 1961, **118,** 398–404.

153 Miller, N., D. T. Campbell, H. Twedt, and E. J. O'Connell: Similarity, contrast and complementarity in friendship choice. *J. Pers. soc. Psychol.,* 1966, **3,** 3–12.

154 Mitchell, S., and M. Shepherd: The child who dislikes going to school. *Brit. J. educ. Psychol.,* 1967, **37,** 32–40.

155 Moller, N., and W. Asher: Comment on "A comparison of dropouts and nondropouts on participation in school activities." *Psychol. Rep.,* 1968, **22,** 1243–1244.

156 Morrison, I. E., and I. Perry: Acceptance of overage children by their classmates. *Elem. Sch. J.,* 1956, **56,** 217–220.

157 Muma, J. R.: Peer evaluation and academic performance. *Personnel Guid. J.,* 1966, **44,** 405–409.

158 Mussen, P. H., J. J. Conger, and J. Kagan: *Child development and personality,* 3d ed. New York: Harper & Row, 1969.

159 Norman, R. D., and M. F. Daley: The comparative personality adjustment of superior and inferior readers. *J. educ. Psychol.,* 1959, **50,** 31–36.

160 Oakland, J. A.: Measurement of personality correlates of academic achievement in high school students. *J. counsel. Psychol.,* 1969, **16,** 452–453.

161 Osborn, D. K.: Saliencies in students' perceptions of teachers. *Dissert. Abstr.,* 1968, **29** (3–A), 816.

162 Packard, V.: *The status seekers.* New York: Pocket Books, 1961.

163 Packard, V.: *The pyramid climbers.* New York: McGraw-Hill, 1962.

164 Parker, J. C.: Comment on children. *Children,* 1960, **7,** 116.

165 Pauley, B. G.: The effects of transportation and part-time employment upon participation in school activities, school offices held, acceptability for leadership positions and grade point average among high school seniors. *J. educ. Res.,* 1958, **52,** 3–9.

166 Pearlin, L. I., M. R. Yarrow, and H. A. Scarr: Unintended effects of parental aspirations: The case of children's cheating. *Amer. J. Sociol.,* 1967, **73,** 73–83.

167 Perelli, D. L.: The effect of teachers on the self-concept of junior high-school students as reported by the students themselves. *Dissert. Abstr.,* 1967, **27,** 1666–1667.

168 Perkes, V. A.: Correlates of teacher satisfaction in junior and senior high schools. *J. educ. Res.,* 1968, **19,** 222–225.

169 Pervin, L. A., and D. B. Rubin: Student dissatisfaction with college and the college dropout: A transactional approach. *J. soc. Psychol.,* 1967, **72,** 285–295.

170 Peterson, H. A.: Teacher and peer acceptance of four student behavioral types. *Calif. J. educ. Res.,* 1968, **19,** 16–27.

171 Phillips, B. N.: Problem behavior in the elementary school. *Child Develpm.,* 1968, **39,** 895–903.

172 Pickup, A. J., and W. S. Anthony: Teachers' marks and pupils' expectations: The short-term effects of discrepancies upon classroom performance in secondary schools. *Brit. J. educ. Psychol.,* 1968, **38,** 302–309.

173 Pielstick, N. L.: Perception of mentally superior children by their classmates. *Percept. mot. Skills,* 1963, **17,** 47–53.

174 Poffenberger, T., and D. Norton: Factors in the formation of attitudes toward mathematics. *J. educ. Res.,* 1959, **52,** 171–176.

175 Porterfield, O. V., and H. F. Schlichting: Peer status and reading achievement. *J. educ. Res.,* 1961, **54,** 291–297.

176 Powers, F.: Pupil acceptance of teacher authority. *Sch. Soc.,* 1962, **40,** 249–250.

177 Pressey, S. L.: Concerning the nature and nurture of genius. *Scient. Monthly,* 1955, **81,** 123–129.

178 Rand, L. P.: Effect of college choice satisfaction of matching students and colleges. *Personnel Guid. J.,* 1968, **47,** 34–39.

179 Ranyard, R. W.: The organizational climate and organizational structure of elementary schools. *Dissert. Abstr.,* 1968, **29,** 449.

180 Regan, G.: Personality characteristics and attitude to school. *Brit. J. educ. Psychol.,* 1967, **37,** 127–129.

181 Remmers, H. H., and D. A. Radler: *The American teenager.* Indianapolis: Bobbs-Merrill, 1957.

182 Rice, J. P.: A comparative study of academic interest patterns among selected groups of exceptional and normal intermediate children. *Calif. J. educ. Res.,* 1963, **14,** 131–137, 144.

183 Rolcik, J. W.: Scholastic achievement of teenagers and parental attitudes toward and interest in schoolwork. *Family Life Coordinator,* 1965, **14,** 158–160.

184 Rosen, B. C.: The achievement syndrome: A psychocultural dimension of social stratification. *Amer. sociol. Rev.,* 1956, **21,** 203–211.

185 Rothney, J. W. M., and N. E. Koopman:

Guidance of the gifted. *57th Yearb. nat. Soc. Stud. Educ.,* 1958, pt. 2, 347–361.

186 Rubenstein, B. O., M. L. Falick, and M. Levitt: Learning impotence: A suggested diagnostic category. *Amer. J. Orthopsychiat.,* 1959, **29,** 315–323.

187 Russell, I. L., and W. A. Thalman: Personality: Does it influence teachers' marks? *J. educ. Res.,* 1955, **48,** 561–564.

188 Ryan, F. J.: Trait ratings of high school students by teachers. *J. educ. Psychol.,* 1958, **49,** 124–128.

189 Ryan, M. S.: *Clothing: A study in human behavior.* New York: Holt, 1966.

190 Sattler, J. M.: A theoretical, developmental and clinical investigation of embarrassment. *Genet. Psychol. Monogr.,* 1965, **71,** 19–59.

191 Scates, D. E.: Significant factors in teachers' classroom attitudes. *J. teacher Educ.,* 1956, **7,** 274–279.

192 Schmuck, R.: Some relationships of peer liking patterns in the classroom to pupil attitudes and achievement. *School Review,* 1963, **71,** 337–359.

193 Schwartz, J.: The portrayal of educators in motion pictures: 1950–1958. *J. educ. Sociol.,* 1960, **34,** 82–90.

194 Scott, J. W., and M. El-Assal: Multiversity, university size, university quality and student protests: An empirical study. *Amer. sociol. Rev.,* 1969, **35,** 702–709.

195 Sears, R. R., E. E. Maccoby, and H. Levin: *Patterns in child rearing.* New York: Harper & Row, 1957.

196 Settlage, C. F.: The values of limits in child rearing. *Children,* 1958, **5,** 175–178.

197 Sharples, D.: Children's attitudes towards junior school activities. *Brit. J. educ. Psychol.,* 1969, **39,** 72–77.

198 Sheldon, P. M.: Isolation as a characteristic of highly gifted children. *J. educ. Sociol.,* 1959, **22,** 215–221.

199 Shelton, J., and J. P. Hall: Effects on cheating of achievement anxiety and knowledge of peer performance. *Develpm. Psychol.,* 1969, **1,** 449–455.

200 Silverman, D.: An evaluation of the relationship between attitudes toward self and attitudes toward a vocational high school. *J. educ. Sociol.,* 1963, **36,** 410–418.

201 Silverman, J. S., M. W. Fite, and M. M. Mosher: Clinical findings in reading disability children: Special cases of intellectual inhibition. *Amer. J. Orthopsychiat.,* 1959, **29,** 298–314.

202 Simon, M. D.: Body configuration and school readiness. *Child Develpm.,* 1959, **30,** 493–512.

203 Simpson, R. L., and L. H. Simpson: The school, the peer group, and adolescent development. *J. educ. Sociol.,* 1958, **32,** 37–41.

204 Slee, F. W.: The feminine image factor in girls' attitudes to school subjects. *Brit. J. educ. Psychol.,* 1968, **38,** 212–214.

205 Smelser, W. T., and L. H. Stewart: Where are the siblings? A re-evaluation of the relationship between birth order and college attendance. *Sociometry,* 1968, **31,** 294–303.

206 Solomon, J. C.: Neuroses of school teachers. *Ment. Hyg., N. Y.,* 1960, **44,** 79–90.

207 Spiegelberger, C. D., and W. G. Kalzenmeyer: Manifest anxiety, intelligence and college grades. *J. consult. Psychol.,* 1959, **23,** 78.

208 Steininger, M., R. E. Johnson, and D. K.

Kirts: Cheating on college examinations as a function of situationally aroused anxiety and hostility. *J. educ. Psychol.*, 1964, **55**, 317–324.

209 Stone, L. J. and J. Church: *Childhood and adolescence.* 2d ed. New York: Random House, 1968.

210 Storey, A. G.: Acceleration, deceleration and self-concepts. *Alberta J. educ. Res.*, 1967, **13**, 135–142.

211 Stout, R. T.: Social class and educational aspirations: A Weberian analysis. *Personnel Guid. J.*, 1969, **47**, 650–654.

212 Strang, R.: *The adolescent views himself.* New York: McGraw-Hill, 1957.

213 Symonds, P. M.: What education has to learn from psychology, IX. Origins of personality. *Teachers Coll. Rec.*, 1960, **61**, 301–317.

214 Tannenbaum, A. J.: *Adolescent attitudes toward academic brilliance.* New York: Teachers College, 1962.

215 Taylor, P. H.: Children's evaluations of the characteristics of the good teacher. *Brit. J. educ. Psychol.*, 1962, **32**, 258–266.

216 Terman, L. M., and M. A. Merrill: *Stanford-Binet Intelligence Scale,* 3d ed. Boston: Houghton Mifflin, 1960.

217 Thelen, M. H., and C. S. Harris: Personality of college underachievers who improve with group therapy. *Personnel Guid. J.*, 1968, **46**, 561–666,

218 Thistlewaite, D.L.: Effects of social recognition upon the educational motivation of talented youth. *J. educ. Psychol.*, 1959, **50**, 111–116.

219 Thompson, G. W.: Children's acceptance of television advertising and the relation of televiewing to school achievement. *J. educ. Res.*, 1964, **58**, 171–174.

220 Toby, J.: Orientation to education as a factor in the school maladjustment of lower-class children. *Soc. Forces*, 1957, **35**, 259–266.

221 Tolor, A., W. L. Scarpetti, and P. A. Lane: Teachers' attitudes toward children's behavior revisited. *J. educ. Psychol.*, 1967, **58**, 175–180.

222 Torrence, E. P.: Changing reactions of preadolescent girls to tasks requiring creative scientific thinking. *J. genet. Psychol.*, 1963, **102**, 217–223.

223 Tulkin, S. R.: Race, class, family and school achievement. *J. Pers. soc. Psychol.*, 1968, **9**, 31–37.

224 Turner, R. H.: Some aspects of women's ambition. *Amer. J. Sociol.*, 1964, **70**, 271–284.

225 Tyler, L. E.: The development of "vocational interests." I. The organization of likes and dislikes in ten-year-old children. *J. genet. Psychol.*, 1955, **86**, 33–34.

226 *U.S. News & World Report:* What's really wrong with colleges. June 16, 1969, pp. 36–38.

227 *U.S. News & World Report:* The "spectacular '70s." June 23, 1969, pp. 42–45.

228 Very, P. S.: Real and ideal characteristics of the teacher-student relationship. *Percept. mot. Skills*, 1968, **27**, 880–882.

229 Walters, Sister A.: The role of the school in personality development. *Education*, 1957, **77**, 214–219.

230 Walz, G., and J. Miller: School climates and student behavior: Implications for counselor role. *Personnel Guid. J.*, 1969, **47**, 859–867.

231 Warriner, C. C., D. A. Foster, and D. K. Trites: Failure to complete as a family

characteristic: A college sample. *J. educ. Res.*, 1966, **59**, 466–468.

232 Watson, G. H.: Emotional problems of gifted students. *Personnel Guid. J.*, 1960, **39**, 98–105.

233 Wattenberg, W. W., and C. Clifford: Relation of self-concepts to beginning achievement in reading. *Child Develpm.*, 1964, **35**, 461–467.

234 Weber, G. H., and A. B. Motz: School as perceived by the dropout. *J. Negro Educ.*, 1968, **37**, 127–134.

235 Weigand, G.: Adaptiveness and the role of parents in academic success. *Personnel Guid. J.*, 1957, **35**, 518–522.

236 Williams, M. F.: Acceptance and performance among gifted and elementary school children. *Educ. Res. Bull.*, 1958, **37**, 216–220, 224.

237 Williams, R. L., and S. Cole: Self-concept and school adjustment. *Personnel Guid. J.*, 1968, **46**, 478–481.

238 Wilson, A. B.: Residential segregation of social classes and aspirations of high school boys. *Amer. sociol. Rev.*, 1959, **24**, 836–845.

239 Witty, P. A.: A study of pupils' interests: Grades 9, 10, 11, 12. *Education*, 1961, **82**, 160–174.

240 Wolman, B. B.: Education and leadership. *Teachers Coll. Rec.*, 1958, **59**, 465–473.

241 Worth, W. H.: Promotion or not promotion? *Educ. Admin. Superv.*, 1960, **46**, 16–26.

242 Yando, R. M., and J. Kagan: The effect of teacher tempo on the child. *Child Develpm.*, 1968, **39**, 27–34.

243 Yee, A. H.: Source and direction of causal influence in teacher-pupil relationship. *J. educ. Psychol.*, 1968, **59**, 275–282.

244 Yee, A. H., and P. J. Runkel: Simplicial structures of middle class and lower class pupils' attitudes toward teachers. *Develpm. Psychol.*, 1969, **1**, 646–652.

245 Ziller, R. C., and R. D. Behringer: Motivational and perceptual effects in orientation toward a newcomer. *J. soc. Psychol.*, 1965, **66**, 79–90.

246 Zimmerman, I. L., and G. N. Allebrand: Personality characteristics and attitudes toward achievement of good and poor readers. *J. educ. Res.*, 1965, **59**, 28–30.

CHAPTER 13

1 Adams, B. N.: The middle-class adult and his widowed or still-married mother. *Soc. Probl.*, 1968, **16**, 50–59.

2 Adams, P. L., J. J. Schwab, and J. F. Aponte: Authoritarian parents and disturbed children. *Amer. J. Psychiat.*, 1965, **121**, 1162–1167.

3 Adler, A.: *The education of children.* New York: Greenberg, 1930.

4 Aldous, J.: Intergenerational visiting patterns: Variation in boundary maintenance as an explanation. *Family Process*, 1967, **6**, 235–251.

5 Alexander, C. N.: Ordinal positon and social mobility. *Sociometry*, 1968, **31**, 285–293.

6 Allen, M. G.: Psychoanalytic theory on infant gratification and adult personality. *J. genet. Psychol.*, 1964, **104**, 265–274.

7 Altus, W. D.: Birth order and its sequelae. *Science*, 1966, **151**, no. 1, 44–49.

8 Amatora, Sister M.: Analyses of certain recreational interests and activities and other variables in the large family. *J. soc. Psychol.*, 1959, **50**, 225–231.

9 Auerbach, A. B.: Meeting the needs of new mothers. *Children*, 1964, **11**, 223–233.

10 Axelson, L. J.: Personal adjustment in the postparental period. *Marriage fam. Living*, 1960, **22**, 66–68.

11 Axelson, L. J.: The marital adjustment and marital role definitions of husbands of working and nonworking wives. *Marriage fam. Living*, 1963, **25**, 189–195.

12 Baker, F., and G. M. St. L. O'Brien: Birth order and fraternity affiliation. *J. soc. Psychol.*, 1969, **78**, 41–43.

13 Baker, L. G.: The personal and social adjustments of the never-married woman. *J. Marriage & Family*, 1968, **30**, 473–479.

14 Ballweg, J. A.: Resolution of conjugal role adjustment after retirement. *J. Marriage & Family*, 1967, **29**, 277–281.

15 Bartlett, E. W., and C. P. Smith: Child rearing practices, birth order and the development of achievement-related motives. *Psychol. Rep.*, 1966, **19**, 1207–1216.

16 Baumrind, D., and A. E. Black: Socialization practices associated with dimensions of competence in preschool boys and girls. *Child Develpm.*, 1967, **38**, 291–327.

17 Baxter, J. C.: Parental complementarity and parental conflict. *J. indiv. Psychol.*, 1965, **21**, 149–153.

18 Bealer, R. C., F. K. Willits, and P. R. Maida: The rebellious youth subculture: A myth. *Children*, 1964, **11**, 42–48.

19 Becker, S. W., M. J. Lerner, and J. Carroll: Conformity as a function of birth order and type of group pressure. *J. Pers. soc. Psychol.*, 1966, **3**, 242–244.

20 Bell, R. Q.: A reinterpretation of the direction of effects in studies of socialization. *Psychol. Rev.*, 1968, **75**, 81–95.

21 Berardo, F. M.: Widowhood status in the United States: Perspective on a neglected aspect of the family life-cycle. *Family Coordinator*, 1968, **17**, 191–203.

22 Bernard, J.: Marital stability and patterns of status variables. *J. Marriage & Family*, 1966, **28**, 421–448.

23 Bishop, B. M.: Mother-child interaction and the social behavior of children. *Psychol. Monogr.*, 1951, **65**, no. 11.

24 Blood, R. O.: Long-range causes and consequences of the employment of married women. *J. Marriage & Family*, 1965, **27**, 43–47.

25 Blood, R. O.: Kinship interaction and marital solidarity. *Merrill-Palmer Quart.*, 1969, **15**, 171–185.

26 Bossard, J. H. S.: Eight reasons why marriages go wrong. *The New York Times*, June 24, 1956.

27 Bossard, J. H. S., and E. S. Boll: *The sociology of child development,* 4th ed. New York: Harper & Row, 1966.

28 Bowerman, C. E., and D. P. Irish: Some relationships of stepchildren to their parents. *Marriage fam. Living*, 1962, **24**, 113–121.

29 Bowerman, C. E., and J. W. Kinch: Changes in family and peer orientation of children between the fourth and tenth grades. *Soc. Forces*, 1959, **37**, 206–211.

30 Bradley, R. W., and M. P. Sanborn: Ordinal position of high school students identified by their teachers as superior. *J. educ. Psychol.*, 1969, **60**, 41–45.

31 Brim, O. G., R. W. Fairchild, and E. F. Borgatta: Relations between family problems. *Marriage fam. Living*, 1961, **23**, 219–226.

32 Burchinal, L. G.: Characteristics of adoles-

cents from unbroken, broken, and reconstituted families. *J. Marriage & Family*, 1964, **26**, 44–51.

33 Burke, M. O.: A search for systematic personality differentiae of the only child in young adulthood. *J. genet. Psychol.*, 1956, **89**, 71–84.

34 Burton, D.: Birth order and intelligence. *J. soc. Psychol.*, 1968, **76**, 199–206.

35 Caldwell, B. M., L. Hersher, E. L. Lipton, J. B. Richmond, G. A. Stern, E. Eddy, R. Drackman, and A. Rothman: Mother-infant interaction in monomatric and polymatric families. *Amer. J. Orthopsychiat.*, 1963, **33**, 653–664.

36 Caplan, G.: Patterns of parental response to the crisis of premature birth. *Psychiatry*, 1960, **23**, 365–375.

37 Carrigan, W. C., and J. W. Julian: Sex and birth-order differences in conformity as a function of need affiliation arousal. *J. Pers. soc. Psychol.*, 1966, **3**, 479–483.

38 Casler, L.: Maternal deprivation. *Monogr. Soc. Res. Child Develpm.*, 1961, **26**, no. 2.

39 Cavan, R. S.: *The American family*, 4th ed. New York: Crowell, 1969.

40 Chen, R.: The dilemma of divorce: Disaster or remedy. *Family Coordinator*, 1968, **17**, 251–254.

41 Chilman, C. S.: Families in development at mid-stage of the family life cycle. *Family Coordinator*, 1968, **17**, 297–312.

42 Chittenden, E. A., A. M. W. Foan, D. M. Zweil, and J. R. Smith: School achievement of first- and second-born siblings. *Child Develpm.*, 1968, **39**, 1123–1128.

43 Chorost, S. B.: Parental child-rearing attitudes and their correlates in adolescent hostility. *Genet. Psychol. Monogr.*, 1962, **66**, 49–90.

44 Christensen, H. T.: Children in the family: Relationship of number and spacing to marital success. *J. Marriage & Family*, 1968, **30**, 283–289.

45 Christensen, H. T., and B. B. Rubinstein: Premarital pregnancy and divorce: A follow-up study by the interview method. *Marriage fam. Living*, 1956, **18**, 114–123.

46 Clark, A. W., and P. vonSommers: Contradictory demands in family relations and adjustment to school and home. *Hum. Relat.*, 1961, **14**, 97–111.

47 Clifford, E.: Discipline in the home: A controlled observational study of parental practices. *J. genet. Psychol.*, 1959, **95**, 45–82.

48 Cobliner, W. G.: Social factors in mental disorders: A contribution to the etiology of mental illness. *Genet. Psychol. Monogr.*, 1963, **67**, 151–215.

49 Coleman, J. S.: *The adolescent society*: New York: Free Press, 1961.

50 Conners, C. K.: Birth order and need for affiliation. *J. Pers.*, 1963, **31**, 408–416.

51 Crowther, B.: Poor Mom. *The New York Times*, Apr. 22, 1962.

52 Cumming, E., and D. M. Schneider: Sibling solidarity: A property of American kinship. *Amer. Anthropologist*, 1961, **63**, 498–507.

53 Cummings, S. T., H. C. Bayley, and H. E. Rie: Effects of the child's deficiency on the mother: A study of mothers of mentally retarded, chronically ill, and neurotic children. *Amer. J. Orthopsychiat.*, 1966, **36**, 595–608.

54 Cushna, B., M. Greene, and B. C. Snider: First born and last born children in a child

development clinic. *J. indiv. Psychol.*, 1964, **20**, 179–182.

55 Dalta, L. E.: Birth order and scientific creativity. *Sociometry*, 1968, **31**, 76–88.

56 Dame, N. G., G. H. Finck, B. S. Reiner, and B. O. Smith: The effect on the marital relationship of the wife's search for identity. *Family Life Coordinator*, 1965, **14**, 133–136.

57 Day, L. H., and A. T. Day: Family size in industrialized countries: An inquiry into the social-cultural determinants of levels of child bearing. *J. Marriage & Family*, 1969, **31**, 242–251.

58 deLint, J. E. E.: A note on Smart's study of birth rank and affiliation in male university students. *J. Psychol.*, 1966, **62**, 177–178.

59 Dick, H. R., H. J. Friedsam, and C. A. Martin: Residential patterns of aged persons prior to institutionalization. *J. Marriage & Family*, 1964, **26**, 96–98.

60 Dien, D. S., and E. W. Vinacke: Self-concept and parental identification of young adults with mixed Caucasian-Japanese parentage. *J. abnorm. soc. Psychol.*, 1964, **69**, 463–466.

61 Doty, C. N., and R. M. Hoeflin: A descriptive study of thirty-five unmarried graduate women. *J. Marriage & Family.*, 1964, **26**, 91–94.

62 Dubbé, M. C.: What parents are not told may hurt. *Family Life Coordinator*, 1965, **14**, 51–118.

63 Duvall, E. M.: Family dilemmas with teenagers. *Family Life Coordinator*, 1965, **14**, 35–38.

64 Dybwad, G.: Family life in a changing world. *Children*, 1959, **6**, 3–9.

65 Ellis, D., and F. I. Nye: The nagging parent. *Family Life Coordinator*, 1959, **8**, 8–10.

66 Emmerich, W.: Variations in the parent role as a function of the parent's sex and the child's sex and age. *Merrill-Palmer Quart.*, 1962, **8**, 3–11.

67 Farber, B.: Effects of a severely mentally retarded child on family integration. *Monogr. Soc. Res. Child Develpm.*, 1959, **24**, no. 2.

68 Farber, B., and L. S. Blackman: Marital role tensions and number and sex of children. *Amer. sociol. Rev.*, 1956, **21**, 596–601.

69 Farley, J.: Maternal employment and child behavior. *Cornell J. soc. Relat.*, 1968, **3**, 58–71.

70 Fast, I., and A. C. Cain: The stepparent role: Potential for disturbance in family functioning. *Amer. J. Orthopsychiat.*, 1966, **36**, 485–491.

71 Finney, J. C.: Some maternal influences on children's personality and character. *Genet. Psychol. Monogr.*, 1961, **63**, 199–278.

72 Fitzgerald, M. P.: Sex differences in the perception of the parental role for middle and working class adolescents. *J. clin. Psychol.*, 1966, **22**, 15–16.

73 Foster, J. E.: Father images: Television and ideal. *J. Marriage & Family*, 1964, **26**, 353–355.

74 Frank, G. H.: The role of the family in the development of psychopathology. *Psychol. Bull.*, 1965, **64**, 191–205.

75 Freedman, D. S., R. Freedman, and P. K. Whelpton: Size of family and preference for children of each sex. *Amer. J. Sociol.*, 1960, **66**, 141–146.

76 Freedman, R., and L. Coombs: Child spacing and family economic position. *Amer. sociol. Rev.*, 1966, **31**, 631–648.

77 Freud, S.: *The standard edition of the complete psychological works of Sigmund Freud*. London, Hogarth, 1953–1962.

78 Friedenberg, E. Z.: The generation gap. *Ann. Amer. Acad. pol. soc. Sci.*, 1969, **382** 32–42.

79 Gebhard, P. H., W. B. Pomeroy, C. E. Martin, and C. V. Christenson: *Pregnancy, birth and abortion*. New York: Harper & Row, 1958.

80 George, E. L., and M. Thomas: A comparative study of children of employed mothers and unemployed mothers. *Psychol. Stud.*, 1967, **12**, 32–38.

81 Gibson, H. B.: The measurement of parental attitudes and their relation to boys' behavior. *Brit. J. educ. Psychol.*, 1968, **38**, 233–239.

82 Glasner, Rabbi S.: Family religion as a matrix of personal growth. *Marriage fam. Living*, 1961, **23**, 291–293.

83 Glasser, P. H., and L. N. Glasser: Role reversal and conflict between aged parents and their children. *Marriage fam. Living*, 1962, **24**, 46–51.

84 Glenn, H. M.: Attitudes of women regarding gainful employment of married women. *J. Home Econ.*, 1959, **51**, 247–252.

85 Goldin, P. C.: A review of children's reports of parent behaviors. *Psychol. Bull.*, 1969, **71**, 222–236.

86 Goode, W. J.: *The family*. Englewood Cliffs, N.J.: Prentice-Hall, 1964.

87 Greenberg, H., R. Quermo, M. Lashan, D. Mayer, and D. Piskowski: Order of birth as a determinant of personality and attitudinal characteristics. *J. soc. Psychol.*, 1963, **60**, 221–230.

88 Grimm, E. R., and W. R. Venet: The relationship of emotional adjustment and attitudes to the course and outcome of pregnancy. *Psychosom. Med.*, 1966, **28**, 34–49.

89 Gulo, E. V.: Attitudes of rural school children toward their parents. *J. educ. Res.*, 1966, **59**, 450–452.

90 Hader, M.: The importance of grandparents in family life. *Family Process*, 1965, **4**, 228–240.

91 Hall, E.: Ordinal positon and success in engagement and marriage. *J. indiv. Psychol.*, 1965, **21**, 154–158.

92 Hall, E., and B. Barger: Attitudinal structures of older and younger siblings. *J. indiv. Psychol.*, 1964, **20**, 59–68.

93 Hall, G. S.: *Aspects of child life and education*. Boston: Ginn, 1907.

94 Handschin-Ninck, M.: Aelterster und Jüngster in Marchen. *Prax. Kinderpsychol. Kinderpsychiat.*, 1956, **7**, 167–173.

95 Harmon, L.: When homes are broken. *J. Home Econ.*, 1959, **51**, 332–335.

96 Harris, D. B.: Parental judgment of responsibility in children and children's adjustment. *J. genet. Psychol.*, 1958, **92**, 161–166.

97 Harris, D. B., and S. C. Tseng: Children's attitudes toward peers and parents as revealed by sentence completions. *Child Develpm.*, 1957, **28**, 401–411.

98 Harris, I. D., and K. I. Howard: Birth order and responsibility. *J. Marriage & Family*, 1968, **30**, 427–432.

99 Hartley, R. E.: Children's perceptions of sex preferences in four culture groups. *J. Marriage & Family*, 1969, **31**, 380–387.

100 Hawkes, G. R., L. Burchinal, and B. Gardner: Size of family and adjustment of

children. *Marriage fam. Living.* 1958, **20**, 65–68.

101 Heilbrun, A. B., and H. K. Orr: Maternal child-rearing control history and subsequent cognitive and personality functioning of the offspring. *Psychol. Rep.*, 1965, **17**, 259–272.

102 Helson, R.: Effects of sibling characteristics and parental values on creative interest and achievement. *J. Pers.*, 1968, **36**, 589–607.

103 Hendershot, G. E.: Familial satisfaction, birth order, and fertility values. *J. Marriage & Family*, 1969, **31**, 27–33.

104 Herrmann, R. O.: Expectations and attitudes as a source of financial problems in teen-age marriages. *J. Marriage & Family*, 1965, **27**, 89–91.

105 Higgins, J., J. C. Peterson, and L. L. Dolby: Social adjustment and familial schema. *J. abnorm. Psychol.*, 1969, **74**, 296–299.

106 Hobbs, D. F.: Transition to parenthood: A replication and extension. *J. Marriage & Family*, 1968, **30**, 413–417.

107 Hurlock, E. B.: The adolescent reformer. *Adolescence*, 1968, **3**, 273–306.

108 Irish, D. P.: Sibling interaction: A neglected aspect of family life research. *Soc. Forces*, 1964, **42**, 279–288.

109 Jackson, L.: Unsuccessful abortions: A study of 40 cases who attended a child guidance clinic. *Brit. J. med. Psychol.*, 1968, **41**, 389–398.

110 Joseph, T. P.: Adolescents: From the views of members of an informal adolescent group. *Genet. Psychol. Monogr.*, 1969, **79**, 3–88.

111 Jourard, S. M., and R. M. Remy: Perceived parental attitudes, the self, and security. *J. consult. Psychol.*, 1955, **19**, 364–366.

112 Kagan, J., and H. A. Moss: *Birth to maturity: A study in psychological development.* New York: Wiley, 1962.

113 Katelman, D. K., and L. D. Barnett: Work orientations of urban, middle-class, married women. *J. Marriage & Family*, 1968, **30**, 80–88.

114 Kavanagh, G.: The influence of a step-mother's motivation in marriage upon her stepchild's symptom formation. *Smith Coll. Stud. soc. Wk.*, 1961, **32**, 65–66.

115 Kenkel, W. F.: Marriage and the family in modern science fiction. *J. Marriage & Family*, 1969, **31**, 6–14.

116 Kent, D. P.: Social and cultural factors affecting the mental health of the aged. *Amer. J. Orthopsychiat.*, 1966, **36**, 680–685.

117 Kerckhoff, A. C.: Husband-wife expectations and reactions to retirement. *J. Geront.*, 1964, **19**, 510–516.

118 Khatri, A. A., and B. B. Siddiqui: "A boy or a girl?" Preferences of parents for sex of offspring as perceived by East Indian and American children: A cross-cultural study. *J. Marriage & Family*, 1969, **31**, 388–392.

119 Kim, C. C., R. J. Dales, P. Connor, J. Walters, and R. Witherspoon: Social interaction of like-sex twins and singletons in relation to intelligence, language and physical environment. *J. genet. Psychol.*, 1969, **114**, 203–214.

120 King, R. C.: Sibling rivalry: The price of misguided democracy in the family. *Aust. Psychologist*, 1967, **2**, 1.

121 Koch, H. L.: The relation of certain formal attributes of siblings to attitudes held toward each other and toward their parents. *Monogr. Soc. Res. Child Develpm.*, 1960, **25**, no. 4.

122 Koch, H. L.: *Twins and twin relations.* Chicago: University of Chicago Press, 1966.

123 Koch, M. B.: Anxiety in preschool children from broken homes. *Merrill-Palmer Quart.*, 1961, **7**, 225–231.

124 Kramer, R.: Phasing out Mom and Dad. *The New York Times*, Nov. 2, 1969.

125 LaBarre, M. B., L. Jessner, and L. Ussery: The significance of grandmothers in the psychopathology of children. *Amer. J. Orthopsychiat.*, 1960, **30**, 175–185.

126 Landis, J. T.: Social correlates of divorce and nondivorce among the unhappy married. *Marriage fam. Living*, 1963, **25**, 178–180.

127 Langsley, D. G., T. P. Burton, M. Griswold, H. Walzer, and R. B. Spinka: Schizophrenia in triplets: A family study. *Amer. J. Psychiat.*, 1963, **120**, 528–532.

128 Laury, G. V., and J. A. M. Meerlo: Subtle types of mental cruelty to children. *Child & Family*, 1967, **6**, no. 2, 28–34.

129 Lee, H.: *To kill a mocking bird.* Philadelphia: Lippincott, 1960.

130 Lehrman, N. S.: Anarchy, dictatorship, and democracy within the family: A biosocial hierarchy. *Psychiatry*, 1962, **36**, 455–474.

131 Levinger, G.: Sources of marital dissatisfaction among applicants for divorce. *Amer. J. Orthopsychiat.*, 1966, **36**, 803–807.

132 Lieberman, E. J.: The case for small families. *The New York Times*, Mar. 8, 1970.

133 Livson, N.: Parental behavior and children's involvement with their parents. *J. genet. Psychol.*, 1966, **109**, 173–194.

134 Locke, H. J., G. Sabagh, and M. M. Thomas: Interfaith marriage. *Soc. Probl.*, 1957, **4**, 329–333.

135 Lowrie, S. H.: Early marriage: Premarital pregnancy and associated factors. *J. Marriage & Family*, 1965, **22**, 48–56.

136 Luckey, E. B.: Number of years married as related to personality perception and marital satisfaction. *J. Marriage & Family*, 1966, **28**, 44–48.

137 Lunneborg, P. W.: Birth order, aptitude and achievement. *J. consult. clin. Psychol.*, 1968, **32**, 101.

138 MacDonald, A. P.: Manifestations of differential levels of socialization by birth order. *Develpm. Psychol.*, 1969, **1**, 485–492.

139 McArthur, C.: Personalities of first and second children. *Psychiatry*, 1956, **19**, 47–54.

140 McCord, J., W. McCord, and E. Thurber: Effects of maternal employment on lower-class boys. *J. abnorm. soc. Psychol.*, 1963, **67**, 177–182.

141 McDermott, J. F.: Parental divorce in early childhood. *Amer. J. Psychiat.*, 1968, **124**, 1424–1432.

142 Mead, M.: The changing American family. *Children*, 1963, **10**, 173–174.

143 Messer, A. A.: The only-child syndrome. *The New York Times*, Feb. 25, 1968.

144 Messer, M.: Age grouping and the family status of the elderly. *Sociol. soc. Res.*, 1968, **52**, 271–279.

145 Montagu, A.: Sex, order of birth and personality. *Amer. J. Orthopsychiat.*, 1948, **18**, 351–353.

146 Montagu, A.: *Human heredity.* New York: Harcourt, Brace & World, 1959.

147 Munz, D. C., A. D. Smouse, and G. Letchworth: Achievement motivation and ordinal position of birth. *Psychol. Rep.*, 1968, **23**, 175–180.

148 Murdock, P. H.: Birth order and age at marriage. *J. soc. clin. Psychol.*, 1966, **5**, 24–29.

149 Murherjee, B. N.: Birth order and verbalized need for achievement. *J. soc. Psychol.*, 1968, **75**, 223–229.

150 Murstein, B. I., and V. Glaudin: The relationship of marital adjustment to personality: A factor analysis of the interpersonal check list. *J. Marriage & Family*, 1966, **29**, 37–43.

151 Mussen, P. H., and A. L. Parker: Mother nurturance and girls' incidental imitative learning. *J. Pers. soc. Psychol.*, 1965, **2**, 94–97.

152 Mussen, P. H., H. B. Young, R. Gaddini, and L. Morante: The influence of father-son relationships on adolescent personality and attitudes. *J. child Psychol. Psychiat.*, 1963, **4**, 3–16.

153 Navran, L.: Communication and adjustment in marriage. *Family Process*, 1967, **6**, 173–184.

154 Nemy, E.: Adolescents today: Are they more disturbed? *The New York Times*, Feb. 20, 1970.

155 Neugarten, B. L., and K. K. Weinstein: The changing American grandparent. *J. Marriage & Family*, 1964, **26**, 199–204.

156 *New York Times* Report: Reaction to multiple births varies among primitives. Oct. 12, 1963.

157 *New York Times* Report: Leisure use called factor in marriage. May 11, 1966.

158 *New York Times* Report: Panel calls help by wife needed for man's success. Mar. 24, 1968.

159 *Newsweek* Report: The divorced woman: American style. Feb. 13, 1967, pp. 64–70.

160 Nichols, R. C.: A factor analysis of parental attitudes of fathers. *Child Develpm.*, 1962, **33**, 791–802.

161 Nisbett, R. E.: Birth order and participation in dangerous sports. *J. Pers. soc. Psychol.*, 1968, **8**, 351–353.

162 Nye, F. I.: Child adjustment in broken and unhappy unbroken homes. *Marriage fam. Living*, 1957, **19**, 356–361.

163 Offner, V. S.: A study of mothers of twins. *Smith Coll. Stud. soc. Wk.*, 1960, **31**, 45–46.

164 Orden, S. R., and N. M. Bradburn: Working wives and marriage happiness. *Amer. J. Sociol.*, 1969, **74**, 392–407.

165 Packard, V.: *The status seekers.* New York: Pocket Books, 1961.

166 Palmer, R. D.: Birth order and identification. *J. consult. Psychol.*, 1966, **30**, 129–135.

167 Parke, R. D., and R. H. Walters: Some factors influencing the efficacy of punishment training for inducing response inhibition. *Monogr. Soc. Res. Child Develpm.*, 1967, **32**, no. 1.

168 Peck, R. F.: Family patterns correlated with adolescent personality structure. *J. abnorm. soc. Psychol.*, 1958, **57**, 347–350.

169 Peck, R. F., and R. J. Havighurst: *The psychology of character development.* New York: Wiley, 1962.

170 Perrucci, C. C.: Mobility, marriage and child-spacing among college graduates. *J. Marriage & Family*, 1968, **30**, 273–282.

171 Perry, J. B., and E. H. Pfuhl: Adjustment of children in "solo" and "remarriage"

homes. *Marriage fam. Living*, 1963, **25**, 221–223.

172 Peterson, D. R., W. C. Becker, L. A. Hellmer, D. J. Shoemaker, and H. C. Quay: Parental attitudes and child adjustment. *Child Develpm.*, 1959, **30**, 119–120.

173 Plank, E. N.: Reactions of mothers of twins in a child study group. *Amer. J. Orthopsychiat.*, 1958, **28**, 196–208.

174 Poffenberger, T.: A research note on father-child relations and father viewed as a negative figure. *Child Develpm.*, 1959, **30**, 489–492.

175 Pohlman, E. W.: Burgess and Cottrell data on "desire for children": An example of distortion in marriage and family textbooks. *J. Marriage & Family*, 1968, **30**, 433–436.

176 Rainwater, L.: Social status differences in the family relationships of German men. *Marriage fam. Living*, 1962, **24**, 12–17.

177 Ralling, E. M.: Family situations of married and never married males. *J. Marriage & Family*, 1966, **28**, 485–490.

178 Rank, O.: *The trauma of birth*. London: Routledge, 1929.

179 Rappaport, E. A.: The grandparent syndrome. *Psychoanal. Quart.*, 1958, **27**, 518–538.

180 Reddy, N.Y.: A study of the relationship between ordinal position of adolescents and their adjustment. *Psychol. Stud., Mysore*, 1967, **12**, 91–100.

181 Reiss, P. J.: The extended kinship system: Correlates of and attitudes on frequency of interaction. *Marriage fam. Living*, 1962, **24**, 333–339.

182 Reiss, P. J.: The trend in interfaith marriages. *J. sci. Stud. Relig.*, 1965, **5**, 64–67.

183 Robins, L. N., and M. Tomanec: Closeness of blood relatives outside the immediate family. *Marriage fam. Living*, 1962, **24**, 340–346.

184 Rodman, H., F. R. Nichols, and P. Voydanoff: Lower-class attitudes toward "deviant" family patterns: A cross cultural study. *J. Marriage & Family*, 1969, **31**, 315–321.

185 Rosenbaum, M.: Psychological effects on the child raised by an older sibling. *Amer. J. Orthopsychiat.*, 1963, **33**, 515–520.

186 Rosenberg, B. G., and B. Sutton-Smith: Sibling association, family size, and cognitive abilities. *J. genet. Psychol.*, 1966, **109**, 271–279.

187 Rosenthal, M. J.: The syndrome of the inconsistent mother. *Amer. J. Orthopsychiat.*, 1962, **32**, 637–644.

188 Rossi, A. S.: Transition to parenthood. *J. Marriage & Family*, 1968, **30**, 26–39.

189 Rothbart, M. K., and E. E. Maccoby: Parents' differential reactions to sons and daughters. *J. Pers. soc. Psychol.*, 1966, **4**, 237–243.

190 Russell, D. H., and A. H. Rosenberg: Single-parent adoptions. *New Eng. J. Med.*, 1968, **279**, 259–260.

191 Sampson, E. E., and F. T. Hancock: An examination of the relationship between ordinal position, personality, and conformity. *J. Pers. soc. Psychol.*, 1967, **5**, 398–407.

192 Scarr, S.: Environmental bias in twin studies. *Eugen. Quart.*, 1968, **15**, 34–40.

193 Schachter, S.: Birth order, eminence and higher education. *Amer. sociol. Rev.*, 1963, **28**, 757–768.

194 Schaefer, E. S.: Children's reports of parental behavior: An inquiry. *Child Develpm.*, 1965, **36**, 413–424.

195 Scheinfeld, A.: *Twins and supertwins*. Philadelphia: Lippincott, 1967.

196 Schleisinger, B.: Remarriage: An inventory of findings. *Family Coordinator*, 1968, **17**, 248–250.

197 Schmuck, R.: Sex of sibling, birth order position, and female dispositions to conform in two-child familes. *Child Develpm.*, 1963, **34**, 913–918.

198 Scott, E. M.: Psychological examination of quadruplets. *Psychol. Rep.*, 1960, **6**, 281–282.

199 Sears, R. R., E. E. Maccoby, and H. Levin: *Patterns of child rearing*. New York: Harper & Row, 1957.

200 Shrader, W. K., and T. Leventhal: Birth order of children and parental report of problems. *Child Develpm.*, 1968, **39**, 1165–1175.

201 Siegel, E. A., and M. B. Haas: The working mother: A review of research. *Child Develpm.*, 1963, **34**, 513–542.

202 Siegelman, M.: College student personality correlates of early parent-child relationships. *J. consult. Psychol.*, 1965, **29**, 558–564.

203 Slater, P. E.: Parental behavior and the personality of the child. *J. genet. Psychol.*, 1962, **101**, 53–68.

204 Smart, R. G.: Social-group membership, leadership, and birth order. *J. soc. Psychol.*, 1965, **67**, 221–225.

205 Smelser, W. T., and L. H. Stewart: Where are the siblings? A re-evaluation of the relationship between birth order and college attendance. *Sociometry*, 1968, **31**, 294–303.

206 Smith, E. E., and J. D. Goodchilds: Some personality and behavioral factors related to birth order. *J. appl. Psychol.*, 1963, **47**, 300–303.

207 Smith, T. E.: Social class and attitudes toward fathers. *Sociol. soc. Res.*, 1969, **53**, 217–226.

208 Stewart, R. H.: Birth order and dependency. *J. Pers. soc. Psychol.*, 1967, **6**, 192–194.

209 Stinnett, N., and J. E. Montgomery: Youths' perceptions of marriage of older people. *J. Marriage & Family*, 1968, **30**, 392–396.

210 Stöckle, O.: The family with many children and its significance for social education. *Heilpädag Werkbl.*, 1954, **23**, 144–149.

211 Stone, F. B., and V. N. Rowley: Children's behavior problems and parental attitudes. *J. genet. Psychol.*, 1965, **107**, 281–287.

212 Stoodley, B. H.: Mother role as a focus of some family problems. *Marriage fam. Living*, 1952, **14**, 13–16.

213 Streib, G. F.: Intergenerational relations: Perspectives of the two generations on the older parent. *J. Marriage & Family*, 1965, **27**, 469–476.

214 Stroup, A. L., and K. J. Hunter: Sibling position in the family and personality of offspring. *J. Marriage & Family*, 1965, **27**, 65–68.

215 Sutton-Smith, B.: Role replication and reversal in play. *Merrill-Palmer Quart.*, 1966, **12**, 285–298.

216 Sutton-Smith, B., and B. G. Rosenberg: Sibling consensus on power tactics. *J. genet. Psychol.*, 1968, **112**, 63–72.

217 Sutton-Smith, B., B. G. Rosenberg, and F. Landy: Father-absence effects in families of different sibling compositions. *Child Develpm.*, 1968, **39**, 1213–1221.

218 Taylor, A. B.: Role perception, empathy and marriage adjustment. *Sociol. soc. Res.*, 1967, **52**, 22–34.

219 Tolchin, M.: Specialist offers guide to parents of an only child. *The New York Times*, Mar. 20, 1959.

220 Toman, V. V.: Family constellation as a basic personality determinant. *J. indiv. Psychol.*, 1959, **15**, 199–211.

221 Tomeh, A. K.: Birth order and kinship affiliation. *J. Marriage & Family*, 1969, **31**, 19–26.

222 Tuckman, J., and R. A. Regan: Size of family and behavioral problems in children. *J. genet. Psychol.*, 1967, **111**, 151–160.

223 Turner, R. H.: Some aspects of women's ambition. *Amer. J. Sociol.*, 1964, **70**, 271–285.

224 Van der Veen, F.: The parent's concept of the family unit and child adjustment. *J. counsel. Psychol.*, 1965, **12**, 196–200.

225 Verger, D.: Birth order and sibling differences in interests. *J. indiv. Psychol.*, 1968, **24**, 56–59.

226 Vernon, G. M.: Interfaith marriages. *Relig. Educ.*, 1960, **55**, 261–264.

227 Walters, J., R. Connor, and M. Zunich: Interaction of mothers and children from lower-class families. *Child Develpm.*, 1964, **35**, 433–440.

228 Warnath, C. F.: The relation of family cohesiveness and adolescent independence to social effectiveness. *Marriage fam. Living*, 1955, **17**, 346–348.

229 Warren, J. R.: Birth order and social behavior. *Psychol. Bull.*, 1966, **65**, 38–49.

230 Welins, E. G.: Some effects of premature parental responsibility on the older sibling. *Smith Coll. Stud. soc. Wk.*, 1964, **35**, 26–40.

231 Weller, L.: The relationship of birth order to cohesiveness. *J. soc. Psychol.*, 1964, **63**, 249–254.

232 Whitmarsh, R. E.: Adjustment problems of adolescent daughters of employed mothers. *J. Home Econ.* 1965, **57**, 201–204.

233 Winestine, M. C.: Twinship and psychological differentiation. *Dissert. Abstr.*, 1966, **26**, 4082–4083.

234 Wittman, H.: The adjustment of twins: An evaluation of the relationship between twinship patterns of identification and adjustment. *Dissert. Abstr.*, 1964, **25**, 3678.

235 Wright, L.: A study of special abilities in identical twins. *J. genet. Psychol.*, 1961, **99**, 245–251.

236 Yarrow, L. J.: Research in dimensions of early maternal care. *Merrill-Palmer Quart.*, 1963, **9**, 101–114.

237 Yourglich, A.: A comparative analysis of two studies on age-sex-differentiations in sibling systems. *Family Life Coordinator*, 1967, **16**, 73–77.

238 Zucker, R. A., M. Manosevitz, and R. I. Lanyon: Birth order, anxiety and affiliation during a crisis. *J. Pers. soc. Psychol.*, 1968, **8**, 354–359.

239 Zunich, M.: Relationship between maternal behavior and attitudes toward children. *J. genet. Psychol.*, 1962, **100**, 155–165.

CHAPTER 14

1 Adams, K. S.: Suicide: A critical review of the literature. *Canad. Psychiat. Ass. J.*, 1967, **12**, 413–420.

2 Adelson, J., B. Green, and R. O'Neil:

Growth of the idea of law in adolescence. *Develpm. Psychol.*, 1969, **1**, 327–332.

3 Adler, N.: The antinomian personality. *Psychiatry*, 1968, **31**, 325–338.

4 Adorno, T. W., E. Frenkel-Brunswik, D. J. Levinson, and R. N. Sanford: *The authoritarian personality.* New York: Harper, 1950.

5 Ainsworth, L. H.: Rigidity, insecurity and stress. *J. abnorm. soc. Psychol.*, 1958, **56**, 67–74.

6 Alexander, C. N.: Alcohol and adolescent rebellion. *Soc. Forces*, 1967, **45**, 542–550.

7 Allen, V. L.: Effect of knowledge of deception on conformity. *J. soc. Psychol.*, 1966, **69**, 101–106.

8 Allport, G. W.: *The nature of prejudice.* Cambridge, Mass.: Addison-Wesley, 1954.

9 Allport, G. W.: *Pattern and growth in personality.* New York: Holt, 1961.

10 Altus, W. D.: Birth order and its sequelae. *Science*, 1966, **151**, 44–49.

11 Amatora, Sister M.: Developmental trends in preadolescence and early adolescence in self-evaluation. *J. genet. Psychol.*, 1957, **91**, 89–97.

12 Apperson, L. B.: Childhood experiences of schizophrenics and alcoholics. *J. genet. Psychol.*, 1965, **106**, 301–313.

13 Asuni, T.: Maladjustment and delinquency: A comparison of two samples. *J. child Psychol. Psychiat.*, 1983, **4**, 219–228.

14 Barker, G. H., and W. T. Adams: Glue sniffers. *Sociol. soc. Res.*, 1963, **47**, 298–310.

15 Barrett-Lennard, G. T.: The mature person. *Ment. Hyg., N. Y.*, 1962, **46**, 98–102.

16 Barter, J. T., D. O. Swabach, and D. Todd: Adolescent suicide attempts. *Arch. gen. Psychiat.*, 1968, **19**, 523–527.

17 Beilin, H.: Teachers' and clinicians' attitudes toward the behavior problems of children: A reappraisal. *Child Develpm.*, 1959, **30**, 9–25.

18 Bennett, E. M.: A socio-cultural interpretation of maladjustive behavior. *J. soc. Psychol.*, 1953, **37**, 19–26.

19 Berecz, J. M.: Phobias of childhood: Etiology and treatment. *Psychol. Bull.*, 1968, **70**, 694–720.

20 Berkowitz, L.: The expression and reduction of hostility. *Psychol. Bull.*, 1958, **55**, 257–284.

21 Black, M. S., and P. London: The dimensions of guilt, religion and personal ethics. *J. soc. Psychol.*, 1966, **69**, 39–54.

22 Blazer, J. A.: Fantasy and daydreams. *Child & Family*, 1966, **5**, no. 3, 22–28.

23 Bossard, J. H. S., and E. S. Boll: *The sociology of child development*, 4th ed. New York: Harper & Row, 1966.

24 Brandt, R. M.: Children who know and like themselves. *Childhood Educ.*, 1957, **33**, 299–303.

25 Breed, W.: Occupational mobility and suicide among white males. *Amer. sociol. Rev.*, 1963, **28**, 179–188.

26 Breger, L., and C. Ruiz: The role of ego-defense in conformity. *J. soc. Psychol.*, 1966, **69**, 73–85.

27 Brehm, M. L., and K. W. Back: Self-image and attitudes toward drugs. *J. Pers.*, 1968, **36**, 299–314.

28 Bruch, H.: Developmental obesity and schizophrenia. *Psychiatry*, 1958, **21**, 65–70.

29 Bühler, C., H. Brind, and A. Horner: Age as a phase of human life. *Hum. Develpm.*, 1968, **11**, 53–63.

30 Burke, P. J.: Scapegoating: An alternative to role differentiation. *Sociometry*, 1969, **32**, 159–168.

31 Cantril, H.: A study of aspirations. *Scient. American*, 1963, **208**, no. 2, 41–45.

32 Clark, J. P., and E. W. Haurek: Age and sex roles of adolescents and their involvement in misconduct: A reappraisal. *Sociol. soc. Res.*, 1966, **50**, 495–508.

33 Coleman, J. S.: *The adolescent society.* New York: Free Press, 1961.

34 Combs, A. W.: New horizons in field research: The self concept. *Educ. Leadership*, 1958, **15**, 315–319, 328.

35 Corsini, R. J.: Appearance and criminality. *Amer. J. Sociol.*, 1959, **65**, 49–51.

36 Cosgrove, M.: School guidance for home and family. *Marriage fam. Living*, 1952, **14**, 26–31.

37 Cottle, T. J.: Self-concepts, ego ideal and the response to action. *Sociol. soc. Res.*, 1965, **50**, 78–88.

38 Craske, S.: A study of the relation between personality and accident history. *Brit. J. med. Psychol.*, 1968, **41**, 399–404.

39 Crow, L. D.: *Psychology of human adjustment.* New York: Knopf, 1967.

40 Cummins, E. J.: Are disciplinary students different? *Personnel Guid. J.*, 1966, **44**, 624–627.

41 Davis, F., and L. Munoz: Heads and Greeks: Patterns and meanings of drug use among Hippies. *J. Hlth. soc. Behav.*, 1968, **9**, 156–164.

42 Davis, J. M.: A reinterpretation of the Barker, Dumbo and Levin study of frustration and aggression. *Child Develpm.*, 1958, **29**, 503–506.

43 Davitz, J. R.: Contributions of research with children to a theory of maladjustment. *Child Develpm.*, 1958, **29**, 3–7.

44 Dinitz, S., F. R. Scarpitti, and W. C. Reckless: Delinquency vulnerability: A cross-group and longitudinal analysis. *Amer. sociol. Rev.*, 1962, **27**, 515–517.

45 Dodge, N., and G. A. Muench: Relationship of conformity and the need for approval in children. *Develpm. Psychol.*, 1969, **1**, 67–68.

46 Douglas, V. I.: Children's responses to frustration: A developmental study. *Canad. J. Psychol.*, 1965, **19**, 161–171.

47 Dubbé, M. C.: What parents are not told may hurt. *Family Life Coordinator*, 1965, **14**, 51–118.

48 Dublin, L. I.: *Suicide.* New York: Ronald, 1963.

49 Dunbar, F.: Homeostasis during puberty. *Amer. J. Psychiat.*, 1958, **114**, 673–682.

50 Edwards, A. E., and D. B. Wine: Personality changes with age: Their dependency on concomitant intellectual decline. *J. Geront.*, 1963, **18**, 182–184.

51 Epstein, E. M.: The self-concept of the delinquent female. *Smith Coll. Stud. soc. Wk.*, 1962, **32**, 220–234.

52 Erikson, E. H.: Youth and the life cycle. *Children*, 1960, **7**, 43–49.

53 Errera, P.: Some historical aspects of the concept, phobia. *Psychiat. Quart.*, 1962, **36**, 325–336.

54 Eysenck, H. J., M. Tarrant, M. Woolf, and L. England: Smoking and personality. *Brit. med. J.*, 1960, **1**, 1456–1460.

55 Eysenck, S. B. G.: A new scale for personality measurement in children. *Brit. J. educ. Psychol.*, 1965, **35**, 362–367.

56 Farina, A., J. G. Allen, and B. B. Saul: The role of the stigmatized person in affecting social relationships. *J. Pers.*, 1968, **38**, 169–182.

57 Freud, S.: *The standard edition of the complete psychological works of Sigmund Freud.* London: Hogarth, 1953–1962.

58 Gallenkamp, C. R., and J. F. Rychlak: Parental attitudes of sanction in middle-class adolescent male delinquency. *J. soc. Psychol.*, 1968, **75**, 255–260.

59 *Geriatric Focus* Report: Suicide rate in old age linked to social crises. Oct. 15, 1966, pp. 1–5.

60 Gibbs, D. N.: Student failure and social maladjustment. *Personnel Guid. J.*, 1964, **43**, 580–585.

61 Gibbs, J. P.: Marital status and suicide in the United States: A special test of the status integration theory. *Amer. J. Sociol.*, 1969, **74**, 521–533.

62 Gilbert, J. G., and D. N. Lombardi: Personality characteristics of young male narcotic addicts. *J. consult. Psychol.*, 1967, **31**, 536–538.

63 Glaser, K.: Attempted suicide in children and adolescents: Psychodynamic observations. *Amer. J. Psychother.*, 1965, **19**, 220–227.

64 Glueck, S., and E. Glueck: *Family environment and delinquency.* Boston: Houghton Mifflin, 1962.

65 Goslin, D. A.: Accuracy of self perception and social acceptance. *Sociometry*, 1962, **25**, 283–296.

66 Gould, R. E.: Suicide problems in children and adolescents. *Amer. J. Psychother.*, 1965, **19**, 228–246.

67 Greene, J. E.: Alleged "misbehaviors" among senior high school students. *J. soc. Psychol.*, 1962, **58**, 371–382.

68 Haider, I.: Suicidal attempts in children and adolescents. *Brit. J. Psychiat.*, 1968, **114**, 1133–1134.

69 Hampton, M. C., L. R. Shapiro, and R. L. Huenemann: Helping teen-age girls improve their diets. *J. Home Econ.*, 1961, **53**, 835–838.

70 Hardyck, C. D.: Sex differences in personality changes with age. *J. Geront.*, 1964, **19**, 78–82.

71 Harp, J., and P. Taietz: Academic integrity and social structure: A study of cheating among college students. *Soc. Probl.*, 1966, **13**, 365–373.

72 Harris, D. B., A. M. Rose, K. E. Clark, and F. Valasek: Personality differences between responsible and less responsible children. *J. genet. Psychol.*, 1955, **87**, 103–106.

73 Havighurst, R. J.: Conditions productive of superior children. In R. E. Grinder (ed.), *Studies in adolescence.* New York: Macmillan, 1963.

74 Havighurst, R. J.: Personality and patterns of aging. *Gerontologist*, 1968, **8**, 20–23.

75 Havighurst, R. J., and R. Albrecht: *Older people.* New York: Longmans, 1953.

76 Heilbrun, A. B.: Parental model attributes, nurturant reinforcement, and consistency of behavior in adolescents. *Child Develpm.*, 1964, **35**, 151–167.

77 Henry, W. E., and E. Cumming: Personality development in adulthood and old age. *J. proj. Tech.*, 1959, **23**, 383–390.

78 Hicks, N.: Drugs to fight depression. *The New York Times*, Dec. 14, 1969.

79 Hillson, J. S., and P. Worchel: Self concept and defensive behavior in the maladjusted. *J. consult. Psychol.*, 1957, **21**, 83–88.

80 Hirsh, J.: Suicide. *Ment. Hyg., N.Y.*, 1959, **43**, 516–525.

81 Hoffman, M. L.: Conformity as a defense mechanism and a form of resistance to genuine group influence. *J. Pers.*, 1957, **25**, 412–424.

82 Hollingshead, A. B., and F. C. Redlich: *Social class and mental illness.* New York: Wiley, 1958.

83 Horney, K.: On feeling abused. *Amer. J. Psychoanal.*, 1951, **11**, 5–12.

84 Hurwitz, J. I.: Three delinquent types: A multivariate analysis. *J. crim. Law Criminol. police Sci.*, 1965, **56**, 328–334.

85 Inselberg, R. M.: Social and psychological factors associated with high school marriages. *J. Home Econ.*, 1961, **53**, 766–772.

86 Jackson, L.: Anxiety in adolescents in relation to school refusal. *J. child Psychol. Psychiat.*, 1964, **5**, 59–73.

87 Jacobziner, H.: Attempted suicides in adolescence by poisoning. *Amer. J. Psychother.*, 1965, **19**, 247–252.

88 Jamieson, B. D.: The influence of birth order, family size and sex differences on risk-taking behavior. *Brit. J. soc. clin. Psychol.*, 1969, **8**, 1–8.

89 Jenkins, R. L.: Classification of behavior problems of children. *Amer. J. Psychiat.*, 1969, **125**, 1032–1039.

90 Jersild, A. T.: Self-understanding in childhood and adolescence. *Amer. Psychologist*, 1951, **8**, 122–126.

91 Jersild, A. T.: *The psychology of adolescence*, 2d ed. New York: Macmillan, 1963.

92 Jersild, A. T.: *Child psychology*, 6th ed. Englewood Cliffs, N.J.: Prentice-Hall, 1969.

93 Johnson, H. H.: Some effects of discrepancy level on responses to negative information about one's self. *Sociometry*, 1966, **29**, 52–66.

94 Jones, M. C.: Psychological correlates of somatic development. *Child Develpm.*, 1965, **36**, 899–911.

95 Jourard, S. M.: *Personality development: An approach through the study of healthy personality.* New York: Macmillan, 1958.

96 Kagan, J., and H. A. Moss: *Birth to maturity: A study in psychological development.* New York: Wiley, 1962.

97 Kahn, M. W.: A comparison of personality, intelligence and social history of two criminal groups. *J. soc. Psychol.*, 1959, **49**, 33–40.

98 Kaufman, I., and L. Heims: The body image of the juvenile delinquent. *Amer. J. Orthopsychiat.*, 1958, **28**, 146–159.

99 Keeve, J. P.: Perpetuating phantom handicaps in school age children. *Except. Children*, 1967, **33**, 539–544.

100 Kelly, E. L.: Consistency of the adult personality. *Amer. Psychologist*, 1955, **10**, 659–681.

101 Kent, D. P.: Social and cultural factors affecting the mental health of the aged. *Amer. J. Orthopsychiat.*, 1966, **36**, 680–685.

102 King, G. F., and M. Schiller: Ego strength and type of defensive behavior. *J. counsel. Psychol.*, 1960, **24**, 215–217.

103 Konapka, G.: Adolescent delinquent girls. *Children*, 1964, **11**, 21–26.

104 Kulik, J. A., K. B. Stein, and T. R. Sarbin: Dimensions and patterns of adolescent antisocial behavior. *J. consult. clin. Psychol.*, 1968, **32**, 375–382.

105 LaGrone, C. W.: Sex and personality differences in relation to fantasy. *J. consult. Psychol.*, 1963, **27**, 270–272.

106 Lane, E. A., and G. W. Albee: Early childhood intellectual differences between schizophrenic adults and their siblings. *J. abnorm. soc. Psychol.*, 1964, **68**, 193–195.

107 Lane, H.: The meaning of disorder among youth. *Education*, 1955, **76**, 214–217.

108 Lang, B.: When teen-agers start to drink. *The New York Times*, July 19, 1964.

109 LaPouse, R.: The epidemiology of behavior disorders in children. *Amer. J. Dis. Children*, 1966, **111**, 594–599.

110 Lawson, R., and M. H. Marx: Frustration: Theory and experiment. *Genet. Psychol. Monogr.*, 1958, **57**, 393–464.

111 Lerman, P.: Individual values, peer values, and subcultural delinquency. *Amer. sociol. Rev.*, 1968, **33**, 219–235.

112 Lester, D.: Suicide as an aggressive act: A replication with a control for neuroticism. *J. gen. Psychol.*, 1968, **79**, 83–86.

113 Levy, N. J.: The use of drugs by teenagers for sanctuary and illusion. *Amer. J. Psychoanal.*, 1968, **28**, 48–58.

114 Linden, M. E.: The older person in the family. *Soc. Casewk.*, 1956, **37**, 75–81.

115 London, E. S.: An inquiry into boredom and thrill seeking. *Dissert. Abstr.*, 1966, **26**, 4853.

116 Lorber, N. M.: Inadequate social acceptance and disruptive classroom behavior. *J. educ. Res.*, 1966, **59**, 360–362.

117 Lövaas, O. I.: The effect of exposure to symbolic aggression on aggressive behavior. *Child Develpm.*, 1961, **32**, 37–44.

118 Lowrie, S. H.: Early marriage: Premarital pregnancy and assorted factors. *J. Marriage & Family*, 1965, **27**, 48–56.

119 Lynn, R., and B. Hayes: Some international comparisons of tobacco consumption and personality. *J. soc. Psychol.*, 1969, **79**, 13–17.

120 Malefijt, A. deW.: Dutch joking patterns. *Trans. N.Y. Acad. Sci.*, 1968, **30**, 1181–1186.

121 Manheimer, D. I., and G. D. Mellinger: Personality characteristics of the child accident repeater. *Child Develpm.*, 1967, **38**, 491–513.

122 Marcus, I. M., W. Wilson, I. Kraft, S. Swander, F. Southerland, and E. Schulhofer: An interdisciplinary approach to accident patterns in children. *Monogr. Soc. Res. Child Develpm.*, 1960, **25**, no. 2.

123 Martinson, F. M.: Ego deficiency as a factor in marriage: A male sample. *Marriage fam. Living*, 1959, **21**, 48–52.

124 Matarazzo, J. D., and G. Saslow: Psychological and related characteristics of smokers and nonsmokers. *Psychol. Bull.*, 1960, **57**, 493–513.

125 Matteson, R. W.: Self-estimates of college freshmen. *Personnel Guid. J.*, 1956, **34**, 280–284.

126 Matza, D., and G. M. Sykes: Juvenile delinquency and subterranean values. *Amer. sociol. Rev.*, 1961, **26**, 712–719.

127 Maurer, D. W., and V. H. Vogel: *Narcotics and narcotic addiction.* Springfield, Ill.: Charles C Thomas, 1962.

128 McCord, J., W. McCord, and A. Howard: Family interaction as antecedent to the direction of male aggressiveness. *J. abnorm. soc. Psychol.*, 1963, **66**, 239–242.

129 McDonald, R. L.: Effects of sex, race, and class on self, ideal-self, and parental ratings in Southern adolescents. *Percept. mot. Skills*, 1968, **27**, 15–25.

130 McGlothlin, W. H., and L. J. West: The marijuana problem: An overview. *Amer. J. Psychiat.*, 1968, **125**, 370–379.

131 Mednick, S. A., and J. B. P. Shaffer: Mothers' retrospective reports in child-rearing research. *Amer. J. Orthopsychiat.*, 1963, **33**, 457–461.

132 Menninger, W. C.: Tensions in family life. *Pastoral Psychol.*, 1953, **4**, 11–18.

133 Mitchell, S., and M. Shepherd: A comparative study of children's behavior at home and at school. *Brit. J. educ. Psychol.*, 1966, **36**, 248–254.

134 Morgan, C. T.: *Physiological psychology*, 3d ed. New York: McGraw-Hill, 1965.

135 Moss, J. J., and R. Gingles: The relationship of personality to the incidence of early marriage. *Marriage fam. Living*, 1959, **21**, 373–377.

136 Murphy, L. B.: Coping devices and defense mechanisms in relation to autonomous ego functions. *Bull. Menninger Clinic*, 1960, **24**, 144–153.

137 Musgrove, F.: Role conflict in adolescence. *Brit. J. educ. Psychol.*, 1964, **34**, 34–42.

138 Mussen, P. H., and J. Kagan: Group conformity and perceptions of parents. *Child Develpm.*, 1958, **29**, 57–60.

139 Nettler, G.: Antisocial sentiment and criminality. *Amer. sociol. Rev.*, 1959, **24**, 202–208.

140 Neuringer, C., and L. W. Wandke: Interpersonal conflicts in persons of high self-concept and low self-concept. *J. soc. Psychol.*, 1966, **68**, 313–322.

141 *New York Times* Report: Student drug use is laid to tension. Feb. 2, 1969.

142 *New York Times* Report: Briton says illness can impair judgment of world's leaders. Sept. 28, 1969.

143 *New York Times* Report: 12% of Americans in twenties say they've tried marijuana. Oct. 26, 1969.

144 *New York Times* Report: Dr. Mead calls marijuana ban more perilous than marijuana. Oct. 28, 1969.

145 Noyes, R.: The taboo of suicide. *Psychiatry*, 1968, **31**, 173–183.

146 Offer, D.: *The psychological world of the teenager.* New York: Basic Books, 1969.

147 Okrongley, W. D.: Attitude development and accident prevention. *Personnel J.*, 1966, **45**, 169–177.

148 Packard, V.: *The status seekers.* New York: Pocket Books, 1961.

149 Palmai, G., P. B. Storey, and O. Briscoe: Social class and the young offender. *Brit. J. Psychiat.*, 1967, **113**, 1073–1082.

150 Parker, E.: *The seven ages of woman.* Baltimore: Johns Hopkins, 1960.

151 Peck, R. F., and R. J. Havighurst: *The psychology of character development.* New York: 1962.

152 Peterson, H. A.: Teacher and peer acceptance of four student behavior types. *Calif. J. educ. Psychol.*, 1968, **19**, 16–27.

153 Philip, A. E., and J. W. McCulloch: Some psychological features of persons who have attempted suicide. *Brit. J. Psychiat.*, 1968, **114**, 1299–1300.

154 Phillips, B. N.: Age changes in accuracy of self-perception. *Child Develpm.*, 1963, **34**, 1041–1046.

155 Piers, E. V., and D. B. Harris: Age and other correlates of self-concept in children. *J. educ. Psychol.*, 1964, **55**, 91–85.

156 Pine, G. J.: Social class, social mobility, and delinquent behavior. *Personnel Guid. J.*, 1965, **43**, 770–774.

157 Powell, W. J., and S. M. Jourard: Some objective evidence of immaturity in underachieving college students. *J. counsel. Psychol.*, 1963, **10**, 276–282.

158 Quay, H. C., and L. C. Quay: Behavior problems in early adolescence. *Child Develpm.*, 1965, **36**, 215–220.

159 Reckless, W. C., and S. Dinitz: Pioneering with self-concept as a vulnerability factor in delinquency. *J. crim. Law Criminol. police Sci.*, 1967, **58**, 515–523.

160 Reimanis, G.: Relationship of childhood experience memories and anomie later in life. *J. genet. Psychol.*, 1965, **106**, 245–252.

161 Rennie, T. A. C., L. Srole, M. K. Opler, and T. S. Langner: Urban life and mental health. *Amer. J. Psychiat.*, 1957, **113**, 831–837.

162 Resnick, H. E. (ed.): *Suicidal behaviors: Diagnosis and management.* Boston: Little, Brown, 1968.

163 Rich, G. J.: Childhood as a preparation for delinquency. *J. educ. Sociol.*, 1954, **27**, 404–413.

164 Riester, A. E., and R. A. Zucker: Adolescent social structure and drinking behavior. *Personnel Guid. J.*, 1968, **47**, 304–312.

165 Robey, A., R. J. Rosenwald, J. E. Snell, and R. E. Lee: The runaway girl: A reaction to family stress. *Amer. J. Orthopsychiat.*, 1964, **34**, 762–767.

166 Roff, M.: Childhood social interactions and young adult psychosis. *J. clin. Psychol.*, 1963, **19**, 152–157.

167 Rogers, K. D., and G. Reese: Smoking and high school performance. *Amer. J. Dis. Children*, 1964, **108**, 117–121.

168 Rose, A. A.: The homes of homesick girls. *J. child Psychiat.*, 1948, **1**, 181–189.

169 Rose, A. M.: Class differences among the elderly: A research report. *Sociol. soc. Res.*, 1966, **50**, 356–360.

170 Ryle, A., D. A. Pond, and M. Hamilton: The prevalence and patterns of psychological disturbance in children of primary age. *J. child Psychol. Psychiat.*, 1965, **6**, 101–113.

171 Sarbin, F. R.: On the distinction between social roles and social types, with special reference to the Hippie. *Amer. J. Psychiat.*, 1969, **125**, 1024–1031.

172 Schrut, A.: Some typical patterns in the behavior and background of adolescent girls who attempt suicide. *Amer. J. Psychiat.*, 1968, **125**, 69–74.

173 Seltzer, C. C.: Masculinity and smoking. *Science*, 1959, **130**, 1706–1707.

174 Shaffer, L. F., and E. J. Shoben: *The psychology of adjustment*, 2d ed. Boston: Houghton Mifflin, 1956.

175 Shanley, F. J.: Middle-class delinquency as a social problem. *Sociol. soc. Res.*, 1967, **51**, 185–198.

176 Shaw, M. C.: A note on parent attitudes toward independence training and the academic achievement of their children. *J. educ. Psychol.*, 1964, **55**, 371–374.

177 Shellow, R., J. R. Schamp, E. Liebow, and E. Unger: Suburban runaways of the 1960's. *Monogr. Soc. Res. Child Develpm.*, 1967, **32**, no. 3.

178 Short, J. P., and F. L. Strodtbeck: The response of gang leaders to status threats: An observation of group process and delinquent behavior. *Amer. J. Sociol.*, 1963, **48**, 571–579.

179 Shrader, W. K., and T. Leventhal: Birth order of children and parental reports of problems. *Child Develpm.*, 1968, **39**, 1165–1175.

180 Siegel, A. E.: The influence of violence in the mass media upon children's role expectations. *Child Develpm.*, 1958, **29**, 35–56.

181 Singer, J. L., and R. Rowe: An experimental study of some relationships between daydreams and anxiety. *J. consult. Psychol.*, 1962, **26**, 446–454.

182 Singer, J. L., and R. A. Schonbar: Correlates of daydreaming: A dimension of self-awareness. *J. consult. Psychol.*, 1961, **25**, 1–6.

183 Slater, P. E., and H. A. Scarr: Personality in old age. *Genet. Psychol. Monogr.*, 1964, **70**, 229–269.

184 Slovic, P.: Risk-taking in children: Age and sex differences. *Child Develpm.*, 1966, **37**, 169–176.

185 Smith, G. M.: Personality correlates of cigarette smoking in students of college age. *Ann. N.Y. Acad. Sci.*, 1967, **142**, 308–321.

186 Smith, M. E.: A comparison of certain personality traits rated in the same individuals in childhood and fifty years later. *Child Develpm.*, 1952, **23**, 159–180.

187 Smith, S. L., and C. Sander: Food craving, depression and premenstrual problems. *Psychosom. Med.*, 1969, **31**, 281–287.

188 Sperling, O. E.: An imaginary playmate representing a pre-stage of the super-ego. *Psychoanal. Stud. Child*, 1954, **9**, 252–258.

189 Steiner, I. D.: Reactions to adverse and favorable evaluations of one's self. *J. Pers.*, 1968, **36**, 553–563.

190 Steininger, M., R. E. Johnson, and D. K. Kirts: Cheating on college examinations as a function of situationally aroused anxiety and hostility. *J. educ. Psychol.*, 1964, **55**, 317–324.

191 Stewart, L., and N. Livson: Smoking and rebelliousness: A longitudinal study from childhood to maturity. *J. consult. Psychol.*, 1966, **30**, 225–229.

192 Strang, R.: *The adolescent views himself.* New York: McGraw-Hill, 1957.

193 Strecker, E. A.: *Their mothers' sons.* Philadelphia: Lippincott, 1946.

194 Stricker, G.: Scapegoating: An experimental investigation. *J. abnorm. soc. Psychol.*, 1963, **67**, 125–131.

195 Sutton-Smith, B., and B. G. Rosenberg: Peer perceptions of impulsive behavior. *Merrill-Palmer Quart.*, 1961, **7**, 233–238.

196 Thompson, G. G., and E. F. Gardner: Adolescents' perceptions of happy-successful living. *J. genet. Psychol.*, 1969, **115**, 107–120.

197 *Time* Report: Kids and heroin: The adolescent epidemic. Mar. 16, 1970, pp. 16–25.

198 Toigo, R. Social status and schoolroom aggression in third-grade children. *Genet. Psychol. Monogr.*, 1965, **71**, 221–268.

199 Tuckman, J.: College students' judgment of the passage of time over the life span. *J. genet. Psychol.*, 1965, **107**, 43–48.

200 Tuckman, J., and R. A. Regan: Size of family and behavioral problems in children. *J. genet. Psychol.*, 1967, **111**, 151–160.

201 Tuckman, J., and R. Ziegler: Language usage and social maturity as related to suicide notes. *J. soc. Psychol.*, 1966, **68**, 139–142.

202 Turner, R. H., and R. H. Vanderlippe: Self-ideal congruence as an index of adjustment. *J. abnorm. soc. Psychol.*, 1958, **57**, 202–206.

203 *U. S. News & World Report*: Drug problem among students—how bad—what's back of it. Mar. 24, 1969, pp. 90–92.

204 Wagman, M.: Daydreaming frequency and some personality measures. *J. consult. Psychol.*, 1965, **29**, 395.

205 Walker, H. M.: Empirical assessment of deviant behavior in children. *Psychology in the Schools*, 1969, **6**, 93–97.

206 Washburn, W. C.: Patterns of protective attitudes in relation to differences in self evaluation and anxiety level among high school students. *Calif. J. educ. Res.*, 1962, **13**, 84–94.

207 Watley, D. J.: Personal adjustment and prediction of academic achievement. *J. appl. Psychol.*, 1965, **49**, 20–23.

208 Watson, G.: Some personality differences in children related to strict or permissive parental discipline. *J. Psychol.*, 1957, **44**, 227–249.

209 Weatherley, D.: Maternal response to childhood aggression and subsequent anti-Semitism. *J. abnorm. soc. Psychol.*, 1963, **66**, 183–185.

210 Wertheimer, M.: The defense mechanisms that students report in their own behavior. *J. genet. Psychol.*, 1958, **92**, 111–112.

211 Williams, A. F.: Self-concepts of college problem drinkers. II. Heilbrun Need Scales. *Quart. J. Stud. Alcohol*, 1967, **28**, 267–277.

212 Williams, K. L., and H. Byars: Negro self-esteem in a transitional society. *Personnel Guid. J.*, 1968, **47**, 120–125.

213 Willie, C. V.: The relative contribution of family status and economic status to juvenile delinquency. *Soc. Probl.*, 1967, **14**, 326–335.

214 Willis, R. H.: Conformity, independency and anticonformity. *Hum. Relat.*, 1965, **18**, 373–388.

215 Windholz, G.: Discrepancy of self and ideal-self and frequency of daydreams reported by male subjects. *Psychol. Rep.*, 1968, **23**, 1121–1122.

216 Winkler, R. C., and R. A. Myers: Some concomitants of self-ideal discrepancy measures of self-acceptance. *J. counsel. Psychol.*, 1963, **10**, 83–86.

217 Wirt, R. D., and P. F. Briggs: Personality and environmental factors in the development of delinquency. *Psychol. Monogr.*, 1959, **73**, no. 15.

218 Witryol, S. L., and J. E. Calkins: Marginal social values of rural school children. *J. genet. Psychol.*, 1958, **92**, 81–93.

219 Witty, P. A.: Children's interests: A brief summary. *Elem. Eng.*, 1960, **31**, 469–475.

220 Wolff, S.: Symptomatology and outcome of pre-school children with behavior disorders attending a child guidance clinic. *J. child Psychol. Psychiat.*, 1961, **2**, 269–276.

221 Wylie, R. C.: Some relationships between defensiveness and self-concept discrepancies. *J. Pers.*, 1957, **25**, 600–616.

222 Zeitlin, H.: High school discipline. *Calif. J. educ. Res.*, 1962, **13**, 116–125.

CHAPTER 15

1 Amatora, Sister M.: Comparisons in self-evaluation in personality. *J. soc. Psychol.*, 1955, **42**, 315–321.

2 Angrist, S. S.: Role conception as a predictor of adult female roles. *Sociol. soc. Res.*, 1966, **50**, 448–459.

3 Bain, R.: Making normal people. *Marriage fam. Living*, 1954, **16**, 27–31.

4 Barrett, R. L.: Changes in accuracy of self-estimates. *Personnel Guid. J.*, 1968, **47**, 353–357.

5 Barrett-Lennard, G. T.: The mature person. *Ment. Hyg., N.Y.*, 1962, **46**, 98–102.

6 Bayley, N.: Research in child development: A longitudinal perspective. *Merrill-Palmer Quart.*, 1965, **11**, 183–208.

7 Becker, H. S.: Personal changes in adult life. *Sociometry*, 1964, **27**, 40–53.

8 Bellah, R. N.: Religious evolution. *Amer. sociol. Rev.*, 1964, **29**, 358–374.

9 Bernhardt, K. S.: Laying the foundations of mental health in childhood. *Relig. Educ.*, 1956, **51**, 328–331.

10 Blau, Z. S.: Class structure, mobility, and change in child rearing. *Sociometry*, 1965, **28**, 216–219.

11 Bledsoe, J. C.: Self-concepts of children and their intelligence, achievements, interests and anxiety. *J. indiv. Psychol.*, 1964, **20**, 55–58.

12 Blood, R. C.: Long range causes and consequences of the employment of married women. *J. Marriage & Family*, 1965, **27**, 43–47.

13 Bossard, J. H. S., and E. S. Boll: *The sociology of child development*, 4th ed. New York: Harper & Row, 1966.

14 Bowerman, C. E., and J. W. Kinch: Changes in family and peer orientation of children between the fourth and tenth grades. *Soc. Forces*, 1959, **37**, 205–211.

15 Brandt, R. M.: The accuracy of self-estimate: A measure of self-concept reality. *Genet. Psychol. Monogr.*, 1958, **58**, 55–99.

16 Brien, H.: London: Looking back at the future. *The New York Times*, Nov. 17, 1969.

17 Britton, J. H.: Dimensions of adjustment of older adults. *J. Geront.*, 1963, **18**, 60–65.

18 Brower, D.: Child psychology: A look at tomorrow. *J. genet. Psychol.*, 1963, **102**, 45–50.

19 Brown, R. G.: Family structure and social isolation of older people. *J. Geront.*, 1960, **15**, 170–174.

20 Bruce, P.: Relationship of self-acceptance to other variables with sixth grade children oriented in self-understanding. *J. educ. Psychol.*, 1958, **49**, 229–238.

21 Bühler, C., A. Brind, and A. Horner: Old age as a phase of human life. *Hum. Develpm.*, 1968, **11**, 53–63.

22 Busse, E. W., et al: Studies of the process of aging: Factors that influence the psyche of elderly persons. *Amer. J. Psychiat.*, 1954, **110**, 897–903.

23 Canter, G. J., and J. B. Trost: The speech handicapped. *Rev. educ. Res.*, 1966, **36**, 56–74.

24 Cantril, H.: A study of aspirations. *Scient. American*, 1963, **208**, no. 2, 41–45.

25 Caplan, S. W.: The effect of group counseling on junior high school boys' concepts of themselves in school. *J. counsel. Psychol.*, 1957, **4**, 124–128.

26 Cavan, R. S.: Personal adjustment in old age. In A. I. Lansing (ed.), *Cowdry's problems of aging.* Baltimore: Williams & Wilkins, 1952, pp. 1032–1052.

27 Clark, W. H., and C. M. Warner: The relation of church attendance to honesty and kindness in a small community. *Relig. Educ.*, 1955, **50**, 340–342.

28 Cole, L., and I. N. Hall: *Psychology of adolescence*, 6th ed. New York: Holt, 1964.

29 Coleman, J. S.: *The adolescent society.* New York: Free Press, 1961.

30 Combs, A. W.: New horizons in field research: The self-concept. *Educ. Leadership*, 1958, **15**, 315–319, 328.

31 Coombs, R. H.: Social participation, self-concept and interpersonal valuation. *Sociometry*, 1969, **32**, 273–286.

32 Cowan, E. L.: The "negative self-concept" as a personality measure. *J. consult. Psychol.*, 1954, **18**, 138–142.

33 Crandall, V. J., and A. Preston: An assessment of personal-social adjustments of a group of middle-class mothers. *J. genet. Psychol.*, 1956, **89**, 239–249.

34 Crow, L. D., and A. Crow: *Adolescent development and adjustment*, 2d ed. New York: McGraw-Hill, 1965.

35 Cruickshank, W. M., and G. O. Johnson: *Education of exceptional children and youth*, 2d ed. Englewood Cliffs, N.Y.: Prentice-Hall, 1967.

36 DeFleur, M. L.: Mass communication and social change. *Soc. Forces*, 1966, **44**, 314–326.

37 DeJung, J. E., and E. F. Gardner: The accuracy of self-role perception: A developmental study. *J. exp. Educ.*, 1962, **31**, 27–41.

38 Douvan, E.: Independence and identity in adolescence. *Children*, 1957, **4**, 186–190.

39 Dreyer, A. S., and D. Haupt: Self-evaluation in young children. *J. genet. Psychol.*, 1966, **108**, 185–197.

40 Dunbar, F.: Homeostasis during puberty. *Amer. J. Psychiat.*, 1958, **114**, 673–682.

41 Duncan, O. D.: The trend of occupational mobility in the United States. *Amer. sociol. Rev.*, 1965, **30**, 491–498.

42 Dunn, H. L.: Dynamic maturity and purposeful living. *Geriatrics*, 1966, **21**, 205–208.

43 Elkind, D.: Egocentrism in adolescence. *Child Develpm.*, 1967, **38**, 1025–1034.

44 Ellis, R. A., and W. C. Lane: Social mobility and career orientation. *Sociol. soc. Res.*, 1966, **50**, 280–296.

45 Epperson, D. C.: Some interpersonal and performance correlates of classroom alienation. *School Review*, 1963, **71**, 360–376.

46 Eysenck, S. B. G.: A new scale for personality measurement in children. *Brit. J. educ. Psychol.*, 1965, **35**, 362–367.

47 Fellows, E. W.: A study of factors related to a feeling of happiness. *J. educ. Res.*, 1956, **50**, 231–234.

48 Frandsen, A., and M. Sorenson: Interests as motives in academic achievement. *J. sch. Psychol.*, 1968–1969, **7**, no. 1, 52–56.

49 Frank, L. K.: Genetic psychology and its prospects. *Amer. J. Orthopsychiat.*, 1951, **21**, 506–522.

50 Gallagher, J. R., and H. I. Harris: *Emotional problems of adolescents.* Fair Lawn, N. J.: Oxford, 1962.

51 Gardner, D. B., G. R. Hawkes, and L. G. Burchinal: Noncontinuous mothering in infancy and development in later childhood. *Child Develpm.*, 1961, **32**, 225–234.

52 Geiken, K. F.: Expectations concerning husband-wife responsibilities in the home. *J. Marriage & Family*, 1964, **26**, 349–352.

53 Gesell, A., F. L. Ilg, and L. B. Ames: *Youth: The years from ten to sixteen.* New York: Harper & Row, 1956.

54 Gibson, R. M.: Trauma in early infancy and later personality development. *Psychosom. Med.*, 1965, **27**, 229–237.

55 Goldman, S.: Profile of an adolescent. *J. Psychol.*, 1962, **54**, 229–240.

56 Goode, W. J.: The theoretical importance of love. *Amer. sociol. Rev.*, 1959, **24**, 38–47.

57 Grater, H.: Changes in self and other attitudes in a leadership training group. *Personnel Guid. J.*, 1959, **37**, 493–496.

58 Gruenther, Gen. A. W.: An address at Christ Church in Philadelphia, June 16, 1968. *The Beacon of Christ Church*, 1968, **17**, no. 39.

59 Hanawalt, N. G.: Feelings of security and of self-esteem in relation to religious belief. *J. soc. Psychol.*, 1963, **59**, 347–353.

60 Harrison, F.: Aspirations as related to school performance and socioeconomic status. *Sociometry*, 1969, **32**, 70–79.

61 Havighurst, R. J.: Factors which control the experience of aging. *Gawein*, 1965, **13**, 242–248.

62 Havighurst, R. J.: Personality and patterns of aging. *Gerontologist*, 1968, **8**, 20–23.

63 Havighurst, R. J., and R. Albrecht: *Older people.* New York: Longmans, 1953.

64 Havighurst, R. J., and A. deVries: Life styles and free time activities of retired men. *Hum. Develpm.*, 1969, **12**, 34–54.

65 Hechinger, G., and F. M. Hechinger: *Teen-age tyranny.* New York: Morrow, 1963.

66 Hoffman, L. W.: The father's role in the family and the child's peer-group adjustment. *Merrill-Palmer Quart.*, 1961, **7**, 97–106.

67 Horowitz, E.: Reported embarrassment memories of elementary school, high school, and college students. *J. soc. Psychol.*, 1962, **56**, 317–325.

68 Horwitz, J.: This is the age of the aged. *The New York Times*, May 16, 1965.

69 Illingworth, R. S.: How to help a child to achieve his best. *J. Pediat.*, 1968, **73**, 61–68.

70 Jersild, A. T.: Self-understanding in childhood and adolescence. *Amer. Psychologist*, 1951, **8**, 122–126.

71 Jersild, A. T.: *The psychology of adolescence*, 2d ed. New York: Macmillan, 1963.

72 Jourard, S. M.: A study of self-disclosure. *Scient. American*, 1958, **198**, no. 5, 77–82.

73 Jourard, S. M.: *Personal adjustment.* New York: Macmillan, 1958.

74 Jourard, S. M.: Healthy personality and self-disclosure. *Ment. Hyg., N. Y.*, 1959, **43**, 499–507.

75 Jourard, S. M.: Age trends in self-disclosure. *Merrill-Palmer Quart.*, 1961, **7**, 191–197.

76 Keene, J. J.: Religious behavior and neuroticism, spontaneity and world-mindedness. *Sociometry*, 1967, **30**, 137–157.

77 Kennedy, W. A.: School phobia: Rapid treatment of fifty cases. *J. abnorm. Psychol.*, 1965, **70**, 285–289.

78 Kent, D. P.: Social and cultural factors affecting the mental health of the aged. *Amer. J. Orthopsychiat.*, 1966, **36**, 680–685.

79 Lawton, G.: *Aging successfully.* New York: Columbia, 1951.

80 Lemkau, P. V.: The influence of handicapping conditions on child development. *Children*, 1961, **8**, 43–47.

81 Lesure, T. B.: U. S. retirement cities. *Travel*, March 1965, pp. 36–40.

82 Lowe, W. L.: Religious beliefs and religious delusions. *Amer. J. Psychother.*, 1955, **9**, 54–61.

83 MacIver, R. M.: Juvenile delinquency. In E. Ginzberg (ed.), *The nation's children.* New York: Columbia, 1960, vol. 3, pp. 103–123.

84 Maddox, G., and C. Eisdorfer: Some correlates of activity and morale among the elderly. *Soc. Forces*, 1962, **40**, 254–260.

85 Maslow, A. H.: *Motivation and personality.* New York: Harper & Row, 1954.

86 McCammon, R. W.: The concept of normality. *Ann. N.Y. Acad. Sci.*, 1966, **134**, 559–562.

87 McCord, W., J. McCord, and A. Howard: Familial correlates of aggression in nondelinquent male children. *J. abnorm. soc. Psychol.*, 1961, **62**, 79–93.

88 Meltzer, H.: Age and sex differences in workers' perceptions of happiness for self and others. *J. genet. Psychol.*, 1964, **105**, 1–11.

89 Morgan, C. T.: *Physiological psychology*, 3d ed. New York: McGraw-Hill, 1964.

90 Muse, M.: Homes for old age. *J. Home Econ.*, 1965, **57**, 183–187.

91 Nahinsky, I. D.: The self-ideal correlation as a measure of generalized self-satisfaction. *Psychol. Rec.*, 1966, **16**, 55–64.

92 Neuringer, C., and L. W. Wandke: Interpersonal conflicts in persons of high self-concept and low self-concept. *J. soc. Psychol.*, 1966, **68**, 313–322.

93 *New York Times* Report: Depression often mistaken for illness, a doctor says. Nov. 14, 1969.

94 O'Reilly, C. T.: Religious practices and personal adjustment of older people. *Sociol. soc. Res.*, 1958, **42**, 119–121.

95 Packard, V.: *The status seekers.* New York: Pocket Books, 1961.

96 Packard, V.: *The pyramid climbers.* New York: McGraw-Hill, 1962.

97 Pannes, E. D.: The relationship between self-acceptance and dogmatism in junior-senior high school students. *J. educ. Sociol.*, 1963, **36**, 419–426.

98 Parker, E. *The seven ages of woman.* Baltimore: Johns Hopkins, 1960.

99 Peck, R. F., and R. J. Havighurst: *The psychology of character development.* New York: Wiley, 1962.

100 Pederson, D. M., and V. J. Breglio: Personality correlates of actual self-disclosure. *Psychol. Rep.*, 1968, **22**, 495–501.

101 Perkins, H. V.: Factors influencing changes in children's self-concepts. *Child Develpm.*, 1958, **29**, 221–230.

102 Pressey, S. L.: Most important and most neglected topic: Potentials. *Gerontologist*, 1963, **3**, 69–70.

103 Pressey, S. L., and A. D. Pressey: Two insiders searching for the best in life in old age. *Gerontologist*, 1966, **6**, 14–17.

104 Reese, H. W.: Relationships between self-acceptance and sociometric choice. *J. abnorm. soc. Psychol.*, 1961, **62**, 472–474.

105 Reese, H. W.: Attitudes toward the opposite sex in late childhood. *Merrill-Palmer Quart.*, 1966, **12**, 157–163.

106 Robinowitz, M.: The relationship of self regard to the effectiveness of life experiences. *Dissert. Abstr.*, 1966, **26**, 4800–4801.

107 Rose, A. M.: Factors associated with the life satisfaction of middle-class, middle-aged persons. In C. B. Vedder (ed.), *Problems of the middle-aged.* Springfield, Ill.: Charles C Thomas, 1965, pp. 59–67.

108 Rose, A. M.: Class differences among the elderly: A research report. *Sociol. soc. Res.*, 1966, **50**, 356–360.

109 Rosenthal, M. J.: The syndrome of the inconsistent mother. *Amer. J. Orthopsychiat.*, 1962, **32**, 637–644.

110 Scarpitti, F. R., E. Murray, S. Dinitz, and W. C. Reckless: The "good" boy in a high delinquency area: Four years later. *Amer. sociol. Rev.*, 1960, **25**, 555–558.

111 Schaefer, E. S., and N. Bayley: Maternal behavior, child behavior and their intercorrelations from infancy through adolescence. *Monogr. Soc. Res. Child Develpm.*, 1963, **28**, no. 3.

112 Simonson, E.: The concept and definition of normality. *Ann. N.Y. Acad. Sci.*, 1966, **134**, 541–558.

113 Smith, G. M.: Six measures of self-concept discrepancy and instability: Their interrelations, reliability, and relations to other personality measures. *J. consult. Psychol.*, 1958, **22**, 101–112.

114 Sorenson, R.: Youth's need for challenge and place in society. *Children*, 1962, **9**, 131–138.

115 Spaights, E.: Accuracy of self-estimation of junior high school students. *J. educ. Res.*, 1965, **58**, 416–419.

116 Steiner, I. D.: Reactions to adverse and favorable evaluations of one's self. *J. Pers.*, 1968, **36**, 553–563.

117 Stevenson, L.: Is the human personality more plastic in infancy and childhood? *Amer. J. Psychiat.*, 1957, **114**, 152–161.

118 Stiller, A., H. A. Schwartz, and E. L. Cowen: The social desirability of trait-descriptive terms among nursery-school students. *Child Develpm.*, 1965, **36**, 981–1002.

119 Strang, R.: *The adolescent views himself.* New York: McGraw-Hill, 1957.

120 Thompson, G. G.: *Child psychology*, 2d ed. Boston: Houghton Mifflin, 1962.

121 Thompson, G. G., and E. F. Gardner: Adolescents' perceptions of happy-successful living. *J. genet. Psychol.*, 1969, **115**, 107–120.

122 *Time* Report: The command generation. July 29, 1966, pp. 50–54.

123 Toby, J.: Criminal motivation: A sociocultural analysis. *Brit. J. Criminol.*, 1962, **2**, 317–336.

124 Tuckman, J.: College students' judgment of the passage of time over the life span. *J. genet. Psychol.*, 1965, **107**, 43–48.

125 Tuckman, J.: Older people's judgment of the passage of time over the life span. *Geriatrics*, 1965, **20**, 136–140.

126 Tuckman, J., and I. Lorge: The best years of life: A study in ranking. *J. Psychol.*, 1952, **34**, 137–149.

127 Tuddenham, R. D.: Constancy of personal morale over a fifteen-year interval. *Child Develpm.*, 1962, **33**, 663–673.

128 Turner, R. H., and R. H. Vanderlippe: Self-ideal congruence as an index of adjustment. *J. abnorm. soc. Psychol.*, 1958, **57**, 202–206.

129 *U.S. News & World Report*: How women's role in U.S. is changing. May 30, 1966, pp. 58–60.

130 Vedder, C. B. (ed.): *Problems of the middle-aged.* Springfield, Ill.: Charles C Thomas, 1965.

131 Weiner, P. S.: Personality correlates of accuracy of self-appraisals in four-year-old children. *Genet. Psychol. Monogr.*, 1964, **70**, 329–365.

132 Whitman, H.: Let go of the dream. In C. B. Vedder (ed.); *Problems of the middle-aged.* Springfield, Ill.: Charles C Thomas, 1965, pp. 199–202.

133 Wilson, F. M.: The best of life at any age. *Ment. Hyg., N.Y.*, 1955, **39**, 483–488.

134 Wilson, W.: Correlates of avowed happiness. *Psychol. Bull.*, 1967, **67**, 294–306.

135 Yasuda, S.: A methodological inquiry into social mobility. *Amer. sociol. Rev.*, 1964, **29**, 16–23.

index